Holt Online Assessment

Let the POWER of Holt technology work for you– and make the MOST of your day!

1 ASSESS

- Use Holt's pre-made tests with built-in audio links to assess all skill areas including listening comprehension.

- Create and administer your own tests online with **ExamView® Version 5 Assessment Suite**.

2 GRADE

- Select guidelines for automated scoring and save countless hours.

3 REPORT

- Generate reports for students, parents or administrators with ease.

- Track academic progress to focus instruction.

4 REMEDIATE

- Access addition[...] help each and [...]

TEACHER'S EDITION

HOLT FRENCH 3

Bien dit!™

John DeMado

Séverine Champeny

Marie Ponterio

Robert Ponterio

HOLT, RINEHART AND WINSTON

A Harcourt Education Company

Orlando • **Austin** • New York • San Diego • London

Teacher to Teacher Contributors

Jeanne S. Jendrzejewski
LSU Lab School
Baton Rouge, LA

Sylvia Koester
Lakeland High School
LaGrange, IN

Deborah Zoernig
Bayless Senior High School
St. Louis, MO

Karen Query
Lincoln High School
Vincennes, IN

Norah L. Jones
Rustburg HS
Rustburg, VA

Todd Losié
Renaissance HS
Detroit, MI

Geneviève Delfosse
Thomas Jefferson High School for
Science and Technology
Alexandria, VA

Rachel Norwood
374 Flint St.
Athens, GA 30601

Sharon Telich
Westside MS
Omaha, NE

Sue DiGiandomenico
Wellesley MS
Wellesley, MA

ISBN 13: 978-0-03-079624-1

ISBN 10: 0-03-079624-5

2 3 4 5 6 7 048 10 09 08 07

Contributing Authors

John DeMado

John DeMado has been a vocal advocate for second-language acquisition in the United States for many years. He started his career as a middle/high school French and Spanish teacher, before entering the educational publishing profession. Since 1993, Mr. DeMado has directed his own business, John DeMado Language Seminars, Inc., a company devoted exclusively to language acquisition issues. He has authored numerous books in both French and Spanish that span the K–12 curriculum. Mr. DeMado served as the lead consultant for program content at all levels. He created and recorded the **On rappe!** songs for Level 1.

Séverine Champeny

Séverine Champeny, a native of Provence, has been involved in the development of French language educational programs for over 12 years. She has worked on print and media products ranging from introductory middle-school texts to advanced college-level texts. She created activities for the core sections of the chapters. She authored the **Télé-roman** scripts and wrote activities for the DVD Tutor.

Marie Ponterio

Marie Ponterio is a native of France and teaches French language and civilization at the State University of New York College at Cortland. She's the author of the web site **Civilisation française** and the recipient of several awards from Multimedia Educational Resource for Learning and Online Resources. She has co-authored video activities for several high-school textbooks for Harcourt. She has co-authored the culture notes in the program and reviewed all the **Géoculture** sections.

Robert Ponterio

Bob Ponterio is Professor of French at the State University of New York College at Cortland where he teaches all levels of French. He is a moderator of FLTEACH, the Foreign Language Teaching Forum e-mail list. He has published numerous articles and is a recipient of the Anthony Papalia Award for Outstanding Article on Foreign Language Education and the Dorothy S. Ludwig Award for Service to the FL profession. He has co-authored the culture notes in the program and reviewed all the **Géoculture** sections.

Student Edition

Contributing Writers

Elizabeth Baird
Garfield Heights, OH

Rhonda Brunson
Grand Prairie, TX

Dianne Harwood
Austin, TX

Christian Hiltenbrand
Austin, TX

Serge Laîné
Austin, TX

Karine Letellier
Paris, France

Stephanie Mitchel
Austin, TX

Annick Penant
Austin, TX

Mayanne Wright
Austin, TX

Reviewers

These educators reviewed one or more chapters of the Student Edition.

Todd Bowen
Barrington HS
Barrington, IL

J. Blake Carpenter
Department of Modern Languages
The University of Texas at Arlington
Arlington, TX

Mari Kathryn Drefs
Butler MS
Waukesha, WI

David Graham
Morrisonville, NY

Magda Khoury
West Covina HS
West Covina, CA

Todd Losie
Renaissance High School
Detroit, MI

Linda Mercier
Conestoga Valley HS
Lancaster, PA

Colleen Turpin
Scarsdale HS
Scarsdale, NY

Jennifer Wells
Hamilton HS
Hamilton, IN

Thomasina I. White
School district of Philadelphia
Philadelphia, PA

Lori Wickert
Wilson HS
West Lawn, PA

Teacher's Edition

Contributing Writers

Joan Altobelli
Cedar Park, TX

Elizabeth Baird
Garfield Heights, OH

Jason Demetri
Austin, TX

Chris Hiltenbrand
Austin, TX

Todd Losie
Detroit, MI

Rachel Norwood
Athens, GA

Annick Penant
Austin, TX

Marci Reed
Buda, TX

Renate Wise
Round Rock, TX

Mayanne Wright
Austin, TX

Penelope Wynns
Austin, TX

Erika Zettl
Austin, TX

Reviewers

These individuals reviewed one or more chapters of the Teacher's Edition.

Robert Didsbury
Raleigh, NC

Richard Lindley
Dripping Springs, TX

Field Test Participants

Carmel McDonnell
Mills HS
Millbrae, CA

Cynthia Driesner
Triad HS
Troy, IL

Cynthia Madsen
St. Joseph HS
Lakewood, CA

Jennifer Cox
The Harpeth Hall School
Nashville, TN

Joanne Capek
Sidney HS
Sidney, NY

Karen Simmons
Troy Buchanan HS
Troy, MO

Lenee Soto
St. Victor HS
Arlington Heights, IL

Linda Masterson
Granby HS
Norfolk, VA

Linda Stone
Marshfield HS
Marshfield, MA

Lynn Rau
Brentwood HS
Brentwood, TN

Magalie Danier-O'Connor
William Allen HS
Allentown, PA

Maria Bonito
Sanderson HS
Raleigh, NC

Mary Ellen Gianturco
Depew HS
Depew, NY

Melanie L. Calhoun
Sullivan South HS
Kingsport, TN

Melody Bennett
DeForest HS
DeForest, WI

Patricia D. Shanahan
Swampscott HS
Swampscott, MA

Ramona Ngolla
Christopher Columbus HS
Bronx, NY

Samantha Godden-Chmielowicz
Carl Shurz HS
Chicago, IL

Stephen Lynch
St. Marks School
Southborough, MA

Suzanne Polo
Pittsfield HS
Pittsfield, MA

Valerie Hughey
Starr's Mill HS
Fayetteville, GA

Teacher's Edition
Sommaire

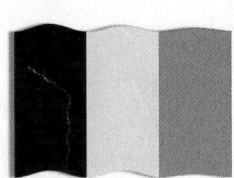

To the Teacher

Bien dit!—a new program with real-world photos, on-location video, animated grammar, and solid pedagogy—is an exciting, motivational, and effective French series that will appeal to all types of learners and keep them coming back for more. Based on the "five C's" of the national standards, this new program has an easy-to-use format that allows students to achieve success, and gives teachers a host of teaching tools to make sure all students can focus on each lesson's goals.

Connections

Links to other subject areas, such as social studies, math, language arts, music, and fine arts are found throughout each chapter of *Bien dit!* Additional opportunities for connections are found at point of use in the *Teacher's Edition.*

Communication

Bien dit! engages students right from the start of each lesson and carefully leads them from structured practice to open-ended communication. Unique image-based **Vocabulaire** presentations introduce a thematic context and provide a reason and motivation for using the language. Colorful **Grammaire** presentations, accompanied by **animated grammar** explanations, help students achieve accuracy in their communication.

Comparisons

To enable students to acquire a broader and a deeper understanding of language and culture, *Bien dit!* offers them multiple opportunities to compare the new language and culture with their own.

Communities

The ultimate goal of learning to communicate in a new language should be the ability to function in an increasingly diverse community and an increasingly demanding world market. *Bien dit!* is built on the theory that the global community has its roots in the second language classroom. If learning language and culture is enjoyable and accessible, all students will become productive members of their community.

For any language program to be successful, the needs of teachers and students have to be the primary consideration. From suggestions for differentiated instruction to the latest in technology products, *Bien dit!* provides an abundance of teacher support and learning tools to help ensure success for all teachers and students.

Culture

The **Géoculture** feature that precedes every other chapter, hands-on projects, realia-based readings and activities, and culture notes in each chapter offer high-interest cultural information and a chance to learn about the **products, practices,** and **perspectives** of the target cultures.

Sommaire

La France
Chapitres 1 et 2

Chapitre 1 Retour de vacances 4

Objectifs

In this chapter you will learn to
- express likes, dislikes, and preferences
- ask about plans
- tell when and how often you did something
- describe a place in the past

DVD Géoculture

Online Practice
go.hrw.com
Online Edition

KEYWORD: BD3 CH1

Chapitre 2 Le monde du travail 42

Objectifs

In this chapter you will learn to
• ask about future plans
• make polite requests
• make a phone call
• write a formal letter

Online Practice
go.hrw.com
Online Edition

KEYWORD: BD3 CH2

L'Afrique francophone
Chapitres 3 et 4

┌─────────────── **Chapter Interleaf with Teaching Resources** ───────────────┐

└──┘

Objectifs

In this chapter you will learn to
- set the scene for a story
- continue and end a story
- relate a sequence of events
- tell what happened to someone else

Géoculture

Online Practice
go.hrw.com
Online Edition

KEYWORD: BD3 CH3

Chapitre 4 Amours et amitiés 132

Objectifs

In this chapter you will learn to
• say what happened
• ask for and give advice
• share good and bad news
• renew old acquaintances

Online Practice
go.hrw.com
Online Edition
KEYWORD: BD3 CH4

L'Amérique francophone

Chapitres 5 et 6

Chapitre 5 En pleine nature 184

Objectifs

In this chapter you will learn to
- express astonishment and fear
- forbid and give warning
- give general directions
- complain and offer encouragement

DVD Géoculture

Online Practice

go.hrw.com
Online Edition

KEYWORD: BD3 CH5

Chapitre 6 La presse

Chapter Interleaf with Teaching Resources

Objectifs

In this chapter you will learn to
• express certainty and possibility
• express doubt and disbelief
• break news
• ask about information

Online Practice
go.hrw.com
Online Edition

KEYWORD: BD3 CH6

L'Europe francophone

Chapitres 7 et 8

Objectifs

In this chapter you will learn to
- caution
- tell why something happened
- make predictions and express assumptions
- express and support an opinion

Géoculture

Online Practice
go.hrw.com
Online Edition

KEYWORD: BD3 CH7

T14

Chapitre 8 La société 312

Objectifs

In this chapter you will learn to
• express a point of view
• speculate about what happened
• ask for assistance
• get information and explain

Online Practice

go.hrw.com
Online Edition

KEYWORD: BD3 CH8

L'outre-mer

Chapitres 9 et 10

Chapitre 9 L'art en fête 364

Objectifs

In this chapter you will learn to
- ask for and give opinions
- introduce and change a topic of conversation
- make suggestions and recommendations
- give an impression

Géoculture
DVD

Online Practice
go.hrw.com
Online Edition

KEYWORD: BD3 CH9

Chapitre 10 Bon voyage! 402

Objectifs

In this chapter you will learn to
• ask for and give information
• remind and reassure
• ask for and give help
• ask for directions

Online Practice
go.hrw.com
Online Edition
KEYWORD: BD3 CH10

Pacing and Planning
Bien dit! Levels 1, 2 and 3

Base your pacing on your schedule...

If you are teaching on a traditional schedule, spend two days on each **Géoculture** and 16 days on each chapter.

Traditional Schedule

Days of Instruction: 180		
Géoculture	2 days of instruction per **Géoculture** x 5 **Géoculture**	10 days
Chapter	16 days per chapter (including assessment) x 10	160 days
Chroniques	1 day per reading x 10	10 days
Total days of instruction using **Bien dit!**:		**180 days**

Block Schedule

Blocks of instruction: 90		
Géoculture	1 block of instruction per **Géoculture** x 5 **Géoculture**	5 blocks
Chapter	8 blocks per chapter (including assessment) x 10	80 blocks
Chroniques	1/2 block per reading x 10	5 blocks
Total blocks of instruction using **Bien dit!**:		**90 blocks**

If you are teaching on a block schedule, spend one block on each **Géoculture** and eight blocks on each chapter.

...and plan your lessons to fit.

Suggested pacing:	Traditional Schedule	Block Schedule
Vocabulaire/Grammaire/Application 1	5 days	2 blocks
Culture	1 day	1 block
Vocabulaire/Grammaire/Application 2	5 days	2 blocks
Lecture	1 day	1/2 block
L'atelier de l'écrivain	1 day	1/2 block
Prépare-toi pour l'examen	1/2 day	1/2 block
Activités préparatoires	1/2 day	1/2 block
Examen	1 day	1/2 block
Révisions cumulatives	1 day	1/2 block

Pacing Suggestions	Essential	Recommended	Optional
Vocabulaire 1 • Relationships and friends • Flash culture	✔		
Grammaire 1 • Reciprocal verbs • The past conditional	✔		
Application 1 • **Un peu plus:** The verbs **manquer** and **plaire**	✔		
Culture • **Lecture culturelle: Maroc: nouveau code de la famille** • **Comparaisons** • **Communauté et professions**		✔	
Vocabulaire 2 • Family history and life events • Flash culture	✔		
Grammaire 2 • Review: The subjunctive • The subjunctive with necessity, desire, and emotions • Flash culture	✔		
Application 2 • **Un peu plus:** Disjunctive (stress) pronouns	✔		
Lecture • **Le fils d'Agatha Moudio** **L'atelier de l'écrivain** • **Une histoire d'amour**		✔	
Prépare-toi pour l'examen • **Résumé de vocabulaire et grammaire**		✔	
Activités préparatoires		✔	
Révisions cumulatives			✔
Chroniques			✔

ʌ|ʎ One-Stop Planner® CD-ROM

Use the One-Stop Planner to make *Bien dit!* work for you...

- **Calendar planning tool** for both short-term and long-term planning

- **PDF format lesson plans** with links to **all** teaching resources, including video and audio

- **Editable tests and lesson plans** are available for all chapters on the *One-Stop Planner.*

- **ExamView® Pro Test Generator**

- **Clip art Library**

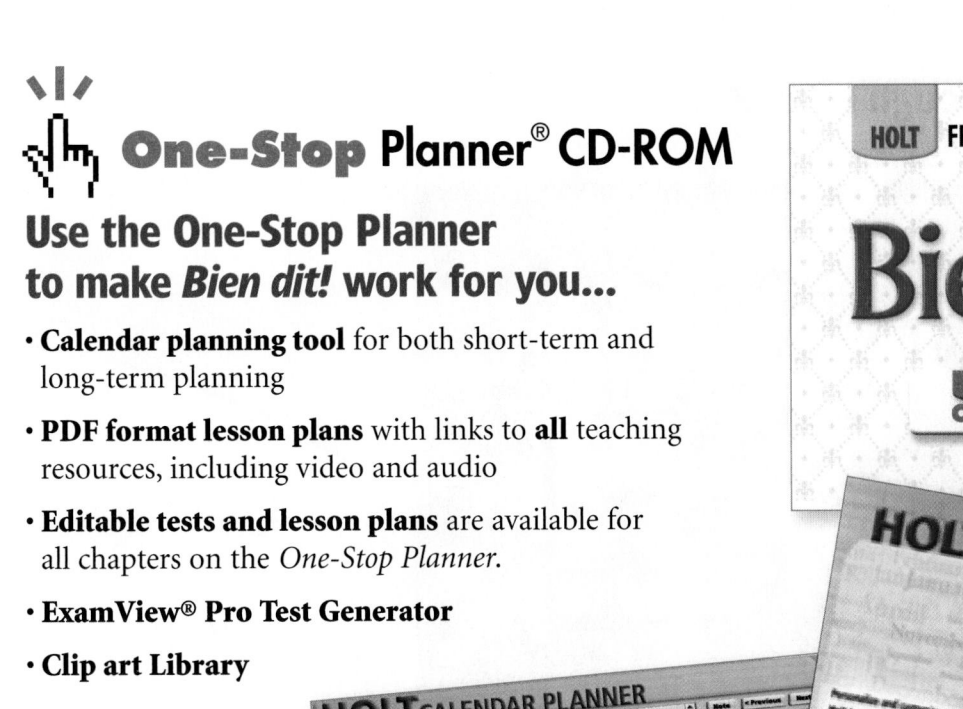

...or customize lesson plans to suit your style or individual classes.

Lesson Plans are available for both 50-minute and 90-minute classes.

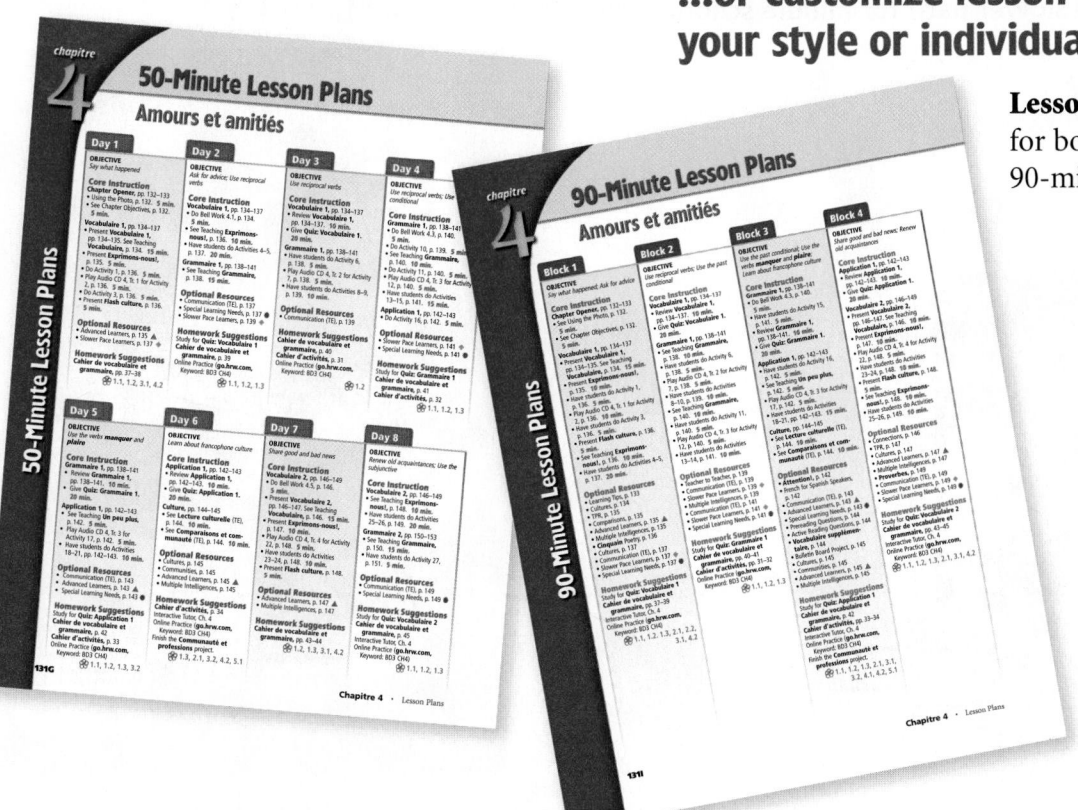

Pacing and Planning

T19

Articulation Across Levels

From Middle School through Level 3

Begin the learning experience with **Level 1**

...or

set a slower pace for middle school with **Level 1A** and **Level 1B**

Level 1A

Level 1B

Level 2 thoroughly reviews the basics and continues to build a solid foundation for communication.

Level 3 begins with a review of the major points covered in Level 2, then builds student skills to the Intermediate Proficiency level.

Scope and Sequence
Bien dit! Level 1

Scope and Sequence

Vocabulary	Functions	Grammar	Culture	Strategies
Chapitre 1 Salut, les copains! pp. 4–37				
• Greetings • Numbers 0–30	• Greet someone and say goodbye • Ask how someone is • Introduce someone • Ask how old someone is	• Subjects and verbs • Subject pronouns	• Kissing or shaking hands while greeting • Personal space and formal versus informal greetings • **Culture appliquée: Les gestes** • **Comparaisons:** Greetings • **Communauté:** Join a French club	• **Video Strategy:** Analyzing the opening • **Reading Strategy:** Recognizing cognates • **Writing Strategy:** Making a list
• Classroom objects and expressions • Accents and special characters	• Ask about things in a classroom • Give classroom commands and ask the teacher something • Ask how words are spelled • Ask for and give e-mail addresses	• Indefinite articles and plural of nouns • The verb **avoir** and negation	• Saying "hello" in the street **FINE ART** • ***Dans la classe,*** Théophile Duverger	
Review/Re-Entry	• **Révisions cumulatives,** pp. 36–37			
Chapitre 2 Qu'est-ce qui te plaît? pp. 38–71				
• Likes and dislikes	• Ask about likes or dislikes • Agree and disagree	• Definite articles • **-er** verbs • Irregular plurals	• Music in France • French-language comic books • **Culture appliquée: Danses traditionnelles** • **Comparaisons: On joue au foot?** • **Communauté:** Folk dances	• **Video Strategy:** Gathering information • **Reading Strategy:** Using visual clues • **Writing Strategy:** Cluster diagrams
• Leisure activites	• Ask how often you do an activity • Ask how well you do an activity and talk about preferences	• Contractions with **à** • Conjunctions • **Est-ce que**	• Movie theaters in France **FINE ART** • ***Une baignade, Asnières,*** Georges Seurat	
Review/Re-Entry	• **Révisions cumulatives,** pp. 70–71	• Irregular plurals		

L'Île-de-France

La gastronomie
Les beaux-arts
L'histoire
Les loisirs

La tour Eiffel

Notre Dame de Chartres

La province de Québec

La gastronomie
Les sports
Les fêtes et
les festivals
L'histoire

La biosphère de Montréal

	Vocabulary	Functions	Grammar	Culture	Strategies
Chapitre 3 Comment est ta famille? pp. 76–109					
	• Physical descriptions and personality traits	• Ask about and describe people • Ask for and give opinions	• The verb **être** • Adjective agreement • More irregular adjectives 	• Last names • Motto of Quebec • **Culture appliquée: Le blason familial** • **Comparaisons: En famille** • **Communauté:** Your city's coat of arms	• **Video Strategy:** Separating essential information from non-essential information • **Reading Strategy:** Using genre to set expectations • **Writing Strategy:** Graphic organizers
	• Family and pets	• Identify family members • Ask about someone's family	• Possessive adjectives • Contractions with **de** • **C'est** versus **Il/Elle est** 	• **Festival d'été et Fête de la famille** • **Carnaval de Québec**  **FINE ART** • *Le traditionnel gâteau des Rois,* Edmond-Joseph Massicotte	
	Review/Re-Entry	• **Révisions cumulatives,** pp. 108–109			

Vue panoramique de Québec

	Vocabulary	Functions	Grammar	Culture	Strategies
Chapitre 4 Mon année scolaire pp. 110–143					
	• School subjects • Days of the week • Time	• Ask about classes • Ask for and give an opinion	• **-re** verbs • **-ger** and **-cer** verbs • **Le** with days of the week 	• Bill 101 • 24-hour clock • **Culture appliquée: Les jours de la semaine** • **Comparaisons: Les délégués de classe** • **Communauté:** Vacations	• **Video Strategy:** Understanding a character's motives • **Reading Strategy:** Using background knowledge • **Writing Strategy:** Using chronology
	• School supplies • Colors and numbers 31–201	• Ask others what they need and tell what you need • Inquire about and buy something	• The verbs **préférer** and **acheter** • Adjectives as nouns • Agreement with numbers 	• The school system • The **Cégep** **FINE ART** • *La Danseuse créole,* Henri Matisse	
	Review/Re-Entry	• **Révisions cumulatives,** pp. 142–143			

L'Ouest de la France

L'histoire
L'architecture
La gastronomie
Les sports

Le château de Chambord

	Vocabulary	Functions	Grammar	Culture	Strategies
Chapitre 5 Le temps libre pp. 148–181					
	• Sports and activities • Seasons and months of the year	• Ask about interests • Ask how often someone does an activity	• The verb **faire** • Question words • Adverbs 	• School sports • **Sports de glisse** • French sports teams • **Culture appliquée: La pétanque** • **Comparaisons: Vive le sport!** • **Communauté: Un club de pétanque**	• **Video Strategy:** Looking for clues • **Reading Strategy:** Making predictions • **Writing Strategy:** An outline
	• Places in town • Weather	• Extend, accept, and refuse an invitation • Make plans	• **Aller** and the **futur proche** • **Venir** and the **passé récent** • Idioms with **avoir**	• The Celsius scale **FINE ART** • *Sur la plage à Trouville,* Claude Monet	
	Review/Re-Entry	• **Révisions cumulatives,** pp. 180–181	• Likes and dislikes		

LIAISON

Vocabulary	Functions	Grammar

Liaison Bien dit! Level 1B pp. xxii–L33

Les Champs-Elysées et l'Arc de Triomphe

Vocabulary	Functions	Grammar
• Greetings • Physical descriptions and personality traits • Likes and dislikes • Sports and leisure activities • Weather • School supplies • Time • School subjects	• Ask for personal information • Ask for and give an opinion • Ask about one's interests • Make plans • Ask about school and classes • Ask and tell about family relationships	• The verbs **être** and **avoir** • Adjective agreement • **aller** and the **futur proche** • Contractions with **à** and **de** • Possessive adjectives • The present tense of **-er** and **-re** verbs

Vocabulary	Functions	Grammar	Culture	Strategies

Chapitre 6 Bon appétit! pp. 182–215

Maisons à poutres apparentes

Vocabulary	Functions	Grammar	Culture	Strategies
• Breakfast foods and drinks • Place settings	• Offer, accept, and refuse food • Ask for and give an opinion	• The partitive • **-ir** verbs • The verb **vouloir** 	• A typical breakfast • Table manners in France • **Viennoiseries** • **Culture appliquée: La tarte** • **Comparaisons: À table!** • **Communauté: Des desserts**	• **Video Strategy:** Keeping track of the plot • **Reading Strategy:** Context clues and visual clues • **Writing Strategy:** Organizing via charts
• **Café** foods	• Inquire about food and place an order • Ask about prices and pay the check	• The verb **prendre** • The imperative • The verb **boire** 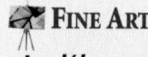	• Tipping in France • The euro • **Menu à prix fixe** 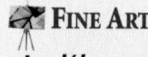 **FINE ART** • *Le déjeuner des canotiers,* Pierre Auguste Renoir	
Review/Re-Entry	• Contractions with **de** • **Révisions cumulatives,** pp. 214–215		• Sports and pastime activities	

Chapitre 7 On fait les magasins? pp. 220–253

Le Sénégal

L'artisanat
La musique
Les sports
La gastronomie

Marché en plein air

Vocabulary	Functions	Grammar	Culture	Strategies
• Clothing and accessories	• Offer and ask for help in a store • Ask for and give opinions	• Demonstrative adjectives • Interrogative adjectives • The verb **mettre** 	• Clothing sizes • **Batik** • Bargaining in Senegal • **Culture appliquée: Le boubou** • **Comparaisons: Les soldes** • **Communauté: Des costumes traditionnels**	• **Video Strategy:** Recognizing different points of view • **Reading Strategy:** Facts and opinions • **Writing Strategy:** Using charts to visualize and contrast
• Sports equipment, leather goods, and jewelry • Numbers 1,000–1,000,000	• Ask about and give prices • Make a decision	• The **passé composé** of **-er** verbs • The **passé composé** of irregular verbs • Adverbs with the **passé composé** 	• The Senegalese **franc CFA** **FINE ART** • *Un souwère,* M'Bida	
Review/Re-Entry	• Giving opinions • **Révisions cumulatives,** pp. 252–253		• Adjective agreement • **Avoir**	

	Vocabulary	Functions	Grammar	Culture	Strategies

Chapitre 8 À la maison pp. 254–287

Le lac Rose, Sénégal

Vocabulary	Functions	Grammar	Culture	Strategies
• Chores	• Ask for, give or refuse permission • Tell how often you do things	• The verbs **pouvoir** and **devoir** • The **passé composé** of -ir and -re verbs • Negative expressions	• Tea ceremony in Senegal • **Culture appliquée: La cérémonie du thé** • **Comparaisons: Où sont les toilettes?** • **Communauté: C'est comment chez toi?**	• **Video Strategy:** Making deductions • **Reading Strategy:** Scanning for specific information • **Writing Strategy:** Using visuals
• House and furniture	• Describe a house • Tell where things are	• The verbs **dormir, sortir,** and **partir** • The **passé composé** with **être** • -yer verbs	• Numbering floors in Senegal • Senegalese **cases** 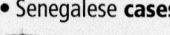 **FINE ART** • *La chambre de Van Gogh à Arles,* Vincent Van Gogh	
Review/Re-Entry	• Places and activities • **Révisions cumulatives,** pp. 286–287		• The **passé composé** of regular -er verbs • The past participles of -er, -ir, and -re verbs	

Chapitre 9 Allons en ville! pp. 292–325

Le Midi

L'artisanat
Les fêtes et les festivals
La gastronomie
Les arts

Marché en plein air à Nice

Vocabulary	Functions	Grammar	Culture	Strategies
• Places in the city • Means of transportation	• Plan your day • Ask for and give directions	• The verb **voir** • The verbs **savoir** and **connaître** • The imperative 	• **Code de la route** • Public transportation • The metric system • **Culture appliquée: La ville en chanson** • **Comparaisons: Les médicaments** • **Communauté: Plan de ta ville**	• **Video Strategy:** Making predictions • **Reading Strategy:** Reading aloud • **Writing Strategy:** Using a map to write directions
• At the pharmacy, bank, and post office	• Tell what you need • Make and respond to requests	• The present tense • Inversion • The partitive 	• **La carte bleue** • **Pharmacie** versus **droguerie** • Banking at the post office 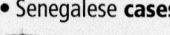 **FINE ART** • *La rue,* Marc Chagal	
Review/Re-Entry	• The imperative • The partitive	• The present tense • **Révisions cumulatives,** pp. 324–325	• Questions with intonation and **est-ce que**	

Chapitre 10 Enfin les vacances! pp. 326–359

La gare de Nice

Vocabulary	Functions	Grammar	Culture	Strategies
• Travel items • At the hotel	• Give advice • Get information	• The verb **appeler** • Prepositions with countries and cities • Idioms with **faire** 	• **Gîtes** • Hotel ratings • **Culture appliquée: Les santons** • **Comparaisons: L'électricité** • **Communauté: Souvenirs**	• **Video Strategy:** Summarizing • **Reading Strategy:** Improving comprehension • **Writing Strategy:** Create a timeline
• At the train station and airport	• Ask for information • Buy tickets and make a transaction	• The **passé composé** with **avoir** • The **passé composé** with **être** • Ordinal numbers	• **SNCF** and **TGV** • **Un composteur** 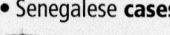 **FINE ART** • *La gare,* Daniel Lordey	
Review/Re-Entry	• Contractions with **à** and **de** • Cardinal numbers • Places		• **Passé composé** with **avoir** • **Passé composé** with **être** • **Révisions cumulatives,** pp. 358–359	

Scope and Sequence
Bien dit! Level 2

Paris
Les sports
Les sciences
La gastronomie
La mode

Le Louvre

Les Invalides

	Vocabulary	Functions	Grammar	Culture	Strategies
Chapitre 1 Ma famille et mes copains pp. 4–39					
	• Describing friends and family	• Describe yourself and ask about others • Talk about your likes and dislikes	• The verbs **avoir** and **être** • Adjective agreement • The adjectives **beau, nouveau, and vieux** 	• Sundays • Family nicknames • **La cursive** • **La famille au Maroc** • **Le français et l'enseignement**	• **Video Strategy:** Looking for clues • **Reading Strategy:** Genre of a text • **Writing Strategy:** Writing plan
	• After-school activities	• Inquire • Tell when you do something	• **-er** verbs • **-ir** and **-re** verbs • Verbs like **dormir** 	• After-school activities • Cafés 🎨 **FINE ART** • *Yvonne et Christine Lerolle au piano,* Renoir	
Review/Re-Entry	• **Tu** vs. **Vous** • The verbs **avoir** and **être** • Adjective agreement • The adjectives **beau, nouveau, and vieux** • Days and months			• **-er** verbs • **-ir** and **-re** verbs • Verbs like **dormir** • **Révisions cumulatives,** pp. 38–39	
Chapitre 2 On fait la fête pp. 40–75					
	• Celebrations	• Wish someone a good time • Ask for and give advice	• Direct object pronouns • Indirect object pronouns • The verb **offrir** 	• **L'épiphanie, le jour des rois** • **Le 14 juillet** • **Le carnaval** • **Invitation à manger** • **Spécialités pour les fêtes**	• **Video Strategy:** Gathering information • **Reading Strategy:** Using cognates • **Writing Strategy:** Good use of dialogue
	• Party preparations	• Ask for help • Check if things have been done	• The **passé composé** with **avoir** • The **passé composé** with **être** • Negative expressions 	• **Noël** • Holidays 🎨 **FINE ART** • *La Rue Montorgueil, la Fête du 30 juin 1878,* Claude Monet	
Review/Re-Entry	• The **passé composé** • The **passé composé** with **avoir**			• The **passé composé** with **être** • **Révisions cumulatives,** pp. 74–75	

Vocabulary	Functions	Grammar	Culture	Strategies

Chapitre 3 Faisons les courses pp. 80–115

Québec

L' architecture
La gastronomie
Les fêtes et festivals
Les arts

Le château Frontenac

Vocabulary	Functions	Grammar	Culture	Strategies
• Fruits, vegetables, and cooking	• Ask about food preparation • Make requests	• The partitive • The pronoun **y** • Question formation 	• The metric system • Typical foods of Quebec • **Le sirop d'érable** • **Le couscous** • **Le français dans les cuisines**	• **Video Strategy:** Comparing attitudes • **Reading Strategy:** Making inferences • **Writing Strategy:** Arranging your ideas chronologically
• Food shopping	• Shop for groceries • Ask where things are in a store	• The pronoun **en** • Placement of object pronouns • Contractions with **à** and **de**	• Shopping **FINE ART** • *La rue des abesses,* Maximilien Luce	

Review/Re-Entry	• Indefinite articles **un**, **une**, **des** • The partitive • Question formation • Prepositions	• In town • Contractions with **à** and **de** • **Révisions cumulatives,** pp. 114–115

Chapitre 4 Au lycée pp. 116–151

Bâtiment gouvernemental

Vocabulary	Functions	Grammar	Culture	Strategies
• School places and events	• Ask how something turned out • Wonder what happened	• Object pronouns with the **passé composé** • **Quelqu'un, quelque chose, ne...personne, ne... rien, ne...que** • The verb **recevoir**	• **Diplôme d'études collégiales (Québec)** • School books • **La ringuette** • **On mange où?** • **Être professeur de français**	• **Video Strategy:** Understanding subtext • **Reading Strategy:** The genre of a text • **Writing Strategy:** Answering the five "W" questions
• Computer terms	• Ask for information • Express frustration	• The verb **suivre** • **Depuis, il y a, ça fait...** • The verb **ouvrir** 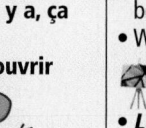	• Computer keyboards • Web sites **FINE ART** • *Le Hockey,* Henri Masson	

Review/Re-Entry	• Direct and indirect object pronouns • **ne...personne; ne...rien**	• Party preparations • **Révisions cumulatives,** pp. 150–151

Chapitre 5 Une journée typique pp. 156–191

Rennes

L'architecture
Les fêtes et festivals
La musique
Les arts

L'Opéra de Rennes

Vocabulary	Functions	Grammar	Culture	Strategies
• Morning routine	• Talk about your routine • Express impatience	• Reflexive verbs • **tout, tous, toute, toutes** • The verbs **s'appeler** and **se lever** 	• Typical French teen's day • The **métro** in Rennes • **La faïence de Quimper** • **À pied, à vélo ou en bus?** • **Le français et les produits de beauté**	• **Video Strategy:** Evaluating choices • **Reading Strategy:** Using the context • **Writing Strategy:** Identifying your audience
• Daily routine	• Say when you do things • Make recommendations	• Reflexive verbs in the **passé composé** • The imperative with reflexive verbs • Reflexive verbs with infinitives	• **Le goûter** • Shopping **FINE ART** • *Nana,* Edouard Manet	

Review/Re-Entry	• Verbs like **balayer** and **essayer** • **Tu, vous, nous** commands	• **Révisions cumulatives,** pp. 190–191

Scope and Sequence

	Vocabulary	Functions	Grammar	Culture	Strategies

Chapitre 6 Le bon vieux temps pp. 182–227

Place de la Mairie

Vocabulary	Functions	Grammar	Culture	Strategies
• Childhood activities	• Talk about when you were a child • Tell about an event in the past	• The **imparfait** • The **passé composé** and the **imparfait** • Adverb placement	• Children's games • Comic books • **Les comptines** • **À la ferme** • **Au pair**	• **Video Strategy:** Making deductions • **Reading Strategy:** Using images and symbols • **Writing Strategy:** Symbols, imagery, metaphors, similes
• Country life	• Compare life in the country and in the city • Describe life in the country	• The comparative with adjectives and nouns • The superlative with adjectives • Irregular comparatives and superlatives	• Living in the country versus the city • Summer camps **FINE ART** • *Paysage du Pont-Aven*, Paul Gauguin	
Review/Re-Entry	• The **passé composé** • Adverbs • Adverb placement	• Contractions with **de** • **Révisions cumulatives,** pp. 226–227		

Chapitre 7 Un week-end en plein air pp. 232–267

Dakar

Les arts
La mode
Les fêtes et festivals
Le cinéma

Bateaux de pêche

Vocabulary	Functions	Grammar	Culture	Strategies
• Camping	• Say what happened • Describe circumstances	• The **passé composé** and the **imparfait** • **être en train de** • Verbs with **être** or **avoir** in the **passé composé**	• Camping • Nautical sports • **Le Parc national de la Langue de Barbarie** • **Le camping** • **Le français dans le monde du tourisme**	• **Video Strategy:** Getting confirmation • **Reading Strategy:** Focusing on ideas • **Writing Strategy:** Create the setting
• Nature, animals, and activities	• Tell what you will do • Wonder what will happen	• The future • The future of irregular verbs • The verb **courir**	• Fishing • The **pirogue** **FINE ART** • Jean Metzinger	
Review/Re-Entry	• The **passé composé** and the **imparfait** • Childhood activities • Verbs with **être** in the **passé composé** • **Révisions cumulatives,** pp. 266–267			

Chapitre 8 Es-tu en forme? pp. 268–303

La porte du troisième millénaire

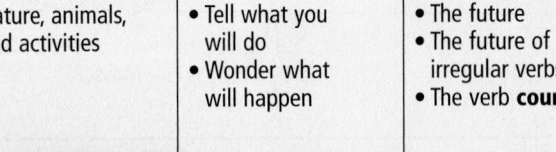

Vocabulary	Functions	Grammar	Culture	Strategies
• Parts of the body; injuries and illnesses	• Ask and tell how you feel • Describe symtoms and give advice	• The subjunctive of regular verbs • The subjunctive of irregular verbs • More expressions with the subjunctive	• Health care • **L'awalé** • **Malade en France** • **Le français dans le monde médical**	• **Video Strategy:** Following the plot • **Reading Strategy:** Using background knowledge • **Writing Strategy:** Providing specific details
• Improving one's health	• Complain about health and give advice • Sympathize with someone	• The conditional • **Si** clauses • The conditional to make polite requests	• Gyms • Senegalese foods **FINE ART** • *Un souwère du Sénégal*	
Review/Re-Entry	• Body parts • Family • Future stems of irregular verbs	• **Imparfait** endings • Fruits and vegetables • **Révisions cumulatives,** pp. 302–303		

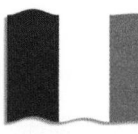

	Vocabulary	Functions	Grammar	Culture	Strategies

Chapitre 9 On s'amuse! pp. 308–342

Nice

Les arts
Les fêtes et festivals
L'architecture
La gastronomie

La FNAC

	Vocabulary	Functions	Grammar	Culture	Strategies
	• Movies and books	• Describe a movie or a book • Ask for and give information	• The relative pronouns **qui, que,** and **dont** • Present participles • **C'est** and **Il/Elle est** 	• Movies • The **TVA** (French tax) • **Le Festival de Cannes** • **La télévision en France** • **Être traducteur ou interprète**	• **Video Strategy:** Predicting • **Reading Strategy:** Recognizing the main idea • **Writing Strategy:** Using conjunctions and relative pronouns
	• Television shows and music	• Ask about preferences • Recommend and advise against something	• Interrogative pronouns • Demonstrative pronouns • Comparatives and superlatives 	• The TVA • Television  **FINE ART** • **Pont de Langlois,** Vincent Van Gogh	
Review/Re-Entry	• Expressions followed by **de** • **C'est** and **Il/Elle est** • **Quel**		• Comparatives and superlatives • **Révisions cumulatives,** pp. 342–343		

Chapitre 10 Partons en vacances! pp. 344–379

Musée d'Art Moderne et d'Art Contemporain (MAMAC)

	Vocabulary	Functions	Grammar	Culture	Strategies
	• Vacation	• Ask about a vacation • Say what you would do if you could	• Object pronouns • The conditional • **Si** clauses 	• Tourism • Vacations • **Le tourisme à Nice** • **En vacances!** • **Le français et le tourisme**	• **Video Strategy**: Putting the pieces together • **Reading Strategy:** Personification • **Writing Strategy:** Purpose for writing
	• Making preparations for vacation	• Express necessity • Ask about what has been done	• The subjunctive • The **passé composé** and the **imparfait** • **être en train de** 	• School holidays • Vacation schedules  **FINE ART** • **Femme sur la terrasse,** Henri Matisse	
Review/Re-Entry	• To say in, to, from a country • Object pronouns • The conditional • Clothes and accessories • **Révisions cumulatives,** pp. 378–379		• The **passé composé** and the **imparfait** • **être en train de** • **Si** clauses • The subjunctive		

Scope and Sequence
Bien dit! Level 3

Vocabulary	Functions	Grammar	Culture	Strategies
Chapitre 1 Retour de vacances pp. 4–41				
La France **La géographie** **L'histoire** *Marché aux fleurs*	• Back-to-school activities and classes • After-school activities	• Express likes, dislikes, and preferences • Ask about plans	• Regular verbs in the present • Irregular verbs in the present • Verbs followed by the infinitive	• The **baccalauréat** and professional studies • The **baccalauréat** • **Chevaux de polo** • **Les moniteurs** • **Le français et le développement des loisirs et du tourisme**	• **Reading Strategy:** Creating mental images • **Writing Strategy:** Sensory details
	• What you did last summer: activities, things, and places	• Tell when and how often you did something • Describe a place in the past	• The **passé composé** • The **passé composé** and the **imparfait** • Reflexive verbs in the **passé composé**	• Summer vacation for French youth • Festivals in France 📷 **FINE ART** • *Un dimanche après-midi à l'Île de la Grande Jatte* de Georges Seurat	
Review/Re-Entry	• Regular verbs in the present • Irregular verbs in the present • Verbs followed by the infinitive • The **passé composé**		• The **passé composé** and the **imparfait** • Reflexive verbs in the **passé composé** • **Révisions cumulatives,** pp. 40–41	
Chapitre 2 Le monde du travail pp. 42–79				
Fontaine et fleurs	• Professions and services	• Ask about future plans • Make polite requests	• The future • Feminine forms of nouns • The verb **conduire**	• The three parts of the French economy • The French work year • **Designer olfactif** • **Curriculum vitae** • **Le français et la publicité**	• **Reading Strategy:** Summarizing ideas • **Writing Strategy:** Details and organization
	• Telephone and formal letter vocabulary	• Make a phone call • Write a formal letter	• The future perfect • The present participle • **Conditionnel de politesse**	• Finding a job in France, the ANPE • Unions and strikes in France 📷 **FINE ART** • *Les constructeurs* de Fernand Léger	
Review/Re-Entry	• The future • Present participles		• The **conditionnel de politesse** • **Révisions cumulatives,** pp. 78–79	

Scope and Sequence

S1 - Ch 1, 2B, 4, ... (If time avail; 10.2)

Increase work on P.C. or imparfait

S2 — Chapters 5, 6, 7, 8, 9 / 10.1

	Vocabulary	Functions	Grammar	Culture	Strategies
Chapitre 3 Il était une fois... pp. 94–131					
L'Afrique francophone **La géographie** **L'histoire** Femmes en costume traditionnel	• Legends, fairy tales, and fables	• Set the scene for a story • Continue and end a story	• The **passé simple** • Relative pronouns with **ce** • Adjective placement and meaning	• Oral tradition • The **médina** • **La littérature maghrébine en français** • **Écrire en français** • **Doubleur — un métier en plein boum**	• **Reading Strategy:** Using chronology • **Writing Strategy:** Using realistic dialogue
	• Historical accounts from Africa	• Relate a sequence of events • Tell what happened to someone else	• The past perfect • Sequence of tenses in indirect discourse • The past infinitive	• French colonists in Algeria **FINE ART** • Cave art painting from Aounrhet, Tassili, Algeria	
Review/Re-Entry	• **Imparfait et passé composé** • The pronouns **qui, que,** and **dont**			• Reflexive verbs in the **passé composé** • **Révisions cumulatives,** pp. 130–131	
Chapitre 4 Amours et amitiés pp. 132–169					
Perles et colliers sur un marché à Dakar	• Reciprocal actions and emotions	• Say what happened • Ask for and give advice	• Reciprocal verbs • The past conditional • The verbs **manquer** and **plaire**	• Hospitality in Africa • **Maroc: nouveau code de la famille** • **Sorties entre copains!** • **Les formateurs multiculturels**	• **Reading Strategy:** Using background knowledge • **Writing Strategy:** Using similes
	• Life events and emotions	• Share good and bad news • Renew old acquaintances	• The subjunctive • The subjunctive with necessity, desire, and emotions • Disjunctive (stress) pronouns	• Weddings in North Africa • Family politics **FINE ART** • **La Noce** d'Henri-Julien Félix Rousseau dit Le Douanier	
Review/Re-Entry	• Reflexive verbs in the **passé composé** • The conditional • **Révisions cumulatives,** pp. 168–169			• The subjunctive • Activities	
Chapitre 5 En pleine nature pp. 184–221					
L'Amérique francophone **La géographie** **L'histoire** Bâtiment gouvernemental	• Nature and animals	• Express astonishment and fear • Forbid and give warning	• The subjunctive with expressions of fear • The imperative • The verbs **voir** and **regarder**	• Parks in Louisiana • French and Cajun influence • **Les oies voyageuses** • **Les parcs publics en France** • **Moniteurs/ Guides de sports extrêmes**	• **Reading Strategy:** Using inferences • **Writing Strategy:** Using multiple techniques
	• Exploration (hiking, rafting, extreme outdoor sports)	• Give general directions • Complain and offer encouragement	• **Apporter, amener, emporter** and **emmener** • Verbs followed by **à/de** and the infinitive • Verbs with idioms	• Canadian sports **FINE ART** • **Louisiana heron** de Jean-Jacques Audubon	
Review/Re-Entry	• The subjunctive • The imperative • **Révisions cumulatives,** pp. 220–221			• **Voir** and **regarder** • Idiomatic expressions	

Vocabulary	Functions	Grammar	Culture	Strategies

Chapitre 6 La presse pp. 222–259

Pont piétonnier de
Sainte-Anne-du-Nord

Vocabulary	Functions	Grammar	Culture	Strategies
• Francophone newspapers and magazines	• Express certainty and possibility • Express doubt and disbelief	• The subjunctive with doubt and uncertainty • The verbs **croire** and **paraître** • **Quelque part, quelqu'un, quelque chose** et **quelquefois**	• The Francophone press in the US • Becoming a journalist in Quebec • **Mon quotidien, un journal pour les 10–14 ans** • **Créole ou français en Haïti?** • **Le français et le journalisme**	• **Reading Strategy:** Background knowledge and context clues • **Writing Strategy:** Defining your style
• The news	• Break news • Ask about information	• Object pronouns • **Qui est-ce qui, qui est-ce que, qu'est-ce qui** and **qu'est-ce que** • More negative expressions	• Blogs **FINE ART** • *Le snobisme* de Toulouse-Lautrec	
Review/Re-Entry	• Subjunctive forms, regular and irregular • **quelque** • Sequence of tenses		• Direct object agreement of the past participle • Object pronouns • **Révisions cumulatives,** pp. 258–259	

Chapitre 7 Notre planète pp. 274–311

L'Europe francophone

**La géographie
L'histoire**

Les Alpes françaises

Vocabulary	Functions	Grammar	Culture	Strategies
• Natural phenomena	• Caution • Tell why something happened	• The comparative and superlative • The passive voice • Prepositions	• The climate • **Dépollution par le lombric** • **La minuterie** • **Le français et le monde de la recherche**	• **Reading Strategy:** Identifying the main idea • **Writing Strategy:** Defining your audience
• Environmental issues and solutions	• Make predictions and express assumptions • Express and support an opinion	• **Quand, lorsque,** and **dès que** • Subjunctive after a conjunction • The verb **éteindre**	• Kyoto treaty for Environmental protection • Electric cars **FINE ART** • **La Jetée du Havre** par mauvais temps de Claude Monet	
Review/Re-Entry	• Irregular comparative and superlative of **bon** and **bien** • The future and future perfect • **Révisions cumulatives,** pp. 310–311		• The subjunctive • The verb **éteindre**	

Vocabulary	Functions	Grammar	Culture	Strategies

Chapitre 8 La société pp. 312–349

Place Masséna

Vocabulary	Functions	Grammar	Culture	Strategies
• Political campaign, government	• Express a point of view • Speculate about what happened	• Contractions with **lequel** (**auquel** and **duquel**) • The past subjunctive • Adverbs	• Traveling in the EU • Belgium's three cultures • **Cité de la paix et de l'intégration** • **Les juges en France** • **Le français et les organisations internationales**	• **Reading Strategy:** Taking notes • **Writing Strategy:** Good introductions and conclusions
• Government services (police, firefighter, adminstration)	• Ask for assistance • Get information and explain	• The conditional • The verb **vaincre** • **Chacun/chacune**	• Swiss government **FINE ART** • *Les Représentants des puissances étrangères venant saluer la République en signe de paix* d'Henri Rousseau	

Review/Re-Entry	• The interrogative pronoun **lequel** • The subjunctive • Adverbs	• The **imparfait** • The conditional • **Révisions cumulatives,** pp. 348–349

Chapitre 9 L'art en fête pp. 364–401

L'outre-mer

**La géographie
L'histoire**

Forteresse à la Martinique

Vocabulary	Functions	Grammar	Culture	Strategies
• Types of fine arts	• Ask for and give opinions • Introduce and change a topic of conversation	• The inversion • Present participles used as adjectives • **Si** and **oui**	• Tahitian crafts • **La sculpture, l'âme des Marquises** • **Les musées en France** • **Le français et la musique**	• **Reading Strategy:** Dialoguing with the text • **Writing Strategy:** Using note cards
• Music and other performing arts	• Make suggestions and recommendations • Give an impression	• The comparative and superlative • Demonstrative pronouns • **Savoir** and **connaître**	• Music of the Antilles • Tahitian song and dance **FINE ART** • *Le jongleur* de Marc Chagall	

Review/Re-Entry	• Intonation • Inversion • Present participles used as adjectives • Adjective agreement	• The comparative and superlative • Demonstrative pronouns • **Savoir** and **connaître** • **Révisions cumulatives,** pp. 400–401

Chapitre 10 Bon voyage! pp. 402–439

Bateaux à la Martinique

Vocabulary	Functions	Grammar	Culture	Strategies
• At the airport	• Ask for and give information and clarifications • Remind and reassure	• Prepositions with places • The subjunctive	• DROM • **A380 Naissance d'un géant** • **Les autoroutes en France** • **Le français et les métiers du tourisme**	• **Reading Strategy:** Combining strategies • **Writing Strategy:** Creating mood
• Travel by car	• Ask for and give help • Ask for directions	• The future • The past perfect • The causative **faire**	• French driver's license • French driver's license — the point system **FINE ART** • *Interior in Nice* d'Henri Matisse	

Review/Re-Entry	• Gender of countries • Preposition with places • The subjunctive • Adverbs and adverb placement	• The future • The **plus-que-parfait** • The causative **faire** • **Révisions cumulatives,** pp. 438–439

Student Edition

Bien dit! gives students the confidence to express themselves!

With ever-growing class sizes and more ability levels than ever before in the French classroom, it takes a special French program to engage your students. *Bien dit!* immerses students in the French-speaking world and makes them want to communicate!

Cross-curricular connections make material relevant to students

The *Géoculture* video brings each location to life.

The *Géoculture* pages introduce students to a new Francophone region. Students make connections with geography, art, architecture, and history.

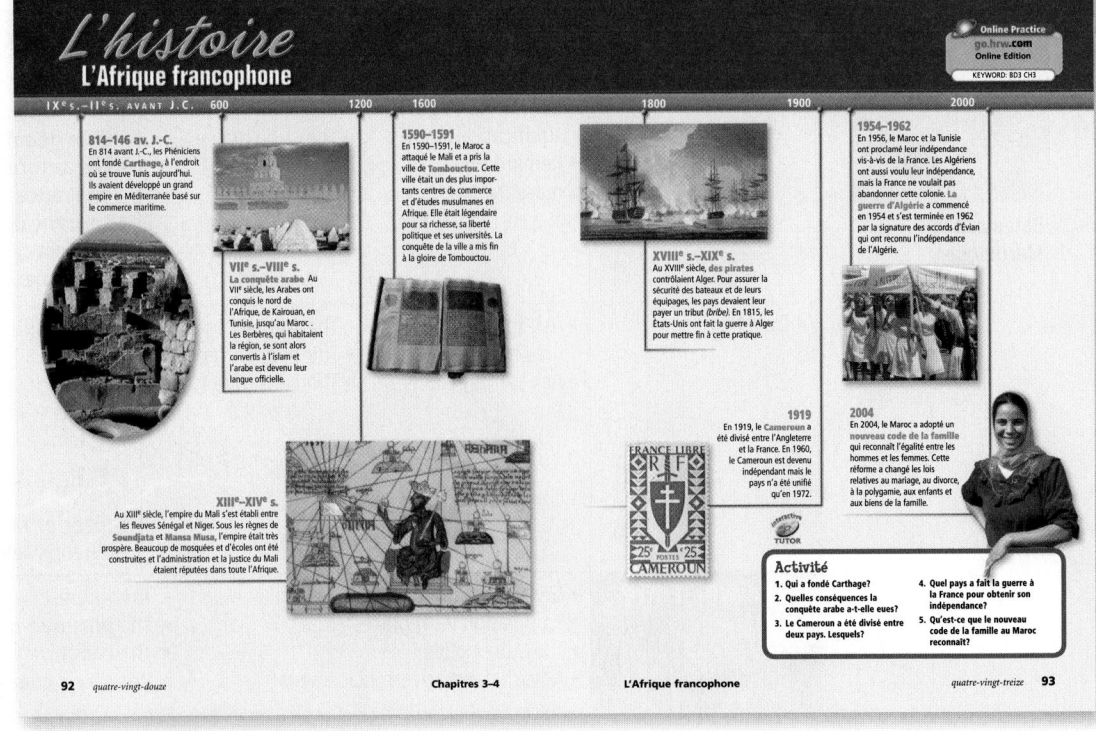

Colorful and vivid presentations that hold students' attention

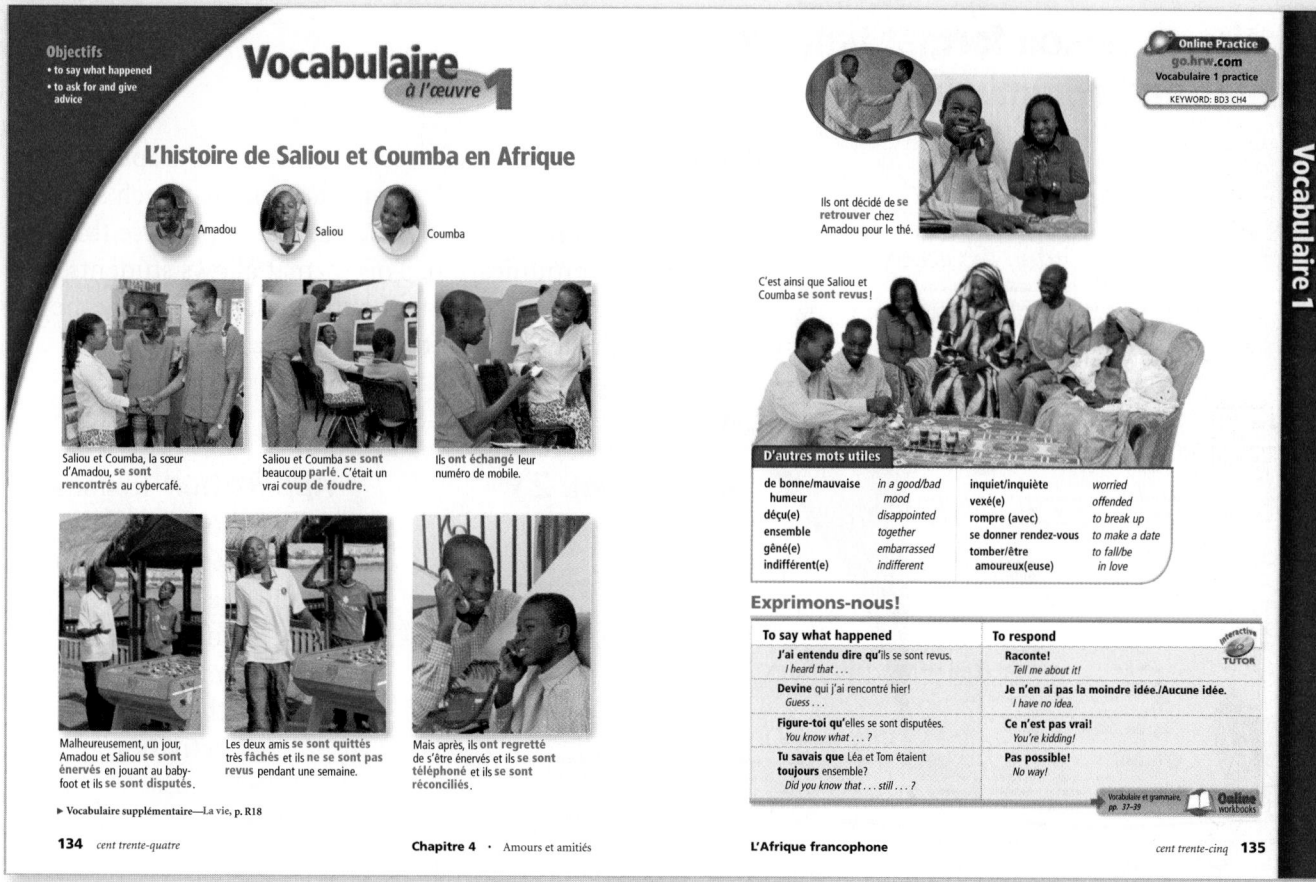

Vocabulary and functional phrases are the foundation of meaningful communication. The large, real-life photos in the vocabulary sections help students connect learning French to their world.

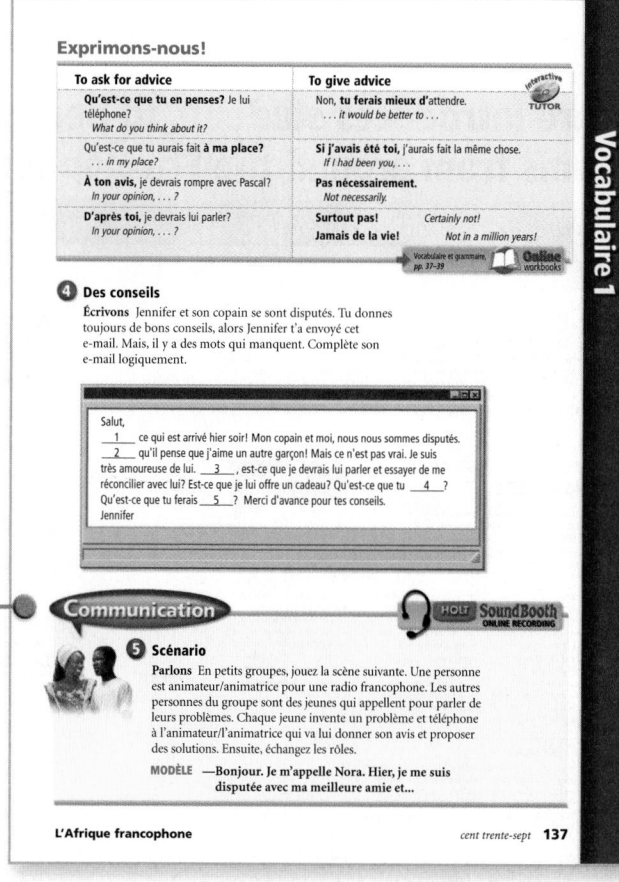

Communication is the goal of every presentation. The consistent placement of features helps all students recognize the pattern and easily comprehend the chapter format.

Student Edition

A consistent lesson format balances grammar and communication

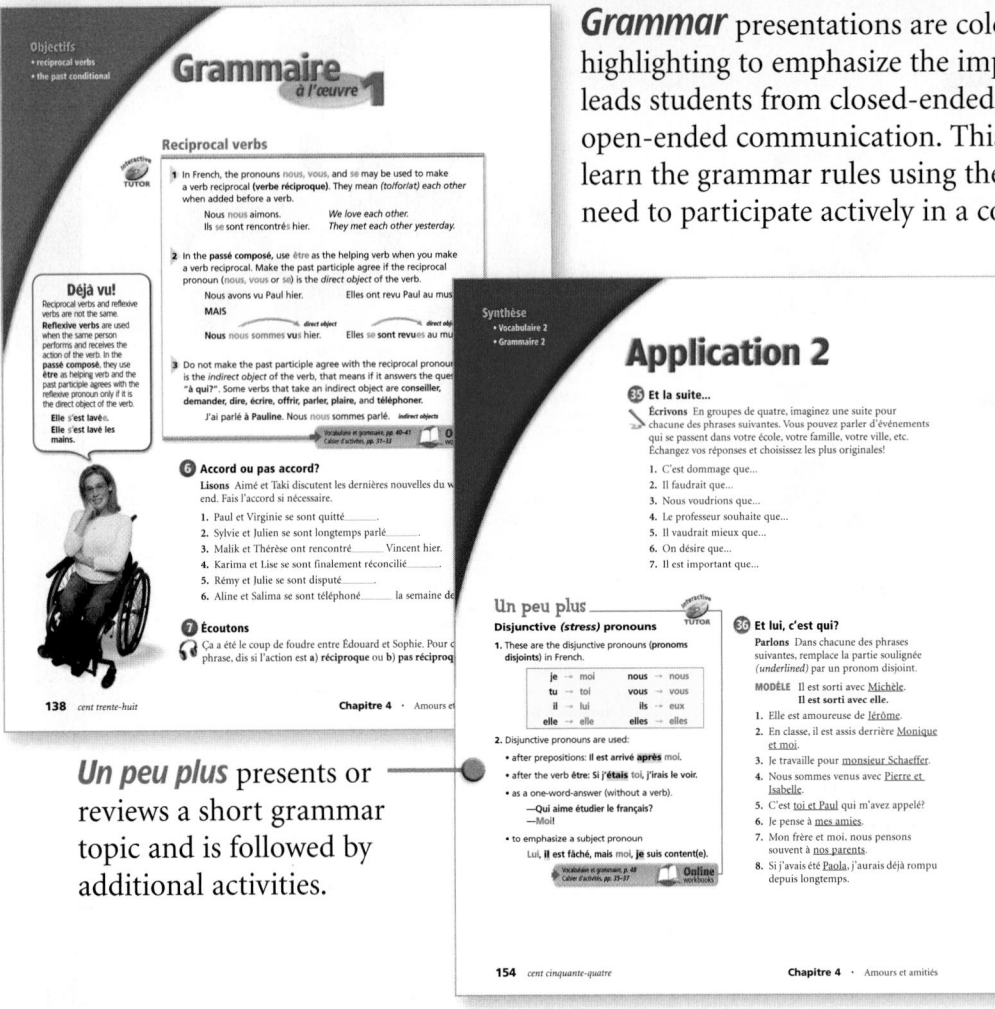

Grammar presentations are color-coded with graphics and highlighting to emphasize the important points. Each section leads students from closed-ended, structured practice through open-ended communication. This format allows students to learn the grammar rules using the thematic vocabulary they need to participate actively in a communicative situation.

Application sections follow the vocabulary and grammar. Here students synthesize what they have learned to that point. These sections begin with integrated practice activities.

Un peu plus presents or reviews a short grammar topic and is followed by additional activities.

Culture introduces students to people and customs from around the Francophone world

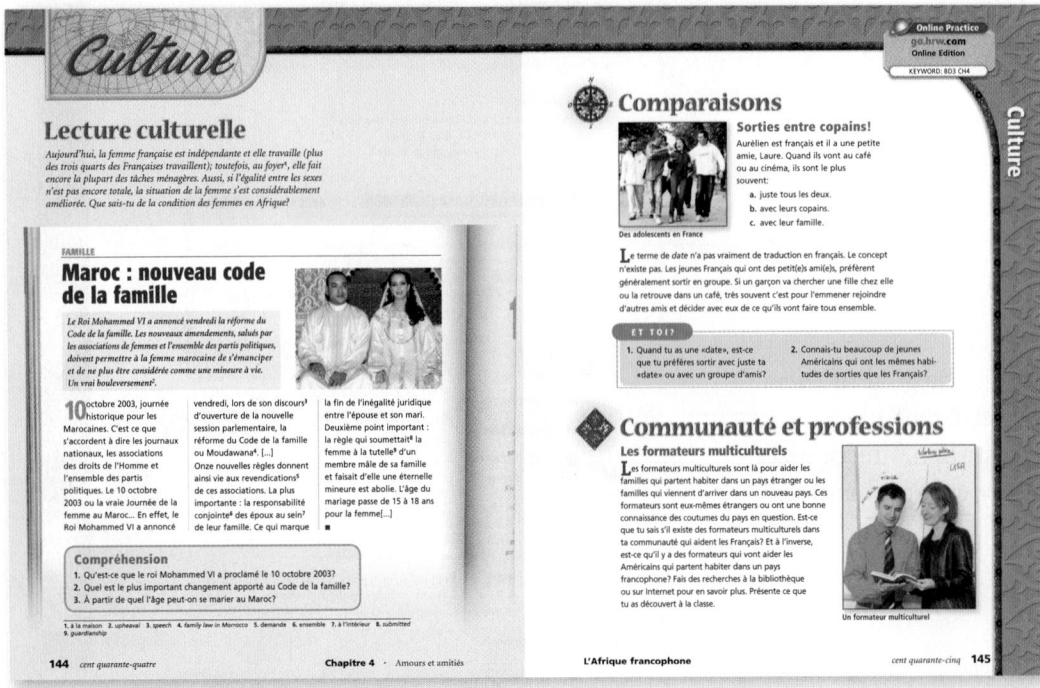

Culture engages students while they learn more about cultural products and practices in the French-speaking world.

Comparaisons challenges students to compare the culture studied with their own.

Communauté et professions asks students to think critically about career choices and their community.

Reading and writing practice build student comprehension and written communication

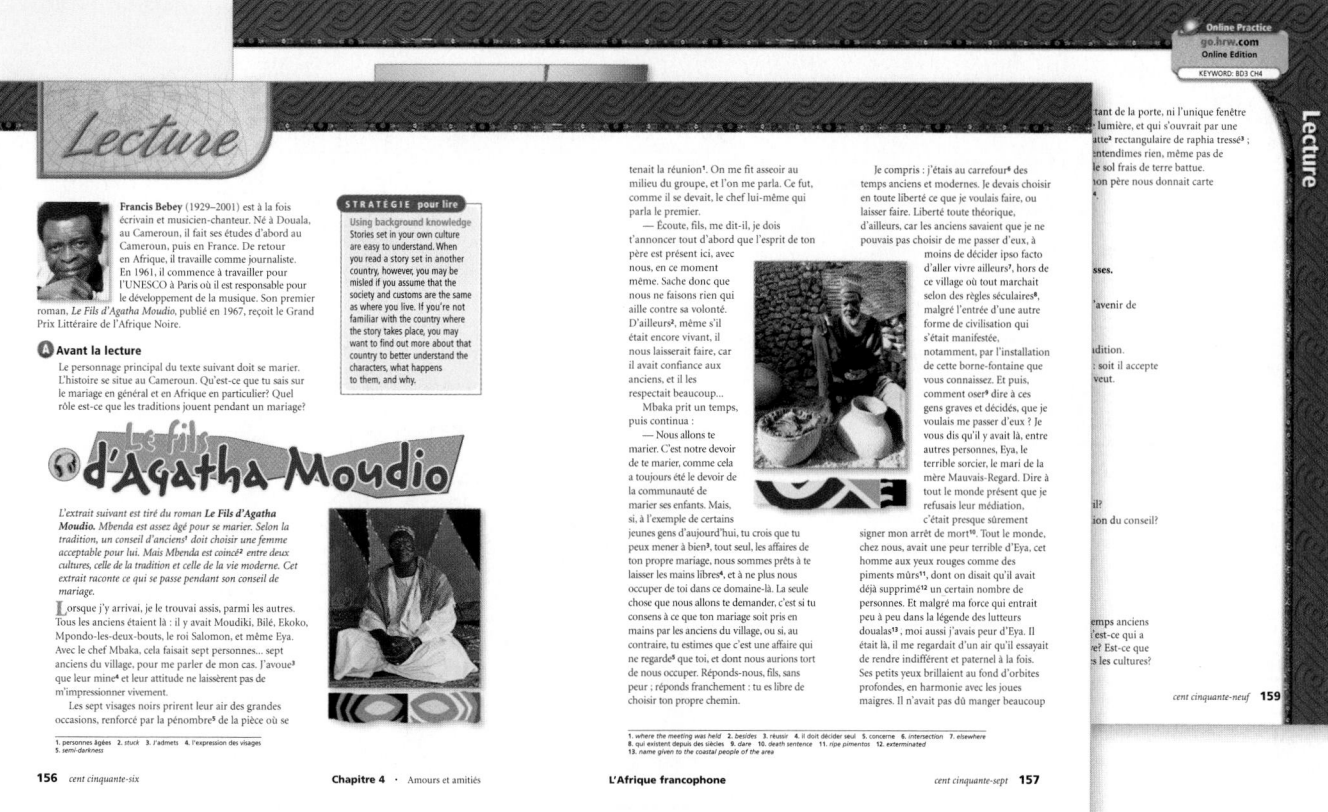

The *Lecture* section provides students with readings from informational texts to literature. Every reading has a corresponding strategy and active reading questions to help students tackle reading confidently.

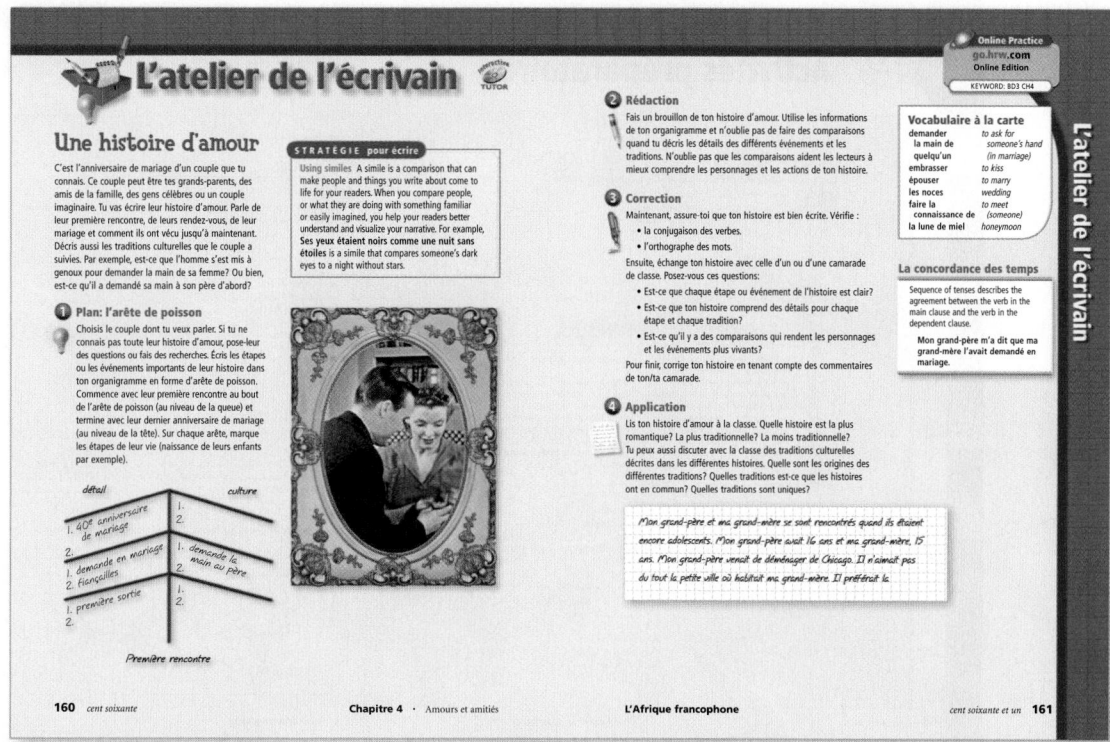

L'atelier de l'écrivain follows each reading section and steps students through the writing process, gradually building their writing skills in French.

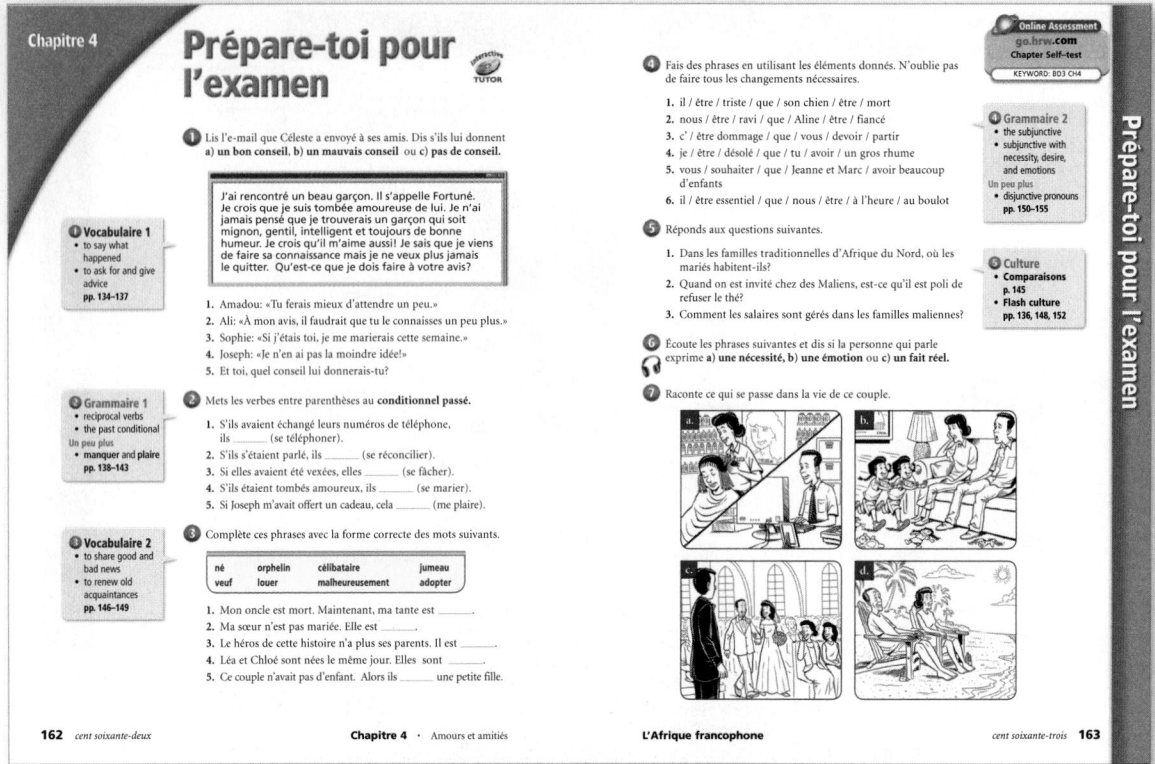

The ***Prépare-toi pour l'examen*** review section offers
discrete, chapter-specific practice with references back into
the chapter if students need further review.

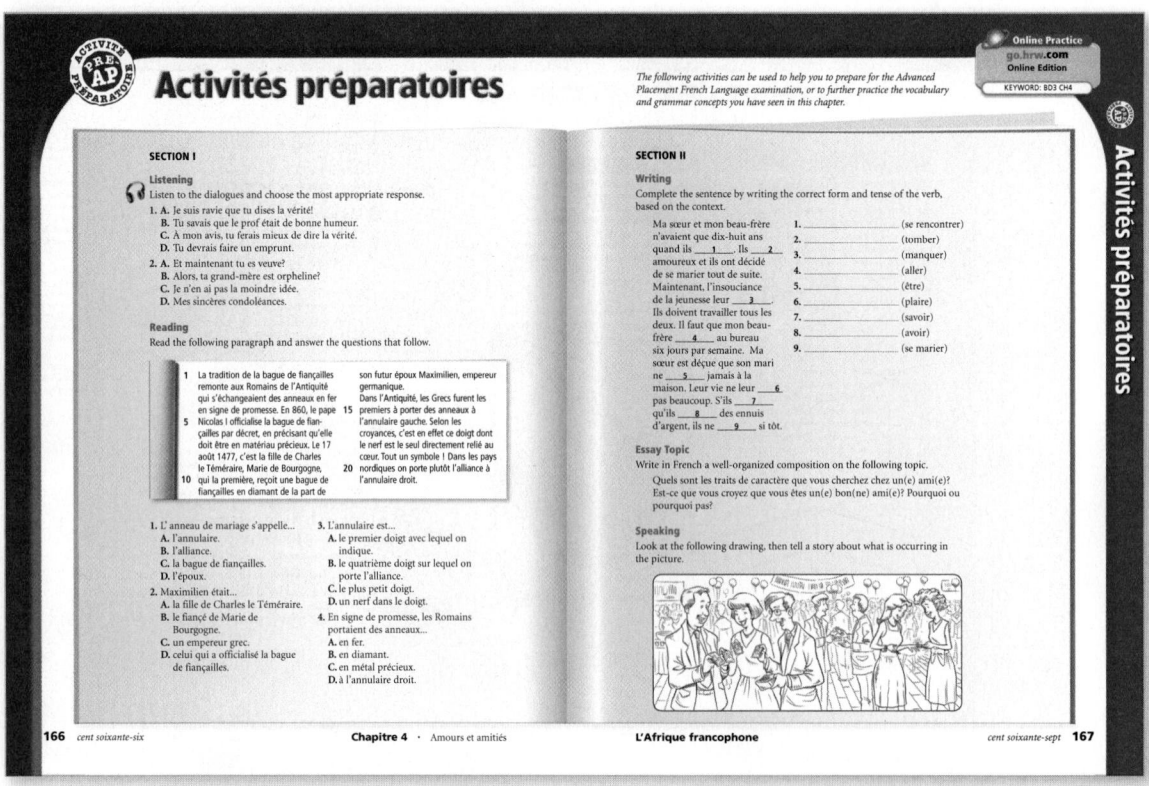

Activités préparatoires provide activities similar to those in
the Advanced Placement French Language Exam. The activities are
based on materials taught up to and including the current chapter.

Cumulative Review

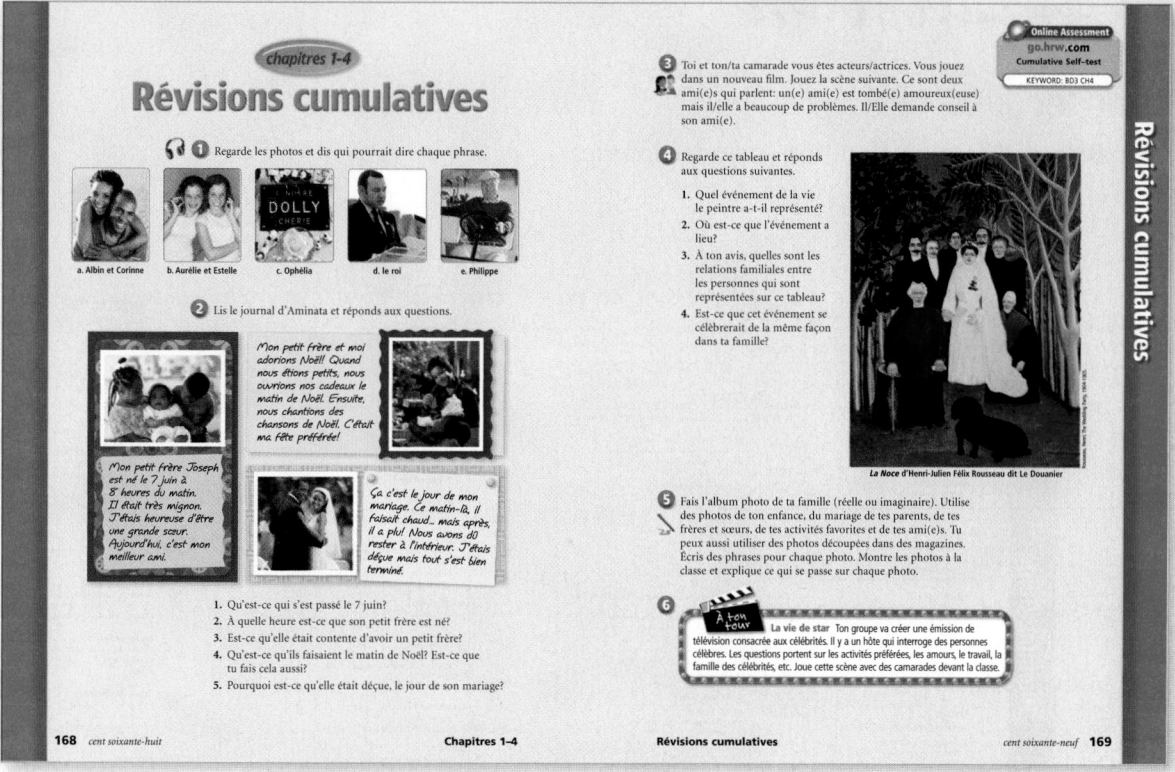

The **Révisions cumulatives** section provides students with **cumulative practice after every chapter.** Students are ready for a cumulative test at any time.

Additional Cultural Readings

Chroniques are inserted after every two chapters and provide students with a large variety of informative, cultural, and literary readings from around the Francophone world. Topics range from current events, sports, politics to art and history.

Teacher's Edition

Using the Chapter Interleaf

Each chapter of the *Bien dit!* Teacher's Edition includes interleaf pages to help you plan, teach, and expand your lessons.

Planning Guide
is a snapshot of the material presented, as well as the additional practice resources available. Pacing Suggestions list **Essential**, **Recommended**, and **Optional** sections.

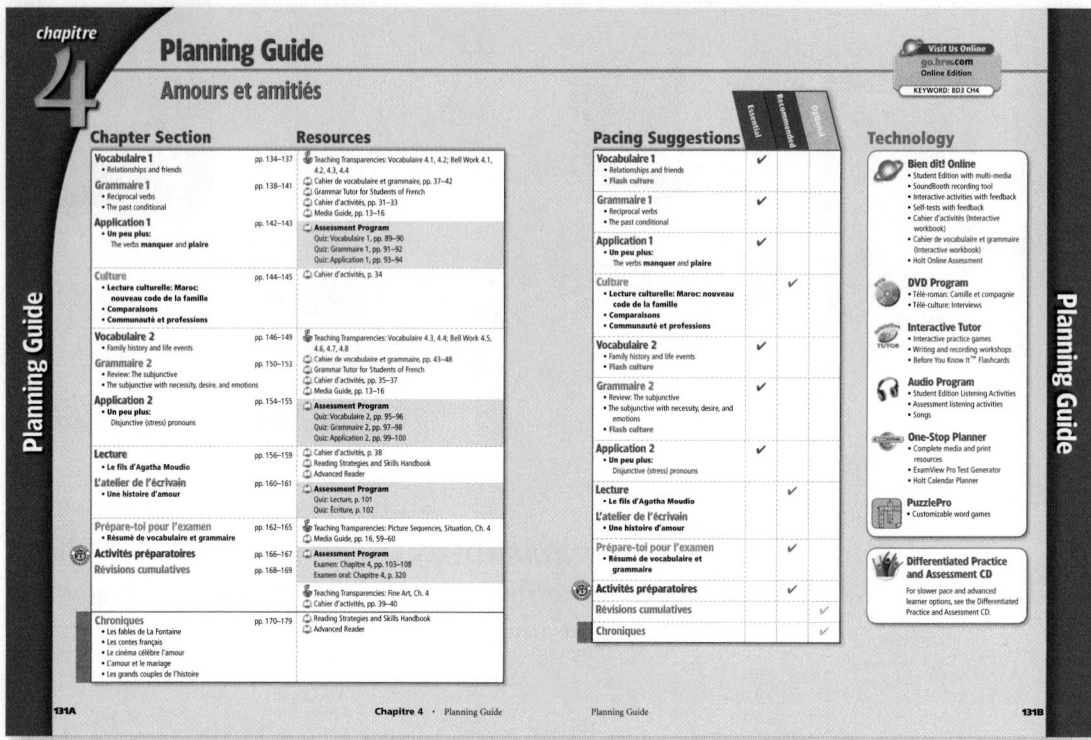

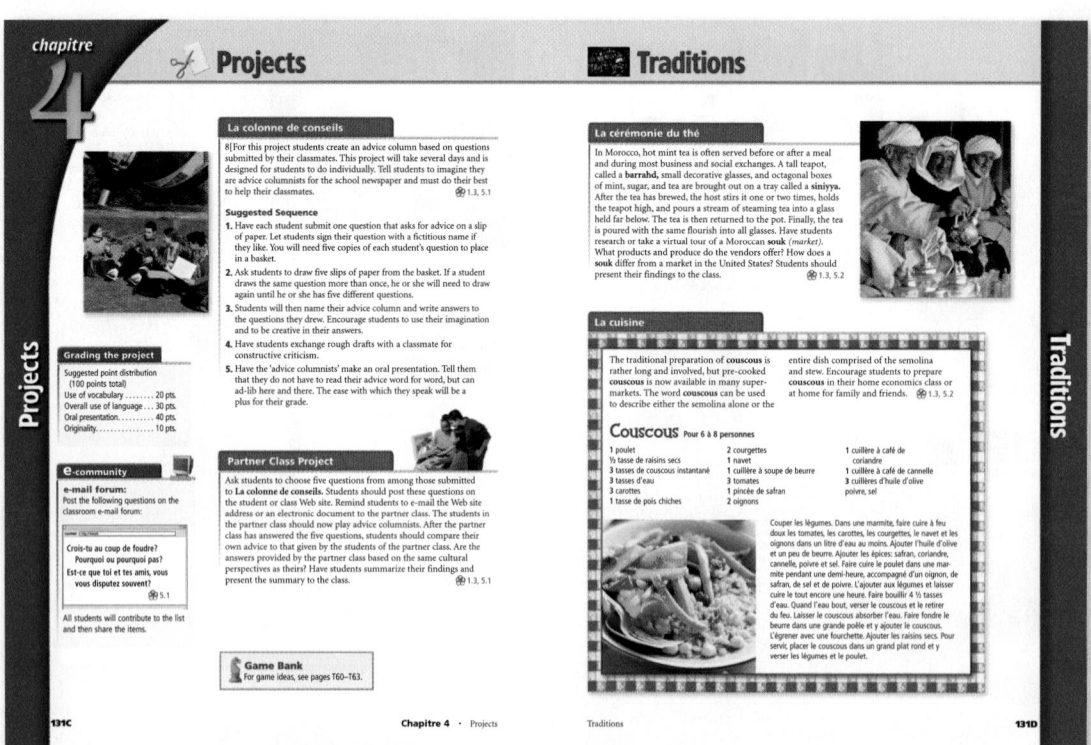

Projects and Traditions allow students to work at different levels to expand on the information in the chapter—individually, in pairs or groups, or with a partner class.

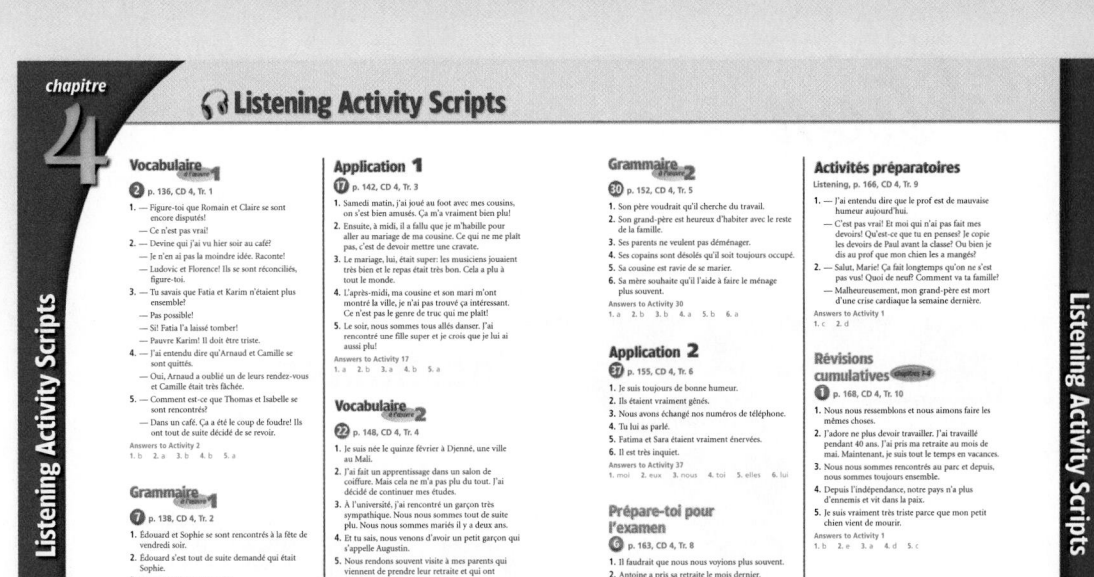

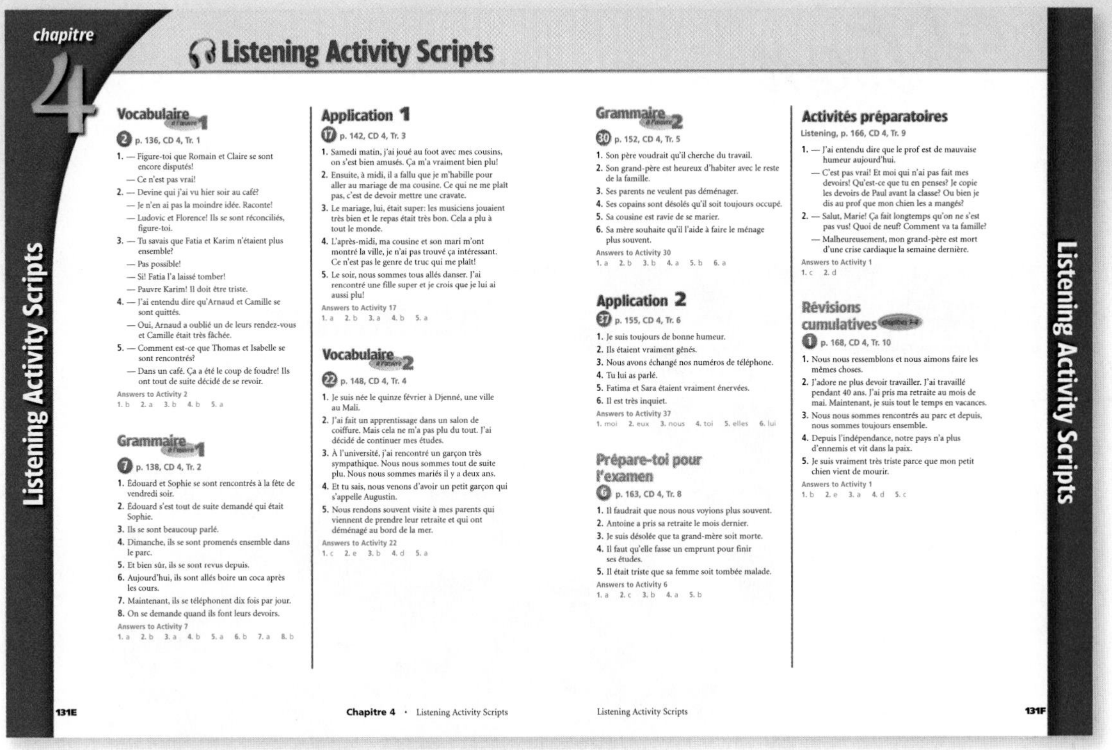

Listening Activity Scripts are placed at point of use throughout each chapter. In addition, all scripts and answers for listening activities are on these pages for easy reference. The activity masters for listening activities are in the *Media Guide*.

Ideas and suggestions for differentiated instruction are marked with the icons ▲ ◆ ●.

KEY

▲ Advanced Learners
◆ Slower Pace Learners
● Special Learning Needs

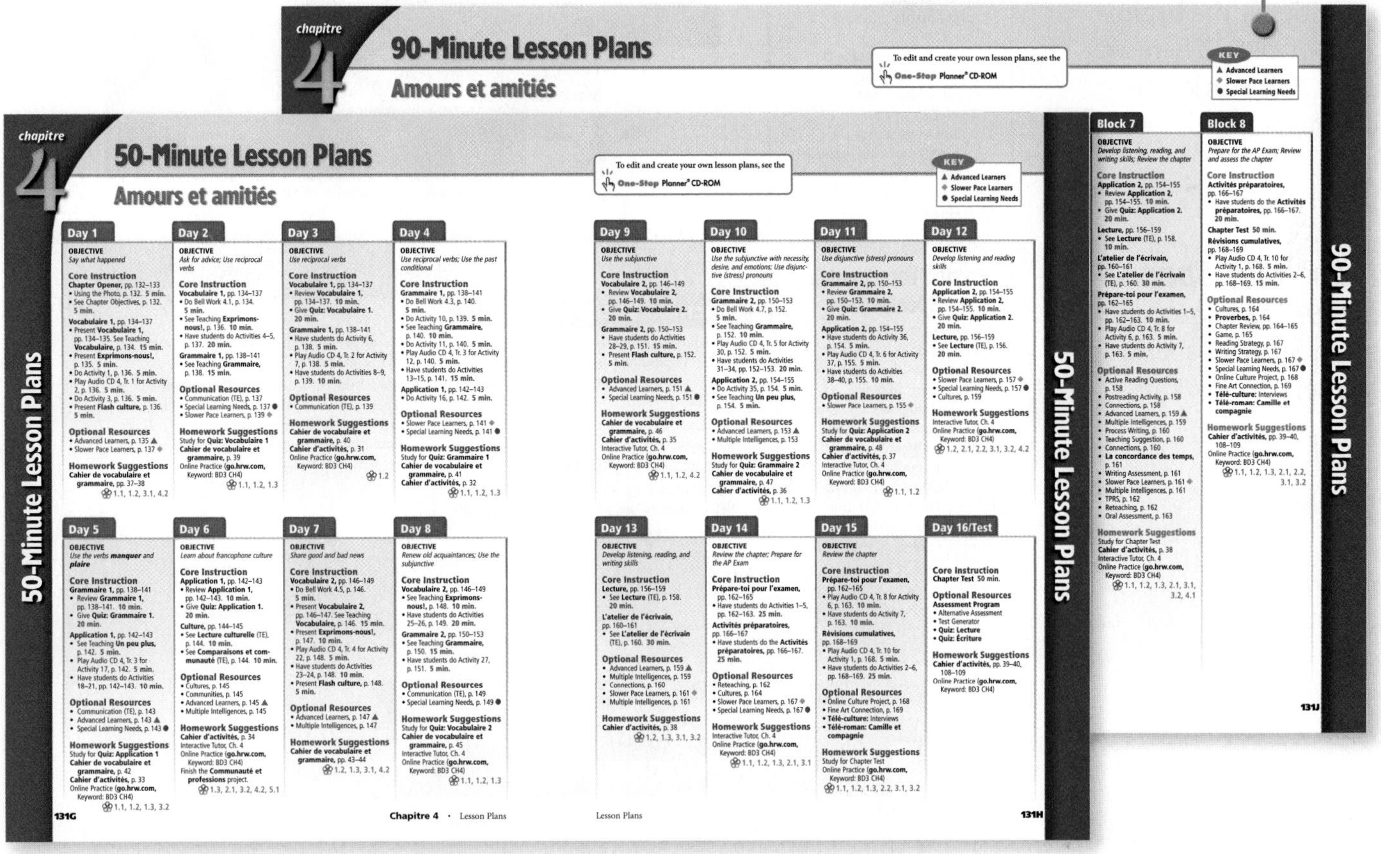

Suggested Lesson Plans provide a logical sequence of instruction along with suggestions for optional practice and homework. Both **50-minute** and **90-minute** block plans are provided.

Teacher's Edition *continued*

Using the Wrap-Around Teacher Text

Resources

Here you find a quick list of all resources available for each chapter section.

Bell Work transparencies can be used for warm-up activities at the beginning of class. There are eight Bell Work transparencies per chapter.

French for Spanish Speakers helps you reach Spanish-speaking learners.

Chapitre 5
Vocabulaire 1

Resources

Planning:
Lesson Planner
One-Stop Planner

Presentation:
Teaching Transparencies
Vocabulaire 5.1, 5.2

Practice:
Cahier de vocabulaire et grammaire

Differentiated Practice and Assessment CD-ROM

Media Guide
Teaching Transparencies
Bell Work 5.1

Interactive Tutor, Disc 1

Bell Work
Use Bell Work 5.1 in the *Teaching Transparencies* or write this activity on the board.
Réponds en remplaçant les mots soulignés avec un **pronom disjoint.**
1. Est-ce que Roméo est amoureux de Juliette? Oui, il...
2. Est-ce que tu as travaillé avec Nicolas? Non, je...
3. Ces chaussures sont à toi? Non, elles...
4. Pensez-vous souvent à Julie et à moi? Oui, nous...
5. Tu habites chez tes parents? Oui, j'... ✿1.2

French for Spanish Speakers
Ask Spanish speakers which animal names look or sound similar to Spanish names? **(aigle/águila, animaux sauvages/animales salvajes, espèces/especies, dauphin/delfín, corail/coral, abeille/abeja, baleine/ballena)** What other words are similar? **(liberté/libertad, mordre/morder, piquer/picar)** ✿4.1

186 *cent quatre-vingt-six*

Objectifs
• to express astonishment and fear
• to forbid and give warning

Vocabulaire à l'œuvre 1

Les animaux sauvages

un aigle · un castor · un loup · un orignal · un ours

Dans les parcs naturels du Québec, quand on a de la patience, on peut observer des animaux sauvages vivre en liberté.

un papillon · un alligator · un héron · une écrevisse

De nombreuses espèces vivent dans les bayous de Louisiane.

Core Instruction

TEACHING VOCABULAIRE

1. Introduce the vocabulary using transparencies **Vocabulaire 5.1** and **5.2**. Model the pronunciation of each noun, using **Ça c'est...** **(3 min.)**
2. Ask students to point to various animals on the transparency: **un ours, un papillon, un loup, un alligator, ...** **(3 min.)**
3. Ask students questions about their fears. **Est-ce que tu as peur des...? Est-ce que tu as peur que les... te piquent/mordent/mangent? (3 min.)**
4. Model the expressions in **Exprimons-nous!** Then have students react to everything you say, with either astonishment or fear. **Il n'y aura plus d'examens dans ce cours. Il y a un serpent sous ta chaise! (3 min.)**

Chapitre 5 · En pleine nature

Core Instruction

TEACHING VOCABULAIRE

Timed suggestions for each presentation in the chapter provide guidance to newer teachers and a quick reference for more experienced teachers.

Online Practice
go.hrw.com
Grammaire 2 practice
KEYWORD: BD3 CH8

Chapitre 8
Grammaire 2

28 Si ça arrivait 1.2

Écrivons/Parlons Qu'est-ce qui se passe dans les situations suivantes?

1. S'il y avait un incendie, les pompiers ______ .
2. J'appellerais la police si je ______ un voleur.
3. Si tu perdais tes papiers, il ______ les faire refaire.
4. S'il pouvait, il ______ fonctionnaire.
5. Si c'était un accident grave, on ______ les sirènes.

Entre copains

une contredance/ une prune	*fine*
un flic/un poulet	*policeman*
être en tôle	*to be in jail*
un rond-de-cuir	*civil servant*

29 Si j'avais une sœur... 1.2

Écrivons Reconstruis ces phrases en utilisant **le conditionnel**.

1. je / une sœur / si / avoir / parler / nous / nous / tous les jours
2. au / ensemble / aller / nous / centre commercial
3. en / emmener / parents / à la mer / nos / nous / vacances
4. un cadeau / lui / je / acheter / son / pour / anniversaire
5. voir / partout / nous / on / ensemble

30 On peut rêver, non? 1.2

Parlons Ces gens parlent de ce qu'ils feraient s'ils étaient riches. Regarde les illustrations et imagine ce qu'ils disent.

MODÈLE **Tu donnerais de l'argent à la Croix Rouge.**

tu

1. je

2. mes parents

3. nous

4. ma sœur

Communication

HOLT SoundBooth ONLINE RECORDING

31 Scénario 1.1

Parlons Demande à un(e) camarade tout ce qu'il/elle ferait s'il/si elle était un jour élu(e) président(e) des États-Unis. Puis dis-lui tout ce que tu ferais si tu étais élu(e).

MODÈLE **—Qu'est-ce que tu ferais si tu devenais président(e)?**

Grammaire 2

27 Script

See script on p. 311F.

28 Answers

1. viendraient
2. voyais
3. faudrait
4. serait
5. entendrait

29 Answers

1. Si j'avais une sœur, nous nous parlerions tous les jours.
2. Nous irions au centre commercial ensemble.
3. Nos parents nous emmèneraient en vacances à la mer.
4. Je lui achèterais un cadeau pour son anniversaire.
5. On nous verrait partout ensemble.

30 Possible Answers

1. J'achèterais une voiture de sport.
2. Mes parents feraient le tour du monde à voile.
3. Nous habiterions à la campagne.
4. Ma sœur voyagerait en Europe.

Answers at point of use are a quick reference for all *Student Edition* activities.

Communication

Group Activity: Interpersonal

Form small groups. Each student writes a sentence that includes a **si** clause with the **imparfait** and the **conditionnel**. Students take turns reading their **si** clause. The other group members each respond with a **si** clause of their own that either expands the possibility of the original statement or points out possible negative consequences of the hypothetical situation. 1.1

Communication

The activities suggested here focus on one of the three kinds of communication: **interpersonal, interpretive,** or **presentational.**

Differentiated Instruction

SLOWER PACE LEARNERS

Additional Practice Before introducing the forms of the conditional, tell students that the conditional tense indicates that an action is dependent on something else. Ask students to give examples of the present conditional in English. Then introduce the form of the conditional and ask students to give the French equivalents of the English examples they have just provided. 1.2, 4.1

SPECIAL LEARNING NEEDS

Students with Language Impairments When reviewing **Déjà vu!**, make sure that students with language challenges have understood the concept of forming a particular tense with the verb stem and its appropriate endings. Have students create several examples before you present the conditional. 1.2

COMMON ERROR ALERT
ATTENTION !

If students are not careful, they may confuse the **conditionnel** with the **futur,** since they use the same stems or the **conditionnel** with the **imparfait,** since they use the same endings.

COMMON ERROR ALERT
ATTENTION !

helps you alert students to errors they should watch for and avoid, such as false cognates.

Differentiated Instruction

suggests ways to address the diversity of any classroom. The suggestions on the left provide support for teaching advanced or slower-pace learners. Those on the right help accomodate students with special learning needs or reach learners through multiple intelligences.

Teacher's Edition

STUDENT *Resources*

Media

Marius
Côte d'Ivoire

Leisure time   School

Timer   Scoring
Min. Sec.   0   0   10
Correct Incorrect Remaining

Click the image that best matches what you hear.

DVD PROGRAM

- Comprehensive Video Program
- Video Activities

BIEN DIT! ONLINE EDITION

- Interactive Student Edition
- All Video and Audio Files at Point of Use
- Audio Recordings for all Vocabulary and Expressions
- Searchable Glossaries
- Self-Tests

INTERACTIVE TUTOR

- Chapter Practice Games with Video Support
- Writing and Recording Workshops
- Glossaries and Grammar Reference Tool
- Teacher Management System

HOLT SoundBooth

Interactive Tutor on CD-ROM

HOLT FRENCH 3

Bien dit!

HOLT, RINEHART AND WINSTON

SOUNDBOOTH ONLINE RECORDING TOOL

- Record, Save, Listen

WORKBOOKS ONLINE

- Interactive Self-correcting Activities

MP3

- Downloadable Audio and Video Files

MP3

MEDIA GUIDE

- Video Activities
- Response Forms for Listening Activities

Practice and Activities

CAHIER DE VOCABULAIRE ET GRAMMAIRE

- Presentations of Major Grammar Points
- Additional Practice Activities

CAHIER D'ACTIVITÉS

- Additional Reading and Writing Activities

GRAMMAR TUTOR

- Comparisons of Grammar Concepts in English and French

MORE PRACTICE ACTIVITIES ONLINE

- Additonal Interactive Activities for Every Chapter Section, Located at **go.hrw.com**

Reading

BEGINNING/INTERMEDIATE/ADVANCED READERS

- Illustrated Readings
- Scaffolded Reading Support Activities

READING STRATEGIES AND SKILLS HANDBOOK

- Reading Strategies
- Strategy Activity Masters

Student Resources

TEACHER *Resources*

Media

Télé-culture

Télé-roman

DVD Program

HOLT FRENCH 3

Bien dit!

VIDEO – DVD PROGRAM

- Animated Grammar Presentations
- Optional French and English Captions for All Segments
- Comprehension Activities
- **Télé-culture** Interviews
- *Camille et compagnie* **Télé-roman** soap opera
- Downloadable Files

ONE-STOP PLANNER WITH MEDIA AND PRINT RESOURCES

- All Resources in One Place

PUZZLEPRO®

- Interactive Crossword, Jumble, and Word Search Puzzles with Pre-loaded Vocabulary for All Chapters
- Instant Correction and Feedback

TEACHING TRANSPARENCIES

- Colorful Transparencies with Activity Suggestions for **Vocabulary and Grammar Practice**
- Bell Work Activities
- Fine Art Transparencies
- Picture Sequences Transparencies
- **Activités préparatoires** Transparencies

AUDIO PROGRAM

- Student Edition Listening Activities
- Assessment Program Listening Activities
- MP3 Formatted Files
- Songs

Assessment

ASSESSMENT PROGRAM

- Quizzes for All Chapter Sections
- Chapter Tests
- Speaking Tests
- Midterm and Final Exams
- Diagnostic Section
- Alternative Assessment Suggestions
- Rubrics, Portfolio Checklists, Evaluation Forms

INTERACTIVE TUTOR CD-ROM

- Teacher Management System for Evaluating Proficiency and More

EXAMVIEW PRO TEST GENERATOR, VERSION 5.0 WITH ASSESSMENT SUITE

- Pre-loaded, Customizable Assessment Items

DIFFERENTIATED INSTRUCTION/ ADDITIONAL PRACTICE

- **Cahier de vocabulaire et grammaire** for Advanced and Slower-Pace Students
- Assessment Program for Advanced and Slower-Pace Students

HOLT ONLINE ASSESSMENT

- Pre-loaded Quizzes, Tests, Midterm and Final Exams
- Online Grading
- Online Reporting

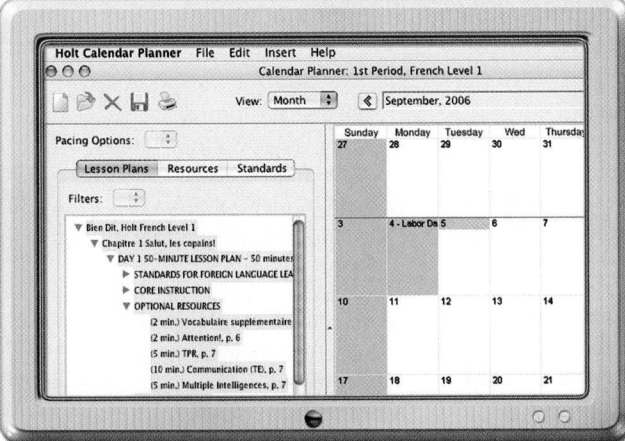

Calendar Planner

Géoculture video

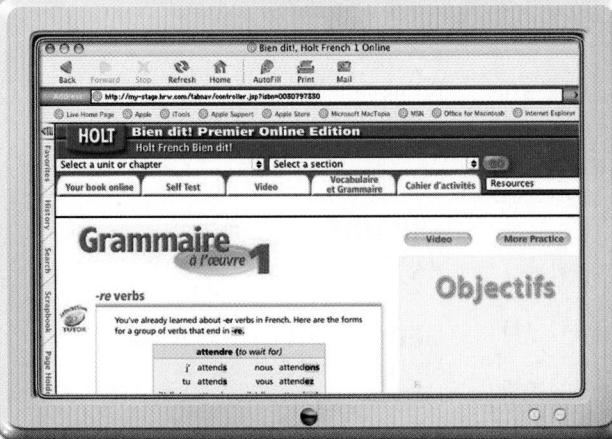

Bien dit! **Interactive Online Edition**

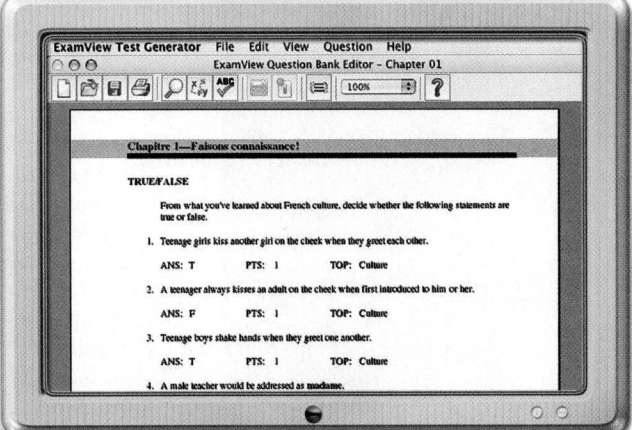

Editable tests and ExamView

One-Stop Planner

- One-Stop Planner Tools and Links
- ExamView® Pro Test Generator
- Interactive Teacher's Edition with Links to Print and Media Resources
- Links to Online Edition and Online Assessment
- Clip Art
- Calendar Planning Tool for Customized Lesson Plans
- Complete Video Program
- Complete Audio Program
- **Cahier de vocabulaire et grammaire**
  Teacher's Edition
- **Cahier d'activités**
  Teacher's Edition
- Assessment Program
  with Editable Tests
  and Quizzes

Teacher Resources

Cultural References

Page numbers referring to material in the Student Edition appear in regular type. For material located in the Teacher's Edition, page numbers appear in **boldface type**.

PRODUCTS AND ECONOMY

RECIPES

SCHOOL LIFE

SEASONS, WEATHER, AND TIME

SHOPPING

SOCIAL AND POLITICAL CUSTOMS

SPORTS AND FITNESS

TRADITIONS

TRANSPORTATION

Network, Promote, and Advocate to Increase French Enrollment

Margot M. Steinhart

Dr. Steinhart, President of the American Association of Teachers of French (AATF) and lecturer in French at Northwestern University, taught French in high school for many years. She is national task force co-chair of "Standards for the Learning of French" in Standards for Foreign Language Learning in the 21st Century.

Dear Colleague,

Dickens refers to the French Revolution in the opening line of *A Tale of Two Cities*: "It was the best of times; it was the worst of times." Hyperbole aside, this could describe the status of foreign language study in the United States. Between the publication of Paul Simon's *The Tongue-tied America: Confronting the Foreign Language Crisis* and Thomas Friedman's *The World is Flat,* Americans have grasped incrementally the need to communicate with the rest of the world. Still, only 43.6% of students in Grades 9–12 are enrolled in a foreign language class.

The gradual recognition of foreign languages as part of the core curriculum with national and state standards is a plus, but the commitment accorded foreign language study remains precarious and uneven across the 50 states, making language courses vulnerable to school boards' chopping blocks. In addition, while the Federal Government has identified critical languages to create or expand K–12 programs, French and other most commonly taught languages do not fall within the current definition of "critical languages."

The good news for us in the 21st century is that French remains strongly positioned. For reasons of history, literature, culture, and now globalization, French is identified with **la Francophonie,** comprised of 53 nations and governments on five continents. French stands as the most studied foreign language, after English, in the world. In fact, more people use French today than at any time in history.

I'd like to propose that as teachers of world languages and of French that we amass our resources both individually and collectively to maintain and to extend language programs K–12 and, ultimately, to increase enrollment in French classes. This strategy focuses on Networking, Promotion, and Advocacy.

In solidarity,

Margot M. Steinhart

Networking

Networking becomes an invaluable tool when teachers reach beyond the classroom and the school to find solutions to classroom challenges and to collaborate on lesson planning, curriculum development, and special projects. Professional organizations can help fill this role, not only through meetings and conferences, but through more formal mentoring structures. This can even take place on-line in chat rooms, e.g., FLTEACH and BABILLARD of the American Association of Teachers of French (AATF). By attending conferences, one learns about new resources, meets colleagues who want to share, and acquires ideas and materials for one's own classes. By joining professional foreign language organizations, especially those that reflect the interests of French teachers, opportunities become identifiable for scholarships to study in French-speaking countries, for workshops with a special focus, and for professional reading. The web sites for state, regional, and national foreign language associations, as well as those for Title VI National Language Resource Centers, <http://nflrc.msu.edu/>, organize workshops for teachers and offer valuable resources relating to foreign language acquisition.

Promotion

What we do every day with students constitutes promotion of French. It is the cumulative effect of the various initiatives undertaken that creates a reputation for our French program in the school and larger community. What is essential is that our community SEE evidence of that success and that French be taken outside of the classroom INTO the community.

Sometimes teachers create events, but they also take advantage of occasions announced in the school calendar. For example, an open house for incoming students or parent conferences provide opportunities to distribute promotional flyers and to highlight programs through photo displays, PowerPoint, or French promotional clips. When school or community events lend themselves to additional participation, consider how French students or Francophone Club members might be involved, e.g., presentations at meetings of community service clubs, or celebrations, like Homecoming or Mardi Gras.

National French Week (NFW) and **la Fête de la Francophonie** provide instances to celebrate everything French. Requesting a proclamation from the mayor and having it presented at a town meeting is a very public way to validate French studies. Having students present a program, teach a game or song, or introduce French expressions to students at a sending school in the district can attract prospective students. When recruiting students *per se* is discouraged, events planned to coincide with NFW may garner more administrative support. Whatever the event, it is important to invite school administrators and board members, counselors, and local officials. AATF, <www.frenchteachers.org>, has a plethora of ideas that French teachers have developed to promote French.

An effective promotional activity incorporates a learning component and can be linked to the national standards. Many teachers organize excursions to art exhibits and restaurants, trips to French-speaking countries, and immersion days with both instructional and promotional elements. Another way to connect French with the "Communities" standard is through service or fund-raising projects for international organizations like Doctors without Borders or the Red Cross. It is important to take the extra step to collect photographs and write articles for the local and school newspapers, for the parents' bulletins or the principal or headmaster's newsletter about students' experiences. Where available, the French program can be featured on the local cable station, if not the area public stations.

Students need reassurance that their study of French has value beyond their immediate studies or college admission. Incorporate a lesson on career opportunities, using some of the web resources, like <www.monster.com>. Make the connections for students in terms of where French is used and expressions that can enrich their speaking and writing in English.

Advocacy

Language advocacy frequently surfaces in response to a proposed or actual program reduction as a way to influence public policy or to redistribute financial resources. The reasons for such devastating announcements are frequently attributed to failed school referenda, budget cuts, other funding priorities, declining enrollment, teacher retirement, politics of a local school board member or community leader, a bias that language choice is not important or that another language is more useful, or no identified need for foreign languages in the region. Ideally, the French teacher has been networking and knows where to find resources, both people and materials, and has been building community support for the French program. This makes it harder to eliminate a visibly successful French program and easier to find support when the advocacy card needs to be played.

When any of the danger signs mentioned appear, the time is right to align a support team, engaging as many influential people in the community as possible. Parents and students can be very effective supporters, for they are important stakeholders in the decision. Over time, the French teacher should consider building and updating a data base of students who have completed the capstone French course and who can provide effective testimonials or be part of a letter writing campaign to save programs. In addition, professional organizations are poised to provide materials and to supply letters in support of French programs. The AATF web site provides a number of links to data that can be used to produce arguments and talking points for supporting French. State foreign language associations and the Joint National Committee for Languages and the National Council for Languages and International Studies (JNCL-NCLIS) can also provide tips, strategies, and sample models for directing an advocacy campaign.

Being an effective French teacher requires more than being a good teacher. It demands that we observe and research our community, that we identify resources, and that we develop the knowledge and skills to network, promote, and advocate for French. The efficient French teacher sees how to initiate and share responsibilities, for a strong French program benefits students, a whole community, and potentially, the world.

Professional Development

Holt, Rinehart and Winston is dedicated to enabling America's students to study world languages and culture. The educators who developed *Bien dit!* know that professional development begins with the instructional resources that teachers use every day. To that end, *Bien dit!* Teacher's Editions include:

Differentiated Instruction

ADVANCED LEARNERS
Bring several clothing catalogues to class and have students choose a page with an outfit that

SPECIAL LEARNING NEEDS
Students with Learning Disabilities/Dyslexia Students with learning disabilities

- Instructions for adapting activities to meet the needs of a diverse student population with a wide range of ability levels and interests

Meeting the National Standards

Communication
Communication, pp. 187, 189, 191, 193, 199, 201, 203, 205

- Specific suggestions for building the national standards into the instructional program

TPR
TOTAL PHYSICAL RESPONSE
Have students help you gather a variety of clothing items made of various fabrics. Ask individual students to respond to these commands.

- Instructions for using methods, such as TPR, that appeal to specific types of learners

Cahier d'activités

HOLT FRENCH 3

Bien dit!

This book contains:
- Reading and writing activities
- Puzzles
- Creative learning practice

ALSO AVAILABLE ONLINE!

- Ancillaries such as the *Cahier d'activités* help teachers learn to use reading strategies to help struggling readers become more effective readers.

The No Child Left Behind (NCLB) legislation considers foreign language a "core academic subject," which means foreign language teachers must be "highly qualified"; therefore states and districts can use their Title II teacher quality grant money on professional development and other initiatives to get their teachers, including foreign language teachers, to become highly qualified in their field.

ACTFL introduced policy directives to increase the international focus of the Department of Education. In response, the Fulbright-Hays Group Projects Abroad includes a request for seminars that develop and improve foreign language and area studies at elementary and secondary schools. Holt Speaker's Bureau Institutes can help local schools and districts increase their focus.

For the first time, the Title VI Undergraduate International Studies and Foreign Language competition has asked for projects that provide in-service training for K-12 teachers in foreign languages and international studies. Holt Professional Development courses can provide teachers with research-based, data-driven teacher education programs that are highly effective in improving performance.

Several Holt Professional Development Workshops are available for foreign language teachers.

Holt Professional Development Workshops

- **TPR Storytelling**

- **Teaching for Proficiency**

- **Culture in the World Languages Classroom**

- **Meeting the Needs of Diverse Learners and Students with Special Needs**

- **Assessment Options for World Languages**

- **Balancing the Four Skills and Culture**

- **The "What, Why, and How" of No Child Left Behind**

- **Teaching and Technology**

Implementing National Standards

Paul Sandrock
World Language Consultant, Wisconsin Department of Public Instruction Madison, Wisconsin

RESEARCH

National Standards in Foreign Language Education Project. (1999) *Standards for Foreign Language Learning in the 21st Century.* Lawrence, KS: Allen Press.

Phillips, June K., ed. (1999) *Foreign Language Standards: Linking Research, Theories, and Practice.* Lincolnwood, IL: National Textbook Company. (ACTFL Foreign Language Education Series)

Sandrock, Paul. (2002) *Planning Curriculum for Learning World Languages.* Madison, WI: Wisconsin Department of Public Instruction.

Shrum, Judith and Eileen Glisan. (2000) *Teacher's Handbook: Contextualized Language Instruction,* 2nd Edition. Heinle & Heinle.

Wiggins, Grant, and Jay McTighe. (1998) *Understanding by Design.* Alexandria, VA: Association for Supervision and Curriculum Development.

To implement the five goals of the national standards—communication, cultures, connections, comparisons, and communities—requires a shift from emphasizing the means to focusing on the ends.

Instead of simply planning a series of activities, today's world language teacher focuses on what and how the student is learning. Rather than teaching and testing the four skills of listening, speaking, reading, and writing in isolation, teachers need to make their instructional decisions based on the three purposes directing the communication (interpersonal, interpretive, and presentational) and within a cultural context. Our standards answer why we are teaching various components of language.

Since the publication of the standards, many states have developed more specific performance standards that provide evidence of the application of the national content standards, and teachers have carried the standards into the classroom. Textbook writers and materials providers are also responding to the shift brought about by the standards, providing an organization, creating a context, and modeling the kind of instruction that leads students to successfully demonstrate the communication strategies envisioned in our standards. Textbooks can bring authentic materials into the classroom, real cultural examples that avoid stereotypes, and a broader exposure to the variety of people who speak the language being studied. Standards provide the ends; teachers use textbooks and materials to help students practice the means.

Assessment is the jigsaw puzzle that shows students what they can do with their new language. If we only test students on the means of vocabulary and grammar, students simply collect random puzzle pieces. We have to test, and students have to practice, putting the pieces together in meaningful and purposeful ways. When they are truly communicating, students will know they've achieved the standards.

Communication Communicate in Languages Other Than English	**Standard 1.1 Interpersonal** Students engage in conversations, provide and obtain information, express feelings and emotions, and exchange opinions. **Standard 1.2 Interpretive** Students understand and interpret written and spoken language on a variety of topics. **Standard 1.3 Presentational** Students present information, concepts, and ideas to an audience of listeners or readers on a variety of topics.
Cultures Gain Knowledge and Understanding of Other Cultures	**Standard 2.1 Practices** Students demonstrate an understanding of the relationship between the practices and perspectives of the culture studied. **Standard 2.2 Products** Students demonstrate an understanding of the relationship between the products and perspectives of the culture studied.
Connections Connect with Other Disciplines and Acquire Information	**Standard 3.1 Across Disciplines** Students reinforce and further their knowledge of other disciplines through the foreign language. **Standard 3.2 Added Perspective** Students acquire information and recognize the distinctive viewpoints that are only available through the foreign language and its cultures.
Comparisons Develop Insight into the Nature of Language and Culture	**Standard 4.1 Language** Students demonstrate understanding of the nature of language through comparisons of the language studied and their own. **Standard 4.2 Culture** Students demonstrate understanding of the concept of culture through comparisons of the cultures studied and their own.
Communities Participate in Multilingual Communities at Home and Around the World.	**Standard 5.1 Practical Applications** Students use the language both within and beyond the school setting. **Standard 5.2 Personal Enrichment** Students show evidence of becoming life-long learners by using the language for personal enjoyment and enrichment.

Teaching Comprehension

Kylene Beers, PhD.
Clinical Associate Professor
University of Houston
Houston, Texas

RESEARCH

Baumann, J. 1984
"Effectiveness of a Direct Instruction Paradigm for Teaching Main Idea Comprehension." *Reading Research Quarterly,* 20: 93–108.

Beers, K. 2002.
When Kids Can't Read—What Teachers Can Do. Portsmouth: Heinemann.

Dole, J., Brown, K., and Trathen, W. 1996.
The Effects of Strategy Instruction on the Comprehension Performance of At-Risk Students," *Reading Research Quarterly,* 31: 62–89.

Duffy, G. 2002
"The Case for Direct Explanation of Strategies." *Comprehension Instruction: Research-Based Best Practices.* Eds. C. Block and M. Pressley. New York: Guilford Press. 28–41.

Pearson, P. D. 1984
"Direct Explicit Teaching of Reading Comprehension." *Comprehension Instruction: Perspectives and Suggestions.* Eds. G. Duffy, L. Roehler, and J. Mason. New York: Longman, 222–233

"Comprehension is both a product and a process, something that requires purposeful, strategic effort on the reader's part as he or she predicts, visualizes, clarifies, questions, connects, summarizes, and infers."

—Kylene Beers

When the Text is Tough

"Comprehension is only tough when you can't do it," explained the eleventh grader. I almost dismissed his words until I realized what truth they offered. We aren't aware of all the thinking we do to comprehend a text until faced with a difficult text. Then, all too clearly, we're aware of what words we don't understand, what syntax seems convoluted, what ideas are beyond our immediate grasp. As skilled readers, we know what to do; we slow our pace, re-read, ask questions, connect whatever we do understand to what we don't understand, summarize what we've read thus far, make inferences about what the author is saying. In short, we make that invisible act of comprehension visible as we consciously push our way through the difficult text. At those times, we realize that, indeed, comprehension is tough.

Reading Strategies for Struggling Readers

It's even tougher if you lack strategies that would help you through the difficult text. Many struggling readers believe they aren't successful readers because that's just the way things are (Beers, 2002); they believe successful readers know some secret that they haven't been told (Duffy, 2002). While we don't mean to keep comprehension a secret, at times we do. For instance, though we tell students to "re-read," we haven't shown them how to alter their reading. We tell them to "make inferences," or "make predictions," but we haven't taught them how to do such things. In other words, we tell them what to do, but don't show them how to do it, in spite of several decades of research showing the benefit of direct instruction in reading strategies to struggling readers. (Baumann, 1984; Pearson, P.D., 1984; Dole, et al., 1996; Beers, 2002).

Direct Instruction

Direct instruction means telling students what you are going to teach them, modeling it for them, providing assistance as they practice it, then letting them practice it on their own. It's not saying, "Visualize while you read," but, instead, explaining, "Today, I'm going to read this part aloud to you. I'm going to focus on seeing some of the action in my mind as I read. I'm going to stop occasionally and tell you what I'm seeing and what in the text helped me see that." When we directly teach comprehension strategies to students via modeling and repeated practice, we show students that good readers don't just get it. They work hard to get it. ***Bien dit!*** takes the secret out of comprehension as it provides teachers the support they need to reach struggling readers.

Differentiated Instruction

arol Ann omlinson
e University of irginia

Cindy Strickland
The University of Virginia

RESEARCH

Tomlinson, C., and Eidson, C. *Design for Differentiation: Curriculum for the Differentiated Classroom,* Grades 5–9. Alexandria, VA: Association for Supervision and Curriculum Development (in press).

Tomlinson, C. 2001. *How to Differentiate Instruction in Mixed-Ability Classrooms,* 2/e. Alexandria, VA: Association for Supervision and Curriculum Development

Tomlinson, C. and Allan, S. 2001. *Leadership for Differentiating Schools and Classrooms.* Alexandria, VA: Association for Supervision and Curriculum Development, 2000.

Winebrenner, S. 1996. *Teaching Kids with Learning Difficulties in the Regular Classroom.* Minneapolis, MN: Free Spirit, 1996.

Teachers who differentiate their instruction recognize that students are at different points in their learning journeys, will grow at different rates, and will need different kinds and amounts of support to reach their goals.

Differentiation and Varied Approaches

Differentiated classrooms offer varied approaches to **content** (what students learn), **process** (how students go about making sense of essential knowledge and practicing essential skills), **product** (how students demonstrate what they have learned), and **learning environment** (the setting in which students learn). Differentiation is based on an ongoing diagnosis of student interest, learning profile, and readiness.

Differentiation and the World Language Teacher

World language teachers are natural differentiators for learning profile. We provide opportunities for students to acquire proficiency in the target language through a variety of means: speaking, listening, writing, and reading. Through this variety of approaches, we recognize that students' proficiency in each of these skill areas will vary. Good language teachers work hard to help students improve in areas in which they struggle, and revel in areas of strength.

Systematic differentiation for readiness provides many world language teachers with a bit more of a challenge. Students come to us with a huge range in amount and type of language experience, including, for example, first-year students who have had no exposure to the target language, who have had an exploratory class, who have studied another target language, or who are native speakers.

Key Principles of Differentiated Instruction

There are several key principles to follow when differentiating instruction in the language classroom. First, start by clearly defining what is most essential for students to know, understand, and be able to do in the target language. Second, hold high expectations for all students and make sure that they are engaged in **respectful work.** Third, use **flexible grouping,** an excellent tool to ensure that all students learn to work independently, cooperatively and collaboratively in a variety of settings and with a variety of peers.

A final principle of differentiated instruction is **ongoing assessment.** To this end, the teacher constantly monitors student interest, learning profile, and readiness in order to adjust to the growing and changing learner. Teachers must not assume that a student will have the same readiness or interest in every unit of study or in every skill area. Preassessment is a must, particularly in the areas of knowledge and facility with vocabulary and grammatical constructions.

The Role of the Teacher in Academically Diverse Classrooms

Good teachers have always recognized that "one size fits all" instruction does not serve students well. To be effective, teachers must find ways consistently to **reach more kinds of learners more often**—by recognizing and responding to students' varied readiness levels, by honoring their diverse interests, and by understanding their preferences for how they learn information and practice new skills.

Technology and Foreign Language Instruction

Robert Ponterio,
Professor of French, SUNY Cortland

Jean W. LeLoup,
Professor of Spanish, SUNY Cortland

RESEARCH

Binkley, S. C. (2004). "Using digital video of native speakers to enhance listening comprehension and cultural competence." In Lomicka, L., & Cooke-Plagwitz, J., Eds. *Teaching with Technology*. Boston, MA: Heinle & Heinle; 115–120.

LeLoup, J. W. & Ponterio, R. (2003). *Second Language Acquisition and Technology: A Review of the Research*. ERIC Digest EDO-FL-03-11.

Omaggio Hadley, A. (2001). *Teaching Language in Context*. Boston, MA: Heinle & Heinle.

Phillips, J. K. (1998). "Changing teacher/learner roles in Standards-driven contexts." In Harper, J., Lively, M., & Williams, M., Eds. *The coming of age of the profession: Issues and emerging ideas for the teaching of foreign languages*. Boston, MA: Heinle & Heinle; 3–14.

Scott, V. M. (1996). *Rethinking foreign language writing*. Boston, MA: Heinle & Heinle.

Shrum, J. L., & Glisan, E. W. (2000). *Teacher's Handbook: Contextualized Language Instruction*. Boston, MA: Heinle & Heinle.

Standards for foreign language learning in the 21st century. (1999). Lawrence, KS: Allen Press, Inc.

Terry, R. M. (1998). Authentic tasks and materials for testing in the foreign language classroom. In Harper, J., Lively, M., & Williams, M., Eds. *The coming of age of the profession: Issues and emerging ideas for the teaching of foreign languages*. Boston, MA: Heinle & Heinle; 277–290.

$\mathbf{N}$ew technologies make it possible for foreign language teachers to bring the world into their classroom as never before and to make direct connections between their students and the speakers and culture of the target language.

From the World to the Classroom

Communication technologies are of prime interest to foreign language professionals because communication is the main thrust in foreign language teaching (Omaggio Hadley, 2001; Phillips, 1998). The present emphasis on using language, not just learning about language, calls for materials that prepare students for authentic communicative situations and lead them quickly to work with real information in the target language. In addition, the ready access to authentic materials, native speakers, and rich target language input that these new media can provide facilitates the creation of lessons that have tremendous potential in the foreign language classroom for directly addressing many of the goal areas of the national Standards for Foreign Language Learning (Shrum & Glisan, 2000).

The Standards, Cultural Knowledge, and Multimedia

The Standards stress the importance of cultural knowledge as an integral part of language learning; the tri-part examination of cultural products, practices and the perspectives underlying them is greatly enhanced by using Internet materials that help students better connect with different cultural realities (Standards, 1999). Multimedia—by mixing together realia, photos, video, and sounds from the native environment—contributes significantly to creating a culturally and linguistically authentic context for language learning. Multimedia visual materials also offer a window to nonlinguistic cues that are vital to second language comprehension and learning (Binkley, 2003).

Technology Is a Tool

Technology is a powerful tool when properly integrated in the curriculum (LeLoup & Ponterio, 2003). Computers, audio, and video are an adjunct to language learning objectives and not an end in themselves; they offer many benefits for expanding options in the instructional process. Access to the materials through Internet sites can significantly increase the time spent working with the language as well as the quality of homework activities. Electronic materials are easily updated for continued accuracy and adapted to correspond to current lesson topics and themes. Computer-based exercises that offer immediate feedback to the learner reflect a student-centered approach to language instruction that can help reinforce accuracy in the written language and provide for self-paced learning. For example, the use of hypertext allows an individual to find clarification of meaning or to examine an idea in more depth by connecting to additional materials beyond the text. It puts the power to control this exploration squarely in the student's hands. Current writing tools, both assisted writing environments and word processors, help develop the skills needed for communication in the real world (Scott, 1996). Finally, because of its flexibility and ease of use, technology provides the optimal vehicle for creating authentic assessments, which parallels the use of authentic materials and complements a proficiency-based orientation (Terry, 1998).

Classroom Management

Nancy Humbach
*Associate Professor,
Miami University*

RESEARCH

Cangelosi, James (1997). *Classroom Management Strategies: Gaining and Maintaining Students' Cooperation.* New York: Addison Wesley Longman. Third Edition.

Danforth, Scot and Joseph R. Boyle (2000). *Cases in Behavior Management.* Upper Saddle River: Pearson Education (Merrill Prentice Hall).

McEwan Landau, Barbara (2004). *The Art of Classroom Management: Building Equitable Learning Communities.* Pearson Education (Merrill Prentice Hall).

McEwan, Barbara (2000). *The Art of-Classroom Management: Effective Practices for Buiding Equitable Learning Communities.* Upper Saddle River: Pearson Education (Merrill Prentice Hall).

Palmer, Parker (1998). *The Courage to Teach: Exploring the Inner Landscape of a Teacher's Life.* San Francisco: Jossey-Bass Publishers.

Schmuck, Richard A. and Patricia A. Schmuck (2001). *Group Processes in the Classroom.* Boston: McGraw Hill. Eighth Edition.

Shrum, Judith and Eileen Glisan. *Teachers' Handbook: Contextualized Language Instruction.* Boston: Heinle and Heinle. Any edition.

Successful classes are created by teachers who are motivated, have high expectations, demonstrate enthusiasm for their students and for content, and who maintain organization, flexibility, and the ability to mediate.

Managing Your Class Successfully

Managing the classroom so that students stay on task, understand the concepts being taught, and have their needs addressed is one of the most daunting challenges facing a teacher. The beginning of the year is the best time to let students know what you expect of them and what they can expect of you. Inform students what they will need to bring to class and discuss with them required behaviors, such as respect for others. For more effective participation, allow students to brainstorm behaviors that would help them learn.

Present your expectations in writing and on your Web site, if you have one, keeping rules and regulations simple and clear. State them in positive terms, such as "Come to class with textbook, paper, etc.," instead of "Don't come to class without…"

Plans and Organization

To keep your class running smoothly, create lesson plans that have a variety of activities, plans for transitions between activities, a varied pace, and attention to time-on-task. Effective lesson plans take into account the ability level of the students. They present a challenge that is within reach of the students but holds their interest, and they include advance organizers, presentations, checks, and evaluations.

Begin class on a positive note by having an activity (some type of advance organizer) on the board, the overhead, or on paper. Such an activity will allow you to take attendance and check homework and still be ready to begin class as the bell rings.

Task-based activities enlist the creativity of students and may be done either alone, in pairs, or in groups. Problem-solving tasks with time limits allow students to be involved actively in learning, as do those that require students to discover solutions or outcomes.

Pair and Group Work

Group work is important in a language class. If you plan well, train students to work in groups, and have a sound evaluation plan, group work can be rewarding and a highly productive part of the learning process. No matter how you establish your groups, the process of moving into groups must be rapid and cause as little disruption as possible. Systematic monitoring is essential for successful pair and group work, evaluation, and teacher feedback.

Be Prepared—But Stay Flexible

No two teaching situations are alike. What works for one teacher or one class may not work in all situations. However, motivation, preparation, interest in the students and in the content, and sensible ground rules for such things as pair and group work can help you maintain a successful class.

Game Bank

Loto!

This game, played much like Bingo, lets students practice numbers, colors, body parts, clothing, or other objects in French.

Materials Index cards (or paper) and markers

Procedure Students prepare their own **Loto!** card by drawing a card similar to a Bingo card with five horizontal and vertical spaces. Students write a number, color a square a certain color, or draw a body part, piece of clothing, or other object in each space. Read a number or one of the other themed vocabulary words in French and record it. Students cover or cross off the spaces as the items in them are called until a player has filled an entire row or column. He or she then says **Loto!** The student who reads the vocabulary back correctly wins. You may laminate the cards for later use with water-based markers, or use paper scraps to cover the numbers.

\multicolumn{5}{c}{LOTO}
12	18	41	47	66
7	26	39	54	70
6	27	LIBRE	49	63
5	23	35	58	73
3	30	36	52	75

Cerveau

This game, played like Concentration®, helps students learn and review through concentration and recall. This game can be used to reinforce vocabulary, questions and answers, and verbs.

Materials Index cards

Procedure Have students make three pairs of cards. On a card have them write a question, a verb, or another vocabulary word. On the card's mate, the student writes the answer to the question, draws the action of the verb, or draws the vocabulary item. Divide the class into pairs or small groups. Have one student combine and shuffle all the group's cards together and then lay them out in a grid on the desk, blank side up. Players take turns turning over two cards each. If they match, the player takes them. If they don't, they are returned, face down, to their original place. Play continues until all the cards are paired. The player with the most matches wins.

Ils aiment manger de la pizza.

Catégories

This game is patterned after the game Scattergories®. It should be played in teams and is good for reinforcing vocabulary from various categories.

Materials A timer, index cards, and pencils and paper for scoring

Procedure Make index cards with the letters of the alphabet on them. Write a list of three categories on the board that the class has learned: classes, school supplies, names, descriptive adjectives or other themed vocabulary. Have teams prepare a paper with three columns, one for each category. One team chooses a letter from the stack of index cards and calls out the letter to be used in this round. The timer is set for one minute and the round begins. For each category, teams quickly fill in the answer sheet with vocabulary words that begin with the key letter. When the timer rings, students must stop writing. Have one team read its answers. If any other team has that word, everyone crosses it off their list. The next team reads any words remaining on their lists, and again any duplicates are crossed off all lists. Repeat this process for the remaining teams. The winning team is the one with the highest number of unique, unduplicated words.

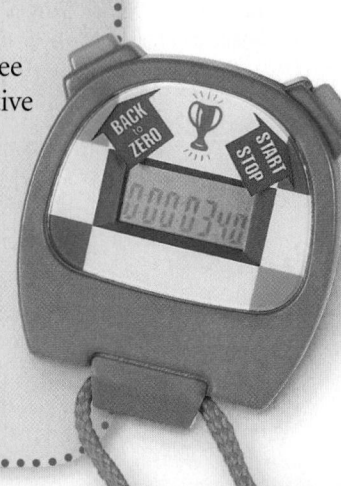

Scrabble®

Similar to Scrabble®, this game is excellent for review of all learned vocabulary and verbs.

Materials Heavy paper or card stock.

Procedure Cut the paper into one-inch squares. Leave a third of them blank and write the French alphabet on the rest. Make extra squares with the most common letters: vowels, s, t, etc. A blank may serve as any letter. Place the letters face down in one pile and the blanks in another pile. Each student picks ten letters and five blanks. Using learned vocabulary, students arrange letters and blanks to form as many words as possible on their desk. The student with the most words, and the student with the longest word, are the winners. This game may be played in pairs with students taking turns and building their words off of the already played words on the desk.

Charade

Played like charades, this game reviews active verbs. It is an excellent activity for kinesthetic learners.

Materials Index cards

Procedure Write action verbs or phrases from chapter themes on index cards, (things you like to do, school activities, preparing for a party, preparing and serving food, staying healthy, or vacation activities). Divide the class into teams and give one card to each student. Taking turns, students act out their word or phrase without speaking, while the other team guesses in French. You may consider limiting the time that each team has to guess. As a challenge, have the teams combine a number of students' cards to create sentences, assigning nouns and other necessary parts of speech to individuals. The team acts out its string of words while the other team tries to figure out the sentence that is being presented.

faire de la musculation

aller au ciné

jouer à des jeux vidéo

La patate chaude

This exciting game quickly practices vocabulary and phrases while getting the entire class involved.

Materials A small box, a wind-up timer or battery-operated alarm clock

Procedure Make a **patate chaude** by placing an alarm clock or a timer in a small box. Be sure the alarm or timer ticks loudly. Have students sit in a circle. Call out a category based on a vocabulary category, (**fruits, le petit-déjeuner,** etc.). As you name the category, hand the **patate** to a student who must then say a related vocabulary word. After saying a word, that student then passes the **patate** to the student to the right, who is to name a different item from the category. If a student is left holding the **patate** when the timer goes off, he or she is out of the game. You decide when a category has been exhausted and change it accordingly. The winner is the last student remaining who could think of a new vocabulary word, and pass the **patate** on without getting caught by the buzzer.

Lettres dans le désordre

This game is good for tactile learners. The goal is for students to construct French vocabulary words from scrambled letters.

Materials Small squares of paper for each student

Procedure Divide the class into two teams. Each person on the team finds a different French vocabulary word from the chapter and writes each letter of that word on one of the pieces of paper. After everyone is finished, team members exchange their letters with a person on the other team. Students quickly try to arrange the letters to form the word. The student who unscrambles a word before his or her counterpart wins a point for his or her team.

Un mot de plus

This game helps students build on words and ideas to make complete sentences. The sentences can be odd or funny, but they should be grammatically correct.

Procedure Create any number of teams. Begin a sentence on the board with a word. For example, (**Mon**). Have one player write a word to continue the sentence, (**frère**). The next team's player writes another word, (**a**). Once the sentence becomes complicated, students may add words before or after others. For example, **petit** could go between **mon** and **frère**. Players score one point for each logical contribution.

Mon frère a...

Dessine-le!

This game provides a thorough review of nouns, verbs, and adjectives and creates team spirit within the class.

Materials Index cards and colored markers

Procedure Divide the class into five equal groups of students. Each group selects 10 vocabulary items from a chapter or various chapters already learned and writes one vocabulary word on each card. A more challenging version can be played with phrases or short sentences. Combine all cards from each group and shuffle. Divide the class into two teams. You will need one scorekeeper and one timekeeper. Give the first team a card with the French word written on it. That team member goes to the board and must illustrate the word within 15 seconds. The next three people in line from that person's team are allowed one guess each. If one of the three people guesses correctly, the team scores a point. If they cannot guess, the question goes to the next person on the other team. The other team is allowed only one guess. If the student shown the card does not know what the French désord means, the team defaults its turn, and the opportunity to play the word goes to the other team. *Dessine-le!* can be played by the whole class, or a small group, for vocabulary review.

Mon anniversaire est le 13 septembre.

D'une syllabe à un mot

This game provides an opportunity to practice pronunciation and can be used to review vocabulary from any chapter.

Materials Index cards and pens or markers

Procedure Review the definition of a syllable as a short unit of speech. Break up the vocabulary words from the chapter into syllables and have the students write each syllable on an index card using large letters. For example, make three cards for **por-ta-ble,** two cards for **ca-hier,** etc. Shuffle the cards and pass them out among students. Say **"D'une syllabe à un mot"**. Give the students a specific amount of time (one minute), to find other people with whom they can form a word. Tell students to call out **"Mot!"** when they have formed a word. The group must say their word in unison as you point to them. Collect all the index cards, shuffle them, and redistribute to play again.

Le base-ball avec des mots

With this game students will practice the new vocabulary words and expressions and review previously learned vocabulary.

Preparation Develop a list of questions whose answers require the students to use words and phrases from the current and previous chapters. (Examples: **Pour ne pas être stressé (e), je fais ____. Pour avoir de gros muscles, il faut faire ____. Tu dois dormir pour ne pas être ____. Avant de faire de l'exercice, il faut ____.**

Procedure Divide the class into two teams. Assign a student scorekeeper. Draw a baseball diamond with bases on the board. Set a number of innings for playing. The batter is the first player on Team A. You serve as the pitcher and ask the batter a question. If the batter gives a correct answer, he or she moves to first base. The scorekeeper places a mark on first base. If the batter cannot answer, he or she is out. You then ask a question of the second batter on Team A. If the second batter answers correctly, he or she goes to first base. If there is a player on first base, he or she advances to second base and the scorekeeper places a mark on second base. A team scores a run by advancing a player to home plate. Team A continues batting until it has three outs. Then Team B goes to bat. When Team B has three outs, the first inning is over. Teams get one point for each run, and the team with the most points wins.

Enchaînement

This game, which helps students review vocabulary, is good for auditory learners.

Procedure Have all students stand up. Announce a vocabulary theme, (school classes, clothing, household items, etc.). Say a sentence with one word from the theme. For example, **J'étudie les mathématiques à l'école.** The first student then repeats the sentence saying what you said and adding another word that follows the theme. **J'étudie les mathématiques et le français à l'école.** When someone says the "chain" incorrectly, he or she sits down. This sequence continues until no one can add any more words to the sentence. At this time you might select another theme. The winners are the last three students to be left standing.

Why Study French?
French Can Take You around the World!

Margot M. Steinhart, Ph.D.

Chers élèves,

Formidable! You have chosen to learn French, the most frequently studied world language after English, and are becoming a citizen of the world. Your sphere immediately expands to include 175 million French speakers in more than 50 countries and millions of people who have studied French on five continents. And did you know that about 2 million people speak French as a first language in the U.S.?

In addition to learning the language, you will discover the uniqueness of many cultures from around the world. You will have the opportunity to explore Quebec, the Caribbean, West and North Africa, Europe, and the Pacific Ocean islands, to name a few. It is remarkable that through one language, French, the richness of these diverse regions can be learned and experienced. You can connect to the Francophone world through e-mail correspondence or by travel and study experiences.

Did you select French because it is a language associated with renowned artists, literary giants, medical, scientific, and techno-logical break-through discoveries, and an enviable sense of style? French can also improve your English-language skills since French is more like English than is any other Romance language, such as Italian and Spanish. More than 30% of English vocabulary is derived from French. How many French expressions related to government, law, food, art, music, dance, cinema, literature,

Browse the flower market in Rennes. It's a visual delight!

Take the bullet train from Paris to Nice. It can be fun!

Buy souwère paintings by local artisans in markets all over Senegal.

xvi

architecture, fashion, or diplomacy do you already know: *coup d'état, bon appétit, faux pas, genre, à la mode, pas de deux, carte blanche,* and *déjà vu?*

As you plan your future, French can lead to fulfilling careers in many fields: manufacturing, finance, law, government, education, the sciences, journalism, advertising, telecommunications, tourism and hospitality. Your language skills will also benefit you in working with international agencies like the International Red Cross, UNESCO, the World Health Organization, and the International Olympic Committee. Did you know that the majority of U.S. exports are to countries having French as a national language? Exports to bilingual Canada alone are greater than the combined exports to all countries south of the United States. Approximately $1 billion in commercial transactions take place between the U.S. and France each day. In terms of emerging markets, French-speaking Africa occupies an area larger than the U.S.

You undoubtedly chose French for very personal reasons. Imagine yourself as a fluent speaker of the language, communicating in French with people all around the globe, being an international student in a French-speaking country, or attending the Cannes Film Festival. How about serving in the Peace Corps in a Sub-Saharan African country, working with **Médecins sans Frontières** *(Doctors Without Borders),* or negotiating a business deal for a multinational company?

As you continue your journey as a French speaker, and as you open doors to opportunities that become possible just because you have chosen to communicate in French, let me wish you **Bonne chance!** *(Good luck!).* May you enjoy the adventure that awaits you.

Bonne Continuation,

Margot M. Steinhart

Discover modern art at the MAMAC museum in Nice!

Meet French-speaking teens from around the world.

Ride the funicular in Quebec!

Stop at a crêperie in Paris for a tasty treat!

xvii

Le monde francophone
Welcome to the French-speaking World

Did you know that French is spoken not only in France but in many other countries in Europe (Belgium, Switzerland, Andorra and Monaco), North America (New England, Louisiana and Quebec province), Asia (Vietnam, Laos and Cambodia), and over twenty countries in Africa? French is also the official language of France's overseas territories like Martinique, Guadeloupe, French Guiana, and Reunion.

As you look at the map, what other places can you find where French is spoken? Can you imagine how French came to be spoken in these places?

La France

Saint-Pierre-et-Miquelon

QUÉBEC

NOUVELLE-ANGLETERRE

ÉTATS-UNIS

OCÉAN ATLANTIQUE

LOUISIANE

Antilles françaises

HAÏTI

Le Québec

OCÉAN PACIFIQUE

GUYANE FRANÇAISE

Polynésie française

La Louisiane

N
O · E
S

La Martinique

xviii

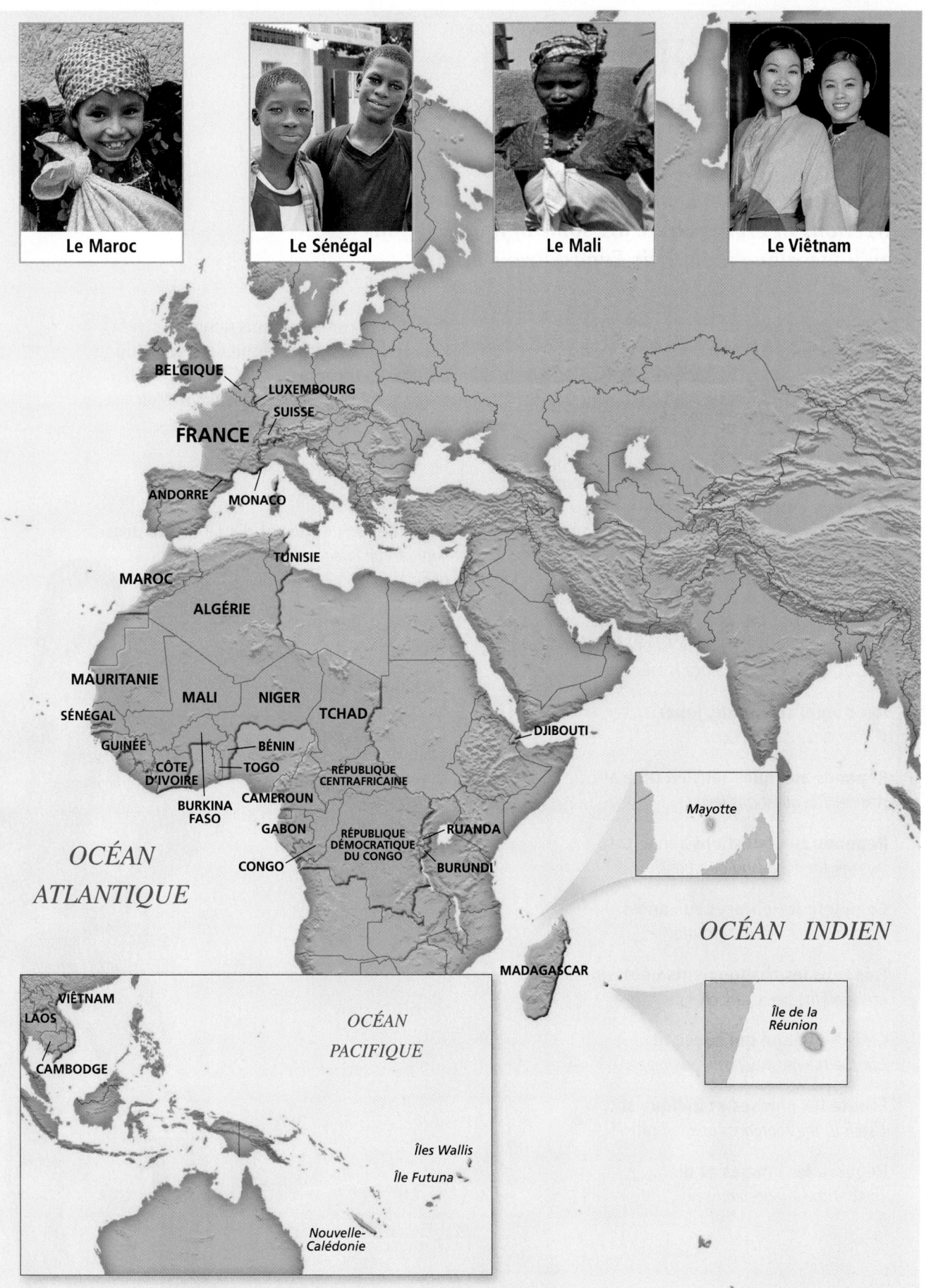

Le Maroc

Le Sénégal

Le Mali

Le Viêtnam

BELGIQUE

LUXEMBOURG

SUISSE

FRANCE

ANDORRE

MONACO

TUNISIE

MAROC

ALGÉRIE

MAURITANIE

MALI

NIGER

TCHAD

SÉNÉGAL

DJIBOUTI

GUINÉE

BÉNIN

CÔTE
D'IVOIRE

TOGO

RÉPUBLIQUE
CENTRAFRICAINE

BURKINA
FASO

CAMEROUN

GABON

RÉPUBLIQUE
DÉMOCRATIQUE
DU CONGO

RUANDA

CONGO

BURUNDI

OCÉAN

ATLANTIQUE

Mayotte

OCÉAN   INDIEN

MADAGASCAR

*Île de la
Réunion*

VIÊTNAM

LAOS

OCÉAN

PACIFIQUE

CAMBODGE

Îles Wallis

Île Futuna

*Nouvelle-
Calédonie*

xix

Instructions

Directions

Throughout the book, many activities will have directions in French. Here are some of the directions you'll see, along with their English translations.

Complète... avec un mot/une expression de la boîte.
Complete . . . with a word/expression from the box.

Complète le paragraphe avec...
Complete the paragraph with . . .

Complète les phrases avec la forme correcte du verbe entre parenthèses.
Complete the sentences with the correct form of the verb in parentheses.

D'après..., réponds aux questions suivantes par *vrai* ou *faux*. Si la phrase est fausse, corrige-la.
Based on . . ., respond to the following questions with true or false. If the sentence is false, correct it.

Avec un(e) camarade, jouez...
With a classmate, act out . . .

Réponds aux questions en utilisant...
Answer the questions using . . .

Réponds aux questions suivantes.
Answer the following questions.

Complète les phrases suivantes.
Complete the following sentences.

Fais tous les changements nécessaires.
Make all the necessary changes.

Choisis l'image qui convient.
Choose the most appropriate image.

Écoute les phrases et indique si...
Listen to the sentences and indicate if . . .

Regarde les images et dis...
Look at the images and say . . .

Écoute les conversations suivantes. Fais correspondre chaque conversation à l'image appropriée.
Listen to the following conversations. Match each conversation with the appropriate image.

En groupe de..., discutez...
In groups of . . ., discuss . . .

Regarde les images et dis ce qui se passe.
Look at the images and say what is happening.

Remets... en ordre.
Put . . . in order.

Demande à ton/ta camarade...
Ask your classmate . . .

Échangez les rôles.
Switch roles.

Directions

xx

Suggestions pour apprendre le français
Tips for learning French

Do you remember everything you learned last year? It's easy to forget your French when you don't use it for a while. Here are some tips to help you in French class this year.

Listen

When someone else is speaking, ask yourself what that person is saying. Listen for specific words or phrases that either support or do not support your guess. If you don't hear or understand a word, don't panic or give up. Try to figure out its meaning from the sentences that follow it.

Speak

Have you ever tried to say something in English, but then you forgot a certain word? Chances are you did not let that stop you. You simply thought of another way of saying the same thing. Use that same trick when speaking French.

With a classmate, practic short conversations on topics you learned about last year. If you can't remember how to say something in French, look in the glossary or ask someone, **"Comment dit-on...?"** You can also try using words you do know or gestures to explain what you mean.

Read

Sometimes you might feel anxious when you read in French because understanding the entire text seems to be an overwhelming task. One easy way to reduce this anxiety is to break the reading up into parts. With the reading divided into small sections, you can focus all your attention on one section at a time.

If you look up specific words or phrases in an English-French dictionary, be careful about choosing the meaning. Many words can have several different meanings in English or in French. Be sure to look closely at the context, if one is given, before choosing a word.

Write

Before you begin writing, organize your ideas. Write a sentence that states the main idea. Then choose the details that support it. List them in an order that makes sense to you. After you have listed all of your ideas, you can write about the ones that appeal to you most.

One way to make the task of writing easier is to make sure you know most of the words you will need to use. With a classmate, make a list of words you will probably need to complete your task. Then look up the words you don't know in the dictionary. Look at the charts in the back of this book to refresh your memory on important grammar points.

Learning a foreign language is like any other long-term project, such as getting into shape or taking up a new sport: it will take some time to see the results you want. Remember, knowing another language is a valuable asset, and you've already come a long way. Keep up your French and...

Bonne chance! (Good luck!)

xxi

Géoculture Overview

La France

Bienvenue! This section is designed to familiarize the students with the geographic location, history, and cultural practices of the region to be explored. It provides a guide for classroom discussion and discovery of the differences and similarities of the student's own culture and that of the French-speaking world.

Géoculture

50-Minute Lesson Plans

Day 1

Lesson Sequence
Géoculture: La France, pp. T72–1
- Ask students what they have read or heard about France. Have they or a family member visited France? What stereotypes do students have about France? Share experiences and thoughts.
  12 min.
- Go over the photos and captions with the students. **10 min.**
- See Map Activities, p. T72. **5 min.**
- Talk about geographic features on the map. Discuss the differences between the regions of France.
  9 min.
- Complete **Géo-quiz. 1 min.**
- Show **Géoculture** video. **3 min.**
- Have students answer **Questions,** p. 1. **10 min.**

Optional Resources
- Background Information, p. T72
- **Savais-tu que...?,** p. 1
- Thinking Critically, p. T71
- Research Online!, p. T71

Homework Suggestions
Online Practice (**go.hrw.com,** Keyword: BD3 CH1)
Interactive Tutor, Ch. 1 ❀1.3, 3.1

Day 2

Lesson Sequence
Géoculture: La France, pp. 2–3
- Briefly revisit main points about geography. **5 min.**
- Go over the photos and captions with the students. **8 min.**
- Ask students to choose a century and discuss what important event(s) happened in that century. **5 min.**
- Have students answer **As-tu compris?** questions, p. 2. **7 min.**
- Play the Map Game on p. T71. **25 min.**

Optional Resources
- Advanced Learners, p. T71 ▲
- Special Learning Needs, p. T71 ●
- Interdisciplinary Links, pp. 2–3
- **Prépare-toi pour le quiz,** p. T71
- Connections, p. 1
- Products and Perspectives, p. 1
- Practices and Perspectives, p. 3

Homework Suggestions
Activité, p. 3
Study for the **Géoculture** quiz.
   ❀1.1, 1.3, 2.1, 3.1, 3.2, 4.2, 5.2

90-Minute Lesson Plan

Block 1

Lesson Sequence
Géoculture: La France, pp. T72–3
- Ask students what they have heard or read about France. Have they or a family member visited France? What stereotypes do students have about France? Share experiences and thoughts.
  10 min.
- Go over the photos and captions with students. **20 min.**
- See Map Activities, p. T72. **5 min.**
- Talk about geographic features on the map. Discuss the differences between the regions of France.
  10 min.
- Complete **Géo-quiz. 1 min.**
- Show **Géoculture** video. **4 min.**
- Have students answer **Questions,** p. 1. **5 min.**
- Have students answer **As-tu compris?** questions, p. 2. **5 min.**
- Ask students if they have learned anything about France that surprised them. Why? **5 min.**
- Play the Map Game on p. T71. **25 min.**

Optional Resources
- Background Information, p. T72
- **Savais-tu que...?,** pp. T72, 1
- Advanced Learners, p. T71 ▲
- Special Learning Needs, p. T71 ●
- Thinking Critically, p. T71
- Research Online!, p. T71
- Interdisciplinary Links, pp. 2–3
- **Prépare-toi pour le quiz,** p. T71
- Connections, p. 1
- Products and Perspectives, p. 1
- Practices and Perspectives, p. 3

Homework Suggestions
Online Practice (**go.hrw.com,** Keyword: BD3 CH1)
Interactive Tutor, Ch. 1
Activité, p. 3
Study for the **Géoculture** quiz.
   ❀1.3, 2.2, 3.1, 4.2, 5.2

KEY

▲ **Advanced Learners**   ◆ **Slower Pace Learners**   ● **Special Learning Needs**

Differentiated Instruction

Advanced Learners

Challenge Have partners create a conversation in which they plan a five-day sightseeing tour in France. They may use the information presented in the **Géoculture** as a start and then look up specific information on the Internet about sights, accommodations, transportation, and restaurants. Have partners present their conversation to the class. ✿ 1.3, 3.1

Special Learning Needs

Students with Dyslexia Students with dyslexia may find it difficult to understand the text that accompanies each photo. Ask the class to scan each photo for visual clues. Then have volunteers read the text with emphasis on the terms that are most descriptive of the photo. The class should underline the stressed terms, asking for clarifications if necessary. Encourage students with dyslexia to use the underlined terms in a sentence to describe the corresponding photo. ✿ 1.1, 3.1

Thinking Critically

Analyzing France has four climatic zones: an oceanic, humid climate in the west, a semi-continental climate in the east and in the mountainous massifs, an intermediate climate in the north, and a Mediterranean climate in the south. Ask students to analyze the impact geographic location and climate have on the economy of a region and on the food and clothing of its inhabitants. ✿ 3.1

Quiz Preparation/Enrichment

Map Game

For this game you will need a large map of France and two pins with different-colored heads. Divide the class into two groups; each group has a pin with a different color. Both pins are placed on the map at Biarritz. When a group answers correctly a **Géoculture** question asked by the other group, it can move its pin from Biarritz to the closest city north. The groups take turns asking and answering questions. The group that reaches Lille first, wins. The questions should be limited to information that can be gleaned from the map and material covered in the **Géoculture** pages. If a group asks a question that it itself cannot answer, it has to move its pin one city back. **Bon voyage.**

Prépare-toi pour le quiz

1. Form groups of three to four students and have each group create a puzzle. They should glue a map of France on a piece of cardboard and cut the map into at least 20 pieces. Each group should put together the puzzle created by another group.

2. Have students work with a partner. One will name a city on the map and the other will describe it in two complete sentences.

3. Copy and attach the photos that illustrate the timeline on pp. 2–3 to a set of index cards. Write the dates introducing the captions on another set of cards. Ask students to match the photos with the appropriate dates. ✿ 1.3, 3.1

Research Online!

Les régions Ask students to imagine that they are travel agents. A client plans to take a trip to France and wants information about a French region. The travel agent researches the region and addresses climate and geographical features; sports and leisure activities offered; major historic sights; festivals and traditions. Students should document their sources by noting the names and the URLs of all the sites they consulted. ✿ 1.3, 3.1

Géoculture

Resources

Planning:

Lesson Planner

 One-Stop Planner

Presentation:

Teaching Transparencies
Cartes 1, 2, 3, 6

DVD Program, Disc 1
Géoculture

Practice:

Cahier d'activités

Media Guide

Interactive Tutor, Disc 1

Map ACTIVITIES

1. Have students look at the map of France and name the countries that border France. **(la Belgique, l'Allemagne, la Suisse, l'Italie, l'Espagne)** Then have them identify the four mountain ranges and four bodies of water that form part of France's borders. **(les Vosges, le Jura, les Alpes, les Pyrénées; la Mer du Nord, La Manche, l'Océan Atlantique, la Mer Méditerranée)**

2. Tell students that France was the first nation in Europe to become unified. Ask them how they think France's geography may have contributed to that. (France has definite boundaries, almost completely surrounded by water and high mountains. The definite boundaries kept some people in while keeping others out.)

DVD
Géoculture

Géoculture
La France

> **La Corse,** lieu de naissance de Napoléon Bonaparte, est une île située dans la mer Méditerranée. C'est un lieu touristique qui mérite son surnom d'«île de beauté». ❸

Les grottes de Lascaux sont parmi les sites préhistoriques les plus importants d'Europe. On y trouve des dessins de taureaux, de chevaux et de cerfs qui datent de près de 17.000 ans. ❷

Avignon a été la capitale de l'Europe chrétienne au XIVe siècle. Les papes y ont résidé pendant près de 70 ans. Le palais des Papes est le plus important palais gothique du monde. ❶

Savais-tu que...?
On surnomme la France «l'Hexagone» parce qu'elle a six côtés.

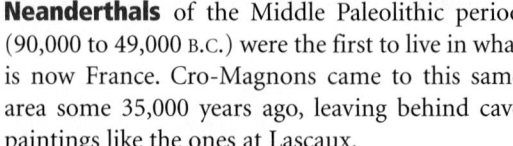

Background Information

Geography

France is almost twice the size of Colorado. Plains, low plateaus, and rolling hills make up two-thirds of the country. Mountainous areas lie primarily to the east and southeast, with the exception of the Pyrenees and the Massif Central. The highest point in France is the Mont Blanc at 4,807 meters. Rivers and streams criss-cross every region of France. The Seine is the most important river. The Loire is the longest. Three other major rivers, the Rhine, the Rhone, and the Garonne, are important sources of hydroelectricity.

History

Neanderthals of the Middle Paleolithic period (90,000 to 49,000 B.C.) were the first to live in what is now France. Cro-Magnons came to this same area some 35,000 years ago, leaving behind cave paintings like the ones at Lascaux.

Napoleon ruled France from 1799 until 1815. During his rule, he proclaimed himself emperor of France and, through a series of wars, gained control over most of Europe. He was finally overthrown after his defeat to the English at Waterloo. He died in exile in 1821.

VIDEO OPTION

▶ Géoculture

◀ **Annecy** se trouve dans les Alpes, au bord du lac d'Annecy. C'est de là que partent certaines expéditions pour le Mont-Blanc, la montagne la plus haute d'Europe de l'ouest. **4**

▲ **Strasbourg** est passée de la France à l'Allemagne plusieurs fois au cours de son histoire. La culture, la cuisine et l'architecture de la ville reflètent les influences de ces deux pays. Aujourd'hui, c'est le siège du Parlement européen. **5**

▲ **Lyon** se trouve au carrefour de régions riches en produits agricoles. Cette ville est réputée pour sa gastronomie. **6**

▲ **À Poitiers,** le Futuroscope est un parc qui présente des spectacles et des expositions futuristes, comme par exemple des voyages simulés et des films en trois dimensions. **7**

◀ **Biarritz** est le rendez-vous des amateurs de surf en Europe. **8**

Géo-quiz Strasbourg ✿3.1
Quelle ville française a été influencée par la culture allemande?

Connections

Language Note

Strasbourg is the capital of Alsace, a region in eastern France that has its own local language, called Alsatian. Alsatian is an Allemannic dialect that closely resembles Swiss German with French influences. Since it has no official written form, spelling can vary widely from place to place. Pronunciation also varies throughout the region. Despite attempts by both the French and German governments to restrict or ban the use of Alsatian and impose their own language, the dialect has survived. It is used in everyday life by both young and old. Many street signs in Strasbourg appear in both French and Alsatian. Ask students how they think the people of Alsace have managed to preserve their language and why they have done so. You might also ask students if they can think of any region in the United States where the inhabitants have struggled to preserve a local language or dialect. ✿ 3.2, 4.2

Cultures

✿ Products and Perspectives

Lyon's culinary tradition owes much to the women cooks, or **mères,** who worked for middle-class families in the 19th century. Their delicious dishes became well known after men staying with these families while working on the Tour de France spread the word. The tradition is now carried on largely by men, such as the world famous chef Paul Bocuse, and by eateries called **bouchons.** Have students research Paul Bocuse and lyonnais cuisine.
✿2.2

Savais-tu que…?

- France is the most visited country in the world, with some 75 million tourists visiting in a given year.
- France, a world leader in the aerospace industry, is the headquarters of the European Space Agency.
- The French consume more cheese than anyone else in the world. They also produce more than 400 different varieties.
- The French national anthem, **La Marseillaise,** was written in Strasbourg in 1792. It was made popular by volunteer soldiers from Marseilles, marching off to war with Austria.

Questions ✿1.2

1. **D'où les expéditions partent-elles pour le Mont Blanc? (d'Annecy)**
2. **Qu'est-ce qu'on peut voir à Poitiers? (des expositions et des spectacles futuristes au Futuroscope)**
3. **Quel sport est-ce qu'on peut faire à Biarritz? (du surf)**
4. **Quel français célèbre est né en Corse? (Napoléon)**
5. **Pourquoi est-ce qu'Avignon a été une ville importante au XIV siècle? (Les papes y habitaient.)**

L'histoire
La France

Comparing and Contrasting

In August 1789, the **Déclaration des droits de l'homme et du citoyen** was released. This document, modeled after the United States Declaration of Independence, proclaimed the rights of all French citizens, including those of **liberté, égalité, fraternité,** a trio that became the motto of the revolution and continues to be France's motto today. Ask students if they know what the original motto of the United States was and what it is today. (**E pluribus unum**; In God We Trust). Then tell students that **E pluribus unum** means *from many, one* or *out of many, one.* Have them share their thoughts regarding the values represented by France's motto and the two mottos of the United States. How are the values similar? How are they different? ✿ 3.2, 4.2

As-tu compris?

You might ask the following questions to check comprehension of the **Géoculture.**
1. **Qu'est-ce qui s'est passé en 52 avant J.-C.? (Les Romains ont vaincu les Gaulois.)**
2. **Qu'est-ce qui a mené à la construction des grandes cathédrales? (un réveil réligieux dû en partie aux croisades)**
3. **Quelle a été une des contributions de François Ier à la France? (Il a introduit la Renaissance italienne.)**
4. **Qu'est-ce que le gouvernement révolutionnaire a fait en 1792 et 1793? (Il a aboli la monarchie et a guillotiné le roi Louis XVI et Marie-Antoinette.)**
5. **Qu'est-ce que les pays de l'Union Européenne ont en commun? (des réglementations politiques et économiques; l'euro)**
✿ 1.2

52 avant J.-C.–Ve s.
Jules César a mis fin à la résistance du chef gaulois Vercingétorix. Les Romains ont gouverné les Gaulois pendant cinq siècles. Ils ont construit de grandes villes et ils ont introduit un système juridique, les impôts, le christianisme et le latin.

1515–1547
À son retour des guerres d'Italie, le roi de France François Ier a introduit la Renaissance italienne en France. Il a invité des artistes italiens à décorer tous les châteaux royaux. Léonard de Vinci a même passé les dernières années de sa vie près du roi, à Amboise.

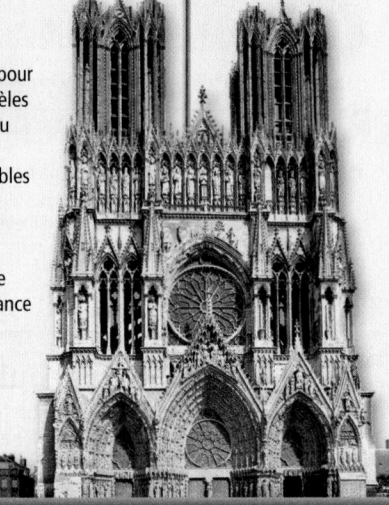

XIe s.–XIIIe s.
Les chrétiens de France sont partis en croisade pour faire la guerre aux infidèles à Jérusalem au milieu du XIe siècle. Les croisades sont en partie responsables du réveil religieux qui a mené à la construction de vastes cathédrales. La plus riche est celle de Reims où les rois de France étaient couronnés.

1793
Pendant la Révolution, en 1792, le gouvernement révolutionnaire a aboli la monarchie et a établi la première République. Sa devise était *liberté, égalité, fraternité*. En 1793, Louis XVI, roi de France, et sa femme Marie-Antoinette, ont été guillotinés.

TEACHING L'HISTOIRE

1. Have students look at the dates on the timeline. Then ask them to think about the history of western civilization over the past 2,000 years. Have them name the important civilizations, events, and accomplishments that they remember for this period. Ask how many of these involved France.

2. Before students read the captions in the timeline, discuss the pictures. Have students predict what the captions will say based on the pictures and the highlighted words. Call on volunteers to read the captions.

3. Check comprehension with the **As-tu compris?** questions and by having students summarize the captions in English or French in their own words.

4. Have students read the captions again silently and do the **Activité** individually. Go over the answers with the class.

5. Ask students if they have already studied any of the events in the timeline in another class? You might also discuss what the consequences of these events were for France and the world.

La France

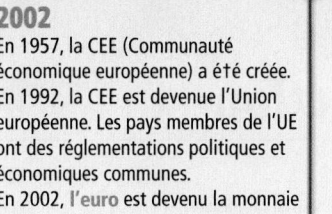

1862

Napoléon III, l'empereur de France, a envoyé Maximilien d'Autriche au Mexique pour établir un empire. Les Mexicains ont vaincu les Français à Puebla le 5 mai 1862, date que les Mexicains continuent à fêter aujourd'hui.

2002

En 1957, la CEE (Communauté économique européenne) a été créée. En 1992, la CEE est devenue l'Union européenne. Les pays membres de l'UE ont des réglementations politiques et économiques communes.

En 2002, **l'euro** est devenu la monnaie commune à la majorité de ces pays. En France, il a remplacé le franc, utilisé depuis 1360.

1944

En août 1944, vers la fin de la Seconde Guerre mondiale, les Alliés ont libéré Paris. **Le général de Gaulle** est entré dans Paris avec les Forces Françaises qui ont repris la ville avec l'aide de la Résistance.

1968

En **mai 68**, la révolte des étudiants, suivie de grèves ouvrières, provoque une crise politique. En 1969, le général de Gaulle quitte le pouvoir après l'échec d'un référendum sur la régionalisation et la réforme du Sénat.

Interactive TUTOR

Activité · 3.1

1. Quelles sont les contributions romaines à la civilisation gauloise?

2. Comment est-ce que la Renaissance italienne est arrivée en France?

3. Où est-ce que les Français ont essayé d'établir un empire?

4. En quelle année Paris a été libérée?

5. Qu'est-ce que la France a adopté en 2002?

Cultures

Practices and Perspectives

Many believe that the student revolts and worker strikes of 1968 were an example of France's "revolutionary tradition." In fact, it is said that a tradition of protest is part of the French national identity. Some other examples of the people rising up against the government are the French Revolution in 1789, the Paris Commune in 1871, general labor strikes in the 1930's, and the student protests in 2006 over a labor law affecting those under the age of 26. Have students research one of these events to find out its causes and consequences. Have them share their findings with the class. Discuss whether they agree or disagree that the tradition of protest is part of the French national identity. · 2.1

Answers

1. un système juridique, les impôts, le christianisme, le latin
2. Le roi François I a invité des artistes italiens pour décorer les châteaux.
3. au Mexique
4. 1944
5. l'euro

INTERDISCIPLINARY LINKS

Le gouvernement · 3.2

Government Link One of Rome's legacies to France was its legal system. In fact, Roman law was practiced throughout Europe until the 18th century. This is why many European civil law systems today reflect Roman law, in particular the type called *Jus commune*. Today, *Jus commune* is seen by some members of the European Union as a model that would help unification. Have students find out more about *Jus commune*, its basic principles, and where forms of it are practiced.

Les maths · 3.1

Math Link The euro is the currency of France and other European Union countries. There are seven banknotes (5, 10, 20, 50, 100, 200, 500) and eight coins (1, 2, 5, 10, 20, and 50 euro cents, 1 and 2 euro). Have students find the exchange rate for the euro against the U.S. dollar. Then have them calculate the dollar amount of each euro denomination.

Assess

Assessment Program
Quiz: Géoculture
Differentiated Practice and Assessment CD-ROM

Online Assessment
my.hrw.com

Test Generator

Planning Guide

Retour de vacances

Chapter Section		Resources
Vocabulaire 1	pp. 6–9	📺 Teaching Transparencies: Vocabulaire 1.1, 1.2; Bell Work 1.1, 1.2, 1.3, 1.4
• Back-to-school activities and classes		📖 Cahier de vocabulaire et grammaire, pp. 1–6
• After-school activities		📖 Grammar Tutor for Students of French
Grammaire 1	pp. 10–13	📖 Cahier d'activités, pp. 1–3
• Review: Regular verbs in the present		📖 Media Guide, pp. 1–4
• Review: Irregular verbs in the present		
Application 1	pp. 14–15	📖 **Assessment Program**
• **Un peu plus:**		Quiz: Vocabulaire 1, pp. 3–4
Review: Verbs followed by the infinitive		Quiz: Grammaire 1, pp. 5–6
		Quiz: Application 1, pp. 7–8
Culture	pp. 16–17	📖 Cahier d'activités, p. 4
• **Lecture culturelle: Chevaux de polo**		
• **Comparaisons**		
• **Communauté et professions**		
Vocabulaire 2	pp. 18–21	📺 Teaching Transparencies: Vocabulaire 1.3, 1.4; Bell Work 1.5, 1.6, 1.7, 1.8
• What you did last summer: activities, things, and places		📖 Cahier de vocabulaire et grammaire, pp. 7–12
Grammaire 2	pp. 22–25	📖 Grammar Tutor for Students of French
• Review: The **passé composé**		📖 Cahier d'activités, pp. 5–7
• Review: The **passé composé** and the **imparfait**		📖 Media Guide, pp. 1–4
Application 2	pp. 26–27	📖 **Assessment Program**
• **Un peu plus:**		Quiz: Vocabulaire 2, pp. 9–10
Review: Reflexive verbs in the **passé composé**		Quiz: Grammaire 2, pp. 11–12
		Quiz: Application 2, pp. 13–14
Lecture	pp. 28–31	📖 Cahier d'activités, p. 8
• **Un papillon dans la cité**		📖 Reading Strategies and Skills Handbook
L'atelier de l'écrivain	pp. 32–33	📖 Advanced Reader
• **Des vacances extraordinaires**		📖 **Assessment Program**
		Quiz: Lecture, p. 15
		Quiz: Écriture, p. 16
Prépare-toi pour l'examen	pp. 34–37	📺 Teaching Transparencies: Picture Sequences, Situation, Ch. 1
• **Résumé de vocabulaire et grammaire**		📖 Media Guide, pp. 4, 53–54
Activités préparatoires	pp. 38–39	📖 **Assessment Program**
Révisions cumulatives	pp. 40–41	Examen: Chapitre 1, pp. 17–22
		Examen oral: Chapitre 1, p. 317
		📺 Teaching Transparencies, Fine Art, Ch. 1
		📖 Cahier d'activités, pp. 9–10
Chroniques	pp. 80–89	📖 Reading Strategies and Skills Handbook
• Travailler pour vivre ou vivre pour travailler?		📖 Advanced Reader
• Le système scolaire français		
• Les femmes au travail		
• L'artisanat sans frontière		
• Inventions et découvertes		

Visit Us Online
go.hrw.com
Online Edition

KEYWORD: BD3 CH1

Pacing Suggestions

	Essential	Recommended	Optional
Vocabulaire 1 • Back-to-school activities and classes • After-school activities • **Flash culture**	✔		
Grammaire 1 • Review: Regular verbs in the present • Review: Irregular verbs in the present • **Flash culture**	✔		
Application 1 • **Un peu plus:** Review: Verbs followed by the infinitive	✔		
Culture • **Lecture culturelle: Chevaux de polo** • **Comparaisons** • **Communauté et professions**		✔	
Vocabulaire 2 • What you did last summer: activities, things, and places • **Flash culture**	✔		
Grammaire 2 • Review: The **passé composé** • Review: The **passé composé** and the **imparfait** • **Flash culture**	✔		
Application 2 • **Un peu plus:** Review: Reflexive verbs in the **passé composé**	✔		
Lecture • **Un papillon dans la cité**		✔	
L'atelier de l'écrivain • **Des vacances extraordinaires**			
Prépare-toi pour l'examen		✔	
Activités préparatoires		✔	
Révisions cumulatives			✔
Chroniques			✔

Technology

Bien dit! Online
• Student Edition with multi-media
• SoundBooth recording tool
• Interactive activities with feedback
• Self-tests with feedback
• Cahier d'activités (Interactive workbook)
• Cahier de vocabulaire et grammaire (Interactive workbook)
• Holt Online Assessment

DVD Program
• Télé-roman: Camille et compagnie
• Télé-culture: Interviews

Interactive Tutor
• Interactive practice games
• Writing and recording workshops
• Before You Know It™ Flashcards

Audio Program
• Student Edition Listening Activities
• Assessment listening activities
• Songs

One-Stop Planner
• Complete media and print resources
• ExamView Pro Test Generator
• Holt Calendar Planner

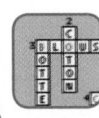

PuzzlePro
• Customizable word games

Differentiated Practice and Assessment CD

For slower pace and advanced learner options, see the Differentiated Practice and Assessment CD.

Planning Guide

✂️ Projects

Grading the project

Suggested point distribution
   (100 points total)

Preparation

Vocabulary use . . . . .45 pts.

Creativity and appearance . . . . .25 pts.

Oral presentation

Comprehensibility . . . . .10 pts.

Vocabulary use . . . . .10 pts.

Delivery .10 pts.

e-community

e-mail forum:

Post the following questions on the classroom e-mail forum:

| Location: | http://french |

> **Qu'est-ce que tu as fait cet été?**
>
> **Qu'est-ce que tu penses faire pendant l'année scolaire?**
>
> 5.1

All students will contribute to the list and then share the items.

Activités d'été

In this activity students will use all four skills as they create magazine advertisements for summer activities and vacations, present them, and read and listen to classmates' ads. Have students discuss seasonal advertising, how advertising influences them, and how it targets certain consumers. Have them tell what kinds of ads they prefer.

🍀 1.3, 5.1

Suggested Sequence

1. Have students work individually or in groups to create an ad. They will need pictures of vocabulary items found in magazines or brochures. (Encourage artistic students to create their own.) Each item should include a price in euros reflecting the exchange rate, which they can find in the newspaper or on the Internet.

2. Remind students to use the chapter vocabulary in both a written and an oral context. Encourage them to be creative, yet accurate, in their ad.

3. Assign due dates for the rough draft, the completed ad, and the oral presentation. The rough draft may be a sketch with drawings labeled in French.

4. Allow for peer review after completion of the first draft.

5. Collect rough drafts from the students.

6. Have students do the final draft and present their ad to the class.

Partner Class Project

Have students work together to develop a survey about the travel habits of a partner class in a French-speaking country. The survey should consist of five multiple-choice questions. Students should post the survey on the student or class Web site. Remind students to e-mail the Web site address or an electronic document to the partner class. Each student in the partner class should complete the survey. The class then evaluates the answers. Are the travel habits of the partner class similar to or different than their own? In what ways? Students should work in groups to summarize the results in French. Have students present their summaries to the class.

🍀 1.3, 4.2

 Game Bank
For game ideas, see pages T60–T63.

La pétanque

«**Tu tires ou tu pointes?**» is a question you might hear quite often in Provence. It is asked when people play the game of **pétanque**, or **boules**. Players form teams of two (**doublettes**) or three (**triplettes**). The object of the game is to get as many **boules** as close as possible to the **cochonnet** (literally *piglet*). The boules are steel balls that measure a little over 3 inches in diameter. Each team has a set of **boules** marked with a distinctive pattern. The **cochonnet** is a small wooden ball. The player can **pointer**, which means to aim at the **cochonnet**, or, if an adversary already has a **boule** close to the **cochonnet**, the player must **tirer**, to try to hit the opponent's ball out of the way. Have students research the history of **pétanque** and ask them if the rules are similar to those of any game played in the United States. Encourage students to explain the rules of this game to friends or family and then play the game. ✿ 4.2, 5.2

La cuisine

The **Quiche Lorraine** is said to have been created in the sixteenth century in Nancy, France. The original recipe contained only eggs, smoked bacon, and butter, and the crust was made out of bread. Cheese was added to the recipe later on. A quiche can be prepared with a variety of ingredients, including spinach and salmon. Usually, French people eat quiche as an appetizer or sometimes as a main dish with a salad. It is also a favorite lunch dish. Cafés and restaurants serve a single helping of quiche for lunch. Quiches fall under the fast-food category for the French. Encourage students to make quiche in their home economics class or at home. ✿ 2.2, 5.2

Quiche Lorraine Pour 6 personnes

Pâte brisée
2 tasses de farine
une pincée de sel
1 cuillère à soupe de sucre
½ tasse de beurre froid

3 cuillères à soupe d'eau
(ou acheter la pâte toute faite)

Garniture
5 œufs
2 tasses de crème fraîche

1 tranche épaisse de jambon coupée en cubes
des champignons coupés et du fromage râpé (au choix)

Pâte brisée
Mettre la farine, le sucre et le sel dans un bol. Couper le beurre en petits morceaux. Mélanger le beurre et la farine avec les doigts. Ajouter l'eau petit à petit. Faire une boule avec la pâte. Laisser reposer pendant 30 minutes.

Garniture
Dans un bol, mélanger les oeufs et la crème fraîche. Ajouter le jambon (les champignons et le fromage). Rouler la pâte et la mettre dans le moule. Ajouter la garniture. Mettre dans le four à 375°F pendant 45 minutes.

Vocabulaire à l'œuvre 1

2 p. 8, CD 1, Tr. 1

1. — Oh non, c'est encore du poulet aujourd'hui!

— Oui, pourquoi? Tu n'aimes pas le poulet?

— Si, j'aime le poulet, mais pas tous les jours!

2. — Tu as choisi un livre?

— Oui, je vais emprunter *Le comte de Monte Cristo*.

3. — Je ne comprends rien à cette expérience.

— Moi non plus. La chimie, je trouve ça difficile!

4. — Oh non! Je n'ai pas mes baskets!

— Alors, tu ne peux pas jouer avec nous aujourd'hui.

5. — Hé Simon, tu as vu? On a cinq nouveaux ordinateurs!

— Ah! Génial!

Answers to Activity 2

1. b   **2.** a   **3.** d   **4.** c   **5.** e

Grammaire à l'œuvre 1

9 p. 10, CD 1, Tr. 2

1. Tous les matins, je [STATIC] le bus à la même heure.

2. On [STATIC] quand on mange trop de chocolat.

3. Vous [STATIC] souvent au basket?

4. Je [STATIC] bien français!

5. Tu [STATIC] cette chanson à la radio? C'est ma chanson préférée.

Answers to Activity 9

1. a   **2.** c   **3.** e   **4.** g   **5.** i

Application 1

18 p. 14, CD 1, Tr. 3

1. — Nathalie, à table! On t'attend!

— Maman, je n'ai pas faim. Je viens de manger une glace!

2. — Nathalie, n'oublie pas de donner à manger au chat.

— Non papa, je vais donner à manger à Pompon maintenant.

3. — Tu as fait tes devoirs?

— Non, je vais finir mes devoirs après le dîner.

4. — Regarde, maman, je viens d'acheter la dernière BD de Gaston Lagaffe.

— Ah oui? Fais voir!

5. — Hé maman, je viens de parler à Élodie. Est-ce qu'elle peut venir dîner avec nous ce soir?

— Bien sûr, dis-lui d'être là à sept heures.

Answers to Activity 18

1. a   **2.** b   **3.** b   **4.** a   **5.** a

Vocabulaire à l'œuvre 2

24 p. 20, CD 1, Tr. 4

1. J'avais une grande tente et un nouveau sac de couchage.

2. Je suis allée à la ferme de mon grand-père.

3. J'ai attrapé quatre poissons le premier jour!

4. J'ai fait de la planche à voile. C'était super!

5. J'ai fait du ski tous les jours.

6. On était en demi-pension.

Answers to Activity 24

1. c   **2.** f   **3.** e   **4.** d   **5.** a   **6.** b

Grammaire à l'œuvre 2

29 p. 22, CD 1, Tr. 5

1. Pendant les vacances, je vais chez mes grands-parents.

2. Moi, chaque année, je rends visite à mes cousins à la campagne.

3. Malika a fait de la planche à voile cet été.

4. Patrick et Vincent ne font jamais rien pendant les vacances.

5. Tous les étés, nous allons au bord de la mer.

6. Le week-end dernier, tu es allé à la pêche avec ta famille, n'est-ce pas?

7. En général, nous faisons de la randonnée quand il fait beau.

Answers to Activity 29

1. a   **2.** a   **3.** b   **4.** a   **5.** a   **6.** b   **7.** a

Application 2

38 p. 26, CD 1, Tr. 6

1. Nous allions toujours en vacances chez des amis, les Spoletti.
2. Une fois, nous sommes arrivés chez eux très tard.
3. Il faisait nuit et il n'y avait pas de lumière.
4. Nous étions tous très fatigués.
5. Soudain, quelqu'un a ouvert la porte.
6. Ce n'était pas monsieur Spoletti mais un homme grand et très mince.
7. On a tous eu très peur.

Answers to Activity 38

1. a **2.** b **3.** a **4.** a **5.** b **6.** a **7.** b

Prépare-toi pour l'examen

6 p. 35, CD 1, Tr. 8

1. Quand j'étais petite, j'allais chez ma tante chaque été.
2. Elle habitait au bord de la mer.
3. Un jour, nous sommes allées à la pêche.
4. Vers midi, il a commencé à pleuvoir.
5. À ce moment-là, j'ai attrapé un gros poisson.
6. Ma tante est rentrée, mais moi, je suis restée là sous la pluie, avec mon beau poisson.

Answers to Activity 6

1. a **2.** a **3.** b **4.** b **5.** b **6.** b

Activités préparatoires

Listening, p. 38, CD 1, Tr. 9

1. — Tu suis un cours de géo cette année?
   — Oui, j'ai cours le lundi, le mercredi et le vendredi.
2. — J'adore les montagnes, mais j'aime aussi la campagne. J'aime bien aussi aller au bord de la mer.
   — Où vas-tu passer tes vacances, alors?

Answers to Listening

1. b **2.** d

Révisions cumulatives chapitre 1

1 p. 40, CD 1, Tr. 10

1. — Salut, Sandrine! Enfin le week-end! Pourquoi on n'irait pas au cinéma?
   — Je voudrais bien, mais je dois étudier parce que j'ai un examen de chimie la semaine prochaine.
2. — Est-ce que tu faisais du skate quand tu étais petit, papi?
   — Non! Il n'y avait pas de skate quand j'étais petit!
   — Qu'est-ce que tu faisais comme sport?
   — Tous les jours, après l'école, je jouais au foot.
3. — Regarde cette brochure! Il y a beaucoup de choses à faire!
   — Oui, je sais! Je n'arrive pas à me décider!
   — Je crois que je vais faire du ski ce matin. Tu viens?
   — Bon, j'aime bien faire du ski, mais je préfère faire de la randonnée.
   — Alors, à plus tard!
4. — Allô?
   — Madame Boucher? C'est Hélène. Est-ce que Véronique est là?
   — Bonjour, Hélène! Je regrette. Elle n'est pas là. Elle monte à cheval cet après-midi.

Answers to Activity 1

1. b **2.** c **3.** a **4.** d

50-Minute Lesson Plans

Retour de vacances

50-Minute Lesson Plans

Day 1

OBJECTIVE
Express likes, dislikes, and preferences

Core Instruction
Chapter Opener, pp. 4–5
- See Using the Photo, p. 4. **5 min.**
- See Chapter Objectives, p. 4. **5 min.**

Vocabulaire 1, pp. 6–9
- Present **Vocabulaire 1,** pp. 6–7. See Teaching **Vocabulaire,** p. 6. **15 min.**
- Present **Exprimons-nous!,** p. 7. **5 min.**
- Do Activity 1, p. 8. **5 min.**
- Play Audio CD 1, Tr. 1 for Activity 2, p. 8. **5 min.**
- Do Activities 3–4, p. 8. **10 min.**

Optional Resources
- Slower Pace Learners, p. 7 ◆
- Multiple Intelligences, p. 7

Homework Suggestions
Cahier de vocabulaire et grammaire, pp. 1–2
Interactive Tutor, Ch. 1
❀ 1.1, 1.2, 1.3, 3.1, 4.2

Day 2

OBJECTIVE
Ask about plans; Use regular verbs in the present

Core Instruction
Vocabulaire 1, pp. 6–9
- Do Bell Work 1.1, p. 6. **5 min.**
- Present **Flash culture,** p. 8. **5 min.**
- See Teaching **Exprimons-nous!,** p. 8. **10 min.**
- Have students do Activities 5–7, p. 9. **20 min.**

Grammaire 1, pp. 10–13
- See Teaching **Grammaire,** p. 10. **10 min.**

Optional Resources
- Communication (TE), p. 9
- Advanced Learners, p. 9 ▲
- Special Learning Needs, p. 9 ●

Homework Suggestions
Study for **Quiz: Vocabulaire 1**
Cahier de vocabulaire et grammaire, p. 3
Online Practice (**go.hrw.com,** Keyword: BD3 CH1)
❀ 1.1, 1.2, 1.3, 4.2

Day 3

OBJECTIVE
Use regular verbs in the present

Core Instruction
Vocabulaire 1, pp. 6–9
- Review **Vocabulaire 1,** pp. 6–9. **10 min.**
- Give **Quiz: Vocabulaire 1.** **20 min.**

Grammaire 1, pp. 10–13
- Have students do Activity 8, p. 10. **5 min.**
- Play Audio CD 1, Tr. 2 for Activity 9, p. 10. **5 min.**
- Have students do Activities 10–11, p. 11. **10 min.**

Optional Resources
- Connections, p. 11
- Slower Pace Learners, p. 11 ◆
- Special Learning Needs, p. 11 ●

Homework Suggestions
Cahier de vocabulaire et grammaire, p. 4
Cahier d'activités, p. 1
Online Practice (**go.hrw.com,** Keyword: BD3 CH1)
❀ 1.2, 4.1

Day 4

OBJECTIVE
Use regular verbs in the present; Use irregular verbs in the present; Use verbs followed by the infinitive

Core Instruction
Grammaire 1, pp. 10–13
- Do Activity 12, p. 11. **5 min.**
- Present **Flash culture,** p. 12. **5 min.**
- See Teaching **Grammaire,** p. 12. **10 min.**
- Do Activities 13–16, pp. 12–13. **20 min.**

Application 1, pp. 14–15
- Have students do Activity 17, p. 14. **5 min.**
- See Teaching **Un peu plus,** p. 14. **5 min.**

Optional Resources
- Slower Pace Learners, p. 13 ◆
- Special Learning Needs, p. 13 ●

Homework Suggestions
Study for **Quiz: Grammaire 1**
Cahier de vocabulaire et grammaire, p. 5
Cahier d'activités, p. 2
❀ 1.1, 1.2, 1.3, 2.1

Day 5

OBJECTIVE
Use verbs followed by the infinitive

Core Instruction
Grammaire 1, pp. 10–13
- Review **Grammaire 1,** pp. 10–13. **10 min.**
- Give **Quiz: Grammaire 1.** **20 min.**

Application 1, pp. 14–15
- Play Audio CD 1, Tr. 3 for Activity 18, p. 14. **5 min.**
- Have students do Activities 19–23, pp. 14–15. **15 min.**

Optional Resources
- Advanced Learners, p. 15 ▲
- Special Learning Needs, p. 15 ●

Homework Suggestions
Study for **Quiz: Application 1**
Cahier de vocabulaire et grammaire, p. 6
Cahier d'activités, p. 3
Online Practice (**go.hrw.com,** Keyword: BD3 CH1)
❀ 1.1, 1.2, 1.3

Day 6

OBJECTIVE
Learn about francophone culture

Core Instruction
Application 1, pp. 14–15
- Review **Application 1,** pp. 14–15. **10 min.**
- Give **Quiz: Application 1.** **20 min.**

Culture, pp. 16–17
- See **Lecture culturelle** (TE), p. 16. **10 min.**
- See **Comparaisons et communauté** (TE), p. 16. **10 min.**

Optional Resources
- Advanced Learners, p. 17 ▲
- Multiple Intelligences, p. 17

Homework Suggestions
Cahier d'activités, p. 4
Interactive Tutor, Ch. 1
Online Practice (**go.hrw.com,** Keyword: BD3 CH1)
Finish the **Communauté et professions** project
❀ 1.1, 1.3, 2.1, 4.2, 5.1

Day 7

OBJECTIVE
Tell when and how often you did something

Core Instruction
Vocabulaire 2, pp. 18–21
- Do Bell Work 1.5, p. 18. **5 min.**
- Present **Vocabulaire 2,** pp. 18–19. See Teaching **Vocabulaire,** p. 18. **15 min.**
- Present **Exprimons-nous!,** p. 19. **10 min.**
- Play Audio CD 1, Tr. 4 for Activity 24, p. 20. **5 min.**
- Have students do Activities 25–26, p. 20. **10 min.**
- Present **Flash culture,** p. 20. **5 min.**

Optional Resources
- Advanced Learners, p. 19 ▲
- Multiple Intelligences, p. 19
- Slower Pace Learners, p. 21 ◆

Homework Suggestions
Cahier de vocabulaire et grammaire, pp. 7–8
❀ 1,1. 1.2, 1.3, 4.2

Day 8

OBJECTIVE
Describe a place in the past; Use the passé composé

Core Instruction
Vocabulaire 2, pp. 18–21
- See Teaching **Exprimons-nous!,** p. 20. **10 min.**
- Have students do Activities 27–28, p. 21. **20 min.**

Grammaire 2, pp. 22–25
- See Teaching **Grammaire,** p. 22. **10 min.**
- Play Audio CD 1, Tr. 5 for Activity 29, p. 22. **5 min.**
- Do Activity 30, p. 23. **5 min.**

Optional Resources
- Special Learning Needs, p. 21 ●
- French for Spanish Speakers, p. 23

Homework Suggestions
Study for **Quiz: Vocabulaire 2**
Cahier de vocabulaire et grammaire, p. 9
Interactive Tutor, Ch. 1
Online Practice (**go.hrw.com,** Keyword: BD3 CH1)
❀ 1.1, 1.2, 4.1

Day 9

OBJECTIVE
Use the passé composé

Core Instruction
Vocabulaire 2, pp. 18–21
• Review **Vocabulaire 2,**
 pp. 18–21. **10 min.**
• Give **Quiz: Vocabulaire 2.**
 20 min.

Grammaire 2, pp. 22–25
• Present **Flash culture,** p. 22.
 5 min.
• Have students do Activities
 31–33, p. 23. **15 min.**

Optional Resources
• Communication (TE), p. 23
• Slower Pace Learners, p. 23 ◆
• Multiple Intelligences, p. 23

Homework Suggestions
**Cahier de vocabulaire et
 grammaire,** p. 10
Cahier d'activités, p. 5
Interactive Tutor, Ch. 1
Online Practice (**go.hrw.com,**
 Keyword: BD3 CH1)
 ❀ 1.1, 1.2, 1.3, 4.2

Day 10

OBJECTIVE
*Use the passé composé and the
imparfait*

Core Instruction
Grammaire 2, pp. 22–25
• Do Bell Work 1.7, p. 24. **5 min.**
• See Teaching **Grammaire,**
 p. 24. **10 min.**
• Have students do Activities
 34–37, pp. 24–25. **25 min.**

Application 2, pp. 26–27
• Play Audio CD 1, Tr. 6 for Activity
 38, p. 26. **5 min.**
• Do Activity 39, p. 26. **5 min.**

Optional Resources
• Slower Pace Learners, p. 25 ◆
• Special Learning Needs, p. 25 ●

Homework Suggestions
Study for **Quiz: Grammaire 2**
**Cahier de vocabulaire et
 grammaire,** p. 11
Cahier d'activités, p. 6
 ❀ 1.1, 1.2, 1.3

Day 11

OBJECTIVE
*Use reflexive verbs in the passé
composé*

Core Instruction
Grammaire 2, pp. 22–25
• Review **Grammaire 2,**
 pp. 22–25. **10 min.**
• Give **Quiz: Grammaire 2.**
 20 min.

Application 2, pp. 26–27
• See Teaching **Un peu plus,**
 p. 26. **5 min.**
• Have students do Activities
 40–43, pp. 26–27. **15 min.**

Optional Resources
• Communication (TE), p. 27
• Advanced Learners, p. 27 ▲
• Special Learning Needs, p. 27 ●

Homework Suggestions
Study for **Quiz: Application 2**
**Cahier de vocabulaire et
 grammaire,** p. 12
Cahier d'activités, p. 7
Online Practice (**go.hrw.com,**
 Keyword: BD3 CH1)
 ❀ 1.1, 1.2, 1.3

Day 12

OBJECTIVE
*Develop listening and reading
skills*

Core Instruction
Application 2, pp. 26–27
• Review **Application 2,**
 pp. 26–27. **10 min.**
• Give **Quiz: Application 2.**
 20 min.

Lecture, pp. 28–31
• See **Lecture** (TE), p. 28.
 20 min.

Optional Resources
• Connections, p. 29
• Multiple Intelligences, p. 29

Homework Suggestions
Interactive Tutor, Ch. 1
Online Practice (**go.hrw.com,**
 Keyword: BD3 CH1)
 ❀ 1.1, 1.3, 4.2

Day 13

OBJECTIVE
*Develop listening, reading, and
writing skills*

Core Instruction
Lecture, pp. 28–31
• See **Lecture** (TE), p. 30.
 20 min.

L'atelier de l'écrivain,
pp. 32–33
• See **L'atelier de l'écrivain**
 (TE), p. 32. **30 min.**

Optional Resources
• Advanced Learners, p. 29 ▲
• Slower Pace Learners, p. 31 ◆
• Special Learning Needs, p. 31 ●
• Slower Pace Learners, p. 33 ◆
• Special Learning Needs, p. 33 ●

Homework Suggestions
Cahier d'activités, p. 8
L'atelier de l'écrivain, Activity
 4, p. 33 ❀ 1.1, 1.2, 1.3

Day 14

OBJECTIVE
*Review the chapter; Prepare for
the AP Exam*

Core Instruction
Prépare-toi pour l'examen,
pp. 34–37
• Have students do Activities 1–5,
 pp. 34–35. **25 min.**

Activités préparatoires,
pp. 38–39
• Have students do the **Activités
 préparatoires,** pp. 38–39.
 25 min.

Optional Resources
• Reteaching, p. 34
• Slower Pace Learners, p. 39 ◆
• Special Learning Needs, p. 39 ●
• **Télé-culture:** Interviews

Homework Suggestions
Interactive Tutor, Ch. 1
Online Practice (**go.hrw.com,**
 Keyword: BD3 CH1)
 ❀ 1.2, 1.3, 2.1, 4.1

Day 15

OBJECTIVE
Review the chapter

Core Instruction
Prépare-toi pour l'examen,
pp. 34–37
• Play Audio CD 1, Tr. 8 for Activity
 6, p. 35. **10 min.**
• Have students do Activity 7,
 p. 35. **10 min.**

Révisions cumulatives,
pp. 40–41
• Play Audio CD 1, Tr. 10 for
 Activity 1, p. 40. **5 min.**
• Have students do Activities 2–6,
 pp. 40–41. **25 min.**

Optional Resources
• Online Culture Project, p. 40
• Fine Art Connection, p. 41
• **Télé-roman: Camille et
 compagnie**

Homework Suggestions
Study for Chapter Test
Online Practice (**go.hrw.com,**
 Keyword: BD3 CH1)
 ❀ 1.1, 1.2, 1.3, 2.2, 3.1, 3.2

Day 16/Test

Core Instruction
Chapter Test 50 min.

Optional Resources
Assessment Program
• Alternative Assessment
• Test Generator
• **Quiz: Lecture**
• **Quiz: Écriture**

Homework Suggestions
Cahier d'activités, pp. 9–10,
 102–103
Online Practice (**go.hrw.com,**
 Keyword: BD3 CH1)

50-Minute Lesson Plans

90-Minute Lesson Plans

Retour de vacances

Block 1

OBJECTIVE
Express likes, dislikes, and preferences; Ask about plans

Core Instruction
Chapter Opener, pp. 4–5
• See Using the Photo, p. 4. **5 min.**
• See Chapter Objectives, p. 4. **5 min.**

Vocabulaire 1, pp. 6–9
• Present **Vocabulaire 1**, pp. 6–7. See Teaching **Vocabulaire**, p. 6. **15 min.**
• Present **Exprimons-nous!**, p. 7. **5 min.**
• Have students do Activity 1, p. 8. **5 min.**
• Play Audio CD 1, Tr. 1 for Activity 2, p. 8. **5 min.**
• Have students do Activities 3–4, p. 8. **10 min.**
• Present **Flash culture**, p. 8. **5 min.**
• See Teaching **Exprimons-nous!**, p. 8. **10 min.**
• Have students do Activities 5–7, p. 9. **25 min.**

Optional Resources
• Learning Tips, p. 5
• **Attention!**, p. 6
• TPR, p. 7
• Comparisons, p. 7
• Slower Pace Learners, p. 7 ◆
• Multiple Intelligences, p. 7
• Teacher to Teacher, p. 9
• Communication (TE), p. 9
• Advanced Learners, p. 9 ▲
• Special Learning Needs, p. 9 ●

Homework Suggestions
Study for **Quiz: Vocabulaire 1**
Cahier de vocabulaire et grammaire, pp. 1–3
Interactive Tutor, Ch. 1
Online Practice (**go.hrw.com**, Keyword: BD3 CH1)
❀ 1.1, 1.2, 1.3, 3.1, 4.1, 4.2

Block 2

OBJECTIVE
Use regular verbs in the present; Use irregular verbs in the present

Core Instruction
Vocabulaire 1, pp. 6–9
• Review **Vocabulaire 1**, pp. 6–9. **10 min.**
• Give **Quiz: Vocabulaire 1**. **20 min.**

Grammaire 1, pp. 10–13
• See Teaching **Grammaire**, p. 10. **10 min.**
• Have students do Activity 8, p. 10. **5 min.**
• Play Audio CD 1, Tr. 2 for Activity 9, p. 10. **5 min.**
• Have students do Activities 10–12, p. 11. **10 min.**
• Present **Flash culture**, p. 12. **5 min.**
• See Teaching **Grammaire**, p. 12. **10 min.**
• Have students do Activities 13–15, pp. 12–13. **15 min.**

Optional Resources
• Communication (TE), p. 11
• Connections, p. 11
• Slower Pace Learners, p. 11 ◆
• Special Learning Needs, p. 11 ●
• French for Spanish Speakers, p. 12
• Slower Pace Learners, p. 13 ◆
• Special Learning Needs, p. 13 ●

Homework Suggestions
Study for **Quiz: Grammaire 1**
Cahier de vocabulaire et grammaire, pp. 4–5
Cahier d'activités, pp. 1–2
Interactive Tutor, Ch. 1
Online Practice (**go.hrw.com**, Keyword: BD3 CH1)
❀ 1.1, 1.2, 1.3, 2.1, 4.1

Block 3

OBJECTIVE
Use irregular verbs in the present; Use verbs followed by the infinitive; Learn about francophone culture

Core Instruction
Grammaire 1, pp. 10–13
• Do Bell Work 1.3, p. 12. **5 min.**
• Have students do Activity 16, p. 13. **5 min.**
• Review **Grammaire 1**, pp. 10–13. **10 min.**
• Give **Quiz: Grammaire 1**. **20 min.**

Application 1, pp. 14–15
• Have students do Activity 17, p. 14. **5 min.**
• See Teaching **Un peu plus**, p. 14. **5 min.**
• Play Audio CD 1, Tr. 3 for Activity 18, p. 14. **5 min.**
• Have students do Activities 19–23, pp. 14–15. **15 min.**

Culture, pp. 16–17
• See **Lecture culturelle** (TE), p. 16. **10 min.**
• See **Comparaisons et communauté** (TE), p. 16. **10 min.**

Optional Resources
• Communication (TE), p. 13
• Communication (TE), p. 15
• Advanced Learners, p. 15 ▲
• Special Learning Needs, p. 15 ●
• Prereading Questions, p. 16
• Active Reading Questions, p. 16
• **Vocabulaire supplémentaire**, p. 16
• Cultures, p. 17
• Communities, p. 17
• Connections, p. 17
• Advanced Learners, p. 17 ▲
• Multiple Intelligences, p. 17

Homework Suggestions
Study for **Quiz: Application 1**
Cahier de vocabulaire et grammaire, p. 6
Cahier d'activités, pp. 3–4
Interactive Tutor, Ch. 1
Online Practice (**go.hrw.com**, Keyword: BD3 CH1)
Finish the **Communauté et professions** project
❀ 1.1, 1.2, 1.3, 2.1, 2.2, 3.1, 4.2, 5.1

Block 4

OBJECTIVE
Tell when and how often you did something; Describe a place in the past

Core Instruction
Application 1, pp. 14–15
• Review **Application 1**, pp. 14–15. **10 min.**
• Give **Quiz: Application 1**. **20 min.**

Vocabulaire 2, pp. 18–21
• Present **Vocabulaire 2**, pp. 18–19. See Teaching **Vocabulaire**, p. 18. **15 min.**
• Present **Exprimons-nous!**, p. 19. **10 min.**
• Play Audio CD 1, Tr. 4 for Activity 24, p. 20. **5 min.**
• Have students do Activities 25–26, p. 20. **10 min.**
• Present **Flash culture**, p. 20. **5 min.**
• See Teaching **Exprimons-nous!**, p. 20. **5 min.**
• Have students do Activities 27–28, p. 21. **10 min.**

Optional Resources
• Connections, p. 18
• TPR, p. 19
• Connections, p. 19
• Advanced Learners, p. 19 ▲
• Multiple Intelligences, p. 19
• Communication (TE), p. 21
• Slower Pace Learners, p. 21 ◆
• Special Learning Needs, p. 21 ●

Homework Suggestions
Study for **Quiz: Vocabulaire 2**
Cahier de vocabulaire et grammaire, pp. 7–9
Interactive Tutor, Ch. 1
Online Practice (**go.hrw.com**, Keyword: BD3 CH1)
❀ 1.1, 1.2, 1.3. 3.1, 4.2

Block 5

OBJECTIVE
*Use the **passé composé**; Use the **passé composé** and the **imparfait***

Core Instruction
Vocabulaire 2, pp. 18–21
• Review **Vocabulaire 2,** pp. 18–21. **10 min.**
• Give **Quiz: Vocabulaire 2.** **20 min.**

Grammaire 2, pp. 22–25
• Present **Flash culture,** p. 22. **5 min.**
• See Teaching **Grammaire,** p. 22. **10 min.**
• Play Audio CD 1, Tr. 5 for Activity 29, p. 22. **5 min.**
• Have students do Activities 30–33, p. 23. **20 min.**
• See Teaching **Grammaire,** p. 24. **10 min.**
• Have students do Activities 34–35, pp. 24–25. **10 min.**

Optional Resources
• **Attention!,** p. 22
• Communication (TE), p. 23
• French for Spanish Speakers, p. 23
• Slower Pace Learners, p. 23 ◆
• Multiple Intelligences, p. 23
• Connections, p. 24
• Slower Pace Learners, p. 25 ◆
• Special Learning Needs, p. 25 ●

Homework Suggestions
Study for **Quiz: Grammaire 2**
Cahier de vocabulaire et grammaire, pp. 10–11
Cahier d'activités, pp. 5–6
Interactive Tutor, Ch. 1
Online Practice (**go.hrw.com,** Keyword: BD3 CH1)
❀ 1.1, 1.2, 1.3, 4.1, 4.2

Block 6

OBJECTIVE
*Use the **passé composé** and the **imparfait;** Use reflexive verbs in the **passé composé;** Develop listening and reading skills*

Core Instruction
Grammaire 2, pp. 22–25
• Have students do Activities 36–37, p. 25. **10 min.**
• Review **Grammaire 2,** pp. 22–25. **10 min.**
• Give **Quiz: Grammaire 2.** **20 min.**

Application 2, pp. 26–27
• Play Audio CD 1, Tr. 6 for Activity 38, p. 26. **5 min.**
• Have students do Activity 39, p. 26. **5 min.**
• See Teaching **Un peu plus,** p. 26. **5 min.**
• Have students do Activities 40–43, pp. 26–27. **15 min.**

Lecture, pp. 28–31
• See **Lecture** (TE), p. 28. **20 min.**

Optional Resources
• Communication (TE), p. 25
• Communication (TE), p. 27
• Advanced Learners, p. 27 ▲
• Special Learning Needs, p. 27 ●
• AP Reading Suggestion, p. 28
• Applying the Strategies, p. 28
• Active Reading Questions, p. 29
• Comparing and Contrasting, p. 29
• Connections, p. 29
• Multiple Intelligences, p. 29

Homework Suggestions
Study for **Quiz: Application 2**
Cahier de vocabulaire et grammaire, p. 12
Cahier d'activités, p. 7
Interactive Tutor, Ch. 1
Online Practice (**go.hrw.com,** Keyword: BD3 CH1)
❀ 1.1, 1.2, 1.3, 3.1, 4.2

Block 7

OBJECTIVE
Develop listening, reading, and writing skills; Review the chapter

Core Instruction
Application 2, pp. 26–27
• Review **Application 2,** pp. 26–27. **10 min.**
• Give **Quiz: Application 2.** **20 min.**

Lecture, pp. 28–31
• See **Lecture** (TE), p. 30. **10 min.**

L'atelier de l'écrivain, pp. 32–33
• See **L'atelier de l'écrivain** (TE), p. 32. **30 min.**

Prépare-toi pour l'examen, pp. 34–37
• Have students do Activities 1–5, pp. 34–35. **10 min.**
• Play Audio CD 1, Tr. 8 for Activity 6, p. 35. **5 min.**
• Have students do Activity 7, p. 35. **5 min.**

Optional Resources
• Active Reading Questions, p. 30
• Postreading Activity, p. 30
• Comparisons, p. 31
• Slower Pace Learners, p. 30 ◆
• Special Learning Needs, p. 30 ●
• Process Writing, p. 32
• Teaching Suggestion, p. 32
• Connections, p. 32
• **Le passé composé et l'imparfait,** p. 33
• Writing Assessment, p. 33
• Slower Pace Learners, p. 33 ◆
• Special Learning Needs, p. 33 ●
• TPRS, p. 34
• Reteaching, p. 34
• Oral Assessment, p. 35
• Cultures, p. 36
• Chapter Review, pp. 36–37
• Game, p. 37

Homework Suggestions
Study for Chapter Test
Cahier d'activités, p. 8
L'atelier de l'écrivain, Activity 4, p. 33
Interactive Tutor, Ch. 1
Online Practice (**go.hrw.com,** Keyword: BD3 CH1)
❀ 1.1, 1.2, 1.3, 2.1, 2.2, 3.1, 4.2

Block 8

OBJECTIVE
Prepare for the AP Exam; Review and assess the chapter

Core Instruction
Activités préparatoires, pp. 38–39
• Have students do the **Activités préparatoires,** pp. 38–39. **20 min.**

Chapter Test 50 min.

Révisions cumulatives, pp. 40–41
• Play Audio CD 1, Tr. 10 for Activity 1, p. 40. **5 min.**
• Have students do Activities 2–6, pp. 40–41. **15 min.**

Optional Resources
• Reading Strategy, p. 38
• Writing Strategy, p. 39
• Slower Pace Learners, p. 39 ◆
• Special Learning Needs, p. 39 ●
• Online Culture Project, p. 40
• Fine Art Connection, p. 41
• **Télé-culture:** Interviews
• **Télé-roman: Camille et compagnie**

Homework Suggestions
Cahier d'activités, pp. 9–10, 102–103
Interactive Tutor, Ch. 1
Online Practice (**go.hrw.com,** Keyword: BD3 CH1)
❀ 1.1, 1.2, 1.3, 2.2, 3.1, 3.2, 4.1

90-Minute Lesson Plans

Meeting the National Standards

Communication
Communication, pp. 9, 11, 13, 15, 21, 23, 25, 27

À ton tour, p. 41

Cultures
Flash culture, pp. 8, 12, 20, 22

Comparaisons, p. 17

Practices and Perspectives, p. 17

Products and Perspectives, p. 36

Connections
Language Note, p. 24

Science Link, p. 17

Health Link, pp. 18, 19

Geography Link, p. 18

Literature Link, pp. 29, 32

Comparisons
Comparing and Contrasting, pp. 7, 9

Comparaisons, p. 17

Comparisons, pp. 7, 31

Communities
Communauté, p. 17

Career Path, p. 17

Using the Photo
The photo shows **la plage du Lupin** in the old coastal town of Rothéneuf in Brittany. It is named after a family of corsairs and is famous for its sculpted rocks, **rochers sculptés**, sculptures of pirates and sea monsters depicting the history of the Rothéneuf family. This seaport is also famous for Jacques Cartier, the explorer of the St. Lawrence River, who was born here in 1491. The photo shows the English riding style. Have students compare the riding clothes shown in the photos to those worn by Western riders.
🏵 3.1, 4.2

chapitre **1**

Retour de vacances

Objectifs

In this chapter, you will learn to
- express likes, dislikes, and preferences
- ask about plans
- tell when and how often you did something
- describe a place in the past

And you will review
- the present
- verbs followed by the infinitive
- the **passé composé**
- the **passé composé** and the **imparfait**
- reflexive verbs in the **passé composé**

▶ *Que vois-tu sur la photo?*

Où se trouvent ces adolescents?

Qu'est-ce qu'ils font?

Et toi, qu'est-ce que tu aimes faire en vacances?

Suggested pacing:	Traditional Schedule	Block Schedule
Vocabulaire/Grammaire/Application 1	4 days	1 1/2 blocks
Culture	1 day	1 block
Vocabulaire/Grammaire/Application 2	6 days	2 1/2 blocks
Lecture	1 day	1/2 block
L'atelier de l'écrivain	1 day	1/2 block
Prépare-toi pour l'examen	1/2 day	1/2 block
Activités préparatoires	1/2 day	1/2 block
Examen	1 day	1/2 block
Révisions cumulatives	1 day	1/2 block

Vocabulaire supplémentaire

Students might use these terms to discuss the photo.

les rênes	*reins*
la selle	*saddle*
la culotte de cheval	*riding breeches*
la toque	*riding cap*

Learning Tips

A good way to learn new vocabulary is to read in French. Encourage students to read the online version of French newspapers, such as **Le Monde** or **Le Figaro**. Remind students that they do not have to be able to understand every word, but seeing new words used in context will help them increase their vocabulary as they study French.

Language Lab

You might want to use your language lab to have students:
- listen to all target vocabulary and phrases in the chapter
- use Holt SoundBooth to practice pronunciation of vocabulary and phrases and save their work for evaluation
- complete the listening activities in this chapter

Des cavaliers sur une plage de Bretagne

LISTENING PRACTICE

Vocabulaire
Activity 2, p. 8, CD 1, Tr. 1
Activity 24, p. 20, CD 1, Tr. 4

Grammaire
Activity 9, p. 10, CD 1, Tr. 2
Activity 29, p. 22, CD 1, Tr. 5

Application
Activity 18, p. 14, CD 1, Tr. 3
Activity 38, p. 26, CD 1, Tr. 6

Language Lab and Classroom Activities

Prépare-toi pour l'examen
Activity 6, p. 35, CD 1, Tr. 8
Télé-culture: Interviews, Chapter 1

Activités préparatoires
Section I, Listening, p. 38, CD 1, Tr. 9
Télé-roman: *Camille et compagnie*, Épisode 1

Révisions cumulatives
Activity 1, p. 40, CD 1, Tr. 10

Lecture
p. 28, CD 1, Tr. 7

Bell Work

Use Bell Work 1.1 in the *Teaching Transparencies* or write this activity on the board.

Complète les phrases avec le mot juste.

1. Dans le laboratoire, les élèves mettent une (blouse / chemise).
2. On emprunte des livres à la (librairie / bibliothèque).
3. Les élèves / jouent dans la (cantine / cour de récré).
4. Nous avons gagné la (compétition / documentaliste).
5. On se plante quand on (réussit / rate) un examen.

 1.2

Objectifs
- to express likes, dislikes, and preferences
- to ask about plans

Vocabulaire
à l'œuvre 1

Révisions Voici mon lycée

J'ai **un emploi du temps chargé** cette année.

Au CDI, on peut **emprunter des livres** et parler **au conseiller d'éducation.**

C'est dans **le laboratoire** qu'on a cours de **physique-chimie** et de **biologie.**

Ça, c'est **la salle de classe** où j'ai mes cours de **maths, de français, d'histoire-géo** et **d'anglais.**

Dans **la salle d'informatique,** il y a **des ordinateurs.**

On déjeune **à la cantine** à midi.

Ça, c'est **le gymnase** où on a sport.

Pendant **la récréation,** on peut lire.

▶ Vocabulaire supplémentaire—À l'école, p. R16

Core Instruction

TEACHING VOCABULAIRE

1. Introduce the vocabulary, using transparencies **Vocabulaire 1.1** and **Vocabulaire 1.2.** Model the pronunciation of each noun as you point to the appropriate picture. **Ça, c'est...** and **Il(s)/Elle(s)...** **(3 min.)**

2. Model the pronunciation of the phrases in **Exprimons-nous!** Ensure that students see that **mon... préféré** will agree in gender with the noun. **(3 min.)**

3. Ask students questions about places in a high school. **Où est-ce qu'on déjeune? Où est-ce qu'on a sport?** Then act out the activities presented in **Vocabulaire** and ask, **Qu'est-ce que j'aime faire?** (For **aller au cinéma**, stare at a screen while eating popcorn and drinking a soda; act scared if it is **un film d'horreur.**) **(5 min.)**

4. Point out to students the use of **au** before some names of places and **dans la** before others. **(1 min.)**

Les passe-temps préférés de mes copains

Online Practice
go.hrw.com
Vocabulaire 1 practice
KEYWORD: BD3 CH1

Mehdi **joue de la guitare.**

Le mercredi après-midi, Agnès aime **faire du skate.**

Deux fois par semaine, Rémi **fait de la photo** en noir et blanc.

Céline et Jeanne **vont** souvent **au cinéma.** Elles adorent les **films d'horreur.**

D'autres mots utiles

les arts plastiques	*visual arts*	faire de la vidéo amateur	*to make amateur videos*
un devoir	*homework*	monter à cheval	*to go horseback riding*
une matière	*school subject*	jouer	*to play*
faire la fête	*to party*	au basket/au volley	*basketball/volleyball*
faire les magasins (m.)	*to go shopping*	aux échecs	*chess*

Exprimons-nous!

To express likes, dislikes, and preferences

Interactive TUTOR

Mon sport **préféré, c'est** la natation.
Ma matière **préférée, c'est** l'anglais.
My favorite . . . is . . .

Ce que j'aime, c'est faire la fête avec mes copains.
What I like is . . .

J'aime bien manger à la cantine, **mais je préfère** manger à la maison.
I like . . . but I prefer . . .

Je déteste me lever tôt pendant la semaine et **j'adore** dormir tard le dimanche.
I hate . . . I love . . .

Vocabulaire et grammaire, pp. 1–3
Online workbooks

T P R
TOTAL PHYSICAL RESPONSE

Have students respond to these commands.

Lève-toi si tu empruntes souvent des livres au CDI.

Assieds-toi si tu préfères aller au gymnase.

Lève la main si tu aimes la salle de classe où tu suis le cours de français.

Mets les deux mains sur la tête si tu détestes faire les devoirs.

Viens au tableau et dessine ce qui est dans la salle d'informatique.

Then have them mime the following situations.

Tu es au cinéma, tu regardes un film d'horreur.

Tu fais de la photo.

Tu montes à cheval.

Tu joues de la guitare.

Tu as sport. 1.2

Comparisons

Comparing and Contrasting

The French phrase for 'on the first (ground) floor' of a building is **au rez-de-chaussée**, which means literally *right at the level of the street*. The second floor is called **le premier étage.** Ask students for the French equivalent of the third floor. ❀4.1

Proverbes

For French proverbs and activities related to the chapter theme and vocabulary, see **Proverbes et expressions,** pp. R6–R7.

Differentiated Instruction

SLOWER PACE LEARNERS

Additional Practice Have groups of three or four students draw a simplified floor plan of their own high school. Ask them to label five different rooms and draw objects that identify each room's purpose. They should also write a sentence about the purpose of each room. Have a group present its floor plan to the class. The other groups should comment on the presentation and ask for clarifications, if needed. ❀1.1

MULTIPLE INTELLIGENCES

Visual Learners To assist students in learning new vocabulary, create a "Word Wall" by attaching butcher paper to a wall of the classroom. Have students copy new vocabulary words directly onto the butcher paper from the **Vocabulaire** sections of each chapter. Use the posted list to give visual cues to students when they are searching for or using a new vocabulary word. ❀3.1

Resources

Planning:

Lesson Planner

One-Stop Planner

Presentation:

Teaching Transparencies
Vocabulaire 1.1, 1.2

Practice:

Cahier de vocabulaire et
grammaire

Differentiated Practice and
Assessment CD-ROM

Media Guide

Audio CD 1, Tr. 1

Interactive Tutor, Disc 1

❷ Script

1. — Oh non, c'est encore du poulet
 aujourd'hui!
 — Oui, pourquoi? Tu n'aimes pas le
 poulet?
 — Si, j'aime le poulet, mais pas
 tous les jours!
2. — Tu as choisi un livre?
 — Oui, je vais emprunter *Le comte
 de Monte Cristo.*
3. — Je ne comprends rien à cette
 expérience.
 — Moi non plus. La chimie, je
 trouve ça difficile!
4. — Oh non! Je n'ai pas mes baskets!
 — Alors, tu ne peux pas jouer avec
 nous aujourd'hui.
5. — Hé, Simon, tu as vu? On a cinq
 nouveaux ordinateurs!
 — Ah! Génial!

❸ Answers

1. la salle d'informatique
2. faire de la vidéo amateur
3. emprunter des livres
4. les arts plastiques
5. La cantine
6. jouer de la guitare
7. la récréation

❺ Answers

1. Qu'est-ce que tu vas
2. Quel film
3. Je n'arrive pas
4. je n'ai pas le temps
5. Pourquoi on n'irait pas
6. Bonne idée!

---

❶ Où doit-elle aller? 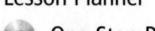1.2

Lisons C'est le jour de la rentrée et Chloé ne connaît pas son
lycée. Aide Chloé à trouver l'endroit où elle doit aller.

d **1.** Où est-ce qu'on déjeune?   **a.** la salle de classe

e **2.** J'ai besoin d'un ordinateur.   **b.** le CDI

            c. le gymnase

b **3.** Je dois rendre des livres.   **d.** la cantine

c **4.** J'ai sport cet après-midi.   **e.** la salle d'informatique

a **5.** J'ai maths à 8h30.   **f.** le laboratoire

❷ Écoutons   CD 1, Tr. 1 1.2   **1.** b **2.** a **3.** d **4.** c **5.** e

Écoute les élèves du lycée Voltaire et dis si ceux qui parlent sont
a) au CDI, b) à la cantine, c) au gymnase, d) au laboratoire ou
e) dans la salle d'informatique.

❸ La vie scolaire 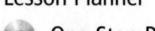1.2

Lisons/Écrivons Complète les phrases avec les mots de la boîte.

jouer de la guitare	la récréation
les arts plastiques	faire de la vidéo amateur
la cantine	la salle d'informatique
emprunter des livres	monter à cheval

1. Je fais beaucoup de recherche sur Internet. Je suis tout
 le temps dans _____.
2. J'ai acheté un caméscope pour _____.
3. Il faut aller au CDI pour _____.
4. J'adore _____, surtout la sculpture.
5. On va manger au café aujourd'hui? _____ est fermée.
6. J'aime bien _____ mais je déteste le piano.
7. Ce que j'aime, c'est parler avec mes copains pendant _____.

❹ Et toi? 1.3

Écrivons/Parlons Réponds aux questions suivantes.

1. Quelle matière est-ce que tu n'aimes pas?
2. Qu'est-ce que tu aimes manger à la cantine?
3. Est-ce que tu préfères aller au cinéma ou faire tes devoirs?
4. Quel est ton cours préféré?
5. Qu'est-ce que tu fais quand tu fais la fête avec tes amis?

Flash culture

À 15 ans, les élèves vont
au lycée ou suivent une
formation professionnelle.

Ceux qui vont au lycée
préparent le baccalauré-
at. Ils ont des cours communs et des cours qu'ils
choisissent en fonction de
ce qu'ils veulent devenir.

D'autres suivent une for-
mation professionnelle et
font un apprentissage.
Après deux ans, ils ont un
CAP (certificat d'aptitude
professionnelle) et après
trois ans, un **BEP** (brevet
d'études professionnelles).
Y a-t-il des écoles
professionnelles dans
ta ville? 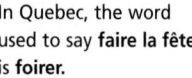4.2

À la québécoise

In Quebec, the word
used to say **faire la fête**
is **foirer.**

But in other franco-
phone countries, the
verb **foirer** means *to
mess up.*

Core Instruction

TEACHING EXPRIMONS-NOUS!

1. Model the pronunciation of the expressions
 in **Exprimons-nous!** With the vocabulary in
 Vocabulaire 1 use these expressions to ask
 students what their plans are. First, model
 an indecisive answer and then, have students
 come up with indecisive responses. **(4 min.)**

2. Extend different invitations to various students. Tell them if you give a thumbs-up sign
 to accept the invitation.

If you show thumbs-down, they should
decline, and if you waggle your open hand,
they should respond indecisively. **(5 min.)**

3. Have partners take turns extending invitations
 and accepting or declining them. **(3 min.)**

Exprimons-nous!

To ask about plans	To respond
Qu'est-ce que tu veux faire **comme** sport cette année? *What . . . do you want to . . . ?*	**Je n'arrive pas à me décider.** *I can't decide.*
Quel film **tu vas** voir ce soir? *What . . . are you going to . . . ?*	**Je n'en sais rien.** *I have no idea.*
Pourquoi on n'irait **pas** à Nice pour le week-end? *How about / Why not . . . ?*	**Bonne idée!** *Great idea!* **Non, désolé(e), je n'ai pas le temps.** *Sorry, I don't have time.*

Interactive TUTOR

Vocabulaire et grammaire, pp. 1–3 — **Online** workbooks

5 **Qu'est-ce qu'on fait samedi?** 🎬1.2

Lisons/Écrivons Ali et Tom parlent de leur projet de week-end. Complète leur conversation logiquement.

TOM ___1___ faire ce week-end?

ALI Samedi soir, je vais au cinéma.

TOM ___2___ tu vas voir?

ALI ___3___ à me décider. Tu veux venir avec moi?

TOM Non, désolé, ___4___. ___5___ au café dimanche?

ALI ___6___!

6 **Qu'est-ce que tu vas faire?** 🎬1.3

Écrivons Écris un e-mail à un(e) camarade et demande -lui ce qu'il/elle va faire ce week-end. Pose-lui au moins trois questions.

Communication

HOLT **SoundBooth** ONLINE RECORDING

7 **Scénario** 🎬1.1

Parlons Demande à un(e) camarade s'il/si elle aime les activités représentées et propose-lui d'en faire une. Il/Elle va accepter ou refuser. S'il/Si elle refuse, suggère une autre activité.

1.　　2.　　3.　　4.

Vocabulaire 1

Comparisons
Comparing and Contrasting

Tell students that sometimes languages borrow words from other languages but do not use these words in their original meaning. For example, in German, a term for ground floor is **Parterre**. Ask students for the literal meaning of **Parterre**. If a language borrows a term from another language and uses it in its original meaning, this term is called a loanword. For example, in French as well as in English, a **pied-à-terre** refers to a lodging or dwelling that is used only part-time or temporarily. What is the literal meaning of this term?

🎬4.1

Communication
Pair Activity: Interpersonal

Briefly review the four forms of **quel** and the difference between **c'est** and **ce sont**. Then, on the board, write the following list: **une matière, un film, un magasin, les céréales** Have the class interview three students about their preferences in each category. Students should listen and then write the responses.

MODÈLE
— **Quelle est ta matière préférée?**
— **Ma matière préférée, c'est la physique.**
(written) **Sa matière ...**

🎬1.1, 1.2

Differentiated Instruction

ADVANCED LEARNERS

Have partners create a poster for their school to advertise after-school club activities. It should address fellow students, encouraging them to participate in a variety of activities after school. **Après ton cours de physique-chimie, joue de la guitare avec des amis.** Encourage students to make their poster as attractive as possible and present it to the class. 🎬1.1, 1.3

SPECIAL LEARNING NEEDS

2 Students with Auditory/Language Impairments To support students with auditory or language impairments, allow them to use a copy of the script for listening activities, such as this. This will increase their ability to process the conversation and respond to comprehension questions regarding the content. 🎬1.2

Assess
Assessment Program
Quiz: Vocabulaire 1
Alternative Assessment
Differentiated Practice and Assessment CD-ROM
Online Assessment
my.hrw.com
Test Generator

Resources

Planning:

Lesson Planner

 One-Stop Planner

Practice:

Grammar Tutor for Students of French, Chapter 1

Cahier de vocabulaire et grammaire

Differentiated Practice and Assessment CD-ROM

Cahier d'activités

Media Guide

 Teaching Transparencies
Bell Work 1.2

 Audio CD 1, Tr. 2

 Interactive Tutor, Disc 1

Bell Work

Use Bell Work 1.2 in the *Teaching Transparencies* or write this activity on the board.

Complète les phrases suivantes logiquement.

1. Mon sport préféré...

2. J'emprunte souvent des livres...

3. On fait des expériences de chimie...

4. Dans la salle d'informatique...

5. Le midi, nous déjeunons...

 1.2

⑨ Script

1. Tous les matins, je [STATIC] le bus à la même heure.

2. On [STATIC] quand on mange trop de chocolat.

3. Vous [STATIC] souvent au basket?

4. Je [STATIC] bien français!

5. Tu [STATIC] cette chanson à la radio? C'est ma chanson préférée.

Objectifs
- regular verbs in the present
- irregular verbs in the present

Révisions — Regular verbs in the present

1 To conjugate **-er**, **-ir**, and **-re** verbs in the present tense (to say that something *is happening* or *happens*), drop the last two letters from the infinitive and add the endings below.

	aimer	choisir	attendre
je/j'	aim**e**	chois**is**	attend**s**
tu	aim**es**	chois**is**	attend**s**
il/elle/on	aim**e**	chois**it**	attend
nous	aim**ons**	chois**issons**	attend**ons**
vous	aim**ez**	chois**issez**	attend**ez**
ils/elles	aim**ent**	chois**issent**	attend**ent**

2 To make a sentence negative, place **ne/n'... pas** around the conjugated verb.

Il attend le bus. Il **n'**attend **pas** le bus.

Vocabulaire et grammaire, *pp. 4–5*
Cahier d'activités, *pp. 1–3*

Online workbooks

Déjà vu!

You already know that in English any verb, for example *to play*, can be conjugated in the present tense three different ways:

I play chess.
I do play chess.
I am playing chess.

Do you remember how you would say the same sentences in French?

Je joue aux échecs.

---

⑧ Suite logique 1.2

Lisons Complète chaque début de phrase logiquement.

f **1.** Paul et moi, nous...   **a.** attends mon fils.

c **2.** Aline...   **b.** grossissent facilement.

a **3.** Je/J'...   **c.** ne perd jamais ses devoirs.

e **4.** Fabrice et toi, vous...   **d.** téléphones souvent à tes copains?

d **5.** Tu...   **e.** choisissez un cadeau pour Laurent.

b **6.** Mes chiens...   **f.** attendons le bus pour aller en ville.

⑨ Écoutons CD 1, Tr. 2 1.2 **1.** a **2.** c **3.** e **4.** g **5.** i

Tu es à la cantine et tu entends des bouts de conversation parce qu'il y a trop de bruit. Pour chaque phrase choisis le bon verbe.

a. prends   **c.** grossit   **e.** jouez   **g.** parle   **i.** entends

b. prend   **d.** grossis   **f.** jouer   **h.** parlent   **j.** entend

---

Core Instruction

TEACHING GRAMMAIRE

1. Go over **Déjà vu!** with students. Review **-er**, **-ir**, and **-re** conjugations by asking students to help three volunteers write one conjugation each (**aimer, choisir,** and **attendre**) on the board. **(4 min.)**

2. Model the pronunciation of all forms of each conjugation.

Point out that the three singular forms have the same pronunciation, as well as the third person plural of the **-er** conjugation. (**aime, aimes, aime, aiment**) **(2 min.)**

3. Practice the forms by asking students questions about themselves and other people. **John, qu'est-ce que tu aimes faire? Nathalie, est-ce que toi et tes amis finissez toujours vos devoirs? (5 min.)**

10 Devoirs pour lundi 🏵1.2

Écrivons Isabelle et ses amis ont des devoirs à faire ce week-end. Complète leur conversation avec la forme correcte des verbes entre parenthèses.

JEAN-MARC   Tous mes copains ___1___ le dimanche soir pour faire leurs devoirs. (attendre) attendent

ISABELLE   Marie ___2___ tous ses devoirs le samedi soir. Et moi aussi! (finir) finit

FRANÇOISE   Oui, avant le week-end, elle ___3___ toujours plein de livres au CDI. (emprunter) emprunte

JEAN-MARC   Oh là là... moi, je ___4___ faire mes devoirs le samedi. (détester) déteste

ISABELLE   Oui, mais Marie et moi, nous ___5___ toujours réussissons aux interros du lundi. (réussir)

11 Qu'est-ce qu'ils font? 🏵1.2

Écrivons Regarde les photos et dis ce que ces gens font.

MODÈLE   **Sylvestre attend son amie.**

Sylvestre

1. ils

2. Lucas

3. Koffi et son oncle

4. Laurie

Communication

HOLT **SoundBooth**
ONLINE RECORDING

12 Interview personnelle 🏵1.1

Parlons Ton/Ta camarade est très curieux/curieuse et te pose des questions. Réponds à toutes ses questions, puis échangez les rôles.

> toi / préférer le français ou les maths
> tes copains et toi / aimer tous vos cours
> tes amis / attendre le dimanche soir pour étudier
> toi / perdre quelquefois ton stylo ou ton cahier
> tes professeurs / finir leur cours à l'heure

MODÈLE   —**Est-ce que tu préfères le français ou les maths?**

Grammaire 1

11 Possible Answers

1. Ils attendent le bus.
2. Lucas emprunte des livres au CDI.
3. Koffi et son oncle jouent aux échecs.
4. Laurie choisit une robe.

Teacher to Teacher

Jeanne S. Jendrzejewski
LSU Lab School
Baton Rouge, LA

Students e-mail me comments about their day twice a week using the grammar that we are focusing on in class. I do not correct them, but I do respond in the correct form to reinforce the structure. E-mails can review vocabulary and functions from the current chapter.

Communication

Pair Activity: Interpersonal
Write the following question prompts on the board.

> **Que / choisir / typiquement**
> **Qui / désobéir / parents**
> **Qui / attendre / bus**
> **Que / perdre / souvent**

Students write the questions, skipping four lines between each question. Then they should use the questions to interview three classmates, and write the responses on their sheet in the **il/elle** form.

MODÈLE
— **Qu'est-ce que tu choisis typiquement au centre commercial?**
— **Je choisis un lecteur MP3.** (written) **Il choisit ...**

🏵1.1, 1.2

Differentiated Instruction

SLOWER PACE LEARNERS

10 Additional Practice Before they do this activity, have students conjugate the verbs in parentheses. They may refer to the conjugation table in **Révisions** for guidance. Then ask students to identify the subject in each sentence.
🏵1.2

SPECIAL LEARNING NEEDS

Students with Learning Disabilities/ Dyslexia Have students remember new grammar concepts by keeping a **Grammaire** notebook. Each time grammar rules and examples appear in the textbook, ask students to copy the rules and examples provided. Be sure each student understands each concept by asking them to add their own example for each rule. Whenever possible, make connections to English grammar rules to help students to remember the French rules.
🏵4.1

Chapitre 1
Grammaire 1

Resources

Planning:

Lesson Planner

 One-Stop Planner

Practice:

Grammar Tutor for Students of French, Chapter 1

Cahier de vocabulaire et grammaire

Differentiated Practice and Assessment CD-ROM

Cahier d'activités

Media Guide

 Teaching Transparencies Bell Work 1.3

 Interactive Tutor, Disc 1

Bell Work

Use Bell Work 1.3 in the *Teaching Transparencies* or write this activity on the board.

Complète les phrases en mettant les verbes entre parenthèses au présent.

1. Pendant les vacances, Mélanie et toi _____ (grossir) toujours un peu.
2. Éric _____ (finir) ses devoirs avant d'aller au cinéma.
3. Louis et moi _____ (jouer) au tennis tous les week-ends.
4. Les élèves _____ (attendre) leur professeur.
5. Tu _____ (descendre) du bus devant l'école. ✿1.2

French for Spanish Speakers

Ask Spanish speakers what the verbs **être** and **aller** are in Spanish. (**ser/estar** and **ir**) Ask them why they think they are among the most irregular verbs in both languages. (frequently used and therefore easier to memorize) ✿4.1

Flash culture

Il y a plusieurs sortes de bac: le bac L (littéraire), le bac S (scientifique) et le bac STT (Sciences technologiques et tertiaires). Pour ceux qui préfèrent une formation pratique, il y a le bac ES (Sciences économiques et sociales) ou le bac pro (professionnel). Pour réussir, il faut une moyenne générale de 10/20. Si le lycéen échoue, il peut le repasser l'année suivante. Le bac permet d'entrer à l'université.

Dans ton état, y a-t-il un examen d'entrée à l'université? ✿2.1

Révisions — Irregular verbs in the present

1 You've already learned many irregular verbs. Do you remember how to conjugate these verbs?

	avoir	être	aller
je/j'	ai	suis	vais
tu	as	es	vas
il/elle/on	a	est	va
nous	avons	sommes	allons
vous	avez	êtes	allez
ils/elles	ont	sont	vont

Vous **avez** raison!
Tu **es** vraiment sympa!
Je **vais** en Grèce cet été.

	faire	prendre	venir
je	fais	prends	viens
tu	fais	prends	viens
il/elle/on	fait	prend	vient
nous	faisons	prenons	venons
vous	faites	prenez	venez
ils/elles	font	prennent	viennent

Julien **fait** ses devoirs.
Tu **prends** l'avion pour aller en Angleterre?
Vous **venez** avec moi?

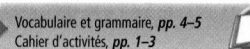 Vocabulaire et grammaire, pp. 4–5
Cahier d'activités, pp. 1–3
 **Online** workbooks

13 **Le bon verbe** ✿1.2

Lisons Complète chaque phrase avec la forme correcte du verbe.

1. Ali et moi, nous (sont / <u>sommes</u>) dans la même classe.
2. Nous (<u>avons</u> / ont) un beau gymnase dans notre lycée.
3. Tu (comprend / <u>comprends</u>) les explications du professeur?
4. Tu (va / <u>vas</u>) au cinéma ce soir?
5. Mes parents (<u>font</u> / faisons) les magasins le week-end.
6. Tu (fait / <u>fais</u>) souvent du skate?
7. Vous (<u>prenez</u> / prends) du sucre dans votre thé?

Core Instruction

TEACHING GRAMMAIRE

1. Ask students which forms within each conjugation have the same pronunciation and which have the same spelling. Model the pronunciation of all forms. **(4 min.)**

2. Ask students questions about themselves and other people, using irregular verbs.

Begin with yes/no questions. Then proceed with more open-ended questions. **Doug, quel âge as-tu? D'où es-tu? Comment viens-tu en cours? Et Jennifer? Et tes amis? (5 min.)**

14 **Hein? Quoi?** 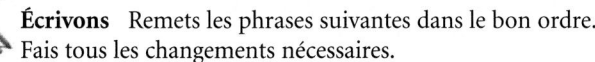1.2

Écrivons Remets les phrases suivantes dans le bon ordre. Fais tous les changements nécessaires.

1. à la MJC / tu / de la photo / faire / les cours / après
2. mes / être / copains / intelligent / vraiment
3. venir / ils / souvent / nous / chez
4. je / pas / ne / aller / soir / au / ce / cinéma
5. les / prendre / tous / mes / le métro / parents / jours
6. avoir / nouveau / une / tu / guitare
7. ma / cette / cousine / apprendre / année / l'allemand

15 **Et toi?** 1.3

Parlons/Écrivons Réponds aux questions suivantes.

1. Vous êtes combien dans ta classe de français?
2. Tu as beaucoup de devoirs à faire le week-end?
3. Tes amis et toi, vous prenez le bus pour aller à l'école?
4. Qu'est-ce que tu fais après les cours?
5. Tes copains et toi, vous allez souvent au centre commercial?
6. Est-ce que ton/ta meilleur(e) ami(e) vient souvent chez toi?

Communication

HOLT **SoundBooth**
ONLINE RECORDING

16 **Scénario** 1.1

Parlons Tes copains et toi, vous voulez faire quelque chose ensemble ce week-end. Fais un emploi du temps pour ce week-end et dis-leur si tu es libre. Si tu es occupé(e), propose un autre moment.

MODÈLE —Tu viens jouer au foot avec nous samedi matin?
—Non, j'ai...

Vendredi	Samedi	Dimanche
18h: photos à la MJC	10h: cours de tennis	16h: chez mes grands-parents
	12h: déjeuner avec Sara	
	20h: cinéma	

14 Answers

1. Tu fais de la photo à la MJC après les cours.
2. Mes copains sont vraiment intelligents.
3. Ils viennent souvent chez nous.
4. Je ne vais pas au cinéma ce soir.
5. Mes parents prennent le métro tous les jours.
6. Tu as une nouvelle guitare.
7. Ma cousine apprend l'allemand cette année.

Communication

16 Group Activity: Presentational

Have students start a question-and-answer chain with the verbs **aller** and **venir de**. Student A starts by saying what he or she is going to do, using **aller** + infinitive, and then calls on student B. Using **venir de,** Student B says that he or she has just done that activity and then says what he or she is going to do instead, using **aller**. Continue the cycle.

MODÈLE
A — Je vais faire la vaisselle.
B — Je viens de faire la vaisselle. Je vais lire un roman. 1.3

Differentiated Instruction

SLOWER PACE LEARNERS

14 **Building on Previous Skills** Some students may have trouble building sentences. Help these students by reviewing the structure of simple sentences and the correct word order. Encourage students to write the scrambled terms in the appropriate columns of a graphic organizer that groups subjects, verbs, objects, and circumstantial complements. 1.2

SPECIAL LEARNING NEEDS

14 **Students with AD(H)D** Before they begin the activity, prepare, or ask students to prepare, note cards with the suggested sentence parts, one word or phrase on each note card. Ask students to use the cards to create the sentence they will then write for the assignment. This hands-on activity is effective for improving student attention and understanding. 1.2

Assess

Assessment Program
Quiz: Grammaire 1
Alternative Assessment
Differentiated Practice and Assessment CD-ROM

Online Assessment
my.hrw.com

Test Generator

Bell Work

Use Bell Work 1.4 in the *Teaching Transparencies* or write this activity on the board.

Complète les phrases avec un verbe qui convient.

1. Au lycée, tu _____ des profs intéressants?

2. Le matin, vous _____ le bus pour aller en cours?

3. Édouard et moi _____ de la photo tous les week-ends.

4. Mes amies _____ intelligentes et sympa.

5. Aurélie _____ chez moi ce soir. 🍀1.2

⑰ Possible Answers

1. Nous allons au musée.

2. Bernard et ses copains jouent au foot.

3. Toi, tu surfes sur Internet.

4. Amélie mange à la cantine.

⑱ Script

See script on p. 3E.

Synthèse
- Vocabulaire 1
- Grammaire 1

Application 1

⑰ Que font-ils? 🍀1.2

Parlons Regarde les photos et dis ce que font ces jeunes en ce moment.

MODÈLE Je vais au lycée.

je

1. nous

2. Bernard et ses copains

3. toi, tu

4. Amélie

Un peu plus — Révisions

Verbs followed by the infinitive

In French, as in English, many verbs are often followed by an infinitive. Some of those verbs are **vouloir**, **devoir**, and **pouvoir**.

> Je **dois finir** mes devoirs.

Use the verb **aller** with an infinitive to indicate that something *is going to happen.*

> Je **vais étudier** les arts plastiques cette année.

Use the verb **venir** (followed by **de**) with an infinitive to indicate that something *just happened.*

> Caroline **vient de partir** en vacances.

Vocabulaire et grammaire, *p. 6*
Cahier d'activités, *pp. 1–3*

Online workbooks

1. a **2.** b **3.** b **4.** a **5.** a

⑱ Écoutons CD 1, Tr. 3 🍀1.2

Écoute les conversations entre Nathalie et ses parents et décide si Nathalie **a) vient de faire** ou **b) va faire** quelque chose.

⑲ Des phrases à faire 🍀1.2

Écrivons Remets les phrases dans le bon ordre et fais les changements nécessaires.

MODÈLE Je / voir un bon film / venir de
Je viens de voir un bon film.

1. Ali / téléphoner à sa tante / devoir

2. Mes amis et moi, nous / manger une glace / aller

3. Mes parents / partir en vacances / vouloir

4. Mon cousin / rentrer à l'université / venir de

5. Madame Gantois, vous / faire les magasins / vouloir / ne... pas

6. Tu / acheter le dernier CD de Zouk / aller

7. Et moi, je / finir cet exercice / venir de

Core Instruction

INTEGRATED PRACTICE

1. Have students do Activity 17 to practice vocabulary and grammar already presented. **(5 min.)**

2. Introduce **Un peu plus.** (See presentation suggestions at right.) **(4 min.)**

3. Continue with integrated practice Activities 18–23. **(30 min.)**

TEACHING UN PEU PLUS

1. Review the conjugation of **aller, venir,** and **devoir** by asking students to write a few short sentences about themselves and other people. Before they write sentences with **devoir**, tell them the verb also means *to owe* and can be used with **de l'argent** or **le respect.** **(5 min.)**

2. Go over **Un peu plus.** Call out infinitives and expressions, like **avoir une bonne note à l'examen**, and have students make complete sentences. **(4 min.)**

㉒ L'emploi du temps de Laura 1.2

Lisons/Parlons Regarde l'emploi du temps de Laura et réponds aux questions qui suivent.

Lycée Victor Hugo
18 boulevard Berthier
29000 Brest
Fax: 02.92.03.10
Tel: 02.92.10.10

	lundi	mardi	mercredi	jeudi	vendredi
8h	anglais	informatique		sport	biologie
9h	maths	histoire	informatique	physique	biologie
10h	français	histoire	maths	géographie	espagnol
11h	français	maths	physique	géographie	informatique
12h			DÉJEUNER		
13h					
14h	sport	anglais		français	histoire
15h	sport	français		chimie	maths
16h	informatique	espagnol		espagnol	anglais

1. Où est Laura à midi?
2. Quand est-ce qu'elle est au gymnase?
3. Où est-ce qu'elle est le lundi à huit heures du matin?
4. Est-ce qu'elle va au laboratoire le mardi?
5. Qu'est-ce qu'elle fait le vendredi à 11h?
6. Est-ce que Laura peut aller au cinéma le jeudi après-midi?

1. Elle est à la cantine.
2. le lundi après-midi et le jeudi matin
3. Elle est en classe.
4. Non.
5. Elle travaille sur ordinateur.
6. Non.

㉑ Mon école 1.3

Écrivons Écris un petit paragraphe pour expliquer ce qu'il y a dans ton école, les cours que tu as cette année, ceux que tu préfères et ceux que tu n'aimes pas trop.

Communication

 HOLT **SoundBooth**
ONLINE RECORDING

㉒ Scénario 1.1

Parlons Tu viens d'arriver dans un nouveau lycée. Pose cinq questions à un(e) camarade de classe pour lui demander ce qu'on peut ou ne peut pas faire et ce qu'on doit faire dans ce lycée.

MODÈLE **—On peut faire du skate pendant la récréation?**

㉓ Préférences personnelles 1.1

Parlons Avec un(e) camarade, parlez de ce que vous aimez et n'aimez pas faire et de ce que vous allez faire ce week-end.

MODÈLE **—J'adore lire et je viens d'acheter une BD, alors, ce week-end, je vais...**

㉙ Answers
1. Ali doit téléphoner à sa tante.
2. Mes amis et moi, nous allons manger une glace.
3. Mes parents veulent partir en vacances.
4. Mon cousin vient de rentrer à l'université.
5. Madame Gantois, vous ne voulez pas faire les magasins?
6. Tu vas acheter le dernier CD de Zouk.
7. Et moi, je viens de finir cet exercice!

Communication

Group Activity: Interpersonal
Review the conjugations of **vouloir, pouvoir,** and **devoir**. Then have each student write a list of five things he or she wants to do. Each student asks two classmates if they want to do one of his or her listed activities. The classmates should decline with an excuse. Ask them to use the verbs **vouloir, pouvoir,** and **devoir**.

MODÈLE
— Tu veux aller au ciné ce week-end?
— Je ne peux pas. Je dois ranger ma chambre.

1.1

Differentiated Instruction

ADVANCED LEARNERS

㉑ Challenge When students have completed the activity, ask groups of four students to create a survey of five questions related to school subjects. For example, groups could ask their classmates about the courses they are currently taking, which subjects they like, or which ones they like less. Have students summarize the survey results and present them to the class.
1.1

SPECIAL LEARNING NEEDS

㉙ Students with Learning Disabilities
Copy, enlarge, and cut apart the sentence pieces in this activity. Color code the pieces of each sentence. Have students move the pieces into the correct order to form each sentence. Then have them find the correct conjugation of the verb. With practice, students will become familiar with the step-by-step process. 1.2

Assess

Assessment Program
Quiz: Application 1
Audio CD 1, Tr. 11
Alternative Assessment
Differentiated Practice and Assessment CD-ROM

Online Assessment
my.hrw.com

Test Generator

Prereading Questions

You might ask these questions before students read the selection.

1. **Est-ce que tu as déjà vu un match de polo?**
2. **Est-ce que tu vas quelquefois voir des courses de chevaux?**
3. **Est-ce que tu montes à cheval?**
4. **Est-ce que tu as déjà caressé (petted) un cheval?**

Active Reading Questions

1. **Où est-ce que les chevaux s'entraînent? (sur la plage)**
2. **À quoi Mme Belisha compare-t-elle les chevaux de polo? (à des athlètes)**
3. **De combien de chevaux est-ce qu'un joueur de polo débutant a besoin pour un match? (de deux ou trois chevaux)**
4. **Combien de chevaux faut-il pour un joueur de polo de haut niveau au cours d'un match? (jusqu'à 16 chevaux)**

✿1.2

Vocabulaire supplémentaire

You might wish to use these terms to discuss the text.

un éperon *spur*
la bride *bridle*
le mors *bridle bit*
la selle *saddle*
un étrier *stirrup*

Culture

Lecture culturelle

La mer reste la destination préférée des Français et les sports nautiques y sont très populaires. Toutefois, d'autres formes de loisirs se développent. C'est ainsi que depuis plusieurs années, de plus en plus de clubs équestres s'installent sur le littoral. Tôt le matin ou tard le soir, on peut voir des chevaux galoper sur la plage ou nager dans la mer. Que penses-tu de l'activité ci-dessous?

Chevaux de polo

Judith Belisha, propriétaire du club de l'Oxer depuis 7 ans, s'est lancée dans l'élevage[1] et le dressage[2] de 10 chevaux de polo. La plage à marée[3] basse lui fournit[4] un excellent terrain d'entraînement pour l'initiation, destinée à tout bon cavalier[5] : « Les chevaux de polo sont de véritables athlètes. Ils naissent en Amérique du Sud, principalement en Argentine, issus[6] d'une jument[7] de la Pampa et d'un pur-sang[8], pour la vitesse. Les chevaux doivent être extrêmement intelligents, rapides et endurants. Un joueur débutant a besoin de 2 ou 3 bêtes[9] pour un match, mais au plus haut niveau, il faut jusqu'à 16 chevaux. » Le club propose par ailleurs des baignades[10] en mer, « là où les chevaux n'ont plus pied », avec tangage[11] garanti.

Compréhension ✿2.1
1. Quelle est l'activité de Judith Belisha?
2. Quelles sont les qualités d'un bon cheval de polo?
3. D'où viennent ces chevaux?

1. l'élevage et le dressage de chevaux de polo
2. intelligent, rapide et endurant
3. d'Argentine (d'Amérique du Sud)

1. *breeding* 2. entraîner 3. *low tide* 4. donne 5. personne qui monte à cheval 6. né de 7. femelle du cheval 8. *thoroughbred horse* 9. *animals* 10. *bain* 11. balance d'un côté et de l'autre

Core Instruction

LECTURE CULTURELLE

1. Read and discuss the introductory paragraph as a class. **(3 min.)**
2. Ask students where they usually spend their vacations and which activities they prefer when on vacation. **(2 min.)**
3. Have volunteers read the selection aloud and then have partners answer the **Compréhension** questions. **(5 min.)**

COMPARAISONS ET COMMUNAUTÉ

1. Have students read the first paragraph of **Comparaisons** and answer the question. **(3 min.)**
2. Have students read the second paragraph. Then have them answer the **Et toi?** questions. **(4 min.)**
3. Go over **Communauté et professions** with students. Have them answer the research questions with a partner. **(3 min.)**

Online Practice
go.hrw.com
Online Edition
KEYWORD: BD3 CH1

Chapitre 1
Culture

Comparaisons

Les moniteurs 🎴4.2

Imagine que tu es champion de ski et que tu donnes des cours de ski depuis deux ans dans le Colorado. Tu décides d'aller travailler en France pour une saison. Tu dois...

- **a.** envoyer une lettre de recommandation.
- **b.** montrer les médailles (*medals*) que tu as gagnées.
- **c.** obtenir un monitorat de ski (*ski diploma*).

Un moniteur de ski

En France, la planche à voile, le ski, le tennis, l'équitation et de nombreux autres sports sont enseignés le plus souvent par des moniteurs. Pour être moniteur, il faut avoir 18 ans et obtenir une Attestation de Formation de Premier Secours (AFPS). Il faut aussi être titulaire du Brevet d'État d'Éducateur Sportif (BEES). Ce diplôme est délivré par le Ministère des Sports et comprend des épreuves théoriques (niveau bac) et pratiques.

🎴 4.2, 1.3

ET TOI?

1. Est-ce qu'il existe un diplôme similaire au BEES aux États-Unis?

2. Est-ce que tu crois qu'il est nécessaire d'avoir un diplôme pour enseigner un sport?

Communauté et professions

Le français et le développement des loisirs et du tourisme 🎴5.1

Le développement des loisirs et du tourisme a permis la création de nouveaux métiers. Le plus souvent ces métiers requièrent la connaissance d'une langue étrangère, comme le français. Quels sont les centres d'intérêt touristique de ton état? Fais des recherches sur le tourisme dans ton état. En faisant tes recherches, as-tu trouvé des renseignements sur ta région en français? Présente ce que tu as trouvé à ta classe.

Un guide à New York

Objectifs
- to tell when and how often you did something
- to describe a place in the past

Vocabulaire à l'œuvre 2

Révisions
Une carte postale de Damien

Chers mamie et papi,
Les vacances à la montagne, c'est génial! Hier, je suis allé à la pêche avec papa pendant que maman faisait la sieste, et j'ai même attrapé un poisson! Papa, lui, n'a rien pris. On fait de la randonnée en forêt tous les jours. Merci encore pour le sac à dos et la gourde que vous m'avez offerts. Je les utilise beaucoup. J'ai plein de copains à l'hôtel. La semaine dernière, on est allés camper.
J'ai pris beaucoup de photos. Je vous les montrerai à mon retour.

Grosses bises,
Damien

M. et Mme Noiret
10, place des Platanes
71240 Châtenoy-le-Royal

▶ Vocabulaire supplémentaire—À la montagne, p. R16

Resources

Planning:
Lesson Planner

 One-Stop Planner

Presentation:
 Teaching Transparencies
Vocabulaire 1.3, 1.4

Practice:
Cahier de vocabulaire et grammaire

Differentiated Practice and Assessment CD-ROM

Media Guide
 Teaching Transparencies
Bell Work 1.5

 Interactive Tutor, Disc 1

 Bell Work

Use Bell Work 1.5 in the *Teaching Transparencies* or write this activity on the board.

Mets les phrases suivantes dans le bon ordre.

1. examen / Alix / venir / réussir / de / son
2. difficile / finir / devoir / exercice / cet / nous
3. russe / aller / prochaine / année / étudier / je / l' / le
4. venir / cinéma / soir / pouvoir / tu / au / ce / ?
5. tennis / ils / demain / vouloir / avec / jouer / moi / au ✿ 1.2

Connections

Geography Link

Biarritz, on the **Côte Basque**, became famous in 1854 when Empress Eugenie, wife of Napoleon III, built a palace on the beach, now the **Hôtel du Palais.** Biarritz became a popular winter resort for European and Russian nobility. Today, surfers from all over the world come to the annual Surf Festival. Have students list reasons for Biarritz's popularity, first among aristocrats and then among surfers. ✿ 3.1

Core Instruction

TEACHING VOCABULAIRE

1. Introduce the vocabulary, using transparencies **Vocabulaire 1.3** and **1.4**. Model the pronunciation of each word. Ça, c'est à la montagne/un sac de couchage. Il/Elle a attrapé un poisson/fait de la randonnée. (3 min.)

2. Ask students to point out various items (**la tente**), locations (**la campagne**), and activities (**la planche à voile**) on the transparency. (2 min.)

3. Ask students questions about their last vacation. **Où est-ce que tu es allé(e) en vacances? Qu'est-ce que tu as fait? Qu'est-ce que tu as utilisé pour faire de la randonnée? (3 min.)**

4. Model the pronunciation of the expressions in **Exprimons-nous!** Then provide students practice by asking them questions with **quand. Quand est-ce que tu as dormi sous la tente? Quand as-tu fait de la randonnée? (4 min.)**

Mes copains aussi sont partis en vacances

Vocabulaire 2

Johanna est allée **au bord de la mer.**
Elle **a fait de la planche à voile.**

Léna est allée **au Canada** avec ses
parents. Elle **a adoré!**

Mathilde **a rendu visite** à ses cousins
à la campagne.

Nicolas **est parti** à Paris pour **une semaine.**

D'autres mots utiles

la canne à pêche	*fishing rod*	la lotion anti-moustiques	*insect repellent*
les chaussures de randonnée	*hiking shoes*	le sac de couchage	*sleeping bag*
la demi-pension	*room with breakfast and 1 meal included*	le sac de voyage	*traveling bag*
		la tente	*tent*
la pension complète	*room with 3 meals*		

Exprimons-nous!

To tell when and how often you did something		*Interactive* **TUTOR**
Je me suis baigné(e) **tous les jours** pendant les vacances.	*. . . every day . . .*	
Quand il faisait beau, j'allais à la plage.	*When . . .*	
Le soir, on faisait un feu de camp et on jouait de la guitare.	*Every evening/In the evening, . . .*	
Tous les deux jours, on allait à la pêche avec mon grand-père.	*Every other day, . . .*	

Vocabulaire et grammaire, pp. 7–9
**Online** workbooks

▶ Vocabulaire supplémentaire—À la mer, **p. R16**

Resources

Planning:
Lesson Planner
 One-Stop Planner

Presentation:
 Teaching Transparencies
Vocabulaire 1.3, 1.4

Practice:
Cahier de vocabulaire et grammaire
Differentiated Practice and Assessment CD-ROM
Media Guide
 Audio CD 1, Tr. 4
 Interactive Tutor, Disc 1

24 Script

1. J'avais une grande tente et un nouveau sac de couchage.
2. Je suis allée à la ferme de mon grand-père.
3. J'ai attrapé quatre poissons le premier jour!
4. J'ai fait de la planche à voile. C'était super!
5. J'ai fait du ski tous les jours.
6. On était en demi-pension.

25 Answers

1. Il te faut une gourde et un sac à dos.
2. Il te faut une canne à pêche et une planche à voile.
3. Il vous faut des sacs de couchage, de la lotion anti-moustiques et une tente.
4. Il vous faut une canne à pêche, une gourde et un sac à dos.

26 Answers

1. semaines
2. bord de la mer
3. tous les jours
4. pêche
5. gourde
6. soir
7. Quand
8. planche à voile
9. rendre visite
10. tente
11. sac de couchage

Entre copains

le cinoche	movie theater
la cambrousse	countryside
faire la teuf	to party
s'éclater	to have a blast
aller prendre un pot	to go to a café

Flash culture

Les jeunes Français sont en vacances en juillet et en août. Ce sont «les grandes vacances».

Ils vont à la mer, à la montagne ou à l'étranger pour se perfectionner dans la langue du pays.

La plupart ne travaillent pas l'été, mais certains ont un diplôme qui leur permet d'être moniteur et de s'occuper d'enfants dans des centres aérés en ville ou dans des colonies de vacances. 4.2

Que fais-tu pendant tes vacances?

---

24 Écoutons CD 1, Tr. 4 1.2

Écoute ce que disent ces personnes et décide où elles sont allées ou ce qu'elles ont fait en vacances.

5 **a.** la montagne   4 **d.** le bord de la mer
6 **b.** l'hôtel   3 **e.** la pêche
1 **c.** le camping   2 **f.** la campagne

25 Qu'est-ce qu'il leur faut? 1.2

Lisons/Parlons Dis à ces personnes quels objets de la liste ils doivent emporter avec eux.

MODÈLE Léa: Je vais à Rome. (un sac de voyage / une tente / un dictionnaire / une planche à voile / des skis)
Il te faut un sac de voyage et un dictionnaire.

1. **Julien:** Je vais faire une randonnée. (une gourde / une canne à pêche / un sac de voyage / un sac à dos / un dictionnaire)
2. **Max:** Je vais à la mer. (des chaussures de randonnée / des skis / une canne à pêche / un ordinateur / une planche à voile)
3. **Éloïse:** Vincent et moi, nous allons camper cet été. (des sacs de couchage / une planche à voile / des skates / de la lotion anti-moustiques / une tente)
4. **Lucas:** Avec des copains, on va pêcher cet après-midi. (une planche à voile / une canne à pêche / une tente / un livre d'histoire / une gourde / un sac à dos)

26 Un petit mot d'Ibrahim 1.2

Écrivons Choisis des mots de la boîte pour compléter le mot d'Ibrahim à son amie Clara.

bord de la mer	soir	rendre visite
pêche	planche à voile	demi-pension
gourde	semaines	sac de couchage
quand	tous les jours	tente

Je passe deux __1__ chez mes cousins, au __2__. On va __3__ à la plage. C'est vraiment super! Hier, je suis allé à la __4__ avec Soliman mais on n'a pas attrapé de poisson. Il faisait très chaud. Heureusement, j'avais ma __5__. Le __6__, on a joué de la guitare et on a dansé. C'était très sympa. __7__ il fait beau, on fait de la __8__. Demain, nous allons __9__ à mon frère qui campe dans la région. Il a une super __10__. Je voulais rester camper avec lui, mais j'ai oublié mon __11__ à la maison.

Core Instruction

TEACHING EXPRIMONS-NOUS!

1. Model the expressions in **Exprimons-nous!** **(2 min.)**
2. Remind students that they can also use these expressions in the present: **il y a..., les paysages me rappellent..., il fait froid, c'est super. (2 min.)**
3. Ask students to describe the places where they spent their last vacation. You may want to ask them questions with **comment. Comment était la plage où tu es allé(e)? (3 min.)**

Exprimons-nous!

To describe a place in the past	
Il y avait beaucoup de monde à l'hôtel.	*There was/were . . .*
Les paysages **me rappelaient** la Corse	*. . . reminded me of . . .*
Il faisait froid le soir.	*The weather was . . .*
C'était super/génial, les châteaux de la Loire.	*It was . . .*

Interactive TUTOR

Vocabulaire et grammaire, pp. 7–9

Online workbooks

27 C'était comment? 1.2

Parlons/Écrivons Regarde ces photos et imagine ce que ces personnes disent de leurs vacances.

MODÈLE —J'ai fait des randonnées en montagne. C'était super.

1. nous

2. Julie

3. André

4. Alain et Lise

5. ils

6. je

Communication

HOLT SoundBooth ONLINE RECORDING

28 Sondage 1.1

Parlons Tu dois écrire un article sur les vacances des jeunes. Prépare une liste de 10 questions sur les vacances (lieux, activités, comment c'était, etc.) à poser à tes camarades de classe. Présente les résultats de ton sondage à la classe.

MODÈLE —Où est-ce que tu es allée en vacances? Qu'est-ce que tu as fait? Est-ce que c'était bien?

27 Possible Answers

1. Nous avon joué au volley sur la plage.
2. Julie est allée à la pêche. Elle a attrapé un gros poisson!
3. André a campé au bord de la mer. Il faisait beau et il y avait beaucoup de monde sur la plage.
4. Alain et Lise sont montés à cheval.
5. Ils sont allées à la montagne. Il neigeait et il faisait froid.
6. J'ai fait de la planche à voile. C'était cool!

Communication

28 Pair Activity: Presentational

Students may need to research some of the necessary vocabulary before the activity. Write the following vacation destinations on the board:

à la Martinique, à Paris, en Afrique, dans les Alpes, à la campagne

Have partners choose a place and create a conversation between a traveler preparing for a trip and a sales clerk. The traveler should buy five items and include adjectives. The sales clerk can ask questions about the traveler's plans and what he or she is going to do with the items. Have partners act out their conversations in front of the class. 1.3

Differentiated Instruction

SLOWER PACE LEARNERS

26 Additional Practice Before students begin this activity, ask them to close their books. Read the letter with the answers included. Students should focus on understanding the content of the letter. Ask volunteers to summarize the letter. Then ask students to open their books and complete the activity. 1.2

SPECIAL LEARNING NEEDS

27 Students with Visual Impairments The photographs in this activity may not be large enough for students with visual impairments to see. If the pictures in an activity are difficult to see, try enlarging them or have students use their magnifying assistive technology. As an alternative, have students work with a partner who describes the picture in detail. 1.2

Assess

Assessment Program

Quiz: Vocabulaire 2

Alternative Assessment

Differentiated Practice and Assessment CD-ROM

Online Assessment

my.hrw.com

Test Generator

Objectifs
- the *passé composé*
- using the *passé composé* and the *imparfait*

Resources

Planning:

Lesson Planner

 One-Stop Planner

Practice:

Grammar Tutor for Students of French, Chapter 1

Cahier de vocabulaire et grammaire

Differentiated Practice and Assessment CD-ROM

Cahier d'activités

Media Guide

 Teaching Transparencies
Bell Work 1.6

 Audio CD 1, Tr. 5

 Interactive Tutor, Disc 1

Bell Work

Use Bell Work 1.6 in the *Teaching Transparencies* or write this activity on the board.

Complète ce texte avec le vocabulaire approprié.

1. Aujourd'hui, nous faisons une randonnée et je ne dois oublier ni ma _____ ni mon _____.
2. Demain, nous allons à la pêche et je vais prendre ma _____.
3. Le soir, je rigole avec mes copains autour d'un feu de camp, puis je me couche sous la _____ dans mon _____. ✿1.2

COMMON ERROR ALERT
///ATTENTION !

Agreement of past participles with direct object pronouns is obvious when the direct object pronoun is **le, la** or **les**. It is not as obvious with the pronouns **me, te, nous, vous,** and the reflexive **se,** which may be direct or indirect object pronouns.

29 Script

See script on p. 3E.

 Interactive TUTOR

Grammaire
à l'œuvre 2

Révisions The *passé composé*

1. Use the **passé composé** to say that something happened at a specific time. The **passé composé** has two parts: the helping verb (**avoir** or **être**) and the past participle of the main verb. To make a sentence negative, place **ne/n'… pas** around the helping verb.

2. The helping verb **avoir** is used with most verbs in the **passé composé**.

   The helping verb **être** is used with verbs of transition and motion and with reflexive verbs.

3. To form the past participle of regular verbs, drop the last two letters of the infinitive and add the following endings to the stem.

   -er → **-é**   **-ir** → **-i**   **-re** → **-u**

   Here are the past participles of some irregular verbs you already know.

aller	→ allé	être	→ été	pouvoir	→ pu
avoir	→ eu	faire	→ fait	prendre	→ pris
connaître	→ connu	lire	→ lu	venir	→ venu
croire	→ cru	mettre	→ mis	voir	→ vu
devoir	→ dû	pleuvoir	→ plu	vouloir	→ voulu

4. If the helping verb is **être**, the past participle agrees in gender and number with the subject.

   Elles sont **allées** au cinéma.

   If the helping verb is **avoir**, the past participle agrees in gender and number with a preceding direct object.

   Tu as **lu les livres** de Pagnol?   Non, je ne **les** ai pas **lus**.

    Vocabulaire et grammaire, *pp. 10–11*
   Cahier d'activités, *pp. 5–7*
   Online workbooks

29 Écoutons CD 1, Tr. 5 ✿1.2 **1.** a **2.** a **3.** b **4.** a **5.** a **6.** b **7.** a

Émilie parle avec ses amis. Dis si ce qu'ils disent...
a) se passe habituellement ou **b) s'est passé une seule fois.**

Flash culture

La plupart des familles voyagent en France pendant les vacances. Beaucoup de villes organisent des festivals: de musique comme à Antibes, de théâtre comme à Avignon, de bandes dessinées comme à Angoulême, etc. Et bien sûr, chaque année, il y a Paris Plages qui attire de plus en plus de vacanciers.

Est-ce qu'il y a des festivals dans des villes de ta région? ✿4.2

Core Instruction

TEACHING GRAMMAIRE

1. To review the use of the **passé composé**, ask volunteers to tell the class three things they did last weekend and one thing they did not do. **Qu'est-ce que tu as fait ce week-end, Cassie? Qu'est-ce que tu n'as pas fait? (2 min.)**

2. Point out that verbs of transition and motion take **être** in the **passé composé**. You might want to use DR & MRS VANDERTRAMPP as a mnemonic device to list all the verbs students have learned. **(3 min.)**

3. Go over Points 3 and 4. Ask volunteers to form one sentence in the **passé composé** with each of the verbs and write it on the board. Ask the class to check for spelling and agreement. **(4 min.)**

4. Point out to students that when the helping verb is **avoir**, the past participle will always agree with its direct object. Give them **La femme que j'ai vue**, as an example. **(2 min.)**

Online Practice
go.hrw.com
Grammaire 2 practice
KEYWORD: BD3 CH1

Chapitre 1
Grammaire 2

30 **Souvenirs de vacances** 🌸1.2

Lisons/Écrivons Complète les souvenirs de vacances de Paul. Utilise **le passé composé**.

Un jour, pendant les vacances, Denis et moi, nous ___1___ (aller) à la pêche. Nous ___2___ (attraper) beaucoup de poissons. Nous les ___3___ (manger) le soir même! Véronique et Liliane ___4___ (venir) nous rendre visite un week-end. Nous ___5___ (faire) une grande randonnée. Elles ___6___ (rentrer) chez elles très fatiguées. Nous les ___7___ (revoir) le week-end suivant. Cette fois, elles ___8___ (ne pas vouloir) venir avec nous! Nous les ___9___ (voir) au parc avec d'autres garçons!

1. sommes allés
2. avons attrapé
3. avons mangés
4. sont venues
5. avons fait
6. sont rentrées
7. avons revues
8. n'ont pas voulu
9. avons vues

31 **Vacances en famille** 🌸1.2

Parlons Pascale part souvent en vacances avec sa famille. Regarde les images et imagine ce qu'elle dit.

MODÈLE J'ai attrapé des poissons.

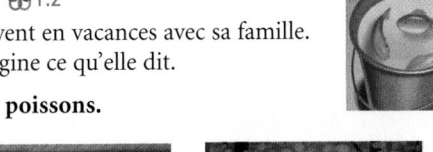

1. mes parents et moi   2. je   3. mes parents   4. ma sœur

32 **Le week-end dernier** 🌸1.3

Écrivons Écris un paragraphe pour dire cinq choses que tu as faites ou qui se sont passées le week-end dernier.

MODÈLE J'ai rendu visite à ma tante et je suis allé(e) au cinéma avec mes cousins...

**Communication**

HOLT **SoundBooth**
ONLINE RECORDING

33 **Expérience personnelle** 🌸1.1

Parlons Demande à tes camarades ce qu'ils ont fait pendant leurs vacances: s'ils ont rendu visite à leur famille, s'ils sont allés camper, s'ils ont fait du sport, etc. Ensuite, échangez les rôles.

MODÈLE —Qu'est-ce que tu as fait? Tu es allé(e) camper?

Grammaire 2

31 **Possible Answers**

1. Mes parents et moi, nous sommes partis en vacances à la campagne.
2. J'ai rendu visite à ma grand-mère.
3. Mes parents ont fait de la randonnée.
4. Ma sœur est montée à cheval.

Communication

33 **Group Activity: Presentational**

Have students interview each other, as in Activity 33, but have them get as many details as possible. Then have two interview pairs form a group of four. Ask each student to talk about his or her respective partner's vacation. **Il/Elle....** Students may use notes for details, but they should try to speak as freely as possible.

🌸1.3

French for Spanish Speakers

Remind Spanish speakers that the **passé composé** corresponds very closely to the **pretérito perfecto** in Spanish. Ask students what the auxiliary verb is in Spanish that corresponds to **avoir. (haber)** What are some differences between the **passé composé** in French and the **pretérito perfecto** in Spanish? (In French it has two auxiliary verbs, **avoir** and **être**. In Spanish only **haber** is used) Have students make a chart with two columns in order to compare the present tense conjugations of **avoir** and **haber**. Which forms are most alike in spelling? (**a** and **ha, as** and **has**) Which forms are most alike in pronunciation? (**a** and **ha, ai** and **he**) 🌸4.1

Differentiated Instruction

SLOWER PACE LEARNERS

31 **Variation** Some students may not remember the correct vocabulary to complete this activity. Before students do this activity, have volunteers describe what is happening in the pictures. Write the verbs they use in the descriptions on the board and ask students to form the **passé composé** of these verbs. Students should refer to these verbs as they complete the activity. 🌸1.2

MULTIPLE INTELLIGENCES

Intrapersonal Ask students to create a journal-type entry that describes a dream vacation. The journal should include the location, the reason they chose the location, activities they experienced, weather conditions, souvenirs they obtained, and people they met. Journal writing can be an ongoing activity that may be used throughout the semester to enter personal thoughts and ideas related to the lessons in each chapter. 🌸1.3

Resources

Planning:

Lesson Planner

 One-Stop Planner

Practice:

Grammar Tutor for Students of French, Chapter 1

Cahier de vocabulaire et grammaire

Differentiated Practice and Assessment CD-ROM

Cahier d'activités

Media Guide

 Teaching Transparencies Bell Work 1.7

 Interactive Tutor, Disc 1

Bell Work

Use Bell Work 1.7 in the *Teaching Transparencies* or write this activity on the board.

Mets les verbes entre parenthèses au **passé composé**.

1. Quand nous _____ (partir) en vacances en Tunisie, nous _____ (préparer) nos valises et nous _____ (prendre) l'avion.
2. Pendant le voyage mes parents _____ (lire) et j'_____ (dormir).
3. Quand on _____ (arriver), mes parents _____ (trouver) l'hôtel facilement. ✿1.2

Comparisons

Comparing and Contrasting

Point out that, **Je jouais au football,** can mean *I played soccer, I would play soccer,* or *I used to play soccer.* All imply that playing soccer took place often and over an indefinite period of time. Some expressions, such as **toujours** and **de temps en temps,** indicate repeated action and require the **imparfait.** Ask students for other expressions that signal the **imparfait.** ✿4.1

Révisions — The *passé composé* and the *imparfait*

Interactive TUTOR ✿4.1

En anglais

In English, to say that you used to do something repeatedly, you use a variety of expressions in the past tense:

When I was young,
- I **used to play** soccer.
- I **would play** soccer.
- I **played** soccer.

What is the difference between the above sentences and "Last weekend, I played soccer"?

In French, the imparfait includes all these expressions:
Quand j'étais petit(e), je jouais au foot.

I did play, I had played

1 To conjugate verbs in the **imparfait** take the present tense **nous** form of the verb, minus **-ons**, and add the following endings: **-ais, -ais, -ait, -ions, -iez, -aient**.
Être is the only verb that has an irregular stem in the **imparfait: ét-.**

2 To talk about events that *used to happen* or *were happening,* and to describe people, things, and situations in the past, use the **imparfait.**

Quand j'étais enfant, on allait souvent à la montagne.

Il faisait beau et la mer était bleue.

3 To talk about past events that happened at a *specific time in the past* or during a *well-defined period of time*, use the **passé composé.**

Hier, Fabrice est parti en vacances.

Sonia a rendu visite à ses grands-parents *l'été dernier.*

4 When a continuous action is interrupted by an event, use the **imparfait** to describe the continuous action and the **passé composé** to describe the interrupting event.

Élisa faisait sa valise quand son copain lui a téléphoné.

Vocabulaire et grammaire, *pp. 10–11*
Cahier d'activités, *pp. 5–7*
Online workbooks

34 Les vacances de Martin ✿1.2

Lisons Martin vient de rentrer de vacances et il te raconte tout ce qu'il a fait. Complète ses phrases correctement.

1. _____ en vacances en Corse.
   a. Je suis parti **b.** Je partais
2. En général, le matin, _____ à la plage.
   a. j'allais **b.** je suis allé
3. _____ qu'une fois pendant toute la semaine.
   a. Il n'a plu **b.** Il ne pleuvait
4. _____ visite à mes cousins.
   a. Je rendais **b.** J'ai rendu
5. Un jour, _____ de la plongée avec eux.
   a. je faisais **b.** j'ai fait
6. _____ vraiment super!
   a. C'était **b.** Ça a été

Core Instruction

TEACHING GRAMMAIRE

1. Go over **En anglais** with students. **(2 min.)**
2. Review the use of the **passé composé** by asking students about things they did in the past. **Qu'est-ce que tu as fait hier, Denise? (2 min.)**
3. Review the forms of the **imparfait** by asking students about things they and other people used to do in the past. **Qu'est-ce que tu faisais quand tu avais trois ans, Mike? Et tes parents? Et vous, John et Bryan? (3 min.)**

4. Finally, ask students what they were doing when something happened. **Jenna et Kendra, qu'est-ce que vous faisiez quand je suis entré(e) en classe? (2 min.)**

---

35 Vacances à la mer 🌸1.2

Écrivons Didier raconte ses vacances. Complète ses phrases avec **le passé composé** ou **l'imparfait** des verbes entre parenthèses.

1. Quand nous _____ (arriver) à la plage, il n'y _____ (avoir) personne.   sommes arrivés, avait

2. Il y _____ (avoir) beaucoup de vent et la mer _____ (être) dangereuse.   avait, était

3. Ce jour-là, je _____ (rester) à l'hôtel.   suis resté

4. Le jour suivant, comme il _____ (faire) beau, nous _____ (retourner) à la plage.   faisait, sommes retournés

5. Nous _____ (faire) de la planche à voile tout l'après-midi.   avons fait

6. Quand il avait mon âge, papa _____ (venir) tous les étés au même endroit.   venait

36 Raconte, maman! 🌸1.2

Parlons Anne a trouvé de vieilles photos de famille. Sa mère lui raconte l'histoire de chaque photo. Imagine ce qu'elle dit.

MODÈLE Oncle Lucien avait faim, alors il a attrapé un poisson.

oncle Lucien / avoir
faim / alors...

1. tes tantes / devoir acheter un cadeau / alors....

2. je / être à une fête / et...

3. faire beau / alors, papa et moi,...

4. tu / passer les vacances à la mer / et...

Communication

HOLT **SoundBooth** ONLINE RECORDING

37 Expérience personnelle 🌸1.1

Parlons Demande à un(e) camarade ce qu'il/elle faisait en vacances quand il/elle était petit(e) ou ce qu'il/elle a fait ces vacances-ci. Ensuite, dis à la classe ce que tu as appris.

MODÈLE —Où est-ce que tu allais en vacances quand tu étais petit(e)? Est-ce que tu es allé(e)...?

Communication

Pair Activity: Interpersonal

Write the following on the board.

Toi et tes amis, qu'est-ce que vous faisiez...

— **pendant les vacances d'été?**

— **après l'école?**

— **le week-end?**

— **pendant les vacances de Noël?**

Then have students interview one another about their childhood friends and activities. Students should recount what they used to do with friends during the periods indicated, using the **nous** form of the **imparfait**. You might ask students to write down the information they receive. **Ils/Elles**...   🌸1.1

Differentiated Instruction

SLOWER PACE LEARNERS

36 Additional Practice Have students bring in six to eight pictures of vacation activities (their own or cut from magazines.) Ask them to arrange the pictures in pairs. Then have students form sentences, connecting the pictured activities to say that one activity interrupted the other. **Je faisais les magasins quand j'ai vu ma copine manger dans le bistro.**   🌸1.2

MULTIPLE INTELLIGENCES

Logical-Mathematical Ask students to use their skills to describe past events in French. Have them report on the expenses of a vacation described in the lesson or one taken personally. The expenses should include amounts spent on travel, food, hotels, souvenirs, and activities. Ask students to research the approximate cost of these expenses. Have students create a poster to use when they report to the class on the expenses.   🌸1.3

Assess

Assessment Program

Quiz: Grammaire 2

Alternative Assessment

Differentiated Practice and Assessment CD-ROM

Online Assessment

my.hrw.com

Test Generator

Synthèse
- Vocabulaire 2
- Grammaire 2

Application 2

38 Écoutons CD 1, Tr. 6 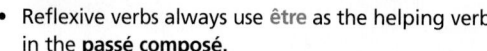1.2 **1.** a **2.** b **3.** a **4.** a **5.** b **6.** a **7.** b

Anaïs raconte une histoire qui lui est arrivée il y a bien longtemps. Écoute et décide si c'est **a) une habitude ou une description,** ou **b) une action qui s'est passée à un moment précis.**

39 Que se passait-il quand...? 1.2

Écrivons Lis les premières phrases de la rédaction d'Amélie où elle raconte ces dernières vacances. Imagine un événement qui leur est arrivé. Utilise le **passé composé** et **l'imparfait** pour raconter cet événement. Tu peux t'inspirer des mots de la boîte.

tomber	soudain	quand	génial
monter à cheval	pleuvoir	perdre	pendant

MODÈLE L'été dernier, je suis partie en vacances avec ma meilleure amie et sa famille. Nous faisions une randonnée quand...

Un peu plus — Révisions

Reflexive verbs in the passé composé

- Reflexive verbs always use **être** as the helping verb in the **passé composé.**

- When the main verb is a reflexive verb AND the reflexive pronoun is a direct object, the past participle agrees in gender and number with the direct object.

  Alice s'est lavée.

- If the direct object of the reflexive verb is placed after the verb, there is no agreement of the past participle.

  Alice s'est lavé les cheveux.

Vocabulaire et grammaire, p. 12
Cahier d'activités, pp. 5–7
Online workbooks

40 Ce matin 1.2

Écrivons Bénédicte a fait beaucoup de choses ce matin. Complète ses phrases avec le **passé composé** du verbe indiqué.

1. Mes parents et moi, nous _____ (se lever) à sept heures.
2. Ensuite, je/j' _____ (prendre) un bain.
3. Je _____ (se laver) les cheveux.
4. Je _____ (se sécher).
5. Puis, je _____ (se peigner).
6. Et je _____ (se brosser) les dents.
7. Finalement, je _____ (s'habiller).
8. Et je _____ (se dépêcher) de partir.

1. nous sommes levés **2.** ai pris **3.** me suis lavé **4.** me suis séchée **5.** me suis peignée **6.** me suis brossé **7.** me suis habillée **8.** me suis dépêchée

Bell Work

Use Bell Work 1.8 in the *Teaching Transparencies* or write this activity on the board.

Complète les phrases logiquement en utilisant **le passé composé** ou **l'imparfait.**

1. Quand j'étais jeune, tous les ans nous...
2. Ce matin il faisait beau, alors nous...
3. Ce midi, j'avais très faim, alors...
4. Les élèves s'amusaient quand le prof... 1.2

Cinquain Poetry

Have students write a **cinquain** poem using the new vocabulary.

Line 1 A verb that titles the poem
Line 2 Two nouns
Line 3 Three expressions of time
Line 4 A sentence with the verb
Line 5 An adjective

Sample answer

J'adore
Les livres, la pêche
Quand, aujourd'hui, toujours
J'adore attraper des poissons.
Relaxant

Core Instruction

INTEGRATED PRACTICE

1. Have students do Activities 38 and 39 to practice previously taught uses of **passé composé** and **imparfait. (6 min.)**

2. Introduce **Un peu plus.** (See presentation suggestions at right.) **(5 min.)**

3. Continue with integrated practice Activities 40–43. For more practice with reflexive verbs in the **passé composé,** have students write five sentences to describe what they did this morning to get ready for school. **(30 min.)**

TEACHING UN PEU PLUS

1. Go over **Un peu plus.** Review how to make reflexive verbs negative and go over placement of direct object pronouns. **(3 min.)**

2. Ask students at what time they and other people did certain things this morning. **À quelle heure tu t'es réveillé(e) ce matin? Et ton frère? À quelle heure tes parents se sont brossé les dents?** You might ask volunteers to write on the board, so you can check agreement. **(2 min.)**

41 Quelle aventure! 1.2

Lisons/Écrivons Pendant ses vacances, Gilles a tenu un journal. Lis ce passage de son journal et réponds aux questions.

Online Practice
go.hrw.com
Application 2 practice
KEYWORD: BD3 CH1

> *Hier, je suis allé faire une randonnée avec des copains. On a marché dans les bois et après un moment, on ne savait plus où on était! On n'avait pas de carte et on commençait à avoir peur quand on a vu des gens qui nous ont dit comment rentrer au village. On était très fatigués quand on est arrivés au village, mais super-contents! La prochaine fois, je vais prendre une carte de la région! Ça, c'est sûr!*

1. Est-ce que Gilles est parti faire une randonnée tout seul?
2. Qu'est-ce qui s'est passé?
3. Qu'est-ce qu'il n'avait pas avec lui?
4. Comment est-ce qu'il était quand il est rentré?

1. Non, il est parti avec ses copains.
2. Ils ne savaient pus où ils étaient.
3. Il n'avait pas de carte.
4. Il était content mais fatigué.

42 Carte postale 1.3

Écrivons Tu es en vacances. Écris une carte postale à un(e) ami(e). Raconte-lui quatre choses que tu as faites.

MODÈLE Salut de Paris! Aujourd'hui nous avons visité...

Communication

HOLT **SoundBooth** ONLINE RECORDING

43 Histoire à raconter 1.3

Parlons Regarde les illustrations et raconte le week-end d'Élodie et de son amie.

38 Script
See script on p. 3F.

PRÉPARATOIRE AP Language Examination

To display the drawings to the class, use the Picture Sequences Transparency for Chapter 1.

43 Sample answer

a. — Marie-Christine et son amie sont allées à la plage. Elles ont joué au volley.

b. — Elles ont décidé de camper sur la plage. Elles ont monté leur tente.

c. — Pendant la nuit, il y a eu un gros orage.

Communication

Group Activity: Presentational

Ask students to describe an occasion when they were interrupted by someone. Remind them to use verbs they know. They should use the **imparfait** and the **passé composé**.

MODÈLE
— J'étais frustré(e)! Je parlais à un ami au téléphone quand ma mère m'a appelé(e). 1.3

Differentiated Instruction

ADVANCED LEARNERS

41 Extension After they complete this activity, have students write an entry for Gilles's journal. They should write about another incident that could have happened during Gilles's vacation. Encourage students to use both the **passé composé** and the **imparfait** in their narration and to write at least ten sentences. Have some students present their entry to the class. Students should consider using photos to illustrate their presentation. 1.3

SPECIAL LEARNING NEEDS

43 Interpersonal As an alternate to this activity, ask students with strong interpersonal skills to interview other students about the events of their weekend. The interviewer should then write an account of the events described by his or her classmates. 1.1

Assess

Assessment Program
Quiz: Application 2
Audio CD 1, Tr. 12
Alternative Assessment
Differentiated Practice and Assessment CD-ROM

Online Assessment
my.hrw.com

Test Generator

Lecture

AP Reading Suggestion

Ask students to create a character sketch of the author. Ask them to provide passages from the reading to support their ideas.

Applying the Strategies

For more practice with finding the main idea, you might have students use the "Think Aloud" strategy from the *Reading Strategies and Skills Handbook*.

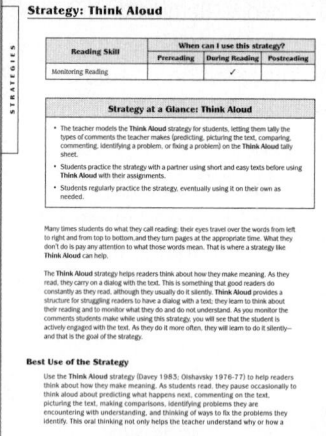

READING PRACTICE

Strategy: Think Aloud

Reading Skill	When can I use this strategy?		
	Prereading	During Reading	Postreading
Monitoring Reading		✓	

Strategy at a Glance: Think Aloud

- The teacher models the Think Aloud strategy for students, letting them tally the types of comments the teacher makes (predicting, picturing the text, comparing, commenting, identifying a problem, or fixing a problem) on the Think Aloud tally sheet.
- Students practice the strategy with a partner using short and easy texts before using Think Aloud with their assignments.
- Students regularly practice the strategy, eventually using it on their own as needed.

Many times students do what they call reading: their eyes travel over the words from left to right and from top to bottom, and they turn pages at the appropriate time. What they don't do is pay any attention to what those words mean. That is where a strategy like Think Aloud can help.

The Think Aloud strategy helps readers think about how they make meaning. As they read, they carry on a dialog with the text. This is something that good readers do constantly as they read, although they usually do it silently. Think Aloud provides a structure for struggling readers to have a dialog with a text: they learn to think about their reading and to monitor what they do and do not understand. As you monitor the comments students make while using this strategy, you will see that the student is actively engaged with the text. As they do it more often, they will learn to do it silently—and that is the goal of the strategy.

Best Use of the Strategy

Use the Think Aloud strategy (Davey 1983; Olshavsky 1976-77) to help readers think about how they make meaning. As students read, they pause occasionally to think aloud about predicting what happens next, commenting on the text, picturing the text, making comparisons, identifying problems they are encountering with understanding, and thinking of ways to fix the problems they identify. This oral thinking not only helps the teacher understand why or how a

---

Gisèle Pineau est née à Paris en 1956, de parents guadeloupéens. Elle a passé son enfance en France. Les Pineau se sont installés[1] à la Martinique en 1970, puis à la Guadeloupe deux ans plus tard. Gisèle Pineau est retournée en France pour finir ses études et ensuite elle a regagné[2] la Guadeloupe. Elle réside à Paris depuis 2000. Elle a aussi écrit *L'Exil selon Julia* (1996), *Caraïbes sur Seine* (1999), *C'est la règle* (2002), *Les Colères du volcan* (2004).

A Avant la lecture 4.2

Comment est-ce que tu imagines les «banlieues[3]» en France? Et la Guadeloupe, à quoi est-ce que cela ressemble d'après toi? Quelles images te viennent à l'esprit? Écris les mots qui te viennent à l'esprit pour décrire la Guadeloupe.

CD 1, Tr. 7

Un papillon dans la cité

*Dans l'extrait suivant d'**Un papillon dans la cité**, Félicie (Féli) est une adolescente qui vient de déménager[4] de la Guadeloupe dans une banlieue pauvre de Paris Elle raconte à Mohamed (Mo), un copain, comment elle passait ses vacances à la Guadeloupe dans la maison de sa grand-mère, Man Ya.*

D es fois, je pense à Laurine, aux belles vacances qu'elle doit vivre à Haute-Terre[5]. Je songe à tous mes amis que j'ai laissés là-bas. Et mon cœur se serre.

---

1. sont partis habiter   2. retourné   3. suburb
4. changer de maison   5. La Guadeloupe est divisée entre Haute-Terre *(high land)* et Basse-Terre *(low land)*

Core Instruction

LECTURE

1. Read **Stratégie pour lire** aloud for students. Ask students if they enjoy this freedom to mentally create their own picture, or if they would rather watch a movie where the scene has been set by someone else? **(5 min.)**

2. Have students do **Avant la lecture.** Ask volunteers to write their words on the board or an overhead transparency. You might bring photographs of Guadeloupe and of low-income French suburbs downloaded from the

Internet. How do they compare to the mental images students had formed? **(10 min.)**

3. Have students read pages 28–29 of *Un papillon dans la cité* in small groups. Ask them to make a list of adjectives the author associates with Guadeloupe. (**bon, chaud, sucré, orange**) What color does she associate with her suburb? (**le gris**) **(15 min.)**

J'imagine Laurine en train de grimper dans le manguier[1] de la cour pour ramener des tas de mango-ponm[2] tout ronds. Je vois sa bouche barbouillée[3] du bon jus orangé, épais et sucré. Je ferme les yeux très fort et je prie pour me réveiller à Haute-Terre, au pied de ce même manguier, après une sieste habitée par un rêve qui m'aurait fait atterrir dans la Cité grise de maman. Je me souviens... je me souviens aussi des bains de rivière que nous prenions avec toute la marmaille[4] des alentours. On rassemblait nos sous[5] pour acheter une grosse bouteille de Fanta orange ou de Coca-Cola. Après le bain, on en buvait à tout de rôle, en tenant le coude des plus voraces. Pendant les vacances, Man Julia criait toujours qu'elle deviendrait folle par ma faute. Elle n'aimait pas les filles qui suivaient les garçons dans toutes les monté et désann[6]. Mais quand je lui demandais la permission, elle ne savait pas refuser. Un peu comme madame Fathia. Elle faisait toujours semblant d'être fâchée. Elle promettait des coups de ceinture et des raclées[7] phénoménales, mais son cœur était chaud et bon comme le soleil de midi qui sèche en trois minutes le linge étalé sur l'herbe, devant la case. C'est bizarre, quand je vivais auprès d'elle, je n'entendais que les « bête, sotte, couillon[8] » qu'elle me lançait. Aujourd'hui que la mer nous sépare, d'autres mots me reviennent en mémoire. Oui, chacune de ses phrases finissait par « p'tit a manman[9], doudou en mwen[10], Féfé doudou » Une fois, j'ai appelé ainsi Mimi : « Ti doudou en mwen ». Il s'est arrêté net de gigoter[11] et m'a fixée longuement de ses gros yeux noirs, bouche bée. On ne parle pas créole dans l'appartement. Il n'est pas interdit de cité, mais il n'est pas non plus invité.

---

1. *mango tree*   2. mangue-pomme *(mango)*   3. *smeared*
4. *un groupe d'enfants*   5. *argent*   6. *aller et venir*
7. *hiding*   8. *idiot*   9. créole pour petite chérie de maman
10. créole pour: ma chérie à moi   11. *bouger*

Active Reading Questions

1. **Qui est Laurine? (une amie de Féli)**
2. **Où habitent Laurine et les autres amis de Féli? (à Haute-Terre)**
3. **Qu'est-ce que Féli veut? (se réveiller/être à Haute-Terre)**
4. **Qui est Man Julia? (la grand-mère)**
5. **Comment est la personnalité de Man Julia? (gentille et bonne)**
6. **Est-ce que Féli aimait ou n'aimait pas Man Julia? (Elle l'aimait.)**
7. **Quelle langue est-ce que Féli parlait à Haute-Terre? à Paris? (créole, français)**

Comparisons

Comparing and Contrasting

Ask students to compare and contrast Féli's life in Guadeloupe with her life in Paris. Have students use examples from the text to show how her life is different now that she lives in Paris and how it has remained the same 🌼 1.2

PRE-AP ACTIVITÉ PRÉPARATOIRE — Language Examination

Lecture helps students prepare for Section 1, Part B: **Reading Comprehension**. The audio recording helps them prepare for Part A: **Listening —Short Narratives**.

Differentiated Instruction

ADVANCED LEARNERS

Challenge Ask students to create a conversation between Féli and Mo that is based on the information provided in the story. Students should perform their conversations for the class, using facial expressions and gestures to emphasize their statements. 🌼 1.1

MULTIPLE INTELLIGENCES

Linguistic Ask students to recall a memorable day from their childhood. Ask them to narrate this day in the first person and include details that made it memorable. The narration could be fictional. 🌼 1.1

Active Reading Questions

1. Qu'est-ce que Féli a décrit à Mo? (ses vacances à Haute-Terre)
2. Qu'est-ce que Mo n'a jamais connu? (la mer)
3. Comment est-ce que Féli réagit à cette déclaration de Mo? (Elle ne le croit pas.)
4. Qu'est-ce que Féli a compris après cette conversation? (qu'elle a eu de la chance d'habiter en Guadeloupe)
5. Qu'est-ce que Féli a eu de la chance de connaître en Guadeloupe? (la nature: les rivières, la mer, les bois, et cetera)
6. Pourquoi est-ce que la Guadeloupe n'est pas un paradis? (parce qu'il y a des cyclones et un volcan)
7. Que'est-ce que Féli veut faire un jour? (retourner en Guadeloupe) 1.2

Postreading Activity

Ask students to think about the metaphor of the butterfly used in the title of the selection and in the text. Ask them to explain the metaphor and why they think the author chose it.

Connections

Literature Link

Gisèle Pineau is a prominent member of the **Créolité** movement, which focuses on oral tradition and seeks to validate the popular culture of Caribbean societies. Many **Créolité** authors attempt to combine the oral language of Creole with the written language of French. They emphasize popular music, folk traditions, and folk tales. Have students research, in the library or on the Internet, other authors that belong to the **Créolité** movement. Students should also report on major themes in the works of these authors. 3.1

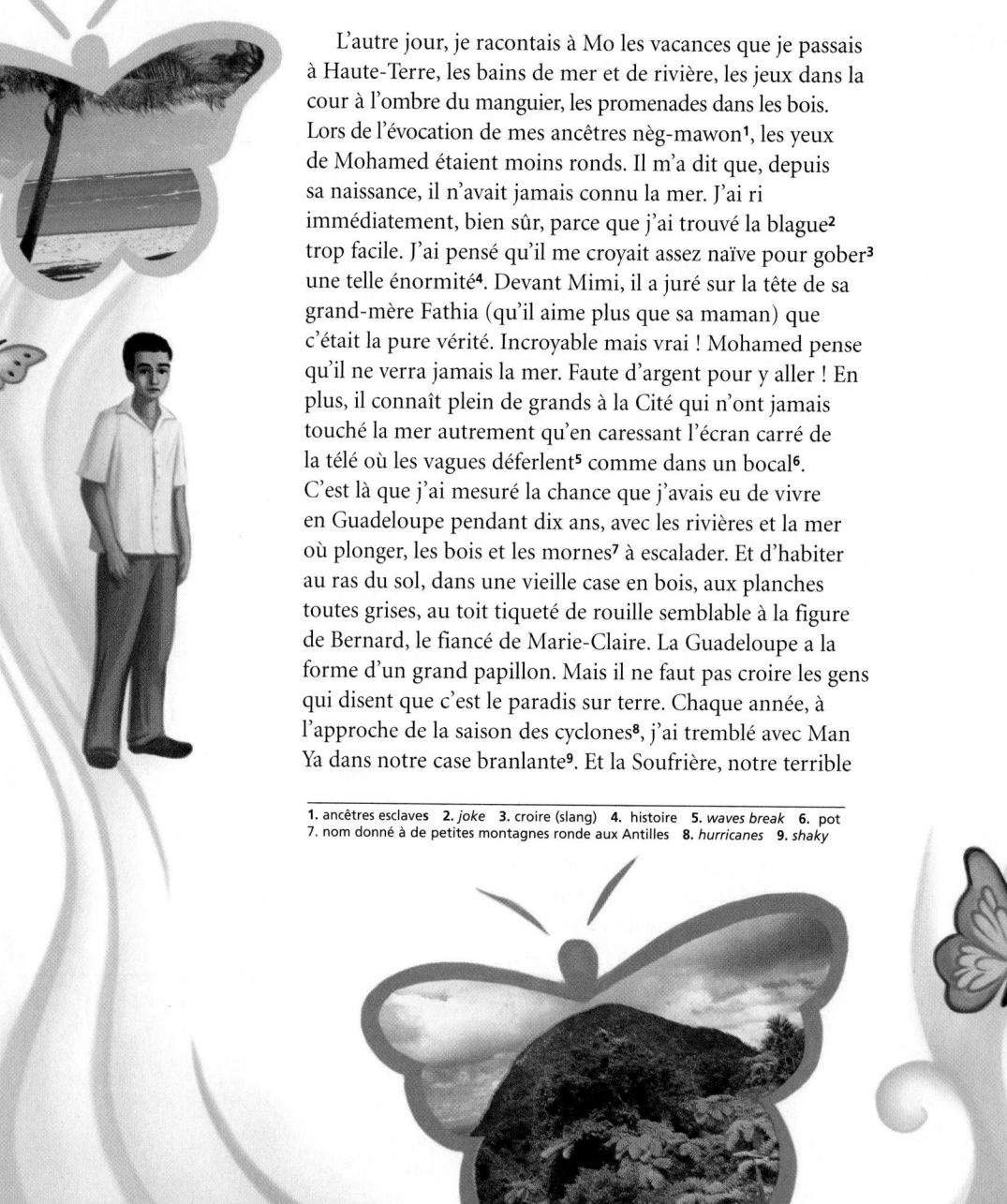

L'autre jour, je racontais à Mo les vacances que je passais à Haute-Terre, les bains de mer et de rivière, les jeux dans la cour à l'ombre du manguier, les promenades dans les bois. Lors de l'évocation de mes ancêtres nèg-mawon[1], les yeux de Mohamed étaient moins ronds. Il m'a dit que, depuis sa naissance, il n'avait jamais connu la mer. J'ai ri immédiatement, bien sûr, parce que j'ai trouvé la blague[2] trop facile. J'ai pensé qu'il me croyait assez naïve pour gober[3] une telle énormité[4]. Devant Mimi, il a juré sur la tête de sa grand-mère Fathia (qu'il aime plus que sa maman) que c'était la pure vérité. Incroyable mais vrai ! Mohamed pense qu'il ne verra jamais la mer. Faute d'argent pour y aller ! En plus, il connaît plein de grands à la Cité qui n'ont jamais touché la mer autrement qu'en caressant l'écran carré de la télé où les vagues déferlent[5] comme dans un bocal[6]. C'est là que j'ai mesuré la chance que j'avais eu de vivre en Guadeloupe pendant dix ans, avec les rivières et la mer où plonger, les bois et les mornes[7] à escalader. Et d'habiter au ras du sol, dans une vieille case en bois, aux planches toutes grises, au toit tiqueté de rouille semblable à la figure de Bernard, le fiancé de Marie-Claire. La Guadeloupe a la forme d'un grand papillon. Mais il ne faut pas croire les gens qui disent que c'est le paradis sur terre. Chaque année, à l'approche de la saison des cyclones[8], j'ai tremblé avec Man Ya dans notre case branlante[9]. Et la Soufrière, notre terrible

1. ancêtres esclaves 2. *joke* 3. croire (slang) 4. histoire 5. *waves break* 6. pot
7. nom donné à de petites montagnes ronde aux Antilles 8. *hurricanes* 9. *shaky*

Core Instruction

LECTURE

1. Have students finish reading *Un papillon dans la cité.* Point out to students the opposing themes of freedom (the butterfly) and captivity (the ocean in a jar). **(15 min.)**

2. Complete **Compréhension** and **Après la lecture** as a class. Have students reflect on whether their childhood experiences were as nice as they now remember them to have been? **(10 min.)**

Online Practice
go.hrw.com
Online Edition
KEYWORD: BD3 CH1

Chapitre 1

Lecture

Lecture

volcan, peut aussi se réveiller, sur un coup de tête, et tous nous engloutir[1]. Et la terre peut se mettre à danser sous nos pieds, et puis nous faire chavirer[2]; c'est comme si le papillon battait des ailes pour un envol impossible et désespéré. Pourtant, il ne se passe pas un jour sans que je ne songe à ma vie de là-bas. Y retourner, voilà ce qui me travaille[3].

Compréhension

B Est-ce que les phrases suivantes sont **a) vraies** ou **b) fausses?** Si la phrase est fausse, dis pourquoi. 🌸1.2

1. Laurine est une amie de Féli.
2. Laurine aime manger des mangues.
3. Féli rêve qu'elle habite encore à la Guadeloupe.
4. Man Julia était très sévère avec Féli. Féli n'avait pas le droit de sortir.
5. Mo va à la mer tous les étés.
6. La Guadeloupe est un paradis.

C Réponds aux questions suivantes. 🌸1.2

1. Qu'est-ce que Féli faisait pendant ses vacances à Haute-Terre?
2. Est-ce que Féli était heureuse à Haute-Terre? Est-ce qu'elle est heureuse maintenant? Pourquoi? Pourquoi pas?
3. Comment est la Cité? Comment imagines-tu la vie de Mohamed et des gens de la Cité?
4. Mo pense qu'il ne verra jamais la mer. Pourquoi?
5. Mo dit à Féli qu'il ne verra sans doute jamais la mer. Qu'est-ce que Féli réalise après cette conversation?
6. Qu'est-ce que Féli veut faire un jour?

Après la lecture 🌸1.3

D Qu'est-ce que tu penses des vacances de Féli à Haute-Terre? Est-ce qu'elles te semblent agréables? Quels souvenirs as-tu de tes vacances quand tu étais enfant? Où les passais-tu? Qu'est-ce que tu faisais?

---

1. faire disparaître   2. to capsize
3. j'y pense

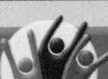

Comparisons

Comparing and Contrasting

Ask students to reread the last part of the story and think about childhood fears of their own concerning natural disasters. Have students describe how their fears were similar to or different than what the author describes.

🌸4.1

Differentiated Instruction

SLOWER PACE LEARNERS

B **Variation** Before students decide if a statement is true or false, ask them to read the text indicating whether the statement is true or false. Then call on volunteers to complete the activity. 🌸1.1, 1.2

SPECIAL LEARNING NEEDS

Students with Learning Disabilities Have students listen to the audio recording of the reading. Play a section at a time, stopping at intervals. Have students tell you the main idea of each section. Once students have summarized all the sections, have them make an overall summary of the reading. 🌸1.2

Assess

Assessment Program

Quiz: Lecture

Online Assessment

    my.hrw.com

Test Generator

L'atelier de l'écrivain

Process Writing

Tell students that they may remember more details about their childhood incident once they actually begin writing. Remind them to write the basic story first, following the suggestions in **Rédaction.** Ask them to go back later to add specific details.

Teaching Suggestion

Brainstorm with students the qualities of a good autobiographical narrative, such as a clear story line, interesting characters, convincing details, and the feeling that the author is telling the truth. Have students review their **organigramme** before writing to insure their composition will have these qualities.

Connections

Literature Link

There are only few examples of autobiographical literature in antiquity and the Middle Ages. It was not until the Renaissance in the fifteenth century that this genre started to flourish. There are roughly four different types of autobiographical writing. These are thematic, religious, intellectual, and fictionalized. Students should also research an autobiography written by a Francophone author and determine to which type it belongs. Have students present their findings to the class. 🍀1.3, 3.1

L'atelier de l'écrivain

Des vacances extraordinaires

Tu vas écrire un récit autobiographique dans lequel tu vas décrire un incident qui t'est arrivé. Pense aux vacances d'été de ton enfance. Qu'est-ce que tu faisais? Avec qui est-ce que tu jouais? Maintenant, essaie de te rappeler d'un incident en particulier — un jeu que tu as gagné, un accident que tu as eu... Décris cet incident et explique son importance.

STRATÉGIE pour écrire

Including sensory details help your reader imagine how an experience looks, sounds, feels, smells, and tastes. When you think of an event or incident to describe, try to remember what sights come to mind. What colors and objects did you notice? What smells were in the air? What was the weather like? As you write, incorporate these details into your description.

🍀1.3

① **Plan: un organigramme de base** 🍀1.3

Une fois que tu as décidé quel incident de vacances tu veux décrire, crée un organigramme comme celui ci-dessous. Divise ta feuille de papier en deux colonnes. Dans la première colonne, écris les questions suivantes: *Qui?, Où?, Quand?, Qu'est-ce qui s'est passé?, Pourquoi?* et *Comment?* Réponds aux questions dans la deuxième colonne.

Ajoute des détails qui font appel aux cinq sens (la vue, l'odorat, le goût, le toucher et l'ouïe). Qu'est-ce que tu as vu? Quelles odeurs y avait-il? Qu'est-ce que tu as entendu? Puis, décide de l'ordre logique des actions et des détails.

Qui?	
Où?	
Quand?	
Qu'est-ce qui s'est passé?	
Pourquoi?	
Comment?	

Core Instruction

L'ATELIER DE L'ÉCRIVAIN

1. Read the introduction and have students answer the questions about childhood summer vacations. Ask them if they recall any events that changed their life. **(4 min.)**

2. Discuss **Stratégie pour écrire** and have students give examples of sensory details. Have students complete step 1. **(8 min.)**

3. Go over **Vocabulaire à la carte.** Review **Le passé** by telling about an incident from your own life and having students state which tense to use for each verb. **(5 min.)**

4. Have students complete steps 2 and 3 and find illustrations to accompany it (step 4) as homework. **(30 min.)**

2 Rédaction ❀1.3

Tout d'abord, fais un brouillon *(draft)* de ton récit. Commence avec une phrase de description qui va captiver l'attention du lecteur, comme par exemple:

Il m'est arrivé quelque chose de bizarre ce jour-là.

Puis, écris les actions et les détails d'une manière logique. N'oublie pas d'utiliser des expressions telles que **à ce moment-là, ensuite, tout d'un coup**, etc. pour lier les différents moments de ton récit.

Écris une conclusion qui explique l'importance de l'incident.

3 Correction ❀1.3

Maintenant, lis ton récit pour t'assurer qu'il raconte les faits d'un seul incident.

• Est-ce que l'introduction est intéressante?
• Est-ce que les actions suivent un ordre chronologique?
• Est-ce qu'il y a assez de détails qui font appel aux cinq sens?
• As-tu expliqué l'importance de l'incident?

Ensuite, échange ton récit avec celui d'un ou d'une camarade de classe. Demande-lui de vérifier l'emploi de l'imparfait et du passé composé et de corriger les fautes d'orthographe. Fais les corrections et écris la version finale de ton récit.

4 Application ❀1.3

Trouve des photos de toi et des personnes qui ont joué un rôle dans ton récit autobiographique. Ou bien, dessine des images pour illustrer l'incident que tu as décrit. Organise les images et le texte de ton récit. Tu peux partager ta composition avec tes camarades.

Vocabulaire à la carte

Quand j'avais... ans,...	When I was . . . years old, . . .
Quand j'étais petit(e),...	When I was little, . . .
Au moment où...	As . . .
J'étais sur le point de...	I was about to . . .
Ça sentait mauvais/bon.	It smelled bad/good.
Ça avait un goût de (poulet).	It tasted like (chicken)

Le passé

Use the **passé composé** to tell what happened in the past. It is used to describe an action.

Je suis allé(e) chez ma grand-mère.

Use the **l'imparfait** to describe something in the past. It set the scene in which the action occured.

Le ciel était bleu.

Je me levais tous les jours à 6 heures.

Le tour de l'Europe en 10 jours

La Suisse

La tour Eiffel

Pendant l'été, je suis allée en Europe avec mes parents, ma soeur et mes cousins. Nous avons pris l'avion de

L'atelier de l'écrivain

Le passé

Ask students to change the verbs to the correct form of the **passé composé** or **imparfait** in the following fragments, and then finish each sentence.

1. **L'été que j'(avoir) 10 ans...**
2. **Cet été-là nous (aller) à la plage pour...**
3. **Tous les matins, maman (préparer)...**
4. **Au moment où mes parents (savoir)...** ❀1.2

Writing Assessment

To assess **L'atelier de l'écrivain,** you can use the following rubric. For additional rubrics, see the *Assessment Program.*

Writing Rubric	4	3	2	1
Content (Complete—Incomplete)				
Comprehensibility (Comprehensible—Seldom comprehensible)				
Accuracy (Accurate—Seldom accurate)				
Organization (Well-organized—Poorly organized)				
Effort (Excellent effort—Minimal effort)				

18-20: A 14-15: C Under
16-17: B 12-13: D 12: F

Differentiated Instruction

SLOWER PACE LEARNERS

Before students decide on an incident they want to describe, they should work in pairs, telling each other about incidents that have happened during their last vacations. This will help students remember incidents and narrow down their options. ❀1.1, 1.2

SPECIAL LEARNING NEEDS

Students with AD(H)D After they read **Stratégie pour écrire,** have students gather sensory details for a class writing example before they begin writing independently. Ask students to take a trip to the school cafeteria to take notes describing the multi-sensory experiences they encounter. Alternatively, provide students with pictures of places such as a beach or a restaurant. Lead a class activity to practice the four-part writing process on the board, using the notes taken for the example. ❀1.3

Assess

Assessment Program

Quiz: Écriture

Online Assessment my.hrw.com

Test Generator

Chapitre 1

Prépare-toi pour l'examen

Resources

Planning:

Lesson Planner

 One-Stop Planner

Practice:

Cahier d'activités

Media Guide

 Teaching Transparencies
Situation, Chapitre 1
Picture Sequences, Chapter 1

 Audio CD 1, Tr. 8

 Interactive Tutor, Disc 1

VIDEO OPTIONS

▶ **Télé-culture: Interviews**

TPRS

You may wish to use the Picture Sequences Transparency that accompanies Activity 7 for a TPRS activity.

---

② Answers

1. Angélique et Camille empruntent des livres au CDI.
2. Robert attend son copain dans la cour de récréation.
3. Tu ne joues pas aux échecs.
4. Samir et Annick, vous faites une expérience au laboratoire cet après-midi.
5. Vincent et moi, nous prenons toujours un croque-monsieur à la cantine.
6. Ils viennent au cinéma avec nous ce soir.
7. Nous allons nager ce week-end.

---

① Vocabulaire 1
- to express likes, dislikes, and preferences
- to ask about plans
pp. 6–9

② Grammaire 1
- regular verbs in the present
- irregular verbs in the present
Un peu plus
- verbs followed by the infinitive
pp. 10–15

③ Vocabulaire 2
- to tell when and how often you did something
- to describe a place in the past
pp. 18–21

1. C'était 2. Le matin
3. les jours
4. faisait 5. Il y avait
6. me rappelaient

---

① Mets ces activités par ordre de préférence. Dis celle que tu préfères et celle que tu détestes. Pour chaque activité, explique pourquoi. 🌀1.3

 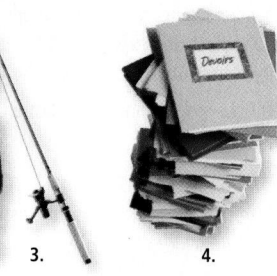

1.   2.   3.   4.

② Fais des phrases avec les éléments donnés. Utilise le présent et n'oublie pas de faire les changements nécessaires. 🌀1.2

1. CDI / Angélique / emprunter / Camille / livres / et
2. dans / attendre / copain / la cour / son / Robert / de récréation
3. tu / ne / jouer / échecs / pas
4. expérience / cet après-midi / laboratoire / vous / Samir / Annick / faire / et
5. et / prendre / cantine / Vincent / moi / croque-monsieur / toujours / nous
6. ils / nous / ce / cinéma / venir / soir / avec
7. nous / ce / nager / week-end / aller

③ Complète le journal de Lucas avec les expressions de la boîte. 🌀1.2

Il y avait	échecs	me rappelaient	faisait
C'était	jouer	les jours	le matin

Me voilà de retour après mes vacances au bord de la mer. ___1___ incroyable! ___2___ , je me levais très tôt et j'allais à la plage. Je me baignais tous ___3___ . Mais un jour, je me suis senti mal, alors, je ne me suis pas baigné. Et une autre fois, il ___4___ très froid, je ne me suis pas baigné non plus. Mais, j'ai adoré la plage. ___5___ beaucoup de gens qui faisaient de la planche à voile. Ils ___6___ les beaux oiseaux sur l'eau.

Preparing for the Exam

RETEACHING

Have students review the **Exprimons-nous!** expressions for likes, dislikes, and preferences. (**Mon sport préféré, c'est la natation.**) Ask students to talk to a partner about past vacation activities in order to practice the **passé composé.** They should pay special attention to the use of the auxiliary verbs **avoir** and **être.** (**Ils sont allés au cinéma. Elle a lu le livre.**)

TEST-TAKING STRATEGY

Tell students that when taking the test, they should be sure to check number and gender agreement of past participles and subjects.

---

1. dormait, suis arrivé(e) **2.** a lavé **3.** s'est coupée, préparait
4. se sont maquillées **5.** nous sommes brossé

4 Complète les phrases suivantes avec **le passé composé** ou **l'imparfait** des verbes entre parenthèses. 🍀1.2

1. Sophie _____ (dormir) quand je _____ (arriver).
2. Ce matin, Camille _____ (laver) le chien.
3. Maman _____ (se couper) quand elle _____ (préparer) le repas.
4. Mes amies _____ (se maquiller) pour aller à la fête d'Ali.
5. Nous _____ (se brosser) les dents après le dîner.

5 Réponds aux questions suivantes. 🍀2.1

1. Comment s'appelle l'examen qu'on passe à la fin du lycée?
2. Qu'est-ce qu'un moniteur?
3. Qu'y a-t-il dans certaines villes en été? Donne deux exemples.

6 Marie raconte ses souvenirs de vacances. Dis si elle parle d'un événement **a) habituel** ou **b) occasionnel.** CD 1, Tr. 8 🍀1.2
1. a **2.** a **3.** b **4.** b **5.** b **6.** b

7 Élodie, son cousin Mathias et Julie parlent de leurs vacances. Avec des camarades, créez une conversation pour chaque image. 🍀1.1

Online Assessment
go.hrw.com
Chapter Self–test
KEYWORD: BD3 CH1

4 Grammaire 2
• the **passé composé**
• using the **passé composé** and the **imparfait**
Un peu plus
• reflexive verbs in the **passé composé** pp. 22–27

5 Culture
• Comparaisons p. 17
• Flash culture pp. 8, 12, 20, 22

Prépare-toi pour l'examen

Prépare-toi pour l'examen

5 Answers
1. Le bac
2. Il s'occupe d'enfants dans des colonies de vacances.
3. des festivals; de musique à Antibes, de théâtre à Avignon, de bandes dessinées à Angoulême.

6 Script
1. Quand j'étais petite, j'allais chez ma tante chaque été.
2. Elle habitait au bord de la mer.
3. Un jour, nous sommes allées à la pêche.
4. Vers midi, il a commencé à pleuvoir.
5. À ce moment-là, j'ai attrapé un gros poisson.
6. Ma tante est rentrée, mais moi, je suis restée là sous la pluie, avec mon beau poisson.

PRÉPARATOIRE / PRE-AP
Language Examination

To display the drawings to the class, use the Picture Sequences Transparency for Chapter 1.

7 Sample answer
a. **Julie et Élodie parlent de leurs vacances. Élodie est allée à la montagne où elle a fait du ski.**
b. **Julie est allée au bord de la mer. Elle a fait de la planche à voile.**
c. **Élodie demande à Mathias ce qu'il a fait pendant les vacances.**
d. **Mathias lui répond qu'il est allé à la campagne où il a travaillé dans une ferme.**

Oral Assessment
To assess the speaking activities in this section, you might use the following rubric. For additional speaking rubrics, see the Alternative Assessment section of the *Assessment Program.*

Speaking Rubric	4	3	2	1
Content (Complete—Incomplete)				
Comprehension (Total—Little)				
Comprehensibility (Comprehensible—Incomprehensible)				
Accuracy (Accurate—Seldom Accurate)				
Fluency (Fluent—Not Fluent)				

18-20: A   16-17: B   14-15: C   12-13: D   Under 12: F

Grammar Review
For more practice with the grammar topics in this chapter, see the *Grammar Tutor*, the *Interactive Tutor*, or the *Cahier de vocabulaire et grammaire*.

Online Edition
Students might use the online textbook and Holt SoundBooth to practice pronunciation of the **vocabulaire.**

Cultures

 Products and Perspectives

Carp fishing, or carping, is very popular in France. Almost all French lakes, manmade as well as natural, hold carp. It is considered a delicacy in France and many other European countires. In some regions of France, carp may even be the focus of Christmas dinner. Carp were first brought to North America from Europe in the early 1800s as a food fish. Today, carp inhabit many rivers and lakes in the United States. Ask students if they eat carp. Why or why not?

🌼 2.2, 4.2

Proverbes

For French proverbs and activities related to the chapter theme and vocabulary, see **Proverbes et expressions,** pp. R6–R7.

Grammaire 1
- regular verbs in the present
- irregular verbs in the present

Un peu plus
- verbs followed by the infinitive
pp. 10–15

Résumé: Grammaire 1

Most verbs ending in **-er**, **-ir**, and **-re** are regular and have the following endings in the present:

aimer: j'aim**e**, tu aim**es**, il aim**e**
nous aim**ons**, vous aim**ez**, ils aim**ent**

choisir: je chois**is**, tu chois**is**, il chois**it**
nous chois**issons**, vous chois**issez**, ils chois**issent**

attendre: j'attend**s**, tu attend**s**, il attend
nous attend**ons**, vous attend**ez**, ils attend**ent**

To make a sentence negative, place **ne/n'... pas** around the conjugated verb: **Je n'attends pas le bus.**

Here are some verbs that have irregular forms in the present:
aller, avoir, voir, être, faire, prendre, venir.

Some verbs can be followed by an infinitive:
Je dois parler à Luc. Je vais aller au parc. Je viens de faire du tennis.

Grammaire 2
- the **passé composé**
- using the **passé composé** and the **imparfait**

Un peu plus
- reflexive verbs in the **passé composé**
pp. 22–27

Résumé: Grammaire 2

The **passé composé** is made up of a helping verb (**avoir** or **être**) and the past participle of the main verb. The helping verb **avoir** is used with most verbs. The helping verb **être** is used with most verbs of *motion* and *reflexive verbs.*

To form the past participles of regular vers, drop the two last letters of the infinitive and add these endings: **-er → é, -ir → i, -re → u.**

To form the **imparfait,** take the **nous** form of the verb in the present, drop the ending **-ons,** and add these endings: **-ais, -ais, -ait, -ions, -iez, -aient.**

Use the passé composé	Use the imparfait
• to talk about an event that happened at a specific time in the past	• to talk about an event that used to happen • to describe • to set a scene in the past

When a continuous action is interrupted by an event, use the **imparfait** for the continuous action and the **passé composé** for the event.

Je regardais la télé quand Julien est arrivé.

With reflexive verbs, the past participle agrees in gender and number with a preceding direct object. There is no agreement if the direct object is placed after the verb:

Claire s'est lavée. but **Claire s'est lavé les cheveux.**

Chapter Review

Teacher Management System
Password: admin
For more details, log on to www.hrw.com/CDROMTUTOR.

Create a variety of puzzles to review chapter vocabulary.

DVD Program	Interactive Tutor	PuzzlePro

Résumé: Vocabulaire 1

HOLT SoundBooth ONLINE RECORDING

To express likes, dislikes, and preferences

aller au cinéma	to go to the movies
la biologie	biology
les arts plastiques (m.)	visual arts
l'anglais (m.)	English
la cantine	school cafeteria
la classe/la salle de classe	classroom
le/la conseiller(-ère) d'éducation	school counselor
un devoir	homework
un emploi du temps (m.) chargé	busy schedule
emprunter des livres	to borrow books
faire la fête	to party
faire de la photo	to do photography
faire de la vidéo amateur	to make amateur videos
faire du skate	to skateboard
faire les magasins (m.)	to go shopping
le film d'horreur	horror movie
le français	French
le gymnase	gymnasium

l'histoire-géo(graphie) (f.)	history/geography
jouer au basket/au volley (m.)	to play basketball/volleyball
jouer aux échecs (m.)	to play chess
jouer de la guitare	to play guitar
le laboratoire	laboratory
le lycée	school
les maths (f.)	math
une matière	school subject
monter à cheval	to do horseback riding
la physique-chimie	physics/chemistry class
la récréation (récré)	break
la salle d'informatique	computer lab
Ce que j'aime, c'est...	What I like is . . .
J'aime bien... mais je préfère...	I like . . . but I prefer . . .
Je déteste... j'adore...	I hate . . . I love . . .
Mon/Ma... préféré(e), c'est...	My favorite . . . is . . .

**To ask about plans
and respond** .... *See p. 9*

Résumé: Vocabulaire 2

To tell when and how often you did something

adorer	to love
aller à la pêche	to go fishing
attraper un poisson	to catch a fish
le bord de la mer	the seashore
la campagne	countryside
camper	to camp
la canne à pêche	fishing rod
les chaussures de randonnée (f.)	hiking shoes
la demi-pension	room with breakfast and 1 meal
faire de la randonnée	to go hiking
la gourde	canteen
l'hôtel (m.)	hotel
la lotion anti-moustiques	insect repellant
la montagne	mountain
partir en vacances	to go on vacation
la pension complète	room with 3 meals included
la planche à voile	surfboard

rendre visite à	to visit (a person)
le retour	return
le sac à dos	backpack
le sac de couchage	sleeping bag
le sac de voyage	traveling bag
une semaine	week
la tente	tent
utiliser	to use
Le soir...	Every evening . . .
Quand...	When . . .
Tous les jours/deux jours...	Every day/other day . . .

To describe a place in the past

C'était...	It was . . .
Il faisait...	The weather was . . .
Il y avait...	There were . . .
...me rappelait/rappelaient...	. . . reminded me of . . .

Prépare-toi pour l'examen

♟ Game

Réponse-Question Draw a grid on a transparency with these categories across the top: likes, dislikes, preferences, plans, and past activities. Down the left-hand side, write point values from 100 to 500. In the squares, write answers to questions that might be asked in each category. **(Ma matière préférée, c'est l'anglais.)** Then cover each square with an adhesive note. Form two teams. Have a member of one team choose a category and a point value. Remove the note to show the answer. The student has ten seconds to ask a question that would elicit that response. **(Quelle est ta matière préférée?)** Teams take turns.

❀ 1.2

Online Edition

Transparency: Vocabulaire

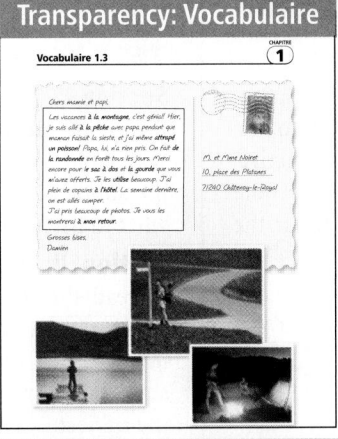

Transparency: Situation

Assess

Assessment Program
Examen: Chapitre 1
Audio CD 1, Trs. 13–14
Examen oral: Chapitre 1
Alternative Assessment
Differentiated Practice and Assessment CD-ROM

Online Assessment
my.hrw.com

Test Generator

Activités préparatoires

Resources

Planning:

Lesson Planner

 One-Stop Planner

Practice:

Cahier de vocabulaire et grammaire

Cahier d'activités

Differentiated Practice and Assessment CD-ROM

 Teaching Transparencies Picture Sequences, Chapter 1

 Audio CD 1, Tr. 9

VIDEO OPTIONS

▶ **Télé-culture: Interviews**

The AP French Language Exam

Activités préparatoires provide students with activities similar to those found in the Advanced Placement French Language exam. The activities are based on material taught up to and including this chapter and concentrate on the chapter grammar and vocabulary. In the Teacher's Edition you will find test-taking strategies, as well as strategies for succeeding in the four skills. Students who plan on taking the exam should already have a good grasp of French vocabulary and grammar. They also should possess adequate competence in listening, reading, writing, and speaking.

Listening Script

1. — Tu suis un cours de géo cette année?

— Oui, j'ai cours le lundi, le mercredi et le vendredi.

2. — J'adore les montagnes, mais j'aime aussi la campagne. J'aime bien aussi aller au bord de la mer.

— Où vas-tu passer tes vacances, alors?

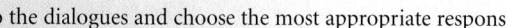

SECTION I

 Listening CD 1, Tr. 9 🎬1.2

Listen to the dialogues and choose the most appropriate response.

1. **A.** Alors, tu as cours de géo tous les jours.
   B. Alors, tu as cours de géo tous les deux jours.
   C. Alors, tu as cours de géo deux fois par semaine.
   D. Alors, tu as toujours cours de géo.

2. **A.** Bonne idée.
   B. Je fais un feu de camp.
   C. J'allais à la pêche.
   D. Je n'arrive pas à me décider.

Reading 🎬1.2

Read the following paragraph and answer the questions that follow.

> Amboise, ville symbole de la Renaissance française, est située entre le Cher et la Loire. Elle est le témoin privilégié de l'empreinte laissée par
> 5 l'influence italienne en Touraine. Le château Royal d'Amboise offre une perspective privilégiée sur la vieille ville et une vue imprenable sur la Loire. Autrefois résidence régulière de
> 10 François Ier, le château possède une intéressante collection de meubles (gothique, Renaissance et Empire). La tombe de Léonard de Vinci se trouve dans la chapelle Saint-Hubert. Les
> 15 jardins Renaissance sont aussi l'occasion d'une promenade au charme délicieusement italien.

1. La Loire c'est...
   A. un fleuve.
   B. un château.
   C. une ville.
   D. un édifice.

2. La ville d'Amboise se trouve...
   A. où le Cher rencontre la Loire.
   B. près de Paris.
   C. en Italie.
   D. à plusieurs kilomètres du château Royal.

3. Le château Royal d'Amboise...
   A. est un château médiéval.
   B. était le château de François Ier.
   C. était à Léonard de Vinci.
   D. a influencé l'art gothique.

4. On voit partout à Amboise, l'influence...
   A. de François Ier.
   B. de Léonard de Vinci.
   C. italienne.
   D. de la Loire.

Preparing for the Exam

ADDITIONAL PRACTICE

Have volunteers tell about their last vacation. Ask students to pay specific attention to the correct tense when they recount vacation activities or events. On the board, you might note the verbs used and review their forms in the **imparfait** and **passé composé**. 🎬1.1

TEST-TAKING STRATEGIES

Section I: Listening Remind students to read the four choices before they listen to the dialogs. If the choices are similar, tell them to look for the subtle differences so they know specifically what to listen for.

Section II: Writing You might tell students to read through the paragraph first and note which tense to use in each blank. They should then go back and write each verb form, making sure their verb form corresponds correctly to the subject.

Activités préparatoires

The following activities can be used to help you to prepare for the Advanced Placement French Language examination, or to further practice the vocabulary and grammar concepts you have seen in this chapter.

SECTION II

Writing 🍀1.2

In the following paragraph, some verbs have been omitted. Complete each sentence by writing the correct form and tense of the verb, based on the context.

Aujourd'hui, c'___**1**___ la rentrée. Les grandes vacances ___**2**___ finies. Cet été, mes amis et moi, nous ___**3**___ du sport presque tous les jours. Le samedi soir nous ___**4**___ au cinéma ou nous ___**5**___ au restaurant. Le premier août, je ___**6**___ en vacances avec ma famille. On ___**7**___ visite à mon grand-père. Il ___**8**___ en Provence. Un jour, nous ___**9**___ à la plage à Nice. Après un bon séjour en Provence, nous ___**10**___ chez nous le 15 août.

1. <u>est</u> (être)
2. <u>sont</u> (être)
3. <u>avons fait</u> (faire)
4. <u>allions</u> (aller)
5. <u>dînions</u> (dîner)
6. <u>suis parti(e)</u> (partir)
7. <u>a rendu</u> (rendre)
8. <u>habite</u> (habiter)
9. <u>sommes allés</u> (aller)
10. <u>sommes rentrés</u> (rentrer)

Essay Topic 🍀1.3

Write in French a well-organized and coherent composition of substantial length (at least 10 to 15 sentences) on the following topic.

Décrivez ce que vous avez fait pendant vos dernières vacances. Est-ce que vous faites le même genre d'activités en vacances et pendant l'année scolaire? Pourquoi ou pourquoi pas?

Speaking 🍀1.2

Look at the following drawing, then tell a story about what is occurring in the picture.

Reading Strategy

Preparing to read Remind students to read through the questions before reading the paragraph. They will be better able to ignore extraneous information as they read the paragraph and focus on the details they need to know.

Writing Strategy

Essay topic Tell students to read the essay topic and take a few moments to list all the French words they can think of on that topic. They can then build their paragraph with the familiar vocabulary.

Language Examination

To display the drawing to the class, use the **Activités préparatoires** Transparency for Chapter 1.

Speaking: Sample answer

Trois amis sont allés à la montagne pour camper pendant le week-end. Ils ont déjà monté la tente et ils ont mis leurs sacs de couchage dedans. Maintenant, deux amis font de la randonnée. Ils portent des chaussures de randonnée, des sacs à dos et des gourdes. Le troisième ami va à la pêche; il est en train d'attraper un poisson.

You may also want to ask students the following.

Est-ce que tu aimes faire du camping? Pourquoi ou pourquoi pas?

Differentiated Instruction

SLOWER PACE LEARNERS

Before attempting the essay topic, encourage students to draw a chart with three columns titled **Activités pendant les vacances**, **Activités pendant l'année scolaire**, and **Pourquoi? Pourquoi pas?** Students should brainstorm activities and fill in the chart. Ask students to list transitional expressions in English. Then have students provide the English equivalents for the transitional expressions **pourtant, toutefois, aussi, d'ailleurs, en plus, en outre,** and **finalement**. 🍀1.2, 4.1

SPECIAL LEARNING NEEDS

Students with Learning Disabilities/Dyslexia Prior to assigning **Activités préparatoires,** make copies of the paragraph to be read. If possible, enlarge the paragraph to make it easier to read for students with reading difficulties. Work with students to highlight the proper nouns and vocabulary that may be new or difficult in the paragraph. Read these words aloud and explain their meanings.

VIDEO OPTIONS

▶ **Géoculture**

▶ **Télé-roman: Camille et compagnie, Épisode 1**

❶ Script

1. — Salut, Sandrine! Enfin le week-end! Pourquoi on n'irait pas au cinéma?

— Je voudrais bien, mais je dois étudier parce que j'ai un examen de chimie la semaine prochaine.

2. — Est-ce que tu faisais du skate quand tu étais petit, papi?

— Non! Il n'y avait pas de skate quand j'étais petit!

— Qu'est-ce que tu faisais comme sport?

— Tous les jours, après l'école, je jouais au foot.

3. — Regarde cette brochure! Il y a beaucoup de choses à faire!

— Oui, je sais! Je n'arrive pas à me décider!

— Je crois que je vais faire du ski ce matin. Tu viens?

— Bon, j'aime bien faire du ski, mais je préfère faire de la randonnée.

— Alors, à plus tard!

4. — Allô?

— Madame Boucher? C'est Hélène. Est-ce que Véronique est là?

— Bonjour, Hélène! Je regrette. Elle n'est pas là. Elle monte à cheval cet après-midi.

Révisions cumulatives

CD 1, Tr. 10

❶ Choisis la photo qui correspond à chaque conversation. ✿1.2

3. a.

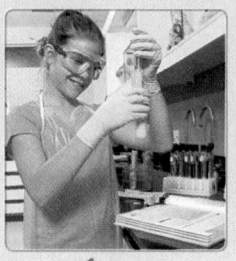
1. b.

2. c.

4. d.

❷ Lis cette brochure qui décrit une école d'été en France. Ensuite, décide si les personnes suivantes **a) devraient aller à cette école** ou **b) ne devraient pas y aller.** ✿3.2

L'École d'Été de Pau

L'École d'été de Pau est située dans la ville historique de Pau, la « porte des Pyrénées ».

L'école est destinée à tous les élèves de secondaire désirant s'améliorer dans les matières suivantes :

- **informatique • physique • anglais**
- **histoire-géo • SVT • français**
- **mathématiques • arts plastiques**
- **espagnol • chimie**

Cependant, l'école n'est pas seulement un camp pédagogique, mais aussi un camp de vacances, où les participants peuvent faire des sports et des activités divers :

- **photo • ski • pêche • randonnée**
- **foot • stage de vidéo**
- **camping • tennis • stage de guitare**

Quand : du 4 juillet au 5 août

- Les cours seront donnés en intensifs d'une semaine ou le week-end.
- Horaire des cours : de 9h à 12h de 13h à 15h
- Activitiés et sports : après 15h

Pour s'inscrire : Remplir le formulaire et le renvoyer à :
L'ÉCOLE D'ÉTÉ DE PAU, 20 Rue Louis-Barthon, 64000 Pau (France)

a **1.** Ce que Nicole aime, c'est la nature. Elle adore faire des randonnées.

a **2.** Raphaël adore les ordinateurs.

b **3.** Lise n'aime ni aller à la pêche ni camper. Ce qu'elle aime, c'est faire les magasins.

b **4.** Le sport préféré de Simon, c'est le basket.

a **5.** Mélodie aime parler anglais et espagnol.

b **6.** Félix déteste le sport et les devoirs! Il préfère aller au cinéma.

Online Culture Project

Tell students to imagine they are spending the year in a high school in Rennes, France. Have students search the Web for French stores that sell school supplies online. Have students create a poster displaying supplies French students need for school. All supplies should be labeled in French and should include the price in euros. On the labels, have students document the URLs of the Web sites they used. ✿2.2

3 Ton/Ta camarade et toi, vous assistez à l'École d'été de Pau de l'activité 2. Demande-lui quelles activités il/elle préfère et dis-lui lesquelles tu aimes. Puis, invite-le/la à faire une des activités que l'école offre. Il/Elle va accepter ou refuser. 1.1

Online Assessment
go.hrw.com
Cumulative Self–test
KEYWORD: BD3 CH1

4 Regarde ce tableau et décris les activités de ces gens. Dis où et en quelle saison cette scène se passe. Nomme au moins trois activités différentes. Est-ce que tu fais des activités semblables le week-end? Pourquoi ou pourquoi pas? 1.3, 2.2

Un dimanche après-midi à l'Île de la Grande Jatte de Georges Seurat

Seurat, Georges; A Sunday Afternoon on the Island of La Grande Jatte, 1884-86. ©The Granger Collection, New York

5 Imagine que tu es en vacances à la montagne ou au bord de la mer. Dessine une carte postale de l'endroit où tu es et envoie-la à un(e) ami(e) pour lui raconter ce que tu fais pendant tes vacances. 1.3

6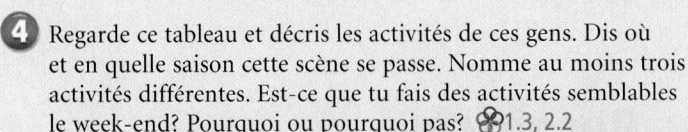

Le nouveau/La nouvelle Tu es chargé(e) de faire visiter ton école à un(e) nouvel/nouvelle étudiant(e). Indique les salles où les différentes matières sont enseignées et demande à l'étudiant(e) ce qu'il/elle pense de chaque matière. 1.1

FINE ART CONNECTION

Introduction After turning away from Impressionism, painter Georges-Pierre Seurat (1859-1891) became the founder of Neo-Impressionism, or pointillism. One of the most famous paintings of the nineteenth century, **Un dimanche après-midi à l'Île de la Grande Jatte** took Seurat two years to finish. It is now displayed at the Art Institute of Chicago. Seurat conducted color studies to maximize the luminosity of the painting. Motivated by scientific studies of color, optical effects, and perception, the artist created this masterpiece by juxtaposing tiny dots or strokes of primary, often contrasting, colors. This allows the eye of the viewer to blend colors optically, rather than having the colors blended as pigment. This form of painting, known as pointillism, makes colors more brilliant and powerful than standard brush strokes.

Analyzing
Seurat concentrated on the issues of color, light, and form in **Un dimanche après-midi à l'Île de la Grande Jatte.** To help students discuss the painting, you might use the following questions.
1. **Quelles sont les couleurs primaires dans ce tableau?**
2. **Comment l'artiste a-t-il créé des couleurs non-primaires?**
3. **Comment Seurat a-t-il dépeint la lumière?** 3.1

Extension
Most color television receivers and computer screens can be considered a kind of pointillism. Ask students to research how color television and computer screens generate pictures. (Both use tiny dots of primary red, green, and blue to render color.) 3.1

ACTFL Performance Standards

The activities in Chapter 1 target the communicative modes as described in the Standards.

Interpersonal	Two-way communication using receptive skills and productive skills	**Communication (SE),** pp. 9, 11, 13, 15, 21, 23 **Communication (TE),** pp. 9, 11, 15, 25 **À ton tour,** p. 41
Interpretive	One-way communication using receptive skills	**Culture,** pp. 16–17 **Lecture,** pp. 29-31
Presentational	One-way communication using productive skills	**Communication (SE),** pp. 25, 27 **Communication (TE),** pp. 13, 21, 23, 27

chapitre 2

Planning Guide

Le monde du travail

Chapter Section	Resources
Vocabulaire 1 pp. 44–47 • Jobs and professions **Grammaire 1** pp. 48–51 • Review: The future • The feminine forms of nouns **Application 1** pp. 52–53 • **Un peu plus:** The verb **conduire**	Teaching Transparencies: Vocabulaire 2.1, 2.2; Bell Work 2.1, 2.2, 2.3, 2.4 Cahier de vocabulaire et grammaire, pp. 13–18 Grammar Tutor for Students of French Cahier d'activités, pp. 11–13 Media Guide, pp. 5–8 **Assessment Program** Quiz: Vocabulaire 1, pp. 31–32 Quiz: Grammaire 1, pp. 33–34 Quiz: Application 1, pp. 35–36
Culture pp. 54–55 • **Lecture culturelle: Designer Olfactif** • **Comparaisons** • **Communauté et professions**	Cahier d'activités, p. 14
Vocabulaire 2 pp. 56–59 • Talking on the telephone and writing a formal letter **Grammaire 2** pp. 60–63 • The future perfect • The resent participle **Application 2** pp. 64–65 • **Un peu plus:** Review: **Conditionnel de politesse**	Teaching Transparencies: Vocabulaire 2.3, 2.4; Bell Work 2.5, 2.6, 2.7, 2.8 Cahier de vocabulaire et grammaire, pp. 19–24 Grammar Tutor for Students of French Cahier d'activités, pp. 15–17 Media Guide, pp. 5–8 **Assessment Program** Quiz: Vocabulaire 2, pp. 37–38 Quiz: Grammaire 2, pp. 39–40 Quiz: Application 2, pp. 41–42
Lecture pp. 66–69 • **Le petit prince** **L'atelier de l'écrivain** pp. 70–71 • **Ta lettre de motivation**	Cahier d'activités, p. 18 Reading Strategies and Skills Handbook Advanced Reader **Assessment Program** Quiz: Lecture, p. 43 Quiz: Écriture, p. 44
Prépare-toi pour l'examen pp. 72–75 • **Résumé de vocabulaire et grammaire** **Activités préparatoires** pp. 76–77 **Révisions cumulatives** pp. 78–79	Teaching Transparencies: Picture Sequences, Situation, Ch. 2 Media Guide, pp. 8, 75–76 **Assessment Program** Examen: Chapitre 2, pp. 45–50 Examen oral: Chapitre 2, p. 318 Teaching Transparencies: Fine Art, Ch. 2 Cahier d'activités, pp. 19–20
Chroniques pp. 80–89 • Travailler pour vivre ou vivre pour travailler? • Le système scolaire français • Les femmes au travail • L'artisanat sans frontière • Inventions et découvertes	Reading Strategies and Skills Handbook Advanced Reader

Pacing Suggestions

	Essential	Recommended	Optional
Vocabulaire 1 • Jobs and professions • **Flash culture**	✔		
Grammaire 1 • Review: The future • The feminine forms of nouns	✔		
Application 1 • **Un peu plus:** The verb **conduire** • **Flash culture**	✔		
Culture • **Lecture culturelle: Designer Olfactif** • **Comparaisons** • **Communauté et professions**		✔	
Vocabulaire 2 • Talking on the telephone and writing a formal letter • **Flash culture**	✔		
Grammaire 2 • The future perfect • The resent participle • **Flash culture**	✔		
Application 2 • **Un peu plus:** Review: **Conditionnel de politesse**	✔		
Lecture • **Le petit prince**		✔	
L'atelier de l'écrivain • **Ta lettre de motivation**			
Prépare-toi pour l'examen		✔	
Activités préparatoires		✔	
Révisions cumulatives			✔
Chroniques			✔

Technology

Bien dit! Online
• Student Edition with multi-media
• SoundBooth recording tool
• Interactive activities with feedback
• Self-tests with feedback
• Cahier d'activités (Interactive workbook)
• Cahier de vocabulaire et grammaire (Interactive workbook)
• Holt Online Assessment

DVD Program
• Télé-roman: Camille et compagnie
• Télé-culture: Interviews

Interactive Tutor
• Interactive practice games
• Writing and recording workshops
• Before You Know It™ Flashcards

Audio Program
• Student Edition Listening Activities
• Assessment listening activities
• Songs

One-Stop Planner
• Complete media and print resources
• ExamView Pro Test Generator
• Holt Calendar Planner

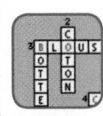

PuzzlePro
• Customizable word games

Differentiated Practice and Assessment CD

For slower pace and advanced learner options, see the Differentiated Practice and Assessment CD.

Planning Guide

Projects

Les carrières

Students will create a poster to advertise a particular career of their choice. They will also give an oral presentation in which they act as a representative of that field, encouraging other students to consider it as a career. ❀ 1.3, 5.1

Suggested Sequence

1. Have students choose a profession that is listed in the **Vocabulaire.** They might refer to French-English dictionaries to find additional professions.

2. Have students research their profession. They might interview a friend, relative, or community member in that field, check the Internet for a definition and history of the profession, and find information in magazines or college catalogues about the necessary training, employment opportunities, average salary, and so on.

3. Have students organize their oral presentation and plan the layout of their poster. Remind them that they are acting as a representative of their profession during a "career day" at school. If they choose to be a doctor, they should be prepared to tell the class why they chose to be a doctor, what training is necessary, what it is like to be a doctor, and what their everyday duties and responsibilities are.

4. Have students give their oral presentation to the class, using their posters to encourage their classmates to choose their profession. Class members should ask questions, just as they would if a guest were visiting the class.

Grading the project

Suggested point distribution
(100 points total)
Content . . . . 20 pts.
Creativity of visuals . . . . 20 pts.
Oral presentation . . . . 20 pts.
Language use . . . . 20 pts.
Participation . . . . 20 pts.

e-community

e-mail forum:

Post the following questions on the classroom e-mail forum:

Location:	http://french

Qu'est-ce que tu voudrais faire plus tard?

Que fait un avocat? Un mécanicien? Un médecin? ❀ 5.1

All students will contribute to the list and then share the items.

Partner Class Project

Have students imagine that they work for a job placement center. They should prepare a questionnaire that asks the students in their partner class about their interests and strengths, their career goals, and the type of company they would like to work for. Students should ask their partner class questions, such as **Qu'est-ce que tu aimes faire? Qu'est-ce que tu sais faire?** and **Quelle sorte de métier est-ce que tu voudrais faire?** Students should post the questionnaire on the student or class Web site. Remind students to e-mail the Web site address or an electronic document to the partner class. When the survey comes back from the partner class, students should try to match each student with a job. Students should list the jobs they recommended for students in the partner class. They then should list the jobs they themselves would like to have and compare the two lists. As a class, do students in the partner class have similar or different career goals? Why? ❀ 1.2, 4.2

Game Bank
For game ideas, see pages T60–T63.

Le Tour de France

One of the most popular sporting traditions in France is cycling. France ranks number one in the world in track cycling competition and has an impressive record in mountain biking, but it is best known for the road cycling of the famous **Tour de France.** Each July, the French and tourists alike put everything on hold to watch **le Tour,** the world's most prestigious bicycle race, covering over 3,000 kilometers of varied terrain. Everyone wants to know who will wear the coveted yellow jersey awarded to the cyclist who leads the race (**le maillot jaune**), has the most points (**le maillot vert**), and rules the mountains (**le maillot à pois rouges**). Although long dominated by the French, two Americans won the tour: Greg LeMond (1986) and Lance Armstrong (1999–2005). Have students research the history of the **Tour de France.** What is its cultural significance for the French? What sporting events in the United States carry cultural significance for Americans? Have students present their conclusions to the class. ✿ 3.1, 4.2

La cuisine

Lentils come from the Mediterranean countries and have been cultivated for more than 2,000 years. There are three varieties of lentils: blond, brown, and green (most commonly found in France). Green lentils are dried in the sun while still in the fields. France produces 20,000 tons of green lentils per year. Encourage students to make **petit salé** in their home economics class or at home for family and friends. ✿ 2.2, 5.2

Petit Salé aux Lentilles

pour 6 personnes

4 livres de porc	**2** oignons
½ livre de lard	**2** cuillères à soupe de beurre
1 livre de lentilles	sel, poivre
4 carottes	

Mettre le porc et le lard dans un faitout. Recouvrir d'eau et laisser cuire pendant 1 heure 30. Éplucher et couper les carottes. Éplucher les oignons et les couper en petits morceaux. Ajouter les lentilles, les carottes et les oignons à la viande. Laisser cuire 30 minutes à feu doux. Retirer du faitout. Garder le bouillon de cuisson. Faire fondre le beurre dans une marmite. Ajouter la viande. Saler et poivrer. Ajouter les légumes. Verser une louche du bouillon de cuisson. Laisser cuire pendant 20 minutes. Servir très chaud.

Traditions

Listening Activity Scripts

Vocabulaire à l'œuvre 1

2 p. 46, CD 2, Tr. 1

LAURE   Dis, Maxence, qu'est-ce que tu as l'intention de faire après le lycée?

MAXENCE   J'aimerais travailler tout de suite. Je crois que je vais devenir mécanicien. Et toi, Laure?

LAURE   Moi, j'adore les ordinateurs. J'aimerais être informaticienne. Mais ma mère aimerait que je devienne pharmacienne, comme mon père. Et toi, Mélanie, qu'est-ce que tu vas faire plus tard?

MÉLANIE   Moi, mes parents voudraient que je devienne cuisinière pour travailler dans leur restaurant. Mais moi, j'aime voyager et je voudrais apprendre l'espagnol et l'allemand. Je préférerais devenir interprète.

Answers to Activity 2

1. a   2. b   3. b   4. a   5.

Grammaire à l'œuvre 1

7 p. 48, CD 2, Tr. 2

1. Plus jeune, je travaillais dans le restaurant de mes parents.
2. Je serai cuisinier plus tard.
3. Est-ce que vous choisirez la profession de vos parents?
4. Moi, je voudrais être avocate.
5. Je travaillerai dans l'informatique.
6. Je faisais mes études à Paris cette année-là.
7. J'avais un bon métier.
8. Moi, je serai vétérinaire.

Answers to Activity 7

1. a   2. b   3. b   4. b
5. b   6.a   7. a   8. a

Application 1

15 p. 52, CD 2, Tr. 3

1. J'aime beaucoup ce pâtissier. Ses tartes sont excellentes.
2. Quand on était jeunes, on allait chercher du beurre chez la fermière.
3. Notre professeur nous a donné un devoir difficile à faire.
4. Ce vétérinaire est très sympa avec les animaux.
5. La journaliste qui écrit pour ce journal est très connue.

Answers to Activity 15

1. b   2. a   3. c   4. c   5. a

Vocabulaire à l'œuvre 2

21 p. 58, CD 2, Tr. 4

1. Mon frère a été licencié. C'est dommage parce qu'il aimait bien son travail.
2. Lucas est allé à un entretien pour une place de comptable dans une grande société. Je crois que cela s'est bien passé parce qu'il avait l'air très content en sortant.
3. J'ai envoyé des lettres de demande de stage et j'ai déjà reçu des réponses très intéressantes.
4. Monsieur Lermitte cherche un travail à plein temps depuis plus de trois mois mais il n'a toujours rien trouvé. Pourtant, il lit les journaux tous les jours!

Answers to Activity 21

1. d   2. b   3. c   4. a

Grammaire à l'œuvre 2

26 p. 60, CD 2, Tr. 5

1. Je téléphonerai à Michel quand j'aurai écrit ma lettre de motivation.
2. Quand ils auront déjeuné, ils iront au cinéma.
3. Elle ira voir Alice quand elle aura parlé à Stéphanie.
4. Nous viendrons vous rendre visite dès que nous serons arrivés.
5. Vous comprendrez la leçon quand vous aurez fini les exercices.

Answers to Activity 26
1. écrire la lettre de motivation
2. déjeuner   3. parler à Stéphanie
4. arriver   5. finir les exercices

Application 2

37 p. 64, CD 2, Tr. 6

— Hé, vous pouvez laver ma voiture ce matin?
— Pourriez-vous réparer ma télévision?
— C'est possible de se faire couper les cheveux ici?
— Livrez-moi une pizza au fromage pour dix-neuf heures.
— Ça vous ennuierait de m'aider à repasser le linge?
— Il faudrait que vous fassiez aussi le ménage.
— Nettoyez-moi bien ce pantalon, hein.
— Vous serait-il possible de garder ma petite Émilie?

Answers to Activity 37
1. b   2. a   3. b   4. b
5. a   6. a   7. b   8. a

Prépare-toi pour l'examen

6 p. 73, CD 2, Tr. 8

1. Bonjour monsieur Delforges, vous serait-il possible de réparer mon ordinateur? Il plante tout le temps.
2. Donnez-moi la carte.
3. Ça vous ennuierait de garder mon chat ce week-end?
4. Je veux un gâteau d'anniversaire pour ce soir.

Answers to Activity 6
1. a   2. b   3. a   4. b

Activités préparatoires

Listening, p. 76, CD 2, Tr. 9

1. — Désolé, mais je ne peux pas aller au cinéma avec toi demain après-midi.
   — Ah oui, c'est vrai. Tu as un job d'été, n'est-ce pas?
2. — Qu'est-ce que tu as? Tu as l'air stressé.
   — Je dois faire réparer ma voiture. J'ai demandé de l'argent à mes parents, mais mon père est au chômage et ils ne peuvent pas m'aider. Et moi, je n'ai pas d'argent.

Answers to Listening Activity
1. c   2. a

Révisions cumulatives *chapitres 1-2*

1 p. 78, CD 2, Tr. 10

1. Il est teinturier. Il lave et repasse les vêtements des gens.
2. Ils adorent préparer de bons plats. Ils travaillent dans un restaurant.
3. C'est un bon comptable. Il travaille pour une grande société.
4. Il aime soigner les animaux.
5. Il travaille dans sa ferme et vend ses légumes.

Answers to Activity 1
1. Albin   2. Léa et Albert   3. Joseph
4. Martin   5. Éric

50-Minute Lesson Plans

Le monde du travail

Day 1

OBJECTIVE
Ask about future plans

Core Instruction
Chapter Opener, pp. 42–43
• See Using the Photo, p. 42. **5 min.**
• See Chapter Objectives, p. 42. **5 min.**

Vocabulaire 1, pp. 44–47
• Present **Vocabulaire 1,** pp. 44–45. See Teaching **Vocabulaire,** p. 44. **15 min.**
• Present **Exprimons-nous!,** p. 45. **5 min.**
• Do Activity 1, p. 46. **5 min.**
• Play Audio CD 2, Tr. 1 for Activity 2, p. 46. **5 min.**
• Do Activity 3, p. 46. **5 min.**
• Present **Flash culture,** p. 47. **5 min.**

Optional Resources
• Advanced Learners, p. 45 ▲
• Special Learning Needs, p. 45 ●
• Slower Pace Learners, p. 47 ◆

Homework Suggestions
Cahier de vocabulaire et grammaire, pp. 13–14
✿ 1.1, 1.2, 1.3, 4.2

Day 2

OBJECTIVE
Make polite requests; Use the future

Core Instruction
Vocabulaire 1, pp. 44–47
• Do Bell Work 2.1, p. 44. **5 min.**
• See Teaching **Exprimons-nous!,** p. 46. **10 min.**
• Have students do Activities 4–6, p. 47. **25 min.**

Grammaire 1, pp. 48–51
• See Teaching **Grammaire,** p. 48. **10 min.**

Optional Resources
• Communication (TE), p. 47
• Multiple Intelligences, p. 47
• Advanced Learners, p. 49 ▲

Homework Suggestions
Study for **Quiz: Vocabulaire 1**
Cahier de vocabulaire et grammaire, p. 15
Online Practice (**go.hrw.com,** Keyword: BD3 CH2)
✿ 1.1, 1.2, 1.3

Day 3

OBJECTIVE
Use the future

Core Instruction
Vocabulaire 1, pp. 44–47
• Review **Vocabulaire 1,** pp. 44–47. **10 min.**
• Give **Quiz: Vocabulaire 1.** **20 min.**

Grammaire 1, pp. 48–51
• Play Audio CD 2, Tr. 2 for Activity 7, p. 48. **5 min.**
• Have students do Activities 8–10, p. 49. **15 min.**

Optional Resources
• Communication (TE), p. 49
• Multiple Intelligences, p. 49

Homework Suggestions
Cahier de vocabulaire et grammaire, p. 16
Cahier d'activités, p. 11
Online Practice (**go.hrw.com,** Keyword: BD3 CH2)
✿ 1.1, 1.2, 1.3

Day 4

OBJECTIVE
Use feminine forms of nouns

Core Instruction
Grammaire 1, pp. 48–51
• See Teaching **Grammaire,** p. 50. **10 min.**
• Have students do Activities 11–14, pp. 50–51. **25 min.**

Application 1, pp. 52–53
• Present **Flash culture,** p. 52. **5 min.**
• Play Audio CD 2, Tr. 3 for Activity 15, p. 52. **5 min.**
• Have students do Activity 16, p. 52. **5 min.**

Optional Resources
• Advanced Learners, p. 51 ▲
• Multiple Intelligences, p. 51

Homework Suggestions
Study for **Quiz: Grammaire 1**
Cahier de vocabulaire et grammaire, p. 17
Cahier d'activités, p. 12
✿ 1.1, 1.2, .1.3, 4.2

Day 5

OBJECTIVE
Use the verb **conduire**

Core Instruction
Grammaire 1, pp. 48–51
• Review **Grammaire 1,** pp. 48–51. **10 min.**
• Give **Quiz: Grammaire 1.** **20 min.**

Application 1, pp. 52–53
• See Teaching **Un peu plus,** p. 52. **5 min.**
• Have students do Activities 17–20, pp. 52–53. **15 min.**

Optional Resources
• Communication (TE), p. 53
• Slower Pace Learners, p. 53 ◆
• Multiple Intelligences, p. 53

Homework Suggestions
Study for **Quiz: Application 1**
Cahier de vocabulaire et grammaire, p. 18
Cahier d'activités, p. 13
Online Practice (**go.hrw.com,** Keyword: BD3 CH2)
✿ 1.1, 1.2, 1.3, 3.2

Day 6

OBJECTIVE
Learn about francophone culture

Core Instruction
Application 1, pp. 52–53
• Review **Application 1,** pp. 52–53. **10 min.**
• Give **Quiz: Application 1.** **20 min.**

Culture, pp. 54–55
• See **Lecture culturelle** (TE), p. 54. **10 min.**
• See **Comparaisons et communauté** (TE), p. 54. **10 min.**

Optional Resources
• Cultures, p. 55
• Communities, p. 55
• Advanced Learners, p. 55 ▲
• Multiple Intelligences, p. 55

Homework Suggestions
Cahier d'activités, p. 14
Interactive Tutor, Ch. 2
Online Practice (**go.hrw.com,** Keyword: BD3 CH2)
Finish the **Communauté et professions** project
✿ 1.1, 1.3, 2.1, 4.2, 5.1

Day 7

OBJECTIVE
Make a phone call

Core Instruction
Vocabulaire 2, pp. 56–59
• Do Bell Work 2.5, p. 56. **5 min.**
• Present **Vocabulaire 2,** pp. 56–57. See Teaching **Vocabulaire,** p. 56. **15 min.**
• Present **Exprimons-nous!,** p. 57. **10 min.**
• Play Audio CD 2, Tr. 4 for Activity 21, p. 58. **5 min.**
• Have students do Activities 22–23, p. 58. **10 min.**
• Present **Flash culture,** p. 58. **5 min.**

Optional Resources
• Slower Pace Learners, p. 57 ◆
• Multiple Intelligences, p. 57

Homework Suggestions
Cahier de vocabulaire et grammaire, pp. 19–20
✿ 1.1, 1.2, 4.2

Day 8

OBJECTIVE
Write a formal letter; Use the future perfect

Core Instruction
Vocabulaire 2, pp. 56–59
• See Teaching **Exprimons-nous!,** p. 58. **10 min.**
• Have students do Activities 24–25, p. 59. **20 min.**

Grammaire 2, pp. 60–63
• See Teaching **Grammaire,** p. 60. **10 min.**
• Play Audio CD 2, Tr. 5 for Activity 26, p. 60. **5 min.**
• Have students do Activity 27, p. 60. **5 min.**

Optional Resources
• Advanced Learners, p. 59 ▲
• Special Learning Needs, p. 59 ●
• Slower Pace Learners, p. 61 ◆

Homework Suggestions
Study for **Quiz: Vocabulaire 2**
Cahier de vocabulaire et grammaire, p. 21
✿ 1.1, 1.2, 1.3

50-Minute Lesson Plans

Day 9

OBJECTIVE
Use the future perfect

Core Instruction
Vocabulaire 2, pp. 56–59
• Review **Vocabulaire 2,** pp. 56–59. **10 min.**
• Give **Quiz: Vocabulaire 2.** **20 min.**

Grammaire 2, pp. 60–63
• Have students do Activities 28–30, p. 61. **15 min.**
• Present **Flash culture,** p. 62. **5 min.**

Optional Resources
• Communication (TE), p. 61
• Special Learning Needs, p. 61 ●

Homework Suggestions
Cahier de vocabulaire et grammaire, p. 22
Cahier d'activités, p. 15
Interactive Tutor, Ch. 2
Online Practice (**go.hrw.com,** Keyword: BD3 CH2)
❀ 1.1, 1.2, 1.3, 4.2

Day 10

OBJECTIVE
Use the present participle; Use the ***conditionnel de politesse***

Core Instruction
Grammaire 2, pp. 60–63
• Do Bell Work 2.7, p. 62. **5 min.**
• See Teaching **Grammaire,** p. 62. **10 min.**
• Have students do Activities 31–35, pp. 62–63. **25 min.**

Application 2, pp. 64–65
• Have students do Activity 36, p. 64. **5 min.**
• See Teaching **Un peu plus,** p. 64. **5 min.**

Optional Resources
• Slower Pace Learners, p. 63 ◆
• Multiple Intelligences, p. 63

Homework Suggestions
Study for **Quiz: Grammaire 2**
Cahier de vocabulaire et grammaire, p. 23
Cahier d'activités, p. 16
❀ 1.1, 1.2, 4.1

Day 11

OBJECTIVE
Use the ***conditionnel de politesse***

Core Instruction
Grammaire 2, pp. 60–63
• Review **Grammaire 2,** pp. 60–63. **10 min.**
• Give **Quiz: Grammaire 2.** **20 min.**

Application 2, pp. 64–65
• Play Audio CD 2, Tr. 6 for Activity 37, p. 64. **5 min.**
• Have students do Activities 38–41, pp. 64–65. **15 min.**

Optional Resources
• Advanced Learners, p. 65 ▲
• Multiple Intelligences, p. 65

Homework Suggestions
Study for **Quiz: Application 2**
Cahier de vocabulaire et grammaire, p. 24
Cahier d'activités, p. 17
Online Practice (**go.hrw.com,** Keyword: BD3 CH2)
❀ 1.1, 1.2, 1.3, 3.2, 5.1

Day 12

OBJECTIVE
Develop listening and reading skills

Core Instruction
Application 2, pp. 64–65
• Review **Application 2,** pp. 64–65. **10 min.**
• Give **Quiz: Application 2.** **20 min.**

Lecture, pp. 66–69
• See **Lecture** (TE), p. 66. **20 min.**

Optional Resources
• Advanced Learners, p. 67 ▲
• Special Learning Needs, p. 67 ●
• Connections, p. 69

Homework Suggestions
Interactive Tutor, Ch. 2
Online Practice (**go.hrw.com,** Keyword: BD3 CH2)
❀ 1.1, 1.2, 3.1, 3.2

Day 13

OBJECTIVE
Develop listening, reading, and writing skills

Core Instruction
Lecture, pp. 66–69
• See **Lecture** (TE), p. 68. **20 min.**

L'atelier de l'écrivain, pp. 70–71
• See **L'atelier de l'écrivain** (TE), p. 70. **30 min.**

Optional Resources
• Slower Pace Learners, p. 69 ◆
• Special Learning Needs, p. 69 ●
• Slower Pace Learners, p. 71 ◆
• Special Learning Needs, p. 71 ●

Homework Suggestions
Cahier d'activités, p. 18
❀ 1.1, 1.2, 1.3, 3.1

Day 14

OBJECTIVE
Review the chapter; Prepare for the AP Exam

Core Instruction
Prépare-toi pour l'examen, pp. 72–75
• Have students do Activities 1–5, pp. 72–73. **25 min.**

Activités préparatoires, pp. 76–77
• Have students do the **Activités préparatoires,** pp. 76–77. **25 min.**

Optional Resources
• Reteaching, p. 72
• Connections, p. 77
• Slower Pace Learners, p. 77 ◆
• Multiple Intelligences, p. 77
• **Télé-culture:** Interviews

Homework Suggestions
Interactive Tutor, Ch. 2
Online Practice (**go.hrw.com,** Keyword: BD3 CH2)
❀ 1.2, 1.3, 2.1, 2.2, 3.1, 4.1

Day 15

OBJECTIVE
Review the chapter

Core Instruction
Prépare-toi pour l'examen, pp. 72–75
• Play Audio CD 2, Tr. 8 for Activity 6, p. 73. **10 min.**
• Have students do Activity 7, p. 73. **10 min.**

Révisions cumulatives, pp. 78–79
• Play Audio CD 2, Tr. 10 for Activity 1, p. 78. **5 min.**
• Have students do Activities 2–6, pp. 78–79. **25 min.**

Optional Resources
• Online Culture Project, p. 78
• Fine Art Connection, p. 79
• **Télé-roman: Camille et compagnie**

Homework Suggestions
Study for Chapter Test
Online Practice (**go.hrw.com,** Keyword: BD3 CH2)
❀ 1.1, 1.2, 1.3, 2.1, 2.2, 3.1, 3.2

Day 16/Test

Core Instruction
Chapter Test 50 min.

Optional Resources
Assessment Program
• Alternative Assessment
• Test Generator
• Quiz: Lecture
• Quiz: Écriture

Homework Suggestions
Cahier d'activités, pp. 19–20, 104–105
Online Practice (**go.hrw.com,** Keyword: BD3 CH2)

chapitre

90-Minute Lesson Plans

Le monde du travail

90-Minute Lesson Plans

Block 1

OBJECTIVE
Ask about future plans; Make polite requests

Core Instruction
Chapter Opener, pp. 42–43
• See Using the Photo, p. 42. **5 min.**
• See Chapter Objectives, p. 42. **5 min.**

Vocabulaire 1, pp. 44–47
• Present **Vocabulaire 1,** pp. 44–45. See Teaching **Vocabulaire,** p. 44. **15 min.**
• Present **Exprimons-nous!,** p. 45. **10 min.**
• Have students do Activity 1, p. 46. **5 min.**
• Play Audio CD 2, Tr. 1 for Activity 2, p. 46. **5 min.**
• Have students do Activity 3, p. 46. **5 min.**
• Present **Flash culture,** p. 47. **5 min.**
• See Teaching **Exprimons-nous!,** p. 46. **10 min.**
• Have students do Activities 4–6, p. 47. **25 min.**

Optional Resources
• Learning Tip, p. 43
• TPR, p. 45
• Connections, p. 45
• Advanced Learners, p. 45 ▲
• Special Learning Needs, p. 45 ●
• Communication (TE), p. 47
• Slower Pace Learners, p. 47 ◆
• Multiple Intelligences, p. 47

Homework Suggestions
Study for **Quiz: Vocabulaire 1**
Cahier de vocabulaire et grammaire, pp. 13–15
Interactive Tutor, Ch. 2
Online Practice (**go.hrw.com,** Keyword: BD3 CH2)
❀ 1.1, 1.2, 1.3, 3.1, 4.2

Block 2

OBJECTIVE
Use the future; Use feminine forms of nouns

Core Instruction
Vocabulaire 1, pp. 44–47
• Review **Vocabulaire 1,** pp. 44–47. **10 min.**
• Give **Quiz: Vocabulaire 1.** **20 min.**

Grammaire 1, pp. 48–51
• See Teaching **Grammaire,** p. 48. **10 min.**
• Play Audio CD 2, Tr. 2 for Activity 7, p. 48. **5 min.**
• Have students do Activities 8–10, p. 49. **15 min.**
• See Teaching **Grammaire,** p. 50. **10 min.**
• Have students do Activities 11–13, pp. 50–51. **20 min.**

Optional Resources
• Communication (TE), p. 49
• Advanced Learners, p. 49 ▲
• Multiple Intelligences, p. 49
• **Attention!,** p. 50
• Communication (TE), p. 51
• Advanced Learners, p. 51 ▲
• Multiple Intelligences, p. 51

Homework Suggestions
Study for **Quiz: Grammaire 1**
Cahier de vocabulaire et grammaire, pp. 16–17
Cahier d'activités, pp. 11–12
Online Practice (**go.hrw.com,** Keyword: BD3 CH2)
❀ 1.1, 1.2, 1.3

Block 3

OBJECTIVE
*Use feminine forms of nouns; Use the verb **conduire;** Learn about francophone culture*

Core Instruction
Grammaire 1, pp. 48–51
• Do Bell Work 2.3, p. 50. **5 min.**
• Have students do Activity 14, p. 51. **5 min.**
• Review **Grammaire 1,** pp. 48–51. **10 min.**
• Give **Quiz: Grammaire 1.** **20 min.**

Application 1, pp. 52–53
• Present **Flash culture,** p. 52. **5 min.**
• Play Audio CD 2, Tr. 3 for Activity 15, p. 52. **5 min.**
• Have students do Activity 16, p. 52. **5 min.**
• See Teaching **Un peu plus,** p. 52. **5 min.**
• Have students do Activities 17–20, pp. 52–53. **10 min.**

Culture, pp. 54–55
• See **Lecture culturelle** (TE), p. 54. **10 min.**
• See **Comparaisons et communauté** (TE), p. 54. **10 min.**

Optional Resources
• French for Spanish Speakers, p. 52
• Communication (TE), p. 53
• Slower Pace Learners, p. 53 ◆
• Multiple Intelligences, p. 53
• Prereading Questions, p. 54
• Active Reading Questions, p. 54
• **Vocabulaire supplémentaire,** p. 54
• Bulletin Board Project, p. 55
• Cultures, p. 55
• Communities, p. 55
• Advanced Learners, p. 55 ▲
• Multiple Intelligences, p. 55

Homework Suggestions
Study for **Quiz: Application 1**
Cahier de vocabulaire et grammaire, p. 18
Cahier d'activités, pp. 13–14
Interactive Tutor, Ch. 2
Online Practice (**go.hrw.com,** Keyword: BD3 CH2)
Finish the **Communauté et professions** project
❀ 1.1, 1.2, 1.3, 2.1, 2.2, 3.2, 4.2, 5.1

Block 4

OBJECTIVE
Make a phone call; Write a formal letter

Core Instruction
Application 1, pp. 52–53
• Review **Application 1,** pp. 52–53. **10 min.**
• Give **Quiz: Application 1.** **20 min.**

Vocabulaire 2, pp. 56–59
• Present **Vocabulaire 2,** pp. 56–57. See Teaching **Vocabulaire,** p. 56. **15 min.**
• Present **Exprimons-nous!,** p. 57. **10 min.**
• Play Audio CD 2, Tr. 4 for Activity 21, p. 58. **5 min.**
• Have students do Activities 22–23, p. 58. **10 min.**
• Present **Flash culture,** p. 58. **5 min.**
• See Teaching **Exprimons-nous!,** p. 58. **5 min.**
• Have students do Activities 24–25, p. 59. **10 min.**

Optional Resources
• TPR, p. 57
• Connections, p. 57
• Slower Pace Learners, p. 57 ◆
• Multiple Intelligences, p. 57
• Cultures, p. 58
• Communication (TE), p. 59
• Advanced Learners, p. 59 ▲
• Special Learning Needs, p. 59 ●

Homework Suggestions
Study for **Quiz: Vocabulaire 2**
Cahier de vocabulaire et grammaire, pp. 19–21
Interactive Tutor, Ch. 2
Online Practice (**go.hrw.com,** Keyword: BD3 CH2)
❀ 1.1, 1.2, 1.3, 2.1, 3.1, 4.2

Block 5

OBJECTIVE
Use the future perfect; Use the present participle

Core Instruction
Vocabulaire 2, pp. 56–59
• Review **Vocabulaire 2,** pp. 56–59. **10 min.**
• Give **Quiz: Vocabulaire 2.** **20 min.**

Grammaire 2, pp. 60–63
• See Teaching **Grammaire,** p. 60. **10 min.**
• Play Audio CD 2, Tr. 5 for Activity 26, p. 60. **5 min.**
• Have students do Activities 27–30, pp. 60–61. **15 min.**
• Present **Flash culture,** p. 62. **5 min.**
• See Teaching **Grammaire,** p. 62. **10 min.**
• Have students do Activities 31–34, pp. 62–63. **15 min.**

Optional Resources
• Communication (TE), p. 61
• Slower Pace Learners, p. 61 ◆
• Special Learning Needs, p. 61 ●
• French for Spanish Speakers, p. 62
• Slower Pace Learners, p. 63 ◆
• Multiple Intelligences, p. 63

Homework Suggestions
Study for **Quiz: Grammaire 2**
Cahier de vocabulaire et grammaire, pp. 22–23
Cahier d'activités, pp. 15–16
Interactive Tutor, Ch. 2
Online Practice (**go.hrw.com,** Keyword: BD3 CH2)
❀ 1.1, 1.2, 1.3, 4.1, 4.2

Block 6

OBJECTIVE
*Use the present participle; Use the **conditionnel de politesse;** Develop listening and reading skills*

Grammaire 2, pp. 60–63
• Do Bell Work 2.7, p. 62. **5 min.**
• Have students do Activity 35, p. 63. **5 min.**
• Review **Grammaire 2,** pp. 60–63. **10 min.**
• Give **Quiz: Grammaire 2.** **20 min.**

Application 2, pp. 64–65
• Have students do Activity 36, p. 64. **5 min.**
• See Teaching **Un peu plus,** p. 64. **5 min.**
• Play Audio CD 2, Tr. 6 for Activity 37, p. 64. **5 min.**
• Have students do Activities 38–41, pp. 64–65. **15 min.**

Lecture, pp. 66–69
• See **Lecture** (TE), p. 66. **20 min.**

Optional Resources
• Communication (TE), p. 63
• Communication (TE), p. 65
• Advanced Learners, p. 65 ▲
• Multiple Intelligences, p. 65
• AP Reading Suggestion, p. 66
• Applying the Strategies, p. 66
• Active Reading Questions, p. 67
• Finding the Main Idea, p. 67
• Advanced Learners, p. 67 ▲
• Special Learning Needs, p. 67 ●
• Connections, p. 69

Homework Suggestions
Study for **Quiz: Application 2**
Cahier de vocabulaire et grammaire, p. 24
Cahier d'activités, p. 17
Interactive Tutor, Ch. 2
Online Practice (**go.hrw.com,** Keyword: BD3 CH2)
❀ 1.1, 1.2, 1.3, 3.1, 3.2, 5.1

Block 7

OBJECTIVE
Develop listening, reading, and writing skills; Review the chapter

Core Instruction
Application 2, pp. 64–65
• Review **Application 2,** pp. 64–65. **10 min.**
• Give **Quiz: Application 2.** **20 min.**

Lecture, pp. 66–69
• See **Lecture** (TE), p. 68. **10 min.**

L'atelier de l'écrivain, pp. 70–71
• See **L'atelier de l'écrivain** (TE), p. 70. **30 min.**

Prépare-toi pour l'examen, pp. 72–75
• Have students do Activities 1–5, pp. 72–73. **10 min.**
• Play Audio CD 2, Tr. 8 for Activity 6, p. 73. **5 min.**
• Have students do Activity 7, p. 73. **5 min.**

Optional Resources
• Active Reading Questions, p. 68
• Postreading Activity, p. 68
• Slower Pace Learners, p. 69 ◆
• Special Learning Needs, p. 69 ●
• Process Writing, p. 70
• Teaching Suggestion, p. 70
• Cultures, p. 70
• **The futures,** p. 71
• Writing Assessment, p. 71
• Slower Pace Learners, p. 71 ◆
• Special Learning Needs, p. 71 ●
• TPRS, p. 72
• Teacher to Teacher, p. 72
• Reteaching, p. 72
• **Attention!,** p. 73
• Oral Assessment, p. 73
• Cultures, p. 74
• Game, p. 75
• **Télé-culture:** Interviews

Homework Suggestions
Study for Chapter Test
Cahier d'activités, p. 18
Interactive Tutor, Ch. 2
Online Practice (**go.hrw.com,** Keyword: BD3 CH2)
❀ 1.1, 1.2, 1.3, 2.1, 2.2, 3.1

Block 8

OBJECTIVE
Prepare for the AP Exam; Review and assess the chapter

Core Instruction
Activités préparatoires, pp. 76–77
• Have students do the **Activités préparatoires,** pp. 76–77. **20 min.**

Chapter Test 50 min.

Révisions cumulatives, pp. 78–79
• Play Audio CD 2, Tr. 10 for Activity 1, p. 78. **5 min.**
• Have students do Activities 2–6, pp. 78–79. **15 min.**

Optional Resources
• Reading Strategy, p. 76
• Preparing for the Exam, p. 76
• Writing Strategy, p. 77
• Connections, p. 77
• Slower Pace Learners, p. 77 ◆
• Multiple Intelligences, p. 77
• Online Culture Project, p. 78
• Fine Art Connection, p. 79
• **Télé-roman: Camille et compagnie**

Homework Suggestions
Cahier d'activités, pp. 19–20, 104–105
Online Practice (**go.hrw.com,** Keyword: BD3 CH2)
❀ 1.1, 1.2, 1.3, 2.2, 3.1, 3.2, 4.1

90-Minute Lesson Plans

Meeting the National Standards

Communication
Communication, pp. 47, 49, 51, 53, 59, 61, 63, 65

À ton tour, p. 79

Cultures
Flash culture, pp. 47, 52, 58, 62

Comparaisons, p. 55

Practices and Perspectives, pp. 55, 58, 70, 74

Connections
Social Studies Link, pp. 45, 57

Science Link, p. 69

Math Link, p. 77

Comparisons
Comparaisons, p. 55

Comparing and Contrasting, p. 51

Communities
Communauté, p. 55

Career Path, p. 55

Using the Photo
Have students look at the photo and describe the scene. Then have them read the caption and discuss the questions. Tell students that the **Ministre de l'Économie, des Finances et de l'Industrie** is one of the most prominent positions in the cabinet of France, after the Prime Minister. Two of the most important tasks of the Minister of Finance are preparing the budget and formulating taxation policies. Ask students what position in the Federal Government of the United States is analogous to the **Ministre de l'Économie, des Finances et de l'Industrie**.
3.1, 4.2

chapitre **2**

Le monde du travail

Objectifs

In this chapter, you will learn to
- ask about future plans
- make polite requests
- make a phone call
- write a formal letter

And you will use and review
- the future
- the feminine forms of nouns
- the verb **conduire**
- the future perfect
- the present participle
- the **conditionnel de politesse**

▶ *Que vois-tu sur la photo?*

Où se trouvent ces jeunes gens?

À ton avis, quel genre de travail est-ce qu'ils font?

Et toi, qu'est-ce que tu voudrais faire plus tard comme travail?

Suggested pacing:	Traditional Schedule	Block Schedule
Vocabulaire/Grammaire/Application 1	4 1/2 days	1 3/4 blocks
Culture	1 day	1 block
Vocabulaire/Grammaire/Application 2	5 1/2 days	2 1/4 blocks
Lecture	1 day	1/2 block
L'atelier de l'écrivain	1 day	1/2 block
Prépare-toi pour l'examen	1/2 day	1/2 block
Activités préparatoires	1/2 day	1/2 block
Examen	1 day	1/2 block
Révisions cumulatives	1 day	1/2 block

Visit Us Online
go.hrw.com
Online Edition
KEYWORD: BD3 CH2

Vocabulaire supplémentaire

Students might use these terms to discuss the photo.

les impôts	*taxes*
le budget	*budget*
la dette	*debt*
la politique fiscale	*fiscal policy*
l'actif financier	*financial assets*

Learning Tip

Ask students to visit the Web site of the **Ministère de l'Économie, des Finances et de l'Industrie** and make a list of cognates they find on this site. Write some of the cognates on the board and have students practice these new words in a class discussion about the economy.

Language Lab

You might want to use your language lab to have students:

- listen to all target vocabulary and phrases in the chapter
- practice pronunciation of vocabulary and phrases, using Holt SoundBooth and their work for evaluation
- complete the listening activities in this chapter

De jeunes professionnels devant le ministère de l'Économie, des Finances et de l'Industrie, à Paris

---

LISTENING PRACTICE

Vocabulaire
Activity 2, p. 46, CD 2, Tr. 1
Activity 21, p. 58, CD 2, Tr. 4

Grammaire
Activity 7, p. 48, CD 2, Tr. 2
Activity 26, p. 60, CD 2, Tr. 5

Application
Activity 15, p. 52, CD 2, Tr. 3
Activity 37, p. 64, CD 2, Tr. 6

Language Lab and Classroom Activities

Prépare-toi pour l'examen
Activity 6, p. 72, CD 2, Tr. 8
Télé-culture: Interviews, Chapter 2

Activités préparatoires
Section I, Listening, p. 76, CD 2, Tr. 9
Télé-roman: *Camille et compagnie*, Episode 2

Révisions cumulatives
Activity 1, p. 78, CD 2, Tr. 10

Lecture
p. 66, CD 2, Tr. 7

Resources

Planning:

Lesson Planner

One-Stop Planner

Presentation:

Teaching Transparencies **Vocabulaire 2.1, 2.2**

Practice:

Cahier de vocabulaire et grammaire

Differentiated Practice and Assessment CD-ROM

Media Guide

Teaching Transparencies Bell Work 2.1

Interactive Tutor, Disc 1

Bell Work

Use Bell Work 2.1 in the *Teaching Transparencies* or write this activity on the board.

Complète les phrases avec le **passé composé** des verbes entre parenthèses.

1. **Nous ____ (se retrouver) au restaurant.**
2. **Anne et Jean ____ (se laver) les mains.**
3. **Mathilde ____ (se maquiller) devant la miroir.**
4. **Andréa et toi, vous ____ (se mettre) à table.**
5. **Nous ____ (se relaxer) et nous avons dîné.** 1.2

Proverbes

For French proverbs and activities related to the chapter theme and vocabulary, see **Proverbes et expressions,** pp. R6–R7.

Objectifs
- to ask about future plans
- to make polite requests

Vocabulaire à l'œuvre 1

Métiers et professions

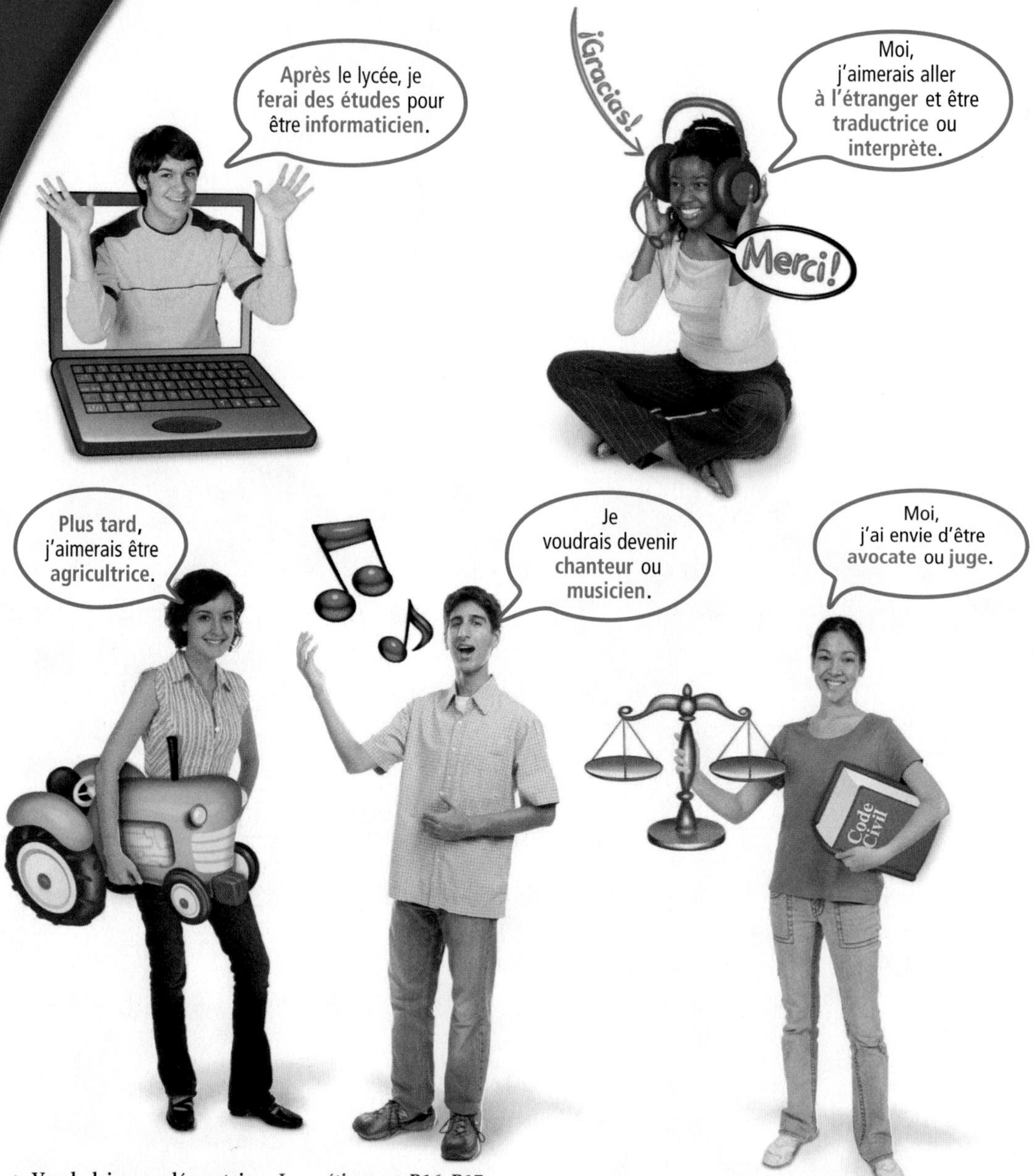
¡Gracias!
Après le lycée, je ferai des études pour être informaticien.
Moi, j'aimerais aller à l'étranger et être traductrice ou interprète.
Merci!
Plus tard, j'aimerais être agricultrice.
Je voudrais devenir chanteur ou musicien.
Moi, j'ai envie d'être avocate ou juge.
Code Civil

▶ Vocabulaire supplémentaire—Les métiers, pp. R16–R17

Core Instruction

TEACHING VOCABULAIRE

1. Introduce the vocabulary, using transparencies **Vocabulaire 2.1** and **2.2.** Model the pronunciation of all words and expressions, including **D'autres mots utiles**. Point out that **moniteur/monitrice** is mainly an instructor of sports or outdoor activities. **(3 min.)**
2. Ask students what their plans are for the future and what they need to have done.

   Qu'est-ce que tu voudrais faire plus tard? Qu'est-ce que tu dois faire faire? (3 min.)
3. Model the sentences in **Exprimons-nous!** Then have students ask each other about their future plans. **Qu'est-ce que tu comptes faire comme métier? Aucune idée! (3 min.)**

On doit...

Online Practice
go.hrw.com
Vocabulaire 1 practice
KEYWORD: BD3 CH2

faire réparer sa voiture

un mécanicien/
une mécanicienne

se faire couper les cheveux

une coiffeuse/un coiffeur

faire soigner son chat

un(e) vétérinaire

faire faire un gâteau

un pâtissier/
une pâtissière

D'autres mots utiles

un(e) couturier/couturière	*tailor*	un plombier	*plumber*
un(e) cuisinier/cuisinière	*cook*	un(e) teinturier/teinturière	*dry cleaner*
un diplôme	*degree*	un(e) tuteur/tutrice	*tutor*
un(e) libraire	*book seller*	faire livrer/garder...	*to have . . .*
un médecin	*doctor*		*delivered/watched*
un(e) moniteur/monitrice	*instructor*		

Exprimons-nous!

To ask about future plans	To respond
Qu'est-ce que tu as l'intention de faire après le bac? *What do you intend to . . . ?*	**Ça me plairait d'**être dentiste. *I'd like to . . .*
Qu'est-ce que tu comptes/vous comptez faire comme métier? *What are you planning to do . . . as a . . . ?*	Quand j'aurai mon diplôme, je voudrais **travailler dans** l'informatique. *. . . to work in . . .*
Quels sont tes projets d'avenir? *What are your plans for the future?*	J'aimerais faire le **même** métier **que** mon père. *. . . same . . . as . . .*
	Aucune idée. *No idea.*

Interactive TUTOR

Vocabulaire et grammaire, pp. 13–15

Online workbooks

Resources

Planning:
Lesson Planner
 One-Stop Planner

Presentation:
 Teaching Transparencies
Vocabulaire 2.1, 2.2

Practice:
Cahier de vocabulaire et grammaire
Differentiated Practice and Assessment CD-ROM
Media Guide
🎧 Audio CD 2, Tr. 1
 Interactive Tutor, Disc 1

Teacher Note
Lawyers in France wear long black robes and white collars whenever they appear in court.

② Script
— Dis, Maxence, qu'est-ce que tu as l'intention de faire après le lycée?
— J'aimerais travailler tout de suite. Je crois que je vais devenir mécanicien. Et toi, Laure?
— Moi, j'adore les ordinateurs. J'aimerais être informaticienne. Mais ma mère aimerait que je devienne pharmacienne, comme mon père. Et toi, Mélanie, qu'est-ce que tu vas faire plus tard?
— Moi, mes parents voudraient que je devienne cuisinière pour travailler dans leur restaurant. Mais moi, j'aime voyager et je voudrais apprendre l'espagnol et l'allemand. Je préférerais devenir interprète.

③ Possible Answers
1. Mégane voudrait devenir vétérinaire.
2. Louise aimerait bien être avocate.
3. Bastien a envie d'être professeur.
4. Lynn aimerait être musicienne.
5. Thomas et Sylvain voudraient devenir agriculteurs.
6. Mathilde voudrait être libraire.

D'autres mots utiles

architecte	architect
artiste	artist
chauffeur	driver
comptable	accountant
décorateur (-trice)	interior designer
écrivain	writer
fermier(-ière)	farmer
ingénieur	engineer
journaliste	reporter
serveur(-euse)	waiter
vendeur(-euse)	salesperson

À l'algérienne

Some Arabic words have become part of everyday French language. For example, from North Africa, the word **toubib** meaning **docteur** is used in familiar French.

Je vais chez le toubib.

① Projets d'avenir 🎦1.2
Lisons Remets la conversation de Paul et Maya dans le bon ordre.

2 —J'aimerais être vétérinaire.

6 —Tu devrais parler à la conseillère d'éducation!

4 —Oui, je sais, mais j'aime les animaux. Et toi, tu as des projets?

1 —Dis Paul, qu'est-ce que tu comptes faire après le lycée?

5 —Moi, j'aimerais continuer mes études, mais je ne sais pas quoi faire.

3 —Oh! Ce sont des études difficiles!

② Écoutons CD 2, Tr. 1 🎦1.2
🎧 Ces jeunes parlent de ce qu'ils voudraient faire plus tard. Écoute-les et dis si les phrases suivantes sont **a) vraies** ou **b) fausses.**

a 1. Maxence aimerait être mécanicien.

b 2. Plus tard, Laure voudrait être pharmacienne.

b 3. Laure voudrait avoir la même profession que son père.

a 4. Mélanie voudrait être interprète.

b 5. Mélanie va être cuisinière dans le restaurant de ses parents.

③ À chacun son métier 🎦1.2
Écrivons/Parlons D'après les photos, dis ce que ces jeunes aimeraient faire plus tard.

MODÈLE Serge voudrait être informaticien.

Serge

1. Mégane

2. Louise

3. Bastien

4. Lynn

5. Thomas et Sylvain

6. Mathilde

Core Instruction

TEACHING EXPRIMONS-NOUS!

1. Model the pronunciation of the expressions in **Exprimons-nous! (2 min.)**

2. Make up additional examples of polite requests and ask students to reply appropriately. **(4 min.)**

3. Have partners make up similarly constructed questions and practice making polite requests. **(4 min.)**

Exprimons-nous!

To make polite requests	Interactive TUTOR

Te/Vous serait-il possible de tondre la pelouse?
Would it be possible for you to . . . ?

Ça ne t'/vous ennuierait pas de nettoyer ces chemises?
Would you mind . . . ?

Si possible, pourrais-tu/pourriez-vous faire réparer l'ordinateur?
If possible, could you . . . ?

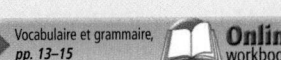
Vocabulaire et grammaire, pp. 13–15 — Online workbooks

④ Une fête d'anniversaire ✿1.2

Parlons/Écrivons Madame Martin prépare l'anniversaire de son fils. Complète ses phrases et dis à qui elle parle. Utilise des expressions différentes.

1. _____ faire un gâteau d'anniversaire pour samedi?

2. Bonjour madame Clément, _____ couper les cheveux de Romain cet après-midi?

3. J'organise une petite fête pour l'anniversaire de Romain et _____ vous veniez chanter «Bon anniversaire», mais chut *(shhh!)*! C'est une surprise!

4. _____ nettoyer tous ces vêtements pour vendredi?

⑤ Que de choses à faire! ✿1.2

Écrivons Tes parents louent leur maison à une famille française. Tu leur demandes poliment de faire (ou de faire faire) ces choses.

faire le ménage	arroser les plantes
tondre la pelouse	promener le chien
donner à manger aux animaux	prendre le courrier

MODÈLE Pourriez-vous faire le ménage régulièrement?

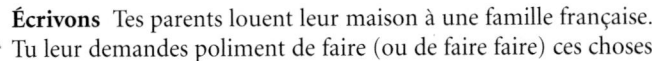 Communication

 HOLT SoundBooth ONLINE RECORDING

⑥ Scénario ✿1.1

Parlons Tu ne sais pas quoi faire après le lycée. Tu vas voir un conseiller/une conseillère d'éducation. Il/Elle te demande ce que tu aimes et te donne des idées. Joue cette scène avec un(e) camarade.

MODÈLE —Tu aimes savoir ce qui se passe dans le monde? Tu pourrais faire des études pour devenir journaliste.

Flash culture

En France, la population active est répartie en 3 secteurs: l'agriculture (le primaire), l'industrie (le secondaire) et les services (le tertiaire). En 2003, 71,55% de la population active travaillait dans le tertiaire, 24,2% dans l'industrie et seulement 4,3% dans l'agriculture, alors que la France est le deuxième pays exportateur de produits agricoles au monde après les États-Unis. ✿4.2

La population active est-elle répartie de la même manière aux États-Unis?

Communication

⑥ Individual Activity: Presentational

Have students research a particular career that interests them. Students should find out what kind of classes they would need to take, which university they would choose to attend, how much they would expect to earn in that career, and if that career and the salary would satisfy their future plans. Have students present their findings to the class. ✿1.3

Differentiated Instruction

SLOWER PACE LEARNERS

② Additional Practice Some students may have trouble completing this activity. You may want to pause the recording after each statement and have a volunteer repeat or paraphrase it, with intonation, facial expressions, and gestures to emphasize the message. ✿1.1, 1.2

MULTIPLE INTELLIGENCES

Interpersonal Ask partners to pretend to call each other to ask for these favors with the **Exprimons-nous!** vocabulary. They might need a ride to school tomorrow, need help understanding a homework assignment, or would like to help with preparations for a dance or party. They should also come up with several more favors to ask of each other. Partners may present one mini conversation to the class. ✿1.1

Assess

Assessment Program

Quiz: Vocabulaire 1

Alternative Assessment

Differentiated Practice and Assessment CD-ROM

Online Assessment
my.hrw.com

Test Generator

Resources

Planning:

Lesson Planner

 One-Stop Planner

Practice:

Grammar Tutor for Students of French, Chapter 2

Cahier de vocabulaire et grammaire

Differentiated Practice and Assessment CD-ROM

Cahier d'activités

Media Guide

 Teaching Transparencies Bell Work 2.2

 Audio CD 2, Tr. 2

 Interactive Tutor, Disc 1

Bell Work

Use Bell Work 2.2 in the *Teaching Transparencies* or write this activity on the board.

Quel est son métier? Complète chaque phrase logiquement.

1. Il vend des médicaments. Il est...
2. Il répare des voitures. Il est...
3. Il coupe les cheveux. Il est...
4. Il nettoie les vêtements. Il est...
5. Il vend des livres. Il est...
6. Il fait des gâteaux. Il est...
7. Il répare les robinets. Il est...
8. Il soigne mon chat. Il est...

a. pâtissier
b. libraire
c. mécanicien
d. coiffeur
e. vétérinaire
f. pharmacien
g. teinturier
h. plombier 1.2

Objectifs
• review of the future
• feminine forms of nouns

Grammaire à l'œuvre 1

Révisions The future

1 To conjugate **-er** and **-ir** verbs in the future, just add the endings listed below to the end of the infinitive. To conjugate **-re** verbs in the future, drop the **-e** from the infinitive before adding the endings. Notice that all the future stems end in **-r.**

	aimer	choisir	attendre
je/j'	aimer**ai**	choisir**ai**	attendr**ai**
tu	aimer**as**	choisir**as**	attendr**as**
il/elle/on	aimer**a**	choisir**a**	attendr**a**
nous	aimer**ons**	choisir**ons**	attendr**ons**
vous	aimer**ez**	choisir**ez**	attendr**ez**
ils/elles	aimer**ont**	choisir**ont**	attendr**ont**

Je travailler**ai** dans le restaurant de mes parents.

Jacques apprendr**a** l'allemand cet été.

2 Many verbs that have a spelling change in the present have the same spelling change in their future stems.

Infinitive		Present tense		Future tense
acheter	→	j'ach**è**te	→	j'ach**è**terai
appeler	→	j'appe**ll**e	→	j'appe**ll**erai

3 Some verbs have **irregular future stems** to which you add the future endings. Here are the stems of the most common ones.

aller → **ir-**	être → **ser-**	venir → **viendr-**
avoir → **aur-**	faire → **fer-**	voir → **verr-**
devoir → **devr-**	pouvoir → **pourr-**	vouloir → **voudr-**
savoir → **saur-**	envoyer → **enverr-**	recevoir → **recevr-**

Vocabulaire et grammaire, *pp. 16–17*
Cahier d'activités, *pp. 11–13*  **Online** workbooks

7 **Écoutons** CD 2, Tr. 2 ✿1.2 **1.** a **2.** b **3.** b **4.** b **5.** b **6.** a **7.** a **8.** b

Ces personnes répondent à des questions sur leur vie professionnelle. Écoute et dis si elles parlent **a) du passé** ou **b) de l'avenir.**

Déjà vu!

In English we use the helping verb *will* with a main verb to indicate a **future** action.

I will finish my homework this evening.

Remember that in French, unlike in English, a verb in the **future** tense does not need a helping verb.

Je finirai mes devoirs ce soir.

Core Instruction

TEACHING GRAMMAIRE

1. Review the future by asking volunteers to write the future forms of **acheter, choisir,** and **attendre** on the board. Point out that the endings are the same as those of the present of **avoir. (4 min.)**

2. Remind students that spelling changes occur in some conjugations when the forms end in a mute *e.*

You might want to point out that **j'achète** and **j'achèterai** would be hard to pronounce without adding an accent. **(2 min.)**

3. Go over Point 3. **(2 min.)**

4. Have students practice the forms by asking questions about their plans. **Où iras-tu pendant les vacances? (2 min.)**

Online Practice
go.hrw.com
Grammaire 1 practice
KEYWORD: BD3 CH2

⑧ **Future carrière** 🌼1.2

Parlons/Écrivons Cathy a des projets très intéressants. Complète sa conversation avec Julien en mettant les verbes entre parenthèses au futur.

JULIEN Qu'est-ce que tu ___1___ (faire) après le lycée?

CATHY Moi, j'___2___ (apprendre) l'espagnol.

JULIEN Tu ___3___ (être) professeur?

CATHY Non, je ___4___ (travailler) comme interprète.

JULIEN Tu ___5___ (devoir) suivre des cours d'espagnol, alors...

CATHY Oui, et ensuite j'___6___ (aller) travailler à Barcelone.

JULIEN J'espère que tu m'___7___ (envoyer) des cartes postales.

CATHY Oui, et toi, tu ___8___ (venir) me rendre visite!

⑨ **Leur métier favori** 🌼1.2

Parlons/Écrivons En te basant sur les photos, dis ce que ces personnes aiment et ce qu'elles feront après le lycée.

MODÈLE Alexandra aime les animaux. Elle sera vétérinaire.

Alexandra

1. Éva

2. Fabien et Louise

3. Jean-Marc

4. Ali et Lise

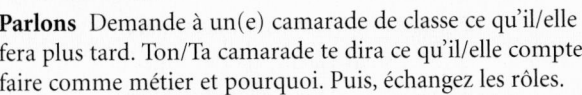

Communication

HOLT **SoundBooth**
ONLINE RECORDING

⑩ **Interview** 🌼1.1

Parlons Demande à un(e) camarade de classe ce qu'il/elle fera plus tard. Ton/Ta camarade te dira ce qu'il/elle compte faire comme métier et pourquoi. Puis, échangez les rôles.

MODÈLE —Dis, Martin, qu'est-ce que tu feras plus tard?
—Moi, j'adore les voitures et je deviendrai mécanicien comme mon père. Je travaillerai avec lui au début et puis j'aurai mon garage.

⑦ **Script**

1. Plus jeune, je travaillais dans le restaurant de mes parents.
2. Je serai cuisinier plus tard.
3. Est-ce que vous choisirez la profession de vos parents?
4. Moi, je voudrais être avocate.
5. Je travaillerai dans l'informatique.
6. Je faisais mes études à Paris cette année-là.
7. J'avais un bon métier.
8. Moi, je serai vétérinaire.

1. feras
2. apprendrai
3. seras
4. travaillerai
5. devras
6. irai
7. enverras
8. viendras

⑨ **Possible Answers**

1. Éva aime voyager. Elle fera des études pour devenir pilote.
2. Fabien et Louise aiment les enfants. Ils deviendront tuteurs.
3. Jean-Marc aime vivre à la campagne. Il sera agriculteur.
4. Ali et Lise sont toujours devant leur ordinateur. Ils seront informaticiens.

Communication

Class Activity: Interpersonal

In groups of three, Student A says what he or she will do this summer, along with a gesture. Student B gestures and restates what Student A said (**Tu...**) and then tells his or her own plans, also with a gesture (**Je...**). Student C retells what Student A will do (**Il/Elle...**), what Student B will do (**Tu...**), and his or her plans (**Je...**), accompanied by the respective gesture. All group members should have a chance to be A, B, and C.

MODÈLE
— **Moi, j'étudierai en France.**
— **Tu étudieras en France, et moi, j'irai à la plage.**
— **Il étudiera en France. Tu iras à la plage, et moi, je regarderai la télé.** 🌼1.2

Differentiated Instruction

👐

ADVANCED LEARNERS

Challenge After presenting the grammar review, have partners make statements about their likes or favorite leisure-time activities. (**J'aime les animaux.**) Students should then make predictions as to what profession the partner will have in the future. (**Tu seras vétérinaire.**) They should take turns making and responding to the statements.
🌼 1.1, 1.2

MULTIPLE INTELLIGENCES

Intrapersonal Ask students to create a journal entry describing their future plans. The entry should include where they will live and work, what trips or vacations they will take, and what hobbies or sports they will pursue in the future. Ask for volunteers to share their journal entries with the class.
🌼 1.3

Resources

Planning:

Lesson Planner

 One-Stop Planner

Practice:

Grammar Tutor for Students of French, Chapter 2

Cahier de vocabulaire et grammaire

Differentiated Practice and Assessment CD-ROM

Cahier d'activités

Media Guide

 Teaching Transparencies
Bell Work 2.3

 Interactive Tutor, Disc 1

Bell Work

Use Bell Work 2.3 in the *Teaching Transparencies* or write this activity on the board.

Mets les verbes entre paren-thèses au **futur**.

1. Après le lycée, je _____ (être) interprète.
2. L'année prochaine, nous _____ (aller) en Allemagne.
3. Mes parents _____ (travailler) dans une banque.
4. Nous _____ (acheter) une nouvelle voiture.
5. On _____ (devoir) habiter à Berlin.
6. J'espère que tu m' _____ (envoyer) souvent des lettres. 🌸1.2

COMMON ERROR ALERT
⫻⫻ATTENTION !⫻⫻

Students may have difficulty with words ending in **-eur** that refer to professions. Such words do not all have the same ending for their feminine form. Some change the **-eur** to **-euse** (**serveur/serveuse**), some change to **-rice** (**traducteur/ traductrice**), and some simply stay the same (**professeur**).

 Interactive **TUTOR**

Feminine forms of nouns

1 To form most feminine nouns add an -e to the masculine noun.

un avocat / une avocate   un marchand / une marchande

2 Masculine nouns with the following endings follow a different pattern to form the feminine form.

MASCULINE	FEMININE
un musicien	une musicienne
un serveur	une serveuse
un acteur	une actrice
un boulanger	une boulangère
un fermier	une fermière

3 Others have only one form that can be masculine or feminine.

un journaliste / une journaliste   un dentiste / une dentiste

un architecte / une architecte   un artiste / une artiste

4 Some nouns of professions which were historically held by men remain masculine whether they refer to a man or a woman.

un auteur   un juge   un écrivain

un ingénieur   un pilote   un médecin

5 However, there are some exceptions to the rules, for example:

un chanteur / une chanteuse   un docteur / une doctoresse

un prince / une princesse   un maître / une maîtresse

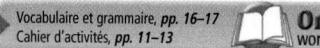
Vocabulaire et grammaire, *pp. 16–17*
Cahier d'activités, *pp. 11–13*
Online workbooks

11 **Des métiers en tout genre** 🌸1.2

Parlons/Écrivons Ces gens ont le même métier que leur époux/ épouse (*spouse*). Dis ce qu'ils font comme métier.

MODÈLE Monsieur Julot est couturier.
Madame Julot est couturière.

1. Monsieur Ripeau est ingénieur.
2. Madame Vermon est cuisinière.
3. Monsieur Galant est décorateur.
4. Monsieur Durant est chanteur.
5. Madame Arman est pharmacienne.
6. Monsieur Julot est médecin.
7. Monsieur Dupont est journaliste.
8. Monsieur Allard voudrait devenir acteur.

À la québécoise

In some parts of the francophone world, like Quebec, people use the feminine form of some words listed as tradition-aly only having a mascu-line form:

une auteure
une écrivaine

Core Instruction

TEACHING GRAMMAIRE

1. Go over Points 1–4. Have pairs of students come up with other names of professions and their feminine forms. (**le mécanicien, la mécanicienne, le coiffeur, la coiffeuse**) **(4 min.)**

2. Go over Point 5. Tell students that this is changing, and that such words as **la juge** and **la ministre** are now commonly used. Point out that while **professeur** has only one form, its familiar version can either be **le prof** or **la prof. (2 min.)**

Grammaire 1 *(side tab)*

12 Ce qu'elles vont faire 🏵1.2

Lisons/Écrivons Floriane et ses amies discutent de ce qu'elles aimeraient faire plus tard. Complète leur conversation.

FLORIANE Moi, je crois que je vais devenir ___1___. Comme ça, je pourrai dessiner ma maison! architecte

THUY Moi, je serai ___2___ parce que j'adore la mode et je ferai de très belles robes. couturière

MAEVA Moi, j'aimerais être ___3___. J'irai en Afrique soigner les malades dans les petits villages! médecin

CAROLE Moi, je veux soigner les animaux. Je serai ___4___. vétérinaire

CHLOÉ Moi, mon rêve, c'est de devenir ___5___ et d'avoir mon avion. pilote

SYLVIANE Et moi, je me marierai *(to marry)* avec un prince et je serai ___6___! princesse

13 Les femmes au travail 🏵1.2

Parlons/Écrivons Dis ce que ces femmes font comme métier.

1. Karima   2. Lise   3. Léa   4. Corinne   5. Marie-Pierre   6. Fabienne

Communication

HOLT **SoundBooth** ONLINE RECORDING

14 Questions personnelles 🏵1.1

Parlons Demande à tes camarades s'ils connaissent des gens qui ont les métiers suivants. Est-ce que ces gens aiment ce qu'ils font? Pourquoi ou pourquoi pas?

ingénieur	musicien	médecin	fermier	plombier
artiste	interprète	avocat	??	chanteur

Communication

Group Activity: Interpersonal

In small groups, have students interview one another and ask about each other's interests, what they do well, and which classes they like. Then have them suggest a career based on that information. **(Tu devrais être...)** Students can share with the class what they learned about their group members and tell what they will become. **(Il/Elle deviendra...)** and why. 🏵1.1, 1.3

Differentiated Instruction

ADVANCED LEARNERS

Extension After presenting the grammar, have students create a graphic organizer that lists the different forms of feminine nouns. Then ask students to find feminine nouns on the Internet or in the dictionary and write these in the appropriate columns of their organizer. Encourage students to use dictionaries on CD because they can search them by word ending. 🏵1.2

MULTIPLE INTELLIGENCES

Visual Have students create a small French children's book of occupations with their own drawings or pictures from the Internet. Have students use the appropriate feminine or masculine noun as a caption for the picture. Each booklet should include at least ten different occupations. You may wish to keep the booklets in class as a resource or study aid. 🏵1.3

Assess

Assessment Program

Quiz: Grammaire 1
Alternative Assessment
Differentiated Practice and Assessment CD-ROM

Online Assessment
my.hrw.com

Test Generator

Synthèse
- Vocabulaire 1
- Grammaire 1

Application 1

15 **Écoutons** CD 2, Tr. 3 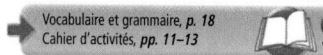1.2 **1.** b **2.** a **3.** c **4.** c **5.** a

Dis si on parle **a) d'une femme, b) d'un homme** ou si **c) on ne peut pas dire.**

16 **Rien ne va plus!** 1.3

Écrivons/Parlons Dis ce que ces gens feront dans ces situations.

1. Le chat de ta sœur est malade.
2. Tes cheveux sont longs.
3. Le chemisier en soie de ta mère est sale.
4. La voiture de tes parents ne marche pas bien.
5. Ta mère voudrait un gâteau pour l'anniversaire de ton père.
6. Tes copains ont besoin d'argent pour partir en vacances.

Un peu plus

Interactive TUTOR

The verb *conduire*

1. The verb **conduire** *(to drive)* is irregular. Its past participle is **conduit.**

conduire	
je cond**uis**	nous cond**uisons**
tu cond**uis**	vous cond**uisez**
il/elle/on cond**uit**	ils/elles cond**uisent**

2. The verbs **traduire** *(to translate)*, **construire** *(to build)*, and **produire** *(to produce)* are conjugated like **conduire**.

Vocabulaire et grammaire, *p. 18*
Cahier d'activités, *pp. 11–13*

Online workbooks

17 **Un choix à faire** 1.2

1. conduit **2.** traduisent **3.** avons construit **4.** produit **5.** conduisez

Écrivons Complète ces phrases logiquement avec la forme correcte des verbes **traduire, conduire, produire** et **construire.**

1. Tous les matins, ma mère _____ mon petit frère à l'école.
2. Tes amis sont interprètes. Ils _____ des textes allemands.
3. Hier, nous _____ une maison pour le chien dans le jardin.
4. Cette région _____ des raisins de bonne qualité.
5. Vous _____ trop vite! J'ai peur!

Bell Work

Use Bell Work 2.4 in the *Teaching Transparencies* or write this activity on the board.

Ils font le même métier!
Complète les phrases suivantes.

1. Henri est boulanger et Joëlle est...
2. Nicole est serveuse et Éric est...
3. Amélie est actrice et Gérard est...
4. Laurent est avocat et Anne est...
5. Nicolas est moniteur et Céline et Thérèse sont...
6. Clément est électricien et Alexandra est... 1.2

Flash culture

En France, les employés ont droit à 5 semaines de congés payés. La semaine de travail est de 35 heures. Et il y a 11 jours fériés par an: le jour de l'an, le lundi de Pâques, la fête du Travail, l'Ascension, la Pentecôte, la fête nationale, l'Assomption, la Tousssaint, l'Armistice de 1918 et Noël. 4.2

En général, combien de jours de congé les Américains ont-ils?

French for Spanish Speakers

Ask Spanish speakers how feminine forms of nouns for professions are formed in Spanish. (words that end in **–o** in the masculine form change to **–a**; **el abogado/la abogada**) Ask them to list Spanish professions that have only one form. **(un/una periodista)** 4.1

Core Instruction

INTEGRATED PRACTICE

1. Have students do Activities 15–16 to practice previously taught material. **(5 min.)**
2. Introduce **Un peu plus.** (See presentation suggestions at right.) **(4 min.)**
3. Continue with integrated practice activities 17–20. **(30 min.)**

TEACHING UN PEU PLUS

1. Go over the forms of **conduire** and model the pronunciation of all forms. **(4 min.)**
2. Point out that the verb **conduire** is conjugated the same way as the verbs **traduire, produire,** and **construire.** Choose one of these verbs and go over its conjugation as a class. Ask students yes-no questions using different forms of one of these verbs. **Beth, est-ce que ton frère conduit sa voiture chaque jour? (4 min.)**

Online Practice
go.hrw.com
Application 1 practice
KEYWORD: BD3 CH2

Chapitre 2
Application 1

Application 1

18 **Faites-le faire!** 🍀3.2

Lisons/Parlons Regarde cette affiche que des jeunes distribuent dans ton quartier et réponds aux questions suivantes. Fais des phrases complètes.

1. Pourquoi ça s'appelle SOS Corvées, à ton avis?
2. Qu'est-ce qu'on peut leur demander de faire?
3. Quelle corvée ajouterais-tu à la liste?
4. Est-ce que tu utiliserais SOS Corvées? Qu'est-ce que tu ferais faire?
5. Est-ce que tu aimerais travailler pour SOS Corvées?

Si vous ne voulez pas:

Appelez le 06. 88. 44. 53. 74
SOS Corvées le fera pour vous!

19 **Tes projets et expériences professionnelles** 🍀1.2

Écrivons/Parlons Tu vas bientôt finir tes études. Tu as peut-être déjà une expérience professionnelle. Quels sont tes projets d'avenir? Réponds en faisant des phrases complètes.

1. Quel métier tu voudrais faire plus tard? Pourquoi?
2. Tu aimerais aller à l'université? Si oui, dans quelle université aimerais-tu aller?
3. Est-ce que tu aimerais faire un stage dans une compagnie?
4. Est-ce que tu aimerais travailler comme moniteur/monitrice avec des enfants? Pourquoi?
5. Est-ce que tu as déjà eu des jobs d'été? Lesquels?
6. Est-ce que tu travailles pendant l'année scolaire? Si oui, qu'est-ce que tu fais?
7. Tu aimerais travailler pour une grande société ou pas?

Communication

HOLT **SoundBooth**
ONLINE RECORDING

20 **Questions personnelles** 🍀1.1

Parlons Demande à un(e) camarade s'il/si elle a fait ou a fait faire des choses récemment et par qui. Ensuite échangez les rôles.

MODÈLE —Tu t'es fait couper les cheveux?
—Oui, tu aimes?
—Tu es allée chez la même coiffeuse que d'habitude?

Communication

Pair Activity: Interpersonal

In pairs, have students ask each other about the driving ability of five family members or friends. **Comment est-ce que ta mère conduit?** The partner responds using the verb **conduire** along with an adverb. Encourage students to be detailed and creative. 🍀1.1

Differentiated Instruction

SLOWER PACE LEARNERS

20 **Variation** Before starting the conversation, students should brainstorm and write at least five questions they want to ask their partners. As students do the activity, encourage them to write down their partners' answers. Have students take turns asking and answering questions. Then have students report to the class what their partners have said. 🍀1.1, 1.3

MULTIPLE INTELLIGENCES

Interpersonal Ask students to select one of the occupations discussed in this chapter that interests them. Give the option of researching this occupation or interviewing a person who currently works in that field. The interview can be done by telephone, in person, or by exchanging letters or e-mail. Have students report, in French, about the qualifications, study, job requirements, salary range, and benefits of working in that occupation. 🍀1.3

Assess

Assessment Program
Quiz : Application 1
Audio CD 2, Tr. 11 🎧
Alternative Assessment
Differentiated Practice and Assessment CD-ROM
Online Assessment
my.hrw.com
Test Generator

Resources

Planning:
Lesson Planner
One-Stop Planner

Practice:
Cahier d'activités

Prereading Questions

You might ask these questions before students read the selection.

1. **Est-ce que tu aimes les parfums?**
2. **Est-ce que tu achètes quelquefois des parfums?**
3. **Est-ce que tu connais des parfums français?**
4. **Est-ce que tu as déjà acheté des parfums français?** 1.2

Active Reading Questions

1. **Quand est-ce que l'auteur a voulu devenir parfumeur? (très jeune)**
2. **Qu'est-ce que l'auteur a remarqué quand elle était jeune? (des nuances, des odeurs)**
3. **Maintenant, travaille-t-elle dans une grande entreprise? (Non, elle travaille à son compte.)**
4. **Qu'est-ce qu'elle fait pour les marques de prêt-à-porter? (des fragrances)** 1.2

Vocabulaire supplémentaire

You might use these terms to discuss the text.

le flacon	*bottle of perfume*
le vaporisateur	*vaporizer*
la senteur	*scent*
un arôme	*aroma, fragrance*

Answers
1. un parfumeur
2. un bac S, un Deug de chimie, l'ISIPCA
3. une personne qui compose des parfums

Culture

Lecture culturelle

Nous sommes entourés par des odeurs: l'odeur du café le matin au réveil, l'odeur de l'herbe coupée, l'odeur d'un toast brûlé ou encore l'odeur de la poubelle. Les odeurs sont plus ou moins agréables et aussi dépendent de la sensibilité de chacun. Et certaines personnes ont un nez plus développé que d'autres. Alors pourquoi ne pas s'en servir? Il existe des métiers, comme celui de parfumeur, où l'odorat[1] est un atout[2]. On surnomme les personnes qui composent des parfums des «nez». 2.1

Designer Olfactif[3]

Karine Chevalier *designer olfactif[3]*

Très jeune, j'ai eu conscience que de même qu'il existe une nuance entre entendre et écouter, il y a plusieurs façons d'être attentif aux odeurs. Depuis, je n'ai jamais perdu l'idée de devenir parfumeur. Je m'en suis donné les moyens[4] : après un bac S[5], j'ai enchaîné avec un Deug[6] de chimie. Sans ce diplôme, impossible de rentrer à l'ISIPCA[7], la seule école de parfumeurs en France. Après deux ans en alternance[8] et plusieurs expériences dans de grandes entreprises, j'ai senti le besoin de me démarquer[9] pour suivre mon propre chemin. Aujourd'hui à mon compte[10], je dessine des logos olfactifs pour des marques de prêt-à-porter[11]. En partant du logo et de ses couleurs, je signe les espaces de vente par une odeur originale. L'important, c'est de faire évoluer la fragrance afin qu'elle devienne la traduction exacte de la commande.

Phosphore, Juin 2005

REPÈRES

Formation : ISIPCA (*Institut supérieur international du parfum, de la cosmétique et de l'aromatique alimentaire*).

Évolution : débutant en tant que préparateurs dans les maisons de compositions, les « nez » les plus talentueux sont formés pour devenir parfumeurs-créateurs.

Compréhension 2.1

1. Designer olfactif, qu'est-ce que c'est?
2. Quelle formation est-ce qu'il faut suivre pour devenir parfumeur?
3. Qu'est-ce qu'un « nez »?

---

1. *sense of smell* 2. *un avantage* 3. *olfactory* 4. *possibilités* 5. Bac en sciences 6. diplôme obtenu après deux ans d'études universitaires 7. école qui forme les «nez» 8. *training which alternates study and work* 9. d'être différente 10. *being self-employed* 11. *ready-to-wear*

Core Instruction

LECTURE CULTURELLE

1. Go over the Prereading questions. Then read and discuss **Lecture culturelle** as a class. Ask students to identify specific smells that they associate with memories of happy times. (hot chocolate, books, new toys) **(8 min.)**

2. Ask students if the way things smell is as important to them as the way things look. **(2 min.)**

3. Read *Designer Olfactif* as a class. Ask volunteers to answer the questions in **Compréhension. (10 min.)**

COMPARAISONS ET COMMUNAUTÉ

1. Read and discuss the introductory question of **Comparaisons** as a class. **(2 min.)**

2. Continue reading **Curriculum vitæ** and discuss the **Et toi?** questions as a class. Ask students why they think French companies want the letter of interest that accompanies the CV to be handwritten. **(6 min.)**

3. Go over **Communauté et professions** with students. Ask volunteers to research American products with French names. **(3 min.)**

Comparaisons

Forum sur le travail

Curriculum vitæ ✿4.2

Tu décides de trouver un travail pour l'été en France, sur ton CV (résumé) tu dois inclure:

a. juste tes études et ton expérience professionnelle.

b. tes études, ton expérience professionnelle et tes activités extra-scolaires.

c. tes études, ton expérience professionnelle, ton âge et une photo d'identité.

Il n'existe pas de modèle type de CV. Il doit tenir sur une page et il doit inclure:

— Nom, adresse, téléphone, fax, e-mail, photo
— Âge, situation de famille
— Études
— Expérience professionnelle
— Langues parlées
— Connaissances en informatique
— Centres d'intérêt (facultatif)

Il est souvent accompagné d'une lettre de motivation manuscrite.

✿4.2

ET TOI?

1. Est-ce que tu travailles? Qu'est-ce que tu as fait pour trouver et obtenir ce travail?

2. As-tu déjà fait un CV pour trouver un travail? Quelles informations as-tu inclues?

Communauté et professions

Le français et la publicité ✿4.2, 5.1

La France est réputée[1] pour la haute couture, les parfums et autres produits de luxe. Certains produits se vendent mieux s'ils ont un nom français ou un slogan publicitaire qui fait référence à la France. Est-ce que tu connais un produit américain qui utilise cette technique? Est-ce qu'il existe un produit unique à ta région? Fais des recherches pour savoir quelle est son origine. D'où vient son nom? Quelles sont les techniques publicitaires[2] utilisées pour le vendre? Fais des recherches et présente ce que tu as trouvé à ta classe.

Produits de luxe

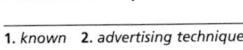

1. known 2. advertising technique

Bell Work

Use Bell Work 2.5 in the *Teaching Transparencies* or write this activity on the board.

Complète les phrases suivantes.

1. Julien _____ très bien. Je n'ai jamais peur en voiture avec lui.
2. Raphaël et Alan parlent très bien allemand. Ils _____ même des textes et des articles de journaux.
3. Ces champs _____ plus de maïs cette année que l'année dernière.
4. Tu _____ un château de sable?
5. Nous pensons faire _____ une nouvelle maison. 1.2

Proverbes

For French proverbs and activities related to the chapter theme and vocabulary, see **Proverbes et expressions,** pp. R6–R7.

Objectifs
• to make a phone call
• to write a formal letter

Vocabulaire
à l'œuvre 2

Une conversation téléphonique

> **Allô,** je voudrais parler à madame Frémion, s'il vous plaît.

un téléphone **sans fil**

Alain Favier **appelle** pour **obtenir un entretien**.

Madame **le directeur dirige la société**.

> Un instant, je vous la passe.

Le **secrétaire répond** au téléphone et **transfère l'appel**.

Dring! Dring!

le combiné

un afficheur

la sonnerie

D'autres mots utiles

un apprentissage/ un stage	apprenticeship/ internship	débutant(e)	beginner
un emploi	job	décrocher/raccrocher	to pick up/hang up
des heures supplémentaires	overtime	être au chômage	to be unemployed
un salaire	salary	être engagé(e)/licencié(e)	to be hired/laid off
un travail à temps plein/partiel	full/part time job	gagner de l'argent	to earn money

▶ Vocabulaire supplémentaire—Au téléphone, **p. R17**

Core Instruction

TEACHING VOCABULAIRE

1. Introduce the vocabulary, using transparencies **Vocabulaire 2.3** and **2.4.** Model the pronunciation of each word or expression. Use **Ça, c'est...** (**un téléphone sans fil, une secrétaire**) whenever possible. Include the words and phrases from **D'autres mots utiles** in your presentation. **(3 min.)**

2. Ask students questions about themselves.

> **Est-ce que tu vas faire un stage pendant les vacances? Est-ce que tu vas chercher un emploi? (3 min.)**

3. Model the pronunciation of the expressions in **Exprimons-nous!** Then ask partners to pretend to call each other on the phone and ask to talk to someone else. **Bonjour, est-ce que je pourrais parler à...? (4 min.)**

Une lettre de motivation

Alain Favier
17, boulevard Jourdan
75013 PARIS
Tél: 01.53.05.00.0

Paris, le 3 septembre

À l'attention de: Monsieur Tevet
Objet: demande de stage

Monsieur,

Étant actuellement étudiant en architecture, je
désirerais effectuer un stage d'une durée d'un
mois dans votre cabinet dans le but d'acquérir
une expérience nécessaire à ma formation.

Vos réalisations m'intéressent et j'aimerais
vivement travailler avec vous.

Veuillez trouver ci-joint mon curriculum vitae.

Dans l'attente d'une réponse qui, je l'espère, me
sera favorable, je vous prie d'agréer, Monsieur,
l'expression de mes salutations distinguées.

A. Favier

m Vitæ

Annecy
Jourdan

des en architecture
l'études professionnelles

NNELLES:
ndeur-caissier

ordinateur inventaire

hui: Directeur des

ATIQUES

QUES:

le couramment
allemand: niveau scolaire

CENTRES D'INTÉRÊT:
• Volley-ball
• Randonnée pédestre

Online Practice
go.hrw.com
Vocabulaire 2 practice
KEYWORD: BD3 CH2

Exprimons-nous!

To make a phone call	To respond
Bonjour, **est-ce que je pourrais parler à** Sylvain/Sylvie, s'il vous plaît? *. . . may I speak with . . . ?*	**Un instant,** je vous **le/la passe.** *Hold on, . . . I'll put him/her on.*
	Désolé(e), il/elle n'est pas là. **Vous pouvez rappeler?** *. . . Could you call back?*
	C'est de la part de qui/Qui est à l'appareil? *May I ask who is calling?*
Est-ce que je peux laisser un message? *Can I leave a message?*	**Un moment,** je prends un papier et un crayon. *One moment, . . .*
Je suis bien chez Patricia? *Is this . . .'s house?*	Non, **vous avez fait le mauvais numéro.** *. . ., you have the wrong number.*
La ligne est occupée. *The line is busy.*	
Ça ne répond pas. *There is no answer.*	

Interactive TUTOR

Vocabulaire et grammaire, pp. 19–21

Online workbooks

▶ **Vocabulaire supplémentaire**—Le monde du travail, p. R17

Vocabulaire 2

T P R
TOTAL PHYSICAL RESPONSE

Have students respond to these commands.

Lève-toi si tu as un télé-phone sans fil chez toi.

Lève le doigt si c'est toi qui réponds au téléphone.

Lève la main si tu voudrais un emploi avec un bon salaire.

Cherche un(e) camarade qui a un travail à temps partiel.

Lève les bras si tu comptes faire un apprentissage.

Then have some students mime the following situations.

Tu es secrétaire. Transfère un appel.

Tu décroches le téléphone, mais il n'y a personne.

Rappelle, maintenant.

La ligne est occupée.

Tu viens d'être licencié(e).

❀ 1.2

Connections
Social Studies Link

Over the last twenty years, youth unemployment has become a major issue for the French labor market. In recent years, the French government has brought overall unemployment down from 10.2 percent to 9.6 percent, but joblessness among the nation's youth stays at 22 percent. Youth joblessness soars to over 50 percent in the suburbs, that are home to many of France's more than five million first- and second-generation African and Arab immi-grants. Comprehensive programs and reforms aimed at reducing youth unemployment have yet to be introduced. Most students do not find a job when they finish school. Ask students to suggest programs and initiatives that could help French students find jobs. ❀ 3.1

Differentiated Instruction

SLOWER PACE LEARNERS

Additional Practice After you finish present-ing **Exprimons-nous!**, have partners make and respond to a phone call. Call on the partners to perform their conversation for the class. Encourage them to use props, as well, as facial expressions and gestures to emphasize their messages. ❀ 1.1, 1.2

MULTIPLE INTELLIGENCES

Bodily–Kinesthetic Set up two desks with toy telephones in front of the class. Ask students to take turns sitting at the desks and making and answering telephone calls. Give students situations, such as calling different businesses to ask about job opportunities, the application process, and salaries for positions or calling a specific person at a place of business that may be unavailable at the moment. ❀ 1.1

Resources

Planning:

Lesson Planner

 One-Stop Planner

Presentation:

 Teaching Transparencies
Vocabulaire 2.3, 2.4

Practice:

Cahier de vocabulaire et
grammaire

Differentiated Practice and
Assessment CD-ROM

Media Guide

 Audio CD 2, Tr. 4

Interactive Tutor, Disc 1

 **Script**

See script on p. 41E.

Cultures

 **Practices and
Perspectives**

In 2006, French students, workers, and would-be workers demonstrated for months against a controversial bill, entitled the **Contrat première embauche (CPE)**. The bill meant to increase employment opportunities for young people by allowing employers to fire workers under age 26 without reason, notice, or severance. The hope was that by making it easier to dismiss workers, employers would hire more workers and youth unemployment would fall. The demonstrations forced the government to withdraw the bill. Ask students to research if a bill similar to the **CPE** exists in their state.

2.1, 3.1, 4.2

21 **Écoutons** CD 2, Tr. 4 1.2 **1.** d **2.** b **3.** c **4.** a

Dis à quelle illustration chaque phrase correspond.

a.

b.

> Alain Favier
> 17, boulevard Jourdan
> 75013 PARIS
> Tél: 01.53.05.00.0
>
> À l'attention de: Monsieur
> Objet: demande de stage
>
> Monsieur,
> Étant actuellement étudiant
> désirerais effectuer un stage
> mois dans votre cabinet da

c.

d.

22 **La bonne définition** 1.2

Lisons Trouve les mots ou expressions de la première colonne qui correspondent aux mots ou expressions de la deuxième colonne.

b **1.** une description des études et de la vie professionnelle   **a.** une formation

d **2.** expression qui termine une lettre officielle   **b.** un curriculum vitae

a **3.** un autre mot pour «études»   **c.** faire un stage

e **4.** situation de quelqu'un qui n'a pas de travail   **d.** mes sentiments distingués

c **5.** travailler dans une compagnie pendant ses études   **e.** être au chômage

   f. un salaire

Flash culture

L'Agence nationale pour l'emploi (ou ANPE) est un organisme créé en 1967 pour centraliser les offres et les demandes d'emploi. Depuis 1997, le site Web de l'ANPE s'est développé et propose aujourd'hui la consultation en ligne de centaines de milliers d'offres d'emploi.

Est-ce qu'il y a une agence semblable dans ton état? 4.2

23 **Au téléphone** 1.2

Écrivons Zachary téléphone pour la première fois à son correspondant français. Complète sa conversation téléphonique.

—Bonjour. ___**1**___ Tanguy Gatineau?

—Non. ___**2**___.

—Excusez-moi.

—DRING! ___**3**___

—Bonjour, madame. ___**4**___ M. et Mme Gatineau?

—Oui.

—___**5**___ Tanguy, s'il vous plaît?

—___**6**___?

—C'est Zachary à l'appareil, son correspondant américain.

—___**7**___, je vous le passe.

Core Instruction

TEACHING EXPRIMONS-NOUS!

1. Model the pronunciation of each expression. Tell students that most of these expressions are used only in writing. Point out the lengthy closing sentence (**Je vous prie d'agréer...**) that is required when writing a formal letter in French. **(2 min.)**

2. Have partners write an outline of a formal letter with these expressions. **(6 min.)**

3. On the board, use one pair's outline as a model to write a formal letter. **(7 min.)**

Exprimons-nous!

To write a formal letter

Suite à notre conversation téléphonique, ...
Following our phone conversation, . . .

En réponse à votre petite annonce du...
In response to your ad of . . .

Dans le cadre de ma formation, je voudrais faire un stage
dans votre société.   *As part of my education, . . .*

Veuillez trouver ci-joint mon curriculum vitæ.
Please, find my resumé attached.

**Je vous prie d'agréer, Monsieur/Madame, l'expression de mes
sentiments distingués.**   *Sincerely.*

Vocabulaire et grammaire, pp. 19–21 | Online workbooks

24 Une lettre officielle 🌸1.2

✏ **Écrivons** Alexandra voudrait faire un stage au *Monde*, un grand journal français. Elle a écrit une lettre mais elle n'a pas utilisé de formules de politesse. Réécris sa lettre de façon polie. Inspire-toi du modèle de la page 57.

> *Bonjour,*
> *Je vous ai parlé au téléphone le 3 septembre. Je vous envoie cette lettre parce que je veux faire un stage chez vous. Je suis étudiante en journalisme et je veux travailler dans votre journal. Voici une description de mes études et de mes expériences professionnelles.*
> *Au revoir.*
> *Alexandra*

Communication

25 Scénario 🌸1.1

Parlons Tu voudrais faire un stage dans une banque en France. Tu appelles la banque et tu demandes à parler à la personne qui s'occupe d'engager le personnel, monsieur Préjean. Joue cette scène avec un(e) camarade.

MODÈLE —Bonjour, madame. Est-ce que je pourrais parler à monsieur Préjean?
—Oui, c'est de la part de qui?

Vocabulaire 2

23 Answers
1. Est-ce que je pourrais parler à
2. Vous avez fait le mauvais numéro.
3. Allô?
4. Je suis bien chez
5. Est-ce que je pourrais parler à
6. C'est de la part de qui?
7. Un instant

Comparisons

Comparing and Contrasting
The **futur antérieur** is frequently used in subordinate clauses with conjunctions, such as **quand, lorsque, dès que,** and **aussitôt que.** For example, **Elle enverra la lettre dès qu'elle l'aura écrite.** Ask students to give the English equivalent of this sentence and provide more examples. 🌸4.1

Communication

Group Activity: Presentational
In small groups, have students prepare a comedy sketch for the class. Have them act out a phone conversation that is comical and full of misunderstanding on a topic of their choosing. For example, someone who is unemployed calls a company to set up an interview with the CEO but encounters a secretary who is not very helpful. Encourage students to be creative. 🌸1.3

Differentiated Instruction

ADVANCED LEARNERS

25 Extension Have students complete this activity. Then tell students that Mr. Préjean has offered them the internship at the bank and that they need to call him back to find out the details (salary, part/full time, overtime, etc.) of the internship. Call on some students to present their phone conversation to the class. 🌸1.1, 1.3

SPECIAL LEARNING NEEDS

Students with Language Impairments An enlarged formal letter in French, created by students on a bulletin board, can be a valuable reference. The parts of the letter should be labeled, and the letter itself should be an exemplary letter with the expressions in **Vocabulaire**. The letter and display should include the date in French, the greeting, the body of text, the closing, and the signature. Use the display as a reference and study guide in class. 🌸1.3

Assess

Assessment Program
Quiz: Vocabulaire 2
Alternative Assessment
Differentiated Practice and
    Assessment CD-ROM

Online Assessment
    my.hrw.com

Test Generator

Resources

Planning:

Lesson Planner

 One-Stop Planner

Practice:

Grammar Tutor for Students of French, Chapter 2

Cahier de vocabulaire et grammaire

Differentiated Practice and Assessment CD-ROM

Cahier d'activités

Media Guide

 Teaching Transparencies Bell Work 2.6

 Audio CD 2, Tr. 5

 Interactive Tutor, Disc 1

Bell Work

Use Bell Work 2.6 in the *Teaching Transparencies* or write this activity on the board.

Écris cette lettre en mettant les phrases dans le bon ordre.

1. **Je vous prie d'agréer, Monsieur,**
2. **...je voudrais faire un stage dans votre société.**
3. **Cher Monsieur,**
4. **Veuillez trouver ci-joint,**
5. **...l'expression de mes sentiments distingués.**
6. **Dans le cadre de ma formation,**
7. **... mon curriculum vitæ.**

✿1.2

26 Script

1. Je téléphonerai à Michel quand j'aurai écrit ma lettre de motivation.
2. Quand ils auront déjeuné, ils iront au cinéma.
3. Elle ira voir Alice quand elle aura parlé à Stéphanie.
4. Nous viendrons vous rendre visite dès que nous serons arrivés.
5. Vous comprendrez la leçon quand vous aurez fini les exercices.

Objectifs
- the future perfect
- the present participle

Grammaire à l'œuvre 2

 Interactive **TUTOR**

The future perfect

> 1 To indicate that one future action precedes another future action, use the future perfect (**futur antérieur**) for the action that will happen first.
>
> 2 To form the future perfect, use **avoir** or **être** in the future and add the **past participle of the main verb.**
>
> Quand j'**aurai** fini mes études, je travaillerai avec ma mère.
> *When I have finished my studies, I will work with my mother.*
>
> Julie te téléphonera quand maman **sera** rentrée.
> *Julie will call you when mom has arrived.*

Vocabulaire et grammaire, pp. 22–23
Cahier d'activités, pp. 15–17

 **Online** workbooks

En anglais ✿4.1

In English, to indicate that one action in the future will happen before another action in the future, you use the future perfect (a form of the verb *have* plus the past participle of the main verb) for the action that will happen first.

> *I will call you as soon as I have had lunch.*
>
> (**having lunch** must happen before **calling**)

How is this shortened in conversational English?

In French also, you use a special tense to indicate that one future action precedes another future action: **le futur antérieur.**

> Je te téléphonerai dès que **j'aurai déjeuné.**

I'll call you as soon as I have lunch.

26 Écoutons CD 2, Tr. 5 ✿1.2

Écoute ces phrases et dis quel événement doit arriver d'abord pour que l'autre puisse se passer.

1. écrire la lettre de motivation / téléphoner à Michel
2. aller au cinéma / déjeuner
3. parler à Stéphanie / aller voir Alice
4. venir vous rendre visite / arriver
5. comprendre la leçon / finir les exercices

27 Et ensuite? ✿1.2

Écrivons Ces choses se passeront quand quelque chose d'autre sera arrivé. Complète les phrases avec les formes correctes des verbes entre parenthèses.

1. Marie _____ (se maquiller) quand elle _____ (prendre) sa douche.
2. Quand l'infirmière _____ (se laver) les mains, elle _____ (aller) aider le docteur.
3. Je _____ (être) contente quand il m'_____ (téléphoner).
4. Nous _____ (venir) quand nous _____ (finir) nos devoirs.
5. Ils _____ (trouver) plus facilement du travail quand ils ____ (faire) leur stage.

Core Instruction

TEACHING GRAMMAIRE

1. Read **En anglais** aloud with students. **(2 min.)**
2. Tell students that the **futur antérieur** is like a **passé composé** with the auxiliary verb in the future. Have volunteers write the **passé composé** forms of **finir** and **aller** on the board. **(4 min.)**
3. Now, ask students to tell you how to change each auxiliary verb from the present to the future. **J'ai fini... J'aurai fini; Je suis allé(e)... Je serai allé(e). (4 min.)**
4. Tell students that all rules of agreement that apply to the **passé composé** also apply to the **futur antérieur. (1 min.)**

28 Dans quel ordre? 🎴1.2

Lisons/Parlons Pour chaque paire d'activités, dis quelle activité ces gens feront logiquement en premier.

MODÈLE Pascaline: faire ses devoirs / aller au cinéma
Pascaline ira au cinéma quand elle aura fait ses devoirs.

1. Laurent et Olivier: finir ses études / travailler
2. Tu: pouvoir se payer des vacances / trouver un travail
3. Vous: être prof d'italien / apprendre l'italien
4. Anaïs: étudier le russe / devenir interprète
5. Je: te la montrer / écrire ma lettre de motivation
6. Nous: sortir avec nos amis / finir les cours
7. Il: s'habiller / se raser
8. Elles: recevoir leur passeport / aller en France

29 Téléphone-moi! 🎴1.2

Écrivons/Parlons Tes camarades te demandent de leur téléphoner. Dis-leur quand tu pourras les appeler.

MODÈLE Je vous téléphonerai quand...
...mon petit frère aura fini ses devoirs.

mon petit frère

1. nous

2. je

3. vous

4. ma sœur

 **Communication**

 HOLT **SoundBooth** ONLINE RECORDING

30 Questions personnelles 🎴1.1

Parlons Demande à un(e) camarade ces projets de week-end. Il/Elle va te dire trois choses qu'il/elle doit faire avant de pouvoir faire ce qu'il/elle a envie de faire. Puis, échangez les rôles.

MODÈLE —Virginie, qu'est-ce que tu vas faire ce week-end?
—Je vais d'abord faire mes devoirs. Quand j'aurai fini mes devoirs, je... Ensuite, quand j'aurai..., je...

27 Answers
1. se maquillera; aura pris
2. se sera lavé; ira
3. serai; aura téléphoné
4. viendrons; aurons fini
5. trouveront; auront fait

28 Answers
1. Laurent et Olivier travailleront quand ils auront fini leurs études.
2. Tu pourras te payer des vacances quand tu auras trouvé un travail.
3. Vous serez prof d'italien quand vous aurez appris l'italien.
4. Anaïs deviendra interprète quand elle aura étudié le russe.
5. Quand j'aurai écrit ma lettre de motivation, je te la montrerai.
6. Nous sortirons avec nos amis quand nous aurons fini les cours.
7. Il s'habillera quand il se sera rasé.
8. Elles iront en France quand elles auront reçu leur passeport.

29 Possible Answers
1. Je vous téléphonerai quand nous aurons fait les magasins.
2. ... quand j'aurai lavé la voiture.
3. ... quand vous aurez dîné.
4. ... quand ma sœur aura fini de parler au téléphone.

Communication

30 Pair Activity: Interpersonal
First, have students write five sentences in the **futur simple** about what they will do this weekend. Have partners role-play a parent and a child. The parent starts by asking, **Qu'est-ce que tu feras ce week-end?** The child will respond with one of his or her activities. Then the parent will grant permission but add a condition, using **dès que + futur antérieur.**

MODÈLE
— **Qu'est-ce que tu feras ce week-end?**
— **J'irai au cinéma avec mes amis.**
— **Tu iras au ciné avec tes amis dès que tu auras rangé ta chambre.** 🎴1.1

Differentiated Instruction

SLOWER PACE LEARNERS

Building on Previous Skills Before presenting the future perfect ask students which verbs use the helping verb **avoir** and which use **être**. Then have students explain the formation of the past participle. Encourage students to ask for clarifications if needed. 🎴1.1, 1.2

SPECIAL LEARNING NEEDS

Students with Language Impairments
When reviewing **En anglais,** ensure that students with language challenges understand the use of the future perfect and past participle in English. Give students more examples and ask them to create others. Discuss a few planned steps in cooking or sports where initial actions must happen before the following actions. Present the **futur antérieur** after students understand how the sequence of tenses works in English. 🎴1.3

Resources

Planning:

Lesson Planner

 One-Stop Planner

Practice:

Grammar Tutor for Students of French, Chapter 2

Cahier de vocabulaire et grammaire

Differentiated Practice and Assessment CD-ROM

Cahier d'activités

Media Guide

 Teaching Transparencies Bell Work 2.7

 Interactive Tutor, Disc 1

Bell Work

Use Bell Work 2.7 in the *Teaching Transparencies* or write this activity on the board.

Mets les verbes entre parenthèses au **futur** ou au **futur antérieur**.

1. Je t' _____ (appeler) quand j' _____ (finir) mon travail.
2. Sylvain _____ (acheter) un ordinateur quand il _____ (trouver) un travail.
3. Les parents _____ (dîner) quand les enfants _____ (s'endormir).
4. Vous _____ (être) avocats quand vous _____ (réussir) vos examens. ✿1.2

French for Spanish Speakers

The future perfect in Spanish is formed with the future form of the auxiliary verb **haber** + the past participle of the verb. How does this compare to the way the **futur antérieur** is formed in French? (Both languages use a conjugated form of the auxiliary verb and the past participle, but French has two auxiliary verbs, **avoir** and **être**) ✿4.1

Flash culture

En France, les syndicats *(unions)* ont beaucoup de pouvoir. En général, ce sont eux qui organisent les grèves *(strikes)* et les manifestations. Le droit de grève est reconnu par la Constitution depuis 1946. Les Français le considèrent comme un élément essentiel de la démocratie et n'hésitent pas à l'utiliser. Même les étudiants font la grève pour protester contre des réformes qu'ils trouvent injustes! ✿4.2

Quel est le rôle des syndicats dans ton état?

Entre copains

une boîte	company
un boulot	job
bosser	to work
un coup de fil	phone call
un job	job

The present participle

Interactive TUTOR

1 As you already know, to form the **present participle** of all regular and most irregular verbs, you remove the **-ons** from the present **nous** form and add the ending **-ant**.

nous écoutons → écout**ant**   nous faisons → fais**ant**

2 **Être, avoir,** and **savoir** have irregular present participles.

être → étant   avoir → ayant   savoir → sachant

3 Use **en** + present participle to say that someone is doing something *at the same time* as something else.

Ils sont partis de chez nous **en chantant**.
They left our house singing.

en + present participle may also express *how* or *why* something is done. This translates as *by* or *through* in these cases.

En étudiant, tu réussiras.
By studying, you'll succeed.

4 The present participle can be used without **en**.

Étant étudiante en art, je voudrais faire un stage.

The present participle may also be used instead of a *relative clause*. This construction is typical of formal speech and writing.

En Chine, les personnes **parlant** *(qui parlent)* français sont rares.

5 You can also use the present participle as *an adjective* to describe someone or something. In this case, it will agree in gender and number with the noun being described.

C'est une histoire **passionnante**.   *It's an exciting story.*

 Vocabulaire et grammaire, *pp. 22–23*
Cahier d'activités, *pp. 15–17*   **Online** workbooks

31 La langue de l'administration ✿1.2

Parlons Remplace les mots soulignés par le participe présent.

1. Les élèves <u>qui passent</u> un examen demain devront arriver à 8h.
2. Les gens <u>qui cherchent</u> du travail devraient lire le journal.
3. Les gens <u>qui ont</u> de l'expérience ont un meilleur salaire.
4. Les personnes <u>qui font</u> une demande d'emploi doivent envoyer leur CV.
5. Voici un plan <u>qui indique</u> les endroits importants de la ville.
6. Les gens <u>qui savent</u> parler anglais trouvent du travail plus facilement.

1. passant 2. cherchant 3. ayant
4. faisant 5. indiquant 6. sachant

Core Instruction

TEACHING GRAMMAIRE

1. Go over Points 1 and 2. **(2 min.)**

2. Go over Point 3. Ask students about their multitasking habits and the way things are done. **Est-ce que tu fais tes devoirs en regardant la télé? Comment est-ce qu'on reste en forme? (3 min.)**

3. Go over Points 4 and 5. Point out that a present-tense verb is used to talk about an ongoing action, and remind students never to use a present participle in this construction. (**Je déjeune...** *I am having lunch.*) **(1 min.)**

Grammaire 2

32 Comment dirais-tu? 🎬1.2

Écrivons/Parlons Pour chaque phrase, écris l'adjectif verbal.

1. En automne, les feuilles ont des couleurs _____.(changer)
2. Les enfants de Laura sont très _____.(obéir)
3. Il a trouvé un travail _____.(intéresser)
4. Il m'a offert une jolie plante _____.(grimper)
5. Cette bande dessinée n'est pas très _____.(amuser)

1. changeantes
2. obéissants
3. intéressant
4. grimpante
5. amusante

33 Voilà comment il faut faire! 🎬1.2

Écrivons Remplace chaque condition par un participe présent.

MODÈLE Si tu étudies bien, tu auras de bonnes notes.
En étudiant bien, tu auras de bonnes notes.

1. Si vous travaillez régulièrement, vous réussirez.
2. S'il fait un apprentissage, il aura plus d'expérience.
3. Si tu pars à 7 heures, tu arriveras à temps au travail.
4. Je gagnerai plus d'argent si je fais des heures supplémentaires.
5. Nous apprendrons beaucoup si nous faisons un stage.

33 Answers

1. En travaillant régulièrement, vous réussirez.
2. En faisant un apprentissage, il aura plus d'expérience.
3. En partant à 7 heures, tu arriveras à temps au travail.
4. En faisant des heures supplémentaires, je gagnerai plus d'argent.
5. En faisant un stage, nous apprendons beaucoup.

34 Answers

1. Tu ne devrais pas regarder la télé en faisant tes devoirs.
2. Il ne devrait pas parler au mobile en conduisant.
3. Elle ne devrait pas lire en marchant.

34 Des conseils 🎬1.2

Parlons/Écrivons Que dirais-tu à ces gens?

MODÈLE **Vous ne devriez pas surfer sur Internet en préparant le repas.**

1. tu

2. il

3. elle

Communication

HOLT **SoundBooth**
ONLINE RECORDING

35 Scénario 🎬1.1

Parlons Un(e) camarade te demande ce qu'il/elle doit faire pour réussir à son cours de français. Tu vas lui donner trois conseils. Ensuite, échangez les rôles.

MODÈLE **Tu apprendras beaucoup en regardant des films français.**

Communication

35 Pair Activity: Interpersonal
Have students list five daily activities or chores, such as brushing teeth or dressing, along with the time of day. Then have partners take turns telling each other what they do and giving advice with **Tu devrais…** or **Tu ne devrais pas…** They can accept or reject the advice.

MODÈLE
— **Chaque matin, je me brosse les dents.**
— **Tu devrais utiliser du dentifrice en te brossant les dents.**
— **Bonne idée.** 🎬1.1, 1.2

Differentiated Instruction

SLOWER PACE LEARNERS

Additional Practice After presenting the present participles, ask students to find additional examples that illustrate Points 3–5 in the grammar presentation. Students should also provide the English equivalent of each example and explain how the French construction differs from the English construction. 🎬1.2, 4.1

MULTIPLE INTELLIGENCES

34 Visual Give students the option of creating three more situations where advice is required. Tell them the situations they illustrate should have complexities that need to be resolved in the future. The illustrations should have captions with the advice they would give the person in that situation and use future tenses appropriately. 🎬1.2

Assess

Assessment Program
Quiz: Grammaire 2
Alternative Assessment
Differentiated Practice and Assessment CD-ROM

Online Assessment
my.hrw.com

Test Generator

Bell Work

Use Bell Work 2.8 in the *Teaching Transparencies* or write this activity on the board.

Donne le contraire des phrases suivantes. Utilise **en + le participe présent**.

1. Il a réussi ses examens *sans étudier.*
2. Je suis partie *sans fermer* la porte.
3. Tu conduis *sans faire* des mots croisés.
4. Nous grossissons *sans manger* trop de chocolats.
5. Il fait du vélo *sans avoir* peur de tomber. 1.2

36 Answers

1. Quand elle aura réussi ses examens, elle finira le lycée.
2. Quand elle aura fini le lycée, elle ira à l'université.
3. Quand elle sera allée à l'université, elle cherchera du travail.
4. Quand elle aura cherché du travail, elle trouvera du travail.
5. Quand elle aura trouvé du travail, elle aura un bon salaire.
6. Quand elle aura eu un bon salaire, ell partira en vacances.

37 Script

See script on p. 41F.

Synthèse
- Vocabulaire 2
- Grammaire 2

Application 2

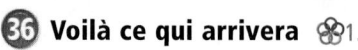

36 **Voilà ce qui arrivera** 1.2

Parlons/Écrivons Dis ce que Christelle aura dû faire pour arriver aux choses suivantes. Utilise le futur antérieur.

MODÈLE   réussir ses examens
Quand elle aura étudié, elle réussira ses examens.

1. finir le lycée
2. aller à l'université
3. chercher du travail
4. trouver du travail
5. avoir un bon salaire
6. partir en vacances

Un peu plus Révisions

The *conditionnel de politesse*

1. To form the conditional, use the future stem and add the **imparfait** endings: **-ais, -ais, -ait, -ions, -iez, -aient**

2. The conditional is used to soften statements, making them sound more polite than the present or a command.

> Je **voudrais** travailler avec vous.
>
> **Pourrais**-tu laver la voiture?
>
> Vous **serait**-il possible de laver les vitres?

 Vocabulaire et grammaire, p. 24
Cahier d'activités, pp. 15–17   **Online** workbooks

37 **Écoutons** CD 2, Tr. 6 1.2

Madame Aubry a beaucoup de choses à faire faire. Dis si elle demande ces services de manière a) **polie** ou b) **impolie**.

1. b **2.** a **3.** b **4.** b **5.** a **6.** a **7.** b **8.** a

38 **Où se trouve...?** 1.2

Parlons/Écrivons Sam est perdu et demande poliment des renseignements à une jeune fille dans la rue.

SAM   Mademoiselle, ___1___-vous (pouvoir) me dire où il y a une station de métro?

LA FILLE Il y en a une juste là, à droite.

SAM   ___2___-vous (savoir) aussi s'il y a une pharmacie près d'ici?

LA FILLE Non, je suis désolée.

SAM   ___3___-vous (connaître) un bon restaurant dans le quartier?

LA FILLE Oui, il y en a un bon près d'ici.

SAM   Je ne ___4___ (savoir) assez vous remercier. ___5___-vous (accepter) une invitation à dîner?

1. pourriez **2.** Sauriez **3.** Connaîtriez
4. saurais **5.** Accepteriez

Core Instruction

INTEGRATED PRACTICE

1. Have students do Activity 36 to practice previously taught expressions. **(4 min.)**

2. Introduce **Un peu plus.** (See presentation suggestions at right.) **(4 min.)**

3. Continue with integrated practice Activities 37–41. **(20 min.)**

TEACHING UN PEU PLUS

1. Go over Point 1. To review the conditional, ask volunteers to write the conditional forms of **pouvoir** or **vouloir** on the board. Point out that whereas the future has the present endings of **avoir**, the conditional has its **imparfait** endings. **(2 min.)**

2. Go over Point 2. Tell students that **Excusez-moi** can be added to the beginning of the sentence and **s'il vous plaît** to the end to further soften a request. **(2 min.)**

Online Practice
go.hrw.com
Application 2 practice
KEYWORD: BD3 CH2

Chapitre 2
Application 2

39 **Offres d'emploi** 3.2

Lisons/Écrivons Lis ces offres d'emploi et réponds aux questions.

1. Quels emplois sont offerts?
2. Est-ce qu'il faut avoir de l'expérience pour être chauffeur?
3. Où faut-il envoyer sa lettre?
4. Combien de langues la/le secrétaire doit-elle/il parler? Lesquelles?
5. Écris une lettre de motivation pour un de ces emplois.

Service Express

RECHERCHE

• **Secrétaire bilingue :** français/espagnol
expérience souhaitée

• **Chauffeurs Poids Lourds**
débutant accepté, salaire motivant

• **Mécaniciens**
Niveau BEP, expérience nécessaire

Envoyer CV et lettre de motivation à
Service-Express
Zone Industrielle Nord, 64100 Pau

40 **Ta petite annonce** 1.2

Écrivons Tu as un restaurant ou une société de ton choix et tu voudrais engager du personnel. Crée une petite annonce disant ce que tu cherches chez les candidats pour cet emploi.

MODÈLE Restaurant des Trois Ponts recherche cuisinier et serveurs/serveuses. Travail à temps partiel...

Communication

HOLT **SoundBooth**
ONLINE RECORDING

41 **Histoire à raconter** 1.2

Parlons Avec un(e) camarade, imaginez ce que les parents de Serge lui demandent et ce que Serge décide de faire.

39 **Answers**
1. secrétaire, chauffeurs, mécaniciens
2. non
3. à Service-Express
4. deux, français et espagnol

Communication

Class Activity: Interpersonal
Have students practice the **conditionnel de politesse** with a class chain. One student makes a statement, request, or command. The next student restates the original sentence in the **conditionnel de politesse** and then makes a new statement to continue the chain. 1.2

ACTIVITÉ PRÉPARATOIRE PRE-AP **Language Examination**

To display the drawings to the class, use the Picture Sequences Transparency for Chapter 2.

41 Sample answer:

a. — Est-ce que tu pourrais laver la voiture?
— Mais papa, il faut que je fasse mes devoirs.

b. — Ça t'ennuierait de faire la lessive?
— Mais maman, je voulais aller au cinéma.

c. — Je vais faire laver la voiture et le linge.

Differentiated Instruction

ADVANCED LEARNERS

40 **Variation** Have students imagine that they work in the department of human resources at a large department store. The store has several job openings. Students should create an ad that announces these openings and gives the requirements for each. Ask students to present their ads to the class. 1.3, 5.1

MULTIPLE INTELLIGENCES

Artistic Have students draw their own three-panel picture story in which they illustrate how someone wants them to do a chore and how they try to get out of it. Ask partners to exchange illustrations and provide captions. You might display the illustrations and captions on the classroom bulletin board. 1.1

Assess

Assessment Program
Quiz : Application 2
Audio CD 2, Tr. 12
Alternative Assessment
Differentiated Practice and Assessment CD-ROM

Online Assessment
my.hrw.com

Test Generator

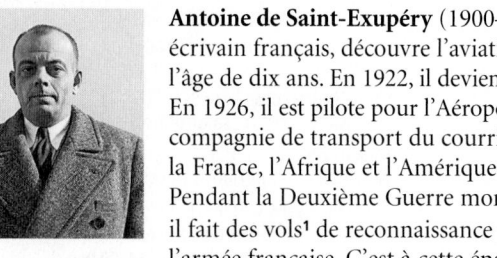

Resources

Planning:

Lesson Planner

 One-Stop Planner

Presentation:

🎧 Audio CD 2, Tr. 7

Practice:

Cahier d'activités

Reading Strategies and Skills Handbook, Chapter 2

Advanced Reader

AP Reading Suggestion

Have students analyze the excerpt from the story by comparing it to other stories they know. What do they have in common? What are some differences?

Applying the Strategies

For practice with summarizing, have students use the "Retellings" strategy from the *Reading Strategies and Skills Handbook*.

READING PRACTICE

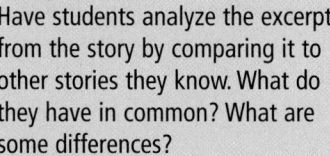

Antoine de Saint-Exupéry (1900–1944) écrivain français, découvre l'aviation à l'âge de dix ans. En 1922, il devient pilote. En 1926, il est pilote pour l'Aéropostale, compagnie de transport du courrier entre la France, l'Afrique et l'Amérique du Sud. Pendant la Deuxième Guerre mondiale, il fait des vols[1] de reconnaissance pour l'armée française. C'est à cette époque qu'il écrit et illustre son récit le plus connu, *Le Petit Prince* publié en 1943. Saint-Exupéry disparaît pendant une mission le 31 juillet 1944. Saint-Exupéry a aussi écrit *Courrier-Sud* (1928), *Vol de Nuit* (1931) et *Terre des Hommes* (1938) entre autres.

> **STRATÉGIE pour lire**
>
> **Summarizing** is an easy way to help you concentrate on what you are reading. After you read a short amount of text, stop and write down *what* has happened and *why* it has happened. If you have any questions, jot them down as well. Repeat this process for the rest of the reading. As you continue reading, the answers will probably become clear.

A Avant la lecture 🔷3.1

Est-ce que tu as déjà entendu parler de l'histoire du petit prince? Qu'est-ce que tu connais de l'histoire? Lis le paragraphe d'introduction au texte. Qui sont les personnages de l'histoire? Où se passe-t-elle?

CD 2, Tr. 7

🎧 Le Petit Prince

L'extrait suivant est tiré du récit
Le Petit Prince. *Un aviateur s'écrase[2] dans le Sahara. Il y rencontre le petit prince qui a quitté sa planète parce qu'il se sentait seul. Le petit prince lui raconte ses aventures. Dans cet extrait, le petit prince arrive sur la cinquième planète où il fait la connaissance d'un allumeur de réverbères[3].*

1. *flights* 2. tombe 3. *street lights*

Core Instruction

LECTURE

1. Read **Stratégie pour lire** aloud for students. Ask students to take notes while they read the author's biography. **(5 min.)**

2. Have students do **Avant la lecture**. On the board, you might want to list everything that students already know about the story. **(10 min.)**

3. Have students take turns reading the first page of *Le Petit Prince*. Help with pronunciation as needed. Stop regularly to monitor comprehension. Have partners summarize what they have read. Ask them to describe the lamplighter's job. **(15 min.)**

La cinquième planète était très curieuse. C'était la plus petite de toutes. Il y avait là juste assez de place pour loger un réverbère et un allumeur de réverbères. Le petit prince ne parvenait[1] pas à s'expliquer à quoi pouvaient servir, quelque part dans le ciel, sur une planète sans maison, ni population, un réverbère et un allumeur de réverbères. Cependant il se dit en lui même :

— Peut-être bien que cet homme est absurde. Cependant il est moins absurde que le roi, que le vaniteux[2], que le businessman et que le buveur. Au moins son travail a-t-il un sens. Quand il allume son réverbère, c'est comme s'il faisait naître une étoile de plus, ou une fleur. Quand il éteint[3] son réverbère ça endort la fleur ou l'étoile. C'est une occupation très jolie. C'est véritablement utile puisque c'est joli.

Lorsqu'il aborda[4] la planète il salua respectueusement l'allumeur :

— Bonjour. Pourquoi viens-tu d'éteindre ton réverbère ?

— C'est la consigne[5], répondit l'allumeur. Bonjour.

— Qu'est-ce que la consigne ?

— C'est d'éteindre mon réverbère. Bonsoir.

Et il le ralluma.

— Mais pourquoi viens-tu de le rallumer ?

— C'est la consigne, répondit l'allumeur.

— Je ne comprends pas, dit le petit prince.

— Il n'y a rien à comprendre, dit l'allumeur. La consigne c'est la consigne. Bonjour.

Et il éteignit son réverbère.

Puis il s'épongea[6] le front avec un mouchoir[7] à carreaux rouges.

— Je fais là un métier terrible. C'était raisonnable autrefois. J'éteignais le matin et j'allumais le soir. J'avais le reste du jour pour me reposer, et le reste de la nuit pour dormir...

— Et, depuis cette époque, la consigne a changé ?

— La consigne n'a pas changé, dit l'allumeur. C'est bien là le drame ! La planète d'année en année a tourné de plus en plus vite, et la consigne n'a pas changé !

— Alors ? dit le petit prince.

— Alors maintenant qu'elle fait un tour par minute, je n'ai plus une seconde de repos. J'allume et j'éteins une fois par minute !

— Ça c'est drôle ! Les jours chez toi durent une minute !

— Ce n'est pas drôle du tout, dit l'allumeur. Ça fait déjà un mois que nous parlons ensemble.

— Un mois ?

— Oui. Trente minutes. Trente jours ! Bonsoir.

Et il ralluma son réverbère.

Le petit prince le regarda et il aima cet allumeur qui était tellement fidèle[8] à la consigne. Il se souvint des couchers de soleil que lui-même allait autrefois

---

1. ne pouvait pas 2. prétentieux 3. *turns off* 4. *landed* 5. ordre 6. s'essuya 7. *handkerchief* 8. *faithful*

Active Reading Questions

1. **Pourquoi est-ce que la cinquième planète est curieuse? (Elle est très petite.)**
2. **Qui habite la cinquième planète? (un allumeur de réverbères)**
3. **Qu'est-ce que le petit prince pense de l'occupation d'allumeur? (C'est utile et joli.)**
4. **Quel est le travail de l'allumeur? (allumer et éteindre le réverbère)**
5. **Pourquoi le travail de l'allumeur est-il terrible? (Il n'a pas le temps pour se reposer ou pour dormir.)**
6. **Qu'est-ce qui se passe chaque année? (la planète tourne de plus en plus vite)**
7. **Un jour dure combien de temps sur cette planète? (une minute)**   1.2

Finding the Main Idea

Remind students that the details in a selection can be used to infer, or guess, the main ideas. Ask them to list key words and details as they read to find the main ideas. Then have them apply **Stratégie pour lire.**

Language Examination

Lecture helps students prepare for Section 1, Part B: **Reading Comprehension.** The audio recording helps them prepare for Part A: **Listening—Short Narratives.**

Differentiated Instruction

ADVANCED LEARNERS

Challenge In *Vol de nuit,* Saint-Exupéry writes, **"Le règlement est semblable aux rites d'une religion, qui semblent absurdes, mais qui façonnent les hommes."** Ask students if this quote applies to the life of the lamplighter. Why or why not?   1.1, 3.2

SPECIAL LEARNING NEEDS

Students with Dyslexia Assist students in using **Stratégie pour lire** by creating a study guide. Prior to reading the selection, ask students to fold a piece of paper into three sections. The headings for the sections should reflect the three suggestions in **Stratégie pour lire:** What has happened? Why did it happen? What questions do I have about the reading? After reading, discuss the items students placed in each category.   1.2

Active Reading Questions

1. Pourquoi est-ce que le petit prince aime l'allumeur? (L'allumeur est fidèle.)
2. Qu'est-ce que le petit prince veut faire pour l'allumeur? (l'aider)
3. Pour se reposer, qu'est-ce que le petit prince propose à l'allumeur? (de marcher lentement)
4. Pourquoi l'allumeur n'aime-t-il pas la suggestion du petit prince? (Il préfère dormir.)
5. Pourquoi l'allumeur n'est-il pas ridicule? (Il s'occupe d'autre chose que de lui-même.)
6. Quelle est la raison pour laquelle le petit prince ne reste pas avec son nouvel ami? (La planète est trop petite pour deux.) ✿ 1.2

Postreading Activity

Ask students to state the moral of this story. Have them quote from the text to support their response. Then ask students if they agree with Saint-Exupéry's views and to explain why or why not. ✿ 1.2

chercher, en tirant sa chaise. Il voulut aider son ami :

— Tu sais... je connais un moyen de te reposer quand tu voudras...

— Je veux toujours, dit l'allumeur.

Car on peut être, à la fois, fidèle et paresseux.

Le petit prince poursuivit :

— Ta planète est tellement petite que tu en fais le tour en trois enjambées[1]. Tu n'as qu'à marcher assez lentement pour rester toujours au soleil. Quand tu voudras te reposer tu marcheras... et le jour durera aussi longtemps que tu voudras.

— Ça ne m'avance pas à grand'chose, dit l'allumeur. Ce que j'aime dans la vie, c'est dormir.

— Ce n'est pas de chance, dit le petit prince.

— Ce n'est pas de chance, dit l'allumeur. Bonjour.

Et il éteignit son réverbère.

Celui-là, se dit le petit prince, tandis qu'il poursuivait plus loin son voyage, celui-là serait méprisé[2] par tous les autres, par le roi, par le vaniteux, par le buveur, par le businessman. Cependant c'est le seul qui ne me paraisse pas ridicule. C'est, peut-être, parce qu'il s'occupe d'autre chose que de soi-même.

Il eut un soupir de regret et se dit encore :

— Celui-là est le seul dont j'eusse pu faire[3] mon ami. Mais sa planète est vraiment trop petite. Il n'y a pas de place pour deux... Ce que le petit prince n'osait pas s'avouer, c'est qu'il regrettait cette planète bénie à cause, surtout, des mille quatre cent quarante couchers de soleil par vingt-quatre heures !

---

1. un grand pas 2. *despised* 3. *could have been*

Core Instruction

LECTURE

1. Have students finish reading *Le Petit Prince*. Have them summarize the ending of the selection. **(10 min.)**
2. Complete **Compréhension** questions as a class.

Have students do **Après la lecture** individually. **(10 min.)**

3. Ask students to revise the list on the board that you made for **Avant la lecture. (5 min.)**

Online Practice
go.hrw.com
Online Edition
KEYWORD: BD3 CH2

Chapitre 2

Lecture

Lecture

B Compréhension 🌸1.2

Complète les phrases suivantes.

1. Le petit prince atterrit sur...
   a. la quatrième planète.
   b. la cinquième planète. *(circled)*
   c. la quinzième planète.

2. L'allumeur de réverbères doit...
   a. éteindre et allumer trois réverbères.
   b. seulement éteindre les réverbères.
   c. éteindre et allumer un seul réverbère. *(circled)*

3. L'allumeur de réverbères allume et éteint le réverbère...
   a. tous les soirs.
   b. toutes les minutes. *(circled)*
   c. tous les mois.

4. L'allumeur de réverbères peut arrêter d'allumer et d'éteindre le réverbère toutes les minutes s'il...
   a. fait trois enjambées.
   b. marche lentement. *(circled)*
   c. marche vite.

5. Le petit prince aime cette planète...
   a. parce qu'il y a beaucoup de couchers de soleil. *(circled)*
   b. parce qu'il y a beaucoup de réverbères.
   c. parce que la planète est petite.

C Réponds aux questions suivantes. 🌸1.2

1. Comment est la cinquième planète?
2. Qu'est-ce qu'il y a sur la planète?
3. Pourquoi le petit prince pense-t-il que l'occupation d'allumeur de réverbères est utile?
4. Quelles sont les consignes de l'allumeur?
5. Quand l'allumeur faisait-il son travail autrefois?
6. Quel est le problème de l'allumeur?
8. Comment le petit prince se sentait-il après avoir quitté la planète? Pourquoi?

Après la lecture 🌸1.2, 3.1

D Relis le texte encore une fois et résume l'histoire. Assure-toi que tous les faits importants de l'histoire se trouvent dans ton résumé. Puis, élimine les détails qui ne sont pas nécessaires.

C Possible Answers

1. La cinquième planète est la plus petite de toutes celles que le petit prince a visitées.
2. Il y a un réverbère et un allumeur de réverbères.
3. C'est utile parce que c'est joli.
4. L'allumeur doit allumer et éteindre son réverbère.
5. Il faisait son métier le matin et le soir.
6. Il n'a plus le temps de se reposer.
7. Le petit prince regrettait la planète parce qu'elle avait beaucoup de couchers de soleil par jour.

Connections

Science Link

Saint-Exupéry was a pioneer of international postal flight in the days when airplanes had few instruments and pilots flew by instinct. Later, he complained that those who flew the more advanced aircraft were more like accountants than pilots. He did not return from a mission to collect data on German troop movements in the Rhone river valley. In 2004, investigators from the French Underwater Archaeological Department confirmed that the wreckage of a Lockheed F-5 photo-reconnaissance aircraft found off the coast of Marseille was Saint-Exupéry's. The cause of the crash remains a mystery. Ask students to research aircraft instruments and their functions. What devices are used today to investigate the cause of a crash?

🌸3.1

Differentiated Instruction

SLOWER PACE LEARNERS

C Variation You may want to convert Activity C into a multiple choice activity. Provide at one correct two incorrect answers for each question. Have slower pace learners choose the correct answer. 🌸1.1, 1.2

SPECIAL LEARNING NEEDS

Students with Dyslexia In Activity B, accommodate reading challenges by reading aloud the questions and answer choices before asking students to select the correct response. The purpose of the activity is to check for comprehension and not reading skills, therefore, providing choices will eliminate the reading requirement from checking for comprehension of the text. 🌸1.2

Assess

Assessment Program

Quiz: Lecture

Online Assessment

my.hrw.com

Test Generator

L'atelier de l'écrivain

Interactive
TUTOR

Resources

Planning:

Lesson Planner

 One-Stop Planner

Practice:

Cahier d'activités

Process Writing

As students correct each other's drafts, have them underline their partner's work experience with one color and his or her skills and qualifications with another. Have them check that all their partner's qualifications fit the job and are listed in the order that will have the greatest impact, according to the **Stratégie pour écrire.** Then have students reread the letters to make sure the language is clear and polite.

Teaching Suggestion

Before students begin writing, discuss with them the differences in register, tone, structure, and language between informal and formal letters. Ask them to provide examples of appropriate language used in each type of letter, first in English, and then in French.

Cultures

Practices and Perspectives

The French application letter is short and handwritten. The greeting would be **Monsieur, Madame,** or **Messieurs,** followed by a comma. The form of address in the greeting is reflected in the closing formula. If the greeting is addressed to **Madame,** the closing could be, **Veuillez agréer, Madame, l'expression de mes sentiments distingués,** followed by the applicant's signature. Ask students to research where addresses and the date are placed on French letters. ✿2.1

Ta lettre de motivation

Tu as vu une offre d'emploi qui t'intéresse sur Internet. Pour poser ta candidature, tu vas écrire une lettre de motivation qui va accompagner ton curriculum vitae. Dans cette lettre, il faut convaincre l'employeur que tu es le meilleur candidat/la meilleure candidate pour le poste.

1 Plan: l'araignée ✿1.2

Choisis un emploi qui t'intéresse. Écris le nom de ce travail dans le cercle de ton organigramme. Sur les lignes à droite du cercle, fais la liste de tes qualifications, compétences et qualités (tu peux les imaginer) pour persuader l'employeur de ton expérience et de l'intérêt que tu portes à ce travail. Ensuite, pense à ce dont l'employeur aura besoin. Écris tes idées sur les lignes à gauche du cercle. Revois les détails que tu as écrit et mets-les par ordre d'importance. Commence par le moins important pour finir par le plus important.

STRATÉGIE pour écrire

Use details and organization to maximize the effect of your persuasive writing. First, try to predict your readers' concerns, and choose facts and supporting examples to address each one. Begin writing by clearly stating your objective, and then proceed to explain and to support your point of view. Back up each statement with specific information that illustrates your point. Be sure to end with your strongest arguments. Your most convincing argument will have the biggest impact if your audience reads it last. ✿3.1

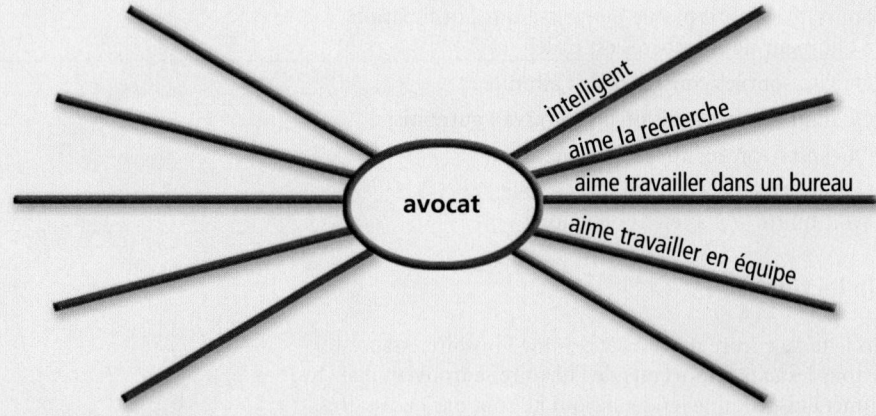

avocat — intelligent / aime la recherche / aime travailler dans un bureau / aime travailler en équipe

Core Instruction

L'ATELIER DE L'ÉCRIVAIN

1. Ask students to list several jobs they would like to have and why. Then discuss the assignment and **Stratégie pour écrire. (5 min.)**

2. Have students do step 1. Then have them use their **organigramme** to role-play a job interview with a partner. Tell them to add any details that came up in the interview that they had not initially included in their **organigramme. (10 min.)**

3. Go over the **Vocabulaire à la carte,** appropriate salutations and closings for a business letter, and the grammar presentation for **The futures. (5 min.)**

4. Assign step 2 as homework.

5. After students revise their letter, ask for volunteers to read their's to the class. Discuss with the class what would make these applicants good employees. **(10 min.)**

L'atelier de l'écrivain

② Rédaction ✿1.3

Fais un brouillon de ta lettre. Commence par une phrase qui explique l'objectif de ta lettre. Puis, essaie de convaincre l'employeur que tu es le ou la meilleur(e) candidat(e) en parlant de ton expérience et de tes qualités. Utilise le futur et le futur antérieur pour lui dire ce que tu apporteras à son entreprise. N'oublie pas d'utiliser les formules de politesse nécessaires.

③ Correction ✿1.2

Échange ta lettre avec celle d'un ou d'une camarade de classe. Posez-vous les questions suivantes pour corriger vos lettres respectives:

• Est-ce que toutes les qualifications, les compétences et les qualités nécessaires pour l'emploi sont remplies?

• Est-ce que les détails et la structure rendent la lettre convaincante?

• Est-ce que la lettre est assez polie et le style adéquat?

Ensuite, assurez-vous de l'emploi correct des temps des verbes et des formules de politesse. Corrigez les fautes d'orthographe.

Fais les corrections suggérées et écris la version finale de ta lettre.

④ Application ✿1.3

Lis ta lettre à un petit groupe de camarades qui va jouer le rôle des employeurs. Ils vont la lire et dire si tu les as persuadés de t'accorder un entretien. Si non, ils vont te suggérer ce que tu dois faire pour améliorer ta candidature.

Vocabulaire à la carte

accorder un entretien	*to grant an interview*
une compétence	*skill, ability*
contribuer	*to contribute*
une lettre de motivation	*cover letter*
poser sa candidature	*to apply for a position*
un emploi	*job*
souhaiter	*to wish*

The futures

The future is used to talk about an event that is going to happen.

Tu seras boulanger.

The future perfect is used to talk about a future event that needs to happen before another future event.

Quand j'aurai fini mes études, je partirai faire le tour du monde.

Alain Favier
17, boulevard Jourdan
75013 PARIS
Tél: 01.53.05.00.01   *Paris, le 3 septembre*

À l'attention de: Monsieur Tevet
Objet: demande de stage

Monsieur,

Étant actuellement étudiant en architecture, je désirerais effectuer un stage d'une durée d'un mois dans votre cabinet dans le but d'acquérir une expérience nécessaire à ma formation.

Vos réalisations m'intéressent et j'aimerais vivement

…lum Vitæ

…embre à Annecy
…oulevard Jourdan

….com
…nçaise

…DIPLÔMES:
…Diplôme d'études en architecture
…DEP Diplôme d'études professionnelles

…ES PROFESSIONNELLES:
…oût 2002: Vendeur-caissier service à la

The futures

Have students write about what they will do when one of the following happens:
finir mes études, avoir mon premier appartement, trouver un emploi que j'aime

Writing Assessment

To assess the **L'atelier de l'écrivain,** you can use the following rubric. For additional rubrics, see the *Assessment Program.*

Writing Rubric	4	3	2	1
Content (Complete—Incomplete)				
Comprehensibility (Comprehensible— Seldom comprehensible)				
Accuracy (Accurate—Seldom accurate)				
Organization (Well-organized—Poorly organized)				
Effort (Excellent effort— Minimal effort)				

18-20: A   14-15: C   Under
16-17: B   12-13: D   12: F

Differentiated Instruction

SLOWER PACE LEARNERS

Building on Previous Skills Before students outline their letter in step 2, ask them to name professions and list these on the board. Next to each profession, have them write a brief description of it and the qualifications it entails. Encourage students to refer to the information on the board when they compose their own letter. As an alternative, you might allow students to research on the Internet the profession that interests them.   ✿1.1

SPECIAL LEARNING NEEDS

Students with Learning Disabilities Allow students with writing challenges to use classified ads for employment opportunities to assist when they write their letter of interest. A classified ad will give general information about the job requirements and assist students in developing their persuasive writing response. Encourage students to highlight their strengths that match the requirements for the job they chose.   ✿1.3

Assess

Assessment Program

Quiz: Écriture

Online Assessment
my.hrw.com

Test Generator 💿

Chapitre 2

Prépare-toi pour l'examen

Interactive TUTOR

① Ces gens te parlent de leurs projets. Dis à quelle photo chaque phrase correspond. Il n'y a pas de photo pour chaque phrase. 1.2

a.

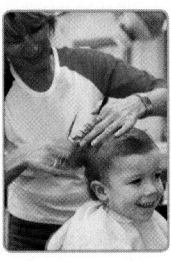
b.

c.

d.

① Vocabulaire 1
• to ask about future plans
• to make polite requests
pp. 44–47

a **1.** Cet été, j'aimerais trouver un job de serveuse.
d **2.** Après ma retraite, je voudrais travailler comme libraire.
3. Moi, j'aimerais travailler dans l'informatique.
c **4.** Ça me plairait d'être avocate, comme mon père.
b **5.** J'aimerais faire un stage chez un coiffeur avant de me décider.

② Mets les verbes entre parenthèses au futur. 1.2

1. Ma sœur _____ (aller) à l'université après le lycée. ira
2. Mon frère _____ (être) cuisinier. sera
3. Vous _____ (finir) vos cours d'anglais au mois de mai. finirez
4. Nous _____ (acheter) une maison cette année. achèterons
5. Je _____ (devenir) plombier comme mon père. deviendrai
6. Mes cousins _____ (conduire) des voitures de sport et _____ (faire) de la compétition. conduiront; feront

② Grammaire 1
• the future
• feminine form of nouns
Un peu plus
• the verb **conduire**
pp. 48–53

③ Sylvie est la secrétaire de monsieur Legrand. Complète la conversation téléphonique entre Sylvie et Lucas, un garçon qui cherche du travail. 1.2

SYLVIE   Bonjour. Le cabinet de M. Legrand.
LUCAS   ___1___ à monsieur Legrand, s'il vous plaît?
YLVIE   ___2___ de qui?
LUCAS   Je m'appelle Lucas Tiemont et je voudrais avoir ___3___ parce que j'aimerais faire ___4___ chez vous.
SYLVIE   Désolée, sa ligne ___5___. Vous pouvez ___6___?

③ Vocabulaire 2
• to make a phone call
• to write a formal letter
pp. 56–59

1. Est-ce que je pourrais parler
2. C'est de la part **3.** une entrevue
4. un stage **5.** est occupée **6.** rappeler

Preparing for the Exam

RETEACHING
Review the use and formation of the present participle, especially the irregular forms of the verbs **avoir**, **être,** and **savoir** (**ayant**, **étant, sachant.**) Ask students to write three sentences with a relative pronoun, such as **Les femmes qui ont de l'expérience ont un meilleur salaire.** Then have partners exchange sentences and replace the relative pronoun and the verb with the present participle. **Les femmes ayant de l'expérience ont un meilleur salaire.**

TEST-TAKING STRATEGY
Remind students that the **futur antérieur** is formed by conjugating **avoir** or **être** in the future tense and adding the past participle of the main verb. This works very similarly as in the already familiar **passé composé. Quand j'aurai fini mes études, je travaillerai avec ma mère.**

Online Assessment
go.hrw.com
Chapter Self–test
KEYWORD: BD3 CH2

Chapitre 2

Prépare-toi pour l'examen

4 Complète les phrases suivantes. Utilise le futur antérieur. ✿1.2

1. Quand… (finir mes études), je serai avocat.
2. M. Petit vous répondra quand… (lire votre lettre de motivation)
3. Il aura un meilleur salaire quand… (finir son stage)
4. Nous ne serons plus au chômage quand… (trouver du travail)
5. Quand… (lire ce livre), je te le prêterai.
6. Vous serez contents quand… (finir cet exercice)

4 Grammaire 2
- the future perfect
- the present participle

Un peu plus
- conditionnel de politesse
  pp. 60–65

5 Réponds aux questions suivantes. ✿2.1, 2.2

1. En France, dans quel secteur est-ce que la majorité de la population active travaille?
2. Depuis quand est-ce que le droit de grève est reconnu par la Constitution française?
3. Qu'est-ce que l'ANPE fait?

5 Culture
- Comparaisons p. 55
- Flash culture pp. 47, 52, 58, 62

6 Écoute les phrases suivantes et dis si elles sont a) **polies** ou b) **impolies.** CD 2, Tr. 8 ✿1.2 **1.** a **2.** b **3.** a **4.** b

7 Regarde les images et raconte ce qui se passe. ✿1.2

Prépare-toi pour l'examen

4 Answers

1. j'aurai fini mes études.
2. il aura lu votre lettre de motivation.
3. il aura fini son stage.
4. nous aurons trouvé du travail.
5. j'aurai lu ce livre
6. vous aurez fini cet exercice!

5 Answers

1. les services (le tertiaire)
2. depuis 1946
3. Elle s'occupe des offres et des demandes d'emploi.

6 Script

See script on p. 41F.

Language Examination
PRÉ-AP PRÉPARATOIRE

📖 To display the drawings to the class, use the Picture Sequences Transparency for Chapter 2.

7 Sample answer

a. Étienne voudrait faire un stage dans une grande société. Il téléphone à la secrétaire pour avoir un entretien avec le directeur.

b. Plus tard, Étienne va au bureau du directeur pour lui parler.

c. Pendant l'entretien, le directeur pose plusieurs questions à Étienne. Étienne lui parle de ses études.

d. À la fin de l'entretien, le directeur engage Étienne.

COMMON ERROR ALERT
///// ATTENTION ! \\\\\

Students will often confuse the **je** form of the future tense with the conditional, since they sound the same, e.g. **je parlerai / je parlerais**.

Oral Assessment

To assess the speaking activities in this section, you might use the following rubric. For additional speaking rubrics, see the Alternative Assessment section of the *Assessment Program*.

Speaking Rubric	4	3	2	1
Content (Complete—Incomplete)				
Comprehension (Total—Little)				
Comprehensibility (Comprehensible—Incomprehensible)				
Accuracy (Accurate—Seldom Accurate)				
Fluency (Fluent—Not Fluent)				

18-20: A   16-17: B   14-15: C   12-13: D   Under 12: F

Prépare-toi pour l'examen

Grammar Review

For more practice with the grammar topics in this chapter, see the *Grammar Tutor*, the *Interactive Tutor*, or the *Cahier de vocabulaire et grammaire*.

Online Edition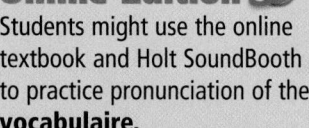

Students might use the online textbook and Holt SoundBooth to practice pronunciation of the **vocabulaire.**

Cultures

 **Products and Perspectives**

Charles Frederick Worth (1826–1895) is considered **"le père de la haute couture."** Born in England, Worth made his mark in the French fashion industry. He worked at several London drapery shops before moving to Paris in 1846. He was hired by Gagelin, a well-known Parisian draper, and opened his own **maison de couture** in 1858. The patronage of **Empress Eugénie** (1826–1920) ensured Worth's success as a popular dressmaker from the 1860s onward. Worth's former apprentice, Paul Poiret, opened his own fashion house in 1904. Following in Worth's and Poiret's footsteps were, among others, Patou, Vionnet, Chanel, Schiaparelli, Balenciaga, and Dior. Ask students who created and designed clothing before fashion houses were established? (anonymous seamstresses) How did people know what clothes were fashionable before the age of fashion designers? (High fashion was what was worn at the royal court.) 🍀 2.1, 2.2

Grammaire 1
- the future
- feminine form of nouns

Un peu plus
- the verb **conduire**
pp. 48–53

Résumé: Grammaire 1

To form the future of **-er** and **-ir** verbs, add the future endings to the infinitive. For **-re** verbs, first drop the **-e** from the infinitive and then add the future endings: **-ai, -as, -a, -ons, -ez, -ont.** Verbs like **appeler** or **jeter** that have spelling changes in the present also have the same spelling changes in the future. Some verbs have irregular future stems:

avoir → **aur-**	être → **ser-**	pouvoir → **pourr-**
aller → **ir-**	faire → **fer-**	vouloir → **voudr-**

Form most **feminine nouns** by adding an -e to the masculine noun. Some nouns have masculine endings and must be changed to a feminine ending.

-ien → -ienne   -eur → -euse   -teur → -trice   -er → -ère   -ier → -ière

Some nouns have one form that can take either masculine or feminine articles (**un/une vétérinaire**). Some nouns are masculine whether they refer to a man or a woman (**un plombier**).

The verb **conduire** is irregular: **je conduis, tu conduis, il/elle/on conduit, nous conduisons, vous conduisez, ils/elles conduisent.** Past participle is **conduit.**

Grammaire 2
- the future perfect
- the present participle

Un peu plus
- the **conditionnel de politesse**
pp. 60–65

Résumé: Grammaire 2

To indicate that one future action will happen before another future action, use the future perfect (**futur antérieur**). To form the future perfect, use **avoir** or **être** in the future and add the past participle of the main verb.

precedes

Quand tu **arriveras,** nous **serons partis.**

To form the **present participle,** remove the **-ons** from the **nous** form and add the ending **-ant.**
Few verbs have irregular present participles:

être → **étant**   avoir → **ayant**   savoir → **sachant**

Use **en** + **present participle** to say that someone *is doing something at the same time as something else* or to express *how or why something is done.* The **present participle** can be used without **en** to replace a relative clause or as an adjective.

The **conditional** can be used to make a statement more polite. To form the conditional, use the future stem and add the **imparfait** endings: **-ais, -ais, -ait, -ions, -iez, -aient.**

Chapter Review

Teacher Management System
Password: admin
For more details, log on to www.hrw.com/CDROMTUTOR.

Create a variety of puzzles to review chapter vocabulary.

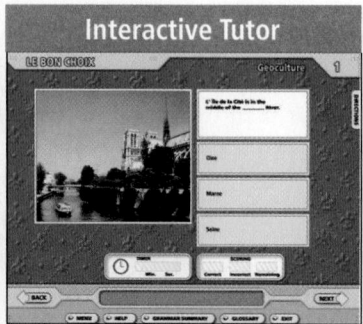

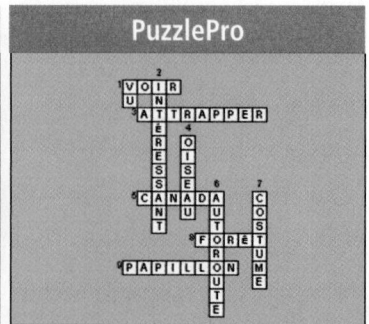

Résumé: Vocabulaire 1

HOLT SoundBooth ONLINE RECORDING

Professions

à l'étranger	abroad
un/une agriculteur(-trice)	farmer
un/une architecte	architect
un/une artiste	artist
un auteur	author
un/une avocat(e)	lawyer
un/une chanteur(-euse)	singer
un chauffeur	driver
un/une coiffeur(-euse)	hair dresser
un/une comptable	accountant
un/une couturier(-ière)	fashion designer
un/une cuisinier(-ière)	cook
un/une décorateur(-trice)	interior designer
un diplôme	degree
faire des études (f.)	to study (university level)
faire livrer/garder	to have . . . delivered/watched
un/une étudiant(e)	student
un/une fermier(-ière)	farmer
un/une informaticien(ne)	programmer
un ingénieur	engineer
un/une interprète	interpreter
un/une journaliste	journalist

un/une juge	judge
un/une libraire	book seller
un/une marchand(e)	salesman
un/une mécanicien(ne)	mechanic
un métier/une profession	job/profession
un/une moniteur(-trice)	instructor
un médecin	doctor
un/une musicien(ne)	musician
un/une pâtissier(-ière)	baker
un plombier	plumber
réparer	to fix
un/une serveur(-euse)	waiter/waitress
soigner	to care for
un/une teinturier(-ière)	dry cleaner
un/une traducteur(-trice)	translator
un/une tuteur(-trice)	tutor
un/une vendeur(-euse)	salesperson
un/une vétérinaire	veterinarian

To ask about future plans
and respond... .... See p. 45

To make polite requests .... See p. 47

Résumé: Vocabulaire 2

A phone conversation

un afficheur	caller ID
Âllo.	Hello.
avoir de l'expérience	to have experience
une (petite) annonce	ad
appeler/répondre	to call/answer
un apprentissage/un stage	apprenticeship/internship
l'architecture (f.)	architecture
un cabinet	office
le combiné	receiver
débutant(e)	beginner
diriger	to lead/to be in charge of
une durée de	a duration of
décrocher/raccrocher	to pick up/hang up the phone
un emploi	job
un entretien/une entrevue	interview
être au chômage	to be unemployed

être engagé(e)/licencié(e)	to be hired/laid off
un/une étudiant(e)	student
gagner de l'argent	to earn money
des heures supplémentaires	overtime
obtenir	to get
un salaire	salary
sans fil	cordless
le/la secrétaire	secretary
la société	company
la sonnerie	ringing
transférer l'appel/passer	to transfer the call/to transfer
un travail à temps plein/ partiel	full time/part time job

To make a phone call
and respond .... See p. 57

To write a formal letter .... See p. 59

Prépare-toi pour l'examen

Prépare-toi pour l'examen

Game

Mots croisés Each student will need two sheets of graph paper to create a crossword puzzle with the chapter vocabulary for a classmate to solve. Students should fit about fifteen vocabulary words into the grid, going across and down. The words should be numbered and a clue is given in French, such as a definition, equivalent word, or fill-in-the-blank sentence. Students will reproduce the puzzle on the other sheet of graph paper with just the numbers, blank squares, and clues. Partners then exchange and solve the puzzles. 1.1

Online Edition

Transparency: Vocabulaire

Transparency: Situation

Assess

Assessment Program

Examen: Chapitre 2

Audio CD 2, Trs. 13–14

Examen oral: Chapitre 2

Alternative Assessment

Differentiated Practice and Assessment CD-ROM

Online Assessment

my.hrw.com

Test Generator

Resources

Planning:

Lesson Planner

 One-Stop Planner

Practice:

Cahier de vocabulaire et grammaire

Cahier d'activités

Differentiated Practice and Assessment CD-ROM

 Teaching Transparencies Picture Sequences, Chapter 2

 Audio CD 2, Tr. 9

VIDEO OPTIONS

▶ **Télé-culture: Interviews**

The AP French Language Exam

Activités préparatoires provide students with activities similar to those found in the Advanced Placement French Language exam. The activities are based on material taught up to and including this chapter and concentrate on the chapter grammar and vocabulary. In the Teacher's Edition you will find test-taking strategies, as well as strategies for succeeding in the four skills. Students who plan on taking the exam should already have a good grasp of French vocabulary and grammar. They also should possess adequate competence in listening, reading, writing, and speaking.

Reading Strategy

Key Words You might tell students to underline or highlight key words as they read. This may help them to find information more quickly when they are answering the questions about the text.

Listening Script

See script on p. 41F.

Activités préparatoires

SECTION I

 Listening CD 2, Tr. 9 🌸1.2

Listen to the dialogues and choose the most appropriate response.

1. A. Oui, je serai avocat.
  B. Oui, je fais nettoyer mes vêtements.
  C. Oui, je suis moniteur au club de tennis des Cèdres.
  D. Oui, je compte être vétérinaire.

2. A. Et, si tu cherchais un boulot à mi-temps?
  B. Aucune idée.
  C. Tu n'as qu'à faire réparer ta voiture.
  D. Tu devrais te reposer.

Reading 🌸1.2

Read the following paragraph and answer the questions that follow.

> 1 «Un génie». Tel est le mot le plus souvent associé au nom de Blaise Pascal. C'était un génie qui a marqué l'histoire de la science, en particulier
> 5 par sa grande rigueur d'analyse et son sens de l'expérience. Il est mort à l'âge de 39 ans. En 1642, il entreprend de développer une machine à calculer
> afin d'aider son père dans son travail
> 10 de comptabilité fiscale. Il n'a alors que 19 ans. Destinée au calcul abstrait et financier, la «Pascaline» additionne, soustrait, multiplie et divise, grâce à un système composé de six roues à
> 15 dix dents.

1. En 1642, Pascal...
  A. avait vingt-huit ans.
  B. est mort.
  C. est né.
  D. a développé une machine à calculer.

2. Pascal est mort...
  A. très jeune.
  B. très vieux.
  C. en 1642.
  D. à l'âge de 39 ans.

3. Le père de Pascal était...
  A. un génie.
  B. dentiste.
  C. homme de sciences.
  D. homme d'affaires.

4. Le meilleur mot pour décrire Pascal est...
  A. Pascaline.
  B. un génie.
  C. prématurée.
  D. fiscal.

5. Pascal a marqué...
  A. la science.
  B. son père.
  C. ses parents.
  D. la comptabilité.

Preparing for the Exam

ADDITIONAL PRACTICE

Have students challenge one another to give the future tense of various verbs. Students may try to trick one another by choosing verbs that they know are irregular. This will give them additional practice with the irregular future stems.

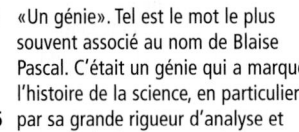 🌸1.1

TEST-TAKING STRATEGIES

Section I: Listening You might remind students to pay attention to the speakers' tone of voice. They may be able to glean information about the speakers' attitudes.

Section II: Writing When students are required to determine the correct verb tense to use in paragraph fill-ins, tell them to underline or highlight any words or phrases that indicate time. These are clues to help them decide which tense is required.

The following activities can be used to help you to prepare for the Advanced Placement French Language examination, or to further practice the vocabulary and grammar concepts you have seen in this chapter.

SECTION II

Writing ❀1.2

In the following paragraph, some verbs have been omitted. Complete each sentence by writing the correct form and tense of the verb, based on context.

Mes amis et moi, nous ____1____ tous nos propres centres d'intérêt et talents. Nous ____2____ tous un métier différent. Moi, je n' ____3____ pas encore _____.

Mon amie Romane, quand elle ____4____ le lycée, elle ____5____ à l'université pour devenir interprète. Elle ____6____ travailler à New York, à l'ONU.

Ahmed ____7____ travailler comme mécanicien. Il ____8____ les voitures.

1. avons___ (avoir)
2. ferons___ (faire)
3. ai décidé (décider)
4. aura fini (finir)
5. ira___ (aller)
6. voudrait (vouloir)
7. aimerait (aimer)
8. réparera (réparer)

Essay Topic ❀1.3

Write in French a well-organized and coherent composition of substantial length (at least 10 to 15 sentences) on the following topic.

À votre avis, est-ce que les adolescents devraient travailler à temps partiel pendant l'année scolaire? Expliquez pourquoi ou pourquoi pas.

Speaking ❀1.2

Look at the following picture, then tell a story about what is occurring in the picture.

Activités préparatoires

Writing Strategy

Tell students to be sure that their introductory paragraph contains a thesis statement, and that each paragraph further develops this thesis. They also need a concluding paragraph that summarizes or restates the thesis. Additionally, each individual paragraph should have a clear beginning (topic sentence), middle, and end.

Language Examination

To display the drawing to the class, use the **Activités préparatoires** Transparency for Chapter 2.

Speaking: Sample answer

Le garçon voudrait faire un stage chez le vétérinaire. Il va avoir un entretien avec lui. La salle où il attend est très propre. Quand le garçon entre dans le bureau du vétérinaire, il y a des animaux partout!

You may also want to ask students the following.

Tu penses que le vétérinaire est un homme gentil? Pourquoi? Pourquoi pas?

Connections

Math Link

Blaise Pascal (1623–1662) was a French mathematician and philosopher. In 1645, he constructed a mechanical currency calculator, called Pascal's calculator or the Pascaline. Because it was a decimal machine and the French currency system at that time was not decimal, additional calculations were necessary. Ask students to research the basic mechanism of the Pascaline and to explain their findings. ❀3.1

Differentiated Instruction

SLOWER PACE LEARNERS

Many scientific terms are cognates and loan words. Ask students to skim the paragraph for words they recognize from English. Have students underline these words before they read the paragraph for comprehension. ❀1.2, 4.1

MULTIPLE INTELLIGENCES

Visual Prior to asking students to complete the speaking activity, prepare several other visual story prompts for students to use. You may allow students to draw prompts for one another or select appropriate cartoons from the newspaper. Remove the inserted words or captions and use cartoons as additional visuals for the impromptu speaking activity. ❀1.3

Révisions cumulatives

VIDEO OPTIONS

▶ **Géoculture**

▶ **Télé-roman: Camille et compagnie, Épisode 2**

❶ Script

1. Il est teinturier. Il lave et repasse les vêtements des gens.

2. Ils adorent préparer de bons plats. Ils travaillent dans un restaurant.

3. C'est un bon comptable. Il travaille pour une grande société.

4. Il aime soigner les animaux.

5. Il travaille dans sa ferme et vend ses légumes.

❷ Answers

1. Alice Perrin

2. 03 56 25 87 91

3. assez bien

4. à Mme Gardé ou à M. Blanc

5. Elle a travaillé comme secrétaire.

Révisions cumulatives

1. Albin 2. Léa et Albert
3. Joseph 4. Martin
5. Éric

CD 2, Tr. 10

  ❶ Écoute ces phrases et dis de qui on parle. 1.2

1. Éric 2. Martin 3. Joseph 4. Léa et Albert 5. Albin

❷ Lis ce curriculum vitæ et répond aux questions suivantes. 3.2

Curriculum Vitæ

État civil :
Nom : Alice Perrin
Née le : 28 octobre 1985 à Paris
Adresse : 46, rue des Templiers
59850 NIEPPE
Téléphone : 03 56 25 87 91
E-mail : aperrin@hrw.com
Nationalité : française

Diplômes :
Diplôme de comptabilité de l'Université de Lille

Expérience professionnelle :
Bureau d'Éducation : a travaillé comme secrétaire, répondu au téléphone, aidé les étudiants et classé des documents.

Références :
Mme Gardé, Bureau d'Éducation
tél : 03 43 70 30 27
M. Blanc, Professeur de comptabilité
tél : 03 12 51 00 42

Connaissances linguistiques :
Français : parlé, lu et écrit
Anglais : parlé, lu et écrit
Espagnol : assez bon (niveau scolaire)

1. Qui cherche un emploi?

2. Quel est son numéro de téléphone?

3. Est-ce qu'elle parle bien espagnol?

4. Pour des renseignements sur Alice, à qui peut-on téléphoner?

5. Qu'est-ce qu'elle a fait pour le Bureau d'Éducation?

Online Culture Project

Tell students to pretend they work for an international job agency. They create a newsletter with job listings in France. Students may work in groups to researc, five prospective French companies on the Internet, noting their specialty field, location, work regulations, and salary (at the current exchange rate with the U.S. dollar). The newsletter should be two pages long and should include an introduction, in addition to the job listings and relevant company information, such as phone numbers and Web site address. 2.2

3 Tu téléphones à un(e) ami(e). C'est son père qui répond. Tu demandes à parler à ton ami(e), mais il/elle n'est pas là. Tu laisses un message. Avec un(e) camarade, jouez cette scène. ✿1.1

4 Regarde ce tableau de Fernand Léger et réponds aux questions qui suivent. ✿2.2, 1.3

1. Qu'est-ce que ces gens font? Est-ce que tu aimerais faire ce métier? Pourquoi ou pourquoi pas?

2. Est-ce que les gens qui font ce métier dans ton état sont habillés comme ceux que tu vois sur ce tableau?

3. Est-ce que c'est un tableau moderne, à ton avis? Pourquoi ou pourquoi pas?

4. Est-ce que tu aimes les couleurs de ce tableau? Est-ce que le choix des couleurs te semble réaliste? Qu'est-ce que cela apporte au tableau?

Léger, Fernand; Les Constructeurs, 1950. ©Art Resource, New York

Les constructeurs de Fernand Léger

5 Écris ton curriculum vitæ. Donne tous les renseignements qui donneraient envie au directeur de t'engager. ✿1.3

6 À ton tour

La Journée des Professions Ton lycée organise une Journée des Professions pendant laquelle des gens viennent parler de leur profession et les jeunes peuvent leur poser des questions. Un groupe d'élèves joue le rôle de ces professionnels et l'autre groupe leur pose des questions sur leur métier. ✿1.1

Révisions cumulatives

FINE ART CONNECTION

Introduction This painting titled *Les constructeurs,* is by Fernand Léger (1881–1955) whose early works were influenced by Impressionism. From 1911–1914, his works were inspired by Cubism. They became increasingly abstract and are dominated by mostly cylindrical forms and the primary colors, as well as black and white. After World War I, in which Léger fought and almost died, his "mechanical" period evolved. Figures and objects are characterized by tubular, machine-like forms. The relations of geo-metric forms and mechanical elements – cranks, pistons, cogs, and robots – were an important part of his creative vision. Léger lived in the United States during World War II. After his return to France in 1945 until his death in 1955, his work became less abstract. He often portrayed scenes of popular life, such as acrobats and divers. In this period, figures retain their robot-like shapes, but are painted in black lines with bold colors filling in the outlined areas.

Analyzing

To help students discuss the painting, you might ask them the following.

Pendant laquelle de ses périodes est-ce que Léger a peint *Les constructeurs*? Explique ta réponse.
✿3.1

Extension

Léger said, "I organize the opposition between colors, lines, and curves. I set curves against straight lines, patches of color against plastic forms, pure colors against subtly nuanced shades of gray." Ask students how Léger realizes this creative directive in *Les constructeurs*. ✿2.2, 3.1

ACTFL Performance Standards

The activities in Chapter 2 target the communicative modes as described in the Standards.

Interpersonal	Two-way communication using receptive skills and productive skills	**Communication (SE)**, pp. 47, 49, 51, 53, 61, 63, 65 **Communication (TE)**, pp. 49, 53, 61, 63, 65 **À ton tour**, p. 79
Interpretive	One-way communication using receptive skills	**Culture**, pp. 54–55 **Lecture**, pp. 66–69
Presentational	One-way communication using productive skills	**Communication (SE)**, pp. 51, 59, 73, 77 **Communication (TE)**, pp. 47, 51, 59

Resources

Practice:

Reading Strategies and Skills Handbook

Advanced Reader

Applying the Strategies

You may want to use the "Anticipation Guide" strategy from the *Reading Strategies and Skills Handbook* to encourage students to examine the text more closely.

READING PRACTICE

Strategy: Anticipation Guide

Reading Skill	When can I use this strategy?		
	Prereading	During Reading	Postreading
Making Predictions	✓		
Using Prior Knowledge	✓		
Analyzing Cause and Effect Relationships		✓	
Analyzing Persuasive Techniques			✓
Making Generalizations			✓

Strategy at a Glance: Anticipation Guide

- The teacher writes the Anticipation Guide, a set of generalizations based on issues in the text and designed to promote discussion and predictions about the selection.
- Students mark whether they agree or disagree with each statement, then discuss their responses.
- While students read, they take notes on the issues in the guide as those issues are revealed in the text.
- After reading, students look at their responses again to see whether they still agree or disagree with the statements.

Both younger and older children do it. They constantly ask what's going on and where they are being taken. They ask what the doctor is going to do before the doctor does it, and they plan what they'll say when they are approaching parents with special requests. Adults do it. We pick up travel brochures before we travel, study maps before we make a car trip, and check out the checkbook before we make a purchase. We all do it—we try to anticipate what's going to happen before it actually happens.

Good readers consciously try to anticipate what a text is about before they begin reading. They look at the cover, art, title, genre, author, headings, graphs, charts, length, print size, inside flaps, and back cover. Some students read the bibliographic information on the copyright page. They ask friends, "Is this any good?" They do anything to find out something about a text before they begin reading.

Struggling readers, on the other hand, often don't do that; they are told to read something, and once the text is in hand, they just begin. They often skip titles and background information, hardly ever read book jackets, and rarely look through the text.

Prereading

To prepare for the **Chroniques** selections, ask volunteers to research this information about labor in the U.S.: average number of hours per work week, days of paid vacation per year, retirement age, and legal minimum wage. Have students bring their findings to class and list them on one side of a 2-column table on the board. Then ask students to scan page 80 to find the same information for France. Write it in the second column and ask students to compare the numbers. ✿3.1

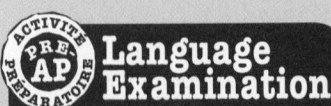

Language Examination

The **Chroniques** section helps students prepare for Section I, Part B: **Reading Comprehension.**

Travailler pour vivre

ou **vivre** pour travailler?

En France, le travail n'est pas considéré comme la chose la plus importante au monde. Beaucoup de Français travaillent seulement parce qu'il faut gagner sa vie[1].

Les loisirs et la vie de famille

En France, on aime souvent mieux gagner moins d'argent et avoir plus de temps libre pour être avec sa famille et ses amis.

Le temps de travail obligatoire est de 35 heures par semaine et les Français ont 5 semaines de congés payés par an. Pour obtenir une retraite complète, il faut avoir travaillé pendant 40 ans. Mais les Français peuvent choisir de prendre leur retraite[2] à 60 ans, ou même de partir en préretraite à 55 ans.

La protection sociale

La France est réputée pour son système de protection sociale. Tout d'abord, il existe un salaire minimum: le SMIC, ou «salaire minimum interprofessionnel de croissance». En 2005, il était de 8,03€ de l'heure.

Ensuite, il y a la Sécurité Sociale, le système français de protection sociale. C'est la Sécurité Sociale qui paie les retraites, l'assurance-maladie et la formation professionnelle. La Sécurité Sociale aide aussi les chômeurs pendant qu'ils cherchent du travail et les familles avant même la naissance de leur enfant.

Tous ces avantages sociaux expliquent les impôts élevés que les Français sont obligés de payer.

---

1. to make a living   2. retirement

Core Instruction

TEACHING CHRONIQUES

1. Ask students to rank the importance of the following when considering a career or job: salary, hours/work schedule, medical insurance, paid vacation. Make a list on the board in the order of importance. **(3 min.)**

2. Have students read the introduction and the first two sections and then answer questions 1 and 2 in **Après la lecture.** Then ask students if they think French people would rank the criteria listed on the board in the same order they did. **(10 min.)**

3. Have students read the last two sections and answer questions 3 and 4 in **Après la lecture. (7 min.)**

Les jobs d'été

En France, les élèves des lycées ne peuvent pas travailler toute l'année pendant qu'ils vont en classe, comme ils le font aux États-Unis. Ils ont seulement le droit de travailler pendant leurs vacances d'été. Il y a beaucoup de chômage en France et les emplois pour les jeunes sont rares et limités (babysitter, moniteur de colonie de vacances, etc.); beaucoup d'employeurs préfèrent faire travailler des jeunes qui sont majeurs[1]. S'ils ont entre 14 et 16 ans, ils doivent obtenir une autorisation officielle de l'Inspection du Travail en plus de la permission de leurs parents et ils n'ont pas le droit de travailler le soir après 20h. Quand ils ont entre 16 et 18 ans, la permission de leurs parents est suffisante mais ils n'ont toujours pas le droit de travailler la nuit après 22h, ni de faire des travaux dangereux.

Les stages en entreprise

Certaines entreprises[2] offrent des stages aux lycéens et aux étudiants pendant les vacances d'été. C'est souvent leur première expérience professionnelle; malheureusement, ces stages ne sont pas toujours rémunérés[3].

Mais c'est l'occasion pour les jeunes de découvrir l'univers de l'entreprise et le monde du travail.

Parfois, ces stages créent des vocations, pour d'autres, cela confirme le choix déjà fait, et pour d'autres encore, ces stages conduisent à des réorientations suite à une expérience décevante[4]. Suite à un stage, certains jeunes qui avaient décidé d'arrêter leurs études choisissent parfois de les continuer pour obtenir un emploi plus satisfaisant.

APRÈS la lecture

🎴1.3, 4.2

1. Dans votre pays, est-ce qu'on travaille plus ou moins qu'en France? Expliquez.

2. Qu'est-ce qui est plus important pour vous, avoir beaucoup d'argent ou du temps libre? Pourquoi?

3. À quel âge est-ce qu'on peut commencer à travailler aux États-Unis?

4. Quels sont les avantages des stages?

---

1. adults, of age   2. companies   3. remunerated, paid   4. disappointing

Answers

1. Answers will vary.
2. Answers will vary.
3. Answers will vary.
4. faire découvrir le monde du travail, créer des vocations, confirmer des choix, se réorienter

Connections

Social Studies Link

In France, the concept of paid vacation appeared in 1936. The **Front populaire,** the alliance of left-wing political parties that was in power at the time, enacted the first law mandating two weeks of paid vacation per year for workers, as a result of **les accords de Matignon** (also known as the "Magna Carta of French labor"). Have students use the Internet or a French encyclopedia to find out more about these agreements and the **Front populaire** government. Have them report their findings to the class. 🎴3.1

Postreading

Ask students how common they think it is for American students to have part-time jobs. Have them list jobs they would typically associate with student work. Ask them if they think it is a good idea to work part-time while going to school, and discuss the pros and cons as a class.

Recherches

Assign the following work-related acronyms to pairs or small groups (one to two acronyms per pair or group). Have them use the Internet to research what each one stands for and to find a short description of what it is. **CDI, CDD, PARE, ANPE, ASSEDIC, RMI, RTT.** Have volunteers present their findings in class. Remind students to document their sources. 🎴5.1

Differentiated Instruction

SLOWER PACE LEARNERS

To help slower pace students answer question 4, you might want to read aloud some of the key statements in the last section, for example, **malheureusement, ces stages ne sont pas toujours rémunérés.** Then ask students whether it is **un avantage** or **un inconvénient.** 🎴1.2

MULTIPLE INTELLIGENCES

Intrapersonal Have students imagine what it would be like to do an internship. Have them think about the kind of internship and/or company that would interest them and why. Ask if they would consider an internship in a French company, or even in a French-speaking country. Finally, ask them to describe the benefits of completing such an internship and the impact it might have on their future life and career. 🎴5.1

Resources

Practice:

Reading Strategies and Skills
  Handbook

Advanced Reader

Applying the Strategies

You may want to use the "Think Aloud" strategy from the *Reading Strategies and Skills Handbook* to encourage students to examine the text more closely.

READING PRACTICE

Strategy: Think Aloud

Reading Skill	When can I use this strategy?		
	Prereading	During Reading	Postreading
Monitoring Reading		✓	

Strategy at a Glance: Think Aloud

- The teacher models the **Think Aloud** strategy for students, letting them tally the types of comments the teacher makes (predicting, picturing the text, comparing, commenting, identifying a problem, or fixing a problem) on the **Think Aloud** tally sheet.
- Students practice the strategy with a partner using short and easy texts before using **Think Aloud** with their assignments.
- Students regularly practice the strategy, eventually using it on their own as needed.

Many times students do what they call reading: their eyes travel over the words from left to right and from top to bottom, and they turn pages at the appropriate time. What they don't do is pay any attention to what those words mean. That is where a strategy like **Think Aloud** can help.

The **Think Aloud** strategy helps readers think about how they make meaning. As they read, they carry on a dialog with the text. This is something that good readers do constantly as they read, although they usually do it silently. **Think Aloud** provides a structure for struggling readers to have a dialog with a text; they learn to think about their reading and to monitor what they do and do not understand. As you monitor the comments students make while using **Think Aloud**, you will see that the student is actively engaged with the text. As they do it more often, they will learn to do it silently—and that is the goal of the strategy.

Best Use of the Strategy

Use the **Think Aloud** (Davey 1983; Olshavsky 1976-77) to help readers think about how they make meaning. As students read, they pause occasionally to think aloud about predicting what happens next, commenting on the text, picturing the text, making comparisons, identifying problems they are encountering with understanding, and planning of ways to fix the problems they identify. This oral thinking not only helps the teacher understand why or how a

Prereading

Before you begin this **Chroniques** section, ask students to list five things they associate with French schools and the French school system, such as **le collège, le bac, les interros,** etc. Collect the lists and form several teams. Play a game of *Jeopardy* with clues you make up based on the information you collected from the students. For example, to elicit **le collège,** say: **L'école où on va avant le lycée.** The student who correctly guesses wins a point for his/her team. (**Qu'est-ce que c'est, le collège?**) 🍀 1.2

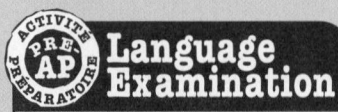

Language Examination

The **Chroniques** section helps students prepare for Section I, Part B: **Reading Comprehension.**

CHRONIQUES

Le système scolaire *français*

En France, l'école est obligatoire[1] de six à seize ans et elle est gratuite sauf dans les écoles privées.

Dans les écoles françaises, il n'y a pas de *graduation*, pas de *prom*, pas de *homecoming*, ni de *cheerleaders*. Par contre, il y a d'autres activités telles que les voyages de fin d'année ou des classes de neige ou de mer.

L'enseignement secondaire

L'enseignement secondaire en France consiste en quatre années de collège et trois années de lycée. Au collège et au lycée, une classe compte de 20 à 30 élèves qui suivent tous les mêmes cours ensemble, à l'exception de quelques options (art, sport, 3ème langue vivante). On entre au collège vers l'âge de onze ans. À la fin de la 5ème deux formes d'enseignement sont offertes: un enseignement général ou un enseignement technique selon les capacités et souhaits des élèves. S'orienter vers un enseignement technique, ne signifie pas nécessairement que l'élève ne peut pas ensuite bénéficier d'un enseignement universitaire.

Le système de notation

Dans le système français, les notes sont sur 20, et il est suffisant d'avoir 10/20 pour réussir à un examen ou à une interrogation écrite[2]. Ce qui est important pour passer dans la classe supérieure ou pour avoir le baccalauréat, c'est la moyenne générale[3]. S'il est encore possible d'avoir un 20/20 en sixième, cela devient presque impossible en seconde, sauf pour certains quiz. 10/20 est l'équivalent d'un C, 13/20 d'un B et 16/20 d'un A.

Le bac

Le baccalauréat, ou bac, est un examen qui a lieu à la fin du mois de juin pour les élèves de terminale. Les épreuves[4] ont lieu sur plusieurs jours. Il y a des épreuves écrites et des épreuves orales. Chaque épreuve écrite dure environ 4 heures. L'examen se déroule dans un lycée d'enseignement public, autre que[5] le lycée fréquenté par les élèves. Les copies sont corrigées par des professeurs autres que les professeurs des élèves. Les copies sont anonymes. Les résultats sont affichés dans le lycée où l'élève a passé le Bac.

Un élève peut avoir son Bac avec:
- mention **Très bien et félicitations du jury** (au moins 18/20)
- mention **Très bien** (au moins 16/20)
- mention **Bien** (entre 14/20 et 16/20)
- mention **Assez bien** (entre 12/20 et 14/20)
- sans mention

Si les résultats ne sont pas suffisants mais supérieurs à 8, l'élève peut aller au «rattrapage[6]». C'est-à-dire qu'il peut repasser deux matières[7] à l'oral.

S'il échoue[8] il peut redoubler son année de terminale.

L'examen du baccalauréat ouvre les portes de l'université et des grandes écoles.

1. mandatory 2. quiz 3. Grade Point Average 4. exams 5. other than 6. make-up exam 7. subjects 8. fail

Core Instruction

TEACHING CHRONIQUES

1. Have students read the introduction and the first section then answer question 1 in **Après la lecture. (4 min.)**

2. Have partners use the visuals to complete question 2. **(4 min.)**

3. Have students read the section entitled **Le système de notation** and answer question 3. Then have students who said they would prefer the French grading system raise their hands. Ask for several volunteers to explain their choice. Do the same with students who chose the American grading system. **(7 min.)**

4. Have students read the section about **le bac** and answer question 4. Finally, ask them to make a list of the various schools and universities French students can attend after **le bac,** as they read the last section of **Chroniques. (10 min.)**

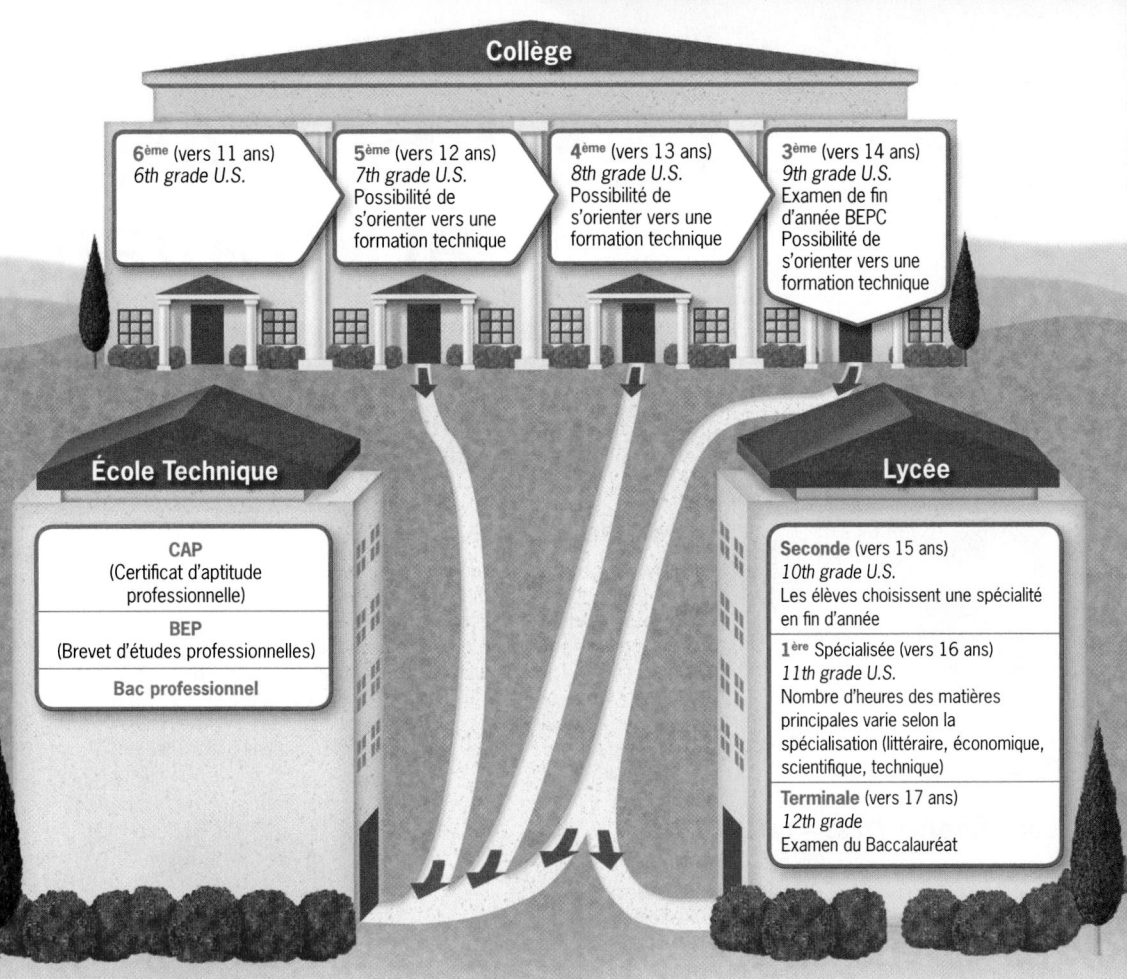

Collège

6ème (vers 11 ans)
6th grade U.S.

5ème (vers 12 ans)
7th grade U.S.
Possibilité de
s'orienter vers une
formation technique

4ème (vers 13 ans)
8th grade U.S.
Possibilité de
s'orienter vers une
formation technique

3ème (vers 14 ans)
9th grade U.S.
Examen de fin
d'année BEPC
Possibilité de
s'orienter vers une
formation technique

École Technique

CAP
(Certificat d'aptitude
professionnelle)

BEP
(Brevet d'études professionnelles)

Bac professionnel

Lycée

Seconde (vers 15 ans)
10th grade U.S.
Les élèves choisissent une spécialité
en fin d'année

1ère Spécialisée (vers 16 ans)
11th grade U.S.
Nombre d'heures des matières
principales varie selon la
spécialisation (littéraire, économique,
scientifique, technique)

Terminale (vers 17 ans)
12th grade
Examen du Baccalauréat

Après le bac

Les élèves qui ont leur bac ont plusieurs options. Si leurs notes au bac sont très bonnes et s'ils réussissent le concours d'entrée[1], il peuvent rentrer dans une grande école, comme polytechnique, HEC, Sciences Po, ENA[2]... Ils peuvent aussi entrer dans une école spécialisée, comme un école de commerce ou de journalisme. Une autre option est l'université. L'université est presque gratuite (les frais d'inscription sont d'environ 180€ par an) et offre beaucoup de choix.

Dans certains cas[3], les élèves qui avaient quitté le cursus[4] scolaire général au collège, peuvent quand même faire des études universitaires. Ils devront pour cela passer un bac professionnel.

1. competitive exam   2. high level school (polytechnique) is a military school, HEC (Haute Ecole de Commerce) is a business school, Science Po is a political/international relations school, ENA (École Nationale d'Administration) high level civil servant school, for diplomate for instance.
3. In some instances   4. school path

APRÈS ▶ la lecture

❀1.3

1. Quelles différences y a-t'il entre les écoles en France et les écoles aux États-Unis?

2. Fais un tableau de comparaison des classes françaises et américaines.

3. Aimerais-tu avoir le système de notes français dans ton lycée? Pourquoi ou pourquoi pas?

4. Est-ce que tu dois passer un examen spécial pour entrer à l'université?

LES FEMMES
au travail

Les femmes jouent un rôle important dans le monde du travail. En France, plus de 81% des femmes entre 25 et 50 ans ont un emploi.

Sylvie Guillem (1965 –)

Sylvie Guillem est née à Paris le 25 février 1965. Enfant, elle fait de la gymnastique de compétition. Puis, à 11 ans, elle découvre la danse classique et entre à l'école de danse de l'Opéra de Paris. À 16 ans, elle commence sa carrière de danseuse professionnelle à Paris. Elle gagne la médaille d'or[1] au Concours international de ballet à 18 ans. À 19 ans, elle devient la plus jeune danseuse étoile[2] de l'Opéra de Paris, après sa performance dans le célèbre ballet *Le Lac des Cygnes*[3]. Elle a aussi dansé au London Royal Ballet et à l'American Ballet Theater de New York.

Coco Chanel (1883 – 1971)

Couturière et styliste de mode à Paris, Coco Chanel a révolutionné la mode féminine. En effet, dans les années 1910, elle crée la mode «à la garçonne», c'est-à-dire une mode pour les femmes qui emprunte beaucoup d'éléments à la mode masculine, comme par exemple le pantalon et le costume. Elle invente aussi le concept du tailleur féminin, qui est encore aujourd'hui synonyme de la maison Chanel. Pour Coco Chanel, le confort est important et ses vêtements sont simples, élégants et classiques.

Gisèle Halimi (1927 –)

Avocate, écrivain et militante[4] pour les droits[5] de la femme, cette Tunisienne se bat[6] pour l'égalité de tous et pour les libertés fondamentales. Après des études de droit[7], elle devient avocate en 1948. C'est dans les années 1970 qu'elle commence surtout à s'intéresser à l'égalité entre les hommes et les femmes. Puis, elle devient ambassadrice de la France à l'UNESCO[8] et conseillère spéciale de la délégation française à l'Assemblée générale de l'ONU[9].

---

1. gold medal 2. prima ballerina 3. Swan Lake 4. activist 5. rights 6. fights 7. law 8. United Nations Educational, Scientific, and Cultural Organization 9. UN

Julie Payette (1963 –)

Après avoir fait des études pour être ingénieur électricienne et informatique et après avoir travaillé comme ingénieur pour plusieurs compagnies internationales, Julie Payette est entrée dans le programme spatial canadien en 1992. Elle a obtenu sa licence de pilote et elle est devenue la première astronaute canadienne à travailler à bord de la Station spatiale internationale.

Euzhan Palcy (1958 –)

Euzhan Palcy est une réalisatrice[1], cinéaste[2] et productrice de cinéma martiniquaise. Passionnée de cinéma depuis son enfance, elle a fait son premier film à l'âge de 17 ans. Parmi ses films les plus célèbres, il faut noter *Rue cases nègres*, un film qui a reçu 17 prix et pour lequel Euzhan Palcy a obtenu le César[3] de la Meilleure première œuvre[4], et *Une saison blanche et sèche*, avec Marlon Brando. Elle est ainsi devenue la première femme noire à avoir réalisé un film à Hollywood.

Assia Djébar (1936 –)

Assia Djébar est l'un des plus grands écrivains du Maghreb. Elle a obtenu de nombreux prix de littérature pour ses livres et elle est la première maghrébine élue à[5] l'Académie française[6]. Après des études en Algérie et en France, elle a habité au Maroc où elle a été professeur à l'université de Rabat. C'est là qu'elle a commencé sa carrière d'écrivain. Plus tard, elle a aussi fait du cinéma. Aujourd'hui, elle vit aussi aux États-Unis où elle est professeur au département d'études françaises de New York University.

APRÈS ▷ la lecture

⌗1.3, 4.2

1. Pourquoi est-ce qu'on appelle le style de Coco Chanel, la mode «à la garçonne»?

2. Pour quelles organisations est-ce que Gisèle Halimi a travaillé?

3. Pourquoi est-ce que Julie Payette est célèbre?

4. Qu'est-ce qu'Assia Djébar et Euzhan Palcy ont en commun?

5. Pourquoi est-ce que le film *Rue cases nègres* a été important pour Euzhan Palcy?

1. director   2. filmmaker   3. the French equivalent of an Oscar   4. work   5. elected to   6. prestigious French institute

Differentiated Instruction

SLOWER PACE LEARNERS

Once students have read all the portraits and each woman's accomplishments have been summarized on the board by volunteers, make statements that describe these women and ask slower pace learners to correctly identify each woman. **Elle a inventé un nouveau style de vêtements. (C'est Coco Chanel.)** If students are still having trouble, give them two to three options to choose from. (**C'est Coco Chanel, Euzhan Palcy ou Julie Payette?**)   ⌗1.2

MULTIPLE INTELLIGENCES

Mathematical/Logical According to the **Chroniques** introduction, a large percentage of French women work outside the home. Have students find out what percentage of women work outside the home in the U.S. and two to three other Francophone countries of your choice. In class, create a graph or chart to display these findings. Ask students to compare the numbers for the various countries and to try to think of reasons for the similarities and differences.   ⌗3.1, 4.2

Answers

1. Il emprunte des éléments à la mode masculine.
2. l'UNESCO, l'ONU
3. Elle est la première astronaute canadienne à travailler à bord de la Station spatiale internationale.
4. Elles font du cinéma.
5. Le film a obtenu 17 prix et un César.

Connection

Social Studies Link

Write the following quote by famous feminist French author Simone de Beauvoir on the board: **"C'est par le travail que la femme a en grande partie franchi la distance qui la séparait du mâle; c'est le travail qui peut seul lui garantir une liberté concrète."** (*Le Deuxième Sexe*, 1949). Explain any difficult words, then ask students whether they agree or disagree with the quote and discuss it as a class.   ⌗3.1

Postreading

Ask students to choose a person whose contributions to society they feel are important. They may select one of the people they came up with in the **Prereading** activity, or they may choose another person (i.e., a family member whose life and accomplishments they admire). Ask them to write a portrait of this person modeled on the portraits in the **Chroniques**. Encourage them to use the adjectives they thought of in the **Prereading** activity.
   ⌗1.3

Recherches

Have students use the Internet to find information about another Francophone woman whose contributions in her field are notable. Have volunteers present "their" woman in class. Remind students to document their sources.   ⌗2.2

Chroniques

Applying the Strategies

You may want to use the "Sketch to Stretch" strategy from the *Reading Strategies and Skills Handbook* to encourage students to examine the text more closely.

READING PRACTICE

Strategy: Sketch to Stretch

Reading Skill	When can I use this strategy?		
	Prereading	During Reading	Postreading
Drawing Conclusions			✓
Making Generalizations			✓
Analyzing Cause and Effect			✓
Summarizing			✓

Strategy at a Glance: Sketch to Stretch

• The teacher introduces **Sketch to Stretch** to students by showing and discussing symbolic pictures based on a text.

• After reading a selection, students work independently or with a partner to create their own symbolic sketches. On the back of the sketches, students write why they drew what they did, using evidence from the text to support their opinions.

• Students share their sketches in small groups, allowing others to comment before revealing explanations of their work.

Many students find it difficult to go beyond the reading selection to talk about the theme, or the symbolism, or to express a generalization about the story that can be applied to their lives. But some students who have difficulty talking about a text can express their ideas visually, far beyond what even they themselves imagine. This strategy, **Sketch to Stretch**, gives students the opportunity to formulate images that represent the ideas they cannot otherwise express. For some students, putting ideas into pictures, rather than words, is the best way to express their responses to the text.

This is a postreading strategy in which students think about what a passage or entire selection means to them and then draw symbolic representations of their interpretations of the text. As students discuss the text and decide what to draw, they think about the theme, draw conclusions, form generalizations, recognize cause-and-effect relationships, and summarize.

Prereading

Before you begin this **Chroniques** section, have students locate the four areas mentioned in the reading on a world map. Ask for volunteers to share what they already know about each area and the culture of its people. Or, form four groups and assign one area to each group before class. Ask them to research their assigned area on the Internet or at the library and then make a short presentation in class. 🏵2.2

Language Examination

The **Chroniques** section helps students prepare for Section I, Part B: **Reading Comprehension.**

L'artisanat[1] sans frontière

Les produits artisanaux qui nous viennent des pays francophones sont aussi variés que les cultures de ces pays.

En Polynésie française

Les coquillages[2] à coquilles de nacre[3] qu'on trouve dans la mer au large de la Polynésie française sont utilisés de deux façons. D'abord, ils produisent la célèbre perle de culture[4] de Tahiti, qui est la principale ressource de ces îles. Ensuite, les artisans utilisent également les coquilles de ces coquillages pour fabriquer des bijoux en nacre (boucles d'oreilles, bagues, bracelets, colliers) et des accessoires (boucles[5] de ceinture, porte-monnaie[6], etc.). Ces bijoux et objets en nacre sont parfois gravés[7] ou bien travaillés avec d'autres matériaux (bois, fibre de coco[8], corail, autres coquillages, etc.).

Au Viêtnam

La laque[9] est une vieille tradition de l'artisanat viêtnamien. Les artisans fabriquent de nombreux objets laqués: des boîtes, des bols, des plats, des vases et toutes sortes d'autres objets décoratifs.

La technique de la laque consiste à appliquer plusieurs couches[10] de laque sur des objets qui sont à l'origine souvent en bambou. Chaque objet reçoit ensuite une couche de vernis[11]. Il faut souvent plusieurs mois à un artisan pour finir un objet en laque parce que le temps de séchage[12] est très long.

1. crafts 2. seashells 3. shells made of mother-of-pearl 4. cultured pearl 5. belt buckles 6. coin purses 7. engraved 8. coconut fiber 9. lacquer 10. layers 11. varnish 12. drying time

Core Instruction

TEACHING CHRONIQUES

1. First, ask students to use their own words to try to define the expression "arts and crafts." You may wish to ask questions to help them. **Ce sont quels types d'objets? Qui crée ces objets? Est-ce que ces objets sont seulement décoratifs ou est-ce qu'ils servent à quelque chose? (5 min.)**

2. Write **Viêtnam, Côte d'Ivoire,** and **Maghreb** on the board. Ask students to look at the three photos on these pages and guess which one goes with each area. Have them give reasons to justify their answers. **(2 min.)**

3. Have students read the questions in **Après la lecture** first. Then ask them to read the text, individually or in pairs, to find the answers to these questions. **(15 min.)**

En Côte d'Ivoire

Les artisans[1] africains sont réputés pour leur travail du bois. Ils le sculptent pour créer des objets divers: des masques, des statuettes ou des objets de tous les jours.

Le masque africain est un objet sacré[2] qui est utilisé dans les cérémonies religieuses et traditionnelles. En Côte d'Ivoire, les Sénoufo (un peuple[3] du nord du pays) et les Baoulé (un peuple du centre et du sud-est du pays) sont réputés pour leurs masques. Les artisans africains produisent aussi beaucoup de statuettes en bois. Celles-ci sont aussi souvent utilisées pendant les cérémonies.

En ce qui concerne les objets de tous les jours, on trouve de magnifiques peignes[4], des outils de tissage[5], des plats, des instruments de musique, des jeux et des assises qui sont des tabourets[6] utilisés aussi pour certaines occasions spéciales, comme les mariages.

Au Maghreb

En général, les artisans du Maghreb vendent leurs produits dans des souks. Les souks sont des marchés qu'on trouve dans la médina (la vieille ville). Ils sont organisés par types de produits vendus: par exemple, le souk des épices, le souk des bijoux en or, etc. Dans les souks, tout le monde marchande[7].

Dans le souk des tapis[8], on peut trouver des tapis berbères magnifiques. Le terme «berbères» décrit les peuples qui parlent la langue berbère et qui vivent dans les pays du Maghreb (Maroc, Tunisie et Algérie) et dans quelques autres pays d'Afrique. Les tapis des artisans berbères sont très réputés. Ils sont faits avec de la laine de mouton et en général, ils sont blancs ou beiges avec des motifs[9] de couleurs chaudes.

Cultures

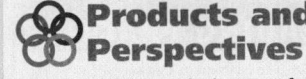

Products and Perspectives

Bring in additional photos of other traditional objects typical of the areas mentioned in the **Chroniques,** as well as of other parts of the Francophone world. Hold each one up and have students describe what they see in the picture. Have them venture guesses as to where these objects were made. Ask them to justify their answers by explaining how each one reflects the culture of the area it represents. ✿ 2.2

APRÈS la lecture

✿ 1.2

1. Quelles sont les deux choses qu'on trouve dans les coquillages de la Polynésie française?
2. Décris la technique utilisée dans le travail de la laque au Viêtnam.
3. Quand est-ce qu'on utilise les masques et les statuettes en Afrique?
4. Cite quatre types d'objets en bois que les artisans africains fabriquent.
5. Décris l'organisation des souks au Maghreb.
6. Comment sont les tapis berbères?

1. craftsmen 2. sacred 3. people 4. combs 5. weaving tools 6. stools 7. haggles 8. carpets 9. patterns

Postreading

Ask students if they have ever purchased a souvenir, a traditional product, or any type of handmade object. Ask what type of object or product it was, where they purchased it, who made it, what attracted them to it, etc. Allow students to bring an object to class to talk about it.

Recherches

Have students select a region of France they have a particular interest in and use the Internet to find information about the traditional products and the typical crafts of that region, such as olive oil products, lavender honey, or **santons** in **Provence.** Have volunteers present their findings in class. Remind students to document their sources.

✿ 2.2

Differentiated Instruction

ADVANCED LEARNERS

Form several small groups with at least one advanced student in each one. Have them interview a local craftsperson about his or her work, or have them research the work of a craftsperson who lives in your community. Each group should then put together a portrait of its craftsperson in French and present it to the class. ✿ 5.1

MULTIPLE INTELLIGENCES

Spatial/Visual You might ask volunteers who enjoy doing arts and crafts projects to bring in one of their creations and present it to their classmates, who will ask questions to find out more about the piece and the process used to create it. ✿ 1.3, 5.2

Resources

Practice:

Reading Strategies and Skills Handbook

Advanced Reader

Applying the Strategies

You may want to use the "Somebody Wanted But So" strategy from the *Reading Strategies and Skills Handbook* to encourage students to examine the text more closely.

READING PRACTICE

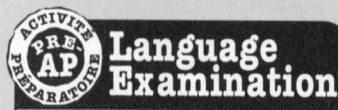

Strategy: Somebody Wanted But So

Reading Skill	When can I use this strategy?		
	Prereading	During Reading	Postreading
Analyzing Cause-and-Effect Relationships			✓
Summarizing			✓

Strategy at a Glance: Somebody Wanted But So

- After students read a story, they work alone or in groups to fill in columns on the **Somebody Wanted But So** chart: who the *someone* in the story is, what he or she *wanted*, *but* what happened that created a problem, and *so* how the problem was resolved.
- Students work together to condense **Somebody Wanted But So** statements into concise summaries or to develop summaries for longer texts.
- To focus on literary elements, students create **Somebody Wanted But So** statements for different characters in the same story or for different types of conflicts.

Summarizing a short story or a novel appears to be too overwhelming for many students who either offer nothing or restate everything in the story. **Somebody Wanted But So** offers students a framework to help them create that summaries. Students read a story and then decide who the *Somebody* is, what that somebody *Wanted*. *But* what happened to keep something from happening, and *So*, finally, how everything worked out.

Somebody Wanted But So also helps students move beyond summary writing. As students choose names for the *Somebody* column, they are deciding which characters are the main characters. In the *Wanted* column, they look at events of the plot and talk about main ideas and details. With the *But* column they are examining conflict. With the *So* column they are identifying the resolution.

Prereading

Before you begin this **Chroniques** section, ask students to suggest important and useful inventions while a volunteer writes them on the board. Then tell students to agree on the five most important inventions from the list. Finally, have them rank these inventions from most important to least important and give reasons for their choices.

Language Examination

The **Chroniques** section helps students prepare for Section I, Part B: **Reading Comprehension**.

CHRONIQUES

D'où vient le cinéma? l'avion? et même le Velcro? Si vous avez répondu «des États-Unis, bien sûr», vous allez être surpris!

Inventions

Louis Pasteur

Louis Pasteur (France, 1822–1895), scientifique français, a fait des recherches dans des domaines très variés mais est surtout connu pour ses découvertes médicales. La plus importante: les microbes provoquent des maladies. De là, il fallait trouver des moyens pour combattre les microbes, surtout dans les hôpitaux. Il a mis au point[1] des méthodes de stérilisation, connues aujourd'hui sous le nom de «pasteurisation». Il est difficile de croire que le milieu médical de l'époque s'est vivement opposé à ses conseils.

En 1879, Pasteur et ses collaborateurs ont découvert que les cultures de certains microbes ne déclenchaient[2] pas de maladie chez les animaux. De plus, ces animaux résistaient à de nouvelles infections. Il avait découvert le principe du vaccin! En 1885, il a réussi à sauver la vie d'un garçon mordu par un chien enragé[3]. En 1888, Pasteur a créé l'Institut Pasteur uniquement pour traiter la rage[4]. Ayant changé à jamais le monde de la médecine, il est resté à la tête de son Institut jusqu'à sa mort.

Louis Braille

Louis Braille (France, 1809–1852) a perdu la vue à l'âge de trois ans. À dix ans, il est rentré à l'école pour aveugles[5] fondée par Valentin Haüy, qui avait développé un système de caractères en relief qui était difficile à lire. Élève doué, Braille est devenu assistant dès l'âge de 15 ans et, plus tard, professeur. À cette époque, il a pris contact avec un monsieur Barbier, inventeur d'un système de lecture nocturne qui permettait aux soldats de lire des messages dans l'obscurité. Cela a inspiré Braille à créer le système actuel[6]: un alphabet tout comme celui des voyants, mais à une différence près: son alphabet était en points[7]. Braille, qui était doué en musique, a aussi créé un système de notation musicale ponctuée pour aveugles.

Clément Ader

Clément Ader (France, 1841–1925), ingénieur et inventeur, a consacré une grande partie de sa vie à la réalisation d'un rêve d'enfant: le vol aérien. Ses études sur le vol des oiseaux l'ont conduit à construire un planeur[8] en plumes d'oie. On ignore si Ader a réussi à voler avec ce planeur. Quoi qu'il en soit[9], il a convaincu le ministre de la Guerre de financer ses travaux, et a réalisé trois appareils entre 1890 et 1897. Le premier, l'Éole, avait un moteur à vapeur ultraléger; le deuxième, le Zéphyr, n'a pas été achevé mais a servi de base au troisième, l'Aquilon, qui était plus stable grâce à ses deux moteurs.

Le 14 octobre 1897, l'Aquilon a effectué un vol de 300 mètres devant un comité militaire. Mais, à cause du mauvais temps, l'appareil a été endommagé lors de son atterrissage. Le ministère de la Guerre a donc retiré son soutien[10], et Ader a dû arrêter la construction de ses prototypes. Contraint[11] au secret militaire, Ader n'a parlé de ses vols qu'en 1906. C'est à cause de son silence qu'est née la controverse: avait-il inventé l'avion avant les **frères Wright** dont le premier vol a eu lieu en 1903?

1. to implement 2. to trigger 3. rabid 4. rabies 5. blind 6. current 7. dots 8. glider 9. in any case 10. support 11. sworn

---

Core Instruction

TEACHING CHRONIQUES

1. Write the names of the inventors on the board. Ask students if they have heard of any of these people. If so, ask them to share what they know about them with the class. **(3 min.)**

2. Write the inventions (in an order different from that of the inventors' names) on the other side of the board. Ask students to try to associate each invention with its inventor(s). Then have them scan the text to see if they were correct in their guesses. **(5 min.)**

3. Finally, have students read the text more carefully and answer the questions in **Après la lecture. (20 min.)**

et découvertes

Les frères Lumière

Les frères Lumière (France : Louis, 1854–1946 / Auguste, 1862–1956) sont connus dans le monde entier pour avoir inventé le cinématoscope. Mais la vérité[1] est plus riche et plus compliquée. D'abord, c'est grâce à leur père que les frères ont appris l'existence du kinétoscope inventé par l'Américain Thomas Edison. Cet appareil destiné au visionnage individuel permettait de visionner[2] des films de quelques secondes. Edison n'avait pas pensé à faire projeter les films... alors les frères Lumière ont pris le relais[3].

Les frères Lumière se sont mis tout de suite à améliorer un appareil existant, le phonoscope. Ils ont créé une machine qui aurait pû marcher s'il n'y avait pas eu un problème d'entraînement de la pellicule[4]. Finalement, Louis a trouvé la solution: utiliser le même principe que les machines à coudre[5], et monter le tout sur une manivelle[6]. Ils ont réalisé des essais sur bandes de papier et ensuite sur celluloïd transparent. Le cinématographe était né! Le public a vu tourner le cinématographe pour la première fois en 1895: *Arrivée d'un train à la Ciotat* montrait une locomotive qui entrait en gare et tous les spectateurs ont eu peur et sont sortis de la salle en courant.

Georges de Mestral

Georges de Mestral (Suisse, 1907–1990) a inventé le Velcro® en s'inspirant de la nature. Un jour, il est revenu d'une promenade en montagne avec ses vêtements couverts de mauvaises herbes[7] très collantes. Il a examiné une de ces herbes au microscope et a distingué une multitude de fibres se terminant par de petits crochets, ce qui permettaient à ces plantes de s'accrocher solidement aux tissus. De là, il a eu l'idée d'un nouveau dispositif de fermeture.

En 1951, de Mestral a déposé une demande pour un brevet sur son nouveau produit, qu'il appelait «Velcro» (la combinaison des mots «velours»[8] et «crochet»[9]).

Zénobe Gramme

Zénobe Gramme (Belgique, 1826–1901), n'était pas un homme de science. C'était un technicien, un bricoleur[10] de génie. Menuisier[11] habile, il a été engagé chez deux entreprises faisant usage de l'électricité. Là, il

a observé des machines magnéto-électriques. Il a travaillé ensuite chez un constructeur d'instruments scientifiques. En 1868, il a construit la première dynamo à courant continu[12]. En 1873, un ami lui a montré que la dynamo était réversible: elle pouvait servir de moteur. C'était le point de départ de l'industrie électrique moderne. En 1881, Gramme aurait dit, «s'il m'avait fallu savoir tout cela, je ne l'aurais jamais inventée».

APRÈS la lecture

1. Quelles découvertes est-ce que Pasteur a faites?
2. Qui est-ce qui a inspiré Braille?
3. Comment s'appelait le premier appareil qui a volé? Quelle distance est-ce qu'il a parcouru?
4. Qu'est-ce que les frères Lumière ont inventé?
5. Comment est-ce que de Mestral a eu l'idée d'inventer le Velcro?

1. truth 2. to screen 3. to take up the idea 4. film 5. sewing machines 6. crank 7. weeds 8. velvet 9. hook 10. handyman 11. carpenter
12. direct current

Differentiated Instruction

SLOWER PACE LEARNERS

To keep slower pace students from feeling overwhelmed with this longer, more difficult text, call on advanced learners to identify and read aloud the sentence(s) or paragraph in the text that contain(s) the answer to each of the **Après la lecture** questions. Then have students give the correct answer to the question. ✿1.2

MULTIPLE INTELLIGENCES

Spatial/Visual You might ask students with artistic and/or conceptual abilities to make drawings, blue prints, or models of some of the inventions students came up with in the Postreading activity, and then present them to the class. ✿3.1

Teaching Suggestion

Form three groups and assign one of the following people to each group: Jacques Daguerre, René Laennec, the Montgolfier brothers. Have each group use the Internet or your library to research its inventor(s) and prepare a short presentation for the class. ✿3.1, 3.2

Postreading

Form small groups and ask them to come up with a useful invention in the field of their choice. Students should first brainstorm ideas for potential new products. Then they should consider the feasibility and usefulness of each one and select the best one. They should then come up with a detailed description of their invention and its application(s). You might give students time outside of class to prepare a presentation. ✿3.1

Recherches

The **Musée des Arts et Métiers,** founded by **l'abbé Grégoire** in 1794 in Paris, houses a huge collection of inventions and scientific instruments. Have students explore this museum by visiting its Web site. Ask them to select one invention they find particularly interesting and write a paragraph in French about it. ✿2.2

Géoculture Overview

L'Afrique francophone

Bienvenue! This section is designed to familiarize the students with the geographic location, history, and cultural practices of the region to be explored. It provides a guide for classroom discussion and discovery of the differences and similarities of the student's own culture and that of the French-speaking world.

Géoculture

50-Minute Lesson Plans

Day 1

Lesson Sequence
Géoculture:
L'Afrique francophone,
pp. 90–91
• Ask students to name African countries. What have they heard or read about Cameroon, Mali, Tunisia, Algeria, or Morocco? Would they like to visit any of these countries? Why or why not? **12 min.**
• Go over the photos and captions with the students. **10 min.**
• See Map Activities, p. 90. **5 min.**
• Discuss Background Information, p. 90. **9 min.**
• Complete **Géo-quiz**, p. 91. **1 min.**
• Show **Géoculture** video. **3 min.**
• Have students answer **Questions**, p. 91. **10 min.**

Optional Resources
• **Savais-tu que...?**, p. 91
• Multiple Intelligences, p. 89B
• Thinking Critically, p. 89B

Homework Suggestions
Online Practice (**go.hrw.com,**
  Keyword: BD3 CH3)
Interactive Tutor, Ch. 3
  ✿ 1.1, 1.3, 3.1

Day 2

Lesson Sequence
Géoculture:
L'Afrique francophone,
pp. 92–93
• Briefly revisit main points about geography. **5 min.**
• Go over the photos and captions with the students. **8 min.**
• Have students write down the dates mentioned in the captions and then ask students what happened or might have happened on these dates in North America. **7 min.**
• Have students answer **As-tu compris?** questions, p. 93. **5 min.**
• Do **Prépare-toi pour le quiz,** p. 89B. **25 min.**

Optional Resources
• Map Game, p. 89B
• Advanced Learners, p. 89B ▲
• Research Online!, p. 89B
• Interdisciplinary Links, pp. 92–93

Homework Suggestions
Activité, p. 93
Study for the **Géoculture** quiz.
  ✿ 1.1, 1.2, 1.3, 2.2, 3.1

90-Minute Lesson Plan

Block 1

Lesson Sequence
Géoculture:
L'Afrique francophone,
pp. 90–93
• Ask students to name African countries. What have they heard or read about Cameroon, Mali, Tunisia, Algeria, or Morocco? Have they visited or would they like to visit any of these countries? Why or why not? **10 min.**
• Go over the photos and captions with the students. **20 min.**
• See Map Activities, p. 90. **5 min.**
• Discuss Background Information, p. 90. **10 min.**
• Complete **Géo-quiz**, p. 91. **1 min.**
• Show **Géoculture** video. **4 min.**
• Have students answer **Questions**, p. 91. **5 min.**
• Have students answer **As-tu compris?** questions, p. 93. **5 min.**
• Write the dates mentioned in the captions on the board. Ask students what happened or might have happened on these dates in America. **5 min.**
• Do **Prépare-toi pour le quiz,** p. 89B. **25 min.**

Optional Resources
• **Savais-tu que ...?**, p. 91
• Advanced Learners, p. 89B ▲
• Multiple Intelligences, p. 89B
• Thinking Critically, p. 89B
• Research Online!, p. 89B
• Interdisciplinary Links, pp. 92–93
• Map Game, p. 89B

Homework Suggestions
Online Practice (**go.hrw.com,**
  Keyword: BD3 CH3)
Interactive Tutor, Ch. 3
Activité, p. 93
Study for the **Géoculture** quiz.
  ✿ 1.1, 1.2, 1.3, 2.2, 3.1

KEY

▲ **Advanced Learners**   ◆ **Slower Pace Learners**   ● **Special Learning Needs**

Differentiated Instruction

Advanced Learners

Extension Ask students to explore Islamic art and architecture in the **Maghreb.** Students should do their research in the library or on the Internet. They should report on features, styles, and types of buildings that are representative of Islamic art and architecture.

🌸 1.3, 2.2

Multiple Intelligences

Naturalist Ask students to compare life in an oasis in the Sahara, such as Tozeur, to life in a rain forest in Cameroon. Students should address the impact of the environment and the climate on the inhabitants. Would students prefer to live in an oasis or in a rain forest? Why?

🌸 1.3, 3.1

Thinking Critically

Analyzing In 1953, the search for new oilfields in the deserts of southern Libya led to the discovery of vast quantities of fresh water trapped in the underlying strata of the Sahara. In the Algerian and Tunisian parts of the Sahara, groundwater from aquifers has been tapped more and more intensively for over fifty years. Efforts to intensify tapping are continuing with over ninety percent of the water being used for agriculture. Students should analyze the impact unlimited access to water would have on the economy of North Africa and on the lives of its inhabitants.

🌸 1.3, 3.1

Quiz Preparation/Enrichment

Map Game

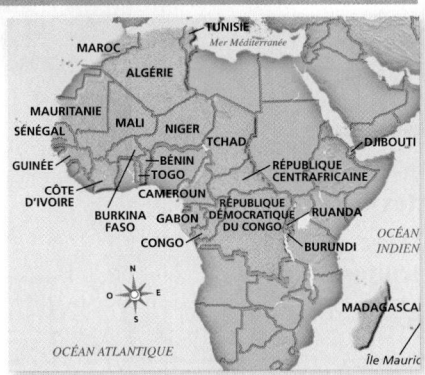

Divide the class into groups and have each group create a crossword puzzle, using the names of countries and geographical features on the map. The puzzles should have at least five columns and five rows. Names consisting of two or more words should be written without spaces between words. Clues are to be given in French. For example:

horizontal

1. pays en Afrique du nord (Maroc)

vertical

2. Cette république a été créée en 1972.

¹M	A	R	O	²C
				A
				M
				E
				R
				O
				U
				N

Students may create clues using the information provided on the map or in the **Géoculture** pages. Each group should solve the crossword puzzle created by another group. You may want to allow students to use crossword-puzzle-maker software.

Prépare-toi pour le quiz

1. Give students a map of Africa without labels, showing only the borders. Students should shade in and label the countries discussed in the **Géoculture** pages.

2. Have students indicate the location of the capital of each of the shaded countries and provide its name.

Research Online!

La Guerre d'Algérie Have students research **la Guerre d'Algérie** (1954–1962). They should draw a timeline of important events and write a brief chronology of the Algerian war of independence. Students should document their sources by noting the names and the URLs of all the sites they consulted. Have students present their chronologies to the class.

🌸 1.3, 3.1

Géoculture

Resources

Planning:
Lesson Planner
 One-Stop Planner

Presentation:
 Teaching Transparencies
Cartes 4, 6
DVD Program, Disc 1
Géoculture

Practice:
Cahier d'activités
Media Guide
 Interactive Tutor, Disc 1

Map
ACTIVITIES

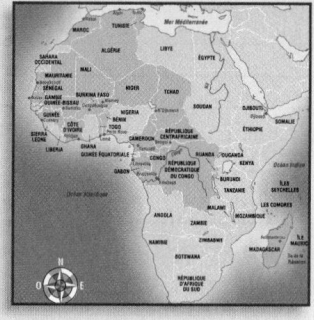

1. Have students find a map of Africa in French and locate: **la Tunisie, l'Algérie, le Maroc, le Mali,** and **le Cameroun.** Then have them locate and name each country's capital city. **(Tunis, Alger, Rabat, Bamako, Yaoundé)**
2. Have students find a map of Africa's land forms. Then have them locate the Sahara desert and the Atlas Mountains. Which countries do the Atlas Mountains cross? **(la Tunisie, l'Algérie, le Maroc)**
3. Ask students which of the countries is landlocked **(Mali).** Ask them how they think this affects Mali's economy. (It has to depend on its neighbor's infrastructure and political stability to get products to market.)

DVD
Géoculture

Géoculture
L'Afrique francophone

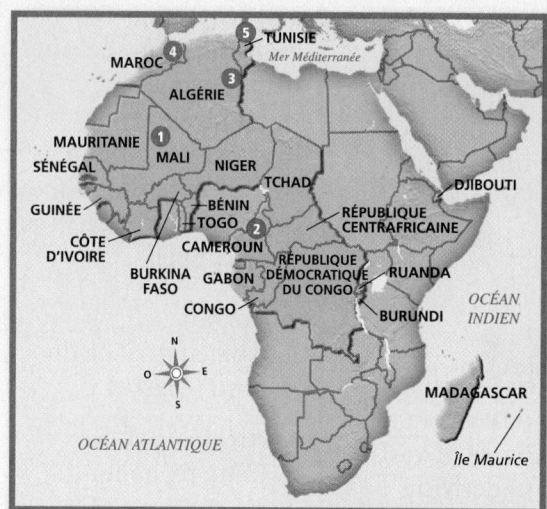

▲ **LE CAMEROUN: Le parc national de Korup** est une forêt tropicale très diversifiée. On y trouve de nombreuses espèces animales et végétales dont plusieurs plantes médicinales. ❷

▲ **LE MALI: Le pays Dogon** abrite une des plus anciennes populations d'Afrique. ❶

➤ **LE MALI: La grande mosquée de Djenné** est célèbre dans toute l'Afrique musulmane. Elle est construite en argile *(adobe).* ❶

Savais-tu que...?
Le Maroc, l'Algérie et la Tunisie forment une unité géographique, religieuse et culturelle qu'on appelle le Maghreb.

Background Information

Geography

Tunisia, Algeria, and Morocco are bordered by the Mediterranean to the north and the Sahara to the south. The Atlas Mountains cross these countries, creating a natural barrier against the expanding desert. Most people live along the coast, at desert oases or near petroleum or mineral deposits.

Mali, the largest country in West Africa, is almost twice the size of Texas. The Sahara extends over most of north Mali. The Niger River flows across the semi-arid south.

History

Tunisia's, Algeria's, and Morocco's original inhabitants were the Berbers. The Berbers are not one but several ethnic groups of people that share similar cultural, economic, and political practices.

The Portuguese landed in Cameroon in the 1500's; however, the area wasn't colonized by Europeans until the late 19th century due to malaria. In 1884, it became a German colony.

Caravans of up to 12,000 camels transporting salt and gold used to travel from the Mediterranean across Mali to West Africa and back.

> ➤ **L'ALGÉRIE: Le Sahara** est le plus grand désert du monde. Il s'étend sur plusieurs pays africains dont les pays du Maghreb. Il couvre presque 90% du territoire algérien. **3**

◄ **LE MAROC: La place Jemaa el Fna** est le cœur de la ville de Marrakech. En fin d'après-midi, on y trouve des marchands de toutes sortes, des acrobates, des musiciens, des conteurs et des charmeurs de serpents. **4**

▲ **LE MAROC: Le Haut-Atlas** est une chaîne de montagnes qui se trouve dans l'est du Maroc. Son sommet le plus élevé est le djebel Toubkal (4.165 m). **4**

▼ **LA TUNISIE: Matmata** Le paysage autour de Matmata ressemble à la lune, mais les cratères sont les patios de maisons souterraines. Ce paysage irréel a servi de décor pour le film *La Guerre des Étoiles.* **5**

▲ **LA TUNISIE: L'oasis de Tozeur** doit sa prospérité aux deux cents sources qui produisent huit cents litres d'eau par seconde. **5**

Géo-quiz 3.1

Comment s'appelle le désert qui couvre une grande partie du territoire algérien? Le Sahara

---

Cultures

Products and Perspectives

The original mosque of **Djenné** oversaw one of the most important Islamic learning centers in Africa during the Middle Ages. Thousands of students came here to study the *Qur'an,* Islam's holy book. Today's mosque, although not the original structure, remains an important symbol of the city and of Mali. The mosque is made entirely of mud and every year suffers damage, primarily due to erosion. To repair this important structure each year, the people of **Djenné** hold a festival to work on the mosque. Days before the festival begins, mud plaster is prepared and cured in pits. Then, on festival day, amidst singing and drumming, men carry the plaster from the pits to workmen who apply it to the mosque. Women and girls help out by carrying water to be used for the plaster's application. Ask students what values of the community are reflected in this festival. Does their community share similar values? **2.2**

Cultures

Practices and Perspectives

The majority of the people in Mali, Algeria, Morocco, and Tunisia belong to the Sunni denomination of Islam. A Sunni Muslim's main responsibilities are laid out in the Five Pillars of Faith. They are: the profession of faith in Allah **(sha-hadah),** prayer **(salat),** paying of alms **(zakat),** fasting **(sawm),** and a pilgrimage to Mecca **(hajj).** Have students research the Five Pillars of Faith and briefly comment on each in French. **2.1**

Savais-tu que…?

Students might be interested in knowing the following facts about Francophone Africa.

- Cameroon is one of the most ethnically diverse countries in Africa with more than 200 different ethnic groups.
- The Sahara desert is almost as large as the United States and is one of the hottest places on Earth.
- Africa's name comes from a Tunisian tribe called the Afri. The Romans were the first to use the name.

Questions 1.2

1. **Qu'est-ce qu'on trouve dans le parc national de Korup? (de nombreuses espèces animales et végétales)**

2. **Qui sont les Dogons? (une des populations les plus anciennes de l'Afrique)**

3. **Qu'est-ce qu'on peut voir sur la place Jemaa el Fna? (des marchands, des acrobates, des charmeurs de serpents, des musiciens, des conteurs)**

4. **Quel paysage a servi de décor pour le film** *La Guerre des Étoiles?* **(Matmata en Tunisie)**

L'histoire
L'Afrique francophone

L'Afrique francophone

IXᵉ S.–IIᵉ S. AVANT J.C.   600   1200   1600

Comparisons

Language Note

The Phoenicians who founded Carthage were great manufacturers, traders, and sailors living along the Mediterranean coast. In order to better keep track of their trade, they abandoned their complex cuneiform writing and adopted a phonetic alphabet made up of 22 letters. This alphabet was later adopted by the Greeks and became the ancestor of the Latin alphabet. Remind students that English and French share the same alphabet. Then ask students how the two languages are different when writing the letters of the alphabet (diacritical marks: ´, `, ^, ç, ¨) and linking of letters, such as œ). Have students look up the Phoenician alphabet online and create a poster of the letters and their pronunciations. They should also show which letters were transformed into the modern alphabet used in French and English.  4.1

Cultures

Practices and Perspectives

The new family law in Morocco is a sweeping reform to the *Moudawana*, a very old code that defined the economic and social status of women. Under the new code: 1) Wives are no longer bound to obey their husbands. Now, husbands and wives share equal responsibility. 2) Men and women may enter into marriage of their own free will. Women no longer need permission of a male guardian. 3) Polygamy is restricted. 4) Divorce is now easier for women. 5) The minimum age for marriage has been raised from 15 to 18 years of age. How do students think the king of Morocco instituted these reforms. Ask them how they think the general public reacted. 2.1

814–146 av. J.-C.
En 814 avant J.-C., les Phéniciens ont fondé **Carthage**, à l'endroit où se trouve Tunis aujourd'hui. Ils avaient développé un grand empire en Méditerranée basé sur le commerce maritime.

VIIᵉ s.–VIIIᵉ s.
La conquête arabe Au VIIᵉ siècle, les Arabes ont conquis le nord de l'Afrique, de Kairouan, en Tunisie, jusqu'au Maroc . Les Berbères, qui habitaient la région, se sont alors convertis à l'islam et l'arabe est devenu leur langue officielle.

1590–1591
En 1590–1591, le Maroc a attaqué le Mali et a pris la ville de **Tombouctou.** Cette ville était un des plus importants centres de commerce et d'études musulmanes en Afrique. Elle était légendaire pour sa richesse, sa liberté politique et ses universités. La conquête de la ville a mis fin à la gloire de Tombouctou.

XIIIᵉ–XIVᵉ s.
Au XIIIᵉ siècle, l'empire du Mali s'est établi entre les fleuves Sénégal et Niger. Sous les règnes de **Soundjata** et **Mansa Musa**, l'empire était très prospère. Beaucoup de mosquées et d'écoles ont été construites et l'administration et la justice du Mali étaient réputées dans toute l'Afrique.

TEACHING L'HISTOIRE

1. Ask students how old they think civilization in North and West Africa is and if they know which ancient civilizations were established there. Then have them look at the timeline and read the words in boldface orange print. Ask them if they have ever heard of any of those people, places, and events, and if so what do they know about them.

2. Have students look at the images and ask them simple questions in French about each one. For example, **Qu'est-ce qu'on voit sur la première photo? Un château? Des ruines? C'est dans le désert ou près de la mer? Dans quel pays est-ce?**

3. Have students read and discuss the captions with a partner. Check comprehension using the **As-tu compris?** questions.

4. Have students do the **Activité** individually and check their answers with a partner.

5. Ask students what their impressions are of Algeria, Morocco, Tunisia, Cameroon, and Mali now that they have read the timeline. What new information did they learn about these countries? What else would they like to know about these places? Why?

Online Practice
go.hrw.com
Online Edition
KEYWORD: BD3 CH3

1800   1900   2000

XVIIIᵉ s.–XIXᵉ s.
Au XVIIIᵉ siècle, **des pirates** contrôlaient Alger. Pour assurer la sécurité des bateaux et de leurs équipages, les pays devaient leur payer un tribut *(bribe)*. En 1815, les États-Unis ont fait la guerre à Alger pour mettre fin à cette pratique.

1954–1962
En 1956, le Maroc et la Tunisie ont proclamé leur indépendance vis-à-vis de la France. Les Algériens ont aussi voulu leur indépendance, mais la France ne voulait pas abandonner cette colonie. **La guerre d'Algérie** a commencé en 1954 et s'est terminée en 1962 par la signature des accords d'Évian qui ont reconnu l'indépendance de l'Algérie.

1919
En 1919, le **Cameroun** a été divisé entre l'Angleterre et la France. En 1960, le Cameroun est devenu indépendant mais le pays n'a été unifié qu'en 1972.

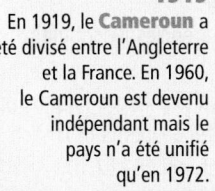

2004
En 2004, le Maroc a adopté un **nouveau code de la famille** qui reconnaît l'égalité entre les hommes et les femmes. Cette réforme a changé les lois relatives au mariage, au divorce, à la polygamie, aux enfants et aux biens de la famille.

Interactive TUTOR

Activité
    ❀3.1

1. Qui a fondé Carthage?
2. Quelles conséquences la conquête arabe a-t-elle eues?
3. Le Cameroun a été divisé entre deux pays. Lesquels?
4. Quel pays a fait la guerre à la France pour obtenir son indépendance?
5. Qu'est-ce que le nouveau code de la famille au Maroc reconnaît?

As-tu compris?
You can use the following questions to check comprehension of the **Géoculture**.

1. **Quelle ville faisait partie d'un grand empire maritime? (Carthage)**
2. **Quel évènement important a eu lieu au Nord de L'Afrique au VIIᵉ et au VIIIᵉ siècle? (la conquête arabe)**
3. **Quels rois ont rendu l'empire du Mali très prospère? (Soundjata et Mansa Musa)**
4. **Pourquoi est-ce que Tombouctou était légendaire? (pour sa richesse, sa liberté politique et ses universités)**
5. **Pourquoi est-ce que les États-Unis ont fait la guerre à Alger? (pour mettre fin au règne des pirates)**
6. **Qu'est-ce qui s'est passé au Cameroun en 1919? (le pays a été divisé entre la France et l'Angleterre)**
7. **Qu'est-ce que l'Algérie a obtenu aux accords d'Évian? (son indépendance)** ❀1.2

Answers
1. les Phéniciens
2. Les Berbères se sont convertis à l'Islam et l'arabe est devenu leur langue.
3. la France et l'Angleterre
4. l'Algérie
5. l'égalité entre les hommes et les femmes

INTERDISCIPLINARY LINKS

La littérature   ❀1.2, 1.3, 3.1
Literature Link Although Soundjata, or Sundiata as he is also known, was a real king of Mali, he is also the hero of a famous legend. "Sundiata, the Lion King" is a legend still told by oral storytellers, **griots,** today and was the basis for the movie and play *The Lion King*. According to the legend, Sundiata was a sickly boy who became a great warrior and united the Mandinka people. Have students find a French version of the legend, read it, and write a short summary of it.

L'histoire
History Link Algeria was the only country to undergo a long and difficult war to obtain its independence. This war left deep scars on both French and Algerian society. Many lives were lost and there was much damage to the cities and land in Algeria. After the war, more than a million Algerians of European descent, Muslim loyalists that supported France, and Jews fled to France. Have students research the Algerian War for Independence and write an essay on the consequences of the war for both Algeria and France.

Assess

Assessment Program
Quiz: Géoculture
Differentiated Practice and Assessment CD-ROM
Online Assessment
my.hrw.com
Test Generator 🖱

Il était une fois...

Chapter Section		Resources
Vocabulaire 1 • Stories, legends, and fables	pp. 96–99	📚 Teaching Transparencies: Vocabulaire 3.1, 3.2; Bell Work 3.1, 3.2, 3.3, 3.4 📖 Cahier de vocabulaire et grammaire, pp. 25–30
Grammaire 1 • The **passé simple** • Relative pronouns with **ce**	pp. 100–103	📖 Grammar Tutor for Students of French 📖 Cahier d'activités, pp. 21–23 📖 Media Guide, pp. 9–12
Application 1 • **Un peu plus:** Adjective placement and meaning	pp. 104–105	📖 **Assessment Program** Quiz: Vocabulaire 1, pp. 61–62 Quiz: Grammaire 1, pp. 63–64 Quiz: Application 1, pp. 65–66
Culture • **Lecture culturelle: La littérature maghrébine en français** • **Comparaisons** • **Communauté et professions**	pp. 106–107	📖 Cahier d'activités, p. 24
Vocabulaire 2 • History of Francophone Africa	pp. 108–111	📚 Teaching Transparencies: Vocabulaire 3.3, 3.4; Bell Work 3.5, 3.6, 3.7, 3.8 📖 Cahier de vocabulaire et grammaire, pp. 31–36
Grammaire 2 • The past perfect • Sequence of tenses (in indirect discourse)	pp. 112–115	📖 Grammar Tutor for Students of French 📖 Cahier d'activités, pp. 25–27 📖 Media Guide, pp. 9–12
Application 2 • **Un peu plus:** The past infinitive	pp. 116–117	📖 **Assessment Program** Quiz: Vocabulaire 2, pp. 67–68 Quiz: Grammaire 2, pp. 69–70 Quiz: Application 2, pp. 71–72
Lecture • **Les origines de l'inimitié entre l'homme et les animaux**	pp. 118–121	📖 Cahier d'activités, p. 28 📖 Reading Strategies and Skills Handbook 📖 Advanced Reader
L'atelier de l'écrivain • **Ta légende à toi**	pp. 122–123	📖 **Assessment Program** Quiz: Lecture, p. 73 Quiz: Écriture, p. 74
Prépare-toi pour l'examen • **Résumé de vocabulaire et grammaire**	pp. 124–127	📚 Teaching Transparencies: Picture Sequences, Situation, Ch. 3 📖 Media Guide, pp. 12, 57–58
Activités préparatoires	pp. 128–129	📖 **Assessment Program** Examen: Chapitre 3, pp. 75–80 Examen oral: Chapitre 3, p. 319
Révisions cumulatives	pp. 130–131	📚 Teaching Transparencies: Fine Art, Ch. 3 📖 Cahier d'activités, pp. 29–30
Chroniques • Les fables de La Fontaine • Les contes français • Le cinéma célèbre l'amour • L'amour et le mariage • Les grands couples de l'histoire	pp. 170–179	📖 Reading Strategies and Skills Handbook 📖 Advanced Reader

Pacing Suggestions

	Essential	Recommended	Optional
Vocabulaire 1 • Stories, legends, and fables	✔		
Grammaire 1 • The **passé simple** • Relative pronouns with **ce** • **Flash culture**	✔		
Application 1 • **Un peu plus:** 　Adjective placement and meaning • **Flash culture**	✔		
Culture • **Lecture culturelle: La littérature 　maghrébine en français** • **Comparaisons** • **Communauté et professions**		✔	
Vocabulaire 2 • History of Francophone Africa • **Flash culture**	✔		
Grammaire 2 • The past perfect • Sequence of tenses (in indirect discourse)	✔		
Application 2 • **Un peu plus:** 　The past infinitive	✔		
Lecture • **Les origines de l'inimitié entre 　l'homme et les animaux**		✔	
L'atelier de l'écrivain • **Ta légende à toi**			
Prépare-toi pour l'examen		✔	
Activités préparatoires		✔	
Révisions cumulatives			✔
Chroniques			✔

Technology

Bien dit! Online
• Student Edition with multi-media
• SoundBooth recording tool
• Interactive activities with feedback
• Self-tests with feedback
• Cahier d'activités (Interactive workbook)
• Cahier de vocabulaire et grammaire (Interactive workbook)
• Holt Online Assessment

DVD Program
• Télé-roman: Camille et compagnie
• Télé-culture: Interviews

Interactive Tutor
• Interactive practice games
• Writing and recording workshops
• Before You Know It™ Flashcards

Audio Program
• Student Edition Listening Activities
• Assessment listening activities
• Songs

One-Stop Planner
• Complete media and print resources
• ExamView Pro Test Generator
• Holt Calendar Planner

PuzzlePro
• Customizable word games

Differentiated Practice and Assessment CD
For slower pace and advanced learner options, see the Differentiated Practice and Assessment CD.

Planning Guide

✂ Projects

Projects

Un conte de fée

Groups of four to five students create a puppet show of a legend or fairy tale from Francophone Africa. They use what they have learned about storytelling: setting the scene, moving the action along, and ending a story. Students then create puppets and perform for the class. As an alternative, you might have students make props and costumes and act out their story. ❀ 3.1, 5.2

Suggested Sequence

1. Have students research in the library or on the Internet legends and fairy tales from Francophone Africa. They should then decide on a legend or fairy tale and write an outline of the story, breaking it down into scenes.

2. Assign students leadership roles: organizer, editor, designer, note-taker, and so on.

3. The group assigns an equal number of scenes to be written by each member. Two other members should proofread the scenes.

4. The editor and note-taker compile the script. Other group members design the set, gather materials, and make the puppets and the stage.

5. Groups rehearse and memorize their lines. Everyone should have approximately the same amount of speaking time.

6. The final script is turned in, and the puppet show is performed for the class. You might have audience members review the performance.

Grading the project

Suggested point distribution
  (100 points total)
Group grade
(written product) . . . . .50 pts.
Individual grade
(performance) . . . . .50 pts.
(25 points each for language use and 25 points for theatrical quality)

e-community

e-mail forum:
Post the following questions on the classroom e-mail forum:

Location:	http:// french

Quand tu étais petit(e), est-ce que tu aimais lire ou écouter des contes de fées?

Quels contes aimais-tu le mieux?
❀ 5.1

All students will contribute to the list and then share the items.

Partner Class Project

Have students prepare a questionnaire about fairy tales for their partner class in a Francophone country. The questionnaire should include questions such as: What are the titles of three fairy tales that you have read? Who are the characters in these tales, and are these characters supernatural beings? What is the plot of each tale? Do the tales have a moral? Students should post the questionnaire on the student or class Web site. Remind students to e-mail the Web site address or an electronic document to the partner class. Students should then fill out the questionnaire themselves and compare their answers to the answers provided by the partner class. Have students evaluate their comparisons and present their conclusions to the class. ❀ 3.1, 4.2

 Game Bank
For game ideas, see pages T60–T63.

Les griots

The **Malinké** of West Africa have a long tradition of transmitting their people's history by word of mouth from one generation to the next. The professional historians and praise singers that perform this task are called **jeli** in the **Malinké** language, or **griots** in French. Their histories are poetic and often accompanied by the **kora,** a lute-like instrument, and a **tam-tam,** or *talking drum.* Considered word-smiths, **griots** form part of the artisan class in **Malinké** society. As with many traditional professions, their role in the community is passed down from generation to generation. Without the stories of the **griots,** we would know very little about the **Malinké,** since their history has only just recently been written down. Have students research and listen to the **kora.** They should describe the instrument and its sound. Do students know of musical instruments or styles in the United States that are associated with certain groups of people or activities? 🏵 3.1, 5.2

La cuisine

There are two words for peanut in French: the scientific term, **arachide,** and the more commonly used term, **cacahouète.** Peanuts originated in South America. The Aztec name for peanut is **tlacacahuatl,** from which **cacahouète** is derived. Peanuts were introduced to Africa by the Spanish and Portuguese during the colonial era. Senegal is one of the top producers of peanuts. Encourage students to prepare **potage à l'arachide** in their home economics class or at home for friends and family. 🏵 2.2, 5.2

Potage à l'arachide

pour 6 personnes

1 tasse d'arachides
2 blancs de poulet
½ tasse de beurre
1 cuillère à soupe de farine

4 tasses de bouillon de volaille
1 tasse de crème fraîche

Faire fondre le beurre dans une casserole. Ajouter la farine. Mélanger. Ajouter un petit peu de bouillon et porter le tout à ébullition. Faire cuire les blancs de poulet, les hacher et mélanger avec la crème fraîche. Passer le poulet au tamis avec le bouillon. Faire griller les cacahouètes et les piler. Ajouter au bouillon et laisser mijoter.

Traditions

Listening Activity Scripts

Vocabulaire *à l'œuvre* 1

2 p. 98, CD 3, Tr. 1

1. Jadis, dans une grande forêt, il y avait un monstre dont tout le village avait peur.
2. Il y a bien longtemps, dans un pays lointain, un roi et une reine étaient très tristes car ils n'avaient pas d'enfant.
3. On raconte qu'autrefois, un géant mangeait tout ce qu'il trouvait sur son chemin.
4. C'est à ce moment-là que la fée a fait apparaître le passage secret.
5. Il était une fois un sorcier qui préparait des potions pour donner des pouvoirs magiques à tous ceux qui en buvaient.
6. Le génie, dont les pouvoirs magiques étaient exceptionnels, a accordé le souhait du jeune sultan: il lui a donné un tapis volant très rapide.

Answers to Activity 2

1. f   2. a   3. e   4. c   5. b   6. d

Grammaire *à l'œuvre* 1

12 p. 103, CD 3, Tr. 2

1. Dis-moi [...] t'ennuie.
2. Je n'ai pas entendu [...] il parlait.
3. Il ne veut pas me dire [...] il a fait hier.
4. Quoi? Répète. Je n'ai pas entendu [...] tu as dit.
5. Je crois que [...] il a peur, c'est qu'elle ne lui dise pas tout.
6. [...] me plaît le plus dans cette histoire, c'est que la princesse sauve le chevalier.

Answers to Activity 12

1. ce qui   2. ce dont   3. ce qu'   4. ce que
5. ce dont   6. Ce qui

Application 1

17 p. 104, CD 3, Tr. 3

Un jour, Ahmed qui venait de gagner beaucoup d'argent, voulut faire un cadeau à son grand ami, Ali Pacha. Il lui offrit une lampe ancienne pour son anniversaire. Le pauvre Ahmed ne savait pas qu'un mauvais génie vivait dans cette lampe. Ali Pacha utilisa la lampe pendant un certain temps et rien ne se passa, mais la dernière fois qu'il l'alluma, le méchant génie sortit de la lampe et transforma le petit Pacha en serpent.

Answers to Activity 17

1. b   2. a   3. b   4. a   5. b   6. b

Vocabulaire *à l'œuvre* 2

24 p. 111, CD 3, Tr. 4

1. On a annoncé que le Japon allait signer un accord important avec les États-Unis.
2. Le président français a déclaré vouloir rendre visite au président tunisien.
3. Il paraît que le roi a finalement décidé d'arrêter les combats.
4. On a rapporté que la reine avait rendu visite aux victimes des combats qui ont eu lieu dans le sud du pays.

Answers to Activity 24

1. e   2. b   3. d   4. a

Grammaire *à l'œuvre* 2

32 p. 114, CD 3, Tr. 5

1. Grand-maman a dit qu'elle pensait à nous.
2. Elle a aussi dit qu'elle viendrait vendredi.
3. Et puis elle a ajouté qu'elle nous avait acheté des cadeaux.
4. Est-ce qu'elle a dit qu'elle prendrait le train?
5. Elle a dit qu'elle avait un billet d'avion.
6. Je lui ai dit que nous l'attendrions à l'aéroport.

Answers to Activity 32

1. a   2. b   3. a   4. b   5. a   6. b

Application 2

 **p. 116, CD 3, Tr. 6**

— Ce matin, après avoir préparé le thé, j'ai télé-phoné à mon fils qui est professeur pour savoir s'il voulait aller à la pêche. Il était d'accord pour y aller mais seulement après avoir fini de préparer sa leçon pour le lendemain. Après avoir déjeuné, je suis allé chez lui et nous sommes partis au lac. Après avoir pris vingt gros poissons, nous avons décidé de faire une grande fête et d'inviter tout le village!

Answers to Activity 37

1. c   **2.** b   **3.** a   **4.** d   **5.** f   **6.** e

Prépare-toi pour l'examen

 **p. 125, CD 3, Tr. 8**

1. Dans l'histoire du petit chaperon rouge, le loup mange la grand-mère.

2. Cendrillon avait une marraine qui était méchante et qui ne voulait pas qu'elle aille au bal.

3. Au vingtième siècle, des explorateurs français ont exploré les pays du Maghreb.

4. Quand il y a un cessez-le-feu les batailles continuent.

5. Dans les contes, les chevaliers sont souvent des héros qui sauvent les princesses.

6. Les fées utilisent des baguettes magiques pour faire apparaître ou disparaître des objets.

7. Après leur indépendance, la Tunisie et le Maroc ont choisi des présidents.

Answers to Activity 6

1. a   **2.** b   **3.** b   **4.** b   **5.** a   **6.** a   **7.** b

Activités préparatoires

Listening, p. 128, CD 3, Tr. 9

1. — Tu as entendu ce qu'on a annoncé à la télévision?

— On dit qu'un conflit a éclaté entre deux pays africains.

— Qui.

2. — Tu connais la princesse Léa?

— Qui, j'ai entendu dire qu'elle avait disparu.

— Elle n'est jamais rentrée au palais?

Answers to Listening Activity

1. c   **2.** c

Révisions cumulatives *chapitres 1-3*

 **p. 130, CD 3, Tr. 10**

1. Tu as vu? Le magicien a fait apparaître un petit lapin blanc. C'est incroyable!

2. La princesse a rendu visite aux soldats.

3. Les deux présidents ont beaucoup travaillé la dernière fois qu'ils se sont vus.

4. Un groupe d'explorateurs est allé en Afrique. Ils ont exploré plusieurs pays et ont fait des cartes de ces régions.

5. On dit qu'on peut voir un fantôme dans cette pièce chaque nuit à minuit!

Answers to Activity 1

1. d   **2.** a   **3.** b   **4.** c   **5.** e

Listening Activity Scripts

50-Minute Lesson Plans

Il était une fois...

Day 1

OBJECTIVE
Set the scene for a story

Core Instruction
Chapter Opener, pp. 94–95
• See Using the Photo, p. 94. **5 min.**
• See Chapter Objectives, p. 94. **5 min.**

Vocabulaire 1, pp. 96–99
• Present **Vocabulaire 1,** pp. 96–97. See Teaching **Vocabulaire,** p. 96. **15 min.**
• Present **Exprimons-nous!,** p. 97. **5 min.**
• Have students do Activity 1, p. 98. **5 min.**
• Play Audio CD 3, Tr. 1 for Activity 2, p. 98. **5 min.**
• Do Activity 3, p. 98. **10 min.**

Optional Resources
• Advanced Learners, p. 97 ▲
• Special Learning Needs, p. 97 ●

Homework Suggestions
Cahier de vocabulaire et grammaire, pp. 25–26
Interactive Tutor, Ch. 3
✿ 1.2, 1.3, 3.1, 4.2

Day 2

OBJECTIVE
Continue and end a story; Use the passé simple

Core Instruction
Vocabulaire 1, pp. 96–99
• Do Bell Work 3.1, p. 96. **5 min.**
• See Teaching **Exprimons-nous!,** p. 98. **10 min.**
• Have students do Activities 4–6, p. 99. **20 min.**

Grammaire 1, pp. 100–103
• Present **Flash culture,** p. 100. **5 min.**
• See Teaching **Grammaire,** p. 100. **10 min.**

Optional Resources
• Slower Pace Learners, p. 99 ◆
• Special Learning Needs, p. 99 ●

Homework Suggestions
Study for **Quiz: Vocabulaire 1**
Cahier de vocabulaire et grammaire, p. 27
Online Practice (**go.hrw.com,** Keyword: BD3 CH3)
✿ 1.1, 1.2, 1.3, 3.1 , 4.2

Day 3

OBJECTIVE
Use the passé simple

Core Instruction
Vocabulaire 1, pp. 96–99
• Review **Vocabulaire 1,** pp. 96–99. **10 min.**
• Give **Quiz: Vocabulaire 1.** **20 min.**

Grammaire 1, pp. 100–103
• Have students do Activities 7–9, pp. 100–101. **20 min.**

Optional Resources
• Communication (TE), p. 101
• French for Spanish Speakers, p. 101
• Slower Pace Learners, p. 101 ◆
• Special Learning Needs, p. 101 ●

Homework Suggestions
Cahier de vocabulaire et grammaire, p. 28
Cahier d'activités, p. 21
Online Practice (**go.hrw.com,** Keyword: BD3 CH3)
✿ 1.1, 1.2, 1.3, 3.2, 4.1

Day 4

OBJECTIVE
Use relative pronouns with ce

Core Instruction
Grammaire 1, pp. 100–103
• See Teaching **Grammaire,** p. 102. **10 min.**
• Have students do Activities 10–11, p. 102. **10 min.**
• Play Audio CD 3, Tr. 2 for Activity 12, p. 103. **5 min.**
• Do Activities 13–15, p. 103. **15 min.**

Application 1, pp. 104–105
• Have students do Activity 16, p. 104. **5 min.**
• Present **Flash culture,** p. 105. **5 min.**

Optional Resources
• Advanced Learners, p. 103 ▲
• Special Learning Needs, p. 103 ●

Homework Suggestions
Study for **Quiz: Grammaire 1**
Cahier de vocabulaire et grammaire, p. 29
Cahier d'activités, p. 22
✿ 1.1, 1.2, 1.3, 3.1, 4.2

Day 5

OBJECTIVE
Use adjective placement and meaning

Core Instruction
Grammaire 1, pp. 100–103
• Review **Grammaire 1,** pp. 100–103. **10 min.**
• Give **Quiz: Grammaire 1.** **20 min.**

Application 1, pp. 104–105
• See Teaching **Un peu plus,** p. 104. **5 min.**
• Play Audio CD 3, Tr. 3 for Activity 17, p. 104. **5 min.**
• Have students do Activities 18–20, p. 105. **10 min.**

Optional Resources
• Communication (TE), p. 105
• Multiple Intelligences, p. 105

Homework Suggestions
Study for **Quiz: Application 1**
Cahier de vocabulaire et grammaire, p. 30
Cahier d'activités, p. 23
Online Practice (**go.hrw.com,** Keyword: BD3 CH3)
✿ 1.1, 1.2, 1.3, 3.2

Day 6

OBJECTIVE
Learn about francophone culture

Core Instruction
Application 1, pp. 104–105
• Review **Application 1,** pp. 104–105. **10 min.**
• Give **Quiz: Application 1.** **20 min.**

Culture, pp. 106–107
• See **Lecture culturelle** (TE), p. 106. **10 min.**
• See **Comparaisons et communauté** (TE), p. 106. **10 min.**

Optional Resources
• Cultures, p. 107
• Communities, p. 107
• Advanced Learners, p. 107 ▲
• Multiple Intelligences, p. 107

Homework Suggestions
Cahier d'activités, p. 24
Interactive Tutor, Ch. 3
Online Practice (**go.hrw.com,** Keyword: BD3 CH3)
Finish the **Communauté et professions** project.
✿ 1.2, 1.3, 2.1, 2.2, 3.2, 4.2, 5.1, 5.2

Day 7

OBJECTIVE
Relate a sequence of events

Core Instruction
Vocabulaire 2, pp. 108–111
• Do Bell Work 3.5, p. 108. **5 min.**
• Present **Vocabulaire 2,** pp. 108–109. See Teaching **Vocabulaire,** p. 108. **15 min.**
• Present **Exprimons-nous!,** p. 109. **10 min.**
• Have students do Activities 21–23, p. 110. **15 min.**
• Present **Flash culture,** p. 110. **5 min.**

Optional Resources
• Advanced Learners, p. 109 ▲
• Special Learning Needs, p. 109 ●
• Slower Pace Learners, p. 111 ◆

Homework Suggestions
Cahier de vocabulaire et grammaire, pp. 31–32
Online Practice (**go.hrw.com,** Keyword: BD3 CH3)
✿ 1.2, 3.1, 3.2

Day 8

OBJECTIVE
Tell what happened to someone else; Use the past perfect

Core Instruction
Vocabulaire 2, pp. 108–111
• See Teaching **Exprimons-nous!,** p. 110. **10 min.**
• Play Audio CD 3, Tr. 4 for Activity 24, p. 111. **5 min.**
• Have students do Activities 25–26, p. 111. **15 min.**

Grammaire 2, pp. 112–115
• See Teaching **Grammaire,** p. 112. **10 min.**
• Have students do Activities 27–28, pp. 112–113. **10 min.**

Optional Resources
• Multiple Intelligences, p. 111
• Multiple Intelligences, p. 113

Homework Suggestions
Study for **Quiz: Vocabulaire 2**
Cahier de vocabulaire et grammaire, p. 33
Interactive Tutor, Ch. 3
Online Practice (**go.hrw.com,** Keyword: BD3 CH3)
✿ 1.1, 1.2, 1.3

To edit and create your own lesson plans, see the

One-Stop Planner® CD-ROM

50-Minute Lesson Plans

Day 9

OBJECTIVE
Use the past perfect

Core Instruction
Vocabulaire 2, pp. 108–111
• Review **Vocabulaire 2,** pp. 108–111. **10 min.**
• Give **Quiz: Vocabulaire 2.** **20 min.**

Grammaire 2, pp. 112–115
• Have students do Activities 29–30, p. 113. **20 min.**

Optional Resources
• Communication (TE), p. 113
• Advanced Learners, p. 113 ▲

Homework Suggestions
Cahier de vocabulaire et grammaire, p. 34
Cahier d'activités, p. 25
Interactive Tutor, Ch. 3
Online Practice (**go.hrw.com,** Keyword: BD3 CH3)
🏵 1.1, 1.2

Day 10

OBJECTIVE
Use sequence of tenses (in indirect discourse)

Core Instruction
Grammaire 2, pp. 112–115
• See Teaching **Grammaire,** p. 114. **10 min.**
• Play Audio CD 3, Tr. 5 for Activity 32, p. 114. **5 min.**
• Do Activity 31, p. 114. **5 min.**
• Have students do Activities 33–35, p. 115. **20 min.**

Application 2, pp. 116–117
• Do Activity 36, p. 116. **5 min.**
• See Teaching **Un peu plus,** p. 116. **5 min.**

Optional Resources
• Slower Pace Learners, p. 115 ◆
• Multiple Intelligences, p. 115

Homework Suggestions
Study for **Quiz: Grammaire 2**
Cahier de vocabulaire et grammaire, p. 35
Cahier d'activités, p. 26
🏵 1.1, 1.2, 1.3, 3.2

Day 11

OBJECTIVE
Use the past infinitive

Core Instruction
Grammaire 2, pp. 112–115
• Review **Grammaire 2,** pp. 112–115. **10 min.**
• Give **Quiz: Grammaire 2.** **20 min.**

Application 2, pp. 116–117
• Play Audio CD 3, Tr. 6 for Activity 37, p. 116. **5 min.**
• Have students do Activities 38–40, p. 117. **15 min.**

Optional Resources
• Communication (TE), p. 117
• Special Learning Needs, p. 117 ●

Homework Suggestions
Study for **Quiz: Application 2**
Cahier de vocabulaire et grammaire, p. 36
Cahier d'activités, p. 27
Interactive Tutor, Ch. 3
Online Practice (**go.hrw.com,** Keyword: BD3 CH3)
🏵 1.1, 1.2, 1.3

Day 12

OBJECTIVE
Develop listening and reading skills

Core Instruction
Application 2, pp. 116–117
• Review **Application 2,** pp. 116–117. **10 min.**
• Give **Quiz: Application 2.** **20 min.**

Lecture, pp. 118–121
• See **Lecture** (TE), p. 118. **20 min.**

Optional Resources
• Slower Pace Learners, p. 119 ◆
• Special Learning Needs, p. 119 ●
• Connections, p. 121

Homework Suggestions
Interactive Tutor, Ch. 3
Online Practice (**go.hrw.com,** Keyword: BD3 CH3)
🏵 1.2, 3.1

Day 13

OBJECTIVE
Develop listening, reading, and writing skills

Core Instruction
Lecture, pp. 118–121
• See **Lecture** (TE), p. 120. **20 min.**

L'atelier de l'écrivain, pp. 122–123
• See **L'atelier de l'écrivain** (TE), p. 122. **30 min.**

Optional Resources
• Advanced Learners, p. 121 ▲ ●
• Special Learning Needs, p. 121 ●
• Connections, p. 122
• Advanced Learners, p. 123 ▲
• Multiple Intelligences, p. 123

Homework Suggestions
Cahier d'activités, p. 28
L'atelier de l'écrivain, Activities 3–4, p. 123
🏵 1.1, 1.2, 1.3, 3.1

Day 14

OBJECTIVE
Review the chapter; Prepare for the AP Exam

Core Instruction
Prépare-toi pour l'examen, pp. 124–127
• Have students do Activities 1–5, pp. 124–125. **25 min.**

Activités préparatoires, pp. 128–129
• Have students do the **Activités préparatoires,** pp. 128–129. **25 min.**

Optional Resources
• Reteaching, p. 124
• Connections, p. 126
• Slower Pace Learners, p. 129 ◆
• Special Learning Needs, p. 129 ●
• Télé-culture: Interviews

Homework Suggestions
Interactive Tutor, Ch. 3
Online Practice (**go.hrw.com,** Keyword: BD3 CH3)
🏵 1.1, 1.2, 1.3, 2.1, 3.1

Day 15

OBJECTIVE
Review the chapter

Core Instruction
Prépare-toi pour l'examen, pp. 124–127
• Play Audio CD 3, Tr. 8 for Activity 6, p. 125. **10 min.**
• Do Activity 7, p. 125. **10 min.**

Révisions cumulatives, pp. 130–131
• Play Audio CD 3, Tr. 10 for Activity 1, p. 130. **5 min.**
• Have students do Activities 2–6, pp. 130–131. **25 min.**

Optional Resources
• Online Culture Project, p. 130
• Fine Art Connection, p. 131
• Télé-roman: Camille et compagnie

Homework Suggestions
Study for Chapter Test
Online Practice (**go.hrw.com,** Keyword: BD3 CH3)
🏵 1.1, 1.2, 1.3, 2.2, 3.1, 3.2, 4.2

Day 16/Test

Core Instruction
Chapter Test 50 min.

Optional Resources
Assessment Program
• Alternative Assessment
• Test Generator
• **Quiz: Lecture**
• **Quiz: Écriture**

Homework Suggestions
Cahier d'activités, pp. 29–30, 106–107
Online Practice (**go.hrw.com,** Keyword: BD3 CH3)

Il étais une fois...

Block 1

OBJECTIVE
Set the scene for a story; Continue and end a story

Core Instruction
Chapter Opener, pp. 94–95
• See Using the Photo, p. 94. **5 min.**
• See Chapter Objectives, p. 94. **5 min.**

Vocabulaire 1, pp. 96–99
• Present **Vocabulaire 1,** pp. 96–97. See Teaching **Vocabulaire,** p. 96. **15 min.**
• Present **Exprimons-nous!,** p. 97. **10 min.**
• Have students do Activity 1, p. 98. **5 min.**
• Play Audio CD 3, Tr. 1 for Activity 2, p. 98. **5 min.**
• Have students do Activity 3, p. 98. **10 min.**
• See Teaching **Exprimons-nous!,** p. 98. **10 min.**
• Have students do Activities 4–6, p. 99. **25 min.**

Optional Resources
• Learning Tips, p. 95
• **Attention!,** p. 97
• TPR, p. 97
• Advanced Learners, p. 97 ▲
• Special Learning Needs, p. 97 ●
• Teacher to Teacher, p. 99
• Communication (TE), p. 99
• Slower Pace Learners, p. 99 ◆
• Special Learning Needs, p. 99 ●

Homework Suggestions
Study for **Quiz: Vocabulaire 1**
Cahier de vocabulaire et grammaire, pp. 25–27
Interactive Tutor, Ch. 3
Online Practice (**go.hrw.com,** Keyword: BD3 CH3)
🍀 1.1, 1.2, 1.3, 3.1, 5.2

Block 2

OBJECTIVE
*Use the **passé simple;** Use relative pronouns with **ce***

Core Instruction
Vocabulaire 1, pp. 96–99
• Review **Vocabulaire 1,** pp. 96–99. **10 min.**
• Give **Quiz: Vocabulaire 1.** **20 min.**

Grammaire 1, pp. 100–103
• Present **Flash culture,** p. 100. **5 min.**
• See Teaching **Grammaire,** p. 100. **10 min.**
• Have students do Activities 7–9, pp. 100–101. **15 min.**
• See Teaching **Grammaire,** p. 102. **10 min.**
• Have students do Activities 10–11, p. 102. **5 min.**
• Play Audio CD 3, Tr. 2 for Activity 12, p. 103. **5 min.**
• Have students do Activities 13–14, p. 103. **10 min.**

Optional Resources
• Connections, p. 100
• Communication (TE), p. 101
• French for Spanish Speakers, p. 101
• Slower Pace Learners, p. 101 ◆
• Special Learning Needs, p. 101 ●
• Comparisons, p. 102
• Communication (TE), p. 103
• Special Learning Needs, p. 103 ●

Homework Suggestions
Study for **Quiz: Grammaire 1**
Cahier de vocabulaire et grammaire, pp. 28–29
Cahier d'activités, pp. 21–22
Interactive Tutor, Ch. 3
Online Practice (**go.hrw.com,** Keyword: BD3 CH3)
🍀 1.1, 1.2, 1.3, 3.2, 4.1, 4.2

Block 3

OBJECTIVE
*Use relative pronouns with **ce;** Use adjective placement and meaning; Learn about francophone culture*

Core Instruction
Grammaire 1, pp. 100–103
• Do Bell Work 3.3, p. 102. **5 min.**
• Have students do Activity 15, p. 103. **5 min.**
• Review **Grammaire 1,** pp. 100–103. **10 min.**
• Give **Quiz: Grammaire 1.** **20 min.**

Application 1, pp. 104–105
• Have students do Activity 16, p. 104. **5 min.**
• See Teaching **Un peu plus,** p. 104. **5 min.**
• Play Audio CD 3, Tr. 3 for Activity 17, p. 104. **5 min.**
• Have students do Activities 18–20, p. 105. **10 min.**
• Present **Flash culture,** p. 105. **5 min.**

Culture, pp. 106–107
• See **Lecture culturelle** (TE), p. 106. **10 min.**
• See **Comparaisons et communauté** (TE), p. 106. **10 min.**

Optional Resources
• Advanced Learners, p. 103 ▲
• Communication (TE), p. 105
• Slower Pace Learners, p. 105 ◆
• Multiple Intelligences, p. 105
• Prereading Questions, p. 106
• Active Reading Questions, p. 106
• **Vocabulaire supplémentaire,** p. 106
• Bulletin Board Project, p. 107
• Cultures, p. 107
• Communities, p. 107
• Advanced Learners, p. 107 ▲
• Multiple Intelligences, p. 107

Homework Suggestions
Study for **Quiz: Application 1**
Finish the **Communauté et professions** project
Cahier de vocabulaire et grammaire, p. 30
Cahier d'activités, pp. 23–24
Interactive Tutor, Ch. 3
Online Practice (**go.hrw.com,** Keyword: BD3 CH3)
🍀 1.1, 1.2, 1.3, 2.1, 2.2, 3.1, 3.2, 4.2, 5.1, 5.2

Block 4

OBJECTIVE
Relate a sequence of events; Tell what happened to someone else

Core Instruction
Application 1, pp. 104–105
• Review **Application 1,** pp. 104–105. **10 min.**
• Give **Quiz: Application 1.** **20 min.**

Vocabulaire 2, pp. 108–111
• Present **Vocabulaire 2,** pp. 108–109. See Teaching **Vocabulaire,** p. 108. **10 min.**
• Present **Exprimons-nous!,** p. 109. **10 min.**
• Have students do Activities 21–23, p. 110. **10 min.**
• Present **Flash culture,** p. 110. **5 min.**
• See Teaching **Exprimons-nous!,** p. 110. **10 min.**
• Play Audio CD 3, Tr, 4 for Activity 24, p. 111. **5 min.**
• Have students do Activities 25–26, p. 111. **10 min.**

Optional Resources
• Connections, p. 108
• TPR, p. 109
• French for Spanish Speakers, p. 109
• Advanced Learners, p. 109 ▲
• Special Learning Needs, p. 109 ●
• Connections, p. 110
• Communication (TE), p. 111
• Slower Pace Learners, p. 111 ◆
• Multiple Intelligences, p. 111

Homework Suggestions
Study for **Quiz: Vocabulaire 2**
Cahier de vocabulaire et grammaire, pp. 31–33
Interactive Tutor, Ch. 3
Online Practice (**go.hrw.com,** Keyword: BD3 CH3)
🍀 1.1, 1.2, 1.3, 3.1, 3.2

Block 5

OBJECTIVE
Use the past perfect; Use sequence of tenses (in indirect discourse)

Core Instruction
Vocabulaire 2, pp. 108–111
• Review **Vocabulaire 2,** pp. 108–111. **10 min.**
• Give **Quiz: Vocabulaire 2.** **20 min.**

Grammaire 2, pp. 112–115
• See Teaching **Grammaire,** p. 112. **10 min.**
• Have students do Activities 27–30, pp. 112–113. **15 min.**
• See Teaching **Grammaire,** p. 114. **10 min.**
• Have students do Activity 31, p. 114. **5 min.**
• Play Audio CD 3, Tr. 5 for Activity 32, p. 114. **5 min.**
• Have students do Activities 33–34, p. 115. **15 min.**

Optional Resources
• Communication (TE), p. 113
• Advanced Learners, p. 113 ▲
• Multiple Intelligences, p. 113
• Slower Pace Learners, p. 115 ◆
• Multiple Intelligences, p. 115

Homework Suggestions
Study for **Quiz: Grammaire 2**
Cahier de vocabulaire et grammaire, pp. 34–35
Cahier d'activités, pp. 25–26
Interactive Tutor, Ch. 3
Online Practice (**go.hrw.com,** Keyword: BD3 CH3)

✿ 1.1, 1.2, 1.3

Block 6

OBJECTIVE
Use sequence of tenses (in indirect discourse); Use the past infinitive; Develop listening and reading skills

Core Instruction
Grammaire 2, pp. 112–115
• Do Bell Work 3.7, p. 114. **5 min.**
• Have students do Activity 35, p. 115. **5 min.**
• Review **Grammaire 2,** pp. 112–115. **10 min.**
• Give **Quiz: Grammaire 2.** **20 min.**

Application 2, pp. 116–117
• Have students do Activity 36, p. 116. **5 min.**
• See Teaching **Un peu plus,** p. 116. **5 min.**
• Play Audio CD 3, Tr. 6 for Activity 37, p. 116. **5 min.**
• Have students do Activities 38–40, p. 117. **15 min.**

Lecture, pp. 118–121
• See **Lecture** (TE), p. 118. **20 min.**

Optional Resources
• Communication (TE), p. 115
• Communication (TE), p. 117
• Advanced Learners, p. 117 ▲
• Multiple Intelligences, p. 117
• AP Reading Suggestion, p. 118
• Applying the Strategies, p. 118
• Active Reading Questions, p. 119
• Using Background Knowledge, p. 119
• Slower Pace Learners, p. 119 ◆
• Special Learning Needs, p. 119 ●
• Connections, p. 121

Homework Suggestions
Study for **Quiz: Application 2**
Cahier de vocabulaire et grammaire, p. 36
Cahier d'activités, p. 27
Interactive Tutor, Ch. 3
Online Practice (**go.hrw.com,** Keyword: BD3 CH3)

✿ 1.1, 1.2, 1.3, 3.1, 3.2

Block 7

OBJECTIVE
Develop listening, reading, and writing skills; Review the chapter

Core Instruction
Application 2, pp. 116–117
• Review **Application 2,** pp. 116–117. **10 min.**
• Give **Quiz: Application 2.** **20 min.**

Lecture, pp. 118–121
• See **Lecture** (TE), p. 120. **10 min.**

L'atelier de l'écrivain, pp. 122–123
• See **L'atelier de l'écrivain** (TE), p. 122. **30 min.**

Prépare-toi pour l'examen, pp. 124–127
• Have students do Activities 1–5, pp. 124–125. **10 min.**
• Play Audio CD 3, Tr. 8 for Activity 6, p. 125. **5 min.**
• Have students do Activity 7, p. 125. **5 min.**

Optional Resources
• Active Reading Questions, p. 120
• Postreading Activity, p. 120
• Advanced Learners, p. 121 ▲
• Special Learning Needs, p. 121 ●
• Process Writing, p. 122
• Teaching Suggestion, p. 122
• Connections, p. 122
• **Le plus-que-parfait,** p. 123
• Writing Assessment, p. 123
• Advanced Learners, p. 123 ▲
• Multiple Intelligences, p. 123
• TPRS, p. 124
• Reteaching, p. 124
• **Attention!,** p. 125
• Oral Assessment, p. 125
• Connections, p. 126
• Game, p. 127

Homework Suggestions
Study for Chapter Test
L'atelier de l'écrivain, Activities 3–4, p. 123
Cahier d'activités, p. 28
Interactive Tutor, Ch. 3
Online Practice (**go.hrw.com,** Keyword: BD3 CH3)

✿ 1.1, 1.2, 1.3, 2.1, 3.1

Block 8

OBJECTIVE
Prepare for the AP Exam; Review and assess the chapter

Core Instruction
Activités préparatoires, pp. 128–129
• Have students do the **Activités préparatoires,** pp. 128–129. **20 min.**

Chapter Test 50 min.

Révisions cumulatives, pp. 130–131
• Play Audio CD 3, Tr. 10 for Activity 1, p. 130. **5 min.**
• Have students do Activities 2–6, pp. 130–131. **15 min.**

Optional Resources
• Reading Strategy, p. 128
• Writing Strategy, p. 129
• Slower Pace Learners, p. 129 ◆
• Special Learning Needs, p. 129 ●
• Online Culture Project, p. 130
• Fine Art Connection, p. 131
• **Télé-culture:** Interviews
• **Télé-roman:** Camille et compagnie

Homework Suggestions
Cahier d'activités, pp. 29–30, 106–107
Online Practice (**go.hrw.com,** Keyword: BD3 CH3)

✿ 1.1, 1.2, 1.3, 2.2, 3.1, 3.2, 4.2

90-Minute Lesson Plans

Meeting the National Standards

Communication
Communication, pp. 99, 101, 103, 105, 111, 113, 115, 117
À ton tour, p. 131

Cultures
Flash culture, pp. 100, 105, 110
Comparaisons, p. 107
Practices and Perspectives, p. 107

Connections
Language-to-Language, p. 100
Literature Link, pp. 96, 121, 122, 126
History Link, pp. 108, 110

Comparisons
Comparaisons, p. 107
Comparing and Contrasting, p. 102

Communities
Communauté, p. 107
Career Path, p. 107

Using the Photo
The Erg Chebbi dunes, near the small Moroccan Berber town of Merzouga on the edge of the Sahara desert, are among the highest in Morocco, reaching heights up to 164 feet. It is said that a huge sandstorm buried the old settlement after its inhabitants had refused to give shelter to a woman and her children during a festival. According to this tale, the cries of the villagers begging for forgiveness can be heard every day at noon. Ask students why hospitality has always carried such importance for the inhabitants of the Sahara. Can students think of other peoples who are known for their hospitality? (for example, the Inuit)   2.1, 3.1, 4.2

chapitre **3**

Il était une fois...

Objectifs

In this chapter, you will learn to
• set the scene for a story
• continue and end a story
• relate a sequence of events
• tell what happened to someone else

And you will use and review
• the **passé simple**
• relative pronouns with **ce**
• adjective placement and meaning
• the past perfect
• sequence of tenses
• the past infinitive

▶ *Que vois-tu sur la photo?*

Où est cette personne?

À quoi est-ce que cette photo te fait penser?

Et toi, est-ce que tu aimerais voyager dans une région retirée *(far away)*? Laquelle? Pourquoi?

Suggested pacing:	Traditional Schedule	Block Schedule
Vocabulaire/Grammaire/Application 1	5 days	2 blocks
Culture	1 day	1 block
Vocabulaire/Grammaire/Application 2	5 days	2 blocks
Lecture	1 day	1/2 block
L'atelier de l'écrivain	1 day	1/2 block
Prépare-toi pour l'examen	1/2 day	1/2 block
Activités préparatoires	1/2 day	1/2 block
Examen	1 day	1/2 block
Révisions cumulatives	1 day	1/2 block

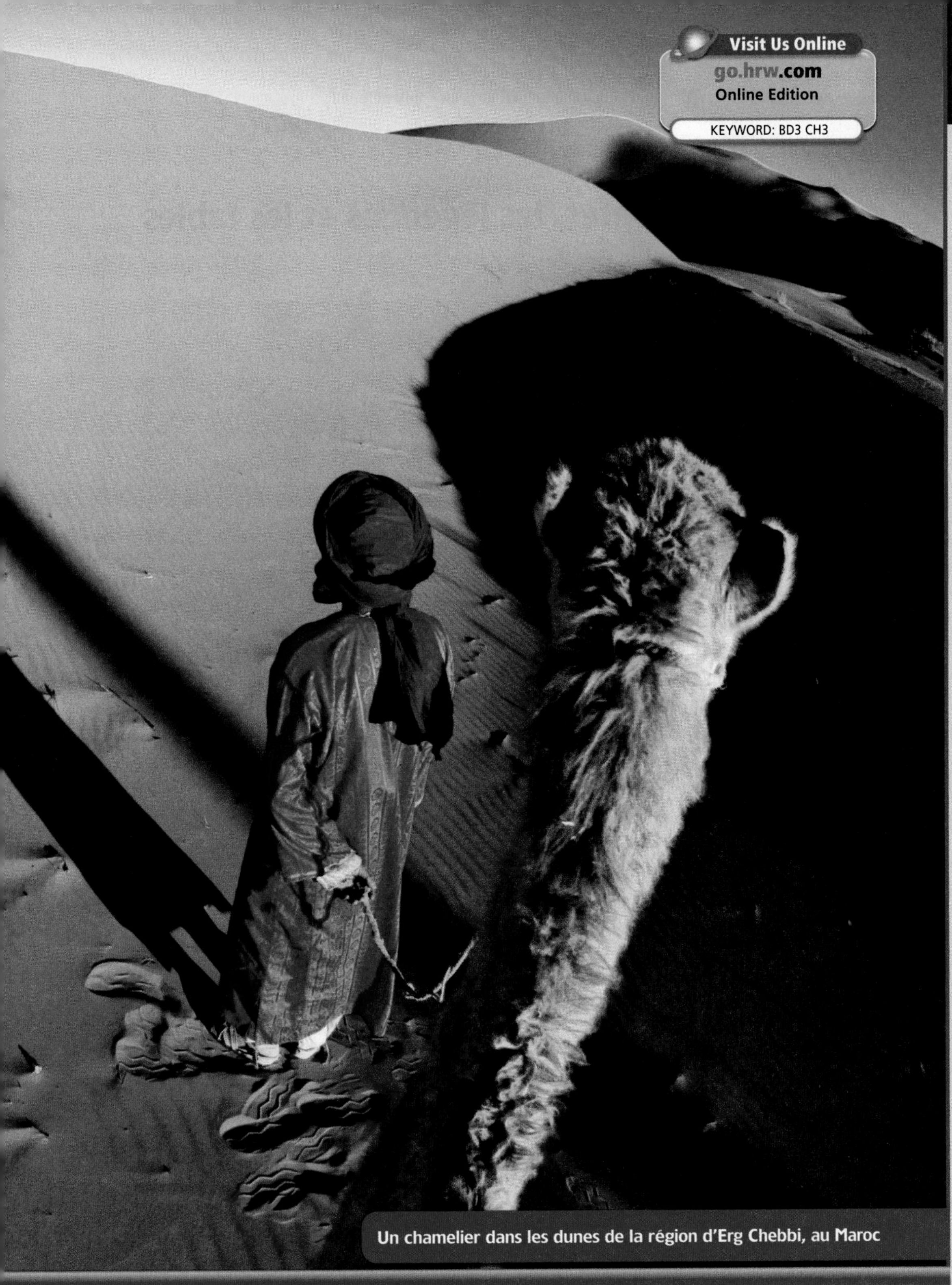

Un chamelier dans les dunes de la région d'Erg Chebbi, au Maroc

Vocabulaire supplémentaire

Students might use these terms to discuss the photo.

l'hospitalité	hospitality
la survie	survival
l'abri	shelter
mourir de faim	to starve
mourir de soif	to die of thirst
le palmier	palm tree
l'oasis	oasis
le turban	turban

Learning Tips

Have students imagine they work as tour guides at the Erg Chebbi dunes. Ask them to write in English a list of twenty terms they would need to know in order to provide tourists with information about the dunes. How many of these terms do they know in French? Have them look up the terms they do not know and write them in a notebook to use as reference.

Language Lab

You might want to use your language lab to have students:
- listen to all target vocabulary and phrases in the chapter
- practice pronunciation of vocabulary and phrases, using Holt SoundBooth to save their work for evaluation
- complete the listening activities in this chapter

LISTENING PRACTICE

Vocabulaire
Activity 2, p. 98, CD 3, Tr. 1
Activity 24, p. 111, CD 3, Tr. 4

Grammaire
Activity 12, p. 103, CD 3, Tr. 2
Activity 32, p. 114, CD 3, Tr. 5

Application
Activity 17, p. 104, CD 3, Tr. 3
Activity 37, p. 116, CD 3, Tr. 6

Language Lab and Classroom Activities

Prépare-toi pour l'examen
Activity 6, p. 125, CD 3, Tr. 8
Télé-culture: Interviews, Chapter 3

Activités préparatoires
Section I, Listening, p. 128, CD 3, Tr. 9
Télé-roman: Camille et compagnie, Épisode 3

Révisions cumulatives
Activity 1, p. 130, CD 3, Tr. 10

Lecture
p. 118, CD 3, Tr. 7

Objectifs
- to set the scene for a story
- to continue and end a story

Vocabulaire
à l'œuvre

Les contes, les légendes et les fables

Chaque culture a des croyances locales d'il y a bien longtemps. Dans ces récits, il y a souvent de la magie et des personnages héroïques et maléfiques.

Dans les contes du **Moyen-Orient**, **le sultan** est **souverain**. Il y a **des génies** qui **accordent des souhaits** au héros ou à l'héroïne. Il y a aussi **le calife** et **le vizir** qui **intriguent** contre le sultan.

D'autres mots utiles

des pouvoirs (m.)	*powers*
une potion	*potion*
le mal	*evil*
un tapis volant	*flying carpet*
un(e) sorcier(-ière)	*sorcerer*
se déplacer	*to get around*

▶ **Vocabulaire supplémentaire**—Les contes de fées, p. R17

Dans les contes, il y a **des ogres**, **des géants** et **des nains**. **La fée** et **le magicien** utilisent **une baguette** ou **une formule magique** pour faire **apparaître**, **disparaître** ou **transformer** des personnes et des objets.

 Bell Work

Use Bell Work 3.1 in the *Teaching Transparencies* or write this activity on the board.

Récris ces phrases poliment.

1. Je veux ce livre.
2. Vous pouvez tondre la pelouse?
3. Appelle-moi à 10h.
4. Je veux un gâteau d'anniversaire.
5. Coupez-moi les cheveux.

 1.2

Connections

Literature Link

The English term fairy tale derives from *Les contes de fées*, the title of a collection of fairy tales by Madame d'Aulnoy (1650/51–1705). Aulnoy is best known for her works *Les contes de fées* (1697) and *Contes nouveaux ou les fées à la mode* (1698). The tales reflect court and salon conversation and, as a result, had to be considerably revised to make them suitable for children. Some versions available in English bear little resemblance to the originals. Encourage students to read some her fairy tales.  3.1, 5.2

Core Instruction

TEACHING VOCABULAIRE

1. Introduce the vocabulary, using transparencies **Vocabulaire 3.1** and **3.2**. Model the pronunciation of each noun, using **Il y a...** or **Ça, c'est...**, as you point to the appropriate picture. **(3 min.)**

2. Model the pronunciation of the expressions in **Exprimons-nous!** Point out that even those that contain a verb in the present tense will be followed by a story in the past. **(3 min.)**

3. Ask students questions, using the vocabulary. **Tu aimes les contes de fées? Tu as peur des sorcières? Tu crois aux fantômes? (4 min.)**

4. Teach students the French names of some fairy tales (*Cendrillon, La belle au bois dormant, Blanche-neige*) and have them tell you the stories with the expressions in **Exprimons-nous!** and the vocabulary they just learned. Have them add, **Il y avait...**, when necessary. **(5 min.)**

Vocabulaire 1

Dans les contes européens, **le roi** et **la reine** habitent dans **un palais**. Il y a aussi **les chevaliers** qui **tuent des monstres** pour **sauver** les princesses **en danger** ou **prisonnières** dans **des tours**.

Dans les légendes et les fables, la nature est souvent **personnifiée**. Les animaux parlent et les éléments naturels, comme les arbres ou **les pierres**, jouent un rôle dans l'histoire. **Le but** des fables, c'est de donner **une leçon de conduite**, appelée **morale**.

D'autres mots utiles

une épée	*sword*		**un sort**	*spell*
un fantôme	*ghost*		**un traître**	*traitor*
une marâtre	*cruel stepmother*		**enchanté(e)**	*enchanted*
une marraine	*godmother*		**combattre**	*to fight*
un passage secret	*secret passage*		**délivrer**	*to set free*
un personnage	*character*		**transformer**	*to transform*

Exprimons-nous!

To set the scene for a story

Interactive TUTOR

Il était une fois... *Once upon a time, . . .*

Il y a bien longtemps, **dans un pays lointain...**   *. . . in a faraway place . . .*

Jadis, dans une tribu reculée,...   *A long time ago, in a remote tribe,. . .*

On raconte qu'autrefois...   *It is said that in times past, . . .*

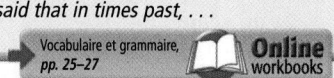
Vocabulaire et grammaire, pp. 25–27
Online workbooks

T P R
TOTAL PHYSICAL RESPONSE

Have students respond to these commands.

Lève le doigt si tu aimais les contes de fées quand tu étais petit(e).

Lève les deux mains si tu avais peur des sorcières.

Lève-toi si tu lis parfois des légendes.

Assieds-toi si tu préfères les récits où tout est bien qui finit bien.

Touche ton oreille si tu crois aux fantômes.

Dessine un tapis volant.

Place figurines and illustrations on a table. Have some students respond to the following commands.

Montre-moi un chevalier.

Amène-moi une princesse.

Va chercher un ogre.

Donne-moi une épée.

Prends la baguette magique. 1.2

COMMON ERROR ALERT
///ATTENTION !\\\

Students may assume that since **héros** and **héroïne** are related in meaning, they should both use the shortened form of the definite article (**l'**). However, **héros** has an aspirated **h** (**le héros**) and **héroïne** does not (**l'héroïne**).

Proverbes

For French proverbs and activities related to the chapter theme and vocabulary, see **Proverbes et expressions,** pp. R6–R7.

Differentiated Instruction

ADVANCED LEARNERS

Extension Legends, fairy tales, fables, romances, parables, and stories of adventures are often presented in a different context, such as a storyteller telling tales to an individual or a group of people. Have students research the context of *The Thousand and One Nights* in the library or on the Internet. Students may want to do their research in English, but should present the context, or frame story, in French. Encourage students to ask for clarifications if needed.
1.3, 3.1

SPECIAL LEARNING NEEDS

Students with Learning Disabilities Before presenting **Vocabulaire 1,** bring several children's books and a collection of fables to class. Review with the students how the author set, developed, and ended some of the stories. Emphasize the common language and characters in the stories to help students comprehend the concepts and vocabulary introduced in this chapter. 3.1

Resources

Planning:
Lesson Planner
 One-Stop Planner

Presentation:
 Teaching Transparencies
Vocabulaire 3.1, 3.2

Practice:
Cahier de vocabulaire et grammaire
Differentiated Practice and Assessment CD-ROM
Media Guide
 Audio CD 3, Tr. 1
Interactive Tutor, Disc 1

② Script

1. Jadis, dans une grande forêt, il y avait un monstre dont tout le village avait peur.
2. Il y a bien longtemps, dans un pays lointain, un roi et une reine étaient très tristes car ils n'avaient pas d'enfant.
3. On raconte qu'autrefois, un géant mangeait tout ce qu'il trouvait sur son chemin.
4. C'est à ce moment-là que la fée a fait apparaître le passage secret.
5. Il était une fois un sorcier qui préparait des potions pour donner des pouvoirs magiques à tous ceux qui en buvaient.
6. Le génie, dont les pouvoirs magiques étaient exceptionnels, a accordé le souhait du jeune sultan: il lui a donné un tapis volant très rapide.

③ Possible Answers

1. Un sultan, c'est le souverain d'un pays d'Afrique du Nord ou du Moyen-Orient.
2. Un génie, c'est quelqu'un de magique qui accorde des souhaits.
3. Une princesse, c'est la fille du roi et de la reine.
4. Un chevalier, c'est un jeune héros qui délivre la princesse.

---

① Associations logiques 🔗1.2

Lisons Associe les mots de la colonne de droite avec un mot ou une expression de la colonne de gauche.

b **1.** un nain   **a.** la maison d'un roi
d **2.** autrefois   **b.** quelqu'un de petit
e **3.** une morale   **c.** une formule magique
f **4.** un beau prince   **d.** il y a bien longtemps
a **5.** un palais   **e.** une leçon de conduite
           f. un héros

② Écoutons CD 3, Tr. 1 🔗1.2

Écoute ces extraits de contes et choisis l'image qui correspond à chaque conte.

a. 2.   **b.** 5.   **c.** 4.

d. 6.   **e.** 3.   **f.** 1.

③ Définitions 🔗1.2

Parlons/Écrivons Donne une courte explication pour chacun des mots suivants.

MODÈLE un ogre: **c'est un homme qui mange beaucoup.**

1. un sultan   **3.** une princesse
2. un génie   **4.** un chevalier

Core Instruction

TEACHING EXPRIMONS-NOUS!

1. Model the pronunciation of the expressions in **Exprimons-nous!** (2 min.)
2. Ask students to close their books while you randomly say the sentences in **Exprimons-nous!** Ask them if the sentences you say are 'to continue a story' or 'to end a story.' (3 min.)
3. Make up sentences that continue a story or end a story. Include the new expressions but use a different context, and have students decide whether you are continuing or ending a story. (3 min.)
4. Have partners create other sentences that use some of these expressions. (5 min.)

Exprimons-nous!

To continue a story	To end a story
Le lendemain, il est parti voir le sorcier. *The following day, . . .*	**Ils vécurent heureux et eurent beaucoup d'enfants.** *They lived happily ever after and had many children.*
La veille de son départ, il a préparé la potion. *On the eve of . . .*	**Tout est bien qui finit bien.** *All is well that ends well.*
Le temps a passé et le prince a grandi. *Time went by and . . .*	**La morale de cette histoire est que...** *The moral of this story is that . . .*
Un an **plus tard,** il est retourné au village. *. . . later . . .*	**Nul ne sait ce qui lui est arrivé.** *No one knows what happened to him/her.*

Interactive TUTOR

Vocabulaire et grammaire, pp. 25–27

Online workbooks

4 **Un conte de fées** 1.2

1. a passé 2. sa marâtre 3. sa marraine 4. pouvoirs magiques
5. une potion magique 6. disparaître 7. nul ne sait 8. tout est bien

Écrivons Complète ce conte avec les expressions de la boîte.

pouvoirs magiques	sa marraine	a passé	morale	sa marâtre
une potion magique	disparaître	nul ne sait	veille	tout est bien

Le temps ___1___ et la princesse a grandi. Mais ___2___ était de plus en plus méchante. Un jour, la princesse a décidé d'aller voir ___3___ qui avait des ___4___. La princesse lui a demandé de préparer ___5___ pour faire ___6___ sa marâtre. Plus tard, au dîner, la princesse a mis la potion dans l'eau de sa marâtre. Tout à coup, la marâtre a disparu et ___7___ ce qui lui est arrivé. Et pour la princesse, ___8___ qui finit bien.

5 **Mon conte préféré** 1.3

Écrivons Écris un paragraphe pour résumer ton conte préféré. Utilise l'imparfait et le passé composé.

Souviens-toi! Imparfait et passé composé, p. 24

MODÈLE Jadis, il y avait un garçon qui s'appelait Aladin...

À la créole

In Haïti, every story starts with **Cric-crac. It is like "Il était une fois..."** that starts every story in French.

Communication

HOLT **SoundBooth** ONLINE RECORDING

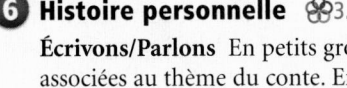

6 **Histoire personnelle** 3.1

Écrivons/Parlons En petits groupes, faites une liste de dix choses associées au thème du conte. Ensuite, échangez votre liste avec un autre groupe. Chaque groupe doit utiliser les mots de la liste pour inventer un conte. Une personne est le narrateur/la narratrice et les autres jouent les rôles des personnages du conte.

Communication

Class Activity: Presentational

Have students do a story chain of a fairy tale with real or imaginary characters. The first student begins a sentence with an opening and calls on another student who continues the story and calls on a third student. This continues until every one in the class has had a turn. Ask students to use the **passé composé** and the **imparfait** as appropriate. 1.3

Differentiated Instruction

SLOWER PACE LEARNERS

4 **Variation** Some students may have difficulty completing this activity. Illustrate, or ask volunteers to illustrate, the fairy tale in three to four frames. Use an overhead projector to show the illustrations to the class. Have students describe what is happening in each frame with the sentences in this activity and the expressions from the word box. 1.1

SPECIAL LEARNING NEEDS

Students with Learning Disabilities/ Dyslexia Ask students to create note cards with each of the phrases and vocabulary introduced in this chapter. The note cards should have the English translation on the back. A sample sentence using the word can be added to the note cards. Students may use the note cards as a classroom resource for studying or practice. 1.2

Assess

Assessment Program

Quiz: Vocabulaire 1

Alternative Assessment

Differentiated Practice and Assessment CD-ROM

Online Assessment
my.hrw.com

Test Generator

Objectifs
• the *passé simple*
• relative pronouns with *ce*

Grammaire
à l'œuvre 1

Interactive TUTOR

Resources

Planning:

Lesson Planner

 One-Stop Planner

Practice:

Grammar Tutor for Students of French, Chapter 3

Cahier de vocabulaire et grammaire

Differentiated Practice and Assessment CD-ROM

Cahier d'activités

Media Guide

 Teaching Transparencies Bell Work 3.2

 Interactive Tutor, Disc 1

 Bell Work

Use Bell Work 3.2 in the *Teaching Transparencies* or write this activity on the board.

Complète les phrases suivantes.

1. Le roi et la reine habitent...
2. Le sultan est...
3. Le sorcier fait...
4. Le magicien transforme...
5. La fée a...

a. les personnes et les animaux.
b. des potions magiques.
c. dans un palais.
d. une baguette magique.
e. un souverain. 🌸1.2

Connections

Language to Language

In English, fairy tales usually begin with the stock phrase "Once upon a time..." and end with "... and they all lived happily ever after." In French, fairy tales begin with "Il était une fois ..." Ask students to research the common ending of fairy tales in French. **("... et se marièrent et eurent beaucoup d'enfants.")** 🌸3.2, 4.1

Flash culture

Autrefois, en Afrique, les griots jouaient le rôle très important d'historiens et de conseillers des rois. Ils racontaient des légendes et transmettaient le savoir et l'histoire d'un peuple. Aujourd'hui, les griots racontent encore des contes et des légendes mais ce sont aussi des chanteurs de chansons traditionnelles.

Est-ce qu'il existe une tradition orale dans ta communauté? Ta famille raconte des histoires anciennes? 🌸4.2

Un griot en Afrique

The *passé simple*

1 In French, the **passé simple** is a past tense, used in place of the **passé composé**, primarily in literary texts. To form the **passé simple** of regular verbs, remove the **-er**, **-ir**, or **-re** ending from the infinitive and add the following endings. Notice that **-ir** and **-re** verbs have the same endings.

	parler	finir	perdre
je	parl**ai**	fin**is**	perd**is**
tu	parl**as**	fin**is**	perd**is**
il/elle/on	parl**a**	fin**it**	perd**it**
nous	parl**âmes**	fin**îmes**	perd**îmes**
vous	parl**âtes**	fin**îtes**	perd**îtes**
ils/elles	parl**èrent**	fin**irent**	perd**irent**

2 Here are the forms of a few verbs with irregular **passé simple** forms.

> **avoir:** j'**eus**, tu **eus**, il **eut**, nous **eûmes**, vous **eûtes**, ils **eurent**
> **être:** je **fus**, tu **fus**, il **fut**, nous **fûmes**, vous **fûtes**, ils **furent**
> **faire:** je **fis**, tu **fis**, il **fit**, nous **fîmes**, vous **fîtes**, ils **firent**
> **venir:** je **vins**, tu **vins**, il **vint**, nous **vînmes**, vous **vîntes**, ils **vinrent**
> **dire:** je **dis**, tu **dis**, il **dit**, nous **dîmes**, vous **dîtes**, ils **dirent**

In the **passé simple**, **aller** is conjugated like a regular **-er** verb.

Here are some verbs that are often used in stories in the **passé simple**:
  naître: il **naquit**   vivre *(to live):* il **vécut**   mourir: il **mourut**

> Vocabulaire et grammaire, *pp. 28–29*
> Cahier d'activités, *pp. 21–23*
>  **Online** workbooks

7 **C'était un rêve?** 🌸1.2

Lisons L'auteur de ce passage a fait un rêve bizarre… mais était-ce un rêve? Souligne les verbes qui sont au **passé simple**.

«Après le dîner, je <u>passai</u> une ou deux heures dans un fauteuil à lire une vieille légende. Soudain, j'<u>entendis</u> sonner minuit. J'en <u>fus</u> surpris, parce qu'il n'y avait pas d'horloge *(clock)* dans la pièce. Alors la porte s'<u>ouvrit</u>, et le fantôme de la princesse Anaïs <u>entra</u>: elle portait une robe blanche et je la <u>trouvai</u> très belle. Elle me <u>dit</u> de me lever et nous <u>allâmes</u> vers un passage secret… à ce moment-là, mon portable <u>sonna</u> et me <u>réveilla</u>…»

Core Instruction

TEACHING GRAMMAIRE

1. Review the present tense of **-er**, **-re**, and **-ir** verbs by having students prompt three volunteers who conjugate one verb each on the board. (**parler**, **finir**, and **perdre**) **(5 min.)**

2. Erase the endings of all three verbs and replace them with those of the **passé simple**. Model their pronunciation. Point out that the three singular forms of **-ir** and **-re** verbs have the same pronunciation, as do the second-person and third-person singular forms of **-er** verbs. **(4 min.)**

3. Go over the forms of irregular verbs and model their pronunciation. Point out that the three singular forms have the same pronunciation. **(2 min.)**

4. Tell students they are not likely to hear these forms unless they are watching a 17th century play. Ask them what forms of the **passé composé** they would use instead. **(2 min.)**

Online Practice
go.hrw.com
Grammaire 1 practice
KEYWORD: BD3 CH3

8 Livres de contes 🌸 1.2

Écrivons Dans les contes, on utilise souvent le **passé simple.**
Récris les phrases suivantes au **passé composé.**

MODÈLE   Le sultan et sa femme arrivèrent au palais.
Le sultan et sa femme **sont arrivés** au palais.

1. Ce jour-là, le sultan vint à la fête.
2. Il parla à ses invités.
3. Vous fûtes héroïques, leur dit-il.
4. Je n'eus jamais de meilleurs amis.
5. Nous combattîmes ensemble le mauvais sort.
6. Vous fîtes obstacle au génie.
7. Et toi, Ali, tu cherchas le traître dans tout le pays.
8. Tu le fis prisonnier.
9. Ensuite, tes hommes le conduisirent dans la tour du palais.
10. Et nous fûmes tous contents de ne plus être en danger.

8 Answers

1. Ce jour-là, le sultan est venu…
2. Il a parlé à ses invités.
3. Vous avez été héroïques, leur a-t-il dit.
4. Je n'ai jamais eu…
5. Nous avons combattu…
6. Vous avez fait…
7. Et toi, Ali, tu as cherché…
8. Tu l'as fait prisonnier.
9. Ensuite, tes hommes l'ont conduit…
10. Et nous avons tous été contents.

Communication

9 Scénario 🌸 1.1, 3.2

Parlons Tu racontes cette histoire à un(e) camarade. Il/Elle ne comprend pas tout parce qu'il y a des verbes au passé simple et te pose des questions.

MODÈLE   —Le roi et la reine arrivèrent au palais.
—Qu'est-ce qu'ils ont fait?

HOLT **SoundBooth**
ONLINE RECORDING

Il était une fois un roi et une reine qui n'avaient pas d'enfant. Ils allèrent voir une sorcière et lui demandèrent de leur donner un fils. La sorcière accepta à une condition: le jour où le prince aurait vingt ans, il devrait se marier avec elle. Le roi et la reine n'acceptèrent pas cette condition et s'en allèrent, très tristes. En rentrant, ils virent une vieille dame qui portait beaucoup de paquets et ne pouvait plus marcher. La reine lui offrit de monter dans sa voiture. Alors, la vieille se transforma en une belle jeune fille. Elle dit que la sorcière l'avait transformée en vieille dame. Seul quelqu'un de gentil pouvait changer le mauvais sort. Et la jeune fille, qui était aussi une fée, accorda son souhait à la reine et quelques mois plus tard, un petit prince naquit.

Communication

Individual/ Group Activity: Presentational

Have students write a short story in the **passé simple.** Encourage them to include some of the new vocabulary from the chapter. Then have students form small groups and exchange stories. After exchanging stories, each student reads the story to the group, but changes the tense from the **passé simple** to the **passé composé** as he or she reads it. 🌸 1.2, 1.3

French for Spanish Speakers

Ask Spanish speakers what tense the **passé simple** seems to correspond with structurally in Spanish? (the **pretérito**) Ask students to identify verbs in this list that seem most similar in pronunciation or spelling to equivalent Spanish verbs in the **pretérito.** (perdre/perder, être/ser) Ask students what the difference in usage is between the **passé simple** and the **pretérito.** (The **passé simple** is hardly ever used in spoken language, whereas the **pretérito** is used in both spoken and written Spanish) 🌸 4.1

Differentiated Instruction

SLOWER PACE LEARNERS

7 **Additional Practice** After students have finished this activity, ask them to conjugate in the **passé simple** the verbs they have marked. They may refer to the grammar presentation above as well as the reference section in the back of their book. 🌸 1.2

MULTIPLE INTELLIGENCES

Bodily-Kinesthetic While reviewing the **passé simple,** ask students to repeat each form of the verb in a choral response. Have students repeat each form chorally a second time and clap with each syllable. The physical act of clapping creates another way to imprint the verb form in their memory. This activity can be useful anytime new verb forms are introduced.

Je (clap) **parl** (clap) **ai** (clap)
Tu (clap) **parl** (lap) **as** (clap) 🌸 1.1

Resources

Planning:

Lesson Planner

 One-Stop Planner

Practice:

Grammar Tutor for Students of French, Chapter 3

Cahier de vocabulaire et grammaire

Differentiated Practice and Assessment CD-ROM

Cahier d'activités

Media Guide

Teaching Transparencies Bell Work 3.3

Audio CD 3, Tr. 2

Interactive Tutor, Disc 1

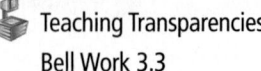

Bell Work

Use Bell Work 3.3 in the *Teaching Transparencies* or write this activity on the board.

Mets les phrases à la forme correcte du **passé simple**.

1. Le sorcier (fit / fut) une potion magique pour la princesse.
2. La princesse (s'endormît / s'endormit).
3. Des chevaliers (verront / vinrent) tuer le monstre.
4. Le prince (délivra / délivrai) la princesse.
5. La princesse (s'éveilla / s'éveillera). 🌼 1.2

Comparisons

Comparing and Contrasting

The pronoun **tout** when used with indefinite relative pronouns changes the meaning to *everything* or *all*. Ask students to give the English equivalents of **Tout ce qu'elle écrit est intéressant.** What is the French equivalent of, "The genie granted the princess everything she wanted"? 🌼 4.1

Relative pronouns with *ce*

Ce qui and **ce que** are relative pronouns that mean *what* (or *that which*) and are used to refer to *a general idea* or *to something that hasn't been mentioned.* For example, in the sentence "I don't understand **what** he means," **what** doesn't refer to anything specifically mentioned.

1 Ce qui is a subject and is usually followed by a **verb**.

> **Ce qui est** incroyable, c'est la fin de la fable.
> *What's incredible is the end of the fable.*

2 Ce que/qu' is an object and is usually followed by a **subject** and a **verb**.

> Le génie a accordé au prince **ce qu'il voulait**.
> *The genie granted the prince what he wanted.*

3 Ce dont also means *what*. It replaces a phrase that follows an expression with **de**.

> Elle parlait **de** quelque chose. Il ne savait pas **ce dont** elle parlait.
> *She talked about something. He did not know what she was talking about.*

Vocabulaire et grammaire, pp. 28–29
Cahier d'activités, pp. 21–23

 **Online** workbooks

Déjà vu!

Do you remember how to use the relative pronouns **qui**, **que**, and **dont**? These pronouns help you avoid repeating a word or phrase previously mentioned.

Qui is the subject of a clause. It is usually followed by a verb.

> C'est la reine **qui** a dit ça.

Que is the direct object of a clause. It is usually followed by a subject and a verb.

> Voici le conte **que** je lis.

Dont replaces a phrase starting with **de**.

> Il a peur **de** ce chien.
> Le chien **dont** il a peur n'est pas méchant.

⑩ Suite logique 🌼 1.2

Lisons Trouve la continuation logique de chaque phrase.

d **1.** Je voudrais savoir ce qui…
f **2.** Les génies accordent tout ce que/qu'…
e **3.** Le héros réussit toujours à trouver ce que/qu'…
a **4.** Une baguette magique, c'est ce dont…
b **5.** La potion magique est ce que…

a. elle aurait besoin.
b. les magiciens utilisent.
c. j'ai peur.
d. est arrivé à la fin de l'histoire.
e. il cherche.
f. on veut.

⑪ Soyons réalistes 🌼 1.2

Lisons/Écrivons Ahmed parle des contes de fées. Complète ses phrases avec **qui, que/qu', dont, ce qui, ce que/qu'** et **ce dont**.

1. Ce qui
2. que
3. que
4. Ce dont
5. qu'
6. ce que
7. qui
8. dont
9. qu'
10. qui

____1____ est fantastique dans cette histoire, c'est ____2____ le prince utilise la chaussure ____3____ Cendrillon a perdue pour la retrouver. ____4____ le prince avait vraiment envie, c'était de danser encore avec Cendrillon ____5____ il trouvait très belle. Moi, ____6____ je n'aime pas, ce sont les histoires peu réalistes, comme l'histoire du prince ____7____ réveille une princesse ____8____ personne ne parlait plus, ____9____ on avait oubliée et ____10____ dormait depuis cent ans.

Core Instruction

TEACHING GRAMMAIRE

1. Go over **Déjà vu!** to review **qui**, **que**, and **dont**. (5 min.)

2. Introduce **ce qui**, **ce que**, and **ce dont**. Tell students that unlike **qui**, **que**, and **dont** they can only refer to an unknown thing and never to people. (5 min.)

3. Ask students to answer questions with **ce qui**, **ce que**, or **ce dont**. Leslie, qu'est-ce qui est important, à ton avis? David, qu'est-ce que tu aimes faire le weekend? Sarah, de quoi est-ce que tu as envie? (5 min.)

12 Écoutons CD 3, Tr. 2 🌐1.2   1. a 2. c 3. b 4. b 5. c 6. a

Tu es dans un endroit où il y a beaucoup de bruit et tu entends des bouts de conversation mais certains mots sont difficiles à entendre. Écoute les phrases suivantes et complète-les avec **a) ce qui, b) ce que/qu'** ou **c) ce dont.**

13 Mille et une nuits 🌐1.2

✏️ **Écrivons** Fais des phrases avec les mots des colonnes.

Je n'ai pas bien compris	ce que/qu'	la légende parle.
C'est le tapis volant	dont	lui a accordé trois souhaits.
Voilà le héros	ce dont	s'est passé.
Il y a un génie	que/qu'	il parle.
	ce qui	le vizir veut.
	qui	le sultan va faire.

14 Un peu de magie 🌐1.2

✏️ **Écrivons/Parlons** Fais une phrase avec chacun des objets représentés. Utilise **ce qui, ce que** et **ce dont.**

MODÈLE   Ce que le magicien a fait apparaître, c'est un lapin.

1.   2.   3.   4.

Communication

HOLT **SoundBooth** ONLINE RECORDING

15 Questions personnelles 🌐1.1

Parlons Pose des questions à un(e) camarade. Il/Elle va te dire ce qu'il/elle aime en littérature, en sport, comme films, ce dont il/elle parle avec ses ami(e)s, et de quoi il/elle a envie ou peur, etc. Ensuite, échangez les rôles.

MODÈLE —De quoi est-ce que tu as envie?
          —Moi, ce dont j'ai envie, c'est…

12 Script
See script on p. 93E.

14 Possible Answers

1. Ce dont la sorcière avait besoin, c'est une potion.
2. Ce qui est arrivé au génie, c'est qu'il n'a pas pu sortir de la lampe.
3. Ce que le prince voulait, c'est un tapis volant.
4. Ce qui est incroyable, c'est que le monstre n'a pas détruit toute la ville.

Communication

15 Group Activity: Interpersonal

Write the following verbs and phrases on the board: **avoir besoin de, être en solde, vouloir acheter, chercher, avoir envie de.** Have partners create a dialog between a customer and a salesperson in a store. The customer describes an item without naming it, starting each statement with **ce que, ce qui,** or **ce dont.** The salesperson identifies what the client is talking about using the same verb the client used along with **que, qui,** or **dont.** Have students discuss five items.

MODÈLE
—Pardon, ce dont j'ai envie est en plastique et me protège quand il pleut.
—C'est un imperméable dont vous avez envie. 🌐1.1

Differentiated Instruction

ADVANCED LEARNERS

15 Variation Ask students to imagine that they are working for a teen magazine. Their task is to create a survey about the interests of teens. The survey should include ten questions with the relative pronoun **ce.** Have students distribute their survey in class. Encourage students to use graphs, charts, or other graphic organizers to illustrate their findings. The class should evaluate the results, addressing issues such as slanted survey questions, non-representative samples, and misleading graphs or charts. 🌐1.3, 3.1

SPECIAL LEARNING NEEDS

Students with AD(H)D Ask students to make a poster to convey the information in **Déjà vu!** Have students list the rules for the use of the relative pronouns **qui, que,** and **dont** and develop additional examples of their use. Display the posters in the classroom to us as a resource when you begin the presentation about relative pronouns with **ce.** 🌐1.3

Assess

Assessment Program

Quiz: Grammaire 1

Alternative Assessment

Differentiated Practice and Assessment CD-ROM

Online Assessment
my.hrw.com

Test Generator

Synthèse
• Vocabulaire 1
• Grammaire 1

Application 1

16 **Plein de questions** 1.3

Parlons/Écrivons Réponds à ces questions en utilisant **ce qui**, **ce que** et **ce dont** dans tes réponses.

MODÈLE De quoi a-t-on besoin pour écrire un bon conte?
Ce dont on a besoin pour écrire un bon conte, c'est d'un prince qui doit sauver une princesse et d'un mauvais génie qui le transforme en...

1. Qu'est-ce qui est arrivé à la fin du conte de Cendrillon?
2. De quoi est-ce que tu avais peur quand tu étais petit(e)?
3. Qu'est-ce que tu préfères, les contes ou les fables? Pourquoi?
4. Qu'est-ce que tu aimes prendre avec toi pour lire quand tu pars en vacances?
5. Qu'est-ce qui se passe en général à la fin d'un conte?

Un peu plus

Adjective placement and meaning

Some French adjectives have a different meaning depending on whether they are placed **before a noun** or **after a noun**. When they are placed **after a noun** adjectives usually have a more *litteral meaning*: un homme **grand** is a *tall man*. If the adjectives are placed **before a noun** the meaning is more *figurative*: un **grand** homme is a *great man*.

un **ancien** professeur	*a former professor*
une légende **ancienne**	*an ancient (old) legend*
un **vrai** cauchemar	*a real nightmare*
une histoire **vraie**	*a true story*

Here are some other adjectives that change meaning:

certain: *certain (some) / sure*
cher: *dear / expensive*
dernier: *last / previous*
pauvre: *poor (unfortunate) / poor (destitute)*
propre: *own / clean*
sale: *nasty / dirty*
seul: *only / lonely*

 Vocabulaire et grammaire, p. 30
Cahier d'activités, pp. 21–23
Online workbooks

17 **Écoutons** CD 3, Tr. 3 1.2

Écoute cette histoire et dis si les phrases suivantes sont
a) **vraies** ou b) **fausses**.

b **1.** Ali Pacha est grand.
a **2.** L'homme lui offre une vieille lampe.
b **3.** L'homme n'a pas beaucoup d'argent.
a **4.** Ali Pacha a utilisé la lampe plusieurs fois sans problème.
b **5.** Le génie est sorti de la lampe la fois dernière.
b **6.** L'histoire que tu viens d'entendre est une histoire vraie!

Resources

Planning:

Lesson Planner

 One-Stop Planner

Practice:

Grammar Tutor for Students of French, Chapter 3

Cahier de vocabulaire et grammaire

Differentiated Practice and Assessment CD-ROM

Cahier d'activités

Media Guide

 Teaching Transparencies
Bell Work 3.4

Audio CD 3, Tr. 3

Interactive Tutor, Disc 1

Bell Work

Use Bell Work 3.4 in the *Teaching Transparencies* or write this activity on the board.

Complète les phrases avec **ce qui, ce que, ce qu'** et **ce dont.**

1. _____ Cendrillon rêve, c'est d'aller au bal.
2. Un superbe carrosse! C'est _____ il lui faut.
3. _____ elle veut, c'est une belle robe.
4. _____ est drôle, c'est que sa marâtre ne l'a pas reconnue.
5. Les contes, c'est _____ je préfère. 1.2

17 Script

Un jour, Ahmed qui venait de gagner beaucoup d'argent, voulut faire un cadeau à son grand ami, Ali Pacha. Il lui offrit une lampe ancienne pour son anniversaire. Le pauvre Ahmed ne savait pas qu'un mauvais génie vivait dans cette lampe. Ali Pacha utilisa la lampe pendant un certain temps et rien ne se passa, mais la dernière fois qu'il l'alluma, le méchant génie sortit de la lampe et transforma le petit Pacha en serpent.

Core Instruction

INTEGRATED PRACTICE

1. Have students do Activity 16 to practice previously taught material. **(5 min.)**
2. Introduce **Un peu plus.** (See presentation suggestions at right.) **(4 min.)**
3. Continue with integrated practice Activities 17–20. **(30 min.)**

TEACHING UN PEU PLUS

1. Review the placement of adjectives by asking students to write a few short sentences that describe people and objects. Ask them to begin their sentences with **C'est un/une...** **(4 min.)**
2. Go over **Un peu plus.** Call out combinations of nouns and adjectives, such as **élève / ancien**, and then have students use them in complete sentences. **(4 min.)**

Online Practice
go.hrw.com
Application 1 practice
KEYWORD: BD3 CH3

Chapitre 3
Application 1

18 À la bonne place 🍀1.2

Écrivons Place les adjectifs correctement dans ces phrases.

1. Pépin le Bref fût un _____ roi _____ mais il était très petit. (grand)
2. Le _____ cours _____ que j'aime, c'est le cours de français! (seul)
3. Cendrillon mit une _____ robe _____ pour aller au bal. (propre)
4. «Mon _____ ami _____!», dit le traître. (cher)
5. Le _____ jour _____ des vacances, j'étais triste. (dernier)

19 La nuit du Sultan 🍀1.3, 3.2

Lisons/Écrivons Regarde ce poster et réponds aux questions.

1. Quel conte de fées est présenté?
2. En quelle saison ce spectacle a-t-il lieu?
3. À quelle heure est-ce que le spectacle commence?
4. Quels jours de la semaine est-ce que cela a lieu?
5. D'après toi, cela se passe dans quel pays? Pourquoi?

La nuit du Sultan

Son et Lumière sur la médina

Pendant tout l'été, venez assister au spectacle son et lumière qui vous transportera au XIVe siècle.

Tous les vendredis et samedis, les sultans, les vizirs et les califes seront vos guides.

Redécouvrez l'histoire d'Ali Baba et des 40 voleurs.

Spectacle à 21h • Entrée gratuite

Communication

HOLT **SoundBooth** ONLINE RECORDING

20 Préférences personnelles 🍀1.1

Parlons Avec un(e) camarade, discutez de ce que vous aimez et n'aimez pas comme contes et parlez de ce qui est essentiel dans un bon conte de fées. Pensez aux contes de votre enfance.

MODÈLE —Moi, ce que j'aime dans les contes, c'est quand il y a des génies qui...

18 Answers

1. un grand roi
2. le seul cours
3. une robe propre
4. mon cher ami
5. le dernier jour

19 Answers

1. L'histoire d'Ali Baba et des 40 voleurs est présentée.
2. Le spectacle a lieu en été.
3. Le spectacle commence à 21h.
4. Cela a lieu le vendredi et le samedi.
5. Answers will vary.

Communication

Pair Activity: Interpersonal

Write the list of adjectives from **Un peu plus** on the board. Partners take turns describing an object or a person with circumlocution to avoid using the adjectives on the board. The partner then uses one of the adjectives on the board to confirm his or her understanding. Have students pay attention to proper placement of the adjective.

MODÈLE
— C'est un homme qui n'a pas d'argent. Il n'a pas de job.
— C'est un homme pauvre?
— Oui, c'est ça. 🍀1.1, 1.2

Differentiated Instruction

SLOWER PACE LEARNERS

16 Building on Previous Skills Have students look at the **modèle**. Remind them to use **ce qui** if a verb follows and **ce que/qu'** if a subject and a verb follow. Tell students to use **ce dont** if a subject and a verb that requires the preposition **de** follow. Ask students to list verbs or verb phrases that require the preposition **de**.

MULTIPLE INTELLIGENCES

19 Visual Learners Students with visual intelligence enjoy creating images or objects. As an alternative to this activity, allow students to create their own poster, questions, and responses. When finished, students may ask classmates to respond to their questions. Students may be more motivated to participate when given the opportunity to use their creativity. 🍀1.1

Assess

Assessment Program
Quiz: Application 1
Audio CD 3, Tr. 11 🎧
Alternative Assessment
Differentiated Practice and Assessment CD-ROM
Online Assessment
my.hrw.com
Test Generator

Lecture culturelle

La littérature maghrébine de langue française prend ses racines dans l'histoire, celle de la colonisation territoriale, politique, linguistique et culturelle; elle est le produit d'écrivains arabes ou berbères[1] nés au Maghreb mais formés à l'école française et dont les textes témoignent de la rencontre des cultures arabo-berbère et occidentale. Que penses-tu d'une culture bilingue comme celle décrite ci-dessous? 🌼2.2

Prereading Questions

You may ask these questions before students read the selection.

1. **Où se trouve le Maghreb? (en Afrique du Nord)**
2. **Peux-tu nommer les pays du Maghreb? (Algérie, Maroc, Tunisie)**
3. **Quel pays a colonisé les pays du Maghreb au XIXème siècle? (la France)**

Active Reading Questions

1. **Quelles cultures est-ce que la littérature maghrébine en langue française englobe? (maghrébine et française)**
2. **Où est-ce qu'on apprend le français dans les pays du Maghreb? (à l'école, au lycée, à l'université)**
3. **Est-ce qu'il y a des auteurs maghrébins qui écrivent dans plusieurs langues? Lesquelles? (oui; en arabe et en français)**
4. **Est-ce que les livres des écrivains maghrébins sont publiés en France? (oui)** 🌼1.2

Vocabulaire supplémentaire

You might use these terms to discuss the text.

Mots arabes utilisés dans la langue française:

bled (village)	*village*
caïd (chef)	*chief*
klebs (chien)	*dog*
souk (marché)	*market*
toubib (médecin)	*doctor*

La littérature Maghrébine en Français

La littérature englobe[2] souvent plusieurs cultures en un seul style d'écriture, comme c'est le cas de la littérature maghrébine de langue française. [...] Les auteurs maghrébins se servent[3] du français, parce que l'histoire de leurs pays l'a voulu ainsi[4]. [...] Le français est la deuxième langue officielle dans tout le Maghreb, elle s'apprend à l'école, au lycée, à l'université. Les gens parlent le français, l'entendent à la télévision, à la radio, bref, le français est partout[5], même[6] dans les administrations.

Par ailleurs[7], il existe des auteurs nouveaux, qui connaissent l'arabe et écrivent aussi bien en arabe qu'en français. D'autres, dominent mieux le français que l'arabe et préfèrent donc s'exprimer en français.

Du reste[8], la langue française leur ouvre une audience plus large que l'arabe, surtout pour les écrivains publiés par de grands éditeurs parisiens.

Compréhension 🌼2.2

1. Quelle est la deuxième langue officielle du Maghreb?
2. Où est-ce que l'on pratique le français?
3. Pourquoi les auteurs maghrébins écrivent-ils en français?

1. le français
2. à l'école, au lycée, à l'université
3. pour avoir une audience plus large

1. habitants d'une région du Maroc et de l'Algérie 2. inclut 3. utilisent 4. *this way* 5. *everywhere* 6. *even* 7. *Moreover* 8. De plus

Core Instruction

LECTURE CULTURELLE

1. Read and discuss the introductory paragraph as a class. **(3 min.)**
2. Continue reading the text of **La littérature maghrébine en français** as a class. **(5 min.)**
3. Have students write the answers to the **Compréhension** questions on the board. Then discuss the selection as a class and go over any questions students might have. **(15 min.)**

COMPARAISONS ET COMMUNAUTÉ

1. Ask students to read the first paragraph of **Écrire en français** and discuss the question. Continue reading. **(6 min.)**
2. Have students answer the **Et toi?** questions in small groups. **(5 min.)**
3. Go over **Communauté et professions.** Ask volunteers to research careers that involve dubbing movies. You might bring in a dubbed French version of an American movie on DVD and show short excerpts. **(5 min.)**

Comparaisons

Écrire en français 🎬4.2

Pièce de Samuel Beckett

Tu es au lycée en France. Pour un cours tu dois lire la pièce de théâtre *En attendant Godot* de Samuel Beckett, un écrivain irlandais. Est-ce que la pièce est écrite à l'origine en anglais ou en français?

　a. en français
　b. en anglais
　c. dans les deux langues

Samuel Beckett, lauréat du Prix Nobel de littérature en 1969, a d'abord écrit en anglais, puis en français, puis dans l'une et l'autre langue. *En attendant Godot* est sa première pièce de théâtre en français. Beaucoup d'écrivains pour des raisons personnelles, économiques ou même politiques quittent[1] leur pays d'origine et s'installent à l'étranger[2]. Lorsque tu penses à des auteurs vivant loin de leur pays natal[3], tu t'imagines qu'ils écrivent automatiquement dans leur langue maternelle[4]. Et pourtant, ce n'est pas toujours le cas.

🎬4.2

ET TOI?

1. Connais-tu des personnes qui viennent d'un autre pays? Dans quelle langue s'expriment-elles?

2. Connais-tu des écrivains, acteurs, chanteurs, politiciens, chercheurs... étrangers qui vivent aux États-Unis? Dans quelle langue s'expriment-ils?

Communauté et professions

Doubleur – un métier en plein boum

🎬5.2

Une séance de doublage

De nos jours, on a souvent besoin de doubler des voix pour la version française de films, de reportages étrangers et même de jeux vidéo. Le doublage est difficile: il faut être juste et fidèle à l'interprétation de l'acteur. Pour devenir doubleur, on passe des castings et on apprend sur le tas[5]. Que faut-il faire pour devenir doubleur aux États-Unis? Y a-t-il des écoles spécialisées? Fais des recherches et présente ce que tu as découvert sur le doublage à ta classe.

1. partent de　2. un autre pays　3. où une personne est née
4. première langue parlée　5. en pratiquant

Culture

Bulletin Board Project

Have groups of students research, on the Internet or in the library, other places in the Francophone world where one or more languages, besides French, are spoken, and where literature is written in those languages. Have each group choose a country and a piece of prose or poetry. Group members should describe how the other language and culture influence the writing. If possible, students should illustrate their selection with pictures that show the influence of culture on the piece. On a bulletin board in the classroom, volunteers can exhibit their work.　🏵3.2

Cultures

🏵 Practices and Perspectives

Every day, people from all over the world are coming to the United States to find work or political asylum. Many of these foreigners do not speak the language. Ask your students if they know of such families in their town. Are there any organizations or agencies that are set up to help these persons integrate into American society? Do you know if these agencies have staff members who can speak French?　🏵2.1

Communities

Career Path

Ask students to name some French or Francophone movies. Have they watched a French movie in the original version or was it dubbed? Ask students to make a list of careers in show business. Are they interested in such careers? Can they think of some instances when French would be an asset in this field?　🏵5.1

Differentiated Instruction

ADVANCED LEARNERS

Extension In 2005, the Algerian author Assia Djebar was the first writer from the Maghreb to be elected to the **Académie française.** She has been nominated repeatedly for the Nobel Prize in literature. Ask students to research one of her novels and discuss its main idea. Students should address perspectives that may be prevalent in Maghrebian literature, such as critism of colonization or of the status of Muslim women. Have students present their research to the class.　🏵1.3, 3.2

MULTIPLE INTELLIGENCES

Linguistic Ask students to bring a favorite movie to class. They should memorize several lines from a scene and prepare to dub the lines in French for the class. With the sound off, play the scene and allow students to dub the French translation of the lines, while the class watches the scene on the video.　🏵1.2

Resources

Planning:

Lesson Planner

 One-Stop Planner

Presentation:

 Teaching Transparencies
Vocabulaire 3.3, 3.4

Practice:

Cahier de vocabulaire et grammaire

Differentiated Practice and Assessment CD-ROM

Media Guide

 Teaching Transparencies
Bell Work 3.5

 Interactive Tutor, Disc 1

Bell Work

Use Bell Work 3.5 in the *Teaching Transparencies* or write this activity on the board.

Mets les phrases suivantes dans le bon ordre.

1. **Napoléon / homme / grand / un / était**
2. **Marine / chère / a acheté / maison / une**
3. **mon / maths / professeur / de / C'est / ancien**
4. **meuble / C'est / ancien / un**
5. **l'année / Décembre / mois / est / dernier / le / de**
6. **dernier / en / suis allé / Je / mois / le / France** 1.2

Connections

History Link

France had colonial possessions from the beginning of the 17th century until the 1960s. Including metropolitan France, the total area of land under French sovereignty in the 1920s and 1930s covered 8.6 percent of the world's land area. Have students research France's colonial history in Africa. They should provide dates and facts as well as report on the main reasons for France's colonization of Africa.

3.1

Objectifs
- to relate a sequence of events
- to tell what happened to someone else

Vocabulaire à l'œuvre 2

Un peu d'histoire franco-africaine

La **conquête** de l'Algérie a commencé en 1830. Ce fut **le commencement** de **la colonisation** française.

Au XIXᵉ siècle, des **explorateurs** français sont allés en Afrique pour **établir des cartes géographiques**. Ils ont **exploré** les pays du **Maghreb** (la Tunisie, le Maroc et l'Algérie) et des pays d'**Afrique de l'Ouest**.

1830	**1940–1945**	**1955**	

Souvent, les pays **colonisés** ont combattu aux côtés de l'armée française. Des **combats** ont eu lieu au Maghreb pendant la **Seconde Guerre mondiale**. Il y a eu beaucoup de **victimes** parmi les soldats.

À la fin des années cinquante, les pays colonisés ont voulu leur **indépendance**. La plupart des **colonies** et **protectorats** français **ont obtenu** leur **autonomie pacifiquement**. Le Maroc est resté une **monarchie** et le sultan Mohammed V est devenu **roi**.

▶ **Vocabulaire supplémentaire—Les conflits, p. R18**

Core Instruction

TEACHING VOCABULAIRE

1. Introduce the vocabulary, using transparencies **Vocabulaire 3.3** and **3.4**. Model the pronunciation of each word. **(3 min.)**
2. Ask students to point out vocabulary items on the transparency as you say them in French. **(2 min.)**
3. Ask students questions about their own country's history. **Quand les États-Unis ont-ils obtenu leur indépendance? Qui avons-nous combattu pendant la Seconde Guerre mondiale? (3 min.)**
4. Model the pronunciation of the expressions in **Exprimons-nous!** Then provide practice by asking students questions with **quand**. **Quand la France a-t-elle occupé le Maroc? (4 min.)**

Online Practice
go.hrw.com
Vocabulaire 2 practice
KEYWORD: BD3 CH3

Chapitre 3

Vocabulaire 2

Vocabulaire 2

Après son indépendance, la Tunisie **a élu** Habib Bourguiba comme **président** et est devenue **une république.**

D'autres mots utiles

une bataille	battle
un cessez-le-feu	ceasefire
un coup d'état	hostile takeover
un drapeau	flag
un empereur	emperor
un(e) ennemi(e)	enemy
une invasion	invasion
le peuple	nation
signer un accord	to sign
un traité (de paix)	(peace) treaty

1957   1962

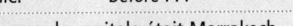

Cependant, **un conflit a éclaté** entre la France et l'Algérie. Il **s'est terminé** en 1962 par l'indépendance de l'Algérie. Ce fut la fin de la **décolonisation** française.

Exprimons-nous!

To relate a sequence of events

Interactive TUTOR

Avant de devenir un protectorat français, le Maroc était une monarchie.   *Before . . .*

À cette époque, la capitale était Marrakech.   *At the time of . . .*

Par la suite, pendant le protectorat français, Rabat est devenue la capitale.   *Later, . . .*

Au moment de l'indépendance, le Maroc est redevenu un royaume.   *During that time . . .*

Après la mort du roi Hasssan II, son fils est devenu roi.   *After . . .*

Une fois qu'il est devenu roi, Mohammed VI a fait de nombreuses réformes.   *Once . . .*

Vocabulaire et grammaire, pp. 31–33

Online workbooks

TPR
TOTAL PHYSICAL RESPONSE

Have students respond to these commands.

Touche ton nez si les États-Unis ont été une colonie.

Lève-toi si nous sommes une monarchie.

Lève le doigt si nous avons un président.

Lève la main si ton grand-père a combattu pendant la Seconde Guerre Mondiale.

Viens au tableau et dessine le drapeau américain.

Then have them mime the following situations.

J'ai annoncé qu'il y aurait un examen demain.

Il paraît que l'examen sera très facile.

Tu es un soldat pendant une bataille. ❀1.2

French for Spanish Speakers

Ask Spanish speakers about words used in Spanish to relate a sequence of events. Which French words look similar to Spanish words? (**moment/momento, avant de/antes de, époque/época**) Have students look closely at the sentence that begins with **Avant de.** What form of the verb follows it? (the infinitive) Is this sentence structured the same as it would be in Spanish? (Yes, the infinitive would also follow **antes de** in Spanish.) What would the first part of that sentence be in Spanish? (**Antes de declarar la guerra...**) ❀4.1

Differentiated Instruction

ADVANCED LEARNERS

Extension Have students write an essay about the colonization of Algeria from the perspective of an Algerian. Encourage students to research the life and works of Frantz Fanon (1925–1961), who wrote extensively about the problems of colonization. His works, especially *Les damnés de la terre,* may help students write their essay. Ask students to present their essay to the class. The class should discuss some essays and ask for clarification if needed. ❀3.1, 3.2

SPECIAL LEARNING NEEDS

Students with Dyslexia Before you ask students to read **Un peu d'histoire franco-africaine,** you might go over the proper nouns that appear in each caption. Explaining the proper nouns and their meaning will assist students with reading disorders to focus on the remaining content and its meaning. This technique will be useful for students prior to any independent reading. ❀1.2

㉒ Answers

1. colonisation
2. Par la suite
3. autonomie
4. pacifiquement
5. monarchie
6. Après
7. président
8. indépendance
9. Une fois que
10. guerre
11. fin
12. décolonisation

Connections

History Link

Thirty years after Algeria's War of Independence, a bloody civil war erupted in Algeria. The conflict began in 1992, when the military-backed government cancelled elections after first results had shown that the religiously conservative Islamic Salvation Front (FIS) party would win. After the FIS was banned, Islamist guerrillas quickly emerged and rebelled against the government. The war ended with a government victory, following the surrender of the Islamic Salvation Army and the 2002 defeat of the Armed Islamic Group. Have students discuss if they agree with the reaction and action of the Algerian government. Why or why not? 🌸3.1

㉑ L'intrus 🎬1.2

Lisons Identifie le terme qui ne va pas avec les autres dans chacune des listes suivantes.

1. un conflit / (un drapeau) / un ennemi / un soldat
2. une colonie / (un soldat) / un protectorat / une monarchie
3. une armée / une bataille / (une colonie) / une guerre
4. le Maroc / (le Sénégal) / l'Algérie / la Tunisie
5. le cessez-le-feu / la paix / (l'empereur) / pacifiquement

㉒ Quelques faits historiques 🌸1.2

Lisons/Parlons Complète les phrases suivantes de façon logique. Attention! Il faut bien respecter les faits historiques!

guerre	indépendance	monarchie	pacifiquement
une fois que	fin	autonomie	colonisation
décolonisation	président	après	par la suite

Au XIXe siècle, ce fut le début de la ___1___ française. ___2___, quand le Maroc a voulu son ___3___, cela s'est passé assez ___4___. Aujourd'hui, le Maroc est une ___5___. ___6___ son indépendance, la Tunisie a élu un ___7___.

L'Algérie, elle, a dû se battre pour son ___8___. ___9___ la ___10___ d'Algérie se termina, ce fut la ___11___ de la ___12___ française.

㉓ Des photos 🎬1.2

Écrivons D'abord, dis ce qui est représenté sur chaque photo. Ensuite, fais une phrase complète et logique qui contient ce terme.

MODÈLE **une carte géographique: Les explorateurs ont fait des cartes géographiques de l'Afrique.**

1.

2.

3.

4.

---

1. un président
2. des soldats
3. un empereur
4. un drapeau
Second part of answers will vary.

Core Instruction

TEACHING EXPRIMONS-NOUS!

1. Model the expressions in **Exprimons-nous!** Point out that proper tense sequence requires that expressions in the **passé composé** be followed by a clause in the **imparfait** when telling what someone said, reported, or announced. **(2 min.)**

2. Tell students that these expressions are used to talk about what they have heard, and that they do not introduce a first-hand account. For each expression, ask them how they would say the same thing if they knew what was reported to be a fact. **(2 min.)**

Exprimons-nous!

To tell what happened to someone else

On **a rapporté que** le président voulait un cessez-le-feu.
It was reported that . . .

Le président **a déclaré qu'**il ne voulait pas de conflit. *. . . declared that . . .*

Le roi **a annoncé que** son fils partait combattre. *. . . announced that . . .*

Il paraît que le prince est malade. *It seems that . . .*

Interactive **TUTOR**

Vocabulaire et grammaire,
pp. 31–33

Online *workbooks*

24 Écoutons CD 3, Tr. 4 ✿1.2

Écoute les nouvelles à la télévision. Dis ce que chaque personne a fait ou dit.

e **1.** Le Japon
b **2.** Le président français
d **3.** Le roi
a **4.** La reine

a. aller à l'hôpital
b. aller en Tunisie
c. visiter le sud du pays
d. signer un cessez-le-feu
e. signer un accord

25 Rumeurs ✿1.2

Écrivons Quelles sont les rumeurs qui circulent dans la classe? Complète chacune des phrases suivantes.

1. On a rapporté que/qu'...
2. Il paraît que/qu'...
3. Les élèves ont annoncé que/qu'...
4. Le conseiller/La conseillère d'éducation a déclaré que/qu'...
5. Le prof a annoncé que/qu'...

Entre copains

le bidasse	*soldier*
le troufion	*soldier*
rempiler	*to re-enlist*

Communication

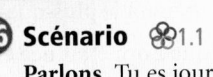

HOLT **SoundBooth**
ONLINE RECORDING

26 Scénario ✿1.1

Parlons Tu es journaliste et ton journal t'envoie dans un pays où il y a eu un coup d'état. À ton retour, on t'interviewe. Joue cette scène avec un(e) camarade. Ton/Ta camarade est le présentateur/ la présentatrice et tu réponds à ses questions.

| peuple | conflit | le président | a annoncé que | après |
| les soldats | victime | l'armée | au moment de | a déclaré |

MODÈLE —Vous étiez au palais au moment du coup d'état?
—Oui, les soldats sont arrivés et après...

24 Script

1. On a annoncé que le Japon allait signer un accord important avec les États-Unis.
2. Le président français a déclaré vouloir rendre visite au président tunisien.
3. Il paraît que le roi a finalement décidé d'arrêter les combats.
4. On a rapporté que la reine avait rendu visite aux victimes des combats qui ont eu lieu dans le sud du pays.

Communication

Individual Activity: Presentational
Have students choose a Francophone country in Africa and conduct some research on its history and independence from France. Ask students to write a brief summary using as many words from **Vocabulaire** as possible. Then have students present their country to the class, give a historical overview, and identify the country on a map.
✿1.3

Differentiated Instruction

SLOWER PACE LEARNERS

21 Variation Some students may have problems deciding which word does not belong in each group. Before you ask students to complete this activity, you may want to go over the sets of words and have students define each one.
✿1.2

MULTIPLE INTELLIGENCES

Interpersonal Ask interested students to create a French news report about current events in their area. Students should write a script, using the vocabulary in **Exprimons-nous!** Students may then present their newscast to the class.
✿1.3

Assess

Assessment Program
Quiz: Vocabulaire 2
Alternative Assessment
Differentiated Practice and Assessment CD-ROM

Online Assessment
my.hrw.com

Test Generator

Objectifs
• the past perfect
• sequence of tenses in indirect discourse

Grammaire
à l'œuvre 2

Déjà vu!

Most verbs are conjugated with avoir in the **passé composé.**

Le prince **a bu** la potion.

Reflexive verbs, verbs of motion (**aller, arriver, descendre, entrer, monter, partir, rentrer, retourner, revenir, sortir, tomber, devenir,** and **venir**), and verbs that indicate a state or condition (**mourir, naître,** and **rester**) are conjugated with être in the **passé composé.**

La reine s'**est** levée, puis elle **est** allée dans le parc.

The past perfect

1 To say that a past event happened before another past event, use the past perfect (**plus-que-parfait**). To form the **plus-que-parfait,** use the helping verbs **avoir** or **être** in the **imparfait** and the past participle of the main verb.

	dire	rentrer
j'	avais **dit**	étais **rentré(e)**
tu	avais **dit**	étais **rentré(e)**
il/elle/on	avait **dit**	était **rentré(e)(s)**
nous	avions **dit**	étions **rentré(e)s**
vous	aviez **dit**	étiez **rentré(e)(s)**
ils/elles	avaient **dit**	étaient **rentré(e)s**

2 The rules for agreement of past participles in the **plus-que-parfait** are the same as those for the **passé composé.**

L'explorateur a dit qu'il **avait** traversé l'océan Atlantique.
The explorer said that he had crossed the Atlantic Ocean.

La princesse **était** déjà partie quand l'armée est arrivée.
The princess had already left when the army arrived.

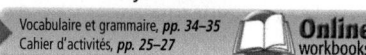
Vocabulaire et grammaire, *pp. 34–35*
Cahier d'activités, *pp. 25–27*
Online workbooks

② Histoire d'une Maghrébine 1.2

Lisons/Écrivons Bénédicte t'a raconté l'histoire de Zora. Et toi, raconte-la à un(e) ami(e) en utilisant le **plus-que-parfait.**

MODÈLE **Bénédicte m'a dit que Zora était née en Algérie...**

Zora est née en Algérie mais ses parents ont dû quitter le pays et sont venus s'installer en France quand elle avait trois ans. À vingt ans, parce qu'elle a décidé de devenir chanteuse, elle a dû quitter sa famille qui ne voulait pas qu'elle soit artiste. Pour gagner sa vie, Zora a d'abord écrit des livres qui racontaient son histoire. Ensuite, elle a aussi essayé de faire du cinéma, malheureusement, sans grand succès. Enfin, elle et sa sœur, Fatima ont formé un groupe musical inspiré par les rythmes et les mélodies de leur pays d'origine. Là, le succès a été immédiat! Zora est finalement arrivée à ce qu'elle voulait!

Core Instruction

TEACHING GRAMMAIRE

1. Read **Déjà vu!** aloud with students. Remind them that if they memorize the names DR & MRS VANDERTRAMPP, they will have the first letter of each verb that takes **être** in the **passé composé. (3 min.)**

2. Go over the **plus-que-parfait** forms of **dire** and **rentrer.** Point out to students that the **plus-que-parfait** is like the **passé composé** in every way, except that its auxil-

iary is in the **imparfait** instead of the **présent.** **J'ai dit. / J'avais dit. Je suis rentré(e). / J'étais rentré(e). (3 min.)**

3. Tell students that the **plus-que-parfait** is often required in French, whereas conversational English tends to avoid the past perfect. **(2 min.)**

28 L'année dernière 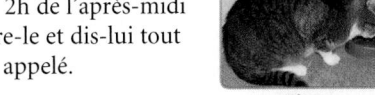 1.2

Écrivons Ta famille et toi, vous vivez à Paris et ton ami Ahmed t'a rendu visite cet été, mais ce n'était pas la première fois. Tu racontes ce qui s'était passé pendant sa première visite. Remets les mots dans le bon ordre et utilise le **plus-que-parfait**.

MODÈLE déjà / Ahmed / en / voyager/ France
Ahmed avait déjà voyagé en France.

1. aller / il / déjà / à / Paris

2. l'année dernière / visiter / Ahmed et Amira / la tour Eiffel

3. avec eux / nous / monter / y

4. au / déjeuner / puis / restaurant / nous

5. Amira / rencontrer / des amis

6. chez Jean-Pierre / dîner / ils / ce soir-là

7. aller / au / pendant ce temps / nous / théâtre

29 Il n'y a pas de mal! 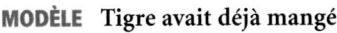 1.2

Parlons Ton ami t'a téléphoné de Marrakech à 2h de l'après-midi mais chez toi, il n'était que 8h du matin! Rassure-le et dis-lui tout ce que toi et ta famille aviez déjà fait quand il a appelé.

Tigre

MODÈLE **Tigre avait déjà mangé.**

1. je   2. nous   3. mon frère   4. ma mère

Communication

HOLT **SoundBooth**
ONLINE RECORDING

30 Interview  1.1

Parlons Fais une liste de cinq choses et demande à un(e) camarade s'il/si elle avait déjà fait ces choses quand il/elle avait neuf ans. Ensuite dis à la classe ce que tu as appris.

MODÈLE —Est-ce que tu avais déjà voyagé en avion?
—Non, je n'avais pas encore voyagé en avion.

Communication

Resources

Planning:

Lesson Planner

 One-Stop Planner

Practice:

Grammar Tutor for Students of French, Chapter 3

Cahier de vocabulaire et grammaire

Differentiated Practice and Assessment CD-ROM

Cahier d'activités

Media Guide

 Teaching Transparencies Bell Work 3.7

 Audio CD 3, Tr. 5

 Interactive Tutor, Disc 1

Bell Work

Use Bell Work 3.7 in the *Teaching Transparencies* or write this activity on the board.

Complète les phrases en mettant les verbes entre parenthèses au **plus-que-parfait.**

1. Astrid _____ (voyager) en France.
2. Elle _____ (aller) à Paris avec moi.
3. Nous _____ (dîner) dans un restaurant excellent.
4. J'_____ (rencontrer) deux amis.
5. Ils _____ (visiter) le Louvre et le musée Rodin.

🏵1.2

32 Script

1. Grand-maman a dit qu'elle pensait à nous.
2. Elle a aussi dit qu'elle viendrait vendredi.
3. Et puis elle a ajouté qu'elle nous avait acheté des cadeaux.
4. Est-ce qu'elle a dit qu'elle prendrait le train?
5. Elle a dit qu'elle avait un billet d'avion.
6. Je lui ai dit que nous l'attendrions à l'aéroport.

 Interactive TUTOR

🏵4.1

En anglais

In English, one way to retell what someone said is to use a quotation:

The president said, "Our army will defeat the enemy."

Can you think of a way to retell what someone said without using a direct quotation?

In French, as in English, you can retell what someone said using a quotation:

Le président a dit, «Notre armée réussira à battre l'ennemi.»

You can also use indirect discourse:

Le président a dit que notre armée réussirait à battre l'ennemi.

The president said <u>that</u> our army <u>would</u> defeat the enemy.

Sequence of tenses (in indirect discourse)

When you're reporting what someone else said without using a direct quotation, you use **indirect discourse.** In indirect discourse, you will have a main clause and a dependent clause.

Sequence of tenses describes the agreement between the verb in the main clause and the verb in the dependent clause.

1 If the verb in the main clause is in the present, the verb in the dependent clause can be in the present, the future, the **passé composé,** or the **imparfait.**

2 If the verb in the main clause is in the **passé composé,** the verb in the dependent clause can be in the **imparfait,** the conditional or the past perfect.

Main clause	Dependent clause
Le roi dit *the king says* (présent)	qu'il travaille. *that he works.* (at the present time)
	qu'il travaillera. *that he will work.* (at some time in the future)
	qu'il a travaillé./qu'il travaillait. *that he worked.* (at some time in the past)
Le roi a dit *the king said* (passé)	qu'il travaillait. *that he was working/worked.* (at some time in the past)
	qu'il travaillerait. *that he would work.* (at some time in the future)
	qu'il avait travaillé. *that he had worked.* (at some time further in the past)

Vocabulaire et grammaire, *pp. 34–35*
Cahier d'activités, *pp. 25–27*

 **Online** workbooks

31 Mauvaise communication 🏵1.2

Lisons Lis ces phrases et dis **a) si on rapporte ce que quelqu'un a dit** ou **b) si on ne rapporte pas ce que quelqu'un a dit.**

a **1.** Mamadou m'a dit qu'il viendrait ce soir.

b **2.** Moi, je crois qu'il viendra.

b **3.** Et toi, Saïd, tu penses qu'il va venir?

a **4.** Oui, il m'a aussi dit qu'il viendrait.

b **5.** Ah bon? Il ne m'a rien dit à moi!

32 Écoutons CD 3, Tr. 5 🏵1.2 1. a 2. b 3. a 4. b 5. a 6. b

La grand-mère de Pauline et de Gérard vient de téléphoner. Écoute ce que Pauline et Gérard disent et dis si l'événement dont ils parlent **a) est déjà arrivé** ou **b) va arriver.**

Core Instruction

TEACHING GRAMMAIRE

1. Read **En anglais** aloud with students, and then go over the sequence of tenses in indirect discourse. Read the examples with students. **(5 min.)**

2. Describe your weekend routine. Next, ask students what they usually do on the weekend. **Qu'est-ce que tu fais le week-end, Susie?** Then report the answer in indirect discourse. **(3 min.)**

3. Tell what you will do next weekend. Next, ask a student what he or she will do. **Qu'est-ce que tu feras le week-end prochain, Jeff?** Then ask the class what that person said. **Qu'est-ce qu'il a dit qu'il ferait le week-end prochain? (3 min.)**

4. Tell what a celebrity did last weekend. Next, ask students what they did last weekend. **Qu'est-ce que tu as fait le week-end passé, Mary?** Have classmates report what they said. **Elle a dit qu'elle avait... (3 min.)**

33 Chagrin d'amour ✿1.2

Écrivons Adrien a des problèmes avec sa copine Nicole. Il en parle à ses amis. Récris ses phrases **au discours indirect.**

> MODÈLE Ali m'a dit: «Je t'aiderai à lui parler.»
> **Ali m'a dit qu'il m'aiderait à lui parler.**

1. Vous m'avez dit: «Nous irons tous au cinéma ce week-end.»
2. Nicole m'a dit: «J'ai trop de devoirs pour aller au ciné.»
3. Nicole m'a aussi dit: «Je suis sortie avec Jean-Charles.»
4. Et elle m'a dit: «Je ne veux pas en parler.»
5. Ses amies m'ont dit: «Ce n'est pas sérieux.»

34 C'est ce qu'ils ont dit ✿1.2

Écrivons/Parlons C'est samedi midi et tu viens d'appeler différentes personnes. Qu'est-ce que ces personnes ont dit qu'elles faisaient quand tu leur as téléphoné à midi? Qu'est-ce qu'elles ont dit qu'elles avaient fait ce matin et qu'elles feraient ce soir?

> MODÈLE **Quand j'ai téléphoné à Aziza, elle a dit qu'elle avait lavé la voiture ce matin et que maintenant elle lisait le journal. Elle a dit qu'elle ferait ses devoirs cet aprèm.**

samedi

10h	laver la voiture
12h	lire le journal
16h	faire mes devoirs

Aziza

samedi

11h	faire du skate
12h	écouter de la musique
20h	regarder la télé

1. Abdul et Tarik

samedi

9h	faire le ménage
12h	laver le chien
14h	faire les magasins

2. Fatima

samedi

9h	jouer au tennis
12h	lire un magazine
13h	aller au restaurant.

3. toi et ton frère

Communication

 HOLT **SoundBooth** ONLINE RECORDING

35 Expérience personnelle ✿1.1

Parlons Demande à un(e) camarade ce que ses parents ont dit la dernière fois qu'il/elle leur a demandé s'il/elle pouvait sortir tard le soir. Ensuite, échangez les rôles.

> MODÈLE —Qu'est-ce que tes parents t'ont dit quand tu leur as demandé de sortir?
> —Ils m'ont dit que...

33 Answers

1. Vous m'avez dit que nous irions tous au cinéma ce week-end-là.
2. Nicole m'a dit qu'elle avait trop de devoirs pour aller au ciné.
3. Nicole m'a aussi dit qu'elle était sortie avec Jean-Charles.
4. Et elle m'a dit qu'elle ne voulait pas en parler.
5. Ses amies m'ont dit que ce n'était pas sérieux.

34 Possible Answers

1. Quand j'ai téléphoné à Abdul et Tarik, ils ont dit qu'ils avaient fait du skate ce matin et que maintenant ils écoutaient de la musique. Ils ont dit qu'ils regarderaient la télé ce soir.
2. Quand j'ai téléphoné à Fatima, elle a dit qu'elle avait fait le ménage ce matin et que maintenant elle lavait le chien. Elle a dit qu'elle ferait les magasins cet après-midi.
3. Quand j'ai téléphoné à toi et ton frère, vous avez dit que vous aviez joué au tennis ce matin et que maintenant vous lisiez un magazine. Vous avez dit que vous iriez au restaurant cet après-midi.

Communication

35 Class Activity: Presentational

Have each student write a quote. Then have Student A read his or her quote to Student B. Student B restates the quote in indirect discourse, calls on Student C and the chain continues. Encourage students to use **Il/Elle a dit que...** to practice the indirect discourse in the past. ✿1.2, 1.3

Assess

Assessment Program

Quiz: Grammaire 2

Alternative Assessment

Differentiated Practice and Assessment CD-ROM

Online Assessment

my.hrw.com

Test Generator 🌐

Differentiated Instruction

SLOWER PACE LEARNERS

Extension Have students work in groups of three. In eight to ten sentences, Student A describes to student B an event that happened in the past. Student B, will now tell Student C what Student A has said, using indirect discourse. Then Student C relates, in direct discourse, what Student A had said to Student B. Are the versions of Student A and Student C of the event identical? What was different?

✿1.1, 1.2

MULTIPLE INTELLIGENCES

Intrapersonal When reviewing **En anglais,** ask students to create a journal entry that retells or quotes what was said by their friends, family members, or teachers. Students should write five direct quotations and five sentences telling what the people said. These can be shared with partners or the whole class. ✿1.3

Resources

Planning:

Lesson Planner

 One-Stop Planner

Practice:

Grammar Tutor for Students of French, Chapter 3

Cahier de vocabulaire et grammaire

Differentiated Practice and Assessment CD-ROM

Cahier d'activités

Media Guide

Teaching Transparencies
Bell Work 3.8

Audio CD 3, Tr. 6

Interactive Tutor, Disc 1

Bell Work

Use Bell Work 3.8 in the *Teaching Transparencies* or write this activity on the board.

Récris les phrases suivantes en utilisant le **discours indirect**.

1. Paul me dit, «J'ai trop de travail.»
2. Des amis m'ont dit, «Nous allons au cinéma.»
3. Tu m'as dit, «Je vais à la bibliothèque.»
4. Vous m'avez dit, «Nous sortirons après les examens.»

🍀 1.2

36 Answers

1. Dans le journal, ils disaient que le roi du Maroc avait parlé du rôle de la femme dans la famille marocaine.
2. que le président avait dit qu'il allait tout faire pour que les jeunes aient une meilleure formation professionnelle et trouvent du travail plus facilement.
3. que le roi et la reine de Suède avaient rendu visite aux familles des victimes de l'accident d'avion qui avait eu lieu la semaine dernière.
4. que le président avait décidé de partir en vacances et que ses médecins lui avaient conseillé de se reposer.

Synthèse
• Vocabulaire 2
• Grammaire 2

Application 2

36 Les nouvelles  3.2

Lisons/Parlons Tu lis le journal et tu racontes ce que tu as lu à tes copains. Commence par: **Dans le journal, ils disaient que...**

> Pendant son voyage en France, le roi du Maroc a parlé du rôle de la femme dans la famille marocaine.
>
> 1.

> Le président a dit qu'il allait tout faire pour que les jeunes aient une meilleure formation professionnelle et trouvent du travail plus facilement.
>
> 2.

> Le roi et la reine de Suède ont rendu visite aux familles des victimes de l'accident d'avion qui a eu lieu la semaine dernière.
>
> 3.

> Le président a décidé de partir en vacances. Ses médecins lui ont conseillé de se reposer.
>
> 4.

Un peu plus

The past infinitive

1. You already know how to use **infinitives** in some sentences.

> Le conflit va **éclater** entre les deux pays.

2. Infinitive phrases can also be used to express past time. To form the past infinitive, use the helping verbs **avoir** or **être** in the **infinitive** and add the **past participle of the main verb**. The rules for agreement with past participles are the same as for the **passé composé.**

> Il a célébré sa victoire après **avoir gagné.**
> *He celebrated its victory after having won.*
> Après **être** rentrée chez elle, la reine s'est couchée.
> *After returning home, the queen went to bed.*
> Il les a trouvés après les **avoir cherchés** partout.
> *He found them after having looked for them everywhere.*

Vocabulaire et grammaire, p. 36
Cahier d'activités, pp. 25–27
Online workbooks

37 Écoutons CD 3, Tr. 6  1.2

Écoute monsieur Darouk parler de ce qu'il a fait aujourd'hui, puis remets les événements dans le bon ordre.

3 **a.** Il déjeune.
2 **b.** Il appelle son fils.
1 **c.** Il prépare le thé.
4 **d.** Il va chez son fils.
6 **e.** Ils décident de faire une fête.
5 **f.** Ils prennent des poissons.

Core Instruction

INTEGRATED PRACTICE

1. Have students do Activity 36 to practice indirect discourse. **(6 min.)**

2. Introduce **Un peu plus.** (See presentation suggestions at right.) **(4 min.)**

3. Continue with integrated practice Activities 37–40. You might provide more practice with the past infinitive by having students write five sentences to describe what they did today after they arrived at school. **Après avoir/(m')être... (30 min.)**

TEACHING UN PEU PLUS

1. Go over **Un peu plus.** Point out to students that the past infinitive is like the **passé composé**, except that the auxiliary is in the infinitive instead of the present tense. **(2 min.)**

2. Model sentences for students that explain that you do something without having done something else. **Je vais parfois en classe sans avoir fait mes devoirs.** Ask students to come up with more examples. **(3 min.)**

38 Et après? 1.2

Écrivons Qu'est-ce qu'on a fait après avoir fait les choses suivantes? Fais des phrases complètes.

1	**2**	**3**	**4**
Après	faire ses devoirs	je	être contents.
	être une monarchie	tu	élire un président.
	laver la voiture	le Cameroun	commencer à les coloniser.
	aller au CDI	Francine	combattre aux côtés des
	explorer les pays	nous	Français.
	africains	vous	aller au centre commercial.
	finir l'examen	les Français	regarder la télé.
	être colonisé	les Marocains	

Communication

HOLT **SoundBooth** ONLINE RECORDING

39 Questions personnelles 1.1

Parlons Demande à un(e) camarade de te dire cinq choses qu'il/elle a faites le week-end dernier. Répète chaque réponse pour demander ce qu'il/elle a fait après. Ensuite, échangez les rôles.

MODÈLE — Qu'est-ce que tu as fait samedi dernier?
— Je me suis levé(e) à neuf heures.
— Et après t'être levé(e)?

40 Histoire à raconter 1.2

Parlons Regarde les images et raconte ce qui s'est passé.

---

37 Script
See script on p. 93F.

PRÉ-AP Language Examination

To display the drawings to the class, use the Picture Sequences Transparency for Chapter 3.

40 Sample answer

a. **Le roi demande au chevalier d'aller sauver sa fille, qui est prisonnière.**

b. **Le chevalier va trouver le magicien et il lui raconte que le roi lui a demandé de sauver sa fille. Il lui donne une épée magique.**

c. **Le chevalier arrive à la tour et il tue le monstre.**

1.2

Communication

Group Activity: Presentational
In small groups, have students tell what they did last weekend. Then ask them to retell another student's story in the third person.

MODÈLE
— **Après m'être levé, j'ai pris une douche.**
— **Après s'être levé, il a pris une douche.**

1.3

Differentiated Instruction

ADVANCED LEARNERS

36 Extension After students have done this activity, ask them to read the headlines of an online newspaper, such as **Le Monde** or **Le Figaro**. Students should read an article that interests them and report the gist of this article in three to five sentences to the class. Classmates may ask for clarifications if needed. 1.2

SPECIAL LEARNING NEEDS

40 Students with AD(H)D Allow students the option of creating their own illustrations of situations like those in this activity. Students may be more motivated to participate or focus their attention when given the opportunity to create their own scenario to retell. Have students present their illustrations and sentences to the class. 1.3

Assess

Assessment Program
Quiz: Application 2
Audio CD 3, Tr. 12
Alternative Assessment
Differentiated Practice and Assessment CD-ROM

Online Assessment
my.hrw.com

Test Generator

Resources

Planning:

Lesson Planner

 One-Stop Planner

Presentation:

 Audio CD 3, Tr. 7

Practice:

Cahier d'activités

Reading Strategies and Skills Handbook, Chapter 3

Advanced Reader

AP Reading Suggestion

Have students research similar legends from around the world. What does this story have in common with them? What sets it apart?

Applying the Strategies

For practice using chronology, have students use the "Somebody Wanted But So" strategy from the *Reading Strategies and Skills Handbook*.

READING PRACTICE

Strategy: Somebody Wanted But So

Reading Skill	When can I use this strategy?		
	Prereading	During Reading	Postreading
Analyzing Cause-and-Effect Relationships			✓
Summarizing			✓

Strategy at a Glance: Somebody Wanted But So

- After students read a story, they work alone or in groups to fill in columns on the Somebody Wanted But So chart: who the someone in the story is, what he or she wanted, but what happened that created a problem, and so how the problem was resolved.
- Students work together to condense Somebody Wanted But So statements into concise summaries or to develop summaries for longer texts.
- To focus on literary elements, students can write Somebody Wanted But So statements for different characters in the same story or for different types of conflicts.

Summarizing a short story or a novel appears to be too overwhelming for many students who either offer nothing or restate everything in the story. Somebody Wanted But So offers students a framework to help them create their summaries. Students read a story and then decide who the Somebody is, what that somebody Wanted, But what happened to keep something from happening, and So, finally, how everything worked out.

Somebody Wanted But So also helps students move beyond summary writing. As students choose names for the Somebody column, they are deciding which characters are the main characters. In the Wanted column, they look at events of the plot and talk about main ideas and details. With the But column they are examining conflict. With the So column they are identifying the resolution.

Lecture

Contes et légendes Les pays d'Afrique ont une tradition orale très riche. Les contes folkloriques et les légendes sont transmis de génération en génération par des conteurs[1]. Beaucoup ont pour but de transmettre des valeurs morales ou une explication pour un phénomène social ou naturel. Les légendes sont fondées sur une histoire vraie. Elles expliquent souvent l'origine de quelque chose, d'une tradition ou d'un peuple[2]. Par contre[3], les contes sont de la pure fiction. Ils ont souvent des éléments magiques et mystiques.

Ⓐ Avant la lecture 🞉3.1

Le texte suivant est une légende marocaine. Lis le titre et regarde les illustrations. De quoi est-ce que ce texte va parler? Imagine l'histoire et sa chronologie. Note tes idées.

> **STRATÉGIE pour lire**
>
> **Using chronology** Keeping track of the order of events, will help you understand and remember information in narratives. As you read, note each main event, when it happens, and why it happens on a graphic organizer, such as a timeline, sequence chart, or fishbone.

CD 3, Tr. 7

Les origines de l'inimitié[4] entre l'homme et les animaux

Les anciens racontent qu'au tout début, l'homme menait[5] une vie de nomade, mais comme sa famille s'agrandissait, il songea[6] à s'installer définitivement.

Il se mit à chercher un site où il aurait de l'eau, des fruits et du gibier[7]. Il trouva son lieu de résidence et s'y établit.

Or, le site qu'il avait choisi n'était autre que le territoire du serpent. Celui-ci vint voir l'homme et lui dit :

1. personne qui raconte une histoire   2. les personnes qui habitent une région   3. *On the other hand*   4. *enmity/hatred*   5. *led*   6. a pensé
7. des animaux

Core Instruction

LECTURE

1. Read **Stratégie pour lire** aloud with students. **(1 min.)**

2. Have students do **Avant la lecture** in small groups. **(10 min.)**

3. Read *Les Origines de l'inimitié entre l'homme et les animaux* as a class to the end of page 119.

As they read have students draw a timeline that shows important events. Ask students what they think of man treating animals like this. Ask whether territory is an unusual source of conflict or not. Have students give examples to support their answer. **(15 min.)**

— Homme, je te conjure[1] ! Cherche-toi un autre site, tu as des enfants et j'en ai aussi, tôt ou tard nous nous disputerons à cause de nos enfants et comme je tiens à garder de bons rapports avec toi, je te conseille d'aller ailleurs[2] !

L'homme qui ne voulait rien entendre lui répondit :

— Tu sais, serpent, je suis fatigué de ma vie d'errance[3] et je ne suis pas prêt à déménager[4], cependant, je te promets que je vais recommander à mes enfants de ne jamais importuner[5] les tiens. De ton côté, tu en feras de même avec tes enfants, et de la sorte nous garderons des relations de bon voisinage !

Il en fut ainsi pendant longtemps, mais un jour, les enfants se querellèrent[6] et le cadet de l'homme tua[7] le cadet du serpent.

Le serpent jura de se venger. Il attendit la nuit et se glissa dans la demeure de l'homme, il le chercha et quand il le trouva, il s'enroula[8] autour de son cou et se mit à l'étrangler[9] en lui disant :

— Tu te souviens de ce que je t'ai dit le jour où tu es venu t'installer sur mon territoire, tu vas payer pour ta fatuité[10] !

L'homme lui rétorqua :

— Je comprends ta douleur, mais je te propose qu'on aille voir un arbitre et je te promets que j'accepterai la sentence quelle qu'elle soit !

Le serpent accepta. Le lendemain ils partirent à la recherche d'un arbitre. Ils trouvèrent un vieux mulet, chétif[11] et usé par le temps. Ils lui racontèrent l'objet de leur litige et demandèrent son avis.

Le mulet, après les avoir écoutés, leur expliqua en s'adressant au serpent :

— Je connais la perfidie de l'homme, tant que j'étais jeune, il m'aimait, il m'entretenait et me faisait travailler dur ; mais dès que j'ai donné les premiers signes de vieillesse, il me chassa[12]. Alors s'il ne tenait qu'à moi, je te conseillerais de le tuer, mais pour être plus juste demandez un second avis !

Le serpent acquiesça et ils continuèrent leur chemin ; ils rencontrèrent un chien. Le serpent lui raconta ses déboires[13] et lui demanda son avis. Le chien répondit :

— La mesquinerie[14] de l'homme, j'en ai souffert ! Que de temps j'ai passé à le distraire, à lui tenir compagnie, à garder sa maison et ses moutons, à subir tous les caprices de ses enfants. Quand j'ai veilli, il me chassa. S'il ne tenait qu'à moi, je le jugerais coupable et passible de mort, mais sachant ta sagesse, consulte un troisième arbitre afin que ta sentence soit sans appel !

1. demande 2. dans un endroit différent 3. voyageur 4. aller habiter dans un nouvel endroit 5. ennuyer 6. *quarreled* 7. *killed*
8. *wrapped himself* 9. *strangled* 10. *self-conceit* 11. petit et maigre 12. *chased me away* 13. difficultés 14. *pettiness*

Active Reading Questions

1. **Qui habitait dans le même endroit que l'homme? (le serpent)**
2. **Qu'est-ce que le serpent a prédit? (que ses enfants et ceux de l'homme se disputeraient)**
3. **Qu'est-ce que le fils de l'homme a fait? (Il a tué le fils du serpent.)**
4. **Quelle solution l'homme et le serpent ont-ils trouvée? (Ils sont allés voir un arbitre.)**
5. **Comment est-ce que l'homme a traité le mulet et le chien? (Il les a fait travailler dur, et il les a chassés quand ils étaient vieux.)**
6. **Qui a accepté d'être l'arbitre? (le hérisson)**
7. **Qu'est-ce que le hérisson a commandé à l'homme? (de tuer le serpent)** 1.2

Using Background Knowledge

Have students read the first three paragraphs of the legend. Discuss how snakes are portrayed in other works of literature and how people feel about them in general. Based on this knowledge and the text they have just read, have students predict what will happen between the snake and man.

Language Examination

Lecture helps students prepare for Section 1, Part B: **Reading Comprehension.** The audio recording helps them prepare for Part A: **Listening—Short Narratives.**

Differentiated Instruction

SLOWER PACE LEARNERS

Extension Explain to students that understanding the chronological order of this story is crucial to understanding its denouement and moral. Encourage students to draw a timeline that depicts the most important events of this story. Are the beginning and the end of the story similar? Why or why not? 1.2

SPECIAL LEARNING NEEDS

Students with Learning Disabilities/ Dyslexia To accommodate students with learning challenges in reading, play the recording of *Les origines de l'inimitié entre l'homme et les animaux.* Allow students to listen as they read the written text. Understanding the text instead of struggling with the reading on their own will be the objective of this accommodation. 1.2

Active Reading Questions

1. **Comment est-ce que l'homme a remercié le hérisson? (Il l'a invité à dîner.)**

2. **Qu'est-ce que la femme de l'homme lui a informé? (qu'il n'y avait rien à manger)**

3. **Qu'est-ce que l'homme voulait faire au hérisson? (Il voulait le manger.)**

4. **Qu'est-ce que le hérisson a suggéré à l'homme? (d'aller chercher toute sa famille)**

5. **Où est-ce que le hérisson habitait? (dans un trou sous un rôcher)**

6. **Qu'est-ce qui est arrivé à l'homme chez le hérisson? (Une vipère l'a mordu et il est mort.)**

 1.2

Postreading Activity

Ask students to think about the different conflicts in the story. Have them describe the conflict each animal has or has had with man. What do these conflicts imply about the general nature of human beings and animals? Do students agree or disagree with what the story implies? Why or why not?

Le duo continua son chemin. Ils rencontrèrent un hérisson[1], le mirent au courant. Celui-ci dit au serpent :

— Tu sais, la justice est sourde, alors approche-toi et parle dans mon oreille pour que je puisse t'entendre et rendre mon jugement en toute équité[2] !

Le serpent s'approcha de l'oreille du hérisson et se mit à renarrer les péripéties du litige qui l'opposait à l'homme. Le hérisson se tourna alors vers l'homme et lui dit :

— De la tête à la tête !

L'homme comprit l'allusion, prit une grosse pierre et écrasa la tête du serpent. Il remercia le hérisson de sa précieuse aide et l'invita à dîner chez lui.

Or, quand ils arrivèrent chez l'homme, la femme lui rappela qu'il s'était absenté toute la journée : ils n'avaient rien à se mettre sous la dent !

L'homme revint auprès du hérisson et lui dit :

— Tu m'excuseras mon cher hérisson, je t'ai invité alors que mon garde-manger est vide et il se trouve que mes enfants ont cruellement faim. Aussi, me vois-je dans l'obligation de te sacrifier !

Le hérisson, connu pour sa ruse, rétorqua :

— Voyons, rien ne me fera plus plaisir que de servir de festin à toi et aux tiens, mais je suis chétif. Pourquoi ne m'accompagnes-tu pas chez moi, tu ramèneras toute ma famille, comme ça, je ne laisserai pas d'orphelins derrière moi et vous aurez de quoi vous rassasier[3] !

L'homme accepta la proposition et accompagna le hérisson chez lui. Arrivés sous un grand rocher, le hérisson dit à l'homme :

— Tu vois ce trou, je vais y entrer et tu vas placer tes mains, juste devant la sortie. Dès que nous sortons tu nous attrapes tous !

L'homme se posta devant le terrier[4] et plaça ses mains comme convenu. C'est alors qu'une grande vipère en sortit et le mordit si fort qu'il en tomba mort. [...]

Voilà le secret de l'inimitié entre l'homme, le serpent, le hérisson et bien d'autres.

---

1. *hedgehog* 2. *égalité* 3. *to satisfy one's hunger* 4. *burrow*

Core Instruction

LECTURE

1. Have students finish reading *Les origines de l'inimitié entre l'homme et les animaux.* Ask them which of the four animals traditionally is characterized as a villain? Who plays that part here? Have students recall other tales with villains. **(8 min.)**

2. Ask students what animal(s) they would expect to play the clever role in European folklore. **(5 min.)**

3. Complete **Compréhension** in small groups. Do **Après la lecture** as a class. **(10 min.)**

Chapitre 3

Lecture

Online Practice
go.hrw.com
Online Edition
KEYWORD: BD3 CH3

Compréhension

B Remets l'histoire dans l'ordre. ✿1.2 **4, 7, 1, 3, 2, 9, 5, 10, 8, 6**

1. L'enfant de l'homme a tué l'enfant du serpent.
2. L'homme et le serpent ont demandé conseil au mulet.
3. Le serpent a essayé d'étrangler l'homme.
4. L'homme a décidé de s'installer sur le territoire du serpent.
5. Le chien a dit à l'homme et au serpent d'aller demander conseil à un troisième animal.
6. L'homme s'est fait piquer par une vipère et il est mort.
7. Le serpent a mis l'homme en garde contre son installation sur son territoire.
8. L'homme a voulu manger le hérisson et sa famille.
9. Le mulet a dit à l'homme et au serpent de demander un second avis.
10. Le hérisson dit à l'homme de tuer le serpent.

C Réponds aux questions suivantes. ✿1.2

1. Pourquoi le serpent veut que l'homme cherche un autre endroit?
2. L'enfant de l'homme a tué l'enfant du serpent. Quelles réactions ont eu leur père?
3. Qu'est-ce que le mulet a conseillé? Pourquoi?
4. Quelle était la solution du troisième arbitre, le hérisson?
5. Qu'est-ce que l'homme voulait faire quand le hérisson est arrivé chez lui?
6. Qu'est-ce qui est arrivé à l'homme devant le terrier?

Après la lecture ✿3.1

D Est-ce que ce texte est une légende ou un conte folklorique? A-t-il une morale? Si oui, quelle est-elle? Connais-tu d'autres textes qui parlent des relations entre l'homme et les animaux? Lesquels?

C Answers

1. Il ne veut pas se disputer avec l'homme à cause de leurs enfants.
2. Le serpent a voulu tuer l'homme, mais l'homme l'a convaincu d'aller voir un arbitre.
3. Le mulet pensait que le serpent devrait tuer l'homme, mais il leur a conseillé de demander un second avis.
4. Le hérisson a recommandé à l'homme de tuer le serpent.
5. L'homme voulait manger le hérisson.
6. Une grande vipère est sortie du terrier et elle a mordu l'homme.

Connections

Literature Link

The Thousand and One Nights is a medieval Middle-Eastern literary epic. During the reign of the Abbasid Caliph Harun al-Rashid in the eighth century, Baghdad had become an important cosmopolitan city. It was during this time that many of the stories were collected orally and later compiled into a single book. The first modern Arabic compilation was published in Cairo in 1835. The first European version (and first printed edition) was a translation into French (1704–1717) by Antoine Galland. This 12 volume book, *Les Mille et une nuits,* includes Arabic stories that were known to the translator but were not included in the Arabic compilation. Have students research the first English translation of this collection of tales. ✿3.1

Differentiated Instruction

ADVANCED LEARNERS

D **Extension** After students have completed this activity, ask them if this story could be considered a fable. Have students research the characteristics of a fable and determine if these apply to this story. Have students present their conclusions to the class. ✿3.1

SPECIAL LEARNING NEEDS

Students with Language Impairments To assist students with the concept of chronology and the use of a timeline, sequence chart, or fishbone, select a familiar story, legend, or folktale and ask a student to summarize the story. While the basic events are summarized, create a graphic organizer on the board to show the chronology of events. A children's story, such as *Cinderella* or *The Three Bears,* can be quickly summarized and the chronology easily recorded.

Assess

Assessment Program

Quiz: Lecture

Online Assessment
  my.hrw.com

Test Generator

 # L'atelier de l'écrivain

Ta légende à toi

C'est à ton tour d'écrire une légende sur les origines de quelque chose. Ton histoire doit avoir des éléments fantastiques et la nature doit être personnifiée. Ta légende peut aussi avoir une morale. La légende africaine que tu viens de lire peut te servir d'exemple ou souviens-toi des contes et légendes que tu lisais quand tu étais petit(e).

STRATÉGIE pour écrire

Using realistic dialogue makes the characters in a story come alive. When writing dialogue, consider who your characters are. What style would they use to express themselves? Are they old? Young? Sophisticated? Shy? Would their tone be emotional or intellectual? Match your characters' forms of expression to their personalities and backgrounds. ✿3.1

① **Plan: chronologie** 1.2

Choisis d'abord un phénomène ou élément dont tu veux expliquer l'origine. Imagine pourquoi il existe. Les causes peuvent être fantastiques ou basées sur la réalité. Parmi les causes, choisis-en une pour commencer ta légende. Écris-la dans ton organigramme. Puis, décide quels événements vont suivre, le point culminant et le dénouement. Écris-les dans ta chronologie. S'il y a une morale, note-la dans le dernier carré de ton organigramme.

```
conflit (problème)
        ↓
   événements
        ↓
 point culminant
        ↓
dénouement (conclusion)
```

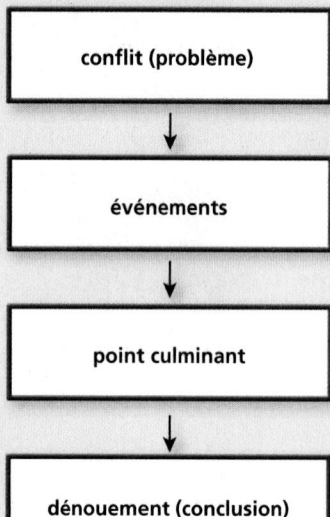

Resources

Planning:

Lesson Planner

 One-Stop Planner

Practice:

Cahier d'activités

Process Writing

Remind students that each event in their legend should build on the previous one. Suggest that in addition to their **organigramme,** they use a timeline to help them organize the events of their legend in a clear, logical order.

Teaching Suggestion

Before students plan their legend, define and discuss with them the following elements of a short story: plot (events that move the story along), conflict (problem the main characters encounter), climax (turning point), and denouement (resolution or tying up loose ends). Use examples from common fairy tales, such as "Little Red Riding Hood," to illustrate the different elements.

Connections

Literature Link

The word legend derives from the Latin **legenda**, *things to be read.* Legends tell about human actions that are perceived to take place within human history. They possess certain characteristics that give the tale the appearance of being true or real. A legend does not include happenings that are outside the realm of possibility, but includes miracles that are perceived as actually having happened. The purpose of the legend is to educate and warn against some danger. Ask students to give examples of legends. *(King Arthur and the Knights of the Round Table, The Holy Grail, The Legend of Sleepy Hollow, Robin Hood)* ✿3.1

Core Instruction

L'ATELIER DE L'ÉCRIVAIN

1. Have students recall other legends they have read or heard and write the titles on the board. Call on volunteers to give a brief summary of each legend and state its moral. **(5 min.)**

2. Read **Stratégie pour écrire.** Have students think of a character from a TV program, movie, or book and give examples of the character's speech. Then, have them imagine how the character would talk if he or she were older or younger, more sophisticated, shy, and so on. **(5 min.)**

3. Go over **Vocabulaire à la carte** and **Le plus-que-parfait. (5 min.)**

4. Have students complete steps 1 and 2 in class. **(30 min.)**

5. Assign steps 3 and 4 for homework. Invite volunteers to read their illustrated legend to the class the next day. Ask students to determine the moral of each legend.

L'atelier de l'écrivain

② Rédaction ❀1.1, 1.3

Fais un brouillon de ta légende. N'oublie pas de suivre ton plan. Ajoute des détails et des dialogues pour rendre tes personnages intéressants.

③ Correction ❀1.2

Relis ton brouillon pour t'assurer que tu as respecté l'ordre de ton plan.

- **Le conflit:** est-ce que le problème est présenté clairement?
- **Les événements:** est-ce que les détails donnent une image claire de la scène et des événements? Est-ce que les dialogues reflètent les personnalités des personnages?
- **Le point culminant:** as-tu oublié quelque chose?
- **Le dénouement:** est-ce que la morale est claire?

Maintenant, assure-toi que les verbes sont bien conjugués et que les temps sont corrects. N'oublie pas de vérifier l'orthographe des mots dont tu n'es pas sûr(e) dans le dictionnaire. Relis ton brouillon une troisième fois. Fais les corrections nécessaires et écris la version finale de ta légende.

④ Application ❀1.3

Copie le texte de ta légende sur plusieurs grandes feuilles de papier. Dessine ou trouve des illustrations pour accompagner le texte. Quand tu auras terminé, tu auras un livre pour enfant. Tu peux lire ta légende illustrée à des élèves d'une école primaire. Tu peux aussi donner une copie de ta légende à la bibliothèque de ta communauté.

Il était une fois un roi qui avait trois fils. Ses deux fils aînés aimaient se battre mais son dernier fils préférait jouer avec les animaux sauvages de la forêt. Il avait pour ami un chat.

Vocabulaire à la carte

heureusement	*fortunately*
malheureusement	*unfortunately*
à cause de	*because of*
s'échapper	*to escape*
avoir de la chance	*to be lucky*

Le plus-que-parfait

To say that a past event happened before another past event, use the **plus-que-parfait,** or the past perfect tense.

> **La sorcière avait déjà transformé la princesse en grenouille quand le prince est arrivé.**

Le plus-que-parfait

Have students put the verbs in the correct form and tense to talk about some of the events in *Cendrillon* (Cinderella).

Les belles-sœurs (sortir) déjà quand la bonne fée (*fairy godmother*) **(arriver) chez Cendrillon. (étaient déjà sorties, est arrivée)**

Le prince (trouver) le soulier de Cendrillon, mais elle (partir) déjà. (a trouvé, était déjà partie)

Le prince (dire) qu'il la (chercher). (a dit, chercherait)

Le prince (dire) qu'il (vouloir) se marier avec Cendrillon. (a dit, voulait)

Writing Assessment

To assess **L'atelier de l'écrivain,** you can use the following rubric. For additional rubrics, see the *Assessment Program.*

Writing Rubric	4	3	2	1
Content (Complete—Incomplete)				
Comprehensibility (Comprehensible—Seldom comprehensible)				
Accuracy (Accurate—Seldom accurate)				
Organization (Well-organized—Poorly organized)				
Effort (Excellent effort—Minimal effort)				

18-20: A	14-15: C	Under 12: F
16-17: B	12-13: D	

Differentiated Instruction

ADVANCED LEARNERS

Extension Ask students to list the characters in their legend and write a short description of each one's looks and personality. Tell students that good writers do not need to provide the names of speakers in dialogs because they have defined their characters so well that readers recognize them when they speak. ❀3.1

MULTIPLE INTELLIGENCES

Musical In addition to the writing assignment, ask students to write a song or poem that can be the theme for their story. Students may wish to use the additional vocabulary and the past perfect tense in their theme song, as well as in their story. Give students the opportunity to perform the song, read the lyrics, or read their poem in class. ❀1.3

Assess

Assessment Program
Quiz: Écriture
Online Assessment
my.hrw.com
Test Generator

Chapitre 3

Prépare-toi pour l'examen

Interactive TUTOR

Resources

Planning:

Lesson Planner,

 One-Stop Planner

Practice:

Cahier d'activités

Media Guide

 Teaching Transparencies
Situation, Chapitre 3
Picture Sequences, Chapter 3

 Audio CD 3, Tr. 8

Interactive Tutor, Disc 1

VIDEO OPTIONS

▶ **Télé-culture: Interviews**

TPRS
You may wish to use the Picture Sequences Transparency that accompanies Activity 7 for a TPRS activity.

① Answers

2. princesse
4. enchantée
1. nain
3. sort

② Answers

1. J'adore ce qu'elle a acheté au centre commercial.
2. Je ne sais pas ce dont elle a peur.
3. Dis-moi ce que tu veux pour Noël.
4. Raconte-moi ce qui est arrivé.
5. Nous ne comprenons pas ce dont le prof parle.

③ Answers

1. armée
2. combattons
3. annoncé
4. ennemi
5. soldats
6. cessez-le-feu
7. Une fois
8. guerre

---

① Utilise les dessins pour compléter les phrases suivantes et ensuite remets l'histoire dans le bon ordre. 🎬1.2

① Vocabulaire 1
• to set the scene for a story
• to continue and end a story
pp. 96–99

1. Elle rencontra un _____ qui la transforma en pierre.
2. Il était une fois une belle _____ qui adorait l'aventure.
3. Un peu plus tard, un beau prince arriva et délivra la princesse du _____.
4. Un jour, elle se promenait dans une forêt _____.

② Récris les phrases suivantes et ajoute **ce que, ce qui** ou **ce dont**. 🎬1.2

② Grammaire 1
• the **passé simple**
• relative pronouns with **ce**
Un peu plus
• adjective placement and meaning
pp. 100–105

1. j'adore / a acheté / au centre commercial / elle
2. ne sais pas / a peur / elle / je
3. tu / dis-moi / pour Noël / veux /
4. est / raconte-moi / arrivé
5. le prof / nous / ne comprenons pas / parle

③ Farida a trouvé une lettre que son grand-père avait écrite à sa grand-mère pendant la guerre. Aide-la à trouver les mots qui manquent. Fais les changements nécessaires. 🎬1.2

③ Vocabulaire 2
• to relate a sequence of events
• to tell what happened to someone else
pp. 108–111

combattre	traité	ennemi	une fois	soldat
cessez-le-feu	paix	guerre	annoncé	armée

Chère Salima,

Notre ___1___ avance. Nous ___2___ avec courage. On a ___3___ que l'___4___ était fatigué. Les autres ___5___ et moi, nous espérons qu'il y aura un ___6___. ___7___ que cette ___8___ sera finie, je rentrerai chez nous!

Mansour

Preparing for the Exam

RETEACHING

Have students review **Vocabulaire 1.** Then have a volunteer start telling a fairy tale, with the expressions introduced in **Exprimons-nous!** (**Il était une fois... On raconte qu'autrefois...**) It can be a story that is made up by the student or one that is well known. Next, have partners continue the story but not finish it. Last, have all students write an ending to the story. Remind them that in fairy tales the primary tense is the **passé simple.**

TEST-TAKING STRATEGY

Remind students that in the **passé simple, aller** is conjugated like a regular verb. (**j'allai, tu allas, il alla, nous allâmes, vous allâtes, ils allèrent**) Ask students to add this to their grammar notebook and to review the notebook regularly.

---

④ Lis ce que ces gens ont fait et dis ce qu'ils avaient fait avant. 🍀1.2

MODÈLE À midi, la reine est allée au parc. (Hier / au palais)
Hier, elle était allée au palais.

1. Lundi, le héros a parlé au roi. (lundi dernier / l'ennemi)
2. Cette année, notre président a visité le Mali. (l'an dernier / le Cameroun)
3. Au XIXᵉ siècle, des explorateurs ont exploré le Maghreb. (avant / d'autres pays)
4. La semaine dernière, la sorcière a utilisé une potion. (le mois dernier / formule magique)
5. Cet été, je suis allé(e) en Afrique. (l'année dernière / France)

⑤ Réponds aux questions suivantes. 🍀2.1

1. Qu'est-ce que c'est, une **médina**?
2. Quel est le nom donné aux colons français qui vivaient en Algérie?
3. Quel était le rôle des **griots**?

⑥ Écoute les phrases suivantes et dis si elles sont a) **vraies** ou
🎧 b) **fausses.** CD 3, Tr. 8 🍀1.2 1. a 2. b 3. b 4. b 5. a 6. a 7. b

⑦ Raconte ce qui se passe sur les illustrations. 🍀1.2

④ **Grammaire 2**
• the past perfect
• sequence of tenses (in indirect discourse)
Un peu plus
• the past infinitive
pp. 112–117

⑤ **Culture**
• Comparaisons p. 107
• Flash culture pp. 100, 105, 110

④ **Answers**
1. Lundi dernier, il avait parlé à l'ennemi.
2. L'an dernier, il avait visité le Cameroun.
3. Avant, ils avaient exploré d'autres pays.
4. Le mois dernier, elle avait utilisé une formule magique.
5. L'année dernière, j'étais allé(e) en France.

⑤ **Answers**
1. La partie ancienne des villes arabes
2. les pieds noirs
3. historiens et conseillers des rois

⑥ **Script**
See script on p. 93F.

COMMON ERROR ALERT
ATTENTION !

Remind students to make participles agree when they are part of past infinitives. All rules of agreement still apply. Verbs with **être** need to agree with the subject. (**Ils sont contents d'être arrivés.**) Verbs with **avoir** agree with preceding direct objects. (**La bague? Je suis triste de l'avoir perdue.**)

ACTIVITÉ PRÉPARATOIRE PRE-AP **Language Examination**

To display the drawings to the class, use the Picture Sequences Transparency for Chapter 3.

⑦ Sample answer

a. **Le chevalier va sauver la princesse qui est prisonnière dans une tour.**
b. **Il utilise l'épée magique que le magicien lui a donnée pour trouver l'escalier.**
c. **Il réussit à délivrer la princesse.**
d. **Le roi invite le héros et le magicien au palais.**

Oral Assessment

To assess the speaking activities in this section, you might use the following rubric. For additional speaking rubrics, see the Alternative Assessment section of the *Assessment Program*.

Speaking Rubric	4	3	2	1
Content (Complete—Incomplete)				
Comprehension (Total—Little)				
Comprehensibility (Comprehensible—Incomprehensible)				
Accuracy (Accurate—Seldom Accurate)				
Fluency (Fluent—Not Fluent)				

18-20: A   16-17: B   14-15: C   12-13: D   Under 12: F

Prépare-toi pour l'examen

Grammar Review

For more practice with the grammar topics in this chapter, see the *Grammar Tutor*, the *Interactive Tutor*, or the *Cahier de vocabulaire et grammaire*.

Online Edition

Students might use the online textbook and Holt SoundBooth to practice pronunciation of the **vocabulaire**.

Connections

Literature Link

Chivalry, a term borrowed from Old French **chevalier** (horseman), is a medieval institution of knighthood that is often associated with ideals of knightly virtues, honor, and courtly love. **Amour courtois** was a late medieval code that prescribed the behavior and emotions of ladies and their knights. It spawned an extensive courtly medieval literature that began with the troubadour poetry of Aquitaine and Provence in southern France toward the end of the eleventh century. The idea of courtly love spread swiftly across Europe. Eleanor of Aquitaine, wife first to Louis VII and then to Henry II of England, and her daughter Marie of Champagne inspired some of the best troubadour poetry. Ask students to read troubadour poetry and report on the real and idealized behaviour that it describes. 3.1

> **Grammaire 1**
> • the **passé simple**
> • relative pronouns with **ce**
> **Un peu plus**
> • adjective placement and meaning
> **pp. 100–105**

Résumé: Grammaire

To form the **passé simple** of regular verbs, remove the **-er**, **-ir**, or **-re** ending, then add the correct endings.

  • For **-er** verbs, add **-ai, -as, -a, -âmes, -âtes, -èrent**.
  • For **-ir** and **-re** verbs, add **-is, -is, -it, -îmes, -îtes, -irent**.

These are some irregular verbs in the **passé simple**:

	avoir	être	faire	venir	dire
je/j'	eus	fus	fis	vins	dis
tu	eus	fus	fis	vins	dis
il/elle/on	eut	fut	fit	vint	dit
nous	eûmes	fûmes	fîmes	vînmes	dimes
vous	eûtes	fûtes	fîtes	vîntes	dites
ils/elles	eurent	furent	firent	vinrent	dirent

The relative pronouns **ce qui, ce que,** and **ce dont** mean *what* and refer to something that hasn't yet been mentioned or to a general idea.

  • **Ce qui** is a subject and is usually followed by a verb.
  • **Ce que/qu'** is an object and is followed by a subject and verb.
  • **Ce dont** replaces a phrase that follows an expression with **de**.

Some French adjectives have a different meaning depending on whether they are placed **before** or **after** the noun. For a list of such adjectives, see p. 104.

> **Grammaire 2**
> • the past perfect
> • sequence of tenses (in indirect discourse)
> **Un peu plus**
> • the past infinitive
> **pp. 112–117**

Résumé: Grammaire 2

To say that one past event happened before another past event, use the **plus-que-parfait**. To form the **plus-que-parfait,** use the **imparfait** of **avoir** or **être** and the past participle of the main verb.

The sequence of tenses for indirect discourse is:

Main clause	Dependent clause	
Le roi dit (présent)	qu'il travaille (present)	
	qu'il travaillera (future)	
	qu'il a travaillé/qu'il travaillait (past)	
Le roi a dit (passé)	qu'il travaillait (imperfect)	
	qu'il travaillerait (conditional)	
	qu'il avait travaillé (past perfect)	

To form the *past infinitive*, use **avoir** or **être** in the infinitive and add the past participle of the main verb. The past infinitive with **être** follows the same agreement rules as the **passé composé**.

Chapter Review

Teacher Management System
Password: admin
For more details, log on to www.hrw.com/CDROMTUTOR.

Create a variety of puzzles to review chapter vocabulary.

DVD Program

Interactive Tutor

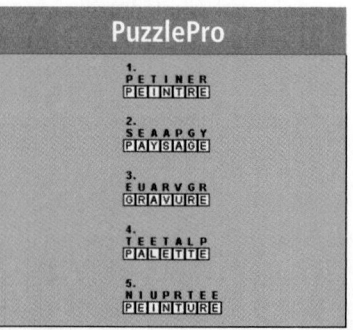

PuzzlePro

Résumé: Vocabulaire 1

To set the scene for a story

apparaître/disparaître	to appear/to disappear
une baguette magique	magic wand
le but	goal
un calife/un vizir	calif/vizir
un chevalier	knight
un conte/une histoire/un récit	story/tale/narrative
combattre	to fight
le danger/en danger	danger/in danger
délivrer/sauver	to rescue
enchanté(e)	enchanted
une épée	sword
une fable	fable, tale
un fantôme	ghost
une fée	fairy
une formule/une potion	formula/potion
un géant	giant
un génie	spirit/genie
héroïque/maléfique	heroic/evil
intriguer	to intrigue
la leçon de conduite/la morale	moral
une légende	legend
un/une magicien(ne)	magician
une marâtre	cruel stepmother

une marraine	godmother
un monstre	monster
le Moyen-Orient	Middle East
un/une nain(e)	dwarf
un/une ogre(sse)	ogre/ogress
un palais	palace
un passage secret	secret passage
un personnage/personnifié(e)	character/personified
la pierre	stone
des pouvoirs magiques (m.)	magic powers
prisonnier(-ière)	imprisoned
la reine/le roi	queen/king
un/une sorcier(-ière)	sorcerer/sorceress
un sort	spell
un souhait	wish
un/une souverain(e)	monarch
le sultan	sultan
un tapis volant	flying carpet
une tour	tower
transformer	to change
un traître	traitor
tuer	to kill

To continue and end a story, ...See p. 99

Résumé: Vocabulaire 2

To relate a sequence of events

un accord/un traité de paix	agreement/peace treaty
une armée	army
l'autonomie (f.)	autonomy
avoir lieu	to take place
une bataille/un combat	battle/fight
un cessez-le-feu	cease fire
une colonie/la colonisation	colony/colonization
le commencement/la fin	beginning/end
un conflit	conflict
la conquête	conquest
un coup d'état	hostile take over
la décolonisation	decolonization
un drapeau	flag
éclater	to break out
élire	to elect
un empereur/un président	emperor/president

un/une ennemi(e)	enemy
un explorateur/explorer	explorer/to explore
l'indépendance (f.)	independence
une invasion	invasion
une monarchie/une république	monarchy/republic
pacifiquement	peacefully
le peuple	nation/people
un protectorat	protectorate
la Seconde Guerre mondiale	World War II
se terminer	to end
un siècle	century
signer	to sign
le soldat	soldier
une victime	victim

To tell what happened to someone else, ...See p. 111

Prépare-toi pour l'examen

Game

Dis-moi! Form groups of three. Write 20 vocabulary words or expressions on a grid of 20 squares. Make and distribute two copies to each group. Have two of the students cut the squares apart and take ten squares each. The third student, who is the judge and timekeeper for the other two, receives a copy with all the words. The two students take turns giving clues to get their partner to say all the words or expressions on the squares within 30 seconds. French words or gestures should be used to convey the meaning. Squares with words that were not guessed are placed into a pile. At the end of the game, the group should write a sentence with each of the words or expressions from this pile. ✿1.2

Online Edition

Transparency: Vocabulaire

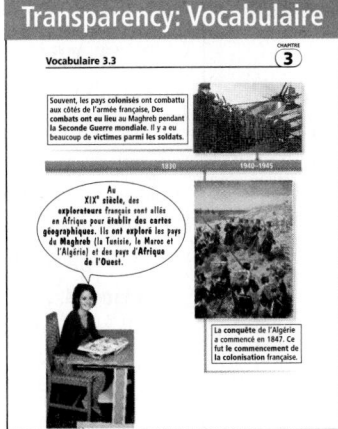

Transparency: Situation

Assess

Assessment Program

Examen: Chapitre 3

Audio CD 3, Trs. 13, 14 🎧

Examen oral: Chapitre 3

Alternative Assessment

Differentiated Practice and Assessment CD-ROM

Online Assessment

my.hrw.com

Test Generator 💿

VIDEO OPTIONS

▶ **Télé-culture: Interviews**

The AP French Language Exam

Activités préparatoires provide students with activities similar to those found in the Advanced Placement French Language exam. The activities are based on material taught up to and including this chapter. They concentrate on the chapter grammar and vocabulary. In the Teacher's Edition you will find test-taking strategies, as well as strategies for succeeding in the four skills. Students who plan on taking the exam should already have a good grasp of French vocabulary and grammar. They also should possess adequate competence in listening, reading, writing, and speaking.

Reading Strategy

Multiple Readings Tell students that it is a good idea to read through a text at least three times. The first reading will give them the general idea, the second will allow them to fill in a few details, and the third should give them a fairly good understanding of the text.

Activités préparatoires

SECTION I

 Listening CD 3, Tr. 9 🌸1.2

Listen to the dialogues and choose the most appropriate response.

1. **A.** Oui, ils ont déclaré un cessez-le-feu.
   B. Oui, ils ont signé un accord.
   C. Oui, ils vont déclarer la guerre.
   D. Oui, ils ont élu un président.

2. **A.** Tout est bien qui finit bien.
   B. Ils vécurent heureux.
   C. Nul ne sait ce qui lui est arrivé.
   D. C'est ça la morale du conte.

Reading 🌸1.2

Read the following paragraph and answer the questions that follow.

> 1 La fée dit alors à Cendrillon :
> — Eh bien, voilà de quoi aller au bal, n'es-tu pas bien aise?
> — Oui, mais est-ce que j'irai comme ça,
> 5 avec mes vilains habits?
> Sa marraine ne fit que la toucher avec sa baguette et aussitôt ses habits furent changés en habits de drap d'or et d'argent tout chamarrés de pierreries;
> 10 elle lui donna ensuite une paire de pantoufles de verre, les plus jolies du monde.
>
> Quand elle fut ainsi parée, elle monta en carrosse; mais sa marraine lui recommanda instamment de ne pas dépasser
> 15 minuit, l'avertissant que si elle demeurait au bal un moment de plus, son carrosse redeviendrait citrouille, ses chevaux des souris, ses laquais des lézards, et que ses vieux habits reprendraient leur première
> 20 forme. Elle promit à sa marraine qu'elle ne manquerait pas de quitter le bal avant minuit.

1. La fée qui parle à Cendrillon est sa...
   A. mère.
   B. marraine.
   C. mer.
   D. marâtre.

2. L'expression «vilains habits» signifie...
   A. vêtements moches.
   B. mauvaises habitudes.
   C. robe élégante.
   D. vieux carrosse.

3. Un synonyme pour le mot «parée» est...
   A. partie.
   B. prête.
   C. habillée.
   D. avertie.

4. Avec sa baguette, la fée a transformé...
   A. le carrosse en citrouille.
   B. des habits en verre.
   C. des chevaux en souris.
   D. des lézards en laquais.

5. Cendrillon promet de...
   A. redevenir citrouille.
   B. ne pas manquer le bal.
   C. ne pas quitter le bal avant dix heures.
   D. quitter le bal avant minuit.

Preparing for the Exam

ADDITIONAL PRACTICE

Give students a variety of sentences that include past participles. Ask them to decide if agreement is necessary and have them explain why or why not. 🌸 1.1

TEST-TAKING STRATEGY

Section I: Listening Understanding a recorded voice requires more concentration than a personal encounter where facial expressions and gestures help convey meaning. Tell students to focus attention on the voices in the recording and to ignore distracting noises.

Section II: Writing Tell students to look closely at all past participles to determine if agreement is necessary. If so, they need to make sure that it agrees with the correct antecedent.

Online Practice
go.hrw.com
Online Edition
KEYWORD: BD3 CH3

Chapitre 3

Activités préparatoires

Activités préparatoires

The following activities can be used to help you to prepare for the Advanced Placement French Language examination, or to further practice the vocabulary and grammar concepts you have seen in this chapter.

SECTION II

Writing ✿1.2

Complete the sentence by writing the correct form and tense of the verb, based on the context.

La princesse ___1___ de ce qui est arrivé quand elle a frotté la lampe; un génie apparût! Le génie ___2___ à la princesse ce qu'elle ___3___. Elle a fermé les yeux, et après avoir réfléchi un moment, elle ___4___! Le génie, connaissant le souhait de la princesse, ___5___ apparaître un coffre plein de bijoux. La princesse ___6___ heureuse d'avoir libéré le génie de sa prison!

1. _était étonnée_ (être étonné)
2. _a demandé_ (demander)
3. _désirait_ (désirer)
4. _s'est décidée_ (décider)
5. _avait fait_ (avoir faire)
6. _était_ (être)

Complete each of the following sentences by writing one of the given adjectives in the blank EITHER before or after the noun.

1. On célèbre Noël la _dernière_ semaine _____ de décembre. (dernier)
2. Marie est une _____ amie _chère_ depuis longtemps. (cher)
3. Une _____ femme _pauvre_ est une femme sans argent. (pauvre)
4. J'ai ma _propre_ voiture _____ . (propre)

Essay Topic ✿1.3

Write in French a well-organized composition on the following topic.
    Est-ce que les contes de fées sont trop violents pour les enfants?

Speaking ✿1.2

Look at the following pictures, then tell a story about what is occurring in the illustrations.

Listening Script

1.
— Tu as entendu ce qu'on vient de rapporter à la télé?
— On dit qu'un conflit a éclaté entre deux pays africains.

2.
— La sorcière a utilisé une potion magique pour faire disparaître la princesse.
— Et elle n'est jamais rentrée au palais?

Writing Strategy

Encourage students to take some time to write a brief, informal outline before they write their essay. This outline may be as simple as a list of their ideas numbered in a logical order.

✿ Language Examination
PRE-AP ACTIVITÉ PRÉPARATOIRE

📖 To display the drawing to the class, use the **Activités préparatoires** Transparency for Chapter 3.

Speaking: Sample answer
Il était une fois, une petite fille qui s'était perdue dans une forêt enchantée. Elle voulait rentrer chez elle, mais les arbres lui faisaient peur. Quand elle est enfin arrivée, sa mère l'a embrassée et tous les animaux sont venus la voir.

You may also want to ask students the following.

Souvent les contes de fées nous apprennent une leçon. Quelles leçons as-tu appris des contes de fées?

Differentiated Instruction

SLOWER PACE LEARNERS

You may want to pause after each conversation in the Listening section and ask advanced learners to paraphrase or summarize it. Encourage students to ask for clarifications if needed. Then have students complete the activity.

SPECIAL LEARNING NEEDS

Students with Auditory/Language Impairments Use the script for the Listening activity as an accommodation for students with auditory and language impairments. Allow students to read the script while they listen to the conversations. Students' auditory memory challenges would also be helped by using the script as a reference when choosing the appropriate rejoinder. ✿1.2

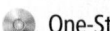

1 Script

1. Tu as vu? Le magicien a fait apparaître un petit lapin blanc. C'est incroyable!
2. La princesse a rendu visite aux soldats.
3. Les deux présidents ont beaucoup travaillé la dernière fois qu'ils se sont vus.
4. Un groupe d'explorateurs est allé en Afrique. Ils ont exploré plusieurs pays et ont fait des cartes de ces régions.
5. On dit qu'on peu voir un fantôme dans cette pièce chaque nuit à minuit!

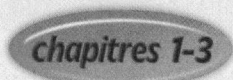

Révisions cumulatives

CD 3, Tr. 10 1.2

1 Choisis l'image qui correspond à chaque phrase.

a. 2. b. 3. c. 4. d. 1. e. 5.

2 Lis cette publicité et réponds aux questions suivantes. 3.2

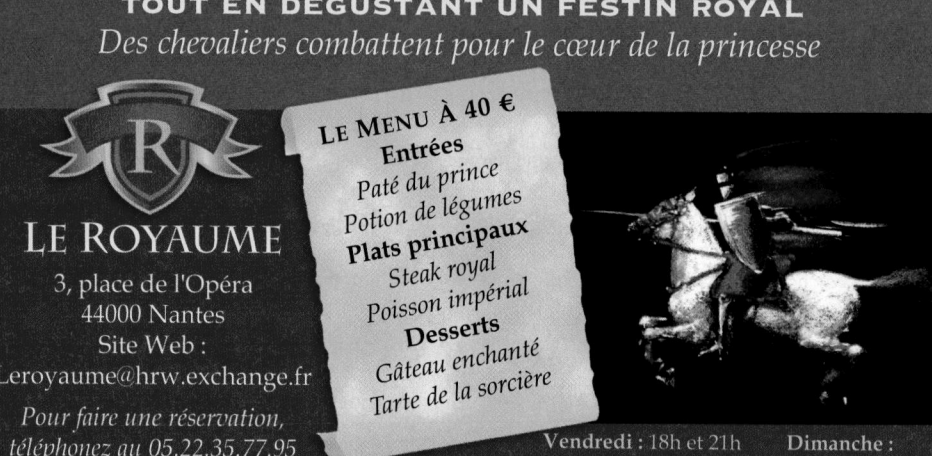

VENEZ ASSISTER À UN SPECTACLE DU MOYEN ÂGE TOUT EN DÉGUSTANT UN FESTIN ROYAL

Des chevaliers combattent pour le cœur de la princesse

LE ROYAUME

3, place de l'Opéra
44000 Nantes
Site Web :
Leroyaume@hrw.exchange.fr

Pour faire une réservation, téléphonez au 05.22.35.77.95

LE MENU À 40 €
Entrées
Paté du prince
Potion de légumes
Plats principaux
Steak royal
Poisson impérial
Desserts
Gâteau enchanté
Tarte de la sorcière

Vendredi : 18h et 21h   Dimanche :
Samedi : 18h et 21h   12h, 15h, 18h et 21h

1. On peut voir un spectacle en mangeant.
2. du pâté ou de la potion de légumes
3. À 40 €
4. un combat de chevaliers
5. téléphonez au 05.22.35.77.95

1. Qu'est-ce qu'on peut faire au Royaume?
2. Qu'est-ce que tu peux prendre comme entrées?
3. À combien est le menu?
4. Quel genre de spectacle est-ce que c'est?
5. Comment peux-tu réserver une table?

Online Culture Project

Have students prepare a two-minute PowerPoint® slide show to introduce their classmates to three customs of the Maghreb region, one custom per slide. Tell students to do their research on the Internet and to find appropriate illustrations to include in their presentation. Students will then compare and contrast each North African custom with a custom in their home country. Students should cite the URLs of the Web sites they consult. 4.2

3 Crée une entrevue entre les chefs d'état *(head of state)* de deux pays francophones. Ils discutent la possibilité de la paix dans le monde. Chacun dit ce qui devrait arriver pour que la paix dans le monde soit possible. 🌼1.1

Online Assessment
go.hrw.com
Cumulative Self–test
KEYWORD: BD3 CH3

4 Regarde ce dessin d'une déesse peint sur les murs d'une grotte *(cave)* en Algérie. 🌼1.3, 2.2

Prehistoric Cave Art, Aounrhet, Tassili, Algeria. ©The Granger Collection, New York

Peinture rupestre d' Aounrhet, Tassili

1. Imagine une légende qui raconte ce que cette déesse faisait.

2. Est-ce qu'à ton avis, c'était un personnage maléfique ou non? Est-ce que les hommes de la tribu représentés sur le dessin avaient peur d'elle?

3. À quelle époque tu crois que ce dessin a été fait? Pourquoi crois-tu que les gens dessinaient de telles scènes sur les murs des grottes?

4. Est-ce que tu connais d'autres endroits dans le monde où il y a des dessins comme celui-ci? Lesquels?

5 Tu as vu un film historique ou un film qui racontait une légende que tu as beaucoup aimé. Écris un petit paragraphe de dix lignes pour raconter l'histoire de ce film. Utilise le passé composé, l'imparfait et le plus-que-parfait. 🌼1.3

6  **Conte pour enfants** Un(e) camarade de classe et toi, vous allez créer un conte pour enfants. Une personne fera les dessins et l'autre créera l'histoire. Ensuite, racontez votre conte à la classe. 🌼1.3

FINE ART CONNECTION

Introduction Located in a strange lunar landscape in the Algerian Sahara, Tassili n'Ajjer *(plateau of the rivers)* is one of the greatest outdoor art museums. This remote massif has more than 15,000 drawings and engravings, that record climatic changes, animal migrations, and the evolution of human life in the Sahara from 6000 B.C. to the first centuries of the present era. Tassili rock art is commonly divided into four chronological periods, based on style and content. 1. The Bubalus (hunter or wild fauna) period extends from the end of the sixth to the mid-fourth millennium B.C. 2. The Cattle period lasts from the mid-fourth to the mid-second millennium B.C. Cattle are depicted with increasing frequency, sometimes in large herds. Herdsmen have replaced hunters. 3. The Horse period begins about 1,200 B.C. Horses with chariots have replaced the herds of the Cattle period. 4. The Camel period begins in the first centuries of the present era. At this time, the Sahara had become increasingly arid, and the camel had replaced the horse as the beast of burden.

Analyzing
Ask students the following.
À quelle période la déesse cornue a-t-elle été probablement peinte? Justifie ta réponse. (la période des pasteurs bovidiens *(Cattle Period)* **Une averse de grain tombe sur la déesse qui est entre les jambes de la déesse cornue.)** 🌼3.1

Extension
Have students research the cave paintings at Lascaux in southwestern France. Students should report on the age and the subjects of the paintings. Have students present their research to the class. 🌼3.1

The activities in Chapter 3 target the communicative modes as described in the Standards.

Interpersonal	Two-way communication using receptive skills and productive skills	**Communication (SE),** pp. 101, 103, 105, 111, 113, 115, 117 **Communication (TE),** pp. 105, 111, 113 **À ton tour,** p. 131
Interpretive	One-way communication using receptive skills	**Culture,** pp. 106–107 **Lecture,** pp. 118–121
Presentational	One-way communication using productive skills	**Communication (SE),** p. 99, 101, 117 **Communication (TE),** pp. 99, 101, 111, 115, 117

Planning Guide

Amours et amitiés

Chapter Section		Resources
Vocabulaire 1 • Relationships and friends	pp. 134–137	Teaching Transparencies: Vocabulaire 4.1, 4.2; Bell Work 4.1, 4.2, 4.3, 4.4
Grammaire 1 • Reciprocal verbs • The past conditional	pp. 138–141	Cahier de vocabulaire et grammaire, pp. 37–42 Grammar Tutor for Students of French Cahier d'activités, pp. 31–33 Media Guide, pp. 13–16
Application 1 • **Un peu plus:** The verbs **manquer** and **plaire**	pp. 142–143	**Assessment Program** Quiz: Vocabulaire 1, pp. 89–90 Quiz: Grammaire 1, pp. 91–92 Quiz: Application 1, pp. 93–94
Culture • **Lecture culturelle: Maroc: nouveau code de la famille** • **Comparaisons** • **Communauté et professions**	pp. 144–145	Cahier d'activités, p. 34
Vocabulaire 2 • Family history and life events	pp. 146–149	Teaching Transparencies: Vocabulaire 4.3, 4.4; Bell Work 4.5, 4.6, 4.7, 4.8
Grammaire 2 • Review: The subjunctive • The subjunctive with necessity, desire, and emotions	pp. 150–153	Cahier de vocabulaire et grammaire, pp. 43–48 Grammar Tutor for Students of French Cahier d'activités, pp. 35–37 Media Guide, pp. 13–16
Application 2 • **Un peu plus:** Disjunctive (stress) pronouns	pp. 154–155	**Assessment Program** Quiz: Vocabulaire 2, pp. 95–96 Quiz: Grammaire 2, pp. 97–98 Quiz: Application 2, pp. 99–100
Lecture • **Le fils d'Agatha Moudio**	pp. 156–159	Cahier d'activités, p. 38 Reading Strategies and Skills Handbook Advanced Reader
L'atelier de l'écrivain • **Une histoire d'amour**	pp. 160–161	**Assessment Program** Quiz: Lecture, p. 101 Quiz: Écriture, p. 102
Prépare-toi pour l'examen • **Résumé de vocabulaire et grammaire**	pp. 162–165	Teaching Transparencies: Picture Sequences, Situation, Ch. 4 Media Guide, pp. 16, 59–60
Activités préparatoires	pp. 166–167	**Assessment Program** Examen: Chapitre 4, pp. 103–108 Examen oral: Chapitre 4, p. 320
Révisions cumulatives	pp. 168–169	Teaching Transparencies: Fine Art, Ch. 4 Cahier d'activités, pp. 39–40
Chroniques • Les fables de La Fontaine • Les contes français • Le cinéma célèbre l'amour • L'amour et le mariage • Les grands couples de l'histoire	pp. 170–179	Reading Strategies and Skills Handbook Advanced Reader

Pacing Suggestions

	Essential	Recommended	Optional
Vocabulaire 1 • Relationships and friends • **Flash culture**	✔		
Grammaire 1 • Reciprocal verbs • The past conditional	✔		
Application 1 • **Un peu plus:** The verbs **manquer** and **plaire**	✔		
Culture • **Lecture culturelle: Maroc: nouveau code de la famille** • **Comparaisons** • **Communauté et professions**		✔	
Vocabulaire 2 • Family history and life events • **Flash culture**	✔		
Grammaire 2 • Review: The subjunctive • The subjunctive with necessity, desire, and emotions • **Flash culture**	✔		
Application 2 • **Un peu plus:** Disjunctive (stress) pronouns	✔		
Lecture • **Le fils d'Agatha Moudio** **L'atelier de l'écrivain** • **Une histoire d'amour**		✔	
Prépare-toi pour l'examen		✔	
Activités préparatoires		✔	
Révisions cumulatives			✔
Chroniques			✔

Technology

Bien dit! Online
• Student Edition with multi-media
• SoundBooth recording tool
• Interactive activities with feedback
• Self-tests with feedback
• Cahier d'activités (Interactive workbook)
• Cahier de vocabulaire et grammaire (Interactive workbook)
• Holt Online Assessment

DVD Program
• Télé-roman: Camille et compagnie
• Télé-culture: Interviews

Interactive Tutor
• Interactive practice games
• Writing and recording workshops
• Before You Know It™ Flashcards

Audio Program
• Student Edition Listening Activities
• Assessment listening activities
• Songs

One-Stop Planner
• Complete media and print resources
• ExamView Pro Test Generator
• Holt Calendar Planner

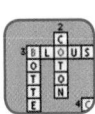

PuzzlePro
• Customizable word games

Differentiated Practice and Assessment CD

For slower pace and advanced learner options, see the Differentiated Practice and Assessment CD.

Planning Guide

✂ Projects

Grading the project

Suggested point distribution
(100 points total)

Use of vocabulary . . . . 20 pts.
Overall use of language . . . 30 pts.
Oral presentation. . . . . 40 pts.
Originality. . . . . 10 pts.

e-community

e-mail forum:
Post the following questions on the classroom e-mail forum:

Location: http://french

**Crois-tu au coup de foudre?
Pourquoi ou pourquoi pas?**

**Est-ce que toi et tes amis, vous
vous disputez souvent?**

 5.1

All students will contribute to the list and then share the items.

La colonne de conseils

For this project students create an advice column based on questions submitted by their classmates. This project will take several days and is designed for students to do individually. Tell students to imagine they are advice columnists for the school newspaper and must do their best to help their classmates. 🕸 1.3, 5.1

Suggested Sequence

1. Have each student submit one question that asks for advice on a slip of paper. Let students sign their question with a fictitious name if they like. You will need five copies of each student's question to place in a basket.

2. Ask students to draw five slips of paper from the basket. If a student draws the same question more than once, he or she will need to draw again until he or she has five different questions.

3. Students will then name their advice column and write answers to the questions they drew. Encourage students to use their imagination and to be creative in their answers.

4. Have students exchange rough drafts with a classmate for constructive criticism.

5. Have the 'advice columnists' make an oral presentation. Tell them that they do not have to read their advice word for word, but can ad-lib here and there. The ease with which they speak will be a plus for their grade.

Partner Class Project

Ask students to choose five questions from among those submitted to **La colonne de conseils.** Students should post these questions on the student or class Web site. Remind students to e-mail the Web site address or an electronic document to the partner class. The students in the partner class should now play advice columnists. After the partner class has answered the five questions, students should compare their own advice to that given by the students of the partner class. Are the answers provided by the partner class based on the same cultural perspectives as theirs? Have students summarize their findings and present the summary to the class. 🕸 1.3, 5.1

 Game Bank
For game ideas, see pages T60–T63.

Traditions

La cérémonie du thé

In Morocco, hot mint tea is often served before or after a meal and during most business and social exchanges. A tall teapot, called a **barrahd,** small decorative glasses, and octagonal boxes of mint, sugar, and tea are brought out on a tray called a **siniyya.** After the tea has brewed, the host stirs it one or two times, holds the teapot high, and pours a stream of steaming tea into a glass held far below. The tea is then returned to the pot. Finally, the tea is poured with the same flourish into all glasses. Have students research or take a virtual tour of a Moroccan **souk** *(market).* What products and produce do the vendors offer? How does a **souk** differ from a market in the United States? Students should present their findings to the class. ✿1.3, 5.2

La cuisine

The traditional preparation of **couscous** is rather long and involved, but pre-cooked **couscous** is now available in many supermarkets. The word **couscous** can be used to describe either the semolina alone or the entire dish comprised of the semolina and stew. Encourage students to prepare **couscous** in their home economics class or at home for family and friends. ✿1.3, 5.2

Couscous Pour 6 à 8 personnes

- **1** poulet
- ½ tasse de raisins secs
- **3** tasses de couscous instantané
- **3** tasses d'eau
- **3** carottes
- **1** tasse de pois chiches

- **2** courgettes
- **1** navet
- **1** cuillère à soupe de beurre
- **3** tomates
- **1** pincée de safran
- **2** oignons

- **1** cuillère à café de coriandre
- **1** cuillère à café de cannelle
- **3** cuillères d'huile d'olive
- poivre, sel

Couper les légumes. Dans une marmite, faire cuire à feu doux les tomates, les carottes, les courgettes, le navet et les oignons dans un litre d'eau au moins. Ajouter l'huile d'olive et un peu de beurre. Ajouter les épices: safran, coriandre, cannelle, poivre et sel. Faire cuire le poulet dans une marmite pendant une demi-heure, accompagné d'un oignon, de safran, de sel et de poivre. L'ajouter aux légumes et laisser cuire le tout encore une heure. Faire bouillir 4 ½ tasses d'eau. Quand l'eau bout, verser le couscous et le retirer du feu. Laisser le couscous absorber l'eau. Faire fondre le beurre dans une grande poêle et y ajouter le couscous. L'égrener avec une fourchette. Ajouter les raisins secs. Pour servir, placer le couscous dans un grand plat rond et y verser les légumes et le poulet.

Vocabulaire à l'œuvre 1

2 p. 136, CD 4, Tr. 1

1. — Figure-toi que Romain et Claire se sont encore disputés!
   — Ce n'est pas vrai!

2. — Devine qui j'ai vu hier soir au café?
   — Je n'en ai pas la moindre idée. Raconte!
   — Ludovic et Florence! Ils se sont réconciliés, figure-toi.

3. — Tu savais que Fatia et Karim n'étaient plus ensemble?
   — Pas possible!
   — Si! Fatia l'a laissé tomber!
   — Pauvre Karim! Il doit être triste.

4. — J'ai entendu dire qu'Arnaud et Camille se sont quittés.
   — Oui, Arnaud a oublié un de leurs rendez-vous et Camille était très fâchée.

5. — Comment est-ce que Thomas et Isabelle se sont rencontrés?
   — Dans un café. Ça a été le coup de foudre! Ils ont tout de suite décidé de se revoir.

Answers to Activity 2
1. b   **2.** a   **3.** b   **4.** b   **5.** a

Grammaire à l'œuvre 1

7 p. 138, CD 4, Tr. 2

1. Édouard et Sophie se sont rencontrés à la fête de vendredi soir.
2. Édouard s'est tout de suite demandé qui était Sophie.
3. Ils se sont beaucoup parlé.
4. Dimanche, ils se sont promenés ensemble dans le parc.
5. Et bien sûr, ils se sont revus depuis.
6. Aujourd'hui, ils sont allés boire un coca après les cours.
7. Maintenant, ils se téléphonent dix fois par jour.
8. On se demande quand ils font leurs devoirs.

Answers to Activity 7
1. a   **2.** b   **3.** a   **4.** b   **5.** a   **6.** b   **7.** a   **8.** b

Application 1

17 p. 142, CD 4, Tr. 3

1. Samedi matin, j'ai joué au foot avec mes cousins, on s'est bien amusés. Ça m'a vraiment bien plu!

2. Ensuite, à midi, il a fallu que je m'habille pour aller au mariage de ma cousine. Ce qui ne me plaît pas, c'est de devoir mettre une cravate.

3. Le mariage, lui, était super: les musiciens jouaient très bien et le repas était très bon. Cela a plu à tout le monde.

4. L'après-midi, ma cousine et son mari m'ont montré la ville, je n'ai pas trouvé ça intéressant. Ce n'est pas le genre de truc qui me plaît!

5. Le soir, nous sommes tous allés danser. J'ai rencontré une fille super et je crois que je lui ai aussi plu!

Answers to Activity 17
1. a   **2.** b   **3.** a   **4.** b   **5.** a

Vocabulaire à l'œuvre 2

22 p. 148, CD 4, Tr. 4

1. Je suis née le quinze février à Djenné, une ville au Mali.

2. J'ai fait un apprentissage dans un salon de coiffure. Mais cela ne m'a pas plu du tout. J'ai décidé de continuer mes études.

3. À l'université, j'ai rencontré un garçon très sympathique. Nous nous sommes tout de suite plu. Nous nous sommes mariés il y a deux ans.

4. Et tu sais, nous venons d'avoir un petit garçon qui s'appelle Augustin.

5. Nous rendons souvent visite à mes parents qui viennent de prendre leur retraite et qui ont déménagé au bord de la mer.

Answers to Activity 22
1. c   **2.** e   **3.** b   **4.** d   **5.** a

Grammaire à l'œuvre 2

30 p. 152, CD 4, Tr. 5

1. Son père voudrait qu'il cherche du travail.
2. Son grand-père est heureux d'habiter avec le reste de la famille.
3. Ses parents ne veulent pas déménager.
4. Ses copains sont désolés qu'il soit toujours occupé.
5. Sa cousine est ravie de se marier.
6. Sa mère souhaite qu'il l'aide à faire le ménage plus souvent.

Answers to Activity 30
1. a **2.** b **3.** b **4.** a **5.** b **6.** a

Application 2

37 p. 155, CD 4, Tr. 6

1. Je suis toujours de bonne humeur.
2. Ils étaient vraiment gênés.
3. Nous avons échangé nos numéros de téléphone.
4. Tu lui as parlé.
5. Fatima et Sara étaient vraiment énervées.
6. Il est très inquiet.

Answers to Activity 37
1. moi **2.** eux **3.** nous **4.** toi **5.** elles **6.** lui

Prépare-toi pour l'examen

6 p. 163, CD 4, Tr. 8

1. Il faudrait que nous nous voyions plus souvent.
2. Antoine a pris sa retraite le mois dernier.
3. Je suis désolée que ta grand-mère soit morte.
4. Il faut qu'elle fasse un emprunt pour finir ses études.
5. Il était triste que sa femme soit tombée malade.

Answers to Activity 6
1. a **2.** c **3.** b **4.** a **5.** b

Activités préparatoires

Listening, p. 166, CD 4, Tr. 9

1. — J'ai entendu dire que le prof est de mauvaise humeur aujourd'hui.

   — C'est pas vrai! Et moi qui n'ai pas fait mes devoirs! Qu'est-ce que tu en penses? Je copie les devoirs de Paul avant la classe? Ou bien je dis au prof que mon chien les a mangés?

2. — Salut, Marie! Ça fait longtemps qu'on ne s'est pas vus! Quoi de neuf? Comment va ta famille?

   — Malheureusement, mon grand-père est mort d'une crise cardiaque la semaine dernière.

Answers to Activity 1
1. c **2.** d

Révisions cumulatives

1 p. 168, CD 4, Tr. 10

1. Nous nous ressemblons et nous aimons faire les mêmes choses.
2. J'adore ne plus devoir travailler. J'ai travaillé pendant 40 ans. J'ai pris ma retraite au mois de mai. Maintenant, je suis tout le temps en vacances.
3. Nous nous sommes rencontrés au parc et depuis, nous sommes toujours ensemble.
4. Depuis l'indépendance, notre pays n'a plus d'ennemis et vit dans la paix.
5. Je suis vraiment très triste parce que mon petit chien vient de mourir.

Answers to Activity 1
1. b **2.** e **3.** a **4.** d **5.** c

50-Minute Lesson Plans

Amours et amitiés

Day 1

OBJECTIVE
Say what happened

Core Instruction
Chapter Opener, pp. 132–133
• Using the Photo, p. 132. **5 min.**
• See Chapter Objectives, p. 132. **5 min.**

Vocabulaire 1, pp. 134–137
• Present **Vocabulaire 1,** pp. 134–135. See Teaching **Vocabulaire,** p. 134. **15 min.**
• Present **Exprimons-nous!,** p. 135. **5 min.**
• Do Activity 1, p. 136. **5 min.**
• Play Audio CD 4, Tr. 1 for Activity 2, p. 136. **5 min.**
• Do Activity 3, p. 136. **5 min.**
• Present **Flash culture,** p. 136. **5 min.**

Optional Resources
• Advanced Learners, p. 135 ▲
• Slower Pace Learners, p. 137 ◆

Homework Suggestions
Cahier de vocabulaire et grammaire, pp. 37–38
🏵 1.1, 1.2, 3.1, 4.2

Day 2

OBJECTIVE
Ask for advice; Use reciprocal verbs

Core Instruction
Vocabulaire 1, pp. 134–137
• Do Bell Work 4.1, p. 134. **5 min.**
• See Teaching **Exprimons-nous!,** p. 136. **10 min.**
• Have students do Activities 4–5, p. 137. **20 min.**

Grammaire 1, pp. 138–141
• See Teaching **Grammaire,** p. 138. **15 min.**

Optional Resources
• Communication (TE), p. 137
• Special Learning Needs, p. 137 ●
• Slower Pace Learners, p. 139 ◆

Homework Suggestions
Study for **Quiz: Vocabulaire 1**
Cahier de vocabulaire et grammaire, p. 39
Online Practice (**go.hrw.com,** Keyword: BD3 CH4)
🏵 1.1, 1.2, 1.3

Day 3

OBJECTIVE
Use reciprocal verbs

Core Instruction
Vocabulaire 1, pp. 134–137
• Review **Vocabulaire 1,** pp. 134–137. **10 min.**
• Give **Quiz: Vocabulaire 1.** **20 min.**

Grammaire 1, pp. 138–141
• Have students do Activity 6, p. 138. **5 min.**
• Play Audio CD 4, Tr. 2 for Activity 7, p. 138. **5 min.**
• Have students do Activities 8–9, p. 139. **10 min.**

Optional Resources
• Communication (TE), p. 139

Homework Suggestions
Cahier de vocabulaire et grammaire, p. 40
Cahier d'activités, p. 31
Online Practice (**go.hrw.com,** Keyword: BD3 CH4)
🏵 1.2

Day 4

OBJECTIVE
Use reciprocal verbs; Use the past conditional

Core Instruction
Grammaire 1, pp. 138–141
• Do Bell Work 4.3, p. 140. **5 min.**
• Do Activity 10, p. 139. **5 min.**
• See Teaching **Grammaire,** p. 140. **10 min.**
• Do Activity 11, p. 140. **5 min.**
• Play Audio CD 4, Tr. 3 for Activity 12, p. 140. **5 min.**
• Have students do Activities 13–15, p. 141. **15 min.**

Application 1, pp. 142–143
• Do Activity 16, p. 142. **5 min.**

Optional Resources
• Slower Pace Learners, p. 141 ◆
• Special Learning Needs, p. 141 ●

Homework Suggestions
Study for **Quiz: Grammaire 1**
Cahier de vocabulaire et grammaire, p. 41
Cahier d'activités, p. 32
🏵 1.1, 1.2, 1.3

Day 5

OBJECTIVE
*Use the verbs **manquer** and **plaire***

Core Instruction
Grammaire 1, pp. 138–141
• Review **Grammaire 1,** pp. 138–141. **10 min.**
• Give **Quiz: Grammaire 1.** **20 min.**

Application 1, pp. 142–143
• See Teaching **Un peu plus,** p. 142. **5 min.**
• Play Audio CD 4, Tr. 3 for Activity 17, p. 142. **5 min.**
• Have students do Activities 18–21, pp. 142–143. **10 min.**

Optional Resources
• Communication (TE), p. 143
• Advanced Learners, p. 143 ▲
• Special Learning Needs, p. 143 ●

Homework Suggestions
Study for **Quiz: Application 1**
Cahier de vocabulaire et grammaire, p. 42
Cahier d'activités, p. 33
Online Practice (**go.hrw.com,** Keyword: BD3 CH4)
🏵 1.1, 1.2, 1.3, 3.2

Day 6

OBJECTIVE
Learn about francophone culture

Core Instruction
Application 1, pp. 142–143
• Review **Application 1,** pp. 142–143. **10 min.**
• Give **Quiz: Application 1.** **20 min.**

Culture, pp. 144–145
• See **Lecture culturelle** (TE), p. 144. **10 min.**
• See **Comparaisons et communauté** (TE), p. 144. **10 min.**

Optional Resources
• Cultures, p. 145
• Communities, p. 145
• Advanced Learners, p. 145 ▲
• Multiple Intelligences, p. 145

Homework Suggestions
Cahier d'activités, p. 34
Interactive Tutor, Ch. 4
Online Practice (**go.hrw.com,** Keyword: BD3 CH4)
Finish the **Communauté et professions** project.
🏵 1.3, 2.1, 3.2, 4.2, 5.1

Day 7

OBJECTIVE
Share good and bad news

Core Instruction
Vocabulaire 2, pp. 146–149
• Do Bell Work 4.5, p. 146. **5 min.**
• Present **Vocabulaire 2,** pp. 146–147. See Teaching **Vocabulaire,** p. 146. **15 min.**
• Present **Exprimons-nous!,** p. 147. **10 min.**
• Play Audio CD 4, Tr. 4 for Activity 22, p. 148. **5 min.**
• Have students do Activities 23–24, p. 148. **10 min.**
• Present **Flash culture,** p. 148. **5 min.**

Optional Resources
• Advanced Learners, p. 147 ▲
• Multiple Intelligences, p. 147

Homework Suggestions
Cahier de vocabulaire et grammaire, pp. 43–44
🏵 1.2, 1.3, 3.1, 4.2

Day 8

OBJECTIVE
Renew old acquaintances; Use the subjunctive

Core Instruction
Vocabulaire 2, pp. 146–149
• See Teaching **Exprimons-nous!,** p. 148. **10 min.**
• Have students do Activities 25–26, p. 149. **20 min.**

Grammaire 2, pp. 150–153
• See Teaching **Grammaire,** p. 150. **15 min.**
• Have students do Activity 27, p. 151. **5 min.**

Optional Resources
• Communication (TE), p. 149
• Special Learning Needs, p. 149 ●

Homework Suggestions
Study for **Quiz: Vocabulaire 2**
Cahier de vocabulaire et grammaire, p. 45
Interactive Tutor, Ch. 4
Online Practice (**go.hrw.com,** Keyword: BD3 CH4)
🏵 1.1, 1.2, 1.3

50-Minute Lesson Plans

Day 9

OBJECTIVE
Use the subjunctive

Core Instruction
Vocabulaire 2, pp. 146–149
- Review **Vocabulaire 2,** pp. 146–149. **10 min.**
- Give **Quiz: Vocabulaire 2.** **20 min.**

Grammaire 2, pp. 150–153
- Have students do Activities 28–29, p. 151. **15 min.**
- Present **Flash culture**, p. 152. **5 min.**

Optional Resources
- Advanced Learners, p. 151 ▲
- Special Learning Needs, p. 151 ●

Homework Suggestions
Cahier de vocabulaire et grammaire, p. 46
Cahier d'activités, p. 35
Interactive Tutor, Ch. 4
Online Practice (**go.hrw.com,** Keyword: BD3 CH4)
❀ 1.1, 1.2, 4.2

Day 10

OBJECTIVE
Use the subjunctive with necessity, desire, and emotions; Use disjunctive (stress) pronouns

Core Instruction
Grammaire 2, pp. 150–153
- Do Bell Work 4.7, p. 152. **5 min.**
- See Teaching **Grammaire,** p. 152. **10 min.**
- Play Audio CD 4, Tr. 5 for Activity 30, p. 152. **5 min.**
- Have students do Activities 31–34, pp. 152–153. **20 min.**

Application 2, pp. 154–155
- Do Activity 35, p. 154. **5 min.**
- See Teaching **Un peu plus,** p. 154. **5 min.**

Optional Resources
- Advanced Learners, p. 153 ▲
- Multiple Intelligences, p. 153

Homework Suggestions
Study for **Quiz: Grammaire 2**
Cahier de vocabulaire et grammaire, p. 47
Cahier d'activités, p. 36
❀ 1.1, 1.2, 1.3

Day 11

OBJECTIVE
Use disjunctive (stress) pronouns

Core Instruction
Grammaire 2, pp. 150–153
- Review **Grammaire 2,** pp. 150–153. **10 min.**
- Give **Quiz: Grammaire 2.** **20 min.**

Application 2, pp. 154–155
- Have students do Activity 36, p. 154. **5 min.**
- Play Audio CD 4, Tr. 6 for Activity 37, p. 155. **5 min.**
- Have students do Activities 38–40, p. 155. **10 min.**

Optional Resources
- Slower Pace Learners, p. 155 ◆

Homework Suggestions
Study for **Quiz: Application 2**
Cahier de vocabulaire et grammaire, p. 48
Cahier d'activités, p. 37
Interactive Tutor, Ch. 4
Online Practice (**go.hrw.com,** Keyword: BD3 CH4)
❀ 1.1, 1.2

Day 12

OBJECTIVE
Develop listening and reading skills

Core Instruction
Application 2, pp. 154–155
- Review **Application 2,** pp. 154–155. **10 min.**
- Give **Quiz: Application 2.** **20 min.**

Lecture, pp. 156–159
- See **Lecture** (TE), p. 156. **20 min.**

Optional Resources
- Slower Pace Learners, p. 157 ◆
- Special Learning Needs, p. 157 ●
- Cultures, p. 159

Homework Suggestions
Interactive Tutor, Ch. 4
Online Practice (**go.hrw.com,** Keyword: BD3 CH4)
❀ 1.2, 2.1, 2.2, 3.1, 3.2, 4.2

Day 13

OBJECTIVE
Develop listening, reading, and writing skills

Core Instruction
Lecture, pp. 156–159
- See **Lecture** (TE), p. 158. **20 min.**

L'atelier de l'écrivain, pp. 160–161
- See **L'atelier de l'écrivain** (TE), p. 160. **30 min.**

Optional Resources
- Advanced Learners, p. 159 ▲
- Multiple Intelligences, p. 159
- Connections, p. 160
- Slower Pace Learners, p. 161 ◆
- Multiple Intelligences, p. 161

Homework Suggestions
Cahier d'activités, p. 38
❀ 1.2, 1.3, 3.1, 3.2

Day 14

OBJECTIVE
Review the chapter; Prepare for the AP Exam

Core Instruction
Prépare-toi pour l'examen, pp. 162–165
- Have students do Activities 1–5, pp. 162–163. **25 min.**

Activités préparatoires, pp. 166–167
- Have students do the **Activités préparatoires,** pp. 166–167. **25 min.**

Optional Resources
- Reteaching, p. 162
- Cultures, p. 164
- Slower Pace Learners, p. 167 ◆
- Special Learning Needs, p. 167 ●

Homework Suggestions
Interactive Tutor, Ch. 4
Online Practice (**go.hrw.com,** Keyword: BD3 CH4)
❀ 1.1, 1.2, 1.3, 2.1, 3.1

Day 15

OBJECTIVE
Review the chapter

Core Instruction
Prépare-toi pour l'examen, pp. 162–165
- Play Audio CD 4, Tr. 8 for Activity 6, p. 163. **10 min.**
- Have students do Activity 7, p. 163. **10 min.**

Révisions cumulatives, pp. 168–169
- Play Audio CD 4, Tr. 10 for Activity 1, p. 168. **5 min.**
- Have students do Activities 2–6, pp. 168–169. **25 min.**

Optional Resources
- Online Culture Project, p. 168
- Fine Art Connection, p. 169
- **Télé-culture:** Interviews
- **Télé-roman: Camille et compagnie**

Homework Suggestions
Study for Chapter Test
Online Practice (**go.hrw.com,** Keyword: BD3 CH4)
❀ 1.1, 1.2, 1.3, 2.2, 3.1, 3.2

Day 16/Test

Core Instruction
Chapter Test 50 min.

Optional Resources
Assessment Program
- Alternative Assessment
- Test Generator
- **Quiz: Lecture**
- **Quiz: Écriture**

Homework Suggestions
Cahier d'activités, pp. 39–40, 108–109
Online Practice (**go.hrw.com,** Keyword: BD3 CH4)

90-Minute Lesson Plans

Amours et amitiés

Block 1

OBJECTIVE
Say what happened; Ask for advice

Core Instruction
Chapter Opener, pp. 132–133
• See Using the Photo, p. 132. **5 min.**
• See Chapter Objectives, p. 132. **5 min.**

Vocabulaire 1, pp. 134–137
• Present **Vocabulaire 1,** pp. 134–135. See Teaching **Vocabulaire,** p. 134. **15 min.**
• Present **Exprimons-nous!,** p. 135. **10 min.**
• Have students do Activity 1, p. 136. **5 min.**
• Play Audio CD 4, Tr. 1 for Activity 2, p. 136. **10 min.**
• Have students do Activity 3, p. 136. **5 min.**
• Present **Flash culture,** p. 136. **5 min.**
• See Teaching **Exprimons-nous!,** p. 136. **10 min.**
• Have students do Activities 4–5, p. 137. **20 min.**

Optional Resources
• Learning Tips, p. 133
• Cultures, p. 134
• TPR, p. 135
• Comparisons, p. 135
• Advanced Learners, p. 135 ▲
• Multiple Intelligences, p. 135
• **Cinquain** Poetry, p. 136
• Cultures, p. 137
• Communication (TE), p. 137
• Slower Pace Learners, p. 137 ◆
• Special Learning Needs, p. 137 ●

Homework Suggestions
Study for **Quiz: Vocabulaire 1**
Cahier de vocabulaire et grammaire, pp. 37–39
Interactive Tutor, Ch. 4
Online Practice (**go.hrw.com,** Keyword: BD3 CH4)
❀ 1.1, 1.2. 1.3, 2.1, 2.2, 3.1, 4.2

Block 2

OBJECTIVE
Use reciprocal verbs; Use the past conditional

Core Instruction
Vocabulaire 1, pp. 134–137
• Review **Vocabulaire 1,** pp. 134–137. **10 min.**
• Give **Quiz: Vocabulaire 1.** **20 min.**

Grammaire 1, pp. 138–141
• See Teaching **Grammaire,** p. 138. **10 min.**
• Have students do Activity 6, p. 138. **5 min.**
• Play Audio CD 4, Tr. 2 for Activity 7, p. 138. **5 min.**
• Have students do Activities 8–10, p. 139. **10 min.**
• See Teaching **Grammaire,** p. 140. **10 min.**
• Have students do Activity 11, p. 140. **5 min.**
• Play Audio CD 4, Tr. 3 for Activity 12, p. 140. **5 min.**
• Have students do Activities 13–14, p. 141. **10 min.**

Optional Resources
• Teacher to Teacher, p. 139
• Communication (TE), p. 139
• Slower Pace Learners, p. 139 ◆
• Multiple Intelligences, p. 139
• Communication (TE), p. 141
• Slower Pace Learners, p. 141 ◆
• Special Learning Needs, p. 141 ●

Homework Suggestions
Study for **Quiz: Grammaire 1**
Cahier de vocabulaire et grammaire, pp. 40–41
Cahier d'activités, pp. 31–32
Online Practice (**go.hrw.com,** Keyword: BD3 CH4)
❀ 1.1, 1.2, 1.3

Block 3

OBJECTIVE
*Use the past conditional; Use the verbs **manquer** and **plaire**; Learn about francophone culture*

Core Instruction
Grammaire 1, pp. 138–141
• Do Bell Work 4.3, p. 140. **5 min.**
• Have students do Activity 15, p. 141. **5 min.**
• Review **Grammaire 1,** pp. 138–141. **10 min.**
• Give **Quiz: Grammaire 1.** **20 min.**

Application 1, pp. 142–143
• Have students do Activity 16, p. 142. **5 min.**
• See Teaching **Un peu plus,** p. 142. **5 min.**
• Play Audio CD 4, Tr. 3 for Activity 17, p. 142. **5 min.**
• Have students do Activities 18–21, pp. 142–143. **15 min.**

Culture, pp. 144–145
• See **Lecture culturelle** (TE), p. 144. **10 min.**
• See **Comparaisons et communauté** (TE), p. 144. **10 min.**

Optional Resources
• **Attention!,** p. 142
• French for Spanish Speakers, p. 142
• Communication (TE), p. 143
• Advanced Learners, p. 143 ▲
• Special Learning Needs, p. 143 ●
• Prereading Questions, p. 144
• Active Reading Questions, p. 144
• **Vocabulaire supplémentaire,** p. 144
• Bulletin Board Project, p. 145
• Cultures, p. 145
• Communities, p. 145
• Advanced Learners, p. 145 ▲
• Multiple Intelligences, p. 145

Homework Suggestions
Study for **Quiz: Application 1**
Cahier de vocabulaire et grammaire, p. 42
Cahier d'activités, pp. 33–34
Interactive Tutor, Ch. 4
Online Practice (**go.hrw.com,** Keyword: BD3 CH4)
Finish the **Communauté et professions** project.
❀ 1.1, 1.2, 1.3, 2.1, 3.1, 3.2, 4.1, 4.2, 5.1

Block 4

OBJECTIVE
Share good and bad news; Renew old acquaintances

Core Instruction
Application 1, pp. 142–143
• Review **Application 1,** pp. 142–143. **10 min.**
• Give **Quiz: Application 1.** **20 min.**

Vocabulaire 2, pp. 146–149
• Present **Vocabulaire 2,** pp. 146–147. See Teaching **Vocabulaire,** p. 146. **10 min.**
• Present **Exprimons-nous!,** p. 147. **10 min.**
• Play Audio CD 4, Tr. 4 for Activity 22, p. 148. **5 min.**
• Have students do Activities 23–24, p. 148. **10 min.**
• Present **Flash culture,** p. 148. **5 min.**
• See Teaching **Exprimons-nous!,** p. 148. **10 min.**
• Have students do Activities 25–26, p. 149. **10 min.**

Optional Resources
• Connections, p. 146
• TPR, p. 147
• Cultures, p. 147
• Advanced Learners, p. 147 ▲
• Multiple Intelligences, p. 147
• **Proverbes,** p. 149
• Communication (TE), p. 149
• Slower Pace Learners, p. 149 ◆
• Special Learning Needs, p. 149 ●

Homework Suggestions
Study for **Quiz: Vocabulaire 2**
Cahier de vocabulaire et grammaire, pp. 43–45
Interactive Tutor, Ch. 4
Online Practice (**go.hrw.com,** Keyword: BD3 CH4)
❀ 1.1, 1.2, 1.3, 2.1, 3.1, 4.2

90-Minute Lesson Plans

Block 5

OBJECTIVE
Use the subjunctive; Use the subjunctive with necessity, desire, and emotions

Core Instruction
Vocabulaire 2, pp. 146–149
- Review **Vocabulaire 2,** pp. 146–149. **10 min.**
- Give **Quiz: Vocabulaire 2. 20 min.**

Grammaire 2, pp. 150–153
- See Teaching **Grammaire,** p. 150. **10 min.**
- Have students do Activities 27–29, p. 151. **15 min.**
- Present **Flash culture,** p. 152. **5 min.**
- See Teaching **Grammaire,** p. 152. **10 min.**
- Play Audio CD 4, Tr. 5 for Activity 30, p. 152. **5 min.**
- Have students do Activities 31–33, pp. 152–153. **15 min.**

Optional Resources
- **Attention!,** p. 150
- Communication (TE), p. 151
- Advanced Learners, p. 151 ▲
- Special Learning Needs, p. 151 ●
- French for Spanish Speakers, p. 152
- Communication (TE), p. 153
- Advanced Learners, p. 153 ▲
- Multiple Intelligences, p. 153

Homework Suggestions
Study for **Quiz: Grammaire 2**
Cahier de vocabulaire et grammaire, pp. 46–47
Cahier d'activités, pp. 35–36
Interactive Tutor, Ch. 4
Online Practice (**go.hrw.com,** Keyword: BD3 CH4)
❀ 1.1, 1.2, 1.3, 4.1, 4.2

Block 6

OBJECTIVE
Use the subjunctive with necessity, desire, and emotions; Use disjunctive (stress) pronouns; Develop listening and reading skills

Grammaire 2, pp. 150–153
- Have students do Activity 34, p. 153. **10 min.**
- Review **Grammaire 2,** pp. 150–153. **10 min.**
- Give **Quiz: Grammaire 2. 20 min.**

Application 2, pp. 154–155
- Have students do Activity 35, p. 154. **5 min.**
- See Teaching **Un peu plus,** p. 154. **5 min.**
- Have students do Activity 36, p. 154. **5 min.**
- Play Audio CD 4, Tr. 6 for Activity 37, p. 155. **5 min.**
- Have students do Activities 38–40, p. 155. **10 min.**

Lecture, pp. 156–159
- See **Lecture** (TE), p. 156. **20 min.**

Optional Resources
- Communication (TE), p. 155
- Slower Pace Learners, p. 155 ◆
- Special Learning Needs, p. 155 ●
- AP Reading Suggestion, p. 156
- Applying the Strategies, p. 156
- Active Reading Questions, p. 157
- Making Predictions, p. 157
- Slower Pace Learners, p. 157 ◆
- Special Learning Needs, p. 157 ●
- Cultures, p. 159

Homework Suggestions
Study for **Quiz: Application 2**
Cahier de vocabulaire et grammaire, p. 48
Cahier d'activités, p. 37
Interactive Tutor, Ch. 4
Online Practice (**go.hrw.com,** Keyword: BD3 CH4)
❀ 1.1, 1.2, 1.3, 2.1, 2.2, 3.1, 3.2, 4.2

Block 7

OBJECTIVE
Develop listening, reading, and writing skills; Review the chapter

Core Instruction
Application 2, pp. 154–155
- Review **Application 2,** pp. 154–155. **10 min.**
- Give **Quiz: Application 2. 20 min.**

Lecture, pp. 156–159
- See **Lecture** (TE), p. 158. **10 min.**

L'atelier de l'écrivain, pp. 160–161
- See **L'atelier de l'écrivain** (TE), p. 160. **30 min.**

Prépare-toi pour l'examen, pp. 162–165
- Have students do Activities 1–5, pp. 162–163. **10 min.**
- Play Audio CD 4, Tr. 8 for Activity 6, p. 163. **5 min.**
- Have students do Activity 7, p. 163. **5 min.**

Optional Resources
- Active Reading Questions, p. 158
- Postreading Activity, p. 158
- Connections, p. 158
- Advanced Learners, p. 159 ▲
- Multiple Intelligences, p. 159
- Process Writing, p. 160
- Teaching Suggestion, p. 160
- Connections, p. 160
- **La concordance des temps,** p. 161
- Writing Assessment, p. 161
- Slower Pace Learners, p. 161 ◆
- Multiple Intelligences, p. 161
- TPRS, p. 162
- Reteaching, p. 162
- Oral Assessment, p. 163

Homework Suggestions
Study for Chapter Test
Cahier d'activités, p. 38
Interactive Tutor, Ch. 4
Online Practice (**go.hrw.com,** Keyword: BD3 CH4)
❀ 1.1, 1.2, 1.3, 2.1, 3.1, 3.2, 4.1

Block 8

OBJECTIVE
Prepare for the AP Exam; Review and assess the chapter

Core Instruction
Activités préparatoires, pp. 166–167
- Have students do the **Activités préparatoires,** pp. 166–167. **20 min.**

Chapter Test 50 min.

Révisions cumulatives, pp. 168–169
- Play Audio CD 4, Tr. 10 for Activity 1, p. 168. **5 min.**
- Have students do Activities 2–6, pp. 168–169. **15 min.**

Optional Resources
- Cultures, p. 164
- **Proverbes,** p. 164
- Chapter Review, pp. 164–165
- Game, p. 165
- Reading Strategy, p. 167
- Writing Strategy, p. 167
- Slower Pace Learners, p. 167 ◆
- Special Learning Needs, p. 167 ●
- Online Culture Project, p. 168
- Fine Art Connection, p. 169
- **Télé-culture:** Interviews
- **Télé-roman: Camille et compagnie**

Homework Suggestions
Cahier d'activités, pp. 39–40, 108–109
Online Practice (**go.hrw.com,** Keyword: BD3 CH4)
❀ 1.1, 1.2, 1.3, 2.1, 2.2, 3.1, 3.2

Meeting the National Standards

Communication
Communication, pp. 137, 139, 141, 143, 149, 151, 153, 155

À ton tour, p. 169

Cultures
Flash culture, pp. 136, 148, 152

Comparaisons, p. 145

Products and Perspectives, pp. 134, 164

Practices and Perspectives, pp. 137, 145, 147, 159

Connections
Language Note, pp. 151, 162

Social Studies Link, p. 135

Geography Link, p. 146

Language Arts Link, p. 160

Comparisons
Comparaisons, p. 145

Communities
Communauté, p. 145

Career Path, p. 145

Using the Photo

Mali has a rich heritage of crafts, including textiles and hair-decorating. The Bamanan people have been making cloth for hundreds of years, using locally grown cotton and natural dyes. Ask students to describe the clothes worn by this wedding party. The traditional music of Mali is based on the songs of the **griots,** or bards, who memorize and recite events of the country's glorious past. One of their traditional instruments is the lute-like **kora**. Ask students to name other instruments Malian musicians may play at festivals and ceremonies, such as this wedding. ❀ 1.1, 3.1

chapitre **4**

Amours et amitiés

Objectifs

In this chapter, you will learn to
• say what happened
• ask for and give advice
• share good and bad news
• renew old acquaintances

And you will use and review
• reciprocal verbs
• the past conditional
• the verbs **manquer** and **plaire**
• the subjunctive
• the subjunctive with necessity, desire, and emotions
• the disjunctive pronouns

▶ *Que vois-tu sur la photo?*

Où sont ces personnes?

Qu'est-ce que ces personnes font?

Et toi, est-ce que tu as déjà assisté à un mariage? Comment est-ce que c'était?

Suggested pacing:

	Traditional Schedule	Block Schedule
Vocabulaire/Grammaire/Application 1	5 days	2 blocks
Culture	1 day	1 block
Vocabulaire/Grammaire/Application 2	5 days	2 blocks
Lecture	1 day	1/2 block
L'atelier de l'écrivain	1 day	1/2 block
Prépare-toi pour l'examen	1/2 day	1/2 block
Activités préparatoires	1/2 day	1/2 block
Examen	1 day	1/2 block
Révisions cumulatives	1 day	1/2 block

Visit Us Online
go.hrw.com
Online Edition
KEYWORD: BD3 CH4

Vocabulaire supplémentaire

Students might use these terms to discuss the photo.

le mariage	*wedding*
la cérémonie	*ceremony*
les tambours	*drums*
les rayures	*stripes*
les boucles d'oreille	*earrings*
les nouveaux mariés	*the bride and groom*

Learning Tips

Tell students that when they listen to spoken French they might not recognize every word. Remind them that they will usually be able to understand the gist of a presentation or conversation, even if they do not know all the words. Remind students to watch for gestures and body language to help them understand when they talk to a French speaker face to face.

Language Lab

You might want to use your language lab to have students:
• listen to all target vocabulary and phrases in the chapter
• practice pronunciation of vocabulary and phrases, using Holt SoundBooth to save their work for evaluation
• complete the listening activities in this chapter

Un mariage traditionnel à Bamako, au Mali

LISTENING PRACTICE

Vocabulaire
Activity 2, p. 136, CD 4, Tr. 1
Activity 22, p. 148, CD 4, Tr. 4

Grammaire
Activity 7, p. 138, CD 4, Tr. 2
Activity 30, p. 152, CD 4, Tr. 5

Application
Activity 17, p. 142, CD 4, Tr. 3
Activity 37, p. 154, CD 4, Tr. 6

Language Lab and Classroom Activities

Prépare-toi pour l'examen
Activity 6, p. 163, CD 4, Tr. 8
Télé-culture: Interviews, Chapter 4

Activités préparatoires
Section I, Listening, p. 166, CD 4, Tr. 9
Télé-roman: *Camille et compagnie*, Épisode 4

Révisions cumulatives
Activity 1, p. 168, CD 4, Tr. 10

Lecture
p. 156, CD 4, Tr. 7

Bell Work

Use Bell Work 4.1 in the *Teaching Transparencies* or write this activity on the board.

Change les phrases et utilise **l'infinitif passé.** Commence chaque phrase avec **Après.**

1. Martin s'est réveillé, puis il s'est levé.
2. Il a déjeuné, puis il s'est brossé les dents.
3. Il a mis un jean, puis il est sorti.
4. Il a acheté le journal, puis il a pris le métro.  1.2

Cultures

Products and Perspectives

Mali has a population of 13.5 million (2005) and a literacy rate of about 20 percent. About 70 percent of the population lives on less than a dollar a day. The little-developed telecommunications infrastructure is heavily skewed to the urban areas. In 2004, 7 out of 1000 people had a landline telephone; 36 had a cell phone; 5 had Internet access. Ask students why they think there are so few Internet subscribers in Mali and how that compares to the U.S.. 2.2, 4.2

Objectifs
- to say what happened
- to ask for and give advice

Vocabulaire à l'œuvre 1

L'histoire de Saliou et Coumba en Afrique

 Amadou  Saliou  Coumba

Saliou et Coumba, la sœur d'Amadou, **se sont rencontrés** au cybercafé.

Saliou et Coumba **se sont** beaucoup **parlé.** C'était un vrai **coup de foudre.**

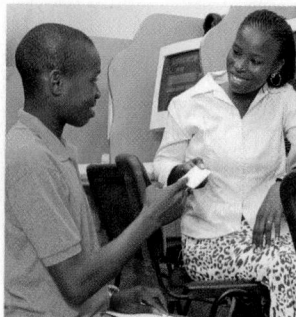
Ils **ont échangé** leur numéro de mobile.

Malheureusement, un jour, Amadou et Saliou **se sont énervés** en jouant au baby-foot et ils **se sont disputés.**

Les deux amis **se sont quittés** très **fâchés** et ils **ne se sont pas revus** pendant une semaine.

Mais après, ils **ont regretté** de s'être énervés et ils **se sont téléphoné** et ils **se sont réconciliés.**

▶ **Vocabulaire supplémentaire—La vie, p. R18**

Core Instruction

TEACHING VOCABULAIRE

1. Introduce the vocabulary, using transparencies **Vocabulaire 4.1** and **4.2.** Model the pronunciation of all words and expressions. **(3 min.)**

2. Ask students questions about the photos on the transparency and have them point to the photo you are talking about. **Quelle photo montre où ils se sont rencontrés? Quelle photo montre où ils se sont quittés fâchés? (3 min.)**

3. Model the sentences from **Exprimons-nous!** Then have students react to everything you say. **J'ai entendu dire qu'il n'y a pas de cours demain. Ce n'est pas vrai! (3 min.)**

Ils ont décidé de **se retrouver** chez Amadou pour le thé.

C'est ainsi que Saliou et Coumba **se sont revus!**

Online Practice
go.hrw.com
Vocabulaire 1 practice
KEYWORD: BD3 CH4

D'autres mots utiles

de bonne/mauvaise humeur	in a good/bad mood	inquiet/inquiète	worried
déçu(e)	disappointed	vexé(e)	offended
ensemble	together	rompre (avec)	to break up
gêné(e)	embarrassed	se donner rendez-vous	to make a date
indifférent(e)	indifferent	tomber/être amoureux(euse)	to fall/be in love

Exprimons-nous!

To say what happened	To respond
J'ai entendu dire qu'ils se sont revus. _I heard that . . ._	**Raconte!** _Tell me about it!_
Devine qui j'ai rencontré hier! _Guess . . ._	**Je n'en ai pas la moindre idée./Aucune idée.** _I have no idea._
Figure-toi qu'elles se sont disputées. _You know what . . . ?_	**Ce n'est pas vrai!** _You're kidding!_
Tu savais que Léa et Tom étaient **toujours** ensemble? _Did you know that . . . still . . . ?_	**Pas possible!** _No way!_

Interactive TUTOR

Vocabulaire et grammaire, pp. 37–39

Online workbooks

TPR
TOTAL PHYSICAL RESPONSE

Have students respond to these commands.

Lève le doigt si tu es de bonne humeur.

Lève-toi si tu sais où tes parents se sont rencontrés.

Lève la main si tes amis et toi, vous vous donnez rendez-vous le week-end.

Montre les dents si tu t'énerves souvent.

Mets la main sur le cœur si tu es déjà tombé(e) amoureux(euse).

Have partners to act out the following situations. Their classmates will guess what is going on.

Ils se disputent.

Vous vous téléphonez.

Ils se regardent... ah... c'est le coup de foudre!

Vous êtes inquiets ou gênés? ❀ 1.2

Connections
Social Studies Link

Although the constitution of Mali prohibits discrimination based on gender, social and cultural factors give men a dominant role. A Malian woman is first and foremost valued in her roles of wife and mother. Socialization into these family roles starts early; five-year-old girls are expected to help with housework and look after younger siblings. Ask students to discuss gender socialization in the United States. ❀ 3.1

Differentiated Instruction

ADVANCED LEARNERS

Extension Have students create a conversation in which they tell a partner about a real or fictitious argument they recently had with a family member or friend. The partner should react appropriately, using expressions presented in **Exprimons-nous!** Ask some partners to role-play their conversation for the class. Encourage students to use facial expressions and gestures to emphasize their statements. ❀ 1.1, 1.3

MULTIPLE INTELLIGENCES

Intrapersonal Ask students to use words and expressions from **Vocabulaire 1** to write a journal entry about their emotional reaction to events in their life. The events may include an embarrassing moment or a time they were offended, disappointed, or worried. This can be a personal entry that is not shared with others. ❀ 1.3

Resources

Planning:

Lesson Planner

 One-Stop Planner

Presentation:

Teaching Transparencies
Vocabulaire 4.1, 4.2

Practice:

Cahier de vocabulaire et grammaire

Differentiated Practice and Assessment CD-ROM

Media Guide

Audio CD 4, Tr. 1

Interactive Tutor, Disc 1

---

② Script

See script on p. 131E.

③ Answers

1. devine
2. Aucune idée
3. Tu savais
4. ensemble
5. Pas possible
6. amoureux
7. entendu dire

④ Answers

1. Devine
2. Figure-toi
3. À ton avis/D'après toi
4. en penses
5. à ma place

Cinquain Poetry

Ask students to create a poem using the new vocabulary.

Line 1 One noun phrase
Line 2 Two adjectives
Line 3 Three verbs
Line 4 An expression
Line 5 One noun that describes the first noun

Sample answer

Un coup de foudre
Amoureuse, inquiète
Se donner rendez-vous,
tomber amoureuse, rompre
Ce n'est pas vrai!
L'amour

Entre copains

draguer	to flirt
casser	to break up
laisser tomber	to dump (someone)
Tu charries!	You're going too far!
Tu rigoles!	You're kidding!

Flash culture

L'hospitalité est très importante en Afrique. C'est un honneur de recevoir des invités et la tradition est de leur servir du thé à la menthe qu'il est mal élevé de refuser.

Le premier verre de thé n'a pas beaucoup de sucre et est appelé **amer comme la mort**; le deuxième plus sucré, **bon comme la vie**, et le troisième, très sucré, **doux comme l'amour.**

Qu'est-ce que ta famille sert aux invités? ✿4.2

---

❶ Sentiments et émotions ✿1.2

Lisons Choisis la réaction qui correspond le mieux à chaque situation.

1. Lola a rencontré un garçon super. Elle est _____.
   a. inquiète   b. déçue   **c.** heureuse

2. La copine de Yann ne l'aime plus. Yann est _____.
   a. triste   b. gêné   c. de bonne humeur

3. Entre Juliette et Sébastien c'est le vrai coup de foudre. Ils sont _____.
   a. vexés   **b.** amoureux   c. de mauvaise humeur

4. La femme de M. Reynaud est très en retard à leur rendez-vous. Il est _____.
   a. inquiet   b. gêné   c. content

5. Aziz et son copain Mohammed se sont disputés et ils ne se parlent plus. Ils sont _____.
   a. fâchés   b. gênés   c. de bonne humeur

6. Mamadou a rompu avec Fatou. Elle est très _____.
   a. amoureuse   b. inquiète   **c.** malheureuse

❷ Écoutons   CD 4, Tr. 1   ✿1.2   **1.** b **2.** a **3.** b **4.** b **5.** a

Les couples suivants ont une relation assez difficile et se disputent souvent. Écoute les conversations et dis si on parle de quelque chose qui est **a) positif** ou **b) négatif**.

❸ Dernières nouvelles ✿1.2

Lisons/Écrivons Lana raconte les dernières nouvelles à son amie Fatia. Complète leur conversation avec les expressions de la boîte. Fais tous les changements nécessaires.

ensemble	deviner	pas possible	entendre dire
amoureux	tu savais	aucune idée	rompre

LANA   Hier, je suis allée au centre commercial et ___1___ qui j'ai vu!

FATIA   ___2___.

LANA   Karim et Lætitia! ___3___ qu'ils sortaient ___4___?

FATIA   ___5___!

LANA   Mais oui! Et ils avaient l'air vraiment ___6___!

FATIA   Pauvre Lætitia! J'ai ___7___ que Karim n'était pas très sérieux!

Core Instruction

TEACHING EXPRIMONS-NOUS!

1. Model the pronunciation of the expressions in **Exprimons-nous!** Tell students that **à ton avis** and **d'après-toi** are interchangeable. Ask them what **à ma place, à ton avis,** and **d'après toi** would become if they were used in one of the answers. (**à ta place, à mon avis, d'après moi**) **(2 min.)**

2. Have partners make up similarly constructed questions and practice asking for and giving advice. **(2 min.)**

Exprimons-nous!

To ask for advice	To give advice
Qu'est-ce que tu en penses? Je lui téléphone? *What do you think about it?*	Non, **tu ferais mieux d'**attendre. *. . . it would be better to . . .*
Qu'est-ce que tu aurais fait **à ma place?** *. . . in my place?*	**Si j'avais été toi,** j'aurais fait la même chose. *If I had been you, . . .*
À ton avis, je devrais rompre avec Pascal? *In your opinion, . . . ?*	**Pas nécessairement.** *Not necessarily.*
D'après toi, je devrais lui parler? *In your opinion, . . . ?*	**Surtout pas!** *Certainly not!* **Jamais de la vie!** *Not in a million years!*

Vocabulaire et grammaire, pp. 37–39 · **Online** workbooks

4 **Des conseils** ✿1.2

Écrivons Jennifer et son copain se sont disputés. Tu donnes toujours de bons conseils, alors Jennifer t'a envoyé cet e-mail. Mais, il y a des mots qui manquent. Complète son e-mail logiquement.

Salut,
  __1__ ce qui est arrivé hier soir! Mon copain et moi, nous nous sommes disputés. __2__ qu'il pense que j'aime un autre garçon! Mais ce n'est pas vrai. Je suis très amoureuse de lui. __3__ , est-ce que je devrais lui parler et essayer de me réconcilier avec lui? Est-ce que je lui offre un cadeau? Qu'est-ce que tu __4__ ? Qu'est-ce que tu ferais __5__ ? Merci d'avance pour tes conseils.
Jennifer

Communication

HOLT **SoundBooth** ONLINE RECORDING

5 **Scénario** ✿1.1

Parlons En petits groupes, jouez la scène suivante. Une personne est animateur/animatrice pour une radio francophone. Les autres personnes du groupe sont des jeunes qui appellent pour parler de leurs problèmes. Chaque jeune invente un problème et téléphone à l'animateur/l'animatrice qui va lui donner son avis et proposer des solutions. Ensuite, échangez les rôles.

MODÈLE —Bonjour. Je m'appelle Nora. Hier, je me suis disputée avec ma meilleure amie et...

Vocabulaire 1

Resources

Planning:

Lesson Planner

 One-Stop Planner

Practice:

Grammar Tutor for Students of French, Chapter 4

Cahier de vocabulaire et grammaire

Differentiated Practice and Assessment CD-ROM

Cahier d'activités

Media Guide

 Teaching Transparencies
Bell Work 4.2

 Audio CD 4, Tr. 2

 Interactive Tutor, Disc 1

Bell Work

Use Bell Work 4.2 in the *Teaching Transparencies* or write this activity on the board.

Complète chaque phrase avec le mot ou l'expression qui convient.

réconciliés, inquiète, coup de foudre, fâchés, bonne humeur

1. Quand il l'a vue, ça a été un vrai...
2. Coumba est heureuse et de très...
3. Hier, ils se sont disputés et ils se sont quittés...
4. Coumba est tombée malade et sa mère est...
5. Ils se sont téléphoné et ils se sont... 🞕1.2

7 Script

1. Édouard et Sophie se sont rencontrés à la fête de vendredi soir.
2. Édouard s'est tout de suite demandé qui était Sophie.
3. Ils se sont beaucoup parlé.
4. Dimanche, ils se sont promenés ensemble dans le parc.
5. Et bien sûr, ils se sont revus depuis.
6. Aujourd'hui, ils sont allés boire un coca après les cours.
7. Maintenant, ils se téléphonent dix fois par jour.
8. On se demande quand ils font leurs devoirs.

Objectifs
• reciprocal verbs
• the past conditional

Grammaire
à l'œuvre 1

Reciprocal verbs

1 In French, the pronouns nous, vous, and se may be used to make a verb reciprocal **(verbe réciproque)**. They mean *(to/for/at) each other* when added before a verb.

Nous nous aimons.	*We love each other.*
Ils se sont rencontrés hier.	*They met each other yesterday.*

2 In the **passé composé,** use être as the helping verb when you make a verb reciprocal. Make the past participle agree if the reciprocal pronoun (nous, vous or se) is the *direct object* of the verb.

Nous avons vu Paul hier.   Elles ont revu Paul au musée.

MAIS

Nous nous sommes vus hier. → *direct object*

Elles se sont revues au musée. → *direct object*

3 Do not make the past participle agree with the reciprocal pronoun if it is the *indirect object* of the verb, that means if it answers the question "à qui?". Some verbs that take an indirect object are **conseiller, demander, dire, écrire, offrir, parler, plaire,** and **téléphoner.**

J'ai parlé à **Pauline.** Nous nous sommes parlé. *indirect objects*

> Vocabulaire et grammaire, *pp. 40–41*
> Cahier d'activités, *pp. 31–33*

Déjà vu!

Reciprocal verbs and reflexive verbs are not the same. **Reflexive verbs** are used when the same person performs and receives the action of the verb. In the **passé composé,** they use **être** as helping verb and the past participle agrees with the reflexive pronoun only if it is the direct object of the verb.

> Elle s'est lavée.
> Elle s'est lavé les mains.

---

6 **Accord ou pas accord?** 🞕1.2

Lisons Aimé et Taki discutent les dernières nouvelles du week-end. Fais l'accord si nécessaire.

1. Paul et Virginie se sont quittés____.
2. Sylvie et Julien se sont longtemps parlé____.
3. Malik et Thérèse ont rencontré____ Vincent hier.
4. Karima et Lise se sont finalement réconciliées____.
5. Rémy et Julie se sont disputés____.
6. Aline et Salima se sont téléphoné____ la semaine dernière.

7 **Écoutons** CD 4, Tr. 2 🞕1.2 **1.** a **2.** b **3.** a **4.** b **5.** a **6.** b **7.** a **8.** b

Ça a été le coup de foudre entre Édouard et Sophie. Pour chaque phrase, dis si l'action est **a) réciproque** ou **b) pas réciproque.**

Core Instruction

TEACHING GRAMMAIRE

1. Go over **Déjà vu!** Then ask volunteers to write two reflexive verb phrases on the board, one in the present and the other in the **passé composé** (e.g. **elle se lève, elle s'est habillée**). **(4 min.)**

2. Tell students that when the action takes place between two or more people, the plural reflexive pronouns they already know become reciprocal.

Tell students that since **se, nous,** and **vous** are used to make a reflexive or reciprocal, **Nous nous aimons** can mean either *We love ourselves* or *We love each other,* depending on the context. **(2 min.)**

3. Practice the forms by asking students questions about themselves and other people. **Tes amis et toi, est-ce que vous vous parlez souvent? Et tes parents? (2 min.)**

Online Practice

go.hrw.com

Grammaire 1 practice

KEYWORD: BD3 CH4

Grammaire 1

8 Une bonne copine 🌸1.2

Écrivons Alexandre raconte comment il a rencontré Martine et ce qui s'est passé depuis leur première rencontre. Complète le texte avec la forme appropriée des verbes entre parenthèses.

> Martine et moi, nous ___1___ (se parler) pour la première fois il y a trois mois. Nous ___2___ (échanger) nos adresses e-mail. Nous ___3___ (se donner) rendez-vous le samedi suivant au centre commercial. Depuis cette fois-là, nous ___4___ (se téléphoner) régulièrement et maintenant, nous ___5___ (se retrouver) chaque week-end. Chaque fois que nous nous voyons, nous ___6___ (beaucoup se parler). Nous ___7___ (se quitter) toujours à six heures, parce qu'elle doit rentrer chez elle pour dîner. Nous ___8___ (se revoir) le week-end prochain à la fête d'anniversaire de Koffi.

1. nous sommes parlé
2. avons échangé
3. nous sommes donné
4. nous sommes téléphoné
5. nous retrouvons
6. nous parlons beaucoup
7. nous quittons
8. nous allons nous revoir

9 Histoire d'amour 🌸1.2

Parlons/Écrivons Utilise des verbes réciproques et les photos pour raconter ce qui se passe dans la vie de Philippe et Rebecca.

la première fois

MODÈLE Ils se sont vus pour la première fois au café.

1. d'abord   2. ensuite   3. hier   4. mais après

Communication

HOLT **SoundBooth** ONLINE RECORDING

10 Opinions personnelles 🌸1.1

Parlons Avec un(e) camarade, choisissez un couple célèbre, réel ou fictif, et discutez de leur relation. Ton/Ta camarade n'est pas toujours d'accord avec toi.

MODÈLE —Je pense que Roméo et Juliette, c'est la plus belle histoire d'amour de tous les temps!
—Tu rigoles! Ils...

Grammaire 1

9 Possible Answers

1. D'abord, ils se sont parlé.
2. Ensuite, ils se sont téléphoné.
3. Hier, ils se sont disputés.
4. Mais après, ils se sont réconciliés.

Teacher to Teacher

Karen Query
Lincoln HS
Vincennes, IN

Put all students' names in a hat and have them draw a name. Each student writes a Dear Abby® letter, asking for advice with an imaginary problem. Ask students to use expressions from **Vocabulaire 1** as much as possible. Encourage them to be creative, even outlandish – but not offensive. Ask them to exchange letters with the partner whose name they drew and write a letter of advice using the subjunctive where appropriate. After teacher edits, volunteers may share their letters with the class.

Communication

Class Activity: Interpersonal

Prepare enough index cards for half of your largest class. On one side of the card, write a sentence with **ils**, **elles**, **nous**, or **vous** as the subject and a person as the direct or indirect object. Below that sentence, write the same sentence but in a reciprocal form. Have half the class form a circle, facing out, holding the cards so that only the cardholder can see the sentences. The other half of the class forms an outside circle facing the inside circle. The student holding the card states the first sentence and the student in the outside circle restates the sentence but in a reciprocal form. When correct, the outside circle rotates one student to the left.

🌸1.2

Differentiated Instruction

SLOWER PACE LEARNERS

Building on Previous Skills Some students may have difficulty distinguishing between direct and indirect objects. Call on students to name verbs that take a direct object and verbs that take an indirect object. (Grammar point 3 lists some verbs that commonly take indirect objects.) List the verbs in two columns on the board. Encourage students to copy this list in their notebook and use it as reference when they do the activities in this chapter.

MULTIPLE INTELLIGENCES

10 Visual Students who are visual learners may benefit from visual cues when they complete this activity. Allow students to use entertainment magazines or newspapers to find pictures of two people interacting. Their responses will describe the activities pictured in the photographs.

🌸1.3

Resources

Planning:

Lesson Planner

 One-Stop Planner

Practice:

Grammar Tutor for Students of French, Chapter 4

Cahier de vocabulaire et grammaire

Differentiated Practice and Assessment CD-ROM

Cahier d'activités

Media Guide

Teaching Transparencies Bell Work 4.3

Audio CD 4, Tr. 3

Interactive Tutor, Disc 1

Bell Work

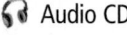

Use Bell Work 4.3 in the *Teaching Transparencies* or write this activity on the board.

Dis ce qui est arrivé à tes amis. Mets les verbes entre parenthèses au **passé composé**.

1. Ils _____ (se rencontrer) au Maroc.
2. Elles _____ (se parler).
3. Ils _____ (ne pas se disputer).
4. Ils _____ (échanger) leurs adresses.
5. Nous _____ (s'écrire).
6. Ils _____ (se retrouver) à Paris. ✿1.2

The past conditional

Interactive TUTOR

1 Use the **past conditional** to state the result in a hypothetical situation. Use the **past perfect** in the **si** clause, and the **past conditional** in the other clause.

       past perfect   *past conditional*

S'il **avait su** la réponse, il **aurait réussi** son examen.

2 To form the **past conditional**, use the **conditional** of the helping verb (**avoir** or **être**) and add the **past participle** of the main verb.

Si nous **avions vu** les Renaud, nous leur **aurions parlé**.
If we had seen the Renauds, we would have spoken with them.

Ils se **seraient réconciliés** s'ils **s'étaient parlé**.
They would have made up if they had spoken to each other.

3 The **past conditional** is also used by itself to state an event that could have taken place in the past, but did not.

Tu **aurais pu** m'aider!   *You could have helped me!*

➤ Vocabulaire et grammaire, *pp. 40–41*
Cahier d'activités, *pp. 31–33* **Online** workbooks

Déjà vu!

Do you remember how to conjugate verbs in the **conditional**? Take the future stem and add the imperfect endings (**-ais, -ais, -ait, -ions, -iez, -aient**).

Je lui parlerais.
I would talk to him/her.

Vous devriez **téléphoner à votre grand-mère.**
You should call your grandmother.

⑪ Rien que des critiques ✿1.2

Lisons Complète les phrases suivantes logiquement.

c **1.** Si Léon était allé chez le médecin…

f **2.** Si je n'avais pas été si timide…

e **3.** Si tu ne t'étais pas disputée avec Pierre…

b **4.** Si vous aviez étudié…

a **5.** Si tu avais rangé ta chambre…

    a. tes parents ne t'auraient pas punie.

    b. vous auriez eu de bonnes notes.

    c. il ne serait plus malade.

    d. Pierre se serait fâché.

    e. vous ne vous seriez pas quittés.

    f. j'aurais parlé à David.

⑫ Si seulement... ✿1.2

Lisons Choisis la forme correcte des verbes entre parenthèses.

1. Si j'(avais / aurais) su, j'(avais / aurais) tout dit à maman.

2. Si Martin t'(avait / aurait) parlé, tu (avais / aurais) compris.

3. Elles (seraient / avaient) venues si tu leur (aurais / avais) dit.

4. Vous (seriez / aviez) allé le voir si vous (aviez / auriez) su.

5. Si nous (avions / aurions) pu, nous (aurions / avions) fait ce qu'il fallait.

6. Ils (avaient / auraient) joué s'ils (auraient / avaient) pu.

Core Instruction

TEACHING GRAMMAIRE

1. Go over **Déjà vu!**

2. Choose one verb that takes **avoir** in the **passé composé** and one that takes **être**. Have volunteers conjugate these verbs in the **passé composé** on the board. Then ask students to rewrite the helping verbs in the conditional. Model the pronunciation of all the past conditional forms they just created. **(4 min.)**

3. Point out to students that a conditional or past conditional should never directly follow **si**. **(2 min.)**

4. Practice past conditional forms by giving students sentence fragments to complete. **Si j'avais eu de la chance... (j'aurais eu une bonne note à l'examen.) (4 min.)**

13 **Avec des «si»...** 🎬1.2

Lisons/Écrivons Patrice dit ce qui se serait passé si...! Complète ses phrases avec la forme correcte du verbe entre parenthèses.

1. Si je n'avais pas fait du skate, je/j'_____ (finir) mes devoirs.

2. Si j'avais fini mes devoirs, je/j'_____ (ne pas avoir) une mauvaise note.

3. Si je n'avais pas eu de mauvaise note, mes parents _____ (ne pas me punir).

4. Si mes parents ne m'avaient pas puni, je/j'_____ (aller) au cinéma.

5. Si j'étais allé au cinéma, je/j'_____ (rencontrer) la sœur d'Ali!

14 **Voilà pourquoi** 🎬1.2

Parlons/Écrivons Explique les sentiments de ces gens et ce qui se serait passé si les choses avaient été différentes.

Amadou

MODÈLE **Amadou est triste. S'il ne s'était pas cassé la jambe, il aurait pu jouer avec ses copains et alors, il n'aurait pas été triste.**

1. madame Dakeyo

2. les parents de Fatia

3. Véronique

4. M. Brutus

15 **Questions personnelles** 🎬1.1

Parlons Demande à un(e) camarade cinq choses qu'il/elle aurait faites pendant ses vacances si les choses avaient été différentes. Ton/Ta camarade va te dire ce qu'il/elle aurait fait. Puis, échangez les rôles.

MODÈLE —Qu'est-ce que tu aurais fait si tu n'étais pas parti(e) en vacances?
—Si je n'étais pas parti(e), j'aurais...

---

13 Answers

1. aurais fini
2. n'aurais pas eu
3. ne m'auraient pas puni
4. serais allé
5. aurais rencontré

14 Possible Answers

1. Madame Dakeyo est inquiète. Si son bébé n'avait pas été malade, elle aurait été heureuse.
2. Les parents de Fatia sont très fâchés. Si elle n'avait pas eu d'accident de voiture, alors, ils n'auraient pas été fâchés.
3. Véronique est déçue. Si Gérard n'avait pas oublié leur rendez-vous, elle n'aurait pas été triste.
4. M. Brutus est content. S'il n'avait pas gagné de voiture, il n'aurait pas été de bonne humeur.

Communication

Class Activity: Interpersonal
Have students describe a problem in a couple of sentences, on a small slip of paper. Then ask them to circulate and tell this problem to a classmate. The classmate should respond with **Tu aurais dû** + infinitive or **Tu aurais pu** + infinitive to advise or admonish the student. 🎬1.1

Differentiated Instruction

SLOWER PACE LEARNERS

Additional Practice Write an infinitive on the board, call out a subject pronoun, and ask a student to give the appropriate **conditionnel passé** form. The student then calls out another pronoun and asks another student to provide the correct form. After several turns write a different infinitive and continue as before. 🎬1.2

SPECIAL LEARNING NEEDS

Students with Dyslexia To help students with reading challenges understand the **conditionnel passé** presentation, ask them to copy the three rules into their grammar notebook. Review each rule with students and give at least one additional example for each rule. Then ask partners to explain the rules to each other and collaborate on their understanding of the concepts. 🎬1.3

Assess

Assessment Program
Quiz: Grammaire 1
Alternative Assessment
Differentiated Practice and Assessment CD-ROM
Online Assessment
my.hrw.com
Test Generator

Synthèse
• Vocabulaire 1
• Grammaire 1

Application 1

16 Encore des «si»... 1.3

Écrivons/Parlons Imagine ce qui se serait passé et quels sentiments ces gens auraient eus si les choses suivantes étaient arrivées.

MODÈLE Si ton prof vous avait donné congé aujourd'hui.
S'il nous avait donné congé, nous ne serions pas venus à l'école et nous aurions été très contents.

1. Si tes amis avaient organisé une fête pour ton anniversaire pour te faire une surprise.
2. Si tes parents avaient gagné un voyage en France l'été dernier.
3. Si ton/ta meilleur(e) ami(e) et toi, vous vous étiez disputés.
4. Si ton frère s'était cassé la jambe la veille d'un match très important et que son équipe avait perdu!
5. Si tu avais oublié d'inviter ton/ta meilleur(e) ami(e) à ta boum.

Un peu plus

The verbs *manquer* and *plaire*

1. Manquer is a regular **-er** verb.

When used with *a direct object,* **manquer** means *to miss something.*

Il a **manqué** *le bus.*

When used with an **indirect object, manquer** à + a *person* or *thing* means *to miss someone or something.*

Ma sœur leur **manque.** (*Ma sœur* **manque** à *mes parents.*)
They (*my parents*) miss *my sister.*

Mes amis me **manquent.** I miss *my friends.*

2. The verb **plaire à** means *to like.* The past participle is **plu.**

Le cours de français **me plaît** mais les maths ne **me plaisent** pas du tout.

As a reflexive verb, **se plaire** means *to enjoy oneself at a place or event.*

Je **me suis** beaucoup **plu** en Tunisie cet été.

As a reciprocal verb, **se plaire** means *to like each other.*

Farid et Malika **se sont plu** tout de suite.

➜ Vocabulaire et grammaire, *p. 42*
Cahier d'activités, *pp. 31–33*
 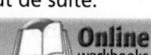 Online workbooks

1. a **2.** b. **3.** a **4.** b **5.** a

17 Écoutons CD 4, Tr. 3 1.2

Écoute ce que Fortuné a fait ce week-end et dis si cela **a) lui a plu** ou **b) ne lui a pas plu.**

18 Souvenirs de camping 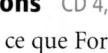1.2

Écrivons Tes amis sont allés camper et te racontent leur expérience! Complète leurs phrases avec la forme appropriée de **manquer.**

1. Les soirées autour du feu de camp me _____.
2. Quand on campait, ce qui m'_____, c'est mon lit!
3. Ce qui va me _____, c'est de dormir jusqu'à midi!
4. Mais les moustiques ne me _____ pas!
5. Tu aurais dû venir avec nous! Tu nous as beaucoup _____.

Resources

Planning:
Lesson Planner
 One-Stop Planner

Practice:
Grammar Tutor for Students of French, Chapter 4
Cahier de vocabulaire et grammaire
Differentiated Practice and Assessment CD-ROM
Cahier d'activités
Media Guide
 Teaching Transparencies Bell Work 4.4
 Audio CD 4, Tr. 3
 Interactive Tutor, Disc 1

Bell Work

Use Bell Work 4.4 in the *Teaching Transparencies* or write this activity on the board.

Complète les phrases avec la forme correcte des verbes entre parenthèses.

1. Si tu avais travaillé, tu _____ (avoir) de meilleures notes.
2. Si Anne m'avait appelé, nous _____ (aller) au cinéma.
3. Si vous aviez bien mangé, vous _____ (ne pas avoir) faim.
4. Si Luc avait vu un médecin, il _____ (être) bien soigné. 1.2

COMMON ERROR ALERT
///ATTENTION !\\\

Students will commonly mistranslate the sentence, "I miss you" as **"Je te manque"**, rather than **Tu me manques**. It might help to compare **manquer** to **plaire** or **intéresser**.

Core Instruction

INTEGRATED PRACTICE

1. Have students do Activity 16 to practice previously taught material. **(5 min.)**
2. Introduce **Un peu plus.** (See presentation suggestions at right.) **(4 min.)**
3. Continue with integrated practice Activities 17–21.

TEACHING UN PEU PLUS

1. Review indirect object pronouns by asking students to write a few short sentences about themselves and their friends with verbs that are followed by à. (**Je lui parle, je leur téléphone.**) **(4 min.)**
2. Go over **Un peu plus.** Call out names of people and places and have students make complete sentences about them with **plaire** and **manquer.** (**ta grand-mère, ton lycée, les vacances**) **(4 min.)**

Online Practice
go.**hrw**.com
Application 1 practice
KEYWORD: BD3 CH4

19 On aime ou on n'aime pas 🌸1.2

Écrivons Jean-René et ses camarades parlent de personnes et de choses qu'ils aiment et qu'ils n'aiment pas. Utilise le verbe **plaire** et le temps qui convient pour récrire leurs commentaires.

MODÈLE J'adore ce CD. → Ce CD me plaît beaucoup.

1. Tarek aime les voitures de sport italiennes.
2. J'ai beaucoup aimé le film que j'ai vu samedi soir.
3. Tu aimes bien la sœur d'Isabelle, hein?
4. Nous n'aimons pas du tout ces gens-là.
5. Je suis sûr que tu vas aimer ce livre.

À la québécoise

In Quebec, people say "**être en amour**" for being in love and refer to a boyfriend as a "**chum**".

20 Ton avis compte 🌸1.3, 3.2

Lisons/Écrivons Lis la lettre de Valentin au courrier du cœur d'un magazine pour adolescents. Qu'est-ce que tu aurais fait si tu avais été à la place de Valentin? Écris un petit paragraphe pour lui dire ce qu'il aurait dû faire d'après toi.

Courrier du cœur

Je suis amoureux.
Dans mon lycée, il y a une fille que j'aime bien. J'aimerais bien lui demander de sortir avec moi, mais je suis plutôt timide. L'autre jour, elle a laissé tomber ses cahiers juste devant moi. Je suis resté pétrifié. J'aurais dû l'aider mais je n'ai pas pu. Maintenant, je suis gêné quand je la vois. Qu'est-ce que je peux faire?
     -Valentin

Communication

HOLT **SoundBooth**
ONLINE RECORDING

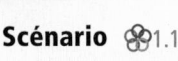

21 Scénario 🌸1.1

Parlons Tu es nouveau/nouvelle dans cette école et un de tes nouveaux camarades te demande ce qui te manque et ce qui te plaît plus dans cette école-ci.

MODÈLE —Est-ce que les amis de ton ancienne école
        te manquent?
        —Oui beaucoup, mais...

---

17 Script

See script on p. 131E.

18 Answers

1. manquent
2. a manqué
3. manquer
4. manquent
5. manqué

19 Answers

1. Les voitures de sport italiennes plaisent à Tarek.
2. Le film que j'ai vu samedi soir m'a beaucoup plu.
3. La sœur d'Isabelle te plaît bien, hein?
4. Ces gens-là ne nous plaisent pas du tout.
5. Je suis sûr que ce livre va te plaire.

Communication

Group Activity: Interpersonal
Have students write down a problem (real or hypothetical) for which they seek advice. Ask them to circulate, state their problem, and ask for advice using the new vocabulary. Those giving advice should tell what they would do in the same situation.

MODÈLE
Si j'avais été toi ...

🌸1.1, 1.2

Differentiated Instruction

ADVANCED LEARNERS

20 Challenge Have students complete this activity and then direct them to the Web site of an online teen magazine that publishes letters of teens seeking advice. Working with a partner, students should write a reply to one of these letters. 🌸1.1, 3.2

SPECIAL LEARNING NEEDS

18 Students with Language Impairments Before asking students to complete the activity, ask them to conjugate the regular verb **manquer**. Check to be sure that all students with language impairments have correctly conjugated the verb on a note card or in their notebook. Allow them to use the notes as a reference as they complete the activity. 🌸1.2

Assess

Assessment Program
Quiz: Application 1
Audio CD, Tr. 11 🎧
Alternative Assessment
Differentiated Practice and Assessment CD-ROM

Online Assessment
my.hrw.com

Test Generator

Prereading Questions

You might ask these questions before students read the selection.

1. **Est-ce que beaucoup de femmes travaillent aux États-Unis?**
2. **Est-ce que les femmes peuvent avoir le même travail que les hommes?**
3. **Est-ce que tu peux nommer et localiser quelques pays africains?**
4. **Est-ce que les femmes africaines sont aussi libres que les femmes américaines?** ✿1.2

Active Reading Questions

1. **Qui a annoncé la réforme du code de la famille? (Mohammed VI)**
2. **Qui est Mohammed VI? (le roi du Maroc)**
3. **Est-ce que la femme marocaine est encore considérée comme une mineure? (non)**
4. **Combien de nouvelles règles ont été ajoutées au code de la famille? (onze)**
5. **Maintenant qui est responsable de la famille? (le mari et la femme)** ✿1.2

Vocabulaire supplémentaire

You might use these terms to discuss the selection.

majeur	*of age*
l'émancipation (f.)	*emancipation*
l'autorité (f.) **parentale**	*parental authority*
le contrat de mariage	*marriage contract*

Lecture culturelle

Aujourd'hui, la femme française est indépendante et elle travaille (plus des trois quarts des Françaises travaillent); toutefois, au foyer¹, elle fait encore la plupart des tâches ménagères. Aussi, si l'égalité entre les sexes n'est pas encore totale, la situation de la femme s'est considérablement améliorée. Que sais-tu de la condition des femmes en Afrique? ✿2.1

FAMILLE

Maroc : nouveau code de la famille

Le Roi Mohammed VI a annoncé vendredi la réforme du Code de la famille. Les nouveaux amendements, salués par les associations de femmes et l'ensemble des partis politiques, doivent permettre à la femme marocaine de s'émanciper et de ne plus être considérée comme une mineure à vie. Un vrai bouleversement².

10 octobre 2003, journée historique pour les Marocaines. C'est ce que s'accordent à dire les journaux nationaux, les associations des droits de l'Homme et l'ensemble des partis politiques. Le 10 octobre 2003 ou la vraie Journée de la femme au Maroc... En effet, le Roi Mohammed VI a annoncé vendredi, lors de son discours³ d'ouverture de la nouvelle session parlementaire, la réforme du Code de la famille ou Moudawana⁴. [...] Onze nouvelles règles donnent ainsi vie aux revendications⁵ de ces associations. La plus importante : la responsabilité conjointe⁶ des époux au sein⁷ de leur famille. Ce qui marque la fin de l'inégalité juridique entre l'épouse et son mari. Deuxième point important : la règle qui soumettait⁸ la femme à la tutelle⁹ d'un membre mâle de sa famille et faisait d'elle une éternelle mineure est abolie. L'âge du mariage passe de 15 à 18 ans pour la femme[...] ■

Compréhension ✿2.1

1. Qu'est-ce que le roi Mohammed VI a proclamé le 10 octobre 2003?
2. Quel est le plus important changement apporté au Code de la famille?
3. À partir de quel l'âge peut-on se marier au Maroc?

1. la réforme du Code de la famille
2. la responsabilité conjointe du mari et de la femme
3. 18 ans

1. à la maison 2. *upheaval* 3. *speech* 4. *family law in Morrocco* 5. demande 6. ensemble 7. à l'intérieur 8. *submitted* 9. *guardianship*

Core Instruction

LECTURE CULTURELLE

1. Read and discuss the introductory paragraph about women in France. **(2 min.)**
2. As a class, read *Maroc: nouveau code de la famille.* **(20 min.)**
3. Ask volunteers to answer the **Compréhension** questions. **(2 min.)**

COMPARAISONS ET COMMUNAUTÉ

1. Have students read **Sorties entre copains!** in small groups. **(5 min.)**
2. Have the class discuss **Et toi?** What do students think of the French system? **(5 min.)**
3. Go over **Communauté et professions** with students. Ask students to research organizations that help acclimate foreigners and then present their findings to the class. **(8 min.)**

Online Practice
go.hrw.com
Online Edition
KEYWORD: BD3 CH4

Chapitre 4
Culture

Comparaisons

Des adolescents en France

Sorties entre copains! 🏵4.2

Aurélien est français et il a une petite amie, Laure. Quand ils vont au café ou au cinéma, ils sont le plus souvent:

a. juste tous les deux.
b. avec leurs copains.
c. avec leur famille.

Le terme de *date* n'a pas vraiment de traduction en français. Le concept n'existe pas. Les jeunes Français qui ont des petit(e)s ami(e)s, préfèrent généralement sortir en groupe. Si un garçon va chercher une fille chez elle ou la retrouve dans un café, très souvent c'est pour l'emmener rejoindre d'autres amis et décider avec eux de ce qu'ils vont faire tous ensemble.

🏵4.2

ET TOI?

1. Quand tu as une «date», est-ce que tu préfères sortir avec juste ta «date» ou avec un groupe d'amis?

2. Connais-tu beaucoup de jeunes Américains qui ont les mêmes habitudes de sorties que les Français?

Communauté et professions

Les formateurs multiculturels 🏵5.1

Les formateurs multiculturels sont là pour aider les familles qui partent habiter dans un pays étranger ou les familles qui viennent d'arriver dans un nouveau pays. Ces formateurs sont eux-mêmes étrangers ou ont une bonne connaissance des coutumes du pays en question. Est-ce que tu sais s'il existe des formateurs multiculturels dans ta communauté qui aident les Français? Et à l'inverse, est-ce qu'il y a des formateurs qui vont aider les Américains qui partent habiter dans un pays francophone? Fais des recherches à la bibliothèque ou sur Internet pour en savoir plus. Présente ce que tu as découvert à la classe.

Un formateur multiculturel

L'Afrique francophone

Bell Work

Use Bell Work 4.5 in the *Teaching Transparencies* or write this activity on the board.

Récris les phrases en utilisant le verbe **plaire.**

1. J'aime beaucoup cette peinture.
2. Vous avez aimé ce livre?
3. Je suis sûr(e) que tu aimeras ce film.
4. Nous allons beaucoup aimer la France.
5. Ils n'ont pas aimé ce restaurant. 1.2

Connections

Geography Link

Ségou or **Segu** was founded by the Bozo people in 1620. It has about 100,000 inhabitants, making it the second largest city in Mali. It is a port city on the Niger River and lies in the **Ségou** region in the Sahel. The climate is semi-arid. Ask students to discuss the influence of geography on the economy of **Ségou.** 3.1

Objectifs
- to share good and bad news
- to renew old acquaintances

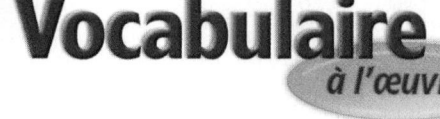
Vocabulaire
à l'œuvre 2

Ma famille au Mali

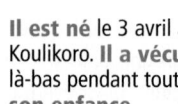

> J'ai fait un **album de photos** de la vie de mon oncle, Habib.

Il est né le 3 avril à Koulikoro. **Il a vécu** là-bas pendant toute **son enfance.**

Après le lycée, **il a fait un apprentissage** à Bamako.

Ensuite, il a **déménagé** et **s'est installé** à Ségou où **il a trouvé du travail.**

▶ **Vocabulaire supplémentaire—La vie, p. R18**

Core Instruction

TEACHING VOCABULAIRE

1. Introduce the vocabulary, using transparencies **Vocabulaire 4.3** and **4.4.** Model the pronunciation of each word or expression. **Il/Elle... (a vécu, a fait un apprentissage). (3 min.)**

2. Ask students to point out various events on the transparency. **Il/Elle s'est marié(e)... il/elle a déménagé... (2 min.)**

3. Ask students questions about their family.

   Où est-ce que ta grand-mère est née? Est-ce que ton grand-père a déjà pris sa retraite? (3 min.)

4. Model pronunciation of the expressions in **Exprimons-nous!** Then share good and bad news that students respond to. **Malheureusement, ma cousine est morte hier. Mes sincères condoléances.** You may want to respond first and let students come up with news that your response might have elicited. **(4 min.)**

Online Practice
go.hrw.com
Vocabulaire 2 practice
KEYWORD: BD3 CH4

Chapitre 4
Vocabulaire 2

Vocabulaire 2

Il s'est marié avec ma tante et ils ont eu cinq enfants.

Lorsqu'il a eu soixante-cinq ans, mon oncle **a pris sa retraite**.

À soixante-dix ans, **il est tombé malade** et il **est mort** un an plus tard.

D'autres mots utiles

un(e) orphelin(e)	orphan
un(e) veuf/veuve	widower/widow
adopter	to adopt
célibataire	single
des jumeaux (m.)/ jumelles (f.)	twins
divorcer	to divorce
faire un emprunt	to take a loan
louer	to rent
poser sa candidature	to apply for (a job)
se fiancer/être fiancé(e)	to get/ be engaged

Exprimons-nous!

To share good and bad news	To respond
À propos, nous allons bientôt nous marier. *By the way, . . .*	**Tous mes vœux de bonheur.** *All my best wishes.*
Vous savez, nous avons eu un petit garçon. *You know, . . .*	**Toutes mes félicitations!/Félicitations!** *Congratulations!*
Malheureusement, mon oncle est mort la semaine dernière. *Unfortunately, . . .*	**Mes sincères condoléances.** *My deepest sympathy.*

Interactive TUTOR

Vocabulaire et grammaire, pp. 43–45

Online workbooks

TPR
TOTAL PHYSICAL RESPONSE

Have students respond to these commands.

Lève la main si tu as vécu dans une autre ville.

Lève le pied si tu es né(e) ici.

Assieds-toi là si tu as déménagé trois fois.

Lève-toi si tu vas te marier un jour.

Mets les mains sur la tête si ça fait longtemps que nous n'avons pas eu d'examen.

Viens ici si tu n'as pas changé depuis ton enfance.

Mets la main devant la bouche si tu tombes parfois malade.

Lève les deux mains si tu vas faire un apprentissage après le lycée. 1.2

Cultures

Practices and Perspectives

The Bambara are the largest and most dominant group in Mali. Most of the Bambara are farmers who live in villages with an average of 600 people. Every Bambara village is made up of many different family units, usually all from one extended family. Some of the Bambara dwellings hold as many as sixty or more people. Each household, or **gwa,** is responsible for providing for all of its members, as well as for helping them with their farming duties. All individuals between the ages of six and thirty have status and roles within the village. Have students discuss the advantages and disadvantages of the extended family versus the nuclear family.

2.1, 4.2

Resources

Planning:

Lesson Planner

 One-Stop Planner

Presentation:

 Teaching Transparencies
Vocabulaire 4.3, 4.4

Practice:

Cahier de vocabulaire et grammaire

Differentiated Practice and Assessment CD-ROM

Media Guide

 Audio CD 4, Tr. 4

 Interactive Tutor, Disc 1

22 Script

1. Je suis née le quinze février à Djenné, une ville au Mali.
2. J'ai fait un apprentissage dans un salon de coiffure. Mais cela ne m'a pas plu du tout. J'ai décidé de continuer mes études.
3. À l'université, j'ai rencontré un garçon très sympathique. Nous nous sommes tout de suite plu. Nous nous sommes mariés il y a deux ans.
4. Et tu sais, nous venons d'avoir un petit garçon qui s'appelle Augustin.
5. Nous rendons souvent visite à mes parents qui viennent de prendre leur retraite et qui ont déménagé au bord de la mer.

24 Answers

1. Tous mes vœux de bonheur.
2. Mes sincères condoléances.
3. Félicitations!
4. Toutes mes félicitations!
5. Mes sincères condoléances.
6. Félicitations!

---

22 Écoutons   CD 4, Tr. 4   🎞1.2   1. c 2. e 3. b 4. d 5. a

Fatou te raconte sa vie. Fais correspondre chaque photo avec ce qu'elle dit.

a.

b.

c.

d.

e.

23 Biographie   🎞1.2

Lisons Voici la fiche biographique de Marcel Duguélec. Complète-là avec les informations appropriées.

des jumelles	mort	né	travail
apprentissage	marié	veuf	louer

Nom : Paul Marcel Duguélec
___1___ le 10 mars 1922 à Quimper
Études/Formation : ___2___ à Paris
___3___ : Employé dans une librairie, écrivain
Situation familiale : S'est ___4___ avec Annie Dupuis en 1950
A eu trois enfants dont un garçon et ___5___ .
Est tombé malade et est ___6___ en 1995.

1. Né 2. Apprentissage
3. Travail 4. marié
5. des jumelles 6. mort

24 Des nouvelles   🎞1.2

Parlons Qu'est-ce que tu dirais à quelqu'un qui t'annonce les choses suivantes?

1. Sylvain et moi, nous nous sommes fiancés. Nous allons nous marier l'été prochain.
2. Mon grand-père est mort le mois dernier.
3. Nous avons gagné le championnat de tennis.
4. J'ai posé ma candidature pour une place de comptable et j'ai été engagé tout de suite!
5. Ma tante vient de perdre son mari.
6. J'ai eu mon bac avec mention «bien»!

Flash culture

En Afrique du Nord, la cérémonie du mariage est très traditionnelle et peut durer plusieurs jours. La mariée porte plusieurs robes chargées de broderies et de paillettes. La mariée a aussi les mains peintes au henné avec des dessins très élaborés. Après le mariage, dans les familles traditionnelles, le couple va habiter chez les parents du marié.   🎞4.2

Quelles sont les traditions dans ta famille quand quelqu'un se marie?

Un mariage au Maroc

Core Instruction

TEACHING EXPRIMONS-NOUS!

1. Model the pronunciation of each expression. Point out to students that another answer to **Comment va...?** could be **Il/Elle va bien.** Tell them that **Comment va...?** and **Quoi de neuf?** can also be used with friends you see every day. **(2 min.)**

2. Address students with the questions and statements on the left (**Quoi de neuf?**) to have them practice appropriate responses. **(3 min.)**

Exprimons-nous!

To renew old acquaintances	
Comment va ton ami Hassan? *How is . . . ?*	**Je ne le vois plus.** Il a déménagé. *I don't see him any more.*
Quoi de neuf? *What's new?*	**Rien de spécial.** **Plein de choses!** *Nothing much.* *A lot!*
Tu n'as pas changé! *You haven't changed!*	**Toi non plus.** *You haven't either.*
Je suis ravi(e) de te revoir. *I am delighted to . . .*	Oui, **ça fait longtemps qu'**on ne s'est pas vu(e)s. *. . . it's been a long time since . . .*

Vocabulaire et grammaire, pp. 43–45

Online workbooks

(25) Conversation dans la rue 🌸1.2

Écrivons Justine rencontre une amie qu'elle n'a pas vue depuis longtemps. Complète leur conversation de façon logique.

JUSTINE   Tiens, Fabienne! ___1___ on ne s'est pas vues!

FABIENNE   Oui, c'est vrai. En tout cas, toi, ___2___!

JUSTINE   Toi non plus! Toujours aussi élégante!

FABIENNE   Alors, ___3___?

JUSTINE   Eh bien, Gilles et moi, nous allons nous marier.

FABIENNE   Ah bon? ___4___.

JUSTINE   Merci. Et toi, ___5___ ton mari?

FABIENNE   Très bien. Et tu sais, nous avons eu des jumeaux.

JUSTINE   Des jumeaux! ___6___!

Communication

HOLT SoundBooth ONLINE RECORDING

(26) Scénario 🌸1.1

Écrivons/Parlons Comment imagines-tu ta vie dans vingt ans? Après le lycée, penses-tu aller à l'université, faire un apprentissage, etc.? Prends quelques notes pour décrire la vie que tu aimerais avoir. Ensuite, imagine que tous tes souhaits se sont réalisés. Joue une scène avec un(e) camarade dans laquelle vous vous rencontrez dans un restaurant. Vous ne vous êtes pas vu(e)s depuis vingt ans et vous parlez de tout ce qui s'est passé pendant ce temps. Chacun(e) doit au moins parler cinq fois.

MODÈLE   —Ah! Patrick! Ça fait longtemps qu'on ne s'est pas vus! Quoi de neuf?

(25) Answers

1. Ça fait longtemps qu'
2. tu n'as pas changé
3. quoi de neuf
4. Tous mes vœux de bonheur
5. comment va
6. Toutes mes félicitations

Proverbes

For French proverbs and activities related to the chapter theme and vocabulary, see **Proverbes et expressions**, pp. R6–R7.

Communication

Pair Activity: Interpersonal

Have partners imagine that they have not seen each other in a long time. One student has had nothing but bad luck all this time, while the other has been very successful. Have partners use the new vocabulary, as well as the vocabulary from **Vocabulaire 1** for asking advice, telling what happened, or gossiping. Have them present their conversation to the class.   🌸1.1

Differentiated Instruction

SLOWER PACE LEARNERS

(25) Additional Practice Some students may have difficulty understanding the conversation in this activity. You may want to pause after each line and ask volunteers to paraphrase or summarize it. Encourage students to ask for clarifications if needed.   🌸1.2

SPECIAL LEARNING NEEDS

Students with AD(H)D Ask students to use the new vocabulary to create greeting cards for different occasions. The cards, funny or serious, may deliver good news, bad news, congratulatory messages, or sentiments of sympathy. Encourage students to enhance the greeting cards with illustrations and decorative writing. The cards may be shared or presented in class.   🌸1.3

Assess

Assessment Program

Quiz: Vocabulaire 2

Alternative Assessment

Differentiated Practice and Assessment CD-ROM

Online Assessment

my.hrw.com

Test Generator

Bell Work

Use Bell Work 4.6 in the *Teaching Transparencies* or write this activity on the board.

Qu'est-ce que tu dis quand on t'annonce ces nouvelles?

1. J'ai un nouveau travail.
2. Mon fils a réussi son bac.
3. Mon grand-père est mort hier.
4. Nous allons nous marier.
5. Ma fille vient d'avoir un petit garçon. ❀1.2

COMMON ERROR ALERT
ATTENTION !

Students may need to be reminded that to use the subjunctive requires a change of subject. **Je veux que tu partes.** Otherwise, a simple infinitive construction is used. **Je veux partir.** French would never allow, "**Je veux que je...**"

Objectifs
- the subjunctive
- subjunctive with necessity, desire, and emotions

 # Grammaire à l'œuvre 2

Révisions — The subjunctive

1 To conjugate most verbs in the subjunctive, take the present indicative **ils/elles** form, drop **-ent**, and add the subjunctive endings.

	regarder	choisir	perdre
je	regarde	choisisse	perde
tu	regardes	choisisses	perdes
il/elle/on	regarde	choisisse	perde
nous	regardions	choisissions	perdions
vous	regardiez	choisissiez	perdiez
ils/elles	regardent	choisissent	perdent

Il faut que tu lises ce roman. **Il faut que tu** finisses tes études.

En anglais ❀4.1

In English, we use the subjunctive, but its forms often look like forms in other tenses and moods.

I wish you were in Paris with me. (subjunctive, same form as past tense)

It is important that he finish his homework. (subjunctive, same as infinitive)

Can you think of other sentences in English that use the subjunctive?

In French, there are specific phrases and expressions that require the use of the subjunctive.

Il faut qu'il finisse ses devoirs.

If I were you, I would stay in school.
Long live the King.
It's important that you be on time.

2 Some verbs, like **prendre, venir,** and **voir** have a different stem for the **nous** and **vous** forms. Take the **nous** form of the present indicative, drop **-ons,** and add the subjunctive endings.

nous **pren**ons → nous prenions, vous preniez
nous **ven**ons → nous venions, vous veniez
nous **voy**ons → nous voyions, vous voyiez

Il faut que vous reveniez avant onze heures.

3 **Être, avoir, aller,** and **faire** are irregular in the subjunctive.

	aller	avoir	être	faire	pouvoir
je/j'	aille	aie	sois	fasse	puisse
tu	ailles	aies	sois	fasses	puisses
il/elle/on	aille	ait	soit	fasse	puisse
nous	allions	ayons	soyons	fassions	puissions
vous	alliez	ayez	soyez	fassiez	puissiez
ils/elles	aillent	aient	soient	fassent	puissent

Vocabulaire et grammaire, *pp. 46–47*
Cahier d'activités, *pp. 35–37*
 **Online** workbooks

Core Instruction

TEACHING GRAMMAIRE

1. Read **En anglais** with students. **(2 min.)**

2. To review the present tense, have students conjugate **choisir, perdre,** and **regarder.** Ask volunteers to come to the board and write the present **ils/elles** form of each verb six times in a column. **(2 min.)**

3. Erase the endings of the **ils/elles** forms the students wrote on the board. Then add subject pronouns and subjunctive endings. **(2 min.)**

4. Go over Points 2 and 3. Model the pronunciation of all irregular forms. Point out the differences between the forms of **aller** and those of **avoir.** **(3 min.)**

5. To provide practice with these forms and their pronunciation, ask students about things they have to do. **Qu'est-ce qu'il faut que tu fasses aujourd'hui? Et ce week-end?** Ask them to try to avoid using **faire** in their answers, which would limit them to certain expressions. **(2 min.)**

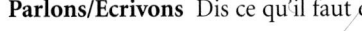

27 Ce qu'il faut faire 🌸1.2

Parlons/Écrivons Dis ce qu'il faut que ces gens fassent.

1. vous: venir nous voir plus souvent
2. nous: louer une voiture pour partir en vacances
3. moi: poser ma candidature avant la fin du mois d'août
4. vous: faire un emprunt pour acheter une maison
5. ton frère: téléphoner à son patron lundi matin
6. Amadou: déménager avant la fin du mois
7. nous: trouver un travail plus intéressant
8. toi: faire un apprentissage pour avoir plus d'expérience
9. mes grands-parents: prendre leurs médicaments régulièrement
10. ma sœur: avoir plus d'argent pour pouvoir partir en vacances

28 Des choses à faire 🌸1.2

Parlons Les personnes suivantes doivent faire certaines choses. Dis ce qu'il faut que chacune d'elles fasse.

MODÈLE **Il faut que tu lises ce livre.**

tu

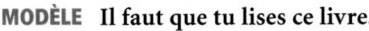

1. ils 2. vous 3. Delphine 4. elles

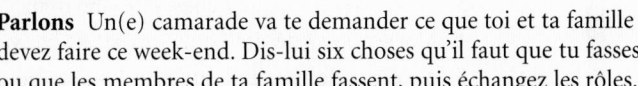

Communication

HOLT **SoundBooth**
ONLINE RECORDING

29 Interview 🌸1.1

Parlons Un(e) camarade va te demander ce que toi et ta famille devez faire ce week-end. Dis-lui six choses qu'il faut que tu fasses ou que les membres de ta famille fassent, puis échangez les rôles.

MODÈLE —Qu'est-ce qu'il faut que tu fasses, ce week-end?
—Oh là là… ce week-end, il faut que je… et puis…

Online Practice
go.hrw.com
Grammaire 2 practice
KEYWORD: BD3 CH4

27 Answers

Il faut que...
1. vous veniez nous voir plus souvent.
2. nous louions une voiture pour partir en vacances.
3. je pose ma canditature avant la fin du mois d'août.
4. vous fassiez un emprunt pour acheter une maison.
5. ton frère téléphone à son patron lundi matin.
6. Amadou déménage avant la fin du mois.
7. nous trouvions un travail plus intéressant.
8. tu fasses un apprentissage pour avoir plus d'expérience.
9. mes grands-parents prennent leurs médicaments régulièrement.
10. ma sœur ait plus d'argent pour pouvoir partir en vacances.

28 Answers

Il faut...
1. qu'ils nettoient la maison.
2. que vous voyiez ce film.
3. que Delphine étudie pour son examen.
4. qu'elles fassent la vaisselle.

Communication

Class Activity: Interpersonal
Review the verb **devoir**. Then have one student make a sentence with **devoir** plus an infinitive. That student directs his or her sentence to a classmate who rephrases the original in the subjunctive with **il faut que**.

MODÈLE
— **Erika, ta mère doit faire la vaisselle.**
— **Oui, il faut que ma mère fasse la vaisselle.** 🌸1.1

Differentiated Instruction

ADVANCED LEARNERS

27 Variation Working with a partner, students should make a list with last-minute chores for family members right before they go on an extended vacation. Encourage students to be creative and make up some comical chores. Ask some volunteers to present their list of chores to the class. 🌸1.1

SPECIAL LEARNING NEEDS

Students with Language Impairments Ask students to create a poster for each of the three grammar rules about the subjunctive. The posters may include additional or different examples to demonstrate each of the rules. The posters can be displayed in class as a resource to accommodate students with language impairments.

Resources

Planning:

Lesson Planner

 One-Stop Planner

Practice:

Grammar Tutor for Students of French, Chapter 4

Cahier de vocabulaire et grammaire

Differentiated Practice and Assessment CD-ROM

Cahier d'activités

Media Guide

 Teaching Transparencies

Bell Work 4.7

 Audio CD 4, Tr. 5

 Interactive Tutor, Disc 1

Bell Work

Use Bell Work 4.7 in the *Teaching Transparencies* or write this activity on the board.

Qu'est-ce qu'il faut que tu fasses ce week-end? Fais cinq phrases en mettant les verbes suivants au **subjonctif**.

1. aller (moi)
2. jouer (mon frère)
3. prendre (mes amis et moi)
4. étudier (vous)
5. se reposer (mes parents)

 1.2

French for Spanish Speakers

Ask Spanish speakers about using the subjunctive with expressions of necessity, desire, and emotion. What are Spanish equivalents for **il faut que/je veux que/je suis désolé(e) que? (es necesario que/ quiero que/ siento que)** Does Spanish use the subjunctive with these expressions? (yes)

🌸 4.1

 **Script**

See script on p. 131F.

 Interactive TUTOR

Subjunctive with necessity, desire, and emotions

1 The subjunctive is used after certain expressions of *necessity, desire,* and *emotion*. Some of these phrases are listed below.

Expressions of necessity:

Il faut que…	**Il est nécessaire que…**
Il est essentiel que…	**Il est important que…**
Il faudrait que…	**Il vaudrait mieux que…**

Expressions of desire:

Je désire que…	**J'ai envie que…**
Je souhaite que…	**Je voudrais que…**

Expressions of emotion:

Je suis désolé(e) que…	**Je suis content(e) que…**
C'est dommage que…	**Je suis ravi(e) que…**
Je suis triste que…	**Je suis heureux(-se) que…**

2 If the subject of both clauses in the sentence is the same, you use the infinitive in the second clause. In the expressions with **être** and **avoir** add **de** before the infinitive.

Nous sommes désolés que **vous** deviez déménager.
We are sorry that you need to move.

Nous sommes désolés **de** devoir déménager.
We are sorry that we need to move.

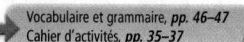 Vocabulaire et grammaire, *pp. 46–47*
Cahier d'activités, *pp. 35–37*  Online workbooks

---

30 **Écoutons** CD 4, Tr. 5 1.2 **1.** a **2.** b **3.** b **4.** a **5.** b **6.** a

Les parents et les amis d'Honoré sont réunis pour fêter ses dix-huit ans. Écoute les conversations et dis s'ils parlent **a) d'Honoré** ou **b) d'eux-mêmes** (*about themselves*).

31 **Qu'est-ce que vous dites?** 1.2

Écrivons/Parlons Reconstitue les phrases suivantes. Fais tous les changements nécessaires!

1. ils / être / ravi / que / tu / faire / apprentissage
2. il / être / important / que / vous / ne pas tomber malade
3. nous / désirer / que / elle / être / heureux
4. Marie / être / désolé / que / nous / ne pas venir / ce / week-end
5. c' / être / dommage / que / on / ne pas pouvoir / rester
6. elle / avoir / peur / que / il / avoir rendez-vous / avec / autre / fille

---

Flash culture

Au Mali, tout se déroule selon une hiérarchie très stricte. La famille, au sens large, est l'unité de base. Le chef de famille est le souverain absolu. Mais c'est la mère qui gère l'argent des salaires (même si la personne est âgée et a sa propre famille). Ce système permet de subvenir aux besoins de beaucoup de personnes au lieu de juste quelques-unes.

Est-ce qu'il y a une telle hiérarchie familiale aux États-Unis ? 🌸 4.2

Core Instruction

TEACHING GRAMMAIRE

1. Go over the expressions of necessity and model their pronunciation. Point out that **Il faut que…** is by far the most commonly used expression of necessity, and that the French are more likely to say **Il faut que je…** than **Je dois….** Also tell students that **Il est nécessaire que…** is not as common as **Il faut que…**, and that **Il est essentiel que…** sounds relatively formal. **(2 min.)**

2. Introduce expressions of desire and emotion. Tell students that **Je veux/voudrais que…** is the most common way of expressing desire, and that **Je désire que…** is more formal. **(3 min.)**

4. Go over Point 2. Ask students to compare this use of the infinitive to the English construction *I am sorry to . . .* (*I am sorry to intrude, I am sorry to have to move*). **(1 min.)**

---

32 **Des choses importantes** 🏵1.2

Parlons/Écrivons Fais des phrases complètes avec les éléments suivants.

1	**2**	**3**	**4**

Il est important
Il faudrait
Je suis ravi(e)
Ma mère désire
Le prof souhaite
Je ne veux pas
J'ai envie
	que
	de
		je
		tu
		mon frère/
		  ma sœur
		nous
		vous
		mes camarades
			s'installer dans un
			  bel appartement
			apprendre le français
			trouver du travail
			avoir beaucoup d'enfants
			être malade
			être heureux
			se marier

33 **Bonheur et tristesse** 🏵1.3

Parlons Quelle est ta réaction dans chacune de ces situations? Dis si tu es content(e) ou désolé(e) pour les personnes suivantes.

MODÈLE **Je suis désolé(e) que Lubin chante mal.**

Lubin

1. John   2. Cyril   3. tu   4. ils

HOLT **SoundBooth** ONLINE RECORDING

Communication

34 **Questions personnelles** 🏵1.1

Parlons Demande à un(e) camarade s'il/si elle ou quelqu'un de sa famille a une raison d'être content(e) ou triste et ce qu'il souhaite. Il/Elle va te donner trois explications différentes. Puis, échangez les rôles.

MODÈLE —Est-ce que tu es triste ou content(e)?
—Je suis triste que..., mais je suis content(e)...,
  et je voudrais vraiment que...

Communication

Pair Activity: Interpersonal

Have partners write and act out a dialog between a disobedient child and a concerned parent. The child states his or her intentions in the present, or **futur proche,** that are against the parent's rules or unacceptable. The parent uses expressions of emotion and desire to try to persuade the child to do the right thing.

MODÈLE
— **Je ne vais pas à l'école aujourd'hui. J'en ai marre!**
— **Je veux que tu ailles à l'école.** 🏵1.1, 1.2

Assess

Assessment Program

Quiz: Grammaire 2

Alternative Assessment

Differentiated Practice and Assessment CD-ROM

Online Assessment
my.hrw.com

Test Generator

Differentiated Instruction

ADVANCED LEARNERS

Challenge Tell students that you are preparing for a trip to Morocco and you need their advice. Ask students, **Qu'est-ce que je dois faire?** Students should give advice, such as **Il faudrait que vous emportiez un appareil-photo.** Encourage students to write the answers in their notebook for reference. 🏵1.1

MULTIPLE INTELLIGENCES

32 **Bodily-Kinesthetic** Copy each of the phrases and words in the four colored puzzle pieces on adhesive notes and give each note to a student. Ask students to circulate and find three partners to form a complete sentence. Have them write the appropriate verb form on the adhesive note that has the verb. In addition, you may want students to write the complete sentences on the board. 🏵1.2

Synthèse
• Vocabulaire 2
• Grammaire 2

Application 2

35 Et la suite... 1.3

Écrivons En groupes de quatre, imaginez une suite pour chacune des phrases suivantes. Vous pouvez parler d'événements qui se passent dans votre école, votre famille, votre ville, etc. Échangez vos réponses et choisissez les plus originales!

1. C'est dommage que...
2. Il faudrait que...
3. Nous voudrions que...
4. Le professeur souhaite que...
5. Il vaudrait mieux que...
6. On désire que...
7. Il est important que...

Bell Work

Use Bell Work 4.8 in the *Teaching Transparencies* or write this activity on the board.

Complète les phrases et mets les verbes entre parenthèses au **subjonctif**.

1. Je suis désolé que vous _____ (être) malade.
2. C'est dommage que tes parents ne _____ (pouvoir) pas venir.
3. Je souhaite que tu _____ (venir) avec ton frère.
4. Il est essentiel que nous ne _____ (faire) pas trop de bruit. 1.2

Un peu plus

Disjunctive (stress) pronouns

Interactive TUTOR

1. These are the disjunctive pronouns (**pronoms disjoints**) in French.

je → moi	nous → nous
tu → toi	vous → vous
il → lui	ils → eux
elle → elle	elles → elles

2. Disjunctive pronouns are used:

• after prepositions: **Il est arrivé après moi.**

• after the verb **être**: **Si j'étais toi, j'irais le voir.**

• as a one-word-answer (without a verb).

—**Qui aime étudier le français?**
—**Moi!**

• to emphasize a subject pronoun

Lui, il est fâché, mais moi, je suis content(e).

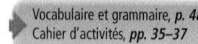 Vocabulaire et grammaire, *p. 48*
Cahier d'activités, *pp. 35–37*

 Online workbooks

36 Et lui, c'est qui? 1.2

Parlons Dans chacune des phrases suivantes, remplace la partie soulignée *(underlined)* par un pronom disjoint.

MODÈLE Il est sorti avec <u>Michèle</u>.
Il est sorti avec elle.

lui   1. Elle est amoureuse de <u>Jérôme</u>.

nous   2. En classe, il est assis derrière <u>Monique et moi</u>.

lui   3. Je travaille pour <u>monsieur Schaeffer</u>.

eux   4. Nous sommes venus avec <u>Pierre et Isabelle</u>.

vous   5. C'est <u>toi et Paul</u> qui m'avez appelé?

elles   6. Je pense à <u>mes amies</u>.

eux   7. Mon frère et moi, nous pensons souvent à <u>nos parents</u>.

elle   8. Si j'avais été <u>Paola</u>, j'aurais déjà rompu depuis longtemps.

37 Script

See script on p. 131F.

38 Answers

1. C'est lui qui a fait un emprunt pour acheter une voiture.
2. C'est elles qui ont loué une maison à la mer cet été.
3. C'est eux qui ont gagné le match.
4. Ce sont elles qui ont été engagées.
5. Ce sont eux qui ont donné rendez-vous à Lucie et Stella.

Core Instruction

INTEGRATED PRACTICE

1. Have students do Activity 35 to practice previously taught expressions. **(4 min.)**

2. Introduce **Un peu plus.** (See presentation suggestions at right.) **(4 min.)**

3. Continue with integrated practice Activities 36–40. **(20 min.)**

TEACHING UN PEU PLUS

1. Go over Points 1 and 2 of **Un peu plus.** **(2 min.)**

2. Ask students questions to be answered with disjunctive pronouns. **C'est qui, Dylan?** (**C'est lui!**) **C'est toi, le prof?** (**Non, c'est vous!**) **(2 min.)**

Online Practice
go.hrw.com
Application 2 practice
KEYWORD: BD3 CH4

Application 2

37 Écoutons CD 4, Tr. 6 🔲1.2

🎧 Écoute les phrases et choisis un pronom disjoint pour insister sur la personne dont on parle. **1.** moi **2.** eux **3.** nous **4.** toi **5.** elles **6.** lui

38 Si c'est pas toi, c'est qui? 🔲1.2

Parlons Dis qui a fait ces choses. Utilise des pronoms disjoints.

MODÈLE demander l'e-mail de Léa / Marcel
C'est lui qui a demandé l'e-mail de Léa.

1. faire un emprunt pour acheter une voiture / Patrick

2. louer une maison à la mer cet été / Francine et Léa

3. gagner le match / mes copains

4. être engagé dans une grosse société / ma copine et moi

5. donner rendez-vous à Lucie et Stella / Lucas et Théo

 **Communication**

 HOLT **SoundBooth** ONLINE RECORDING

39 Interview 🔲1.1

Parlons Demande à un(e) camarade de classe ce qu'il/elle aime faire comme activités, et ce que d'autres membres de sa famille aiment faire. Il/Elle utilisera des pronoms disjoints dans ses réponses.

♻ *Souviens-toi, Les activités, pp. 7, 18–19*

MODÈLE —Qu'est-ce que tu aimes faire comme activités?
—Moi, j'aime…
—Et tes frères?

40 Histoire à raconter 🔲1.2

Parlons Regarde les illustrations et dis ce qui a changé dans la vie d'Asukilé et de Nabila.

PRE-AP **Language Examination**

🖥 To display the drawings to the class, use the Picture Sequences Transparency for Chapter 4.

40 Sample answer

a. Asukilé et Nabila habitaient dans un très petit appartement. Ils n'étaient pas contents et ils voulaient déménager.

b. Ils sont allés à la banque pour faire un emprunt. Ils pensaient acheter une nouvelle maison.

c. Ils ont enfin déménagé! Maintenant, ils ont une belle maison qui leur plaît. Ils sont ravis.

Communication

Group Activity: Interpersonal

Form small groups and assign a topic of discussion, such as school, celebrity lifestyles, music, or politics. Within each group, have students express a desire, emotion, or a necessity with the subjunctive. Then, as a wrap-up activity, have groups share some of the statements that were made. 🔲1.1

Differentiated Instruction

SLOWER PACE LEARNERS

35 Building on Previous Skills Before students do this activity, ask for volunteers to explain the formation of the subjunctive. You may want them to write examples on the board. Then ask them to list on the board expressions that require the subjunctive. Encourage students to refer to these expressions as they do this activity. 🔲1.3

SPECIAL LEARNING NEEDS

39 Students with Auditory Impairments Allow students with auditory impairments to write questions to exchange with a partner. Then allow the partner to create a written response to the interview questions. This accommodation will allow students with auditory impairments to have a visual script to rely upon when they ask or are being asked questions in French. 🔲1.2

Assess

Assessment Program
Quiz: Application 2
Audio CD 4, Tr. 12 🎧
Alternative Assessment
Differentiated Practice and Assessment CD-ROM

Online Assessment
my.hrw.com

Test Generator

Resources

Planning:

Lesson Planner

One-Stop Planner

Presentation:

Audio CD 4, Tr. 7

Practice:

Cahier d'activités

Reading Strategies and Skills
Handbook, Chapter 4

Advanced Reader

AP Reading Suggestion

Remind students that they should
determine the main idea of the
selection, which they can do even
if they do not understand every
detail of it.

Applying the Strategies

For practice using cultural context, have students use the
"Anticipation Guide" strategy
from the *Reading Strategies and
Skills Handbook.*

READING PRACTICE

Strategy: Anticipation Guide

Reading Skill	When can I use this strategy?		
	Prereading	During Reading	Postreading
Making Predictions	✓		
Using Prior Knowledge	✓		
Analyzing Cause and Effect Relationships		✓	
Analyzing Persuasive Techniques			✓
Making Generalizations			✓

Strategy at a Glance: Anticipation Guide

• The teacher writes the Anticipation Guide, a set of generalizations based on issues in the text and designed to promote discussion and predictions about the selection.

• Students mark whether they agree or disagree with each statement, then discuss their responses.

• While students read, they take notes on the issues in the guide as those issues are revealed in the text.

• After reading, students look at their responses again to see whether they still agree or disagree with the statements.

Both younger and older children do it. They constantly ask what's going on and where they are being taken. They ask what the doctor is going to do before the doctor does it, and they plan what they'll say when they are approaching parents with special requests. Adults do it. We pick up travel brochures before we travel, study maps before we make a car trip, and check out the checkbook before we make a purchase. We all do it—we try to anticipate what's going to happen before it actually happens.

Good readers consciously try to anticipate what a text is about before they begin reading. They look at the cover, art, title, genre, author, headings, graphs, charts, length, print size, inside flaps, and back cover. Some students read the bibliographic information on the copyright page. They ask friends, "Is this any good?" They do anything to find out something about a text before they begin reading.

Struggling readers, on the other hand, often don't do that; they are told to read something, and once the text is in hand, they just begin. They often skip titles and background information, hardly ever read book jackets, and rarely look through the text

---

Francis Bebey (1929–2001) est à la fois
écrivain et musicien-chanteur. Né à Douala,
au Cameroun, il fait ses études d'abord au
Cameroun, puis en France. De retour
en Afrique, il travaille comme journaliste.
En 1961, il commence à travailler pour
l'UNESCO à Paris où il est responsable pour
le développement de la musique. Son premier
roman, *Le Fils d'Agatha Moudio*, publié en 1967, reçoit le Grand
Prix Littéraire de l'Afrique Noire.

A Avant la lecture 3.1, 4.2, 2.2

Le personnage principal du texte suivant doit se marier.
L'histoire se situe au Cameroun. Qu'est-ce que tu sais sur
le mariage en général et en Afrique en particulier? Quel
rôle est-ce que les traditions jouent pendant un mariage?

STRATÉGIE pour lire

Using background knowledge
Stories set in your own culture
are easy to understand. When
you read a story set in another
country, however, you may be
misled if you assume that the
society and customs are the same
as where you live. If you're not
familiar with the country where
the story takes place, you may
want to find out more about that
country to better understand the
characters, what happens
to them, and why.

CD 4, Tr. 7 **Le fils d'Agatha Moudio**

*L'extrait suivant est tiré du roman **Le Fils d'Agatha
Moudio**. Mbenda est assez âgé pour se marier. Selon la
tradition, un conseil d'anciens[1] doit choisir une femme
acceptable pour lui. Mais Mbenda est coincé[2] entre deux
cultures, celle de la tradition et celle de la vie moderne. Cet
extrait raconte ce qui se passe pendant son conseil de
mariage.*

Lorsque j'y arrivai, je le trouvai assis, parmi les autres.
Tous les anciens étaient là : il y avait Moudiki, Bilé, Ekoko,
Mpondo-les-deux-bouts, le roi Salomon, et même Eya.
Avec le chef Mbaka, cela faisait sept personnes... sept
anciens du village, pour me parler de mon cas. J'avoue[3]
que leur mine[4] et leur attitude ne laissèrent pas de
m'impressionner vivement.

Les sept visages noirs prirent leur air des grandes
occasions, renforcé par la pénombre[5] de la pièce où se

1. personnes âgées   2. *stuck*   3. J'admets   4. l'expression des visages
5. *semi-darkness*

Core Instruction

LECTURE

1. Read **Stratégie pour lire** aloud with students.
(1 min.)

2. Do **Avant la lecture** as a class. Have students
brainstorm wedding traditions they know of
while volunteers write them on the board.
You may also want to bring in photographs
of traditional African weddings downloaded
from the Internet.

Do they look like the weddings students have
seen? **(10 min.)**

3. Have volunteers take turns reading the first
part of **Le fils d'Agatha Moudio** aloud to the
end of page 157. Pause regularly to monitor
students' comprehension. **(15 min.)**

Lecture

tenait la réunion[1]. On me fit asseoir au milieu du groupe, et l'on me parla. Ce fut, comme il se devait, le chef lui-même qui parla le premier.

— Écoute, fils, me dit-il, je dois t'annoncer tout d'abord que l'esprit de ton père est présent ici, avec nous, en ce moment même. Sache donc que nous ne faisons rien qui aille contre sa volonté. D'ailleurs[2], même s'il était encore vivant, il nous laisserait faire, car il avait confiance aux anciens, et il les respectait beaucoup...

Mbaka prit un temps, puis continua :

— Nous allons te marier. C'est notre devoir de te marier, comme cela a toujours été le devoir de la communauté de marier ses enfants. Mais, si, à l'exemple de certains jeunes gens d'aujourd'hui, tu crois que tu peux mener à bien[3], tout seul, les affaires de ton propre mariage, nous sommes prêts à te laisser les mains libres[4], et à ne plus nous occuper de toi dans ce domaine-là. La seule chose que nous allons te demander, c'est si tu consens à ce que ton mariage soit pris en mains par les anciens du village, ou si, au contraire, tu estimes que c'est une affaire qui ne regarde[5] que toi, et dont nous aurions tort de nous occuper. Réponds-nous, fils, sans peur ; réponds franchement : tu es libre de choisir ton propre chemin.

Je compris : j'étais au carrefour[6] des temps anciens et modernes. Je devais choisir en toute liberté ce que je voulais faire, ou laisser faire. Liberté toute théorique, d'ailleurs, car les anciens savaient que je ne pouvais pas choisir de me passer d'eux, à moins de décider ipso facto d'aller vivre ailleurs[7], hors de ce village où tout marchait selon des règles séculaires[8], malgré l'entrée d'une autre forme de civilisation qui s'était manifestée, notamment, par l'installation de cette borne-fontaine que vous connaissez. Et puis, comment oser[9] dire à ces gens graves et décidés, que je voulais me passer d'eux ? Je vous dis qu'il y avait là, entre autres personnes, Eya, le terrible sorcier, le mari de la mère Mauvais-Regard. Dire à tout le monde présent que je refusais leur médiation, c'était presque sûrement signer mon arrêt de mort[10]. Tout le monde, chez nous, avait une peur terrible d'Eya, cet homme aux yeux rouges comme des piments mûrs[11], dont on disait qu'il avait déjà supprimé[12] un certain nombre de personnes. Et malgré ma force qui entrait peu à peu dans la légende des lutteurs doualas[13], moi aussi j'avais peur d'Eya. Il était là, il me regardait d'un air qu'il essayait de rendre indifférent et paternel à la fois. Ses petits yeux brillaient au fond d'orbites profondes, en harmonie avec les joues maigres. Il n'avait pas dû manger beaucoup

---

1. *where the meeting was held* 2. *besides* 3. *réussir* 4. *il doit décider seul* 5. *concerne* 6. *intersection* 7. *elsewhere*
8. *qui existent depuis des siècles* 9. *dare* 10. *death sentence* 11. *ripe pimentos* 12. *exterminated*
13. *name given to the coastal people of the area*

Active Reading Questions

1. **Pourquoi les anciens du village se réunissent-ils? (pour parler du mariage de Mbenda)**
2. **Comment est l'ambiance du conseil? (très sérieuse)**
3. **Où est le père de Mbenda? (Il est mort, mais son esprit est là.)**
4. **Qu'est-ce que le père de Mbenda, s'il était vivant, penserait des opinions du conseil? (Il serait d'accord.)**
5. **Qu'est-ce que Mbenda doit décider? (de laisser le conseil choisir sa femme ou de se marier avec celle qu'il veut)**
6. **Que se passerait-il si Mbenda n'acceptait pas l'aide du conseil? (Il ne pourrait pas continuer à vivre dans le village)**
7. **De quoi Mbenda a-t-il peur s'il refuse le jugement du conseil? (de mourir par suite des sortilèges d'Eya, le sorcier)** 1.2

Making Predictions

Ask students to stop reading at the bottom of this page, and have them predict what Mbenda's decision will be. Have them explain why they believe he will make this choice, citing information from the text.

Language Examination

Lecture helps students prepare for Section I, Part B: **Reading Comprehension**. The audio recording helps them prepare for Part A: **Listening—Short Narratives.**

Active Reading Questions

1. Pourquoi le roi Salomon inspire-t-il confiance à Mbenda? (parce qu'il est sincère et intelligent)
2. Qu'est-ce que Salomon indique à Mbenda? (qu'il est de l'avis du groupe, que Mbenda doit suivre leurs conseils)
3. Qu'est-ce que Mbenda décide? (de suivre la tradition)
4. Comment réagit le conseil à la déclaration de Mbenda? (Ils sont contents.)
5. Avec qui Mbenda doit se marier? (avec Fanny, la fille de Tanga)
6. Qu'est-ce que le chef demande à l'esprit du père de Mbenda? (d'indiquer s'il est d'accord ou pas)
7. Comment est-ce que l'esprit du père se manifeste? (Il ne fait rien pour protester.)

🍀 1.2

Postreading Activity

Ask students what they think would have happened to Mbenda if he had chosen to ignore the advice of the council. What changes would he have had to make in his life in order to survive? (He would have had to move away from the village; his life might have been in danger.)

Comparisons

Language Note

The French past conditional is used just like the English past conditional. It expresses actions that would have occurred in the past if circumstances had been different. In most cases, the past conditional is translated as *would have.* However, **j'aurais pu** is *I could have* and **j'aurais dû** means *I should have.* Ask students for the English equivalent of **j'aurais voulu**. *(I would have liked)* 🍀 4.1

quand il était jeune. Il était là, devant moi, véritable allégorie de la mort habillée d'un pagne immense, et d'une chemise de popeline moisie[1]. Je n'osai pas le regarder en face. Je pensai, dans mon for intérieur[2], que de tous ces hommes groupés autour de moi, seul le roi Salomon pouvait m'inspirer une certaine confiance. Lui au moins, était un homme sincère. À part les moments où il désirait vraiment inventer des histoires, ce qu'il réussissait d'ailleurs fort bien, à part ces moments-là, il disait les choses qu'il pensait, avec des pointes de sagesse[3] dignes du nom célèbre qu'il portait. C'était, du reste, à cause de cette sagesse que notre village l'avait sacré roi, bien que de toute sa vie, Salomon n'eût connu que son métier de maçon[4]. Je tournai les yeux vers lui, comme pour lui demander conseil. Il secoua affirmativement la tête, assez légèrement pour que les autres ne voient pas, assez cependant pour que je comprenne. Oui, le roi Salomon était de l'avis du groupe, et moi je devais me ranger[5] à son avis, à leur avis à tous.

— Chef Mbaka, et vous autres, mes pères, dis-je, je ne puis vous désobéir. je suis l'enfant de ce village-ci, et je suivrai la tradition jusqu'au bout. Je vous déclare que je laisse à votre expérience et à votre sagesse le soin[6] de me guider dans la vie, jusqu'au jour lointain où moi-même je serai appelé à guider d'autres enfants de chez nous.

Chacun des hommes manifesta sa satisfaction à sa manière [...]

— C'est bien, fils, dit le chef Mbaka. Voilà la réponse que nous attendions de notre fils le plus digne, et nous te remercions de la confiance que tu nous accordes, de ton plein gré[7]. Maintenant, tu vas tout savoir : dès demain, nous irons « frapper à la porte » de Tanga, pour sa fille Fanny... Esprit, toi qui nous vois et qui nous écoutes, entends-tu ce que je dis ? Je répète que nous irons demain frapper à la porte de Tanga, pour lui demander la main de sa fille pour notre fils La Loi[8], comme tu l'as ordonné toi-même avant de nous quitter. Si tu n'es pas d'accord avec nous, manifeste-toi

1. *musty poplin (cloth)* 2. *in my mind* 3. *wisdom* 4. *mason* 5. être d'accord 6. *care* 7. avec ton accord
8. *French translation of the narrator's name (Mbenda)*

Core Instruction

LECTURE

1. Finish reading *Le fils d'Agatha Moudio* as a class. Point out the spiritual symbolism in the text. Ask students who might represent good (**le roi Salomon**), evil (**Eya**), the past (**l'esprit de son père**), and the present (**Mbenda**) at this wedding council. **(15 min.)**

2. Complete **Compréhension** and **Après la lecture** as a class. Would students like their community to choose a spouse for them? Have they heard of cultures where this is still being done? **(10 min.)**

d'une manière ou d'une autre, et nous modifierons aussitôt nos plans...

Il parla ainsi à l'esprit de mon père, qui était présent dans cette pièce, et nous attendîmes une manifestation éventuelle¹, pendant quelques secondes. Elle ne vint point ; rien ne bougea dans la pièce,

ni le battant de la porte, ni l'unique fenêtre avare de lumière, et qui s'ouvrait par une petite natte² rectangulaire de raphia tressé³ ; nous n'entendîmes rien, même pas de pas sur le sol frais de terre battue. Rien : mon père nous donnait carte blanche⁴.

1. possible 2. *mat* 3. *braided palm* 4. libre choix

Compréhension

B Dis si les phrases suivantes sont **a) vraies** ou **b) fausses.** Précise pourquoi elles sont fausses. ✿1.2

1. Les sept anciens du village doivent décider de l'avenir de Mbenda. a.
   b. Le père de Mbenda est mort. C'est le chef du village qui parle le premier.
2. C'est le père de Mbenda qui parle le premier.
3. Les anciens veulent marier Mbenda selon la tradition. a.
4. Les anciens sont prêts à laisser Mbenda choisir: soit il accepte le choix des anciens, soit il se marie avec qui il veut. a.
5. Mbenda est libre de son choix. b. S'il décide de ne pas écouter les anciens, il devra aller vivre ailleurs.
6. Eya est un homme qui fait peur. a.
7. Salomon est le roi du village. b. Il est maçon.
8. Mbenda décide de choisir lui-même sa femme. b. Il décide de laisser les anciens choisir une femme pour lui.

C Réponds aux questions suivantes. ✿1.2

1. Qui est présent au conseil?
2. Quel est le choix donné à Mbenda par le conseil?
3. De quoi Mbenda a-t-il peur s'il refuse la médiation du conseil?
4. Qui est Eya? Comment est-il?
5. Pourquoi le roi Salomon s'appelle-t-il ainsi?
6. Quelle est la décision de Mbenda?

Après la lecture ✿1.3

D Qu'est-ce que la phrase «...j'étais au carrefour des temps anciens et modernes» veut dire dans le texte? À ton avis, qu'est-ce qui a causé cette situation dans laquelle Mbenda se trouve? Est-ce que c'est une situation universelle, qui existe dans toutes les cultures?

C Answers
1. le narrateur et tous les anciens du village
2. Les anciens lui donnent l'occasion de choisir sa propre femme s'il le veut.
3. Il a peur du sorcier Eya.
4. C'est le vieux sorcier aux yeux rouges.
5. C'est un sage.
6. Mbenda décide de laisser les anciens choisir une femme pour lui.

Cultures

Practices and Perspectives

Cameroon law stipulates that no marriage may take place if the girl is younger than 15 or if the boy is younger than 18, unless the President of the Republic grants an exemption for a serious reason. By law the prospective spouses must consent freely to the marriage, and the consent of a minor is valid only if his or her father and mother consent to the marriage. However, forced and arranged marriages of girls and boys below these ages are common in the northern, predominantly Muslim, part of the country and in rural areas. Forced marriage is less common in the urban areas among a younger generation that is more aware of its rights. Ask students to discuss why it may be difficult for some ethnic groups in Cameroon to abandon their customs. Do parents in the U.S. attempt to influence their children's choice of a marital partner? ✿2.1, 3.2

Differentiated Instruction

ADVANCED LEARNERS

Extension Have students write a final paragraph in which they describe a scene where the elders knock on Tanga's door and ask for his daughter's hand in marriage to Mbenda. Students should make the conversations as authentic as possible by using the information and expressions Mbaka provides in his speech. ✿1.3, 3.2

MULTIPLE INTELLIGENCES

Musical According to the author's biography, Francis Bebey is also a **musicien-chanteur.** Allow students to research the music of Francis Bebey on the Internet and present the information they find to the class. If possible play a recording of Bebey's music in class. ✿3.1

Assess

Assessment Program
Quiz: Lecture
Online Assessment
my.hrw.com
Test Generator

Process Writing

Have partner's list the important events that occur in any romantic relationship. Then have them brainstorm cultural traditions, across different cultures they know of, associated with each event. Suggest that students use this information as a guideline for their research about the couple they have chosen.

Teaching Suggestion

When discussing **Stratégie pour écrire** with students, review the following structures for comparisons and superlatives.

— **plus/moins/aussi** + adj./adv. + **que**
   (**Bernard parle aussi vite que le professeur.**)
— **le/la/les** + plus/moins + adj./adv + **de** + noun
   (**Marc est le plus grand de la classe.**)
— noun + **le/la/les** +plus/moins + adj./adv. + **de** + noun
   (**Chantal est l'étudiante la plus intelligente de la classe.**)

Connections

Language Arts Link

Metaphors and similes are rhetorical devices that express comparison. A simile is an explicit comparison between two things using "like"or "as". A metaphor is an implied comparison in which one trait ordinarily associated with one thing is applied to another. Ask students to give examples of similes and metaphors in both, English and French. 3.1

L'atelier de l'écrivain

Une histoire d'amour

C'est l'anniversaire de mariage d'un couple que tu connais. Ce couple peut être tes grands-parents, des amis de la famille, des gens célèbres ou un couple imaginaire. Tu vas écrire leur histoire d'amour. Parle de leur première rencontre, de leurs rendez-vous, de leur mariage et comment ils ont vécu jusqu'à maintenant. Décris aussi les traditions culturelles que le couple a suivies. Par exemple, est-ce que l'homme s'est mis à genoux pour demander la main de sa femme? Ou bien, est-ce qu'il a demandé sa main à son père d'abord?

① Plan: l'arête de poisson 🕸1.2

Choisis le couple dont tu veux parler. Si tu ne connais pas toute leur histoire d'amour, pose-leur des questions ou fais des recherches. Écris les étapes ou les événements importants de leur histoire dans ton organigramme en forme d'arête de poisson. Commence avec leur première rencontre au bout de l'arête de poisson (au niveau de la queue) et termine avec leur dernier anniversaire de mariage (au niveau de la tête). Sur chaque arête, marque les étapes de leur vie (naissance de leurs enfants par exemple).

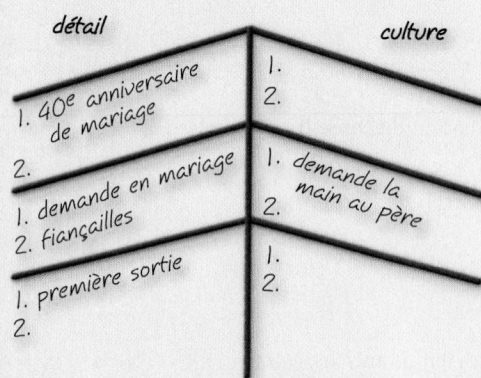

détail — culture

1. 40e anniversaire de mariage
2.
1.
2.

1. demande en mariage
2. fiançailles
1. demande la main au père
2.

1. première sortie
2.
1.
2.

Première rencontre

Core Instruction

L'ATELIER DE L'ÉCRIVAIN

1. Have students think about couples they know and admire and discuss the assignment. **(3 min.)**

2. Read **Stratégie pour écrire.** Have students use comparisons to describe the couples they thought about earlier. **(5 min.)**

3. Go over the additional vocabulary and **La concordance des temps. (5 min.)**

4. Assign steps 1 and 2 as homework. You might have students create a PowerPoint® slide show to illustrate the events in their stories.

5. Have students complete step 3 with a partner. **(15 min.)**

6. Complete step 4 with the class. If students have created a slide show, they can use it as they read their stories to the class. **(15 min.)**

② Rédaction ❀1.3

Fais un brouillon de ton histoire d'amour. Utilise les informations de ton organigramme et n'oublie pas de faire des comparaisons quand tu décris les détails des différents événements et les traditions. N'oublie pas que les comparaisons aident les lecteurs à mieux comprendre les personnages et les actions de ton histoire.

③ Correction ❀1.2

Maintenant, assure-toi que ton histoire est bien écrite. Vérifie :

- la conjugaison des verbes.
- l'orthographe des mots.

Ensuite, échange ton histoire avec celle d'un ou d'une camarade de classe. Posez-vous ces questions :

- Est-ce que chaque étape ou événement de l'histoire est clair ?
- Est-ce que ton histoire comprend des détails pour chaque étape et chaque tradition ?
- Est-ce qu'il y a des comparaisons qui rendent les personnages et les événements plus vivants ?

Pour finir, corrige ton histoire en tenant compte des commentaires de ton/ta camarade.

④ Application ❀1.3

Lis ton histoire d'amour à la classe. Quelle histoire est la plus romantique ? La plus traditionnelle ? La moins traditionnelle ? Tu peux aussi discuter avec la classe des traditions culturelles décrites dans les différentes histoires. Quelles sont les origines des différentes traditions ? Quelles traditions est-ce que les histoires ont en commun ? Quelles traditions sont uniques ?

> Mon grand-père et ma grand-mère se sont rencontrés quand ils étaient encore adolescents. Mon grand-père avait 16 ans et ma grand-mère, 15 ans. Mon grand-père venait de déménager de Chicago. Il n'aimait pas du tout la petite ville où habitait ma grand-mère. Il préférait la

Vocabulaire à la carte

demander la main de quelqu'un	to ask for someone's hand (in marriage)
embrasser	to kiss
épouser	to marry
les noces	wedding
faire la connaissance de	to meet (someone)
la lune de miel	honeymoon

La concordance des temps

Sequence of tenses describes the agreement between the verb in the main clause and the verb in the dependent clause.

> **Mon grand-père m'a dit que ma grand-mère l'avait demandé en mariage.**

L'atelier de l'écrivain

L'atelier de l'écrivain

La concordance des temps

Have students write sentences with these words and the correct tenses.

1. **Robert / être / dans / cafétéria / quand / il / voir / Émilie / première fois**
2. **à ce moment-là / il / décider / que / elle /être / belle fille / monde**
3. **il / faire sa cour / pendant six mois / quand / il / demander sa main**

Writing Assessment

To assess **L'atelier de l'écrivain,** you can use the following rubric. For additional rubrics, see the *Assessment Program.*

Writing Rubric	4	3	2	1
Content (Complete—Incomplete)				
Comprehensibility (Comprehensible—Seldom comprehensible)				
Accuracy (Accurate—Seldom accurate)				
Organization (Well-organized—Poorly organized)				
Effort (Excellent effort—Minimal effort)				

18-20: A   14-15: C   Under
16-17: B   12-13: D   12: F

Differentiated Instruction

SLOWER PACE LEARNERS

② Additional Practice While students are doing **Rédaction,** you might want to discuss their love stories with individuals. Show them examples of comparisons they might use to add life to their descriptions of characters and events.

MULTIPLE INTELLIGENCES

Interpersonal Before they conduct research about a couple's relationship history (step 1), ask students to develop questions that will elicit the type of information they need. For example, how would one partner describe the other partner's features and/or characteristics? A follow-up question could be to compare key features to something familiar, as suggested in **Stratégie pour écrire.** ❀1.3

Assess

Assessment Program

Quiz: Écriture

Online Assessment
my.hrw.com

Test Generator

L'Afrique francophone

cent soixante et un **161**

Prépare-toi pour l'examen

Interactive TUTOR

Chapitre 4

Prépare-toi pour l'examen

Resources

Planning:

Lesson Planner

 One-Stop Planner

Practice:

Cahier d'activités

Media Guide

 Teaching Transparencies
Situation, Chapitre 4
Picture Sequences, Chapter 4

 Audio CD 4, Tr. 8

 Interactive Tutor, Disc 1

VIDEO OPTIONS

▶ **Télé-culture: Interviews**

TPRS
You may wish to use the Picture Sequences Transparency that accompanies Activity 7 for a TPRS activity.

❸ Answers

1. veuve
2. célibataire
3. orphelin
4. jumelles
5. ont adopté

French for Spanish Speakers

Ask Spanish speakers to look at the verb **plaire**. Ask if they can think of a verb that is used similarly in Spanish. (**gustar**) How is this verb different from **aimer**? (What the person likes is the subject of **gustar**. The person is the subject of **aimer**.) Have students identify the subjects of these sentences. **Cette chanson me plaît. / Me gusta esta canción.** (**chanson/canción**) What is the difference in the word order for using **plaire** and **gustar** in these sentences? (The indirect object can start the sentence in Spanish.) ✿ 4.1

---

❶ Lis l'e-mail que Céleste a envoyé à ses amis. Dis s'ils lui donnent
a) **un bon conseil**, b) **un mauvais conseil** ou c) **pas de conseil.** ✿ 1.2, 1.3

> J'ai rencontré un beau garçon. Il s'appelle Fortuné. Je crois que je suis tombée amoureuse de lui. Je n'ai jamais pensé que je trouverais un garçon qui soit mignon, gentil, intelligent et toujours de bonne humeur. Je crois qu'il m'aime aussi! Je sais que je viens de faire sa connaissance mais je ne veux plus jamais le quitter. Qu'est-ce que je dois faire à votre avis?

❶ Vocabulaire 1
• to say what happened
• to ask for and give advice
pp. 134–137

a **1.** Amadou: «Tu ferais mieux d'attendre un peu.»

a **2.** Ali: «À mon avis, il faudrait que tu le connaisses un peu plus.»

b **3.** Sophie: «Si j'étais toi, je me marierais cette semaine.»

c **4.** Joseph: «Je n'en ai pas la moindre idée!»

Answers will vary. **5.** Et toi, quel conseil lui donnerais-tu?

❷ Grammaire 1
• reciprocal verbs
• the past conditional
Un peu plus
• **manquer** and **plaire**
pp. 138–143

❷ Mets les verbes entre parenthèses au **conditionnel passé**. ✿ 1.2

1. S'ils avaient échangé leurs numéros de téléphone, ils _____ (se téléphoner).

2. S'ils s'étaient parlé, ils _____ (se réconcilier).

3. Si elles avaient été vexées, elles _____ (se fâcher).

4. S'ils étaient tombés amoureux, ils _____ (se marier).

5. Si Joseph m'avait offert un cadeau, cela _____ (me plaire).

1. se seraient téléphoné **2.** se seraient réconciliés **3.** se seraient fâchées **4.** se seraient mariés **5.** m'aurait plu

❸ Vocabulaire 2
• to share good and bad news
• to renew old acquaintances
pp. 146–149

❸ Complète ces phrases avec la forme correcte des mots suivants. ✿ 1.2

né	orphelin	célibataire	jumeau
veuf	louer	malheureusement	adopter

1. Mon oncle est mort. Maintenant, ma tante est _____.

2. Ma sœur n'est pas mariée. Elle est _____.

3. Le héros de cette histoire n'a plus ses parents. Il est _____.

4. Léa et Chloé sont nées le même jour. Elles sont _____.

5. Ce couple n'avait pas d'enfant. Alors ils _____ une petite fille.

Preparing for the Exam

RETEACHING

Review the use of reciprocal verbs. In the **passé composé**, **être** is used as the helping verb when a verb is made reciprocal. Point out that the past participle agrees if the reciprocal pronoun is the *direct object* of the verb. The past participle does not agree if the reciprocal pronoun is the indirect object of the verb. Write several examples of each use on the board, leaving out the past participle, and ask students to provide the answers along with the explanation for each.

TEST-TAKING STRATEGY

Remind students that the conditional is conjugated by taking the future stem of the verb and adding the imperfect endings (-**ais**, -**ais**, -**ait**, -**ions**, -**iez**, -**aient**). **Je choisirais la voiture noire.** (See **Déjà vu!** page 140.)

Online Assessment
go.hrw.com
Chapter Self–test
KEYWORD: BD3 CH4

Chapitre 4

Prépare-toi pour l'examen

Prépare-toi pour l'examen

4 Fais des phrases en utilisant les éléments donnés. N'oublie pas de faire tous les changements nécessaires. ✿1.2

1. il / être / triste / que / son chien / être / mort
2. nous / être / ravi / que / Aline / être / fiancé
3. c' / être dommage / que / vous / devoir / partir
4. je / être / désolé / que / tu / avoir / un gros rhume
5. vous / souhaiter / que / Jeanne et Marc / avoir beaucoup d'enfants
6. il / être essentiel / que / nous / être / à l'heure / au boulot

5 Réponds aux questions suivantes. ✿2.1

1. Dans les familles traditionnelles d'Afrique du Nord, où les mariés habitent-ils?
2. Quand on est invité chez des Maliens, est-ce qu'il est poli de refuser le thé?
3. Comment les salaires sont gérés dans les familles maliennes?

6 Écoute les phrases suivantes et dis si la personne qui parle exprime **a) une nécessité, b) une émotion** ou **c) un fait réel.**
CD 4, Tr. 8 ✿1.2 **1.** a **2.** c **3.** b **4.** a **5.** b

7 Raconte ce qui se passe dans la vie de ce couple. ✿1.2

4 Grammaire 2
• the subjunctive
• subjunctive with necessity, desire, and emotions
Un peu plus
• disjunctive pronouns
pp. 150–155

5 Culture
• **Comparaisons** p. 145
• **Flash culture** pp. 136, 148, 152

4 Answers

1. Il est triste que son chien soit mort.
2. Nous sommes ravis qu'Aline soit fiancée.
3. C'est dommage que vous deviez partir.
4. Je suis désolé(e) que tu aies un gros rhume.
5. Vous souhaitez que Jeanne et Marc aient beaucoup d'enfants.
6. Il est essentiel que nous soyons à l'heure au boulot.

5 Answers

1. chez les parents du mari
2. non
3. la mère gère l'argent

6 Script

1. Il foudrait que nous nous voyions plus souvent.
2. Antoine a pris sa retraite le mois dernier.
3. Je suis désolée que ta grand-mère soit morte.
4. Il faut qu'elle fasse un emprunt pour finir ses études.
5. Il était triste que sa femme soit tombée malade.

ACTIVITÉ PRÉPARATOIRE PRE-AP Language Examination

📋 To display the drawings to the class, use the Picture Sequences Transparency for Chapter 4.

7 Sample answer

a. **Nabila a trouvé du travail comme coiffeuse et Asukilé comme informaticien.**

b. **Ils ont eu des jumelles. Ils étaient vraiment fatigués!**

c. **Une de leurs filles s'est mariée.**

d. **Récemment, ils ont pris leur retraite. Ils se sont installés dans une maison au bord de la mer.**

Oral Assessment

To assess the speaking activities in this section, you might use the following rubric. For additional speaking rubrics, see the Alternative Assessment section of the *Assessment Program.*

Speaking Rubric	4	3	2	1
Content (Complete—Incomplete)				
Comprehension (Total—Little)				
Comprehensibility (Comprehensible—Incomprehensible)				
Accuracy (Accurate—Seldom Accurate)				
Fluency (Fluent—Not Fluent)				

18-20: A   16-17: B   14-15: C   12-13: D   Under 12: F

Prépare-toi pour l'examen

Grammar Review

For more practice with the grammar topics in this chapter, see the *Grammar Tutor*, the *Interactive Tutor*, or the *Cahier de vocabulaire et grammaire*.

Online Edition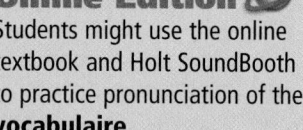

Students might use the online textbook and Holt SoundBooth to practice pronunciation of the **vocabulaire**.

Cultures

Products and Perspectives

Mali and Cameroon, like most countries of West Africa, have a large Muslim population. Both countries have civil laws, but Islam exerts a strong influence on customary law and women's issues. Marriage, divorce, and property laws continue to discriminate against women. Thus, all forms of divorce sanctioned by Islamic law are allowed, with repudiation, or the refusal to honor the marriage contract, being the most common. Women who initiate divorce must return the bride price their husband paid at the time of marriage. Once a woman is divorced, she will generally remarry within a few months, as most Muslims consider it socially unacceptable for a woman of childbearing age to remain single. Ask students to research the rights of women in divorce according to Islamic law.  2.1, 3.1

Proverbes

For French proverbs and activities related to the chapter theme and vocabulary, see **Proverbes et expressions**, pp. R6–R7.

Grammaire 1
- reciprocal verbs
- the past conditional

Un peu plus
- manquer and plaire
  pp. 138–143

Résumé: Grammaire 1

The pronouns **nous**, **vous**, and **se** are used to make a verb reciprocal. Reciprocal verbs use **être** as the helping verb in the **passé composé**. The past participle agrees with a preceding direct object.

agreement ⟶ ⟶ no agreement

Elles **se** sont vu**es** samedi et **se** sont parl**é** pendant des heures!

After a **si** clause with the **plus-que-parfait** use the past conditional to state the result. The past conditional is formed with the **conditional** of the helping verb plus the **past participle** of the main verb.

si clause — result clause

Si j'**avais su**, je ne **serais** pas **venu(e)**!

Manquer means *to miss something* when used with a direct object.
  Ils ont manqué leur train.

When **manquer** is used with an indirect object, it means *to miss someone or something*.
  Mes amis me manquent!

Plaire means *to like*. **Se plaire** means *to like each other* or *to enjoy oneself at a place or event*.

Grammaire 2
- the subjunctive
- subjunctive with necessity, desire, and emotions

Un peu plus
- disjunctive pronouns
  pp. 150–155

Résumé: Grammaire 2

To form the subjunctive, take the **ils/elles** form of the present, drop the **-ent**, and add **-e, -es, -e, -ions, -iez, -ent**.
Some verbs have a different stem for the **nous** form of the present. In this case, drop the **-ons** and add the subjunctive endings.
Some verbs are irregular in the subjunctive:

	aller	avoir	être	faire	pouvoir
je/j'	aille	aie	sois	fasse	puisse
tu	ailles	aies	sois	fasses	puisses
il/elle/on	aille	ait	soit	fasse	puisse
nous	allions	ayons	soyons	fassions	puissions
vous	alliez	ayez	soyez	fassiez	puissiez
ils/elles	aillent	aient	soient	fassent	puissent

Some phrases and expressions require the subjunctive. They usually express an emotion, desire or necessity:
Je suis désolé(e) que…, Je désire que…, Il faut que…

The disjunctive pronouns are used after prepositions, the verb **être**, or to emphasize.

- **moi, toi, lui, elle, nous, vous, eux, elles**

Chapter Review

Teacher Management System
Password: admin
For more details, log on to www.hrw.com/CDROMTUTOR.

Create a variety of puzzles to review chapter vocabulary.

DVD Program

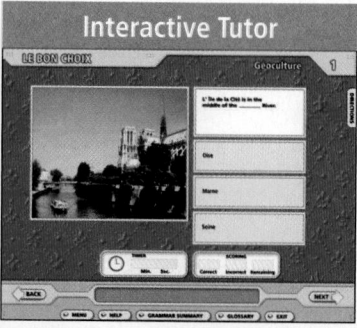

Interactive Tutor

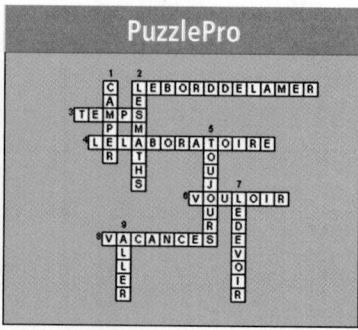

PuzzlePro

Résumé: Vocabulaire 1

To say what happened

un coup de foudre	love at first sight
de bonne/mauvaise humeur	in a good/bad mood
déçu(e)	disappointed
échanger	to exchange
ensemble	together
être/tomber amoureux(-euse)	to be/fall in love
fâché(e)	mad
gêné(e)	embarrassed
indifférent(e)	indifferent
inquiet/inquiète	worried
manquer	to miss
regretter	to be sorry
rompre (avec)	to break up (with)
se disputer	to argue
se donner rendez-vous	to have a date
s'énerver	to get annoyed
se parler	to talk (to each other)
se plaire	to like each other/enjoy oneself
se quitter	to leave (each other)
se réconcilier	to make up (with each other)
se rencontrer	to meet
se retrouver	to meet again
se revoir	to see (each other)

se téléphoner	to call (each other)
vexé(e)	offended
Devine…	Guess …
J'ai entendu dire que…	I hear that …
Figure-toi que…	You know what …
Tu savais que… toujours	Did you know that … still … ?
Ce n'est pas vrai!	You're kidding!
Je n'en ai pas la moindre idée. Aucune idée!	I have no idea.
Pas possible!	Really?
Raconte!	Tell me about it!

To ask for and give advice

Qu'est-ce que tu en penses?	What do you think about it?
…à ma place?	… in my place?
À ton avis…	In your opinion …
D'après toi…	In your opinion …
… tu ferais mieux de…	… it would be better to …
Si j'avais été toi…	If I had been you …
Pas nécessairement.	Not necessarily.
Surtout pas!	Certainly not!
Jamais de la vie!	Not in a million years!

Résumé: Vocabulaire 2

To share good and bad news and respond

adopter	to adopt
célibataire	single
déménager	to move
divorcer	to divorce
l'enfance (f.)	childhood
faire un emprunt	to apply for a loan
des jumeaux (m.)/jumelles (f.)	twins
louer	to rent
naître/mourir	to be born/to die
un orphelin/une orpheline	orphan
poser sa candidature	to apply for a job
prendre sa retraite	to retire
se fiancer/être fiancé(e)	to get/be engaged
s'installer	to move in

se marier	to be married
tomber malade	to fall ill
trouver du travail	to find work
un veuf/une veuve	widower/widow
vivre	to live
À propos…	By the way …
Vous savez…	You know …
malheureusement	unfortunately
Tous mes vœux de bonheur.	I wish you all the best.
Toutes mes félicitations!/ Félicitations!	Congratulations!
Mes sincères condoléances.	My deepest sympathy.

To renew old acquaintances …………… See p. 149

Prépare-toi pour l'examen

Game

Cercle de mots Ask students to make two identical sets of 20 note cards with words or expressions from **Vocabulaire 1** and **2** on one side and the English equivalents on the other. Form two teams and have each team sit in a circle. Give one card to each student. One student on each team begins by showing the English equivalent on his or her card to the teammate on the left. That student gives the French expression. Then, he or she shows the English equivalent on his or her card to the student on his or her left. The first team to complete the circle wins. ❀1.1

Online Edition

Transparency: Vocabulaire

Transparency: Situation

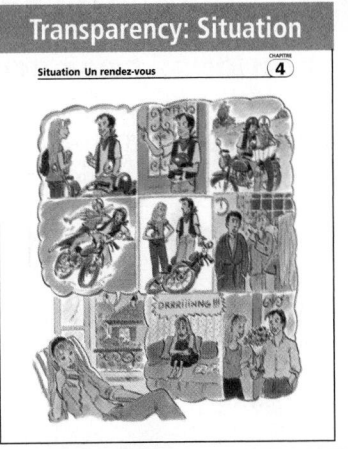

Assess

Assessment Program

Examen: Chapitre 4

Audio CD 4, Trs. 13, 14

Examen oral: Chapitre 4

Alternative Assessment

Differentiated Practice and
Assessment CD-ROM

Online Assessment

my.hrw.com

Test Generator

Activités préparatoires

Resources

Planning:
Lesson Planner

 One-Stop Planner

Practice:
Cahier de vocabulaire et grammaire

Differentiated Practice and Assessment CD-ROM

 Teaching Transparencies

Picture Sequences, Chapter 4

Cahier d'activités

 Audio CD 4, Tr. 9

VIDEO OPTIONS

▶ Télé-culture: Interviews

The AP French Language Exam
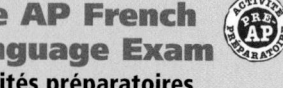

Activités préparatoires provide students with activities similar to those found in the Advanced Placement French Language exam. The activities are based on material taught up to and including this chapter and concentrate on the chapter grammar and vocabulary.

Listening Script

1.
— J'ai entendu dire que le prof est de mauvaise humeur aujourd'hui.
— C'est pas vrai! Et moi qui n'ai pas fait mes devoirs! Qu'est-ce que tu en penses? Je copie les devoirs de Paul avant la classe? Ou bien je dis au prof que mon chien les a mangés?

2.
— Salut, Marie! Ça fait longtemps qu'on ne s'est pas vus! Quoi de neuf? Comment va ta famille?
— Malheureusement, mon grand-père est mort d'une crise cardiaque la semaine dernière.

SECTION I

 Listening CD 4, Tr. 9 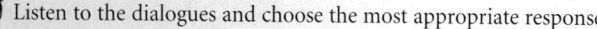 1.2

Listen to the dialogues and choose the most appropriate response.

1. A. Je suis ravie que tu dises la vérité!
  B. Tu savais que le prof était de bonne humeur.
  (**C.**) À mon avis, tu ferais mieux de dire la vérité.
  D. Tu devrais faire un emprunt.

2. A. Et maintenant tu es veuve?
  B. Alors, ta grand-mère est orpheline?
  C. Je n'en ai pas la moindre idée.
  (**D.**) Mes sincères condoléances.

Reading 1.2

Read the following paragraph and answer the questions that follow.

1 La tradition de la bague de fiançailles remonte aux Romains de l'Antiquité qui s'échangeaient des anneaux en fer en signe de promesse. En 860, le pape 5 Nicolas I officialise la bague de fiançailles par décret, en précisant qu'elle doit être en matériau précieux. Le 17 août 1477, c'est la fille de Charles le Téméraire, Marie de Bourgogne, 10 qui la première, reçoit une bague de fiançailles en diamant de la part de	son futur époux Maximilien, empereur germanique. Dans l'Antiquité, les Grecs furent les 15 premiers à porter des anneaux à l'annulaire gauche. Selon les croyances, c'est en effet ce doigt dont le nerf est le seul directement relié au cœur. Tout un symbole ! Dans les pays 20 nordiques on porte plutôt l'alliance à l'annulaire droit.

1. L'anneau de mariage s'appelle...
  A. l'annulaire.
  (**B.**) l'alliance.
  C. la bague de fiançailles.
  D. l'époux.

2. Maximilien était...
  A. la fille de Charles le Téméraire.
  (**B.**) le fiancé de Marie de Bourgogne.
  C. un empereur grec.
  D. celui qui a officialisé la bague de fiançailles.

3. L'annulaire est...
  A. le premier doigt avec lequel on indique.
  (**B.**) le quatrième doigt sur lequel on porte l'alliance.
  C. le plus petit doigt.
  D. un nerf dans le doigt.

4. En signe de promesse, les Romains portaient des anneaux...
  (**A.**) en fer.
  B. en diamant.
  C. en métal précieux.
  D. à l'annulaire droit.

Preparing for the Exam

ADDITIONAL PRACTICE

Write some scenarios on note cards. Have students choose a card at random and tell you what they would have done in that situation. This will give them a chance to practice the past conditional tense. 1.1

TEST-TAKING STRATEGY

Section I: Listening Tell students to listen for background sounds on the recording that might help indicate where the speakers are and what they are doing. This may give them context and help them narrow down their choices.

Section II: Writing If students are uncertain about an answer, tell them to skim through other parts of the test that are written in French. They may find a similar structure on which they can base their answer.

The following activities can be used to help you to prepare for the Advanced Placement French Language examination, or to further practice the vocabulary and grammar concepts you have seen in this chapter.

Activités préparatoires

Activités préparatoires

SECTION II

Writing ❀1.2

Complete the sentence by writing the correct form and tense of the verb, based on the context.

Ma sœur et mon beau-frère n'avaient que dix-huit ans quand ils ___1___. Ils ___2___ amoureux et ils ont décidé de se marier tout de suite. Maintenant, l'insouciance de la jeunesse leur ___3___. Ils doivent travailler tous les deux. Il faut que mon beau-frère ___4___ au bureau six jours par semaine. Ma sœur est déçue que son mari ne ___5___ jamais à la maison. Leur vie ne leur ___6___ pas beaucoup. S'ils ___7___ qu'ils ___8___ des ennuis d'argent, ils ne ___9___ si tôt.

1. <u>se sont rencontrés</u> (se rencontrer)
2. <u>sont tombés</u> (tomber)
3. <u>manque</u> (manquer)
4. <u>aille</u> (aller)
5. <u>soit</u> (être)
6. <u>plaît</u> (plaire)
7. <u>avaient su</u> (savoir)
8. <u>auraient</u> (avoir)
9. <u>se seraient pas mariés</u> (se marier)

Essay Topic ❀1.3

Write in French a well-organized composition on the following topic.

Quels sont les traits de caractère que vous cherchez chez un(e) ami(e)? Est-ce que vous croyez que vous êtes un(e) bon(ne) ami(e)? Pourquoi ou pourquoi pas?

Speaking ❀1.2

Look at the following drawing, then tell a story about what is occurring in the picture.

Reading Strategy

Recognizing Cognates You may want to remind students to look for cognates. Ask students to skim the paragraph for words they recognize as cognates in English. Students should underline these words before reading the paragraph for comprehension.

Writing Strategy

Tell students to write a first draft of their essay without worrying about grammar mistakes. Once they have their ideas down, they can go back and correct grammar and spelling. It is a good idea to skip lines as they write in order to leave room for insertions later.

Language Examination

📖 To display the drawing to the class, use the **Activités préparatoires** Transparency for Chapter 4.

Speaking: Sample answer
Tout le monde se réunit dans le gymnase de leur ancien lycée. Ça fait longtemps qu'ils ne se sont pas vus. Des amis se rencontrent pour la première fois depuis des années: "Tu n'as pas changé!" "Toi non plus." "Quoi de neuf?" "Plein de choses!" Ils parlent de leurs enfants et de leurs métiers. Ils se souviennent du bon vieux temps.

You may also want to ask students the following.

Qu'est-ce que tu feras dans dix ans? Penses-tu que tes camarades de classe auront beaucoup changé? Comment?

Differentiated Instruction

SLOWER PACE LEARNERS

Additional Practice Before completing the sentences in the Writing activity, students should review the grammar presentations in this chapter, especially the reciprocal verbs, the past conditional, the forms of the verbs **manquer** and **plaire,** and the subjunctive. You may want to ask volunteers to present these grammar points to the class, using examples and illustrations if possible. Encourage the class to ask for clarification if needed. ❀1.1, 1.2

SPECIAL LEARNING NEEDS

Dyslexia Accommodate students who have reading challenges by previewing the text for the Reading activity. Before class, make copies of the paragraph with a slightly larger font. Ask students to use highlighters to mark the proper nouns, questions, and answer options in the paragraph. Review the meaning and purpose of the proper nouns to lessen the struggle of reading and understanding the passage, questions, and answer options. ❀1.2

VIDEO OPTIONS

▶ **Géoculture**

▶ **Télé-roman: Camille et compagnie, Épisode 4**

❶ Script

1. Nous nous ressemblons et nous aimons faire les mêmes choses.
2. J'adore ne plus devoir travailler. J'ai pris ma retraite au mois de mai. Maintenant, je suis tout le temps en vacances.
3. Nous nous sommes rencontrés au parc et depuis, nous sommes toujours ensemble.
4. Depuis l'indépendance, notre pays n'a plus d'ennemis et vit dans la paix.
5. Je suis vraiment très triste parce que mon petit chien vient de mourir.

Révisions cumulatives

CD 4, Tr. 10 🌀1.2

🎧 ❶ Regarde les photos et dis qui pourrait dire chaque phrase.

a. Albin et Corinne	b. Aurélie et Estelle	c. Ophélia	d. le roi	e. Philippe
3	1	5	4	2

❷ Lis le journal d'Aminata et réponds aux questions. 🌸3.2

Mon petit frère et moi adorions Noël! Quand nous étions petits, nous ouvrions nos cadeaux le matin de Noël. Ensuite, nous chantions des chansons de Noël. C'était ma fête préférée!

Mon petit frère Joseph est né le 7 juin à 8 heures du matin. Il était très mignon. J'étais heureuse d'être une grande sœur. Aujourd'hui, c'est mon meilleur ami.

Ça c'est le jour de mon mariage. Ce matin-là, il faisait chaud... mais après, il a plu! Nous avons dû rester à l'intérieur. J'étais déçue mais tout s'est bien terminé.

1. Son petit frère est né.
2. Il est né à 8h du matin.
3. Oui, elle était heureuse.
4. Ils ouvraient les cadeaux, prenaient leur petit-déjeuner et chantaient des chansons de Noël. Answer will vary.
5. Il a plu.

1. Qu'est-ce qui s'est passé le 7 juin?
2. À quelle heure est-ce que son petit frère est né?
3. Est-ce qu'elle était contente d'avoir un petit frère?
4. Qu'est-ce qu'ils faisaient le matin de Noël? Est-ce que tu fais cela aussi?
5. Pourquoi est-ce qu'elle était déçue, le jour de son mariage?

Online Culture Project

Have students imagine they are respected history scholars who must write a passage on a topic of African history for their new book, *L'indépendance du Mali*. Students should do research on the Internet, gathering enough information to write half of a page on their topic. Tell students to document their sources and to write their passage in French. They should also select an appropriate photo and create a caption beneath it. 🌸2.1

Online Assessment
go.hrw.com
Cumulative Self–test
KEYWORD: BD3 CH4

Chapitres 1–4
Révisions cumulatives

 3 Toi et ton/ta camarade vous êtes acteurs/actrices. Vous jouez dans un nouveau film. Jouez la scène suivante. Ce sont deux ami(e)s qui parlent: un(e) ami(e) est tombé(e) amoureux(euse) mais il/elle a beaucoup de problèmes. Il/Elle demande conseil à son ami(e). 🎞️1.1

4 Regarde ce tableau et réponds aux questions suivantes. 🎞️1.3, 2.2

1. Quel événement de la vie le peintre a-t-il représenté?
2. Où est-ce que l'événement a lieu?
3. À ton avis, quelles sont les relations familiales entre les personnes qui sont représentées sur ce tableau?
4. Est-ce que cet événement se célèbrerait de la même façon dans ta famille?

La Noce d'Henri-Julien Félix Rousseau dit Le Douanier

5 Fais l'album photo de ta famille (réelle ou imaginaire). Utilise des photos de ton enfance, du mariage de tes parents, de tes frères et sœurs, de tes activités favorites et de tes ami(e)s. Tu peux aussi utiliser des photos découpées dans des magazines. Écris des phrases pour chaque photo. Montre les photos à la classe et explique ce qui se passe sur chaque photo. 🎞️1.3

6

À ton tour **La vie de star** Ton groupe va créer une émission de télévision consacrée aux célébrités. Il y a un hôte qui interroge des personnes célèbres. Les questions portent sur les activités préférées, les amours, le travail, la famille des célébrités, etc. Joue cette scène avec des camarades devant la classe.

🎞️1.1

ACTFL Performance Standards

The activities in Chapter 4 target the communicative modes as described in the Standards.

Interpersonal	Two-way communication using receptive skills and productive skills	**Communication (SE),** pp. 137, 139, 141, 143, 149, 151, 153, 155 **Communication (TE),** pp. 139, 141, 143, 153, 155 **À ton tour,** p. 169
Interpretive	One-way communication using receptive skills	**Culture,** pp. 144–145 **Lecture,** pp. 156–159
Presentational	One-way communication using productive skills	**Communication (SE),** pp. 155, 163 **Communication (TE),** pp. 137, 149, 151, 153, 155

FINE ART CONNECTION

Introduction Henri Julien Rousseau (1844 – 1910), a French Post-impressionist painter, is also known as **Le Douanier Rousseau** (the customs inspector) after his place of employment. The artist's child-like way of painting, bright colors, and attention to detail are characteristic of naïve or primitive art. **Le Douanier Rousseau** had a unique technique, painting the different colors one by one—first the blues, then the greens and so on. **La Noce** *(The Wedding Party)* is one of his most famous works. The artist is depicted to the right behind the bride. **Le Douanier Rousseau** probably based this painting on a photograph, superimposing the figures on a stylized background.

Analyzing
You may want to draw students' attention to the positioning of the figures in the painting and ask them the following questions.

1. **Penses-tu que le vieil homme à gauche est assis sur la souche, qu'il s'appuie contre elle, ou qu'il se tient debout devant elle?**
2. **Comment Rousseau a-t-il fait poser la jeune mariée? Est-ce que ses pieds touchent le sol?**
3. **Crois-tu que Rousseau ait voulu faire poser ses personnages ainsi? Pourquoi?** 🎞️3.1

Extension
Rousseau said to Picasso, **"Nous sommes les deux plus grands peintres de notre temps, toi dans le genre égyptien et moi dans le genre moderne."** By "Egyptian style" Rousseau refers to the elements of African tribal art on which Picasso and other artists based cubism. Ask students if they agree with Rousseau's assessment. Why or why not? 🎞️2.2, 3.1

Les fables de La Fontaine

Resources

Practice:

Reading Strategies and Skills
Handbook

Advanced Reader

Applying the Strategies

You may want to use the "Save the Last Word For Me" strategy from the *Reading Strategies and Skills Handbook* to encourage students to examine the text more closely.

READING PRACTICE

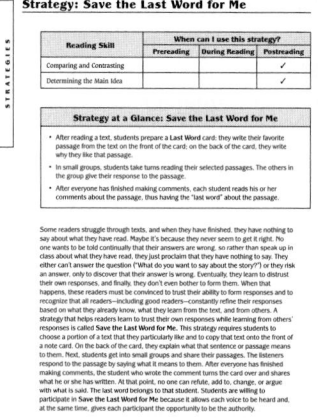

Strategy: Save the Last Word for Me

Prereading

To prepare for this **Chroniques** section, ask students to explain what fables are and what makes them different from other types of literary works. Have them consider the length of a fable, the typical characters involved, and the goal or moral of the story. Ask them if they know any fables and authors who are known for their fables. Ask volunteers to briefly summarize in French a fable they know and to explain its moral.

Language Examination

The **Chroniques** section helps students prepare for Section I, Part B: **Reading Comprehension.**

Nous avons tous un jour appris une fable. Ce sont des histoires simples qui mettent en scène, le plus souvent, des animaux et parfois, des hommes ou des objets. Il s'agit de leçons de morale ayant un caractère symbolique.

Le premier auteur de fables connu de tous est Ésope, un esclave grec affranchi[1] et boiteux[2] (son nom signifie "pieds inégaux[3]"). Il est né au VIIe siècle avant Jésus-Christ. C'était un conteur qui, n'a sans doute jamais écrit ses fables. Celles-ci ont été recueillies plus tard par *Démétrios de Phalère* (IVe siècle avant J.-C.).

Le plus célèbre des fabulistes français, Jean de la Fontaine, s'est inspiré des fables d'Ésope, d'Horace (poète lyrique de l'Antiquité romaine) et de la Panchatantra (collection de fables en sanskrit[4]). La Fontaine, né en Champagne en 1621, était poète et fréquentait les salons parisiens. Il a publié ses premières fables, "Les Fables Choisies", en 1668, contenant 124 fables mises en vers. Pendant sa vie, il en a écrit 243. La Fontaine a été élu à l'Académie française[5] en 1683.

« Je me sers des animaux pour instruire les hommes », dit-il. Chaque fable utilise une histoire courte pour souligner une vertu et un vice La vertu triomphe à la fin. *La Cigale et la Fourmi, Le Corbeau et le Renard, Le Laboureur et ses Enfants* sont parmi les plus connues de ses fables.

1. freed 2. lame 3. unequal feet 4. the classical old Indian literary language 5. a prestigious society of writers founded in 1635 by Richelieu

Core Instruction

TEACHING CHRONIQUES

1. Have students read the introductory paragraph and the background information on page 170. Ask for volunteers to summarize what they have learned about fables. **(6 min.)**

2. Have students reread the last paragraph on page 170. Ask them to describe the typical features of La Fontaine's fables. Then have them answer question 2 in **Après la lecture. (4 min.)**

3. Draw a table on the board with the row heads, *Le Laboureur et ses Enfants* and *Le Corbeau et le Renard,* and the column heads, **personnages, résumé de l'histoire, morale.** Have students read each fable and provide the information called for. **(20 min.)**

4. Have students compare the two fables. Ask them if they agree with the morals. Then take a poll to see which of the two fables students prefer and why. Finally, have students answer the remaining questions in **Après la lecture. (4 min.)**

Le Laboureur et ses Enfants

Travaillez, prenez de la peine[1] :
C'est le fonds qui manque le moins.
Un riche Laboureur, sentant sa mort prochaine,
Fit venir ses enfants, leur parla sans témoins.
Gardez-vous[2], leur dit-il, de vendre l'héritage
Que nous ont laissé nos parents.
Un trésor est caché dedans.
Je ne sais pas l'endroit ; mais un peu de courage
Vous le fera trouver, vous en viendrez à bout.
Remuez[3] votre champ dès qu'on aura fait l'Oût.
Creusez[4], fouillez[5], bêchez[6] ; ne laissez nulle place
Où la main ne passe et repasse.
Le père mort, les fils vous retournent le champ
Deçà, delà[7], partout ; si bien qu'au bout de l'an
Il en rapporta davantage[8].
D'argent, point de caché. Mais le père fut sage[9]
De leur montrer avant sa mort
Que le travail est un trésor.

Le Corbeau et le Renard

Maître Corbeau, sur un arbre perché,
Tenait en son bec un fromage.
Maître Renard, par l'odeur alléché[10],
Lui tint à peu près ce langage :
« Hé ! bonjour, Monsieur du Corbeau,
Que vous êtes joli ! que vous me semblez beau !
Sans mentir, si votre ramage[11]
Se rapporte à votre plumage,
Vous êtes le phénix des hôtes de ces bois. »
À ces mots le Corbeau ne se sent pas de joie ;
Et pour montrer sa belle voix,
Il ouvre un large bec, laisse tomber sa proie[12].
Le Renard s'en saisit, et dit : « Mon bon Monsieur,
Apprenez que tout flatteur
Vit aux dépens de[13] celui qui l'écoute :
Cette leçon vaut bien un fromage, sans doute. »
Le Corbeau, honteux[14] et confus[15],
Jura[16], mais un peu tard, qu'on ne l'y prendrait plus[17].

APRÈS ▶ **la lecture**

🌼1.2, 4.2

1. Connaissez-vous les titres de ces fables en anglais ? Les avez-vous lues en vers ou en prose ?

2. À quelles sources La Fontaine a-t-il puisé ses fables ?

3. Quelle est la morale du *Laboureur et ses Enfants* ?

4. Que fait le renard pour manger le fromage du corbeau ?

1. to make an effort 2. take care not to 3. stir up 4. dig 5. dig up 6. turn over 7. here and there 8. was more profitable 9. wise 10. lured
11. song 12. prey 13. at the expense of 14. shameful 15. embaressed 16. swore 17. wouldn't be fooled again

Differentiated Instruction

SLOWER PACE LEARNERS

If slower pace students are having difficulty with these authentic, more complicated literary readings, read each fable aloud slowly for the class, pausing after every two to three sentences. Take questions and explain difficult vocabulary. Have advanced students summarize key ideas and/or paraphrase important sentences with simpler vocabulary. Then ask slower pace students simple comprehension questions. 🌼1.2

MULTIPLE INTELLIGENCES

Bodily-Kinesthetic Form several groups. Have group members select their favorite fable from among those they wrote for the Postreading activity. Ask them to turn this fable into a short play, with group members taking on the roles of actor(s), narrator, director, and costume/prop designer. Have the groups present their play to the class. 🌼1.3, 3.1

Answers

1. *The Farmer and His Sons, The Fox and the Raven.* Answers will vary.
2. Il s'est inspiré d'Ésope, d'Horace et de la Panchatantra.
3. Ça vaut la peine de travailler.
4. Il flatte le corbeau.

Connections

Social Studies Link

Anthropomorphism, a form of personification comes from the Greek **anthropos**, meaning *human*, and **morph**, meaning *form*. It is the attribution of human characteristics and qualities to non-humans. The term anthropomorphism is widely used in literature, where animals often take on the personality traits of human beings. Have students use the library or the Internet to find out more about anthropomorphism. Ask them to find another work of Francophone literature in which personification is used. 🌼3.1

Postreading

Have partners or small groups create their own fable. First, they should select a moral or a principle they would like to feature. Then they should create a story line to illustrate their moral and choose appropriate characters. Have students exchange their fables for editing and review before they turn in their final draft. 🌼1.3

ℝecherches

Have students search the Internet for free domain Web sites that feature other fables by La Fontaine. Ask them to print one fable they like and write a summary of the story and the moral. Then have them bring their fable to class and read it aloud to their classmates. Ask the class to repeat the moral of each fable. Remind students to document their sources. 🌼1.3

LES CONTES FRANÇAIS

CHRONIQUES

Resources

Practice:

Reading Strategies and Skills Handbook

Advanced Reader

Applying the Strategies

You may want to use the "Most Important Word" strategy from the *Reading Strategies and Skills Handbook* to encourage students to examine the text more closely.

READING PRACTICE

Strategy: Most Important Word

Reading Skill	When can I use this strategy?		
	Prereading	During Reading	Postreading
Identifying the Main Idea			✓
Making Generalizations			✓
Summarizing			✓

Strategy at a Glance: Most Important Word

- After reading a text, students discuss their responses to the theme of the work.
- Students decide either independently or in small groups what they think the Most Important Word in the text is, basing their answers on evidence from the reading.
- Students share and explain their choices.

Many times when you ask students to find the main idea of a story, or to make a generalization, or simply, "What did the story mean to you?", they can't do it, because they find the question too broad. One strategy that students can use to help them answer the question is **Most Important Word**. **Most Important Word** is a postreading strategy in which students decide which word in a text they think is the most important based on specific evidence in the text. As students decide which word is the most important, they begin to formulate their responses to the question: "What did the story mean to you?" **Most Important Word** leads to revealing discussions that encourage students to use this skill while they read and later reflect on what they have read.

Best Use of the Strategy

Most Important Word (Bleich 1975) is a good strategy to help students identify the theme of a reading and to make generalizations about it by breaking down the selection and deciding which word in the text carries the message that speaks to them.

Prereading

Ask students to name their favorite fairy tales and stories from their childhood. Write the French equivalents of the titles on the board. Then summarize these stories simply and have students identify them. **C'est l'histoire d'une jeune fille qui a deux demi-sœurs très méchantes, (Cendrillon).** ✿ 1.2

Language Examination

The **Chroniques** section helps students prepare for Section I, Part B: **Reading Comprehension.**

Les contes de fées, issus du folklore populaire, n'étaient pas destinés aux enfants. À leur origine, c'étaient des histoires racontées entre femmes et ayant leur racine dans l'imaginaire médiéval.

Charles Perrault est le plus connu des auteurs de contes. Contemporain de La Fontaine, Perrault est né à Paris en 1628. Ses contes les plus connus sont *La Belle au bois dormant*, *Les Contes de ma mère l'Oye*[1], *Cendrillon*, *Barbe-bleue*, *Le Chat botté*, *Peau d'Ane*, *Les Fées* et *Le Petit Chaperon rouge*. Perrault est élu a l'Académie française en 1671.

La Belle au bois dormant

Une jeune princesse, fille unique[2], est condamnée à une mort accidentelle par une méchante fée vexée de n'avoir pas été invitée au baptême de la Belle. Grâce à[3] l'intervention d'une bonne fée, au lieu de subir[4] la mort prédite, elle s'endort pour un sommeil de cent ans. Au terme des cent ans, un Prince l'éveille[5] puis l'épouse en secret. La Belle donne naissance[6] à une fille, l'Aurore, et à un garçon, le Jour, que sa belle-mère, l'Ogresse, cherche à dévorer: une ruse de son maître d'hôtel l'en empêche[7] et l'Ogresse meurt[8], victime de l'horrible vengeance qu'elle avait préparée.

1. goose 2. only daughter 3. Thanks to 4. to be subjected to 5. awakens her 6. gives birth 7. prevents 8. dies

Core Instruction

TEACHING CHRONIQUES

1. Have students read the introduction and the background information. Then ask them to tell who Charles Perrault was and why he is famous. **(5 min.)**

2. Have partners read the summary of *La belle au bois dormant*. Ask them to write their own summary of the story. **(10 min.)**

3. Have students read the summary of *Cendrillon* individually. Ask them to create five true-false statements about the story. As volunteers read their statements aloud, the class decides whether each one is true or false. Volunteers correct the false statements. **(12 min.)**

4. Finally, have students answer the questions in **Après la lecture. (6 min.)**

Cendrillon

Il existerait pas moins de 345 versions du conte de *Cendrillon*. La plus ancienne serait une histoire chinoise écrite au IXe siècle avant Jésus-Christ. Depuis celle de Perrault, écrite en 1697, *Cendrillon* a été largement reprise à la scène[1]. Un gentilhomme peiné par le deuil[2] de sa première épouse se remarie à la plus méchante des femmes. Cendrillon, sa première fille, est maltraitée par cette belle-mère dominatrice et ses deux filles. Elle doit s'occuper des tâches les plus pénibles de la maison. Un jour, un bal organisé par le Prince convie[3] toutes les jeunes femmes du royaume à s'y rendre.

Les sœurs se préparent tandis que Cendrillon pleure de ne pas pouvoir y aller. Sa marraine la fée vient la consoler et l'habiller somptueusement[4] pour qu'elle puisse se rendre au bal. Le Prince tombe tout de suite amoureux d'elle. À minuit, cependant, elle doit fuir[5] car l'enchantement[6] doit s'éteindre. En s'enfuyant, elle laisse tomber l'une de ses pantoufles de verre[7]. Le lendemain, le prince fait rechercher la propriétaire de la pantoufle dans tout le royaume. Personne ne peut la mettre sauf... Cendrillon. C'est ainsi qu'elle épouse le Prince.

APRÈS la lecture

🌸1.2

1. Est-ce que les contes ont été écrits pour les enfants?

2. Quels sont les points communs entre les contes et les fables?

3. Quelle est la différence entre le conte de La *Belle au bois dormant* et la version de Disney?

4. D'où viendrait la première version de *Cendrillon?*

---

1. remade into plays and movies 2. mourning 3. invites 4. lavishly 5. flee 6. speel 7. glass slippers

Differentiated Instruction

ADVANCED LEARNERS

Extension Ask advanced learners to imagine what happens to **Cendrillon** and the prince, as well as to her stepmother and stepsisters, after **Cendrillon** marries the prince. Have students write a paragraph to describe these characters' future life. You might have students read their paragraph to the class and have the class choose the most original or interesting one. 🌸1.3

MULTIPLE INTELLIGENCES

Visual Bring in a French illustrated children's version of another fairy tale or story to class, such as **Les trois petits cochons** or **Le petit chaperon rouge.** Show the illustrations one at a time in sequence and have students "tell" the story in French, with the illustrations as cues. You may wish to write important vocabulary words students will need on the board.

🌸1.3, 3.2

Answers

Answers will vary.
1. Non
2. La vertu triomphe.
3. La belle a des enfants dans le conte de Perrault.
4. d'une histoire chinoise ancienne

Comparisons

Comparing and Contrasting

Bring in the French version of either **La belle au bois dormant** or **Cendrillon,** preferably from a simplified, illustrated children's book. Read aloud several important segments, or have volunteers read them, showing the appropriate illustrations. Pause after each segment. Check comprehension, with true-false statements or simple questions. Then have students compare the French version of the story with the English version that they are familiar with. 🌸4.2

Postreading

Form several groups and have each one create a different version of **Cendrillon,** for example a modern day version, a version set in Africa, a science fiction version, or a version where the main character is a boy instead of a girl. Have groups present their story to the class. 🌸1.3

Recherches

Have students search the Internet for other fairy tales and stories by Charles Perrault or other Francophone authors and write a summary of one of them. Remind students to document their sources. 🌸3.2

Resources

Practice:

Reading Strategies and Skills
    Handbook

Advanced Reader

Applying the Strategies

You may want to use the "Say Something" strategy from the *Reading Strategies and Skills Handbook* to encourage students to examine the text more closely.

READING PRACTICE

Strategy: Say Something

Reading Skill	When can I use this strategy?		
	Prereading	During Reading	Postreading
Using Prior Knowledge (Drawing from Your Own Experience)	✓		
Monitoring Reading		✓	

Strategy at a Glance: Say Something

- The teacher models the strategy by "saying something" about a text with a colleague or by reading and discussing a typed **Say Something** dialogue with students.
- Students read a short text, stopping occasionally to discuss the text with a partner. In their conversations, they must make a prediction, ask a question, make a comment, or make a connection.
- Students practice **Say Something** using very short texts before using the strategy with longer assignments.

Often readers are unable to discuss something they have just finished reading because while they were reading, their eyes were merely moving over the words, their minds moving to thoughts of weekend plans, last night's phone conversations, or after-school sports events. They don't focus on what they are reading. To help students break that habit, we need to help them pay attention to what they are reading. **Say Something** is a very simple strategy that keeps readers focused on a text. **Say Something** helps students think about what they are reading by helping them see where they aren't paying attention.

Best Use of the Strategy

Say Something (Horste, Short, and Burke 1988) is a strategy in which students occasionally pause and "say something" to a partner about what they have read. This strategy helps students comprehend what they are reading by helping them to stay focused. Telling students to say something about the text, or giving them specific types of things they can say, keeps them interacting with the text and from that interaction comes meaning.

Getting the Strategy to Work

1. First, model the strategy. In order to model the **Say Something** strategy, it is best if you can recruit a colleague to help you demonstrate the strategy. Read aloud each piece of text you will comment on to the students, so they can understand what you

Prereading

Have students brainstorm the characteristics and features that make a movie a great love story. Then ask them to come up with their five favorite love stories in the history of cinema. Have volunteers summarize each movie and tell why they think it needs to be included in the top five.

Language Examination

The **Chroniques** section helps students prepare for Section I, Part B: **Reading Comprehension.**

CHRONIQUES
Quand le cinéma célèbre l'amour...

Le cinéma est riche en histoires d'amour. Voici quatre films français qui ont l'amour pour thème.

Cyrano de Bergerac

de Jean-Paul Rappeneau, avec Gérard Depardieu, Anne Brochet et Vincent Perez

Cyrano de Bergerac est une comédie dramatique de Jean-Paul Rappeneau.

Sorti en 1990, le film est une adaptation de la célèbre pièce en vers[1] que l'écrivain Edmond Rostand avait écrit en 1897.

Roxanne est belle et elle est aimée par deux hommes. L'un, Christian, est beau, mais il est timide et il n'ose pas avouer[2] son amour à Roxanne. L'autre, Cyrano, maîtrise[3] les mots et il sait parler aux femmes mais il n'est pas beau. Cyrano décide d'aider Christian à conquérir Roxanne[4].

Avec *Cyrano de Bergerac*, Jean-Paul Rappeneau a réussi une adaptation magnifique d'un grand classique de la littérature française, et le film a reçu de nombreux prix.

La Belle et la Bête

un film de Jean Cocteau, avec Jean Marais et Josette Day

La Belle et la Bête est la première adaptation cinématographique du conte de fées écrit en 1757 par Mme Leprince de Beaumont. C'est un film fantastique[5] en noir et blanc qui a été tourné[6] par Jean Cocteau en 1945.

À la suite d'un sort dont elle a été victime, la Bête vit seule dans un château sombre. Sa laideur[7] est repoussante[8] et la Bête en souffre[9]. Un jour, ignorant[10] qu'il est dans le jardin de la Bête, un homme cueille[11] une rose pour sa fille (la Belle). La Bête s'offense et, pour sauver son père, la Belle accepte d'aller vivre au château de la Bête.

La Belle et la Bête a remporté un immense succès et reste un grand moment du cinéma français, un magnifique conte de fées pour adultes qui est riche en émotion et en poésie.

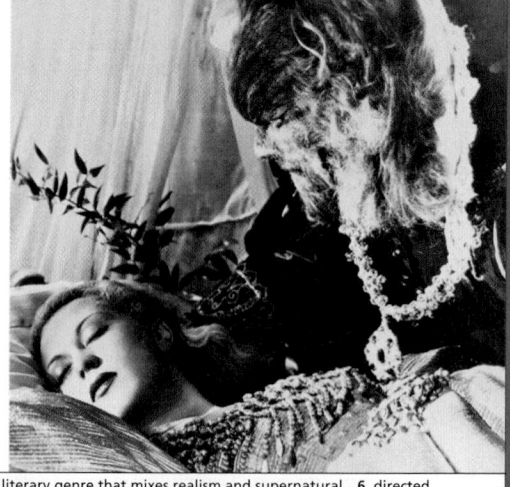

1. play in verse   2. doesn't dare reveal   3. masters   4. win Roxanne's love   5. literary genre that mixes realism and supernatural   6. directed   7. ugliness   8. repulsive   9. suffers from it   10. not knowing   11. picks

Core Instruction

TEACHING CHRONIQUES

1. Ask students to look at the titles of the movies and the photos on these pages. Ask if they've seen or heard of any of these movies, or if they're familiar with any of these stories or the actors mentioned. **(3 min.)**

2. Have students read the four movie summaries and jot down important keywords. **(15 min.)**

3. Have students work with a partner to answer questions 1–4 in **Après la lecture.** They should use their notes as needed. **(10 min.)**

4. Have volunteers answer question 5 in **Après la lecture** orally. **(5 min.)**

Un long dimanche de fiançailles

un drame de Jean-Pierre Jeunet
sorti en 2004, avec Audrey Tautou,
Gaspard Ulliel et Albert Dupontel

En 1919, Mathilde a 19 ans. Un jour, on lui annonce que son fiancé, Manech, qui était parti à la guerre, est mort.

Mathilde refuse de le croire car son intuition lui dit que Manech est toujours en vie. Mathilde commence alors une véritable enquête[1] pour découvrir la vérité sur le sort[2] de Manech.

Sorti en 2004 et adapté d'un roman de Sébastien Japrisot, *Un long dimanche de fiançailles* est l'histoire émouvante[3] d'une quête[4] désespérée pour retrouver un amour perdu.

Un homme et une femme

un film de Claude Lelouch,
avec Anouk Aimée et Jean-Louis Trintignant

Un homme et une femme est une comédie dramatique qui est sortie en 1966.

C'est l'histoire de la rencontre, sur une plage, d'une femme dont le mari est mort, et d'un homme dont la femme est morte. Les deux personnages vont se découvrir et de cette rencontre, une histoire d'amour d'une grande beauté va naître.

Pour beaucoup, *Un homme et une femme* est un des chefs-d'œuvre[5] du cinéma français.

De l'interprétation exceptionnelle des acteurs à la mise en scène[6] originale de Lelouch, qui choisit de filmer certaines scènes en couleur et d'autres en noir et blanc, *Un homme et une femme* est un film troublant[7] et inoubliable[8] à voir et à revoir. Le film a gagné la Palme d'Or du Festival de Cannes[9] en 1966.

APRÈS la lecture

 1.2, 1.3

1. Comment sont les trois personnages principaux du film *Cyrano de Bergerac?*

2. Décris la vie de la Bête avant l'arrivée de la Belle dans son château.

3. Dans le film *Un homme et une femme,* qu'est-ce qui est original dans la mise en scène de Claude Lelouch?

4. Résume la quête de Mathilde dans le film *Un long dimanche de fiançailles.*

5. Lequel de ces films aimerais-tu voir? Pourquoi?

1. investigation 2. fate 3. moving 4. quest 5. masterpiece 6. directing 7. unsettling 8. unforgettable
9. French equivalent to the Sundance Film Festival

Differentiated Instruction

SLOWER PACE LEARNERS

To help slower pace learners with the answers to questions 1–5 in **Après la lecture,** provide several multiple-choice options for them.
🌸 1.2

SPECIAL LEARNING NEEDS

**Students with Learning Disabilities/
Dyslexia** As students begin the Postreading activity, suggest they answer what, who, where, when, and why to help them with their movie plot summary. Encourage them also to use timelines and charts to organize their ideas and describe the events in the movie in chronological order.
🌸 1.3

Answers

1. Roxanne est belle. Christian est beau, mais timide. Cyrano maîtrise les mots, mais il n'est pas beau.
2. Sa vie est sombre.
3. Claude Lelouch choisit de filmer certaines scènes en couleur et d'autres en noir et blanc.
4. Mathilde commence une enquête pour decouvrir le sort de Manech, son fiancé.
5. Answers will vary.

Teaching Suggestion

If available at your school or your local video store, you might watch and discuss an excerpt from one of the movies mentioned here, or any other appropriate Francophone movie available. Be sure to preview the excerpt you intend to show to make sure it is appropriate. 🌸 5.2

Postreading

Ask students to write a review of a movie they really like. They should give the title, the director, and the main actors. They should also summarize the plot and if applicable, mention any awards this movie has received. Finally, they should give and justify their personal opinion of the movie.
🌸 5.2

Recherches

Have students use the Internet to research Francophone cinema. You might give them a list of topics to choose from, such as well-known movies that you feel are appropriate, famous directors and actors, or the Cannes film festival. Have volunteers present their findings in class. Remind students to document their sources. 🌸 1.2

L'amour et le mariage

« Le respect et l'amour doivent être si bien proportionnés qu'ils se soutiennent[1] sans que ce respect étouffe[2] l'amour. » Citation de l'écrivain Pascal au sujet du mariage dans le *Discours sur les passions de l'amour*

Où se marie-t-on en France?

En France, on doit obligatoirement se marier à la mairie[3], devant le maire[4], avec deux témoins[5] (un pour le marié et un pour la mariée). C'est la cérémonie civile. Si on le souhaite, on peut aussi avoir une cérémonie religieuse. Aujourd'hui, environ 40% des mariés choisissent d'avoir une cérémonie religieuse en plus du mariage civil.

Les jeunes Français et l'amour

Contrairement aux jeunes Américains, les jeunes Français ne sortent pas souvent en couple. Le rendez-vous à l'américaine, ou *date*, n'existe pas vraiment. On préfère sortir avec un groupe de copains. En général, les jeunes Français se retrouvent en ville et ils vont au café, au cinéma, au restaurant ou au concert. Ils aiment aussi organiser des soirées chez eux.

1. complement each other 2. suffocates 3. city hall 4. mayor 5. witnesses

---

Resources

Practice:
Reading Strategies and Skills Handbook
Advanced Reader

Applying the Strategies

You may want to use the "Anticipation Guide" strategy from the *Reading Strategies and Skills Handbook* to encourage students to examine the text more closely.

READING PRACTICE

Strategy: Anticipation Guide

Reading Skill	When can I use this strategy?		
	Prereading	During Reading	Postreading
Making Predictions	✓		
Using Prior Knowledge	✓		
Analyzing Cause and Effect Relationships		✓	
Analyzing Persuasive Techniques			✓
Making Generalizations			✓

Strategy at a Glance: Anticipation Guide

• The teacher writes the Anticipation Guide, a set of generalizations based on issues in the text and designed to promote discussion and predictions about the selection.
• Students mark whether they agree or disagree with each statement, then discuss their responses.
• While students read, they take notes on the issues in the guide as those issues are revealed in the text.
• After reading, students look at their responses again to see whether they still agree or disagree with the statements.

Both younger and older children do it. They constantly ask what's going on and where they are being taken. They ask what the doctor is going to do before the doctor does it, and they plan what they'll say when they are approaching parents with special requests. Adults do it. We pick up travel brochures before we travel, study maps before we make a car trip, and check out the checkbook before we make a purchase. We all do it—we try to anticipate what's going to happen before it actually happens.

Good readers consciously try to anticipate what a text is about before they begin reading. They look at the cover, art, title, genre, author, headings, graphs, charts, length, print size, inside flaps, and back cover. Some students read the bibliographic information on the copyright page. They ask friends, "Is this any good?" They do anything to find out something about a text before they begin reading.

Struggling readers, on the other hand, often don't do that; they are told to read something, and once the text is in hand, they just begin. They often skip titles and background information, hardly ever look read book jackets, and rarely look through the text

Prereading

Before you begin this **Chroniques** section, ask students to brainstorm words and ideas they associate with love and marriage. Ask them to name factors that they think can contribute to a good relationship and those that they feel can create contention. Have a volunteer take notes on the board for future reference.

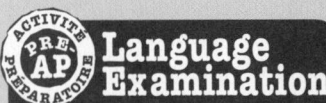

ACTIVITÉ PRÉPARATOIRE PRE AP Language Examination

The **Chroniques** section helps students prepare for Section I, Part B: **Reading Comprehension.**

Core Instruction

TEACHING CHRONIQUES

1. Have students read the articles on page 176. Ask them to find the two differences between French and American customs that are mentioned in the text. **(4 min.)**

2. Have students read the articles on page 177. Then have them look at the photos and ask them to describe what they see, using the information they gathered from reading the text. **(15 min.)**

3. Have students answer the questions in **Après la lecture.**

4. Finally, ask volunteers to tell you which one of the traditions presented here they find most interesting or unusual and to explain why. **(6 min.)**

Quelques traditions du monde francophone:

En Polynésie française

Les Polynésiennes portent souvent une fleur à l'oreille. Le côté où elles portent cette fleur révèle leur situation maritale. Si la fleur est portée à l'oreille droite, la jeune femme est célibataire[1]. Si la fleur est portée à l'oreille gauche, cela veut dire que son coeur est pris.

En Haïti

Dans certaines parties de l'île d'Haïti, la demande en mariage doit être écrite. Le jeune homme explique ses désirs et ses intentions dans sa lettre. Il met ensuite la lettre dans une enveloppe et il écrit son nom sur l'enveloppe. Son frère ou sa sœur apporte la lettre à la jeune fille. Si elle ouvre l'enveloppe tout de suite, cela veut dire qu'elle accepte. Si elle ne l'ouvre pas, cela veut dire qu'elle refuse.

En Tunisie

Avant la cérémonie du mariage, les femmes se retrouvent et appliquent du henné[2] sur les cheveux, les mains et les pieds de la future mariée tout en chantant des chants traditionnels et en buvant du thé. Les peintures corporelles[3] au henné sont souvent très élaborées.

Au Maroc

La tradition de la negafa existe depuis plusieurs centaines d'années. La negafa est l'habilleuse de la mariée[4] au Maroc. Elle lui loue des vêtements et des bijoux. Son rôle est de s'assurer que la mariée sera magnifique au moment de la cérémonie.

APRÈS ▶ la lecture

🎴 1.2, 1.3

1. Est-ce qu'en France, il est possible d'avoir seulement une cérémonie de mariage religieuse? Explique ta réponse.

2. Si une jeune Polynésienne porte une fleur à l'oreille droite, elle est mariée?

3. Que doit faire une jeune Haïtienne qui n'accepte pas une demande en mariage?

4. Que fait la negafa au Maroc?

---

1. single   2. henna   3. body paintings   4. the woman who dresses the bride

---

Cultures

🎴 Practices and Perspectives

With the class, prepare a list of questions about traditions and customs related to love and marriage. If your class corresponds with a school in a Francophone country, e-mail your questions to that school and ask that the students there e-mail back their answers. Read and discuss their responses in class. Or, have your students use their list of questions to interview Francophone pen pals on an appropriate Web site and report back to the class. 🎴 5.1

Postreading

Organize a class debate on the topic of marriage. Have students refer to the notes they wrote on the board in the Prereading activity. Ask them to come up with 10 "rules" couples should follow to ensure a long and happy marriage. 🎴 3.1

Recherches

Have students use the Internet to research additional culture-specific traditions related to dating and marriage in the Francophone world and to share their findings with the class. Remind students to document their sources. 🎴 3.2

Differentiated Instruction

ADVANCED LEARNERS

Challenge Write on the board the following quote by famous French author Françoise Sagan: «**Aimer, ce n'est pas seulement 'aimer bien'; c'est surtout comprendre.**» Have advanced students explain what Sagan means. Then ask students whether they agree or not with Sagan and have them justify their position. 🎴 1.2, 3.2

MULTIPLE INTELLIGENCES

Interpersonal If you have exchange students, or students with different cultural backgrounds in your class or school, you might ask them if they would be willing to share anecdotes and information about marriage and love in their cultures. They could make short presentations to the class, followed by a question and answer forum. 🎴 1.3, 2.1, 4.2

Les grands couples de l'histoire

Voici les portraits de quelques couples célèbres de l'histoire de France

Louis XVI et Marie-Antoinette

Louis XVI a 20 ans quand il devient roi de France, en 1774. Sa femme, Marie-Antoinette d'Autriche, a 19 ans. C'est une période difficile pour le jeune roi qui a peu d'expérience et qui hérite d'un royaume où le peuple a faim et où le mécontentement[1] augmente[2] de jour en jour. La reine, elle, aime le luxe et elle dépense des sommes d'argent énormes, ce qui la rend impopulaire. Elle est aussi mêlée[3] à plusieurs scandales. De plus, elle est contre les réformes demandées par le peuple et contre l'abolition des privilèges. On l'accuse même de pousser le roi à résister aux changements. Quand la Révolution éclate[4], le couple s'enfuit[5], mais Louis XVI et Marie-Antoinette seront tous les deux arrêtés, puis guillotinés en 1793.

Henri II et Diane de Poitiers

Henri II, qui est né en 1519, a été roi de France de 1547 à 1559. C'est le deuxième fils du célèbre roi François Ier. En 1533, Henri II se marie avec Catherine de Medicis, une Italienne, mais quelques années plus tard, il tombe amoureux de Diane de Poitiers, une veuve plus âgée que lui dont la beauté était célèbre et avec laquelle il va avoir une liaison pendant toute sa vie. Intelligent et passionnée, Diane de Poitiers a eu beaucoup d'influence sur Henri II. Pour lui montrer son amour, Henri II lui a offert le magnifique château de Chenonceau, un geste qui a rendu la reine, Catherine de Médicis, furieuse. À la mort du roi, la reine a repris le château et fait construire la magnifique salle de bal au-dessus du Cher.

1. discontent 2. increases 3. mixed up 4. breaks out 5. flees

---

Resources

Practice:

Reading Strategies and Skills Handbook

Advanced Reader

Applying the Strategies

You may want to use the "It Says. . . I Say. . ."strategy from the *Reading Strategies and Skills Handbook* to encourage students to examine the text more closely.

READING PRACTICE

Strategy: It Says ... I Say

Reading Skill	When can I use this strategy?		
	Prereading	During Reading	Postreading
Making Inferences		✓	
Making Generalizations and Drawing Conclusions			✓

Strategy at a Glance: It Says ... I Say

- The teacher creates a model **It Says ... I Say** chart for the classroom. The chart consists of four columns: a question that requires an inference (**Question**), what the text says about the question (**It Says**), what students already know about that information (**I Say**), and their inference (**And So**).
- The teacher models the strategy using an inferential question based on a familiar story.
- Students practice making inferences by using the chart regularly to explain their answers to inferential questions.

Please read the following: The bridnic scroffled the ibnic. The ibnic scroffled the flibberond. The flibberond scroffled the webernet. Now answer the following questions:

1. What did the bridnic scroffle?
2. Did the ibnic scroffel the flibberond or the bridnic?
3. What scroffled the webernet?

Here are the answers:

a. The bridnic scroffled the ibnic.
b. The ibnic scroffled the flibberond.
c. The flibberond scroffled the webernet.

You were probably able to answer all those questions correctly, because to do so, you didn't have to understand what a bridnic or an ibnic, or even a flibberond, is. You just needed to match words in the questions to words in the text. But look at the next question:

4. Would you rather be a bridnic, an ibnic, or a flibberond?

Prereading

Before you begin this **Chroniques** section, have students describe the illustrations on these pages. Then ask them if they've heard of any of the French historical figures in the titles. Have volunteers share what they already know about these people.

Language Examination

The **Chroniques** section helps students prepare for Section I, Part B: **Reading Comprehension.**

Core Instruction

TEACHING CHRONIQUES

1. Write the following on the board **la Révolution, Catherine de Médicis, Chenonceau, la Martinique, la Deuxième Guerre mondiale, le général de Gaulle.** Ask students to quickly scan the reading to find out what or who they are or with what or with whom they are associated. **(4 min.)**

2. Have students read the articles one at a time and answer the corresponding question(s) in **Après la lecture.** Encourage them to ask questions if they are having difficulty and explain any words or expressions students are having trouble with. Have volunteers read aloud their answers to the questions in **Après la lecture. (25 min.)**

3. Finally, have students select one of the famous couples mentioned in the reading and write a short paragraph in which they summarize why they are famous. **(5 min.)**

Napoléon Bonaparte et Joséphine de Beauharnais

Joséphine de Beauharnais est née à la Martinique en 1763. En 1796, elle épouse Napoléon Bonaparte, un jeune officier de l'armée française d'origine corse[1]. Napoléon se distingue[2] rapidement par ses victoires militaires. Leur vie de couple est tumultueuse. Napoléon est très jaloux et Joséphine refuse de le suivre dans ses campagnes[3]. En 1804, Napoléon se proclame empereur des Français et Joséphine devient ainsi impératrice, mais en 1809, Napoléon répudie Joséphine parce qu'elle ne lui a pas donné d'héritier[4]. Elle va cependant garder son titre d'impératrice et elle restera, malgré leur séparation, l'unique grand amour de Napoléon.

Lucie et Raymond Aubrac

Lucie et Raymond Aubrac ont fait partie de la Résistance pendant la Deuxième Guerre mondiale. La Résistance est le mouvement qui a lutté contre[5] l'occupation des armées de l'Allemagne nazie. En 1943, Raymond Aubrac est arrêté par la Gestapo, la police secrète allemande. C'est sa femme, Lucie, qui va former un commando armé pour le libérer. Ils quittent alors la France et rejoignent[6] le général de Gaulle[7], chef de la France libre, à Londres pour continuer à organiser la Résistance.

APRÈS › la lecture

🌼1.2

1. Pourquoi Marie-Antoinette n'était-elle pas une reine populaire?

2. Pourquoi est-ce que Napoléon a répudié Joséphine en 1809?

3. Qu'est-ce que c'est, la Résistance?

4. Pourquoi est-ce que Lucie et Raymond Aubrac sont allés à Londres?

1. who was originally from Corsica 2. distinguishes himself 3. military campaigns 4. heir 5. fought against 6. join
7. a famous general who encouraged the French to fight back and later became president.

Differentiated Instruction

ADVANCED LEARNERS

Extension Have advanced learners interview Francophone pen pals or native speakers of French in your area to find out who these people think were the most influential historical figures in their country. Have students report their findings to the class. 🌼3.2, 5.1

MULTIPLE INTELLIGENCES

Visual Prepare a list of the important events mentioned in the reading, such as **Henri II devient roi, Louis XVI et Marie-Antoinette sont guillotinés, Napoléon devient empereur, Raymond Aubrac est arrêté,** etc. Ask students to find the corresponding dates in the reading and have a volunteer create a timeline of these events on the board. 🌼1.2

Answers

1. Elle aime le luxe et elle dépense des sommes d'argent énormes.
2. Elle ne lui a pas donné d'héritier.
3. la lutte contre l'occupation des Allemands
4. pour échapper à la Gestapo et rejoindre le général de Gaulle

Comparisons

History Link

Ask students to identify the important dates and events mentioned in the reading. Have a volunteer write these on the board. Then ask students what was happening around the same dates in America. You might bring a history book or an encyclopedia to help students. Have the volunteer at the board take notes. Finally, ask students to comment on all these historical events and to compare them.

🌼4.2

Postreading

Form several groups and assign one of these periods in French history to each one: **le Moyen Âge, la Renaissance, l'ancien régime (la monarchie absolue), le Premier empire, la Première Guerre mondiale, la Deuxième Guerre mondiale et la Résistance.** Have groups use the Internet or your library's resources to research the important events that took place during those times. Have them prepare an oral presentation for the class. 🌼3.1

Recherches

Louis XVI (1754–1793) was King of France and Navarre from 1774 until 1791, and then King of the French from 1791 to 1792, when he was arrested and tried for treason. He was executed in January of 1793, signaling the end of absolutist monarchy in France and eventually leading to the rise of Napoleon. Have students use the Internet to research other French kings and report their findings. Remind them to document their sources. 🌼3.1

Géoculture Overview

L'Amérique francophone

Bienvenue! This section is designed to familiarize the students with the geographic location, history, and cultural practices of the region to be explored. It provides a guide for classroom discussion and discovery of the differences and similarities of the student's own culture and that of the French-speaking world.

50-Minute Lesson Plans

Day 1

Lesson Sequence

Géoculture: L'Amérique francophone, pp. 180–181

- Ask students to locate Canada, Louisiana, and Haiti on the map. Basing their conjectures on geographic location and features, students should discuss differences in climate, architecture, and economy among the three places. **10 min.**
- Go over the photos and captions with the students. **10 min.**
- See Map Activities, p. 180. **5 min.**
- Discuss Background Information, p. 180. **11 min.**
- Complete **Géo-quiz. 1 min.**
- Show **Géoculture** video. **3 min.**
- Have students answer **Questions,** p. 181. **10 min.**

Optional Resources

- **Savais-tu que...?,** p. 181
- Thinking Critically, p. 179B
- Multiple Intelligences, p. 179B

Homework Suggestions

Online Practice (**go.hrw.com,** Keyword: BD3 CH5)
Interactive Tutor, Ch. 5

1.1, 2.2, 3.1, 4.2

Day 2

Lesson Sequence

Géoculture: L'Amérique francophone, pp. 182–183

- Briefly revisit main points about geography. **5 min.**
- Go over the photos and captions with the students. **8 min.**
- Ask students to compare the history of Haiti and Canada. How did these two countries become independent?, What forms of government did and do these two nations have? **5 min.**
- Have students answer **As-tu compris?** questions, p. 183. **7 min.**
- Play the Map Game on p. 179B. **25 min.**

Optional Resources

- Slower Pace Learners, p. 179B ◆
- Interdisciplinary Links, pp. 182–183
- Research Online!, p. 179B
- **Prépare-toi pour le quiz,** p. 179B

Homework Suggestions

Activité, p. 183
Study for the **Géoculture** quiz.

1.2, 3.1, 3.2, 4.2

90-Minute Lesson Plan

Block 1

Lesson Sequence

Géoculture: L'Amérique francophone, pp. 180–183

- Ask students to locate Canada, Louisiana, and Haiti on the map. Basing their conjectures on geographic location and features, students should discuss differences in climate, architecture, and economy among the three places. **10 min.**
- Go over the photos and captions with the students. **20 min.**
- See Map Activities, p. 180. **5 min.**
- Discuss Background Information, p. 180. **10 min.**
- Complete **Géo-quiz. 1 min.**
- Show **Géoculture** video. **4 min.**
- Have students answer **Questions,** p. 181. **5 min.**
- Have students answer **As-tu compris?** questions, p. 183. **5 min.**
- Ask students to compare the history of Haiti and Canada. How did these two countries become independent? What forms of government did and do these two nations have?. **5 min.**
- Play the Map Game on p. 179B. **25 min.**

Optional Resources

- **Savais-tu que ...?,** p. 181
- Slower Pace Learners, p. 179B ◆
- Multiple Intelligences, p. 179B
- Thinking Critically, p. 179B
- Research Online!, p. 179B
- Interdisciplinary Links, pp. 182–183
- **Prépare-toi pour le quiz,** p. 179B

Homework Suggestions

Online Practice (**go.hrw.com,** Keyword: BD3 CH5)
Interactive Tutor, Ch. 5
Activité, p. 183
Study for the **Géoculture** quiz.

1.2, 2.2 3.1, 3.2, 4.2

KEY

▲ Advanced Learners ◆ Slower Pace Learners ● Special Learning Needs

Géoculture

Differentiated Instruction

Slower Pace Learners

Building on Previous Skills Before reading **L'histoire: L'Amérique francophone,** students should create a graphic organizer, grouping persons, events, and dates they would expect to find on the timeline. As students read the timeline, they should fill in their organizers with information they did not include previously.

personnes	événements	dates
Christophe Colomb	la découverte de l'Amérique	1492

🏵 3.1

Multiple Intelligences

Kinesthetic Form groups of three students. Assign each group either Canada, Haiti, or Louisiana. Have students role-play a trip to the assigned state or country to include a tour guide and two tourists.

🏵 1.1, 3.1

Thinking Critically

Comparing and contrasting Quebec is Canada's northernmost province. Winter usually lasts from November to April. Have students compare life in Montreal or Quebec City to life in their own city or town. Students should consider the impact the climate has on the activities and traditions of the inhabitants. They should also investigate the influence the climate has on housing and infrastructure in general.

🏵 2.2, 4.2

Quiz Preparation/Enrichment

Map Game

This game is similar to Scrabble®. Cut heavy paper into one-inch squares. Leave a third of them blank and write the French alphabet on the rest. Make extra squares with the most common letters: vowels, s, t, etc. A blank may serve as any letter and as a hyphen. Place the letters face down in one pile and the blanks in another pile. Each student picks ten letters and five blanks. Students arrange letters and blanks to form the name of a geographical feature shown on the map. Once students have formed a name, they should write it down and reuse the letters and blanks to form new names. The student with the most names and the student with the longest word are the winners.

Prépare-toi pour le quiz

1. Form three to four groups. Give each group a map of America without labels. Students should shade in Louisiana, Canada, and Haiti and indicate the location of the capital of each of the shaded areas and provide its name.

2. Have students work in groups of three to discuss the sights and history of Haiti, Canada, and Louisiana. One member of the group should play a Haitian; another, a citizen of Quebec; and another, a Cajun. Students should praise the sights and history of their assigned country or state. 🏵 1.1, 3.1

Research Online!

Journaux Students compare an article about a political or historical event published in the online version of their local newspaper with an article about the same event published in the online version of a Quebec or Haitian newspaper. Are the descriptions similar or different? What cultural values and attitudes might influence the interpretation of events? Have students present their conclusions to the class. Students should document their sources by noting the names and the URLs of all sites they consulted. 🏵 3.2, 4.2

Resources

Planning:
Lesson Planner
 One-Stop Planner

Presentation:
 Teaching Transparencies
Cartes 1, 5
 DVD Program, Disc 1
Géoculture

Practice:
Cahier d'activités
Media Guide
 Interactive Tutor, Disc 1

Map
ACTIVITIES

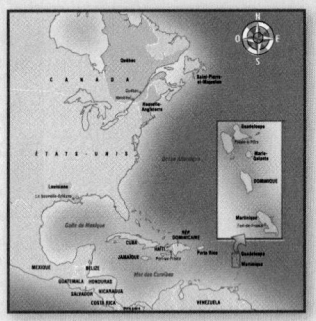

1. Have students find a map of Louisiana and locate New Orleans. Ask them to name the river that forms part of the eastern state border (**le Mississippi**). Then have them name two major cities on the river (**Baton Rouge, La Nouvelle-Orléans**). Ask why they think New Orleans has long been one of the most important ports in the south. (It is located on the Mississippi River leading to the Gulf of Mexico; it can handle traffic back and forth between the northern U.S. and the Caribbean.)

2. Have students look at the map of **L'Amérique francophone** and ask them which country shares an island with Haiti (**la République dominicaine**).

DVD
Géoculture

Géoculture
L'Amérique francophone

▲ **LA LOUISIANE: Les bayous** se trouvent dans tout le sud de la Louisiane. Un bayou est un cours d'eau qui passe lentement à travers les marais ou les terrains bas. **1**

▼ **LA LOUISIANE: La plantation Melrose** est remarquable parce qu'elle a été établie par une ancienne esclave africaine et son fils. **1**

➤ **LA LOUISIANE: Le Vieux Carré** est l'ancien quartier français de La Nouvelle-Orléans. Son architecture, ses restaurants et ses clubs de jazz en ont fait le cœur touristique et historique de la ville. **1**

Savais-tu que...?

Une grande partie de La Nouvelle-Orléans se trouve au-dessous (*under*) du niveau de la mer. Entourée d'eau, la ville a été inondée après l'ouragan Katrina, en 2005.

Background Information

Geography

Haiti is a mountainous country, shaped like a horseshoe on its side. About the size of the state of Maryland, it shares the island of Hispaniola with the Dominican Republic.

Canada is the second largest country in the world, stretching north to the Arctic Circle. It is divided into ten provinces and three territories.

Louisiana is made up primarily of prairie land, marshland, and rolling hills. Altitude ranges from 535 feet at its highest to eight feet below sea level.

History

Port Royale, established on the east coast in 1605, was the first French settlement in Canada. Quebec City and Montreal were settled a few decades later. The French developed the fishing industry on the east coast and the fur trade inland. They ruled until 1763 when they lost the colony to the British. One year later, the Quebec Act was passed giving French Canadians the right to practice their religion (Catholicism), to use French in courts of law, and the right to hold public office.

L'Amérique francophone

VIDEO OPTION

▶ **Géoculture**

marée basse   marée haute

➤ **LE CANADA: La baie de Fundy** a des marées spectaculaires. Elle a aussi un riche écosystème marin. Plusieurs espèces de baleines y vivent. ❷

◀ **LE CANADA: La forêt acadienne** abrite une grande variété d'arbres et d'oiseaux migrateurs. Elle est aussi la base économique de la région. ❷

▲ **LE CANADA: Saint-Laurent,** dans le Manitoba, est une communauté de Métis, un des grands peuples aborigènes du Canada. ❷

▲ **HAÏTI: La Citadelle** a été construite au début du XIXᵉ siècle pour défendre Haïti. C'est un important symbole national. ❸

Géo-quiz 1.2, 3.1
Qu'est-ce que c'est, un bayou?
Où est-ce qu'il y en a?
Dans le sud de la Louisiane.

Cultures

Products and Perspectives

Jazz was born in New Orleans around the turn of the 20th century. Jazz blends several Western and African-American musical traditions, including ragtime, marching bands, spirituals, and the blues. Some of the elements that make jazz unique are *blue notes,* notes falling between two other notes on the western scale, *polyrhythm,* putting one pattern of rhythm on top of another with equal emphasis, and *improvisation.* The first Jazz musicians were African-Americans and Creoles who often took familiar songs and used these elements to turn them into something fresh and new. Ask students why many consider jazz uniquely American. 2.2

Language Note

The **Métis** are descendents of the indigenous peoples of Canada and Europeans, mainly French fur trade workers. Many of them once spoke **Michif,** a language that developed over two hundred years ago due to frequent contact between French and Cree speakers. **Michif** is a highly complex mixed language, using grammatical structures from both French and Cree. Although there have been attempts to revive the use of **Michif,** it is now considered an endangered language. Ask students if they know of a mixing of two different languages in the United States. 4.1

Savais-tu que...?

Students might be interested in the following facts about Francophone America.

• English and French are Canada's two official languages. However, there are two types of French spoken in Canada, Quebec French and Acadian French. The latter is the ancestor of Cajun French spoken in Louisiana.

• Haiti's name comes from the Arawak/Taino (the island's original inhabitants) word *ayti* meaning "mountainous land."

• Louisiana is the only state in the U.S. that does not have counties. Instead, it is has parishes.

Questions   1.2

1. **Pourquoi la plantation Melrose est-elle remarquable? (Elle a été établie par une ancienne esclave et son fils.)**

2. **Comment s'appelle le centre historique de La Nouvelle-Orléans? (le Vieux Carré)**

3. **Où est-ce qu'on peut trouver des marées impressionnantes et des baleines? (dans la baie de Fundy)**

4. **Qu'est-ce qui forme la base économique de l'Acadie? (la forêt acadienne)**

L'histoire
L'Amérique francophone

Comparisons

Comparing and Contrasting

Jean-Jacques Dessalines, born a slave, was one of the primary leaders of the Haitian Revolution. After defeating troops sent by Napoleon, he declared Haiti an independent nation on January 1, 1804. A council of generals declared him Governor General, and he became emperor in 1805. He was a harsh ruler, who maintained tight control of the economy. In 1806, he was killed. Although Dessalines was not well thought of for many years, he is now considered the father of the Haitian nation. The day of his death, October 17, is a national holiday, and the national anthem, *La Dessalinienne,* is named for him. Have students look up the French lyrics of *La Dessalinienne,* and if possible, listen to them. Ask them what sentiments the lyrics express. Then have them compare and contrast the anthem to *The Star Spangled Banner.* 🎴 4.1, 4.2

Connections

History Link

The predominantly Francophone Province of **Québec** has long had a rocky relationship with the rest of English-speaking Canada. The beginnings of the separatist movement date back to the mid-18th century. Finally, in 1980, **Québec** voted on whether to separate from the rest of Canada. Sixty percent of the population voted "no". In 1995, the vote was a lot closer. Only 1% more of the people voted "no" than "yes." In honor of struggle and hardships, the province adopted the slogan **"Je me souviens."** *(I remember.)* Have students read about the separatist movement in **Québec** and its underlying causes, then create a cause-and-effect chart reflecting what they learned. 🎴 3.1

1492
En 1492, **Christophe Colomb** a découvert l'île où se trouvent Haïti et la République Dominicaine. Il y a rencontré les indigènes **Taïnos** et **Arawaks.** Colomb leur a donné le nom d'*Indiens* parce qu'il pensait être arrivé en Inde.

1755
Entre 1755 et 1763, les Anglais ont expulsé beaucoup de francophones qui vivaient en Acadie, région de l'est du Canada. La plupart ont émigré à Saint-Domingue (l'actuel Haïti) et en Louisiane. On a appelé cette déportation des Acadiens le **Grand Dérangement.** Les Acadiens établis en Louisiane sont les ancêtres des Cajuns d'aujourd'hui.

1682
En 1682, l'explorateur français **Robert Cavelier de la Salle** a descendu le Mississippi jusqu'au golfe du Mexique. Il a pris possession de ce territoire au nom de la France et l'a appelé Louisiane en l'honneur du roi de France, Louis XIV.

1791–1804
En 1791, il y a eu une révolte des esclaves noirs contre les colons français. Cela a été le début de la guerre pour l'indépendance haïtienne. En 1804, **Jean-Jacques Dessalines,** général de l'armée des esclaves, a déclaré l'indépendance d'Haïti. L'ancienne colonie française a été le premier état noir des temps modernes.

TEACHING L'HISTOIRE

1. Ask students if they remember who the early explorers of the Americas were and list them on the board. Then ask them when the French came to the Americas, how much territory they had, and where was it. Ask them to recall any armed conflicts in the Americas in which the French participated.

2. Discuss each picture in the timeline and call on volunteers to read each caption. Check comprehension with the **As-tu compris?** questions.

3. Have students read the captions again individually and do the **Activité.**

4. Ask students which of these events they feel had the greatest impact on the history of the region and the world and why.

1800	1900	1950	1980	1990	2000

1803

En 1803, **Napoléon** a vendu le territoire de la Louisiane aux États-Unis pour 15 millions de dollars. À cette époque, c'était une vaste région qui comprenait la plus grande partie du centre des États-Unis. Par cet achat, les États-Unis ont doublé leur territoire.

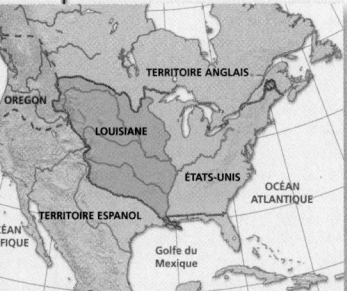

1957–1986

François Duvalier, dit *Papa Doc,* a gagné les élections présidentielles en Haïti en 1957. Il s'est déclaré président à vie en 1964. Sous sa dictature, des milliers de Haïtiens ont été tués ou se sont exilés. Après sa mort, en 1971, son fils, **Jean-Claude Duvalier**, dit *Bébé Doc,* a continué la dictature de la terreur jusqu'en 1986.

1982

En 1982, **le Canada et l'Angleterre** ont signé une loi qui a donné la souveraineté au Canada. Cette loi a établi le français et l'anglais comme les deux langues officielles du pays.

1995

En 1995, **la province francophone du Québec** a décidé pour la seconde fois de son histoire de ne pas se séparer du reste du Canada. Mais le «non à la séparation» ne l'a emporté qu'à une toute petite majorité des voix (50,58% contre 49,42%).

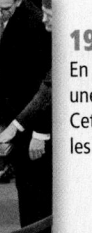

Interactive
TUTOR

Activité

⊛1.2, 3.1

1. Pourquoi Colomb a-t-il donné le nom d'Indiens aux Taïnos et aux Arawaks?

2. Qui sont les ancêtres des Cajuns?

3. Qui a pris possession de la Louisiane pour la France?

4. Comment les États-Unis ont-ils doublé leur territoire en 1803?

5. Qu'est-ce que la loi de 1982 a établi au Canada?

As-tu compris?

You can use the following questions to check comprehension of the Géoculture.

1. **Quels pays se trouvent sur l'île où Colomb est arrivé en 1492? (Haïti et la République dominicaine)**

2. **D'où vient le nom de la Louisiane? (de Louis XIV, roi de France)**

3. **Où est-ce que la plupart des Acadiens sont allés quand les Anglais les ont expulsés du Canada? (à Saint-Domingue et en Louisiane)**

4. **Qu'est-ce qui a commencé la guerre pour l'indépendance de Haïti? (une révolte des esclaves)**

5. **Qu'est-ce que Napoléon a vendu aux États-Unis en 1803? (le territoire de la Louisiane)**

6. **Qu'est-ce qui s'est passé sous la dictature des Duvalier? (des milliers de Haïtiens ont été tués ou se sont exilés)**

7. **Quand est-ce que le Canada est devenu un pays souverain? (1982)**

Answers

1. Il pensait être arrivé en Inde.
2. les Acadiens
3. Robert Cavelier de la Salle
4. Ils ont acheté la Louisiane de la France.
5. le français et l'anglais comme les deux langues officielles

INTERDISCIPLINARY LINKS

La gastronomie

Geography Link The story of many Acadians is one of continuous migration. They originally came from France, settling in Acadia between 1632 and 1654. Many sought to escape violence and hardships in France. About 100 years later the **Grand Dérangement** scattered Acadians across the Americas and even back to Europe. The vast majority traveled south and settled in Louisiana. Have students research **le Grand Dérangement** ancreate a map showing their patterns of migration.

Les maths

Math Link Just prior to the Louisiana Purchase, the territory now known as the United States was divided among several countries. On the map on page 183, the territory in green belonged to the U.S., the purple to Spain, and the orange was claimed by Britain, Russia, Spain, and the United States. The yellow corresponds to the Louisiana Territory, with a total area of 885,000 square miles. Given that the United States paid $15,000,000 for the land, have students calculate how much France received per square mile of land.

Assess

Assessment Program

Quiz: Géoculture

Differentiated Practice and Assessment CD-ROM

Online Assessment
my.hrw.com

Test Generator

Planning Guide

Chapter Section

Resources

Vocabulaire 1 • Nature and animals	pp. 186–189	📀 Teaching Transparencies: Vocabulaire 5.1, 5.2; Bell Work 5.1, 5.2, 5.3, 5.4
Grammaire 1 • The subjunctive with expressions of fear • Review: The imperative	pp. 190–193	📖 Cahier de vocabulaire et grammaire, pp. 49–54 📖 Grammar Tutor for Students of French 📖 Cahier d'activités, pp. 41–43 📖 Media Guide, pp. 17–20
Application 1 • **Un peu plus:** The verbs **voir** and **regarder**	pp. 194–195	📖 **Assessment Program** Quiz: Vocabulaire 1, pp. 119–120 Quiz: Grammaire 1, pp. 121–122 Quiz: Application 1, pp. 123–124
Culture • **Lecture culturelle: Les oies voyageuses** • **Comparaisons** • **Communauté et professions**	pp. 196–197	📖 Cahier d'activités, p. 44
Vocabulaire 2 • Extreme outdoor sports	pp. 198–201	📀 Teaching Transparencies: Vocabulaire 5.3, 5.4; Bell Work 5.5, 5.6, 5.7, 5.8
Grammaire 2 • The verbs **apporter, emporter, amener,** and **emmener** • Verbs followed by **à / de** and the infinitive	pp. 202–205	📖 Cahier de vocabulaire et grammaire, pp. 55–60 📖 Grammar Tutor for Students of French 📖 Cahier d'activités, pp. 45–47 📖 Media Guide, pp. 17–20
Application 2 • **Un peu plus:** Idiomatic expressions	pp. 206–207	📖 **Assessment Program** Quiz: Vocabulaire 2, pp. 125–126 Quiz: Grammaire 2, pp. 127–128 Quiz: Application 2, pp. 129–130
Lecture • **Je viens d'une île de soleil** • **Le Canada**	pp. 208–211	📖 Cahier d'activités, p. 48 📖 Reading Strategies and Skills Handbook 📖 Advanced Reader
L'atelier de l'écrivain • **Hommage à la nature**	pp. 212–213	📖 **Assessment Program** Quiz: Lecture, p. 131, Quiz: Écriture, p. 132
Prépare-toi pour l'examen • **Résumé de vocabulaire et grammaire**	pp. 214–217	📀 Teaching Transparencies: Picture Sequences, Situation, Ch. 5 📖 Media Guide, pp. 20, 61–62
Activités préparatoires	pp. 218–219	📖 **Assessment Program** Examen: Chapitre 5, pp. 133–138 Examen oral: Chapitre 5, p. 321
Révisions cumulatives	pp. 220–221	📀 Teaching Transparencies: Fine Art, Ch. 5 📖 Cahier d'activités, pp. 49–50
Chroniques • Animaux d'Afrique • À la découverte de la nature • Les sports extrêmes • À vos marques! • De grands événements sportifs	pp. 260–269	📖 Reading Strategies and Skills Handbook 📖 Advanced Reader

Pacing Suggestions

	Essential	Recommended	Optional
Vocabulaire 1 • Nature and animals • **Flash culture**	✔		
Grammaire 1 • The subjunctive with expressions of fear • Review: The imperative • **Flash culture**	✔		
Application 1 • **Un peu plus:** The verbs **voir** and **regarder**	✔		
Culture • **Lecture culturelle: Les oies voyageuses** • **Comparaisons** • **Communauté et professions**		✔	
Vocabulaire 2 • Extreme outdoor sports	✔		
Grammaire 2 • The verbs **apporter, emporter, amener,** and **emmener** • Verbs followed by **à / de** and the infinitive • **Flash culture**	✔		
Application 2 • **Un peu plus:** Idiomatic expressions	✔		
Lecture • **Je viens d'une île de soleil,** • **Le Canada** **L'atelier de l'écrivain** • **Hommage à la nature**		✔	
Prépare-toi pour l'examen		✔	
Activités préparatoires		✔	
Révisions cumulatives			✔
Chroniques			✔

Technology

Bien dit! Online
• Student Edition with multi-media
• SoundBooth recording tool
• Interactive activities with feedback
• Self-tests with feedback
• Cahier d'activités (Interactive workbook)
• Cahier de vocabulaire et grammaire (Interactive workbook)
• Holt Online Assessment

DVD Program
• Télé-roman: Camille et compagnie
• Télé-culture: Interviews

Interactive Tutor
• Interactive practice games
• Writing and recording workshops
• Before You Know It™ Flashcards

Audio Program
• Student Edition Listening Activities
• Assessment listening activities
• Songs

One-Stop Planner
• Complete media and print resources
• ExamView Pro Test Generator
• Holt Calendar Planner

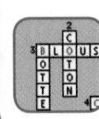
PuzzlePro
• Customizable word games

Differentiated Practice and Assessment CD
For slower pace and advanced learner options, see the Differentiated Practice and Assessment CD.

Planning Guide

✂ Projects

Projects

Excursions de bayou

Have students imagine that they work for a company that offers bayou tours in southern Louisiana. Students will work in groups to create a brochure that advertises one of these tours. The brochure should include illustrations of and information about modes of transportation, routes, animals, and plants tourists will be seeing along the way. It should also include historical and cultural facts about the area and its people. The brochure should offer testimonials of tourists who have previously participated in such a tour. ❀ 1.3, 5.1

Suggested Sequence

1. Have students research in the library or on the Internet bayou tours in southern Louisiana.

2. Students should gather the information they want to include in their brochure: mode of transportation, a map showing the route, pictures or drawings of animals and plants, and historical and cultural facts.

3. Students should create the slogans they want to use to promote their tour. They should write testimonials that express astonishment and encourage readers to take such a tour.

4. Have students plan the layout of their brochure. They should design an attractive cover to catch tourists' attention and should make sure that the pages that follow are colorful and interesting.

5. Have students copy the text of their brochure onto construction paper, tape or glue the illustrations in the appropriate places, and staple the pages of the brochure together.

Grading the project

Suggested point distribution
(100 points total)
Content . . . . 30 pts.
Language use . . . . 30 pts.
Creativity . . . . 20 pts.
Design . . . . 20 pts.

e-community

e-mail forum:
Post the following questions on the classroom e-mail forum:

Location:	http://french

Quels animaux vivent dans la mer? Dans les montagnes? Dans les arbres? ❀ 5.1

All students will contribute to the list and then share the items.

Partner Class Project

Have students prepare a questionnaire to inquire about the favorite sports and leisure activities of their partner class. The questionnaire should have ten, open-ended questions. Students should post the questionnaire on the student or class Web site. Remind students to e-mail the Web site address or an electronic document to the partner class. Students then answer the questionnaire themselves and compare their answers to those of the students in the partner class. Are the answers similar or different? Why? Have students present their conclusions to the class. ❀ 1.3, 4.2

Game Bank
For game ideas, see pages T60–T63.

Le courir de mardi gras

The **Courir de mardi gras,** the rural Mardi Gras celebration of southern Louisiana, dates back to when the Acadians first settled the area. Although altered by frontier influences, it stems from the medieval **fête de la quémande,** a ceremonial begging ritual. Masked and costumed riders on horseback visit farmhouses throughout the countryside, "begging" for contributions to a communal gumbo. Once granted permission to enter a property, the riders charge toward the house, where they dance and sing for donations of chickens, onions, and other ingredients for the gumbo. At the end of the day, a **fais dodo,** or dance, is held in town, where the entire community celebrates and eats the communal gumbo. Have students research in the library or on the Internet other traditions that may also have their roots in the **fête de la quémande.** Have students compare those traditions to the **Courir de mardi gras.** ✿ 4.2, 5.1

La cuisine

Jambalaya is a classic Creole dish made with tomatoes, meat, and chicken broth, and served with French bread and a green salad. To transform a Creole jambalaya into a Cajun version, remove the tomatoes, replace the chicken broth with beef stock, and add a touch of cayenne pepper. Encourage students to make this dish in their home economics class or at home for family and friends. ✿ 3.1, 5.2

Jambalaya

½ litre de saucisse épicée
1 livre d'andouille
¼ tasse de Tasso
2 tasses d'oignon haché
1 poivron vert haché
2 branches de céleri hachées
4 gousses d'ail hachées

1 boîte de tomates en dés en conserve
2 tasses de riz
3 tasses de bouillon de poulet chaud
2 tasses de jambon fumé coupé en cubes

4 échalotes coupées en rondelles
¼ tasse de persil
½ cuillère à café de thym
3 feuilles de laurier
sel, poivre
Tabasco

Faire sauter la saucisse et le Tasso dans une casserole pendant quelques minutes. Ajouter les oignons, le poivron, et le céleri. Laisser cuire jusqu'à ce qu'ils deviennent tendres. Ajouter le thym et les feuilles de laurier. Mélanger le riz à la préparation. Ajouter les tomates, le bouillon, l'ail, l'andouille et la saucisse. Faire bouillir. Recouvrir, baisser le feu, et laisser mijoter jusqu'à ce que le riz soit cuit. Garnir avec de l'échalote et du persil.

Vocabulaire à l'œuvre 1

1 p. 188, CD 5, Tr. 1

1. Je suis jaune et noire. Attention! Je pique!
2. Je suis un cousin du crocodile. On me voit souvent dans les bayous de Louisiane.
3. Je suis un petit animal gris ou marron qui adore se promener dans les arbres.
4. Moi, j'habite dans les grottes et je sors la nuit.
5. On peut me voir dans les parcs du Canada. Je suis un cousin du chien.
6. Et moi, je suis un gros poisson dont tout le monde a peur.

Answers to Activity 1

1. b, une guêpe
2. d, un alligator
3. f, un écureuil
4. c, une chauve-souris
5. e, un loup
6. a, un requin

Grammaire à l'œuvre 1

7 p. 190, CD 5, Tr. 2

1. Éric veut que tu viennes avec nous pour observer les oiseaux.
2. Je crains qu'il y ait des serpents ici.
3. Je suis désolé que tu sois venu pour rien.
4. J'ai peur que nous nous perdions si nous ne suivons pas les sentiers.
5. Il vaudrait mieux que nous rentrions.
6. Est-il possible qu'il y ait des ours?
7. Oui, et je crains que les ours aient faim.
8. Moi aussi, j'ai peur qu'ils veuillent nous manger.

Answers to Activity 7

1. b **2.** a **3.** b **4.** a **5.** b **6.** b **7.** a **8.** a

Application 1

18 p. 194, CD 5, Tr. 3

1. Ne va pas près des ours!
2. Je pense qu'il faut toujours faire attention aux loups, même si on dit qu'il n'y en a plus beaucoup dans ce parc.
3. Regarde cet orignal! Il est magnifique, tu ne trouves pas?
4. Méfie-toi des abeilles! Elles piquent.
5. Le guide ne veut pas qu'on nourrisse les animaux.
6. Fais attention! Tu vas tomber!
7. Je ne crois pas qu'on puisse cueillir les fleurs.

Answers to Activity 18

1. a **2.** b **3.** a **4.** a **5.** b **6.** a **7.** b

Vocabulaire à l'œuvre 2

25 p. 200, CD 5, Tr. 4

1. Pas possible! Il a vraiment fait le tour du monde à la voile en solitaire! C'est vraiment incroyable!
2. Ma famille et moi, on a trouvé des gilets de sauvetage dans un petit magasin près de la plage dans le sud de l'île.
3. Si tu vas plus à l'ouest, il y a un endroit où on peut faire de l'alpinisme.
4. Pauline et Victor sont allés à Tahiti. Ils ont fait de la plongée sous-marine avec des amis.
5. Si tu veux faire du ski, il faut aller dans les Alpes, dans l'est de la France.
6. Julie a oublié son équipement! Regarde! Voilà son masque, sa combinaison et sa bouteille!

Answers to Activity 25

1. a **2.** a **3.** b **4.** a **5.** b **6.** a

Grammaire à l'œuvre 2

31 p. 202, CD 5, Tr. 5

1. Allez, emmenez-le!

2. Vous l'emportez, ou je vous le livre?

3. Amène-la, si tu veux, ça sera intéressant.

4. Tu peux les apporter, si tu as envie.

5. Je ne veux pas les voir, emportez-les!

6. C'est toi qui l'as emmenée là-bas?

Answers to Activity 31

1. a   2. b   3. a   4. b   5. b   6. a

Application 2

41 p. 206, CD 5, Tr. 6

1. — Tu fais souvent la sieste?
   — Oui, le plus souvent possible! J'adore ça!

2. — Est-ce que Marc aime toujours faire la fête?
   — Oui, il ne changera jamais!

3. — Elle va bientôt prendre sa retraite, alors?
   — Dans un an. Elle attend ça avec impatience!

4. — Il aime prendre des risques, celui-là!
   — Oui, et ça fait peur à mes parents!

5. — Elle fait encore des études?
   — Oui, elle veut être prof de russe.

Answers to Activity 41

1. c   2. b   3. a   4. e   5. d

Prépare-toi pour l'examen

6 p. 215, CD 5, Tr. 9

1. L'aigle est le symbole national des États-Unis.

2. Dans les parcs naturels, il est interdit de nourrir les animaux.

3. On n'a pas besoin d'équipement pour faire du parachutisme.

4. Dans les zoos, les animaux ne sont pas en liberté.

5. Quand on fait de la spéléologie, on saute d'un avion.

Answers to Activity 6

1. a   2. a   3. b   4. a   5. b

Activités préparatoires

Listening, p. 218, CD 5, Tr. 10

1. — Est-ce que tu es prêt à partir? Tu as tout ce dont tu as besoin?
   — Oui, maman. J'ai tout mon équipement: ma combinaison de plongée, mon masque et ma bouteille de plongée.

2. — Tu appartiens à un club de spéléologie, n'est-ce pas?
   — Oui, on va explorer des grottes chaque samedi.

Answers to Activity 1

1. a   2. b

Révisions cumulatives *chapitres 1-5*

1 p. 220, CD 5, Tr. 11

1. Brittany a très peur de tomber dans l'eau parce qu'elle a entendu dire qu'il y avait des alligators.

2. Au sud du pays, il y a des bayous.

3. Mon frère aime faire du deltaplane.

4. J'adore les hérons. Je trouve que ce sont de très beaux animaux.

5. Est-ce que tu as vu des aigles en faisant de l'alpinisme?

6. Moi, descendre des rapides, cela me ferait peur.

Answers to Activity 1

1. a   2. a   3. b   4. a   5. b   6. b

50-Minute Lesson Plans

En pleine nature

Day 1

OBJECTIVE
Express astonishment and fear

Core Instruction
Chapter Opener, pp. 184–185
• See Using the Photo, p. 184. **5 min.**
• See Chapter Objectives, p. 184. **5 min.**

Vocabulaire 1, pp. 186–189
• Present **Vocabulaire 1,** pp. 186–187. See Teaching **Vocabulaire,** p. 186. **15 min.**
• Present **Exprimons-nous!,** p. 187. **5 min.**
• Play Audio CD 5, Tr. 1 for Activity 1, p. 188. **5 min.**
• Have students do Activities 2–3, p. 188. **10 min.**
• Present **Flash culture,** p. 188. **5 min.**

Optional Resources
• Advanced Learners, p. 187 ▲
• Slower Pace Learners, p. 189 ◆

Homework Suggestions
Cahier de vocabulaire et grammaire, pp. 49–50
✿ 1.1, 1.2, 1.3, 2.2, 3.1

Day 2

OBJECTIVE
Forbid and give warning; Use the subjunctive with expressions of fear

Core Instruction
Vocabulaire 1, pp. 186–189
• Do Bell Work 5.1, p. 186. **5 min.**
• See Teaching **Exprimons-nous!,** p. 188. **10 min.**
• Have students do Activities 4–6, p. 189. **25 min.**

Grammaire 1, pp. 190–193
• See Teaching **Grammaire,** p. 190. **10 min.**

Optional Resources
• Communication (TE), p. 189
• Special Learning Needs, p. 189 ●

Homework Suggestions
Study for **Quiz: Vocabulaire 1**
Cahier de vocabulaire et grammaire, p. 51
Online Practice (**go.hrw.com,** Keyword: BD3 CH5)
✿ 1.1, 1.2, 1.3

Day 3

OBJECTIVE
Use the subjunctive with expressions of fear

Core Instruction
Vocabulaire 1, pp. 186–189
• Review **Vocabulaire 1,** pp. 186–189. **10 min.**
• Give **Quiz: Vocabulaire 1.** **20 min.**

Grammaire 1, pp. 190–193
• Play Audio CD 5, Tr. 2 for Activity 7, p. 190. **5 min.**
• Have students do Activities 8–11, pp. 190–191. **15 min.**

Optional Resources
• Comparisons, p. 191
• Slower Pace Learners, p. 191 ◆
• Special Learning Needs, p. 191 ●

Homework Suggestions
Cahier de vocabulaire et grammaire, p. 52
Cahier d'activités, p. 41
Online Practice (**go.hrw.com,** Keyword: BD3 CH5)
✿ 1.1, 1.2, 1.3, 3.1, 4.1

Day 4

OBJECTIVE
Use the subjunctive with expressions of fear; Use the imperative

Core Instruction
Grammaire 1, pp. 190–193
• Have students do Activitiy 12, p. 191. **5 min.**
• Present **Flash culture,** p. 192. **5 min.**
• See Teaching **Grammaire,** p. 192. **10 min.**
• Have students do Activities 13–17, pp. 192–193. **20 min.**

Application 1, pp. 194–195
• Play Audio CD 5, Tr. 3 for Activity 18, p. 194. **5 min.**
• Do Activity 19, p. 194. **5 min.**

Optional Resources
• Advanced Learners, p. 193 ▲
• Multiple Intelligences, p. 193

Homework Suggestions
Study for **Quiz: Grammaire 1**
Cahier de vocabulaire et grammaire, p. 53
Cahier d'activités, p. 42
✿ 1.1, 1.2, 1.3, 4.2

Day 5

OBJECTIVE
*Use the verbs **voir** and **regarder***

Core Instruction
Grammaire 1, pp. 190–193
• Review **Grammaire 1,** pp. 190–193. **10 min.**
• Give **Quiz: Grammaire 1.** **20 min.**

Application 1, pp. 194–195
• Have students do Activity 20, p. 194. **5 min.**
• See Teaching **Un peu plus,** p. 194. **5 min.**
• Have students do Activities 21–24, pp. 194–195. **10 min.**

Optional Resources
• Communication (TE), p. 195
• Slower Pace Learners, p. 195 ◆
• Multiple Intelligences, p. 195

Homework Suggestions
Study for **Quiz: Application 1**
Cahier de vocabulaire et grammaire, p. 54
Cahier d'activités, p. 43
✿ 1.1, 1.2, 1.3, 3.2

Day 6

OBJECTIVE
Learn about francophone culture

Core Instruction
Application 1, pp. 194–195
• Review **Application 1,** pp. 194–195. **10 min.**
• Give **Quiz: Application 1.** **20 min.**

Culture, pp. 196–197
• See **Lecture culturelle** (TE), p. 196. **10 min.**
• See **Comparaisons et communauté** (TE), p. 196. **10 min.**

Optional Resources
• Cultures, p. 197
• Communities, p. 197
• Advanced Learners, p. 197 ▲
• Multiple Intelligences, p. 197

Homework Suggestions
Cahier d'activités, p. 44
Interactive Tutor, Ch. 5
Online Practice (**go.hrw.com,** Keyword: BD3 CH5)
Finish the **Communauté et professions** project, p. 197
✿ 1.2, 1.3, 2.1, 2.2, 3.1, 4.2, 5.1

Day 7

OBJECTIVE
Give general directions

Core Instruction
Vocabulaire 2, pp. 198–201
• Do Bell Work 5.5, p. 198. **5 min.**
• Present **Vocabulaire 2,** pp. 198–199. See Teaching **Vocabulaire,** p. 198. **15 min.**
• Present **Exprimons-nous!,** p. 199. **10 min.**
• Play Audio CD 5, Tr. 4 for Activity 25, p. 200. **5 min.**
• Have students do Activities 26–27, p. 200. **15 min.**

Optional Resources
• Advanced Learners, p. 199 ▲
• Multiple Intelligences, p. 199

Homework Suggestions
Cahier de vocabulaire et grammaire, pp. 55–56
✿ 1.2, 1.3, 3.1

Day 8

OBJECTIVE
*Complain and offer encouragement; Use **apporter, amener, emporter,** and **emmener***

Core Instruction
Vocabulaire 2, pp. 198–201
• See Teaching **Exprimons-nous!,** p. 200. **10 min.**
• Have students do Activities 28–29, p. 201. **20 min.**

Grammaire 2, pp. 202–205
• See Teaching **Grammaire,** p. 202. **10 min.**
• Do Activity 30, p. 202. **5 min.**
• Play Audio CD 5, Tr. 5 for Activity 31, p. 202. **5 min.**

Optional Resources
• Advanced Learners, p. 201 ▲

Homework Suggestions
Study for **Quiz: Vocabulaire 2**
Cahier de vocabulaire et grammaire, p. 57
Interactive Tutor, Ch. 5
✿ 1.1, 1.2, 1.3

Day 9

OBJECTIVE
Use apporter, amener, emporter, and emmener

Core Instruction
Vocabulaire 2, pp. 198–201
• Review **Vocabulaire 2,** pp. 198–201. **10 min.**
• Give **Quiz: Vocabulaire 2.** **20 min.**

Grammaire 2, pp. 202–205
• Have students do Activities 32–34, p. 203. **20 min.**

Optional Resources
• Communication (TE), p. 203
• Slower Pace Learners, p. 203 ◆ ●
• Special Learning Needs, p. 203 ●

Homework Suggestions
Cahier de vocabulaire et grammaire, p. 58
Cahier d'activités, p. 45
Interactive Tutor, Ch. 5
Online Practice (**go.hrw.com,** Keyword: BD3 CH5)

❁ 1.1, 1.2

Day 10

OBJECTIVE
Use verbs followed by à/de and the infinitive

Core Instruction
Grammaire 2, pp. 202–205
• Do Bell Work 5.7, p. 204. **5 min.**
• Present **Flash culture,** p. 204. **5 min.**
• See Teaching **Grammaire,** p. 204. **10 min.**
• Have students do Activities 35–38, pp. 204–205. **20 min.**

Application 2, pp. 206–207
• Have students do Activities 39–40, p. 206. **10 min.**

Optional Resources
• Communication (TE), p. 205
• Advanced Learners, p. 205 ▲
• Special Learning Needs, p. 205 ●

Homework Suggestions
Study for **Quiz: Grammaire 2**
Cahier de vocabulaire et grammaire, p. 59
Cahier d'activités, p. 46

❁ 1.1, 1.2, 1.3

Day 11

OBJECTIVE
Use idiomatic expressions

Core Instruction
Grammaire 2, pp. 202–205
• Review **Grammaire 2,** pp. 202–205. **10 min.**
• Give **Quiz: Grammaire 2.** **20 min.**

Application 2, pp. 206–207
• See Teaching **Un peu plus,** p. 206. **5 min.**
• Play Audio CD 5, Tr. 6 for Activity 41, p. 206. **5 min.**
• Have students do Activities 42–43, p. 207. **10 min.**

Optional Resources
• Communication (TE), p. 207
• Slower Pace Learners, p. 207 ◆
• Multiple Intelligences, p. 207

Homework Suggestions
Study for **Quiz: Application 2**
Cahier de vocabulaire et grammaire, p. 60
Cahier d'activités, p. 47
Online Practice (**go.hrw.com,** Keyword: BD3 CH5)

❁ 1.2, 1.3

Day 12

OBJECTIVE
Develop listening and reading skills

Core Instruction
Application 2, pp. 206–207
• Review **Application 2,** pp. 206–207. **10 min.**
• Give **Quiz: Application 2.** **20 min.**

Lecture, pp. 208–211
• See **Lecture** (TE), p. 208. **20 min.**

Optional Resources
• Applying the Strategies, p. 208
• Active Reading Questions, p. 209
• Making Generalizations, p. 209
• Slower Pace Learners, p. 209 ◆
• Multiple Intelligences, p. 209

Homework Suggestions
Interactive Tutor, Ch. 5
Online Practice (**go.hrw.com,** Keyword: BD3 CH5)

❁ 1.2, 1.3, 3.1

Day 13

OBJECTIVE
Develop listening, reading, and writing skills

Core Instruction
Lecture, pp. 208–211
• See **Lecture** (TE), p. 210. **20 min.**

L'atelier de l'écrivain, pp. 212–213
• See **L'atelier de l'écrivain** (TE), p. 212. **30 min.**

Optional Resources
• Active Reading Questions, p. 210
• Postreading Activity, p. 210
• Connections, p. 211
• Advanced Learners, p. 211 ▲
• Multiple Intelligences, p. 211
• Process Writing, p. 212
• Teaching Suggestion, p. 212
• Connections, p. 212
• Slower Pace Learners, p. 213 ◆
• Multiple Intelligences, p. 213

Homework Suggestions
Cahier d'activités, p. 48

❁ 1.1, 1.2, 1.3, 3.1

Day 14

OBJECTIVE
Review the chapter; Prepare for the AP Exam

Core Instruction
Prépare-toi pour l'examen, pp. 214–217
• Have students do Activities 1–4, pp. 214–215. **25 min.**

Activités préparatoires, pp. 218–219
• Have students do the **Activités préparatoires,** pp. 218–219. **25 min.**

Optional Resources
• Connections, p. 214
• Reteaching, p. 214
• Slower Pace Learners, p. 219 ◆
• Special Learning Needs, p. 219 ●
• **Télé-culture:** Interviews

Homework Suggestions
Interactive Tutor, Ch. 5
Online Practice (**go.hrw.com,** Keyword: BD3 CH5)

❁ 1.1, 1.2, 1.3, 3.1

Day 15

OBJECTIVE
Review the chapter

Core Instruction
Prépare-toi pour l'examen, pp. 214–217
• Have students do Activity 5, p. 215. **5 min.**
• Play Audio CD 5, Tr. 10 for Activity 6, p. 215. **5 min.**
• Have students do Activity 7, p. 215. **10 min.**

Révisions cumulatives, pp. 220–221
• Play Audio CD 5, Tr. 11 for Activity 1, p. 220. **5 min.**
• Have students do Activities 2–6, pp. 220–221. **25 min.**

Optional Resources
• Online Culture Project, p. 220
• Fine Art Connection, p. 221
• **Télé-roman: Camille et compagnie**

Homework Suggestions
Study for Chapter Test
Online Practice (**go.hrw.com,** Keyword: BD3 CH5)

❁ 1.1, 1.2, 1.3, 2.1, 2.2, 3.2

Day 16/Test

Core Instruction
Chapter Test **50 min.**

Optional Resources
Assessment Program
• Alternative Assessment
• Test Generator
• **Quiz: Lecture**
• **Quiz: Écriture**

Homework Suggestions
Cahier d'activités, pp. 49–50, 110–111
Online Practice (**go.hrw.com,** Keyword: BD3 CH5)

50-Minute Lesson Plans

90-Minute Lesson Plans

En pleine nature

90-Minute Lesson Plans

Block 1

OBJECTIVE
Express astonishment and fear; Forbid and give warning

Core Instruction
Chapter Opener, pp. 184–185
- See Using the Photo, p. 184. **5 min.**
- See Chapter Objectives, p. 184. **5 min.**

Vocabulaire 1, pp. 186–189
- Present **Vocabulaire 1,** pp. 186–187. See Teaching **Vocabulaire,** p. 186. **15 min.**
- Present **Exprimons-nous!,** p. 187. **10 min.**
- Play Audio CD 5, Tr. 1 for Activity 1, p. 188. **5 min.**
- Have students do Activities 2–3, p. 188. **10 min.**
- Present **Flash culture,** p. 188. **5 min.**
- See Teaching **Exprimons-nous!,** p. 188. **10 min.**
- Have students do Activities 4–6, p. 189. **25 min.**

Optional Resources
- Learning Tips, p. 185
- French for Spanish Speakers, p. 186
- TPR, p. 187
- **Cinquain** Poetry, p. 187
- Advanced Learners, p. 187 ▲
- Multiple Intelligences, p. 187
- Teacher to Teacher, p. 188
- Communication (TE), p. 189
- Slower Pace Learners, p. 189 ◆
- Special Learning Needs, p. 189 ●

Homework Suggestions
Study for **Quiz: Vocabulaire 1**
Cahier de vocabulaire et grammaire, pp. 49–51
Interactive Tutor, Ch. 5
Online Practice (**go.hrw.com,** Keyword: BD3 CH5)
❀ 1.1, 1.2, 1.3, 2.2, 3.1, 4.1

Block 2

OBJECTIVE
Use the subjunctive with expressions of fear; Use the imperative

Core Instruction
Vocabulaire 1, pp. 186–189
- Review **Vocabulaire 1,** pp. 186–189. **10 min.**
- Give Quiz: **Vocabulaire 1.** **20 min.**

Grammaire 1, pp. 190–193
- See Teaching **Grammaire,** p. 190. **10 min.**
- Play Audio CD 5, Tr. 2 for Activity 7, p. 190. **5 min.**
- Have students do Activities 8–12, pp. 190–191. **20 min.**
- Present **Flash culture,** p. 192 **5 min.**
- See Teaching **Grammaire,** p. 192. **5 min.**
- Have students do Activities 13–16, pp. 192–193. **15 min.**

Optional Resources
- Communication (TE), p. 191
- Comparisons, p. 191
- Slower Pace Learners, p. 191 ◆
- Special Learning Needs, p. 191 ●
- **Attention!,** p. 192
- Communication (TE), p. 193
- Advanced Learners, p. 193 ▲
- Multiple Intelligences, p. 193

Homework Suggestions
Study for **Quiz: Grammaire 1**
Cahier de vocabulaire et grammaire, pp. 52–53
Cahier d'activités, pp. 41–42
Interactive Tutor, Ch. 5
Online Practice (**go.hrw.com,** Keyword: BD3 CH5)
❀ 1.1, 1.2, 1.3, 3.1, 4.1, 4.2

Block 3

OBJECTIVE
*Use the imperative; Use the verbs **voir** and **regarder**; Learn about francophone culture*

Core Instruction
Grammaire 1, pp. 190–193
- Do Bell Work 5.3, p. 192. **5 min.**
- Have students do Activity 17, p. 193. **5 min.**
- Review **Grammaire 1,** pp. 190–193. **10 min.**
- Give **Quiz: Grammaire 1.** **20 min.**

Application 1, pp. 194–195
- Play Audio CD 5, Tr. 3 for Activity 18, p. 194. **5 min.**
- Have students do Activities 19–20, p. 194. **5 min.**
- See Teaching **Un peu plus,** p. 194. **5 min.**
- Have students do Activities 21–24, pp. 194–195. **15 min.**

Culture, pp. 196–197
- See **Lecture culturelle** (TE), p. 196. **10 min.**
- See **Comparaisons et communauté** (TE), p. 196. **10 min.**

Optional Resources
- French for Spanish Speakers, p. 195
- Communication (TE), p. 195
- Slower Pace Learners, p. 195 ◆
- Multiple Intelligences, p. 195
- Prereading Questions, p. 196
- Active Reading Questions, p. 196
- Bulletin Board Project, p. 197
- Cultures, p. 197
- Communities, p. 197
- Advanced Learners, p. 197 ▲
- Multiple Intelligences, p. 197

Homework Suggestions
Study for **Quiz: Application 1**
Cahier de vocabulaire et grammaire, p. 54
Cahier d'activités, pp. 43–44
Interactive Tutor, Ch. 5
Online Practice (**go.hrw.com,** Keyword: BD3 CH5)
Finish the **Communauté et professions** project, p. 197
❀ 1.1, 1.2, 1.3, 2.1, 2.2, 3.1, 3.2, 4.1, 4.2, 5.1

Block 4

OBJECTIVE
Give general directions; Complain and offer encouragement

Core Instruction
Application 1, pp. 194–195
- Review **Application 1,** pp. 194–195. **10 min.**
- Give **Quiz: Application 1.** **20 min.**

Vocabulaire 2, pp. 198–201
- Present **Vocabulaire 2,** pp. 198–199. See Teaching **Vocabulaire,** p. 198. **15 min.**
- Present **Exprimons-nous!,** p. 199. **10 min.**
- Play Audio CD 5, Tr. 4 for Activity 25, p. 200. **5 min.**
- Have students do Activities 26–27, p. 200. **10 min.**
- See Teaching **Exprimons-nous!,** p. 200. **10 min.**
- Have students do Activities 28–29, p. 201. **10 min.**

Optional Resources
- **Proverbes,** p. 198
- TPR, p. 199
- **Attention!,** p. 199
- Connections, p. 199
- Advanced Learners, p. 199 ▲
- Multiple Intelligences, p. 199
- Connections, p. 201
- Communication (TE), p. 201
- Advanced Learners, p. 201 ▲
- Multiple Intelligences, p. 201

Homework Suggestions
Study for **Quiz: Vocabulaire 2**
Cahier de vocabulaire et grammaire, pp. 55–57
Interactive Tutor, Ch. 5
Online Practice (**go.hrw.com,** Keyword: BD3 CH5)
❀ 1.1, 1.2, 1.3, 3.1

Block 5

OBJECTIVE
*Use **apporter, amener, emporter,** and **emmener;** Use verbs followed by **à/de** and the infinitive*

Core Instruction
Vocabulaire 2, pp. 198–201
• Review **Vocabulaire 2,** pp. 198–201. **10 min.**
• Give **Quiz: Vocabulaire 2.** **20 min.**

Grammaire 2, pp. 202–205
• See Teaching **Grammaire,** p. 202. **10 min.**
• Have students do Activity 30, p. 202. **5 min.**
• Play Audio CD 5, Tr. 5 for Activity 31, p. 202. **5 min.**
• Have students do Activities 32–34, p. 203. **15 min.**
• Present **Flash culture,** p. 204. **5 min.**
• See Teaching **Grammaire,** p. 204. **5 min.**
• Have students do Activities 35–37, pp. 204–205. **15 min.**

Optional Resources
• Communication (TE), p. 203
• Language Note, p. 203
• Slower Pace Learners, p. 203 ◆
• Special Learning Needs, p. 203 ●
• Communication (TE), p. 205
• Special Learning Needs, p. 205 ●

Homework Suggestions
Study for **Quiz: Grammaire 2**
Cahier de vocabulaire et grammaire, pp. 58–59
Cahier d'activités, pp. 45–46
Interactive Tutor, Ch. 5
Online Practice (**go.hrw.com,** Keyword: BD3 CH5)
❀ 1.1, 1.2

Block 6

OBJECTIVE
*Use verbs followed by **à/de** and the infinitive; Use idiomatic expressions; Develop listening and reading skills*

Grammaire 2, pp. 202–205
• Have students do Activity 38, p. 205. **10 min.**
• Review **Grammaire 2,** pp. 202–205. **10 min.**
• Give **Quiz: Grammaire 2.** **20 min.**

Application 2, pp. 206–207
• Have students do Activities 39–40, p. 206. **10 min.**
• See Teaching **Un peu plus,** p. 206. **5 min.**
• Play Audio CD 5, Tr. 6 for Activity 41, p. 206. **5 min.**
• Have students do Activities 42–43, p. 207. **10 min.**

Lecture, pp. 208–211
• See **Lecture** (TE), p. 208. **20 min.**

Optional Resources
• Advanced Learners, p. 205 ▲
• Communication (TE), p. 207
• Slower Pace Learners, p. 207 ◆
• Multiple Intelligences, p. 207
• AP Reading Suggestion, p. 208
• Applying the Strategies, p. 208
• Active Reading Questions, p. 209
• Making Generalizations, p. 209
• Slower Pace Learners, p. 209 ◆
• Multiple Intelligences, p. 209

Homework Suggestions
Study for **Quiz: Application 2**
Cahier de vocabulaire et grammaire, p. 60
Cahier d'activités, p. 47
Interactive Tutor, Ch. 5
Online Practice (**go.hrw.com,** Keyword: BD3 CH5)
❀ 1.1, 1.2, 1.3, 3.1

Block 7

OBJECTIVE
Develop listening, reading, and writing skills; Review the chapter

Core Instruction
Application 2, pp. 206–207
• Review **Application 2,** pp. 206–207. **10 min.**
• Give **Quiz: Application 2.** **20 min.**

Lecture, pp. 208–211
• See **Lecture** (TE), p. 210. **10 min.**

L'atelier de l'écrivain, pp. 212–213
• See **L'atelier de l'écrivain** (TE), p. 212. **30 min.**

Prépare-toi pour l'examen, pp. 214–217
• Have students do Activities 1–5, pp. 214–215. **10 min.**
• Play Audio CD 5, Tr. 10 for Activity 6, p. 215. **5 min.**
• Have students do Activity 7, p. 215. **5 min.**

Optional Resources
• Active Reading Questions, p. 210
• Postreading Activity, p. 210
• Connections, p. 211
• Advanced Learners, p. 211 ▲
• Multiple Intelligences, p. 211
• Process Writing, p. 212
• Teaching Suggestion, p. 212
• Connections, p. 212
• Slower Pace Learners, p. 213 ◆
• Multiple Intelligences, p. 213
• TPRS, p. 214
• Connections, p. 214
• Reteaching, p. 214
• Oral Assessment, p. 215
• Cultures, p. 216
• **Proverbes,** p. 216
• Game, p. 217

Homework Suggestions
Study for Chapter Test
Cahier d'activités, p. 48
Interactive Tutor, Ch. 5
Online Practice (**go.hrw.com,** Keyword: BD3 CH5)
❀ 1.1, 1.2, 1.3, 2.1, 2.2, 3.1

Block 8

OBJECTIVE
Prepare for the AP Exam; Review and assess the chapter

Core Instruction
Activités préparatoires, pp. 218–219
• Have students do the **Activités préparatoires,** pp. 218–219. **20 min.**

Chapter Test 50 min.

Révisions cumulatives, pp. 220–221
• Play Audio CD 5, Tr. 11 for Activity 1, p. 220. **5 min.**
• Have students do Activities 2–6, pp. 220–221. **15 min.**

Optional Resources
• Reading Strategy, p. 218
• Preparing for the Exam, p. 218
• Writing Strategy, p. 219
• Slower Pace Learners, p. 219 ◆
• Special Learning Needs, p. 219 ●
• Online Culture Project, p. 220
• Fine Art Connection, p. 221
• **Télé-culture:** Interviews
• **Télé-roman:** Camille et compagnie

Homework Suggestions
Cahier d'activités, pp. 49–50, 110–111
Interactive Tutor, Ch. 5
Online Practice (**go.hrw.com,** Keyword: BD3 CH5)
❀ 1.1, 1.2, 1.3, 2.1, 2.2, 3.1

90-Minute Lesson Plans

Meeting the National Standards

Communication
Communication, pp. 189, 191, 193, 195, 201, 203, 205, 207

À ton tour, p. 221

Cultures
Flash culture, pp. 188, 192, 204

Comparaisons, p. 197

Practices and Perspectives, p. 197

Products and Perspectives, p. 216

Connections
Biology Link, p. 214

Geography Link, p. 199

History Link, p. 201

Language Arts Link, p. 212

Literature Link, p. 211

Comparisons
Comparaisons, p. 197

Communities
Communauté, p. 197

Career Path, p. 197

Using the Photo

Lake Martin, near Lafayette, has the largest rookery of wading birds in the United States. Several thousand egrets and several hundred spoonbills nest here during the peak months. A large population of nutria and alligators also live in the swamp, which is referred to as a cypress swamp because of its ancient cypress trees. These trees, with Spanish moss hanging from their branches, grow out of water that is covered with green duckweed. Ask students to describe a scene on Lake Martin they would enjoy photographing. Amateur photographers may also want to mention the type of camera and lens they would use. 🍀 3.1

chapitre **5**

En pleine nature

Objectifs

In this chapter, you will learn to
• express astonishment and fear
• forbid and give warning
• give general directions
• complain and offer encouragement

And you will use and review
• the subjunctive with expressions of fear
• the imperative
• the verbs **voir** and **regarder**
• the verbs **apporter, amener, emporter,** and **emmener**
• verbs followed by **à** or **de** and the infinitive
• idiomatic expressions

▶ *Que vois-tu sur la photo?*

Où se trouvent ces personnes?

Qu'est-ce qu'elles font?

Et toi, est-ce que tu as déjà fait du canoë? Est-ce que tu as déjà été dans les bayous de Louisiane? Si oui, où?

Suggested pacing:	**Traditional Schedule**	**Block Schedule**
Vocabulaire/Grammaire/Application 1	5 days	2 blocks
Culture	1 day	1 block
Vocabulaire/Grammaire/Application 2	5 days	2 blocks
Lecture	1 day	1/2 block
L'atelier de l'écrivain	1 day	1/2 block
Prépare-toi pour l'examen	1/2 day	1/2 block
Activités préparatoires	1/2 day	1/2 block
Examen	1 day	1/2 block
Révisions cumulatives	1 day	1/2 block

Vocabulaire supplémentaire

Students might use these terms to discuss the photo.

le héron	*heron*
l'aigrette (f.)	*egret*
la spatule	*spoonbill*
le chêne	*oak tree*
la mousse	*moss*
le marais	*swamp*
le cyprès	*cypress tree*

Learning Tips

One of the best ways to learn a language is to listen to and communicate with native speakers. If students do not know any native speakers, they may want to watch French films with English subtitles or listen to Francophone radio broadcasts or podcasts over the Internet.

Language Lab

You might want to use your language lab to have students:
- listen to all target vocabulary and phrases in the chapter
- practice pronunciation of vocabulary and phrases, using Holt SoundBooth to save their work for evaluation
- complete the listening activities in this chapter

Visit Us Online
go.hrw.com
Online Edition
KEYWORD: BD3 CH5

Promenade en canoë sur le lac Martin, en Louisiane

LISTENING PRACTICE

Vocabulaire
Activity 1, p. 188, CD 5, Tr. 1
Activity 25, p. 200, CD 5, Tr. 4

Grammaire
Activity 7, p. 190, CD 5, Tr. 2
Activity 31, p. 202, CD 5, Tr. 5

Application
Activity 18, p. 194, CD 5, Tr. 3
Activity 41, p. 206, CD 5, Tr. 6

Language Lab and Classroom Activities

Prépare-toi pour l'examen
Activity 6, p. 215, CD 5, Tr. 9
Télé-culture: Interviews, Chapter 5

Activités préparatoires
Section I, Listening, p. 218, CD 5, Tr. 10
Télé-roman: *Camille et compagnie*, Épisode 5

Révisions cumulatives
Activity 1, p. 220, CD 5, Tr. 11

Lecture
p. 209, CD 5, Tr. 7; p. 210, CD 5, Tr. 8

L'Amérique francophone

Objectifs
- to express astonishment and fear
- to forbid and give warning

Vocabulaire
à l'œuvre **1**

Les animaux sauvages

un aigle

un castor

un loup

un original

un ours

Dans les **parcs naturels** du Québec, quand on **a de la patience**, on peut **observer des animaux sauvages** vivre **en liberté**.

un papillon

un alligator

un héron

une écrevisse

De nombreuses **espèces** vivent dans **les bayous** de Louisiane.

Resources

Planning:

Lesson Planner

 One-Stop Planner

Presentation:

 Teaching Transparencies
Vocabulaire 5.1, 5.2

Practice:

Cahier de vocabulaire et grammaire

Differentiated Practice and Assessment CD-ROM

Media Guide

 Teaching Transparencies
Bell Work 5.1

 Interactive Tutor, Disc 1

Bell Work

Use Bell Work 5.1 in the *Teaching Transparencies* or write this activity on the board.

Réponds en remplaçant les mots soulignés avec un **pronom disjoint**.

1. Est-ce que Roméo est amoureux de <u>Juliette</u>? Oui, il...
2. Est-ce que tu as travaillé avec <u>Nicolas</u>? Non, je...
3. Ces chaussures sont à <u>toi</u>? Non, elles...
4. Pensez-vous souvent à <u>Julie et à moi</u>? Oui, nous...
5. Tu habites chez <u>tes parents</u>? Oui, j'... 1.2

French for Spanish Speakers

Ask Spanish speakers which animal names look or sound similar to Spanish names? **(aigle/águila, animaux sauvages/animales salvajes, espèces/especies, dauphin/ delfín, corail/coral, abeille/ abeja, baleine/ballena)** What other words are similar? **(liberté/libertad, mordre/ morder, piquer/picar)** 4.1

Core Instruction

TEACHING VOCABULAIRE

1. Introduce the vocabulary using transparencies **Vocabulaire 5.1** and **5.2**. Model the pronunciation of each noun, using **Ça c'est...** (3 min.)

2. Ask students to point to various animals on the transparency: **un ours, un papillon, un loup, un alligator, ...** (3 min.)

3. Ask students questions about their fears. **Est-ce que tu as peur des...? Est-ce que**

tu as peur que les... te piquent/mordent/ mangent? (3 min.)

4. Model the expressions in **Exprimons-nous!** Then have students react to everything you say, with either astonishment or fear. **Il n'y aura plus d'examens dans ce cours. Il y a un serpent sous ta chaise!** (3 min.)

Online Practice
go.hrw.com
Vocabulaire 1 practice
KEYWORD: BD3 CH5

Chapitre 5

Vocabulaire 1

Vocabulaire 1

un dauphin

le corail

un requin

une méduse

En Haïti, il y a **une flore** et **une faune** de type **tropical**.

D'autres mots utiles

une abeille	bee
une baleine	whale
un crocodile	crocodile
un écureuil	squirrel
une guêpe	wasp
un(e) guide	guide
un renard	fox
cueillir	to pick
mordre/	to bite/
piquer	sting
se perdre	to get lost

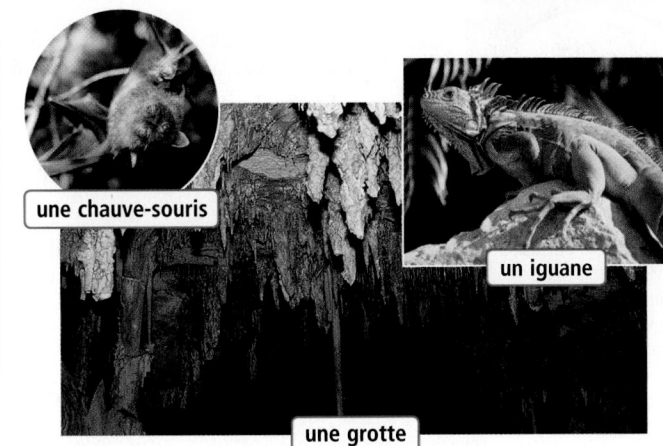

une chauve-souris

un iguane

une grotte

Exprimons-nous!

To express astonishment	To express fear
Ce n'est pas vrai! *It can't be true!*	**Quelle horreur!!** Une araignée! *How horrible!*
C'est incroyable! *It's incredible!*	**J'ai peur des** alligators! *I'm afraid of . . . !*
Pas possible! *Impossible!*	**J'ai peur qu'**il me pique! *I'm afraid that . . . !*
Je n'en reviens pas! *I can't get over it!*	**Au secours!/À l'aide!** *Help!*

Interactive TUTOR

Vocabulaire et grammaire, pp. 49–51

Online workbooks

▶ **Vocabulaire supplémentaire—La faune, pp. R18–R19**

Resources

Planning:

Lesson Planner

 One-Stop Planner

Presentation:

 Teaching Transparencies
Vocabulaire 5.1, 5.2

Practice:

Cahier de vocabulaire et grammaire

Differentiated Practice and Assessment CD-ROM

Media Guide

 Audio CD 5, Tr. 1

 Interactive Tutor, Disc 1

Teacher to Teacher

Norah L. Jones
Rustburg HS
Rustburg, VA

Try a "transparency race" to complete activities in the chapter. Form teams, and give each a transparency, pen, and tissues. Call out the number of an activity and one of the sentences in the activity. Team members should take turns writing the correct sentence on the transparency as you call it out. The first team to project their correct transparency on the overhead is the winner.

❶ Script

See script on p. 183E.

❷ Possible Answers

1. Ce n'est pas vrai!
2. J'ai peur...
3. Quelle horreur!
4. pique
5. Au secours!

---

❶ Écoutons CD 5, Tr. 1 ✿1.2

Devine quel animal est décrit et donne son nom en français.

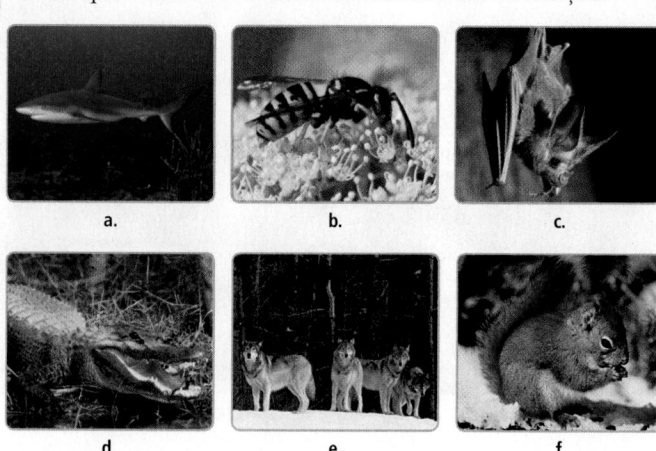

a. b. c.

d. e. f.

1. b, une guêpe 2. d, un alligator 3. f, un écureuil 4. c, une chauve-souris
5. e, un loup 6. a, un requin

❷ Oh là là! ✿1.2

Lisons/Écrivons Jonas et Noémie sont dans un parc national. Complète leur conversation.

JONAS   Regarde! Un orignal!

NOÉMIE   ___1___

JONAS   Mais si! Et là-bas, il y a un loup aussi!

NOÉMIE   Oh là là! ___2___ des loups, moi!

JONAS   Il est déjà parti. Oh! Il y a une araignée près de toi!

NOÉMIE   ___3___

JONAS   Oh! Elle est toute petite et elle ne ___4___ pas!

NOÉMIE   ___5___ Jonas! Viens vite! Je suis tombée!

❸ Une visite dans une école française ✿1.3

Parlons/Écrivons Tu es en France et on te demande quels animaux on peut voir aux États-Unis. Réponds aux questions.

1. Est-ce qu'il y a des parcs naturels dans ta région? Quels animaux est-ce qu'on peut voir dans ces parcs?
2. Quel est ton animal sauvage préféré? Pourquoi?
3. De quels animaux est-ce que tu as peur?
4. Qu'est-ce qu'on peut voir dans les bayous en Louisiane?
5. Est-ce que tu as déjà vu (ou bien est-ce que tu aimerais voir) un requin? Pourquoi ou pourquoi pas?

Flash culture

En Louisiane, les parcs comme le Parc Régional et Réserve Historique Jean-Lafitte offrent des refuges aux alligators et à de nombreux oiseaux. Les visiteurs peuvent y faire du canoë et aller à la pêche aux écrevisses. Certains parcs racontent aussi l'histoire de la région, de l'esclavage, des plantations, de l'influence des Acadiens venus s'installer en Louisiane. ✿2.2

Est-ce que tu as déjà visité un parc national? Lequel? Quel parc natio-nal aimerais-tu visiter?

Core Instruction

TEACHING EXPRIMONS-NOUS!

1. Model the pronunciation of the expressions in **Exprimons-nous!** Point out to students that **Interdiction/Défense de...** and **Prière de ne pas...** are usually found on signs. Explain that when talking to someone, the correct usage is **Il est interdit/défendu de...** and **Veuillez ne pas... (2 min.)**

2. Have partners make up similar sentences to practice forbidding and giving warnings, in different contexts, such as school life. **(2 min.)**

Exprimons-nous!

To forbid	To give warning
Il est interdit de cueillir les fleurs. *It is forbidden to . . .*	**Fais/Faites attention,** il y a un serpent! *Watch out, . . .*
Prière de ne pas nourrir les animaux. *Please don't . . .*	**Prends/Prenez garde** à tes/vos affaires. *Pay attention to . . .*
Interdiction de prendre des photos. *. . . is not allowed.*	**Méfie-toi/Méfiez-vous des** araignées. *Look out for . . .*
Défense de sortir de votre voiture. *You cannot . . .*	**Surtout,** ne va pas près des alligators. *Above all, . . .*

 Interactive TUTOR

Vocabulaire et grammaire, pp. 49–51 | Online workbooks

④ Au zoo 🏵1.2

Écrivons Tu es directeur/directrice d'un zoo. Tu dois écrire le nouveau règlement pour les futurs visiteurs. Crée des interdictions ou des avertissements *(warnings)* pour les choses suivantes.

1. donner à manger aux loups
2. marcher sur la pelouse
3. les serpents
4. jeter des papiers par terre *(on the ground)*
5. déranger les petits avec leurs mamans
6. la marche *(step)*
7. faire du bruit

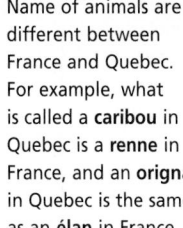

À la française

Name of animals are different between France and Quebec. For example, what is called a **caribou** in Quebec is a **renne** in France, and an **orignal** in Quebec is the same as an **élan** in France.

⑤ Tout est interdit! 🏵1.3

Parlons Dis cinq choses que tu aimerais interdire si tu le pouvais.

MODÈLE **Défense de nourrir mon poisson rouge!**

Communication

⑥ Scénario 🏵1.1

HOLT **SoundBooth** ONLINE RECORDING

Parlons En petits groupes, jouez la scène suivante. Une personne est guide dans un parc naturel. Le/La guide accompagne un groupe d'élèves pour une visite guidée du parc mais les élèves ne respectent pas les règles du parc!

MODÈLE ÉLÈVE 1   **Ces fleurs sont très belles.**
          GUIDE   **Léa! Il est interdit de cueillir les fleurs!**

Differentiated Instruction

SLOWER PACE LEARNERS

① Building on Previous Skills Before you play the audio recording, ask students to look at the photos and identify each animal in English. Have students brainstorm expressions that describe each photo. Then have students complete this activity.   🏵1.1

SPECIAL LEARNING NEEDS

Students with Auditory Impairments Ask students who know or use sign language to demonstrate the signs for the warnings in **Exprimons-nous!** The facial expression of the person signing should match the serious nature of the warnings. The signs for the animal vocabulary may be of interest to the class. Many animal signs accentuate the physical attributes of the animal they communicate.   🏵1.2

Vocabulaire 1

Resources

Planning:

Lesson Planner

 One-Stop Planner

Practice:

Grammar Tutor for Students of French, Chapter 5

Cahier de vocabulaire et grammaire

Differentiated Practice and Assessment CD-ROM

Cahier d'activités

Media Guide

 Teaching Transparencies Bell Work 5.2

🎧 Audio CD 5, Tr. 2

💿 Interactive Tutor, Disc 1

 Bell Work

Use Bell Work 5.2 in the *Teaching Transparencies* or write this activity on the board.

Reconstitue les phrases suivantes. Fais les changements nécessaires.

1. **de / être / il / papillons / attraper / les / interdit**
2. **bayous / alligators / les / les / dans / vivre**
3. **ours / poissons / manger / aimer / les / cet**
4. **être / nourrir / interdit / dauphins / de / les / il**
5. **requins / faire / avoir / y / il / attention / des / ici** 🌼1.2

7 **Script**

1. Éric veut que tu viennes avec nous pour observer les oiseaux.
2. Je crains qu'il y ait des serpents ici.
3. Je suis désolé que tu sois venu pour rien.
4. J'ai peur que nous nous perdions si nous ne suivons pas les sentiers.
5. Il vaudrait mieux que nous rentrions.
6. Est-il possible qu'il y ait des ours?
7. Oui, et je crains que les ours aient faim.
8. Moi aussi, j'ai peur qu'ils veuillent nous manger.

Objectifs
• the subjunctive with expressions of fear
• the imperative

The subjunctive with expressions of fear

1 As you already know the subjunctive is used with expressions of *necessity, desire,* and *emotion.* It is also used with expressions of *fear* like **avoir peur que...** *(to be afraid that . . .)* and **craindre que...** *(to fear that . . .).*

craindre			
je	crains	nous	craignons
tu	crains	vous	craignez
il/elle/on	craint	ils/elles	craignent

The past participle of **craindre** is **craint.**

> J'ai **peur** qu'il y **ait** des ours.   Je **crains** que cette guêpe te **pique.**

2 With expressions of fear, the dependent clause is in the subjunctive regardless of the tense of the main clause.

> Je n'aimerais pas nager là où il y a des requins. J'aurais peur qu'ils m'**attaquent.**

3 Remember that if the subject is the same in both clauses of the sentence, you use **de** with the **infinitive** instead of the **subjunctive.**

> J'ai **peur que** vous vous **blessiez. MAIS** J'ai **peur de me blesser.**

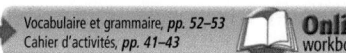 Vocabulaire et grammaire, *pp. 52–53* Cahier d'activités, *pp. 41–43*   **Online** workbooks

7 **Écoutons**   CD 5, Tr. 2 🌼1.2   **1.** b **2.** a **3.** b **4.** a **5.** b **6.** b **7.** a **8.** a

🎧 Éric est allé dans un parc avec ses amis. Écoute ce qu'ils disent et décide si **a) quelqu'un a peur** ou **b) personne n'a peur.**

8 **Une faune hostile** 🌼1.2
1. sont **2.** ait **3.** rencontrer
4. fassions **5.** soit

Écrivons Éva et ses amies se sont perdues dans les bayous. Complète ces phrases avec la forme correcte des verbes donnés.

1. Tu sais que les bayous _____ (être) plein d'alligators?
2. J'ai peur qu'il y _____ (avoir) aussi des loups ici.
3. J'ai vraiment peur de _____ (rencontrer) un alligator.
4. Il faut que nous _____ (faire) très attention.
5. Tu n'as pas peur que ça _____ (être) un peu difficile, la nuit?

En anglais

In English, one way you can complete a sentence that expresses fear is by using the future.

> *I'm afraid that we'll be late.*

Can you think of another tense that could logically complete the sentence:

> *I'm afraid that . . . ?*

In French, however, an expression of fear is always followed by the subjunctive or an infinitive.

> *J'ai peur que nous soyons en retard.*

The conditional: we would be late.

Core Instruction

TEACHING GRAMMAIRE

1. Review the subjunctive by asking volunteers to write the conjugations of **regarder, choisir, perdre, prendre, être, avoir, aller** and **faire** on the board. **(6 min.)**

2. Go over Points 1 and 2. **(2 min.)**

3. Practice using the subjunctive with these expressions by asking students questions about their fears. **Qu'est-ce que tu crains? (Je crains que...) De quoi est-ce que tu as peur? (J'ai peur que...) (2 min.)**

9 **Que d'angoisses!** 🌸1.2

Parlons/Écrivons Dis ce que les gens représentés craignent.

1. Fabien

2. Laurent

3. Théo

Online Practice
go.hrw.com
Grammaire 1 practice
KEYWORD: BD3 CH5

10 **Expédition dans la nature** 🌸1.2

Parlons/Écrivons Tu vas aller observer la faune locale avec un groupe de touristes. Fais des phrases complètes avec ces éléments.

1	2	3	4	5
Il faut	(que)	(je)	ne... pas	des loups
Il a peur	(de)	(tu)	voir	un alligator
Il est important		(elle)	rencontrer	un orignal
Je veux		(nous)	y avoir	des hérons
Je crains		(vous)	faire des photos	un requin
Elle est contente		(ils)	se perdre	un iguane
Mes parents ont peur			nourrir	un ours
			se baigner	

Communication

11 **Sondage** 🌸1.1

Parlons Demande à tes camarades de quoi ils/elles ont peur. Ils/Elles te répondront. Ensuite présente ce que tu as appris à la classe.

MODÈLE —De quoi as-tu peur?
—Je crains d'avoir une mauvaise note. Et toi?

12 **Scénario** 🌸1.1

Parlons Demande à un(e) camarade quel animal il/elle aimerait voir dans la nature et de quel animal il/elle aurait peur et pourquoi. Ensuite, échangez les rôles.

MODÈLE —J'aimerais voir... quand... Mais je n'aimerais pas... J'aurais peur que... Et toi?

Grammaire 1

Communication

Pair Activity: Interpersonal
Have partners share what their mother, father, or other family member is afraid of, especially in regard to themselves. Students should use the subjunctive with expressions of fear.

MODÈLE
— **De quoi ta mère a-t-elle peur?**
— **Elle a peur que je boive de l'alcool, mais ce n'est pas mon truc.** 🌸1.1

Comparisons

Comparing and Contrasting
Most of the functions of the Old English subjunctive have been taken over by auxiliary verbs, such as *may* and *should*. In the Romance languages, the subjunctive remains prominent, mainly because the subjunctive forms of many common verbs are strongly marked phonetically **(je sais/que je sache)**. Ask students to give examples of sentences that have the subjunctive in French but the indicative or future tense in English. **Je crains qu'elle ne vienne pas.** *I am afraid she won't come.* 🌸4.1

Differentiated Instruction

SLOWER PACE LEARNERS

Additional Practice Before you present the grammar, write an infinitive on the board. Call out a subject pronoun and ask a student to provide the correct form of the verb in the subjunctive. This student then says another pronoun and asks a classmate to give the correct verb form. After a few turns, write another infinitive on the board and repeat the procedure. 🌸1.2

SPECIAL LEARNING NEEDS

10 Students with Learning Disabilities/ Dyslexia This activity may be reduced to fewer choices as an accommodation. Prior to asking students with reading challenges to complete this activity, reduce the number of words in categories 1–5 so that the remaining elements will make four meaningful sentences. 🌸1.3

Resources

Planning:

Lesson Planner

 One-Stop Planner

Practice:

Grammar Tutor for Students of French, Chapter 5

Cahier de vocabulaire et grammaire

Differentiated Practice and Assessment CD-ROM

Cahier d'activités

Media Guide

Teaching Transparencies
Bell Work 5.3

Interactive Tutor, Disc 1

Bell Work

Use Bell Work 5.3 in the *Teaching Transparencies* or write this activity on the board.

Complète les phrases suivantes avec la forme correcte des verbes entre parenthèses.

1. J'ai peur qu'il y _____ (avoir) des loups dans le parc.
2. Nous craignons que les enfants _____ (se perdre).
3. Mes parents ont peur que je _____ (nourrir) les ours.
4. Il faut que vous _____ (prendre) des photos de l'orignal.
5. Je voudrais que tu _____ (pouvoir) admirer le corail.
🍀 1.2

COMMON ERROR ALERT
/// **ATTENTION !** \\\

To write commands, students learned to drop the **s** from the **tu** form of **–er** verbs. Sometimes, they mistakenly drop the **s** from the **tu** form of **–ir** and **–re** verbs.

Interactive TUTOR

The imperative

1 To form the imperative of most verbs, use the **tu, nous,** or **vous** form of the present indicative without the subject. Drop the final **-s** from the **tu** form of verbs that end in **-er,** including **aller.**

> Va au parc!   Prenons des photos!   Faites attention!

When the **tu** command form of an **-er** verb is followed by y or en don't drop the final **-s**.

> Vas-y!   Parles-en!
>   z   z

2 In an **affirmative command,** place object pronouns after the verb. Place a **hyphen** between the verb and pronoun. The pronouns **me** and **te** become moi and toi.

> Tu me la donnes? Donne-la-moi!
> Tu en prends? Prends-en!

3 In a **negative command,** object pronouns precede the verb. Place ne... pas around the conjugated verb and the object pronouns.

> Ne donne pas la lampe à Louis. Ne la lui donne pas.

4 The verbs **être** and **avoir** have irregular imperative forms.

> **être:** sois, soyons, soyez   **avoir:** aie, ayons, ayez
> Sois patient!   N'ayez pas peur!

> Vocabulaire et grammaire, *pp. 52–53*
> Cahier d'activités, *pp. 41–43*   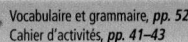  **Online** workbooks

13 **De bonnes résolutions** 1.2

Écrivons Toi et tes amis visitez les parcs naturels. Dis-leur ce qu'il faut et ce qu'il ne faut pas que vous fassiez.

> **MODÈLE** nous: nourrir les animaux (non)
> **Ne nourrissons pas les animaux!**

1. tu: faire attention aux ours (oui)
2. vous: déranger les guêpes (non)
3. nous: sortir de la voiture dans le parc (non)
4. tu: attraper des papillons (non)
5. vous: se reposer (oui)
6. nous: prendre des photos où ce n'est pas interdit (oui)
7. tu: avoir un peu de patience (oui)
8. nous: être prudents (oui)
9. vous: faire du bruit (non)

Flash culture

L'influence française et cajun est encore visible aujourd'hui en Louisiane, par exemple dans les noms des villes comme Baton Rouge et Lafayette ou les noms de famille d'origine française. Il y a aussi des lois de l'état *(state laws)* dont certaines sont basées sur le Code Napoléon. En Louisiane, on ne trouve pas de *counties* comme dans les autres états, mais des *parishes* du mot français «paroisse». 🍀4.2

Quelle influence est-ce que le français a eu dans ton état? Est-ce qu'il y a une autre communauté qui a eu ou a encore de l'influence dans ton état?

Core Instruction

TEACHING GRAMMAIRE

1. Go over Points 1–4. Point out three things to students. First, the final –s, dropped from the **tu** form of verbs ending in –er, reappears when the verb is followed by an object pronoun beginning with a vowel. **Vas-y! Manges-en!** Can students guess why? Next, the pronouns **me** and **te** will change to **moi** and **toi** when placed after the verb. **Regarde-moi! Peigne-toi!** Finally, you cannot leave the subject in a French imperative as you sometimes do in English (*You be quiet!*). **(6 min.)**

2. To practice, write sentences in the **tu, nous** and **vous** forms of the present tense on the board. **Tu laves le chien. Nous parlons au (à) (la) prof. Vous écoutez vos parents.** Then ask students to change them into commands first, and second to replace the direct or indirect objects in these commands with pronouns. Finally, have students make the commands negative. **(4 min.)**

14 **Tout un programme** 1.2

Écrivons/Parlons Ton ami(e) voudrait faire ces choses pendant ses vacances. Dis-lui de les faire seulement si tu penses que c'est une bonne idée. Récris les phrases à l'impératif.

MODÈLE attraper des guêpes **N'attrape pas de guêpes!**

1. aller à la mer
2. prendre beaucoup de photos
3. nourrir les pélicans
4. visiter les grottes
5. nager avec les dauphins
6. allumer un feu

15 **Il faut le savoir** 1.2

Parlons Il y a beaucoup de choses qu'on n'est pas autorisé à faire dans ce parc. Dis à tes amis ce qu'ils ne doivent surtout pas faire.

MODÈLE **Surtout, ne faites pas de vélo!**

à Louis et Rémy

1. à Théo
2. à Lucas et Mia
3. à Tristan
4. à Margot et Luc

16 **Juste le contraire** 1.2

Écrivons/Parlons Pour chaque ordre que Félix donne, dis le contraire. Remplace les mots soulignés par un pronom.

MODÈLE Regarde Julie. **Ne la regarde pas!**

1. Donnons à manger <u>aux requins</u>.
2. Va <u>au zoo</u>.
3. Ne prenez pas <u>de photos</u>.
4. Faisons peur <u>aux hérons</u>.
5. Attrape <u>des méduses</u>.
6. Jouons avec <u>les loups</u>.

Communication

HOLT **SoundBooth**
ONLINE RECORDING

17 **Scénario** 1.1

Parlons Tu guides un groupe de touristes et tu leur dis ce qu'il faut qu'ils fassent et ce qu'il ne faut pas qu'ils fassent. Suggère-leur aussi des choses intéressantes à faire. Joue cette scène avec des camarades.

MODÈLE —C'est incroyable, je n'ai jamais vu d'ours de si près!
—Méfiez-vous! Ils sont très dangereux! Surtout quand il y a des petits!

Differentiated Instruction

ADVANCED LEARNERS

17 **Variation** Have students look at the posters they created in the **Extension** activity on page 187. Ask them to make a positive or negative command relative to each photo. You may want to ask the class to vote on the most creative command(s). 1.1

MULTIPLE INTELLIGENCES

Linguistic Ask students to copy the rules from the imperative grammar presentation onto a sheet of poster board. Next to the rule, they should write example sentences. Work closely with the class to compose the first example for each rule. Allow student volunteers to provide additional examples for each of the rules. Display the posters in the classroom as resources and reference material. 1.2

Communication

Pair Activity: Interpersonal
Have each student write five sentences in the subjunctive, telling others what he or she wants them to do or not to do. Have partners take turns reading their sentences. The partner has to restate the desire in the imperative, using object pronouns.

MODÈLE
— **Je veux que tu fasses la vaisselle.**
— **Fais-la!** 1.2

Assess

Assessment Program
Quiz : Grammaire 1
Alternative Assessment
Differentiated Practice and Assessment CD-ROM

Online Assessment
my.hrw.com

Test Generator

Synthèse
- Vocabulaire 1
- Grammaire 1

Application 1

18 Écoutons CD 5, Tr. 3 🌼1.2 **1.** a **2.** b **3.** a **4.** a **5.** b **6.** a **7.** b

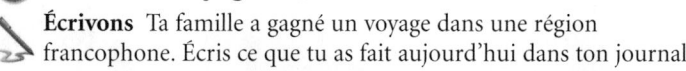 Jacques donne des conseils à ses camarades. Dans chacune des phrases que tu entends, décide si Jacques **a) leur donne un ordre** ou **b) ne leur donne pas d'ordre.**

19 Des conseils 🌼1.3

Parlons/Écrivons Quels conseils donnerais-tu à quelqu'un qui va aller en vacances à la montagne? à la mer? Dis quatre choses qui sont interdites là où cette personne va aller et dis-lui deux choses dont elle doit se méfier.

20 Carnet de voyages 🌼1.3

Écrivons Ta famille a gagné un voyage dans une région francophone. Écris ce que tu as fait aujourd'hui dans ton journal.

MODÈLE Haïti, le 9 juillet
Aujourd'hui, on a fait un tour en bateau. Le guide nous a montré...! C'était...!

Un peu plus

The verbs *voir* and *regarder*

You've already learned the verbs **voir** *(to see)* and **regarder** *(to look at* or *to watch)*. Be careful to choose the appropriate verb when creating sentences in French.

> **Regarde** cet ours!
> *Look at that bear!*
>
> Tu **vois** cet ours?
> *Do you see that bear?*

Vocabulaire et grammaire, *p. 54*
Cahier d'activités, *pp. 41–43*

 **Online** workbooks

21 Le bon verbe 🌼1.2

Lisons/Écrivons Julien et son copain sont dans un parc au Canada. Complète ce passage avec **voir** ou **regarder** au temps correct.

____1____, Julien! Cet ours va attraper un poisson! Tu ____2____ ça! Il l'a attrapé! Je n'ai jamais ____3____ ça! Tu sais, je ____4____ souvent des émissions sur les animaux à la télévision, mais pouvoir les ____5____ dans leur milieu naturel, c'est incroyable! Tu ____6____, c'est pour cela que j'aime passer mes vacances dans des parcs naturels!
1. Regarde **2.** as vu **3.** vu
4. regarde **5.** voir **6.** vois

💻 Bell Work

Use Bell Work 5.4 in the *Teaching Transparencies* or write this activity on the board.

Dis à ton copain ce qu'il doit ou ne doit pas faire. Récris les phrases à **l'impératif.**

1. aller voir les dauphins
2. nager avec les requins
3. prendre une photo d'un iguane
4. jouer avec les ours
5. être prudent 🌼1.2

18 Script

See script on p. 183E.

22 Answers

1. Eric ne pourrait pas y aller parce qu'il ne peut pas prendre son chien.
2. Yanis pourrait y aller parce qu'on peut camper.
3. Léa pourrait y aller parce qu'on peut y faire du vélo.
4. Maya ne pourrait pas y aller parce qu'on ne peut pas nourrir les animaux.

Core Instruction

INTEGRATED PRACTICE

1. Have students do Activities 18–20 to practice previously taught material. **(5 min.)**
2. Introduce **Un peu plus.** (See presentation suggestions at right.) **(4 min.)**
3. Continue with integrated practice Activities 21–24. **(30 min.)**

TEACHING UN PEU PLUS

1. Review the conjugation of **voir** by asking students to write a few sentences about themselves and other people. **Nous nous voyons au centre commercial. (4 min.)**
2. Ask students to complete your sentences, with **voir** or **regarder.**

   Le soir, je suis dans un fauteuil et je... (regarde la télé.) (Mime using the remote.)
   Hé! Là... (Regarde!) (Point with your finger.) **(2 min.)**

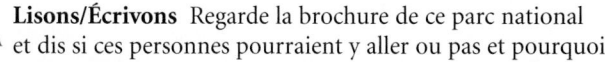
Online Practice
go.**hrw**.com
Application 1 practice
KEYWORD: BD3 CH5

22 **Regarde les panneaux** 3.2

Lisons/Écrivons Regarde la brochure de ce parc national et dis si ces personnes pourraient y aller ou pas et pourquoi.

Règlement du parc des Eaux Claires

 Les feux doivent être allumés dans les endroits prévus en utilisant le bois fourni à cette fin.

 Il est interdit de faire de l'escalade.

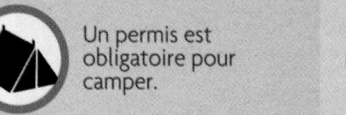 Un permis est obligatoire pour camper.

 Les animaux domestiques sont interdits.

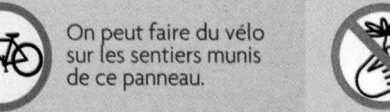 On peut faire du vélo sur les sentiers munis de ce panneau.

 Il est défendu de prélever tout élément naturel (faune, flore, fossile, roche, etc.)

Aucun déchet ne doit être laissé dans le parc.

 Il est défendu de nourrir les animaux sauvages.

1. Éric a un chien.
2. Yanis a pris sa tente.
3. Léa veut faire du vélo.
4. Maya aime nourrir les animaux.

23 **Ton propre panneau** 1.3

Écrivons Crée un panneau pour interdire ou permettre quelque chose. Ensuite montre-le à tes camarades. Est-ce qu'ils comprennent ce que ton panneau veut dire?

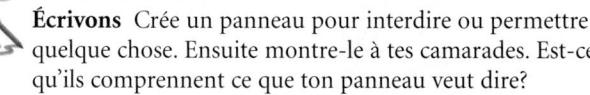**Communication**

 HOLT **SoundBooth** ONLINE RECORDING

24 **Scénario** 1.1

Parlons Tu organises des safaris photos et des touristes te posent des questions pour savoir les animaux qu'ils vont voir. Ils sont très étonnés. Tu leur dis aussi quelles précautions ils vont devoir prendre. Joue cette scène avec des camarades.

Communication

Group Activity: Interpersonal

Have students write down three fears they might have concerning a trip to Quebec, Haiti, or Louisiana. Have them use **avoir peur que** or **craindre que** with the subjunctive. In small groups, students take turns telling where they are going and what they're afraid of. A group member gives advice, using the imperative.

MODÈLE

— **Je vais en Louisiane et je crains que les alligators me mordent.**
— **Ne nage pas dans les bayous!** 1.1

Differentiated Instruction

SLOWER PACE LEARNERS

24 Before students prepare their conversations, ask them to brainstorm and write down the statements they want to make. You may want to call on some partners to present their conversation for the class. 1.1, 1.3

MULTIPLE INTELLIGENCES

24 **Technologist** Before doing this activity, ask students to create a PowerPoint show with a variety of animals. They can scan in the photographs the photographs they took for an earlier project. Each slide should have a brief caption in French. Students can use these slides to help them during their conversation. 1.3

Assess

Assessment Program
Quiz : Application 1
Audio CD 5, Tr. 12
Alternative Assessment
Differentiated Practice and Assessment CD-ROM

Online Assessment
my.hrw.com

Test Generator

Resources

Planning:
Lesson Planner
 One-Stop Planner

Practice:
Cahier d'activités

Prereading Questions

You may ask these questions before students read the selection.

1. **Est-ce que tu es déjà allé dans un grand parc? Lequel?**
2. **Est-ce que tu as déjà fait une randonnée à vélo ou à cheval dans un parc?**
3. **Es-tu déjà allé sur une rivière en bateau?**
4. **Aimes-tu observer les animaux quand tu te promènes?**

Active Reading Questions

1. **Qu'est-ce que vous pouvez observer deux fois par an sur les berges du Saint-Laurent? (oies voyageuses)**
2. **Quel autre nom donne-t-on aux oies blanches? (oies des neiges)**
3. **Pourquoi est-ce que ces oies s'arrêtent sur les berges du Saint-Laurent? (pour se reposer et y prendre des forces)**
4. **En automne, où vont-elles? (au sud, dans les pays chauds)**
5. **Au printemps, où vont-elles? (dans le Grand Nord: aux îles Baffin et Bylot)**

Vocabulaire supplémentaire

You might wish to use these terms to discuss the text.

la migration	*migration*
un oiseau migrateur	*migratory bird*
les jumelles	*binoculars*
la gourde	*gourd*
la barque	*boat*

Culture

Lecture culturelle

Les parcs d'Amérique francophone offrent des activités variées: randonnées à pied ou à vélo, escalade ou encore descentes de rivières en kayak, etc. Au Québec, on peut admirer les ours, les loups et les orignaux en pleine nature, observer les baleines dans l'estuaire du Saint-Laurent ou faire des ballades en traîneau à chiens dans le Grand Nord. Dans le pays cajun au climat subtropical, on peut parcourir les bayous et les rives du Mississippi et y découvrir une faune pittoresque. Observes-tu souvent les animaux? Que penses-tu de l'activité ci-dessous? 1.3, 3.1

NATURE

LES OIES[1] VOYAGEUSES

*Des allers-retours à ne pas manquer
C'est un spectacle unique!*

Des centaines de milliers[2] d'oies des neiges (oies blanches) font escale deux fois l'an sur les berges[3] du Saint-Laurent.

À l'automne, de retour des îles Baffin et Bylot[4], elles viennent y prendre des forces avant de poursuivre le grand voyage qui les mènera[5] vers leurs chauds quartiers d'hiver. Puis elles reviennent au printemps, en route[6] vers le Grand Nord, où elles vont passer l'été. Un périple[7] annuel de près de 4.000 km! Surveillez[8] leur vol dans le ciel[9] ou, encore mieux, allez les observer dans leurs trois haltes de prédilection : Cap-Tourmente, Baie-du-Febvre et Montmagny.

Compréhension 1.2

1. Où peut-on observer la migration des oies sauvages?
2. Combien de fois par an font-elles escale sur les berges du Saint-Laurent?
3. D'où viennent-elles et où vont-elles?
4. Combien de kilomètres parcourent-elles chaque année?

1. au Québec
2. 2 fois par an
3. Elles viennent des îles Baffin et Bylot. Elles vont vers des pays chauds.
4. 4.000 km

1. *geese* 2. *hundreds of thousands* 3. *banks* 4. *des îles proches du Groenland* 5. *dirigera* 6. *vers* 7. *voyage* 8. *Observez* 9. *sky*

Core Instruction

LECTURE CULTURELLE

1. Read and discuss the introductory paragraph. **(2 min.)**
2. Read *Les oies voyageuses* aloud with the class. **(20 min.)**
3. Ask partners to answer the **Compréhension** questions. **(3 min.)**

COMPARAISONS ET COMMUNAUTÉ

1. Read *Les parcs publics en France* as a class. Pause after the first paragraph to let students choose the right answer to the question, then finish reading the article. **(5 min.)**
2. Have the class discuss **Et toi? (5 min.)**
3. Go over **Communauté et professions** with students. Ask volunteers to research extreme sports instructor training in your state and to present their findings to the class. **(8 min.)**

Online Practice
go.hrw.com
Online Edition
KEYWORD: BD3 CH5

Chapitre 5
Culture

Comparaisons

Une pancarte dans un parc en France

Les parcs publics en France 🏵2.2

Tu te promènes avec tes amis au jardin du Luxembourg. Il est midi et vous décidez de manger dans le parc.

a. Vous mettez les chaises sur la pelouse et vous vous installez.
b. Vous vous asseyez sur les chaises qui sont dans l'allée.
c. Vous vous asseyez sur la pelouse.

Dans les villes françaises, il y a beaucoup de parcs publics. Les gens s'y promènent, y lisent, y font du jogging. Il y a des bancs[1] où l'on peut s'asseoir, des bacs à sable[2] et des balançoires pour les tout-petits. Ces parcs sont agréables avec leurs parterres[3] de fleurs et leurs pelouses bien vertes. Malheureusement, il est très souvent interdit de marcher sur les pelouses. Elles sont bien trop fragiles!

🏵4.2

ET TOI?

1. Est-ce qu'il y a des parcs dans ta ville? Ils sont comment?
2. Peut-on jouer, pique-niquer ou même marcher sur les pelouses près de chez toi?

Communauté et professions

Moniteurs/Guides de sports extrêmes 🏵4.2, 5.1

Les sports extrêmes sont de plus en plus populaires et les accrocs[4] à ces sports partent souvent à l'étranger à la recherche de sensations fortes. Est-ce qu'il y a des activités sportives proposées dans ton état (rafting, escalade...)? Quelle formation ont les moniteurs, accompagnateurs ou guides? Est-ce qu'ils doivent savoir parler français ou une autre langue étrangère? Fais des recherches et présente ce que tu as découvert à ta classe.

1. benches   2. sandboxes   3. flower beds   4. addicted

Canyoning dans le Colorado

Culture

Bulletin Board Project

Ask students to create French signs that tell visitors what to do and what not to do in the park or, alternatively, in your classroom. The signs should be creative and can be funny. Ask volunteers to post the signs on a classroom bulletin board. Discuss the entries as a class. 🏵1.3

Cultures

Products and Perspectives

Quebec's 27 national parks provide opportunities for many activities, such as hiking, camping, bicycling, skiing, dog sledding, or wildlife observation. Each park has its unique personality due to its location, flora, and fauna. They all boast a large diversity of natural sites and scenery. Ask students if there are any wilderness parks in their area. Have them discuss the activities people enjoy at these parks and the wildlife that can be observed. 🏵2.1

Communities

Career Path

Ask the students to investigate careers in sports involving the use of the French language. Have volunteers tell whether or not this is a job that might interest them and explain why. 🏵5.1

Differentiated Instruction

ADVANCED LEARNERS

Extension Ask students to choose one of Quebec's 27 national parks and write an advertisement for it. The ad should include a description of the park's location, its scenery and wildlife, and the activities the park has to offer. Does the park provide overnight accommodations? Does it have picnic areas or restaurants? Students should illustrate their ads with photos and charts if possible. After students have presented all the ads, they should vote on a park they would like to visit. 🏵1.3, 3.1

MULTIPLE INTELLIGENCES

Linguistic Ask students to research an extreme sport they would like to try. In French, they should compose a paragraph explaining the sport, the equipment needed, and the potential dangers of the sport. The paragraphs could be collected and displayed on the classroom bulletin board for all to read. 🏵1.3

Bell Work

Use Bell Work 5.5 in the *Teaching Transparencies* or write this activity on the board.

Complète les phrases avec la forme correcte de **voir** ou **regarder**.

1. Hier, j'_____ des loups dans ce parc.
2. Fais attention, _____ où tu mets les pieds.
3. Tu _____ souvent des alligators dans ce bayou?
4. Simon et Théo, _____ cette araignée, comme elle est mignonne!
5. Vous _____ ça! Il a attrapé ce papillon avec sa main.

🌸 1.2

Proverbes

For French proverbs and activities related to the chapter theme and vocabulary, see **Proverbes et expressions,** pp. R6–R7.

Objectifs
- to give general directions
- to complain and offer encouragement

Les sports extrêmes

Ah, au fait, j'ai fait de la plongée sous-marine en Haïti.

J'ai fait de la spéléologie.

une corde

J'ai fait de l'alpinisme (m.) au Québec, cet été.

un VTT

Et j'ai parcouru les Alpes en VTT.

Moi, je rêve de faire le tour du monde à la voile en solitaire!

Core Instruction

TEACHING VOCABULAIRE

1. Introduce the vocabulary with transparencies **Vocabulaire 5.3** and **5.4**. Model the pronunciation of each word or expression, using **Il/Elle a fait... (du rafting, de la spéléologie). (3 min.)**

2. Ask students to point to various activities **(de la plongée sous-marine, du VTT)** on the transparency. **(2 min.)**

3. Ask students questions about their activities and those of family members. **Qu'est-ce que tu as déjà fait comme activités? Et tes parents? (3 min.)**

4. Model the pronunciation of the expressions in **Exprimons-nous!** Have partners write similar sentences about places in your area. **(4 min.)**

On peut aussi...

faire du deltaplane

faire du parachutisme

Online Practice
go.hrw.com
Vocabulaire 2 practice
KEYWORD: BD3 CH5

faire du canoë-kayak

un canoë

descendre des rapides (m.)

Exprimons-nous!

To give general directions

Interactive TUTOR

Les rapides se trouvent/sont **dans le nord de** l'île.
... *in the north of* ...

Au sud de la ville, il y a des montagnes où on fait de l'alpinisme.
South of ...

Si tu vas plus à l'est, tu arriveras aux grottes.
If you go further east, ...

Continue **vers l'ouest,** ce n'est plus très loin.
... *toward the west,* ...

C'est à environ trois kilomètres **d'ici.**
It's about ... *from* ...

D'autres mots utiles

une bouteille de plongée	*scuba tank*
une combinaison de plongée	*wetsuit*
un équipement	*equipment*
une île	*island*
un parachute	*parachute*
du rafting	*rafting*

Vocabulaire et grammaire, pp. 55–57

Online workbooks

▶ Vocabulaire supplémentaire—Le matériel pour les sports extrêmes, p. R19

25 Script

See script on p. 193F.

26 Answers

1. Fort Liberté
2. Les Cayes
3. La République Dominicaine
4. Saint-Louis-du-Nord
5. Port-au-Prince
6. L'île de la Vache

27 Answers

1. Il va faire du parachutisme.
2. Vous allez faire de la plongée sous-marine.
3. Elle va faire de la spéléologie.
4. Il va faire du rafting.
5. Elles vont faire du VTT (vélo tout terrain).
6. Il va faire de l'alpinisme.

28 Possible Answers

1. environ
2. au sud
3. trop
4. est presque
5. n'en peux plus/meurs de soif
6. courage
7. effort
8. en vaut la peine
9. le vertige

25 Écoutons CD 5, Tr. 4 1.2 **1.** a **2.** a **3.** b **4.** a **5.** b **6.** a

Indique si on parle d'activités qu'on fait **a) à la mer** ou **b) à la montagne.**

26 Vacances en Haïti 3.1

Lisons Tu passes des vacances chez Maurice, un ami haïtien. Identifie les endroits qu'il mentionne en utilisant la carte d'Haïti.

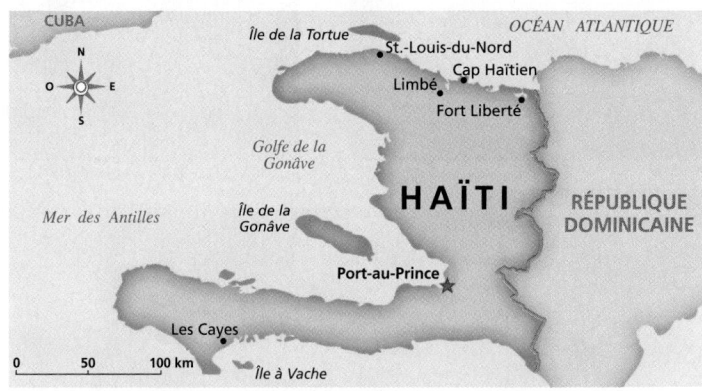

1. Cette ville est dans le nord de l'île, à l'est de Cap Haïtien.
2. De Port-au-Prince, si tu vas plus à l'ouest, tu arriveras dans cette ville.
3. C'est le pays qui est à l'est d'Haïti.
4. Cette ville est juste au sud de l'île de la Tortue.
5. La capitale est à environ 150 km au sud de Cap Haïtien.
6. Cette île est au sud du pays.

27 Envie d'extrême 1.2

Lisons/Écrivons Ces jeunes ont envie d'essayer une nouvelle activité sportive. Quel sport est-ce qu'ils vont faire, d'après toi?

MODÈLE Léo adore la mer et il veut aller dans le monde entier. **Il va faire le tour du monde à la voile en solitaire.**

1. Luc a envie de sauter d'un avion.
2. Patrick et moi, nous voulons voir des requins.
3. Stéphanie veut visiter des grottes.
4. Le cousin de Laurent veut descendre des rapides.
5. Sylvia et Nadine adorent faire du vélo, mais pas en ville.
6. Joshua a pris des cordes et il est parti à la montagne.

Entre copains

une bestiole	bug
casse-cou	daredevil
être casse-cou	to be a daredevil
crever de soif	to die of thirst
faire gaffe	to be careful

Core Instruction

TEACHING EXPRIMONS-NOUS!

1. Model the pronunciation of each expression. **(2 min.)**
2. Name activities. (**Tu fais un marathon. Tu fais de l'alpinisme.**) Ask students to tell you a complaint they might make while doing the activity. (**Je meurs de soif!**)

In response to each complaint, other students offer encouragement, using the expressions introduced in **Exprimons-nous! (3 min.)**

Exprimons-nous!

To complain	To offer encouragement
C'est trop loin! *That's too . . . !*	Oui, mais **ça en vaut la peine.** *. . . it's worth it.*
J'ai le vertige! *I'm dizzy!*	**Allez, encore un petit effort!** *Come on, one last effort!*
Je meurs de soif! *I'm dying of . . . !*	**Tu y es presque!** *You're almost there!*
Je n'en peux plus! *I can't do any more!*	**Courage, on est presque arrivés!** *Hang in there/Cheer up, . . .*

Interactive TUTOR

Vocabulaire et grammaire, pp. 55–57 **Online** workbooks

28 Que tout est difficile! 🌸1.1

Écrivons/Parlons Samir fait visiter la région où il habite à son ami Fabien. Aujourd'hui, Samir a décidé d'emmener son ami voir de magnifiques grottes. Complète leur conversation de manière logique.

FABIEN   Où sont les grottes dont tu parlais?

SAMIR   Elles sont à ___1___ 10 km ___2___ de la ville.

FABIEN   10 km! C'est ___3___ loin!

SAMIR   Mais non! On y ___4___.

FABIEN   Et en plus, il fait si chaud! Je ___5___.

SAMIR   Allez, ___6___ ! Encore un petit ___7___ ! Tu verras, ça ___8___ !

FABIEN   J'espère qu'elles ne sont pas trop grandes, ces grottes, parce que tu sais, j'ai ___9___ !

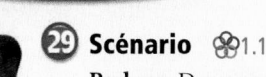

29 Scénario 🌸1.1

HOLT **SoundBooth** ONLINE RECORDING

Parlons Deux ami(e)s ont décidé de passer le week-end à faire de la randonnée dans une région qu'ils/elles ne connaissent pas. Un(e) des deux ami(e)s critique tout et se plaint *(complains)* tout le temps! L'autre ami(e) essaie de l'encourager et de le/la rassurer. Joue cette scène avec un(e) camarade.

MODÈLE   —Mais il n'y a pas d'animaux ici!
—Mais si! Si on va plus à l'ouest, il y a...
Je suis sûr(e) qu'on va voir des...
—Ah non! C'est...

Differentiated Instruction

ADVANCED LEARNERS

26 Extension Ask students to research Haiti on the Internet and add five cities or other places to the map. Then have them write a clue, similar to the clues in this activity, for each new place. Have partners exchange and answer the clues. 🌸1.2

MULTIPLE INTELLIGENCES

Linguistic Have students use the chapter vocabulary to write to an advice columnist about a common complaint of teenagers. Ask students to exchange letters and write responses with advice and encouragement. Have partners share their letters and responses with the class. 🌸1.2

Connections

History Link

The **Île de la Tortue**, discovered by Christopher Columbus in 1494, was a haven for pirates in the seventeenth century. The island was originally settled by a few Spanish colonists and later by French and English colonists. From 1630 on, the island was divided into French and English colonies, allowing buccaneers, more commonly known as pirates, to use the island as their main base of operations. The Treaty of Ratisbon, signed 1684 by the European powers, forbade sailing under foreign flags and was a major legal blow to Caribbean pirates. Within a few years, the age of buccaneers had ended. Have students research piracy in the Caribbean. Ask them if piracy still exists today. 🌸3.1

Communication

Pair Activity: Interpersonal

Have partners act out a conversation in which one pretends to be a travel agent and the other a student who wants to go on an adventurous trip. Have them discuss interests, activities, supplies needed, and location of certain destinations or attractions. Then have the partners act out their conversation in front of the class. 🌸1.1, 1.3

Assess

Assessment Program
Quiz: Vocabulaire 2
Alternative Assessment
Differentiated Practice and Assessment CD-ROM

Online Assessment
my.hrw.com

Test Generator

Bell Work

Use Bell Work 5.6 in the *Teaching Transparencies* or write this activity on the board.

Dis ce qu'il fait!

1. **Il voit souvent des requins.**
2. **Il descend dans des grottes.**
3. **Il descend des rapides.**
4. **Il saute de l'avion.**
5. **Il fait du vélo dans les Alpes.**
6. **Il a pris des cordes à la montagne.**

a. **Il fait du VTT.**
b. **Il fait de l'alpinisme.**
c. **Il fait de la spéléologie.**
d. **Il fait du rafting.**
e. **Il fait de la plongée sous-marine.**
f. **Il fait du parachutisme.**

🌀1.2

31 Script

1. Allez, emmenez-le!
2. Vous l'emportez, ou je vous le livre?
3. Amène-la, si tu veux, ça sera intéressant.
4. Tu peux les apporter, si tu as envie.
5. Je ne veux pas les voir, emportez-les!
6. C'est toi qui l'as emmenée là-bas?

Objectifs
- *apporter, amener, emporter,* and *emmener*
- verbs + *à/de* + infinitive

Grammaire
à l'œuvre

Interactive TUTOR

Apporter, amener, emporter and emmener

1 In French, there are two verbs that mean *to bring,* **apporter** and **amener**. Use **apporter** to say that someone is *bringing something to someone.*

> François m'a **apporté** des fleurs.

Use **amener** to say that someone is *bringing someone to where the speaker is.* Amener has the same spelling change as **acheter**.

> Pauline **amène** son chien chez moi tous les week-ends.

2 There are also two verbs that mean *to take,* **emporter** and **emmener**. Use **emporter** to say that *something is being taken somewhere.*

> J'**emporte** toujours mon portable avec moi quand je fais du jogging.

Use **emmener** to say that *a person is being taken somewhere.* Emmener has the same spelling change as **amener**.

> Pauline **emmènera** Charles à la gare demain matin.
> *(she's dropping him off there)*

🌀4.1
En anglais

In English, *bring* is generally used when an object or person is being moved towards someone. *Take* is generally used when an object or person is being moved away.

Which verb would you use in each of these sentences?

1. *Would you_____me another soft drink?*
2. *The flight attendant is going to_____ your ticket.*

In French also the verb you choose depends on whether the movement is towards or away from someone.

1. bring 2. take

Vocabulaire et grammaire, *pp. 58–59*
Cahier d'activités, *pp. 45–47*
Online workbooks

30 Transport 1.2

Lisons Rita et ses sœurs parlent des personnes et des choses qu'il faut transporter. Complète leurs phrases de manière logique.

e **1.** J'ai besoin de tes dictionnaires, …

a **2.** Maman viendra aussi à la fête, …

b **3.** Voici tes lunettes, …

f **4.** Julien veut aller au cinéma avec toi, …

d **5.** C'est l'anniversaire de mariage de papa et maman, …

a. tu peux l'amener?

b. n'oublie pas de les emporter.

c. apporte-le!

d. emmenons-les au resto!

e. tu peux me les apporter?

f. emmène-le, s'il te plaît.

31 Écoutons CD 5, Tr. 5 1.2 **1.** a **2.** b **3.** a **4.** b **5.** b **6.** a

 Pour chaque phrase que tu entends, dis si on parle a) **d'une personne ou d'un animal** ou b) **d'une chose.**

Core Instruction

TEACHING GRAMMAIRE

1. Read **En anglais** aloud with students. **(2 min.)**

2. Go over the presentation with students. Point out that **apporter** and **emporter** are reserved for objects, because they contain the verb **porter**, which means *to carry.* Tell students that **amener** and **emmener** are used with people and animals, because they contain **mener**, which means *to lead.* **(3 min.)**

3. To have students practice using the right verb, name a person or an object, and a direction, either **ici** or **là-bas**. Students will respond appropriately. **Nathalie, là-bas… (Emmène-la!) Ton livre, ici… (Apporte-le!) (2 min.)**

Online Practice
go.hrw.com
Grammaire 2 practice
KEYWORD: BD3 CH5

Chapitre 5
Grammaire 2

Grammaire 2

32 À ne pas oublier 🏵1.2

Écrivons/Parlons Il y a certaines personnes et certaines choses qu'il ne faut pas oublier. Complète les phrases avec **amener, emmener, apporter** et **emporter**. Attention aux temps des verbes!

♻ *Souviens-toi!* *Subjunctive, p. 150*

1. Le prof a demandé qu'on _____ notre livre de maths en classe demain.

2. Toi, il faut que tu _____ ton petit frère à l'école.

3. Si nous faisons une promenade ce soir, il faudra que nous _____ le chien.

4. Il va sûrement pleuvoir. Si tu sors, _____ ton parapluie!

5. Oh... vous m'avez _____ un cadeau? Qu'est-ce que c'est?

6. N'oublie pas d'_____ ton appareil photo quand tu pars en vacances.

1. apporte
2. emmènes
3. emmenions
4. emporte
5. apporté
6. emporter

33 Qu'ont-ils fait? 🏵1.2

Parlons Isabelle raconte ce que certains de ses amis ont fait récemment. Choisis le bon verbe pour décrire ce que ces gens ont fait.

MODÈLE **Véronique a amené sa grand-mère à l'aéroport.**

Déposez ici vos passagers / Kiss

Véronique / sa grand-mère

1. Vincent / canoë 2. le mécanicien / voiture 3. Amélie / amis 4. Valérie / sa fille

Communication

34 Expérience personnelle 🏵1.1

Parlons Demande à un(e) camarade ce qu'il/elle apporte/amène quand il/elle va à une fête, part en vacances, quand il pleut, etc.

MODÈLE —Qu'est-ce que tu apportes quand tu vas à une fête?
—Oh, quelquefois j'apporte...

HOLT **SoundBooth**
ONLINE RECORDING

33 Possible Answers

1. Vincent a apporté son canoë au parc.
2. Le mécanicien a emporté la voiture à la station-service.
3. Amélie a amené des amis à la fête.
4. Valérie a emmené sa fille à l'école.

Communication

Class Activity: Interpretive

Inside/Outside Circles Prepare enough index cards for half of the class. On the front, write a prompt in this format: Subject → (take) or ← (bring) person/thing. On the back, write the answer. **J'amène des amis.** Then half the class forms a circle, holding the cards with the prompts facing out. The remaining half of the class forms an outside circle. Students in the outside circle form the sentence, based on the prompt, in the present or **passé composé**. The inside circle verifies for accuracy. Students in the outside circle then rotate to the left. After a full rotation, have circles switch roles.

🏵1.2

Language Note

According to the rules, the verb **emmener** should be used in **Il faut que tu emmènes ton petit frère à l'école**, since someone is being taken somewhere. However, the French commonly say, **Il faut que tu amènes ton frère à l'école**, in the sense that someone is bringing someone else somewhere. Sometimes the French say, **J'ai emmené mes affaires.** Ask students if the use of **emmener** is grammatically correct in this sentence. Why or why not? Have students give the correct sentence. (**J'ai emporté mes affaires.**)

🏵1.2

Differentiated Instruction

SLOWER PACE LEARNERS

32 Extension Before students fill in the blanks in this activity, write the following four categories on the board: bring, thing → **apporter**; bring, person/animal → **amener**; take, thing → **emporter**; take, person/animal → **emmener**. Ask students to determine to which category each statement belongs and then have them write the correct form of the verb in each blank. 🏵1.2

SPECIAL LEARNING NEEDS

34 Students with Speech Impairments Give students the option of writing a journal entry about the topic before talking to a classmate. Impromptu speaking can be difficult for students with speech impairments and preparing a script through the journal or completing the assignment through journaling alone may be an appropriate accommodation. 🏵1.1

Resources

Planning:

Lesson Planner

 One-Stop Planner

Practice:

Grammar Tutor for Students of French, Chapter 5

Cahier de vocabulaire et grammaire

Differentiated Practice and Assessment CD-ROM

Cahier d'activités

Media Guide

 Teaching Transparencies Bell Work 5.7

 Interactive Tutor, Disc 1

 Bell Work

Use Bell Work 5.7 in the *Teaching Transparencies* or write this activity on the board.

Complète les phrases avec **apporter, amener,** ou **emporter, emmener.**

1. Vous ne pouvez pas _____ votre chien ici.
2. Audrey _____ Laurent chez le dentiste.
3. Le dimanche nous _____ nos enfants à la plage.
4. Quand je suis invité, j'_____ des fleurs.
5. Est-ce que tu _____ ton appareil photo en voyage? 🌸1.2

Flash culture

Le Canada avec ses grands espaces et sa géographie très diversifiée est un lieu idéal pour certains sports extrêmes : rafting, trecks, escalade et sports de neige. Un des sports pratiqués au Canada est le *mushing* ou sport du chien de traîneau. Il existe des courses de chiens de traîneau dont la plus célèbre est La Grande Odyssée, 1.000 km de course en 10 étapes. Il y a aussi la Yukon Quest qui relie Whitehorse au Canada à Fairbanks en Alaska (16.000 km). 🌸1.2

Est-ce que tu as déjà pratiqué un sport extrême? Lequel? Si non, lequel te tenterait?

 Interactive TUTOR

Verbs followed by *à/de* and the infinitive

1 Some **verbs** are directly followed by an infinitive.

aimer	espérer	préférer
aller	falloir (il faut)	savoir
devoir	pouvoir	vouloir

Je **vais** faire du parachutisme avec ma cousine.

2 Some **verbs** are followed by **à** + infinitive.

aider à	arriver à	encourager à
s'amuser à	commencer à	penser à
apprendre à	continuer à	réussir à

Jean-François m'a **aidé** à trouver le livre que je cherchais.

3 Some **verbs** and **expressions** are followed by **de** + infinitive.

(s')arrêter de	craindre de	mourir de
avoir peur/raison de	décider de	offrir de
choisir de	dire de	oublier de
conseiller de	essayer de	venir de

J'ai **peur** de tomber quand je fais de l'alpinisme.

> Vocabulaire et grammaire, pp. 58–59
> Cahier d'activités, pp. 45–47
> **Online** workbooks

35 **Passionnés de sport** 🌸1.2

Lisons/Écrivons Ces gens-là pratiquent tous des sports plus ou moins extrêmes. Complète les phrases suivantes avec **à** ou **de**, mais seulement si c'est nécessaire.

1. Vous aimeriez ___—___ descendre des rapides?
2. Elle a choisi __de__ faire du deltaplane.
3. Ses parents lui ont dit __de__ faire attention.
4. Le mois prochain, il commencera __à__ suivre des cours de voile.
5. Moi, j'ai décidé __de__ parcourir les routes de France à vélo.
6. Toi, tu préfères ___—___ faire de la spéléologie, n'est-ce pas?
7. En ce moment, nous apprenons __à__ faire du parachutisme.
8. Pour faire de la plongée, il faut ___—___ avoir un masque, des palmes et une bouteille.
9. Vous me conseillez __de__ ne pas faire de la plongée ici?
10. Mes parents ont essayé __de__ faire du rafting! Quelle aventure!

Core Instruction

TEACHING GRAMMAIRE

1. Go over Points 1–3. Point out to students that **demander** can take either **à** or **de**. **J'avais demandé à laver la voiture, mais maman m'a demandé de faire la vaisselle. (2 min.)**

2. To have students practice using the correct preposition—if one is needed—ask them questions to be answered with an infinitive. **Qu'est-ce que tu apprends? Qu'est-ce que tu as décidé? (2 min.)**

---

36 **Travail et loisirs** ✿1.2

Écrivons Fais des phrases complètes avec les éléments suivants.

1	**2**	**3**	**4**
Je	savoir	(à)	faire du parachutisme
Tu	avoir raison	(de)	parler français
Bruno	aimer		faire de la plongée
Mes amis et moi	apprendre		sous-marine
Toi et moi	oublier		descendre les rapides
Tes amis et toi	vouloir		voir des animaux sauvages
Magalie et toi	réussir		faire ses devoirs
Mes amis	essayer		aller dans des pays
			francophones
			bien travailler en classe

37 **Que font-ils?** ✿1.2

Parlons/Écrivons Fais des phrases pour dire ce que ces gens font.

MODÈLE **Éric et Émilie commencent à faire du ski.**

Éric et Émilie / commencer

1. il / avoir peur   2. nous / devoir   3. ils / apprendre   4. je / oublier

Communication

HOLT **SoundBooth** ONLINE RECORDING

38 **Interview** ✿1.1

Parlons Avec des camarades, discutez des sports extrêmes que vous avez envie d'essayer et pourquoi. Utilisez des verbes qui demandent les prépositions **à** et **de** dans votre conversation.

MODÈLE —Quel sport est-ce que tu as décidé de pratiquer?
—Un jour, j'aimerais... parce que...

Differentiated Instruction

ADVANCED LEARNERS

38 **Challenge** Ask partners to create a skit in which two fans of extreme sports try to outdo each other by coming up with more and more challenging sports they plan to do. Have some partners perform their skit for the class. Encourage them to use intonation, facial expressions, and gestures to emphasize their statements. ✿1.1, 1.3

SPECIAL LEARNING NEEDS

Students with Learning Disabilities Assign one of the verbs in the grammar presentation to each student in the class. Ask students to conjugate their verb and then use each form in a sentence that illustrates the rule for that verb. Give volunteers an opportunity to conjugate their verb aloud. The extra practice in conjugating that verb and forming sentences may be a beneficial accommodation for students with learning challenges. ✿1.2

Grammaire 2

1. Il a peur de faire du parachutisme.
2. Nous devons (faire) laver la voiture.
3. Ils apprennent à faire de la plongée sous-marine.
4. J'ai oublié de donner à manger au chien.

Communication

Class Activity: Interpersonal

Assign each student a verb from the grammar box. Then have them write a question in the following format: **Qu'est-ce que tu ____ à / de faire?** Have students circulate and ask their question. The response should be a complete sentence. All students should write down the responses they get using **il/elle**. ✿1.1, 1.2

Assess

Assessment Program

Quiz : Grammaire 2

Alternative Assessment

Differentiated Practice and Assessment CD-ROM

Online Assessment
my.hrw.com

Test Generator

Resources

Planning:

Lesson Planner

 One-Stop Planner

Practice:

Grammar Tutor for Students of French, Chapter 5

Cahier de vocabulaire et grammaire

Differentiated Practice and Assessment CD-ROM

Cahier d'activités

Media Guide

 Teaching Transparencies
Bell Work 5.8

 Audio CD 5, Tr. 6

Interactive Tutor, Disc 1

Bell Work

Use Bell Work 5.8 in the *Teaching Transparencies* or write this activity on the board.

Complète les phrases suivantes avec **à** ou **de** quand c'est nécessaire.

1. Édouard apprend _____ nager.
2. Nous avons peur _____ sauter.
3. Il a décidé _____ faire le tour du monde.
4. Vous savez _____ faire du deltaplane?
5. Il commence _____ faire de la plongée. 1.2

41 Script

1. — Tu fais souvent la sieste?
   — Oui, le plus souvent possible! J'adore ça!
2. — Est-ce que Marc aime toujours faire la fête?
   — Oui, il ne changera jamais!
3. — Elle va bientôt prendre sa retraite, alors?
   — Dans un an. Elle attend ça avec impatience!
4. — Il aime prendre des risques, celui-là!
   — Oui, et ça fait peur à mes parents!
5. — Elle fait encore des études?
   — Oui, elle veut être prof de russe.

Application 2

39 Un peu de géographie 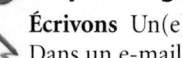1.3

Écrivons Un(e) élève francophone va passer un mois chez toi. Dans un e-mail, décris-lui ta région et les sports qu'on y fait.

MODÈLE J'habite à... C'est dans le... Ma région est super parce qu'on peut faire...

40 Mes projets 1.3

Parlons Parle de tes projets de vacances. Dis où tu voudrais aller, ce que tu as décidé de faire là-bas et ce que tes amis te conseillent d'emporter avec toi. Dis aussi ce que tu voudrais essayer de faire comme sport extrême mais ce dont tu as un peu peur, etc.

MODÈLE Cette année, je vais aller..., dans le sud de... pour faire du... Mes copains m'ont dit..., et mes parents m'ont conseillé...

Un peu plus — Révisions

Idiomatic expressions

An idiom is an expression that can't be translated literally. Here are some that use verbs you know.

avoir	besoin de	to need
	envie de	to feel like
	l'intention de	to intend to
	lieu	to take place
	peur de	to be afraid of
être	en retard	to be late
	en train de	to be in the middle of
faire	des études de	to study
	la fête	to party
	la queue	to wait in line
	la sieste	to take a nap
mettre	la table	to set the table
prendre	le petit-déjeuner	to have breakfast
	sa retraite	to retire
	des risques	to take chances

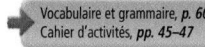 Vocabulaire et grammaire, *p. 60*
Cahier d'activités, *pp. 45–47*  Online workbooks

41 Écoutons CD 5, Tr. 6 1.2

Écoute Tatiana parler de sa famille et fais correspondre chaque conversation à une des personnes suivantes.

3 **a.** Ma tante a 59 ans et elle va bientôt arrêter de travailler.

2 **b.** Mon cousin aime sortir avec ses amis et aller danser.

1 **c.** Moi, j'aime me reposer après le déjeuner.

5 **d.** Ma sœur apprend une langue étrangère.

4 **e.** Mon frère aime les sports extrêmes.

f. Ma mère aimerait vraiment aller au Sénégal cette année.

Core Instruction

INTEGRATED PRACTICE

1. Have students do Activities 39-40 to practice previously taught material. **(4 min.)**
2. Introduce **Un peu plus.** (See presentation suggestions at right.) **(4 min.)**
3. Continue with integrated practice Activities 41–43. **(20 min.)**

TEACHING UN PEU PLUS

1. Model the pronunciation of all idiomatic expressions in **Un peu plus** in a sentence, using mime whenever possible. **Il fait la sieste. Je suis en train de lire. (2 min.)**
2. To practice these expressions, ask students questions about themselves. **Qu'est-ce que tu as envie de faire ce week-end? Qui met la table chez toi? (2 min.)**

Online Practice
go.hrw.com
Application 2 practice
KEYWORD: BD3 CH5

(42) Qu'est-ce qui manque? 1.2

Écrivons Complète les phrases suivantes avec les expressions qui manquent. Fais les changements nécessaires.

faire chaud	mettre la table	être en train de
avoir lieu	faire la queue	avoir peur de
être en retard	prendre le petit-déjeuner	prendre sa retraite

1. Mes parents et moi, nous _____ ensemble tous les matins.
2. Ohhhh... il _____, aujourd'hui! Il fait plus de 30 degrés Celsius!
3. Mon petit frère fait du vélo pour la première fois. Il _____ tomber.
4. Ne me dérange pas! Tu ne vois pas que je _____ faire mes devoirs?
5. Je sais, il est déjà trois heures. Je suis désolé de/d'_____.
6. Il y a trop de gens à la caisse. Je ne veux pas _____. Je reviendrai demain matin.
7. C'est généralement papa qui _____ avant le dîner.
8. Mon grand-père a arrêté de travailler. Il _____.
9. Cette année, la fête de fin d'année _____ dans le gymnase.

1. prenons le petit-déjeuner
2. fait chaud
3. a peur de
4. suis en train de
5. être en retard
6. faire la queue
7. met la table
8. a pris sa retraite
9. aura lieu

Communication

HOLT **SoundBooth**
ONLINE RECORDING

(43) Histoire à raconter 1.2, 1.3

Parlons Christian est parti à vélo pour la ville de Québec. Avec un(e) camarade, imaginez ce qu'il pense et ce que vous pourriez lui dire pour l'encourager.

a. Québec 177km/110 miles

b. Québec 125km/77 miles

c. Québec 20km/12.5 miles

Application 2

Chapitre 5
Application 2

ACTIVITÉ PRÉPARATOIRE PRE-AP **Language Examination**

To display the drawings to the class, use the Picture Sequences Transparency for Chapter 5.

(43) Sample answer

a. Christian a décidé d'aller à Québec en VTT. Il était très content.

b. Il a commencé à être fatigué. Il a pensé, « Oh là là. C'est trop loin! C'est à 125 kilomètres! » On pourrait lui dire que ça en vaut la peine!

c. Il faisait très chaud et Christian était vraiment fatigué. Il avait aussi soif. Il pensait, « Je n'en peux plus! Je meurs de soif! » Moi, je lui dirais, « Allez, courage! »

Communication

Class Activity: Interpersonal
Have students do a question and answer chain with the **Un peu plus** idioms. Student A starts but does not finish a question. **Kyle, est-ce que tu as....?** Student B answers in a complete sentence. **Oui, j'ai l'intention de déjeuner tout de suite.** Then Student B poses the beginning of another question to Student C. This way, all students should have a chance to ask and respond. 1.1

Assess

Assessment Program
Quiz : Application 2
Audio CD 5, Tr. 13
Alternative Assessment
Differentiated Practice and Assessment CD-ROM
Online Assessment
my.hrw.com
Test Generator

Differentiated Instruction

SLOWER PACE LEARNERS

(43) Additional Practice Some students may not remember expressions they need to describe the drawings. Ask the class to suggest appropriate expressions and write these on the board. Encourage students to use these expressions when they complete this activity. 1.2

MULTIPLE INTELLIGENCES

Visual Ask students to illustrate the French idioms in **Un peu plus**. Each idiom can be illustrated on a page with the idiom written at the bottom of the page. The collection might be a reference and study aid or a children's picture book. 1.2

Resources

Planning:

Lesson Planner

 One-Stop Planner

Presentation:

Audio CD 5, Trs. 7, 8

Practice:

Cahier d'activités

Reading Strategies and Skills
Handbook, Chapter 5

Advanced Reader

AP Reading Suggestion

Tell students to take note of literary devices, such as metaphors, analogies, and similes while they read the selection.

Applying the Strategies

For practice with making inferences, have students use the "It Says . . . I Say" strategy from the *Reading Strategies and Skills Handbook.*

READING PRACTICE

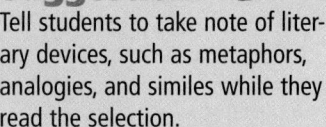

Poète et journaliste, Anthony Phelps, est né à Port-au-Prince en Haïti en 1928. Il étudie aux États-Unis et au Canada. Il retourne en Haïti en 1953 où il écrit pour plusieurs revues et journaux. En 1964, il est obligé de s'exiler. Il trouve asile à Montréal où il fait du journalisme et du théâtre. Phelps est l'auteur de romans, de pièces de théâtre et de plus d'une dizaine de recueils de poèmes, qui ont été traduits en plusieurs langues. Sa poésie est marquée par son expérience de l'exil. Il a écrit entre autres: *Été* (1960), *Points cardinaux* (1967), *Mon pays que voici* (1968) et *Une phrase lente de violoncelle* (2005).

STRATÉGIE pour lire

Using inferences Poets use figurative language and symbols to express their ideas. Readers must make inferences in order to understand the poet's message. An inference is an informed guess based on evidence or clues from a text. Remember, many poets choose their words so that more than one interpretation of their message is possible.

 A Avant la lecture 3.1

Le poème *Je viens d'une île de soleil* parle de l'expérience du poète comme immigrant haïtien au Canada. Qu'est-ce que tu sais sur Haïti? Et sur le Québec? Imagine la vie d'un immigrant haïtien au Canada.

Port-au-Prince, Haïti

Cap-Haïtien, Haïti

Core Instruction

LECTURE

1. Read and discuss **Stratégie pour lire** and **Avant la lecture** with the students. Write what students know about Haiti on the board. How different is the climate of Haiti from that of Canada? Compare the major cities. **(10 min.)**

2. Ask volunteers to read aloud *Je viens d'une île de soleil.* Pause regularly to monitor students' pronunciation and comprehension. **(10 min.)**

3. Complete **Compréhension** questions as a class. **(5 min.)**

CD 5, Tr. 7

🎧 Je viens d'une île de soleil

Je viens d'une île de soleil une île au nom indien
Haïti ? connaissez-vous ?
et je vous dis à la manière de mon peuple
« Honneur ». Répondez-moi

5 « Respect ».
Et laissez-moi m'asseoir auprès[1] de vous
Je ne réclame[2] point
dans ce premier matin de ma nouvelle naissance
le secret de vos fusées

10 encore moins la recette du sirop d'érable.
Je n'ai pas d'atouts maîtres[3].
En fait, je n'ai même pas de cartes
étant très peu joueur
mais j'ai des mots à vous offrir.

15 Des mots puissance de vent puissance de mer
des mots tant que vous en voudrez
et j'échangerai les miens contre les vôtres.
(Sur le mur d'un garage
j'ai vu des mots hâtifs écrits en rouge

20 Main malhabile[4] qui teniez le pinceau
vous avez épaissi mon sang et j'ai pressé le pas
car il m'arrive d'oublier
que Montréal est une Cité
où l'arbre a le droit de chanter

25 selon ses branches et la distance entre ses feuilles.)

Extrait de *Mais c'est le feu qui fait l'acier*, Points cardinaux (1966)

1. à côté **2.** demande **3.** *master trumps* **4.** *clumsy*

Anse-Blanchette, en Gaspésie

Vue sur le centre de Montréal

Compréhension

🌸1.2

B Relis *Je viens d'une île de soleil*. Ensuite, utilise la stratégie pour choisir la réponse qui complète les phrases suivantes.

1. Le poète veut savoir si les lecteurs _____.
   a. savent où se trouve Haïti   b.) ont entendu parler d'Haïti

2. Le poète veut que les gens _____.
   a.) l'acceptent   b. l'admirent

3. Le poète offre _____ aux lecteurs.
   a. son amitié   b.) sa poésie

4. Le poète oublie qu'au Canada tout le monde _____.
   a.) peut vivre en liberté   b. n'est pas complètement libre

Active Reading Questions

1. Qu'est-ce que le poète demande aux lecteurs? (s'ils connaissent Haïti)
2. Qu'est-ce que le poète veut? (s'asseoir auprès du lecteur et le respect)
3. Quels sont deux symboles du Canada dont le poète parle? Qu'est-ce qu'ils représentent? (les fusées et le sirop d'érable)
4. Qu'est-ce que le poète offre aux Canadiens? (des mots, la poésie, la littérature)
5. Comment sont les mots du poète? (puissants)
6. Comment le poète a-t-il réagi quand il a vu le graffiti sur le mur? (Il a eu peur.)
7. Qu'est-ce qu'on a le droit de faire au Canada? (de parler en liberté)

🌸1.2

Making Generalizations

Tell students that when they make broad statements based on information they have gathered, they are making generalizations. For example, a generalization based on *Je viens d'une île de soleil* might be that honor and respect are important values. Ask students to make generalizations about Canada as they read each poem.

Language Examination

Lecture helps students prepare for Section 1, Part B: **Reading Comprehension**. The audio recording helps them prepare for Part A: **Listening—Short Narratives**.

Differentiated Instruction 🙌

SLOWER PACE LEARNERS

Additional Practice Some students may have difficulty understanding the poems. Have them reread the poems and list the expressions they do not understand. Go over their lists as a class and provide synonyms or antonyms for each expression. 🌸1.2

MULTIPLE INTELLIGENCES

Naturalist Ask students to research the natural environments of Haiti and Canada. After they find the types of geography, landforms, weather, or population patterns of both countries, have students compare and contrast the differences and similarities. Have them present their findings to the class. 🌸3.1

Active Reading Questions

1. **Comment est le sol du Canada? (unique, très beau, géant)**
2. **Quelles sont deux caractéristiques géographiques du Canada que le poète mentionne? (des forêts et des lacs)**
3. **Pourquoi est-ce que le poète appelle la France la mère du Canada? (C'est la France qui a colonisé le Canada.)**
4. **Qu'est-ce que la France a laissé au Canada? (la marque de sa gloire)**
5. **Dans quelle direction va le Saint-Laurent? (vers l'océan Atlantique, vers la France)**
6. **D'après le poète, comment est la vie au Canada? (heureuse)**
7. **Qu'est-ce que le poète pense de son pays? (Il l'aime beaucoup.)** ✿1.2

Postreading Activity

Have students identify the references to nature in the poems. Then ask students to compare and contrast the role nature plays in each one. How is nature represented? Is it a positive or negative force in the poems? What does nature symbolize?

Octave Crémazie, poète national du Canada, est né à Québec en 1827. Après avoir terminé ses études, il travaille dans la librairie de son frère. En 1849, il devient secrétaire de l'Institut Canadien à Québec, une organisation littéraire et philosophique. En 1862, il a des problèmes financiers et il part pour la France où il passe les dernières années de sa vie dans la misère[1]. Il meurt en 1879. Crémazie n'a écrit que 25 poèmes, mais il est considéré comme le poète le plus important du Canada francophone du XIXe siècle. Ses poèmes expriment[2] sa fidélité à son héritage francophone et à son pays natal[3], le Canada.

Ⓐ Avant la lecture ✿3.1, 1.3

Le poème suivant s'appelle *Le Canada*. Qu'est-ce que tu sais sur le Canada? Quels pays l'ont colonisé? Quelles sont les traces (langues, traditions, culture) laissées par ces pays? Quelles sont les caractéristiques géographiques les plus importantes du pays?

CD 5, Tr. 8

🎧 Le Canada

Parc national Jasper

La rivière Rouge en automne près de Lanaudière

Ⅱl est sous le soleil un sol unique au monde,
Où le ciel a versé ses dons les plus brillants,
Où, répandant ses biens, la nature féconde[4]
À ses vastes forêts mêle ses lacs géants.

5 Sur ces bords enchantés notre mère, la France,
A laissé de sa gloire un immortel sillon[5] ;
Précipitant ses flots vers l'Océan immense,
Le noble Saint-Laurent redit encor son nom.

Heureux qui le connaît, plus heureux qui l'habite,
10 Et, ne quittant jamais pour chercher d'autres cieux
Les rives du grand fleuve où le bonheur l'invite,
Sait vivre et sait mourir où dorment ses aïeux[6].

---

1. pauvreté 2. disent 3. où il est né 4. fertile 5. *furrow* 6. ancêtres

---

Core Instruction

LECTURE

1. Read **Avant la lecture** as a class. Have students discuss their background knowledge of Canada. **(10 min.)**

2. Ask three volunteers to each read aloud one verse of *Le Canada*. **(5 min.)**

3. Complete **Compréhension** and **Après la lecture** as a class. Ask the students if the two poems talk about the same Canada (urban environment vs. nature). Do they think a Haitian would feel more at home in Octave Crémazie's Canada? **(15 min.)**

Lecture

Compréhension

B Relis *Le Canada*. Ensuite, utilise la stratégie (p. 208) pour déterminer si chaque phrase suivante est **a) vraie** ou **b) fausse**. 1.2

1. Il y a toujours du soleil au Canada. b
2. Le Canada est un pays d'une grande beauté naturelle. a
3. D'après l'auteur, la France a joué un rôle plus important que la Grande-Bretagne dans l'histoire du Canada. a
4. D'après l'auteur, le Canada regrette la présence française. a
5. On peut être heureux en habitant au Canada. a

C Auquel de ces poèmes est-ce que les phrases suivantes correspondent: **a)** *Je viens d'une île de soleil,* **b)** *Le Canada* ou **c) aux deux?** 1.2

1. On ressent de la nostalgie pour un temps passé. b
2. Le ton du poème est très personnel. a
3. Les idées canadiennes font du Canada un pays unique. a
4. Les images de la nature représentent des caractéristiques positives. c
5. Le poète est fier (*proud*) de ses origines francophones. b

Après la lecture

D Lequel des deux poèmes aimes-tu le plus? Pourquoi? Qu'est-ce que le poème te dit? Comment est-ce que tu t'identifies avec les sentiments, les images ou les symboles du poème? Est-ce que le poème a changé ta perspective sur Haïti ou sur le Canada? Explique. 1.3

Les Laurentides

Online Practice
go.hrw.com
Online Edition
KEYWORD: BD3 CH5

Connections
Literature Link
Although Octave Crémazie and Anthony Phelps were born in different centuries and at opposite corners of North America, both poets were instrumental in promoting and advancing the literature of their countries. In Quebec, Crémazie started a bookshop in 1848 that became the center of an influential literary circle. In 1860, he and his friends founded the first literary school of Quebec and in 1861, they began issuing a monthly magazine of literature and history to preserve the folklore of French Canada. Similarly, Phelps was a founding member of the 1960 group **Haïti-Littéraire.** He promoted Haitian authors for over forty years through his company, **Les Productions Caliban**, which has recorded a number of Haitian poets. Both poets left their native countries, albeit for different reasons, but their poems convey their love for their countries. Crémazie is called "the father of French-Canadian poetry" for his patriotic verse. One of his poems *Le Drapeau de Carillon* (1858) almost became a national song of Canada. Ask students to research a US-born poet whose works are known for their patriotism.

3.1

Assess

Assessment Program
Quiz: Lecture

Online Assessment
my.hrw.com

Test Generator

Process Writing

After students complete their detailed **organigramme,** have them look for sound patterns among the words they plan to use in their composition. Suggest that they group the words according to these patterns and then use the reference books mentioned in **Stratégie pour écrire** to find other words with the same sounds to include in their poem.

Teaching Suggestion

Have students listen for alliteration, rhyme, and rhythm when editing their poem. Do they hear any words, phrases, or lines that just do not sound right? What corrections could they make so that they sound better?

Connections

Language Arts Link

In addition to rhyme, poets often use sound-based techniques such as alliteration, assonance, consonance, and onomatopoeia to convey emotions. While alliteration is the repetition of a consonant sound at the beginning of words, consonance is the repetition of a middle or final consonant sound following different vowel sounds, so that the words do not rhyme. Assonance is the repetition of vowel sounds, followed by different consonant sounds, so that the words don't rhyme. Onomatopoeia is a word that imitates a sound, such as 'buzz', 'moo' and 'beep.' Ask students to give examples for each of these sound-based techniques. ❀ 3.1

L'atelier de l'écrivain

Interactive TUTOR

Hommage à la nature

Dans cette activité, tu vas écrire un poème qui rend hommage à la nature en utilisant des techniques poétiques. Tu peux parler de la nature en général, des animaux, des caractéristiques naturelles de ta ville ou de ton état qui inspirent de la fierté ou d'autres émotions, d'une expérience que tu as eue dans la nature. Ton poème doit avoir au moins vingt vers.

① Plan : les cinq doigts de la main ❀ 1.3

Choisis le sujet de ton poème et écris-le dans «la paume» de ton organigramme. Écris les idées dont tu veux parler dans chaque «doigt». Ajoute des détails pour chaque idée dans les doigts. Puis, décide de l'ordre dans lequel tu veux parler de tes idées.

STRATÉGIE pour écrire

Using multiple techniques can help you communicate a variety of ideas and emotion, and create interesting effects with the sound of language. Poets often use **figurative language** and **imagery** to create vivid descriptions of a subject. Poets may also use **alliteration, rhyme, repetition,** and **rhythm** to convey a feeling or mood. Try experimenting with these poetic techniques and see how they add to the depth and intensity of your poem. To help you with your experimentation, use reference books in French, such as a dictionary and a thesaurus, to find synonyms, antonyms, and homonyms. ❀ 3.1

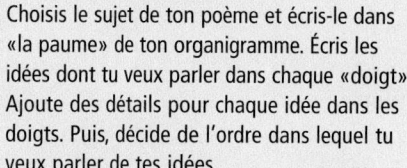

Idée 1: description

Sujet: les montagnes de mon état

Idée 2: saisons/climat

Idée 3: activités

Idée 4: mauvaises expériences

Idée 5: bonnes expériences

Cascade dans le jardin botanique de Montréal

Core Instruction

L'ATELIER DE L'ÉCRIVAIN

1. Have students bring in their favorite poem. Discuss **Stratégie pour écrire.** Call on volunteers to read their poem and have the class point out poetic techniques mentioned in the strategy. **(5 min.)**
2. Go over **Vocabulaire à la carte** and **Le subjonctif. (5 min.)**
3. Have students complete steps 1–3. **(30 min.)**
4. As homework, have students revise their poem and find illustrations to accompany it.

You might also suggest that students memorize their poem to recite for the class.

5. Complete step 4 with the class. To reduce possible anxiety, you might place students in a circle and have them recite their poem while seated. **(20 min.)**

L'atelier de l'écrivain

② Rédaction ✿1.3

Fais un brouillon de ton poème en utilisant les idées et les détails qui sont dans ton organigramme. Tu peux utiliser:

- les verbes avec prépositions que tu as vus dans ce chapitre
- le subjonctif pour exprimer des émotions
- les mots du **Vocabulaire à la carte**

Tu peux aussi utiliser différentes techniques poétiques comme:

- la répétition des sons ou des mots
- l'allitération (série de mots qui commencent par le même son)
- les rimes (série de mots qui se terminent par le même son)

N'oublie pas de te servir d'un dictionnaire bilingue ou d'un dictionnaire des synonymes.

③ Correction ✿1.3

Relis ton brouillon.

- As-tu utilisé deux ou trois techniques poétiques de la stratégie? Par exemple, as-tu utilisé l'allitération, les rimes et la répétition?
- Est-ce que tu as utilisé toutes les idées de ton organigramme?

Échange ton poème avec celui d'un(e) camarade. Relisez vos poèmes ensemble et discutez de la manière de les améliorer.

Corrige les fautes d'orthographe, de vocabulaire et de grammaire. Puis, écris la version finale de ton poème.

④ Application ✿1.3

Trouve des images pour accompagner ton poème. Les images peuvent illustrer les idées principales de ton poème ou elles peuvent représenter les émotions décrites. Projète-les sur un écran ou montre-les d'une autre manière pendant que tu lis ton poème à la classe. Après ta récitation, demande à tes camarades quelles sont leurs réactions. Est-ce qu'ils ont compris ton message? Quelles émotions est-ce qu'ils ont ressenties?

> Dans mon jardin, il y a une montagne
> Tous les matins, je la regarde
> Ma montagne

Vocabulaire à la carte

au milieu de	*in the middle of*
partout	*everywhere*
au pied de	*at the foot of*
quelque part	*somewhere*
au sommet de	*at the top/ summit/height of*
repérer	*to spot, locate, find*
nulle part	*nowhere*
se situer	*to be located*

Le subjonctif

The subjunctive is used with expressions of emotion.

J'ai peur des requins.

J'ai peur qu'ils me mordent.

L'atelier de l'écrivain

Le subjonctif

Have students complete the following sentences with the subjunctive. All completions should have something to do with nature.

1. **Les gens ont peur que...**
2. **Je suis heureux (-euse) que...**
3. **Le gouvernement est furieux que...**
4. **Nous sommes surpris que...**

Writing Assessment

To assess **L'atelier de l'écrivain,** you can use the following rubric. For additional rubrics, see the *Assessment Program.* ✿1.3

Writing Rubric	4	3	2	1
Content (Complete—Incomplete)				
Comprehensibility (Comprehensible— Seldom comprehensible)				
Accuracy (Accurate—Seldom accurate)				
Organization (Well-organized—Poorly organized)				
Effort (Excellent effort— Minimal effort)				

18-20: A	14-15: C	Under
16-17: B	12-13: D	12: F

Differentiated Instruction

SLOWER PACE LEARNERS

② Some students may have difficulty coming up with rhyming words in this activity. Tell them that the library might have a dictionary of rhyming words on a CD, which is useful because they can search for words by ending. Remind students that they can always use the infinitives of verbs with the same ending.

MULTIPLE INTELLIGENCES

Musical Allow students the option of writing their poem as lyrics to a song. The song should follow the suggestions and process in the writing assignment. Students may plan for the song to be sung to a familiar tune, or if musically inclined, they may create original music to accompany the song. You might give students the option of performing or playing a recording of the song. ✿1.2

Assess

Assessment Program

Quiz: Écriture

Online Assessment
my.hrw.com

Test Generator

Chapitre 5
Prépare-toi pour l'examen

 Interactive TUTOR

🌐 1.2, 1.3

1 Tes copains te racontent des histoires incroyables. Choisis une image pour chaque histoire et puis raconte ton histoire incroyable à toi!

1 Vocabulaire 1
- to express astonishment and fear
- to forbid and give warning
pp. 186–189

a.   b.   c.

b **1.** Je suis allé à la plage et j'ai vu des requins jouer à la balle!

c **2.** C'est incroyable! Moi, quand je pêchais avec mon frère, j'ai vu un poisson sauter en dehors de la rivière et attraper un aigle.

a **3.** Pas possible! Moi, j'ai vu un ours qui avait peur d'un castor!

Answers will vary. **4.** Ce n'est pas vrai! Eh bien moi, j'ai _____!

2 Grammaire 1
- the subjunctive with expressions of fear
- the imperative
Un peu plus
- **voir** and **regarder**
pp. 190–195

2 Tu es guide et tu dis à des touristes ce qu'il doivent ou ne doivent pas faire. Remplace les mots soulignés par des pronoms. 🌐 1.2

MODÈLE attraper un papillon   Ne l'attrapez pas!

1. ne pas donner à manger aux animaux sauvages

2. regarder ces ours

3. visiter le parc national des Cent Cascades

4. ne pas faire peur aux dauphins

5. ne pas avoir peur des chauves-souris

1. Ne leur donnez pas à manger!
2. Regardez-les!
3. Visitez-le!
4. Ne leur faites pas peur!
5. N'en ayez pas peur!

3 Vocabulaire 2
- to give general directions
- to complain and offer encouragement
pp. 198–201

3 Sylvie dit ce qu'elle a fait en Haïti. De quels sports parle-t-elle? 🌐 1.2

1. Tout d'abord, j'ai pris un avion et j'ai sauté de l'avion.

2. Après, avec une corde, j'ai grimpé en haut d'une montagne.

3. Ensuite, j'ai descendu la rivière dans un canoë.

4. À la plage, j'ai loué une combinaison de plongée, une bouteille de plongée et un masque. Dans l'eau, j'ai vu du corail.

5. Finalement, j'ai rencontré un ami et nous sommes descendus dans une grotte où j'ai vu beaucoup de chauves-souris!

1. le parachutisme **2.** l'alpinisme **3.** le canoë-kayak
4. la plongée sous-marine **5.** la spéléologie

Preparing for the Exam

RETEACHING

Review with students that in addition to expressions of necessity, desire, and emotion, the **subjonctif** is used with expressions of fear. **J'ai peur qu'il y ait des crocodiles.** Have partners tell each other what they are afraid of. Tell them to pay close attention to the number of clauses.

TEST-TAKING STRATEGY

Remind students that in French some verbs are followed directly by the infinitive of another verb (**aimer, aller, pouvoir**), some are followed by **à** (**aider à, s'amuser à, penser à**), and some by **de** (**avoir peur de, conseiller de, dire de**). It is best to memorize the verb together with the preposition.

④ Choisis le bon verbe ou la bonne préposition pour compléter ces phrases. Fais tous les changements nécessaires. ✿1.2

1. La mère de Michelle lui (apporter / amener) son déjeuner.
2. Il faut que j'(emporter / emmener) mon masque de plongée.
3. Au zoo, les employés (apporter / amener) les repas aux animaux.
4. J'ai peur que mon frère (apporter / amener) son iguane chez moi.
5. Nous (emporter / emmener) nos cousins faire un tour dans les bayous.
6. Julien m'a conseillé (de / à) visiter les grottes.
7. Est-ce que tu pourrais m'aider (à / de) chercher mes lunettes?

⑤ Réponds aux questions suivantes. ✿2.1, 2.2

1. Cite deux sports extrêmes qu'on peut pratiquer au Canada.
2. Quels sont les rôles de certains parcs nationaux louisianais?
3. Peut-on marcher sur les pelouses dans les parcs en France?

CD 5, Tr. 9

⑥ Écoute les phrases et dis si elles sont **a) vraies** ou **b) fausses.** ✿1.2   **1.** a **2.** a **3.** b **4.** a **5.** b

⑦ Dis où Christian est allé, ce qu'il a vu et ce qu'il a fait pendant ses vacances. ✿1.2

a.

b.

c.

d.

Oral Assessment

To assess the speaking activities in this section, you might use the following rubric. For additional speaking rubrics, see the Alternative Assessment section of the *Assessment Program*.

Speaking Rubric	4	3	2	1
Content (Complete—Incomplete)				
Comprehension (Total—Little)				
Comprehensibility (Comprehensible—Incomprehensible)				
Accuracy (Accurate—Seldom Accurate)				
Fluency (Fluent—Not Fluent)				

18-20: A   16-17: B   14-15: C   12-13: D   Under 12: F

L'Amérique francophone

Prépare-toi pour l'examen

Prépare-toi pour l'examen

④ **Grammaire 2**
- apporter, amener, emporter, emmener
- verbs + **à/de** + infinitive
Un peu plus
- idiomatic expressions
pp. 202–207

⑤ **Culture**
- Comparaisons p. 197
- Flash culture pp. 188, 192, 204

④**Answers**

1. apporte
2. j'emporte
3. apportent
4. amène
5. emmenons
6. de
7. à

⑤**Possible Answers**

1. rafting, trecks
2. raconter l'histoire de la région
3. non

⑥**Script**

1. L'aigle est le symbole national des États-Unis.
2. Dans les parcs naturels, il est interdit de nourrir les animaux.
3. On n'a pas besoin d'équipement pour faire du parachutisme.
4. Dans les parcs naturels, les animaux ne sont pas en liberté.
5. Quand on fait de la spéléologie, on saute d'un avion.

PRE-AP PREPARATORY ACTIVITÉ
Language Examination

To display the drawings to the class, use the Picture Sequences Transparency for Chapter 5.

⑦ Sample answer

a. Pendant ses vacances, Christian est allé dans un parc national au Québec. Le premier jour, il a vu un orignal et un ours. C'était incroyable!

b. Christian a décidé de faire de l'alpinisme. Pendant qu'il grimpait, il a vu un aigle!

c. Plus tard, Christian est retourné à la montagne pour faire du deltaplane. Il a eu peur de tomber, mais cela en valait la peine!

d. Il a fait du rafting, mais il n'a pas aimé. C'était trop dangereux!

Grammar Review

For more practice with the grammar topics in this chapter, see the *Grammar Tutor*, the *Interactive Tutor*, or the *Cahier de vocabulaire et grammaire*.

Online Edition

Students might use the online textbook and Holt SoundBooth to practice pronunciation of **vocabulaire**.

Products and Perspectives

Crayfish, also called crawfish or crawdad, are closely related to the lobster. The name, "crayfish", does not derive from the word "fish", but from the Old French word **escrevisse,** meaning "crevice", and referring to the habitat of the animal. More than half of the more than 500 species occur in North America, particularly in Kentucky and Louisiana. The crustacean, usually boiled in a huge pot with heavy seasoning and other items, such as potatoes, sausage, corn, onions, and garlic bulbs, is one of the main staples of Cajun cuisine. Louisianans even call their state the "crawfish capital of the world." Crayfish are often served at a gathering known as a crawfish boil, which is also a traditional Easter event throughout Louisiana. Ask students to research other traditional festivals in Louisiana. Have them report their findings to the class. ❀ 2.1, 2.2

Grammaire 1
- the subjunctive with expressions of fear
- the imperative

Un peu plus
- **voir** and **regarder** pp. 190–195

Résumé: Grammaire 1

The **subjunctive** can be used with *expressions of fear*: **avoir peur que** and **craindre que**. If the subject is the same in both clauses of the sentence, use **de + infinitive** instead of the subjunctive.

J'ai peur qu'il y ait des requins.
J'ai peur de nager avec des dauphins.

To form the **imperative**, use the **tu**, **nous**, or **vous**, form of the verb in the present and drop the subject. For **-er**, verbs, drop the final **-s**, of the **tu**, form. To make the command negative, place the **ne… pas** around the verb. The verbs **être** and **avoir** both have irregular command forms.

être	sois	soyons	soyez
avoir	aie	ayons	ayez

In an **affirmative command**, **object pronouns** follow the verb using a hyphen. In a **negative command**, **object pronouns** come before the verb.

Écris-lui!　　**Ne lui téléphone pas!**

The verb **voir** means *to see*; the verb **regarder** means *to look at* or *to watch*.

Grammaire 2
- **apporter, amener, emporter, emmener**
- verbs + **à/de** + infinitive

Un peu plus
- idiomatic expressions pp. 202–207

Résumé: Grammaire 2

The verbs **apporter** and **amener** mean *to bring*.

The verbs **emporter** and **emmener** mean *to take*.

Use verbs with **-porter** when talking about *things*.

Use verbs with **-mener** when talking about *people* or *animals*.

Some **verbs** are followed immediately by an **infinitive**. Some need **à** or **de** before an infinitive.

An *idiom* is an expression which can not be translated literally. Many idiomatic expressions use the verbs **avoir, être, faire, mettre,** and **prendre**. See p. 206 for a list of idiomatic expressions.

Chapter Review

Teacher Management System
Password: admin
For more details, log on to www.hrw.com/CDROMTUTOR.

Create a variety of puzzles to review chapter vocabulary.

DVD Program	Interactive Tutor	PuzzlePro
		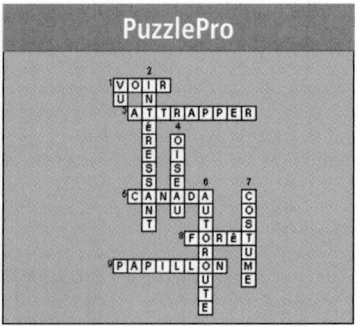

Résumé: Vocabulaire 1

HOLT SoundBooth ONLINE RECORDING

To express astonishment and fear

une **abeille**	bee	en **liberté**	free
un **aigle**	eagle	un **loup**	wolf
un **alligator**	alligator	une **méduse**	jellyfish
avoir de la patience	to have patience	**mordre/piquer**	to bite/sting
une **baleine**	whale	**observer**	to watch
un **bayou**	bayou	un **orignal**	moose
un **castor**	beaver	un **ours**	bear
une **chauve-souris**	bat	un **papillon**	butterfly
le **corail**	coral	un **parc naturel**	nature reserve
craindre	to fear	**se perdre**	to get lost
un **crocodile**	crocodile	un **renard**	fox
cueillir	to pick/gather	un **requin**	shark
un **dauphin**	dolphin	**sauvage**	wild
une **écrevisse**	crayfish	**tropical(e)**	tropical
un **écureuil**	squirrel	**C'est incroyable!**	It's incredible!
une **espèce**	species	**Ce n'est pas vrai!**	It can't be true!
la **faune/la flore**	fauna/flora	**Je n'en reviens pas!**	I can't get over it!
une **grotte**	grotto/cave	**Pas possible !**	Impossible!
une **guêpe**	wasp	**Quelle horreur!**	How horrible!
un/une **guide**	guide	**J'ai peur de/que...**	I'm afraid of/that . . .
un **héron**	heron	**Au secours! À l'aide!**	Help!
un **iguane**	iguana		

To forbid and give warning .... *See p. 189*

Résumé: Vocabulaire 2

To give general directions

une **bouteille de plongée**	scuba tank	**parcourir**	to travel across
une **combinaison de plongée**	wetsuit	la **plongée sous-marine**	scuba diving
une **corde**	rope	**rêver de**	to dream of
descendre des rapides (m.)	to shoot the rapids	la **spéléologie**	caving
un **équipement**	equipment	un **sport extrême**	extreme sport
faire de l'alpinisme (m.)	mountain climbing	un **vélo tout terrain (VTT)**	mountain bike
faire du canoë/kayak (m.)	canoeing/kayaking	**au sud de...**	south of . . .
faire du deltaplane (m.)	hang gliding	**C'est à environ... de/d'...**	It's about . . . from . . .
faire du parachutisme (m.)	parachuting	**... dans le nord de/d'...**	. . . in the north of . . .
faire du rafting (m.)	rafting	**Si tu vas plus à l'est...**	If you go farther east . . .
faire le tour du monde à la voile en solitaire	to sail around the world alone	**... vers l'ouest...**	. . . toward the west . . .
une **île**	island	To complain and offer	
un **parachute**	parachute	encouragement .... *See p. 201*	

Préparer pour l'examen

Prépare-toi pour l'examen

Game

À toi! Have students form a circle. Start by saying a sentence that includes the name of an animal. (**J'ai peur qu'il y ait des alligators dans le parc.**) Then toss a beach ball to a student as you say the name of a different animal (**ours**). The student catches the ball and says a new sentence. (**Il est important que l'ours n'ait pas faim.**) Then he or she tosses the ball to another student, naming another animal. A student who does not respond within five seconds is out of the game, but may get back in by correcting another's error. After several tosses, start a new sentence.

🌸 1.2

Online Edition

Transparency: Vocabulaire

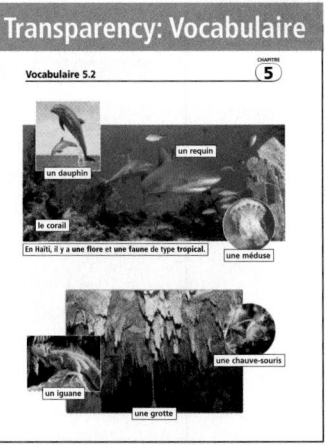

Transparency: Situation

Assess

Assessment Program

Examen: Chapitre 5
Audio CD 5, Trs. 14, 15

Examen oral: Chapitre 5
Alternative Assessment

Examen partial: Chapitres 1–5
Audio CD 5, Trs. 16, 17

Differentiated Practice and Assessment CD-ROM

Online Assessment
my.hrw.com

Test Generator

Activités préparatoires

Resources

Planning:
Lesson Planner

 One-Stop Planner

Practice:
Cahier de vocabulaire et grammaire

Differentiated Practice and Assessment CD-ROM

 Teaching Transparencies
Picture Sequences, Chapter 5

Cahier d'activités

 Audio CD 5, Tr. 10

VIDEO OPTIONS
▶ Télé-culture: Interviews

The AP French Language Exam

Activités préparatoires provide students with activities similar to those found in the Advanced Placement French Language exam. The activities are based on material taught up to and including this chapter and concentrate on the chapter grammar and vocabulary.

Listening Script

1. — Est-ce que tu es prêt à partir? Tu as tout ce dont tu as besoin?
   — Oui, maman. J'ai tout mon équipement: ma combinaison de plongée, mon masque et ma bouteille de plongée.
2. — Tu appartiens à un club de spéléologie, n'est-ce pas?
   — Oui, on va explorer des grottes chaque samedi.

Reading Strategy

Topic Sentence Tell students to identify the topic sentence of the paragraph, first. This will help them pinpoint where to look for answers to the questions.

SECTION I

Listening CD 5, Tr. 10 1.2

Listen to the dialogues and choose the most appropriate response.

1. **A.** N'oublie pas ton gilet de sauvetage.
   B. Tu aimeras faire de l'alpinisme.
   C. Oui, tu as besoin de tout cet équipement pour faire du deltaplane.
   D. Apporte aussi ton VTT.

2. **A.** Vous y rencontrez souvent des baleines?
   B. Je n'en reviens pas! Moi, j'aurais peur des chauve-souris!
   C. Tu dois te méfier des hérons!
   D. Tu ne crains pas qu'une grenouille te pique?

Reading 1.2

Read the following paragraph and answer the questions that follow.

> Le canyoning est un sport à sensations... La règle du jeu en canyoning est simple. Parcourir des canyons, des cascades, des défilés, des 5 gorges, des rivières, des ruisseaux, etc. en alternant marche, nage, escalade, descente en rappel, sauts et glissades. Le succès du canyoning auprès du grand public est lié à son 10 caractère ludique et à son accessibilité d'apparence facile. Cependant la pratique du canyoning est exigeante. De plus, si cette activité est certes accessible à tous, elle ne doit pas faire 15 oublier qu'elle fait évoluer ses pratiquants dans un environnement de montagne où certaines consignes de sécurité ne doivent pas être négligées.

1. Le canyoning est un sport...
   A. tranquille.
   B. extrême.
   C. facile.
   D. ennuyeux.

2. Le canyoning consiste en l'exploration...
   A. de son jardin.
   B. de canyons.
   C. de grottes.
   D. de la mer.

3. Une personne qui fait du canyoning...
   A. reste chez elle et regarde la télévision.
   B. fait des exercices de relaxation.
   C. fait de la marche et de l'escalade.
   D. fait de la voile.

4. Le canyoning peut se pratiquer...
   A. en ville.
   B. au bord de la mer.
   C. n'importe où.
   D. à la montagne.

5. Le canyoning peut être...
   A. amusant et sûr.
   B. ennuyeux et dangereux.
   C. amusant mais dangereux.
   D. ennuyeux et sûr.

Preparing for the Exam

ADDITIONAL PRACTICE

Have volunteers tell one another what extreme sports to try. Ask them to use the imperative. On the board you might want to keep track of the verbs used and review their forms. 1.1

TEST-TAKING STRATEGIES

Section I: Listening If more than one of the choices seems like a correct answer, remind students that they are supposed to pick the one that is most appropriate.

Section II: Writing Tell students that once they fill in a blank, it can be helpful to read the sentence aloud (quietly) to themselves. Sometimes a sentence will sound correct or incorrect to the ear, when simply looking at it does not help.

The following activities can be used to help you to prepare for the Advanced Placement French Language examination, or to further practice the vocabulary and grammar concepts you have seen in this chapter.

Activités préparatoires

SECTION II

Writing ✿1.2

In the following sentences, some prepositions have been omitted. Complete each sentence. If the sentence does not require a preposition, write an X.

1. J'espère ____X____ pouvoir aller au parc avec eux.
2. Le prof nous a dit ____de____ faire cet exercice pour demain.
3. Nous avons réussi ____à____ trouver le chien perdu.
4. N'oublions pas ____d'____ emporter notre équipement.

Complete the sentence by writing the correct form and tense of the verb.

— Maman, est-ce que je peux ____1____ du camping avec mes copains?

— D'accord, mais ____2____ garde, mon fils. ____3____ des serpents! ____4____ bien autour de ton sac de couchage avant de te coucher! En plus, je crains que tu ____5____ froid.

1. ____faire____ (faire)
2. ____prends____ (prendre)
3. ____Méfie-toi____ (se méfier)
4. ____Regarde____ (regarder)
5. ____aies____ (avoir)

Essay Topic ✿1.3

Write in French a well-organized and coherent composition (of at least 10 to 15 lines) on the following topic.

Si vous pouviez être n'importe quel animal, quel animal seriez-vous? Quelles caractéristiques de cet animal aimeriez-vous avoir?

Speaking ✿1.2

Look at the following drawing, then tell a story about what is occurring in the picture.

Activités préparatoires

Writing Strategy

Tell students never to write their essay in English first with the idea of translating it into French. Word-for-word translation will only lead to awkward sentence structure and misinterpretations, especially if they try to translate idioms.

Language Examination

To display the drawing to the class, use the **Activités préparatoires** Transparency for Chapter 5.

Speaking: Sample answer

Au bord de la mer, deux amis se préparent à faire de la plongée sous-marine. Ils emportent une combinaison de plongée et ils vont mettre des palmes. Ils ont apporté des bouteilles de plongée. Ils espèrent voir des dauphins. Un pélican est assis près d'eux. Quelqu'un fait du deltaplane au loin.

You might also ask students the following.

Est-ce que tu aimerais faire de la plongée sous-marine? Pourquoi ou pourquoi pas?

Differentiated Instruction

SLOWER PACE LEARNERS

Additional Practice Some students may not remember expressions and phrases they need in order to complete the speaking activity. Ask the class to suggest expressions and phrases that describe the drawing and list these on the board. Encourage students to refer to the list when they tell their story. ✿1.2

SPECIAL LEARNING NEEDS

Students with Learning Disabilities Provide samples of student essays that are examples of well-organized, coherent compositions of substantial length. Display them or allow students to read them individually prior to completing the Essay Topic activity. Discuss and point out the organization, coherence, and appropriate length that are evident in the samples prior to asking students to write their own essay. ✿1.2

Resources

Planning:
Lesson Planner
 One-Stop Planner

Practice:
Cahier d'activités
 Teaching Transparencies
Fine Art, Chapter 5
 Audio CD 5, Tr. 11
 Interactive Tutor, Disc 1

 **VIDEO OPTIONS**

▸ **Géoculture**
▸ **Télé-roman: Camille et compagnie, Épisode 5**

❶ Script

1. Brittany a très peur de tomber dans l'eau parce qu'elle a entendu dire qu'il y avait des alligators.
2. Au sud du pays, il y a des bayous.
3. Mon frère aime faire du deltaplane.
4. J'adore les hérons. Je trouve que ce sont de très beaux animaux.
5. Est-ce que tu as vu des aigles en faisant de l'alpinisme?
6. Moi, descendre des rapides, cela me ferait peur.

❷ Answers

1. le Parc des Trois Lacs et le Parc Alain Travier
2. au Parc du Mont Pointu et au Parc des Cascades
3. le Parc du Mont Pointu
4. On peut faire du rafting, du VTT et du deltaplane.
5. Answers will vary.

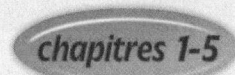

Révisions cumulatives

CD 5, Tr. 11 ✿1.2 **1.** a **2.** a **3.** b **4.** a **5.** b **6.** b

❶ Écoute et dis si on parle **du dessin a** ou **du dessin b.**

a.

b.

✿3.2

❷ Lis cette brochure des parcs nationaux et réponds aux questions.

Découvrez nos PARCS NATIONAUX

	alpinisme	rafting	location de VTT	deltaplane	observation de la faune	période d'ouverture	Tarif adulte	Tarif enfant	Tarif groupe
Parc des Trois Lacs	●		●		●	mai à octobre	15$	7$	30$
Parc du Mont Pointu		●	●	●	●	toute l'année	10$	55$	–
Parc Alain Travier			●		●	juin à août	10$	7$	40$
Parc des Cascades		●			●	juin à septembre	12$	6$	–

1. Quels parcs ont des prix spéciaux pour les groupes?
2. Où est-ce qu'on peut faire du rafting?
3. Quel parc est-ce qu'on peut visiter en avril?
4. Qu'est-ce qu'on peut faire au parc du Mont Pointu?
5. Dans quel parc est-ce que tu aimerais aller? Pourquoi?

Online Culture Project

Have students imagine they are curators for an art museum that specializes in Haitian art. They are to write a plaque to accompany a work of art that will be put on display at an upcoming exhibit. Students should research a piece of art and provide in French the title of the work, the approximate date it was created, the name of the artist, and an explanation of why it should be displayed. Have students document their sources.

✿3.1, 3.2

Online Assessment
go.hrw.com
Cumulative Self–test

KEYWORD: BD3 CH5

Chapitres 1–5

Révisions cumulatives

③ Tu annonces à tes parents que tu vas faire un sport extrême (de la spéléologie ou de l'alpinisme, par exemple) avec tes copains et ils te disent de prendre des précautions. Joue cette scène avec un(e) camarade. ✿1.1

④ Regarde ce tableau et dis quel endroit est représenté. Est-ce que tu as déjà vu cet animal en vrai ou dans un zoo? Quels autres animaux y aurait-il dans l'endroit représenté sur ce tableau? ✿1.3, 2.2

An illustration engraved by Robert Havell, Jr. and published in The Birds of America by John James Audubon.

Louisiana Heron de Jean-Jacques Audubon

⑤ Après avoir parlé avec tes parents, tu as décidé de faire un sport extrême. Écris une lettre à un(e) ami(e) où tu lui expliques où tu vas aller, ce que tu vas faire et ce que tes parents craignent et les avertissements qu'ils t'ont donnés. ✿1.3

⑥ **À ton tour** **Découvrez la Louisiane!** Avec des camarades, créez un poster pour attirer des touristes en Louisiane. Faites une recherche sur la nourriture, les animaux, les activités de plein air, les festivals, la culture cajun, etc. Ensuite, présentez votre poster. ✿1.3, 2.1

✎ FINE ART CONNECTION

Introduction John James Audubon (1785–1851), an ornithologist, naturalist, and painter, was born in Haiti and raised in Nantes. In 1803, his father arranged for him to travel to the United States to avoid the Napoleonic Wars. In order to draw the birds, Audubon had to shoot them first and then use wires to set them in a natural position. In 1826, he took his drawings to London, where he came to be called "The American Woodsman." Eventually, he was able to publish his *Birds of America,* which contains life-size portraits of 1,065 individual birds. It was published in four volumes between 1827 and 1838.

Analyzing

Have students read Audubon's description of the Louisiana heron in *Birds of America.* This work is published on the Web site of the National Audubon Society. Ask students to answer the following questions.

1. **Quel nom Audubon a-t-il donné au héron de la Louisiane?**
2. **Dans quelles parties de l'Amérique du nord est-ce qu'Audubon a rencontré ce héron?**
3. **Comment Audubon décrit-il cet oiseau?**
4. **Comment décrit-il son nid et ses œufs?**
5. **Qu'est-ce que cet oiseau mange?** ✿3.1

Extension

Have students research the National Audubon Society. When and where was this organization founded? What is its mission? What services does it offer? Students should present their research to the class. ✿3.1

ACTFL Performance Standards

The activities in Chapter 5 target the communicative modes as described in the Standards.

Interpersonal	Two-way communication using receptive skills and productive skills	**Communication (SE),** pp. 189, 191, 193, 195, 201, 203, 205 **Communication (TE),** pp. 189, 191, 193, 195, 201, 207 **À ton tour,** p. 221
Interpretive	One-way communication using receptive skills	**Culture,** pp. 196–197 **Lecture,** pp. 208–211
Presentational	One-way communication using productive skills	**Communication (SE),** p. 191, 207 **Communication (TE),** pp. 201

chapitre 6

Planning Guide

La presse

Chapter Section		Resources

Vocabulaire 1 — pp. 224–227
- Newspapers and magazines

Grammaire 1 — pp. 228–231
- The subjunctive with doubt and uncertainty
- The verbs **croire** and **paraître**

Application 1 — pp. 232–233
- **Un peu plus:**
  Quelque part, quelqu'un,
  quelque chose, quelquefois

Resources:
- Teaching Transparencies: Vocabulaire 6.1, 6.2; Bell Work 6.1, 6.2, 6.3, 6.4
- Cahier de vocabulaire et grammaire, pp. 61–66
- Grammar Tutor for Students of French
- Cahier d'activités, pp. 51–53
- Media Guide, pp. 21–24

Assessment Program
Quiz: Vocabulaire 1, pp. 154–155
Quiz: Grammaire 1, pp. 156–157
Quiz: Application 1, pp. 158–159

Culture — pp. 234–235
- **Lecture culturelle: « Mon Quotidien »,**
  un journal pour les 10–14 ans
- **Comparaisons**
- **Communauté et professions**

Resources:
- Cahier d'activités, p. 54

Vocabulaire 2 — pp. 236–239
- News and information

Grammaire 2 — pp. 240–243
- Review: Object pronouns
- **Qui est-ce qui, qui est-ce que...**

Application 2 — pp. 244–245
- **Un peu plus:**
  Negative expressions

Resources:
- Teaching Transparencies: Vocabulaire 6.3, 6.4; Bell Work 6.5, 6.6, 6.7, 6.8
- Cahier de vocabulaire et grammaire, pp. 67–72
- Grammar Tutor for Students of French
- Cahier d'activités, pp. 55–57
- Media Guide, pp. 21–24

Assessment Program
Quiz: Vocabulaire 2, pp. 160–161
Quiz: Grammaire 2, pp. 162–163
Quiz: Application 2, pp. 164–165

Lecture — pp. 246–249
- **Profession journaliste**

L'atelier de l'écrivain — pp. 250–251
- **Reportage: entrer dans le vif**

Resources:
- Cahier d'activités, p. 58
- Reading Strategies and Skills Handbook
- Advanced Reader

Assessment Program
Quiz: Lecture, p. 166
Quiz: Écriture, p. 167

Prépare-toi pour l'examen — pp. 252–255
- **Résumé de vocabulaire et**
  grammaire

Activités préparatoires — pp. 256–257

Révisions cumulatives — pp. 258–259

Resources:
- Teaching Transparencies: Picture Sequences, Situation, Ch. 6
- Media Guide, p. 24, 63–64

Assessment Program
Examen: Chapitre 6, pp. 168–173
Examen oral: Chapitre 6, p. 313

- Teaching Transparencies: Fine Art, Ch. 6
- Cahier d'activités, pp. 59–60

Chroniques — pp. 260–269
- Animaux d'Afrique
- À la découverte de la nature
- Les sports extrêmes
- À vos marques!
- De grands événements sportifs

Resources:
- Reading Strategies and Skills Handbook
- Advanced Reader

Pacing Suggestions

	Essential	Recommended	Optional
Vocabulaire 1 • Newspapers and magazines • **Flash culture**	✔		
Grammaire 1 • The subjunctive with doubt and uncertainty • The verb **croire** and **paraître** • **Flash culture**	✔		

Application 1
• **Un peu plus:**
  Quelque part, quelqu'un, quelque
  chose, quelquefois
	✔		

Culture
• **Lecture culturelle:**
  « Mon Quotidien »,
  un journal pour les 10–14 ans
• **Comparaisons**
• **Communauté et professions**
		✔	

Vocabulaire 2 • News and information • **Flash culture**	✔		
Grammaire 2 • Review: Object pronouns • **Qui est-ce qui, qui est-ce que...**	✔		
Application 2 • **Un peu plus:** More negative expressions	✔		
Lecture • **Profession journaliste** **L'atelier de l'écrivain** • **Reportage: entrer dans le vif**		✔	
Prépare-toi pour l'examen		✔	
Activités préparatoires		✔	
Révisions cumulatives			✔
Chroniques			✔

Technology

Bien dit! Online
• Student Edition with multi-media
• SoundBooth recording tool
• Interactive activities with feedback
• Self-tests with feedback
• Cahier d'activités (Interactive workbook)
• Cahier de vocabulaire et grammaire (Interactive workbook)
• Holt Online Assessment

DVD Program
• Télé-roman: Camille et compagnie
• Télé-culture: Interviews

Interactive Tutor
• Interactive practice games
• Writing and recording workshops
• Before You Know It™ Flashcards

Audio Program
• Student Edition Listening Activities
• Assessment listening activities
• Songs

One-Stop Planner
• Complete media and print resources
• ExamView Pro Test Generator
• Holt Calendar Planner

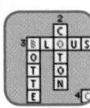

PuzzlePro
• Customizable word games

Differentiated Practice and Assessment CD

For slower pace and advanced learner options, see the Differentiated Practice and Assessment CD.

Planning Guide

Projects

Les informations

The class will create and videotape a French television newscast, using news and sports stories they have written. 🎬 1.3, 5.1

Suggested Sequence

1. First, the class decides on the content of the newscast. The news stories should be a mixture of serious and humorous incidents.

2. Partners write news stories to submit for the newscast. They should keep their identities secret by using pen names.

3. Post the articles around the classroom and have students vote for their five favorite stories, ranking each from one to five, with one being the best.

4. Tally the points for each story and select the seven to nine most popular ones. Of these, choose two or three lead stories, three or four on-the-spot stories, and two or three sports stories. Then form groups and distribute one story to each group for editing. Have students recopy and submit the edited stories for final corrections.

5. Ask for volunteers to read the stories "on the air." There may be as many as two anchor people, three or four reporters, and two sportscasters. Next, ask for three volunteers to write scripts to open the newscast, to introduce the on-the-spot stories and sports, and to end the newscast. Assign a student to select background music for the beginning and end of the show, and another student to tape the broadcast. The remaining students will create the set.

6. Allow students time in class to rehearse the show. Then, videotape the broadcast and show the final product to the class and to other French classes.

Grading the project

Suggested point distribution
(100 points total)

Content . . . . 25 pts.
Language use . . . . 25 pts.
Overall presentation . . . . 25 pts.
Effort/Participation . . . . 25 pts.

e-community

e-mail forum:

Post the following question on the classroom e-mail forum:

Location: http://french

Est-ce que tu préfères lire le journal, écouter la radio, regarder la télé ou surfer sur Internet pour savoir ce qui se passe dans le monde? 🎬 5.1

All students will contribute to the list and then share the items.

Partner Class Project

Have students work together to develop a survey about people's preferred sources of information. Does their partner class prefer television, radio, newspapers, or the Internet? Why? The survey should consist of five, open-ended questions. The survey should be filled out by each student of the partner class. Upon receiving the completed surveys, the class will evaluate the answers and compare the results with their own preferences. Students will then work in groups to summarize the results and present their summaries to the class. 🎬 1.3, 4.2

Game Bank
For game ideas, see pages T60–T63.

Traditions

La ville souterraine

Ever since the pioneers settled the area in the 16th and 17th centuries, the people of Quebec have used their ingenuity to find ever more efficient ways to deal with the region's cold weather. One such effort is Montreal's Underground City, begun in the 1960s as a refuge from the city's bitter winters and humid summers. Today, the underground network consists of 22 kilometers of passages lined with shops, movie theaters, concert halls, restaurants, offices, hotels, and apartments. The passages connect people to everything, from the city's subway and train system to the stock exchange. It is said that soon Montrealers will have no need ever to go outside, due to the Underground City's continuing expansion. Have students discuss in French the advantages and disadvantages of living, working, and engaging in leisure activities in an underground city.

✿ 2.1, 3.2

La cuisine

Another staple of Creole cuisine, gumbo is a thick stew made with meat, poultry, seafood, or vegetables, and often thickened with okra or roux. Gumbo is served over plain white rice. Among the ancestors of the Creole gumbo is the French **bouillabaisse,** or *fish stew*, which was modified by Spanish, African, and native ingredients. Encourage students to make **gumbo créole** in their home economics class or at home for family and friends.

✿ 3.1, 5.2

Gumbo Créole

2 cuillères à soupe d'huile de maïs
2 cuillères à soupe de farine
2 livres d'okras coupés en rondelles
1 oignon haché
1 poivron vert haché
1 branche de céleri hachée

3 livres de poulet coupé en morceaux
¾ tasse de saucisse fumée de dinde coupée en dés
½ tasse de jambon coupé en dés
2 gousses d'ail hachées

2 tomates coupées en dés
8 ½ tasses d'eau
sel, poivre, cayenne
1 cuillère à soupe de sauce Worcestershire

Faire griller l'huile et la farine pendant 15 minutes à haute densité pour faire un roux foncé. Laisser cuire à feu doux pendant une heure. Ajouter les oignons, le poivron et le céleri. Laisser cuire pendant cinq minutes. Ajouter le jambon, l'ail, les tomates, la saucisse, le poulet, et la moitié des okras. Faire sauter pendant 20 minutes. Mêler le reste des okras, l'eau, le sel, le poivre, le poivre de cayenne et la sauce Worcestershire à la préparation. Faire bouillir. Baisser le feu. Laisser mijoter pendant 30 minutes.

Traditions

Vocabulaire 1
à l'œuvre

2 p. 226, CD 6, Tr. 1

1. — Josyane, tu vas en ville?

— Oui.

— Tu peux me prendre *Zurban* au kiosque au coin de la rue?

2. — Est-ce que vous allez vous abonner à ce magazine?

— Je ne sais pas. Il n'est pas terrible. Je crois que je vais plutôt m'abonner à ce magazine féminin. J'aime beaucoup leurs articles sur la mode.

3. — Qu'est-ce que tu lis, Paul?

— Oh, rien de très sérieux. Je regarde les dessins humoristiques et les BD. Parfois, c'est vraiment amusant.

4. — On m'a dit que Nadja travaillait pour un magazine?

— Oui, oui. Elle est rédactrice en chef d'un magazine féminin.

5. — Patrick, tu as vu les gros titres à la une du *Monde* ce matin?

— Non, je ne lis jamais les quotidiens.

6. — Tu as vu la couverture du dernier *Animal*?

— Laquelle? Celle avec le chien?

Answers to Activity 2
1. d   **2.** a   **3.** b   **4.** c   **5.** e   **6.** f

Grammaire 1
à l'œuvre

8 p. 229, CD 6, Tr. 2

1. Monsieur Branconnier est sûr que ce sera dans le journal.

2. Pensez-vous que quelqu'un soit mort?

3. Non, moi je ne pense pas que ce soit sérieux.

4. Je suis persuadé(e) que la presse n'en parlera pas.

5. Moi, je ne suis pas sûr(e) que ce soit dans le journal demain.

6. Je pense qu'il faudra attendre de lire les dernières nouvelles.

Answers to Activity 8
1. a   **2.** b   **3.** b   **4.** a   **5.** b   **6.** a

Application 1

18 p. 233, CD 6, Tr. 3

1. — Tu as le dernier Bonjour, les copains?

— Oui, il doit être là [...].

2. — Tu achètes aussi Le temps des ados?

— Oui, [...], pourquoi?

3. — [...] m'a dit qu'il y avait un article intéressant sur la mode. Tu pourrais me prêter le dernier numéro si tu l'as?

4. — Oui, je l'ai, mais je crois que je l'ai déjà prêté à [...].

5. — Je vois [...] sur ton bureau. Ce ne serait pas le numéro que je cherche?

6. — Tu as raison. [...], je ne sais plus ce que je fais de mes affaires!

Answers to Activity 18
1. a   **2.** c   **3.** b   **4.** b   **5.** d   **6.** c

Vocabulaire 2
à l'œuvre

23 p. 238, CD 6, Tr. 4

1. À voir absolument: L'exposition des œuvres d'Ousmane Sow.

2. Air Aquitaine: La grève des pilotes dure et les passagers sont en colère.

3. Selon le ministre du travail, le chômage est en baisse.

4. Un enfant d'un an est tombé du premier étage de l'appartement de ses parents, mais il n'a pas été blessé!

5. Jeux olympiques: Trois médailles pour la France.

6. Côte d'Azur: Temps lourd et très chaud. Des records de température ont été enregistrés.

Answers to Activity 23
1. g   **2.** a   **3.** d   **4.** e   **5.** b   **6.** h

Grammaire à l'œuvre 2

32 p. 243, CD 6, Tr. 5

1. Qu'est-ce que tu as vu à la bibliothèque?

2. Qu'est-ce qui te dit que ce n'est pas vrai?

3. Qui est-ce que tu vas étudier dans ton cours d'histoire cette année?

4. Qu'est-ce qui ne va pas?

5. Qui est-ce que tu as invité?

6. Qui est-ce qui t'a dit ça?

Answers to Activity 32

1. b   **2.** b   **3.** a   **4.** b   **5.** a   **6.** a

Application 2

36 p. 244, CD 6, Tr. 6

1. — Ils m'ont trouvé un beau jean.

2. — Mon père s'est acheté des tee-shirts.

3. — Mes parents m'en ont aussi pris un.

4. — Ils me l'ont apporté hier soir.

5. — Ma mère y a aussi choisi quelque chose pour toi.

6. — Elle va t'offrir ce chemisier.

7. — Ma sœur va te le donner demain.

Answers to Activity 36

1. a   **2.** b   **3.** a   **4.** a   **5.** b   **6.** b   **7.** b

Prépare-toi pour l'examen

6 p. 253, CD 6, Tr. 8

1. Elle donne le temps qu'il va faire.

2. On peut y acheter des journaux et des magazines.

3. C'est quand les gens refusent de travailler.

4. C'est la première page d'un journal.

5. C'est fait pour faire rire.

Answers to Activity 6

1. e   **2.** d   **3.** c   **4.** f   **5.** a

Activités préparatoires

Listening, p. 256, CD 6, Tr. 9

1. — Regarde cet article sur la plongée. Il est génial!

— Et en voici un autre sur la planche à voile! C'est un magazine qui traite de tous les sports nautiques. Je voudrais m'y abonner. Et il paraît chaque semaine, n'est-ce pas?

2. — Oh non, le musée est fermé. Tu sais pourquoi?

Answers to Activity 1

1. a   **2.** c

Révisions cumulatives *chapitres 1-6*

1 p. 258, CD 6, Tr. 10

1. — Notre équipe a gagné le match!

J'espère qu'ils vont gagner le championnat maintenant!

2. — Nous voulons une augmentation de salaire ou nous continuerons la grève!

3. — Bonjour, combien coûte *Le monde*?

— 1 euro vingt. Vous le prenez?

— Oui, s'il vous plaît. Merci!

4. — Tu regardes toujours les Jeux olympiques?

— Oui, bien sûr!

5. — Je voudrais un journal en chinois.

— Désolé, je n'en ai pas.

Answers to Activity 1

1. b   **2.** c   **3.** a   **4.** b   **5.** a

50-Minute Lesson Plans

La presse

Day 1

OBJECTIVE
Express certainty and possibility

Core Instruction
Chapter Opener, pp. 222–223
• See Using the Photo, p. 222. **5 min.**
• See Chapter Objectives, p. 222. **5 min.**

Vocabulaire 1, pp. 224–227
• Present **Vocabulaire 1,** pp. 224–225. See Teaching **Vocabulaire,** p. 224. **15 min.**
• Present **Exprimons-nous!,** p. 225. **5 min.**
• Do Activity 1, p. 226. **5 min.**
• Play Audio CD 6, Tr. 1 for Activity 2, p. 226. **5 min.**
• Do Activity 3, p. 226. **5 min.**
• Present **Flash culture,** p. 226. **5 min.**

Optional Resources
• Advanced Learners, p. 225 ▲
• Multiple Intelligences, p. 225

Homework Suggestions
Cahier de vocabulaire et grammaire, pp. 61–62

✿ 1.1, 1.2, 1.3, 3.1, 3.2, 4.2

Day 2

OBJECTIVE
Express doubt and disbelief

Core Instruction
Vocabulaire 1, pp. 224–227
• Do Bell Work 6.1, p. 224. **5 min.**
• See Teaching **Exprimons-nous!,** p. 226. **10 min.**
• Have students do Activities 4–5, p. 227. **20 min.**

Grammaire 1, pp. 228–231
• See Teaching **Grammaire,** p. 228. **15 min.**

Optional Resources
• Advanced Learners, p. 227 ▲
• Multiple Intelligences, p. 227

Homework Suggestions
Study for **Quiz: Vocabulaire 1**
Cahier de vocabulaire et grammaire, p. 63
Online Practice (**go.hrw.com,** Keyword: BD3 CH6)

✿ 1.1, 1.2, 1.3, 3.1

Day 3

OBJECTIVE
Use the subjunctive with doubt, disbelief and uncertainty

Core Instruction
Vocabulaire 1, pp. 224–227
• Review **Vocabulaire 1,** pp. 224–227. **10 min.**
• Give **Quiz: Vocabulaire 1. 20 min.**

Grammaire 1, pp. 228–231
• Have students do Activities 6–7, pp. 228–229. **5 min.**
• Play Audio CD 6, Tr. 2 for Activity 8, p. 229. **5 min.**
• Have students do Activities 9–10, p. 229. **10 min.**

Optional Resources
• Slower Pace Learners, p. 229 ◆
• Multiple Intelligences, p. 229

Homework Suggestions
Cahier de vocabulaire et grammaire, p. 64
Cahier d'activités, p. 51
Online Practice (**go.hrw.com,** Keyword: BD3 CH6)

✿ 1.1, 1.2, 1.3

Day 4

OBJECTIVE
*Use the verbs **croire** and **paraître;** Use **quelque part, quelqu'un, quelque chose** and **quelquefois***

Core Instruction
Grammaire 1, pp. 228–231
• Present **Flash culture,** p. 230. **5 min.**
• See Teaching **Grammaire,** p. 230. **10 min.**
• Have students do Activities 11–15, pp. 230–231. **25 min.**

Application 1, pp. 232–233
• Do Activity 16, p. 232. **5 min.**
• See Teaching **Un peu plus,** p. 232. **5 min.**

Optional Resources
• Slower Pace Learners, p. 231 ◆
• Special Learning Needs, p. 231 ●

Homework Suggestions
Study for **Quiz: Grammaire 1**
Cahier de vocabulaire et grammaire, p. 65
Cahier d'activités, 52

✿ 1.1, 1.2, 1.3, 1.4

Day 5

OBJECTIVE
*Use **quelque part, quelqu'un, quelque chose** and **quelquefois***

Core Instruction
Grammaire 1, pp. 228–231
• Review **Grammaire 1,** pp. 228–231. **10 min.**
• Give **Quiz: Grammaire 1. 20 min.**

Application 1, pp. 232–233
• Do Activity 17, p. 232. **5 min.**
• Play Audio CD 6, Tr. 3 for Activity 18, p. 233. **5 min.**
• Have students do Activities 19–21, p. 233. **10 min.**

Optional Resources
• Advanced Learners, p. 233 ▲
• Special Learning Needs, p. 233 ●

Homework Suggestions
Study for **Quiz: Application 1**
Cahier de vocabulaire et grammaire, p. 66
Cahier d'activités, p. 53
Online Practice (**go.hrw.com,** Keyword: BD3 CH6)

✿ 1.1, 1.2, 1.3

Day 6

OBJECTIVE
Learn about francophone culture

Core Instruction
Application 1, pp. 232–233
• Review **Application 1,** pp. 232–233. **10 min.**
• Give **Quiz: Application 1. 20 min.**

Culture, pp. 234–235
• See **Lecture culturelle** (TE), p. 234. **10 min.**
• See **Comparaisons et communauté** (TE), p. 234. **10 min.**

Optional Resources
• Cultures, p. 235
• Communities, p. 235
• Advanced Learners, p. 235 ▲
• Special Learning Needs, p. 235 ●

Homework Suggestions
Cahier d'activités, p. 54
Interactive Tutor, Ch. 6
Online Practice (**go.hrw.com,** Keyword: BD3 CH6)
Finish the **Communauté et professions** project.

✿ 1.2, 1.3, 2.1, 2.2, 3.1, 3.2, 4.2

Day 7

OBJECTIVE
Break news

Core Instruction
Vocabulaire 2, pp. 236–239
• Do Bell Work 6.5, p. 236. **5 min.**
• Present **Vocabulaire 2,** pp. 236–237. See Teaching **Vocabulaire,** p. 236. **15 min.**
• Present **Exprimons-nous!,** p. 237. **10 min.**
• Have students do Activity 22, p. 238. **5 min.**
• Play Audio CD 6, Tr. 4 for Activity 23, p. 238. **5 min.**
• Have students do Activity 24, p. 238. **5 min.**
• Present **Flash culture,** p. 238. **5 min.**

Optional Resources
• Advanced Learners, p. 237 ▲
• Special Learning Needs, p. 237 ●

Homework Suggestions
Cahier de vocabulaire et grammaire, pp. 67–68

✿ 1.2, 1.3, 4.2

Day 8

OBJECTIVE
Ask for information; Use object pronouns

Core Instruction
Vocabulaire 2, pp. 236–239
• See Teaching **Exprimons-nous!,** p. 238. **10 min.**
• Have students do Activities 25–26, p. 239. **20 min.**

Grammaire 2, pp. 240–243
• See Teaching **Grammaire,** p. 240. **10 min.**
• Do Activities 27–28, pp. 240–241. **10 min.**

Optional Resources
• Slower Pace Learners, p. 239 ◆
• Multiple Intelligences, p. 239

Homework Suggestions
Study for **Quiz: Vocabulaire 2**
Cahier de vocabulaire et grammaire, p. 69
Interactive Tutor, Ch. 6
Online Practice (**go.hrw.com,** Keyword: BD3 CH6)

✿ 1.1, 1.2, 3.2

50-Minute Lesson Plans

Day 9

OBJECTIVE
Use object pronouns

Core Instruction
Vocabulaire 2, pp. 236–239
- Review **Vocabulaire 2,** pp. 236–239. **10 min.**
- Give **Quiz: Vocabulaire 2.** **20 min.**

Grammaire 2, pp. 240–243
- Have students do Activities 29–30, p. 241. **20 min.**

Optional Resources
- Communication (TE), p. 241
- Special Learning Needs, p. 241 ●

Homework Suggestions
Cahier de vocabulaire et grammaire, p. 70
Cahier d'activités, p. 55
Interactive Tutor, Ch. 6
Online Practice (**go.hrw.com,** Keyword: BD3 CH6)

🌼 1.1, 1.2

Day 10

OBJECTIVE
*Use **qui est-ce qui, qui est-ce que, qu'est-ce qui,** and **qu'est-ce que***

Core Instruction
Grammaire 2, pp. 240–243
- Do Bell Work 6.7, p. 242. **5 min.**
- See Teaching **Grammaire,** p. 242. **10 min.**
- Do Activity 31, p. 242. **5 min.**
- Play Audio CD 6, Tr. 5 for Activity 32, p. 243. **5 min.**
- Have students do Activities 33–35, p. 243. **15 min.**

Application 2, pp. 244–245
- Play Audio CD 6, Tr. 6 for Activity 36, p. 244. **5 min.**
- Do Activity 37, p. 244. **5 min.**

Optional Resources
- Special Learning Needs, p. 243 ●

Homework Suggestions
Study for **Quiz: Grammaire 2**
Cahier de vocabulaire et grammaire, p. 71
Cahier d'activités, p. 56

🌼 1.1, 1.2

Day 11

OBJECTIVE
Use more negative expressions

Core Instruction
Grammaire 2, pp. 240–243
- Review **Grammaire 2,** pp. 240–243. **10 min.**
- Give **Quiz: Grammaire 2.** **20 min.**

Application 2, pp. 244–245
- See Teaching **Un peu plus,** p. 244. **5 min.**
- Have students do Activities 38–41, pp. 244–245. **15 min.**

Optional Resources
- Advanced Learners, p. 245 ▲
- Multiple Intelligences, p. 245

Homework Suggestions
Study for **Quiz: Application 2**
Cahier de vocabulaire et grammaire, p. 72
Cahier d'activités, p. 57
Interactive Tutor, Ch. 6
Online Practice (**go.hrw.com,** Keyword: BD3 CH6)

🌼 1.1, 1.2, 1.3, 3.1

Day 12

OBJECTIVE
Develop listening and reading skills

Core Instruction
Application 2, pp. 244–245
- Review **Application 2,** pp. 244–245. **10 min.**
- Give **Quiz: Application 2.** **20 min.**

Lecture, pp. 246–249
- See **Lecture** (TE), p. 246. **20 min.**

Optional Resources
- Slower Pace Learners, p. 247 ◆
- Multiple Intelligences, p. 247
- Connections, p. 249

Homework Suggestions
Interactive Tutor, Ch. 6
Online Practice (**go.hrw.com,** Keyword: BD3 CH6)

🌼 1.3, 3.1, 5.1

Day 13

OBJECTIVE
Develop listening, reading, and writing skills

Core Instruction
Lecture, pp. 246–249
- See **Lecture** (TE), p. 248. **20 min.**

L'atelier de l'écrivain, pp. 250–251
- See **L'atelier de l'écrivain** (TE), p. 250. **30 min.**

Optional Resources
- Advanced Learners, p. 249 ▲ ●
- Special Learning Needs, p. 249 ●
- Connections, p. 250
- Slower Pace Learners, p. 251 ◆
- Special Learning Needs, p. 251 ●

Homework Suggestions
Cahier d'activités, p. 58

🌼 1.1, 1.2, 1.3, 3.1, 3.2

Day 14

OBJECTIVE
Review the chapter; Review for the AP Exam

Core Instruction
Prépare-toi pour l'examen, pp. 252–255
- Have students do Activities 1–5, pp. 252–253. **25 min.**

Activités preparatoires, pp. 256–257
- Have students do the **Activités preparatoires,** pp. 256–257. **25 min.**

Optional Resources
- French for Spanish Speakers, p. 252
- Slower Pace Learners, p. 257 ◆
- Special Learning Needs, p. 257 ●
- **Télé-culture:** Interviews

Homework Suggestions
Interactive Tutor, Ch. 6
Online Practice (**go.hrw.com,** Keyword: BD3 CH6)

🌼 1.2, 1.3, 2.1, 3.2, 4.1

Day 15

OBJECTIVE
Review the chapter

Core Instruction
Prépare-toi pour l'examen, pp. 252–255
- Play Audio CD 6, Tr. 8 for Activity 6, p. 253. **10 min.**
- Have students do Activity 7, p. 253. **10 min.**

Révisions cumulatives, pp. 258–259
- Play Audio CD 6, Tr. 10 for Activity 1, p. 258. **5 min.**
- Have students do Activities 2–6, pp. 258–259. **25 min.**

Optional Resources
- Cultures, p. 254
- Game, p. 255
- Online Culture Project, p. 258
- Fine Art Connection, p. 259
- **Télé-roman:** Camille et compagnie

Homework Suggestions
Study for Chapter Test
Online Practice (**go.hrw.com,** Keyword: BD3 CH6)

🌼 1.1, 1.2, 1.3, 2.2, 3.1. 3.2

Day 16/Test

Core Instruction
Chapter Test 50 min.

Optional Resources
Assessment Program
- Alternative Assessment
- Test Generator
- **Quiz: Lecture**
- **Quiz: Écriture**

Homework Suggestions
Cahier d'activités, pp. 59–60, 112–113
Online Practice (**go.hrw.com,** Keyword: BD3 CH6)

90-Minute Lesson Plans

La presse

90-Minute Lesson Plans

Block 1

OBJECTIVE
*Express certainty and possibility;
Express doubt and disbelief*

Core Instruction
Chapter Opener, pp. 222–223
- See Using the Photo, p. 222.
  5 min.
- See Chapter Objectives, p. 222.
  5 min.

Vocabulaire 1, pp. 224–227
- Present **Vocabulaire 1,**
  pp. 224–225. See Teaching
  Vocabulaire, p. 224. **20 min.**
- Present **Exprimons-nous!,**
  p. 225. **10 min.**
- Have students do Activity 1,
  p. 226. **5 min.**
- Play Audio CD 6, Tr. 1 for
  Activity 2, p. 226. **5 min.**
- Have students do Activity 3,
  p. 226. **5 min.**
- Present **Flash culture,** p. 226.
  5 min.
- See Teaching **Exprimons-
  nous!,** p. 226. **10 min.**
- Have students do Activities 4–5,
  p. 227. **20 min.**

Optional Resources
- Learning Tips, p. 223
- TPR, p. 225
- Teaching Suggestion, p. 225
- **Proverbes,** p. 225
- Advanced Learners, p. 225 ▲
- Multiple Intelligences, p. 225
- Cultures, p. 227
- Communication (TE), p. 227
- Advanced Learners, p. 227 ▲
- Multiple Intelligences, p. 227

Homework Suggestions
Study for **Quiz: Vocabulaire 1**
**Cahier de vocabulaire et
  grammaire,** pp. 61–63
Cahier d'activités, p. 51
Interactive Tutor, Ch. 6
Online Practice (**go.hrw.com,**
  Keyword: BD3 CH6)
❀ 1.1, 1.2, 1.3, 2.2, 3.1,
  3.2, 4.2

Block 2

OBJECTIVE
*Use the subjunctive with doubt,
disbelief and uncertainty; Use the
verbs **croire** and **paraître***

Core Instruction
Vocabulaire 1, pp. 224–227
- Review **Vocabulaire 1,**
  pp. 224–227. **10 min.**
- Give **Quiz: Vocabulaire 1.**
  20 min.

Grammaire 1, pp. 228–231
- See Teaching **Grammaire,**
  p. 228. **10 min.**
- Have students do Activities 6–7,
  pp. 228–229. **5 min.**
- Play Audio CD 6, Tr. 2 for
  Activity 8, p. 229. **5 min.**
- Have students do Activities
  9–10, p. 229. **10 min.**
- Present **Flash culture,** p. 230.
  5 min.
- See Teaching **Grammaire,**
  p. 230. **10 min.**
- Have students do Activities
  11–14, pp. 230–231. **15 min.**

Optional Resources
- Comparisons, p. 228
- Communication (TE), p. 229
- Slower Pace Learners, p. 229 ◆
- Multiple Intelligences, p. 229
- Slower Pace Learners, p. 231 ◆
- Special Learning Needs, p. 231 ●

Homework Suggestions
Study for **Quiz: Grammaire 1**
**Cahier de vocabulaire et
  grammaire,** pp. 64–65
Cahier d'activités, pp. 51–52
Online Practice (**go.hrw.com,**
  Keyword: BD3 CH6)
❀ 1.1, 1.2, 1.3, 4.1

Block 3

OBJECTIVE
*Use the verbs **croire** and
paraître; Use **quelque part,
quelqu'un, quelque chose**
and **quelquefois**; Learn about
francophone culture*

Core Instruction
Grammaire 1, pp. 228–231
- Do Bell Work 6.3, p. 230. **5 min.**
- Have students do Activity 15,
  p. 231. **5 min.**
- Review **Grammaire 1,**
  pp. 228–231. **10 min.**
- Give **Quiz: Grammaire 1.**
  20 min.

Application 1, pp. 232–233
- Have students do Activity 16,
  p. 232. **5 min.**
- See Teaching **Un peu plus,**
  p. 232. **5 min.**
- Have students do Activity 17,
  p. 232. **5 min.**
- Play Audio CD 6, Tr. 3 for
  Activity 18, p. 233. **5 min.**
- Have students do Activities
  19–21, p. 233. **10 min.**

Culture, pp. 234–235
- See **Lecture culturelle** (TE),
  p. 234. **10 min.**
- See **Comparaisons et
  communauté** (TE), p. 234.
  10 min.

Optional Resources
- Communication (TE), p. 231
- **Attention!,** p. 232
- Communication (TE), p. 233
- Advanced Learners, p. 233 ▲
- Special Learning Needs, p. 233 ●
- Prereading Questions, p. 234
- Active Reading Questions,
  p. 234
- Vocabulaire supplémentaire,
  p. 234
- Bulletin Board Project, p. 235
- Cultures, p. 235
- Communities, p. 235
- Advanced Learners, p. 235 ▲
- Special Learning Needs, p. 235 ●

Homework Suggestions
Study for **Quiz: Application 1**
**Cahier de vocabulaire et
  grammaire,** p. 66
Cahier d'activités, pp. 53–54
Interactive Tutor, Ch. 6
Online Practice (**go.hrw.com,**
  Keyword: BD3 CH6)
Finish the **Communauté et
  professions** project.
❀ 1.1, 1.2, 1.3, 2.1, 2.2,
  3.1, 3.2, 4.2, 5.1

Block 4

OBJECTIVE
Break news; Ask for information

Core Instruction
Application 1, pp. 232–233
- Review **Application 1,**
  pp. 232–233. **10 min.**
- Give **Quiz: Application 1.**
  20 min.

Vocabulaire 2, pp. 236–239
- Present **Vocabulaire 2,**
  pp. 236–237. See Teaching
  Vocabulaire, p. 236. **15 min.**
- Present **Exprimons-nous!,**
  p. 237. **5 min.**
- Have students do Activity 22,
  p. 238. **5 min.**
- Play Audio CD 6, Tr. 4 for
  Activity 23, p. 238. **5 min.**
- Have students do Activity 24,
  p. 238. **5 min.**
- Present **Flash culture,** p. 238.
  5 min.
- See Teaching **Exprimons-
  nous!,** p. 238. **10 min.**
- Have students do Activities
  25–26, p. 239. **10 min.**

Optional Resources
- Cultures, p. 236
- TPR, p. 237
- Teacher to Teacher, p. 237
- Advanced Learners, p. 237 ▲
- Special Learning Needs, p. 237 ●
- **Cinquain** Poetry, p. 238
- Communication (TE), p. 239
- Slower Pace Learners, p. 239 ◆
- Multiple Intelligences, p. 239

Homework Suggestions
Study for **Quiz: Vocabulaire 2**
**Cahier de vocabulaire et
  grammaire,** pp. 67–69
Interactive Tutor, Ch. 6
Online Practice (**go.hrw.com,**
  Keyword: BD3 CH6)
❀ 1.1, 1.2, 1.3, 2.2, 3.2, 4.2

Block 5

OBJECTIVE
Use object pronouns; Use **qui est-ce qui, qui est-ce que, qu'est-ce qui,** *and* **qu'est-ce que**

Core Instruction
Vocabulaire 2, pp. 236–239
- Review **Vocabulaire 2,** pp. 236–239. **10 min.**
- Give **Quiz: Vocabulaire 2.** **20 min.**

Grammaire 2, pp. 240–243
- See Teaching **Grammaire,** p. 240. **10 min.**
- Have students do Activities 27–30, pp. 240–241. **20 min.**
- See Teaching **Grammaire,** p. 242. **10 min.**
- Have students do Activity 31, p. 242. **5 min.**
- Play Audio CD 6, Tr. 5 for Activity 32, p. 243. **5 min.**
- Have students do Activities 33–34, p. 243. **10 min.**

Optional Resources
- Communication (TE), p. 241
- French for Spanish Speakers, p. 241
- Slower Pace Learners, p. 241 ◆
- Special Learning Needs, p. 241 ●
- Advanced Learners, p. 243 ▲
- Special Learning Needs, p. 243 ●

Homework Suggestions
Study for **Quiz: Grammaire 2**
Cahier de vocabulaire et grammaire, pp. 70–71
Cahier d'activités, pp. 55–56
Interactive Tutor, Ch. 6
Online Practice (**go.hrw.com,** Keyword: BD3 CH6)
　🌼 1.1, 1.2

Block 6

OBJECTIVE
Use **qui est-ce qui, qui est-ce que, qu'est-ce qui,** *and* **qu'est-ce que;** *Use more negative expressions; Develop listening and reading skills*

Core Instruction
Grammaire 2, pp. 240–243
- Have students do Activity 35, p. 243. **10 min.**
- Review **Grammaire 2,** pp. 240–243. **10 min.**
- Give **Quiz: Grammaire 2.** **20 min.**

Application 2, pp. 244–245
- Play Audio CD 6, Tr. 6 for Activity 36, p. 244. **5 min.**
- Have students do Activity 37, p. 244. **5 min.**
- See Teaching **Un peu plus,** p. 244. **5 min.**
- Have students do Activities 38–41, pp. 244–245. **15 min.**

Lecture, pp. 246–249
- See **Lecture** (TE), p. 246. **20 min.**

Optional Resources
- Communication (TE), p. 243
- Communication (TE), p. 245
- Advanced Learners, p. 245 ▲
- Multiple Intelligences, p. 245
- AP Reading Suggestion, p. 246
- Applying the Strategies, p. 246
- Active Reading Questions, p. 247
- Fact or Opinion, p. 247
- Slower Pace Learners, p. 247 ◆
- Multiple Intelligences, p. 247

Homework Suggestions
Study for **Quiz: Application 2**
Cahier de vocabulaire et grammaire, p. 72
Cahier d'activités, p. 57
Interactive Tutor, Ch. 6
Online Practice (**go.hrw.com,** Keyword: BD3 CH6)
　🌼 1.1, 1.2, 1.3, 3.1, 5.1

Block 7

OBJECTIVE
Develop listening, reading, and writing skills; Review the chapter

Core Instruction
Application 2, pp. 244–245
- Review **Application 2,** pp. 244–245. **10 min.**
- Give **Quiz: Application 2.** **20 min.**

Lecture, pp. 246–249
- See **Lecture** (TE), p. 248. **10 min.**

L'atelier de l'écrivain, pp. 250–251
- See **L'atelier de l'écrivain** (TE), p. 250. **30 min.**

Prépare-toi pour l'examen, pp. 252–255
- Have students do Activities 1–5, pp. 252–253. **10 min.**
- Play Audio CD 6, Tr. 8 for Activity 6, p. 253. **5 min.**
- Have students do Activity 7, p. 253. **5 min.**

Optional Resources
- Active Reading Questions, p. 248
- Postreading Activity, p. 248
- Connections, p. 249
- Advanced Learners, p. 249 ▲
- Special Learning Needs, p. 249 ●
- Process Writing, p. 250
- Teaching Suggestion, p. 250
- Connections, p. 250
- The infinitive, p. 251
- Writing Assessment, p. 251
- Slower Pace Learners, p. 251 ◆
- Special Learning Needs, p. 251 ●
- TPRS, p. 252
- French for Spanish Speakers, p. 252
- Reteaching, p. 252
- Oral Assessment, p. 253
- **Proverbes,** p. 254
- Cultures, p. 254
- **Attention!,** p. 254
- Chapter Review, pp. 254–255
- Game, p. 255

Homework Suggestions
Study for Chapter Test
Cahier d'activités, p. 58
Interactive Tutor, Ch. 6
Online Practice (**go.hrw.com,** Keyword: BD3 CH6)
　🌼 1.1, 1.2, 1.3, 2.1, 2.2, 3.1, 3.2, 4.1

Block 8

OBJECTIVE
Prepare for the AP Exam; Review and assess the chapter

Core Instruction
Activités preparatoires, pp. 256–257
- Have students do the **Activités preparatoires,** pp. 256–257. **20 min.**

Chapter Test 50 min.
Révisions cumulatives, pp. 258–259
- Play Audio CD 6, Tr. 10 for Activity 1, p. 258. **5 min.**
- Have students do Activities 2–6, pp. 258–259. **15 min.**

Optional Resources
- Reading Strategy, p. 256
- Writing Strategy, p. 257
- Slower Pace Learners, p. 257 ◆
- Special Learning Needs, p. 257 ●
- Online Culture Project, p. 258
- Fine Art Connection, p. 259
- **Télé-culture:** Interviews
- **Télé-roman: Camille et compagnie**

Homework Suggestions
Cahier d'activités, pp. 59–60, 112–113
Interactive Tutor, Ch. 1
Online Practice (**go.hrw.com,** Keyword: BD3 CH6)
　🌼 1.1, 1.2, 1.3, 2.2, 3.2

90-Minute Lesson Plans

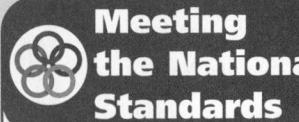

Meeting the National Standards

Communication
Communication, pp. 227, 229, 231, 233, 239, 241, 243, 245

À ton tour, p. 259

Cultures
Flash culture, pp. 226, 230, 238

Comparaisons, p. 235

Products and Perspectives, pp. 227, 231, 235, 236, 254

Connections
History Link, p. 249

Comparing and Contrasting, p. 228

Comparisons
Comparaisons, p. 235

Communities
Communauté, p. 235

Career Path, p. 235

Using the Photo
Among the major French-language newspapers in Quebec are *Le Soleil, Le Journal de Québec,* and *Le Devoir.* The daily, *Le Soleil,* is published in Quebec City. Its main competitor is the tabloid, *Le Journal de Québec.* The influential *Le Devoir* is distributed in Quebec and the rest of Canada. *Le Canard enchaîné* and *Charlie Hebdo* are both satirical newspapers published weekly in France. Ask students what sections and features they would expect to find in the two satirical newspapers.

❀ 1.1, 3.1

chapitre **6**

La presse

Objectifs

In this chapter, you will learn to
- express certainty and possibility
- express doubt and disbelief
- break news
- ask for information

And you will use and review
- the subjunctive with doubt, disbelief, and uncertainty
- the verbs **croire** and **paraître**
- **quelque part, quelqu'un, quelque chose,** and **quelquefois**
- the object pronouns
- **qui est-ce qui, qui est-ce que, qu'est-ce qui** and **qu'est-ce que**
- more negative expressions

▶ *Que vois-tu sur la photo?*

Où sont ces personnes?
Qu'est-ce qu'elles font?
Et toi, est-ce que tu as déjà lu un journal ou un magazine de langue française?

Suggested pacing:	Traditional Schedule	Block Schedule
Vocabulaire/Grammaire/Application 1	6 days	2 1/2 blocks
Culture	1 day	1 block
Vocabulaire/Grammaire/Application 2	4 days	1 1/2 blocks
Lecture	1 day	1/2 block
L'atelier de l'écrivain	1 day	1/2 block
Prépare-toi pour l'examen	1/2 day	1/2 block
Activités préparatoires	1/2 day	1/2 block
Examen	1 day	1/2 block
Révisions cumulatives	1 day	1/2 block

Visit Us Online
go.hrw.com
Online Edition
KEYWORD: BD3 CH6

Chapitre 6
Chapter Opener

Vocabulaire supplémentaire

Students might use these terms to discuss the photo.

les actualités	*the news*
le journal à sensation	*tabloid (newspaper)*
le journal quotidien	*daily newspaper*
le dessin humoristique	*cartoon*
l'hebdomadaire (m.)	*weekly (magazine)*

Learning Tip

Have students practice the new vocabulary from this chapter by starting each class with a discussion about the latest news. This will help students use the new vocabulary in a real-world context. Encourage students to watch the news videos of French online newspapers.

Language Lab

You might want to use your language lab to have students:
- listen to all target vocabulary and phrases in the chapter
- practice pronunciation of vocabulary and phrases, using Holt SoundBooth to save their work for evaluation
- complete the listening activities in this chapter

Un marchand de journaux, à Québec

LISTENING PRACTICE

Vocabulaire
Activity 2, p. 226, CD 6, Tr. 1
Activity 23, p. 238, CD 6, Tr. 4

Grammaire
Activity 8, p. 229, CD 6, Tr. 2
Activity 32, p. 243, CD 6, Tr. 5

Application
Activity 18, p. 233, CD 6, Tr. 3
Activity 36, p. 244, CD 6, Tr. 6

Language Lab and Classroom Activities

Prépare-toi pour l'examen
Activity 6, p. 253, CD 6, Tr. 8
Télé-culture: Interviews, Chapter 6

Activités préparatoires
Section I, Listening, p. 256, CD 6, Tr. 9
Télé-roman: *Camille et compagnie*, Épisode 6

Révisions cumulatives
Activity 1, p. 258, CD 6, Tr. 10

Lecture
p. 246, CD 6, Tr. 7

Resources

Planning:
Lesson Planner
 One-Stop Planner

Presentation:
 Teaching Transparencies
Vocabulaire 6.1, 6.2

Practice:
Cahier de vocabulaire et grammaire

Differentiated Practice and Assessment CD-ROM

Media Guide
 Teaching Transparencies Bell Work 6.1

 Interactive Tutor, Disc 2

 Bell Work

Use Bell Work 6.1 in the *Teaching Transparencies* or write this activity on the board.

Complète les phrases avec les expressions qui manquent et fais les changements nécessaires.
prendre le petit déjeuner, avoir envie de, faire la sieste, faire chaud, prendre sa retraite, faire un stage, faire la fête, faire ses études

1. L'année prochaine, quand Victor ____, ses collègues ____.
2. Tous les après-midi, le bébé de ma sœur ____.
3. Mon frère ____ ____ de droit à Yale.
4. D'habitude, quand il ____, nous ____ dehors.
5. Cet été mon fils va ____ dans une entreprise internationale. ✿ 1.2

Objectifs
• to express certainty and possibility
• to express doubt and disbelief

Vocabulaire 1
à l'œuvre

La presse francophone

un kiosque à journaux

Le marchand de journaux vend des journaux et des magazines.

Les **quotidiens paraissent** tous les jours.

la couverture

La **presse spécialisée** est très développée; il y a par exemple de nombreux **magazines féminins.**

Les magazines sont souvent **hebdomadaires** ou **mensuels**.

▶ Vocabulaire supplémentaire—La presse, p. R19

Core Instruction

TEACHING VOCABULAIRE

1. Introduce the vocabulary, using transparencies **Vocabulaire 6.1** and **6.2**. Model the pronunciation of each word or expression. **(3 min.)**

2. Ask students to point to various items on the transparency as you name them. (**un kiosque, un quotidien**) **(3 min.)**

3. Ask students about their reading habits. **Est-ce que tu lis un quotidien? Est-ce que tu es abonné(e) à des magazines? (3 min.)**

4. Model the sentences in **Exprimons-nous!** Then ask questions, to elicit expressions of certainty or possibility. **Est-ce que l'examen sera difficile? Est-ce que tu auras une bonne note? (3 min.)**

Online Practice
go.hrw.com
Vocabulaire 1 practice
KEYWORD: BD3 CH6

Chapitre 6
Vocabulaire 1

Vocabulaire 1

La première page (la une)

le (gros) titre

FRANCE-ÉCHO
JEUDI 12 JANVIER 2007

Le Salon de l'auto a ouvert ses portes

la légende

...onomiques ont de plus en plus de succès !

D'autres mots utiles

un(e) chômeur(-euse)	*unemployed person*
l'édition (f.)	*edition/issue*
un extraterrestre	*extraterrestrial*
les nouvelles (f.)	*news*
la vérité	*truth*
le numéro précédent	*previous issue*
la presse à sensation	*tabloids*
le/la rédacteur(-trice) en chef	*editor-in-chief*
la revue	*journal*
s'abonner à	*to subscribe*
publier	*to publish*

...des prix

...prix de plusieurs produits de consommation de base: la baguette, le litre de lait, la farine et le sel. Le prix du pain a ainsi doublé en dix ans. Quant au prix du lait, il a triplé!

Les dépê...

Catastrophe à Neuilly : un immeuble s'effondre. p.4

Attentat en Corse : deux suspects arrêtés. p.8

le dessin humoristique

l'article

Exprimons-nous!

To express certainty	To express possibility
Je suis sûr(e) qu'il va faire beau! *I am sure that . . .*	**Il me semble qu'**il devrait lire cet article. *It seems to me that . . .*
Je suis certain(e) qu'il viendra. *I am sure that . . .*	**Il se peut/est possible que** cet article paraisse demain. *It's possible that . . .*
Il/Elle est persuadé(e) que ce film te plaira. *He/She is convinced that . . .*	**Il paraît que** c'est le meilleur film de l'année. *It seems that . . .*

Interactive TUTOR

Vocabulaire et grammaire, pp. 61–63

Online workbooks

---

② Script

1. — Josyane, tu vas en ville?
— Oui.
— Tu peux me prendre *Zurban* au kiosque au coin de la rue?
2. — Est-ce que vous allez vous abonner à ce magazine?
— Je ne sais pas. Il n'est pas terrible. Je crois que je vais plutôt m'abonner à ce magazine féminin. J'aime beaucoup leurs articles sur la mode.
3. — Qu'est-ce que tu lis, Paul?
— Oh, rien de très sérieux. Je regarde les dessins humoristiques. Regarde celui-là! Il est vraiment amusant.
4. — On m'a dit que Nadja travaillait pour un magazine?
— Oui, oui. Elle est rédactrice en chef d'un magazine féminin.
5. — Patrick, tu as vu les gros titres à la une du *Monde* ce matin?
— Non, je ne lis jamais les quotidiens.
6. — Tu as vu la couverture du dernier *Animal*?
— Laquelle? Celle avec le chien?

④ Possible Answers

1. m'étonnerait
2. doute
3. crois
4. pense
5. peut
6. possible
7. étonnerait

Entre copains

un canard/ une feuille de chou	*newspaper*
un hebdo	*weekly newspaper*
une pub	*ad*

Flash culture

Il existe aux États-Unis un journal en langue française: Le Journal Français. Il est édité et publié depuis environ 30 ans et est lu par 35.000 personnes dont des Français, des francophones et des Américains francophiles. Les origines de ce journal remontent à la ruée vers l'or en Californie. En 1850, des chercheurs d'or français se sont installés à San Francisco. Ils ont ouvert des restaurants, des pâtisseries et ont créé des journaux. ✿4.2

Est-ce qu'il existe des journaux publiés dans une langue autre que l'anglais dans ta communauté?

① Des définitions ✿1.2

Lisons Trouve la définition de chaque mot.

b **1.** une légende   **a.** Il paraît tous les mois.

a **2.** un mensuel   **b.** C'est ce qui explique la photo.

c **3.** un quotidien   **c.** Il paraît tous les jours.

d **4.** un hebdomadaire   **d.** Il paraît toutes les semaines.

② Écoutons CD 6, Tr. 1 ✿1.2   **1.** d **2.** a **3.** b **4.** c **5.** e **6.** f

Dis à quelle conversation chaque illustration correspond.

a.

b.

c.

d.

e.

f.

③ Certitude ou possibilité? ✿1.2

Lisons/Écrivons Complète les phrases suivantes en te basant sur les indices donnés. Utilise les expressions d'**Exprimons-nous!**

1. Aline _____ que Marc aime cette revue. (certitude)
2. Il _____ que cet article soit intéresssant. (possibilité)
3. Adrien est _____ que j'ai encore le dernier numéro. (certitude)
4. Il me _____ que vous êtes fatigués! (possibilité)
5. Victoria est _____ que tu trouveras ce livre génial. (certitude)
6. Il est _____ qu'elle devienne rédactrice en chef du journal. (possibilité)
7. Il se _____ que la sœur de Victor soit en couverture des *Copains d'abord* cette semaine. (possibilité)

Core Instruction

TEACHING EXPRIMONS-NOUS!

1. Model the pronunciation of the expressions in **Exprimons-nous!** Point out the use of the sujunctive with expressions of doubt. **(2 min.)**

2. Review the forms of the subjunctive of **-er, -ir,** and **-re** verbs, briefly.

3. Have pairs of students make up similar sentences about unlikely events of their choice and practice expressing doubt and disbelief. **Le prof est un agent secret. (2 min.)**

Exprimons-nous!

To express doubt and disbelief

Je ne crois pas qu'il connaisse la nouvelle.   *I don't think that . . .*

Je ne pense pas qu'il lise des BD.   *I don't think that . . .*

Je doute que cela soit vrai.   *I doubt that . . .*

Ça m'étonnerait qu'il puisse venir!   *It would surprise me if . . .*

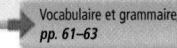 Interactive TUTOR

Vocabulaire et grammaire, pp. 61–63   Online workbooks

4 **Conversation** 🏵1.2

Lisons/Écrivons Complète la conversation de Tanguy et de son ami Mehdi qui doute toujours de tout. Utilise les expressions d'**Exprimons-nous!**

TANGUY   Tu sais que Luc lit régulièrement le journal?

MEHDI   Ça ___1___ qu'il lise le journal. Il ne l'achète jamais!

TANGUY   Oui, mais il connaît toujours toutes les dernières nouvelles!

MEHDI   Je ___2___ qu'il lise les journaux. Il regarde la télé toute la journée!

TANGUY   Je ne ___3___ pas que ce soit vrai. Il doit faire réparer sa télé. Ça fait des mois qu'elle ne marche plus!

MEHDI   Alors, je ne sais pas. Mais je ne ___4___ toujours pas qu'il lise les journaux!

TANGUY   Il se ___5___ qu'il lise les journaux en ligne. Il est toujours devant son ordinateur!

MEHDI   Pour une fois, il est ___6___ que tu aies raison!

TANGUY   Ça m' ___7___ que tu le penses vraiment!

 HOLT **SoundBooth** ONLINE RECORDING

Communication

5 **Interview** 🏵1.1

Écrivons/Parlons Pour gagner un peu d'argent, tu as décidé de faire des sondages pour un groupe de presse spécialisée. D'abord, fais une liste de questions à poser à tes camarades sur la presse écrite. Demande-leur aussi des suggestions pour le nouveau magazine.

MODÈLE   —Marc, est-ce que tu lis un quotidien, un hebdomadaire ou un mensuel?
—Je lis un...
—Quels articles tu aimes lire dans...?

Cultures

Products and Perspectives

The *Quebec Chronicle-Telegraph* may be the oldest newspaper in North America. This weekly is a descendant of several newspapers published during the last three centuries in Quebec. The first, *The Quebec Gazette,* was founded by William Brown (1737-1789) in 1764 and had 150 subscribers. It ceased printing in 1775. The *Chronicle-Telegraph* started as a weekly, but in 1832 it began appearing in English on Monday, Wednesday, and Friday, and in French on Tuesday, Thursday, and Saturday. Today, it is published every Wednesday and has a circulation of 1,800. Have students research when and where the first newspaper was published in the United States.   🏵2.2, 3.1, 4.2

Communication

5 **Individual Activity: Presentational**

Have students bring in a copy of a magazine, newspaper, journal, tabloid, or comic book. Then have them tell what it is, its name, how often it is published, who the target market is, if they subscribe to it, and who the editor-in-chief is. Also, have them describe the cover, the types of articles, and the features.   🏵1.3

Assess

Assessment Program

Quiz: Vocabulaire 1

Alternative Assessment

Differentiated Practice and Assessment CD-ROM

Online Assessment
my.hrw.com

Test Generator

Resources

Planning:

Lesson Planner

 One-Stop Planner

Practice:

Grammar Tutor for Students of French, Chapter 6

Cahier de vocabulaire et grammaire

Differentiated Practice and Assessment CD-ROM

Cahier d'activités

Media Guide

 Teaching Transparencies Bell Work 6.2

 Audio CD 6, Tr. 2

 Interactive Tutor, Disc 2

Bell Work

Use Bell Work 6.2 in the *Teaching Transparencies* or write this activity on the board.

Complète les phrases avec les mots de vocabulaire qui conviennent.

1. **Toutes les semaines, ma mère achète un magazine au _____ à journaux.**
2. **Les _____ sont des journaux qui paraissent tous les jours.**
3. **On trouve des histoires scandaleuses dans la _____.**
4. **Pour recevoir un magazine, il faut _____.**
5. **Les _____ paraissent toutes les semaines.** 🏵1.2

Comparisons

Comparing and Constrasting

The French word **croire**, the Spanish word **creer**, and the Italian word **credere** come from the Latin **credere**, *to believe*. Ask students to brainstorm English words that also can be traced back to **credere**. (credibility, credible, credulous, credentials, credit, creed) 🏵4.1

Objectifs
- the subjunctive with doubt, disbelief, and uncertainty
- the verbs *croire* and *paraître*

Grammaire à l'œuvre 1

The subjunctive with doubt, disbelief and uncertainty

Interactive TUTOR

1 As you've already seen, you use the subjunctive in French with expressions of *necessity, desire, emotion,* and *fear.* You also use the subjunctive with expressions of *doubt, disbelief* and *uncertainty.*

> Je **doute que** ce film **ait** du succès.
> Ça m'**étonnerait que** ces articles **soient** publiés.

2 With most expressions of *possibility,* use the subjunctive.

> Il **se peut que** nous **allions** au cinéma ce soir.
> Il **est possible que** Martin **vienne** avec nous.

3 With **il me semble que** and expressions of *certainty* like: **je suis sûr(e)/ certain(e) que, je crois que, il/elle est persuadé(e) que, je pense que,** use the **indicative.**

> Je **pense que** c'**est** le meilleur film de l'année.
> Il **me semble que** nous **passerons** une soirée amusante!

4 When expressions of *certainty* are used in negative sentences or questions, they become expressions of *uncertainty,* so they take the **subjunctive.**

> Je **ne pense pas que** ce **soit** le meilleur film de l'année.

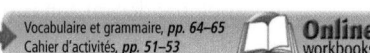
Vocabulaire et grammaire, *pp. 64–65*
Cahier d'activités, *pp. 51–53*   **Online** workbooks

---

6 **La presse écrite** 🏵1.2   **1.** b **2.** b **3.** b **4.** a

Lisons Lis les articles suivants et dis s'ils parlent **a) d'un fait certain** ou **b) d'une possibilité.**

> Il se peut que le président des États-Unis rencontre le président du Mexique avant la fin du mois.
>
> 1.

> Il est possible que la situation s'améliore si les deux parties signent un accord de paix.
>
> 2.

> Il n'est pas certain que l'équipe de France gagne la Coupe du monde cette année.
>
> 3.

> Il est certain que le nombre de chômeurs va encore augmenter pendant la période des vacances.
>
> 4.

Core Instruction

TEACHING GRAMMAIRE

1. Go over Point 1. Point out that the present subjunctive replaces both the indicative present and future after expressions of doubt. **Je pense que ce film a/aura/va avoir du succès. Je doute que ce film ait du succès cette année/l'année prochaine. (2 min.)**

2. Go over Points 2 and 3. Tell students that **Il me semble que...,** is followed by the indicative because it expresses a quasi-certainty. **(2 min.)**

3. Go over Point 4. Emphazise that a negative expression of doubt or uncertainty still takes the subjunctive. **Je ne doute pas qu'elle soit intelligente. (2 min.)**

4. Tell students that asking a question may suggest a doubt and trigger the subjunctive, but only in a formal question with inversion. **Pensez-vous qu'il vienne?** Tell them that in an informal question you would still say, **Est-ce que vous pensez qu'il viendra? (2 min.)**

Online Practice
go.hrw.com
Grammaire 1 practice
KEYWORD: BD3 CH6

Grammaire 1

7 Des gens difficiles 🌼1.2

Lisons Léa et Luc pensent aller au cinéma et ils proposent à Ali de venir avec eux. Mais Ali est difficile et sa copine Mia aussi.

LUC   Il se peut que nous (irons / <u>allions</u>) au cinéma.

ALI   Je doute qu'il y (a / <u>ait</u>) un bon film à voir. Qu'est-ce que vous voulez aller voir?

LÉA   *Les choristes.* Je suis sûre que ce film te (<u>plaira</u> / plaise).

ALI   Non, je ne crois pas qu'il (est / <u>soit</u>) très intéressant.

LUC   Je suis persuadé que tu le (<u>trouveras</u> / trouves) formidable.

ALI   Je ne crois pas que Mia (veut / <u>veuille</u>) venir.

LÉA   Ça m'étonnerait qu'elle ne (vient / <u>vienne</u>) pas si tu viens.

8 Écoutons   CD 6, Tr. 2   🌼1.2   **1.** a **2.** b **3.** b **4.** a **5.** b **6.** a

Il y a eu un accident et les gens parlent de ce qui s'est passé. Décide si la personne qui parle **a) est certaine** ou **b) n'est pas certaine** de quelque chose.

9 Le doute dans les esprits   🌼1.2

Écrivons Récris les phrases suivantes à la forme négative.

♻ *Souviens-toi,* Subjunctive forms, regular and irregular p.150

MODÈLE   Je pense que tous les kiosques ont ce journal.
Je ne pense pas que tous les kiosques aient ce journal.

1. Ils sont sûrs que cette photo fait partie de l'article.

2. Monsieur Loriot pense que la presse nous dit toujours tout.

3. Gaby est persuadé que cette revue est intéressante.

4. Je crois qu'elle choisit cette revue parce que la couverture lui plaît.

5. Nous sommes certaines qu'il a toutes les BD de Tintin.

Communication

HOLT **SoundBooth** ONLINE RECORDING

10 Scénario   🌼1.1

Écrivons/Parlons En groupes de trois, préparez des titres d'articles incroyables et lisez-les à un autre groupe qui va réagir en utilisant les expressions de doute, de possibilité ou de certitude.

MODÈLE   —Un homme est resté trois ans tout seul sur une île déserte.
—Je doute que cela soit possible.

8 Script

1. Monsieur Branconnier est sûr que ce sera dans le journal.
2. Pensez-vous que quelqu'un soit mort?
3. Non, moi je ne pense pas que ce soit sérieux.
4. Je suis persuadé(e) que la presse n'en parlera pas.
5. Moi, je ne suis pas sûr(e) que ce soit dans le journal demain.
6. Je pense qu'il faudra attendre de lire les quotidiens.

9 Answers

1. Ils ne sont pas sûrs que cette photo fasse partie de l'article.
2. Monsieur Loriot ne pense pas que la presse nous dise toujours tout.
3. Gaby n'est pas persuadé que cette revue soit intéressante.
4. Je ne crois pas qu'elle choisisse cette revue parce que la couverture lui plaît.
5. Nous ne sommes pas certaines qu'il ait toutes les BD de Tintin.

Communication

Class Activity: Interpersonal
Have each student think of, or write, a sentence that expresses certainty with the indicative. Then, as a mixer activity, each student makes the statement of certainty to a classmate who restates it as a statement of uncertainty, changing the verb to the subjunctive.

MODÈLE
— **Je suis certain(e) que ma mère connaît ta mère.**
— **Et moi, je ne suis pas certain(e) que ta mère connaisse ma mère.**

🌼 1.1, 1.2

Differentiated Instruction

SLOWER PACE LEARNERS

8 Some students may have trouble following the statements. You may want to stop the recording after each statement and call on volunteers to repeat the sentence(s). Encourage students to ask for clarifications if needed. Ask volunteers to provide clarifications by using synonyms, antonyms, or circumlocution.   🌼1.2

MULTIPLE INTELLIGENCES

Linguistic To assist students in using the subjunctive with doubt and uncertainty, have students write poetry in French. Remind students that poems do not have to rhyme but that you want them to use as many colorful, descriptive, and emotional words as possible in their poems. When students have completed their poems, stage a poetry reading, maybe in a French coffee house style, so that ambiance is appropriate for the activity.   🌼1.3

Resources

Planning:

Lesson Planner

 One-Stop Planner

Practice:

Grammar Tutor for Students of French, Chapter 6

Cahier de vocabulaire et grammaire

Differentiated Practice and Assessment CD-ROM

Cahier d'activités

Media Guide

 Teaching Transparencies
Bell Work 6.3

 Interactive Tutor, Disc 2

 Bell Work

Use Bell Work 6.3 in the *Teaching Transparencies* or write this activity on the board.

Reconstitue les phrases suivantes et fais les changements nécessaires.

1. Il se peut / aller / théâtre / je / que / ce / au / soir
2. Ça m'étonnerait / venir / moi / que / avec / Christophe
3. Je doute / restaurant / pouvoir / aller / nous / que / au
4. Je pense / travail / intéressant / que / son / être / nouveau
5. Il se peut / faire / voyage / Mexique / que / amis / un / au / mes ✿1.2

⑪ Answers

1. Est-ce que ton magazine préféré paraît tous les mois?
2. Nous croyons que cet article est intéressant.
3. Les revues paraissent toutes les semaines.
4. Croyez-vous que cela soit vrai?
5. Moi, je crois que cette histoire est vraie.

The verbs *croire* and *paraître*

 Interactive TUTOR

1 The verb **croire** is irregular. It is conjugated like the verb **voir**.

croire *(to think* or *to believe)*		
je crois	nous	croyons
tu crois	vous	croyez
il/elle/on croit	ils/elles	croient
past participle: cru		

Croire used with the preposition **à** means *to believe in*.

2 When **croire** expresses *certainty*, it is followed by the indicative. When **croire** expresses *doubt*, it is followed by the subjunctive.

Ils **croient** qu'il viendra.   Elle **ne croit pas** qu'il soit malade.

3 The verb **paraître** is irregular.

paraître *(to appear, to be released)*		
je parais	nous	paraissons
tu parais	vous	paraissez
il/elle/on paraît	ils/elles	paraissent
past participle: paru		

 Vocabulaire et grammaire, *pp. 64–65*
Cahier d'activités, *pp. 51–53*
Online workbooks

⑪ **Des phrases à faire** ✿1.2

Écrivons Fais des phrases avec **le présent** des verbes donnés.

1. est-ce que / ton / magazine préféré / paraître / tout / les mois
2. nous / ce / croire que / article / être / intéressant
3. ces revues / paraître / tout / les semaines
4. vous / croire que / cela / être / vrai / ?
5. moi / être / je / croire que / cette histoire / vrai

⑫ **La presse et nous** ✿1.2

Écrivons Forme des phrases complètes avec les éléments donnés.

Mon quotidien préféré	ne... (pas)	ce qui est écrit dans cette revue.
Toi, tu	croire	que ce soit vrai.
Édouard	paraître	toutes les semaines.
Les journaux		que les journalistes sachent ce qu'ils disent.
Chloé et Luc		jamais le dimanche.

Core Instruction

TEACHING GRAMMAIRE

1. Go over the conjugation of **croire** and **paraître**. Mention to students that **apparaître** and **naître** are conjugated just like **paraître**. Model the pronunciation of all forms. Tell students that **croire** tends to be used more often than **penser** whenever the meaning is *to believe*. **Il croit tout savoir. (2 min.)**

2. Go over the uses of **croire** and the tenses that follow it. You may want to tell students that although *to believe in* is **croire à**, *to believe in God* is **croire en Dieu. (2 min.)**

3. Ask students questions to be answered in the indicative or the subjunctive. **Est-ce que tu crois que le cours est difficile? (Crois-tu que le cours soit difficile?) Oui, je crois qu'il est difficile. (Non, je ne crois pas qu'il soit difficile.) (2 min.)**

13 **Histoire policière** 1.2 **1.** croyais **2.** a cru **3.** croira **4.** paraît **5.** croyiez **6.** croiriez

Écrivons Complète cette conversation entre une personne et un policier *(policeman)* avec la forme correcte des verbes **croire** et **paraître.**

LE POLICIER	Je ___1___ que vous vouliez juste lui demander l'heure.
LA VICTIME	Oui, mais lui, quand il m'a vu il ___2___ que j'avais de l'argent.
LE POLICIER	L'inspecteur ne vous ___3___ pas. Votre histoire ne me ___4___ pas très vraisemblable *(believable)*.
LA VICTIME	Je suis innocent, il faut absolument que vous me ___5___ !
LE POLICIER	Et vous, vous me ___6___ si je vous racontais une histoire aussi incroyable?

14 **On y croit ou pas** 1.3

Écrivons/Parlons Regarde les titres parus dans les journaux. Réagis à ces titres en utilisant les verbes **croire** et **paraître.**

1.

2.

3.

4.

Communication

HOLT **SoundBooth** ONLINE RECORDING

15 **Scénario** 1.1

Parlons Il y a un nouveau magazine pour jeunes qui vient de paraître. Ton/Ta camarade et toi, vous en discutez. Toi, tu es sûr(e) qu'il est bien, ton/ta camarade en doute. Jouez cette scène.

MODÈLE —Je suis certain(e) que c'est un magazine intéresssant.
          —Je ne crois pas que...

Cultures

 Products and Perspectives

The Musée d'Orsay was originally a railway station. The Gare d'Orsay was finished in time for the Universal Exhibition (World Fair) in 1900 and was the first Parisian train station to have electric power. In 1977, the French government decided to convert the station into a museum, which was opened in 1980 by then President François Mitterrand. The museum is dedicated to the artistic creation of the nineteenth century (1848–1914). Encourage students to take a virtual tour of the Musée d'Orsay. 2.2, 5.2

Communication

Pair Activity: Interpersonal
Have each student write a sentence with **croire**. Ask partners to take turns stating their sentence. The other partner should respond by agreeing or disagreeing and give a detailed reason.

MODÈLE
— Moi, je crois au père Noël.
— Moi, non. Je ne crois pas que le père Noël existe parce que j'ai vu ma mère mettre les cadeaux sous le sapin de Noël. 1.1

Differentiated Instruction

SLOWER PACE LEARNERS

Building on Previous Skills Before students begin the activities, have them conjugate the verb **croire** in different tenses (**imparfait, passé composé, futur**) and moods (indicative, subjunctive, conditional). Ask students to discuss when to use these tenses and moods. Then have students complete the activities. 1.2

SPECIAL LEARNING NEEDS

Students with Learning Disabilities If students need assistance with the different uses of **croire,** create additional examples in English. Check for mastery of these concepts by asking students to write examples of each use of the verb **croire** in their grammar notebook. 1.2

Assess

Assessment Program
Quiz: Grammaire 1
Alternative Assessment
Differentiated Practice and Assessment CD-ROM

Online Assessment
my.hrw.com

Test Generator

Resources

Planning:

Lesson Planner

 One-Stop Planner

Practice:

Grammar Tutor for Students of French, Chapter 6

Cahier de vocabulaire et grammaire

Differentiated Practice and Assessment CD-ROM

Cahier d'activités

Media Guide

 Teaching Transparencies
Bell Work 6.4

 Audio CD 6, Tr. 3

 Interactive Tutor, Disc 2

Bell Work

Use Bell Work 6.4 in the *Teaching Transparencies* or write this activity on the board.

Complète les phrases avec la forme correcte du verbe **croire**.

1. Tu _____ qu'il lit tous ces journaux?
2. Il ne faut pas que vous _____ tout ce que vous lisez.
3. Patrick _____ que nous allions venir.
4. Il m' _____ quand je lui ai dit que nous arrivions.
5. Et toi, tu me _____ si je te racontais une histoire.

 1.2

COMMON ERROR ALERT

///// ATTENTION ! \\\\\

Students may mistake the word **quelquefois** for the phrase **quelque temps,** but their use is similar to English usage. **Quelquefois** means *sometimes* (on some occasions), and **quelque temps** means *some time* (an undetermined length of time).

Application 1

16 À ton avis? 1.3

Écrivons Réponds aux questions suivantes pour parler de tes goûts personnels et de ceux des jeunes en matière de presse écrite.

1. Quel journal te semble le plus sérieux? Pourquoi?
2. Quels journaux est-ce que tu penses que les jeunes lisent?
3. Est-ce que la couverture d'un magazine est importante? Est-ce que tu crois qu'une belle couverture fait vendre les magazines?
4. Qu'est-ce qui est à la une des journaux aujourd'hui?
5. Est-ce que tu crois que le métier de journaliste est intéressant? Si tu étais journaliste pour quel journal aimerais-tu travailler? Pourquoi?

Un peu plus

Quelque part, quelqu'un, quelque chose and quelquefois

Quelque means *some.* You've already seen quelque in words and phrases like quelquefois *(sometimes),* quelque chose *(something),* and quelqu'un *(someone).*

Quelquefois, j'aime lire des articles sur la mode. Allons manger quelque chose! Quelqu'un m'a téléphoné à deux heures du matin.

Quelque is also used in the expression quelque part which means *somewhere.*

—Tu vois le journal?
—Je l'ai laissé quelque part, mais je ne sais plus où.

→ Vocabulaire et grammaire, *p. 66*
Cahier d'activités, *pp. 51–53*

Online workbooks

17 Rencontre matinale 1.2

Écrivons Le grand-père de Jean-Marie perd un peu la mémoire. Complète ce qu'il dit avec **quelqu'un, quelque chose, quelquefois** ou **quelque part.**

____1____, le matin, après avoir acheté le journal, je prends le petit-déjeuner à la terrasse d'un café. Ce jour-là, je mourais de faim, il fallait que je mange ____2____. Je suis allé à ma table habituelle, il y avait déjà ____3____. J'avais déjà vu cette fille ____4____, mais je ne savais pas où. C'est ____5____ qui m'arrive souvent car j'ai mauvaise mémoire. Je lisais le journal quand j'ai compris ____6____ : la personne assise en face de moi était ____7____ de connu et faisait la une du journal que je venais d'acheter. Alors, je lui ai demandé de signer l'article. Maintenant, je sais que j'ai mis ce journal ____8____ mais je ne sais plus où!

1. Quelquefois **2.** quelque chose **3.** quelqu'un **4.** quelque part
5. quelque chose **6.** quelque chose **7.** quelqu'un **8.** quelque part

Core Instruction

INTEGRATED PRACTICE

1. Have students do Activity 16 to practice previously taught material. **(3 min.)**
2. Introduce **Un peu plus.** (See the presentation suggestions at right.) **(4 min.)**
3. Continue with integrated practice Activities 17–21. **(30 min.)**

TEACHING UN PEU PLUS

1. Go over **Un peu plus.** Tell students that these expressions are invariable and cannot be made plural or feminine. **(2 min.)**
2. To provide practice, ask students to give evasive answers to all your questions. **Où vas-tu après le cours?... Quelque part! Avec qui sors-tu? Avec quelqu'un! (2 min.)**

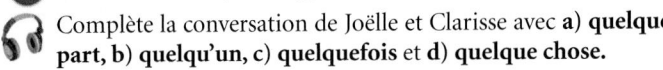

18 Écoutons CD 6, Tr. 3 🍀1.2 **1. a 2. c 3. b 4. b 5. d 6. c**

Complète la conversation de Joëlle et Clarisse avec **a) quelque part, b) quelqu'un, c) quelquefois** et **d) quelque chose.**

19 Publications variées 🍀1.3

Parlons Regarde les couvertures suivantes et dis

1. quel genre de magazines/journaux ce sont,
2. de quoi tu crois qu'ils parlent,
3. qui les lit
4. quand tu crois qu'ils paraissent.

MODÈLE **Je crois/Il me semble que c'est un magazine pour jeunes. Il doit paraître tous les semaines.**

1.

2.

3.

4.

20 Qu'est-ce que tu lis? 🍀1.3

Écrivons/Parlons Écris un petit paragraphe pour expliquer tes goûts en matière de journaux et de magazines. Qu'est-ce que tu lis? Pourquoi? Est-ce qu'il y a des magazines spécialisés auxquels tu es abonné(e)?

MODÈLE **Je ne lis pas les journaux mais je lis des revues de sport parce que je suis un(e) fan de foot. Etc.**

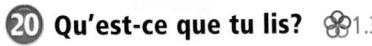 **Communication**

 HOLT **SoundBooth** ONLINE RECORDING

21 Scénario 🍀1.1

Parlons Ta sœur veut savoir tout ce que tu vas faire et te pose des questions. Tu n'as pas envie de le lui dire. Utilise quelque fois, quelqu'un, quelque part et quelque chose dans tes réponses.

MODÈLE —Avec qui est-ce que tu vas sortir ce soir?
—Avec quelqu'un... que tu ne connais pas.

18 Script

1. — Tu as le dernier *Bonjour, les copains*?
— Oui, il doit être là [NOISE].
2. — Tu achètes aussi *Le temps des ados*?
— Oui, [NOISE], pourquoi?
3. — [NOISE] m'a dit qu'il y avait un article intéressant sur la mode. Tu pourrais me prêter le dernier numéro si tu l'as?
4. — Oui, je l'ai, mais je crois que je l'ai déjà prêté à [NOISE].
5. — Je vois [NOISE] sur ton bureau. Ce ne serait pas le numéro que je cherche?
6. — Tu as raison. [NOISE], je ne sais plus ce que je fais de mes affaires!

Communication

Pair Activity: Interpersonal

Have students write six sentences that include **quelque part, quelqu'un, quelque chose,** and **quelquefois** to state that they do not know where something or someone is. For each statement, they should write a question to ask for help. **Tu sais où, ...quand, ...avec qui, ...quoi?** Then partners take turns stating each sentence along with the question. The partner answers the question, using an object pronoun in the appropriate tense.

MODÈLE

— **J'ai laissé ma montre quelque part. Tu sais où?**
— **Tu l'as laissée chez toi sur ton bureau.** 🍀1.1

Differentiated Instruction

ADVANCED LEARNERS

19 Extension After they complete this activity, have students look at the magazine covers they created in the Extension activity on page 225. Ask students to guess the content of each magazine. The student who designed the cover should agree or disagree with the conjectures, elaborating on the content he or she had envisioned when creating the cover. 🍀1.1

SPECIAL LEARNING NEEDS

Students with Language Impairments Go over **Un peu plus** with students and create a wall chart on poster board or butcher paper. Title the chart "**Quelque**" and divide the chart into four categories, **quelque chose, quelquefois, quelqu'un,** and **quelque part.** Ask students to write four sentences, one with each expression, on adhesive notes and place them on the chart. Use the wall chart as a class reference for the usage of these words. 🍀1.3

Assess

Assessment Program
Quiz: Application 1
Audio CD 6, Tr. 11 🎧
Alternative Assessment
Differentiated Practice and Assessment CD-ROM

Online Assessment
my.hrw.com

Test Generator

Lecture culturelle

Presse, radio, télévision, Internet... autant de moyens qui permettent de s'informer, de se faire une opinion et d'agir. En France, il existe beaucoup de magazines et de journaux d'information pour les jeunes. Certains magazines et journaux ont à la fois une version adulte et une version jeune. D'autres, comme Mon Quotidien, ciblent[1] des tranches d'âge différentes avec un format similaire mais adapté au public. 2.2, 3.2

MON QUOTIDIEN, UN JOURNAL POUR LES 10-14 ANS

Mon Quotidien est un journal d'actualité destiné aux 10–14 ans et diffusé à 59.000 exemplaires.

Ce quotidien de huit pages, édité du lundi au vendredi, a été lancé le 5 janvier 1995

par Play-Bac[2]. C'est l'un des rares quotidiens pour enfants dans le monde. L'idée de départ était que les jeunes devraient pouvoir se tenir au courant[3] de l'actualité tous les jours et avoir accès à un journal qui leur est destiné. L'actualité y est racontée du point de vue des jeunes. Il y a un bon équilibre entre les articles sérieux

et les articles plus récréatifs. Une des particularités de *Mon Quotidien* est de faire régulièrement participer ses lecteurs aux réunions de la rédaction[4]. Par exemple, les enfants peuvent préparer des questions à poser à des personnalités du monde politique. Celles-ci sont ensuite posées par un journaliste. C'est instructif et c'est une bonne expérience pour les jeunes. Depuis sa création, *Mon Quotidien* a fait des petits[5] : *Le Petit Quotidien* pour les 6–9 ans et *l'Actu* pour les 14–17 ans.

Compréhension 1.2, 2.2

1. *Mon Quotidien*, qu'est-ce que c'est?
2. Quel est le but de *Mon Quotidien*?
3. Quelle est l'une des particularités de *Mon Quotidien*?

1. Un journal d'actualité destiné aux jeunes.
2. Le but est de tenir les jeunes au courant de l'actualité.
3. Les lecteurs participent aux réunions de la rédaction.

1. target   2. name of the publisher   3. to be kept informed   4. editorial meeting   5. has given birth to

---

Resources

Planning:
Lesson Planner
One-Stop Planner

Practice:
Cahier d'activités

Prereading Questions

You might ask these questions before students read the selection.

1. **Est-ce que tu lis quelquefois des magazines?**
2. **Est-ce que tu as déjà lu le journal de ta ville, ou un journal national?**
3. **Est-ce que tu connais le nom des magazines ou des journaux pour jeunes?**
4. **Est-ce qu'il y a un journal dans ton école?** 1.2

Active Reading Questions

1. *Mon Quotidien* est **diffusé à combien d'exemplaires? (59.000)**
2. **Est-ce que** *Mon Quotidien* **est édité tous les jours? (non, pas le week-end)**
3. **Quand est-ce que ce journal pour les jeunes a été lancé? (le 5 janvier 1995)**
4. **Est-ce que les articles sont sérieux ou récréatifs? (les deux)**
5. **Est-ce que** *Mon Quotidien* **est le seul journal pour les jeunes? (Non. Il y a** *Le Petit Quotidien* **et** *l'Actu.***)** 1.2

Vocabulaire supplémentaire

You might use these terms to discuss the text.

l'abonnement   *subscription*
le blog   *blog*
**le rédacteur,
 la rédactrice**   *editor*
le cyberespace   *cyber space*

Core Instruction

LECTURE CULTURELLE

1. Read the introductory paragraph and discuss it with the class. **(3 min.)**
2. Read *Mon quotidien* as a class. **(5 min.)**
3. Have students work in small groups to answer the questions in **Compréhension**. **(5 min.)**
4. Ask students if there are any equivalent American newspapers. Are American students interested in news and politics? **(5 min.)**

COMPARAISONS ET COMMUNAUTÉ

1. Have students read **Comparaisons** and discuss it in small groups. **(8 min.)**
2. Have students answer the **Et toi?** questions with a partner. **(5 min.)**
3. Go over **Communauté et professions** with students. Ask volunteers to research the requirements to become a journalist and to present their findings to the class. **(8 min.)**

Comparaisons

Piétonville, Haïti.

Créole ou français en Haïti? ✿2.1

Tu passes des vacances à Port-au-Prince et tu veux acheter un journal. En Haïti, on écrit les journaux:

  a. en français seulement.
  b. en créole seulement.
  c. dans les deux langues.

En Haïti, le français et le créole sont les langues officielles. Le créole est la langue maternelle de tous les Haïtiens. 5% d'entre eux parlent aussi français. La presse écrite est très majoritairement en langue française. Les quotidiens tels que *Le Matin* ne paraissent qu'en français. Parmi les revues, hebdomadaires et mensuels, quelques rares journaux sont publiés en créole, parmi lesquels *Boukan, Bon Nouvèl,* etc. Quelques périodiques consacrent régulièrement une ou deux pages au créole. Un périodique paraît en anglais, le *Haitian Times.*

✿4.2

ET TOI?

1. Est-ce qu'il y a des états bilingues aux États-Unis? Est-ce que la presse dans ta région est bilingue?

2. Est-ce qu'il y a des états où l'on parle créole aux États-Unis? Lesquels? Pourquoi?

Communauté et professions

Le français et le journalisme ✿4.2, 5.1

Qui n'a pas rêvé d'être un jour grand reporter. Les reporters voyagent dans le monde entier et parler français peut être un avantage dans de nombreux pays. En France, il existe 9 écoles de journalisme. Pour y entrer, il y a une sélection sur concours[1]. On peut aussi devenir journaliste avec une licence en communication et un DESS[2] de journalisme. Dans ton état comment peut-on devenir journaliste? Fais des recherches et présente ce que tu as découvert à ta classe.

1. *competitive exam* 2. Diplôme d'Éducation Supérieur Spécialisé *(equivalent to a PhD)*

Des journalistes interviewant Peggy Bouchet.

Differentiated Instruction

ADVANCED LEARNERS

Challenge Have students imagine they work as reporters for the daily, **Mon Quotidien.** Their assignment is to create a survey about the use of the Internet by teens. Students should ask at least ten questions such as: Why do you use the Internet? How often do you use the Internet? Do you have any favorite sites? Ask them to evaluate the answers and present the results in graphs or diagrams to the class. ✿1.3, 3.1

SPECIAL LEARNING NEEDS

Students with AD(H)D Ask students to research French teenage magazines, radio stations, and Internet sites for typical teenage activities. What do French teenagers find of interest in their music? Are they allowed to go to clubs at a younger age than American teenagers? Which teenage celebrities do they follow in the tabloids? Students should report the results of their research to the class. Discuss differences between being a teenager in France and in the United States. ✿3.2

Online Practice
go.hrw.com
Online Edition
KEYWORD: BD3 CH6

Culture

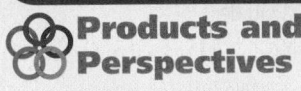

Bulletin Board Project

Have students create a Creole-French dictionary. Have groups of two or three research on the Internet Creole terms used in Haiti and their French equivalents. Each group should come up with five terms. Ask volunteers to compile all the terms, alphabetize them, and post the dictionary on a classroom bulletin board. Go over all entries as a class. ✿2.2

Cultures

✿ **Products and Perspectives**

One can learn a lot about a culture through its newspapers and magazines. Ask students if they have ever looked at French magazines or magazines from French-speaking countries. (You might bring in clippings from different magazines that you have selected.) Did the pictures reveal anything about the culture or the society of these countries? ✿2.1

Communities

Career Path

On the board or on a transparency, list some fields related to communications. (Advertising, journalism, radio, television, film) Ask students to think about careers in each of these fields. (graphic designer, disc jockey, broadcast journalist, film director, script writer, speech pathologist) How might French be useful in these careers? What role does technology play in these careers? ✿5.1

Teacher Note

You might ask students to research other youth magazines, such as **L'Actu 14-17** and **Le Monde des Ados.**

Bell Work

Use Bell Work 6.5 in the *Teaching Transparencies* or write this activity on the board.

Complète les phrases avec **quelque part, quelqu'un, quelque chose** ou **quelquefois.**

1. — Il y a ____ chez toi?
   — Non, il n'y a personne.
2. — Tu sais où sont mes clés?
   — Je les ai mises ____ ce matin.
3. — Tu veux prendre ____?
   — Non, je ne veux rien.
4. — J'entends ____ qui parle derrière la porte.
5. — Je joue ____ au tennis avec Christian.   🎴1.2

Cultures

Products and Perspectives

The broadsheet *Le Soleil* and the tabloid *Le Journal de Québec* are Quebec City's main daily newspapers. Ask students to research the difference in format as well as content between these two newspapers. How would they describe the target audience of each of these papers?   🎴2.2, 3.2

Objectifs
• to break news
• to ask about information

Vocabulaire
à l'œuvre 2

Les différentes rubriques

Sports

Une patineuse en or !

L'équipe canadienne **remporte** une **médaille d'or** et **grâce à cette victoire,** Cindy devient une **des athlètes** les plus médaillées du monde.

Société

Grève des pilotes

Des **centaines de passagers en colère** attendent leur avion pour partir en vacances. Les pilotes sont **en grève** parce qu'ils veulent une **augmentation de salaire.** On ne sait pas combien de temps cette grève va **durer.**

▶ Vocabulaire supplémentaire—L'actualité, p. R19

Météo

Une vague de chaleur s'est abattue sur tout le pays !

Lundi	Mardi	Mercredi

36°C	38°C	40°C

Des **records de température** ont été **enregistrés** hier au Québec. Les agriculteurs sont les seuls à ne pas se réjouir de ces températures inespérées pour la saison !

Petites annonces

Maison à vendre. Beau séjour, 3 chambres, 2 salles de bain, grand jardin, quartier résidentiel. Prix : 178.000 €

Villa 3 chambres, 2 salles de

Actualité internationale

Sommet international pour la paix dans le monde

Le sommet s'est terminé sur une note optimiste.

Core Instruction

TEACHING VOCABULAIRE

1. Introduce the vocabulary, using transparencies **Vocabulaire 6.3** and **6.4.** Model the pronunciation of each word or expression, beginning with **Il y a eu...** (**une grève, un vol**) or **Ça, c'est...** (**une petite annonce.**) **(3 min.)**

2. Ask students to point to various news sections on the transparency. (**la météo, les faits divers**) **(2 min.)**

3. Ask students about their reading habits and recent news. **Qu'est-ce que tu aimes lire comme rubrique dans le journal? Qu'est-ce qui s'est récemment passé? (3 min.)**

4. Model the pronunciation of the expressions in **Exprimons-nous!** Have partners write similar sentences about recent events in your area. **(4 min.)**

Online Practice
go.hrw.com
Vocabulaire 2 practice
KEYWORD: BD3 CH6

Culture

Les critiques sont tous d'accord !

Le nouveau roman de Jean-Pierre Beaupré connaît déjà un grand **succès** en librairie.

Économie

Baisse du **chômage**

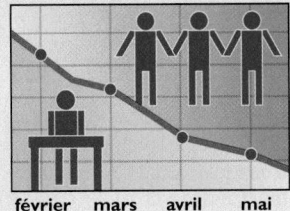

février   mars   avril   mai

Pour la troisième fois depuis le début de l'année, le chômage est en baisse. Le **ministre** du travail a dit que ces chiffres reflétaient le travail de son **équipe**.

D'autres mots utiles

un accident	accident
un attentat	terrorist attack
une catastrophe	catastrophe
le courrier des lecteurs	letters to the Editor
une œuvre	work of art
gratuit(e)	free

Faits divers

Vol au musée du Louvre

Les voleurs avaient du goût : ils ont emporté les plus beaux **tableaux** de la collection italienne du XIVe siècle.

Exprimons-nous!

To break news	To respond
Tu as vu la photo de l'accident? *Did you see . . . ?*	**Fais voir!** *Let me see!*
Devine qui est en couverture du *TV 7 Jours. Guess . . .*	**Montre-moi!** *Show me!*
Tu connais la dernière? *Have you heard the latest?*	Non, **raconte!** *. . . tell me!*
Tu es au courant de ce qui est arrivé à Chloé? *Are you aware of . . . ?*	Non, **je t'écoute!** *. . . I'm listening!*
Tu sais quoi? *Do you know what?*	Non, **qu'est-ce qui s'est passé?** *. . . what happened?*
Tu as entendu parler du vol de voitures? *Have you heard about . . . ?*	

Interactive TUTOR

Vocabulaire et grammaire, pp. 67–69 — Online workbooks

Vocabulaire 2

TPR
TOTAL PHYSICAL RESPONSE

Have students respond to these commands.

Lève-toi si tu es au courant des activités internationales.

Lève les bras si tu lis le courrier des lecteurs.

Lève le pied si tu préfères les faits divers.

Mets les mains sur la tête s'il y a eu des attentats cette semaine.

Then bring in a newspaper and have students respond to these commands.

Fais voir la météo.

Montre-moi une petite annonce.

Cherche un article qui parle d'une catastrophe.

Finally, have students mime the following situations.

Tu es en colère.

Il y a une vague de chaleur.

Tu es un voleur. 🌸1.2

Teacher to Teacher

Todd Losié
Renaissance HS
Detroit, MI

Form eight groups and assign a different section of an imaginary newspaper to each group. Have each group prepare an article about something that could appear in their section. Then collect the articles and display them on the bulletin board. 🌸1.3

Differentiated Instruction

ADVANCED LEARNERS

Extension Ask students to visit the site of an online French newspaper, such as *Le Monde* or *Le Figaro* to find information for each of the rubrics featured in **Vocabulaire 2.** Have students to present their research to the class. 🌸1.3

SPECIAL LEARNING NEEDS

Students with Learning Disabilities/ Dyslexia If you have students with writing challenges, give them the option of responding orally to show their understanding. Have students record three different news reports. Each report should include the who, what, when, where, and why of a school or local event that would fit each news category. 🌸1.3

Resources

Planning:

Lesson Planner

 One-Stop Planner

Presentation:

 Teaching Transparencies
Vocabulaire 6.3, 6.4

Practice:

Cahier de vocabulaire et grammaire

Differentiated Practice and Assessment CD-ROM

Media Guide

 Audio CD 6, Tr. 4

 Interactive Tutor, Disc 2

㉓ Script

1. À voir absolument: L'exposition des œuvres d'Ousmane Sow.
2. Air France: La grève des pilotes dure et les passagers sont en colère.
3. Selon le ministre du travail, le chômage est en baisse.
4. Grave accident sur la Nationale 7 près d'Orange: 8 blessés.
5. Jeux olympiques: Trois médailles pour la France.
6. Côte d'Azur: Temps lourd et très chaud; records de température.

Cinquain Poetry

Ask students to create a poem with the new chapter vocabulary.

Line 1 A noun
Line 2 Two verbs
Line 3 Three past participles
Line 4 An expression
Line 5 Another word for the noun

Sample answer

**La grève
Durer, s'abattre
Développée, rétablie, persuadé
Tu connais la dernière?
La catastrophe**

㉒ Des extraits ✿1.2

Lisons Lis chaque extrait de journal ou de magazine et indique dans quelle rubrique il est probablement paru.

Je vous écris au sujet de votre article paru dans le numéro du 19 janvier...

1. e

À louer : Appartement 2 pièces, centre-ville...

2. a

Pluie et mauvais temps sur tout le nord du pays

3. f

À voir absolument ! Dans son dernier film, Audrey Tautou montre tout son talent.

4. g

Le président des États-Unis en visite officielle en France

5. c

Une dame retrouve son chien qu'elle avait perdu il y a 10 ans!

6. b

a. les petites annonces
b. les faits divers
c. l'actualité internationale
d. les sports
e. le courrier des lecteurs
f. la météo
g. la culture
h. l'économie

㉓ Écoutons   CD 6, Tr. 4   ✿1.2   **1.** g **2.** a **3.** d **4.** e **5.** b **6.** h

Écoute ces personnes qui lisent les gros titres du journal et dis dans quelle rubrique on va trouver chaque article.

a. actualité
b. sports
c. petites annonces
d. économie
e. faits divers
f. courrier des lecteurs
g. culture
h. météo

㉔ Au café ✿1.2

Lisons/Écrivons Éric et Charlotte discutent à la terrasse d'un café. Complète leur conversation de façon logique avec les mots et les expressions du vocabulaire.

1. Devine
2. fais
3. tu sais quoi
4. t'écoute
5. Montre

ÉRIC _____1_____ qui est en couverture du journal *L'Équipe!*
CHARLOTTE Je ne sais pas, ___2___ voir!
ÉRIC Ma cousine Ophélie! Elle a remporté une médaille aux Jeux olympiques!
CHARLOTTE Ouah! C'est une patineuse incroyable, ta cousine!
ÉRIC Oui, c'est vrai. Et ___3___ ?
CHARLOTTE Non, je ___4___ !
ÉRIC Elle a vu Ivan Trosky, le champion de patinage russe et elle lui a demandé un autographe pour moi!
CHARLOTTE Génial! ___5___-moi!

Flash culture

Le blog ou cyberjournal est un phénomène de société. Certains blogs à vocation professionnelle partagent des observations et des commentaires de spécialistes en tout genre, comme des journalistes, des informaticiens, etc. Beaucoup d'adolescents ont leur blog qui parle de leur vie personnelle et de leurs passions. Le langage des blogs varie autant que les thèmes. On peut trouver des abréviations en langage texto de style SMS: ✿4.2

JTM = Je t'aime.

Est-ce qu'il existe un langage similaire en anglais?

Core Instruction

TEACHING EXPRIMONS-NOUS!

1. Model the pronunciation of each expression. **(2 min.)**

2. Ask students the questions in **Exprimons-nous!** and have them give an appropriate answer. They can be one-word answers. **(3 min.)**

3. Make various statements. **Jacques m'a téléphoné. Nous avons fait nos devoirs ensemble.** Have students ask the corresponding questions. **Qui est-ce qui t'a téléphoné? Qu'est-ce que vous avez fait? (5 min.)**

Exprimons-nous!

To ask for information	
Qui est-ce qui a gagné le match de foot?	Who (as subject) . . . ?
Qui est-ce que tu as rencontré à la soirée de Patrick?	Whom (as object) . . . ?
Qu'est-ce qui lui est arrivé?	What (as subject) . . . ?
Qu'est-ce que le voleur a emporté?	What (as direct object) . . . ?

Vocabulaire et grammaire, pp. 67–69

Online workbooks

Interactive TUTOR

㉕ Answers

1. Qui est-ce qui...
2. Qui est-ce que...
3. Qu'est-ce que...
4. Qu'est-ce qui...

㉕ Un vol au Musée d'Orsay ✿3.2

Lisons/Écrivons Lis cet article et réponds aux questions.

Un Monet volé à Orsay

Hier après-midi, deux voleurs ont réussi à entrer dans une salle du Musée d'Orsay qui était fermée au public. Ils étaient en train de voler deux tableaux de Claude Monet quand un employé du musée les a surpris. Il a tout de suite essayé d'appeler la police, mais malheureusement, les voleurs ont gravement blessé l'employé du musée. Ils ont ensuite réussi à quitter le musée avec un des deux tableaux avant que la police arrive. On a emmené l'employé du musée d'urgence à l'hôpital.

1. _____ est entré dans le musée?
2. _____ l'employé a appelé?
3. _____ l'article raconte?
4. _____ est arrivé à la fin?

Communication

Scénario ✿1.1

Parlons Tu as lu quelque chose d'incroyable dans le journal et tu en parles à tes copains.

♻ *Souviens-toi,* Sequence of tenses, p. 114

MODÈLE —Tu connais la dernière?
—Non, raconte!
—Eh bien, dans le journal, ils disaient que...

HOLT **SoundBooth** ONLINE RECORDING

Communication

㉖ Group Activity: Presentational

Have groups of three prepare a conversation in which each student has a bit of gossip or breaking news to share. Students should use the vocabulary for breaking news and responding to news. In addition, they should describe the news or gossip in detail. Then have them repeat the conversation for the class. Encourage the listeners to respond with disbelief or other appropriate responses. You may want the class to write a summary of what they heard. ✿1.2, 1.3

Differentiated Instruction

SLOWER PACE LEARNERS

㉕ Some students may have difficulty understanding the article. As volunteers read it aloud, students should make a list of expressions they do not understand. Go over the lists and ask volunteers to use synonyms, antonyms, or circumlocution to explain problematic expressions. Then have students complete this activity. ✿1.1

MULTIPLE INTELLIGENCES

Bodily-Kinesthetic Divide the class into two teams and place the teams at opposite sides of the room. The first person on one team tosses a soft ball to a person on the other team while asking a who, whom, or what question. The person who catches the ball, answers the question and tosses it to the other team while asking his or her question. ✿1.2

Assess

Assessment Program

Quiz: Vocabulaire 2

Alternative Assessment

Differentiated Practice and Assessment CD-ROM

Online Assessment
my.hrw.com

Test Generator

Resources

Planning:

Lesson Planner

 One-Stop Planner

Practice:

Grammar Tutor for Students of French, Chapter 6

Cahier de vocabulaire et grammaire

Differentiated Practice and Assessment CD-ROM

Cahier d'activités

Media Guide

 Teaching Transparencies

Bell Work 6.6

 Interactive Tutor, Disc 2

Bell Work

Use Bell Work 6.6 in the *Teaching Transparencies* or write this activity on the board.

Dans quelles rubriques trouve-t-on les articles suivants?

1. **Une vague de froid s'est abattue sur le nord de la France.**
2. **Voiture à vendre. Peugeot 2002. 56.000 km. Parfait état. 7.800€.**
3. **Le lauréat du Prix Goncourt pour le meilleur roman de l'année.**
4. **L'équipe de France de football s'est qualifiée pour les championnats.**
5. **Vol dans l'église Saint Sulpice d'un tableau datant du XVIIème siècle.**
6. **Sommet International aux Nations unies sur les changements climatiques.**

 1.2

Objectifs
- object pronouns
- *qui est-ce qui, qui est-ce que, qu'est-ce qui* and *qu'est-ce que*

Grammaire à l'œuvre 2

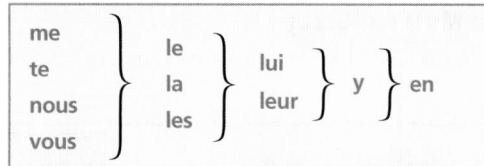 **Révisions** **Object pronouns**

1 If there is more than one object pronoun in a sentence, use the following pronouns, preceding the verb, in the order indicated:

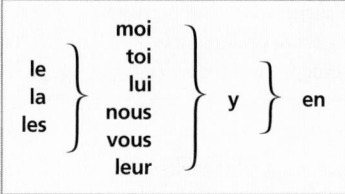

—Tu donnes du chocolat aux enfants? —Oui, je leur en donne.

2 In negative commands, use the same pronouns in front of the verb.

Ne m'en parle pas!   *Don't talk to me about it!*

3 In affirmative commands, the object pronoun follows the verb and is connected to it by a hyphen. **Me** becomes **moi**, and **te** becomes **toi**. When there is more than one pronoun, the order is:

La revue? Donne-la-moi. Donne-lui le journal.

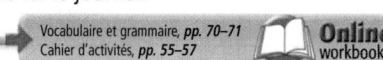

Vocabulaire et grammaire, *pp. 70–71*
Cahier d'activités, *pp. 55–57*

Online workbooks

Déjà vu!

In compound tenses like the **passé composé**, the past participle agrees with the preceding <u>direct</u> object (noun or pronoun).

La clé? Je l'ai donnée à mon père.

I gave it to my father.

---

27 **Le bon pronom** 🎀 1.2

Parlons Complète les phrases suivantes avec le bon pronom.

1. Prête ton livre à Johan. Prête-(les / <u>le</u>)-(la / <u>lui</u>).
2. Je peux aider Camille? Je peux (<u>l'</u> / la) aider?
3. Jonas a offert des fleurs à Lise. Jonas (la / <u>lui</u>) (y / <u>en</u>) a offertes.
4. Mia ne va pas au resto. Mia n'(en / <u>y</u>) va pas.
5. Nous n'avons pas parlé de la fête aux profs. Nous ne (les / <u>leur</u>) (le / <u>en</u>) avons pas parlé.

Core Instruction

TEACHING GRAMMAIRE

1. Read **Déjà vu!** aloud with students. **(2 min.)**
2. Go over Point 1. Point out that the order is first indirect object pronoun, then direct object pronoun, except in the third person singular and plural. Tell students that a good way to remember the order of **y** and **en** is to think of the sound a donkey makes. **(3 min.)**

3. Go over Points 3 and 4. You might point out that in affirmative commands the order of pronouns is reversed, and that **me** and **te** change to **moi** and **toi. Tu me le donnes** becomes **Donne-le moi!**

Online Practice
go.hrw.com
Grammaire 2 practice
KEYWORD: BD3 CH6

Chapitre 6
Grammaire 2

28 Faits divers ✿1.2

Écrivons/Parlons Remplace les mots soulignés par des pronoms.

> **MODÈLE** Julien a donné <u>la revue</u> <u>à Pauline</u>.
> **Il la lui a donnée.**

1. J'ai prêté <u>ma nouvelle BD</u> <u>à mes cousins</u>.
2. Mes parents n'ont pas envoyé <u>de cartes postales</u> <u>à leurs amis</u>.
3. Voudrais-tu acheter <u>du chocolat</u> si tu vas <u>au marché</u>?
4. J'ai rencontré <u>mon prof d'espagnol</u> <u>au Mexique</u> cet été.
5. Le prof explique souvent <u>la politique internationale</u> <u>aux élèves</u>.

29 Exercices de maths ✿1.2

Parlons Jacques fait ses devoirs de maths avec un copain. D'abord, il répond «oui» à chacune de ses questions. Mais, ensuite il change d'avis et dit «non». Utilise **l'impératif**.

> **MODÈLE** —Je peux <u>te</u> poser <u>une question</u>?
> —**Oui, pose-m'en une. Non, ne m'en pose pas!**

1. Tu veux que je <u>te</u> prête <u>ma calculatrice</u>?
2. Je peux <u>te</u> montrer <u>mes réponses</u>?
3. Il faut que j'aille <u>à la bibliothèque</u>?
4. Est-ce que je devrais téléphoner <u>aux autres</u>?
5. J'achète <u>des crayons</u> pour le cours de maths?

Communication

HOLT **SoundBooth**
ONLINE RECORDING

30 Interview ✿1.1

Parlons Demande à un(e) camarade s'il/si elle a fait certaines choses récemment. Utilise les images pour t'inspirer. Ton/Ta camarade utilisera des pronoms pour te répondre.

> **MODÈLE** —**Est-ce que tu as écrit une lettre à ta tante?**
> —**Oui, je lui en ai écrit une la semaine dernière.**

1.   2.   3.   4.

28 Answers
1. Je la leur ai prêtée.
2. Ils ne leur en ont pas envoyé.
3. Voudrais-tu en acheter si tu y vas?
4. Je l'y ai rencontré cet été.
5. Le prof la leur explique souvent.

29 Answers
1. Oui, prête-la-moi! Non, ne me la prête pas!
2. Oui, montre-les moi! Non, ne me les montre pas!
3. Oui, vas-y! Non, n'y va pas!
4. Oui, téléphone-leur! Non, ne leur téléphone pas!
5. Oui, achètes-en! Non, n'en achète pas!

Communication

Class Activity: Interpersonal
Challenge students to write three questions that require a direct and an indirect object. Have them also write the affirmative and the negative answers to these questions with object pronouns. Then have students circulate to see if they can answer each other's questions with double object pronouns in the correct order. Have volunteers ask you their questions. Model the correct answers for all students. ✿1.2

French for Spanish Speakers
Ask Spanish speakers to create a chart that compares and contrasts object pronouns in French and Spanish. Students could start with similarities in the object pronouns, **me/me, te/te, nous/nos,** and then move on to differences, such as the placement of the object pronoun in sentences like **Vamos a verlo/Lo vamos a ver,** which in French can only be, **Nous allons le voir.** ✿4.1

Differentiated Instruction

SLOWER PACE LEARNERS

28 Additional Practice To break down the process, ask students to replace the first underlined phrase in each sentence with a pronoun. Go over each sentence and review the order of pronouns when there are more than one. Then ask them to replace the second underlined phrase with a pronoun. ✿1.2

SPECIAL LEARNING NEEDS

30 Students with Speech Impairments Allow these students to write a script of questions and responses prior to interviewing a classmate. The script may help students with fluency or articulation challenges to practice the sentence and increase confidence before conversing. Another accommodation would be to exempt students from the interview and have them submit the script only. ✿1.2

Resources

Planning:

Lesson Planner

 One-Stop Planner

Practice:

Grammar Tutor for Students of French, Chapter 6

Cahier de vocabulaire et grammaire

Differentiated Practice and Assessment CD-ROM

Cahier d'activités

Media Guide

 Teaching Transparencies
Bell Work 6.7

 Audio CD 6, Tr. 5

 Interactive Tutor, Disc 2

Bell Work

Use Bell Work 6.7 in the *Teaching Transparencies* or write this activity on the board.

Réponds aux questions en remplaçant les mots soulignés par les pronoms qui conviennent.

1. Avez-vous lu <u>les journaux</u> ce matin?
2. Trouve-t-on beaucoup <u>de kiosques à journaux à Paris</u>?
3. Arthr collectionne-t-il toujours <u>des bandes dessinées</u>?
4. Vas-tu acheter <u>ces magazines</u>?
5 Est-ce que tu t'es abonné <u>à ce mensuel avec Rémi</u>?

1.2

(31) Answers

1. Qu'est-ce que le voleur a emporté?
2. Qui est-ce que la police a demandé?
3. Qu'est-ce qu'il a fait?
4. Qu'est-ce qui s'est passé?
5. Qui est-ce qui est en grève?
6. Qui est-ce qui a écrit cet article?
7. Qu'est-ce que tu as lu dans le journal?
8. Qui est-ce que tu as rencontré au kiosque?

4.1

Qui est-ce qui, qui est-ce que, qu'est-ce qui, and *qu'est-ce que*

1 Which word you use in French for *what, who,* and *whom* depends on whether the question word is the **subject** or the **object** of the sentence.

	PERSON	THING
SUBJECT	qui est-ce qui	qu'est-ce qui
OBJECT	qui est-ce que	qu'est-ce que

2 Use **qui est-ce** qui for *who,* when the question word is the **subject** of the sentence. **Qui (est-ce qui)** will usually be followed by a verb. **Qui est-ce** qui is often shortened to **qui.**

> **Qui (est-ce** qui) a volé la voiture?   *Who stole the car?*

Use **qui est-ce** que for *whom* (the **object** of the verb). **Que** becomes **qu'** before a word beginning with a vowel sound. **Qui est-ce** que will usually be followed by a noun or pronoun. There is no short form for **qui est-ce** que.

> **Qui est-ce** que tu as vu dans le parking hier soir?
> *Whom did you see in the parking lot yesterday evening?*

3 Use **qu'est-ce** qui when *what* is the **subject** of the verb. **Qu'est-ce** qui will usually be followed by a verb.

> **Qu'est-ce** qui se passe?   *What is happening?*

Use **qu'est-ce** que when *what* is the **object** of the verb. **Qu'est-ce** que will usually be followed by a subject. **Que** becomes **qu'** before a word beginning with a vowel sound.

> **Qu'est-ce** que tu vas faire?   *What are you going to do?*

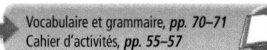
Vocabulaire et grammaire, pp. 70–71
Cahier d'activités, pp. 55–57
Online workbooks

(31) Actualités régionales 1.2

Écrivons Forme des questions logiques et correctes.

Qui est-ce qui	Qui est-ce que/qu'
Qu'est-ce qui	Qu'est-ce que/qu'

1. ... le voleur a emporté?
2. ... la police a demandé?
3. ... il a fait?
4. ... s'est passé?
5. ... est en grève?
6. ... a écrit cet article?
7. ... tu as lu dans le journal?
8. ... tu as rencontré au kiosque?

En anglais

In English, we use *who* if the question word is the **subject** of the sentence and *whom* if the question word is the **object.**

> *Who stole the painting?*
> *Whom did you see at the museum?*

Would you use *who* or *whom* to complete the following sentences?

1. _____ won the game?
2. _____ did she beat to win the title?
3. _____ wants to go see her next match?

In French, there are also different question words for *who* and *whom.*
1. Who **2.** Whom **3.** Who
Qui est-ce qui **a volé le tableau?**

Qui est-ce que **tu as vu au musée?**

Core Instruction

TEACHING GRAMMAIRE

1. Read **En anglais** aloud with students. **(2 min.)**

2. Go over Point 1. Tell students that the first **qui/que** in the sentence shows whether the question is about a person or a thing. **Qui** (person) **est-ce que tu aimes bien?**, **Qu'** (thing) **est-ce que tu aimes bien?** Tell students that the second **qui/que** shows whether this person or thing is the subject or the object of the verb. **Qu'est-ce qui** (subject) **est important?**, **Qu'est-ce que** (object) **tu aimes bien? (4 min.)**

3. Go over Points 2 and 3. Tell students that the questions can be shortened whenever the first and second **qui/que** words are the same. **Qui est-ce qui parle? Qui parle?** Point out that the short version following **que** requires an inversion. **Qu'est-ce que tu dis? Que dis-tu? (2 min.)**

32 Écoutons CD 6, Tr. 5 🎬1.2   **1.** b **2.** b **3.** a **4.** b **5.** a **6.** a

🎧 Écoute et dis si on parle a) **d'une personne** ou b) **d'une chose.**

33 Réponses sans questions 🎬1.2

✏️ **Écrivons/Lisons** Il y a des gens qui parlent sur leur portable. Écris la question qui correspond à chacune de leurs réponses. Utilise la construction **qui/qu'est-ce qui/que.**

> **MODÈLE** —Le lundi? Je travaille, bien sûr.
> **Qu'est-ce que tu fais le lundi?**

1. C'est Philippe de Saintonges qui est ministre des Affaires Étrangères.

2. J'ai vu la sœur de Pascale à l'aéroport.

3. Les araignées me font peur.

4. Ce que je ne comprends pas, c'est comment un accident comme ça peut arriver.

5. Je crois que Thu Hông, elle, elle parle vietnamien.

34 On se le demande 🎬1.2

Parlons Il se passe des choses pas ordinaires. Imagine les questions que ces gens pourraient poser. Utilise la construction **qui est-ce qui, qui est-ce que, qu'est-ce qui** ou **qu'est-ce que.**

> **MODÈLE** **Mais, qu'est-ce que tu fais?**

faire

1. appeler

2. arriver

3. lancer

4. manger

Communication

HOLT **SoundBooth** ONLINE RECORDING

35 Scénario 🎬1.1

Parlons Tu es journaliste et on te demande d'écrire un article sur des faits divers dans ta ville. Invente six questions et pose-les à trois camarades qui vont jouer le rôle des personnes interrogées.

> **MODÈLE** —Qu'est-ce que vous avez vu?
> —J'ai vu quelqu'un entrer par cette fenêtre et...

32 Script

1. Qu'est-ce que tu as vu à la bibliothèque?

2. Qu'est-ce qui te dit que ce n'est pas vrai?

3. Qui est-ce que tu vas étudier dans ton cours d'histoire cette année?

4. Qu'est-ce qui ne va pas?

5. Qui est-ce que tu as invité?

6. Qui est-ce qui t'a dit ça?

33 Answers

1. Qui (est-ce qui) est ministre des Affaires étrangères?

2. Qui est-ce que tu as vu à l'aéroport?

3. Qu'est-ce qui te fait peur?

4. Qu'est-ce que tu ne comprends pas?

5. Qui (est-ce qui) parle vietnamien?

34 Possible Answers

1. Qui est-ce que j'appelle?

2. Qu'est-ce qui est arrivé?

3. Qui est-ce qui a lancé la balle?

4. Qu'est-ce que tu manges?

Communication

Group Activity: Interpersonal
Form small groups. Have each student tell what he or she did this past weekend. Have the other group members take turns asking as many related questions as possible. 🎬1.1

Differentiated Instruction

SLOWER PACE LEARNERS

31 Before they do this activity, ask students to decide if the missing question word is the subject or object of the verb. Remind students that subjects are followed by verbs and objects by subjects. Then ask students if the question word represents a person or a thing. Allow students to use the chart in the grammar presentation to complete this activity. 🎬1.2

SPECIAL LEARNING NEEDS

Students with Auditory/Language Impairments Make sure that students with language challenges understand the English grammar concepts of subject and object before you introduce the rules for the French equivalents of who and whom. Review **En anglais.** Discuss the examples and why these answers are correct. Allow students to create more examples and work with a small group if the concept is not mastered by all students. 🎬1.2

Assess

Assessment Program
Quiz: Grammaire 2
Alternative Assessment
Differentiated Practice and Assessment CD-ROM

Online Assessment
my.hrw.com

Test Generator 🌐

Synthèse
- Vocabulaire 2
- Grammaire 2

Resources

Planning:

Lesson Planner

 One-Stop Planner

Practice:

Grammar Tutor for Students of French, Chapter 6

Cahier de vocabulaire et grammaire

Differentiated Practice and Assessment CD-ROM

Cahier d'activités

Media Guide

 Teaching Transparencies
Bell Work 6.8

 Audio CD 6, Tr. 6

Interactive Tutor, Disc 2

Bell Work

Use Bell Work 6.8 in the *Teaching Transparencies* or write this activity on the board.

Écris les questions qui correspondent à ces réponses en utilisant **qui est-ce qui, qui est-ce que, qu'est-ce qui, qu'est-ce que.**

1. J'ai vu mon prof de physique ce matin.
2. Albert Camus a écrit *La Peste.*
3. La tour Eiffel a plus de cent ans.
4. Le chômage me fait peur.
5. Travis est américain. 1.2

36 Script

See script on p. 221F.

38 Answers

1. Non, je ne fais jamais le ménage.
2. Non, il n'a aucun ami.
3. Non, personne ne m'a téléphoné hier.
4. Non, je ne vais nulle part en vacances cette année.
5. Non, je n'ai rien à faire ce week-end.
6. Non, je n'ai pas encore fini mes devoirs.
7. Non, je n'ai plus d'argent.
8. Aucun magazine n'a la photo de cette actrice...

Application 2

 Écoutons CD 6, Tr. 6 1.2

Sybille parle de sa famille, qui est allée au centre commercial. Décide s'ils ont acheté quelque chose a) **pour Sybille** ou b) **pour quelqu'un d'autre.** **1.** a **2.** b **3.** a **4.** a **5.** b **6.** b **7.** b

37 Devinettes 1.2

Écrivons/Parlons Tu veux savoir si tes copains sont au courant *(aware of)* des actualités. Fais une liste de cinq questions sur des sujets de ton choix et pose tes questions à la classe.

MODÈLE **Qui est-ce qui a gagné la Coupe du monde de football cette année?**

Un peu plus

More negative expressions

1. You've learned about some negative expressions. Two other negative expressions are ne... aucun(e) *(no, not any)* and ne... nulle part *(nowhere)*.

2. When ne... aucun(e) is used with a verb, it is placed around the verb like **ne... pas.** In the **passé composé**, aucun(e) goes after the past participle.

   Notre équipe n'avait aucune chance.
   Il n'a écrit aucun article intéressant.

   When *no* or *none* is the subject of the verb, use Aucun(e)... ne

   Aucun journal ne parle de cette histoire.

3. Ne...nulle part goes around the verb like **ne... pas.**

   J'ai le journal, mais je ne le vois nulle part.

   In the **passé composé** and other compound tenses, nulle part goes after the direct object.

   Je n'ai trouvé tes clés nulle part.

→ Vocabulaire et grammaire, *p. 72*
Cahier d'activités, *pp. 55–57*
 **Online** workbooks

38 Mais non... 1.2

Écrivons/Parlons Tes amis sont vraiment trop curieux. Utilise **ne** et une expression de la boîte pour répondre **non** à chacune de leurs questions.

rien	pas encore	jamais	plus
personne	nulle part	aucun	

1. Est-ce que tu fais souvent le ménage?
2. Est-ce que ton frère a beaucoup d'amis?
3. Est-ce que quelqu'un t'a téléphoné hier?
4. Est-ce que tu vas quelque part en vacances, cette année?
5. Est-ce que tu as quelque chose à faire ce week-end?
6. Est-ce que tu as déjà fini tes devoirs?
7. Est-ce que tu as encore de l'argent?
8. Quel magazine a la photo de cette actrice en couverture?

Core Instruction

INTEGRATED PRACTICE

1. Have students do Activities 36–37 to practice previously taught material. **(10 min.)**
2. Introduce **Un peu plus.** (See presentation suggestions at right.) **(4 min.)**
3. Continue with integrated practice Activities 38–41. **(20 min.)**

TEACHING UN PEU PLUS

1. Model the pronunciation of all the negative expressions in **Un peu plus** by using each of them in a sentence. **Je ne comprends pas, Je ne comprends rien, Je ne comprends jamais. (2 min.)**
2. To practice these expressions, ask students to give a negative answer all your questions. **Est-ce que tu sors, quelquefois? Je ne sors jamais. (2 min.)**

Online Practice
go.hrw.com
Application 2 practice
KEYWORD: BD3 CH6

39 Toujours non! 🌸1.2

Écrivons/Parlons Réponds négativement à ces questions. Utilise des pronoms dans tes réponses si possible.

1. Est-ce que tu as déjà lu des livres en français?
2. Est-ce que tu connais quelqu'un qui parle chinois?
3. Est-ce que tu as beaucoup de bandes dessinées françaises?
4. Est-ce que tu as déjà été dans un pays où on parle français?
5. Est-ce que quelqu'un t'a offert un cadeau aujourd'hui?
6. Qu'est-ce qui te plaît?

40 Et toi? 🌸1.3

Écrivons Écris un petit paragraphe pour dire quels magazines et journaux chaque membre de ta famille lit. Êtes-vous abonnés à des journaux ou à des revues? Lesquels? Est-ce que ce sont des quotidiens ou des revues mensuelles? Quelles rubriques intéressent les différents membres de ta famille?

MODÈLE Mon père lit *Le Monde* tous les jours. Ma mère préfère lire des magazines féminins sur la mode. Ma sœur ne lit jamais le journal.

À la créole

In Creole, people refer to **un journal** as **un nouvelté** and to **un journaliste** as **un nouveltis**.

Communication

41 Histoire à raconter 🌸1.1

Parlons C'était l'anniversaire de Sébastien. Avec un(e) camarade, raconte ce qui s'est passé ce jour-là.

---

39 Answers
1. Non, je n'en ai jamais lu.
2. Non, je ne connais personne qui parle chinois.
3. Non, je n'en ai aucune.
4. Non, je n'y suis jamais allé(e).
5. Non, personne ne m'en a offert.
6. Rien ne me plaît.

Language Examination

To display the drawings to the class, use the Picture Sequences Transparency for Chapter 6.

41 Sample answer
a. C'était l'anniversaire de Sébastien. Des extraterrestres sont arrivés.
b. L'extraterrestre a apporté un cadeau.
c. Le lendemain, Sébastien était à la une du journal.

Communication

Class Activity: Interpersonal
Prepare index cards with a question that includes **quelqu'un, quelque part,** or **quelque chose.** Hand the card to students. In pairs, students take turns asking and answering the questions, using negative expressions from **Un peu plus.** 🌸1.2

Differentiated Instruction

ADVANCED LEARNERS

40 Personalization Have students complete this activity. Then ask them to tell a story about an event that is unlikely to have happened. You may want to bring some tabloids to class and allow students to base their stories on the headlines of these tabloids. Students should present their stories to the class. Have students vote on the most creative story. 🌸1.3, 3.1

MULTIPLE INTELLIGENCES

Linguistic Give a controversial subject for debate to a group of four students. Assign two students to argue one side of the controversy and two students to argue the other side. Ask students to reference **Un peu plus** for the correct usage of negative expressions in their debate. Topics might include current issues at school, local news, or topics of national or worldwide controversy. 🌸1.2

Assess

Assessment Program
Quiz: Application 2
Audio CD 6, Tr. 12
Alternative Assessment
Differentiated Practice and Assessment CD-ROM

Online Assessment
my.hrw.com

Test Generator

AP Reading Suggestion

Remind students how important it is to know the context of a reading selection. It will help them read with better understanding and increase their recollection. Knowing when and under what circumstances the author lived and wrote will improve reading comprehension in general.

Applying the Strategies

For practice with using background knowledge and context clues, have students use the "Story Impressions" strategy from the Reading Strategies and Skills Handbook.

READING PRACTICE

Strategy: Story Impressions

Reading Skill	When can I use this strategy?		
	Prereading	During Reading	Postreading
Making Predictions	✓		
Analyzing Cause-and-Effect Relationships		✓	
Making Inferences		✓	
Analyzing Chronological Order			✓
Identifying Purpose			✓
Comparing and Contrasting			✓

Strategy at a Glance: Story Impressions

- The teacher chooses key words or phrases from the story the students are going to read and arranges them in a linked order.
- The class discusses the pronunciation and meaning of each word.
- Using the key words or phrases in the order they were given, students write brief summaries of what they think the story will be about.
- After reading, students compare their predictions with the actual story.

We often get impressions about texts before we read them. Sometimes those impressions are right, and sometimes they are wrong, but they help us begin to think about the text. Impressions, vague and imprecise as they are, help us predict what may happen in the text.

Some readers never form these predictions. They begin reading with no thought of what might happen; therefore, they are not using their prior experiences to help them understand the text. Predicting, or thinking ahead, is based on the ability to bring previous knowledge to a new situation. If students don't predict, they aren't using what they already know to help them understand what they are about to encounter.

The **Story Impressions** strategy helps students form an overall impression of a text. The teacher gives students 10–15 words taken from a text, keeping these words in the order that the teacher prescribed. students write a brief paragraph that uses each word and summarizes what they think the text will be about. Creating the summary helps students

---

Françoise Giroud, écrivain, journaliste et femme politique française est née à Genève en 1916. Elle a 14 ans quand son père meurt. Elle arrête alors l'école. À 16 ans, elle devient sténodactylo, puis *script-girl*, assistante metteur en scène et scénariste au cinéma. Après la Seconde Guerre mondiale, elle se lance dans le journalisme. En 1953, elle fonde *L'Express®*, avec Jean-Jacques Servan-Schreiber, le premier magazine hebdomadaire d'actualité en France. Françoise Giroud meurt en 2003 à l'âge de 86 ans. Elle a écrit entre autres *Nouveaux portraits* (1954), *Si je mens* (1972), *Le bon plaisir* (1979) et *Profession journaliste* (2001).

Ⓐ Avant la lecture 🌐1.3

Tu vas lire un texte sur le journalisme et l'art d'écrire. Quels journaux, revues ou sites Internet lis-tu? Est-ce que le style des articles est différent de celui d'autres textes que tu lis? Explique. À ton avis, quelles sont les caractéristiques d'un bon article?

CD 6, Tr. 7

Profession journaliste

*L'extrait suivant est tiré de **Profession journaliste**, une biographie de Françoise Giroud écrite sous forme de conversation entre elle-même et Martine de Rabaudy. Dans cet extrait, Françoise Giroud parle de l'écriture.*

L'ÉCRITURE

« Le plaisir que j'ai à poser mes banderilles[1]. »
Émile Henriot, de l'Académie française.

FRANÇOISE GIROUD.   Je répondrai à la phrase d'Émile Henriot par une citation, de Malraux : « On sent les coups[2] que l'on reçoit, jamais ceux qu'on

---

1. *banderillas- darts decorated with streamers that are used in bullfight* 2. *the blows*

Core Instruction

LECTURE

1. Read **Stratégie pour lire** aloud for students. **(1 min.)**

2. Have students read the biographical sketch and use their background knowledge and content clues to guess the meaning of **scénariste. (5 min.)**

3. Do **Avant la lecture** as a class. Take notes on the board while students tell what they know about the way articles are written in newspapers and weekly magazines.

You might also bring copies of periodicals to class. **(10 min.)**

4. Have volunteers take turns reading **Profession journaliste** aloud, to the end of page 247. Pause regularly to monitor students' comprehension. **(15 min.)**

Lecture

donne. » Il m'est arrivé[1] d'écrire des articles virulents et par conséquent de blesser les personnes que je mettais en cause. Il m'est arrivé d'être attaquée aussi et donc de sentir la morsure[2] des mots. Je dirais que c'est le jeu, en tout cas la règle qui s'applique aux personnes qui sont exposées, spécialement en politique où tous les coups semblent permis. Les journaux d'aujourd'hui, si on les compare avec ceux du siècle dernier, sont moins violents, du moins dans la forme. Il n'existe plus de grands polémistes[3]. Le dernier fut François Mauriac et c'était à *L'Express* entre 1956 et 1960. Son *Bloc-notes*[4] demeure un modèle dans l'art de « poser les banderilles ».

MARTINE DE RABAUDY.   *Le scénario qui a été votre formation est, dites-vous, la meilleure école d'écriture du journalisme.*

Attention, ce n'est plus vrai. Je parle d'une époque, celle où j'étais scénariste[5] dans les années 1940 où un bon film devait toujours raconter une histoire avec des ressorts[6] dramatiques. Le cinéma américain a conservé cette règle.

En France, la Nouvelle Vague et ses séquelles l'ont détruite, pour le meilleur

et pour le pire, jugeant que c'était du cinéma d'autrefois. J'ai appris à écrire un film avec Henri Georges Clouzot, entre autres. Un article bien construit, c'est un bon scénario. Il prend le lecteur par la main et celui-ci n'a plus envie de la lâcher[7]. Voilà en quoi je suis redevable[8] à cette formation.

Dans Le Voleur et la Maison vide, *Jean-François Revel témoigne*[9] : « *Françoise Giroud avait joué longtemps la couturière aux doigts de fée qui ravaudait les articles les plus bancals*[10] *et sirupeux. Elle raccourcissait*[11] *les phrases, supprimait les chevilles, éliminait les transitions pesantes*[12], *rajoutait des attaques et des conclusions frappantes*[13], *coupait et intervertissait les paragraphes, pressait le récit. Elle avait contribué à expurger le journalisme de son ton déclamatoire, didactique, raisonneur, pompeux et prolixe qui terrassait le lecteur.* » *Est-ce ça, la griffe*[14] *Giroud ?*

Ce que dit Revel est flatteur, ses remarques m'honorent. Avec l'équipe du journal, nous avions conscience d'avoir électrisé le style journalistique, trop souvent empêtré[15] dans des tics universitaires. Le journalisme n'est pas un sous-produit de la littérature, mais une discipline particulière, dont un magazine comme *Time* avait la totale maîtrise. On a tout cassé jusqu'à faire école en France. Et ça a marché !

---

1. *I happened to* 2. *bite* 3. *a polemist is someone who practices the art of disputation or controversy* 4. « *Scratch pad* » 5. *personne qui écrit des scénario de film* 6. *twists* 7. *to let go* 8. *indebted* 9. *declares* 10. *badly written* 11. *cuts short* 12. *heavy* 13. *striking* 14. *a trademark* 15. *tangled up in*

Active Reading Questions

1. **Qu'est-ce que représentent "les coups" qu'on sent? (les critiques)**
2. **Qu'est-ce qu'on peut faire aux personnes célèbres? (On peut les attaquer.)**
3. **Comment sont les journaux d'aujourd'hui par rapport à ceux du passé? (Ils sont moins violents.)**
4. **Qu'est-ce que Giroud faisait avant de devenir journaliste? (Elle écrivait des scénarios.)**
5. **D'après Giroud, comment est-ce qu'on doit écrire un article? (comme un bon scénario)**
6. **Quelle influence est-ce que Giroud a eu sur l'écriture journalistique? (Elle a changé et électrisé le style journalistique.)**
7. **Quel magazine est-ce que Giroud cite comme un bon modèle de journalisme? (*Time*)**

Fact or Opinion

As students read the article, have them stop periodically and summarize the main points. Then have them determine whether each point made is a fact or an opinion. Ask students if they agree with each opinion or not, and why.
✿ 1.2

 **Language Examination**

Lecture helps students prepare for Section 1, Part B: **Reading Comprehension**. The audio recording helps them prepare for Part A: **Listening—Short Narratives**.

Differentiated Instruction

SLOWER PACE LEARNERS

Extension Françoise Giroud is referring to a number of people in the interview (André Malraux, François Mauriac, Henri Georges Clouzot, Jean-François Revel, Gustave Flaubert, Jacques Duquesne). Assign one of these people to each student. Have students research the person's life and work in encyclopedias or on the Internet and report their findings to the class. This background knowledge may help students understand the main idea as well as details.
✿ 1.3, 3.1

MULTIPLE INTELLIGENCES

Interpersonal Ask students to imagine what their life would be like if they were to choose journalism as a career. What stories would they want to report? What countries would they dream of visiting? What skills would they need to have to be successful? Is this career dangerous, exciting, easy, or fun? Have students write in French and then have a class discussion. Focus on the interpersonal skills one must possess to be successful in this career.
✿ 1.3, 5.1

Active Reading Questions

1. **D'après Giroud, comment est-ce qu'on apprend l'écriture? (On ne l'apprend pas. On la travaille.)**

2. **Qui sont les personnes qui peuvent bien écrire? (les personnes qui ont un don et qui travaillent beaucoup)**

3. **Comment est-ce qu'on doit écrire pour éviter les assonances? (avec l'oreille)**

4. **Comment est-ce qu'on sait qu'un article est trop long? (si on peut couper dix lignes sans enlever une idée)**

5. **Quel est l'objectif d'un journal? (de répondre aux questions du lecteur)**

6. **Pourquoi est-ce que l'écriture est comme la danse? (Si on l'arrête, c'est difficile la reprendre.)**

7. **Qui est Jacques Duquesne? (l'autre "réparateur de style" à *L'Express*)**

8. **Pour Giroud, quand est-ce qu'un article est fini? (quand il est imprimé)**

❀ 1.2

Postreading Activity

Françoise Giroud was a very powerful public personality in France. Ask students how they would describe her personality and her attitude toward her work. What about her do they think contributed to her success? Ask them if they can think of anyone in the public eye at present who compares with her.

« *L'écriture ne s'apprend pas, elle se travaille* », *affirmez-vous.*

L'écriture ne s'apprend pas, donc ne s'enseigne pas. C'est une disposition naturelle. Comme pour le piano, on a le don[1] ou on ne l'a pas. Si on l'a, il faut travailler dur. Savoir qu'un adverbe est presque toujours superflu, un « qui » ou un « que » par phrase le maximum autorisé. Il faut écrire avec l'oreille, comme le faisait Flaubert, pour éviter[2] les assonances et les hiatus. Respecter la musique personnelle de chacun, cette qualité si rare. J'avais édicté[3] un certain nombre de règles simples. Numéro 1 : inutile d'avoir du talent à la cinquième ligne si le lecteur vous a lâché à la quatrième. Numéro 2 : si on peut couper dix lignes dans un article sans enlever une idée, c'est qu'elles étaient en trop. Numéro 3 : jamais de point d'interrogation dans un titre, cette vilaine manie[4] de la presse française. Un journal est là pour répondre aux questions des lecteurs, non pour en poser. Numéro 4 : par contre, placer un verbe dans un titre le renforce. Numéro 5 : suivre le conseil de Paul Valéry : de deux mots, choisir le moindre. Et le

moindre ne signifie pas le plus mou[5], le plus plat mais celui qui a... comment dire.. la taille la plus fine.

Ne pas oublier que l'écriture est comme la danse, il ne faut jamais arrêter les exercices à la barre. Après une interruption un peu prolongée, la reprise[6] est dure. À *L'Express*, je n'étais pas seule à effectuer le métier de « réparateur de style[7] », ainsi défini par Revel. Jacques Duquesne était excellent. Les soirs de « bouclage[8] », il reprenait toute la copie ayant besoin d'une remise en forme. C'était précieux. Cette façon de travailler importée de la presse anglo-saxonne porte le nom de « rewriting ». Elle demeure, je crois.

Angelo Rinaldi raconte qu'un soir où il vous avait accompagnée à la Comédie-Française, dès le spectacle terminé, vous lui aviez dit : « Je retourne au journal changer un mot dans mon papier », il ajoute « Avec elle, un papier n'était jamais fini. »

C'est amusant ce que raconte Rinaldi, et vrai... Chaque mot doit être le mieux approprié, le moins banal[9], sans être précieux. Le premier n'est pas toujours le bon et ça vous obsède. Il m'est arrivé plus d'une fois, l'ayant enfin trouvé, d'aller au journal, à toute heure, l'inscrire dans un de mes articles ou dans celui d'un autre. Tant que le journal n'est pas calé sur machine[10], la tentation est permanente de perfectionner un papier, un titre, une légende...

---

1. *the gift* **2.** *to avoid* **3.** décidé **4.** habitude **5.** *weakest* **6.** revenir **7.** réécrire **8.** *finalizing your article* **9.** commun **10.** *on press*

Core Instruction

LECTURE

1. Finish reading *Profession journaliste* as a class from "**L'écriture ne s'apprend pas** [...]", at the top of page 248. Do students agree that writing cannot be learned? **(15 min.)**

2. Complete **Compréhension** and **Après la lecture** as a class. **(10 min.)**

Chapitre 6

Lecture

Online Practice
go.hrw.com
Online Edition
KEYWORD: BD3 CH6

Compréhension 🌸1.2

B Complète les phrases suivantes selon la lecture.

1. Mme Giroud a appris à bien écrire en écrivant...
2. Jean-François Revel dit que Mme Giroud a changé...
3. Le magazine *Time* illustre que le journalisme est...
4. La meilleure façon d'apprendre à bien écrire est...
5. Les premières lignes d'un article doivent...
6. L'objectif d'un article est...
7. Mme Giroud compare l'écriture avec deux arts: ... et ...
8. Selon Mme Giroud, il est important de toujours choisir le mot...

Answers may vary. Possible answers:

1. des scénarios / films
2. le style du journalisme
3. une discipline particulière
4. d'écrire / de pratiquer
5. capter l'attention du lecteur
6. d'informer
7. la musique; la danse
8. juste / exact

C Utilise **la stratégie pour lire** pour deviner le sens des mots en gras dans les phrases suivantes. 🌸1.2

1. « Je dirais que c'est le jeu, en tout cas la règle qui s'applique aux personnes qui sont **exposées...**»
   a. connues   **b.** responsables   **c.** timides
2. «Un article bien **construit,** c'est un bon scénario.»
   a. lu   **b.** dessiné   **c.** écrit
3. « Avec l'équipe du journal, nous avions conscience d'avoir **électrisé** le style journalistique... »
   a. crée   **b.** revitalisé   **c.** travaillé
4. « ...cette **vilaine** manie de la presse française. »
   a. mauvaise   **b.** ridicule   **c.** bonne
5. «...l'**inscrire** dans un de mes articles...»
   a. enrôler   **b.** écrire   **c.** lire

Après la lecture 🌸1.2, 1.3

D D'après Françoise Giroud, quelles sont les caractéristiques d'un bon article? Maintenant, compare ce que tu as écrit dans **Avant la lecture** avec les commentaires de Mme Giroud. Sur quels points est-ce que vous êtes d'accord? Sur quels points vos opinions sont différentes?

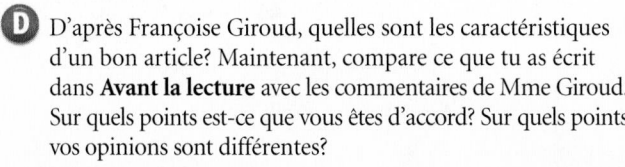

Connections
History Link

The political orientation of *L'Express* was defined largely by Jean-Jacques Servan-Schreiber, who was against colonization and wrote a series of articles on the Indochinese conflict. Servan-Schreiber was an ardent supporter of Pierre Mendès-France, who strongly opposed the French military effort in Indochina. The election of Mendès-France as prime minister was on top of the agenda of *L'Express*. Because of government seizures and censorship, the magazine quickly became popular with the youth and the intellectuals of the 1950s and 1960s. Servan-Schreiber opposed General de Gaulle's return to power in 1958. Thus, when De Gaulle became president anyway, *L'Express* lost some of its political clout. Later, however, *L'Express* soared in popularity once again with its coverage of women's liberation. Today, the magazine has a right-of-center orientation and a circulation of 542,900. Have students research France's involvement in Indochina. 🌸3.1, 3.2

Differentiated Instruction

ADVANCED LEARNERS

Challenge Giroud states that good writing follows five basic rules. Ask students to read some of the articles in the online version of *L'Express* and decide whether or not the authors follow Giroud's guidelines. Students should present their conclusions to the class, citing examples from the articles that comply or do not comply with each guideline. 🌸1.3, 3.2

SPECIAL LEARNING NEEDS

Students with Learning Disabilities To help students with learning disabilities in reading the significant amount of text in **Lecture,** pair students based on reading ability so that advanced and slower readers are partnered up. Pairs take turns reading the text and answering the **Compréhension** questions together. Both students share the same grade as both put forth equal effort in the assignment. 🌸1.2

Assess

Assessment Program
Quiz: Lecture
Online Assessment
my.hrw.com
Test Generator

L'atelier de l'écrivain

Interactive TUTOR

Resources

Planning:
Lesson Planner
 One-Stop Planner
Practice:
Cahier d'activités

Process Writing
When students exchange their articles for review, encourage them to read each other's article twice. During the first reading, they should consider only the content of the article, checking that all necessary information has been included. During the second reading, they should read for style.

Teaching Suggestion
Have students find a French news article online and bring a copy to class. Ask students to read the headline and the first sentence of their article to the class. Discuss the components and style of the headline. Then decide as a class whether the first sentence "hooks" the reader or not, and why.

Connections

History Link
The French novelist Émile Zola (1840–1902) has written the news article that has caused more controversy in France than any other article ever has. Zola risked his career and his life when his article, *J'accuse,* was published in the Paris daily *L'Aurore* on January 13, 1898. An open letter to the French President, the article accused the French government of anti-Semitism and of wrongfully jailing Alfred Dreyfus. One of its most memorable quotes is, **"la vérité est en marche et rien ne l'arrêtera"**. Have students research the Dreyfus Affair and its impact on French law and society.   3.1, 3.2

Reportage: entrer dans le vif

Tu viens de lire une entrevue avec Françoise Giroud, une journaliste très célèbre. C'est à ton tour d'imaginer que tu es journaliste. Tu travailles pour un hebdomadaire dont Mme Giroud est la rédactrice en chef. Tu dois écrire un article sur l'actualité, l'économie, les faits divers, les sports, la culture ou le monde des spectacles. Suis les règles mentionnées dans la lecture et utilise la stratégie pour écrire.

1 **Plan: causes à effets**   1.3

Choisis le sujet de ton article. Il est important que ton reportage soit informatif et très clair. Organise tes informations dans un tableau. Dessine un carré sur une feuille de papier. Sur la première ligne du carré, écris *Cause* et ce qui s'est passé. Au-dessous, écris des détails. Tu dois mentionner ce qui s'est passé, quand, où et comment. Dessine au moins trois flèches. Dessine un carré au bout de chaque flèche. Dans chaque carré, écris le mot *Effet* et une conséquence.

STRATÉGIE pour écrire

Defining your style Style is a term for the distinctive features that characterize a piece of writing. What you are writing, whether it be a letter to a friend or an academic report, determines the style to use. Journalistic style often includes short sentences that get right to the point with precise words and action verbs. Headlines, captions, and the first sentence in an article usually "hook" the reader. They state what the article is about and make the reader want to know more.   3.1

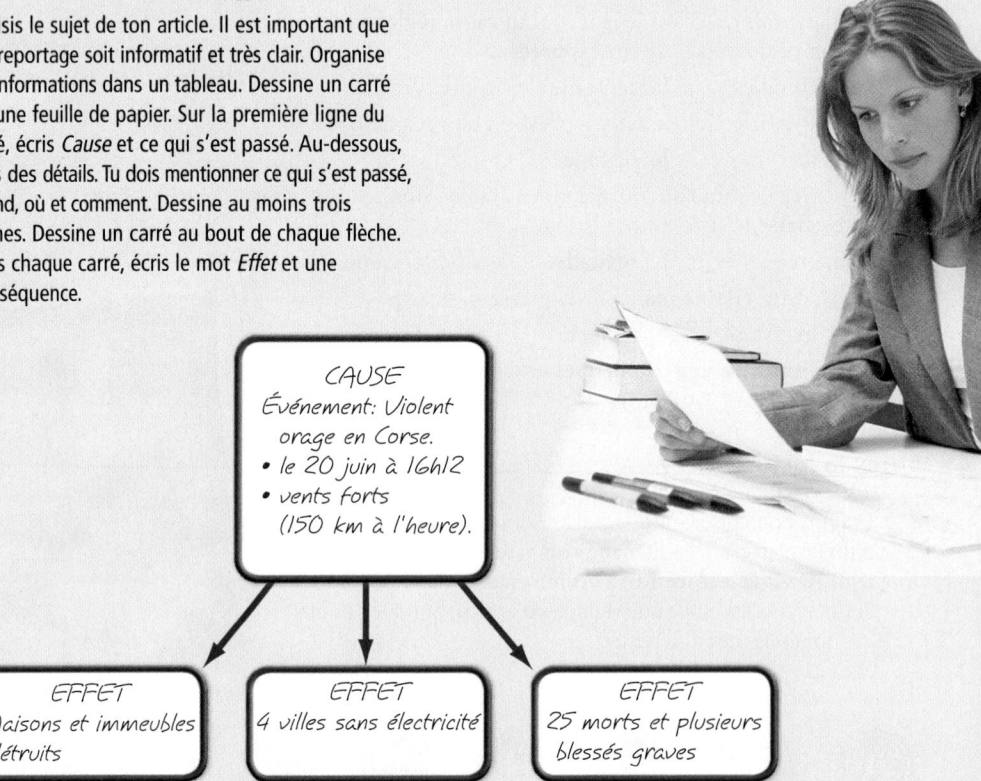

CAUSE
Événement: Violent orage en Corse.
• le 20 juin à 16h12
• vents forts (150 km à l'heure).

EFFET
Maisons et immeubles détruits

EFFET
4 villes sans électricité

EFFET
25 morts et plusieurs blessés graves

Core Instruction

L'ATELIER DE L'ÉCRIVAIN

1. Read aloud the assignment and have students choose their topic. Make sure that all areas of the news (sports, entertainment, the economy, and so on) are covered. **(5 min.)**

2. Review the writing rules in *Profession journaliste.* Have students paraphrase the rules to make sure they understand them. Discuss **Stratégie pour écrire. (10 min.)**

3. Go over the additional vocabulary and **L'infinitif. (5 min.)**

4. Assign steps 1 and 2 as homework. Suggest that students find illustrations to accompany their articles.

5. Have students complete step 3. **(30 min.)**

6. Lead a class discussion to complete step 4. Once the magazine is posted online, you might announce its availability in your community to foster interest in French. **(10 min.)**

L'atelier de l'écrivain

② Rédaction ✿1.3

Fais un brouillon de ton article. Utilise la structure et les informations de ton tableau des causes à effets. Ajoute:

- des faits,
- des descriptions précises,
- des statistiques,
- des citations de témoins ou d'experts.

Essaie d'écrire de manière organisée et logique. Après avoir écrit le corps de ton article, écris le gros titre. Choisis les images que tu veux inclure et écris les légendes qui les accompagneront.

③ Correction ✿1.3

Maintenant, c'est le moment de corriger ton article. Échange ton article avec celui d'un(e) camarade. Vérifiez que:

- la première phrase engage l'attention du lecteur,
- l'article explique ce qui s'est passé, où, quand et comment,
- les phrases sont courtes et directes avec des mots précis et des verbes d'action,
- il n'y a pas de mots ou de phrases superflus,

Ensuite, fais les corrections sugérées par ton/ta camarade. Corrige les fautes d'orthographe, de vocabulaire et de grammaire. Assure-toi que tu as employé correctement les infinitifs et que tu as bien conjugué les verbes. Écris la version finale de ton article. N'oublie pas les photos ou les dessins avec leurs légendes.

④ Application ✿1.3

Compilez tous les articles de la classe pour en faire un magazine. Décidez ensemble du nom du magazine ainsi que des images et des gros titres qui apparaîtront en couverture. Une fois fini, distribuez votre magazine aux autres classes de français ou téléchargez-le sur le site Web de la classe.

Gagner impérativement !

L'équipe des Spurs doit absolument gagner ce samedi si elle veut encore avoir une chance d'être en finale.

L'équipe des Spurs n'a plus le droit à l'erreur

Vocabulaire à la carte

à cause de	because of
aboutir à	to lead to
avoir lieu	to take place
la crise	crisis
être en jeu	to be at stake
la question	issue, matter
selon les derniers sondages	according to the latest polls

The infinitive

The infinitive can be used as:

- the **subject** of a sentence.

  Avoir un diplôme n'assure pas un travail.

- the complement to the main verb, placed directly after the main verb or after the preposition **à** or **de**

  L'équipe française doit gagner la Coupe du monde de football.

  Le ministre de l'économie a réussi à gérer la crise.

  Le président risque de perdre les élections.

L'atelier de l'écrivain

L'infinitif

Have students use the words to make complete sentences.

1. jouer bien / être / plus important / que / gagner
   (**Bien jouer est plus important que gagner.**)
2. nous / avoir besoin / sauvegarder / planète
   (**Nous avons besoin de sauvegarder la planète.**)
3. président / espérer / sortir / crise
   (**Le président espère sortir de la crise.**)
4. orages / continuer / s'abattre / côte
   (**Des orages continuent à s'abattre sur la côte.**)

✿1.2

Writing Assessment

To assess **L'atelier de l'écrivain,** you can use the following rubric. For additional rubrics, see the *Assessment Program.*

Writing Rubric	4	3	2	1
Content (Complete—Incomplete)				
Comprehensibility (Comprehensible— Seldom comprehensible)				
Accuracy (Accurate—Seldom accurate)				
Organization (Well-organized—Poorly organized)				
Effort (Excellent effort— Minimal effort)				

18-20: A	14-15: C	Under 12: F
16-17: B	12-13: D	

Differentiated Instruction

SLOWER PACE LEARNERS

① Additional Practice Before they complete step 1, have students suggest French conjunctions that are commonly used to explain the consequences or effects of an action (**ainsi, alors, donc**) and conjunctions that are used to draw conclusions or relate a cause or explanation with a result or conclusion (**parce que, car, puisque, comme**). Encourage students to use these conjunctions in their articles. ✿1.1, 1.2

SPECIAL LEARNING NEEDS

Students with AD(H)D Ask students to imagine that they are sports writers. Have them write a captivating title and opening line about the weekend's top five sporting events. Students may choose any five sporting events they wish, but their assignment is to create, in French, a catchy title and opening first sentence for the news article. Ask students to illustrate their assignment with photos or art work. ✿1.3

Assess

Assessment Program

Quiz: Écriture

Online Assessment
my.hrw.com

Test Generator

VIDEO OPTIONS

▶ **Télé-culture: Interviews**

TPRS
You may wish to use the Picture Sequences Transparency that accompanies Activity 7 for a TPRS activity.

French for Spanish Speakers

Ask Spanish speakers how they would translate **quelque** as it is used in **Elle a quelques amis.** (**Ella tiene algunos amigos**) How would students translate **quelquefois**? (**A veces** or **de vez en cuando** could be used.) Ask students how they would translate, **Quelqu'un a laissé quelque chose sur la table.** (**Alguien dejó algo sobre la mesa.**) 🍀4.1

---

② Answers

1. Je ne suis pas certaine que le magazine paraisse...
2. Je doute que tu t'abonnes...
3. Je ne pense pas qu'il fasse...
4. Je ne suis pas sûre que tu aies...
5. Ça m'étonnerait que ton voisin soit...

① Regarde les photos et trouve leur légende. 🍀1.2 **1.** d **2.** b **3.** c **4.** a

① Vocabulaire 1
• to express certainty and possibility
• to express doubt and disbelief
pp. 224–227

 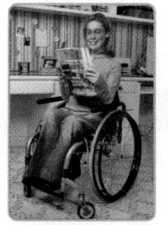  
a.   b.   c.   d.

1. Il doit acheter le journal parce qu'il n'est pas abonné.
2. Les revues de mode lui plaisent.
3. Il lit le journal tous les jours.
4. Il trouve les dessins humoristiques amusants.

② Grammaire 1
• the subjunctive with doubt, disbelief, and uncertainty
• the verbs **croire** and **paraître**
Un peu plus
• **quelque part, quelqu'un, quelque chose,** and **quelquefois**
pp. 228–233

② Sara doute de tout ce que Léa dit. Varie les expressions de doute. 🍀1.2

MODÈLE Je suis sûre qu'il a le dernier numéro.
Je doute qu'il ait le dernier numéro.

1. Je suis certaine que ce magazine paraît tous les mois.
2. Je vais m'abonner à une revue de science-fiction.
3. Il fait ses devoirs avant de lire les dessins humoristiques.
4. Je suis sûre que tu as la dernière édition.
5. Je pense que mon voisin est rédacteur en chef au *Monde*.

③ À quelle section ces articles appartiennent? Trouve-leur un titre. 🍀1.2, 3.2

③ Vocabulaire 2
• to break news
• to ask for information
pp. 236–239

Des artistes québécois montreront et vendront leurs œuvres. C'est l'occasion d'acheter une œuvre originale à un prix raisonnable.

1.

L'empereur du Japon en visite au Québec.

2.

Answers will vary.
1. art: L'art pour tous
2. actualité internationale: Vive l'empereur!
3. sports: Enfin, une victoire!
4. météo: L'hiver est là!

L'équipe de France a gagné le match contre l'Allemagne. C'est seulement la deuxième victoire française cette saison.

3.

Des records de température ont été enregistrés hier. Il faisait -15 degrés! Et on ne prévoit pas de changement d'ici la fin de la semaine.

4.

Preparing for the Exam

RETEACHING

Review the use of the subjunctive with doubt and uncertainty. **Je doute que ce film ait du succès.** Remind students that the verb **croire** can be followed by the subjunctive or by the indicative, depending on whether is expresses uncertainty or disbelief, or certainty. To practice, begin a sentence **Je crois...** or **Je ne crois pas...** Have students finish the sentence with the subjunctive or the indicative. Explain the correct response after each sentence.

TEST-TAKING STRATEGY

Remind students to recall the chart on page 242 when they are trying to figure out when to use **qui est-ce qui, qui est-ce que, qu'est-ce qui,** or **qu'est-ce que.** Ask students to remember one simple sentence with each form.

4 Réponds aux questions. Utilise des pronoms dans tes réponses. 🍀1.3

> **MODÈLE** —Est-ce que tu as acheté déjà le journal?
> **—Oui, je l'ai déjà acheté.**

1. Veux-tu aller au parc? (non)
2. Est-ce que tu t'es abonné(e) à ce magazine? (oui)
3. Est-ce que ton copain a téléphoné à la personne qui s'occupe du courrier des lecteurs? (non)
4. Est-ce que tu as lu la météo pour ce week-end? Je sais que tu veux aller faire du camping. (oui)
5. As-tu parlé de ton idée à la rédactrice en chef? (non)

5 Réponds aux questions suivantes. 🍀2.1

1. Qu'est-ce que c'est, un **blog?**
2. Qu'est-ce qu'il faut pour être journaliste au Québec?
3. Quelles sont les langues officielles en Haïti?

CD 6, Tr. 8   **1.** e **2.** d **3.** c **4.** f **5.** a

6  Quel est le mot qui correspond à chaque définition? 🍀1.2

a. le dessin humoristique	**c.** une grève	**e.** la météo
b. une couverture	**d.** le kiosque	**f.** la une

7 Dis ce qui se passe sur ces illustrations. 🍀1.3

Oral Assessment

To assess the speaking activities in this section, you might use the following rubric. For additional speaking rubrics, see the Alternative Assessment section of the *Assessment Program*.

Speaking Rubric	4	3	2	1
Content (Complete—Incomplete)				
Comprehension (Total—Little)				
Comprehensibility (Comprehensible—Incomprehensible)				
Accuracy (Accurate—Seldom Accurate)				
Fluency (Fluent—Not Fluent)				

18-20: A   16-17: B   14-15: C   12-13: D   Under 12: F

Online Assessment
go.hrw.com
Chapter Self–test
KEYWORD: BD3 CH6

Chapitre 6

Prépare-toi pour l'examen

Prépare-toi pour l'examen

4 Grammaire 2
- object pronouns
- **qui est-ce qui, qui est-ce que, qu'est-ce qui,** and **qu'est-ce que**

Un peu plus
- more negative expressions
pp. 240–245

5 Culture
- Comparaisons p. 235
- Flash culture pp. 226, 230, 238

4 Answers
1. Non, je ne veux pas y aller.
2. Oui, je m'y suis abonné(e).
3. Non, il ne lui a pas téléphoné.
4. Oui, je l'ai lue.
5. Non, je ne lui en ai pas parlé.

5 Answers
1. C'est un cyberjournal.
2. Il ne faut pas faire d'études.
3. Le français et le créole.

6 Script
1. Elle donne le temps qu'il va faire.
2. On peut y acheter des journaux et des magazines.
3. C'est quand les gens refusent de travailler.
4. C'est la première page d'un journal.
5. C'est fait pour faire rire.

PRE-AP PRÉPARATOIRE Language Examination

To display the drawings to the class, use the Picture Sequences Transparency for Chapter 6.

7 Sample answer

a. Sébastien lit la météo. On prévoit de la pluie, mais il fait du soleil dehors.

b. Sébastien lit la section sports qui dit que l'Italie a gagné le match. À la télé, on montre que la France a gagné.

c. Sébastien lit qu'on passe un nouveau film au cinéma cette semaine, mais le film est déjà à la télé.

d. Son copain regarde la date du journal. C'est une vieille édition!

Prépare-toi pour l'examen

Grammar Review

For more practice with the grammar topics in this chapter, see the *Grammar Tutor*, the *Interactive Tutor*, or the *Cahier de vocabulaire et grammaire*.

Online Edition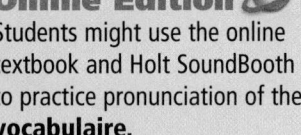

Students might use the online textbook and Holt SoundBooth to practice pronunciation of the **vocabulaire**.

Proverbes

For French proverbs and activities related to the chapter theme and vocabulary, see **Proverbes et expressions**, pp. R6–R7

Cultures

Products and Perspectives

Elle is a women's magazine that was founded in France in 1945 by Helene Lazareff. Françoise Giroud was editor-in-chief of *Elle* from 1945 to 1953. The magazine aimed to be provocative. Beginning with its first issue, *Elle* tried to change the French view of female domesticity in the postwar period. Although the magazine promoted images of women as voters and professionals, it stressed women's primary roles as mothers and wives. Today, *Elle* is read worldwide with 37 editions and more than 20 million readers. Ask students to research a recent copy of *Elle* and report on its portrayal of French women. ✿ 2.2, 3.2

COMMON ERROR ALERT
//// ATTENTION !

Students may erroneously think it is necessary to add **pas** to negative expressions such as **ne... nulle part** and **ne ... aucun(e)**. They may write, "**Je n'ai pas aucune idée**," or "**Je ne le trouve pas nulle part.**"

Grammaire 1
- the subjunctive with doubt, disbelief, and uncertainty
- the verbs **croire** and **paraître**

Un peu plus
- **quelque part, quelqu'un, quelque chose,** and **quelquefois**
pp. 228–233

Résumé: Grammaire 1

Use the **subjunctive** with expressions of *doubt* and *uncertainty*. Use the **indicative** with expressions of *certainty*,

Je ne pense pas qu'il puisse venir ce soir.
Je pense qu'il viendra ce soir.

The verb **croire** is conjugated like **voir**

paraître			
je	parais	nous	paraissons
tu	parais	vous	paraissez
il/elle/on	paraît	ils/elles	paraissent
past participle: paru			

Quelque, meaning *some*, is used in many expressions.

quelquefois *sometimes* **quelque chose** *something*,
quelqu'un *someone* **quelque part** *somewhere*.

Grammaire 2
- object pronouns
- **qui est-ce qui, qui est-ce que, qu'est-ce qui,** and **qu'est-ce que**

Un peu plus
- more negative expressions
pp. 240–245

Résumé: Grammaire 2

Object pronouns (**me, te, nous, vous, le, la, les, lui, leur, y, en**) replace the nouns that are being used as direct and indirect objects. They follow a specific order if there is more than one in a sentence.

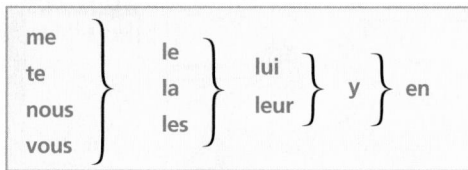

The words for *what*, *who*, and *whom* depend on whether the question word is the *subject* or *object* of a sentence.

	PERSON	THING
SUBJECT	qui est-ce qui	qu'est-ce qui
OBJECT	qui est-ce que	qu'est-ce que

Two negative expressions are **ne...aucun(e)** and **ne... nulle part**.

Chapter Review

Teacher Management System
Password: admin
For more details, log on to www.hrw.com/CDROMTUTOR.

Create a variety of puzzles to review chapter vocabulary.

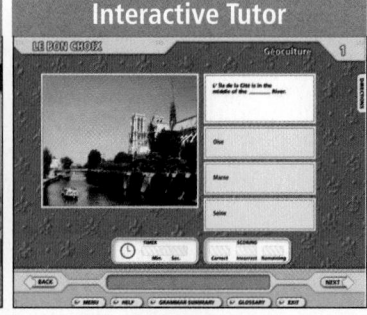

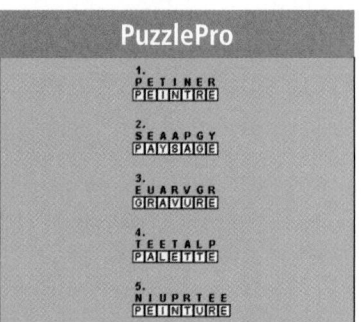

Résumé: Vocabulaire 1

 HOLT SoundBooth ONLINE RECORDING

To express certainty

s'abonner à	to subscribe
un article	article
un/une chômeur(-euse)	unemployed person
consacré(e)	established/accepted
la couverture	cover
le dessin humoristique	cartoon
développer	to develop
l'édition (f.)	edition/issue
un extraterrestre	extraterrestrial
un hebdomadaire	weekly
un kiosque à journaux	news stand
la légende	caption
le magazine féminin	women's magazine
le marchand de journaux	news stand attendant
un mensuel	monthly (magazine)
les nouvelles (f.)	news
le numéro précédent	previous issue

paraître	to be published/to appear
la première page/la une	front page
la presse (spécialisée)	(specialized) press
la presse à sensation	tabloids
publier	to publish
un quotidien	daily (newspaper)
le rédacteur/la rédactrice en chef	editor-in-chief
une revue	journal
le (gros) titre	headline
la vérité	truth
Je suis certain(e) que ...	I am sure that . . .
Je suis sûr(e) que...	I am sure that . . .
Il/Elle est persuadé(e) que...	He/She is convinced that . . .

To express possibility .... *See p. 225*
To express doubt and disbelief .... *See p. 227*

Résumé: Vocabulaire 2

Rubrics

l'actualité internationale (f.)	current events
un accident	accident
un/une athlète	athlete
un attentat	terrorist attack
une augmentation	raise
une catastrophe	catastrophe
le chômage	unemployment
la collection	collection
le courrier des lecteurs	letters to the Editor
le/la critique	critic
la culture	culture
durer	to last
l'économie (f.)	economy
être en baisse	to be falling
être en colère	to be angry
enregistrer	to record
une équipe	crew/team
les faits divers (m.)	news items
grâce à	thanks to
gratuit(e)	free
une grève/être en grève	strike/to be on strike
une médaille d'or	gold medal

la météo	weather forecast
le ministre du travail	secretary of Labor
une œuvre	work of art
un/une patineur(-euse)	skater
les petites annonces (f.)	classified ads
un record	record
refléter	to reflect
remporter	to carry away
une rubrique	section of a magazine
s'abattre (sur)	to strike
se réjouir	to delight
la société	society
le succès	success
le tableau	painting
la température	temperature
une vague de chaleur	heat wave
une victoire	victory
un vol/le voleur	theft/thief

To break news and to respond .... *See p. 237*
To ask about information .... *See p. 239*

Game

Chaîne Have all students stand up. Announce the vocabulary theme for this game: "News in print." Say a sentence with one word from the theme. For example, **Chaque jour je lis les faits divers.** The first player must repeat your sentence in the first person and adds another word that follows the theme. **Chaque jour je lis les faits divers et la météo.** When a player says the 'chain' incorrectly, he or she sits down. The last three students left standing are the winners of the game. 1.1

Online Edition

Transparency: Vocabulaire

Transparency: Situation

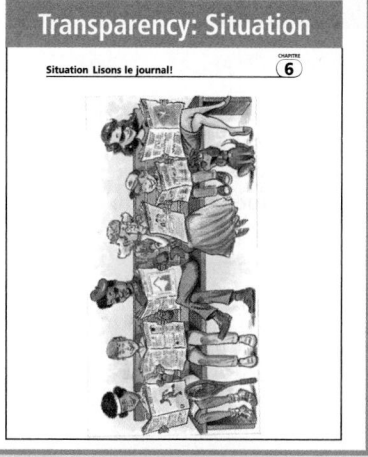

Assess

Assessment Program

Examen: Chapitre 6
Audio CD 6, Trs. 13, 14

Examen oral: Chapitre 6
Alternative Assessment
Differentiated Practice and
   Assessment CD-ROM

Online Assessment
   my.hrw.com

Test Generator

Activités préparatoires

Resources

Planning:
Lesson Planner
 One-Stop Planner

Practice:
Cahier de vocabulaire et grammaire
Differentiated Practice and Assessment CD-ROM
 Teaching Transparencies Picture Sequences, Chapter 6
Cahier d'activités
 Audio CD 6, Tr. 9

VIDEO OPTIONS

▶ **Télé-culture: Interviews**

The AP French Language Exam

Activités préparatoires provide students with activities similar to those found in the Advanced Placement French Language exam. The activities are based on material taught up to and including this chapter and concentrate on the chapter grammar and vocabulary.

Listening Script

1. — Regarde cet article sur la plongée. Il est génial!
   — Et en voici un autre sur la planche à voile! C'est un magazine qui traite de tous les sports nautiques. Je voudrais m'y abonner. Et il paraît chaque semaine, n'est-ce pas?
2. — Oh non, le musée est fermé. Tu sais pourquoi?

Reading Strategy

Tell students to look for words or phrases in the selection that match those in the questions. Caution them, however, that a particular choice is not necessarily correct just because it contains words that appear in the selection.

SECTION I

Listening CD 6, Tr. 9 1.2

Listen to the dialogues and choose the most appropriate response.

1. **A.** Oui, c'est une publication hebdomadaire
   B. Oui, c'est une publication quotidienne.
   C. Oui, c'est une publication mensuelle.
   D. Oui, c'est une publication annuelle.

2. **A.** Ah oui, c'était à cause d'une vague de chaleur.
   B. Ah oui, il y a eu un accident de voiture.
   C. Ah oui, deux tableaux de maître ont disparu.
   D. Ah oui, c'était à cause du chômage.

Reading 1.2

Read the following paragraph and answer the questions that follow.

> **Sept alpinistes français et onze Népalais sont morts dans l'Himalaya**
>
> Sept Français et onze Népalais, portés disparus depuis jeudi, ont trouvé la mort au cours d'une tempête de neige dans le massif de l'Annapurna
> 5 (nord-ouest du Népal), selon des informations diffusées, dimanche 23 octobre, par des chaînes de télévision locales. L'expédition était dirigée par un professeur de l'École
> 10 nationale de ski et d'alpinisme (ENSA) de Chamonix (Haute-Savoie), Daniel Stolzenberg, a-t-on appris dimanche auprès de son entourage... Les alpinistes, accompagnés par onze
> 15 porteurs et guides népalais, avaient l'intention de gravir le mont Kang Guru (6.981 m) dans le nord-ouest de l'Himalaya, au Népal, près de l'Annapurna (8.091 m). Ils ont été
> 20 surpris par une tempête de neige.

1. Combien de personnes sont mortes?
   A. 7
   B. 11
   C. 23
   D. 18

2. Un «massif» c'est...
   A. une chaîne de montagnes.
   B. une chaîne de télévision.
   C. un pays.
   D. une tempête.

3. La destination de l'expédition était...
   A. l'Annapurna.
   B. le mont Kang Guru.
   C. Chamonix.
   D. les Alpes.

4. L'expédition est morte...
   A. de soif.
   B. de faim.
   C. dans une tempête de neige.
   D. de surprise.

Preparing for the Exam

ADDITIONAL PRACTICE

Ask a question, using **qu'est-ce que, qu'est-ce qui, qui est-ce que, qui est-ce qui**. Tell students to give you an evasive answer. Use **quelqu'un** or **quelque chose**. (Qu'est-ce que tu vois? – Je vois quelque chose. Qui est-ce qui parle? – Quelqu'un parle.)   1.1

TEST-TAKING STRATEGIES

Section I: Listening Encourage students to focus their attention on the content of the listening selection, rather than on the sound of the readers' voices.

Section II: Writing Tell students to read the directions very carefully. If the directions say to fill in the blank with one word, using more than one word will result in an incorrect answer.

Online Practice
go.hrw.com
Online Edition

KEYWORD: BD3 CH6

The following activities can be used to help you to prepare for the Advanced Placement French Language examination, or to further practice the vocabulary and grammar concepts you have seen in this chapter.

Activités préparatoires

Activités préparatoires

SECTION II

Writing ✿1.2

In the following conversation, some phrases have been omitted. Complete each sentence by using the correct QUELQUE form according to the context.

> —J'ai lu _quelque chose_ d'intéressant dans le journal ce matin. Il y a vingt ans, _quelqu'un_ a volé un objet d'art. La police l'a trouvé _quelque part_ dans une collection privée.

> —Ça arrive _quelquefois_. Ce n'est pas sans précédent.

> —Oui, mais cette fois-ci, on l'a trouvé chez mon ancien prof de français!

In the following conversation, fill in each blank with the two object pronouns that correctly complete the meaning and context of the sentence:

> —Chéri, tu pourrais donner de l'argent à Laurent.

> —Oui, je _lui en_ donne avant de partir.

> —Et, cette lettre que j'ai écrite à mes parents, tu _la leur_ as envoyée?

> —Oui. Ah, le journal vient d'arriver. Donne-_le-moi_, s'il te plaît.

> —Je _te le_ donne tout de suite.

Essay Topic ✿1.3

Write in French a well-organized and coherent composition (10 to 15 lines) on the following topic.

> À votre avis, la presse écrite sera-t-elle remplacée un jour par la télévision et par Internet? Pourquoi ou pourquoi pas?

Speaking ✿1.2

Look at the following drawing, then tell a story about what is occurring in the picture.

Writing Strategy

Tell students to make sure they address the question that was asked. As they prepare to write, they need to look for key words in the questions that tell them what to do, such as, "explain", "discuss", "compare", or "describe".

Language Examination

To display the drawings to the class, use the **Activités préparatoires** Transparency for Chapter 6.

7 Speaking: Sample answer

Il fait mauvais et il pleut. Alors, toute la famille reste à l'intérieur. Le père est assis dans un fauteuil. Il lit la rubrique économie. Il n'est pas content parce que le prix des actions est en baisse. La mère lit la rubrique culture. Le petit garçon rit à cause du dessin humoristique. La jeune fille est allongée sur le sofa. Elle lit plusieurs magazines féminins. L'autre garçon cherche la météo sur Internet. Il devrait faire beau partout en France. Il ne comprend pas pourquoi il pleut.

You might also ask students the following question.

Selon vous, est-ce qu'il vaut mieux lire ou regarder la télé quand vous devez rester à l'intérieur? Pourquoi?

Differentiated Instruction

SLOWER PACE LEARNERS

Additional Practice Before students fill in the blanks in the second conversation of the Writing activity, ask volunteers to draw on the board a table that shows the placement of pronouns. Have students provide examples of the order of pronouns in commands and questions. Encourage them to refer to the table and the examples when completing the Writing activity. ✿1.2

SPECIAL LEARNING NEEDS

Students with Learning Disabilities In Section II, students might benefit from the use of a computer. Allow students to prepare notes and an outline of the Essay Topic and then type their final essay on a computer. The spelling and grammar check features assist students with the mechanics. The text should be double-spaced with a large font, so that it is easier to read for students as they are typing. ✿1.3

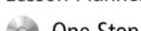

VIDEO OPTIONS

▶ **Géoculture**

▶ **Télé-roman: Camille et compagnie, Épisode 6**

❶ Script

1. — Notre équipe a gagné le match!
   — Oui, j'espère qu'ils vont gagner le championnat.
2. — Nous voulons une augmentation de salaire ou nous continuerons la grève!
3. — Bonjour, combien coûte *Le monde?*
   — 1 euro vingt. Vous le prenez?
   — Oui, s'il vous plaît. Merci!
4. — Tu regardes toujours les Jeux olympiques?
   — Oui, bien sûr!
5. — Je voudrais un journal en chinois.
   — Désolé, je n'en ai pas.

❷ Answers

1. Dans un magazine spécialisé qui s'adresse aux jeunes.
2. Il parle de l'amitié.
3. Answers will vary.
4. Answers will vary.

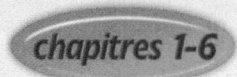
chapitres 1-6

Révisions cumulatives

CD 6, Tr. 10 ❀1.2 **1.** b **2.** c **3.** a **4.** b **5.** a

❶ Écoute les conversations et dis si on parle du dessin **a, b,** ou **c.**

a.   b.   c.

❷ Lis cet article et réponds aux questions suivantes.   ❀1.2, 1.3

L'ami(e) parfait(e), c'est quoi ?

Fais ce petit test pour savoir si tu es un(e) ami(e) parfait(e) :

1 Qu'est-ce que tu demandes à un(e) ami(e) :
★ de te dire la vérité
🌀 de faire la fête avec toi
⚠ tu ne sais pas

2 Ton ami(e) t'appelle au milieu de la nuit :
★ tu l'écoutes
🌀 tu lui dis de rappeler plus tard
⚠ tu ne réponds pas

3 Qu'est-ce qui détruit l'amitié :
★ être trop possessif
🌀 les histoires d'amour
⚠ les petites disputes

4 Ton/Ta meilleure ami(e) vient de rompre :
★ tu arrêtes tout pour l'écouter
🌀 tu penses qu'il/elle viendra te voir s'il/elle veut
⚠ tu lui dis : «un(e) de perdu(e), dix de retrouvé(e)s»

+ de ★ tu es l'ami(e) idéal(e)
+ de 🌀 tu devrais être plus sympa !
+ de ⚠ tu n'es vraiment pas sympa !

1. Dans quel genre de magazine paraît ce type d'article?
2. De quoi parle cet article? À qui s'adresse-t-il?
3. Est-ce que tu fais ce genre de test quand tu lis des magazines?
4. Fais le test et dis quel genre d'ami(e) tu es.

Online Culture Project

Have students research French newspapers and journals to find how the pages of various sections are formatted and how the articles are written. Then ask them to write an article, accompanied by a photo, for one particular section of the paper. The article should be approximately half a page long and should be based on the photo. Remind students to title their article and to document the names of the journals they researched.   ❀3.2

3 Un(e) de tes camarades te raconte quelque chose qu'il/elle a lu dans le journal. Tu mets en doute ce qu'il/elle te raconte. 🌸1.1

1.3,2.2

4 Regarde ce dessin de Toulouse-Lautrec et réponds aux questions.

1. Qu'est-ce que c'est *Le Rire*, à ton avis?

2. Où est-ce que la scène a lieu?

3. Crée une histoire pour expliquer ce qui se passe entre les deux personnes représentées sur cette illustration.

4. Est-ce que tu connais d'autres artistes qui ont illustré des revues ou des magazines? Lesquels?

Le snobisme de Toulouse-Lautrec

Snobbery caricature from the front cover of the magazine 'Le Rire', 4/24/1897. Henri Toulouse-Lautrec

5 Tu as des correspondants dans plusieurs pays et tu voudrais que tous tes amis puissent correspondre ensemble. Crée un blog en français dans lequel tu partages les événements de ta vie d'étudiant avec eux. 🌸1.3

6

Le journal local Avec des camarades, préparez un journal local. Chacun choisit une de ces rubriques:
- une demande d'emploi
- l'actualité internationale
- une rubrique sur les sports extrêmes
- la météo
- un fait divers
- un événement culturel

Ensuite présentez votre journal à la classe. 🌸1.3

ACTFL Performance Standards

The activities in Chapter 6 target the communicative modes as described in the Standards.

Interpersonal	Two-way communication using receptive skills and productive skills	**Communication (SE),** pp. 231, 233, 239, 241, 243, 245 **Communication (TE),** pp. 229, 231, 233, 241, 243, 245 **À ton tour,** p. 259
Interpretive	One-way communication using receptive skills	**Culture,** pp. 234–235 **Lecture,** pp. 246–249
Presentational	One-way communication using productive skills	**Communication (SE),** p. 227, 229 **Communication (TE),** pp. 227, 239

Révisions cumulatives

🖋 FINE ART CONNECTION

Introduction Henri de Toulouse-Lautrec (1864–1901) was born into an aristocratic family. As a child, he had fractured both legs, and a genetic disorder caused him to grow up with abnormally short legs. Lautrec coped with his disability by devoting himself to his art. He spent much of his life in the Parisian suburb of Montmartre, the center of bohemian life at the end of the nineteenth century. Lautrec became an important Post-impressionist painter, art nouveau illustrator, and lithographer. He contributed illustrations to the humourous magazine, **Le Rire.** Since his death in 1901, his paintings and posters have been in great demand, and they have sold for as much as $14.5 million.

Analyzing

Tell students that the lines below the painting read:

— **Jeanne, prends, sans qu'on te voie, mon porte-monnaie dans la poche gauche de mon pardessus.**

— **Et puis après?**

— **Tu me le passeras ostensiblement, au moment de payer, comme si c'était le tien.**

Ask students these questions.

1. **Pourquoi le monsieur demande-t-il à Jeanne de lui donner le porte-monnaie au moment de payer?**

2. **Pourquoi cette peinture est-elle intitulée "Snobisme"?** 🌸3.1

Extension

Le Rire was a successful humor magazine published between 1894 and the **Belle Époque.** Ask students to research how the contents of this magazine reflect the views that characterize the **Belle Époque.** 🌸3.1

Resources

Practice:

Reading Strategies and Skills Handbook

Advanced Reader

Applying the Strategies

You may want to use the "Say Something" strategy from the *Reading Strategies and Skills Handbook* to encourage students to examine the text more closely.

READING PRACTICE

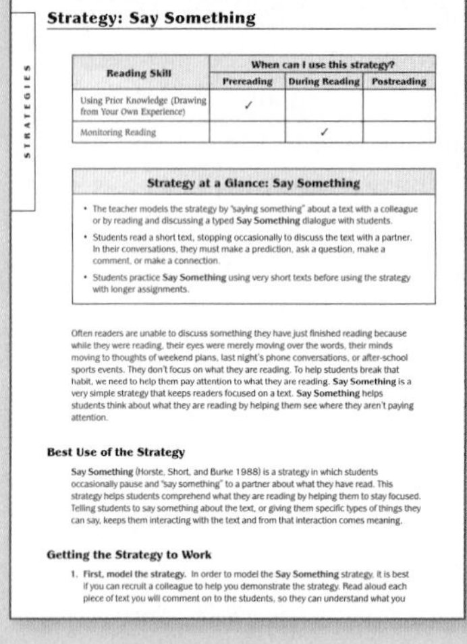

Strategy: Say Something

STRATEGIES

Reading Skill	When can I use this strategy?		
	Prereading	During Reading	Postreading
Using Prior Knowledge (Drawing from Your Own Experience)	✓		
Monitoring Reading		✓	

Strategy at a Glance: Say Something

- The teacher models the strategy by "saying something" about a text with a colleague or by reading and discussing a typed **Say Something** dialogue with students.
- Students read a short text, stopping occasionally to discuss the text with a partner. In their conversations, they must make a prediction, ask a question, make a comment, or make a connection.
- Students practice **Say Something** using very short texts before using the strategy with longer assignments.

Often readers are unable to discuss something they have just finished reading because while they were reading, their eyes were merely moving over the words, their minds moving to thoughts of weekend plans, last night's phone conversations, or after-school sports events. They don't focus on what they are reading. To help students break that habit, we need to help them pay attention to what they are reading. **Say Something** is a very simple strategy that keeps readers focused on a text. **Say Something** helps students think about what they are reading by helping them see where they aren't paying attention.

Best Use of the Strategy

Say Something (Horste, Short, and Burke 1988) is a strategy in which students occasionally pause and "say something" to a partner about what they have read. This strategy helps students comprehend what they are reading by helping them to stay focused. Telling students to say something about the text, or giving them specific types of things they can say, keeps them interacting with the text and from that interaction comes meaning.

Getting the Strategy to Work

1. **First, model the strategy.** In order to model the **Say Something** strategy, it is best if you can recruit a colleague to help you demonstrate the strategy. Read aloud each piece of text you will comment on to the students, so they can understand what you

Prereading

Before class, prepare three to five simple statements describing each animal in the **Chroniques** section. Before you begin, write the names of these animals on the board. Then read the statements you prepared, one at a time, and have students guess which animal each one describes. **Il a de très grandes oreilles. (C'est l'éléphant.)** 1.2

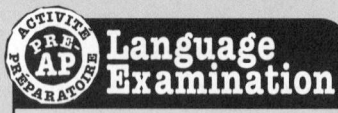

Language Examination

ACTIVITÉ PRÉ-AP PRÉPARATOIRE

The **Chroniques** section helps students prepare for Section I, Part B: **Reading Comprehension.**

CHRONIQUES

ANIMAUX D'AFRIQUE

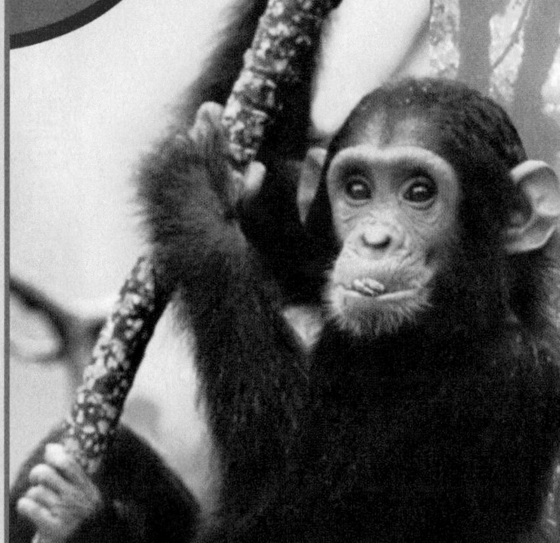

L'Afrique est un vrai paradis pour les amateurs d'animaux sauvages. Les spécimens suivants se retrouvent dans plusieurs pays francophones d'Afrique, comme le Mali, le Cameroun et le Sénégal.

Le gorille et le chimpanzé

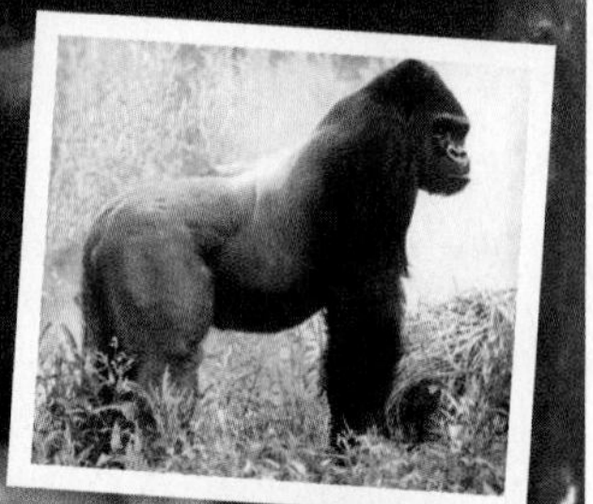

Le gorille et le chimpanzé se distinguent des autres singes par leur poids plus important, leur taille (de 70 cm à 1,90 m selon les espèces), mais surtout par un cerveau[1] plus développé et par certaines particularités physiques comme l'absence de queue[2].

Leur vue est meilleure que celle des autres primates et leurs membres antérieurs («bras») sont plus longs que leurs membres postérieurs.

Comme nous, ces grands singes ont un taux de reproduction bas[3] et vivent longtemps, quand ils ne sont pas menacés par l'intervention de l'homme, comme la guerre ou la chasse!

L'éléphant

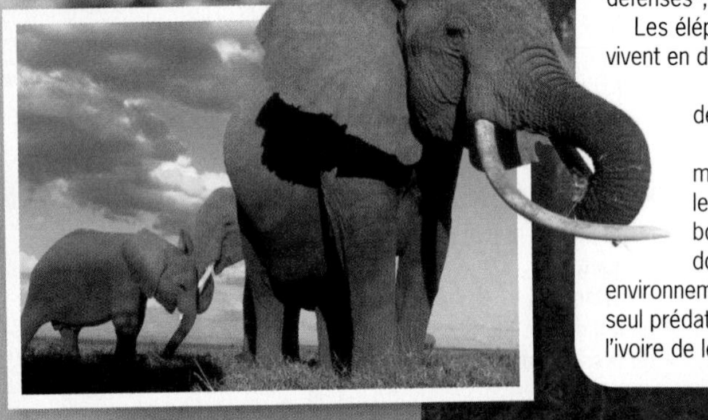

L'éléphant d'Afrique est plus grand que l'éléphant indien. Ses oreilles sont très grandes et il a d'énormes défenses[4], qui peuvent dépasser 3 mètres.

Les éléphants vivent en société matriarcale, les mâles vivent en dehors des groupes de femelles et de jeunes.

Les éléphants adultes peuvent manger plus de 200 kg de végétaux par jour.

La trompe des éléphants contient 40. 000 muscles! Elle est très puissante et agile. Elle leur sert à manger, à boire et à s'arroser de boue[5] pour se protéger des parasites. Cela donne à leur peau la même couleur que leur environnement, contribuant ainsi à leur camouflage. Leur seul prédateur, c'était l'homme qui les chassait pour l'ivoire de leurs défenses. Aujourd'hui, ils sont protégés.

1. brain 2. tail 3. low 4. tusks 5. mud

Core Instruction

TEACHING CHRONIQUES

1. Ask for volunteers to explain where Mali, Cameroon, and Senegal are located and to share what they know about these countries. Point out the exact location of these countries on a map of Africa. Ask students what they imagine the fauna and flora are like. **(4 min.)**
2. Ask students which wild animal among those in the **Chroniques** they prefer and why. Group students according to their favorite animal and have them read the corresponding section. Then ask for a volunteer to summarize his or her group's section. **(8 min.)**
3. Have students read the questions in **Après la lecture** and scan the text to find the answers. Call on individual students to provide the correct answers. **(7 min.)**
4. Have students select an animal from the **Chroniques** other than their favorite. Have them read the corresponding section and share one interesting new fact they learned about this animal. **(6 min.)**

Le lion

Le lion, même s'il est connu sous le nom de «roi de la jungle», est un animal des plaines. Le lion est réputé être le «roi des paresseux», mais c'est une idée reçue[1] qui vient du fait qu'il chasse la nuit (températures plus basses et avantage important de l'obscurité) et qu'il est donc difficile à observer. Il fait la sieste au moment de la journée où il fait le plus chaud, ce qui facilite la digestion des grandes quantités de viandes mangées la nuit.

L'hippopotame

L'hippopotame est un animal beaucoup plus dangereux qu'il ne paraît. Il a tué plus d'hommes que n'importe quel animal en Afrique. Ses canines mesurent 50 centimètres de long et il peut charger à 45 kilomètres à l'heure. Sa peau est très fragile et il est très vulnérable aux coups de soleil. C'est pour cela qu'il passe ses journées dans l'eau douce et boueuse. Il peut fermer ses naseaux[2] et rester complètement immergé pendant dix minutes. Grâce à la grande capacité de ses poumons, il flotte[3] et se révèle très adroit dans l'eau. En revanche, il se nourrit sur la terre ferme, surtout la nuit.

Le crocodile

Le crocodile vit dans des rivières lentes et se nourrit d'une grande variété de mammifères et de poissons vivants et morts. Les crocodiles chassent à l'affût[4] et sont très rapides sur de courtes distances même hors de l'eau. Ils ont des mâchoires[5] très puissantes et des dents coupantes mais ils ne peuvent pas ouvrir leur gueule[6] si on la tient fermée. Comme il s'agit d'animaux à sang froid, ils peuvent rester de longues périodes sans manger. Les crocodiles sont protégés dans de nombreuses parties du monde.

APRÈS la lecture

 1.2, 3.1

1. En quoi les grands singes sont-ils différents des autres primates?

2. Quelles différences y a-t-il entre les éléphants d'Afrique et d'Asie?

3. Quand est-ce que les lions chassent? Pourquoi?

4. Pourquoi l'hippopotame est-il souvent dans l'eau?

5. Pourquoi les crocodiles sont-ils de bons chasseurs?

1. common misconception   2. nostrils   3. floats   4. lie and wait   5. jaws   6. mouth

Teaching Suggestion

Form three groups and assign a country mentioned in the **Chroniques** to each one. Ask them to "plan" an eco-safari there. Students should first research their assigned country's geographical features and interesting sites. They should then decide on an itinerary and look into airfare and accommodations and other travel-related information. Have the groups create a brochure to promote their safari. 🌾 5.2

Postreading

Ask partners to write desciptions of the animals found in your region. Provide their names in French and relevant French vocabulary students may need. Then, as a class, put the descriptions together in an illustrated brochure for potential Francophone visitors to your area. 🌾 1.3, 3.1

Recherches

Have students search the Internet to find out about endangered species, wildlife preserves, and conservation efforts in Africa. Have volunteers present their findings to the class. Remind students to document their sources. 🌾 1.3

Differentiated Instruction

ADVANCED LEARNERS

Ask students to imagine that while on eco-safari (see Teaching Suggestion on this page) they had an incredible, life-changing encounter with a wild animal. Have them tell their story to the class with gestures, props, and pictures. Encourage students to react to the stories and ask questions. 🌾 1.3

MULTIPLE INTELLIGENCES

Naturalist Have students use the library or the Internet to research the fauna and flora in an area of the Francophone world of their choice and present their findings to the class. 🌾 1.3, 3.1

Applying the Strategies

You may want to use the "Read, Rate, Reread" strategy from the *Reading Strategies and Skills Handbook* to encourage students to examine the text more closely.

READING PRACTICE

Strategy: Read, Rate, Reread

Reading Skill	When can I use this strategy?		
	Prereading	During Reading	Postreading
Making Inferences		✓	
Identifying the Main Idea		✓	✓
Determining the Writer's Purpose		✓	✓

Strategy at a Glance: Read, Rate, Reread

- Students read a short text three times, rating their understanding of the text and writing down any questions they have after each reading.
- After the third reading, students discuss with a partner or in a small group any unanswered questions. Then students rate their understanding a fourth and final time.
- As a class, students discuss how their ratings changed between readings, as well as asking any questions they still have.

Many struggling readers don't think rereading the same passage or text again does them any good. That is partly because they operate under the misconception that other readers read something once, read it somewhat effortlessly, and "get it" every time, the first time. Rereading doesn't look any different from reading, so struggling readers don't see how many times proficient readers pause, loop back a few sentences, reread up to a point, reflect, start over completely, and then perhaps proceed slowly. Moreover, as we discuss texts with students, we rarely bring up the issue of how to understand: we are too busy focusing on what students understand. Therefore, struggling readers don't hear teachers or other students talk about the words—or even chapters—that they sometimes reread several times before formulating a meaning. We need to help these students understand that rereading is something good readers do and that it is an important strategy to use when trying to understand a text.

Best Use of the Strategy

Use this strategy to offer students concrete evidence that comprehension does improve with repeated reading. We often tell students that rereading will increase their understanding of a text, but struggling readers need proof. They have years of evidence that reading does not work; therefore, they reason, why would rereading work any better? The structure provided by the **Read, Rate, Reread** strategy (Blau 1992)— the rating and questioning – provides the proof.

Prereading

Have students prepare for class by selecting an interesting natural site, anywhere in the world, that they've had a chance to visit or that they would like to visit. Ask them to find a picture of this site and bring it to class. Have students show their picture and ask the class to guess the name and location of the site. Then have students describe their experiences while visiting the site, or if they haven't been there, have them explain why they would like to go there.

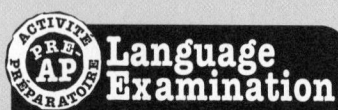

Language Examination

The **Chroniques** section helps students prepare for Section I, Part B: **Reading Comprehension.**

CHRONIQUES

À la découverte de la nature

La France, métropolitaine et d'outre-mer, est un pays d'une grande diversité géographique qui offre de nombreux sites naturels exceptionnels valant la peine[1] d'être explorés.

Le parc naturel de la Soufrière

Le parc naturel de la Soufrière est situé sur l'île de Basse Terre en Guadeloupe. Ce parc est un véritable paradis tropical où on peut admirer plusieurs sortes de paysages: volcanique, forestier et maritime. La végétation du parc est composée d'une forêt tropicale luxuriante et de mangroves[1] qu'on peut découvrir en se promenant sur les 250 kilomètres de chemins de randonnée. On y trouve toutes sortes de fleurs et de plantes tropicales. Le parc possède aussi des rivières et des chutes d'eau[2], dont les très impressionnantes chutes du Carbet. Un des endroits les plus visités du parc est La Soufrière, un volcan actif qui, à 1.467 mètres, est l'endroit le plus élevé[3] des Petites Antilles.

Les gorges du Verdon

Les gorges du Verdon sont un canyon creusé[4] par le Verdon, une rivière qui coule[5] en Provence. Elles sont étroites[6] (de 6 à 10 mètres de large au niveau de la rivière) et très profondes[7] (de 250 à 700 mètres de profondeur). Les gorges du Verdon sont considérées comme le plus beau canyon d'Europe et elles attirent de nombreux touristes. Elles constituent également une destination très appréciée des grimpeurs[8] car elles offrent plus de 1.500 parcours d'escalade. Parmi les autres sports pratiqués dans la région, on peut citer également le canoë-kayak, le parapente, les randonnées et la pêche à la mouche[9].

1. mangrove swamps 2. waterfalls 3. highest 4. hollowed out 5. flows 6. narrow 7. deep 8. climbers 9. fly-fishing

Core Instruction

TEACHING CHRONIQUES

1. Have students read the introduction and the title of each section. Ask them if they've heard of any of these places and if so, have volunteers share what they already know with the class. **(4 min.)**

2. Have students describe the photos. Ask if these places resemble any other places they know, and if so which ones. Ask them to describe what they have in common. **(4 min.)**

3. Have students read the text, one section at a time. Pause after each section and ask simple comprehension questions. Then have students answer the questions in **Après la lecture. (15 min.)**

4. Finally, have volunteers share their answers to question 6 in **Après la lecture** with the class. **(4 min.)**

Le massif du Mont-Blanc

Le Mont-Blanc est une montagne située dans la chaîne des Alpes, entre la France et l'Italie. Avec ses 4.807 mètres d'altitude, c'est le plus haut sommet d'Europe occidentale. La première ascension du Mont-Blanc a marqué les débuts de l'alpinisme et a eu lieu en 1786. Depuis, chaque année, des milliers d'alpinistes essaient de réaliser cet exploit.

La Camargue

La Camargue est une région du sud de la France qui est née de la rencontre du Rhône, un grand fleuve, et de la mer Méditerranée. La Camargue est composée de marais[1] et d'étangs[2] pleins de sel qu'on appelle des sansouires. Dans cette région très sauvage, on trouve de nombreux animaux. Il y a environ 350 espèces d'oiseaux, dont le flamant rose qui est le symbole de la Camargue. On peut aussi voir des troupeaux[3] de taureaux[4] noirs et des chevaux sauvages.

APRÈS la lecture

1.2, 3.1

1. Nomme et décris deux endroits célèbres du parc naturel de la Soufrière.

2. Comment est-ce que les gorges du Verdon ont été formées?

3. Quels sports sont pratiqués dans la région des gorges du Verdon?

4. Quelle est la particularité du Mont-Blanc?

5. Quels animaux est-ce qu'on peut voir en Camargue?

6. Lequel de ces sites aimerais-tu le plus explorer? Pourquoi?

1. swamps 2. ponds 3. herds 4. bulls

Cultures

Practices and Perspectives

Tell students that **gardians,** the traditional "cowboys" of Camargue, have lived in the region for centuries, riding their famous white **Camarguais** horses and rearing the region's bulls. Have students use the library or the Internet to research the history and culture of the **gardians** and then compare them to American cowboys. Have volunteers share their findings with the class.

4.2

Postreading

Have students write a journal entry about a day they spent visiting the place they selected in their answer to question 6 in **Après la lecture.** They should tell what they did and saw, and give their impressions of the site. Have volunteers read their journal entry to the class.　1.3

Recherches

Have students use the Internet to research additional natural sites of interest in various areas of the Francophone world. Have them present the place they find most interesting to the class. Remind students to document their sources　3.2

Differentiated Instruction

SLOWER PACE LEARNERS

Variation You may want to convert **Après la lecture** into a multiple-choice activity. On the board or on a transparency, write the questions with three possible answers for each one, one correct and two incorrect. Call on slower pace learners to choose the correct answer.　1.2

SPECIAL LEARNING NEEDS

Students with Speech Impairments To help students with speech impairments, complete the Prereading activity, have them make a post card of the picture they brought to class. Instead of doing the activity orally, have them do it in writing on the back of their "postcard." Have volunteers show and read it out loud to the class.

1.3

Chroniques

Resources

Practice:

Reading Strategies and Skills Handbook

Advanced Reader

Applying the Strategies

You may want to use the "Retellings" strategy from the *Reading Strategies and Skills Handbook* to encourage students to examine the text more closely.

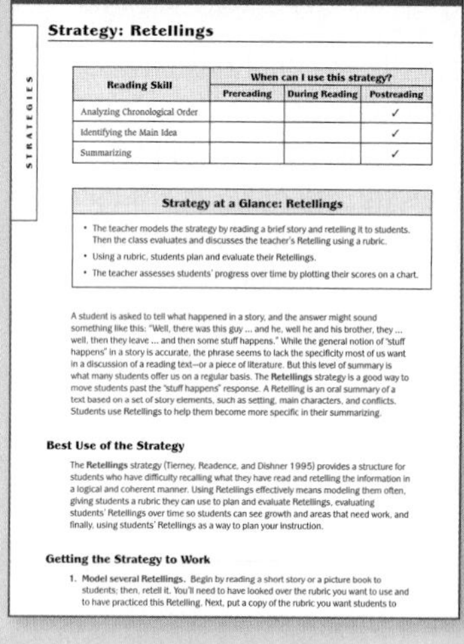

READING PRACTICE

Strategy: Retellings

STRATEGIES

Reading Skill	When can I use this strategy?		
	Prereading	During Reading	Postreading
Analyzing Chronological Order			✓
Identifying the Main Idea			✓
Summarizing			✓

Strategy at a Glance: Retellings

- The teacher models the strategy by reading a brief story and retelling it to students. Then the class evaluates and discusses the teacher's Retelling using a rubric.
- Using a rubric, students plan and evaluate their Retellings.
- The teacher assesses students' progress over time by plotting their scores on a chart.

A student is asked to tell what happened in a story, and the answer might sound something like this: "Well, there was this guy ... and he, well he and his brother, they ... well, then they leave ... and then some stuff happens." While the general notion of "stuff happens" in a story is accurate, the phrase seems to lack the specificity most of us want in a discussion of a reading text—or a piece of literature. But this level of summary is what many students offer us on a regular basis. The **Retellings** strategy is a good way to move students past the "stuff happens" response. A Retelling is an oral summary of a text based on a set of story elements, such as setting, main characters, and conflicts. Students use Retellings to help them become more specific in their summarizing.

Best Use of the Strategy

The **Retellings** strategy (Tierney, Readence, and Dishner 1995) provides a structure for students who have difficulty recalling what they have read and retelling the information in a logical and coherent manner. Using Retellings effectively means modeling them often, giving students a rubric they can use to plan and evaluate Retellings, evaluating students' Retellings over time so students can see growth and areas that need work, and finally, using students' Retellings as a way to plan your instruction.

Getting the Strategy to Work

1. **Model several Retellings.** Begin by reading a short story or a picture book to students; then, retell it. You'll need to have looked over the rubric you want to use and to have practiced this Retelling. Next, put a copy of the rubric you want students to

Prereading

Before you begin this **Chroniques** section, ask students to define "extreme sports" and to give examples of sports they consider extreme. Ask if any of your students participate in extreme sports, and if so, have them share their experience with the class, if they are willing to do so.

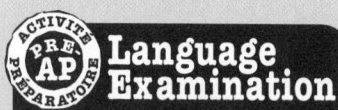

ACTIVITÉ PRÉPARATOIRE PRE-AP Language Examination

The **Chroniques** section helps students prepare for Section I, Part B: **Reading Comprehension.**

CHRONIQUES

Les sports extrêmes

Le terme «sports extrêmes» s'applique aux sports qui sont associés à la vitesse[1], à l'altitude ou au danger.

Le kitesurf

Le kitesurf a été développé dans les années 1990 par Manu Bertin, un Français qui vivait alors à Hawaï. C'est un sport nautique de traction qui consiste à être tiré par un cerf-volant, appelé aile[2] ou voile, et à glisser[3] sur l'eau sur une petite planche de surf. Le surfeur porte un harnais[4] et il contrôle la voile grâce à une barre qui est attachée à son harnais. Il peut ainsi faire des sauts de 15 à 20 mètres au-dessus de l'eau. Une variante de ce sport, le snowkite, est pratiquée en montagne.

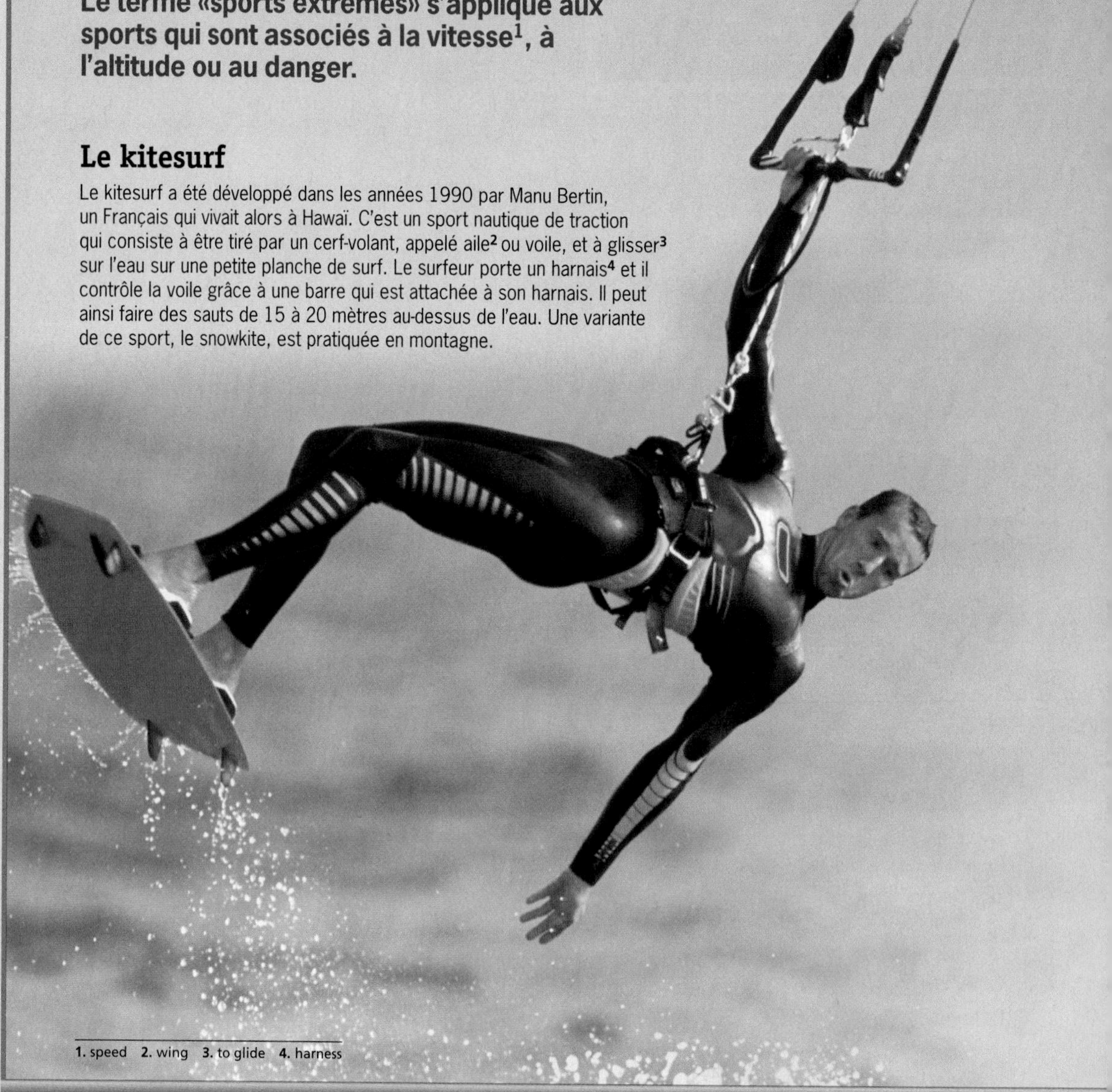

1. speed **2.** wing **3.** to glide **4.** harness

Core Instruction

TEACHING CHRONIQUES

1. Write the words **vitesse, altitude,** and **danger** on the board and ask students to define them. Then have them look at the photos and quickly scan the descriptions of these extreme sports to see which of the three words on the board apply to each sport. **(4 min.)**
2. Have students read the sections one at a time, pausing after each one. Ask a volunteer to summarize each section. Then have students answer the questions in **Après la lecture. (25 min.)**
3. Ask students which one of these sports they find most extreme and why. **(5 min.)**

Le parkour

Le parkour ou *free running*, est décrit comme étant l'art du déplacement[1]. C'est une pratique sportive extrême qui consiste à se déplacer, toujours en avant[2], en franchissant[3] tous les obstacles que l'on rencontre. Ce sport a été développé dans la banlieue parisienne. Son fondateur, David Belle, s'est inspiré des arts martiaux et de l'expérience militaire de son père. D'autres Français, comme Sébastien Foucan et Jérôme Ben Aoues, ont aussi beaucoup contribué au développement du parkour, qui est aujourd'hui un sport pratiqué dans le monde entier.

Le traceur—c'est le nom donné à une personne qui pratique le parkour—se déplace en milieu[4] urbain ou naturel, d'une manière fluide et toujours rapide. Ses mouvements[5] doivent démontrer une grande esthétique et il doit y avoir une harmonie entre le traceur et les obstacles qu'il franchit.

Qu'il soit dans la rue ou dans un milieu naturel, le traceur va toujours rencontrer des obstacles à surmonter[6]. Il doit pouvoir rapidement analyser son parcours[7] pour trouver la meilleure route à suivre. Il doit improviser et décider comment il va franchir les divers obstacles rencontrés. Il utilise des techniques de course, de saut, d'escalade, de gymnastique et d'arts martiaux.

L'escalade

L'escalade remonte à la fin du XIXe siècle. C'est en 1897, dans la forêt de Fontainebleau que l'escalade commence en France. Mais il faut attendre les années 70 pour que l'escalade devienne plus populaire. En effet, l'escalade a pendant longtemps souffert de la médiatisation de l'alpinisme. Dans les années 60, le Belge Claudio Barbier étonne en grimpant les voies rocheuses des Dolomites, en Italie. Patrick Edlinger est sans doute le grimpeur le plus connu et le plus médiatique en France. Dans les années 80, il a marqué le monde de l'escalade et il en a fait profiter le grand public en réalisant plusieurs films avec J-P. Janssen: *La Vie au bouts des doigts, Opéra vertical*. Les autres grands noms de l'escalade en France sont Jean-Christophe Lafaille, Isabelle Patissier et Catherine Destivelle (elle a réalisé le premier 7a féminin). Les sites les plus réputés pour l'escalade sont: Fontainebleau et les gorges du Verdon en France et le rocher de Freyr en Belgique.

APRÈS la lecture

🌸 1.2, 1.3

1. De quel équipement a-t-on besoin pour faire du kitesurf?

2. Qu'est-ce que la voile permet de faire à la personne qui la contrôle?

3. En quelques phrases, décris ce qu'est le parkour et explique ses origines.

4. Quelles doivent être les qualités fondamentales des mouvements dans le parkour?

5. Voudrais-tu pratiquer un de ces sports? Pourquoi ou pourquoi pas?

1. moving 2. forward 3. by jumping over 4. environment 5. moves 6. to overcome 7. route

---

Answers

1. un cerf-volant, une planche de surf, un harnais, une barre
2. des sauts
3. On franchit des obstacles en ville; il a été développé dans la banlieue parisienne.
4. une esthétique, une harmonie
5. Answers will vary.

Cultures

Products and Perspectives

The popularity of extreme sports has evolved into what can be considered an "extreme sports culture" with its own clothing lines, video games, movies, TV shows, and even its own slang. Have students analyze and discuss this extreme sports culture in the U.S. and then compare it with the situation in France, using the Internet. Are Tony Hawk video games popular in France? Do French teens wear surf fashion by famous U.S. designers? Do Francophone "extreme athletes" make up their own slang or do they sometimes use English terms? 🌸 2.2

Postreading

Have students prepare and act out a skit that involves a teenager who wants to participate in an extreme sport and a parent who strongly disapproves. The teen should offer arguments in favor of the sport while the parent should give reasons opposing it.

🌸 1.1

Recherches

Have students use the Internet to research the career of an extreme sports athlete from a Francophone country. They may select one of the people mentioned in the **Chroniques** or any other extreme sports athlete they like. Ask them to prepare a short portrait of him or her and present it to the class. Remind students to document their sources. 🌸 3.2

Applying the Strategies

You may want to use the "Logographic Cues" strategy from the *Reading Strategies and Skills Handbook* to encourage students to examine the text more closely.

READING PRACTICE

Strategy: Logographic Cues

Reading Skill	When can I use this strategy?		
	Prereading	During Reading	Postreading
Understanding Text Structure	✓	✓	
Analyzing Chronological Order		✓	✓
Making Generalizations and Understanding Text Structure		✓	✓

Strategy at a Glance: Logographic Cues

- Logographs are graphic representations of ideas. The Logographic Cues strategy uses simple pictures that represent or symbolize key ideas in a text.
- Students can use logographs to identify textual elements or organize and remember information.

Dr. Kylene Beers explains the Logographic Cues strategy with the following story:

I sat in the train station in Chaumont, France, wondering why I had taken Latin instead of French in high school and college. At that moment, I wanted to know if my train to Dijon was leaving when I thought it was. Blank stares and pitying shakes of the head were all I received when people realized that I was limited to English. Finally, I took out my map of the region, drew a train, circled my destination, and wrote the date and time of my departure. Underneath it all I put a big question mark. The clerk behind the window finally understood my question: Is the train from Chaumont to Dijon still departing today from this station at 3:48? "Oui," she said, nodding her head.

Hours later, as I sat on the train, I realized that although I couldn't read French words, I could read musical notation, numbers, and international signs. I could read information that was presented logographically, but not information presented alphabetically. A Logographic Cue was worth a million French words.

"And why not?" I thought. Our first understanding of written language is a logographic understanding. Three- and four-year-olds who recognize their names in print rarely do so because they attach sounds to letters; instead, they simply recognize the shape of their printed names. Logographs, or picture cues, remain helpful when students are confronted with an alphabetic principle or text that they don't understand.

Prereading

Begin class by asking students to come up with a definition, in French, of "athlete". Have them suggest qualities a good athlete should have. Then ask who their favorite athletes are, what sports they are associated with, and what their main accomplishments are in their fields.

ACTIVITÉ PRE AP PREPARATORY | Language Examination

The **Chroniques** section helps students prepare for Section I, Part B: **Reading Comprehension.**

À vos marques!

Voici quelques sportifs venus des quatre coins du monde francophone. Certains noms sont inattendus!

Maud Fontenoy

Maud Fontenoy est la première femme à avoir réussi la traversée de l'Atlantique Nord en bateau à rames[1]. En 2003, lorsqu'elle avait 25 ans, elle a ramé pendant 4 mois sur plus de 6.700 km.

La traversée de Maud a été suivie par des élèves de classes primaires et secondaires qui ont ainsi appris des tas de choses sur l'océan, sa faune, sa protection et les différentes parties du monde. L'écologie est au coeur du projet pédagogique de Maud.

Tony Parker

Savais-tu que Tony Parker, le basketteur américain des Spurs de San Antonio, était francophone? C'est parce qu'il est né à Bruges, en Belgique, et qu'il a grandi en France où son père jouait déjà au basket-ball. (Son père, qui était originaire de Chicago, a joué dans les championnats[2] de basket-ball en Hollande et en Belgique, avant de finir sa carrière de joueur de basket en France et de gagner la Coupe de France[3] en 1984. Il a ensuite commenté les matchs de la NBA sur une chaîne de télévision française.)

En 2001 et en 2003, Tony Parker a joué pour la France dans les championnats d'Europe de basket-ball.

---

1. rowing boat 2. championships 3. French Cup

Core Instruction

TEACHING CHRONIQUES

1. Have students look at the photos and describe the sports pictured. Then have them brainstorm a list of words and expressions they associate with each sport. You might go over the text ahead of class to provide and explain additional words students may not know. **(5 min.)**

2. Have students read each portrait and jot down the main accomplishments of the athlete. Then have a volunteer summarize each portrait orally for the class. **(15 min.)**

3. Have students answer the questions in **Après la lecture** in writing. Collect the papers and read aloud each answer. Have students identify the corresponding question. **(10 min.)**

4. Ask volunteers to tell which of these sports they like and/or engage in and why. **(4 min.)**

Françoise Mbango Etone

Françoise Mbango Etone est une championne d'athlétisme camerounaise. Elle a fini deuxième aux Championnats d'Afrique de 1999 avec un saut en longueur[1] de 6 mètres 55, et en 2004, elle a gagné la médaille d'or du triple saut[2] aux Jeux olympiques d'Athènes, avec un saut à 15 mètres 30. C'est la première athlète du Cameroun à gagner des médailles aux Championnats du Monde, aux Jeux du Commonwealth et aux Jeux olympiques.

Patrick Vieira

Patrick Vieira est un grand joueur de football. Il est né à Dakar au Sénégal, mais sa famille a déménagé à Paris quand il avait 8 ans. Il a joué pour une équipe française (A.S. Cannes), italienne (A.C. Milan) et anglaise (Arsenal F.C.) ainsi que pour l'équipe de France, avec laquelle il a gagné la Coupe du monde en 1998. Il joue maintenant pour une autre équipe italienne, le Juventus de Turin[3]. Mais il a joué avec l'équipe de France en finale de le Coupe de monde en 2006.

Chantal Petitclerc

Médaillée[4] des Jeux paralympiques de Barcelone, d'Atlanta, de Sydney et d'Athènes et détentrice[5] de plusieurs records du monde, Chantal Petitclerc est championne de course en fauteuil roulant[6]. Elle est aussi animatrice de télévision au Canada et elle fait de nombreuses conférences. Elle a beaucoup contribué à la participation des femmes et des personnes handicapées en athlétisme.

APRÈS la lecture

1. Pourquoi Tony Parker parle-t-il français?
2. Pour quels pays Patrick Vieira a-t-il joué au football?
3. Pourquoi Maud Fontenoy, Françoise Mbango Etone et Chantal Petitclerc sont-elles exceptionnelles?

✤1.2, 1.3

4. Quel champion est-ce que tu admires le plus? Pourquoi?
5. Et toi, quel sport fais-tu?

---

1. long jump 2. triple jump 3. Torino, Italy 4. medal winner 5. holder 6. wheelchair

Teaching Suggestion

Ask students what they think are the most popular sports among teenagers in two to three Francophone countries. Have them poll at least five teenagers per country via a Francophone pen pal Web site to verify their guesses. Or, if your class corresponds with a class in a Francophone country on a regular basis, have students poll the entire class to see which sport "is king" in that particular country. ✤5.2

Postreading

Tell students that "athlete" comes from the Greek *athlêtês,* which was used to refer to the participants in the Ancient Olympic games. Have students use your library resources or the Internet to research the history of the Olympic games, particularly their revival by the **Baron de Coubertin,** a French nobleman, in the late 19th century. ✤3.1

Recherches

Have students research another famous Francophone athlete of their choice. Have students prepare a short portrait of their athlete like those in the **Chroniques** and present it to the class. Remind them to document their sources. ✤3.1

Differentiated Instruction

ADVANCED LEARNERS

Challenge On the board, write this famous quote about sports by **Baron de Coubertin,** the Frenchman who revived the Olympic games in the 19th century: «**L'important, c'est de participer.**» Have advanced students discuss this idea. Ask them whether or not they agree with **Baron de Coubertin** and have them justify their answers. ✤1.2, 1.3

SPECIAL LEARNING NEEDS

Students with Visual Impairments/ Learning Disabilities/Dyslexia Using a different color for each person, write the names of the five athletes and the most important facts about each one in large letters on a transparency or on the board. Give students five colored cards representing the five athletes. Then, using the facts you listed under the athletes' names, make simple statements about them. Have students hold up the card that represents each person you are describing. ✤1.2

Resources

Practice:

Reading Strategies and Skills Handbook

Advanced Reader

Applying the Strategies

You may want to use the "Probable Passage" strategy from the *Reading Strategies and Skills Handbook* to encourage students to examine the text more closely.

READING PRACTICE

Strategy: Probable Passage

Reading Skill	When can I use this strategy?		
	Prereading	During Reading	Postreading
Identifying Purpose	✓		
Making Predictions	✓		
Comparing and Contrasting			
Analyzing Chronological Order			✓

Strategy at a Glance: Probable Passage

- The teacher chooses key words or phrases from the text students will read, then develops categories for the words and writes the Probable Passage (a cloze passage with key words omitted).
- Before students read the text, they arrange the key words and phrases in the categories. Then they fill in the blanks in the cloze passage with the key words.
- After students read the text, they discuss how their passages were similar to or different from the actual text.

Many readers struggle because they don't predict what a selection might be about and don't think about what they already know about a topic. These students simply open a book, look at words, and begin turning pages. **Probable Passage** is a strategy that helps stop those poor reading habits by encouraging students to make predictions and to activate their prior knowledge about a topic.

Best Use of the Strategy

Probable Passage (Wood 1984) is a brief preview of a text from which key words and phrases have been omitted. The teacher chooses these key words from the text and presents them to the students. In some cases, it might be necessary to discuss the meaning of the words; many times, students can figure this out for themselves. Students arrange the words in categories according to their probable functions in the story (such as Setting, Characters, or Conflicts), then use the words to fill in the blanks of the Probable Passage. After reading the story, students compare it to their passages and discuss differences. As students work through this process, they use what they know about story structure, think about vocabulary, practice making predictions, and compare their predictions to the story line.

Prereading

Read aloud the names of the four sporting events described in the **Chroniques.** Ask students if they have ever heard of these events and if so, what they know about them. Then ask if they are familiar with other internationally known sporting events and if so, which ones. Have volunteers briefly describe these events for the class.

Language Examination

The **Chroniques** section helps students prepare for Section I, Part B: **Reading Comprehension.**

Un grand nombre d'événements sportifs nationaux et internationaux ont lieu chaque année en France.

De grands événements sportifs

Le Tour de France

Tu as peut-être entendu parler de l'Américain Lance Armstrong qui a gagné le Tour de France sept fois, de 1999 à 2005. Le Tour de France a été créé en 1903 et il a lieu au mois de juillet, en 20 étapes[1], sur plus de 3.000 km. Il y a des étapes de plaine, des étapes de montagne et des étapes contre la montre[2]. Le Tour de France passe maintenant par d'autres pays européens. En 2006, par exemple, il est parti de Strasbourg et est arrivé à Paris après être passé par le Luxembourg, la Belgique, les Pays-Bas et l'Espagne. Les leaders des différentes catégories portent des maillots[3] de couleur: il y a le maillot jaune pour le classement général au temps, le maillot vert pour le classement général aux points, le maillot blanc à pois[4] rouges pour le meilleur grimpeur[5], et le maillot blanc pour le meilleur jeune coureur de moins de 26 ans. On appelle le coureur qui est dernier au classement général "la lanterne rouge"[6].

1. legs 2. time trials 3. jerseys 4. polka dots 5. climber 6. the red lantern

Core Instruction

TEACHING CHRONIQUES

1. Have students look at the photos and answer simple questions, such as **Le Paris-Dakar, c'est en ville? Non? C'est où, d'après la photo? (3 min.)**

2. Have students read the questions in **Après la lecture** before they read the text and clarify anything students are having trouble understanding. **(2 min.)**

3. Have students read the 4 sections and answer the questions in **Après la lecture.** Have volunteers supply the correct answers and read the sentence in the text that supports each one. **(20 min.)**

4. Finally, ask students which of these events they would be most interested in seeing and why.

Le Paris-Dakar

Le Paris-Dakar est une course de voitures, de motos et de camions qui à l'origine rejoignait Paris à Dakar.

Le premier rallye Paris-Dakar a eu lieu en 1979. Il s'appelle maintenant Le Dakar, parce que depuis 1995 il ne part plus toujours de Paris. Récemment, de 2002 à 2004, il est parti d'autres villes françaises, Arras, Marseille et Clermont-Ferrand, et en 2005 et 2006, le départ a été dans d'autres villes européennes. C'est un événement très important qui a lieu au début du mois de janvier. Plus de 450 véhicules et plus de 1.400 personnes (80% d'amateurs et 20% de professionnels) participent à cette compétition.

Il y a généralement 18 avions pour le transport des personnes, 8 hélicoptères qui observent la course, 27 voitures qui suivent les participants et 11 camions qui les assistent. Le Dakar est très contesté, parce que de 1979 à 2006, 48 personnes, dont 8 enfants, sont mortes dans les villages où les concurrents passaient à grande vitesse. Un événement de cette importance peut bien sûr aussi avoir de mauvais effets pour la région dans les domaines écologique et humanitaire.

Le Tournoi de Roland Garros

De mai à juin, c'est au stade Roland Garros à Paris qu'ont lieu les Internationaux de France[1] de tennis, un tournoi de tennis sur terre battue[2]. Certains grands joueurs de tennis qui jouent habituellement sur surfaces rapides (dures ou gazon[3]) ont parfois des difficultés sur la terre battue de Roland Garros qui est une surface lente.

Roland Garros fait partie des tournois du Grand Chelem[4], au même titre que l'Open d'Australie, Wimbledon et l'US Open.

Les premiers Internationaux de France, qui s'appelaient alors Championnat de France International de Tennis, ont eu lieu à Paris en 1891.

Le stade Roland Garros a été inauguré en 1928 et porte le nom d'un aviateur français qui a fait la première traversée de la Méditerranée en avion en 1913.

Les 24 Heures du Mans

Depuis 1923, les 24 Heures du Mans ont lieu chaque année au Mans (à 200 km au sud-ouest de Paris). La course, qui a lieu maintenant au mois de juin, est réservée aux voitures de sport et Sport-Prototypes, sur une piste[5] qui mesure un peu plus de 13 km.

C'est la course d'endurance la plus ancienne et la plus prestigieuse. Elle permet aux constructeurs automobiles de tester la résistance de la mécanique de leur voiture pendant une période de 24 heures. Le film *Le Mans*, avec Steve McQueen, a été filmé pendant les 24 Heures du Mans de 1970. La course est suivie au Mans par plus de 200.000 spectateurs et aussi par 228 millions de téléspectateurs[6] dans le monde. Comme la course a un succès énorme, il y a aussi maintenant Les 24 Heures Moto[7] en avril, «Les 24 Heures Camion[8]» en octobre, et finalement «Les 24 Heures Karting[9]».

APRÈS la lecture ✿1.2

1. Au Tour de France, quel maillot porte-t-on quand on a le plus de points au classement général?
2. Sur quelle distance est cette course cycliste?
3. Depuis quand le Dakar existe-t-il?
4. Quels tournois composent le «Grand Chelem»?
5. Pourquoi certains joueurs ont-ils des difficultés à Roland Garros?

---

1. the "French Open"   2. red clay   3. turf, grass   4. Grand Slam   5. track   6. TV viewers   7. motorcycle   8. truck   9. go-kart

Cultures

✿✿ Products and Perspectives

Have partners create and act out an interview between a journalist and the winner of one of the events in the **Chroniques.** The journalist should ask the winner how he or she prepared for the event, how everything went during the event, if he or she encountered any specific difficulties or problems, what he or she plans on doing next, etc.   ✿1.1

Postreading

Tell students to imagine they won an all-expenses-paid trip to attend one of the sporting events in the **Chroniques.** Ask them to write a letter back home about their trip and the event.   ✿1.3

®echerches

While Lance Armstrong has had the most Tour de France victories, several other cyclists, including three Francophone champions, have also had multiple victories. Have students use the Internet to research information about these cyclists: Jacques Anquetil (5 wins), Eddy Merckx (5 wins), and Bernard Hinault (5 wins). Have volunteers present their findings in class. Remind students to document their sources.   ✿3.2

Differentiated Instruction

SLOWER PACE LEARNERS

To help slower pace learners complete **Après la lecture,** you might use true-false statements in place of the questions. **Les tournois du Grand Chelem sont Roland Garros, l'Open d'Australie, Wimbledon et l'US Open. Vrai ou faux? (Vrai)**   ✿1.2

MULTIPLE INTELLIGENCES

Linguistic Assign a different year of the Tour de France to partners and have them research the Tour of that particular year on the official Web site of the Tour de France (www.letour.fr). Ask students to print out a map of their year's Tour and to jot down important information. Then, in class, have students give an oral report, as if they were sportscasters covering the Tour de France. For more variety, assign the Dakar race to half of the class (www.dakar.com).   ✿1.3, 3.2

Géoculture Overview

L'Europe francophone

Bienvenue! This section is designed to familiarize the students with the geographic location, history, and cultural practices of the region to be explored. It provides a guide for classroom discussion and discovery of the differences and similarities of the student's own culture and that of the French-speaking world.

50-Minute Lesson Plans

Day 1

Lesson Sequence
Géoculture: L'Europe franco-phone, pp. 270–271
- What do students know about Belgium, Switzerland, and Monaco? Have the class discuss any stereotypes students may have about these countries. **10 min.**
- Go over the photos and captions with the students. **10 min.**
- See Map Activities, p. 270. **5 min.**
- Discuss Background Information, p. 270. **11 min.**
- Complete **Géo-quiz.** **1 min.**
- Show **Géoculture** video. **3 min.**
- Have students answer **Questions,** p. 271. **10 min.**

Optional Resources
- **Savais-tu que...?,** p. 271
- Thinking Critically, p. 269B
- Research Online!, p. 269B

Homework Suggestions
Online Practice (**go.hrw.com,** Keyword: BD3 CH7)
Interactive Tutor, Ch. 7

🌼 1.2, 1.3, 3.1

Day 2

Lesson Sequence
Géoculture: L'Europe franco-phone, pp. 272–273
- Briefly revisit main points about geography. **5 min.**
- Go over the photos and captions with the students. **8 min.**
- Ask students to compare the forms of government of the three countries. **5 min.**
- Have students answer **As-tu compris?** questions, p. 273. **7 min.**
- Do **Prépare-toi pour le quiz,** p. 269B. **25 min.**

Optional Resources
- Slower Pace Learners, p. 269B ◆
- Special Learning Needs, p. 269B ●
- Map Game, p. 269B
- Interdisciplinary Links, pp. 272–273

Homework Suggestions
Activité, p. 273
Study for the **Géoculture** quiz.

🌼 1.1, 1.2, 3.1

90-Minute Lesson Plan

Block 1

Lesson Sequence
Géoculture: L'Europe franco-phone, pp. 270–273
- What do students know about Belgium, Switzerland, and Monaco? Have the class discuss any stereotypes students may have about these countries. **10 min.**
- Go over the photos and captions with the students. **20 min.**
- See Map Activities, p. 270. **5 min.**
- Discuss Background Information, p. 270. **10 min.**
- Complete **Géo-quiz.** **1 min.**
- Show **Géoculture.** **4 min.**
- Have students answer **Questions,** p. 271. **5 min.**
- Have students answer **As-tu compris?** questions, p. 273. **5 min.**
- Ask students to compare the forms of government of the three countries. **5 min.**
- Do **Prépare-toi pour le quiz,** p. 269B. **25 min.**

Optional Resources
- **Savais-tu que ...?,** p. 271
- Slower Pace Learners, p. 269B ◆
- Special Learning Needs, p. 269B ●
- Thinking Critically, p. 269B
- Research Online!, p. 269B
- Interdisciplinary Links, pp. 272–273
- Map Game, p. 269B

Homework Suggestions
Online Practice (**go.hrw.com,** Keyword: BD3 CH7)
Interactive Tutor, Ch. 7
Activité, p. 273
Study for the **Géoculture** quiz.

🌼 1.1, 1.2, 1.3, 3.1

KEY

▲ **Advanced Learners**   ◆ **Slower Pace Learners**   ● **Special Learning Needs**

Differentiated Instruction

Slower Pace Learners

Additional Practice Divide the class into three groups. Assign each group one of the three countries introduced in **Géoculture**. Each group reads the **Géoculture** pages and collects information about its assigned country. Each group reports on the sights and historical events of its assigned country. 🏵 1.1, 3.1

Special Learning Needs

Students with Visual Impairments Students with visual impairments may have trouble seeing how the photos relate to the text on the **Géoculture** pages. Have volunteers describe the photos in French. The students with visual impairments should ask for clarifications if necessary. 🏵 1.1, 3.1

Thinking Critically

Observing The Ardennes has been a battleground for centuries. It was the scene of three major battles during the world wars, notably the Battle of the Bulge in World War II. Ask students why military powers chose the rugged and heavily wooded terrain of the Ardennes as battleground. (The Ardennes is strategically located; parts or all of the Belgian Ardennes belonged at one time or another to France, Germany, the Spanish Netherlands, or the United Kingdom of the Netherlands.) 🏵 3.1

Quiz Preparation/Enrichment

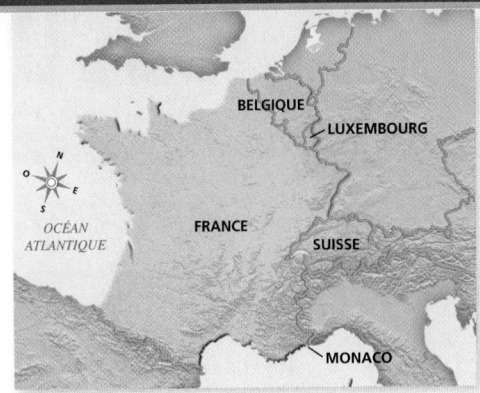

Map Game

Students should play this game with a partner. One of the partners will choose a geographical feature that is shown on the map or mentioned on the **Géoculture** pages. The other will find this feature by asking a maximum of five yes-no questions. **Est-ce une ville? (oui) Cette ville est-elle en Belgique? (oui) Cette ville est-elle la capitale de la Belgique? (oui) Cette ville est Bruxelles.** Partners take turns playing this game. They should have at least three turns each. 🏵 1.1

Prépare-toi pour le quiz

1. Give each student a map of Europe, without labels, that shows only the borders of countries. Students should shade in Belgium, Switzerland, and Monaco.

2. Have students indicate cities, bodies of water, and mountain ranges in the shaded countries.

3. Ask students to choose the event they think was most important in the history of each country introduced in the **Géoculture.** Encourage students to give a reason for each of their choices. 🏵 1.1, 3.1

Research Online!

Monaco With an area of 1.95 sq. km. and a population of 32,400, Monaco has the world's highest population density. Monaco's major industry is tourism. Students should investigate how Monaco tries to solve its environmental problems, especially atmospheric and marine pollution, caused by its citizens and visitors. Have them present their research to the class. Ask for documentation of all used sources. 🏵 1.3, 3.1

Géoculture

Resources

Planning:
Lesson Planner
 One-Stop Planner

Presentation:
 Teaching Transparencies
Cartes 1, 3
DVD Program, Disc 2
Géoculture

Practice:
Cahier d'activités
Media Guide
 Interactive Tutor, Disc 2

Map ACTIVITIES

1. Have students locate Belgium, Switzerland, and Monaco on a map. Ask them to name the surrounding countries and bodies of water. **(Belgique: la France, le Luxembourg, l'Allemagne, les Pays-Bas, la mer du Nord; Suisse: la France, l'Italie, l'Allemagne, l'Autriche, le Liechtenstein; Monaco: la France, l'Italie, la mer Méditerranée)**

2. Tell students that in Belgium and Switzerland more than two languages are spoken. Given the location, can students guess the other languages? **(Belgique: français, néerlandais, allemand; Suisse: français, allemand, italien, romanche)**

Chapitres 7 et 8

DVD
Géoculture

Géoculture
L'Europe francophone

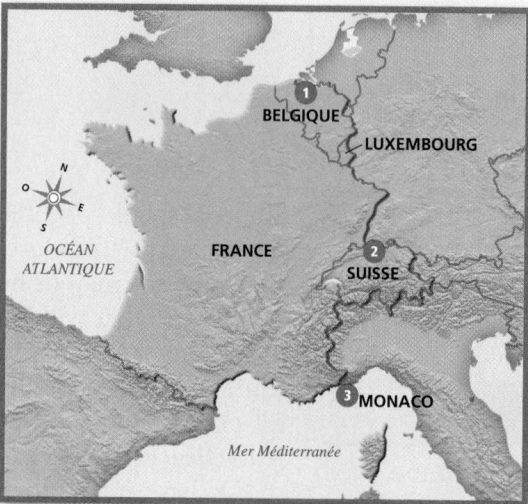

▲ **LA BELGIQUE: Bruxelles,** capitale de la Belgique, est le siège de l'Union européenne. La Grand-Place de Bruxelles est classée au patrimoine mondial de l'Unesco. ❶

▼ **LA BELGIQUE: Han-sur-Lesse,** dans les Ardennes est connu pour ses magnifiques grottes calcaires. ❶

▼ **LA BELGIQUE: Bruges** est une ville flamande réputée pour sa dentelle, ses canaux et ses édifices du Moyen Âge. C'est la ville la plus visitée de Belgique. ❶

Savais-tu que...?

Pour traverser la frontière entre Monaco et la France, il n'y a pas de contrôle. Il faut tout simplement traverser la rue.

Background Information

Geography

Belgium lies at the crossroads of Western Europe. Many Western European capitals lie within 1,000 km of Brussels. Belgium's terrain includes flat coastal plains in the northwest, rolling hills in the center, and mountains in the southeast.

Switzerland is a landlocked, mountainous country. The Alps and Pre-Alps make up about 60% of the terrain. Glaciers cover an area of around 2,000 sq. km. Switzerland has many lakes as well as the Rhine and Rhône river sources.

History

The Protestant Reformation, began in Switzerland during the 16th century when Martin Luther posted his *95 Theses.* This document challenged several teachings of the Roman Catholic Church and sparked a debate that led to the formation of many of today's protestant traditions.

Prince Albert I of Monaco (1848–1922) was considered by many the "father of oceanography." He established many scientific institutions, such as the Oceanographic Institute of Monaco and the Institute for Human Paleontology. He also established the principality's first constitution in 1911.

L'Europe francophone

VIDEO OPTION

▶ Géoculture

▲ **LA SUISSE: Les Alpes** sont les montagnes les plus élevées d'Europe occidentale. On peut y admirer de nombreux glaciers. Les Alpes offrent aux skieurs de la neige même en été. ②

➤ **LA SUISSE: La riviera suisse** se trouve au bord du lac Léman. Réputée pour sa beauté, elle a toujours attiré des artistes et des écrivains. ②

▲ **LA SUISSE: Genève** est dans la région francophone de la Suisse. Elle accueille près de 200 organisations internationales, comme par exemple, la Croix-Rouge Internationale et l'Organisation des Nations unies. ②

➤ **MONACO: Le Rocher de Monaco** abrite le musée océanographique qui possède une remarquable collection de faune marine. ③

▼ **MONACO: Monte-Carlo** Chaque année depuis 1929, le Grand Prix de Monaco a lieu à Monte-Carlo. Le circuit automobile est long de plus de 3 kilomètres et passe à travers la ville et le port. ③

Géo-quiz 🌐 1.2, 3.1
Où se trouve le siège de l'Union européenne? à Bruxelles

Connections

Thinking Critically

Belgium has three official languages—French, Flemish, and German—and is divided into two distinct regions, Flanders and Wallonia. Flanders makes up the northern part of the country. Its people are called Flemings and speak a regional version of Dutch. Wallonia is located in the south. The inhabitants are called Walloons and speak French, except for a small area where German is spoken. Francophone Walloons make up about 33% of the population, while German-speakers make up about 1%. Around 8% of the population is officially bilingual. Ask students what challenges they think Belgium has faced as a result of its multiculturalism. Then ask how they think Belgium has been enriched by it. 🌐 3.2, 4.2

Communities

Community Link

The ideas that would later become the basis for the International Red Cross were first published by Swiss philanthropist Henri Dunant in *Un Souvenir de Solférino*. He urged that voluntary aid societies for war victims be formed. In 1863, the *Société genevoise d'utilité publique* set up a committee to explore Dunant's ideas and later called an international conference to urge the formation of voluntary aid units. These units eventually became the National Red Cross Societies around the world. Have students visit the International Red Cross website at http://www.icrc.org and read the organization's mission in French. 🌐 5.1

Savais-tu que...?

• Switzerland has one of the best recycling programs in the world. For years, Swiss cities have recycled over 40% of their solid waste. In 2003, they recycled 70% of their paper and 95% of their glass.
• *Smurfs*, the blue cartoon characters, were created by the Belgian artist Peyo.
• The word *spa* comes from the Belgian city of Spa. Luxury spas are found throughout the country.
• Monaco, the second smallest country in the world, covers less than two square miles.

Questions 🌐 1.2

1. Qu'est-ce qu'on peut voir à Bruges? (**des canaux et des édifices du Moyen Âge**)

2. Qu'est-ce qu'on peut trouver dans les Alpes? (**des glaciers, des skieurs en été, les montagnes les plus élevées d'Europe occidentale**)

3. Combien d'organisations internationales est-ce que Genève accueille? (**près de 200**)

4. Qu'est-ce qui se passe tous les ans à Monte-Carlo? (**le Grand Prix de Monaco**)

5. Qu'est-ce qu'il y a sur le rocher de Monaco? (**le musée océanographique**)

L'histoire
L'Europe francophone

Connections

History Link

Prior to Charlemagne there were no schools in the modern sense. Even priests and rulers could not read and write Latin, the language of literacy at the time. Charlemagne began educational reform by changing the focus of the schools in the palaces from military tactics and courtly manners to the study of grammar, rhetoric, dialectic, geometry, astronomy, and music. He also created schools next to churches and monasteries. To carry out his reforms, he invited scholars to come from other lands. Charlemagne's goals were to create a literate clergy able to read and understand the scriptures, create literate civil servants that could read government documents, and to unify linguistically and culturally the diverse groups of people who made up his empire. Education was available to peasants and noblemen alike and teachers were prohibited from charging for their services. Ask students what aspects of Charlemagne's educational reforms they think still hold true.

🌸 2.2, 3.2

Cultures

🌸 **Practices and Perspectives**

Switzerland has remained neutral during international conflicts for over 400 years. Despite this neutrality, every able-bodied Swiss male over the age of 20 is required to perform 15 month military service. Ask students why they think the Swiss feel that it is necessary to be prepared for armed conflict even though their intention is to remain neutral.

🌸 2.1, 3.2

VIᵉ S. AVANT J.C. — 800 — 1200 — 1500

VIᵉ s. avant J.-C. – Iᵉʳ s.
Les Belgae et les Helvètes, d'origine celtique, habitaient les territoires de la Belgique et la Suisse actuelles avant la conquête romaine. Les noms «Belgique» et «Helvétie» (nom latin de la Suisse) rappellent ces deux tribus.

XVIᵉ s. – XVIIᵉ s.
En 1648, **le traité de Westphalie** a mis fin à la guerre de Trente Ans, conflit religieux et politique entre certains pays européens. La Suisse est restée neutre pendant ce conflit. Le traité a reconnu cette neutralité et a accordé l'indépendance à la Suisse.

1297
En 1297, **François Grimaldi (le Malizia),** chassé d'Italie, s'est déguisé en moine pour monter une attaque surprise contre la citadelle de Monaco. Il a pris possession du rocher où il a établi la souveraineté de la famille Grimaldi qui règne toujours à Monaco.

768–814
Au VIIIᵉ siècle, **Charlemagne** a unifié l'Europe et en a fait un empire. La Suisse et la Belgique faisaient partie de cet empire et la Belgique en était le centre politique et économique. Une des innovations de Charlemagne a été la création d'écoles à côté des églises et des monastères, pour les nobles et les paysans.

TEACHING L'HISTOIRE

1. Have students look at the timeline and then read the dates above each caption. Ask students what they recall having learned about each of the time periods. You might refer them back to what they learned in previous **Géocultures.**

2. Have students look at each picture and the words in boldface in the caption. Ask students to predict what each caption will be about. Read the captions as a class. Help students use context clues to decipher unfamiliar vocabulary. Check comprehension with the **As-tu compris?** questions.

3. Ask students which of the historical events in the timeline they believe has had the greatest impact on world history, and why.

4. Have students reread pages 272–273 and do the **Activité** questions as homework.

Online Practice
go.hrw.com
Online Edition
KEYWORD: BD3 CH7

1800   1900   2000

1830
En 1830, la Belgique obtient son indépendance des Pays-Bas. Au XIXᵉ siècle, elle connaît une révolution industrielle grâce à la **colonisation du Congo**, riche en matières premières.

1949–2005
Rainier III de Monaco, (1923–2005), a transformé la principauté en centre financier et touristique de renommée mondiale. Le monde se souvient de lui comme du prince qui a créé Monte-Carlo et qui a épousé l'actrice américaine Grace Kelly.

1944–1945
Pendant l'hiver 1944–1945, une des batailles les plus importantes de la Seconde Guerre mondiale a eu lieu en Belgique. C'est la **bataille des Ardennes** avec le siège de Bastogne. Elle s'est terminée par une victoire décisive des Alliés et a contribué à mettre fin à la guerre.

1971–présent
Le suffrage féminin est introduit en Suisse en 1971. En 1999, **Ruth Dreifuss** est la première femme élue présidente de la Confédération helvétique (la Suisse). Quelques années plus tard, en 2002, la Suisse devient le 190ᵉ membre des Nations Unies.

Interactive
TUTOR

Activité   1.2, 3.1

1. Qu'est-ce que le traité de Westphalie a accordé à la Suisse?
2. Qu'est-ce que la colonisation du Congo a permis à la Belgique?
3. Pourquoi est-ce que la bataille des Ardennes a été importante?
4. Quelles sont les contributions de Rainier III à Monaco?

As-tu compris?
You can use the following questions to check comprehension of the Géoculture.
1. **D'où viennent les noms «Belgique» et «Helvétie»? (des tribus celtes qui habitaient ces territoires)**
2. **Quelle innovation importante Charlemagne a-t-il établi dans son empire? (des écoles)**
3. **Qu'est-ce qu'a fait François Grimaldi? (Il a pris possession de Monaco et il y a établi la souveraineté de sa famille.)**
4. **Quand est-ce que la Suisse est devenue indépendante? (en 1648 avec la traité de Westphalie)**
5. **Qu'est-ce qui s'est passé en Belgique après son indépendance? (une révolution industrielle grâce à la colonisation du Congo)**
6. **Qu'est-ce qui a contribué à mettre fin à la Seconde Guerre mondiale? (la bataille des Ardennes)**
    1.2

Answers
1. son indépendance et sa neutralité
2. une révolution industrielle
3. La bataille a été une victoire qui a contribué à mettre fin à la guerre.
4. Il a transformé Monaco en centre financier et touristique; il a créé Monte-Carlo.

INTERDISCIPLINARY LINKS

Les sciences sociales   3.1
Social Studies Link As the industrial revolution in Belgium and other countries grew, so did the need for raw materials and new markets. This led in part to the colonization of Africa. Some also argue that one of the most important reasons for colonizing Africa was the belief that trade and commerce, as well as the introduction of Christianity, were important to the development of the continent. Have students find out what types of economic activity Belgium undertook in the Congo and which raw materials they obtained.

L'histoire   3.1
History Link On December 16, 1944, Germany sent a quarter of a million troops across 85 miles of Allied lines from Belgium to Luxembourg. The troops advanced 50 miles, creating a "bulge" in the lines, hence, the popular name of the conflict, Battle of the Bulge. This battle was perhaps the biggest and most costly in human lives that the United States Army has ever fought. Have students find out more about the battle by reading first-hand accounts of it in English and/or French online.

Assess

Assessment Program
Quiz: Géoculture
Differentiated Practice and Assessment CD-ROM

Online Assessment
my.hrw.com

Test Generator

Planning Guide

Notre planète

Planning Guide

Chapter Section		Resources
Vocabulaire 1 • Natural phenomena	pp. 276–279	Teaching Transparencies: Vocabulaire 7.1, 7.2; Bell Work 7.1, 7.2, 7.3, 7.4
Grammaire 1 • The comparative and superlative • The passive voice	pp. 280–283	Cahier de vocabulaire et grammaire, pp. 73–78 Grammar Tutor for Students of French Cahier d'activités, pp. 61–63
Application 1 • **Un peu plus:** Prepositions	pp. 284–285	Media Guide, pp. 25–28 **Assessment Program** Quiz: Vocabulaire 1, pp. 183–184 Quiz: Grammaire 1, pp. 185–186 Quiz: Application 1, pp. 187–188
Culture • **Lecture culturelle: Dépollution par le lombric** • **Comparaisons** • **Communauté et professions**	pp. 286–287	Cahier d'activités, p. 64
Vocabulaire 2 • Natural resources in danger	pp. 288–291	Teaching Transparencies: Vocabulaire 7.3, 7.4; Bell Work 7.5, 7.6, 7.7, 7.8
Grammaire 2 • **quand, lorsque,** and **dès que** • Subjunctive after a conjunction	pp. 292–295	Cahier de vocabulaire et grammaire, pp. 79–84 Grammar Tutor for Students of French Cahier d'activités, pp. 65–67
Application 2 • **Un peu plus:** The verb **éteindre**	pp. 296–297	Media Guide, pp. 25–28 **Assessment Program** Quiz: Vocabulaire 2, pp. 189–190 Quiz: Grammaire 2, pp. 191–192 Quiz: Application 2, pp. 193–194
Lecture • **Jean de Florette**	pp. 298–301	Cahier d'activités, p. 68 Reading Strategies and Skills Handbook Advanced Reader
L'atelier de l'écrivain • **Lettre à Jean**	pp. 302–303	**Assessment Program** Quiz: Lecture, p. 195 Quiz: Écriture, p. 196
Prépare-toi pour l'examen • **Résumé de vocabulaire et grammaire**	pp. 304–307	Teaching Transparencies: Picture Sequences, Situation, Ch. 7 Media Guide, pp. 25, 65–66
Activités préparatoires	pp. 308–309	**Assessment Program** Examen: Chapitre 7, pp. 197–202 Examen oral: Chapitre 7, p. 323
Révisions cumulatives	pp. 310–311	Teaching Transparencies, Fine Art, Ch. 7 Cahier d'activités, pp. 69–70
Chroniques • Plus loin, plus vite • Une technologie de pointe • SOS Terre • La Ve République • L'Europe francophone	pp. 350–359	Reading Strategies and Skills Handbook Advanced Reader

Pacing Suggestions

	Essential	Recommended	Optional
Vocabulaire 1 • Natural phenomena • **Flash culture**	✔		
Grammaire 1 • The comparative and superlative • The passive voice	✔		
Application 1 • **Un peu plus:** Prepositions	✔		
Culture • **Lecture culturelle: Dépollution par le lombric** • **Comparaisons** • **Communauté et professions**		✔	
Vocabulaire 2 • Natural resources in danger • **Flash culture**	✔		
Grammaire 2 • **quand, lorsque,** and **dès que** • Subjunctive after a conjunction	✔		
Application 2 • **Un peu plus:** The verb **éteindre** • **Flash culture**	✔		
Lecture • **Jean de Florette**		✔	
L'atelier de l'écrivain • **Lettre à Jean**			
Prépare-toi pour l'examen		✔	
Activités préparatoires		✔	
Révisions cumulatives			✔
Chroniques			✔

Technology

Bien dit! Online
• Student Edition with multi-media
• SoundBooth recording tool
• Interactive activities with feedback
• Self-tests with feedback
• Cahier d'activités (Interactive workbook)
• Cahier de vocabulaire et grammaire (Interactive workbook)
• Holt Online Assessment

DVD Program
• Télé-roman: Camille et compagnie
• Télé-culture: Interviews

Interactive Tutor
• Interactive practice games
• Writing and recording workshops
• Before You Know It™ Flashcards

Audio Program
• Student Edition Listening Activities
• Assessment listening activities
• Songs

One-Stop Planner
• Complete media and print resources
• ExamView Pro Test Generator
• Holt Calendar Planner

PuzzlePro
• Customizable word games

Differentiated Practice and Assessment CD
For slower pace and advanced learner options, see the Differentiated Practice and Assessment CD.

Planning Guide

Projects

Grading the project

Suggested point distribution
(100 points total)

Inclusion of requirements.. 20 pts.
Language use............ 20 pts.
Creativity/overall appearance 20 pts.
Effort/Participation......... 20 pts.
Oral presentation.......... 20 pts.

e-community

e-mail forum:
Post the following questions on the classroom e-mail forum:

Location: http://french

> Comment est-ce que tu crois que tu réagirais si tu étais pris(e) dans une tornade? Dans un tremblement de terre? Dans un ouragan? 5.1

All students will contribute to the list and then share the items.

L'environnement

Groups of students will create posters in French that describe an environmental problem in a French-speaking country and propose solutions. They will also give an oral presentation to the class based on their poster. 1.3, 5.1

Suggested Sequence

1. Have students form small groups and select a topic related to the environment. Students should address an environmental concern in a city, region, or country in the Francophone world.

2. Students should research the problem, using current magazines, newspapers, and the Internet, to find relevant statistics and popular opinions about the issue. They should also find or draw pictures to illustrate the problem.

3. Have group members share and compile their research, propose a solution, and plan the graphics and layout. Encourage them to create charts and graphs to present the statistics that they have gathered.

4. Have groups exchange their rough draft and layout to check French spelling and grammar, as well as the content and design of the poster. They might make suggestions for additional or alternative graphics and illustrations.

5. Have groups plan the final layout. They should arrange their illustrations and copy the text onto the poster.

6. Have group members present their poster to the class. Each member should take part in describing the environmental problem and explaining the proposed solutions.

Partner Class Project

Have students work in groups to create a survey on the environmentally sensitive behavior of teenagers. The survey should consist of ten, open-ended questions covering topics, such as the students' choice of products based on packaging, what they do with drink or food packaging at school, or their personal efforts to influence others to live more environmentally conscious lives. Students should answer the survey themselves and compare their answers to those given by the students of the partner class. Are they similar or different? How? Have students present their conclusions to the class. 1.3, 4.2

Game Bank
For game ideas, see pages T60–T63.

Traditions

Traditions écologistes

The Swiss have a long-standing tradition of environmental protection, dating back to 1876 when they enacted a federal forestry law protecting timber against over-cutting. Even Swiss industry reflects the country's desire to preserve its natural resources. For example, one of Switzerland's most important industries is clock and watch making, a trade that uses few raw materials. First fostered in the seventeenth century by French religious **émigrés,** called **Huguenots,** the Swiss clock and watch industry today comprises a large portion of the world's trade in timepieces. Other important industries, that reflect the Swiss penchant for using resources other than nature's raw materials, are banking and pharmaceuticals. Have students investigate Switzerland's top five industries and determine the resources they require. Then have them compare their findings with the top five industries in the United States. ❁ 3.1, 4.2

La cuisine

Raclette is a cheese produced in the Savoie region in the Alps. Its name originates from the French verb **racler** *(to scrape)*, because you scrape the cheese off the dish it is melted on. Traditionally, **raclette** was melted on a wood fire. Nowadays, one can use an electric device **(un appareil à raclette)** with individual pans in which to melt the cheese. Boiled potatoes or slices of smoked meat are used to scrape the cheese off the pans. Encourage students to make this dish in their home economics class or at home for family and friends. ❁ 3.1, 5.2

Raclette
pour 4 personnes

2 livres de raclette
1 livre de jambon de pays coupé en tranches (prosciutto, par exemple)

8 grosses pommes de terre
sel
poivre

Faire cuire les pommes de terre à l'eau. Couper les pommes de terre en lamelles. Mettre un petit peu d'huile d'olive ou de pépin de raisin dans une poêle. Mettre les pommes de terre dans la poêle. Ajouter le jambon. Recouvrir avec le fromage qui aura été coupé en fines tranches préalablement. Laisser cuire jusqu'à ce que le fromage soit fondu. Servir.

Vocabulaire à l'œuvre 1

2 p. 278, CD 7, Tr. 1

1. Cette région est connue pour ses glissements de terrain.
2. La coulée de lave a détruit tout sur son passage.
3. Ce week-end, prenez garde aux avalanches dans les Alpes.
4. Méfiez-vous des tempêtes de neige si vous allez skier cette semaine.
5. Le raz-de-marée a causé de graves inondations.
6. Les habitants sont partis avant l'arrivée du cyclone.

Answers for Activity 2
1. c   2. b   3. a   4. a   5. d   6. e

Grammaire à l'œuvre 1

12 p. 282, CD 7, Tr. 2

1. Hier matin, Jacques s'est blessé avec un couteau.
2. Il a été emmené à l'hôpital.
3. Il a demandé aux infirmières de téléphoner à ses parents.
4. Ensuite, il a été vu par le médecin de service.
5. Heureusement, Jacques a été vacciné contre le tétanos le mois dernier.
6. Il est rentré chez lui aujourd'hui.

Answers for Activity 12
1. a   2. b   3. a   4. b   5. b   6. a

Application 1

19 p. 284, CD 7, Tr. 3

1. Je pense que tu as raison [NOISE] aller en vacances en Floride maintenant. Ce n'est plus la saison des ouragans.
2. Est-ce que tu as ramené un cadeau [NOISE] tes parents la dernière fois que tu es parti en vacances?
3. [NOISE] avoir lu ce guide touristique, ils ont voulu aller à Hawaii pour voir les volcans.
4. Marcel m'a dit qu'il était parti en vacances [NOISE] son chien et qu'il avait eu beaucoup de problèmes à l'hôtel à cause de lui.

5. Est-ce que tu ne m'as pas dit que tu viendrais [NOISE] vélo parce que tu voulais faire de l'exercice?
6. Je ne trouve plus mes lunettes et [NOISE] elles je ne vois rien. Tu ne les aurais pas vues quelque part?
7. Anaïs suit des cours de chinois [NOISE] deux ans. Tu ne savais pas?
8. Tu as vu cet homme! Il a mis quelque chose [NOISE] sa poche et il ne l'a pas montré à la caissière. C'est du vol!

Answers for Activity 19
1. h   2. g   3. a   4. f   5. l   6. e   7. j   8. k

Vocabulaire à l'œuvre 2

24 p. 290, CD 7, Tr. 4

— Je suis convaincue que si tout le monde recyclait, il n'y aurait plus problème de pollution.
— Moi, je parie qu'il est déjà trop tard. Les dégâts sont faits! La déforestation a provoqué le réchauffement de la planète.
— Je suis sûre qu'on peut arrêter l'effet de serre en plantant des arbres pour remplacer ceux qu'on a coupés!
— Oui, mais même si on plante des arbres, il faudra des années pour réparer les dégâts, j'en suis sûr. Et il n'y a pas que la déforestation, je suppose! Il y a aussi les fumées des usines qui polluent l'atmosphère et les marées noires!
— Je parie qu'on va trouver de nouvelles sources d'énergie. Regardez, il y a déjà les voitures hybrides...
— Oh! Mais ça m'étonnerait que ces voitures aient beaucoup de succès! Elles sont bien trop chères!
— Peut-être, mais avec le temps, les prix vont descendre, vous verrez. Et bientôt, il y aura même des bateaux hybrides. Qui sait?

Answers for Activity 24
1. a   2. a   3. b   4. b   5. a   6. a   7. a   8. a

Grammaire à l'œuvre 2

(29) p. 292, CD 7, Tr. 5

1. Quand j'ai le temps, j'emporte les bouteilles en verre au recyclage.
2. Dès que tu auras assez d'argent, achète une voiture hybride!
3. Lorsque les maisons sont équipées de panneaux solaires, elles consomment beaucoup moins d'énergie.
4. Quand je serai au supermarché, je demanderai un sac en papier.
5. Lorsque tu auras ta propre maison, est-ce que tu économiseras l'énergie?
6. Dès que nous avons un sac en plastique, nous le recyclons.

Answers for Activity 29
1. a   2. b   3. a   4. b   5. b   6. a

Application 2

(40) p. 297, CD 7, Tr. 6

1. — Mais, Antoine, tu jettes tes papiers par terre maintenant?
   — Oh, c'était juste un tout petit morceau de papier. C'est pas grave.
2. — J'essaie de ne pas utiliser trop d'électricité.
   — Tu as raison, Valentin. D'abord, ça coûte cher et puis, tu ne gaspilles pas les ressources naturelles!
3. — Alors Ophélie, ta nouvelle maison est finie?
   — Non, pas encore. Il faut encore installer les panneaux solaires.
4. — Tu as vu la nouvelle voiture de Pascale?
   — Oui, c'est une de ces grosses voitures qui consomment beaucoup d'essence! Elle aurait dû acheter une voiture hybride!

Answers for Activity 40
1. b   2. a   3. a   4. b

Prépare-toi pour l'examen

(6) p. 305, CD 7, Tr. 8

1. Les écologistes seront heureux quand il n'y aura plus de pollution.

2. On peut améliorer le problème de l'accumulation des déchets en recyclant.
3. Il a tellement plu qu'il y a des inondations dans toute la région.
4. Un pétrolier a fait naufrage et a causé une marée noire.
5. On prévoit une tempête de neige. Gare aux avalanches!
6. Il faut recycler le verre et l'aluminium. C'est bon pour l'environnement.
7. Les fumées des usines polluent l'air et les écologistes disent que cela cause l'effet de serre.

Answers for Activity 6
1. b   2. b   3. a   4. b   5. a   6. b   7. b

Activités préparatoires

Listening, p. 308, CD 7, Tr. 9

1. Tu as lu cet article dans le journal? Il y a eu un tremblement de terre au Japon suivi d'un raz-de-marée! Plusieurs villages ont été complètement détruits et les dégâts sont importants. C'est un désastre! Une vraie catastrophe!
2. — Salut, Anne! Qu'est-ce que tu fais ce week-end?
   — Je vais travailler chez un vétérinaire pour soigner les animaux blessés pendant la marée noire.

Answers to the Listening Activity
1. a   2. b

Révisions cumulatives *chapitres 1-7*

(1) p. 310, CD 7, Tr. 10

1. Depuis qu'ils ont fermé l'usine, l'air est pur ici.
2. C'est vraiment difficile de nettoyer les plages polluées par des marées noires. Et en plus, beaucoup d'oiseaux meurent!
3. Tu as entendu le tonnerre? J'ai peur de l'orage, moi!
4. C'est une vraie catastrophe! La marée noire a endommagé toutes les plus belles plages de la région!
5. Attention, les éclairs peuvent causer des incendies!

50-Minute Lesson Plans

Notre planète

Day 1

OBJECTIVE
Caution

Core Instruction
Chapter Opener, pp. 274–275
• See Using the Photo, p. 274.
  5 min.
• See Chapter Objectives, p. 274.
  5 min.

Vocabulaire 1, pp. 276–279
• Present **Vocabulaire 1,**
  pp. 276–277. See Teaching
  Vocabulaire, p. 276. **20 min.**
• Present **Exprimons-nous!,**
  p. 277. **5 min.**
• Do Activity 1, p. 278. **5 min.**
• Play Audio CD 7, Tr. 1 for Activity
  2, p. 278. **5 min.**
• Do Activity 3, p. 278. **5 min.**

Optional Resources
• Advanced Learners, p. 277 ▲
• Slower Pace Learners, p. 279 ◆
• Special Learning Needs, p. 279 ●

Homework Suggestions
**Cahier de vocabulaire et
  grammaire,** pp. 73–74

  ❀ 1.1, 1.2, 1.3, 3.1

Day 2

OBJECTIVE
*Tell why something happened; Use
the comparative and superlative*

Core Instruction
Vocabulaire 1, pp. 276–279
• Do Bell Work 7.1, p. 276.
  5 min.
• See Teaching **Exprimons-
  nous!,** p. 278. **10 min.**
• Have students do Activities 4–6,
  p. 279. **20 min.**
• Present **Flash culture,** p. 279.
  5 min.

Grammaire 1, pp. 280–283
• See Teaching **Grammaire,**
  p. 280. **10 min.**

Optional Resources
• Communication (TE), p. 279
• Slower Pace Learners, p. 281 ◆

Homework Suggestions
Study for **Quiz: Vocabulaire 1**
**Cahier de vocabulaire et
  grammaire,** p. 75
Online Practice (**go.hrw.com,**
  Keyword: BD3 CH7)

  ❀ 1.1, 1.2, 4.2

Day 3

OBJECTIVE
*Use the comparative and
superlative*

Core Instruction
Vocabulaire 1, pp. 276–279
• Review **Vocabulaire 1,**
  pp. 276–279. **10 min.**
• Give **Quiz: Vocabulaire 1.**
  20 min.

Grammaire 1, pp. 280–283
• Have students do Activities
  7–11, pp. 280–281. **20 min.**

Optional Resources
• Communication (TE), p. 281
• Special Learning Needs, p. 281 ●

Homework Suggestions
**Cahier de vocabulaire et
  grammaire,** p. 76
Cahier d'activités, p. 61
Interactive Tutor, Ch. 7
Online Practice (**go.hrw.com,**
  Keyword: BD3 CH7)

  ❀ 1.1, 1.2, 1.3, 3.2

Day 4

OBJECTIVE
*Use the passive voice; Use prepo-
sitions*

Core Instruction
Grammaire 1, pp. 280–283
• See Teaching **Grammaire,**
  p. 282. **10 min.**
• Play Audio CD 7, Tr. 2 for Activity
  12, p. 282. **5 min.**
• Have students do Activities
  13–17, pp. 282–283. **25 min.**

Application 1, pp. 284–285
• Do Activity 18, p. 284. **5 min.**
• See Teaching **Un peu plus,**
  p. 284. **5 min.**

Optional Resources
• Advanced Learners, p. 283 ▲
• Slower Pace Learners, p. 285 ◆

Homework Suggestions
Study for **Quiz: Grammaire 1**
**Cahier de vocabulaire et
  grammaire,** p. 77
Cahier d'activités, p. 62

  ❀ 1.1, 1.2, 1.3, 3.1

Day 5

OBJECTIVE
Use prepositions

Core Instruction
Grammaire 1, pp. 280–283
• Review **Grammaire 1,**
  pp. 280–283. **10 min.**
• Give **Quiz: Grammaire 1.**
  20 min.

Application 1, pp. 284–285
• Play Audio CD 7, Tr. 3 for Activity
  19, p. 284. **5 min.**
• Have students do Activities
  20–22, p. 285. **15 min.**

Optional Resources
• French for Spanish Speakers,
  p. 284
• Communication (TE), p. 285
• Multiple Intelligences, p. 285

Homework Suggestions
Study for **Quiz: Application 1**
**Cahier de vocabulaire et
  grammaire,** p. 78
Cahier d'activités, p. 63
Online Practice (**go.hrw.com,**
  Keyword: BD3 CH7)

  ❀ 1.1, 1.2, 1.3, 4.1

Day 6

OBJECTIVE
Learn about francophone culture

Core Instruction
Application 1, pp. 284–285
• Review **Application 1,**
  pp. 284–285. **10 min.**
• Give **Quiz: Application 1.**
  20 min.

Culture, pp. 286–287
• See **Lecture culturelle** (TE),
  p. 286. **10 min.**
• See **Comparaisons et communauté** (TE), p. 286. **10 min.**

Optional Resources
• Cultures, p. 287
• Communities, p. 287
• Advanced Learners, p. 287 ▲
• Multiple Intelligences, p. 287

Homework Suggestions
Cahier d'activités, p. 64
Interactive Tutor, Ch. 7
Online Practice (**go.hrw.com,**
  Keyword: BD3 CH7)
Finish the **Communauté et
  professions** project, p. 287

  ❀ 1.2, 1.3, 2.1, 3.1, 4.2, 5.1

Day 7

OBJECTIVE
*Make predictions and express
assumptions*

Core Instruction
Vocabulaire 2, pp. 288–291
• Do Bell Work 7.5, p. 288.
  5 min.
• Present **Vocabulaire 2,**
  pp. 288–289. See Teaching
  Vocabulaire, p. 288. **15 min.**
• Present **Exprimons-nous!,**
  p. 289. **10 min.**
• Have students do Activity 23,
  p. 290. **5 min.**
• Play Audio CD 7, Tr. 4 for Activity
  24, p. 290. **5 min.**
• Have students do Activity 25,
  p. 290. **5 min.**
• Present **Flash culture,** p. 290.
  5 min.

Optional Resources
• Advanced Learners, p. 289 ▲
• Special Learning Needs, p. 289 ●

Homework Suggestions
**Cahier de vocabulaire et
  grammaire,** pp. 79–80

  ❀ 1.2, 1.3, 3.1, 3.2, 4.2

Day 8

OBJECTIVE
*Express and support an opinion; Use
quand, lorsque, and **dès que***

Core Instruction
Vocabulaire 2, pp. 288–291
• See Teaching **Exprimons-nous!,**
  p. 290. **10 min.**
• Have students do Activities
  26–28, p. 291. **20 min.**

Grammaire 2, pp. 292–295
• See Teaching **Grammaire,**
  p. 292. **10 min.**
• Play Audio CD 7, Tr. 5 for Activity
  29, p. 292. **5 min.**
• Do Activity 30, p. 292. **5 min.**

Optional Resources
• Slower Pace Learners, p. 291 ◆
• Special Learning Needs, p. 291 ●
• Slower Pace Learners, p. 293 ◆

Homework Suggestions
Study for **Quiz: Vocabulaire 2**
**Cahier de vocabulaire et
  grammaire,** p. 81
Interactive Tutor, Ch. 7
Online Practice (**go.hrw.com,**
  Keyword: BD3 CH7)

  ❀ 1.1, 1.2, 1.3, 3.1, 3.2, 4.1

50-Minute Lesson Plans

50-Minute Lesson Plans

Day 9

OBJECTIVE
*Use **quand, lorsque,** and **dès que***

Core Instruction
Vocabulaire 2, pp. 288–291
• Review **Vocabulaire 2,** pp. 288–291. **10 min.**
• Give **Quiz: Vocabulaire 2.** **20 min.**

Grammaire 2, pp. 292–295
• Have students do Activities 31–33, p. 293. **20 min.**

Optional Resources
• French for Spanish Speakers, p. 293
• Communication (TE), p. 293
• Special Learning Needs, p. 293 ●

Homework Suggestions
Cahier de vocabulaire et grammaire, p. 82
Cahier d'activités, p. 65
Interactive Tutor, Ch. 7
Online Practice (**go.hrw.com,** Keyword: BD3 CH7)
❀ 1.1, 1.2, 1.3, 4.1

Day 10

OBJECTIVE
Use the subjunctive after a conjunction

Core Instruction
Grammaire 2, pp. 292–295
• Do Bell Work 7.7, p. 294. **5 min.**
• See Teaching **Grammaire,** p. 294. **15 min.**
• Have students do Activities 34–37, pp. 294–295. **20 min.**

Application 2, pp. 296–297
• Do Activity 38, p. 296. **5 min.**
• Present **Flash culture,** p. 297. **5 min.**

Optional Resources
• Communication (TE), p. 295
• Advanced Learners, p. 295 ▲
• Special Learning Needs, p. 295●

Homework Suggestions
Study for **Quiz: Grammaire 2**
Cahier de vocabulaire et grammaire, p. 83
Cahier d'activités, p. 66
❀ 1.1, 1.2, 1.3, 4.2

Day 11

OBJECTIVE
Use the verb *éteindre*

Core Instruction
Grammaire 2, pp. 292–295
• Review **Grammaire 2,** pp. 292–295. **10 min.**
• Give **Quiz: Grammaire 2.** **20 min.**

Application 2, pp. 296–297
• See Teaching **Un peu plus,** p. 296. **5 min.**
• Do Activity 39, p. 296. **5 min.**
• Play Audio CD 7, Tr. 6 for Activity 40, p. 297. **5 min.**
• Do Act. 41–43, p. 297. **5 min.**

Optional Resources
• Communication (TE), p. 297
• Advanced Learners, p. 297 ▲
• Multiple Intelligences, p. 297

Homework Suggestions
Study for **Quiz: Application 2**
Cahier de vocabulaire et grammaire, p. 84
Cahier d'activités, p. 67
❀ 1.1, 1.2, 1.3

Day 12

OBJECTIVE
Develop listening and reading skills

Core Instruction
Application 2, pp. 296–297
• Review **Application 2,** pp. 296–297. **10 min.**
• Give **Quiz: Application 2.** **20 min.**

Lecture, pp. 298–301
• See **Lecture** (TE), p. 298. **20 min.**

Optional Resources
• Special Learning Needs, p. 299 ●
• Connections, p. 301

Homework Suggestions
Interactive Tutor, Ch. 7
Online Practice (**go.hrw.com,** Keyword: BD3 CH7)
❀ 1.2, 1.3, 3.2

Day 13

OBJECTIVE
Develop listening, reading, and writing skills

Core Instruction
Lecture, pp. 298–301
• See **Lecture** (TE), p. 300. **20 min.**

L'atelier de l'écrivain, pp. 302–303
• See **L'atelier de l'écrivain** (TE), p. 302. **30 min.**

Optional Resources
• Slower Pace Learners, p. 299 ◆
• Advanced Learners, p. 301 ▲
• Special Learning Needs, p. 301 ●
• Advanced Learners, p. 303 ▲
• Multiple Intelligences, p. 303

Homework Suggestions
Cahier d'activités, p. 68
❀ 1.1, 1.2, 1.3, 3.1

Day 14

OBJECTIVE
Review the chapter; Prepare for the AP Exam

Core Instruction
Prépare-toi pour l'examen, pp. 304–307
• Have students do Activities 1–5, pp. 304–305. **25 min.**

Activités préparatoires, pp. 308–309
• Have students do the **Activités préparatoires,** pp. 308–309. **25 min.**

Optional Resources
• Reteaching, p. 304
• Slower Pace Learners, p. 309 ◆
• Special Learning Needs, p. 309 ●
• **Télé-culture:** Interviews

Homework Suggestions
Interactive Tutor, Ch. 7
Online Practice (**go.hrw.com,** Keyword: BD3 CH7)
❀ 1.2, 1.3, 2.1, 2.2, 3.1

Day 15

OBJECTIVE
Review the chapter

Core Instruction
Prépare-toi pour l'examen, pp. 304–307
• Play Audio CD 7, Tr. 8 for Activity 6, p. 305. **10 min.**
• Have students do Activity 7, p. 305. **10 min.**

Révisions cumulatives, pp. 310–311
• Play Audio CD 7, Tr. 10 for Activity 1, p. 310. **5 min.**
• Have students do Activities 2–6, pp. 310–311. **25 min.**

Optional Resources
• Online Culture Project, p. 310
• Fine Art Connection, p. 311
• **Télé-roman: Camille et compagnie**

Homework Suggestions
Study for Chapter Test
Online Practice (**go.hrw.com,** Keyword: BD3 CH7)
❀ 1.1, 1.2, 1.3, 3.1, 3.2

Day 16/Test

Core Instruction
Chapter Test 50 min.

Optional Resources
Assessment Program:
• Alternative Assessment
• Test Generator
• **Quiz: Lecture**
• **Quiz: Écriture**

Homework Suggestions
Cahier d'activités, pp. 69–70, 114–115
Online Practice (**go.hrw.com,** Keyword: BD3 CH7)

90-Minute Lesson Plans

Notre planète

Block 1

OBJECTIVE
Caution; Tell why something happened

Core Instruction
Chapter Opener, pp. 274–275
• See Using the Photo, p. 274. **5 min.**
• See Chapter Objectives, p. 274. **5 min.**

Vocabulaire 1, pp. 276–279
• Present **Vocabulaire 1,** pp. 276–277. See Teaching **Vocabulaire,** p. 276. **20 min.**
• Present **Exprimons-nous!,** p. 277. **10 min.**
• Have students do Activity 1, p. 278. **5 min.**
• Play Audio CD 7, Tr. 1 for Activity 2, p. 278. **5 min.**
• Have students do Activity 3, p. 278. **5 min.**
• See Teaching **Exprimons-nous!,** p. 278. **10 min.**
• Have students do Activities 4–6, p. 279. **20 min.**
• Present **Flash culture,** p. 279. **5 min.**

Optional Resources
• Learning Tips, p. 275
• **Attention!,** p. 276
• TPR, p. 277
• Connections, p. 277
• Advanced Learners, p. 277 ▲
• Multiple Intelligences, p. 277
• Connections, p. 279
• Communication (TE), p. 279
• Slower Pace Learners, p. 279 ◆
• Special Learning Needs, p. 279 ●

Homework Suggestions
Study for **Quiz: Vocabulaire 1**
Cahier de vocabulaire et grammaire, pp. 73–75
Interactive Tutor, Ch. 7
Online Practice (**go.hrw.com,** Keyword: BD3 CH7)
✿ 1.1, 1.2, 1.3, 3.1, 4.2

Block 2

OBJECTIVE
Use the comparative and superlative; Use the passive voice

Core Instruction
Vocabulaire 1, pp. 276–279
• Review **Vocabulaire 1,** pp. 276–279. **10 min.**
• Give **Quiz: Vocabulaire 1.** **20 min.**

Grammaire 1, pp. 280–283
• See Teaching **Grammaire,** p. 280. **10 min.**
• Have students do Activities 7–11, pp. 280–281. **20 min.**
• See Teaching **Grammaire,** p. 282. **10 min.**
• Play Audio CD 7, Tr. 2 for Activity 12, p. 282. **5 min.**
• Have students do Activities 13–16, pp. 282–283. **15 min.**

Optional Resources
• Teacher to Teacher, p. 281
• Communication (TE), p. 281
• Slower Pace Learners, p. 281 ◆
• Special Learning Needs, p. 281 ●
• Communication (TE), p. 283
• Advanced Learners, p. 283 ▲
• Multiple Intelligences, p. 283

Homework Suggestions
Study for **Quiz: Grammaire 1**
Cahier de vocabulaire et grammaire, pp. 76–77
Cahier d'activités, pp. 61–62
Interactive Tutor, Ch. 7
Online Practice (**go.hrw.com,** Keyword: BD3 CH7)
✿ 1.1, 1.2, 1.3, 3.1, 3.2

Block 3

OBJECTIVE
Use the passive voice; Use prepositions; Learn about francophone culture

Core Instruction
Grammaire 1, pp. 280–283
• Do Bell Work 7.3, p. 282. **5 min.**
• Have students do Activity 17, p. 283. **5 min.**
• Review **Grammaire 1,** pp. 280–283. **10 min.**
• Give **Quiz: Grammaire 1.** **20 min.**

Application 1, pp. 284–285
• Have students do Activity 18, p. 284. **5 min.**
• See Teaching **Un peu plus,** p. 284. **5 min.**
• Play Audio CD 7, Tr. 3 for Activity 19, p. 284. **5 min.**
• Have students do Activities 20–22, p. 285. **15 min.**

Culture, pp. 286–287
• See **Lecture culturelle** (TE), p. 286. **10 min.**
• See **Comparaisons et communauté** (TE), p. 286. **10 min.**

Optional Resources
• French for Spanish Speakers, p. 284
• Communication (TE), p. 285
• Slower Pace Learners, p. 285 ◆
• Multiple Intelligences, p. 285
• Prereading Questions, p. 286
• Active Reading Questions, p. 286
• **Vocabulaire supplémentaire,** p. 286
• Bulletin Board Project, p. 287
• Cultures, p. 287
• Communities, p. 287
• Advanced Learners, p. 287 ▲
• Multiple Intelligences, p. 287

Homework Suggestions
Study for **Quiz: Application 1**
Cahier de vocabulaire et grammaire, p. 78
Cahier d'activités, pp. 63–64
Interactive Tutor, Ch. 7
Online Practice (**go.hrw.com,** Keyword: BD3 CH7)
Finish the **Communauté et professions** project, p. 287.
✿ 1.1, 1.2, 1.3, 2.1, 3.1, 4.2, 5.1

Block 4

OBJECTIVE
Make predictions and express assumptions; Express and support an opinion

Core Instruction
Application 1, pp. 284–285
• Review **Application 1,** pp. 284–285. **10 min.**
• Give **Quiz: Application 1.** **20 min.**

Vocabulaire 2, pp. 288–291
• Present **Vocabulaire 2,** pp. 288–289. See Teaching **Vocabulaire,** p. 288. **10 min.**
• Present **Exprimons-nous!,** p. 289. **5 min.**
• Have students do Activity 23, p. 290. **5 min.**
• Play Audio CD 7, Tr. 4 for Activity 24, p. 290. **5 min.**
• Have students do Activity 25, p. 290. **5 min.**
• Present **Flash culture,** p. 290. **5 min.**
• See Teaching **Exprimons-nous!,** p. 290. **10 min.**
• Have students do Activities 26–28, p. 291. **15 min.**

Optional Resources
• **Cinquain** Poetry, p. 288
• TPR, p. 289
• Comparisons, p. 289
• Advanced Learners, p. 289 ▲
• Special Learning Needs, p. 289 ●
• Communities, p. 291
• Communication (TE), p. 291
• Slower Pace Learners, p. 291 ◆
• Multiple Intelligences, p. 291

Homework Suggestions
Study for **Quiz: Vocabulaire 2**
Cahier de vocabulaire et grammaire, pp. 79–81
Interactive Tutor, Ch. 7
Online Practice (**go.hrw.com,** Keyword: BD3 CH7)
✿ 1.1. 1.2, 1.3, 2.1, 3.1, 3.2, 4.2, 5.1

Block 5

OBJECTIVE
*Use **quand, lorsque,** and **dès que;** Use the subjunctive after a conjunction*

Core Instruction
Vocabulaire 2, pp. 288–291
- Review **Vocabulaire 2,** pp. 288–291. **10 min.**
- Give **Quiz: Vocabulaire 2.** **20 min.**

Grammaire 2, pp. 292–295
- See Teaching **Grammaire,** p. 292. **10 min.**
- Play Audio CD 7, Tr. 5 for Activity 29, p. 292. **5 min.**
- Have students do Activities 30–33, pp. 292–293. **20 min.**
- See Teaching **Grammaire,** p. 294. **10 min.**
- Have students do Activities 34–36, pp. 294–295. **15 min.**

Optional Resources
- French for Spanish Speakers, p. 293
- Communication (TE), p. 293
- Slower Pace Learners, p. 293 ◆
- Special Learning Needs, p. 293 ●
- **Attention!,** p. 294
- Communication (TE), p. 295
- Advanced Learners, p. 295 ▲
- Special Learning Needs, p. 295 ●

Homework Suggestions
Study for **Quiz: Grammaire 2**
Cahier de vocabulaire et grammaire, pp. 82–83
Cahier d'activités, pp. 65–66
Interactive Tutor, Ch. 7
Online Practice (**go.hrw.com,** Keyword: BD3 CH7)

✿ 1.1, 1.2, 1.3, 4.1

Block 6

OBJECTIVE
*Use the subjunctive after a conjunction; Use the verb **éteindre;** Develop listening and reading skills*

Core Instruction
Grammaire 2, pp. 292–295
- Have students do Activity 37, p. 295. **10 min.**
- Review **Grammaire 2,** pp. 292–295. **10 min.**
- Give **Quiz: Grammaire 2.** **20 min.**

Application 2, pp. 296–297
- Have students do Activity 38, p. 296. **5 min.**
- Present **Flash culture,** p. 297. **5 min.**
- See Teaching **Un peu plus,** p. 296. **5 min.**
- Have students do Activity 39, p. 296. **5 min.**
- Play Audio CD 7, Tr. 6 for Activity 40, p. 297. **5 min.**
- Have students do Activities 41–43, p. 297. **5 min.**

Lecture, pp. 298–301
- See **Lecture** (TE), p. 298. **20 min.**

Optional Resources
- Communication (TE), p. 297
- Advanced Learners, p. 297 ▲
- Multiple Intelligences, p. 297
- AP Reading Suggestion, p. 298
- Applying the Strategies, p. 298
- Active Reading Questions, p. 299
- Understanding Character, p. 299
- Slower Pace Learners, p. 299 ◆
- Special Learning Needs, p. 299 ●

Homework Suggestions
Study for **Quiz: Application 2**
Cahier de vocabulaire et grammaire, p. 84
Cahier d'activités, p. 67
Interactive Tutor, Ch. 7
Online Practice (**go.hrw.com,** Keyword: BD3 CH7)

✿ 1.1, 1.2, 1.3, 3.1

Block 7

OBJECTIVE
Develop listening, reading, and writing skills; Review the chapter

Core Instruction
Application 2, pp. 296–297
- Review **Application 2,** pp. 296–297. **10 min.**
- Give **Quiz: Application 2.** **20 min.**

Lecture, pp. 298–301
- See **Lecture** (TE), p. 300. **10 min.**

L'atelier de l'écrivain, pp. 302–303
- See **L'atelier de l'écrivain** (TE), p. 302. **30 min.**

Prépare-toi pour l'examen, pp. 304–307
- Have students do Activities 1–5, pp. 304–305. **10 min.**
- Play Audio CD 7, Tr. 8 for Activity 6, p. 305. **5 min.**
- Have students do Activity 7, p. 305. **5 min.**

Optional Resources
- Active Reading Questions, p. 300
- Postreading Activity, p. 300
- Connections, p. 301
- Advanced Learners, p. 301 ▲
- Special Learning Needs, p. 301 ●
- Process Writing, p. 302
- Teaching Suggestion, p. 302
- The conditional, p. 303
- Writing Assessment, p. 303
- Advanced Learners, p. 303 ▲
- Multiple Intelligences, p. 303
- TPRS, p. 304
- Reteaching, p. 304
- Oral Assessment, p. 305
- Connections, p. 306
- **Proverbes,** p. 306
- Chapter Review, pp. 306–307
- Game, p. 307

Homework Suggestions
Study for Chapter Test
Cahier d'activités, p. 68
Interactive Tutor, Ch. 7
Online Practice (**go.hrw.com,** Keyword: BD3 CH7)

✿ 1.1, 1.2, 1.3, 2.1, 2.2, 3.1, 3.2

Block 8

OBJECTIVE
Prepare for the AP Exam; Review and assess the chapter

Core Instruction
Activités préparatoires, pp. 308–309
- Have students do the **Activités préparatoires,** pp. 308–309. **20 min.**

Chapter Test 50 min.

Révisions cumulatives, pp. 310–311
- Play Audio CD 7, Tr. 10 for Activity 1, p. 310. **5 min.**
- Have students do Activities 2–6, pp. 310–311. **15 min.**

Optional Resources
- Reading Strategy, p. 309
- Writing Strategy, p. 309
- Slower Pace Learners, p. 309 ◆
- Special Learning Needs, p. 309 ●
- Online Culture Project, p. 310
- Fine Art Connection, p. 311
- **Télé-roman: Camille et compagnie**

Homework Suggestions
Cahier d'activités, pp. 69–70, 114–115
Interactive Tutor, Ch. 7
Online Practice (**go.hrw.com,** Keyword: BD3 CH7)

✿ 1.1, 1.2, 1.3, 3.1, 3.2

90-Minute Lesson Plans

Meeting the National Standards

Communication
Communication, pp. 279, 281, 283, 285, 291, 293, 295, 297

À ton tour, p. 311

Cultures
Flash culture, pp. 279, 290, 297

Comparaisons, p. 287

Practices and Perspectives, p. 287

Connections
Science Link, p. 277

Health Link, p. 279

Film Link, p. 301

Social Studies Link, p. 306

Comparisons
Comparaisons, p. 287

Comparing and Contrasting, p. 289

Communities
Communauté, p. 287

Career Path, p. 287

Community Link, p. 291

Using the Photo

H. A. Schult was born in 1939 in Mecklenburg, Germany. Among his most famous sculptures are *Trash People, Peace for Trees,* and *Hotel Europa.* His exhibit, *Trash People,* was shown in New York, Paris, Moscow, at the Great Wall of China, and at the pyramids of Giza. The 1,000 soldiers in *Trash People* were created from consumer refuse, such as tin cans and metal containers. Schult describes his army of trash people as "silent witnesses to a consumer age that has created an ecological imbalance worldwide." Ask students why they think *Trash People* was displayed at many famous places.
2.2

---

chapitre **7**

Notre planète

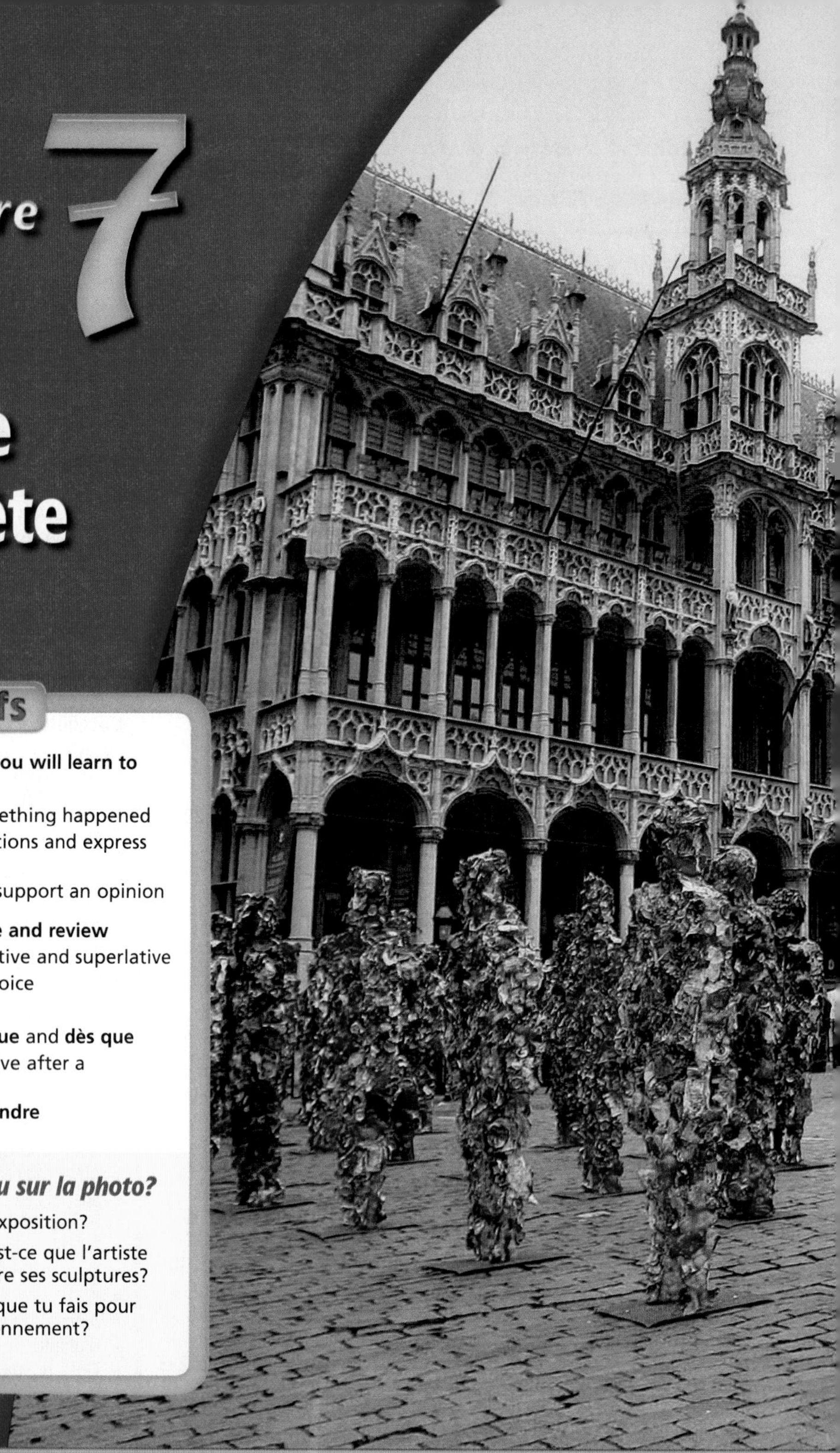

Objectifs

In this chapter, you will learn to
- caution
- tell why something happened
- make predictions and express assumptions
- express and support an opinion

And you will use and review
- the comparative and superlative
- the passive voice
- prepositions
- **quand, lorsque** and **dès que**
- the subjunctive after a conjunction
- the verb **éteindre**

▶ *Que vois-tu sur la photo?*

Où a lieu cette exposition?

D'après toi, qu'est-ce que l'artiste a utilisé pour faire ses sculptures?

Et toi, qu'est-ce que tu fais pour protéger l'environnement?

Suggested pacing:	Traditional Schedule	Block Schedule
Vocabulaire/Grammaire/Application 1	51/2 days	2 blocks
Culture	1 day	1 block
Vocabulaire/Grammaire/Application 2	41/2 days	2 blocks
Lecture	1 day	1/2 block
L'atelier de l'écrivain	1 day	1/2 block
Prépare-toi pour l'examen	1/2 day	1/2 block
Activités préparatoires	1/2 day	1/2 block
Examen	1 day	1/2 block
Révisions cumulatives	1 day	1/2 block

Visit Us Online
go.hrw.com
Online Edition
KEYWORD: BD3 CH7

Chapitre 7

Chapter Opener

Les « Trash People » de l'artiste allemande,
H. A. Schult sur la Grand-Place, à Bruxelles

Vocabulaire supplémentaire

Students might use these terms to discuss the photo.

les détritus (m.)	*trash*
l'exposition (f.)	*exhibition*
le consommateur	*consumer*
l'environnement (m.)	*environment*
la pollution	*pollution*
les ressources naturelles	*natural resources*

Learning Tips

Remind students that intonation is an important aspect of spoken language. French speakers, like English speakers, use different intonation to express emotions, such as excitement or annoyance. The same words can mean something completely different when spoken with different intonation. When they learn new expressions, students should pay attention to intonation.

Language Lab

You might want to use your language lab to have students:
• listen to all target vocabulary and phrases in the chapter
• practice pronunciation of vocabulary and phrases, using Holt SoundBooth to save their work for evaluation
• complete the listening activities in this chapter

LISTENING PRACTICE

Vocabulaire
Activity 2, p. 278, CD 7, Tr. 1
Activity 24, p. 290, CD 7, Tr. 4

Grammaire
Activity 12, p. 282, CD 7, Tr. 2
Activity 29, p. 292, CD 7, Tr. 5

Application
Activity 19, p. 284, CD 7, Tr. 3
Activity 39, p. 296, CD 7, Tr. 6

Language Lab and Classroom Activities

Prépare-toi pour l'examen
Activity 6, p. 305, CD 7, Tr. 8
Télé-culture: Interviews, Chapter 7

Activités préparatoires
Section I, Listening, p. 308, CD 7, Tr. 9
Télé-roman: *Camille et compagnie*, Épisode 7

Révisions cumulatives
Activity 1, p. 310, CD 7, Tr. 10

Lecture
p. 298, CD 7, Tr. 7

L'Europe francophone

Vocabulaire
à l'œuvre 1

Les phénomènes naturels

Un incendie a ravagé la forêt.

Un **tremblement de terre** a secoué la ville. Heureusement, l'**alerte** avait été donnée et les habitants ont eu le temps d'**évacuer la région sinistrée.**

Un **raz-de-marée** a provoqué **des inondations** sur la côte.

▶ Vocabulaire supplémentaire—Les phénomènes naturels, p. R20

Bell Work

Use Bell Work 7.1 in the *Teaching Transparencies* or write this activity on the board.

Réponds négativement aux questions suivantes:

1. **Est-ce que tu vois mon journal quelque part?**
2. **Est-ce que tu lis encore ce magazine de sport?**
3. **Es-tu déjà allé(e) voir un match de polo?**
4. **Est-ce que cette équipe a des chances de gagner?**
5. **Est-ce que tu connais quelqu'un qui joue au polo?**

COMMON ERROR ALERT
/// **ATTENTION !**

When students use dictionaries, they often choose **parce que** when they really mean **à cause de**. **Parce que** means *because* and is followed by a clause. **À cause de** means *because of* and is followed by a noun.

Core Instruction

TEACHING VOCABULAIRE

1. Introduce the vocabulary, using transparencies **Vocabulaire 7.1** and **7.2**. Model the pronunciation of each word or expression. **(3 min.)**

2. Ask students to point out various items on the transparency. (**un incendie, un volcan**) **(3 min.)**

3. Ask students questions about natural disasters in the news. **Où est-ce qu'il y a eu un cyclone récemment? Où est-ce qu'il y a parfois des tremblements de terre aux États-Unis? (3 min.)**

4. Model the sentences from **Exprimons-nous!** Then describe situations and have students caution you about possible dangers. **Il pleut beaucoup. Prenez garde aux inondations. Il va y avoir des orages. Méfiez-vous des éclairs. (3 min.)**

Quand il y a **des orages**, on peut voir **des éclairs** et entendre **le tonnerre**.

Une tornade a détruit plusieurs maisons.

Online Practice

go.hrw.com
Vocabulaire 1 practice

KEYWORD: BD3 CH7

Le volcan est entré en **éruption** mais **la coulée de lave** n'est pas arrivée jusqu'au village.

Les dégâts causés par **le glissement de terrain** sont estimés à plusieurs **millions** d'euros.

Exprimons-nous!

To caution

On prévoit de l'orage **pour** cet après-midi.
They are predicting . . . for . . .

Surtout, ne sortez pas pendant la tornade.
Above all . . .

Prenez garde aux avalanches quand vous irez skier.
Watch out for . . .

Méfie-toi de la grêle. **Elle peut provoquer** des dégâts.
Beware of . . . It could cause . . .

Protégez bien vos fenêtres **au cas où** il y aurait une tempête.
. . . in case . . .

Interactive TUTOR

Vocabulaire et grammaire, pp. 73–75 | Online workbooks

D'autres mots utiles

une avalanche	avalanche
le climat	climate
le courant	current
un désastre	disaster
le désert	desert
la grêle	hail
un ouragan/ un cyclone	hurricane
une précaution	precaution
la sécheresse	drought
une tempête (de sable/ de neige)	(sand/snow) storm
abîmer/ endommager	to damage
empirer	to get worse

Resources

Planning:

Lesson Planner

 One-Stop Planner

Presentation:

 Teaching Transparencies
Vocabulaire 7.1, 7.2

Practice:

Cahier de vocabulaire et grammaire

Differentiated Practice and Assessment CD-ROM

Media Guide

🎧 Audio CD 7, Tr. 1

💿 Interactive Tutor, Disc 2

② Script

See script on p. 273E.

④ Answers

1. à cause
2. dû à
3. C'est pour ça
4. Donc

Cultures

Products and Perspectives

The Sahara, one of the hottest and driest regions of the world, is swept by strong, dry, dust-laden winds, called **simoom,** *poison wind,* in the summer months. Nevertheless, it is home to 2,5 million people, who have adjusted to the harsh environment by wearing clothes such as white robes, cloaks, veils, and turbans. These clothes not only comply with the Islamic code of modesty but protect against heat, wind, and sand. Ask students to research the architecture of the Sahara. What architectural features protect from heat, wind, and sand? 🌐 2.2, 3.1

À la française

Depending on the region of the world where it happens, the same natural disaster can have different names. For example, **un ouragan** is called **un typhon** when it happens in the Pacific Ocean.

---

① C'est quoi? 🌐 1.2

Lisons/Parlons Trouve la définition des mots suivants.

d **1.** C'est une grande lumière dans le ciel pendant un orage.

c **2.** C'est quand il y a de l'eau partout.

e **3.** C'est ce qui sort d'un volcan en éruption.

b **4.** C'est quand il ne pleut pas pendant longtemps.

a **5.** C'est une montagne qui produit du feu.

a. un volcan

b. la sécheresse

c. une inondation

d. un éclair

e. la lave

f. le tonnerre

② Écoutons   CD 7, Tr. 1   🌐 1.2   **1.** c **2.** b **3.** a **4.** a **5.** d **6.** e

🎧 Écoute les nouvelles à la radio et dis de quelle photo on parle.

a.

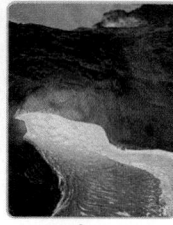
b.

c.

d.

e.

③ La tempête de sable 🌐 1.2

Lisons/Écrivons Complète la lettre d'Ali avec les mots ci-dessous.

tempête	l'alerte	précautions	au cas où	éruption	dégâts
sable	désastre	a détruit	surtout	garde	prévoit

1. tempête
2. l'alerte
3. précautions
4. au cas où
5. dégâts
6. a détruit
7. désastre
8. prévoit
9. Surtout

Ici, on a eu très peur! Il y a eu une grosse ___1___ de sable près de chez moi. Quand on a entendu ___2___, on a dû quitter le village tout de suite et on n'a pas eu le temps de prendre beaucoup de ___3___ pour protéger notre maison avant de partir. On a quand même bien fermé nos fenêtres ___4___ la tempête arriverait jusqu'à notre village, mais cela n'est pas arrivé et il n'y a pas eu de ___5___. Mais la tempête ___6___ plusieurs maisons dans le village voisin. Ça a été un vrai ___7___! Malheureusement, on ___8___ un ouragan pour ce week-end! ___9___ ne viens pas nous rendre visite maintenant!

Core Instruction

TEACHING EXPRIMONS-NOUS!

1. Model the pronunciation of the expressions in **Exprimons-nous! (2 min.)**

2. Write several pairs of sentences on the board and ask students to connect them with words and phrases in **Exprimons-nous! (4 min.)**

3. Have partners make up similarly constructed sentences similar to those in **Exprimons-nous!** to tell what happened and explain why. **(2 min.)**

Exprimons-nous!

To tell why something happened	
Il a beaucoup plu. **C'est pour ça qu'**il y a eu une inondation. *. . . That's why . . .*	
Il y a eu un raz-de-marée **à cause d'**un tremblement de terre. *. . . because of . . .*	
Ces dégâts sont **dûs à** un ouragan. *. . . due to . . .*	
Il y a eu une avalanche. **Donc,** la piste de ski est fermée. *. . . Therefore, . . .*	

Vocabulaire et grammaire, pp. 73–75 — **Online** workbooks

4 **Causes et conséquences** ✿1.2

Écrivons Complète cette conversation entre Raphaël et Mia qui discutent d'une catastrophe naturelle qui vient d'arriver.

RAPHAËL   Tu sais que cette ville a été partiellement détruite ____1____ d'un au raz-de-marée ____2____ tremblement de terre qui a ravagé le nord du pays.

MIA   Oui mais grâce à l'alerte, les habitants ont eu le temps d'évacuer. ____3____ qu'il n'y a pas eu de victimes. ____4____, on peut dire qu'il y a eu plus de peur que de mal!

5 **Que sais-je?** ✿1.2

 **Écrivons** Écris une phrase pour expliquer les causes des phénomènes suivants. Utilise les expressions d'**Exprimons-nous!**

MODÈLE   un glissement de terrain
Un glissement de terrain est dû à beaucoup de pluie.

1. un raz-de-marée
2. un incendie
3. une coulée de lave
4. la sécheresse

Flash culture

La Belgique, la Suisse et Monaco, grâce à leur situation géographique, sont préservés des grands cataclysmes naturels. Par exemple, la Belgique connaît un climat tempéré grâce au Gulfstream qui baigne ses côtes. Mais parfois, dans les Alpes suisses et françaises, il y a des avalanches et des glissements de terrain dus aux pluies torrentielles et à la fonte des glaciers. Est-ce qu'il y a beaucoup de catastrophes naturelles dans ta région? Lesquelles?

✿4.2

Communication

 HOLT **SoundBooth** ONLINE RECORDING

6 **Expérience personnelle** ✿1.1

Parlons Tu viens de survivre à un désastre. Un(e) journaliste te pose des questions sur cette terrible expérience. Réponds à ses questions et explique en détails ce qui s'est passé. Un(e) camarade va jouer le rôle du/de la journaliste, puis échangez les rôles.

MODÈLE   —Vous étiez là quand il y a eu la tempête de neige?
—Oui, il y avait tellement de neige qu'on ne pouvait plus ouvrir la porte, donc... , c'est pour ça que...

Differentiated Instruction

Resources

Planning:

Lesson Planner

 One-Stop Planner

Practice:

Grammar Tutor for Students of French, Chapter 7

Cahier de vocabulaire et grammaire

Differentiated Practice and Assessment CD-ROM

Cahier d'activités

Media Guide

 Teaching Transparencies Bell Work 7.2

Interactive Tutor, Disc 2

Bell Work

Use Bell Work 7.2 in the *Teaching Transparencies* or write this activity on the board.

Finis chaque phrase logiquement.

1. Le tremblement de terre...
2. L'incendie a ravagé...
3. Après l'éruption du volcan...
4. Surtout quand vous skiez...
5. Quand il pleut énormément...

a. ce parc avec des arbres anciens.
b. méfie-toi des routes inondées.
c. la coulée de lave a endommagé plusieurs maisons.
d. a détruit des ponts et des bâtiments.
e. prenez garde aux avalanches! 1.2

---

❾ Possible Answers

1. Je suis meilleur qu'elle en math.
2. Je parle le mieux italien.
3. J'ai fait moins d'erreurs qu'eux à l'examen.
4. J'ai de meilleures notes qu'Aline.
5. J'ai plus de jeux vidéo qu'eux.

Objectifs
• review of the comparative and superlative
• the passive voice

Interactive TUTOR

The comparative and superlative

1 To form the **comparative of nouns** in French, add **plus de** *(more of)*, **moins de** *(less/fewer of)*, or **autant de** *(as many/much of)* before the noun. Use **que** after the noun to continue the comparison.

> Il y a **moins de** tremblements de terre en **France** qu'au Japon.

2 To form the **comparative of adjectives and adverbs**, add **plus** *(more)*, **moins** *(less)*, or **aussi** *(as)* before the adjective or adverb. Use **que** to continue the comparison. The adjective agrees with the first noun in the comparison.

> *agrees*
> À mon avis, un **raz-de-marée** est **plus dangereux** qu'une tempête.

3 To form the **superlative of adjectives**, add the definite article before **plus**, or **moins**. To say *in/of* after the superlative, use **de**.

> C'était la **plus grande** tempête **de** l'hiver.

If the adjective follows the noun, use the following construction:

> **definite article + noun + definite article + plus/moins + adjective**
> C'est le **jour** le **plus long de** l'année.

4 To form the **superlative of adverbs**, use the definite article **le** with the comparative form.

> Le cyclone a frappé **le plus violemment** la côte sud du pays.

Vocabulaire et grammaire, *pp. 76–77*
Cahier d'activités, *pp. 61–63*

Online workbooks

Déjà vu!

Do you remember the irregular comparative and superlative forms for **bon** and **bien**?

> **bon → meilleur**
> **bien → mieux**

Don't forget that **meilleur** agrees with the noun it modifies.

> **Les meilleures pistes de ski sont en Suisse.**

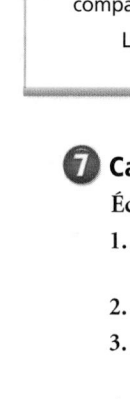

---

❼ Catastrophes naturelles ✿1.2

Écrivons Fais les comparaisons suivantes.

1. Ce tremblement de terre a été _____ important _____ celui du siècle dernier. (−)
2. Mais le raz-de-marée qui l'a suivi a été _____ violent. (+)
3. Cette catastrophe a fait _____ victimes _____ l'éruption du volcan. (+)
4. Les glissements de terrain sont souvent _____ dangereux _____ les avalanches. (=)
5. Et puis surtout, ils peuvent faire _____ dégâts. (=)

1. moins; que 2. plus 3. plus de; que
4. aussi; que 5. autant de

Core Instruction

TEACHING GRAMMAIRE

1. Read **Déjà vu!** aloud with students. **(2 min.)**

2. Go over Points 1–3. You might tell students that when the adjective normally precedes the noun, they actually have the choice of placing its superlative before or after that noun. **la plus grande maison / la maison la plus grande. (4 min.)**

3. Go over Point 4. Tell students that when the adverb is short enough to be placed between the auxiliary and past participle in the **passé composé**, its superlative should be placed there as well. **Il a bien réussi. C'est en maths qu'il a le mieux réussi. (2 min.)**

Online Practice

go.hrw.com

Grammaire 1 practice

KEYWORD: BD3 CH7

8 La carte de France 🍀1.2 **1.** a **2.** b **3.** b **4.** a **5.** a **6.** a

Lisons/Parlons Camille et ses amies comparent des villes de France. Dis si ce qu'elles disent est **a) vrai** ou **b) faux.**

1. Lille est la ville qui est le plus près de la Belgique.
2. Lyon est plus loin de Paris que Grenoble.
3. Brest est la ville la plus à l'est de la France.
4. Nice est plus à l'est que Marseille.
5. Le temps est meilleur dans le sud de la France qu'à Paris.
6. Biarritz est moins loin de l'océan que Bordeaux.

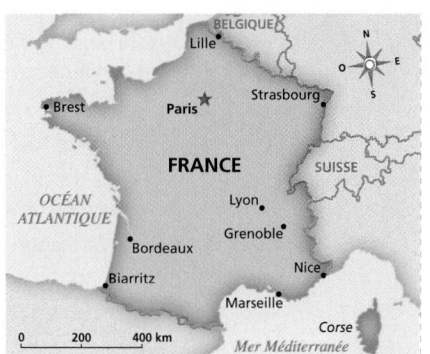

9 C'est moi le meilleur! 🍀1.2

Écrivons/Parlons Ludovic est très prétentieux. Imagine ce qu'il répondrait aux phrases suivantes. Utilise des comparatifs et des superlatifs.

MODÈLE —Léa est très intelligente.
—**Je suis plus intelligent qu'elle./Je suis le plus intelligent.**

1. Léa est bonne en maths.
2. Luc parle bien italien.
3. Rémy et Tom n'ont pas fait beaucoup d'erreurs à l'examen.
4. Aline n'a pas de mauvaises notes.
5. Yanis et Hugo ont beaucoup de jeux vidéo.

10 Et toi?! 🍀1.3

Écrivons Décris tes amis, ta ville ou ton école en utilisant des comparatifs et des superlatifs.

MODÈLE —**Ma ville est plus animée que...**

Communication

 HOLT **SoundBooth** ONLINE RECORDING

11 Opinions personnelles 🍀1.1

Parlons Demande à un(e) de tes camarades qui il/elle admire et pourquoi. Ensuite échangez les rôles.

MODÈLE —**Qui est ton sportif/acteur/etc. préféré et pourquoi?**
—**Je trouve que... C'est le plus... Il est plus... que...**

Communication

Group Activity: Interpersonal
Have each student think of a place he or she is going to visit. Then, in groups of three, one student announces his or her chosen destination. The others express caution about possible natural phenomena and compare natural phenomena of their destination with that in other places. Each group member takes a turn.

MODÈLE
— **Je vais voyager en Caroline du Sud.**
— **Prends garde aux tremblements de terre.**
— **Ne t'inquiète pas, il y a moins de tremblements de terre en Caroline du Sud qu'en Californie.**
— **Tu as raison. Et, il y a plus de glissements de terrain.**
🍀1.1, 1.2

Differentiated Instruction

SLOWER PACE LEARNERS

Additional Practice After presenting the comparative and superlative, ask students to provide at least two more sample sentences for each of the four points in the grammar presentation. Encourage students to use expressions from **Vocabulaire 1.** Students should write the sample sentences in their notebook for future reference. 🍀1.2

SPECIAL LEARNING NEEDS

Students with Learning Disabilities To help students learn French adverbs and adjectives, ask them to find an article about a natural disaster on the Internet written in French within the past year. Students should print the article. Then they should circle all adverbs and adjectives and underline the verbs and nouns they modify. Once students have completed their articles, they should exchange them and review their partner's work. 🍀3.1

Resources

Planning:

Lesson Planner

 One-Stop Planner

Practice:

Grammar Tutor for Students of French, Chapter 7

Cahier de vocabulaire et grammaire

Differentiated Practice and Assessment CD-ROM

Cahier d'activités

Media Guide

 Teaching Transparencies
Bell Work 7.3

 Audio CD 7, Tr. 2

Interactive Tutor, Disc 2

Bell Work

Use Bell Work 7.3 in the *Teaching Transparencies* or write this activity on the board.

Fais les comparaisons suivantes.

1. J'ai ____ peur ____ toi des avalanches. (−)
2. Cette année, il y a eu ____ incendies ____ l'année dernière. (+)
3. Ce deuxième cyclone a été ____ dangereux ____ le premier. (=)
4. La grêle a causé ____ dégâts ____ le cyclone. (=)
5. Cet incendie a fait ____ victimes ____ le précédent. (−) ✿ 1.2

⑫ Script

See script on p. 273E.

⑬ Answers

1. L'énergie doit être économisée.
2. Les déchets doivent être recyclés.
3. La nature doit être préservée.
4. La faune doit être protégée.
5. La pollution doit être combattue.

⑭ Answers

1. a été détruit
2. ont été emmenées
3. ont été évacués
4. ont été estimés
5. être construites

 TUTOR

The passive voice

1 The **passive voice** is used when the subject of the sentence *receives the action*. To form a sentence in the passive voice in French, use a form of **être** plus the **past participle** of the main verb. The past participle agrees in *gender* and *number* with the subject of the sentence.

receives the action

Cette tour a été **construite** en 2005.

2 To tell *who* or *what is doing the action* use **par**.

La maison a été **détruite** par un cyclone.

 Vocabulaire et grammaire, pp. 76–77 · Cahier d'activités, pp. 61–63 · **Online** workbooks

⑫ Écoutons CD 7, Tr. 2 ✿ 1.2 **1.** a **2.** b **3.** a **4.** b **5.** b **6.** a

 Jacques a eu un accident pendant qu'il cuisinait. Pour chaque phrase, dis si **a) c'est Jacques qui a fait quelque chose** ou **b) c'est quelqu'un d'autre qui a fait quelque chose à Jacques.**

⑬ Sauvons la planète ✿ 1.2

Parlons/Écrivons Qu'est-ce qu'il faut faire pour sauver la planète? Mets les phrases suivantes à la voix passive.

MODÈLE On doit respecter la nature.
La nature doit être respectée.

1. On doit économiser l'énergie.
2. On doit recycler les déchets.
3. On doit préserver la nature.
4. On doit protéger la faune.
5. On doit combattre la pollution

⑭ C'était dans les journaux! ✿ 1.2

Lisons/Écrivons Complète les phrases suivantes avec la forme correcte des verbes à la voix passive.

Le village __1__ (détruire) par un tremblement de terre. Les victimes __2__ (emmener) dans les hôpitaux les plus proches. Tous les autres habitants __3__ (évacuer) de la région sinistrée. Les dégâts __4__ (estimer) à plus de trois millions d'euros. Pour éviter un autre désastre de ce genre, les habitants ont décidé que les maisons allaient __5__ (construire) plus solidement à l'avenir.

Core Instruction

TEACHING GRAMMAIRE

1. Tell students that the passive voice is not used as much in French as it is in English, and that the French often avoid it by using **on** or by changing the order of the sentence. **On a créé ce parc l'année dernière. Un cyclone a détruit la maison. (2 min.)**

2. Point out that in the **passé composé,** it is the past participle of the main verb that agrees with the subject, and that the past participle of **être** is invariable. **(2 min.)**

15 **Un cataclysme** ✿1.2

Écrivons Reconstruis les phrases suivantes. Fais tous les changements nécessaires.

MODÈLE famille / l'alarme / toute / réveiller / par
Toute la famille a été réveillée par l'alarme.

1. par / secouer / tremblement de terre / région
2. incendie / ravager / ville / par
3. feu / par / endommager / maison
4. par / flamme *(flame)* / détruire / voiture
5. causer / par / inondation / dégât / beaucoup / par
6. heureusement / alerte / tout de suite / donner
7. rapidement / évacuer / région / sinistré

16 **Qu'est-ce qui s'est passé?** ✿1.3

Écrivons/Parlons Regarde les photos et explique ce qui s'est passé. Utilise la voix passive.

a. les pistes de ski

b. la ville

c. la maison

d. les champs

e. la forêt

f. le village

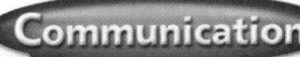
Communication

HOLT SoundBooth
ONLINE RECORDING

17 **Scénario** ✿1.1

Parlons Un(e) de tes camarades et toi vous discutez d'une récente catastrophe naturelle dont on a parlé à la télévision ou dans les journaux. Chacun de vous raconte ce qu'il a appris.

15 Answers

1. La région a été secouée par un tremblement de terre.
2. La ville a été ravagée par l'incendie.
3. Des maisons ont été endommagées par le feu.
4. Des voitures ont été détruites par les flammes.
5. Beaucoup de dégâts ont été causés par des inondations.
6. Heureusement, l'alerte a été donnée tout de suite.
7. La région sinistrée a été évacuée rapidement.

16 Possible Answers

1. Les pistes de ski ont été emportées par une avalanche.
2. Dues aux fortes pluies, la ville a été inondée.
3. La maison a été endommagée par un raz-de-marée.
4. À cause de la sécheresse, les champs ont été dévastés.
5. La forêt a été ravagée par une éruption.
6. Il y a eu un ouragan et le village a été détruit.

Communication

Group Activity: Presentational

Partners recall a school event or holiday and take turns describing what happened using the passive voice. You might have partners present their description to the class.

MODÈLE

— **Les biscuits ont été mangés par Père Noël.**

✿1.3

Assess

Assessment Program

Quiz: Grammaire 1

Alternative Assessment

Differentiated Practice and Assessment CD-ROM

Online Assessment

my.hrw.com

Test Generator

Differentiated Instruction

ADVANCED LEARNERS

16 Extension Once students have completed this activity, ask them to choose one of the photos and write a newspaper article about the event pictured in the photo. Students should provide a title for their article and a caption for the photo. The article should have at least ten sentences. Encourage students to use the passive voice when possible. ✿1.3

MULTIPLE INTELLIGENCES

14 Interpersonal Have students work in groups of three to illustrate the news article presented. Students should complete the text from the book and reformat it as a newspaper article as directed. Students will add illustrations to the article. If students prefer, they may find pictures on the Internet that would provide better illustrations for their article. ✿3.2

Bell Work

Use Bell Work 7.4 in the *Teaching Transparencies* or write this activity on the board.

Mets les phrases suivantes à la forme passive.

1. **Un tremblement de terre a secoué la ville.**
2. **Des incendies ont ravagé plusieurs maisons.**
3. **On a emmené les victimes à l'hôpital.**
4. **On a rapidement donné l'alerte.** 1.2

French for Spanish Speakers

Ask Spanish speakers to look at the prepositions for cognates. Which are closest in spelling and meaning to Spanish? (**à, de, en, par, pour** correspond closely with **a, de, en, por,** and **para**) Ask which preposition is a false cognate. (**depuis / después**) Although French and Spanish have much in common, preposition use can be very different. Ask them how they would translate **Je pense à toi.** (**Pienso en ti**) 4.1

Synthèse
• Vocabulaire 1
• Grammaire 1

Application 1

18 Un incendie 1.2

Écrivons Il y a eu un incendie en ville la nuit dernière. Forme des phrases complètes avec les éléments donnés. Pour certaines phrases, la colonne 3 ne sera pas nécesssaire.

1	**2**	**3**	**4**
Cet article	ont été causés	à	un problème électrique
L'incendie	a téléphoné	à cause de	l'incendie
C'	a commencé	après	la police
Quelqu'un	ne restait plus	de/d'	des faits divers
Il	rien	derrière	l'inondation
Les dégâts	parle	par	la maison
	était		

Un peu plus

Prepositions

1. Prepositions show the relationship between a noun and another word in a sentence. In some cases, you will use a different preposition in French from English.

   À quoi est-ce que tu penses? *What are you thinking about?*

2. In some cases, a preposition can be omitted in one language, but not in the other.

   J'écris une lettre à Luc. (**à** is required)
   I'm writing (to) my parents tonight. (**to** is optional)

   Vocabulaire et grammaire, *p. 78*
   Cahier d'activités, *pp. 61–63*

19 Écoutons   CD 7, Tr. 3   1.2   **1.** h **2.** d/g **3.** a **4.** f **5.** g **6.** e **7.** j **8.** k

 Tu écoutes ces conversations mais tu n'entends pas clairement ce que les gens disent. Dis quelle préposition compléterait logiquement chacune des phrases que tu entends.

a. après	**d.** pour	**g.** à	**j.** depuis
b. devant	**e.** sans	**h.** de/d'	**k.** dans
c. chez	**f.** avec	**i.** par	**l.** en

Core Instruction

INTEGRATED PRACTICE

1. Have students do Activity 18 to practice previously taught material. **(3 min.)**

2. Introduce **Un peu plus.** (See presentation suggestions at right.) **(4 min.)**

3. Continue with integrated practice Activities 19–22. **(30 min.)**

TEACHING UN PEU PLUS

1. Go over **Un peu plus.** Tell students that some verbs can be used with different prepositions, depending on their intended meaning; for example, **penser à** (*to think about*), **penser de** (*to think of, to have an opinion of.*) **(2 min.)**

2. To practice, call out verbs and nouns and have students make complete sentences with prepositions. **Tu vas... Georges... Tu vas avec Georges. Je parle... Amélie... Je parle à/avec/ d'Amélie. (2 min.)**

---

20 Quelques précautions 🎞️1.2

Lisons/Écrivons Lis cette brochure et réponds aux questions.

Il vaut mieux prévenir que guérir!

Quelques précautions à prendre pour protéger votre maison contre:

* les incendies
* les dégâts des eaux
* les intempéries (orages, tempêtes)

* Fermez vos fenêtres quand il y a de l'orage
* N'oubliez pas de fermer vos robinets
* Éteignez les bougies
* Ne laissez pas de casserole sur le feu
* Coupez les branches mortes de vos arbres

1. De quoi est-ce que cette brochure parle?
2. Que faut-il faire pour éviter les incendies?
3. Pourquoi faut-il couper les branches des arbres?
4. Est-ce que tu pourrais donner un autre conseil?
5. Est-ce que tu prends certaines de ces précautions chez toi? Lesquelles?

21 Message des autorités 🎞️1.3

Écrivons/Parlons Parfois la communication avec le public ne se fait plus très bien quand il y a une catastrophe naturelle. Imagine une suite logique à chacun des messages suivants.

1. Méfiez-vous...
2. Prenez garde...
3. On prévoit...
4. C'est au cas où...
5. C'est pour ça...

Communication

HOLT **SoundBooth** ONLINE RECORDING

22 Scénario 🎞️1.1

Parlons Tu vis dans un pays francophone (Martinique, Suisse, Mali, etc.) où il peut y avoir des catastrophes naturelles. Un(e) camarade te demande ce qui pourrait arriver dans cette région et les précautions que tu prends pour éviter des dégâts.

MODÈLE **Tu vis en Suisse? Est-ce qu'il y a souvent des catastrophes naturelles là où tu habites? Oui, il y a parfois des avalanches, alors on a toujours...**

19 Script

See script on p. 273E.

20 Possible Answers

1. de prévention pour protéger sa maison
2. éteindre les bougies, ne pas laisser de casserole sur le feu
3. pour éviter qu'elles endommagent la maison
4. Answers will vary.
5. Answers will vary.

Communication

Class Activitiy: Interpersonal

On the board, write a list of verbs that take prepositions. Have students write five or more sentences, circling the preposition. Then students circulate and read one of their sentences to a classmate omitting the preposition. The classmate repeats the sentence supplying the correct preposition.

🎞️1.2

Differentiated Instruction

SLOWER PACE LEARNERS

19 Variation Some students may have trouble understanding the audio. You may want to stop the recording after each remark and ask volunteers to repeat or paraphrase it. Encourage students to ask for clarifications if necessary. Volunteers should use synonyms, antonyms, or circumlocution to explain problematic expressions. Then have students complete this activity. 🎞️1.2

MULTIPLE INTELLIGENCES

Naturalist Ask students to imagine that they have to prepare for a natural disaster. What materials and natural resources would they need to sustain themselves and their family for one week? What plans would they make for accommodations? Have them make a list in French, along with explanations, of the materials needed and natural resources available. Have students present their completed emergency plans to the class. 🎞️1.3

Assess

Assessment Program
Quiz: Application 1
Audio CD 7, Tr. 3 💿
Alternative Assessment
Differentiated Practice and Assessment CD-ROM

Online Assessment
my.hrw.com

Test Generator 💿

Culture

Lecture culturelle

L'eau continue à être une ressource vitale dans les régions agricoles françaises, comme partout dans le monde[1]. C'est pourquoi les centres de recherche comme l'Inra (Institut national de la recherche agronomique) cherchent des solutions parfois très originales pour aider les communautés agricoles à recycler leurs eaux. Que penses-tu de la méthode de recyclage décrite dans l'article ci-dessous? ✿1.3, 3.1

Dépollution par le lombric[2]

Après six mois d'expérimentation, la commune[3] de Comباillaux (près de Montpellier, 1.400 habitants) se félicite d'avoir adopté, pour la purification de ses eaux usées, un « *lombrifiltre* » unique au monde. Basé sur une technique imaginée par une équipe de l'Inra à Montpellier, le procédé consiste à confier le traitement des eaux sales à... des centaines de milliers[4] de vers de terre[5]. Ces animaux se nourrissent des impuretés. En pullulant[6], ils creusent[7] dans les substrats[8] des kilomètres de galeries, apportant ainsi l'oxygène nécessaire aux bactéries qui collaborent à l'épuration[9] et achèvent le travail. Élaborée dès 1998, la lombrifiltration n'avait jusqu'ici fonctionné qu'en laboratoire, et n'avait jamais été expérimentée à grande échelle[10].

Compréhension ✿1.2, 1.3

1. Qu'est-ce que les lombrics nettoient?
2. Quel est l'autre mot pour «lombric»?
3. Avec un(e) camarade, fais une liste des avantages et des inconvénients de la lombrifiltration. D'après vous, est-ce que c'est une bonne méthode de purification?

1. Ils nettoient les eaux sales.
2. ver de terre
3. Answers will vary.

1. *world* 2. *earthworm* 3. *town* 4. *hundreds of thousands* 5. *earthworms* 6. *swarming* 7. *dig* 8. *substrata*
9. *purification* 10. *on grand scale*

Core Instruction

LECTURE CULTURELLE

1. Read the introductory paragraph and discuss it with the class. **(3 min.)**
2. Read *Dépollution par le lombric* as a class. **(5 min.)**
3. Ask volunteers to answer the questions in **Compréhension. (5 min.)**
4. Ask students if it would bother them to drink this water. Are there any other uses for worms? (e.g. medical use of maggots to clean wounds) **(5 min.)**

COMPARAISONS ET COMMUNAUTÉ

1. Have students read *La minuterie* and discuss it. Ask students why they think it might be important to keep lights turned off. **(8 min.)**
2. Have students complete the **Et toi?** questions with a partner. **(5 min.)**
3. Go over **Communauté et professions** with students. Ask volunteers to find out how scientific research is done in the U.S. and to present their findings to the class. **(8 min.)**

Online Practice
go.hrw.com
Online Edition
KEYWORD: BD3 CH7

Chapitre 7

Culture

Culture

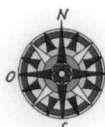

Comparaisons

La minuterie 2.1

Un interrupteur muni d'une minuterie

Tu vas dîner chez un(e) ami(e) qui habite un immeuble à Paris. Quand tu arrives, il fait nuit. Tu allumes la lumière et tu montes l'escalier. Tout à coup, tu te retrouves dans le noir...

   a. La lampe est cassée.

   b. Il y a le feu et l'électricité est coupée.

   c. Il y a une minuterie et tout est normal.

En France, il y a des minuteries dans tous les immeubles. Une minuterie est un petit appareil muni d'un système d'horloge[1]. La minuterie est installée sur un interrupteur[2]. Ce système permet, quand on allume une lumière, qu'elle s'éteigne automatiquement au bout de quelques minutes. Sans minuterie, les lumières dans l'entrée et les couloirs des immeubles resteraient allumées tout le temps!

   4.2

> **ET TOI?**
>
> **1.** Y a-t-il des minuteries dans ton école? Dans les immeubles de ta ville? Où?
>
> **2.** Peux-tu penser à l'usage de minuteries dans la vie quotidienne? (feux/ordinateurs/électroménager...)

Communauté et professions

Le français et le monde de la recherche 5.1

Certains des plus grands chercheurs étaient français: Pasteur et les Curie entre autres. La recherche en France tient encore un rôle prépondérant. L'un des centres de recherche les plus connus est le CNRS (centre national de recherches scientifiques). Est-ce qu'il y a une agence ou un bureau comme le CNRS aux États-Unis? Fais des recherches et présente ce que tu as découvert à ta classe.

Un chercheur du centre de recherche de l'Hôpital de la Pitié-Salpêtrière, Paris.

1. *clock* 2. *switch*

Culture

Bulletin Board Project

Have students bring in an example of recyclable material. Each student should label his or her piece with its French name and where in his or her town it can be recycled (centrally located containers, individual recycling bins provided by the local waste service). Ask volunteers to collect one example for each category (paper, aluminum, cardboard, glass, and others) and display them, with their labels, on a classroom bulletin board. Discuss all entries as a class. 1.3

Cultures

Practices and Perspectives

Eighty per cent of France's energy originates from nuclear power plants. Today, however, the government is developing the use of renewable energy, such as hydropower, wind power, and solar energy. In addition, the government is encouraging citizens to save energy by installing double-pane windows, using low-consumption bulbs, and so forth. Ask students what they do to save energy. Have them research what their community is doing. 2.1

Communities

Career Path

Ask students to research information about careers in ecology. What international organizations deal with environmental issues? What positions require knowledge of a second language? Are there organizations in the United States that work with Francophone countries that deal with environmental issues? 5.1

Differentiated Instruction

ADVANCED LEARNERS

Extension Have students research the scientific discoveries of the microbiologist and chemist Louis Pasteur (1822–1895). As an alternative, student may want to research the work of the two-time Nobel laureate Marie Curie (1867–1934). Students should write a ten-sentence summary and present it to the class. Classmates may ask for clarifications if needed. 1.3, 3.1

MULTIPLE INTELLIGENCES

Naturalist Ask students to make a list of earth conservation and preservation activities they like to do with their families or their friends, such as recycling (items to be recycled should be listed), water conservation, neighborhood/beach clean-ups, and so forth. Have students present their activities to the class. As students present, have them explain how each activity is beneficial for earth conservation and/or preservation. 1.3

Resources

Planning:

Lesson Planner

 One-Stop Planner

Presentation:

 Teaching Transparencies
Vocabulaire 7.3, 7.4

Practice:

Cahier de vocabulaire et grammaire

Differentiated Practice and Assessment CD-ROM

Media Guide

 Teaching Transparencies Bell Work 7.5

 Interactive Tutor, Disc 2

Bell Work

Use Bell Work 7.5 in the *Teaching Transparencies* or write this activity on the board.

Réponds aux questions.

1. À quoi penses-tu?
2. Avec qui étudies-tu?
3. De quoi parles-tu avec tes amis?
4. Depuis quand vas-tu à cette école? 🍀 1.2

Cinquain Poetry

Ask students to create a poem with the new expressions in **Vocabulaire 1** and **2.**

Line 1 One noun
Line 2 Two verbs
Line 3 Three nouns
Line 4 An expression from **Exprimons-nous!**
Line 5 A past participle that refers to the first noun

Sample answer

**L'environnement
Endommager, empirer
Le désastre, les fumées, les pesticides
Je suis convaincue que notre environnement va empirer.
Détruit**

Objectifs
- to make predictions and express assumptions
- to express and support an opinion

Vocabulaire à l'œuvre 2

Les ressources naturelles en danger

Les fumées des usines polluent l'air.

Certains disent que **la déforestation a pour conséquence le réchauffement** de **l'atmosphère** appelé «**l'effet de serre**».

Un pétrolier a fait **naufrage. Une marée noire menace** les côtes.

Les pesticides utilisés en agriculture sont la cause de nombreuses maladies.

▶ Vocabulaire supplémentaire—Les problèmes de l'environnement, p. R20

Core Instruction

TEACHING VOCABULAIRE

1. Introduce the vocabulary, using transparencies **Vocabulaire 7.3** and **7.4.** Model the pronunciation of each word or expression. **(3 min.)**

2. Have students point to specific illustrations on the transparency as you refer to each one. (**la déforestation, une marée noire**, etc.) **(2 min.)**

3. Ask students questions about protecting themselves and the environment. **Qu'est-ce qu'on peut faire pour réduire l'accumulation des déchets/la pollution/l'effet de serre/ certaines maladies? (3 min.)**

4. Model the pronunciation of the expressions in **Exprimons-nous!** Have partners write similar sentences about topics of their choice. **(4 min.)**

Protégeons l'environnement!

Le recyclage **du papier, du verre et de** l'aluminium réduit l'accumulation des déchets.

Certaines maisons sont équipées de panneaux solaires.

Les éoliennes utilisent la force **du vent pour** produire de l'énergie.

De plus en plus, les **compagnies** automobiles produisent **des voitures qui** consomment **moins** d'essence.

Online Practice

go.hrw.com

Vocabulaire 2 practice

KEYWORD: BD3 CH7

Chapitre 7
Vocabulaire 2

Vocabulaire 2

D'autres mots utiles

un(e) écologiste
environmentalist
la conservation
preservation
le gaz
natural gas
la pollution
pollution
la source d'énergie
energy source
(s')améliorer
to improve
empirer
to worsen
gaspiller
to waste
planter
to plant
recycler
to recycle

T P R
TOTAL PHYSICAL RESPONSE

Have students respond to these commands.

Lève la main s'il y a beaucoup de pollution dans cette ville.

Viens ici si la voiture de tes parents ne consomme pas beaucoup d'essence.

Va au tableau et dessine une éolienne.

Lève-toi si tu n'es pas convaincu(e) que l'effet de serre empire.

Cherche quelqu'un qui est écologiste.

Place photos on a table and have some students respond to these commands.

Trouve-moi une voiture hybride.

Montre-nous des panneaux solaires.

Où est la photo de la marée noire?

Fais voir où on recycle le verre et l'aluminium. 1.2

Exprimons-nous!

To make predictions and express assumptions

Interactive TUTOR

Ça ne m'étonnerait pas que l'énergie solaire ait du succès.
It wouldn't surprise me if . . .

Je parie qu'il y aura bientôt des bateaux hybrides.
I bet that . . .

Quand on arrêtera la déforestation, ça ira mieux, **j'en suis sûr(e).**
. . . I'm sure of it.

Je suis convaincu(e) que notre **environnement** va s'améliorer.
I'm convinced that . . . environment . . .

Je suppose qu'on consommera moins d'essence à l'avenir.
I assume that . . .

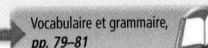

Vocabulaire et grammaire, pp. 79–81

Online workbooks

Comparisons
Comparing and Contrasting

Switzerland is a worldwide leader in preventing carbon dioxide emissions and in recycling efforts. The Swiss government introduced voluntary measures, as well as taxes, to encourage corporate responsibility for minimizing damage to the environment. The taxes are levied on products that cause stress to the environment. The tax revenues are paid back to Swiss residents in the form of discounts on health insurance premiums. Have students compare Switzerland's approach to environmental protection to that of the United States. 2.1, 4.2

Resources

Planning:

Lesson Planner

 One-Stop Planner

Presentation:

 Teaching Transparencies
Vocabulaire 7.3, 7.4

Practice:

Cahier de vocabulaire et grammaire

Differentiated Practice and Assessment CD-ROM

Media Guide

 Audio CD 7, Tr. 4

Interactive Tutor, Disc 2

24 Script

Madame Gemblinne: Je suis convaincue que si tout le monde recyclait, il n'y aurait plus problème de pollution.

Monsieur Bilouet: Moi, je parie qu'il est déjà trop tard. Les dégâts sont faits! La déforestation a provoqué le réchauffement de la planète.

Madame Gemblinne: Je suis sûre qu'on peut arrêter l'effet de serre en plantant des arbres pour remplacer ceux qu'on a coupés!

Monsieur Bilouet: Oui, mais même si on plante des arbres, il faudra des années pour réparer les dégâts, j'en suis sûr. Et il n'y a pas que la déforestation, je suppose! Il y a aussi les gaz et les fumées des usines qui polluent l'atmosphère, les marées noires!

Madame Gemblinne: Je parie qu'on va trouver de nouvelles sources d'énergie. Regardez, il y a déjà les voitures hybrides...

Monsieur Bilouet: Oh! Mais ça m'étonnerait que ces voitures aient beaucoup de succès! Elles sont bien trop chères!

Madame Gemblinne: Peut-être, mais avec le temps, les prix vont descendre, vous verrez. Et bientôt, il y aura même des bateaux hybrides. Qui sait?

26 Answers

1. À priori
2. En principe
3. ce que je sais
4. D'un côté
5. d'un autre,

23 Qu'est-ce que c'est? 1.2

Lisons Finis chaque phrase logiquement.

c **1.** Le recyclage   **a.** polluent l'atmosphère.

e **2.** La déforestation   **b.** consomment moins d'essence.

d **3.** Les éoliennnes   **c.** réduit l'accumulation des déchets.

a **4.** Les fumées des usines   **d.** utilisent la force du vent.

b **5.** Les voitures hybrides   **e.** produit l'effet de serre.

24 Écoutons   CD 7, Tr. 4   1.2 **1.** a **2.** a **3.** b **4.** b **5.** a **6.** a **7.** a **8.** a

 Ce soir, il y a un débat sur la protection de l'environnement à la télévision. Écoute madame Gemblinne et monsieur Bilouet discuter et dis si les phrases suivantes sont a) **vraies** ou b) **fausses**.

1. Madame Gemblinne pense que tout le monde devrait recycler.

2. Ça n'étonnerait pas monsieur Bilouet qu'il soit trop tard.

3. Madame Gemblinne ne croit pas qu'on puisse arrêter l'effet de serre.

4. Monsieur Bilouet ne pense pas que les dégâts soient déjà faits.

5. Ça étonnerait monsieur Bilouet qu'il n'y ait que le problème de la déforestation.

6. Madame Gemblinne est convaincue qu'on va trouver de nouvelles sources d'énergie.

7. Monsieur Bilouet n'est pas sûr que les voitures hybrides soient très populaires.

8. Madame Gemblinne pense qu'il y aura un jour des bateaux hybrides.

25 Des solutions 1.2, 1.3

Parlons/Écrivons Explique ce qui se passe sur ces photos et dis si, à ton avis, cela améliore l'environnement. Utilise les expressions d'Exprimons-nous!

1.   **2.**   **3.**   **4.**

Core Instruction

TEACHING EXPRIMONS-NOUS!

1. Model the pronunciation of the expressions in **Exprimons-nous!** (2 min.)

2. Have students ask your opinion on environmental issues. Answer them, using the new expressions. (4 min.)

3. For more practice with these expressions, ask students to give you their opinion about different topics. **Qu'est-ce que tu penses de...? À priori,...** (3 min.)

Exprimons-nous!

To express and support an opinion

A priori, l'essence pollue plus que le gaz naturel.
At first glance, . . .

D'un côté, on a besoin d'énergie, **d'un autre,** il faut protéger la planète.
On the one hand, . . . on the other hand, . . .

En principe, on devrait avoir moins de marées noires à l'avenir.
Theoretically, . . .

Ce que je sais, c'est qu'il faut mieux conserver l'énergie.
What I know is that . . .

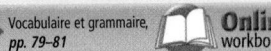
Vocabulaire et grammaire, pp. 79–81 **Online** workbooks

26 Question d'opinion 🍀1.2

Lisons/Écrivons Jean et Léon ont des opinions différentes. Complète leur conversation avec les expressions d'**Exprimons-nous!**

JEAN ___1___ on vit mieux aujourd'hui que dans le temps!

LÉON ___2___ oui, mais ___3___, c'est qu'il y a plus de maladies aujourd'hui que quand j'étais jeune!

JEAN ___4___, c'est vrai mais ___5___ les gens mouraient plus jeunes aussi.

27 Mon point de vue 🍀1.3

Écrivons Choisis un problème environnemental qui t'intéresse et écris un paragraphe pour le décrire et donner ton avis sur le sujet.

MODÈLE **Je pense que les pesticides sont un gros problème. A priori, on en a besoin pour...**

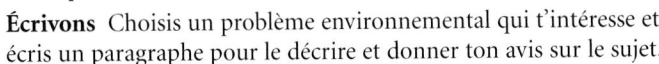

Communication

HOLT **SoundBooth** ONLINE RECORDING

28 Opinions personnelles 🍀1.1

Écrivons/Parlons En groupes, organisez un débat sur un problème de l'environnement. D'abord, choisissez un sujet qui vous intéresse. Faites une liste des «pour» et des «contre» du problème.

MODÈLE Sujet: l'énergie nucléaire
—A priori, l'énergie nucléaire est très dangereuse.
—Oui, c'est vrai, mais d'un autre côté, on dit que...
—Ah bon? Moi, ça ne m'étonnerait pas que...

Differentiated Instruction

SLOWER PACE LEARNERS

Variation Before they begin this activity, have students decide on an environmental problem. Ask partners to come up with terms and expressions they need in order to discuss this problem. You might ask students to write some of these terms and expressions on the board to which they can refer as they complete this activity. 🍀1.1, 3.1

MULTIPLE INTELLIGENCES

Naturalist So that students may fully comprehend how critical the issue of deforestation is becoming to our world, have them each "adopt" a rain forest animal. Ask students to identify a rain forest animal in danger of losing its home to deforestation and to research the animal on the Internet, in encyclopedias, or in other reference material. They should write a brief report in French about their findings and include a picture of the animal. Final reports and pictures can be displayed around the classroom. 🍀3.2

Resources

Planning:

Lesson Planner

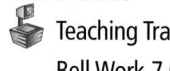 One-Stop Planner

Practice:

Grammar Tutor for Students of French, Chapter 7

Cahier de vocabulaire et grammaire

Differentiated Practice and Assessment CD-ROM

Cahier d'activités

Media Guide

 Teaching Transparencies

Bell Work 7.6

Audio CD 7, Tr. 5

Interactive Tutor, Disc 2

Bell Work

Use Bell Work 7.6 in the *Teaching Transparencies* or write this activity on the board.

Complète les phrases avec les mots de vocabulaire qui conviennent.

1. Les voitures _____ consomment moins d'essence.
2. Les _____ utilisent la force du vent pour produire de l'énergie.
3. Le _____ permet de réduire les déchets.
4. Les _____ utilisés en agriculture causent des maladies.
5. Le pétrolier a fait _____, et maintenant une _____ menace les côtes. 🍀 1.2

29 Script

See script on p. 273F.

Objectifs

- *quand, lorsque,* and *dès que*
- subjunctive after a conjunction

quand, lorsque, and dès que

1 Use the **present** after **quand** *(when)*, and **lorsque** *(when, at the moment of)* when discussing a situation *in general.*

> **Quand** j'ai des sacs en plastique, je les **recycle.**
>
> **Lorsqu'il** **fait** beau, je **vais** en ville en vélo. } *en général*

2 Use the **future** or the **future perfect** after **quand, lorsque,** and **dès que** *(as soon as)* when the event occurs in the future.

> Les écologistes **seront** contents **quand** tout le monde **recyclera.**
>
> **Dès que** les usines ne **pollueront** plus, l'environnement **s'améliorera.** } *dans le futur*
>
> **Lorsque** tu **auras acheté** une voiture hybride, tu **consommeras** moins d'essence.

Vocabulaire et grammaire, *pp. 82–83*
Cahier d'activités, *pp. 65–67*

Online workbooks

En anglais

🍀 4.1

In English, you use the present after expressions like *when, as soon as,* even if the event takes place *in the future.*

> *When I arrive, I'll call you.*

Do you ever use the future after "when"?

In French, however, you will use the future whenever the event occurs in the future.

Yes, if "when" is a question word.

29 Écoutons   CD 7, Tr. 5   🍀 1.2   1. a 2. b 3. a 4. b 5. b 6. a

Écoute ces élèves et dis s'ils parlent d'actions **a) qu'ils font généralement** ou **b) qu'ils feront dans le futur.**

30 Chaque chose en son temps   🍀 1.2

Parlons Lisons Complète les phrases avec la forme correcte du verbe entre parenthèses.

♻ *Souviens-toi,* The future and future perfect, pp. 48, 60

1. J'achèterai une voiture de sport lorsque j'(<u>aurai</u> / ai) un meilleur salaire.
2. Je m'habillerai dès que je/j'(<u>aurai pris</u> / prends) une douche.
3. Tu consommeras moins d'essence quand tu (as / <u>auras</u>) ta nouvelle voiture.
4. Je saurai ma note dès que le prof (rend / <u>aura rendu</u>) les examens.
5. Mes parents iront vivre à la campagne quand ils (sont / <u>seront</u>) à la retraite.
6. Quand nous (<u>dînons</u> / dînerons), nous ne regardons jamais la télévision.

Core Instruction

TEACHING GRAMMAIRE

1. Read **En anglais** aloud with students. Point out that ... *when I arrive* should be ... **quand je serai arrivé(e),** not **quand j'arriverai,** because the action of arriving will have to be completed before the phone call will take place. **(3 min.)**

2. Go over Points 1 and 2. Tell students that **quand** is frequently used in casual conversation, and that **lorsque** tends to be more formal. **(4 min.)**

Grammaire 2

31 Projets de voyage 🎞1.2

Écrivons Julien va aller en Belgique. Complète ce que disent ses amis avec les formes correctes des verbes entre parenthèses. Utilise le futur **seulement si l'action va se passer dans le futur.**

MODÈLE   Quand je __serai__ en Europe, je prendrai l'autobus.
Quand j'__ai__ de l'argent, j'achète des souvenirs.

1. Quand tu _____ (être) en Belgique, envoie-moi des cartes postales!

2. J'aime me promener dans les rues de Bruxelles lorsqu'il _____ (faire) beau.

3. Tu nous téléphoneras dès que tu _____ (arriver) chez Jean-Michel, n'est-ce pas?

4. Lorsque tu _____ (voir) Raoul, dis-lui bonjour de notre part!

5. Rends aussi visite à Véronique dès que tu _____. (pouvoir)

6. Quand je _____ (être) là-bas, j'adore manger du chocolat.

1. seras
2. fait
3. arriveras/seras arrivé
4. verras
5. pourras
6. suis

32 Combattre la pollution 🎞1.3

Parlons/Écrivons L'environnement s'améliorera quand nous ferons ce qu'il faut. Regarde les images et dis quand cela arrivera.

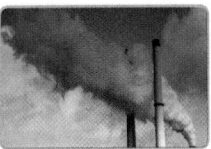

MODÈLE   **Il y aura moins de pollution dès que les fumées des usines ne pollueront plus l'air.**

1.

2.

3.

4.

French for Spanish Speakers

Ask Spanish speakers which verb tense or mode they use after **cuando**. For example, how would they translate **Les écologistes seront contents quand tout le monde recyclera?** (**Los ecólogos estarán contentos cuando todos reciclen**). What is the tense or mode of **reciclen**? (present subjunctive) Ask students if the rules for using the present indicative after **quand** are the same as in Spanish. (yes, when talking about everyday, general activities) 🎞4.1

Communication

Class Activity: Interpersonal
Students write a question that begins **Quand est-ce que tu...** and is followed by a verb in the future tense. Students circulate and ask their question. Students respond with **quand, lorsque,** or **dès que** along with the **futur** and/or the **futur antérieur**. As they respond, the interviewer writes the response beginning with **il** or **elle.**

MODÈLE
— **Quand est-ce que tu seras riche?**
— **Je serai riche dès que je gagnerai à la loterie.**
(written) **Il sera riche dès qu'il gagnera à la loterie.** 🎞1.1

Communication

33 Scénario 🎞1.1

Parlons Avec un des tes camarades, imaginez comment sera la vie dans vingt ans. Est-ce que les problèmes de l'environnement seront résolus ou auront empirés?

Differentiated Instruction

SLOWER PACE LEARNERS

30 Building on Previous Skills Before students complete this activity, read aloud each sentence and have them provide its English equivalent. Ask students if the subordinate clause expresses a situation in the present or an event in the future. Remind students that French, unlike English, uses the future tense after the conjunctions **quand, lorsque,** and **dès que** if the event takes place in the future. Then have students fill in the correct form of the verb in parentheses. 🎞1.2

SPECIAL LEARNING NEEDS

Students with Language Impairments Ask students to write a short paragraph in French about an event in their lives in the past. Then have them underline all words that indicate the past tense. Next, students will rewrite their paragraph twice, changing the underlined words first to indicate the present tense and then again to indicate the future tense. All three paragraphs should be examined with the teacher. 🎞1.2

Resources

Planning:

Lesson Planner

 One-Stop Planner

Practice:

Grammar Tutor for Students of French, Chapter 7

Cahier de vocabulaire et grammaire

Differentiated Practice and Assessment CD-ROM

Cahier d'activités

Media Guide

 Teaching Transparencies
Bell Work 7.7

 Interactive Tutor, Disc 2

Bell Work

Use Bell Work 7.7 in the *Teaching Transparencies* or write this activity on the board.

Mets les verbes entre parenthèses au temps qui convient.

1. Quand j'____ (acheter) une voiture, je choisirai une hybride.
2. Je me sens mieux quand je ____ (manger) des produits bio.
3. Lorsque les usines ne ____ (polluer) plus, l'environnement s'améliorera.
4. Quand vous ____ (aller) faire vos courses, vous emportez toujours un panier.
5. Quand les éoliennes ____ (être) plus populaires, on économisera de l'énergie.

1.2

COMMON ERROR ALERT
////ATTENTION !////

Students may think that the verb **empirer** is related to the noun **empire**. It is actually related to the adjective **pire** (worse).

Interactive TUTOR

The subjunctive after a conjunction

1 As you've already learned, you use the subjunctive with *expressions of necessity, desire, emotion,* and *disbelief* or *doubt.*

You also use the subjunctive after conjunctions like:

à condition que *(provided that)*	en attendant que *(while, until)*
à moins que *(unless)*	jusqu'à ce que *(until)*
afin que *(so that)*	malgré que *(in spite of)*
avant que *(before)*	pour que *(in order that)*
bien que *(although)*	pourvu que *(provided that)*
de sorte que *(so that)*	sans que *(without)*

Je vais nettoyer les bouteilles avant que nous les recyclions.
La déforestation continuera jusqu'à ce qu'il n'y ait plus d'arbres.

2 In some cases, if the subject of both clauses is the same, you can change que to de and use an **infinitive.**

Conjunction		Preposition
à condition que	→	à condition de
à moins que	→	à moins de
afin que	→	afin de
avant que	→	avant de
en attendant que	→	en attendant de
pour que	→	pour
sans que	→	sans

different subjects

Il achètera une voiture avant que nous partions en vacances.
subjunctive

same subject (il va partir)

Il achètera une voiture avant de partir en vacances.
infinitive

3 Remember to use **the indicative** after conjunctions like *parce que, pendant que, depuis que, dès que, quand,* and *lorsque.*

Je recycle *parce que* c'est important.

Vocabulaire et grammaire, pp. 82–83
Cahier d'activités, pp. 65–67

 Online workbooks

34 **Quel est le bon verbe?** 1.2

Lisons/Parlons Complète les phrases avec la forme correcte du verbe.

1. Venez me voir avant (de partir / que vous partiez).
2. J'irai à condition que tu (viennes / venir) avec moi.
3. Je ne t'endends pas bien que tu (parler / parles) fort.
4. Vous êtes contents quand vous (pourrez / pouvez) dormir.
5. Tu planteras des arbres afin (d'améliorer / tu amélioreras) l'environnement.

Déjà vu!

To conjugate French verbs in the subjunctive for most verbs, take the present indicative **ils/elles** form, drop **-ent** and add the endings **-e, -es, -e, -ions, -iez, -ent.**

With some verbs the stem for **nous** and **vous** comes from the **nous** form of the present indicative.

prennent → prenn-→ que je prenne

prenons → pren-→ que nous prenions

Some verbs—including **aller, avoir, être, faire, savoir, pouvoir,** and **vouloir**— have irregular subjunctive forms that you will have to memorize.

Core Instruction

TEACHING GRAMMAIRE

1. Read **Déjà vu!** aloud with students. If needed, ask volunteers to write a few sentences with irregular verbs in the subjunctive on the board. **(2 min.)**

2. Go over Points 1–2. Give additional example sentences contrasting conjunctions and prepositions. **(2 min.)**

3. Then, for more practice, ask students to finish your sentences. **Il faut bien apprendre le subjonctif parce que... c'est important. Je vais vous donner une bonne note pour... avoir étudié/que vos parents sachent que vous êtes un bon étudiant. (5 min.)**

4. Review the usage of the indicative after conjunctions with a few example sentences. **(2 min.)**

35 Un moyen de transport économique 1.2

Lisons/Écrivons Nadine a envoyé un e-mail à Pascale pour lui demander d'emprunter son vélo. Complète la réponse de Pascale avec la forme correcte des verbes entre parenthèses.

> Bon, d'accord, je te prête mon vélo à condition que tu me le ___1___ (rendre) le mois prochain. Ma sœur et moi, nous allons partout à pied depuis que nous ___2___ (habiter) en ville. Nous trouvons qu'il faut combattre la pollution afin que nos enfants ___3___ (pouvoir) encore sortir de chez eux! Donc, tu peux le garder jusqu'à ce que tu ___4___ (partir) en vacances, pourvu que tu n'___5___ pas (avoir) d'accident. Je vais le laver avant que tu ___6___ (venir) le chercher. Téléphone-moi pour que je ___7___ (savoir) quand tu vas venir. À moins que tu ___8___ (vouloir) que je te l'___9___ (amener)...?

36 Dans ce cas-là... 1.2

Écrivons/Parlons Regarde les photos et complète chaque phrase logiquement. Utilise différentes conjonctions dans tes phrases.

MODÈLE J'irai au parc à moins qu'il ne pleuve!

Je

1. Léa   2. Tanguy   3. ils   4. Huang

Communication

37 Interview 1.1

Parlons Avec des camarades posez-vous des questions pour savoir ce que vous faites pour protéger l'environnement. Utilisez des conjonctions dans vos réponses.

| recycler | gaspiller | utiliser des pesticides |
| laisser la télé allumée | ??? | |

35 Answers
1. rendes
2. habitons
3. puissent
4. partes
5. aies
6. viennes
7. sache
8. veuilles
9. amène

36 Possible Answers
1. Léa lit un magazine en attendant que l'autobus arrive.
2. Tanguy aimerait aller au cinéma à condition d'avoir de l'argent.
3. Ils devront faire la vaisselle avant d'aller chez leurs amis.
4. J'ai donné mon numéro de téléphone à Huang pour qu'il puisse me téléphoner.

Communication

Class Activity: Presentational
Prepare a deck of note cards, some with conjunctions that take the subjunctive and others with those that do not. Then form teams and have one team member at a time, construct a sentence in the subjunctive or indicative as appropriate. If correct, his or her team wins a point. 1.3

Differentiated Instruction

ADVANCED LEARNERS

35 Challenge Ask students to write Nadine's response to Pascale's conditions. They should mimic Pascale's style by using conjunctions that require the subjunctive and by giving detailed instructions. Have students read their answer to the class. You may want to ask students to vote on the wittiest response. 1.3

SPECIAL LEARNING NEEDS

Students with Language Impairments
Have students create a set of note cards. On one side they should write the conjunctions that require the subjunctive and the first half of an example sentence. On the other side, they should write the second half of the sentence. Ask students to work with a partner. One partner draws a card from the deck and reads aloud the conjunction and the sentence starter. The other finishes the sentence, while his or her partner verifies the correct verb form. 1.3

Assess

Assessment Program
Quiz: Grammaire 2
Alternative Assessment
Differentiated Practice and Assessment CD-ROM

Online Assessment
my.hrw.com

Test Generator

Synthèse
• Vocabulaire 2
• Grammaire 2

Application 2

38 Pour une planète plus propre 1.2

Lisons/Écrivons Qu'est-ce que ces gens disent au sujet de la pollution? Forme des phrases complètes.

1

On gaspillera moins d'électricité
J'économiserai de l'énergie
Il y aura moins de pollution
Les plages resteront propres
Il faut régulièrement emmener sa voiture chez le mécanicien

2

dès que
quand
afin que
à condition que
malgré que
pourvu que

3

les usines (produire) moins de déchets.
cela (contribuer à) l'effet de serre.
(polluer) moins.
ma maison (avoir) des panneaux solaires.
il (ne pas y avoir) de marées noires.

Un peu plus

The verb *éteindre*

The verb **éteindre** *(to put out or switch off)* is irregular, and is conjugated like **craindre**. Notice that the plural forms have a **g** in the stem while the singular forms do not.

éteindre			
j'	**éteins**	nous	**éteignons**
tu	**éteins**	vous	**éteignez**
il/elle/on	**éteint**	ils/elles	**éteignent**
Past participle: éteint			

Éteins la lumière avant de quitter la maison.

Peindre *(to paint)* is conjugated like **éteindre**.

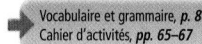 Vocabulaire et grammaire, *p. 84*
Cahier d'activités, *pp. 65–67*
 Online workbooks

39 Halte au gaspillage! 1.2

Lisons/Écrivons Sonia et ses amis parlent des économies d'énergie qu'ils font. Complète leurs phrases avec la forme correcte du verbe entre parenthèses.

1. Tu _____ (éteindre) la climatisation, toi, quand il ne fait pas trop chaud?
2. Nous, nous _____ (éteindre) les lumières quand nous sortons d'une pièce.
3. Je fais cela aussi, parce que je _____ (craindre) de gaspiller l'électricité.
4. Mon frère est écologiste et artiste. Il _____ (peindre) de beaux posters.
5. Certaines personnes _____ (éteindre) leur moteur quand ils sont arrêtés pendant plus de trente secondes.
6. Et vous, est-ce que vous _____ (craindre) le réchauffement de l'atmosphère?

1. éteins 2. éteignons 3. crains 4. peint 5. éteignent 6. craignez

Resources

Planning:

Lesson Planner

One-Stop Planner

Practice:

Grammar Tutor for Students of French, Chapter 7

Cahier de vocabulaire et grammaire

Differentiated Practice and Assessment CD-ROM

Cahier d'activités

Media Guide

Teaching Transparencies Bell Work 7.8

Audio CD 7, Tr. 6

Interactive Tutor, Disc 2

Bell Work

Use Bell Work 7.8 in the *Teaching Transparencies* or write this activity on the board.

Mets les verbes au temps qui convient.

1. Je sortirai pourvu que tu _____ (venir) avec moi.
2. Bien que ce _____ (être) interdit, les enfants jouent avec des allumettes.
3. Depuis que je _____ (prendre) conscience des problèmes, je gaspille moins.
4. Dès que nous _____ (faire) des efforts, nous verrons des améliorations.
5. La pollution continuera à moins que nous _____ (faire) des efforts. 1.2

41 Script

See script on p. 273F.

Core Instruction

INTEGRATED PRACTICE

1. Have students do Activity 38 to practice previously taught expressions. **(4 min.)**
2. Introduce **Un peu plus.** (See presentation suggestions at right.) **(4 min.)**
3. Continue with integrated practice Activities 39–43. **(20 min.)**

TEACHING UN PEU PLUS

1. Model the pronunciation of all forms of **éteindre**. **(2 min.)**
2. Make statements that contain **éteindre, craindre,** or **peindre**. Then call out other subject pronouns and have students use them to modify the statements. **J'éteins toujours la lumière. Nous... Nous éteignons toujours la lumière.** Occasionally, you can include a **passé composé. Hier, j'ai éteint la lumière...** **(2 min.)**

40 Écoutons CD 7, Tr. 6 ✿1.2 **1.** b **2.** a **3.** a **4.** b

Écoute ce que ces gens disent et dis si **a) ils protègent** ou
b) ils ne protègent pas l'environnement.

1. Antoine   3. Ophélie
2. Valentin   4. Pascale

41 Des conseils écologiques ✿1.3

Écrivons Écris un paragraphe en mentionnant au moins
six choses que tu peux faire dans la vie quotidienne pour
protéger l'environnement.

42 Planète en péril ✿1.3

Lisons/Parlons Lis ces phrases et donne une solution au problème.

1. Il n'y a presque plus d'éléphants dans certains pays d'Afrique.
2. On a détruit une grande partie de la forêt en Amérique du sud.
3. Les voitures consomment trop d'essence et polluent
   l'atmosphère.
4. Les gens jettent leurs journaux dans la poubelle.
5. Beaucoup de jeunes laissent la lumière allumée quand
   ils quittent un endroit.

Communication

HOLT **SoundBooth** ONLINE RECORDING

43 Histoire à raconter ✿1.1

Parlons Alex ne s'intéresse pas du tout à l'écologie. Ses copains
lui disent ce qu'il devrait faire. Imagine leur conversation.

 a.

 b.

 c.

Flash culture

La Belgique, la Suisse et
Monaco, comme d'autres
pays de l'Europe de
l'ouest, sont très actifs
pour promouvoir, entre
autres, l'utilisation de
voitures électriques.
Actuellement, 11.000
voitures électriques
circulent en Europe,
dont 8.000 en France.

Y a-t-il des voitures
électriques aux États-Unis?

 24/24

recharge véhicules électriques

✿4.2

Communication

Pair Activity: Interpersonal
Have students write four sentences that use **craindre que** +
the subjunctive with four different
verb forms. Then partners take
turns stating their sentence using
the expressions for predicting or
making assumptions to allay the
other's fear.

MODÈLE
— **Mes parents craignent
  que les pesticides soient
  la cause du cancer.**
— **Je suis convaincu que
  les fermiers arrêteront
  d'utiliser les pesticides.**

✿1.1

PRE-AP ACTIVITÉ PRÉPARATOIRE **Language Examination**

To display the drawings
to the class, use the Picture
Sequences Transparency for
Chapter 7.

43 Sample answer

a. — Alex, tu devrais
recycler l'aluminium
pour aider à protéger
l'environnement.

b. — Alex, arrête de
gaspiller de l'électricité!

c. — Alex, tu ferais bien de
prendre le bus, d'aller
en vélo ou d'acheter une
voiture hybride!

Differentiated Instruction

ADVANCED LEARNERS

43 Personalization Once students have completed this activity, have them create a skit that is
based on the conversation between Alex and his
friend. Students should use appropriate facial
expressions and gestures. Encourage them to
use props and sound effects. Students should
replace the scene that is pictured in the third
drawing with a scene in which Alex uses an
aerosol product.   ✿1.1, 1.3

MULTIPLE INTELLIGENCES

Artistic Have students identify an environmental project at your school. Ask them to get
in touch with the people responsible for the
project and gather information about it. Then
have each student design a poster in French to
advertise the project in the French classroom.
It should explain the project and encourage all
students to participate. You might display the
finished posters in the classroom.   ✿1.3

Assess

Assessment Program
Quiz: Application 2
Audio CD 7, Tr. 12
Alternative Assessment
Differentiated Practice and
Assessment CD-ROM

Online Assessment
my.hrw.com

Test Generator

Resources

Planning:

Lesson Planner

One-Stop Planner

Presentation:

Audio CD 7, Tr. 7

Practice:

Cahier d'activités

Reading Strategies and Skills
Handbook, Chapter 7

Advanced Reader

AP Reading Suggestion

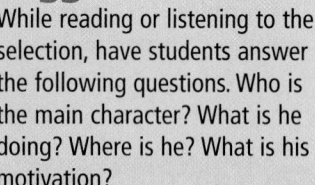

While reading or listening to the selection, have students answer the following questions. Who is the main character? What is he doing? Where is he? What is his motivation?

Applying the Strategies

For practice with recognizing the main idea, have students use the "Logographic Cues" strategy from the *Reading Strategies and Skills Handbook*.

READING PRACTICE

Strategy: Logographic Cues

Reading Skill	When can I use this strategy?		
	Prereading	During Reading	Postreading
Understanding Text Structure	✓		✓
Analyzing Chronological Order		✓	✓
Making Generalizations and Understanding Text Structure		✓	✓

Strategy at a Glance: Logographic Cues

- Logographs are graphic representations of ideas. The **Logographic Cues** strategy uses simple pictures that represent or symbolize key ideas in a text.
- Students can use logographs to identify textual elements or organize and remember information.

Dr. Kylene Beers explains the **Logographic Cues** strategy with the following story:

I sat in the train station in Chaumont, France, wondering why I had taken Latin instead of French in high school and college. At that moment, I wanted to know if my train to Dijon was leaving when I thought it was. Blank stares and pitying shakes of the head were all I received when people realized that I was limited to English. Finally, I took out my map of the region, drew a train, circled my destination, and wrote the date and time of my departure. Underneath it all I put a big question mark. The clerk behind the window finally understood my question: Is the train from Chaumont to Dijon still departing today from this station at 3:48? "Oui," she said, nodding her head.

Hours later, as I sat on the train, I realized that although I couldn't read French words, I could read musical notation, numbers, and international signs. I could read information that was presented logographically, but not information presented alphabetically. A Logographic Cue was worth a million French words.

"And why not?" I thought. Our first understanding of written language is a logographic understanding. Three- and four-year-olds who recognize their names in print rarely do so because they attach sounds to letters; instead, they simply recognize the shape of their printed names. Logographs, or picture cues, remain helpful when students are confronted with an alphabetic principle or text that they don't understand.

Lecture

Marcel Pagnol (1895–1974) écrivain et cinéaste français, a beaucoup écrit sur sa région natale, la Provence. Il a commencé par écrire des pièces de théâtre. Il a écrit aussi des romans dont une série autobiographique: *La Gloire de mon père, Le Château de ma mère, Le Temps des secrets, Le Temps des amours.* Au cinéma, il a mis en scène *La femme du boulanger, Topaze* ou encore *Le curé de Cucugnan.*

A Avant la lecture 1.3

Tu as un jardin, des plantes chez toi? Qu'est-ce qu'il faut faire pour que les plantes poussent? Est-ce qu'il faut beaucoup les arroser ou pas? Et s'il fait très chaud, qu'est-ce que tu dois faire? Est-ce que toutes les plantes ont besoin de mêmes soins?

Jean de Florette

CD 7, Tr. 7

Jean de Florette raconte l'histoire de Jean, un homme de la ville qui hérite d'une ferme et décide de s'y installer avec sa famille. Jean, qui est bossu, décide de se lancer dans l'élevage[1] des lapins et fait des plantations. Mais la vie est difficile. Les autres personnages mentionnés sont le Papet (qui voudrait avoir la ferme de Jean), Ugolin (le neveu du Papet), Aimée (la femme de Jean), Manon (la fille de Jean) et Batistine et Giuseppe (des fermiers qui aident Jean).

Gérard Depardieu dans le rôle de Jean de Florette

« Finalement, dit-il[2] au Papet, le Bon Dieu est contre nous. Ce bossu de malheur a toute l'eau qu'il veut ; moi, ça m'a fait moisir[3] mes pois chiches[4], et ta vigne a pris un coup de

1. *raising*   2. *It's Ugolin speaking to the Papet.*   3. *to get moldy*
4. *chick peas*

Core Instruction

LECTURE

1. Read **Stratégie pour lire** aloud for students. **(1 min.)**

2. Have volunteers take notes on the board as you do **Avant la lecture** with the class. **(10 min.)**

3. Ask students if they have seen the movie, *Jean de Florette*. Tell them **le Papet** is an elderly neighbor who covets the property Jean (**le bossu**, *the hunchback*) has inherited, because a spring runs through it, and that **Ugolin** is

le Papet's only relative. Have volunteers take turns reading the first part of this excerpt aloud, to the end of page 299. Pause regularly to monitor students' comprehension. **(15 min.)**

4. Ask students to draw a very simple sketch to illustrate each paragraph. **(10 min.)**

STRATÉGIE pour lire

Identifying the Main Idea
Recognizing the overall meaning of a text helps us as readers to understand what we read. The **main idea** is the most important idea that the writer wants readers to remember. The supporting details are the bits of information that the writer includes to further develop, explain, or illustrate the main idea.

Daniel Auteuil et Yves Montand dans les rôles d'Ugolin et du Papet

" pourridié[1] ". Lui, ses coucourdes[2] se gonflent[3] comme si l'ange Bouffareou soufflait dedans... Il va faire fortune, et il ne partira jamais !

— Ne t'inquiète pas, disait Papet, il a eu la chance d'un printemps pourri[4], mais c'est le signe d'un été de feu. Je te dis qu'à la fin de juillet, toute cette verdure, ça sera aussi jaune que du blé mûr, et les feuilles de ce maïs, elle chanteront comme des cigales[5]...

S'il pleut en juin,
Mange ton poing. »

**

Le vieux paysan et les dictons avaient raison.

C'est le 5 juillet que l'été tardif s'installa, avec une brutalité soudaine. Les cigales, jusque-là timides, grésillèrent[6] frénétiquement dans les oliviers, et le soleil énorme monta tout droit au zénith comme un ballon de feu.

À midi, l'ombre des pins était toute ronde autour de leur pied. La terre se mit à fumer, en transparentes volutes bleutées[7] : la végétation s'exalta aussitôt. Le champ de maïs grandit chaque

nuit de quelques centimètres, les courges s'accrochèrent aux troncs des oliviers, comme pour en commencer l'escalade. Leurs fruits étaient déjà plus gros que de petits melons.

« Voilà, expliqua le planteur, le secret de la végétation tropicale : après une pluie insistante et pénétrante, un grand coup de soleil stimule l'activité des tiges et des feuilles, en accélérant les échanges. Ce merveilleux système d'alternance vient de s'installer cet été, et il est visible que la Providence a décidé de récompenser nos efforts. »

Mais dès la troisième journée de soleil, il constata que les feuilles commençaient à perdre leur éclat[8] ; quelques-unes même pendaient[9] en arrière, comme fatiguées : il était grand temps d'utiliser la citerne.

Le soir, devant Ugolin venu aux nouvelles, il exposa son plan.

« La citerne est pleine à ras bord[10]. Elle contient douze mètres cubes. Il m'en faut trois par arrosage[11], et un arrosage tous les deux jours. La citerne m'assure donc huit jours de tranquillité.

1. *mildew* 2. *type of squash* 3. *grossissent* 4. *rainy spring* 5. *cicadas* 6. *chirped* 7. *bluish smoke* 8. brille 9. *were hanging*
10. *nearly full to the rim* 11. donner de l'eau

Active Reading Questions

1. **Qui est le bossu? (Jean)**
2. **Est-ce qu'Ugolin aime Jean ou est-ce qu'il ne l'aime pas? (Il ne l'aime pas.)**
3. **Qu'est-ce que Papet prédit? (un été chaud qui fera mal aux plantes de Jean)**
4. **Qu'est-ce qui s'est passé le 5 juillet? (La chaleur d'été a commencé.)**
5. **Quelles sont les conséquences d'une pluie suivie d'un grand soleil? (Les plantes poussent.)**
6. **Qu'est-ce qu'il a fallu faire après trois jours de soleil? (utiliser la citerne)**
7. **Combien de jours est-ce que l'eau de la citerne durera? (8 jours)** ✿ 1.2

Understanding Character

Tell students that dialog is an important element in stories and novels. It is often used to reveal the personality of the characters and what motivates them. It can also add realism and humor to the narrative. Have students reread the dialog in the text and take notes on Ugolin's, Papet's, and Jean's personality. Create with the class a profile of each character that includes personality, background, and motivation.

Language Examination

Lecture helps students prepare for Section 1, Part B: **Reading Comprehension**. The audio recording helps them prepare for Part A: **Listening—Short Narratives**.

Differentiated Instruction

SLOWER PACE LEARNERS

Building on Previous Skills It may help students understand the main idea of this excerpt if they follow Jean's calculations. Ask students how many liters are in a cubic meter. (1,000 liters) Have students calculate how many liters of water Jean will have to transport on the first day, given that his cistern still contains six cubic meters and he needs two cubic meters every two hours during the day. How many liters will he have to transport on the second day? ✿ 1.2, 3.1

SPECIAL LEARNING NEEDS

Students with Learning Disabilities Ask students to think of a movie they have recently seen and to write in French a paragraph about what they believe is the main idea the screen writer wanted to convey to the audience. Have students share their thoughts with the class. Did students who wrote about the same movie also identify the same main idea? This could lead to an interesting class discussion about what constitutes a 'main idea'. ✿ 1.3

1. Jean aura assez d'eau pour combien de temps? (10 jours)
2. Qu'est-ce que Jean fera s'il ne pleut pas dans dix jours? (Il sacrifiera une partie de la récolte.)
3. Comment est-ce que Jean propose de remplir la citerne? (Il louera le mulet d'Ugolin pour porter de l'eau.)
4. Au mois de juillet, comment poussent les plantes de Jean? (très bien)
5. Quel temps fait-il au mois d'août? (Il continue à faire très chaud et il ne pleut pas.)
6. Qu'est-ce que Jean fait pour sauver ses plantes? (Il les arrose chaque matin et il les recouvre.)
7. Qu'est-ce que Papet pense des efforts de Jean? (qu'ils sont bêtes)
8. Qu'est-ce que Jean fait au dixième jour? (Il refait ses calculs.) ✿1.2

Postreading Activity

Ask students what Papet and Ugolin think of Jean. Which passages in the excerpt express their attitude toward him? Ask students why they think Papet and Ugolin have this attitude. What stereotypes may be reflected in their attitude?

— D'accord, dit Ugolin, mais c'est pas sûr qu'il pleuve dans huit jours !

— Prévu ! dit M. Jean. C'est pourquoi, dès demain, nous allons commencer les voyages au Plantier[1]. Cent litres par voyage, quatre voyages par jour. C'est-à-dire que, dans huit jours, nous aurons versé dans la citerne trois mille deux cents litres, ce qui nous donne deux jours de plus. Soit dix jours.

— Dix jours, c'est bien, dit Ugolin, mais en cette saison, on ne sait jamais.

— Vous avez raison : aussi, j'ai prévu le pire. Si dans dix jours le ciel continue à me trahir[2], je sacrifierai une partie de la récolte, et je vous louerai votre mulet. Il peut porter certainement deux bidons[3] de cinquante litres. Donc, nous pourrons fournir à la citerne, en faisant cinq voyages, un mètre cube par jour, ce qui sera suffisant pour attendre la prochaine pluie.

— C'est bien combiné, dit Ugolin.

— J'espère, dit M. Jean, n'avoir pas besoin d'en venir là. » [...]

**

Ils repartirent donc pour le Plantier, mais sans inquiétude et sans hâte : ces corvées d'eau n'étaient plus qu'une précaution, très probablement inutile.

Grâce à l'orage, qui avait profondément pénétré le sol, grâce à la provision de la citerne, les courges vertes, rayées de blanc, s'arrondissaient à l'ombre de leurs feuilles, les épis du maïs s'enflaient gaillardement, et l'herbe[4] rafraîchie des collines suffisait à la nourriture des lapins.

Cependant, le flamboyant soleil du mois d'août montait chaque matin dans un ciel vide, et aspirait la très légère brume qui flottait au-dessus des herbes et des plantes : vers midi, tout était sec[5], et le sol friable s'écrasait en poussière sous les pas[6] de M. Jean.

Il décida donc de changer de méthode, et de verser chaque matin deux litres d'eau au pied de chaque plante de cucurbita ; puis, pour ralentir[7] l'évaporation, il les recouvrit avec des lambeaux de toile de jute[8], un vieux tapis de table, des draps[9] de lit, des couvertures, des journaux, les portes de la

Ugolin et Jean de Florette

1. *part of property further away from the farm* 2. *to betray* 3. *comme de grosses bouteilles* 4. *l'herbe forme la pelouse*
5. *sec est le contraire d'humide* 6. *le pied* 7. *to slow down* 8. *pieces of fabric* 9. *sheets*

Core Instruction

LECTURE

1. Finish reading *Jean de Florette* as a class. If students have not seen the movie, did this excerpt make them want to see it? **(12 min.)**

2. Have students continue drawing a sketch for each of the remaining paragraphs and discuss their sketches as a class.

The main idea should become apparent through the sketches. **(10 min.)**

3. Complete **Compréhension** and **Après la lecture** as a class. **(10 min.)**

Online Practice
go.hrw.com
Online Edition
KEYWORD: BD3 CH7

Chapitre 7

Lecture

Lecture

remise¹ posées sur quatre pierres, de larges ramures² *d'yeuse* ou de pin. Lorsque le Papet (qui surveillait les opérations) vit pour la première fois cet étalage³ il en pleura de rire : il avait tort⁴, car tant qu'il y eut de l'eau dans la citerne, les plantes ainsi protégées continuèrent à prospérer.

Au dixième jour, le bossu inquiet recommença à faire des problèmes de certificat d'études : « Étant donné qu'une citerne contient encore six mètres cubes d'eau, et que son propriétaire est forcé d'en dépenser deux mètres cubes tous les deux jours ; que, d'autre part, il peut en transporter chaque jour..., etc. »

1. *barn*   2. *foliage*   3. *display*   4. *he was wrong*

Compréhension

B Dis si, d'après la lecture, les phrases suivantes sont **a) vraies** ou **b) fausses.** Justifie ta réponse en écrivant le passage de la lecture qui lui correspond. 1.2

1. D'après le Papet, s'il pleut beaucoup au printemps, l'été sera très chaud.
2. Il a commencé a faire très chaud au mois de juillet.
3. Il fait de plus en plus chaud.
4. Jean s'occupe des plantes tous les jours.
5. La citerne contient assez d'eau pour passer tout l'été.
6. Le Papet pense que les méthodes de Jean sont excellentes.

C Réponds par une phrase aux questions suivantes. 1.2

1. En quelle saison se passe cette histoire?
2. Pourquoi, au début du passage, les plantations de Jean ne sont pas en danger?
3. Pourquoi Jean décide-t-il d'arroser ses plantes chaque matin?
4. Qu'est-ce que Jean décide de faire pour empêcher l'eau de s'évaporer?
5. À ton avis, pourquoi le Papet trouve les méthodes de Jean comiques?

Après la lecture 1.3

D Quelle est l'idée principale du texte que tu viens de lire? Une fois que tu as trouvé l'idée principale du texte, fais un résumé du texte. Mentionne seulement ce qui est important à la compréhension de l'histoire.

C Answers

1. L'histoire se passe en été.
2. Au début, les plantations ne sont pas en danger parce qu'il a beaucoup plu.
3. Il décide d'arroser ses plantes chaque matin parce qu'il fait très chaud.
4. Pour empêcher l'eau de s'évaporer, Jean décide de couvrir ses plantes.
5. Answers will vary.

Differentiated Instruction

ADVANCED LEARNERS

Challenge Jean is the main character and Papet und Ugolin are supporting characters in this excerpt of *Jean de Florette*. Students should describe the interaction between Jean and Papet and Jean and Ugolin. Ask students to analyze the relationship between Jean and le Papet. Are they relatives, friends, or neighbors? (They are neighbors.) 1.1, 1.2

SPECIAL LEARNING NEEDS

Students with Learning Disabilities/ Dyslexia You might provide students with the audio recording of the text ahead of time. This allows them to read and listen to the selection at the same time and become familiar with the content before the class begins reading. You might also recommend the movie version of this selection. 1.2

Assess

Assessment Program
Quiz: Lecture

Online Assessment
my.hrw.com

Test Generator

L'atelier de l'écrivain

Interactive
TUTOR

Process Writing

Remind students that each piece of advice they give to Jean should be linked to one of his actions. Students may feel that some of Jean's actions were appropriate. In this case, suggest that they tell Jean why they believe he acted appropriately. Also suggest that students clarify and justify each piece of advice that they give by supplying supporting examples and evidence.

Teaching Suggestion

Have partners exchange their completed letters. Then have them assume the role of Jean and answer their partner's letter. Or, suggest that some students pretend to be Papet or Ugolin and intercept the letter to Jean. They might read the letter aloud to the class, making comments on each piece of advice from the point of view of their character.

Lettre à Jean

Imagine que tu es un célèbre professeur de génie agricole et que tu habites près du village de Jean de Florette. Il t'a écrit une lettre pour te demander des conseils. Tu veux l'encourager à persister dans ses efforts, mais tu veux aussi le prévenir des risques qu'il prend. Donne-lui ton opinion sur les méthodes qu'il utilise. Si tu préfères, imagine qu'un(e) ami(e) te demande des conseils pour trouver un travail, pour annoncer à ses parents qu'il/elle veut se porter volontaire pour une cause humanitaire ou écologique...

1 **Plan: faits et opinions** 🏵1.3

Pour donner des conseils à Jean ou à ton ami(e), tu dois d'abord organiser les faits. Commence par tracer deux colonnes sur une feuille de papier. Dans la première colonne, liste les faits, c'est-à-dire ce que Jean fait ou ne fait pas, ou encore ce que ton ami(e) doit faire ou veut faire. Ensuite, dans la deuxième colonne, pour chaque fait, donne ton opinion et des conseils.

Faits	Opinions
Maïs	S'il ne pleut pas suffisamment, il faut arroser. Le maïs ne devrait pas être planté en Provence. Vous devriez plutôt planter des oliviers.

STRATÉGIE pour écrire

Defining your audience Just as the way you talk depends on the person to whom you're talking, the way you write should be based on your audience. Ask yourself who your audience is before you begin to write. Are they your classmates? Teachers? A particular person? How much does your audience know about the topic? Should you use formal or informal language? Your writing will be much more effective if you keep your reader in mind. 🏵3.1

Core Instruction

L'ATELIER DE L'ÉCRIVAIN

1. Discuss the assignment and **Stratégie pour écrire.** Remind students that they have already written one formal letter. Ask them how this letter will be similar or different. **(5 min.)**

2. Go over the **Vocabulaire à la carte** and the conditional. **(5 min.)**

3. Have students complete step 1 in class. **(15 min.)**

4. Assign step 2 as homework. Suggest that students look online for information and vocabulary pertaining to agriculture to help add details to their advice.

5. Have students complete steps 3 and 4. You might have volunteers read their letter aloud to the class. **(20 min.)**

L'atelier de l'écrivain

② Rédaction 🌸1.3

Fais un brouillon de ta lettre. Utilise ton organigramme pour être sûr(e) que tu utilises toutes tes idées (faits, opinions et conseils) de manière organisée et logique. N'hésite pas à les classer par ordre d'importance. Attention aussi au ton de ta lettre.
Pose-toi ces questions:

- Est-ce que je connais bien la personne à qui j'écris?
- Est-ce que c'est un bon ami ou juste une connaissance?

Cela devrait t'aider à déterminer le ton de ta lettre.

③ Correction 🌸1.3

Maintenant, c'est le moment de t'assurer que ta lettre est bien écrite. Cherche les mots dans le dictionnaire pour vérifier leur orthographe si tu as des doutes. Assure-toi aussi que tes verbes sont bien conjugués. Échange ta lettre avec celle d'un(e) camarade de classe. Corrigez vos lettres respectives.
Posez-vous les questions suivantes:

- Est-ce qu'il y a des fautes d'orthographe, de grammaire, de vocabulaire?
- Est-ce que la lettre est claire?
- Est-ce que le ton est correct?

Fais les corrections et écris la version finale.

④ Application 🌸1.3

Échangez les lettres entre tous les élèves de la classe. Est-ce qu'il y a des suggestions meilleures que d'autres? Est-ce qu'il y a des suggestions qui sont drôles? Affichez les lettres dans la classe.

> Professeur François Beacco
> 110, avenue du Général de Gaulle
> 13000 Marseille
>
> le 15 juillet 2007
>
> Cher Monsieur,
>
> À votre demande, je vais vous faire part de mon opinion et de mes conseils concernant votre exploitation agricole. Vous devriez d'abord lire les infor-

Vocabulaire à la carte

À mon avis,...	*In my opinion, . . .*
D'après moi,...	*According to me, . . .*
Il est important que...	*It's important that . . .*
Il faudrait que...	*It would be necessary that . .*
Je vous conseille de...	*I recommend that you . . .*

Le conditionnel

The **conditionnel de politesse** is used to make a polite request or suggestion.

À mon avis, vous devriez planter des oliviers.

L'atelier de l'écrivain

Le conditionnel

The **conditionnel de politesse** softens a request. Ask students with which verbs is it most often used. (**aimer, devoir, pouvoir, vouloir**) Have students work in groups of three to use each verb in as many polite suggestions or requests as they can, directed toward Jean. **Pourrais-je vous faire une suggestion? Vous ne devriez pas arroser vos plantes tous les jours.**

Writing Assessment

To assess the **L'atelier de l'écrivain,** you can use the following rubric. For additional rubrics, see the *Assessment Program.*

Writing Rubric	4	3	2	1
Content (Complete—Incomplete)				
Comprehensibility (Comprehensible—Seldom comprehensible)				
Accuracy (Accurate—Seldom accurate)				
Organization (Well-organized—Poorly organized)				
Effort (Excellent effort—Minimal effort)				

18-20: A	14-15: C	Under
16-17: B	12-13: D	12: F

Differentiated Instruction

ADVANCED LEARNERS

Variation Ask students to imagine that Papet has found out about Jean's letter to the professor and has bribed the professor to write Jean a letter in which he strongly advises Jean to give up farming. Have students compose a letter to Jean in which they try to persuade him that he is doomed to fail as a farmer. Using formal and scientific language, students should make exaggerated claims and present opinions as facts. Have students read their letter to the class.
🌸1.3

MULTIPLE INTELLIGENCES

Interpersonal Have students write a persuasive letter in French to their parents to request a desired object or permission to do a certain activity. Students should clearly state why they deserve the fulfillment of their request and why the request would be beneficial for both parties. Make sure that students understand that the letter should not be too personal in nature, as they may be called upon to share their letter with the class.
🌸1.3

Assess

Assessment Program

Quiz: Écriture

Online Assessment
my.hrw.com

Test Generator

① Possible Answers

a. Quand Luc est allé en Californie, un grand tremblement de terre a secoué la région.

b. La dernière fois que Luc a visité les Alpes, il y a eu une avalanche. Il n'a pas pu faire de ski.

c. Le jour où Luc est arrivé à Hawaii, un volcan est entré en éruption. La coulée de lave a détruit son hôtel!

d. Quand Luc est arrivé au bord de la mer un pétrolier a fait naufrage, et une marée noire a recouvert la plage.

② Answers

1. Une tempête est moins sérieuse qu'une avalanche.
2. M. Faulon prévoit mieux le temps que Mme Smith.
3. Il fait aussi chaud au Texas qu'en Iowa.
4. À Paris, il pleut plus qu'à Marseille.
5. Le météorologiste du *Monde* est aussi intelligent que le météorologiste d'*EuroNews.Fr.*

① Chaque fois que Luc est en vacances, quelque chose arrive. Écris une phrase pour dire ce qui arrive sur chaque photo. 🎞 1.2

① Vocabulaire 1
• to caution
• to tell why something happened
pp. 276–279

a.

b.

c.

d.

② Fais des phrases avec les éléments donnés. 🎞 1.2

② Grammaire 1
• review of the comparative and superlative
• the passive voice
Un peu plus
• prepositions
pp. 280–285

MODÈLE Une éruption /être / + dangereux / un orage
Une éruption est plus dangereuse qu'un orage.

1. Une tempête / être / − sérieux / une avalanche
2. M. Faulon / prévoir / + bien / le temps / Mme Smith
3. Il / faire / = chaud / Texas / Iowa
4. À Paris / il / + pleuvoir / Marseille
5. Le météorologiste du *Monde* / être / = intelligent / le météorologiste d'*EuroNews.Fr*

③ Vocabulaire 2
• to make predictions and express assumptions
• to express and support an opinion
pp. 288–291

③ Devine de quoi on parle. 🎞 1.2

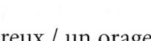
1. les déchets 2. le recyclage
3. les panneaux solaires
4. les éoliennes 5. l'essence

1. C'est quelque chose qu'on jette. Parfois, c'est mauvais pour l'environnement.
2. C'est quand on utilise quelque chose plus d'une fois et qu'on ne le jette pas.
3. Certaines maisons en ont pour utiliser l'énergie du soleil.
4. Elles tournent avec le vent et produisent de l'énergie.
5. Il en faut pour conduire une voiture, même si elle est hybride.

Preparing for the Exam

RETEACHING

Review the use of the passive voice. Remind students that the passive is used when the subject receives the action. A conjugated form of **être** plus the past participle of the main verb combine to form the passive. In pairs, have one student make a statement to the partner. The partner has to form the sentence in the passive voice. Have partners take turns.

TEST-TAKING STRATEGY

Remind students of the use of the subjunctive after a conjunction such as, **avant que, bien que, pour que, sans que.** Have them review the list of conjunctions that are followed by the subjunctive. Ask students to write sample sentences in their grammar notebook.

Online Assessment
go.hrw.com
Chapter Self–test
KEYWORD: BD3 CH7

Chapitre 7

Prépare-toi pour l'examen

Prépare-toi pour l'examen

4 Finis les phrases suivantes. Utilise le subjonctif si nécessaire. 🐾1.2

1. Je te donne de l'argent à condition que tu...
2. Mon père recycle afin que nous...
3. Les voitures hybrides sont économiques bien qu'elles...
4. Les tornades sont dangereuses parce que...
5. Ça ne m'étonnerait pas que...

5 Réponds aux questions suivantes. 🐾2.1, 2.2

1. Comment s'appelle le courant qui baigne les côtes de la Belgique?
2. Donne un exemple de ce que les Français font pour économiser l'électricité.
3. Quel est le nom du protocole que la plupart des pays ont adopté pour la protection de l'environnement?

6 Écoute et dis si on parle **a) de phénomènes naturels** ou **b) de l'environnement.** CD 7, Tr. 8 🐾1.2 **1.** b **2.** b **3.** a **4.** b **5.** a **6.** b **7.** b

7 Alex a décidé de faire des efforts pour protéger l'environnement. Regarde les images et dis ce qu'il fait. 🐾1.2

4 Grammaire 2
- **quand, lorsque,** and **dès que**
- subjunctive after a conjunction

Un peu plus
- the verb **éteindre**
pp. 292–295

5 Culture
- Comparaisons p. 287
- Flash culture pp. 279, 290, 297

5 Answers
1. le Gulf Stream
2. Ils utilisent des minuteries.
3. le protocole de Kyoto

6 Script
1. Les écologistes seront heureux quand il n'y aura plus de pollution.
2. L'accumulation des déchets peut être évitée.
3. Il a tellement plu qu'il y a des inondations dans toute la région.
4. Un pétrolier a fait naufrage et a causé une marée noire.
5. On prévoit une tempête de neige. Gare aux avalanches!
6. Il faut recycler le verre et l'aluminium. C'est bon pour l'environnement.
7. Les fumées des usines polluent l'air et les écologistes disent que cela cause l'effet de serre.

Language Examination
PRE-AP ACTIVITÉ PRÉPARATOIRE

To display the drawings to the class, use the Picture Sequences Transparency for Chapter 7.

7 Sample answer

a. Quand il quitte sa maison, il éteint les lumières pour ne pas gaspiller l'électricité.

b. Après l'école, Alex va au parc avec d'autres écologistes pour nettoyer la terre.

c. Il plante des arbres pour combattre le réchauffement de l'atmosphère.

d. Maintenant, Alex met le verre, le papier et l'aluminium dans le recyclage.

Oral Assessment

To assess the speaking activities in this section, you might use the following rubric. For additional speaking rubrics, see the Alternative Assessment section of the *Assessment Program*.

Speaking Rubric	4	3	2	1
Content (Complete—Incomplete)				
Comprehension (Total—Little)				
Comprehensibility (Comprehensible—Incomprehensible)				
Accuracy (Accurate—Seldom Accurate)				
Fluency (Fluent—Not Fluent)				

18-20: A   16-17: B   14-15: C   12-13: D   Under 12: F

Prépare-toi pour l'examen

Grammar Review

For more practice with the grammar topics in this chapter, see the *Grammar Tutor,* the *Interactive Tutor,* or the *Cahier de vocabulaire et grammaire.*

Online Edition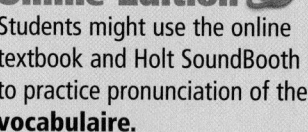

Students might use the online textbook and Holt SoundBooth to practice pronunciation of the **vocabulaire.**

Connections

Social Studies Link

The Red Cross was founded in1863 in Geneva. It won the Nobel Peace Prize in 1917, 1944, and 1963. Henri Dunant, one of its founders, also won in 1901. The Red Cross is composed of three organizations. The self-governing National Red Cross Societies exist in nearly every country in the world. The League of Red Cross Societies, a coordinating world federation of these societies, leads and organizes relief assistance missions responding to large-scale emergencies. The International Committee of the Red Cross (ICRC), a private, independent group of mostly Swiss citizens, has been awarded observer status by the UN. Ask students to research the mission statement of the Red Cross and its recent national or international relief efforts. 3.1

Proverbes

For French proverbs and activities related to the chapter theme and vocabulary, see **Proverbes et expressions,** pp. R6–R7.

Grammaire 1
- review of the comparative and superlative
- the passive voice

Un peu plus
- prepositions
pp. 280–285

Résumé: Grammaire 1

To form the **comparative of nouns,** use

plus de moins de autant de	+	**noun**	+	que

To form the **comparative of adjectives and adverbs,** use

plus moins aussi	+	**adjective/adverb**	+	que

To form the **superlative of adjectives,**

definite article	+	plus meilleur(e) moins	+	**adjective**	+	de

To form the **superlative of adverbs,** use

definite article	+	plus moins	+	**adverb**

In the *passive voice,* the subject of the sentence receives the action. To form the passive voice, use **être** plus the past participle of the main verb. The past participle will agree in number and gender with the subject. To tell *who* or *what* is doing the action use **par.**

La maison a été détruite **par un cyclone.**

Sometimes you will use a different preposition in French than you would in English, or it could be omitted in one language but not in the other.

Grammaire 2
- **quand, lorsque,** and **dès que**
- subjunctive after a conjunction

Un peu plus
- the verb **éteindre**
pp. 292–297

Résumé: Grammaire 2

After **quand** or **lorsque,** use the **present** when discussing a *general situation.* Use the **future** after **quand, lorsque,** and **dès que** when the event *will happen* in the future.

The subjunctive is used after certain conjunctions, see page 294. If the subjects of both clauses are the same, you can use a **preposition** and an infinitive instead of a conjunction and the subjunctive. After conjunctions like **parce que, pendant que, depuis que, dès que, quand,** and **lorsque** use the indicative.

Éteindre is an irregular verb which means *to put out* or *to switch off:* **j'éteins, tu éteins, il éteint, nous éteignons, vous éteignez, ils éteignent.** The past participle is **éteint.**

The verbs **craindre** and **peindre** are conjugated like **éteindre.**

Chapter Review

Teacher Management System
Password: admin
For more details, log on to www.hrw.com/CDROMTUTOR.

Create a variety of puzzles to review chapter vocabulary.

DVD Program

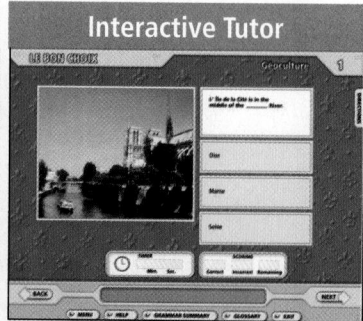

Interactive Tutor

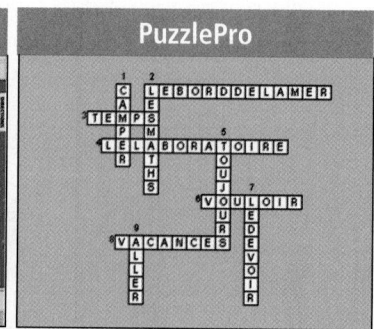

PuzzlePro

Prépare-toi pour l'examen

Résumé: Vocabulaire 1

Natural phenomena

HOLT SoundBooth
ONLINE RECORDING

abîmer/endommager	to damage
une alerte	alert
une avalanche	avalanche
causer/provoquer	to cause
le climat	climate
la côte	coast
une coulée de lave	lava flow
le courant	current
les dégâts (m.)	damage
un désastre	disaster
un désert	desert
détruire/ravager	to destroy
un éclair/le tonnerre	lightning/thunder
empirer	to worsen
une éruption	eruption
estimer	to estimate
évacuer	to evacuate
un glissement de terrain	mudslide

la grêle	hail
un incendie	fire
une inondation	flood
un million	million
un orage	thunderstorm
un ouragan/un cyclone	hurricane
un phénomène naturel	natural phenomenon
une précaution	precaution
un raz-de-marée	tidal wave
une région sinistrée	stricken region
secouer	to shake
une tempête (de sable/neige)	(sand/snow) storm
une tornade	tornado
un tremblement de terre	earthquake
un volcan	volcano

To caution .... *See p. 277*
To tell why something happened .... *See p. 279*

Résumé: Vocabulaire 2

Ressources

l'accumulation (f.)	accumulation
l'air (m.)	air
l'aluminium (m.)	aluminum
(s')améliorer	to improve
l'atmosphère (f.)	atmosphere
la conséquence	consequence
la conservation	preservation
consommer/gaspiller	to use/to waste
le déchet	waste
la déforestation	deforestation
un/une écologiste	environmentalist
l'effet (m.) de serre	the greenhouse effect
l'énergie (f.)	energy
l'environnement (m.)	environment
une éolienne	windmill
équipé(e)	equipped
l'essence (f.)	gasoline
faire naufrage	to wreck
la force	strength
les fumées (f.) des usines (f.)	factory smoke
le gaz	natural gas

hybride	hybrid
une marée noire	oil slick
menacer	to threaten
un panneau solaire	solar panel
un pesticide	pesticide
un pétrolier	oil tanker
planter	to plant
polluer/la pollution	to pollute/pollution
produire	to produce
protéger	to protect
le réchauffement	warming
réduire	to reduce
le recyclage/recycler	recycling/to recycle
les ressources naturelles (f.)	natural resources
la source d'énergie	energy source
utiliser	to use
le verre	glass

To make predictions .... *See p. 289*
To express and support an opinion ..... *See p. 291*

Game

Les manchettes

One student begins by creating a newspaper headline, such as **Un incendie a ravagé la forêt.** The next student must repeat the headline and add another one. **Un incendie a ravagé la forêt. Un tremblement de terre a secoué la ville.** Continue in this manner until someone makes a mistake. The student who makes a mistake is out. Start a new vocabulary round when someone makes a mistake, but the students who are out stay out. The winner is the last one remaining. You might also form small groups to play this game. 🌸 1.1

Online Edition

Transparency: Vocabulaire

Vocabulaire 7.4   CHAPITRE 7
Les nouvelles sources d'énergie

Transparency: Situation

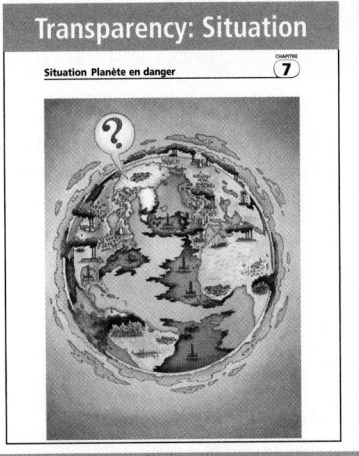
Situation Planète en danger   CHAPITRE 7

Assess

Assessment Program

Examen: Chapitre 7

Audio CD 7, Trs. 13, 14

Examen oral: Chapitre 7

Alternative Assessment

Differentiated Practice and
    Assessment CD-ROM

Online Assessment

my.hrw.com

Test Generator

The AP French Language Exam

Activités préparatoires provide students with activities similar to those found in the Advanced Placement French Language exam. The activities are based on material taught up to and including this chapter and concentrate on the chapter grammar and vocabulary.

Listening Script

1. Tu as lu cet article dans le journal? Il y a eu un tremblement de terre au Japon suivi d'un raz-de-marée! Plusieurs villages ont été complètement détruits et les dégâts sont considérables. C'est un désastre! Une vraie catastrophe!

2. — Salut, Anne! Qu'est-ce que tu fais ce week-end?
   — Je vais travailler dans un refuge pour les animaux blessés pendant la marée noire.

Activités préparatoires

SECTION I

Listening CD 7, Tr. 9 1.2

Listen to the dialogues and choose the most appropriate continuation for each dialogue.

1. **(A.)** Oui, beaucoup de gens sont morts!
   B. C'est vrai. Mais il peut y avoir un ouragan!
   C. C'est vrai. Ici, il n'y a pas de volcans.
   D. C'est pour ça que je te préviens.

2. **A.** C'est bien. Le recyclage, c'est vraiment important!
   (B.) Dis-donc! Tu es une vraie écologiste, toi!
   C. Ah oui, il faut trouver une solution à l'effet de serre.
   D. Je parie que bientôt, l'essence coûtera beaucoup moins cher.

Reading 1.2

Read the following paragraph and answer the questions that follow.

> Comme le suggère leur nom, les aurores polaires sont des phénomènes lumineux que l'on observe dans le ciel, surtout dans les
> 5 régions de latitudes élevées, que ce soit dans l'hémisphère nord - on parle alors d'aurores boréales - ou dans l'hémisphère sud - aurores australes. L'aspect des aurores est très
> 10 variable. Il peut correspondre à celui de simples lueurs colorées, aussi bien qu'à de grandes draperies ondulantes déployées sur une grande partie de la voûte céleste. Ces phénomènes
> 15 auroraux sont rarement visibles aux latitudes moyennes, et se présentent d'ordinaire sous la forme d'une simple coloration du ciel qui semble le reflet d'un incendie. Le plus souvent, ces
> 20 lueurs faiblement brillantes échappent aux regards, à cause de la pollution lumineuse occasionnée par l'urbanisation.

1. Les aurores polaires dans l'hémisphère nord s'appellent...
   (A.) des aurores boréales.
   B. des phénomènes.
   C. des aurores australes.
   D. des latitudes.

2. On voit les aurores polaires...
   A. juste dans l'hémisphère nord.
   (B.) dans les régions de latitudes élevées.
   C. juste dans l'hémisphère sud.
   D. toujours dans les tropiques.

3. Aux latitudes moyennes, elles sont...
   A. comme des étoiles.
   B. comme de la pollution.
   (C.) comme un incendie.
   D. comme des nuages.

4. «échappent aux regards» signifie:
   A. Les lueurs sont belles.
   B. Les lueurs sont très visibles.
   (C.) Les lueurs sont invisibles.
   D. Les lueurs se voient bien.

Preparing for the Exam

ADDITIONAL PRACTICE

In separate sentences, describe two actions that are occurring simultaneously. Have students combine the sentences with **en** + present participle. **Elle étudie. Elle écoute la radio. Elle étudie en écoutant la radio.** 1.2

TEST-TAKING STRATEGIES

Section I: Listening Encourage students to be active listeners, asking themselves questions as they listen to the speakers.

Section II: Writing Tell students not to waste time trying to answer questions they are unsure of. They should go through the section and answer only the questions they feel sure of. Then, as time permits, they can go back and work on the more difficult questions.

Online Practice
go.hrw.com
Online Edition
KEYWORD: BD3 CH7

Activités préparatoires

The following activities can be used to help you to prepare for the Advanced Placement French Language examination, or to further practice the vocabulary and grammar concepts you have seen in this chapter.

Activités préparatoires

SECTION II

Writing ✿1.2

In the following paragraph, some prepositions have been left out. Complete each sentence with the appropriate prepositions.

Notre planète ne pourra pas survivre ____1____ la coopération de tous ses habitants. Qu'est-ce qu'on peut faire ____2____ protéger l'environnement?

• Nous pouvons recycler ____3____ 75% de nos ordures.

• Nous pouvons partager notre véhicule ____4____ nos amis.

• Nous savons que la couche d'ozone est détruite ____5____ les aérosols. Ne les utilisons plus.

1. sans
2. pour
3. environ
4. avec
5. par

In the paragraph below, some verbs have been left out. Complete each sentence by writing the correct form of the verb in parentheses.

Dès que nous ____1____ les dangers qui menacent l'environnement, nous ____2____ essayer de les éliminer. Par exemple, en ____3____ les lumières en sortant d'une pièce, on économise de l'énergie. Pour que l'air ____4____ plus pur, il faut que tout le monde ____5____ à la protection de l'environnement.

1. <u>connaissons</u> (connaître)
2. <u>pouvons</u> (pouvoir)
3. <u>éteignant</u> (éteindre)
4. <u>soit</u> (être)
5. <u>contribue</u> (contribuer)

Essay Topic ✿1.3

Write in French a well-organized and coherent composition (10 to 15 lines) on the following topic.

À ton avis, quelle est la part de responsabilité des hommes dans les changements de l'environnement?

Speaking ✿1.2

Look at the following images and tell what is happening.

Reading Strategy

Factual Details You might tell students to look for numbers, dates, or proper nouns to help locate information quickly within the reading selection.

Writing Strategy

Remind students to pace themselves as they write. Before starting, they should plan their time, allotting one quarter of the total time for planning what to write, one half of the time for writing the essay, and another quarter for proofreading what they have written.

Language Examination

📖 To display the drawing to the class, use the **Activités préparatoires** Transparency for Chapter 7.

Speaking: Sample answer

Anne est une écologiste. Elle a décidé de recycler chez elle pour réduire l'accumulation des déchets dans sa ville. Elle encourage son ami à faire pareil. Malheureusement, l'usine près de la rivière pollue l'air et l'eau. Anne va écrire une lettre au gouvernement local.

You might ask students the following.

Qu'est-ce que tu fais pour protéger l'environnement?

Differentiated Instruction

SLOWER PACE LEARNERS

Building on Previous Skills Remind students that scientific texts often have cognates and loan words. Before students complete the Reading activity, have them list the cognates they find in the paragraph. Ask what they have learned in their science classes about the concepts associated with these cognates. Then have students read the paragraph for comprehension and answer the questions that follow. ✿ **1.2, 3.1**

SPECIAL LEARNING NEEDS

Students with AD(H)D You might reduce the answer choices in the Listening activity from four to two. Have students then work independently to complete the task. In the first Writing activity, give students two prepositions per sentence to choose from and then allow them to work independently to complete the task. In the Essay activity, set clear expectations regarding the length of the essay. ✿ **1.3**

Resources

Planning:

Lesson Planner

 One-Stop Planner

Practice:

Cahier d'activités

 Teaching Transparencies
Fine Art, Chapter 7

 Audio CD 7, Tr. 10

 Interactive Tutor, Disc 2

 **VIDEO OPTIONS**

▶ **Géoculture**

▶ **Télé-roman: Camille et compagnie, Épisode 7**

❶ Script

1. Depuis qu'ils ont fermé l'usine, l'air est pur ici.
2. C'est vraiment difficile de nettoyer les plages polluées par des marées noires. Et en plus, beaucoup d'oiseaux meurent!
3. Tu as vu ces éclairs? J'ai peur de l'orage, moi!
4. C'est une vraie catastrophe! La marée noire a atteint toutes les plus belles plages de la région!
5. Attention, les éclairs peuvent provoquer des incendies!

❷ Possible Answers

1. Il pourrait y avoir des inondations.
2. Il pourrait y avoir une période de sécheresse due à une vague de chaleur.
3. Il pourrait y avoir des avalanches.
4. Il pourrait y avoir un gros orage.
5. Answers will vary.

 *chapitres 1-7*

Révisions cumulatives

CD 7, Tr. 10 🍀1.2 **1.** b **2.** a **3.** c **4.** a **5.** c

❶ Écoute les phrases et décide de quelle photo on parle.

a.

b.

c.

❷ On est en 2025 et le climat est complètement perturbé. Il n'y a plus de saison! Regarde ce site météo sur le Web et réponds aux questions suivantes. 🍀3.2

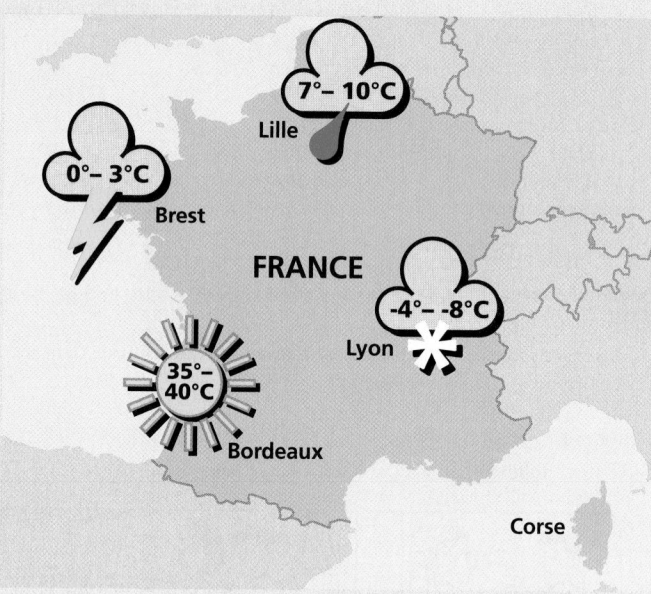

1. Quelle catastrophe naturelle pourrait arriver à Lille?
2. Quelle catastrophe naturelle pourrait arriver à Bordeaux?
3. Quelle catastrophe naturelle pourrait arriver à Lyon?
4. Quelle catastrophe naturelle pourrait arriver à Brest?
5. Quel temps fait-il dans ta région?

Online Culture Project

Using a European environmental organization as a model, students will create a pamphlet for an environmental association that provides recycling services in their neighborhood. The pamphlet should list their organization's services and the residents' responsibilities. Students will work in groups of three and look up Web sites of European environmental organizations and policies. Tell students to focus on the Francophone countries presented in the **Géoculture**. 🍀2.1

Révisions cumulatives

Révisions cumulatives

3 Tu penses qu'il y a trop de déchets dans ta ville. Tu voudrais que les élèves de ton école fassent quelque chose pour améliorer la situation. Tu vas trouver le directeur (la directrice) de ton école pour lui expliquer ton plan. Joue cette scène avec un(e) camarade. 1.1

4 Regarde le tableau et écris un article sur le phénomène naturel dépeint sur ce tableau. Quel a l'air d'être le climat de cette région? Sur quoi tu bases ton opinion? 1.3

Monet, Claude. The Jetty at Le Havre, 1867.

La jetée du Havre par mauvais temps de Claude Monet

5 Il y a eu une catastrophe naturelle dans la région où un(e) de tes ami(e)s habite et sa maison a été détruite. Écris-lui une lettre pour lui dire que tu es désolé(e), donne-lui des conseils et demande-lui comment tu pourrais l'aider. 1.3

6 **À ton tour** **À chaque problème, sa solution** Avec des camarades de classe, faites un tableau des différents problèmes écologiques de votre région et proposez des solutions pour les améliorer. Présentez vos idées à la classe. Vos camarades peuvent choisir les meilleures idées proposées. 1.3

FINE ART CONNECTION

Introduction Claude Monet was born in Paris in 1840. His family moved to Le Havre when he was a child. In 1859, Monet left for Paris, where he developed his own style by rendering outdoor sunlight with a direct, sketch-like application of bright color. In 1872 (or 1873) he painted *Impression, soleil levant.* The term, Impressionism, comes from the title of this painting. In *La jetée du Havre par mauvais temps,* Monet tried to capture the essence of a fleeting moment, the light and reflections on water, the variations in a sky. He said, **"La couleur est mon obsession quotidienne, ma joie et mon tourment."** Monet died in1926 at the age of 86 and is buried in the Giverny church cemetery.

Analyzing
Sometimes Monet painted the same scene again and again, capturing the difference in lighting in different seasons or at different times of the day. Ask students the following questions.
1. **Quelles couleurs Monet aurait utilisé s'il avait peint ce tableau avant la tempête?**
2. **Comment aurait-il peint la jetée après la tempête?**
   1.1, 3.1

Extension
In1862, Monet joined the studio of Charles Gleyre in Paris, where he met Pierre-Auguste Renoir, Frederic Bazille, and Alfred Sisley. The group shared new approaches to art, which later came to be known as Impressionism. Ask students to research Renoir, Bazille, and Sisley and discuss motifs, techniques, and styles they have in common with Monet.
1.3, 3.1

ACTFL Performance Standards

The activities in Chapter 7 target the communicative modes as described in the Standards.

Interpersonal	Two-way communication using receptive skills and productive skills	**Communication (SE),** pp. 279, 281, 283, 285, 291, 293 **Communication (TE),** pp. 279, 281, 285, 291, 293, 297 **À ton tour,** p. 311
Interpretive	One-way communication using receptive skills	**Culture,** pp. 286–287 **Lecture,** pp. 298–301
Presentational	One-way communication using productive skills	**Communication (SE),** p. 297 **Communication (TE),** pp. 279, 283, 295

chapitre 8

Planning Guide

La société

Chapter Section		Resources

Vocabulaire 1
pp. 314–317
- Political campaign and government

Grammaire 1
pp. 318–321
- Contractions with **lequel**
- The past subjunctive

Application 1
pp. 322–323
- **Un peu plus:**
  Review: Adverbs

Resources (right column):

- Teaching Transparencies: Vocabulaire 8.1, 8.2; Bell Work 8.1, 8.2, 8.3, 8.4
- Cahier de vocabulaire et grammaire, pp. 85–90
- Grammar Tutor for Students of French
- Cahier d'activités, pp. 71–73
- Media Guide, pp. 29–32

Assessment Program
Quiz: Vocabulaire 1, pp. 210–211
Quiz: Grammaire 1, pp. 212–213
Quiz: Application 1, pp. 214–215

Culture
pp. 324–325
- **Lecture culturelle: Cité de la paix et de l'intégration**
- **Comparaisons**
- **Communauté et professions**

- Cahier d'activités, p. 74

Vocabulaire 2
pp. 326–329
- Government services

Grammaire 2
pp. 330–333
- Review: The conditional
- The verb **vaincre**

Application 2
pp. 334–335
- **Un peu plus:**
  chacun/chacune

Resources:

- Teaching Transparencies: Vocabulaire 8.3, 8.4; Bell Work 8.5, 8.6, 8.7, 8.8
- Cahier de vocabulaire et grammaire, pp. 91–96
- Grammar Tutor for Students of French
- Cahier d'activités, pp. 75–77
- Media Guide, pp. 29–32

Assessment Program
Quiz: Vocabulaire 2, pp. 216–217
Quiz: Grammaire 2, pp. 218–219
Quiz: Application 2, pp. 220–221

Lecture
pp. 336–339
- De l'esprit des lois

L'atelier de l'écrivain
pp. 340–341
- **La démocratie en pratique**

Resources:

- Cahier d'activités, p. 78
- Reading Strategies and Skills Handbook
- Advanced Reader

Assessment Program
Quiz: Lecture, p. 222
Quiz: Écriture, p. 223

Prépare-toi pour l'examen
pp. 342–345
- **Résumé de vocabulaire et grammaire**

Activités préparatoires
pp. 346–347

Révisions cumulatives
pp. 348–349

Resources:

- Teaching Transparencies: Picture Sequences, Situation, Ch. 8
- Media Guide, pp. 32, 67–68

Assessment Program
Examen: Chapitre 8, pp. 224–229
Examen oral: Chapitre 8, p. 324

- Teaching Transparencies, Fine Art, Ch. 8
- Cahier d'activités, pp. 79–80

Chroniques
pp. 350–359
- Plus loin, plus vite
- Technologie de pointe
- SOS Terre
- La Ve République
- L'Europe francophone

Resources:

- Reading Strategies and Skills Handbook
- Advanced Reader

Pacing Suggestions

	Essential	Recommended	Optional
Vocabulaire 1 • Political campaign and government • **Flash culture**	✔		
Grammaire 1 • Contractions with **lequel** • The past subjunctive • **Flash culture**	✔		
Application 1 • **Un peu plus:** Review: Adverbs	✔		
Culture • **Lecture culturelle: Cité de la paix et de l'intégration** • **Comparaisons** • **Communauté et professions**		✔	
Vocabulaire 2 • Government services • **Flash culture**	✔		
Grammaire 2 • Review: The conditional • The verb **vaincre**	✔		
Application 2 • **Un peu plus:** **chacun/chacune**	✔		
Lecture • **De l'esprit des lois** **L'atelier de l'écrivain** • **La démocratie en pratique**		✔	
Prépare-toi pour l'examen		✔	
Activités préparatoires		✔	
Révisions cumulatives			✔
Chroniques			✔

Technology

Bien dit! Online
• Student Edition with multi-media
• SoundBooth recording tool
• Interactive activities with feedback
• Self-tests with feedback
• Cahier d'activités (Interactive workbook)
• Cahier de vocabulaire et grammaire (Interactive workbook)
• Holt Online Assessment

DVD Program
• Télé-roman: Camille et compagnie
• Télé-culture: Interviews

Interactive Tutor
• Interactive practice games
• Writing and recording workshops
• Before You Know It™ Flashcards

Audio Program
• Student Edition Listening Activities
• Assessment listening activities
• Songs

One-Stop Planner
• Complete media and print resources
• ExamView Pro Test Generator
• Holt Calendar Planner

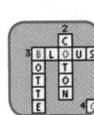
PuzzlePro
• Customizable word games

Differentiated Practice and Assessment CD

For slower pace and advanced learner options, see the Differentiated Practice and Assessment CD.

Planning Guide

Projects

Projects

Grading the project

Suggested point distribution
  (100 points total)
Use of French 30
Vocabulary 30
Creativity of visuals 20
Presentation. 20

Dans la ville de...

In this project, students work in groups of three or four to research a French-speaking city and write a short newscast, reporting on the social and economic challenges faced by that city. You may want to allow a week for groups to collect information on the city they choose. 🞨 1.3, 5.1

Suggested Sequence

1. Form groups of three or four students and have them choose a French-speaking city. Students should research their chosen city in the library or on the Internet.

2. After students have gathered their information, they may begin preparing their written newscast. They should report on the city's current events, cultural resources, recent problems and solutions, and outlook for the near future.

3. Students prepare several icons or pictures that appear behind the shoulder of the newscaster as he or she is introducing the upcoming story. Encourage students to be creative in their representations and to choose an image that depicts the main idea of their reports.

4. Students present their news broadcasts to the class. You may want to record groups' projects on video.

e-community

e-mail forum:
Post the following question on the classroom e-mail forum:

Location: http://french

Que ferais-tu pour résoudre les problèmes sociaux? 🞨 5.1

All students will contribute to the list and then share the items.

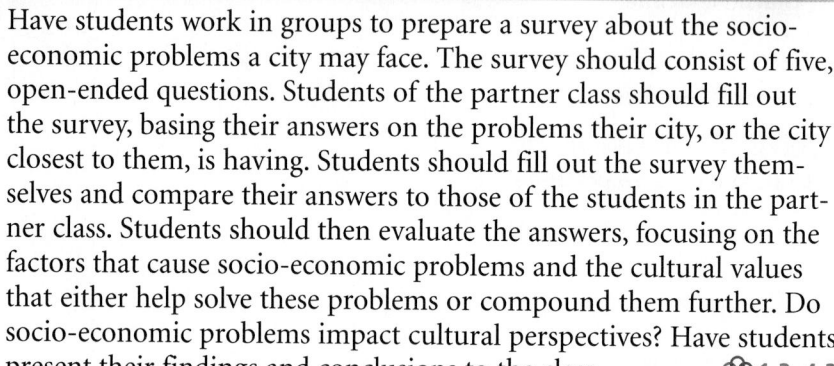

Partner Class Project

Have students work in groups to prepare a survey about the socio-economic problems a city may face. The survey should consist of five, open-ended questions. Students of the partner class should fill out the survey, basing their answers on the problems their city, or the city closest to them, is having. Students should fill out the survey themselves and compare their answers to those of the students in the partner class. Students should then evaluate the answers, focusing on the factors that cause socio-economic problems and the cultural values that either help solve these problems or compound them further. Do socio-economic problems impact cultural perspectives? Have students present their findings and conclusions to the class. 🞨 1.3, 4.2

Game Bank

For game ideas, see pages T60–T63.

Les langues en Belgique

Due to its history and close political and commercial ties with neighboring countries, Belgium has become known as the cross-roads of Europe. Belgians have traditionally learned to speak more than one or two languages. All children in Belgium are required to learn at least a second language in school. Since Brussels is officially a bilingual city, students must learn French and Flemish there. However, in other parts of the country, students may choose to learn German, English, Spanish, or Italian. English and German are the most popular choices, because English is important for advanced study at universities and Germany is a an important trading partner. Ask students why they think knowing foreign languages is more important to Belgians than it is to Americans. Can students think of another country in which knowledge of a foreign language is not deemed important? Allow students to present their conclusions to the class. 🍀 3.2, 4.2

La cuisine

Waterzoï is a Flemish dish. While comparable to the typical Marseilles dish, **bouillabaisse,** it substitutes cream, eggs, and sage for garlic, tomatoes, and saffron. The main ingredient of **waterzoï** is either fish or chicken. Encourage students to make waterzoï in the home economics class or at home for family and friends. 🍀 3.1, 5.2

Waterzoï Pour 6 personnes

1 tasse de branches de céleri
1 gros poireau
3 carottes
1 oignon
4 pommes de terre
1 cuillère à soupe de beurre

1 poulet coupé en morceaux
4 tasses d'eau bouillante
sauge
½ tasse de persil
sel
poivre

1 cuillère à soupe de farine
1 tasse de crème fraîche
2 jaunes d'œufs
1 baguette coupée en tranches

Couper en petits morceaux le céleri, le poireau, les carottes et l'oignon. Dans une marmite, faire revenir les légumes avec le beurre pendant 5 minutes. Ajouter l'eau. Quand l'eau bout, ajouter le poulet coupé en morceaux. Ajouter le persil, le sel et le poivre. Laissez mijoter pendant 45 minutes. À mi-cuisson, ajouter les pommes de terre épluchées. À la fin de la cuisson, prendre 1/2 tasse de bouillon pour préparer la sauce. Pour la sauce, ajouter la farine, la crème fraîche et les jaunes d'œufs au bouillon. Quand la sauce a épaissi, la verser dans la marmite avec le poulet et les légumes. Servir bien chaud avec le pain.

Listening Activity Scripts

Vocabulaire à l'œuvre 1

1 p. 316, CD 8, Tr. 1

1. Les électeurs se rendent au bureau de vote pour voter.
2. Avant la Révolution, la France était une monarchie et Louis XVI était le roi.
3. Allez-y! Mettez votre bulletin dans l'urne, monsieur.
4. En ce qui me concerne, je pense qu'ils ont raison de manifester!
5. C'est à l'Assemblée nationale que le Parlement fait les lois.
6. Pour ma part, je pense que c'était un bon président.

Answers for Activity 1
1. f   2. d   3. b   4. c   5. e   6. a

Grammaire à l'œuvre 1

7 p. 318, CD 8, Tr. 2

1. As-tu parlé au sénateur auquel je t'ai présenté?
2. Le candidat pour lequel j'ai voté a gagné les élections!
3. Les problèmes auxquels il s'intéresse sont la pollution et l'environnement.
4. Les questions auxquelles il n'a pas voulu répondre étaient pourtant intéressantes!

Answers for Activity 7
1. a   2. c   3. d   4. b

Application 1

16 p. 322, CD 8, Tr. 3

1. Mes parents sont contents que leur député préféré ait été réélu.
2. Moi, je ne suis pas sûr qu'ils aient voté pour le meilleur candidat.
3. Je doute qu'il fasse du bon travail.
4. Ça ne m'étonnerait pas qu'il aille en prison!
5. Bien sûr, il est possible que je change d'avis.

Answers for Activity 16
1. b   2. b   3. a   4. a   5. a

Vocabulaire à l'œuvre 2

22 p. 328, CD 8, Tr. 4

1. Bonjour, monsieur, je suis venue chercher mon permis de conduire.
2. J'ai dû regarder des photos pour reconnaître le voleur parce que le policier croit qu'il travaillait pour mon père. Il est possible que je le connaisse.
3. Appelez tout de suite le docteur Maréchal, le blessé est arrivé et a besoin de soins urgents.
4. Ce monsieur était là et il a tout vu. Le policier lui pose des questions pour savoir laquelle des deux voitures ne s'est pas arrêtée au feu.
5. Tu entends la sirène du camion des pompiers? Ils seront là dans une minute.

Answers for Activity 22
1. b   2. e   3. c   4. a   5. d

Grammaire à l'œuvre 2

27 p. 330, CD 8, Tr. 5

1. Il faudrait que je fasse refaire mon passeport si je veux aller en Europe cet été.
2. Ah moi, je dois aller chercher mon permis de conduire à la mairie.
3. Ah! Tu as passé ton permis! Bravo! Si tu avais de l'argent, quelle voiture tu aimerais acheter?
4. Si je pouvais, j'achèterais une voiture hybride.
5. Oh oui, c'est une bonne idée.

Answers for Activity 27
1. a   2. b   3. a   4. a   5. b

Application 2

39 p. 335, CD 8, Tr. 6

1. Les électeurs devaient montrer leurs cartes d'identité avant de pouvoir voter. Chacune d'elles devait avoir une photo récente.

2. Les candidats ont pu présenter leurs idées pendant le débat télévisé. Chacun d'eux a eu dix minutes pour le faire.

3. Les bureaux de vote devaient fermer à 6h pour que les votes puissent être comptés le jour même et chacun d'eux a observé le règlement.

4. Les affiches électorales des candidats avaient été bien préparées. Chacune d'elles présentait bien leurs idées.

5. Les candidates aux élections avaient particulièrement bien soigné leur campagne électorale. Chacune d'elles y avait participé personnellement jusque dans les plus petits détails.

Answers for Activity 39

1. a   2. a   3. a   4. b   5. b

Prépare-toi pour l'examen

6 p. 343, CD 8, Tr. 8

1. S'il y a un accident de la circulation, il faut téléphoner à la police.

2. Quand on entend la sirène des pompiers, il faut laisser le passage.

3. Dans une monarchie, le roi est le chef d'état.

4. Les électeurs votent pour élire le roi.

5. Il faut une carte d'identité pour conduire.

6. Le premier ministre et son cabinet gouvernent le pays.

7. Si on perd ses papiers, il est possible de les faire refaire.

Answers for Activity 6

1. a   2. a   3. a   4. b   5. b   6. a   7. a

Activités préparatoires

Listening, p. 346, CD 8, Tr. 9

1. — Regarde là-bas. Il y a un camion de pompiers de l'autre côté de l'autoroute.

   — C'est une voiture qui est en feu. Les pompiers éteignent l'incendie. Il y a des blessés aussi.

2. — Tu vas au bureau de vote aujourd'hui pour élire ton candidat?

   — Non, je n'y vais pas. J'ai changé d'avis après avoir lu les résultats d'un sondage fait par l'opposition.

Answers to the Listening Activity

1. c   2. a

Révisions cumulatives *chapitres 1-8*

1 p. 348, CD 8, Tr. 10

1. Il faut avoir dix-huit ans pour pouvoir voter.

2. En France, on doit toujours avoir ses papiers sur soi.

3. On a appelé les pompiers parce qu'il y avait un incendie.

4. C'est là que les ambulanciers emmènent les blessés.

5. Tu entends la sirène? Ce sont les pompiers. Laisse-les passer!

6. Tout le monde devrait voter. C'est important d'élire un bon candidat!

7. Je trouve que je suis horrible sur ma photo d'identité!

Answers to Activity 1

1. c   2. b   3. a   4. d   5. a   6. c   7. b

50-Minute Lesson Plans

La société

50-Minute Lesson Plans

Day 1

OBJECTIVE
Express a point of view

Core Instruction
Chapter Opener, pp. 312–313
• See Using the Photo, p. 312. **5 min.**
• See Chapter Objectives, p. 312. **5 min.**

Vocabulaire 1, pp. 314–317
• Present **Vocabulaire 1,** pp. 314–315. See Teaching **Vocabulaire,** p. 314. **15 min.**
• Present **Exprimons-nous!,** p. 315. **10 min.**
• Play Audio CD 8, Tr. 1 for Activity 1, p. 316. **5 min.**
• Have students do Activities 2–3, p. 316. **10 min.**

Optional Resources
• Advanced Learners, p. 315 ▲
• Multiple Intelligences, p. 315
• Advanced Learners, p. 317 ▲

Homework Suggestions
Cahier de vocabulaire et grammaire, pp. 85–86

🌼 1.1, 1.2, 1.3, 3.1, 3.2, 4.2

Day 2

OBJECTIVE
Speculate; Use contractions with **lequel**

Core Instruction
Vocabulaire 1, pp. 314–317
• Do Bell Work 8.1, p. 314. **5 min.**
• Present **Flash culture,** p. 316. **5 min.**
• See Teaching **Exprimons-nous!,** p. 316. **10 min.**
• Have students do Activities 4–5, p. 317. **20 min.**

Grammaire 1, pp. 318–321
• See Teaching **Grammaire,** p. 318. **10 min.**

Optional Resources
• Special Learning Needs, p. 317 ●
• Slower Pace Learners, p. 319 ◆

Homework Suggestions
Study for **Quiz: Vocabulaire 1**
Cahier de vocabulaire et grammaire, p. 87
Online Practice (**go.hrw.com,** Keyword: BD3 CH8)

🌼 1.1, 1.2, 4.1

Day 3

OBJECTIVE
Use contractions with **lequel**

Core Instruction
Vocabulaire 1, pp. 314–317
• Review **Vocabulaire 1,** pp. 314–317. **10 min.**
• Give **Quiz: Vocabulaire 1.** **20 min.**

Grammaire 1, pp. 318–321
• Have students do Activity 6, p. 318. **5 min.**
• Play Audio CD 8, Tr. 2 for Activity 7, p. 318. **5 min.**
• Have students do Activities 8–9, p. 319. **5 min.**
• Present **Flash culture,** p. 319. **5 min.**

Optional Resources
• Communication (TE), p. 319
• Special Learning Needs, p. 319 ●

Homework Suggestions
Cahier de vocabulaire et grammaire, p. 88
Cahier d'activités, p. 71
Interactive Tutor, Ch. 8

🌼 1.2, 3.1

Day 4

OBJECTIVE
Use contractions with **lequel**; *Use the past subjunctive*

Core Instruction
Grammaire 1, pp. 318–321
• Do Activity 10, p. 319. **5 min.**
• See Teaching **Grammaire,** p. 320. **10 min.**
• Have students do Activities 11–15, pp. 320–321. **25 min.**

Application 1, pp. 322–323
• Play Audio CD 8, Tr. 3 for Activity 16, p. 322. **5 min.**
• Do Activity 17, p. 322. **5 min.**

Optional Resources
• Slower Pace Learners, p. 321 ◆
• Special Learning Needs, p. 321 ●

Homework Suggestions
Study for **Quiz: Grammaire 1**
Cahier de vocabulaire et grammaire, p. 89
Cahier d'activités, p. 72

🌼 1.1, 1.2, 1.3

Day 5

OBJECTIVE
Use adverbs

Core Instruction
Grammaire 1, pp. 318–321
• Review **Grammaire 1,** pp. 318–321. **10 min.**
• Give **Quiz: Grammaire 1.** **20 min.**

Application 1, pp. 322–323
• See Teaching **Un peu plus,** p. 322. **5 min.**
• Have students do Activities 18–20, pp. 322–323. **15 min.**

Optional Resources
• Communication (TE), p. 323
• Advanced Learners, p. 323 ▲
• Multiple Intelligences, p. 323

Homework Suggestions
Study for **Quiz: Application 1**
Cahier de vocabulaire et grammaire, p. 90
Cahier d'activités, p. 73
Online Practice (**go.hrw.com,** Keyword: BD3 CH8)

🌼 1.1, 1.2, 1.3, 3.1, 3.2

Day 6

OBJECTIVE
Learn about francophone culture

Core Instruction
Application 1, pp. 322–323
• Review **Application 1,** pp. 322–323. **10 min.**
• **Quiz: Application 1.** **20 min.**

Culture, pp. 324–325
• See **Lecture culturelle** (TE), p. 324. **10 min.**
• See **Comparaisons et communauté** (TE), p. 324. **10 min.**

Optional Resources
• Cultures, p. 325
• Communities, p. 325
• Advanced Learners, p. 325 ▲
• Multiple Intelligences, p. 325

Homework Suggestions
Cahier d'activités, p. 74
Interactive Tutor, Ch. 8
Online Practice (**go.hrw.com,** Keyword: BD3 CH8)
Finish the **Communauté et professions project,** p. 325.

🌼 1.2, 1.3, 2.1, 3.1, 3.2, 4.2, 5.1

Day 7

OBJECTIVE
Ask for assistance

Core Instruction
Vocabulaire 2, pp. 326–329
• Do Bell Work 8.5, p. 326. **5 min.**
• Present **Vocabulaire 2,** pp. 326–327. See Teaching **Vocabulaire,** p. 326. **15 min.**
• Present **Exprimons-nous!,** p. 327. **5 min.**
• Do Activity 21, p. 328. **5 min.**
• Play Audio CD 8, Tr. 4 for Activity 22, p. 328. **5 min.**
• Have students do Activities 23–24, p. 328. **10 min.**
• Present **Flash culture,** p. 328. **5 min.**

Optional Resources
• Advanced Learners, p. 327 ▲
• Special Learning Needs, p. 327 ●

Homework Suggestions
Cahier de vocabulaire et grammaire, pp. 91–92
Online Practice (**go.hrw.com,** Keyword: BD3 CH8)

🌼 1.1, 1.2, 1.3

Day 8

OBJECTIVE
Relate information; Use the conditional

Core Instruction
Vocabulaire 2, pp. 326–329
• See Teaching **Exprimons-nous!,** p. 328. **10 min.**
• Have students do Activities 25–26, p. 329. **10 min.**

Grammaire 2, pp. 330–333
• See Teaching **Grammaire,** p. 330. **20 min.**
• Play Audio CD 8, Tr. 5 for Activity 27, p. 330. **5 min.**
• Do Activity 28, p. 331. **5 min.**

Optional Resources
• Slower Pace Learners, p. 329 ◆
• Special Learning Needs, p. 329 ●
• Slower Pace Learners, p. 331 ◆

Homework Suggestions
Study for **Quiz: Vocabulaire 2**
Cahier de vocabulaire et grammaire, p. 93
Interactive Tutor, Ch. 8

🌼 1.1, 1.2, 4.1

Day 9

OBJECTIVE
Use the conditional

Core Instruction
Vocabulaire 2, pp. 326–329
• Review **Vocabulaire 2,** pp. 326–329. **10 min.**
• Give **Quiz: Vocabulaire 2.** **20 min.**

Grammaire 2, pp. 330–333
• Have students do Activities 29–31, p. 331. **20 min.**

Optional Resources
• Communication (TE), p. 331
• Special Learning Needs, p. 331 ●

Homework Suggestions
Cahier de vocabulaire et grammaire, p. 94
Cahier d'activités, p. 75
Interactive Tutor, Ch. 8
Online Practice (**go.hrw.com,** Keyword: BD3 CH8)

❀ 1.1, 1.2

Day 10

OBJECTIVE
*Use the verb **vaincre**; Use **chacun/chacune***

Core Instruction
Grammaire 2, pp. 330–333
• Do Bell Work 8.7, p. 332. **5 min.**
• See Teaching **Grammaire,** p. 332. **10 min.**
• Have students do Activities 32–36, pp. 332–333. **25 min.**

Application 2, pp. 334–335
• Have students do Activity 37, p. 334. **15 min.**
• See Teaching **Un peu plus,** p. 334. **5 min.**

Optional Resources
• Slower Pace Learners, p. 333 ◆
• Multiple Intelligences, p. 333
• Advanced Learners, p. 335 ▲

Homework Suggestions
Study for **Quiz: Grammaire 2**
Cahier de vocabulaire et grammaire, p. 95
Cahier d'activités, p. 76

❀ 1.1, 1.2, 1.3

Day 11

OBJECTIVE
*Use **chacun/chacune***

Core Instruction
Grammaire 2, pp. 330–333
• Review **Grammaire 2,** pp. 330–333. **10 min.**
• Give **Quiz: Grammaire 2.** **20 min.**

Application 2, pp. 334–335
• Do Activity 38, p. 334. **5 min.**
• Play Audio CD 8, Tr. 6 for Activity 39, p. 335. **5 min.**
• Have students do Activities 40–41, p. 335. **10 min.**

Optional Resources
• Communication (TE), p. 335
• Special Learning Needs, p. 335 ●

Homework Suggestions
Study for **Quiz: Application 2**
Cahier de vocabulaire et grammaire, p. 96
Cahier d'activités, p. 77

❀ 1.1, 1.2, 1.3

Day 12

OBJECTIVE
Develop listening and reading skills

Core Instruction
Application 2, pp. 334–335
• Review **Application 2,** pp. 334–335. **10 min.**
• Give **Quiz: Application 2.** **20 min.**

Lecture, pp. 336–339
• See **Lecture** (TE), p. 336. **20 min.**

Optional Resources
• Slower Pace Learners, p. 337 ◆
• Special Learning Needs, p. 337 ●

Homework Suggestions
Interactive Tutor, Ch. 8
Online Practice (**go.hrw.com,** Keyword: BD3 CH8)

❀ 1.2, 1.3, 3.1

Day 13

OBJECTIVE
Develop listening, reading, and writing skills

Core Instruction
Lecture, pp. 336–339
• See **Lecture** (TE), p. 338. **20 min.**

L'atelier de l'écrivain, pp. 340–341
• See **L'atelier de l'écrivain** (TE), p. 340. **30 min.**

Optional Resources
• Advanced Learners, p. 339 ▲
• Special Learning Needs, p. 339 ●
• Slower Pace Learners, p. 341 ◆
• Special Learning Needs, p. 341 ●

Homework Suggestions
Cahier d'activités, p. 78

❀ 1.1, 1.2, 1.3, 3.1, 4.1

Day 14

OBJECTIVE
Review the chapter; Prepare for AP Exam

Core Instruction
Prépare-toi pour l'examen, pp. 342–345
• Have students do Activities 1–5, pp. 342–343. **25 min.**

Activités préparatoires, pp. 346–347
• Have students do the **Activités préparatoires,** pp. 346–347. **25 min.**

Optional Resources
• Reteaching, p. 342
• Connections, p. 344
• Slower Pace Learners, p. 347 ◆
• Special Learning Needs, p. 347 ●
• **Télé-culture:** Interviews

Homework Suggestions
Interactive Tutor, Ch. 8
Online Practice (**go.hrw.com,** Keyword: BD3 CH8)

❀ 1.1, 1.2, 1.3, 3.1

Day 15

OBJECTIVE
Review the chapter

Core Instruction
Prépare-toi pour l'examen, pp. 342–345
• Play Audio CD 8, Tr. 8 for Activity 6, p. 343. **10 min.**
• Have students do Activity 7, p. 343. **10 min.**

Révisions cumulatives, pp. 348–349
• Play Audio CD 8, Tr. 10 for Activity 1, p. 348. **5 min.**
• Have students do Activities 2–6, pp. 348–349. **25 min.**

Optional Resources
• Game, p. 345
• Online Culture Project, p. 348
• Fine Art Connection, p. 349
• **Télé-roman: Camille et compagnie**

Homework Suggestions
Study for Chapter Test
Online Practice (**go.hrw.com,** Keyword: BD3 CH8)

❀ 1.1, 1.2, 1.3, 2.2, 3.1

Day 16/Test

Core Instruction
Chapter Test **50 min.**

Optional Resources
Assessment Program:
• Alternative Assessment
• Test Generator
• **Quiz: Lecture**
• **Quiz: Écriture**

Homework Suggestions
Cahier d'activités, pp. 79–80, 116–117
Online Practice (**go.hrw.com,** Keyword: BD3 CH8)

50-Minute Lesson Plans

90-Minute Lesson Plans

Block 1

OBJECTIVE
Express a point of view; Speculate

Core Instruction
Chapter Opener, pp. 312–313
• See Using the Photo, p. 312.
  5 min.
• See Chapter Objectives, p. 312.
  5 min.

Vocabulaire 1, pp. 314–317
• Present **Vocabulaire 1,**
  pp. 314–315. See Teaching
  Vocabulaire, p. 314. **15 min.**
• Present **Exprimons-nous!,**
  p. 315. **10 min.**
• Play Audio CD 8, Tr. 1 for Activity
  1, p. 316. **5 min.**
• Have students do Activities 2–3,
  p. 316. **15 min.**
• Present **Flash culture,** p. 316.
  5 min.
• See Teaching **Exprimons-
  nous!,** p. 316. **10 min.**
• Have students do Activities 4–5,
  p. 317. **20 min.**

Optional Resources
• Learning Tips, p. 313
• TPR, p. 315
• Cultures, p. 315
• Advanced Learners, p. 315 ▲
• Multiple Intelligences, p. 315
• Connections, p. 316
• Communication (TE), p. 317
• Advanced Learners, p. 317 ▲
• Special Learning Needs, p. 317 ●

Homework Suggestions
Study for **Quiz: Vocabulaire 1**
**Cahier de vocabulaire et
  grammaire,** pp. 85–87
Interactive Tutor, Ch. 8
Online Practice (**go.hrw.com,**
  Keyword: BD3 CH8)
  ✿ 1.1, 1.2, 1.3, 2.1, 3.1,
    3.2, 4.2

Block 2

OBJECTIVE
*Use contractions with **lequel;** Use
the past subjunctive*

Core Instruction
Vocabulaire 1, pp. 314–317
• Review **Vocabulaire 1,**
  pp. 314–317. **10 min.**
• Give **Quiz: Vocabulaire 1.**
  20 min.

Grammaire 1, pp. 318–321
• See Teaching **Grammaire,**
  p. 318. **10 min.**
• Have students do Activity 6,
  p. 318. **5 min.**
• Play Audio CD 8, Tr. 2 for Activity
  7, p. 318. **5 min.**
• Have students do Activities
  8–10, p. 319. **5 min.**
• Present **Flash culture,** p. 319.
  5 min.
• See Teaching **Grammaire,**
  p. 320. **10 min.**
• Have students do Activities
  11–14, pp. 320–321. **20 min.**

Optional Resources
• Cultures, p. 319
• Communication (TE), p. 319
• Slower Pace Learners, p. 319 ◆
• Special Learning Needs, p. 319 ●
• French for Spanish Speakers,
  p. 320
• Slower Pace Learners, p. 321 ◆
• Special Learning Needs, p. 321 ●

Homework Suggestions
Study for **Quiz: Grammaire 1**
**Cahier de vocabulaire et
  grammaire,** pp. 88–89
Cahier d'activités, pp. 71–72
Interactive Tutor, Ch. 8
Online Practice (**go.hrw.com,**
  Keyword: BD3 CH8)
  ✿ 1.1, 1.2, 2.1, 3.1, 4.1

Block 3

OBJECTIVE
*Use the past subjunctive; Use
adverbs; Learn about francophone
culture*

Core Instruction
Grammaire 1, pp. 318–328
• Do Bell Work 8.3, p. 320.
  5 min.
• Have students do Activity 15,
  p. 321. **5 min.**
• Review **Grammaire 1,**
  pp. 318–321. **10 min.**
• Give **Quiz: Grammaire 1.**
  20 min.

Application 1, pp. 322–323
• Play Audio CD 8, Tr. 3 for Activity
  16, p. 322. **5 min.**
• Have students do Activity 17,
  p. 322. **5 min.**
• See Teaching **Un peu plus,**
  p. 322. **5 min.**
• Have students do Activities
  18–20, pp. 322–323. **15 min.**

Culture, pp. 324–325
• See **Lecture culturelle** (TE),
  p. 324. **10 min.**
• See **Comparaisons et communauté** (TE), p. 324. **10 min.**

Optional Resources
• Communication (TE), p. 321
• Comparisons, p. 323
• Communication (TE), p. 323
• Advanced Learners, p. 323 ▲
• Multiple Intelligences, p. 323
• Prereading Questions, p. 324
• Active Reading Questions, p. 324
• Vocabulaire supplémentaire,
  p. 324
• Bulletin Board Project, p. 325
• Cultures, p. 325
• Communities, p. 325
• Advanced Learners, p. 325 ▲
• Multiple Intelligences, p. 325

Homework Suggestions
Study for **Quiz: Application 1**
**Cahier de vocabulaire et
  grammaire,** p. 90
Cahier d'activités, pp. 73–74
Interactive Tutor, Ch. 8
Online Practice (**go.hrw.com,**
  Keyword: BD3 CH8)
Finish the **Communauté et
  professions** project, p. 325.
  ✿ 1.1, 1.2, 1.3, 2.1, 3.1,
    3.2, 4.1, 4.2, 5.1

Block 4

OBJECTIVE
*Ask for assistance; Relate
information*

Core Instruction
Application 1, pp. 322–323
• Review **Application 1,**
  pp. 322–323. **10 min.**
• Give **Quiz: Application 1.**
  20 min.

Vocabulaire 2, pp. 326–329
• Present **Vocabulaire 2,**
  pp. 326–327. See Teaching
  Vocabulaire, p. 326. **10 min.**
• Present **Exprimons-nous!,**
  p. 327. **5 min.**
• Have students do Activity 21,
  p. 328. **5 min.**
• Play Audio CD 8, Tr. 4 for Activity
  22, p. 328. **5 min.**
• Have students do Activities
  23–24, p. 328. **10 min.**
• Present **Flash culture,** p. 328.
  5 min.
• See Teaching **Exprimons-
  nous!,** p. 328. **10 min.**
• Have students do Activities
  25–26, p. 329. **10 min.**

Optional Resources
• TPR, p. 327
• Teacher to Teacher, p. 327
• Advanced Learners, p. 327 ▲
• Special Learning Needs, p. 327 ●
• Cultures, p. 329
• Communication (TE), p. 329
• Slower Pace Learners, p. 329 ◆
• Special Learning Needs, p. 329 ●

Homework Suggestions
Study for **Quiz: Vocabulaire 2**
**Cahier de vocabulaire et
  grammaire,** pp. 91–93
Interactive Tutor, Ch. 8
Online Practice (**go.hrw.com,**
  Keyword: BD3 CH8)
  ✿ 1.1, 1.2, 1.3, 2.1

Block 5

OBJECTIVE
Use the conditional; Use the verb ***vaincre***

Core Instruction
Vocabulaire 2, pp. 326–329
• Review **Vocabulaire 2,** pp. 326–329. **10 min.**
• Give **Quiz: Vocabulaire 2.** **20 min.**

Grammaire 2, pp. 330–333
• See Teaching **Grammaire,** p. 330. **10 min.**
• Play Audio CD 8, Tr. 5 for Activity 27, p. 330. **5 min.**
• Have students do Activities 28–31, p. 331. **20 min.**
• See Teaching **Grammaire,** p. 332. **10 min.**
• Have students do Activities 32–34, pp. 332–333. **15 min.**

Optional Resources
• French for Spanish Speakers, p. 330
• Communication (TE), p. 331
• **Attention!,** p. 331
• Slower Pace Learners, p. 331 ◆
• Special Learning Needs, p. 331 ●
• **Attention!,** p. 332
• Communication (TE), p. 333
• Slower Pace Learners, p. 333 ◆
• Multiple Intelligences, p. 333

Homework Suggestions
Study for **Quiz: Grammaire 2**
Cahier de vocabulaire et grammaire, pp. 94–95
Cahier d'activités, pp. 75–76
Interactive Tutor, Ch. 8
Online Practice (**go.hrw.com,** Keyword: BD3 CH8)
❀ 1.1, 1.2, 1.3, 4.1

Block 6

OBJECTIVE
Use the verb ***vaincre***; *Use* ***chacun/chacune***; *Develop listening and reading skills*

Core Instruction
Grammaire 2, pp. 330–333
• Have students do Activities 35–36, p. 333. **10 min.**
• Review **Grammaire 2,** pp. 330–333. **10 min.**
• Give **Quiz: Grammaire 2.** **20 min.**

Application 2, pp. 334–335
• Have students do Activity 37, p. 334. **5 min.**
• See Teaching **Un peu plus,** p. 334. **5 min.**
• Have students do Activity 38, p. 334. **5 min.**
• Play Audio CD 8, Tr. 6 for Activity 39, p. 335. **5 min.**
• Have students do Activities 40–41, p. 335. **10 min.**

Lecture, pp. 336–339
• See **Lecture** (TE), p. 336. **20 min.**

Optional Resources
• **Attention!,** p. 334
• Communication (TE), p. 335
• Advanced Learners, p. 335 ▲
• Special Learning Needs, p. 335 ●
• AP Reading Suggestion, p. 336
• Applying the Strategies, p. 336
• Active Reading Questions, p. 337
• Using Context Clues, p. 337
• Slower Pace Learners, p. 337 ◆
• Special Learning Needs, p. 337 ●

Homework Suggestions
Study for **Quiz: Application 2**
Cahier de vocabulaire et grammaire, p. 96
Cahier d'activités, p. 77
Interactive Tutor, Ch. 8
Online Practice (**go.hrw.com,** Keyword: BD3 CH8)
❀ 1.1, 1.2, 1.3, 3.1

Block 7

OBJECTIVE
Develop listening, reading, and writing skills; Review the chapter

Core Instruction
Application 2, pp. 334–335
• Review **Application 2,** pp. 334–335. **10 min.**
• Give **Quiz: Application 2.** **20 min.**

Lecture, pp. 336–339
• See **Lecture** (TE), p. 338. **10 min.**

L'atelier de l'écrivain, pp. 340–341
• See **L'atelier de l'écrivain** (TE), p. 340. **30 min.**

Prépare-toi pour l'examen, pp. 342–345
• Have students do Activities 1–5, pp. 342–343. **10 min.**
• Play Audio CD 8, Tr. 8 for Activity 6, p. 343. **5 min.**
• Have students do Activity 7, p. 343. **5 min.**

Optional Resources
• Active Reading Questions, p. 338
• Postreading Activity, p. 338
• Connections, p. 339
• Advanced Learners, p. 339 ▲
• Special Learning Needs, p. 339 ●
• Process Writing, p. 340
• Teaching Suggestion, p. 340
• **Le subjonctif,** p. 341
• Writing Assessment, p. 341
• Slower Pace Learners, p. 341 ◆
• Special Learning Needs, p. 341 ●
• TPRS, p. 342
• Reteaching, p. 342
• Oral Assessment, p. 343
• Connections, p. 344
• Chapter Review, pp. 344–345
• Game, p. 345

Homework Suggestions
Study for Chapter Test
Cahier d'activités, p. 78
Interactive Tutor, Ch. 8
Online Practice (**go.hrw.com,** Keyword: BD3 CH8)
❀ 1.1, 1.2, 1.3, 3.1, 4.1

Block 8

OBJECTIVE
Prepare for the AP Exam; Review and assess the chapter

Core Instruction
Activités préparatoires, pp. 346–347
• Have students do the **Activités préparatoires,** pp. 346–347. **20 min.**

Chapter Test 50 min.

Révisions cumulatives, pp. 348–349
• Play Audio CD 8, Tr. 10 for Activity 1, p. 348. **5 min.**
• Have students do Activities 2–6, pp. 348–349. **15 min.**

Optional Resources
• Reading Strategy, p. 346
• Writing Strategy, p. 347
• Slower Pace Learners, p. 347 ◆
• Special Learning Needs, p. 347 ●
• Online Culture Project, p. 348
• Fine Art Connection, p. 349
• **Télé-culture:** Interviews
• **Télé-roman: Camille et compagnie**

Homework Suggestions
Cahier d'activités, pp. 79–80, 116–117
Interactive Tutor, Ch. 8
Online Practice (**go.hrw.com,** Keyword: BD3 CH8)
❀ 1.1, 1.2, 1.3, 2.2, 3.1

90-Minute Lesson Plans

Meeting the National Standards

Communication
Communication, pp. 317, 319, 321, 323, 329, 331, 333, 335
À ton tour, p. 349

Cultures
Flash culture, pp. 316, 319, 328
Comparaisons, p. 325
Practices and Perspectives, p. 315, 319, 325, 329

Connections
Government Link, p. 316
Literature Link, p. 339
History Link, p. 344

Comparisons
Comparaisons, p. 325
Comparing and Contrasting, p. 323

Communities
Communauté, p. 325
Career Path, p. 325

Using the Photo

From its founding in 1297 until 1911, the Principality of Monaco has been an absolute monarchy ruled by the House of Grimaldi. In 1911, Prince Albert I promulgated Monaco's first constitution, declaring the principality a constitutional monarchy. The constitution was reformed by Prince Rainier III on December 17, 1962. It states that the succession to the throne passes to the direct and legitimate descendants of the reigning prince. Monaco's military defense is the responsibility of France. Ask students to compare the form of government of Monaco to that of the United States. Have students discuss the history of the constitution of the United States. When was it adopted? Was it ever changed or reformed? ❀ 4.2

chapitre 8

La société

Objectifs

In this chapter, you will learn to
• express a point of view
• speculate
• ask for assistance
• relate information

And you will use and review
• contractions with **lequel**
• the past subjunctive
• adverbs
• the conditional
• the verb **vaincre**
• **chacun** and **chacune**

▶ **Que vois-tu sur la photo?**

Où se passe cette scène?

Qu'est-ce qui se passe?

As-tu déjà assité à une relève de la garde ou à un défilé militaire? Où? Quand?

Suggested pacing:	Traditional Schedule	Block Schedule
Vocabulaire/Grammaire/Application 1	5 1/2 days	2 blocks
Culture	1 day	1 block
Vocabulaire/Grammaire/Application 2	4 1/2 days	2 blocks
Lecture	1 day	1/2 block
L'atelier de l'écrivain	1 day	1/2 block
Prépare-toi pour l'examen	1/2 day	1/2 block
Activités préparatoires	1/2 day	1/2 block
Examen	1 day	1/2 block
Révisions cumulatives	1 day	1/2 block

Visit Us Online
go.hrw.com
Online Edition

KEYWORD: BD3 CH8

Vocabulaire supplémentaire

Students might use these terms to discuss the photo.

la principauté	*the principality*
la monarchie	*monarchy*
la monarchie constitution-nelle	*constitutional monarchy*
la république fédérale	*federal republic*
l'élection (f.)	*election*
la constitution	*constitution*
l'amendement (m.)	*amendment*

Learning Tips

Have students research the history of the House of Grimaldi on French-language Web sites. Ask students to compare notes and practice the new words they learn from their research.   ✿ 2.2

Language Lab

You might want to use your language lab to have students:
- listen to all target vocabulary and phrases in the chapter
- practice pronunciation of vocabulary and phrases, using Holt SoundBooth to save their work for evaluation
- complete the listening activities in this chapter

La relève de la garde des Carabiniers, à Monaco

LISTENING PRACTICE

Vocabulaire
Activity 1, p. 316, CD 8, Tr. 1
Activity 22, p. 328, CD 8, Tr. 4

Grammaire
Activity 7, p. 318, CD 8, Tr. 2
Activity 27, p. 330, CD 8, Tr. 5

Application
Activity 16, p. 322, CD 8, Tr. 3
Activity 39, p. 335, CD 8, Tr. 6

Language Lab and Classroom Activities

Prépare-toi pour l'examen
Activity 6, p. 343, CD 8, Tr. 8
Télé-culture: Interviews, Chapter 8

Activités préparatoires
Section I, Listening, p. 346, CD 8, Tr. 9
Télé-roman: *Camille et compagnie*, Épisode 8

Révisions cumulatives
Activity 1, p. 348, CD 8, Tr. 10

Lecture
p. 336, CD 8, Tr. 7

L'Europe francophone

Resources

Planning:

Lesson Planner

 One-Stop Planner

Presentation:

 Teaching Transparencies
Vocabulaire 8.1, 8.2

Practice:

Cahier de vocabulaire et grammaire

Differentiated Practice and Assessment CD-ROM

Media Guide

 Teaching Transparencies
Bell Work 8.1

Interactive Tutor, Disc 2

Bell Work

Use Bell Work 8.1 in the *Teaching Transparencies* or write this activity on the board.

Complète les phrases avec la forme correcte des verbes **éteindre, peindre** et **craindre.**

1. _____ la lumière, s'il te plaît.
2. Ma sœur et moi _____ souvent en plein air.
3. Les écologistes _____ le réchauffement de l'atmosphère.
4. En Californie, on _____ surtout les tremblements de terre.
5. Vous _____ toujours la climatisation quand vous sortez, n'est-ce pas? 🎴1.2

Proverbes

For French proverbs and activities related to the chapter theme and vocabulary, see **Proverbes et expressions,** pp. R6–R7.

Objectifs
• to express a point of view
• to speculate

Vocabulaire
à l'œuvre 1

Les élections

Les candidats qui **se présentent** aux élections participent à un **débat** télévisé.

Pendant **une campagne électorale**, il y a **des affiches** sur les murs.

un bureau de vote

un électeur

Quand il y a des élections, les électeurs **votent** pour **élire** un candidat.

les bulletins de vote

l'urne (f.)

▶ Vocabulaire supplémentaire—La politique, p. R20

Core Instruction

TEACHING VOCABULAIRE

1. Introduce the vocabulary, using transparencies **Vocabulaire 8.1** and **8.2.** Model the pronunciation of each word or expression. Tell students that **une manifestation** is a demonstration, and that those are a common form of protest in France. **(3 min.)**

2. Ask students to point to various items on the transparency. (**un électeur, un candidat**) **(3 min.)**

3. Ask students questions about recent elections. **Est-ce qu'il y a eu des élections récemment? Qui étaient les candidats? De quels partis politiques étaient-ils? (3 min.)**

4. Model the sentences in **Exprimons-nous!** Then ask students to express their opinions on different topics. **Qu'est-ce que tu penses de... ? Pour ma part/En ce qui me concerne, je crois...** You might also play devil's advocate. **La dictature est le meilleur régime politique! Je ne partage pas votre point de vue. (3 min.)**

Le gouvernement en France

Le Parlement est composé de deux chambres.
Les députés et les sénateurs font les lois.

En France, le premier ministre est le chef
du gouvernement. Il choisit les ministres qui
vont siéger dans son cabinet.

Dans une république, c'est un président qui est le chef
de l'État. Dans une monarchie, c'est un roi.

D'autres mots utiles

une démocratie	democracy
une dictature	dictatorship
un discours	speech
le droit de vote	right to vote
un(e) immigrant(e)	immigrant
une manifestation	protest
l'opposition (f.)	opposition
un parti politique	political party
un régime politique	political regime
un sondage	survey/poll
démissionner	to resign
manifester	to protest

Exprimons-nous!

To express a point of view

En ce qui me concerne, je crois qu'il a raison.
As far as I'm concerned . . .

Pour ma part, je ne pense pas qu'il ait tort.
As for me . . .

Je ne partage pas ton point de vue.
I don't share your point of view.

Interactive TUTOR

Vocabulaire et grammaire,
pp. 85–87
Online workbooks

Vocabulaire 1

TPR
TOTAL PHYSICAL RESPONSE

Have students respond to
these commands.

**Applaudis si nous vivons
dans une démocratie.**

**Lève la main si tu sais qui
est le chef de l'état.**

**Viens ici si tu as déjà voté
pour élire un candidat.**

**Lève-toi si tu ne partages
pas toujours le point de vue
de tes parents.**

**Assieds-toi si tu as entendu
dire que le Président va
démissionner.**

**Lève le doigt si tu trouves
que c'est important
d'accueillir des immigrants.**

**Lève les deux mains si tu
as déjà été dans une
manifestation.**

**Va au tableau et dessine
un bulletin de vote et
une urne.** 🌼1.2

Cultures

🌼🌼 **Practices and
Perspectives**

A national referendum in 1971
gave Swiss women the right to
vote in federal elections and to run
for parliament. More than a third
of the all-male electorate voted
against universal female suffrage,
mostly the rural and traditionally
more conservative German-speaking cantons. The cultural perception of women's role in society
being bound to children, church,
and kitchen remains popular in
the German-speaking regions.
Although Swiss women can now
vote in most regional and national
elections, they still face discrimination under Swiss law. Ask students
to research female suffrage in
Belgium or Monaco and present
their findings to the class.
🌼2.1, 3.1

Differentiated Instruction

ADVANCED LEARNERS

Extension Have students research the government of a French-speaking country. They should
investigate the form of government, the head of
state, the cabinet, elections, and political parties.
They should present their findings to the class.
Encourage them to give their opinion about the
government they have researched.   🌼1.3, 3.1

MULTIPLE INTELLIGENCES

Linguistic In the first part of **Vocabulaire 1**
students learn what **une dictature, le droit
de vote, une manifestation,** and **l'opposition**
mean, but the words have greater meaning
beyond their definition. Have students form
groups and decide on a term to research, on the
Internet or in the library. Ask students to share
their findings with the class.   🌼3.2

Resources

Planning:

Lesson Planner

 One-Stop Planner

Presentation:

 Teaching Transparencies
Vocabulaire 8.1, 8.2

Practice:

Cahier de vocabulaire et grammaire

Differentiated Practice and Assessment CD-ROM

Media Guide

🎧 Audio CD 8, Tr. 1

 Interactive Tutor, Disc 2

Connections

Government Link

In accordance with the 1962 constitution, the principality of Monaco is governed by the ruling prince, who is assisted by a minister of state. The minister presides over a four-member Council of Government (the cabinet). The National Council (parliament) is Monaco's legistlative body. Its 24 members are elected by universal suffrage every five years. The prince may initiate legislation, but all laws must be approved by the National Council. Monaco's local affairs are directed by the Communal Council, which is presided over by the mayor. Ask students to research the political relationship between Monaco and France. ✿3.1

Flash culture

l'Union européenne a pour but la libre circulation des personnes et des biens parmi les pays membres. L'harmonisation de certaines lois est devenue nécessaire car un citoyen de l'UE peut, non seulement voyager librement, mais aussi travailler et vivre dans tous les pays de l'UE. Ces changements parfois difficiles influencent l'attitude des Européens: s'ils sont en général pour l'UE, ils ont ausssi peur de perdre leur autonomie.

Quels sont les pays membres de l'UE aujourd'hui? ✿2.2

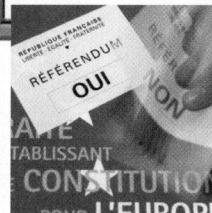

---

1 🎧 **Écoutons** CD 8, Tr. 1 ✿1.2

🎧 Écoute ces phrases et choisis la photo qui correspond à chacune d'entre elles.

6 a.   3 b.   4 c.

2 d.   5 e.   1 f.

2 **Le système politique français** ✿1.2

Lisons/Écrivons Complète le paragraphe suivant pour décrire le système politique de la France. Utilise les mots de la boîte.

un cabinet	chambres	députés	les lois
république	partis politiques	siéger	un président
le chef du gouvernement		le premier ministre	

Aujourd'hui, la France est une ___1___ avec ___2___ qui est le chef de l'état, un premier ministre qui est ___3___ et ___4___ composé des ministres qui sont choisis par ___5___. ___6___ sont faites au Parlement. Le Parlement est composé de deux ___7___. Les hommes politiques qui ___8___ au Parlement font partie de différents ___9___.

3 **Contrôle des connaissances** ✿1.3

Lisons/Parlons Réponds aux questions suivantes pour voir si tu as de bonnes connaissances en politique.

1. Comment s'appelle le chef d'État de ton pays?
2. Quel est le meilleur régime politique, selon ton opinion?
3. À ton avis, à quel âge les jeunes devraient voter?
4. Donne le nom d'un pays qui est une monarchie.
5. Donne le nom d'un pays francophone qui est une république.

---

1 Script

1. Les électeurs se rendent au bureau de vote pour voter.
2. Avant la Révolution, la France était une monarchie et Louis XVI était le roi.
3. Allez-y! Mettez votre bulletin dans l'urne, monsieur.
4. En ce qui me concerne, je pense qu'ils ont raison de manifester!
5. C'est à l'Assemblée nationale que le Parlement fait les lois.
6. Pour ma part, je pense que c'était un bon président.

Core Instruction

TEACHING EXPRIMONS-NOUS!

1. Model the pronunciation of the expressions in **Exprimons-nous!** (2 min.)

2. Ask students questions and have them answer with the expressions in **Exprimons-nous! Tu crois que le président sera ré élu? Il y a peu de chance qu'il soit ré élu!**

3. Have partners make up sentences, similar to those in **Exprimons-nous!** in which they speculate about various events. (2 min.)

Exprimons-nous!

To speculate

À ce que l'on prétend, les agriculteurs ont voté pour lui.	
Allegedly . . .	
Il est probable que le ministre a changé d'avis à cause du président.	
It is probable that . . .	
Il y a peu de chance qu'il soit élu.	*There is little chance that . . .*
J'ai entendu dire que le président ne se représentera pas aux élections.	
I heard that . . .	
À supposer que ce soit vrai, le premier ministre aurait démissionné.	
If what they say is true . . .	
Ça ne m'étonnerait pas qu'il soit malade.	
I would not be surprised if . . .	

Vocabulaire et grammaire, pp. 85–87

Online workbooks

 Parlons politique 🎕1.2

Écrivons Aurélie et son ami Simon parlent de politique, mais ils ne partagent pas les mêmes opinions. Complète leur conversation avec les expressions d'**Exprimons-nous!**

AURÉLIE ____1____ dire que Marine Thibault allait se présenter aux prochaines élections présidentielles!

SIMON À ___2___ que ___3___, il y a ___4___ qu'elle soit élue.

AURÉLIE Pourquoi? À ce que l'on ___5___, elle est très bien. C'est une vraie écolo et je crois que ce serait sympa d'avoir une femme président!

SIMON Je ne partage pas ton ___6___! Je trouve que les femmes sont trop émotives *(emotional)* pour faire de la politique.

AURÉLIE En ce qui me ___7___, je crois que tu as tort.

 **Communication**

HOLT **SoundBooth** ONLINE RECORDING

5 **Opinions personnelles** 🎕1.1

Parlons En petits groupes, choisissez trois événements de l'actualité (locale, régionale, nationale ou internationale) et discutez-en. Échangez vos opinions au sujet de chaque événement.

MODÈLE —Marie Duchamps va se présenter aux élections!
—Ça ne m'étonnerait pas que...! En ce qui me concerne...

Vocabulaire 1

2 Answers
1. république
2. un président
3. le chef du gouvernement
4. un cabinet
5. le premier ministre
6. Les lois
7. chambres
8. siègent
9. partis politiques

4 Answers
1. J'ai
2. supposer
3. ce soit vrai
4. peu de chance
5. prétend
6. point de vue
7. concerne

Communication

5 Pair Activity: Interpersonal
Have partners prepare a script for this scenario. A new citizen is preparing to vote for the first time. He or she came from a country that had a monarchy. A native-born U.S. citizen compares and contrasts democracy to the new citizen's former experience. The American explains what to do when one votes, and may discuss some current political issues and where different candidates stand on them. Partners may volunteer to present their conversation in front of the class. 🎕1.1

Differentiated Instruction

ADVANCED LEARNERS

2 Challenge After completing this activity, have students use the paragraph as a model to describe the political system in the United States. They should title their paragraph **Le système politique américain.** Have some students read their paragraph to the class. 🎕3.1, 4.2

SPECIAL LEARNING NEEDS

Students with Learning Disabilities Students might better understand **Le système politique français** if they can compare it to something they already understand, such as the U.S. system of Government. Likewise, side-by-side diagrams of both systems will probably be more useful than a written summary, as students with disabilities process information more quickly in that format than when written.

Assess

Assessment Program
Quiz: Vocabulaire 1
Alternative Assessment
Differentiated Practice and Assessment CD-ROM

Online Assessment
my.hrw.com

Test Generator

Resources

Planning:

Lesson Planner

 One-Stop Planner

Practice:

Grammar Tutor for Students of French, Chapter 8

Cahier de vocabulaire et grammaire

Differentiated Practice and Assessment CD-ROM

Cahier d'activités

Media Guide

 Teaching Transparencies Bell Work 8.2

 Audio CD 8, Tr. 2

 Interactive Tutor, Disc 2

Bell Work

Use Bell Work 8.2 in the *Teaching Transparencies* or write this activity on the board.

Choisis un terme qui correspond à chacun des termes suivants.

1. monarchie
2. république
3. parlement
4. élection
5. chef de gouvernement

a. chambre
b. roi
c. premier ministre
d. campagne électorale
e. président 🌸1.2

⑦ Script

See script on p. 311E.

⑨ Answers

1. auquel
2. duquel
3. à laquelle
4. auxquelles
5. auxquels
6. à laquelle
7. auquel
8. auxquels
9. lequel
10. auxquelles

Objectifs
- contractions with *lequel*
- the past subjunctive

Grammaire à l'œuvre 1

Interactive TUTOR

Contractions with *lequel*

1 Lequel is the relative or interrogative pronoun that refers to something already mentioned.

> J'aime sa politique. C'est la raison pour **laquelle** j'ai voté pour lui.
> Pour **lequel** de ces candidats tu vas voter?

2 You use the relative or interrogative pronoun **lequel** to take the place of **quel** plus a noun. When the noun is the object of the prepositions **à** or **de**, **lequel**, **lesquels**, and **lesquelles** contract with the preposition.

à + laquelle = à laquelle	de + laquelle = de laquelle
Contraction	*Contraction*
à + lequel = **auquel**	de + lequel = **duquel**
à + lesquels = **auxquels**	de + lesquels = **desquels**
à + lesquelles = **auxquelles**	de + lesquelles = **desquelles**

> J'ai parlé à un des candidats?—**Auquel** as-tu parlé?
> De tous ces partis politiques, **desquels** est-ce qu'ils ont fait partie?
> **Auxquelles** de ces manifestations as-tu assisté?

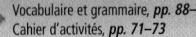 Vocabulaire et grammaire, *pp. 88–89*
Cahier d'activités, *pp. 71–73*  **Online** workbooks

⑥ La suite logique 🌸1.2

Parlons/Lisons Trouve la suite logique de chaque début de phrase.

d **1.** Les travailleurs

c **2.** J'ai reçu une réponse de plusieurs personnes.

b **3.** J'ai jetté les lettres

a **4.** Le candidat

a. auquel tu as parlé ne se présentera pas aux élections.

b. auxquelles tu as déjà répondu.

c. Desquelles?

d. auxquels le président s'est adressé ont dit qu'ils voteraient pour lui.

⑦ Écoutons CD 8, Tr. 2 🌸1.2

Choisis la photo qui correspond à chaque phrase que tu entends.

a. 1   b. 4   c. 2   d. 3

Déjà vu!

Do you remember how to use the interrogative pronoun **lequel**? When you want to avoid repeating a noun that has already been mentioned, use a form of **lequel** *(which one(s))*.

> Voici les candidats: **lequel** est-ce que tu préfères?

(**lequel** replaces **quel candidat**)

Remember that **lequel** agrees with the noun it replaces.

The other forms of **lequel** are **laquelle, lesquels,** and **lesquelles.**

Core Instruction

TEACHING GRAMMAIRE

1. Read **Déjà vu!** with students.

2. Go over the explanation in the box. Point out that the relative pronouns **lequel, laquelle, lesquels,** and **lesquelles** and their contractions refer mainly to objects. It is preferable to use **qui** when referring to people. **La dame à qui j'ai parlé.**

3. You may also choose to tell students that **duquel/de laquelle/desquels/desquelles** (and **de qui**) are often replaced with **dont** when they are not interrogative pronouns. **Le monsieur dont je parle. (6 min.)**

---

8 **Grève générale** 🏵1.2

Lisons Complète les phrases suivantes avec le bon pronom.

1. Les personnes (desquels / <u>auxquelles</u>) tu as parlé vont faire une manifestation demain.

2. Toutes les manifestations (<u>auxquelles</u> / auquel) j'ai assisté étaient pacifiques.

3. Le candidat (<u>auquel</u> / duquel) le journaliste a téléphoné n'avait rien à dire au sujet de la grève.

4. Ceux (desquels / <u>auxquels</u>) on devrait penser quand il y a une grève des médecins, c'est les malades!

5. (Duquel / <u>De laquelle</u>) de ces candidates as-tu le plus entendu parler?

9 **Aux urnes, citoyens!** 🏵1.2

Lisons Complète correctement chaque phrase avec la forme correcte de lequel.

1. Le candidat _____ je pense est le plus jeune de son parti.

2. Le parti _____ ils parlent est dans l'opposition.

3. La personne _____ il a posé cette question est une journaliste célèbre.

4. Les élections _____ elle a participé ont déjà eu lieu.

5. Les députés _____ je t'ai présenté sont certains d'être réélus.

6. Vous n'avez pas vu l'émission _____ il a participé?

7. Le débat _____ les candidats ont assisté était très intéressant.

8. Les députées _____ j'ai écrit ne m'ont pas répondu.

9. Je n'ai pas entendu le discours du président pendant _____ il a parlé de l'augmentation du chômage.

10. Les questions _____ nous avons répondu étaient difficiles!

Communication

HOLT **SoundBooth** ONLINE RECORDING

10 **Interview** 🏵1.1

Parlons Tu veux savoir si tes camarades suivent l'actualité politique. Pose-leur des questions sur les candidats et les partis politiques. Ensuite, présente les résultats de ton sondage à la classe.

MODÈLE —**Tu connais les candidats qui se présentent aux élections? Desquels as-tu le plus entendu parler?**

Online Practice
go.hrw.com
Grammaire 1 practice
KEYWORD: BD3 CH8

Flash culture

La Belgique est composée de trois communautés culturelles: les Flamands qui parlent néerlandais, les Wallons qui parlent français et à l'est, un petit groupe qui parle allemand. Les tensions entre les communautés flamande et francophone provoquent souvent des crises politiques. Pour résoudre ces conflits, le roi Albert II a changé le royaume en un état fédéral.

Est-ce que ton état a plusieurs langues officielles? Lesquelles? Est-ce que c'est une source de conflit? 🏵4.2

Grammaire 1

Cultures

🏵 **Practices and Perspectives**

Is voting a right or a responsibility? In many countries, such as Belgium, voting is considered a responsibility. In Belgium, compulsory voting was introduced for men in 1919 and for women in 1949. The Belgian government strictly enforces its voting law. The non-voter has to provide a legitimate reason for abstaining. The non-voter also faces a fine. It is even possible that after not voting in at least four elections within 15 years, the non-voter will be disenfranchised. There has been a trend of decreasing voter turnout in most established democracies since the 1960s. In the United States and Switzerland scarcely half of the eligible population votes. Ask students if they consider low voter turnout a problem. If yes, would they favor a compulsory voting law? 🏵2.1, 4.2

Communication

Class Activity: Interpersonal

Prepare enough index cards for half of the class. On each card, write a statement with a verb that requires **à, de,** or no preposition. **Ma mère a besoin d'acheter des fruits.** Below the statement, write a contraction with **lequel** that would be an appropriate response. **Desquels est-ce qu'elle a besoin?** Then have half the class form a circle, facing out and holding the cards, blank side out. The other half of the class faces the inside circle. The inside circle makes the statement and the outside circle asks for clarification, using a contraction with **lequel.** Once the response is correctly made, the outside circle rotates one to the left. 🏵1.2

Differentiated Instruction

SLOWER PACE LEARNERS

Extension Before presenting the grammar, tell students that while contractions are optional in English, they are required in French. It is therefore important to learn when and how to make contractions. Have students give examples of French contractions. 🏵4.1

SPECIAL LEARNING NEEDS

8 **9** **Students with Learning Disabilities**

In Activity 8, students might need a partner to read the sentence to them with each of the choices to determine which one best completes the sentence. In Activity 9, students will most likely do better with the aid of a word box and the directive that some words will be used more than once. 🏵1.2

Resources

Planning:

Lesson Planner

 One-Stop Planner

Practice:

Grammar Tutor for Students of French, Chapter 8

Cahier de vocabulaire et grammaire

Differentiated Practice and Assessment CD-ROM

Cahier d'activités

Media Guide

 Teaching Transparencies Bell Work 8.3

 Interactive Tutor, Disc 2

Bell Work

Use Bell Work 8.3 in the *Teaching Transparencies* or write this activity on the board.

Complète chaque phrase avec **lequel, auquel,** ou **duquel.**

1. Aux prochaines élections, il y a deux candidats. _____ préfères-tu?
2. Le candidat _____ je pense n'a aucune chance d'être élu.
3. Peut-être, mais _____ parles-tu?
4. Le débat _____ j'ai assisté était intéressant. ✿1.2

French for Spanish Speakers

Ask Spanish speakers how they would complete the following sentence in Spanish using the equivalent subjunctive form they just learned in French. **Es posible que nuestro candidato _____. (haya perdido)** Ask Spanish speakers if they know of other past-tense forms of the subjunctive in Spanish. (Spanish has two more forms of the past subjunctive, the pluperfect subjunctive and the imperfect subjunctive.) ✿4.1

Interactive TUTOR

The past subjunctive

1 Use the **past subjunctive** to refer to actions and situations that took place in the past after the same expressions and conjunctions that you have used with the present subjunctive.

✿4.1

2 To conjugate verbs in the **past subjunctive,** use the helping verb **avoir** or **être** in the subjunctive, and add the **past participle** of the main verb.

que j'	aie choisi	que je	sois rentré(e)
que tu	aies choisi	que tu	sois rentré(e)
qu'il/elle/on	ait choisi	qu'il/elle/on	soit rentré(e)
que nous	ayons choisi	que nous	soyons rentré(e)s
que vous	ayez choisi	que vous	soyez rentré(e)(s)
qu'ils/elles	aient choisi	qu'ils/elles	soient rentré(e)s

Il est possible que notre candidat **ait perdu** l'élection.
It is possible that our candidate lost the election.

Je suis contente que la reine **soit venue** voir notre nouvelle école.
I'm happy that the queen came to see our new school.

Vocabulaire et grammaire, *pp. 88–89*
Cahier d'activités, *pp. 71–73*
Online workbooks

11 Le président des États-Unis ✿1.2

Lisons Il y a des conditions essentielles pour devenir président des États-Unis. Complète les débuts de phrase logiquement.

d **1.** Il faut que le candidat soit...

a **2.** Il est impossible qu'il ait...

b **3.** Il ne faut pas qu'il soit...

c **4.** Il est essentiel qu'il ait été...

a. moins de 35 ans.

b. allé en prison.

c. élu par la majorité des grands électeurs.

d. né citoyen américain.

12 Ah, la politique...! ✿1.2

Lisons/Écrivons La famille de Luc parle des nouvelles du monde politique. Complète ces phrases avec **le passé du subjonctif** des verbes entre parenthèses.

1. Il n'est pas sûr que ces ministres _____ (partir) volontairement.
2. Je doute qu'ils _____ (être) des ennemis du président.
3. C'était un bon député, bien qu'il _____ (avoir) des idées un peu révolutionnaires.
4. Il a été premier ministre jusqu'à ce qu'il _____ (se disputer) avec le président.
5. Ils ont voté pour ce parti, bien qu'ils _____ (ne pas aimer) sa candidate.
6. Nos amis doutent que nous _____ (voter) pour ce candidat.

1. soient partis
2. aient été
3. ait eu
4. se soit disputé
5. n'aient pas aimé
6. ayons voté

Core Instruction

TEACHING GRAMMAIRE

1. Read **En anglais** with students. **(2 min.)**
2. Point out that the past subjunctive is basically a **passé composé** with the auxiliary verb in the subjunctive. Have volunteers write facts on the board in all forms of the **passé composé** using both, **avoir** and **être,** as the auxiliary verbs. **J'ai fini mes devoirs. Tu as fini..., Je suis allé(e) au cinéma. Tu es allé(e)....**

Then ask the volunteers to add **Il est possible que...** before each sentence and have them change all auxiliaries to the subjunctive. Tell students that any rules of agreement that apply to the **passé composé** will also apply to the past subjunctive. **(4 min.)**

13 Un nouveau cabinet 1.2

Écrivons Le chef du gouvernement vient de choisir de nouveaux ministres. Dans chaque phrase, mets le deuxième verbe **au passé**.

MODÈLE   Je ne pense pas que le président déteste l'ancien cabinet.
Je ne pense pas que le président ait détesté l'ancien cabinet.

1. Il est possible que les ministres arrivent à l'Hôtel Matignon cet après-midi.

2. Je suis ravi que le premier ministre choisisse Gérard de Courneuve comme ministre de la culture.

3. Il est possible qu'on vive un moment historique!

4. Je suis heureux que vous ne doutiez pas des compétences de ce nouveau gouvernement.

5. Je suis triste que tu votes pour l'opposition!

14 Beaucoup de choses à faire 1.2

Parlons/Écrivons Paul travaille pour un parti politique. Regarde les images et dis ce qu'il faudra que son parti ait fait avant la date indiquée pour se préparer pour les prochaines élections.

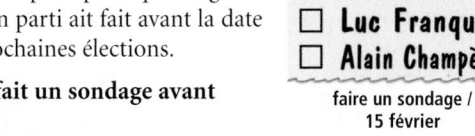

Les candidats
☐ **Henri Vasseur**
☐ **Luc Franquin**
☐ **Alain Champère**

faire un sondage /
15 février

MODÈLE   **Il faudra que son parti ait fait un sondage avant le 15 février.**

1. choisir un candidat / 15 juin

2. faire imprimer des affiches /
1er septembre

3. organiser un débat télévisé /
la fin de l'année

Communication

HOLT SoundBooth
ONLINE RECORDING

15 Scénario 1.1

Parlons Vous préparez une fête pour célébrer l'élection de «l'élève de l'année»! Avec un(e) camarade, expliquez les étapes de l'organisation de la fête et donnez les dates auxquelles elles devront être accomplies.

MODÈLE   —Qu'est-ce qu'il faudra qu'on ait fait avant lundi?
—Il faudra que nous ayons...,

---

13 Answers

1. soient arrivés
2. ait choisi
3. ait vécu
4. n'ayez pas douté
5. aies voté

14 Possible Answers

Il faudra que son parti...
1. ait choisi un candidat avant le 15 juin.
2. ait fait imprimer des affiches avant le 1er septembre.
3. ait organisé un débat télévisé avant la fin de l'année.

Communication

Pair Activity: Interpersonal
Have partners assume the roles of a pessimist and an optimist. Then have them discuss things that have happened in the past year relative to politics, school, or family. They should use the past subjunctive when necessary.

MODÈLE
— **Je suis triste que ma mère se soit remariée.**
— **Mais, es-tu heureux qu'elle ait trouvé un homme responsable?**
1.1

Differentiated Instruction

SLOWER PACE LEARNERS

Building on Previous Skills Before presenting the past subjunctive, have students review the expressions and conjunctions that require the present subjunctive. Ask students to create sentences in the present subjunctive and write these on the board. Once you have introduced the past subjunctive, have students rewrite these sentences in the past subjunctive. 1.2

SPECIAL LEARNING NEEDS

Students with Learning Disabilities Briefly review the function and formation of auxiliaries and past participles. Then write several scrambled sentences on the board that have an auxiliary and a verb in the infinitive form. Ask students to complete them, first in the **passé composé** and then in the past subjunctive. 1.2

Assess

Assessment Program
Quiz: Grammaire 1
Alternative Assessment
Differentiated Practice and Assessment CD-ROM

Online Assessment
my.hrw.com

Test Generator

Synthèse
- Vocabulaire 1
- Grammaire 1

Resources

Planning:

Lesson Planner

 One-Stop Planner

Practice:

Grammar Tutor for Students of French, Chapter 8

Cahier de vocabulaire et grammaire

Differentiated Practice and Assessment CD-ROM

Cahier d'activités

Media Guide

 Teaching Transparencies
Bell Work 8.4

 Audio CD 8, Tr. 3

Interactive Tutor, Disc 2

 **Bell Work**

Use Bell Work 8.4 in the *Teaching Transparencies* or write this activity on the board.

Mets le verbe qui est au subjonctif présent au **subjonctif passé.**

1. Je doute qu'il ait démissionné à cause de sa maladie.
2. Je suis ravie que ce candidat soit élu.
3. Je ne comprends pas que vous votiez pour l'opposition.
4. Je ne pense pas que ce dictateur reconnaisse ses ennemis. 🌐1.2

---

16 Script

See script on p. 311E.

18 Answers

1. récemment
2. mal
3. tristement
4. finalement
5. sérieusement

Application 1

16 Écoutons CD 8, Tr. 3 🌐1.2 **1.** b **2.** b **3.** a **4.** a **5.** a

Décide si on parle **a) du présent** ou **b) du passé.**

17 Des gros titres 🌐1.3

Écrivons Réagis à ces gros titres.

🔄 *Souviens-toi,* The Subjunctive pp. 190, 228, 294

MODÈLE Je doute que le président leur donne le droit de vote!

> Le président va donner le droit de vote à tous les immigrants!

> Les sénateurs proposent de changer l'âge nécessaire pour avoir le droit de vote. On pourra peut-être bientôt voter à 15 ans.
>
> 1.

> Une actrice célèbre vient de créer un nouveau parti politique.
>
> 2.

> Le président a demandé au premier ministre de démissionner.
>
> 3.

> D'après un sondage du mois dernier, 75 % des électeurs ne sont pas d'accord avec les décisions du président.
>
> 4.

> Les professeurs ne sont pas contents de leurs conditions de travail. Ils organisent une grande manifestation demain dans la capitale.
>
> 5.

> Une femme chef de l'état? Marilyne Damery commence sa campagne électorale la semaine prochaine.
>
> 6.

Un peu plus

Adverbs

1. To form most adverbs in French, take the feminine form of the adjective and add **-ment**. If an adjective ends in **-i** or **-e**, form the adverb with the masculine form.

   poli→**poli**ment   joli→**joli**ment

2. For adjectives ending in **-ent** and **-ant**, remove **-nt**, and then add **-mment**.

   récent→**réce**mment

3. Some adverbs are irregular. Here are three of the most common ones:

   mal → *badly*   bien → *well*   trop → *too*

   → Vocabulaire et grammaire, *p. 90*
   Cahier d'activités, *pp. 71–73*   **Online** workbooks

18 L'actualité politique 🌐1.2

Écrivons Complète chaque phrase avec l'adverbe qui correspond à l'adjectif entre parenthèses.

1. Les chefs d'état se sont _____ (récent) rencontrés.
2. La manifestation s'est _____ (mal) terminée.
3. Le ministre de la défense a annoncé _____ (triste) qu'il allait démissionner.
4. Les députés ont _____ (final) adopté le projet de loi.
5. Le gouvernement va _____ (sérieux) examiner sa politique d'immigration.

Core Instruction

INTEGRATED PRACTICE

1. Have students do Activity 16 to practice previously taught material. **(3 min.)**
2. Introduce **Un peu plus.** (See presentation suggestions at right.) **(4 min.)**
3. Continue with integrated practice Activities 17–20. **(30 min.)**

TEACHING UN PEU PLUS

1. Go over Point 1 of **Un peu plus.** Remind students that **actuellement** is a false cognate and that it means *presently*, not *actually*. **(2 min.)**
2. Go over Points 2–4. Remind students that adverbs never go before the verb as they do in English. Tell them that adverbs that are not too long can go between the auxiliary and past participle in compound tenses. (**passé composé, plus-que-parfait, futur antérieur,** past subjunctive) **J'ai bien mangé. (4 min.)**

19 Une campagne électorale 🌸1.3, 3.2

Lisons/Écrivons Ces candidats se présentent aux élections. Regarde leurs affiches électorales et réponds aux questions en utilisant des adverbes si possible.

Online Practice
go.hrw.com
Apppplication 1 practice
KEYWORD: BD3 CH8

1. Quelles sont les principales différences entre ces deux candidats?
2. Quels sont les points communs entre ces deux candidats?
3. Pour qui voterait un écologiste?
4. Pour qui voterait quelqu'un qui est pour l'Europe?
5. Pour qui voterait un chômeur?
6. Pour qui voterais-tu? Pourquoi?

Communication

HOLT **SoundBooth**
ONLINE RECORDING

20 Sondage 🌸1.1

Parlons Demande à tes camarades s'ils participent aux élections scolaires, s'ils regardent les émissions politiques à la télévision, etc. Présente les résultats à la classe.

MODÈLE —Est-ce que tu participes souvent aux élections de ton école?

Differentiated Instruction

ADVANCED LEARNERS

19 Extension Once students have completed this activity, ask them to create a campaign poster for the candidate for whom they would vote in an upcoming election. Students should be able to find photos of their candidate in the newspaper or on the Internet. Encourage students to create catchy slogans and layouts that clearly convey their candidate's political message. Display the posters on the classroom bulletin board. 🌸1.3, 3.1

MULTIPLE INTELLIGENCES

Interpersonal Assign students the task of running for office in a French-speaking country. Students may decide which office they wish to run for, but their task is to create a platform and present it to the class. Ask students to prepare a short speech and a poster in French to convey their qualifications and reasons for running for office. Have them present their platform and poster to the class. 🌸1.3

19 Answers

1. Bonot est plus pour l'écologie et Dupalais pense plus à l'économie.
2. une Europe unie
3. pour Bonot
4. pour les deux
5. pour Dupalais
6. Answers will vary.

Comparisons

Comparing and Constrasting

Adverbs that explain how something happens, are constructed in English by adding *–ly* to an adjective and in French by adding **-ment** to an adjective. However, a number of English *–ly* adverbs are expressed in French with a prepositional phrase plus a noun. **Je vais manger quelque chose en vitesse.** *I am going to eat something quickly.* Ask students to provide other examples of this. 🌸4.1

Communication

Class Activity: Interpersonal

Have students write a question on any topic that would elicit an adverb as the response. Then have students circulate and ask their question to other students. The answer has to be an adverb.

MODÈLE
— **Quand est-ce que les chefs d'État se sont rencontrés?**
— **Récemment.** 🌸1.1

Assess

Assessment Program
Quiz: Application 1
Audio CD 8, Tr. 11 🎧
Alternative Assessment
Differentiated Practice and Assessment CD-ROM

Online Assessment
my.hrw.com

Test Generator 🌐

Resources

Planning:
Lesson Planner
 One-Stop Planner

Practice:
Cahier d'activités

Prereading Questions

You might ask these questions before students read the selection.

1. **Sais-tu où se trouve la Suisse?**
2. **Quelle langue parle-t-on à Genève?**
3. **Connais-tu le nom d'organisations internationales?**
4. **As-tu déjà entendu parler de la Croix-Rouge?**
5. **Le drapeau de la Croix-Rouge, c'est une croix rouge sur fond blanc, et il ressemble beaucoup au drapeau suisse. Comment est le drapeau suisse?**

Active Reading Questions

1. **Qui a créé la Croix-Rouge? (Dunant et des Genevois)**
2. **Peux-tu nommer trois organisations mondiales qui sont à Genève? (ONU, OMS, OMC)**
3. **Quelles sont les ressources économiques de Genève? (l'imprimerie, l'horlogerie, la soie).**
4. **Les étrangers à Genève représentent quel pourcentage de la population? (40%)** 🕸 1.2

Vocabulaire supplémentaire

You might use these terms to discuss the text.

le traducteur	translator
l'ambassadeur (m.)	ambassador
le diplomate	diplomat
le bénévole	volunteer
le traité	treaty
la négociation	negotiation

Culture

Lecture culturelle

La ville de Genève est située au bord du lac Léman et est dominée par le Mont-Blanc. Sports nautiques, golf, tennis, équitation et polo font partie de la vie quotidienne des Genevois¹. La ville est à une heure des plus belles pistes de ski des Alpes! C'est dans ce cadre unique que de nombreuses négociations politiques internationales ont lieu. 🕸3.2

Cité de la paix et de l'intégration

En 1863, Henry Dunant et quelques Genevois créent le Comité International de la Croix-Rouge², dont l'idéal et le rôle sont toujours aussi actuels. Depuis, Genève n'a cessé de s'identifier comme Cité de la Paix et des grandes négociations internationales.

Aujourd'hui, Genève abrite³ quelques 190 organisations internationales, gouvernementales ou non dont l'Organisation des Nations unies (ONU), l'Organisation mondiale de la

santé (OMS), l'Organisation mondiale du commerce (OMC)...

Terre d'asile⁴, Genève a su accueillir, au travers des siècles, des vagues successives de réfugiés, qui ont contribué à son développement (imprimerie, horlogerie ou industrie de la soie⁵, notamment⁶). Cité internationale, comptant⁷ plus de 40% d'habitants étrangers, elle est un formidable *melting-pot,* ouvert à toutes les cultures, toutes les origines.

Compréhension 🕸1.2

1. Quelle organisation a été créée à Genève en 1863?
2. Combien d'organisations internationales y a-t-il à Genève aujourd'hui?
3. Pourquoi peut-on dire que Genève est un *melting pot*?

1. le Comité International de la Croix-Rouge
2. 190
3. Genève accueille des réfugiés du monde entier et sa population est internationale.

---

1. *inhabitants of Geneva in Switzerland* 2. *the Red Cross* 3. *il y a* 4. *place which grants asylum* 5. *silk industry* 6. *entre autres* 7. *ayant*

Core Instruction

LECTURE CULTURELLE

1. Read the introductory paragraph and discuss it with the class. **(3 min.)**
2. Read *Cité de la paix et de l'intégration* as a class. **(5 min.)**
3. Ask students to answer the questions in **Compréhension** in small groups. **(5 min.)**

COMPARAISONS ET COMMUNAUTÉ

1. Have students read *Les juges en France* and discuss it in small groups. **(8 min.)**
2. Have students answer the **Et toi?** questions with a partner. **(5 min.)**
3. Go over **Communauté et professions** with students. Discuss the use of French by local organisations in your area. **(8 min.)**

Comparaisons

Un juge français.

Les juges en France 🏵2.1

Tu discutes avec des amis français des prochaines élections en France et naturellement, tu parles des juges. À ton avis, en France

   a. les juges sont élus.

   b. les juges sont nommés par le président de la République.

   c. les juges sont désignés par le ministre de la Justice.

En France, les juges sont nommés par le président de la République après avis du Conseil supérieur de la magistrature[1]. Ils bénéficient d'un statut à part[2] qui assure l'indépendance et l'impartialité de la justice et de ce fait, ils sont inamovibles[3]. Les juges suivent tous la même formation à l'école de la magistrature de Bordeaux. C'est une école très difficile où l'on est admis sur concours après avoir fait une maîtrise de droit. Il existe des cas où les juges sont élus en France: dans les tribunaux de commerce, les juges sont des commerçants[4] élus par d'autres commerçants pour une période de 2 à 4 ans.

🏵4.2

ET TOI?

1. Comment devient-on juge aux États-Unis?

2. Est-ce que certains juges sont nommés par le président des États-Unis?

Communauté et professions

Le français et les organisations internationales 🏵5.1

Le français est l'une des langues officielles des Jeux olympiques, à l'ONU et dans de nombreuses autres organisations internationales. Est-ce que tu peux penser à des agences gouvernementales, de ta ville ou de ton état où la connaissance du français pourrait être utile? Fais des recherches sur Internet ou à la bibliothèque. Présente ce que tu as découvert à ta classe.

Le siège de L'ONU à New York

1. *Council that oversees the office or position of someone who administers the law* 2. *on its own* 3. *appointed for life* 4. *retailer*

Culture

Bulletin Board Project

Have students research places where the Red Cross has played an important role recently. Each student should bring a photo from a newspaper, magazine, or the Internet that shows a place where the Red Cross has helped. Each photo should have a caption that gives the location and describes the kind of help provided. Ask volunteers to collect all photos and display them with their captions on a classroom bulletin board. Discuss all entries as a class.

🏵3.1

Cultures

🏵 **Practices and Perspectives**

In France, there are no jury trials and only serious criminal cases are decided by a court. **La Cour d'Assises** is a court composed of three professional judges and nine jurors, who retire together to consider the verdict and the appropriate penalty. Decision is by a simple majority. Ask students to point out the differences between this system and the one in their state.

🏵2.1

Communities

Career Path

Have students name some international organizations and the cities that they associate with those organizations. You might have students do research before class. Ask students which languages could be useful in order for them to work in those organizations.

🏵5.1

Differentiated Instruction

ADVANCED LEARNERS

Challenge Why is Geneva the seat of many international organizations such as the Red Cross, the European headquarters of the United Nations, the World Health Organization, and the World Trade Organization? Why does Geneva host so many international negotiations? Working in small groups, students should address these questions and present their answers to the class in French. 🏵 1.3, 3.1

MULTIPLE INTELLIGENCES

Artistic Ask students to compare and contrast the process by which officials are elected in France and how they are elected here in the United States. Have students list in French the steps in the process for both France and the United States and then create a colorful flow chart on a piece of poster board to illustrate their findings. Display the finished products around the classroom and have students discuss their research with the rest of the class. 🏵1.3

Objectifs
- to ask for assistance
- to relate information

Vocabulaire à l'œuvre 2

Les services publics

un accident de la circulation

le camion des pompiers

l'ambulance

Les pompiers éteignent l'incendie.

un policier

Le policier dresse le constat d'accident.

▶ Vocabulaire supplémentaire—Les services publics, pp. R20–R21

Resources

Planning:

Lesson Planner

 One-Stop Planner

Presentation:

 Teaching Transparencies **Vocabulaire 8.3, 8.4**

Practice:

Cahier de vocabulaire et grammaire

Differentiated Practice and Assessment CD-ROM

Media Guide

 Teaching Transparencies Bell Work 8.5

 Interactive Tutor, Disc 2

 Bell Work

Use Bell Work 8.5 in the *Teaching Transparencies* or write this activity on the board.

Complète chaque phrase avec l'adverbe qui correspond à **l'adjectif** entre parenthèses.

1. Ce député est _____ (actuel) en vacances.
2. Les ministres des pays européens se sont _____ (final) retrouvés à Bruxelles.
3. Les manifestations se sont _____ (heureux) passées dans le calme.
4. L'opposition a _____ (récent) choisi un nouveau secrétaire. ✿1.2

Core Instruction

TEACHING VOCABULAIRE

1. Introduce the vocabulary, using transparencies **Vocabulaire 8.3** and **8.4**. Model the pronunciation of each word or expression, beginning with **Ça, c'est... (3 min.)**

2. Have students point to specific illustrations on the transparency as you describe them. (**les pompiers, un policier,** etc.) **(2 min.)**

3. Ask students a few questions to practice the vocabulary. **Qui est-ce qu'on appelle quand il y a un accident? Un feu? Un vol? Qu'est-ce qu'il faut avoir pour conduire une voiture? (3 min.)**

4. Model the pronunciation of the expressions in **Exprimons-nous!** Ask students to react as you describe situations. **Tu es tombé(e) à l'eau et tu ne sais pas nager! Le lycée brûle! Tu as eu un accident! (4 min.)**

Les papiers d'identité

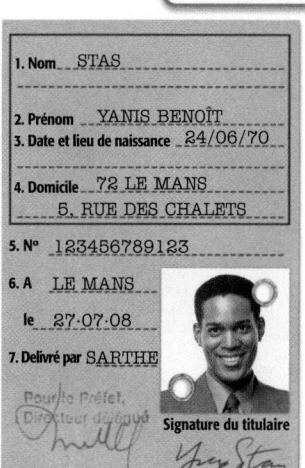

la photo d'identité

la signature

une carte d'identité

un permis de conduire

D'autres mots utiles

un(e) ambulancier (-ière)	*paramedic*
la caserne des pompiers	*fire station*
le commissariat de police	*police station*
une contravention	*fine*
un(e) fonctionnaire	*civil servant*
la police	*police*
la prison	*prison*
la sirène	*siren*
le témoin	*witness*
les urgences (f.)	*emergency*

la mairie

On a dû faire refaire nos **papiers d'identité** à la mairie.

Exprimons-nous!

To ask for assistance

Vous serait-il possible de contacter mes parents?
Would it be possible for you to contact . . . ?

À moi!/Au secours!/À l'aide!   *Help!*

Appelez la police/le 18!   *Call the police!*

Au feu!   *Fire!*

Au voleur!   *Stop thief!*

Vocabulaire et grammaire, pp. 91–93   **Online** workbooks

Online Practice
go.hrw.com
Vocabulaire 2 practice
KEYWORD: BD3 CH8

T P R
TOTAL PHYSICAL RESPONSE

Have students respond to these commands.

Lève la main si tu as apporté ta carte d'identité.

Mets la tête sur la table si tu as déjà eu un accident de la circulation.

Lève-toi si tu as ton permis de conduire.

Viens ici si tu as déjà reçu une contravention.

Lève le doigt si ton père ou ta mère est fonctionnaire.

Then have some students mime the following situations.

Tu es en prison.

Tu es pompier. Mets la sirène.

Tu es policier. Emmène John au commissariat.

Il y a le feu dans la salle de classe!   ✿ 1.2

Teacher to Teacher

Dr. Rachel Norwood
Athens Academy
Athens, GA

I like to ask students to make a list of important events that happened during the school year or calendar year. Then I have them make statements about how they feel about these events, using the past subjunctive. Then students get together and make a timeline of these events and write their statements on the timeline. For example, **10 septembre: Je suis contente que nous ayons gagné le match de foot contre l'équipe du lycée Reagan.**   ✿ 1.3

Differentiated Instruction

ADVANCED LEARNERS

Extension Have partners create a conversation in which a person in distress calls the emergency dispatcher. The caller describes the emergency and the dispatcher contacts the appropriate agency. The dispatcher tries to calm and advise the caller, while waiting for the police, ambulance, or fire truck to arrive at the scene. Ask some partners to present their conversation to the class. Encourage students to use props and appropriate intonation.   ✿ 1.1, 1.3

SPECIAL LEARNING NEEDS

Students with AD(H)D Stage a French emergency room within the classroom. First, assign the role of intake nurse to the most proficient French speaker in the class. Students will then take turns entering the emergency room, giving important information in French to the intake nurse, such as place of birth, date of birth, address, insurance, and so forth, describing the illness or injury that brought them to the hospital.   ✿ 1.1

Resources

Planning:

Lesson Planner

 One-Stop Planner

Presentation:

 Teaching Transparencies
Vocabulaire 8.3, 8.4

Practice:

Cahier de vocabulaire et
grammaire

Differentiated Practice and
Assessment CD-ROM

Media Guide

 Audio CD 8, Tr. 4

 Interactive Tutor, Disc 2

22 Script

1. Bonjour, monsieur, je suis venue chercher mon permis de conduire.
2. J'ai dû regarder des photos pour reconnaître le voleur parce que le policier croit qu'il travaillait pour mon père. Il est possible que je le connaisse.
3. Appelez tout de suite le docteur Maréchal, le blessé est arrivé et a besoin de soins urgents.
4. Ce monsieur était là et il a tout vu. Le policier lui pose des questions pour savoir laquelle des deux voitures ne s'est pas arrêtée au feu.
5. Tu entends la sirène du camion des pompiers? Ils seront là dans une minute.

24 Possible Answers

1. Je crie «Au voleur!»
2. Il doit les faire refaire à la mairie.
3. Le policier lui donne une contravention.
4. Je crie «À l'aide!»
5. Nous crions «Au feu!»
6. Je leur dis «Appelons la police!»
7. Je dis «Vous serait-il possible de contacter mes parents?»

Flash culture

La Suisse est une république fédérale. Le gouvernement fédéral s'occupe, entre autres, de la défense, des finances, de la sécurité sociale, des affaires étrangères, etc. La Suisse est divisée en **cantons**. Chaque canton a sa propre constitution, un conseil d'État et un parlement, «un Grand Conseil». Les cantons et le peuple ont beaucoup d'autonomie et de pouvoir. Les cantons sont responsables, entre autres, de la police cantonale, de la fiscalité, etc. Les Suisses font partie de l'ONU mais pas de l'Union européenne.

En quoi est-ce que la Suisse est comparable aux États-Unis? 1.2

Les nations unies à Genève

---

21 Logique ou illogique? 1.2

Lisons Dans chaque situation décrite dans la première phrase, indique si la deuxième phrase est **a) logique** ou **b) illogique.**

a 1. Cet homme est un voleur. Il va sûrement aller en prison.

a 2. Je veux conduire. J'ai besoin d'un permis de conduire.

b 3. Il y a un voleur chez Noëlle. Elle crie «Vous serait-il possible de contacter mon père?»

b 4. J'ai perdu mes papiers. Je dois aller aux urgences.

a 5. Nous devons aller chercher nos cartes d'identité. Nous allons à la mairie.

b 6. Il y a un incendie au premier étage. Appelez vite la police!

22 Écoutons CD 8, Tr. 4 1.2

Écoute chaque phrase et dis où est la personne qui parle.

4 **a.** sur la scène d'un accident 5 **d.** sur la scène d'un incendie

1 **b.** à la mairie 2 **e.** au commissariat de police

3 **c.** aux urgences **f.** en prison

23 C'est leur travail 1.2

Écrivons/Parlons Explique ce que les personnes suivantes font.

1. les fonctionnaires
2. les policiers
3. les pompiers
4. les ambulanciers
5. les témoins

24 Que faire dans ces situations? 1.2

Écrivons Explique ce que ces gens feraient dans chacune des situations suivantes. Attention! Il faut être logique.

MODÈLE Tu tombes dans une piscine et tu ne sais pas nager.
Je crierais «Au secours!»

1. Quelqu'un que tu ne connais pas part avec ton vélo.
2. Ton ami français a perdu tous ses papiers.
3. Un homme conduit très mal et il a un accident.
4. Tu es dans un ascenseur qui ne marche plus.
5. Il y a un début d'incendie dans la salle de classe.
6. Tes amis et toi, vous voyez des voleurs dans un magasin en ville.
7. Tu as eu un petit accident et les ambulanciers t'emmènent à l'hôpital. Tu n'as pas ton portable et tu ne veux pas que tes parents s'inquiètent.

Core Instruction

TEACHING EXPRIMONS-NOUS!

1. Model the pronunciation of each expression in **Exprimons-nous!**. **(2 min.)**

2. Ask students questions regarding the circumstances of a recent school election. Have students imagine that they only heard about this event and now have to report what they heard.

3. Have partners make up sentences modeled on those in **Exprimons-nous!** to talk about information they were given. **(3 min.)**

Exprimons-nous!

To relate information	
On m'a dit de ne mettre **qu'**un bulletin par enveloppe. *I was told to put only one ballot in each envelope.*	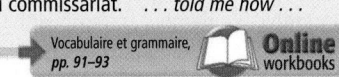 Interactive TUTOR
Il **m'a expliqué qu'**on ne pouvait pas prendre de photos ici. *... explained to me that ...*	
On m'a informé de son accident. *... informed me of ...*	
On m'a montré où était la mairie. *... showed me where ...*	
On m'a indiqué comment aller au commissariat. *... told me how ...*	

Vocabulaire et grammaire, pp. 91–93 — **Online** workbooks

25 **L'accident de mon ami** 🎞1.3

Écrivons Un de tes amis a eu un accident ce matin. Tu n'étais pas là, mais un de tes copains qui était témoin de la scène t'a raconté ce qui s'était passé. Écris cinq phrases pour décrire la scène. Utilise des expressions d'**Exprimons-nous!**

 **Communication**

HOLT **SoundBooth** ONLINE RECORDING

26 **Interview** 🎞1.1

Écrivons/Parlons Imagine que tu as été témoin d'un incendie et un(e) journaliste t'interviewe. Joue cette scène avec un(e) camarade. Ton/Ta camarade joue le rôle du (de la) journaliste. Ensuite, échangez les rôles.

MODÈLE —Où étiez-vous quand c'est arrivé?
—J'étais là-bas, près de ce café. J'ai entendu la sirène...

Cultures

🎞 **Practices and Perspectives**

Swiss neutrality and national sovereignty have allowed the banking sector to develop and prosper. As of 2003, one third of the world's private fortune resides in Swiss banks. One estimate puts the total at $2,500 billion. Banking has contributed a lot to the country's prosperity and is a pillar of its economy. As of 2006, there are 408 authorized banks and securities dealers. The country's tradition of bank secrecy, which dates back to the Middle Ages, is no longer impenetrable. Today, the Swiss government has the power to freeze stolen assets and to return these to the rightful owners. Ask students to research bank secrecy in the United States. 🎞 2.1, 4.2

Communication

Pair Activity: Interpersonal
Have partners select a scenario, such as an automobile accident, a theft, or a physical injury. Then have the partners role-play a scene that involves the incident and obtaining help. Ask students to present their role-play for the class. 🎞 1.1

Differentiated Instruction

SLOWER PACED LEARNERS

Have students imagine that they missed French class last week and that later a schoolmate explained to them what they had missed. Working with a partner, students should tell each other what the schoolmate told them. Encourage students to use expressions from **Exprimons-nous!** 🎞 1.1, 1.2

SPECIAL LEARNING NEEDS

25 **Students with Learning Disabilities**
At times students with learning disabilities have difficulty generating ideas for writing assignments and may need assistance with this activity. Prior to beginning the activity, allow students with learning disabilities to discuss in French with a classmate what they see in the picture. This will give students with learning disabilities the opportunity to work through their ideas before putting them on paper. 🎞 1.2

Assess

Assessment Program
Quiz: Vocabulaire 2
Alternative Assessment
Differentiated Practice and Assessment CD-ROM
Online Assessment
my.hrw.com
Test Generator

Objectifs
• review of the conditional
• the verb *vaincre*

Grammaire à l'œuvre 2

Révisions — The conditional

1 To form the **conditional**, take the **future stem** of the verb and add the appropriate imperfect ending. For most verbs, the future stem is the infinitive. Remember to remove the **-e** from **-re** verbs.

Future Stem	Conditional
parler	je parler**ais**
finir	tu finir**ais**
entendr-	il/elle entendr**ait**

Si tu te présentais aux élections, je **voterais** pour toi.
If you ran for office, I would vote for you.

2 Some verbs that have a spelling change in the **present** tense keep the spelling change in the **future/conditional** stem.

Infinitive	Present	Conditional
acheter	j'ach**è**te	j'ach**è**terais
appeler	j'appe**ll**e	j'appe**ll**erais

Il **appellerait** la police s'il y avait un accident.
He would call the police if there were an accident.

3 Some verbs have an irregular stem in the **future** and the **conditional**. In the list below, you will see the stems for the most common ones.

aller → **ir-**	être → **ser-**	savoir → **saur-**
avoir → **aur-**	faire → **fer-**	venir → **viendr-**
devenir → **deviendr-**	pouvoir → **pourr-**	voir → **verr-**
devoir → **devr-**	recevoir → **recevr-**	vouloir → **voudr-**

Vocabulaire et grammaire, *pp. 94–95*
Cahier d'activités, *pp. 75–77*
Online workbooks

27 **Écoutons** CD 8, Tr. 5 1.2 **1.** a **2.** b **3.** a **4.** a **5.** b

Françoise et Étienne discutent dans la rue après les cours. Pour chacune de leurs phrases, dis a) **s'il y a une condition pour que cela arrive** ou b) **s'il n'y a pas de condition.**

Resources

Planning:

Lesson Planner

 One-Stop Planner

Practice:

Grammar Tutor for Students of French, Chapter 8

Cahier de vocabulaire et grammaire

Differentiated Practice and Assessment CD-ROM

Cahier d'activités

Media Guide

 Teaching Transparencies
Bell Work 8.6

Audio CD 8, Tr. 5

Interactive Tutor, Disc 2

 ## Bell Work

Use Bell Work 8.6 in the *Teaching Transparencies* or write this activity on the board.

Que fais-tu dans les situations suivantes?

1. Tu ne sais pas nager et tu tombes dans l'eau.

2. Dans la rue, quelqu'un te prend ton portable.

3. Tu vois quelqu'un voler une voiture et partir avec.

4. Tu as un accident et on t'emmène en ambulance.

1.2

French for Spanish Speakers

Ask Spanish speakers if any of the stems for the conditional look almost exactly like the infinitives for Spanish verbs. (**ir-/ir**, **ser-/ser**, and **verr-/ver**). Ask students why. (common Latin/Romance roots) 4.1

Core Instruction

TEACHING GRAMMAIRE

1. Read **Déjà vu!** aloud with students. **(2 min.)**

2. Go over Point 1. Point out that the future stem of regular verbs is their infinitive, minus a final mute **e** when there is one. Tell students that the only difference between the future and conditional forms is that the future has the endings of the present of **avoir**, whereas the conditional has the **imparfait** endings of **avoir**. **(2 min.)**

3. Go over Point 2. Remind students that all of these forms would be very difficult to pronounce without the spelling changes. **(2 min.)**

4. Go over Point 3. **(2 min.)**

Déjà vu!

Do you remember how to conjugate verbs in the imperfect? To form the imperfect stem, take the **nous** form of the verb, without **-ons**.

travaillons	→ travaill-
choisissons	→ choisiss-
perdons	→ perd-
croyons	→ croy-
avons	→ av-
faisons	→ fais-

Then add the endings **-ais, -ais, -ait, -ions, -iez, -aient**.

Je **promenais** le chien, quand j'ai vu le voleur.

Être is irregular in the imperfect. The stem is **ét-**.
J'**étais** devant la mairie.

Online Practice
go.hrw.com
Grammaire 2 practice
KEYWORD: BD3 CH8

Chapitre 8
Grammaire 2

Grammaire 2

28 Si ça arrivait 1.2

Écrivons/Parlons Qu'est-ce qui se passe dans les situations suivantes?

1. S'il y avait un incendie, les pompiers _____ .
2. J'appellerais la police si je _____ un voleur.
3. Si tu perdais tes papiers, il _____ les faire refaire.
4. S'il pouvait, il _____ fonctionnaire.
5. Si c'était un accident grave, on _____ les sirènes.

Entre copains

une contredanse/ une prune	fine
un flic/un poulet	policeman
être en tôle	to be in jail
un rond-de-cuir	civil servant

29 Si j'avais une sœur... 1.2

Écrivons Reconstruis ces phrases en utilisant **le conditionnel**.

1. je / une sœur / si / avoir / parler / nous / nous / tous les jours
2. au / ensemble / aller / nous / centre commercial
3. en / emmener / parents / à la mer / nos / nous / vacances
4. un cadeau / lui / je / acheter / son / pour / anniversaire
5. voir / partout / nous / on / ensemble

30 On peut rêver, non? 1.2

Parlons Ces gens parlent de ce qu'ils feraient s'ils étaient riches. Regarde les illustrations et imagine ce qu'ils disent.

MODÈLE Tu donnerais de l'argent à la Croix Rouge.

tu

1. je

2. mes parents

3. nous

4. ma sœur

27 Script
See script on p. 311F.

28 Answers
1. viendraient
2. voyais
3. faudrait
4. serait
5. entendrait

29 Answers
1. Si j'avais une sœur, nous nous parlerions tous les jours.
2. Nous irions au centre commercial ensemble.
3. Nos parents nous emmèneraient en vacances à la mer.
4. Je lui achèterais un cadeau pour son anniversaire.
5. On nous verrait partout ensemble.

30 Possible Answers
1. J'achèterais une voiture de sport.
2. Mes parents feraient le tour du monde à voile.
3. Nous habiterions à la campagne.
4. Ma sœur voyagerait en Europe.

Communication

31 Scénario 1.1

Parlons Demande à un(e) camarade tout ce qu'il/elle ferait s'il/si elle était un jour élu(e) président(e) des États-Unis. Puis dis-lui tout ce que tu ferais si tu étais élu(e).

MODÈLE —Qu'est-ce que tu ferais si tu devenais président(e)?

HOLT **SoundBooth**
ONLINE RECORDING

Communication

Group Activity: Interpersonal
Form small groups. Each student writes a sentence that includes a **si** clause with the **imparfait** and the **conditionnel**. Students take turns reading their **si** clause. The other group members each respond with a **si** clause of their own that either expands the possibility of the original statement or points out possible negative consequences of the hypothetical situation. 1.1

COMMON ERROR ALERT
///// **ATTENTION !** \\\\\

If students are not careful, they may confuse the **conditionnel** with the **futur,** since they use the same stems or the **conditionnel** with the **imparfait,** since they use the same endings.

Differentiated Instruction

SLOWER PACE LEARNERS

Additional Practice Before introducing the forms of the conditional, tell students that the conditional tense indicates that an action is dependent on something else. Ask students to give examples of the present conditional in English. Then introduce the form of the conditional and ask students to give the French equivalents of the English examples they have just provided. 1.2, 4.1

SPECIAL LEARNING NEEDS

Students with Language Impairments
When reviewing **Déjà vu!,** make sure that students with language challenges have understood the concept of forming a particular tense with the verb stem and its appropriate endings. Have students create several examples before you present the conditional. 1.2

Resources

Planning:

Lesson Planner

 One-Stop Planner

Practice:

Grammar Tutor for Students of French, Chapter 8

Cahier de vocabulaire et grammaire

Differentiated Practice and Assessment CD-ROM

Cahier d'activités

Media Guide

 Teaching Transparencies Bell Work 8.7

 Interactive Tutor, Disc 2

Bell Work

Use Bell Work 8.7 in the *Teaching Transparencies* or write this activity on the board.

Reconstruis les phrases suivantes en utilisant le conditionnel. Fais tous les changements nécessaires.

1. être / je / riche / si / voyager / je
2. piscine / si / aller / à / la / souvent / nous / nager / nous / bien / savoir
3. pouvoir / vous / si / acheter / vous / voiture / nouvelle / une
4. voleurs / des / si / entrer / appeler / police / Julie / la

🌸1.2

COMMON ERROR ALERT
⚡ ATTENTION ! ⚡

Students may not trust that the singular forms of **vaincre** are perfectly regular. The **il/elle** form, **vainc**, may seem incomplete, and the **s** ending on **vaincs** may look unusual to them.

The verb *vaincre*

Interactive TUTOR

1 The verb **vaincre** *(to vanquish* or *to conquer)* is irregular. Notice that the **c** in the infinitive changes to **qu** in the plural forms.

vaincre	
je **vaincs**	nous **vainquons**
tu **vaincs**	vous **vainquez**
il/elle/on **vainc**	ils/elles **vainquent**

Past participle: vain**c**u

2 The verb **convaincre** *(to convince)* follows the same pattern.

Le président **convainc** les sénateurs d'adopter son plan.
Il a **convaincu** le candidat de l'opposition.

être convaincu(e) (de/que) means *to be convinced of.*
Je ne **suis** pas **convaincu(e)** qu'il ait raison.
I'm not convinced that he is right.

Vocabulaire et grammaire, *pp. 94–95*
Cahier d'activités, *pp. 75–77*

Online workbooks

À la belge

In Belgium, the cities are divided into **communes** and the city hall is called **une maison communale.**

People get married at **la maison communale** instead of **la mairie,** as in France.

32 **Vaincre et convaincre** 1.2

Parlons/Écrivons Complète les phrases suivantes avec la forme correcte du verbe entre parenthèses.

1. Les pompiers sont arrivés et ils (vainquent / ont vaincu) l'incendie.
2. Ou vous (vainquez / vainc) l'ennemi, ou c'est lui qui vous (vainc / vainquez).
3. Mon père (a convaincu / convaincs) les policiers de faire un constat d'accident.
4. Le chauffeur (n'a pas convaincu / n'est pas convaincu) la police qu'il venait de la droite.
5. Et toi, tu ne (convainc / convaincs) personne quand tu dis que tu as 18 ans.

33 **Convaincre ou être convaincu?** 🌸1.2

Écrivons Complète les phrases suivantes logiquement avec la forme correcte des verbes vaincre ou convaincre.

1. est convaincu
2. suis convaincu(e)
3. convainquent
4. convainc
5. a convaincus
6. convainquent

1. Le président _____ que son parti est le plus fort.
2. Je _____ d'avoir raison!
3. Ils _____ toujours leurs adversaires.
4. Son excuse ne me _____ pas!
5. C'était difficile, mais il les _____!

Core Instruction

TEACHING GRAMMAIRE

1. Go over the conjugation of **vaincre**. Model the pronunciation of all forms. **(2 min.)**
2. Point out to students that the **c** is mute in all three singular forms of **vaincre** and **convaincre**. **(2 min.)**

3. Ask students what they and people they know are convinced of. **Peter, tu es convaincu de quoi? Je suis convaincu que mes parents vont m'acheter une voiture.** **(5 min.)**

34 **Voilà qui est bien dit!** 🌸1.2

Lisons/Écrivons Complète ces citations avec les verbes entre parenthèses.

1. «Je suis venu, j'ai vu, je/j'___1___ (vaincre).» – JULES CÉSAR

2. «On ne souffre (*suffer*) qu'une fois. On ___2___ (vaincre) pour l'éternité.» – SØREN KIERKEGAARD

3. «Si tu ___3___ (vaincre) un ennemi, il sera toujours ton ennemi. Si tu ___4___ (convaincre) un ennemi, il deviendra ton ami.» – MORIHEI UESHIBA

4. «On ne ___5___ (convaincre) pas les masses avec des raisonnements, mais avec des mots.» – BERNARD GRASSET

5. «Pour avoir du talent, il faut être ___6___ (convaincre) qu'on en possède.» – GUSTAVE FLAUBERT

6. «À ___7___ (vaincre) sans péril, on triomphe sans gloire (*suffer*).» – CORNEILLE

1. ai vaincu
2. vainc
3. vaincs
4. convaincs
5. convainc
6. convaincu
7. vaincre

35 **Victoires** 🌸1.3

Parlons/Écrivons Décris ce qui se passe dans chacune des images suivantes. Utilise **vaincre** et **convaincre**.

elle

MODÈLE **Elle vainc son stress.**

1. ils

2. elle

FRANCE 03
BELGIQUE 0
3. l'équipe de France

4. il

Communication

HOLT SoundBooth
ONLINE RECORDING

36 **Interview** 🌸1.1

Parlons Demande à un/une camarade s'il/si elle convainc souvent des gens de faire quelque chose. Il/Elle te dira de quoi il/elle les a convaincus récemment, puis échangez les rôles.

MODÈLE —Est-ce que tu convaincs souvent ton...
—Oui, récemment, je l'ai convaincu...

Differentiated Instruction

SLOWER PACE LEARNERS

Additional Practice Have students conjugate **convaincre** in the **imparfait**, the **futur**, the subjunctive, and the **conditionnel**. Encourage students to write these conjugations in their notebook and to refer to them while completing the activities in **Grammaire 2**. 🌸1.2

MULTIPLE INTELLIGENCES

35 **Linguistic** Have students freewrite about one of the five pictures in French. Students may choose to write a story, a magazine article, a news report, or even a poem. Students should write without any restrictions or limitations. 🌸1.3

---

35 **Possible Answers**

1. Ils ont vaincu le dragon.
2. Elle convainc son fils de se jeter à l'eau.
3. L'équipe de la France a vaincu la Belgique.
4. Il la convainc de l'aimer.

Communication

Individual Activity: Presentational
Have students research a battle, war, or other event in French or Francophone history. Then have them prepare a two-minute PowerPoint® presentation in French that includes the verbs **vaincre** or **convaincre**. Ask the class to take notes. Each presenter should create a a listening comprehension quiz for the class. 🌸1.3

Assess

Assessment Program
Quiz: Grammaire 2
Alternative Assessment
Differentiated Practice and Assessment CD-ROM

Online Assessment
my.hrw.com

Test Generator

Resources

Planning:

Lesson Planner

 One-Stop Planner

Practice:

Grammar Tutor for Students of French, Chapter 8

Cahier de vocabulaire et grammaire

Differentiated Practice and Assessment CD-ROM

Cahier d'activités

Media Guide

 Teaching Transparencies Bell Work 8.8

 Audio CD 8, Tr. 6

Interactive Tutor, Disc 2

 **Bell Work**

Use Bell Work 8.8 in the *Teaching Transparencies* or write this activity on the board.

Complète les phrases suivantes avec la forme correcte des verbes **vaincre** ou **convaincre**.

1. Il faut savoir _____ sa peur.
2. Le président ne _____ personne quand il dit que tout va bien.
3. Nous sommes _____ que ce candidat ne sera pas élu.
4. Ses excuses ne nous _____ pas. ✿1.2

COMMON ERROR ALERT
/// ATTENTION !

Since students know the word **chaque**, they may misspell **chacun** as **chaqu'un**, assuming that it is similar to **quelque**, which becomes **quelqu'un**.

---

39 Script

See script on p. 311F.

Application 2

37 Pouvoirs magiques 1.2

Écrivons Marie-France et ses amis imaginent comment leur vie changerait s'ils trouvaient une baguette magique. Forme des phrases complètes.

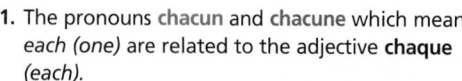

Tu	vaincre	millionnaire(s)
Je	voir	parler français, arabe, russe et chinois
Alice	avoir	tous les problèmes du monde
Vous	faire	une superbe maison
Mes parents	savoir	le futur
Nous	convaincre	des miracles
Didier	être	le prof me donner une bonne note

Un peu plus

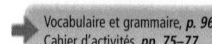 TUTOR

chacun/chacune

1. The pronouns **chacun** and **chacune** which mean *each (one)* are related to the adjective **chaque** *(each)*.

   > **Chacun** de nous avait peur du voleur.
   > *Each (one) of us was afraid of the thief.*

2. **Chacun/chacune** is a singular pronoun, so remember to use the **il/elle** form of the verb. Notice that you use **chacune** when the group includes only females.

   > **Chacune** des étudiantes **devait** aller à la mairie pour obtenir une nouvelle carte d'identité.
   > *Each (one) of the students had to go to the town hall to get a new ID card.*

→ Vocabulaire et grammaire, *p. 96*
Cahier d'activités, *pp. 75–77* **Online** workbooks

1. chacun 2. chacun 3. chacune
4. Chacune 5. Chacun 6. chacune
7. chacune

38 Vos papiers, s'il vous plaît! ✿1.2

Écrivons La police fait un contrôle de routine. Complète chacune des phrases suivantes avec **chacun** ou **chacune**.

1. «Dans la vie, _____ ne fait pas ce qu'il veut, monsieur!»
2. Les policiers ont demandé les permis de conduire de tout le monde et _____ d'eux a été vérifié.
3. Ils ont aussi demandé les cartes d'identité et _____ d'elles a été examinée très atttentivement.
4. _____ des photos a été comparée à la tête du propriétaire des papiers.
5. «_____ de vous, messieurs, doit avoir ses papiers en ordre.», ont-ils dit.
6. Finalement, ils ont donné une contravention à _____ des personnes présentes.
7. Et _____ d'elles est retournée à la maison de mauvaise humeur!

Core Instruction

INTEGRATED PRACTICE

1. Have students do Activity 37 to practice previously taught expressions. **(4 min.)**
2. Go over **Un peu plus.** (See presentation suggestions at right.) **(4 min.)**
3. Continue with integrated practice Activities 38–41. **(20 min.)**

TEACHING UN PEU PLUS

1. Read the explanation with the students. **(2 min.)**
2. Point out that **chacun** and **chacune** are combinations of **chaque** (*each*) and **un/une** (*one*). You might also tell students that the masculine form **chacun** can be used without **de** in the sense of *each man/person*. **Chacun sait qu'il faut travailler pour réussir.** **(2 min.)**

Online Practice
go.hrw.com
Application 2 practice
KEYWORD: BD3 CH8

39 Écoutons CD 8, Tr. 6 🍀1.2

Écoute les phrases suivantes et dis ce que **chacun** ou **chacune** remplace dans chaque situation.

1. (a) les cartes d'identité   b) les électeurs
2. (a) les candidats   b) les idées
3. (a) les bureaux de vote   b) les votes
4. a) les idées   (b) les affiches
5. a) les campagnes électorales   (b) les candidates

40 Et toi? 🍀1.3

Écrivons/Parlons Réponds aux questions suivantes en faisant des phrases complètes.

1. Est-ce que tu es convaincu(e) que les hommes politiques disent toujours la vérité? Pourquoi?
2. Qu'est-ce que tu ferais ou dirais pour convaincre les autres élèves de voter pour toi aux élections de l'école?
3. Qu'est-ce que tu changerais si tu étais élu(e)?
4. Est-ce que tu aimerais faire de la politique plus tard? Pourquoi ou pourquoi pas?
5. Qu'est-ce qui te convainc de voter pour un candidat?.

Communication

HOLT **SoundBooth** ONLINE RECORDING

41 Histoire à raconter 🍀1.3

Parlons Corinne a vécu une vraie aventure aujourd'hui! Avec un(e) camarade, raconte ce qui s'est passé.

Communication

Group Activity: Interpersonal

Form groups of four and assign each group the same discussion topic. Phrase the topic in a conditional sentence that contains a **si** clause. When each group has discussed this topic, ask one student from each group to move to another group and present the results of the discussion. At the end of the presentation in the new group each student states his or her assessment of the topic beginning with, **je suis convaincu(e) de** or **je ne suis pas convaincu(e) de.** 🍀1.1

PRE-AP ACTIVITÉ PRÉPARATOIRE Language Examination

To display the drawings to the class, use the Picture Sequences Transparency for Chapter 8.

41 Sample answer

a. **Un voleur était en train de cambrioler la maison de Corrine quand le chien l'a mordu. Corrine a appelé la police.**

b. **Pendant que l'ambulancier soignait la jambe du voleur, la police est arrivée.**

c. **Les policiers ont emmené le voleur en prison.**

Differentiated Instruction

ADVANCED LEARNERS

37 Personalization Have students imagine that they only need to wave a magic wand to make their wishes come true. What would they wish for themselves, their family, friends, and enemies? Would they be happy if all their wishes were to come true? Why or why not? Have students write an essay in which they address these questions. 🍀1.3

SPECIAL LEARNING NEEDS

Students with Visual Impairments Some students with visual impairments will need assignments enlarged by 150% to 200%. When enlarging activities for a visually impaired student, first make a copy of the page, then cut the activities apart and enlarge each by 150% to 200%. It is best if you have color printouts. Once activities are enlarged, remember to present them in the appropriate order to simulate the page of the book. 🍀1.1

Assess

Assessment Program
Quiz: Application 2
Audio CD 8, Tr. 12 🎧
Alternative Assessment
Differentiated Practice and Assessment CD-ROM

Online Assessment
my.hrw.com

Test Generator 💿

Resources

Planning:

Lesson Planner

 One-Stop Planner

Presentation:

 Audio CD 8, Tr. 7

Practice:

Cahier d'activités

Reading Strategies and Skills
Handbook, Chapter 8

Advanced Reader

AP Reading Suggestion

In order to get accurate notes, ask students to read slowly and, if necessary, to reread sentences that seem more complex and important.

Applying the Strategies

For practice with monitoring comprehension, have students use the "Most Important Word" strategy from the *Reading Strategies and Skills Handbook.*

READING PRACTICE

Strategy: Most Important Word

Reading Skill	When can I use this strategy?		
	Prereading	During Reading	Postreading
Identifying the Main Idea			✓
Making Generalizations			✓
Summarizing			✓

Strategy at a Glance: Most Important Word

- After reading a text, students discuss their responses to the theme of the work.
- Students decide either independently or in small groups what they think the Most Important Word in the text is, basing their answers on evidence from the reading.
- Students share and explain their choices.

Many times when you ask students to find the main idea of a story, or to make a generalization, or simply, "What did the story mean to you?", they can't do it, because they find the question too broad. One strategy that students can use to help them answer the question is Most Important Word. Most Important Word is a postreading strategy in which students decide which word in a text they think is the most important based on specific evidence in the text. As students decide which word is the most important, they begin to formulate their responses to the question: "What did the story mean to you?" **Most Important Word** leads to revealing discussions that encourage students to use this skill while they read and later reflect on what they have read.

Best Use of the Strategy

Most Important Word (Beich 1975) is a good strategy to help students identify the theme of a reading and to make generalizations about it by breaking down the selection and deciding which word in the text carries the message that speaks to them.

Lecture

Charles de Secondat, baron de la Brède et de Montesquieu, (1689–1755), écrivain et philosophe français, s'intéresse à l'histoire et à la politique. En 1721, il publie *Lettres persanes,* une satire de l'Europe vue par deux voyageurs persans[1]. Entre 1728 et 1731, il voyage en Angleterre et en Europe pour étudier l'organisation politique des nations. En 1748, après plusieurs années de travail, Montesquieu publie *De l'esprit des lois.* Les idées sur la liberté et la séparation des pouvoirs au sein[2] d'un gouvernement trouvées dans l'œuvre influenceront les Américains lors de[3] la fondation des États-Unis en 1776.

 A **Avant la lecture** 1.3, 3.1

Dans le texte suivant, Montesquieu parle de la démocratie, de la monarchie et du despotisme. Comment est-ce que tu définirais chaque forme de gouvernement? Lis le texte une première fois, puis relis-le en prenant des notes.

> **STRATÉGIE pour lire**
>
> **Taking notes** as you read will help you monitor your comprehension and determine the main ideas of a text. Your notes should include words and statements that seem important to you. Key words and statements not only tell you what the text is about, they can also contain the main ideas of a reading. You can use your notes later to summarize information or draw conclusions about the text.

CD 8, Tr. 7

De l'esprit des lois

Du principe de la démocratie

Il ne faut pas beaucoup de probité[4] pour qu'un gouvernement monarchique ou un gouvernement despotique se maintienne ou se soutienne[5]. La force des lois dans l'un, le bras du prince toujours levé dans l'autre, règlent ou contiennent tout[6]. Mais, dans un État populaire, il faut un ressort[7] de plus, qui est la VERTU.

Ce que je dis est confirmé par le corps entier de l'histoire, et est très conforme à la nature des choses. Car[8] il est clair que dans une monarchie, où celui qui

La Déclaration universelle des droits de l'homme

---

1. iraniens. **2.** dans **3.** pendant **4.** intégrité **5.** *sustains it self* **6.** *rules and keeps everything* **7.** *level* **8.** Parce que

---

Core Instruction

LECTURE

1. Read **Stratégie pour lire** aloud for students. What would they write down while reading Montesquieu's biography? **(2 min.)**

2. Discuss **Avant la lecture** as a class. Take notes on the board while students define democracy, monarchy, and despotism. Compare these notes to definitions taken from an all-French dictionary. **(8 min.)**

3. Have volunteers read **Du principe de la démocratie** aloud, to the end of page 337. Monitor pronunciation and comprehension **(15 min.)**

---

fait exécuter les lois se juge au-dessus des lois, on a besoin de moins de vertu que dans un gouvernement populaire, où celui qui fait exécuter les lois sent qu'il y est soumis[1] lui-même, et qu'il en portera le poids.

Il est clair encore que le monarque qui, par mauvais conseil ou par négligence, cesse[2] de faire exécuter les lois, peut aisément réparer le mal : il n'a qu'à[3] changer de Conseil, ou se corriger de cette négligence même. Mais lorsque, dans un gouvernement populaire, les lois ont cessé d'être exécutées, comme cela ne peut venir que de la corruption de la république, l'État est déjà perdu. [...]

Les politiques grecs, qui vivaient dans le gouvernement populaire, ne reconnaissaient d'autre force qui pût[4] les soutenir que celle de la vertu. Ceux d'aujourd'hui ne nous parlent que de manufactures, de commerce, de finances, de richesses, et de luxe même.

Lorsque cette vertu cesse, l'ambition entre dans les cœurs qui peuvent la recevoir, et l'avarice[5] entre dans tous. Les désirs changent d'objets : ce qu'on aimait, on ne l'aime plus ; on était libre avec les lois, on veut être libre contre elles ; chaque citoyen est comme un esclave échappé de la maison de son maître ; ce qui était *maxime*, on l'appelle *rigueur* ; ce qui était *règle*, on l'appelle *gêne* ; ce qui était *attention*, on l'appelle *crainte*. C'est la frugalité qui y est l'avarice, et non pas le désir d'avoir. Autrefois le bien des particuliers faisait le trésor public ; mais pour lors le trésor public devient le patrimoine des particuliers. La république est une dépouille[6] ; et sa force n'est plus que le pouvoir de quelques citoyens et la licence de tous.

De l'esprit des lois (livre III, chapitre III)

Marianne, symbole de la République française

La *Liberté éclairant le monde,* plus connue sous le nom de statue de la Liberté, a été offerte aux États-Unis par la France pour célébrer les 100 ans de leur indépendance.

---

1. *subjected* 2. *arrête* 3. *he only has to*
4. *qui pouvait* 5. *greed* 6. *skin*

Active Reading Questions

1. **Quel sont les trois formes de gouvernement dont Montesquieu parle? (monarchie, démocratie, despotisme)**
2. **De quoi est-ce que l'état populaire a besoin? (de vertu)**
3. **Qui exécute les lois dans une monarchie? Dans une démocratie? (le roi; les gens qui les ont faites)**
4. **Qu'est-ce qui se passe si les lois cessent d'être exécutées dans une monarchie? Dans une démocratie? (On change de Conseil; l'État est perdu.)**
5. **Si la vertu cesse dans une république, qu'est-ce qui se passe? (Les gens deviennent trop ambitieux.)**

Using Context Clues

Tell students that they can use context clues and the composition of words to figure out their meaning in the text. Have students note words that they don't know as they read. Then have them go back and reread the sentence in which these words are found. Tell them to first use context to determine what part of speech the word is and determine its general meaning. Next, tell them to look at the root and ending of the word to see if they can guess the word's exact meaning. 1.2

 **Language Examination**

Lecture helps students prepare for Section 1, Part B: **Reading Comprehension.** The audio recording helps them prepare for Part A: **Listening—Short Narratives.**

Differentiated Instruction

SLOWER PACE LEARNERS

Additional Practice Some students may miss or not comprehend statements that are crucial to understanding the main ideas of Montesquieu's treatise. Draw a graphic organizer on the board with columns headed **démocratie, monarchie,** and **gouvernement despotique.** The horizontal rows should be titled **base, forces,** and **faiblesses.** Fill in the table as a class. Allow students to refer to the table while rereading the text and completing the activities. 1.2, 3.1

SPECIAL LEARNING NEEDS

Students with Learning Disabilities Break the note-taking process into two steps. First, as students prepare to take notes, provide them a copy of the reading selection and have them highlight important words or passages rather than try to write the notes. Then, as the second step, ask them to write notes by reviewing the highlighted material. 1.2

Active Reading Questions

1. **Quel est le principe le plus important dans une monarchie? (l'honneur)**
2. **Quelle est l'opinion de Montesquieu sur l'honneur dans une monarchie? (Il est faux, mais utile au public.)**
3. **Quel est le principe important dans un gouvernement despotique? (la crainte)**
4. **Quel principe serait dangereux dans un gouvernement despotique? (l'honneur)**
5. **À part le prince, qui a le pouvoir dans un gouvernement despotique? (les gens à qui il le confie)**
6. **Qu'est-ce qui se passerait sans la crainte dans un gouvernement despotique? (des révolutions)**
7. **Comment est-ce qu'un gouvernement modéré se maintient? (avec des lois et par sa force même)**
8. **Qui souffre si la crainte n'existe plus dans un gouvernement despotique? (le peuple)**

Postreading Activity

Ask students what Montesquieu thought of each type of government. Which form did he believe to be the best? The worst? Or, did each type of government have both positive and negative characteristics? Then ask students if they believe Montesquieu's ideas are relevant today, and why or why not.

Du principe de la monarchie

Le gouvernement monarchique suppose, comme nous avons dit, des prééminences, des rangs[1], et même une noblesse d'origine. La nature de l'HONNEUR est de demander des préférences et des distinctions ; il est donc, par la chose même, placé dans ce gouvernement.

L'ambition est pernicieuse[2] dans une république. Elle a de bons effets dans la monarchie ; elle donne la vie à ce gouvernement ; et on y a cet avantage, qu'elle n'y est pas dangereuse, parce qu'elle y peut être sans cesse réprimée.

La reine Élisabeth II et le prince William

Vous diriez qu'il en est comme du système de l'univers, où il y a une force qui éloigne sans cesse du centre tous les corps, et une force de pesanteur qui les y ramène. L'honneur fait mouvoir[3] toutes les parties du corps politique ; il les lie par son action même et il se trouve que chacun va au bien commun, croyant aller à ses intérêts particuliers.[4]

Il est vrai que, philosophiquement parlant, c'est un honneur faux qui conduit toutes les parties de l'État ; mais cet honneur faux est aussi utile au public, que le vrai le serait aux particuliers qui pourraient l'avoir.

Et n'est-ce pas beaucoup d'obliger les hommes à faire toutes les actions difficiles, et qui demandent de la force, sans autre récompense que le bruit de ces actions ?

De l'esprit des lois (livre III, chapitre VII)

Du principe du gouvernement despotique

Comme il faut de la vertu dans une république, et dans une monarchie, de l'honneur, il faut de la CRAINTE dans un gouvernement despotique : pour la vertu, elle n'y est point nécessaire, et l'honneur y serait dangereux.

Le pouvoir immense du prince y passe tout entier à ceux à qui il le confie[5]. Des gens capables de s'estimer beaucoup eux-mêmes seraient en état d'y faire des révolutions. Il faut donc que la crainte

Staline

1. *ranks*   2. *injurious*   3. *puts in motion*   4. individual
5. gives

Core Instruction

LECTURE

1. Have students take notes while they skim through *Du principe de la monarchie* and **Du principe du gouvernement despotique.** **(10 min.)**

2. Ask volunteers to take turns reading the two sections aloud. Monitor pronunciation and comprehension. **(15 min.)**

3. Complete **Compréhension** and **Après la lecture** as a class. **(10 min.)**

Online Practice
go.hrw.com
Online Edition
KEYWORD: BD3 CH8

Chapitre 8

Lecture

Lecture

y abatte[1] tous les courages, et y éteigne jusqu'au moindre sentiment d'ambition.

Un gouvernement modéré peut, tant qu'il veut, et sans péril, relâcher ses ressorts. Il se maintient par ses lois et par sa force même. Mais lorsque, dans le gouvernement despotique, le prince cesse un moment de lever le bras ; quand il ne peut pas anéantir[2] à l'instant ceux qui ont les premières places, tout est perdu : car le ressort du gouvernement, qui est la crainte, n'y étant plus, le peuple n'a plus de protecteur. [...]

De l'esprit des lois (livre III, chapitre IX).

1. *break down* 2. *to annihilate, destroy*

Compréhension 🌸1.2

B Lis les phrases suivantes. Est-ce qu'elles décrivent **a) une démocratie, b) une monarchie** ou **c) un gouvernement despotique** d'après Montesquieu?

c 1. Pour le maintenir, la force est nécessaire.

a 2. Le gouvernement est élu par le peuple.

a 3. Celui qui exécute les lois doit aussi respecter ces lois.

b 4. Le roi gouverne.

c 5. Les révolutions sont possibles.

c 6. Celui qui gouverne n'est pas obligé de tenir sa parole.

C Répondez aux questions avec des phrases complètes. 🌸1.2

1. Qu'est-ce qu'il faut pour qu'une démocratie existe?

2. Pourquoi est-ce que l'auteur est sûr de ses opinions sur la démocratie?

3. Qu'est-ce qui se passe dans une démocratie corrompue?

4. Sur quel principe est-ce que la monarchie est basée?

5. Qu'est-ce qu'il faut pour maintenir un gouvernement despotique?

6. Qui a le pouvoir dans un gouvernement despotique?

Après la lecture 🌸1.3

D Relis les notes que tu as prises pendant la lecture et tes réponses aux questions de compréhension. Quels sont les mots qui se répètent? Quels sont les phrases principales? Utilise tes notes et tes réponses pour écrire un paragraphe qui résume les idées principales du texte.

C Answers

1. Pour qu'une démocratie existe, il faut de la vertu.
2. Les opinions de l'auteur sont basées sur l'histoire et la nature.
3. Dans une démocratie corrompue, les lois ne sont plus exécutées.
4. La monarchie est basée sur le principe d'honneur.
5. Pour maintenir un gouvernement despotique, il faut de la crainte.
6. Dans un gouvernement despotique, c'est le prince qui a le pouvoir.

Connections

Literature Link

After twenty years of work, Montesquieu published *De l'esprit des lois* anonymously in 1748. In France, this book had a frosty reception from supporters as well as opponents of the regime. The Catholic Church banned the book, along with many of his other works, and included it in its Index Librorum Prohibitorum (list of prohibited books). The rest of Europe, especially England, gave the book the highest praise. It was a great influence on Catherine the Great and the framers of the United States Constitution. Jefferson, the author of the Declaration of Independence, Hamilton, Madison, and Jay were all enthusiastic readers of Montesquieu. Encourage students to read chapters from *De l'esprit des lois* that discuss the relationship between climate and politics (books XIV-XIX).

🌸3.1, 5.2

Differentiated Instruction

ADVANCED LEARNERS

D Challenge After students have completed Activity D, ask them which form of government, they think, suits human nature best. Students should explain their answer by quoting supporting evidence from the excerpts. 🌸1.1

SPECIAL LEARNING NEEDS

Students with Dyslexia To accommodate students with reading challenges who might have difficulty with notetaking, offer 'teacher notes' that you have prepared for this reading selection. You might want to enlarge the print and double-space it as well.

Assess

Assessment Program

Quiz: Lecture

Online Assessment

my.hrw.com

Test Generator 💿

Process Writing

Remind students that their essay will be easier to follow and understand if the ideas they present follow a logical order. The ideas examined in the body of the essay should move from the most important idea to the least important, or vice-versa. Tell students that the introductory paragraph and the conclusion of the essay should also follow the same order.

Teaching Suggestion

Suggest that students invite professionals from the community to hear them read their essays and participate in the class discussion on democracy. Students might invite history and government teachers, individuals in the legal profession, or government officials. Alternatively, tell students that there are many resources available to help them articulate their views on democracy. They can consult dictionaries, encyclopedias, history textbooks, their history or government teacher, local government officials, or U.S. government Web sites. 🌸 5.1

L'atelier de l'écrivain

Interactive TUTOR

La démocratie en pratique

Dans le texte que tu viens de lire, Montesquieu examine la nature de la démocratie et son principe. Maintenant, c'est à toi de jouer le rôle de philosophe. Écris une composition de quatre ou cinq paragraphes dans lesquels tu donnes tes propres opinions sur la démocratie. Commence avec ta définition de la démocratie. Ensuite, explique ce qui est nécessaire à ton avis pour qu'elle existe et puisse se maintenir. Tu peux parler des valeurs indispensables dans une société démocratique et des responsabilités des chefs du gouvernement et du peuple.

1 Plan: les grandes lignes 🌸 1.3

Qu'est-ce que la démocratie? Quelles sont les démocraties que tu as étudiées en classe d'histoire? Quelles sont les caractéristiques qui les définissent? Pour t'aider, consulte un livre d'histoire ou une encyclopédie. Note les informations dont tu auras besoin pour ta composition — des faits, des exemples, des citations et des anecdotes — et tes opinions. Maintenant, organise tes idées en trois sections. La première section représente ton introduction. Note une phrase qui captera l'attention des lecteurs. La deuxième section représente le corps de ta composition. Fais une liste des idées dont tu vas parler. Écris un paragraphe pour chaque idée. La troisième section représente ta conclusion. Résume tes idées et écris un commentaire ou une citation.

Jean-Pierre Raffarin, ancien Premier ministre de la France

I. Introduction
A. Phrase intéressante ou citation
B. Liste des idées

II. Corps
A. Paragraphe 1
• idée
• opinions
• preuve

B. Paragraphe 2
• idée
• opinions
• preuve

C. Paragraphe 3
• idée
• opinions
• preuve

III. Conclusion
A. Résumé des idées principales et conclusion
B. Anecdote ou citation

Core Instruction

L'ATELIER DE L'ÉCRIVAIN

1. Read students a definition of democracy from a dictionary or history book. Then discuss the assignment and **Stratégie pour écrire** with the class. Have the class share ideas for the essay and create a sample outline. **(10 min.)**

2. Go over **Vocabulaire à la carte** and review **Le subjonctif. (5 min.)**

3. Assign steps 1 and 2 as homework. Suggest that, along with the guidelines in step 1, they might also consider the questions in step 3 when they plan their outline.

4. Have students complete steps 3 and 4. Students might formally debate the points over which they disagree, trying to persuade their classmates to adopt their viewpoint. **(40 min.)**

L'atelier de l'écrivain

2 Rédaction ✿1.3

Fais le brouillon de ton essai. Pour écrire une composition comme celle-ci, des fois c'est plus facile de commencer avec le corps de l'essai que l'introduction. Alors, commence avec le premier paragraphe de la deuxième section de ton plan.

- Explique en détails les idées et les opinions que tu y as notées.
- N'oublie pas d'inclure des exemples qui soutiennent tes idées.

Essaie de te concentrer sur le contenu et la structure de ta composition. Une fois le corps de ton essai écrit, écris l'introduction et la conclusion.

3 Correction ✿1.3

Maintenant, tu dois t'assurer que ta composition est claire et organisée. Pose-toi les questions suivantes. Est-ce que tu as:

- donné une définition de la démocratie?
- expliqué comment la démocratie se maintient?
- parlé des valeurs et des responsabilités du peuple et des chefs de gouvernement?
- soutenu tes opinions avec des exemples?
- suivi la structure et le contenu de ton brouillon?

Est-ce que l'introduction et la conclusion sont convaincantes? Ensuite, échange ta composition avec celle d'un(e) camarade de classe. Vérifie l'emploi du subjonctif, l'accord des verbes et des temps. Si tu n'es pas sûr(e) d'avoir employé certains mots correctement, vérifie leur usage et leur orthographe à l'aide d'un dictionnaire. Fais les corrections et écris ta composition finale.

4 Application ✿1.3

Lis ta composition à la classe. Après la lecture de toutes les compositions, discutez de vos réactions. Est-ce que vous partagez les mêmes idées sur la démocratie? Sur quels points n'êtes-vous pas d'accord?

La démocratie

« Tous les êtres humains naissent libres et égaux en dignité et en droits. » Pour qu'un état soit une démocratie, il doit respecter ce principe fondamental de la Déclaration universelle des droits de l'homme. Adoptée en décembre 1948, elle doit garantir l'égalité

Vocabulaire à la carte

à mon avis	in my opinion
un droit	right
égal(e) devant la loi	equal in the eyes of the law
justifier	to justify
maintenir	to maintain
le peuple	people
la puissance	power
sans aucun doute	without a doubt
valable	valid

Le subjonctif

In general, the subjunctive is used in relative clauses after:

- expressions of will
  La démocratie demande que nous votions.

- expressions of necessity
  Il faut que les chefs d'état soient honnêtes.

- expressions of incertitude
  Je ne crois pas que la démocratie puisse exister sans la vertu.

- certain conjunctions like **bien que, pour que, à condition que**
  Pour qu'une démocratie se maintienne, tout le peuple doit participer.

L'atelier de l'écrivain

L'atelier de l'écrivain

Le subjonctif

Form small groups to write as many conclusions to these statements as possible.

1. **On doute qu'une démocratie...**
2. **Nous, le peuple, voulons que...**
3. **Il est nécessaire que le président...**
4. **Bien que la liberté...**

✿3.1

Writing Assessment

To assess **L'atelier de l'écrivain,** you can use the following rubric. For additional rubrics, see the *Assessment Program.*

Writing Rubric	4	3	2	1
Content (Complete—Incomplete)				
Comprehensibility (Comprehensible— Seldom comprehensible)				
Accuracy (Accurate—Seldom accurate)				
Organization (Well-organized—Poorly organized)				
Effort (Excellent effort— Minimal effort)				

18-20: A   14-15: C   Under
16-17: B   12-13: D   12: F

Differentiated Instruction

SLOWER PACE LEARNERS

Extension Before students begin the writing activity, invite a government teacher to talk briefly about the history of democracy and its different forms. This will allow students not only to determine the French words and expressions they will need for the assignment but also to define their ideas about democracy more clearly. Have students write the words and expressions they think they will need on the board. Allow students to refer to the board while they write their essay. ✿3.1

SPECIAL LEARNING NEEDS

Students with AD(H)D To improve writing skills in French, you might use an outline for those students who have difficulty staying on task, or modify the assignment so the student may choose his or her own topic within reason. This deviation from the original assignment may allow a broader range of responses and thereby hold students' attention longer. ✿1.2

Assess

Assessment Program

Quiz: Écriture

Online Assessment
my.hrw.com

Test Generator

Resources

Planning:

Lesson Planner

 One-Stop Planner

Practice:

Cahier d'activités

Media Guide

 Teaching Transparencies
Situation, Chapitre 8
Picture Sequences, Chapter 8

 Audio CD 8, Tr. 8

 Interactive Tutor, Disc 2

VIDEO OPTIONS

▶ **Télé-culture: Interviews**

 TPRS
You may wish to use the Picture Sequences Transparency that accompanies Activity 7 for a TPRS activity.

① Possible Answers

1. Le candidat met son bulletin de vote dans l'urne.
2. Le premier ministre fait un discours devant le parlement.
3. Il y a une manifestation des immigrants dans la rue.
4. Le candidat fait un discours.

③ Answers

1. un permis de conduire
2. les pompiers
3. aux urgences
4. les policiers
5. l'ambulance
6. Au secours!
7. à la mairie
8. pour ma part...

Chapitre 8

Prépare-toi pour l'examen

 Interactive **TUTOR**

① Écris une phrase pour décrire chaque photo. 🕸️1.3

1.　　　　2.　　　　3.　　　　4.

① Vocabulaire 1
• to express a point of view
• to speculate
pp. 314–317

🕸️1.2
② Complète les phrases suivantes avec la bonne forme de **lequel.**

1. —Il a été à cette manifestation?
　—_____ parles-tu?
2. —Tu connais ce candidat?
　— _____ ?
3. Les députés pour _____ j'ai voté n'ont pas été élus.
4. De toutes les candidates que tu as rencontrées, _____ est la plus intelligente?
5. Comment s'appelle le sénateur _____ tu m'as présenté?
6. —Tu as vu le débat entre les deux candidats?
　— _____ parles-tu?
7. —Je crois que ces candidats feront de bons sénateurs.
　— _____ penses-tu ?

1. De laquelle 2. Lequel
3. lesquels 4. laquelle
5. auquel 6. Duquel
7. Auxquels

② Grammaire 1
• contractions with **lequel**
• the past subjunctive
Un peu plus
• adverbs
pp. 318–323

③ Vocabulaire 2
• to ask for and give assistance
• to relate information
pp. 326–329

③ Trouve le mot qui correspond à chaque description. 🕸️1.2

1. Il en faut un pour pouvoir conduire une voiture.
2. On les appelle pour éteindre un incendie.
3. C'est là qu'on emmène les blessés.
4. Ils font le constat quand il y a un accident.
5. Ça sert à emmener les blessés.
6. C'est ce qu'on crie quand on est en danger.
7. C'est là qu'on va quand on doit faire refaire ses papiers.
8. C'est une expression qu'on utilise pour donner son point de vue.

Preparing for the Exam

RETEACHING

Review the contractions with **lequel.** Ask students to go back to the grammar presentation on page 318 and review the forms of **lequel** when preceded by either **à** or **de.** Have partners make statements about politicians, actors, or other famous people or groups. The response should always ask for clarification about the person or group. **J'ai parlé au candidat. Auquel?**

TEST-TAKING STRATEGY

Remind students to recall that the verbs **vaincre** and **convaincre** both have a spelling change in the plural, **c** becomes **qu.**

Prépare-toi pour l'examen

4 Complète les phrases suivantes. N'oublie pas d'utiliser le conditionnel. ✿1.2

1. Si j'étais président, ...
2. Si Joseph avait vu l'accident il...
3. Si ma petite sœur s'était blessée, mes parents...
4. Si les députés et les sénateurs avaient fait une loi injuste, le président...
5. S'il y avait un incendie de forêt, les pompiers...

4 Grammaire 2
- review of the conditional
- **vaincre** and **convaincre**
Un peu plus
- **chacun/chacune** pp. 330–335

5 Réponds aux questions suivantes. ✿2.1, 3.1

1. De combien de communautés culturelles la Belgique est-elle composée?
2. Quel est le but de l'Union européenne?
3. Est-ce que la Suisse fait partie de l'Union européenne?

5 Culture
- **Comparaisons** p. 325
- **Flash culture** pp. 316, 319, 328

CD 8, Tr. 8 ✿1.2
6 Dis si les phrases suivantes sont **a) vraies** ou **b) fausses.**
1. a **2.** a **3.** a **4.** b **5.** b **6.** a **7.** a

7 Corinne va pouvoir voter pour la première fois! Regarde les dessins et dis ce qui se passe. ✿1.2

Prépare-toi pour l'examen

5 Answers
1. trois
2. la libre circulation des personnes et des biens parmi les pays
3. non

6 Script
1. S'il y a un accident de la circulation, il faut téléphoner à la police.
2. Quand on entend la sirène des pompiers, il faut laisser le passage.
3. Dans une monarchie, le roi est le chef d'état.
4. Les électeurs votent pour élire le roi.
5. Il faut une carte d'identité pour conduire.
6. Le premier ministre et son cabinet gouvernent le pays.
7. Si on perd ses papiers, il est possible de les faire refaire.

ACTIVITÉ PRÉPARATOIRE PRE-AP  **Language Examination**

To display the drawings to the class, use the Picture Sequences Transparency for Chapter 8.

7 Sample answer

a. Corinne va voter parce qu'elle a 18 ans. Elle ne soit pas lequel choisir.

b. Elle a regardé un débat à la télé et elle a écouté les discours des candidats.

c. Elle a aussi lu le journal pour savoir de quoi les candidats parlent.

d. Finalement, elle est allée au bureau de vote où elle a mis son bulletin de vote dans l'urne pour la première fois! Elle a décidé de voter pour Mireille Leclerc.

Oral Assessment

To assess the speaking activities in this section, you might use the following rubric. For additional speaking rubrics, see the Alternative Assessment section of the *Assessment Program*.

Speaking Rubric	4	3	2	1
Content (Complete—Incomplete)				
Comprehension (Total—Little)				
Comprehensibility (Comprehensible—Incomprehensible)				
Accuracy (Accurate—Seldom Accurate)				
Fluency (Fluent—Not Fluent)				

18-20: A   16-17: B   14-15: C   12-13: D   Under 12: F

Prépare-toi pour l'examen

Grammar Review

For more practice with the grammar topics in this chapter, see the *Grammar Tutor*, the *Interactive Tutor*, or the *Cahier de vocabulaire et grammaire*.

Online Edition

Students might use the online textbook and Holt SoundBooth to practice pronunciation of the **vocabulaire**.

Connections

History Link

King Leopold II of Belgium owned privately from 1885 until 1908 the Congo Free State that included the entire area now known as the Democratic Republic of the Congo. Under the rule of Leopold II, the Congolese population was brutalized in exchange for rubber, for which there was a growing market given the development of rubber tires. When international pressure against the cruelties of King Leopold II mounted, he was forced to sell his property to the Belgian state in 1908. When the Belgian government took over the administraiton of the Belgian Congo, it made economic and social changes that transformed it into a "model colony." The Congo gained independence in 1960. Have students research Belgian colonial policies. Did colonial policies contribute to the current turmoil in the Congo? Why or why not?  3.1

Proverbes

For French proverbs and activities related to the chapter theme and vocabulary, see **Proverbes et expressions**, pp. R6-R7.

Grammaire 1
- contractions with **lequel**
- the past subjunctive

Un peu plus
- adverbs
  pp. 318–323

Résumé: Grammaire 1

When you do not want to repeat a noun that has already been mentioned, use a form of **lequel** (*which one(s)*). **lequel** agrees with the noun it replaces. Forms of **lequel** are: **laquelle, lesquels,** and **lesquelles.** You can also make contractions with **lequel** if it is the relative or interrogative pronoun that refers to things after a preposition.

à + laquelle = à laquelle   de + laquelle = de laquelle

Contraction		Contraction
à + lequel = **auquel**		de + lequel = **duquel**
à + lesquels = **auxquels**		de + lesquels = **desquels**
à + lesquelles = **auxquelles**		de + lesquelles = **desquelles**

To form the **past subjunctive**, conjugate the helping verb **avoir** or **être** in the subjunctive and add the **past participle** of the main verb. Remember to agree the **past participle** if the helping verb is **être.**

To form most adverbs, add **-ment** to the feminine form of the adjective.

- If the adjective ends in **-i** or **-e,** use the masculine form.

- If the adjective ends in **-nt,** remove the **-nt** and add **-mment.**

- Some adverbs are irregular: **beaucoup, trop, très...**

Grammaire 2
- review of the conditional
- **vaincre** and **convaincre**

Un peu plus
- chacun / chacune
  pp. 330–335

Résumé: Grammaire 2

To form the **conditional,** use the future stem of the verb and add the imperfect ending (**-ais, -ais, -ait, -ions, -iez, -aient**).

- For most verbs, the future stem is the infinitive. Remember to remove the **-e** from the end of verbs ending in **-re.**

- Verbs which have spelling changes in the present tense keep the same spelling changes in the future/conditional stem.

- Some verbs have irregular future stems. For a list of verbs with irregular stem, go to p. 330.

The verb **vaincre** (*to vanquish* or *to conquer*) is an irregular verb.

vaincre	
je **vaincs**	nous **vainquons**
tu **vaincs**	vous **vainquez**
il, elle, on **vainc**	ils, elles **vainquent**

The pronoun **chacun/chacune** means *each (one)*. **Chacun/Chacune** is a singular pronoun. Remember to use the **il/elle** form of the verb. You only use **chacune** when the group includes only females or female nouns.

Chapter Review

Teacher Management System
Password: admin
For more details, log on to www.hrw.com/CDROMTUTOR.

Create a variety of puzzles to review chapter vocabulary.

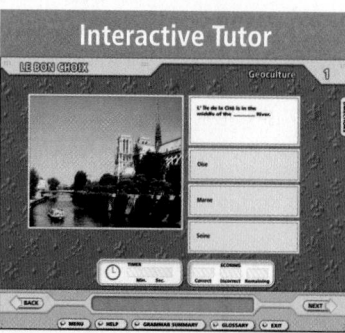

DVD Program — Interactive Tutor

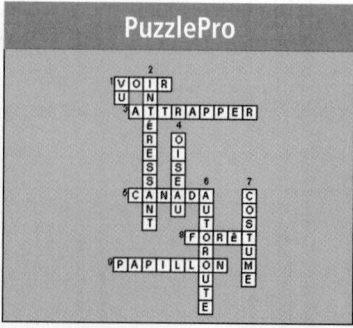

PuzzlePro

Résumé: Vocabulaire 1

To express a point of view

une **affiche (électorale)**	campaign poster
le **bulletin de vote**	ballot
un **bureau de vote**	polling place
un **cabinet**	cabinet
une **campagne électorale**	electoral campaign
un/une **candidat(e)**	candidate
le **chef de l'état**	head of state
un **débat télévisé**	televised debate
démissionner	to resign
une **démocratie**	democracy
un/une **député(e)**	representative
une **dictature**	dictatorship
un **discours**	speech
le **droit de vote**	right to vote
un/une **électeur(-trice)**	voter
une **élection/élire**	election/to elect
le **gouvernement**	government
un/une **immigrant(e)**	immigrant
la **loi**	law
une **manifestation**	protest
une **monarchie**	monarchy

l'**opposition (f.)**	opposition
le **parlement**	parliament
un **parti politique**	political party
participer à	to participate in
un **premier ministre**	prime minister
un **régime politique**	political regime
un/une **sénateur(-trice)**	senator
se **présenter**	to run as a candidate
siéger	to hold a seat
un **sondage**	survey/poll
l'**urne (f.)**	ballot box
voter	to vote
En ce qui me concerne,...	As far as I'm concerned . . .
Je ne partage pas ton point de vue.	I don't share your point of view.
Pour ma part,...	As for me . . .

To speculate .... See p. 317

Résumé: Vocabulaire 2

To ask for assistance

un **accident de la circulation**	traffic accident
l'**ambulance (f.)**	ambulance
un/une **ambulancier(-ière)**	paramedic
le **camion des pompiers**	fire truck
une **carte d'identité**	I.D. card
la **caserne des pompiers**	fire station
une **contravention**	fine
le **commissariat de police**	police station
dresser un constat	to draw up a report
un/une **fonctionnaire**	civil servant
la **mairie**	city hall
les **papiers (m.) d'identité**	personal documents (I.D.)
un **permis de conduire**	driver's license
la **photo d'identité**	I.D. photo
la **police/un policier**	police/policeman

un **pompier**	firefighter
la **prison**	prison
les **services publics (m.)**	government services
la **signature**	signature
la **sirène**	siren
le **témoin**	witness
les **urgences (f.)**	emergency room
Vous serait-il possible de contacter...?	Would it be possible for you to contact . . . ?
À moi!/Au secours!/À l'aide!	Help!
Appelez la police/le 18!	Call the police!
Au feu!	Fire!
Au voleur!	Stop, thief!

To relate information .... See p. 329

Game

Vedettes! To practice the vocabulary of politics and government, write the names of well-known heads of state or politicians on large cards and tape one on each student's back so that he or she cannot see it. Have students circulate, and ask one another students yes-no questions to try to determine their identity. **Je suis chef d'État? Je suis député?** 1.1

Online Edition

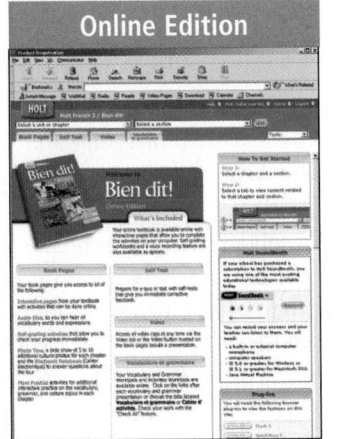

Transparency: Vocabulaire

Transparency: Situation

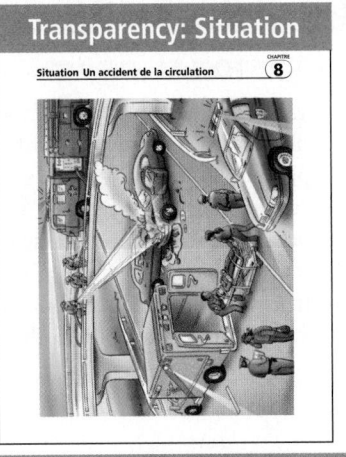

Assess

Assessment Program

Examen: Chapitre 8
Audio CD 8, Trs. 13, 14

Examen oral: Chapitre 8
Alternative Assessment
Differentiated Practice and Assessment CD-ROM

Online Assessment
my.hrw.com

Test Generator

Resources

Planning:

Lesson Planner

 One-Stop Planner

Practice:

Cahier de vocabulaire et grammaire

Differentiated Practice and Assessment CD-ROM

 Teaching Transparencies

Picture Sequences, Chapter 8

Cahier d'activités

 Audio CD 8, Tr. 9

VIDEO OPTIONS

▶ Télé-culture: Interviews

The AP French Language Exam

Activités préparatoires provide students with activities similar to those found in the Advanced Placement French Language exam. The activities are based on material taught up to and including this chapter and concentrate on the chapter grammar and vocabulary.

Listening Script

1. — Regarde là-bas. Il y a un camion de pompiers de l'autre côté de l'autoroute.

— C'est une voiture qui est en feu. Les pompiers éteignent l'incendie. Il y a des blessés aussi.

2. — Tu vas au bureau de vote aujourd'hui pour élire ton candidat?

— Non, je n'y vais pas. J'ai changé d'avis après avoir lu les résultats d'un sondage fait par l'opposition.

Activités préparatoires

SECTION I

Listening CD 8, Tr. 9 1.2

Listen to the dialogues and choose the most appropriate response.

1. A. On les emmène au commissariat de police.
   B. On les emmène à l'église.
   C. On les emmène aux urgences.
   D. On les emmène à la mairie.

2. A. Tu dois voter. C'est ton droit.
   B. Tu dois démissionner.
   C. Les électeurs font une manifestation.
   D. Tu t'es présenté aux élections?

Reading 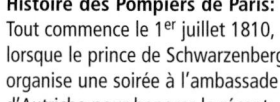1.2

Read the following paragraph and answer the questions that follow.

> **Histoire des Pompiers de Paris:**
> Tout commence le 1er juillet 1810, lorsque le prince de Schwarzenberg organise une soirée à l'ambassade d'Autriche pour honorer le récent mariage de l'Empereur Napoléon Ier.
> 5
> Vers 23 heures, alors que le bal est ouvert, un terrible incendie éclate avec une si soudaine violence que
> 10 la panique désoriente une partie de l'assistance. On déplore une dizaine de morts. À la suite de ce drame, Napoléon Ier décide, par décret impérial du 18 septembre 1811, de
> 15 confier la lutte contre le feu à Paris à un corps militaire, le Bataillon de Sapeurs-Pompiers de Paris.

1. Napoléon Ier s'est marié...
   A. à l'ambassade d'Autriche.
   B. en 1810.
   C. le premier juillet.
   D. en 1811.

2. L'incendie éclate...
   A. vers onze heures du matin.
   B. vers vingt-deux heures.
   C. vers onze heures du soir.
   D. vers treize heures.

3. Le nombre de morts est...
   A. insuffisant.
   B. d'environ dix.
   C. de vingt-trois.
   D. de douze.

4. La première organisation de Sapeurs-Pompiers de Paris était...
   A. un groupe de soldats.
   B. organisée par le prince de Schwarzenberg.
   C. confidentielle.
   D. commandée par Napoléon.

Preparing for the Exam

ADDITIONAL PRACTICE

Make a statement using an impersonal expression followed by **de + infinitive**. (**Il est important de faire...**) Have students use **que + subjunctive** to agree with you. (**Oui, il est important que je fasse/tu fasses...**) To have students vary the forms of the subjunctive they use in their answers, write pronouns on individual flash cards and show one to the student as you ask the question.

TEST-TAKING STRATEGIES

Section I: Listening Tell students that they should only take notes while listening if they are certain that it will not distract their attention from the content.

Section II: Writing Students should familiarize themselves with the scoring system before they take the test. If they will be penalized for incorrect answers, then they should leave questions blank unless they are fairly certain that their answer is correct.

The following activities can be used to help you to prepare for the Advanced Placement French Language examination, or to further practice the vocabulary and grammar concepts you have seen in this chapter.

Activités préparatoires

Reading Strategy

Move along Tell students not to waste time trying to figure out the meaning of an individual word they may not know in the reading selection. Its meaning may not be important, or may become clear later on.

SECTION II

Writing ❀1.2

In the following paragraph, some words have been omitted. When it is a verb, complete the sentence by writing the correct form of the verb. In all other blanks, use CHAQUE or an appropriate form of the word CHACUN.

J'ai dit à mes amis que je ___1___ aux élections présidentielles si j'avais le temps. Ils m'___2___ que ___3___ Américain doit voter. ___4___ d'entre nous a non seulement le droit, mais la responsabilité de voter à ___5___ élection.

1. __voterai__ (voter)
2. __ont convaincu__ (convaincre)
3. __chaque__
4. __Chacun__
5. __chaque__

In the following paragraph, some verbs have been omitted. Complete each sentence by writing the correct form of the verb, based on the context.

Pour obtenir un permis de conduire, il est important de ___1___ avant de passer l'examen. Il est essentiel que chaque candidat ___2___ le code de la route. Il faut aussi qu'on ___3___ avec un conducteur expérimenté pour qu'on ___4___ à l'aise au volant.

1. __se préparer__ (se préparer)
2. __connaisse__ (connaître)
3. __conduise__ (conduire)
4. __se sente__ (se sentir)

Essay Topic ❀1.3

Write in French a well-organized and coherent composition (10 to 15 lines) on the following topic.

Beaucoup d'Américains ne votent pas. À ton avis, pourquoi? Comment peut-on les encourager ou les convaincre à exercer leur droit de vote?

Speaking ❀1.3

Look at the following drawing, then tell a story about what is occurring in the picture.

Writing Strategy

Remind students that varying their sentence style will help add interest to their essay. They should not have every sentence follow the typical 'subject + verb + remainder' structure.

Language Examination

To display the drawing to the class, use the **Activités préparatoires** Transparency for Chapter 8.

Speaking: Sample answer

Il y a eu un accident de la circulation. Le camion des pompiers est arrivé au cas où la voiture prendrait feu. Les ambulanciers emmènent le blessé aux urgences pendant que le policier dresse le constat d'accident.

You may also want to ask students the following.

As-tu jamais eu un accident de voiture? Qu'est-ce que tu as fait?

Differentiated Instruction

SLOWER PACE LEARNERS

Additional Practice Some students may have trouble understanding the dialogs in the Listening section. You might stop the recording after each dialog and ask for volunteers to repeat or paraphrase it. Encourage students to list terms or expressions they do not understand. Go over the lists and have volunteers explain the terms and expressions with synonyms or antonyms, or circumlocution. ❀1.2

SPECIAL LEARNING NEEDS

Students with Dyslexia Copy the reading selection, enlarging it by at least 50%. Then place a piece of clear blue film over the text to dull the brightness of the white paper. Provide each student with a straight edge ruler. (A 3-inch-long, $\frac{1}{2}$-inch-high, rectangular piece of white card stock paper would work.) Have them place it under the line they are reading so that they do not lose their place. ❀1.3

Resources

Planning:

Lesson Planner

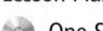 One-Stop Planner

Practice:

Cahier d'activités

 Teaching Transparencies
Fine Art, Chapter 8

 Audio CD 8, Tr. 10

 Interactive Tutor, Disc 2

VIDEO OPTIONS

▸ **Géoculture**

▸ **Télé-roman: Camille et compagnie, Épisode 8**

❶ Script

1. Il faut avoir dix-huit ans pour pouvoir voter.
2. En France, on doit toujours avoir ses papiers sur soi.
3. On a appelé les pompiers parce qu'il y avait un incendie.
4. C'est là que les ambulanciers emmènent les blessés.
5. Tu entends la sirène? Ce sont les pompiers. Laisse-les passer!
6. Tout le monde devrait voter. C'est important d'élire un bon candidat!
7. Je trouve que je suis horrible sur ma photo d'identité!

❷ Answers

1. permis de conduire
2. mairie
3. oui, assez grave
4. parce qu'elle avait le bras cassé
5. l'ambulancier
6. à la fin de la semaine

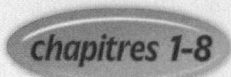

Révisions cumulatives

CD 8, Tr. 10 ✿1.2   **1.** c **2.** b **3.** a **4.** d **5.** a **6.** c **7.** b

❶ Regarde les photos et dis à quelle photo chaque phrase correspond.

a.

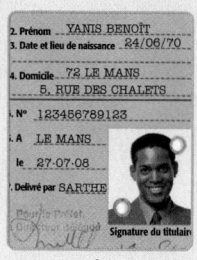

b.

c.

d.

❷ Lis l'e-mail que Sara a écrit à son amie Léa. Réponds aux questions qui suivent. ✿1.2

Chère Léa,
Le jour de mes dix-huit ans, je suis allée à la mairie pour chercher mon permis de conduire, mais j'avais oublié ma carte d'identité. Donc, j'ai dû retourner à la mairie pour le chercher. Finalement, quand je l'ai eu, je suis allée au centre commercial en voiture, mais j'ai eu un accident! J'ai dû aller aux urgences en ambulance! Je me suis cassé le bras et c'est pour cela que je n'ai pas pu t'écrire. Mais, maintenant, tout va bien et je suis à la maison. J'espère retourner au lycée à la fin de la semaine. À bientôt.
Sara

1. Quel papier était-elle allée chercher?
2. Où est-ce qu'elle est allée pour le chercher?
3. Est-ce que l'accident était sérieux?
4. Pourquoi n'a-t-elle pas écrit?
5. Qui est-ce qui a emmené Sara aux urgences?
6. Quand est-ce qu'elle espère retourner au lycée?

Online Culture Project

Ask students to research the current government in Belgium, Switzerland, or Monaco. Encourage students to work in groups and answer questions about the current head of state and the political party he or she is associated with. Who is the current head of foreign affairs? What is a major current political issue under discussion? What were the results of the last elections? Have students create short PowerPoint® presentations about this topic. Students should document all Web sites they use. ✿1.3, 2.2

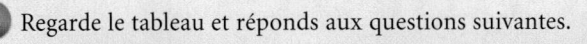

Online Assessment
go.hrw.com
Cumulative Self–test
KEYWORD: BD3 CH8

Chapitres 1–8

Révisions cumulatives

③ Tu veux obtenir ton permis de conduire. Tes parents pensent que tu n'es pas prêt(e). Convaincs-les de te permettre de passer ton permis. Joue cette scène avec un(e) camarade. ✿1.1

④ Regarde le tableau et réponds aux questions suivantes. ✿1.3, 2.2

Rousseau, Henri. Le Douanier. The representatives of the foreign powers coming to hail the Republic as a token of peace.

Les Représentants des puissances étrangères venant saluer la République en signe de paix d'Henri Rousseau

1. Qui sont les personnes représentées sur le tableau?
2. De quels pays est-ce que tu crois qu'ils viennent?
3. Quels drapeaux est-ce que tu reconnais? Nommes-en au moins deux.
4. Est-ce que le peuple a l'air content? Pourquoi?
5. Est-ce que cette scène pourrait arriver, à ton avis?

⑤ Imagine que tu es candidat(e) aux élections présidentielles. Tu as besoin de faire un discours à la télévision. Écris ton discours. Parle des problèmes qui te paraissent importants et propose tes solutions. ✿1.3

⑥ **À ton tour**

Fait divers Il y a eu un accident de la circulation. Ce n'est pas trop grave mais il y a des blessés légers et une voiture est en feu. Tes camarades et toi vous allez jouer cette scène devant la classe. Vous avez besoin d'un policier, d'un ambulancier, d'un pompier, de victimes et d'un témoin. ✿1.1

FINE ART CONNECTION

Introduction Henri Julien Rousseau, known as **Le Douanier Rousseau,** was a self-taught genius who began painting intensively when he was 40 years old. He was often ridiculed during his life by art critics who did not appreciate his naive style. Rousseau worked on each painting for a considerable length of time and, thus, created few paintings. *Les Représentants des puissances étrangères venant saluer la République en signe de paix,* 1907, which Picasso owned, reveals **Le Douanier Rousseau**'s political sympathies. He supported the government of the newly formed Third Republic and courted its cultural authorities with patriotic paintings such as this allegorical work.

Analyzing
This work, painted in 1907, depicts an imaginary gathering hosted by Marianne, the symbol of the French Republic. Ask students these questions.

1. **Les dignitaires sont tous basés sur des personnes réelles. Lesquels peux-tu identifier? (par exemple, Edward VII, Nicholas II, Kaiser Wilhelm II)**
2. **Qu'est-ce que les enfants représentent? (les colonies)**
✿ 1.1, 3.1

Extension
Rousseau enjoyed painting scenes of the jungle and wild animals, but he did not confine himself to a few subjects. His work includes still lifes, genre paintings, portraits, and historical scenes. Ask students to research Rousseau's life to find possible reasons for his extensive repertoire of subjects.
✿ 1.3, 3.1

ACTFL Performance Standards

The activities in Chapter 8 target the communicative modes as described in the Standards.

Interpersonal	Two-way communication using receptive skills and productive skills	**Communication (SE),** pp. 317, 319, 321, 323, 329, 331, 333, 335 **Communication (TE),** pp. 311, 319, 321, 323, 329, 331 **À ton tour,** p. 349
Interpretive	One-way communication using receptive skills	**Culture,** pp. 324–325 **Lecture,** pp. 336–339
Presentational	One-way communication using productive skills	**Communication (SE),** pp. 335 **Communication (TE),** pp. 317, 329, 333, 335

Chroniques

Resources

Practice:

Reading Strategies and Skills Handbook

Advanced Reader

Applying the Strategies

You may want to use the "Sketch to Stretch" strategy from the *Reading Strategies and Skills Handbook* to encourage students to examine the text more closely.

READING PRACTICE

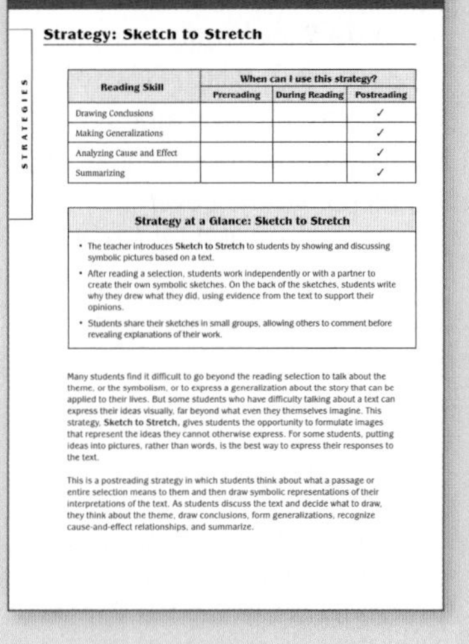

Strategy: Sketch to Stretch

Reading Skill	When can I use this strategy?		
	Prereading	During Reading	Postreading
Drawing Conclusions			✓
Making Generalizations			✓
Analyzing Cause and Effect			✓
Summarizing			✓

Strategy at a Glance: Sketch to Stretch

- The teacher introduces *Sketch to Stretch* to students by showing and discussing symbolic pictures based on a text.
- After reading a selection, students work independently or with a partner to create their own symbolic sketches. On the back of the sketches, students write why they drew what they did, using evidence from the text to support their opinions.
- Students share their sketches in small groups, allowing others to comment before revealing explanations of their work.

Many students find it difficult to go beyond the reading selection to talk about the theme, or the symbolism, or to express a generalization about the story that can be applied to their lives. But some students who have difficulty talking about a text can express their ideas visually, far beyond what even they themselves imagine. This strategy, *Sketch to Stretch*, gives students the opportunity to formulate images that represent the ideas they cannot otherwise express. For some students, putting ideas into pictures, rather than words, is the best way to express their responses to the text.

This is a postreading strategy in which students think about what a passage or entire selection means to them and then draw symbolic representations of their interpretations of the text. As students discuss the text and decide what to draw, they think about the theme, draw conclusions, form generalizations, recognize cause-and-effect relationships, and summarize.

Prereading

Ask students to give all the French terms for means of transportation they can think of. Then ask them the advantages and disadvantages of each one. Finally, ask students their preferred means of transportation and have them explain why.

Language Examination

Chroniques helps students prepare for Section I, Part B: **Reading Comprehension.**

CHRONIQUES

Plus loin, plus vite

Les Français aiment bien chercher des solutions originales pour économiser l'énergie. Dans le domaine des transports, par exemple, la technologie française est très avancée.

Le train à grande vitesse

Le TGV, ou «train à grande vitesse[1]» est un train de conception française qui appartient à la Société nationale des chemins de fer français, la SNCF. Le TGV est entré en service[2] en 1981, sur la ligne Paris-Lyon et il y a maintenant à peu près 400 TGV en France. Ils transportent plus de 85 millions de voyageurs par an. Le TGV est électrique et va à des vitesses de plus de 300 km/h sur des voies spéciales (200 km/h sur les voies normales). Le TGV est devenu un moyen très rapide, confortable et relativement économique de se déplacer en France. À l'intérieur, on n'a pas l'impression de rouler[3] à 300 km/h, et on peut même aller déjeuner ou dîner dans la voiture-bar.

Les avions révolutionnaires

Airbus est une compagnie aéronotique européenne dont le bureau central[4] est à Toulouse, en France. Son dernier modèle, l'Airbus A380, est assemblé en France avec des éléments qui viennent de toute l'Europe. C'est le plus gros avion commercial du monde et il est à la pointe de la technologie. Il a deux étages et peut transporter de 555 personnes pour les vols réguliers à 840 personnes pour les charters, ce qui permettra aux compagnies aériennes d'augmenter leur profit et de réduire la consommation d'énergie. Un gros avion, même s'il est très grand, consomme moins de kérosène[5] que plusieurs petits avions. Il peut parcourir 15.000 km sans escale. L'Airbus A380 a volé pour la première fois le 27 avril 2005 et il a déjà été vendu à plusieurs compagnies aériennes étrangères, principalement en Asie. Certains aéroports doivent être modifiés pour pouvoir recevoir ce géant et le nombre important de passagers qu'il transporte.

1. speed 2. was used 3. go 4. main office 5. gas

Core Instruction

TEACHING CHRONIQUES

1. Have students describe the main photo. Ask for volunteers to share what they know about the **TGV**. Then have students read the first section and ask for a volunteer to summarize the information on the TGV. **(4 min.)**

2. Have students read the second section to find the features of the Airbus A380 that make it different from other commercial aircraft. **(4 min.)**

3. Give students time to read the last two sections. Then have them answer the questions in **Après la lecture.** Have volunteers read their answers aloud. **(10 min.)**

Answers

1. parce qu'il est sur les voies normales
2. en France
3. C'est le plus gros avion commercial du monde et il est à la pointe de la technologie.
4. pour faciliter la circulation dans la vallée du Tarn.
5. Non, on met sa voiture dans un train.

Des voies de communication ultra-modernes

Le viaduc de Millau

Pour faciliter la circulation[1], la France a des ponts et des tunnels très ingénieux. Le viaduc de Millau, par exemple, est un pont pour voitures inauguré en décembre 2004. Il a été construit par le même groupe qui a construit la tour Eiffel, et c'est le deuxième pont pour véhicules le plus haut du monde. Depuis qu'il a été construit, il n'y a plus d'embouteillages[2] dans la vallée du Tarn. Quand on va de Paris à Béziers, on prend aujourd'hui l'autoroute A75 qui passe sur le pont et on économise ainsi beaucoup de temps et d'énergie.

Le tunnel sous la Manche[3]

Le tunnel sous la Manche, qui relie la France à l'Angleterre, mesure 50 km et passe sous la mer pendant 39 km. C'est une construction franco-britannique. On met sa voiture dans un train et on arrive en Angleterre en 35 minutes. L'American Society of Civil Engineers a inscrit le tunnel sous la Manche sur sa liste des sept merveilles du monde moderne.

APRÈS ▶ la lecture

🏵1.2

1. Pourquoi est-ce que la vitesse du TGV est parfois limitée à 200 km/h?

2. Où est assemblé l'Airbus A380?

3. En quoi l'Airbus A380 est-il différent des autres avions?

4. Pourquoi le viaduc de Millau a-t-il été construit?

5. Est-ce qu'on peut conduire sa voiture dans le tunnel sous la Manche?

1. traffic   2. traffic jam   3. channel

Communities

Practices and Perspectives

Have students prepare a survey they will e-mail to a French-speaking class or to francophone e-pals to find out how people get around in their town or city, how they typically travel (short, medium, and long distances), what the most popular means of transportation are and how often they use each one. Have students analyze the results and compare them with their own transportation practices.

🏵5.1

Postreading

Imagine and discuss what it would be like if the United States were linked to Europe by a tunnel like the Channel Tunnel with Europe suddenly less than an hour away.

Recherches

Have groups use the SNCF's travel planning Web site at http://www.voyages-sncf.com to plan a one-week trip to the area of their choice in France that involves different means of transportation.

🏵3.2

Differentiated Instruction

SLOWER PACE LEARNERS

Before they answer the questions in **Après la lecture,** have slower pace students reread the parts of the **Chroniques** with which they had trouble. Allow them to read at their own pace and to ask you for clarifications. Call on advanced learners to paraphrase or summarize sections that prove problematic.   🏵1.2

MULTIPLE INTELLIGENCES

Spatial Working together as a class, have students imagine and design the perfect car of the future. Then have them write a detailed description of it and have students with artistic talents create a drawing or 3-D model of it.   🏵1.1, 1.3

Resources

Practice:

Reading Strategies and Skills
Handbook

Advanced Reader

Applying the Strategies

You may want to use the "Anticipation Guide" strategy from the *Reading Strategies and Skills Handbook* to encourage students to examine the text more closely.

READING PRACTICE

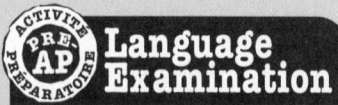

Prereading

Before students begin the **Chroniques** section, ask them to brainstorm a list of technological advances of the last 100 years. Then ask them to select the five most important and rank these on the board, from most to least important. Ask students to explain how they selected the top five and have them describe the significance of each invention they selected.

Language Examination

Chroniques helps students prepare for Section I, Part B: **Reading Comprehension.**

CHRONIQUES

Une technologie de pointe

Les pays européens collaborent de plus en plus à la réalisation de projets communs, comme en témoigne la fusée Ariane.

Un projet européen

La mission de la fusée[1] Ariane n'est pas d'envoyer des hommes et des femmes dans l'espace: elle n'est utilisée que pour mettre des satellites en orbite. Les fusées et les satellites sont fabriqués en Europe et la base de lancement[2] d'Ariane se trouve à Kourou, en Guyane française[3]. C'est la France qui a proposé à l'Europe la construction d'une fusée européenne dans les années 70. Le gouvernement français pensait qu'il était important pour l'Europe d'avoir sa propre fusée et de ne pas dépendre des États-Unis pour placer des satellites européens dans l'espace. L'Agence spatiale européenne (ESA) a alors accepté le projet, et le Centre national d'études spatiales français (CNES) a commencé à travailler sur ce projet.

Les différentes générations de fusées Ariane

La première fusée, Ariane I, a été lancée en 1979. La France a financé les deux tiers du projet et l'Allemagne en a payé 20%. La seconde fusée, Ariane II, ressemblait à Ariane I, mais elle avait un troisième étage plus allongé[4]. Ariane III était identique à Ariane II, mais avec deux propulseurs supplémentaires au premier étage; Ariane III a volé[5] la première en 1984 et Ariane II a finalement été lancée en 1987.

Une fusée plus puissante[6], Ariane IV, a ensuite été lancée en 1988. Elle était non seulement plus puissante, mais aussi plus pratique, car il en existait six versions différentes, équipées d'une grande variété de propulseurs.

Le modèle actuel Ariane V, a volé pour la première fois en 1997. Ariane V permet maintenant de placer en orbite des satellites beaucoup plus lourds qui peuvent peser[7] jusqu'à dix tonnes.

La fusée Ariane

---

1. rocket 2. launching pad 3. French Guyana
4. elongated 5. flew 6. powerful 7. to weigh

Core Instruction

TEACHING CHRONIQUES

1. Ask students why a country would want to develop a space program. Then have them scan the first section to find out why France started its space program. Finally, ask students to find the name of the launching site of the Ariane rockets, explain where it is located, and point it out on a map. **(4 min.)**

2. Have students read the first page. You might have a volunteer come to the board and write a simplified chronology of the French space program with the help of the class. Then have students answer questions 1–3 in **Après la lecture. (15 min.)**

3. Have students read questions 4–6 in **Après la lecture** before they read the second page and clarify anything students are having trouble understanding. Then have them read the rest of the text and answer the remaining questions. **(12 min.)**

L'énergie nucléaire en France

La première source d'énergie

La majorité de l'électricité française (88%) vient de l'énergie nucléaire. En comparaison, l'Allemagne n'utilise le nucléaire que pour 28% de sa production d'électricité, le Japon pour 25%, le Royaume-Uni[1] pour 24% et les États-Unis pour 20%.

Avec ses 58 réacteurs nucléaires d'une puissance de 63.200 mégawatts, la France est à 50% indépendante des autres pays pour sa production d'électricité; elle a des sociétés qui exploitent des mines d'uranium sur presque tous les continents et elle n'a pas besoin d'importer beaucoup de combustibles[2] pour produire de l'électricité. L'électricité française est aussi la plus compétitive d'Europe car elle est moins chère que celle qui est produite par le gaz ou le charbon.

Les avantages et les inconvénients

Les partisans de l'énergie nucléaire insistent sur ses avantages: elle aide à préserver l'environnement parce qu'elle n'émet pas de gaz à effet de serre et ne contribue donc pas au réchauffement climatique; les déchets de l'industrie nucléaire occupent peu de volume et peuvent être traités pour être rendus plus sûrs[3]; les réserves d'énergie nucléaire sont plus importantes que celles de pétrole ou de gaz et peuvent durer[4] des milliers d'années; le coût[5] de l'énergie nucléaire est très stable (le prix de l'uranium ne représente que 5% du coût de production de l'électricité.)

Mais le nucléaire a aussi beaucoup d'adversaires qui en rappellent les inconvénients, comme le problème du stockage[6] à long terme des déchets, les matières très dangereuses (le plutonium) que produisent les centrales nucléaires et leur eau chaude qui va dans les rivières et perturbe l'écosystème. Et puis, il y a toujours les risques d'un accident nucléaire. Par exemple, un réacteur de la centrale russe de Tchernobyl, en Ukraine, a explosé en 1986 et toute une région a été dévastée. On dit même qu'après cet accident, il y a eu des radiations dans toute l'Europe.

APRÈS la lecture

🌸1.2, 4.2

1. Qui a payé la majorité du projet Ariane I?
2. Quelles différences y a-t-il entre Ariane I et Ariane III?
3. Est-ce qu'il y a des fusées similaires dans ton pays? Comment s'appellent-elles et que font-elles?
4. Est-ce que les États-Unis utilisent le nucléaire plus ou moins que la France pour produire de l'électricité?
5. Quel élément radioactif est-ce qu'on utilise pour produire de l'énergie nucléaire?
6. Qu'est-ce qui s'est passé à Tchernobyl?

1. United Kingdom 2. fuel 3. safe 4. last 5. cost 6. storage

Resources

Practice:

Reading Strategies and Skills Handbook

Advanced Reader

Applying the Strategies

You may want to use the "Anticipation Guide" strategy from the *Reading Strategies and Skills Handbook* to encourage students to examine the text more closely.

READING PRACTICE

Strategy: Anticipation Guide

Reading Skill	When can I use this strategy?		
	Prereading	During Reading	Postreading
Making Predictions	✓		
Using Prior Knowledge	✓		
Analyzing Cause and Effect Relationships		✓	
Analyzing Persuasive Techniques			✓
Making Generalizations			✓

Strategy at a Glance: Anticipation Guide

- The teacher writes the Anticipation Guide, a set of generalizations based on issues in the text and designed to promote discussion and predictions about the selection.
- Students mark whether they agree or disagree with each statement, then discuss their responses.
- While students read, they take notes on the issues in the guide as those issues are revealed in the text.
- After reading, students look at their responses again to see whether they still agree or disagree with the statements.

Both younger and older children do it. They constantly ask what's going on and where they are being taken. They ask what the doctor is going to do before the doctor does it, and they plan what they'll say when they are approaching parents with special requests. Adults do it. We pick up travel brochures before we travel, study maps before we make a car trip, and check out the checkbook before we make a purchase. We all do it—we try to anticipate what's going to happen before it actually happens.

Good readers consciously try to anticipate what a text is about before they begin reading. They look at the cover, art, title, genre, author, headings, graphs, charts, length, print size, initial flaps, and back cover. Some students read the bibliographic information on the copyright page. They ask friends, "Is this any good?" They do anything to find out something about a text before they begin reading.

Struggling readers, on the other hand, often don't do that; they are told to read something, and once the text is in hand, they just begin. They often skip titles and background information, hardly ever read book jackets, and rarely look through the text

Prereading

Before you begin this **Chroniques** section, have small groups of students choose and research an environmental issue they are interested in. Have them give a brief oral report in class, with vocabulary they know. You might also wish to provide students with a list of relevant vocabulary. Encourage the class to ask questions. ✿ 1.3

Language Examination

Chroniques helps students prepare for Section I, Part B: **Reading Comprehension.**

L'Europe a adopté une politique pour le protection de l'environnement et a adhéré au protocole de Kyoto. De plus, les Verts, parti écologiste, ont environ 5% des sièges au Parlement européen.

S.O.S. Terre

Le commandant Cousteau

Jacques-Yves Cousteau, né en 1910, est devenu célèbre pour ses recherches océanographiques et l'invention du scaphandre autonome (SCUBA). Il était aussi connu pour ses documentaires extraordinaires sur le monde marin. Mais le commandant Cousteau était aussi un fervent défenseur de l'environnement et surtout, de la protection de l'écosystème marin. Par exemple, deux ans après avoir été nommé président du Conseil[1] pour les droits des générations futures par le président de la République française en 1993, il a démissionné pour protester contre les essais nucléaires menés par la France dans l'océan Pacifique. Cousteau pensait que le nucléaire était une menace pour notre planète. Jusqu'à sa mort, en 1997, cet homme qui avait commencé sa carrière dans l'armée française, a lutté pour la protection de l'environnement.

La France et les essais nucléaires

La France est un des rares pays du monde avec les États-Unis et la Grande-Bretagne, à posséder officiellement des armes nucléaires. Lorsque l'Algérie était une colonie française, les essais nucléaires français étaient menés[2] dans le désert algérien. Après l'indépendance de l'Algérie, en 1962, la France a commencé à effectuer ses essais nucléaires en Polynésie française, sur les atolls[3] de Mururoa et Fangataufa, au milieu de l'océan Pacifique. Ces essais nucléaires ont provoqué beaucoup de controverses depuis 1966. Ceux qui s'y opposent disent que leurs effets sur l'environnement marin et sur les populations locales sont dévastateurs. Malgré[4] un accord international signé en 1986, le président de la République, Jacques Chirac, a décidé de reprendre les essais nucléaires en 1995. Cette décision vaudra[5] à la France des protestations du monde entier, y compris d'une bonne partie de la population française. Finalement, en février 1996, la France a arrêté ses essais nucléaires en Polynésie.

---

1. Counsil 2. conducted 3. small islands 4. despite 5. will bring

Core Instruction

TEACHING CHRONIQUES

1. Ask students if they've ever heard of Jacques-Yves Cousteau and if so, have volunteers share what they know about him with their classmates. Then have them read the section about him. **(5 min.)**

2. Give students time to read the section on nuclear testing. Then ask simple comprehension questions. **Quels pays possèdent des armes nucléaires? Où est-ce que la France a fait des essais nucléaires? (8 min.)**

3. Have students read the section on **les Verts.** Ask for a volunteer to summarize it for the class. Ask students to share what they know about green parties in the U.S. **(10 min.)**

4. Have students read the last section and have them answer the questions in **Après la lecture** with a partner. **(12 min.)**

L'écologie et la Francophonie

La montée[1] des «Verts»

En français, l'expression «les Verts» désigne le mouvement écologiste en général. Depuis 1984, un parti écologiste français a repris le terme «Les Verts» dans son appellation officielle.

Depuis les années soixante-dix, les partis écologistes ont obtenu une place de plus en plus importante sur la scène politique des différents pays francophones, surtout[2] en Europe. En France, le premier événement politique important pour les écologistes a eu lieu en 1974, avec le premier candidat écologiste aux élections présidentielles, René Dumont. C'est en Suisse que le premier «vert» a été élu au Parlement national, en 1979. Le 21 février 2004, le Parti vert européen a été fondé. Aux élections européennes du 13 juin 2004, les «Verts» ont obtenu 7,2% des votes. Cette montée évidente du mouvement écologiste montre que les Européens sont de plus en plus conscients du besoin de protéger l'environnement.

La biodiversité en Afrique

L'Afrique aussi est de plus en plus consciente qu'il faut préserver la biodiversité. Les changements climatiques (l'expansion de régions désertiques comme le Sahara) et la demande commerciale de produits végétaux et animaux (l'ivoire des éléphants, par exemple) entraînent la disparition[3] d'espèces importantes à l'écosystème.

Depuis quelques années, des organisations locales et internationales comme l'AAC (Amis des animaux au Congo) et la SNPN (la Société nationale pour la protection de la nature) luttent[4] pour sauver les espèces africaines en danger. Le CITES (Convention on International Trade of Endangered Species) est un accord signé en 1973 qui définit quelles espèces animales et végétales peuvent et ne peuvent pas être exportées dans un but commercial. De plus en plus de pays, y compris des pays africains, sont membres de cette convention.

APRÈS la lecture

1.2, 1.3

1. Pourquoi Cousteau est-il connu dans le monde entier?
2. À ton avis, pourquoi est-ce que Jacques-Yves Cousteau était contre les armes nucléaires?
3. Est-ce que la France continue à tester ses armes nucléaires en Polynésie?
4. D'après toi, pourquoi est-ce que les écologistes s'appellent «les verts»?
5. Est-ce que la France est le seul pays francophone à lutter pour la protection de l'environnement?
6. Pourquoi les éléphants d'Afrique sont-ils en danger? Que font certaines organisations pour les protéger?

1. rise 2. especially 3. disappearance 4. fight

Differentiated Instruction

SLOWER PACE LEARNERS

Read the questions in **Après la lecture** aloud one at a time, encouraging students to ask questions if they are having difficulty understanding. Clarify or rephrase the questions as needed. Then have advanced students locate and read aloud the sentences in the text that contain the answers to the questions. 1.2

MULTIPLE INTELLIGENCES

Naturalist Have students use your library resources or the Internet to research endangered species in Africa. Have them present their findings to the class. 1.3, 3.1

Answers

1. pour ses recherches océanographiques, l'invention du scaphandre autonome, et ses documentaires sur le monde marin
2. Answers will vary. (Il pensait que le nucléaire était une menace pour le planète.)
3. Non, elle a arrêté en 1996.
4. Answers will vary.
5. Non.
6. demande commerciale de l'ivoire; Elles luttent pour sauver les espèces en danger.

Connections

Science Link

If available, you might show your students a segment from *The Silent World* (**Le Monde du silence**), Cousteau's most famous documentary, which was the first film to use underwater cinematography to show the ocean in color. It received the **Palme d'or** at the Cannes film festival in 1956. 3.2

Postreading

On the board, write the following quote by Nicolas Hulot, a French journalist whose **Fondation Nicolas Hulot** is active in the protection of the environment: **«L'écologie est aussi et surtout un problème culturel. Le respect de l'environnement passe par un grand nombre de changements comportementaux.»** Explain difficult words and ask students to explain what Hulot means, in their own words. Have them brainstorm undesirable behaviors that affect the environment and suggest ways to change them. 1.3

Recherches

Have small groups research green parties in various francophone countries and present their findings to the class. Remind them to document their sources. 3.1

La Vᵉ République

Resources

Practice:

Reading Strategies and Skills
Handbook

Advanced Reader

En France, le président est élu¹ au suffrage universel direct², et peut être ré-élu plusieurs fois. Depuis l'an 2000, son mandat³ est de cinq ans; avant, le mandat présidentiel était de sept ans. Le président détient le pouvoir exécutif. Il est le chef des armées et le plus haut magistrat de France.

Applying the Strategies

You may want to use the "Probable Passage" strategy from the *Reading Strategies and Skills Handbook* to encourage students to examine the text more closely.

READING PRACTICE

Strategy: Probable Passage

Reading Skill	When can I use this strategy?		
	Prereading	During Reading	Postreading
Identifying Purpose	✓		✓
Making Predictions	✓		
Comparing and Contrasting			
Analyzing Chronological Order			✓

Strategy at a Glance: Probable Passage

- The teacher chooses key words or phrases from the text students will read, then develops categories for the words and writes the Probable Passage (a cloze passage with key words omitted).
- Before students read the text, they arrange the key words and phrases in the categories. Then they fill in the blanks in the cloze passage with the key words.
- After students read the text, they discuss how their passages were similar to or different from the actual text.

Many readers struggle because they don't predict what a selection might be about and don't think about what they already know about a topic. These students simply open a book, look at words, and begin turning pages. Probable Passage is a strategy that helps stop these poor reading habits by encouraging students to make predictions and activate their prior knowledge about a topic.

Best Use of the Strategy

Probable Passage (Wood 1984) is a brief preview of a text from which key words and phrases have been omitted. The teacher chooses these key words from the text and presents them to the students. In some cases, it might be necessary to discuss the meaning of the words; many times, students can figure this out for themselves. Students arrange the words in categories according to their probable functions in the story (such as Setting, Characters, or Conflict), then use the words to fill in the blanks of the Probable Passage. After reading the story, students compare it to their passages and discuss differences. As students work through this process, they use what they know about story structure, think about vocabulary, practice making predictions, and compare their predictions to the story line.

La libération de Paris

Charles de Gaulle
(Présidence: 1959–1969)

Le général de Gaulle devient le leader des Forces françaises libres pendant l'occupation de la France par les Allemands au cours de la Seconde Guerre mondiale. Réfugié en Angleterre, de Gaulle participe au mouvement de la Résistance et fait appel aux Français par des messages de la BBC pour combattre l'occupation.

Après la Seconde Guerre mondiale, le général de Gaulle a plusieurs responsabilités au sein du⁴ gouvernement français. En 1958, il devient président du Conseil⁵. Il est alors chargé de préparer un projet de constitution. Cette nouvelle constitution, après approbation par référendum le 28 septembre 1958, devient la Constitution de la Vᵉ République, laquelle donne plus de pouvoir au président.

Prereading

Draw a timeline on the board, from 1789 to today. Ask students to name famous American presidents and have a volunteer write their names on the timeline, according to when they were president. Ask students to share what they know about each president and describe his main accomplishments. Have a volunteer take notes under each president's name. ✿3.1

Georges Pompidou
(Présidence: 1969–1974)

Né de parents enseignants⁶ et enseignant lui-même, Georges Pompidou était un homme d'une grande culture. Après des années de collaboration avec Charles de Gaulle, Pompidou devient premier ministre en 1962. Après la démission de de Gaulle en 1969, Pompidou devient président. Il meurt en 1974 avant la fin de son mandat.

Beaubourg a été construit à l'initiative de Pompidou qui voulait voir le création d'un grand centre culturel à Paris.

1. elected 2. direct suffrage 3. term 4. in 5. Cabinet 6. teacher

Beaubourg

Language Examination

Chroniques helps students prepare for Section I, Part B: **Reading Comprehension.**

Core Instruction

TEACHING CHRONIQUES

1. Ask students to list the powers and functions of the president of the United States. Ask questions about the electoral process: how the president is elected, for how long, etc. Then have students read the introduction and compare the French system to the American system. **(5 min.)**

2. Have students read the information about the five French presidents. Then create a second timeline on the board, below the one you created in the **Prereading** activity. Have volunteers write the names of the five French presidents and their main accomplishments on the timeline. **(20 min.)**

3. Have students compare the two timelines and point out if there are any similarities among the presidents of the two countries. **(5 min.)**

4. Finally, have students answer the questions in **Après la lecture. (4 min.)**

Valéry Giscard d'Estaing
(Présidence: 1974–1981)

Élu à l'âge de 48 ans, Valéry Giscard d'Estaing était à ce jour le plus jeune président français. Sa présidence est marquée par la construction de l'Europe et une volonté de modernisation. Sous sa présidence, la majorité[1] est abaissée à 18 ans. Il apporte un changement dans le protocole en portant des pull-overs en public et en allant déjeuner chez les Français «moyens[2]» le dimanche. En 2003, il a été élu à l'Académie française, au fauteuil de Léopold Sédar Senghor.

Un TGV

François Mitterrand
(Présidence: 1981–1995)

Élu en 1981 et en 1988, François Mitterrand est le premier président à avoir fait deux mandats complets. Contrairement à ses prédécesseurs, Mitterand était socialiste (un parti politique de gauche) et pendant sa première présidence, il a pris de nombreuses mesures sociales, comme l'abolition de la peine de mort[3], l'impôt[4] sur la fortune, la nationalisation des banques, la semaine de 39 heures et la 5e semaine de congés payés. Il a également augmenté les allocations familiales[5] et de logement[6]. Sa deuxième présidence voit l'inauguration du Grand Louvre et de sa pyramide de verre, de l'opéra Bastille et de la nouvelle Bibliothèque nationale.

La pyramide de I.M. Pei au Louvre

Jacques Chirac (Présidence: 1995–2007)

Jacques Chirac est arrivé à la présidence en 1995, après une longue carrière politique. Il a notamment été maire de Paris pendant 18 ans (1977–1995).

Au cours de son premièr mandat, Chirac propose et obtient la modification de la Constitution pour changer la durée du mandat présidentiel de sept ans (le septennat) à cinq ans (le quinquennat). Sa ré-élection en 2002 est un succès sans précédent. Il obtient 82,21% des votes, reflétant le refus des Français de voter pour le candidat du Front National (parti d'extrême droite). Depuis, la situation internationale et la Constitution européenne dominent la scène politique. Chirac a connu une grande défaite avec le rejet de la Constitution européenne au référendum de 2005.

APRÈS la lecture

1.2, 1.3

1. Quel président a fait beaucoup de changements sociaux?
2. Qui est devenu président après le général de Gaulle? Pourquoi est-il connu?
3. Qui a organisé un référendum sur la Constitution européenne?
4. Lequel de ces présidents tu trouves le plus important? Pourquoi?

1. coming of age 2. ordinary 3. death penalty 4. taxes 5. family allowances 6. housing allowances

Answers
1. François Mitterrand
2. Georges Pompidou; la construction de Beaubourg
3. Jacques Chirac
4. Answers will vary.

Connections
Social Studies Link

Have students research the functions of the different institutions that make up the French government and in class, create a diagram representing the French government. Bring in a similar diagram of the American government and have students compare and contrast the two systems. 3.2

Postreading

Ask students to select the American president they admire most or the one whose contributions they feel have been the greatest. Have them write a portrait of this president, using the French presidents' portraits as models. 1.3

Recherches

Have students research the life and political career of a president or head of state from another French-speaking nation. Ask them to make a short oral presentation to the class. Remind students to document their sources. 1.3

Differentiated Instruction

ADVANCED LEARNERS

Have students use the Internet or the library to research additional information about Jacques Chirac and prepare a comprehensive biography of him. The biography should cover the highlights of the president's social backgrounds, education, political career, and accomplishments to date. 1.3, 3.1

MULTIPLE INTELLIGENCES

Musical Play the French national anthem, *La Marseillaise*. The recording is available under **Les symboles de la République** at http://www.elysee.fr. Provide a copy of the lyrics along with an English translation. Then ask students for their opinion of the music and the lyrics and have them compare *La Marseillaise* to the *Star-Spangled Banner*. 3.2

CHRONIQUES

Resources

Practice:

Reading Strategies and Skills Handbook

Advanced Reader

Applying the Strategies

You may want to use the "Think Aloud" strategy from the *Reading Strategies and Skills Handbook* to encourage students to examine the text more closely.

READING PRACTICE

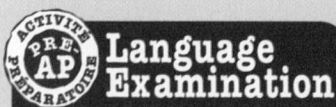

Prereading

Bring to class a large map of Europe (without the countries' names) and put it on the board. Next to it, write the names of the members of the European Union on the board. Ask students to point the countries out on the map. Have volunteers share what they already know about these countries with the class. Then ask them to name the ones where French is spoken and point them out on the map. 🌸 3.1

Language Examination

Chroniques helps students prepare for Section I, Part B: **Reading Comprehension.**

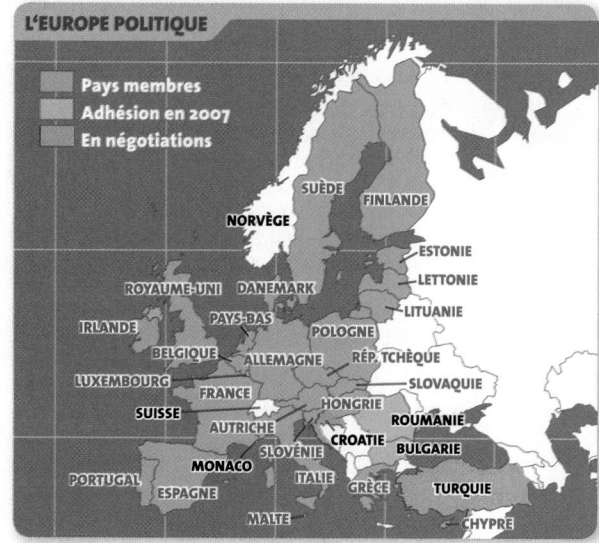

L'EUROPE POLITIQUE

- Pays membres
- Adhésion en 2007
- En négotiations

L'Europe compte cinq pays francophones: la France, la Belgique, le Luxembourg, la Suisse et la principauté de Monaco. La France, la Belgique et le Luxembourg font partie de l'Union européenne. La Suisse et la principauté de Monaco n'en font pas partie.

L'Europe *francophone*

L'Union européenne

En mai 2004, l'Union européenne regroupe 25 pays européens démocratiques: la France, la Belgique, les Pays-Bas, le Luxembourg, l'Allemagne, l'Italie, le Danemark, l'Irlande, le Royaume-Uni, la Grèce, l'Espagne, le Portugal, l'Autriche, la Finlande, la Suède, Chypre, Malte, la Slovénie, la Pologne, la Hongrie, la République tchèque, l'Estonie, la Lettonie, la Lituanie et la Slovaquie.

L'Union européenne a pour but la libre circulation des personnes, des biens[1], des services et des capitaux[2] au sein des pays membres. Ces états ont aussi une politique[3] commune en matière d'agriculture, de politique économique et sociale, de transports, de recherche et de tout autre secteur commun aux pays de l'UE.

Les symboles

le drapeau: un cercle de douze étoiles dorées sur fond bleu
l'hymne[4] européen: l'Ode à la joie de Ludwig van Beethoven
la journée de l'Europe: le 9 mai
la monnaie: Le 1er janvier 2002, l'euro est devenu la monnaie unique europénne dans douze des pays membres: la France, l'Allemagne, l'Autriche, la Belgique, le Luxembourg, l'Italie, l'Espagne, le Portugal, les Pays-Bas, la Grèce, l'Irlande et la Finlande.
la devise[5]: «*In varietate concordia*» (Unie dans la diversité)

1. goods 2. funds 3. policy 4. anthem 5. motto

Core Instruction

TEACHING CHRONIQUES

1. Before class, prepare ten statements describing the four countries in the **Chroniques. On parle quatre langues dans ce pays. Ce pays est neutre. Un prince gouverne ce pays.** Form several teams. Write the ten statements on the board or on a transparency and have the teams compete and scan the text to try to find all the answers as quickly as possible. **(5 min.)**

2. Have students read the first section and ask for a volunteer to summarize the important facts about the European Union. **(5 min.)**

3. Have students read about the individual countries one at a time. Pause and ask simple comprehension questions after each section. Then have students answer the questions in **Après la lecture. (15 min.)**

La Belgique

La Belgique est une monarchie constitutionnelle et un état fédéral. Il y a trois communautés culturelles en Belgique: les Flamands[1], les francophones et les germanophones. Il ne faut pas les confondre[2] avec les quatre zones linguistiques, qui sont la région flamande (néerlandais[3]), la région bruxelloise (bilingue français-néerlandais), la région wallone (français) et les cantons de l'Est (allemand).

Les symboles

l'hymne national: la Brabançonne
la fête nationale: le 21 juillet
la monnaie: avant le 1er janvier 2002, le franc belge; depuis le 1er janvier 2002, l'euro
la devise: «L'union fait la force»

Le grand-duché de Luxembourg

Le Luxembourg est devenu indépendant en 1890. C'est une monarchie constitutionnelle. Avec la Belgique et les Pays-Bas, il forme en 1948 le Benelux (BElgique-NEderland-LUXembourg), une union économique. Le Benelux est à l'origine de l'Union européenne. Au Luxembourg, on parle luxembourgeois, allemand et français.

Les symboles

l'hymne national: Ons Heemecht
la fête nationale: le 23 juin
la monnaie: avant le 1er janvier 2002, le franc luxembourgeois; depuis le 1er janvier 2002, l'euro
la devise: «Nous voulons rester ce que nous sommes»

La Suisse

La Suisse est un état fédéral dont la constitution qui date de 1848, a été modifiée en 1997.

La naissance[4] de la Suisse remonte à 1291. Ce pays n'a pas participé à un conflit européen depuis 1515 mais sa neutralité n'a été reconnue officiellement qu'en 1815 au Congrès de Vienne.

Les symboles

l'hymne national: le Cantique suisse
la fête nationale: le 1er août
la monnaie: le franc suisse
la devise: «Un pour tous, tous pour un»

La principauté de Monaco

Monaco est une monarchie constitutionnelle. Le prince est le chef de l'état.

Selon le traité entre la France et Monaco, signé en 2002, la principauté restera indépendante même s'il n'y a pas de descendant dans la dynastie.

La principauté de Monaco n'est pas membre de l'UE mais elle utilise l'euro comme monnaie officielle. Monaco n'a pas le droit d'émettre[5] des billets en euros, mais peut produire des pièces de monnaie avec une face nationale spécifique à la principauté.

Les symboles

l'hymne national: Hymne monégasque
la fête nationale: le 19 novembre
la monnaie: avant le 1er janvier 2002, le franc français; depuis le 1er janvier 2002, l'euro
la devise: «Avec l'aide de Dieu»

APRÈS la lecture

🏵1.2

1. Est-ce que tous les pays européens sont membres de l'Union européenne?

2. Qu'est-ce que c'est que l'Union européenne?

3. Quel pays utilise l'euro comme monnaie mais ne fait pas partie de l'UE?

4. Quel pays francophone européen n'a pas fait la guerre depuis plus de sept cents ans?

5. Quels sont les pays francophones européens qui sont encore des monarchies?

1. Flemish 2. confuse 3. Dutch 4. birth 5. issue

Answers

1. Non. L'UE regroupe 25 pays.
2. la libre circulation des personnes, des biens, des services et des capitaux dans ses pays membres
3. Monaco
4. la Suisse
5. la Belgique, le Luxembourg et la principauté de Monaco

Teaching Suggestion

Have students select the Francophone country in Europe that they are most interested in. Group students who chose the same country together. Have groups research their their chosen country's history and prepare an oral presentation for the class
🏵 1.3, 3.1

Postreading

In 1876, famous French author Victor Hugo was already envisioning a unified Europe. In his book, *Actes et paroles, Depuis l'exil* (1876), he states, **«Nous aurons ces grands États-Unis d'Europe, qui couronneront le vieux monde comme les États-Unis d'Amérique couronnent le nouveau.»** Discuss Hugo's quote with students. Ask them to compare the European Union with the United States of America. 🏵3.1

Recherches

Have students use the Internet to research the history of the European Union and prepare a chronology of the most important events. Remind students to document their sources. 🏵3.1

Differentiated Instruction

ADVANCED LEARNERS

Challenge Have students write a paragraph about the potential benefits and disadvantages associated with being a member country of the European Union. Have them share their ideas and discuss them in class. 🏵1.3

MULTIPLE INTELLIGENCES

Mathematical Before doing the Postreading activity, have good math students prepare one table for the European Union and one for the United States with facts and information they will be able to use in their discussion. They might include: area, population, government type, natural resources, imports/exports, gross national product, etc. 🏵1.3, 3.1

Géoculture Overview

L'outre-mer

Bienvenue! This section is designed to familiarize the students with the geographic location, history, and cultural practices of the region to be explored. It provides a guide for classroom discussion and discovery of the differences and similarities of the student's own culture and that of the French-speaking world.

Géoculture (sidebar)

50-Minute Lesson Plans

Day 1

Lesson Sequence
Géoculture: L'outre-mer, pp. 360–361
- Have students locate the regions belonging to **L'outre-mer** on the map. Can students guess what the major industries of these areas are? They should give reasons for choosing certain industries. **10 min.**
- Go over the photos and captions with the students. **10 min.**
- Do Map Activities, p. 360. **5 min.**
- Discuss Background Information, p. 360. **11 min.**
- Complete **Géo-quiz. 1 min.**
- Show **Géoculture** video. **3 min.**
- Have students answer **Questions**, p. 361. **10 min.**

Optional Resources
- **Savais-tu que...?**, p. 361
- Research Online!, p. 359B

Homework Suggestions
Online Practice (**go.hrw.com**, Keyword: BD3 CH9)
Interactive Tutor, Ch. 9
🌸 1.2, 1.3, 3.1

Day 2

Lesson Sequence
Géoculture: L'outre-mer, pp. 362–363
- Briefly revisit main points about geography. **5 min.**
- Go over the photos and captions with the students. **8 min.**
- Ask students to put the historical events mentioned in the **Géoculture** in context with events in France. **7 min.**
- Have students answer **As-tu compris?** questions, p. 363. **5 min.**
- Play the Map Game on p. 359B. **25 min.**

Optional Resources
- Advanced Learners, p. 359B ▲
- Multiple Intelligences, p. 359B
- Thinking Critically, p. 359B
- **Prépare-toi pour le quiz**, p. 359B
- Interdisciplinary Links, pp. 362–363

Homework Suggestions
Activité, p. 363
Study for the **Géoculture** quiz.
🌸 1.1, 1.2, 1.3, 3.1

90-Minute Lesson Plan

Block 1

Lesson Sequence
Géoculture: L'outre-mer, pp. 360–363
- Have students locate the regions belonging to **L'outre-mer** on the map. Can students guess what the major industries of these areas are? They should give reasons for choosing certain industries. **10 min.**
- Go over the photos and captions with the students. **20 min.**
- Do Map Activities, p. 360. **5 min.**
- Discuss Background Information, p. 360. **10 min.**
- Complete **Géo-quiz. 1 min.**
- Show **Géoculture** video. **4 min.**
- Have students answer **Questions**, p. 361. **5 min.**
- Have students answer **As-tu compris?** questions, p. 363. **5 min.**
- Ask students to put the historical events mentioned in the **Géoculture** in context with events in France. **5 min.**
- Play the Map Game on p. 359B. **25 min.**

Optional Resources
- **Savais-tu que ...?**, p. 361 ▲
- Advanced Learners, p. 359B ▲
- Multiple Intelligences, p. 359B
- Thinking Critically, p. 359B
- Research Online!, p. 359B
- Interdisciplinary Links, pp. 362-363
- **Prépare-toi pour le quiz**, p. 359B

Homework Suggestions
Online Practice (**go.hrw.com**, Keyword: BD3 CH9)
Interactive Tutor, Ch. 9
Activité, p. 363
Study for the **Géoculture** quiz.
🌸 1.1, 1.2, 1.3, 3.1

KEY

▲ **Advanced Learners** ◆ **Slower Pace Learners** ● **Special Learning Needs**

Differentiated Instruction

Advanced Learners

Extension Have students find three more dates that could be included on the timeline. Students should do their research in the library or on the Internet. They should provide the date and a three-sentence description of each event. Students may also want to include pictures that illustrate the events. 🍀 1.3, 3.1

Multiple Intelligences

Spatial Have students transfer the dates of events discussed on the timeline to their corresponding location on the map. Students should use this map as a guide to describe to the class the events discussed on the timeline. 🍀 1.1, 3.1

Thinking Critically

Analyzing French Polynesia is an administrative division of France called **pays d'outre-mer (POM).** Have students discuss the advantages and disadvantages of this form of government. Have students name other forms of French overseas administration. 🍀 3.1

Quiz Preparation/Enrichment

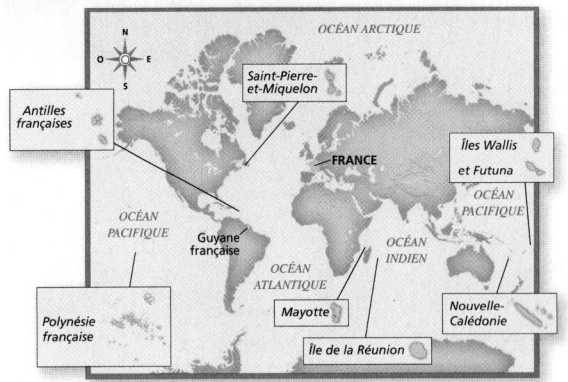

Map Game

Have students work with a partner to create a Word Search puzzle. Students should hide within the grid at least ten terms that are on the map. These terms should be hidden horizontally, vertically, diagonally, backwards or forwards. Names consisting of two or more words should be written without spaces between words. Hyphens should be considered letters. Have partnes make either a list of the hidden terms or a copy of their grid on which all the terms have been shaded in. Partners should complete the Word Search of another pair.

Prépare-toi pour le quiz

1. Working in groups of 3–4, students should describe in French the location of **Les Antilles (Martinique, Dominique, Marie-Galante, Guadeloupe), La Guyane, Saint-Pierre-et-Miquelon,** and **La Polynésie française.**

2. Have a student from each group read his/her group's description of the location of one of the areas without naming the area. The other groups have to guess the area described. If they are unable to guess the area, they may want to make suggestions on how to improve the description. 🍀 1.1, 3.1

Géoculture

Research Online!

Musique et danse Students should investigate the traditional music and dance of Martinique and Tahiti and compare them. They should find Web sites that show pictures of musical instruments and provide links to samples of the music. Ask students to document their sources by noting the names and the URLs of all the sites they consulted. Have students present their research to the class. 🍀 1.3, 3.1

Resources

Planning:
Lesson Planner
 One-Stop Planner

Presentation:
 Teaching Transparencies
Carte 1
DVD Tutor, Disc 2

Practice:
Cahier d'activitiés
Media Guide
Interactive Tutor, Disc 2

Map
ACTIVITIES

1. Have students look at the map on page 360 of their textbook. Ask them which of the overseas locations is not an island (**la Guyane**). Ask students why they think France chose **la Guyane** as a launch site for its space program. (It's on the coast with no large inhabited islands close by.)

2. Ask students which location is the farthest away from France (**la Polynésie**) and which is the closest (**Saint-Pierre-et-Miquelon**). Given the distance of these places, ask students why they think France maintains close ties with them. (They are strategically located, providing France with a foothold in other regions. They also supply agricultural goods or other products for France.)

DVD
Géoculture

Géoculture
L'outre-mer

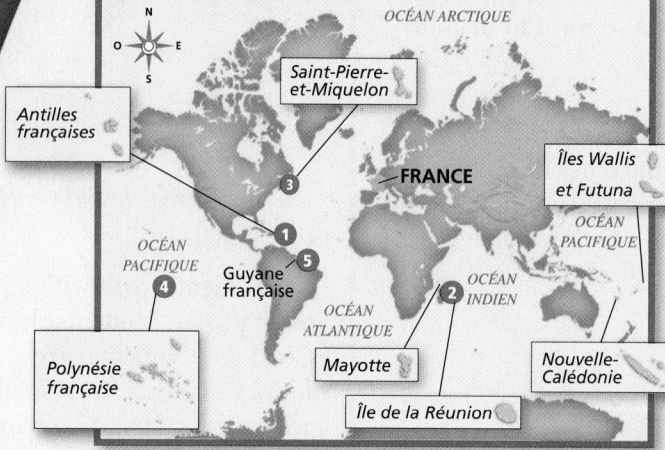

▲ **L'ÎLE DE LA RÉUNION** continue à s'agrandir car son volcan, La Fournaise, est toujours en activité. ❷

▼ **LES ANTILLES: La Martinique** vient du mot arawak «Madinina» qui veut dire «l'île aux fleurs». ❶

▼ **LES ANTILLES: La Guadeloupe** est un vrai paradis pour les amateurs de plongée. La réserve Cousteau protège environ 400 hectares de fonds marins où l'on trouve une impressionnante variété de coraux et de poissons. ❶

Savais-tu que...?
La Martinique, la Guadeloupe, la Guyane et la Réunion sont des DOM (départements d'outre-mer) et sont soumis aux mêmes règles juridiques que la métropole.

Background Information

Geography

La Polynésie française is located in the South Pacific Ocean. It includes five archipelagos. An archipelago is a chain or cluster of islands. There are 118 islands and atolls in all.

Saint-Pierre-et-Miquelon is made up of eight small islands, covering an area just one and one-half times the size of Washington D.C. Mostly barren rock, the islands are cold, wet, and foggy throughout most of the year.

History

Christopher Columbus landed on Guadeloupe in 1493 and on Martinique in 1502. Prior to the arrival of the Europeans, the Arawaks and then the Caribs had lived on the islands. The French arrived in the 17th century and introduced the plantation system, growing crops such as sugar and coffee. After many French "volunteers" and the native population of Caribs died out, slaves were brought from Africa to work on the plantations. In the 18th century, the islands became a center of pirate activity.

SAINT-PIERRE-et-MIQUELON:

Saint-Pierre est le centre administratif et commercial du seul territoire français en Amérique du Nord. La collectivité regroupe deux îles et des îlots au sud de Terre-Neuve. ③

▲ LA POLYNÉSIE FRANÇAISE:

Hiva Oa appartient à l'archipel des Marquises. C'est là que le peintre français Paul Gauguin a vécu à la fin de sa vie. ④

➤ LA POLYNÉSIE FRANÇAISE:

Tahiti est la plus grande île de l'archipel de la Société. Cette île est associée à l'histoire du capitaine Cook et de la mutinerie du Bounty. ④

♥ LA GUYANE: Kourou

abrite le Centre national d'études spatiales (CNES). C'est de là que la fusée européenne Ariane est lancée dans l'espace. ⑤

◄ LA GUYANE:

95% du territoire guyanais est recouvert par une forêt équatoriale très difficile d'accès. ⑤

Géo-quiz

✿1.2, 3.1

Quel est le territoire français situé en Amérique du Nord?

Saint-Pierre-et-Miquelon

Cultures

✿ Products and Perspectives

Paul Gauguin (1848–1903) was one of the most important French masters of Post-impressionist art. His painting style and use of color helped lead the way to 20th century modern art. Born in Paris, Gauguin studied with well-known Impressionist painter Camille Pissarro. Frustrated by lack of recognition in France and eager to find refuge from the West "made rotten by industrial civilization," Gauguin set sail for Polynesia, in 1891. He painted many portraits of Polynesian life; including his masterpiece, *D'où venons-nous? Que sommes-nous? Où allons-nous?* Gauguin called this painting his "testament," including themes of life and death, religion, and fate. Have students search online to find out more about Gauguin's Tahitian paintings.

✿ 1.3, 2.2, 3.1, 3.2

Comparisons

Comparing and Contrasting

The **CNES (Centre National d'Études Spatiales)** is a government agency that develops and carries out France's space policy in Europe. Its objective is to invent space systems for the future, improve existing space technologies, and guarantee independent access to space for France. **CNES** programs focus on gaining access to space, civil applications in space, sustainable development, scientific and technological research, as well as security and defense. Have students compare **CNES** and NASA (National Areonautics and Space Administration), the U.S. equivalent to **CNES**. ✿4.2

Savais-tu que...?

- Cayenne pepper, a hot and spicy member of the capsicum family, takes its name from the capital city of **la Guyane**, where it grows in abundance.
- **Saint-Pierre-et-Miquelon** is a **collectivité d'outre-mer.** This means it has limited freedom in administering its affairs and has a lesser status than a **département**, a governmental division much like a county in the United States.
- Tahiti is the setting for two bestselling books written by American authors. Herman Melville's *Mutiny on the Bounty* and James Michener's *Tales of the South Pacific* were also made into films.

Questions

✿ 1.2

1. **Quel département d'outre-mer continue à s'agrandir grâce à son volcan?** (l'île de la Réunion)

2. **Qu'est-ce que la réserve Cousteau protège?** (environ 400 hectares de fonds marins)

3. **Quelle île est associée avec le capitaine Cook et la mutinerie du Bounty?** (Tahiti)

4. **Qu'est-ce qu'on trouve à Kourou en Guyane?** (le Centre national d'études spatiales)

5. **D'où vient le nom de la Martinique?** (d'un mot arawak qui veut dire «île aux fleurs»)

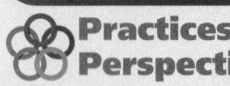

L'histoire
L'outre-mer

Cultures

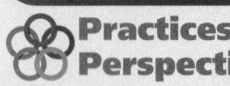 Practices and Perspectives

In 2006, France declared a new national holiday to be celebrated on May 10. The holiday commemorates the abolition of slavery in France's territories in the 19th century. The date chosen for the holiday marks the passage of a law in 2001 declaring slavery and the slave trade, both past and present, a crime against humanity. The 2001 law also requires schools to include lessons in their curriculum about slavery. Ask students how Black heritage is commemorated in the U.S. (Black History Month in February). Then ask if their state has a holiday celebrating the end of slavery, and if so, when is it and how it is celebrated. 🔗 2.1

Connections

Social Studies Link

Louis-Antoine de Bougainville's book, **Voyage autour du monde,** described Tahiti as a place where people lived uncorrupted by civilization. This description lent support to the concept of "the noble savage," a popular idea of the 18th century. This concept is based on the notion that human nature is essentially good and that civilization corrupts it. Many of Rousseau's ideas, as expressed in his work, **Du contrat social,** lay the philosophical groundwork for the French and American Revolutions. Rousseau claims that humankind is born free, but some freedom must be given up in order for society to function properly. He proposes that an agreement be made between the state and its citizens regarding each party's responsibilities and rights. Ask students if they agree or disagree with Rousseau's ideas of the noble savage and the social contract, and why. 🔗 3.2

1690–1763
Entre 1690 et 1763, la France et la Grande-Bretagne se sont disputé l'archipel de Saint-Pierre-et-Miquelon. À plusieurs reprises, tout a été détruit et les habitants ont été déportés. En 1763, la France fête la signature du traité de Paris qui lui a définitivement attribué cet archipel.

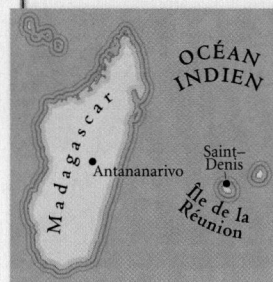

1793
En 1793, l'île de la Réunion a reçu son nom actuel, abandonnant le nom de Bourbon qui était celui des rois de France. Ce nom est probablement une référence aux réunions clandestines des révolutionnaires français.

1768
En 1768, **Louis-Antoine de Bougainville** a fait escale à Tahiti, un an après l'Anglais Samuel Wallis. À son retour en France, il a publié **Voyage autour du monde** dans lequel il décrit l'île comme un paradis sur terre. Sa description de Tahiti a influencé les idées des philosophes de la Révolution française.

1848
En 1848, un décret a aboli l'esclavage dans tous les territoires français et a accordé aux esclaves le statut de citoyen et le droit de vote. Ce décret a été adopté en partie grâce aux efforts de **Victor Schœlcher**, écrivain et homme politique français.

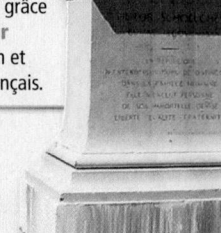

TEACHING L'HISTOIRE

1. Ask students what they expect to learn about the history of these French overseas territories, given their location and their former status as colonies.

2. Before reading each caption, discuss the picture that accompanies it. Then have students read the caption silently. Remind them to focus on key words and information. Ask for a volunteer to summarize the caption. Check comprehension with **As-tu compris?** questions after reading all of the captions.

If any students miss an answer, go over that caption again as a class.

3. Ask students to compare the similarities and differences in the history of these French overseas departments and territories and those Francophone countries that became independent.

4. Assign the **Activité** questions on page 363 as homework.

Online Practice
go.hrw.com
Online Edition
KEYWORD: BD3 CH9

Chapitres 9–10

L'outre-mer

1900   2000

1902
En 1902, la montagne Pelée, volcan de la Martinique, est entrée en éruption et a complètement détruit la ville de Saint-Pierre, appelée le «Paris des Antilles». Une seule personne a survécu à cette catastrophe: le prisonnier!

2004
En 2004, la Polynésie française est devenue un **pays d'outre-mer (POM)**. Un POM est une division administrative de la France qui a plus d'autonomie qu'un territoire. Par exemple, la Polynésie française peut faire ses propres lois et accorder la citoyenneté polynésienne. La France métropolitaine continue à contrôler la défense, la justice et l'économie.

1852–1953
En 1852, la France a commencé à déporter des prisonniers en Guyane. Pendant près de 100 ans, 70.000 personnes environ ont été envoyées au **bagne** (colonie pénitentiaire). Un des bagnards les plus connus était Henri Charrière, dit Papillon. Un livre autobiographique et un film racontent sa vie au bagne et son évasion.

1966
Après l'indépendance de l'Algérie en 1962, la France a dû abandonner le site de ses **essais nucléaires** dans le Sahara et a choisi les atolls polynésiens, Mururoa et Fangataufa, pour servir de nouvelles bases à ses essais nucléaires. Le premier essai a eu lieu en 1966. Ils ont cessé en janvier 1996.

Interactive TUTOR

Activité
🌸1.2, 3.1

1. Quels pays se sont disputé Saint-Pierre-et-Miquelon?
2. Qui a lutté pour l'aboliton de l'esclavage?
3. Comment Bougainville a-t-il décrit Tahiti?
4. Qu'est-ce qu'un POM peut faire?
5. Qu'est-ce qu'on faisait dans les atolls polynésiens de Mururoa et Fangataufa?
6. Qu'est-ce que c'est, le bagne?

As-tu compris?
You can use the following questions to check comprehension of the **Géoculture**.

1. À quoi le nom de l'île de la Réunion fait-il référence? (aux réunions clandestines des révolutionnaires français)
2. Quelle a été la conséquence de l'éruption du volcan la montagne Pelée en 1902? (La ville de Saint-Pierre a été complètement détruite.)
3. Pourquoi est-ce que les habitants de Saint-Pierre-et-Miquelon on beaucoup souffert entre 1690 et 1814? (La Grande-Bretagne et la France se disputaient l'archipel.)
4. Qu'est-ce que le livre de Bougainville a influencé? (les idées des philosophes de la Révolution française)
5. Qu'est-ce que le décret de 1848 a accordé aux anciens esclaves? (le statut de citoyen et le droit de vote)
6. Où est-ce que les prisonniers français ont été envoyés pendant près de 100 ans? (au bagne en Guyane) 🌸1.2

Answers
1. la France et la Grande-Bretagne
2. Victor Schœlcher
3. comme un paradis sur terre
4. Il peut faire ses propres lois et accorder la citoyenneté.
5. des essais nucléaires
6. C'est une colonie pénitentiaire.

INTERDISCIPLINARY LINKS

Les sciences
🌸1.3, 3.1
Science Link Mount Pelée is a stratovolcano, a tall, cone-shaped mountain made up of hardened lava and volcanic ash. It is part of a curved, 530-mile-long chain of volcanos that stretches from Puerto Rico to Venezuela. This is where the Caribbean tectonic plate and the Atlantic plate meet. There are seven major tectonic plates, or pieces of the Earth's crust, that make up the planet's surface. Have students research this volcanic arc and create a diagram in French showing the type of volcanic activity that occurs along it.

Les sciences sociales
Government Link Metropolitan France is divided into 22 **régions** (including Corsica) and subdivided into 96 **départements**. There are four overseas **régions** which are also **départements** (**les DOM-ROM**). Other overseas administrative divisions include overseas territorial collectivities (**les COM**), a collectivity *sui generis*, an overseas territory (**TOM**), and overseas countries (**les POM**). Have students create a chart of France's administrative divisions, the names of the places that correspond to each overseas division, and each division's rights and responsibilites.

Assess

Assessment Program
Quiz: Géoculture
Differentiated Practice and Assessment CD-ROM
Online Assessment
my.hrw.com
Test Generator

Planning Guide

Chapter Section		Resources
Vocabulaire 1 • Fine arts	pp. 366–369	📖 Teaching Transparencies: Vocabulaire 9.1, 9.2; Bell Work 9.1, 9.2, 9.3, 9.4
Grammaire 1 • Review: Inversion • Review: Present participles used as adjectives	pp. 370–373	💻 Cahier de vocabulaire et grammaire, pp. 97–102 💻 Grammar Tutor for Students of French 💻 Cahier d'activités, pp. 81–83
Application 1 • **Un peu plus:** **Si** and **oui**	pp. 374–375	💻 Media Guide, pp. 33–36 💻 **Assessment Program** Quiz: Vocabulaire 1, pp. 239–240 Quiz: Grammaire 1, pp. 241–242 Quiz: Application 1, pp. 243–244
Culture • **Lecture culturelle: La sculpture, l'âme des Marquises** • **Comparaisons** • **Communauté et professions**	pp. 376–377	💻 Cahier d'activités, p. 84
Vocabulaire 2 • Music and the performing arts	pp. 378–381	📖 Teaching Transparencies: Vocabulaire 9.3, 9.4; Bell Work 9.5, 9.6, 9.7, 9.8
Grammaire 2 • Review: The comparative and superlative • Review: Demonstrative pronouns	pp. 382–385	💻 Cahier de vocabulaire et grammaire, pp. 103–108 💻 Grammar Tutor for Students of French 💻 Cahier d'activités, pp. 85–87
Application 2 • **Un peu plus:** The verbs **savoir** and **connaître**	pp. 386–387	💻 Media Guide, pp. 33–36 💻 **Assessment Program** Quiz: Vocabulaire 2, pp. 245–246 Quiz: Grammaire 2, pp. 247–248 Quiz: Application 2, pp. 249–250
Lecture • **Matisse parle** • **Georges Braque**	pp. 388–391	💻 Cahier d'activités, p. 88 💻 Reading Strategies and Skills Handbook 💻 Advanced Reader
L'atelier de l'écrivain • **Un exposé**	pp. 392–393	💻 **Assessment Program** Quiz: Lecture, p. 251 Quiz: Écriture, p. 252
Prépare-toi pour l'examen • **Résumé de vocabulaire et grammaire**	pp. 394–397	📖 Teaching Transparencies Picture Sequences, Situation, Ch. 9 💻 Media Guide, pp. 36, 69–70
Activités préparatoires **Révisions cumulatives**	pp. 398–399 pp. 400–401	💻 **Assessment Program** Examen: Chapitre 9, pp. 253–258 Examen oral: Chapitre 9, p. 325
		📖 Teaching Transparencies, Fine Art, Ch. 9 💻 Cahier d'activités, pp. 89–90
Chroniques • L'impressionnisme • De l'art naïf au surréalisme • La sculpture sous toutes ses formes • Le hit-parade • Au rythme de l'Afrique	pp. 440–449	💻 Reading Strategies and Skills Handbook 💻 Advanced Reader

Pacing Suggestions

	Essential	Recommended	Optional
Vocabulaire 1 • Fine arts	✔		
Grammaire 1 • Review: Inversion • Review: Present participles used as adjectives • Flash culture	✔		
Application 1 • **Un peu plus:** **Si** and **oui**	✔		
Culture • **Lecture culturelle: La sculpture, l'âme des Marquises** • **Comparaisons** • **Communauté et professions**		✔	
Vocabulaire 2 • Music and the performing arts • Flash culture	✔		
Grammaire 2 • Review: The comparative and superlative • Review: Demonstrative pronouns • Flash culture	✔		
Application 2 • **Un peu plus:** The verbs **savoir** and **connaître**	✔		
Lecture • **Matisse parle** • **Georges Braque**		✔	
L'atelier de l'écrivain • **Un exposé**			
Prépare-toi pour l'examen		✔	
Activités préparatoires		✔	
Révisions cumulatives			✔
Chroniques			✔

Technology

Bien dit! Online
• Student Edition with multi-media
• SoundBooth recording tool
• Interactive activities with feedback
• Self-tests with feedback
• Cahier d'activités (Interactive workbook)
• Cahier de vocabulaire et grammaire (Interactive workbook)
• Holt Online Assessment

DVD Program
• Télé-roman: Camille et compagnie
• Télé-culture: Interviews

Interactive Tutor
• Interactive practice games
• Writing and recording workshops
• Before You Know It™ Flashcards

Audio Program
• Student Edition Listening Activities
• Assessment listening activities
• Songs

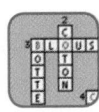

One-Stop Planner
• Complete media and print resources
• ExamView Pro Test Generator
• Holt Calendar Planner

PuzzlePro
• Customizable word games

Differentiated Practice and Assessment CD

For slower pace and advanced learner options, see the Differentiated Practice and Assessment CD.

Planning Guide

chapitre 9

Projects

Couverture de livre

Students will design and make a book jacket for a book of their choice that is written in French. The jacket will be designed as follows:

🏵 3.1, 5.1

Suggested Sequence

1. Have students research, in the library or on the Internet, books written in French. Students should decide on a book and read summaries and reviews of it. (Ideally, students will read the book.) Have students research the author's background, residence, family, hobbies, and other works.

2. Students write the text for the book jacket, including a summary of the story for the inside front flap of the book jacket, a description of the author for the back cover, and three favorable reviews and French titles of other works by the author (if available) for the inside back flap. The back flap should also include a price. The summary should entice others to read the book, without revealing the ending of the story. Students might exchange papers for peer editing.

3. While you correct the rough drafts, have students prepare the illustrations for their book jacket. They might use magazine or catalogue pictures to create a collage or cut out letters to spell the title and the author's name.

4. After students have corrected their rough draft, they should type or write it, cut it apart, and paste the sections in the proper places on the book jacket. You might display the finished jackets in the library.

Grading the project

Suggested point distribution
(100 points total)
Content . . . . 20 pts.
Language use . . . . 20 pts.
Variety of vocabulary . . . . 20 pts.
Creativity/Effort . . . . 20 pts.
Overall appearance . . . . 20 pts.

e-community

e-mail forum:
Post the following questions on the classroom e-mail forum:

> **Location:** http://french
>
> **Quelle sorte de musique te passionne? Pourquoi?**
>
> **Que ressens-tu quand tu écoutes de la musique?** 🏵 5.1

All students will contribute to the list and then share the items.

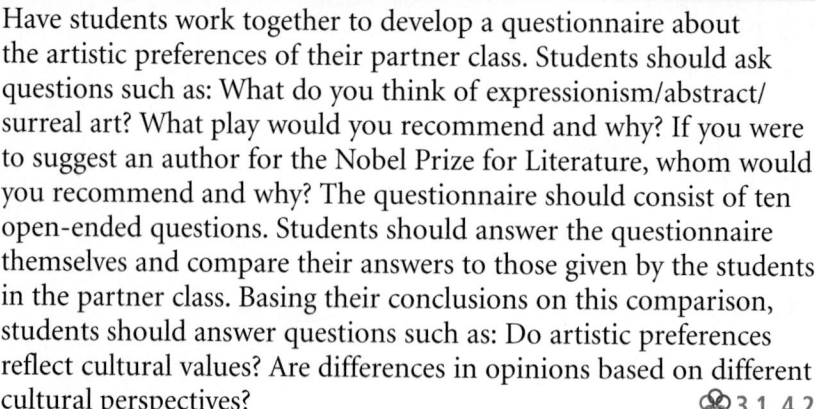

Partner Class Project

Have students work together to develop a questionnaire about the artistic preferences of their partner class. Students should ask questions such as: What do you think of expressionism/abstract/ surreal art? What play would you recommend and why? If you were to suggest an author for the Nobel Prize for Literature, whom would you recommend and why? The questionnaire should consist of ten open-ended questions. Students should answer the questionnaire themselves and compare their answers to those given by the students in the partner class. Basing their conclusions on this comparison, students should answer questions such as: Do artistic preferences reflect cultural values? Are differences in opinions based on different cultural perspectives? 🏵 3.1, 4.2

Game Bank
For game ideas, see pages T60–T63.

Projects

La biguine

Martinique is well-known throughout the Caribbean for its traditional dances and music. Perhaps one of the most important folkdances of the country is **la biguine,** made internationally famous by the American composer Cole Porter in the 1930s when he wrote a song called "Begin the Biguine." **La biguine** is a lively partner dance, which is believed to combine elements from the **calenda,** a dance with African roots, and **le menuet** and **branle,** ballroom dances introduced to the island by the French. **La biguine** has been popular for decades and is still danced everywhere on the island, even though its popularity has been recently challenged by the more modern **zouk.** Have students research the music of Martinique. Students should investigate popular musical instruments and analyze the lyrics of Martinican songs. Do the lyrics have common themes? ✿ 3.1, 3.2

La cuisine

The Aztecs and the Mayas began trading chocolate long ago. Christopher Columbus knew of it, but it was the explorer Hernán Cortés who first brought chocolate to Europe. Originally, chocolate was used as a drink ingredient. The nineteenth century saw the invention of the first chocolate bar. Today, Switzerland and Belgium are reputed to make the best chocolate. Encourage students to prepare creole-style hot chocolate in their home economics class or at home. ✿ 1.2, 3.1, 5.1, 5.2

Chocolat chaud à la créole Pour 4 tasses

4 tasses de lait
1 œuf
4 tasses de chocolat en poudre
6 cuillères à soupe de sucre roux
1 cuillère à soupe de farine de maïs

1 cuillère à café d'extrait de vanille
1 bâton de cannelle
1 tasse de cacahouètes ou d'amandes

Faire chauffer le lait avec la vanille et la cannelle. Dans un bol, mélanger le chocolat en poudre, le sucre, la farine de maïs et l'œuf avec un peu de lait froid. Verser dans le lait chaud et laisser épaissir. Retirer le bâton de cannelle et ajouter les cacahouètes ou les amandes. Servir chaud.

Vocabulaire  à l'œuvre **1**

2 p. 368, CD 9, Tr. 1

1. — Qu'est-ce que tu penses des œuvres de Paul Rimet?

— Elles sont surprenantes! Et son modèle est fantastique! Je la connais. Elle peut poser pendant des heures sans bouger!

2. — Cette exposition t'a plu, Normand?

— Je l'ai trouvée passionnante! J'adore la toile de Maxime Duvallois. Je vais peut-être l'acheter.

— Ah bon? Je ne savais pas que tu aimais tant l'art abstrait.

3. — Alors, comment trouves-tu les tableaux exposés à la galerie Chantelon?

— Ce n'est pas mon style. Je n'aime pas trop les natures mortes, moi. Je préfère les paysages.

4. — Je voudrais offrir quelque chose d'original à ma mère pour son anniversaire. Qu'est-ce que tu penses de ces poteries?

— Bof. Elles ne sont pas terribles. Offre-lui plutôt une poterie de Louis Legrand. Celles-là sont vraiment pas mal. Il expose à la galerie de la rue des Lilas en ce moment.

Answers for Activity 2
1. b   **2.** c   **3.** a   **4.** d

Grammaire à l'œuvre **1**

8 p. 370, CD 9, Tr. 2

1. Elle te plaît, cette sculpture?

2. Que penses-tu de ces aquarelles?

3. Comment est-ce que tu trouves ces natures mortes?

4. À propos, connais-tu ce peintre?

5. Savais-tu que ce tableau était du même artiste?

6. Au fait, il n'a pas aussi peint des natures mortes?

Answers for Activity 8
1. b   **2.** a   **3.** b   **4.** a   **5.** a   **6.** b

Application **1**

19 p. 374, CD 9, Tr. 3

1. — Vous n'êtes pas allés voir l'exposition d'art abstrait, alors.

— Mais si, on y est allé et je l'ai trouvée géniale!

2. — Tu n'as pas trouvé que Mélanie avait l'air malade?

— Si! Je lui ai même conseillé d'aller voir un médecin!

3. — Je ne crois pas que les enfants aient trouvé ces BD très amusantes.

— Mais si, ils ont beaucoup ri en les lisant.

4. — Je pense que cette exposition n'était pas géniale!

— Oui, ils auraient pu faire un effort.

5. — Charles m'a dit que son fils s'était inscrit à un cours de sculpture.

— Oui. Il paraît qu'il est vraiment doué.

Answers for Activity 19
1. a   **2.** a   **3.** a   **4.** b   **5.** b

Vocabulaire à l'œuvre **2**

24 p. 380, CD 9, Tr. 4

1. Oh là là! Tu as vu les trapézistes? C'est incroyable, ce qu'ils font! J'ai peur qu'ils tombent, moi!

2. Moi, ce que j'aime le mieux, c'est ce mélange de danse, de théâtre et de chant. Et puis, celle-ci est vraiment drôle!

3. Je te recommande plutôt d'aller voir Le lac des cygnes. La chorégraphie et les costumes sont magnifiques!

4. Ne va surtout pas le voir! Les décors sont horribles, l'orchestre est nul et les chanteurs chantent faux!

5. Ça vaut vraiment le coup d'aller voir Gilles Martin sur scène. Il chante super bien et son groupe est génial!

Answers for Activity 24
1. d   **2.** a   **3.** c   **4.** f   **5.** e

Grammaire 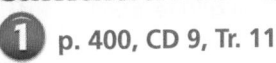à l'œuvre 2

29 p. 382, CD 9, Tr. 5

— Je n'ai pas trouvé la comédie musicale aussi amusante que la pièce de théâtre que nous avons vue la semaine dernière.

— Au cirque, les jongleurs étaient aussi géniaux que les trapézistes.

— Le chapiteau était plus petit que celui de l'autre cirque.

— Le premier clown ne chantait déjà pas très bien, mais alors le deuxième chantait vraiment mal.

— L'orchestre jouait mieux que celui de l'opéra.

Answers for Activity 29
1. a **2.** b **3.** a **4.** b **5.** a

Application 2

39 p. 386, CD 9, Tr. 6

1. Tu [NOISE] ce chef d'orchestre?

Non, mais mes parents le [NOISE].

2. Est-ce que tu [NOISE] à quelle heure le spectacle commence?

Non, je ne [NOISE] pas, mais demande à Martin, lui, il doit [NOISE].

Answers for Activity 39
1. connais, connaissent
2. sais, sais, savoir

Prépare-toi pour l'examen

6 p. 395, CD 9, Tr. 9

1. Le chef d'orchestre donne la mesure aux musiciens.

2. Tu as vu l'affiche à côté du chapiteau?

3. L'artiste a utilisé de la peinture à l'huile pour peindre ce tableau.

4. Les spectateurs ont beaucoup aimé l'acteur principal.

5. Maintenant, c'est un sculpteur, mais il a commencé par faire de la poterie.

6. On n'a pu voir que les œuvres les plus récentes de l'artiste.

Activités préparatoires

Listening, p. 398, CD 9, Tr. 10

1. Que pensez-vous de ces gravures-ci? Ou préférez-vous cette jolie aquarelle?

2. Regarde ce clown! Il est drôle!

Je ne sais pas ce que j'aime mieux: les trapézistes, les clowns ou les jongleurs.

Answers for Listening Activity
1. b **2.** a

Révisions cumulatives  chapitres 1-9

1 p. 400, CD 9, Tr. 11

1. Ce chef d'orchestre est très connu. Si tu en as l'occasion, je te recommande d'aller le voir.

2. Elle utilise un tour pour créer ses œuvres d'art.

3. Le modèle n'a pas bougé pendant que l'artiste faisait son croquis.

4. Elle aime danser et elle suit des cours de ballet.

5. Personnellement, la partition choisie par l'orchestre m'a beaucoup plu.

6. Il est vraiment doué pour le dessin. Il n'a suivi aucun cours.

Answers for Activity 1
1. d **2.** b **3.** c **4.** a **5.** d **6.** c

50-Minute Lesson Plans

L'art en fête

Day 1

OBJECTIVE
Ask for and give opinions

Core Instruction
Chapter Opener, pp. 364–365
• See Using the Photo, p. 364.
  5 min.
• See Chapter Objectives, p. 364.
  5 min.

Vocabulaire 1, pp. 366–369
• Present **Vocabulaire 1,**
  pp. 366–367. See Teaching
  Vocabulaire, p. 366. **15 min.**
• Present **Exprimons-nous!,**
  p. 367. **5 min.**
• Do Activity 1, p. 368. **5 min.**
• Play Audio CD 9, Tr. 1 for Activity
  2, p. 368. **5 min.**
• Have students do Activities 3–4,
  p. 368. **10 min.**

Optional Resources
• Advanced Learners, p. 367 ▲
• Multiple Intelligences, p. 367

Homework Suggestions
**Cahier de vocabulaire et
  grammaire,** pp. 97–98
  ✿ 1.1. 1.2, 1.3, 3.1

Day 2

OBJECTIVE
*Introduce and change a topic of
conversation; Use inversion*

Core Instruction
Vocabulaire 1, pp. 366–369
• Do Bell Work 9.1, p. 366.
  5 min.
• See Teaching **Exprimons-
  nous!,** p. 368. **10 min.**
• Have students do Activities 5–7,
  p. 369. **20 min.**

Grammaire 1, pp. 370–373
• See Teaching **Grammaire,**
  p. 370. **10 min.**
• Present **Flash culture,** p. 371.
  5 min.

Optional Resources
• Advanced Learners, p. 369 ▲
• Special Learning Needs, p. 369 ●

Homework Suggestions
Study for **Quiz: Vocabulaire 1**
**Cahier de vocabulaire et
  grammaire,** p. 99
Online Practice (**go.hrw.com,**
  Keyword: BD3 CH9)
  ✿ 1.1, 1.2, 4.2

Day 3

OBJECTIVE
Use inversion

Core Instruction
Vocabulaire 1, pp. 366–369
• Review **Vocabulaire 1,**
  pp. 366–369. **10 min.**
• Give **Quiz: Vocabulaire 1.**
  20 min.

Grammaire 1, pp. 370–373
• Play Audio CD 9, Tr. 2 for Activity
  8, p. 370. **5 min.**
• Have students do Activities
  9–12, pp. 370–371. **15 min.**

Optional Resources
• Communication (TE), p. 371
• Slower Pace Learners, p. 371 ◆
• Special Learning Needs, p. 371 ●

Homework Suggestions
**Cahier de vocabulaire et
  grammaire,** p. 100
Cahier d'activités, p. 81
Interactive Tutor, Ch. 9
Online Practice (**go.hrw.com,**
  Keyword: BD3 CH9)
  ✿ 1.1, 1.2

Day 4

OBJECTIVE
*Use present participles as
adjectives*

Core Instruction
Grammaire 1, pp. 370–373
• See Teaching **Grammaire,**
  p. 372. **10 min.**
• Have students do Activities
  13–17, pp. 372–373. **30 min.**

Application 1, pp. 374–375
• Have students do Activity 18,
  p. 374. **10 min.**

Optional Resources
• Communication (TE), p. 373
• Slower Pace Learners, p. 373 ◆
• Special Learning Needs, p. 373 ●

Homework Suggestions
Study for **Quiz: Grammaire 1**
**Cahier de vocabulaire et
  grammaire,** p. 101
Cahier d'activités, p. 82
Online Practice (**go.hrw.com,**
  Keyword: BD3 CH9)
  ✿ 1.1, 1.2, 1.3, 4.1

Day 5

OBJECTIVE
*Use **si** and **oui***

Core Instruction
Grammaire 1, pp. 370–373
• Review **Grammaire 1,**
  pp. 370–373. **10 min.**
• Give **Quiz: Grammaire 1.**
  20 min.

Application 1, pp. 374–375
• See Teaching **Un peu plus,**
  p. 374. **5 min.**
• Play Audio CD 9, Tr. 3 for
  Activity 19, p. 374. **5 min.**
• Have students do Activities
  20–23, pp. 374–375. **10 min.**

Optional Resources
• Communication (TE), p. 375
• Advanced Learners, p. 375 ▲

Homework Suggestions
Study for **Quiz: Application 1**
**Cahier de vocabulaire et
  grammaire,** p. 102
Cahier d'activités, p. 83
  ✿ 1.1, 1.2, 1.3, 3.1, 3.2

Day 6

OBJECTIVE
Learn about francophone culture

Core Instruction
Application 1, pp. 374–375
• Review **Application 1,**
  pp. 374–375. **10 min.**
• Give **Quiz: Application 1. 20 min.**

Culture, pp. 376–377
• See **Lecture culturelle** (TE),
  p. 376. **10 min.**
• See **Comparaisons et
  communauté** (TE), p. 376.
  10 min.

Optional Resources
• Cultures, p. 377
• Communities, p. 377
• Advanced Learners, p. 377 ▲
• Multiple Intelligences, p. 377

Homework Suggestions
Cahier d'activités, p. 84
Online Practice (**go.hrw.com,**
  Keyword: BD3 CH9)
Finish the **Communauté et
  professions** project, p. 377.
  ✿ 1.1, 1.2, 1.3, 2.1, 2.2,
  3.1, 4.2, 5.1, 5.2

Day 7

OBJECTIVE
*Make suggestions and
recommendations*

Core Instruction
Vocabulaire 2, pp. 378–381
• Do Bell Work 9.5, p. 378.
  5 min.
• Present **Vocabulaire 2,**
  pp. 378–379. See Teaching
  Vocabulaire, p. 378. **15 min.**
• Present **Exprimons-nous!,**
  p. 379. **10 min.**
• Play Audio CD 9, Tr. 4 for Activity
  24, p. 380. **5 min.**
• Have students do Activities
  25–26, p. 380. **15 min.**

Optional Resources
• TPR, p. 379
• Advanced Learners, p. 379 ▲
• Special Learning Needs, p. 379 ●
• Slower Pace Learners, p. 381 ◆

Homework Suggestions
**Cahier de vocabulaire et
  grammaire,** pp. 103–104
  ✿ 1.1, 1.2, 1.3

Day 8

OBJECTIVE
*Give an impression; Use the
comparative and superlative*

Core Instruction
Vocabulaire 2, pp. 378–381
• See Teaching **Exprimons-nous!,**
  p. 380. **10 min.**
• Have students do Activities
  27–28, p. 381. **15 min.**
• Present **Flash culture,** p. 381.
  5 min.

Grammaire 2, pp. 382–385
• See Teaching **Grammaire,**
  p. 382. **15 min.**
• Play Audio CD 9, Tr. 5 for Activity
  29, p. 382. **5 min.**

Optional Resources
• Special Learning Needs, p. 381 ●
• Advanced Learners, p. 383 ▲

Homework Suggestions
Study for **Quiz: Vocabulaire 2**
**Cahier de vocabulaire et
  grammaire,** p. 105
Interactive Tutor, Ch. 9
  ✿ 1.1, 1.2, 1.3, 4.2

Day 9

OBJECTIVE
Use the comparative and superlative

Core Instruction
Vocabulaire 2, pp. 378–381
• Review **Vocabulaire 2**, pp. 378–381. **10 min.**
• Give **Quiz: Vocabulaire 2**. **20 min.**

Grammaire 2, pp. 382–385
• Have students do Activities 30–32, p. 383. **20 min.**

Optional Resources
• Communication (TE), p. 383
• Special Learning Needs, p. 383 ●

Homework Suggestions
Cahier de vocabulaire et grammaire, p. 106
Cahier d'activités, p. 85
Interactive Tutor, Ch. 9
Online Practice (**go.hrw.com**, Keyword: BD3 CH9)
❀ 1.1, 1.2

Day 10

OBJECTIVE
Use demonstrative pronouns

Core Instruction
Grammaire 2, pp. 382–385
• Do Bell Work 9.7, p. 384. **5 min.**
• Present **Flash culture**, p. 384. **5 min.**
• See Teaching **Grammaire**, p. 384. **10 min.**
• Have students do Activities 33–37, pp. 384–385. **20 min.**

Application 2, pp. 386–387
• Have students do Activity 38, p. 386. **10 min.**

Optional Resources
• Communication (TE), p. 385
• Slower Pace Learners, p. 385 ◆
• Multiple Intelligences, p. 385

Homework Suggestions
Study for **Quiz: Grammaire 2**
Cahier de vocabulaire et grammaire, p. 107
Cahier d'activités, p. 86
❀ 1.1, 1.2, 1.3

Day 11

OBJECTIVE
*Use **savoir** and **connaître***

Core Instruction
Grammaire 2, pp. 382–385
• Review **Grammaire 2**, pp. 382–385. **10 min.**
• Give **Quiz: Grammaire 2**. **20 min.**

Application 2, pp. 386–387
• See Teaching **Un peu plus**, p. 386. **5 min.**
• Play Audio CD 9, Tr. 6 for Activity 39, p. 386. **5 min.**
• Have students do Activities 40–43, pp. 386–387. **10 min.**

Optional Resources
• Slower Pace Learners, p. 387 ◆
• Special Learning Needs, p. 387 ●

Homework Suggestions
Study for **Quiz: Application 2**
Cahier de vocabulaire et grammaire, p. 108
Cahier d'activités, p. 87
❀ 1.1, 1.2

Day 12

OBJECTIVE
Develop listening and reading skills

Core Instruction
Application 2, pp. 386–387
• Review **Application 2**, pp. 386–387. **10 min.**
• Give **Quiz: Application 2**. **20 min.**

Lecture, pp. 388–391
• See **Lecture** (TE), p. 388. **20 min.**

Optional Resources
• Slower Pace Learners, p. 389 ◆
• Special Learning Needs, p. 389 ●
• Connections, p. 391

Homework Suggestions
Interactive Tutor, Ch. 9
Online Practice (**go.hrw.com**, Keyword: BD3 CH9)
❀ 1.1, 1.2, 1.3, 2.2, 3.1, 4.1

Day 13

OBJECTIVE
Develop listening, reading, and writing skills

Core Instruction
Lecture, pp. 388–391
• See **Lecture** (TE), p. 390. **20 min.**

L'atelier de l'écrivain, pp. 392–393
• See **L'atelier de l'écrivain** (TE), p. 392. **30 min.**

Optional Resources
• Advanced Learners, p. 391 ▲
• Multiple Intelligences, p. 391
• Connections, p. 392
• Slower Pace Learners, p. 393 ◆
• Special Learning Needs, p. 393 ●

Homework Suggestions
Cahier d'activités, p. 88
L'atelier de l'écrivain, Activity 4, p. 393
❀ 1.1, 1.2, 1.3, 2.2, 3.1, 3.2

Day 14

OBJECTIVE
Review the chapter; Prepare for the AP Exam

Core Instruction
Prépare-toi pour l'examen, pp. 394–397
• Have students do Activities 1–5, pp. 394–395. **25 min.**

Activités préparatoires, pp. 398–399
• Have students do the **Activités préparatoires**, pp. 398–399. **25 min.**

Optional Resources
• Reteaching, p. 394
• Connections. p. 399
• Slower Pace Learners, p. 399 ◆
• Special Learning Needs, p. 399 ●
• **Télé-culture:** Interviews

Homework Suggestions
Interactive Tutor, Ch. 9
Online Practice (**go.hrw.com**, Keyword: BD3 CH9)
❀ 1.1, 1.2, 1.3, 2.1, 2.2, 3.1

Day 15

OBJECTIVE
Review the chapter

Core Instruction
Prépare-toi pour l'examen, pp. 394–397
• Play Audio CD 9, Tr. 9 for Activity 6, p. 395. **10 min.**
• Have students do Activity 7, p. 395. **10 min.**

Révisions cumulatives, pp. 400–401
• Play Audio CD 9, Tr. 11 for Activity 1, p. 400. **5 min.**
• Have students do Activities 2–6, pp. 400–401. **25 min.**

Optional Resources
• Game, p. 397
• Online Culture Project, p. 400
• Fine Art Connection, p. 401
• **Télé-roman: Camille et compagnie**

Homework Suggestions
Study for Chapter Test
Online Practice (**go.hrw.com**, Keyword: BD3 CH9)
❀ 1.1, 1.2, 1.3, 2.2, 3.2

Day 16/Test

Core Instruction
Chapter Test 50 min.

Optional Resources
Assessment Program
• Alternative Assessment
• Test Generator
• **Quiz: Lecture**
• **Quiz: Écriture**

Homework Suggestions
Cahier d'activités, pp. 89–90, 118–119
Online Practice (**go.hrw.com**, Keyword: BD3 CH9)

50-Minute Lesson Plans

90-Minute Lesson Plans

L'art en fête

Block 1

OBJECTIVE
Ask for and give opinions; Introduce and change a topic of conversation

Core Instruction
Chapter Opener, pp. 364–365
• See Using the Photo, p. 364. **5 min.**
• See Chapter Objectives, p. 364. **5 min.**

Vocabulaire 1, pp. 366–369
• Present **Vocabulaire 1,** pp. 366–367. See Teaching **Vocabulaire,** p. 366. **15 min.**
• Present **Exprimons-nous!,** p. 367. **10 min.**
• Have students do Activity 1, p. 368. **5 min.**
• Play Audio CD 9, Tr. 1 for Activity 2, p. 368. **5 min.**
• Have students do Activities 3–4, p. 368. **15 min.**
• See Teaching **Exprimons-nous!,** p. 368. **10 min.**
• Have students do Activities 5–7, p. 369. **20 min.**

Optional Resources
• Learning Tips, p. 365
• **Proverbes,** p. 366
• TPR, p. 367
• Connections, p. 367
• Advanced Learners, p. 367 ▲
• Multiple Intelligences, p. 367
• Cultures, p. 368
• Communication (TE), p. 369
• Advanced Learners, p. 369 ▲
• Special Learning Needs, p. 369 ●

Homework Suggestions
Study for **Quiz: Vocabulaire 1**
Cahier de vocabulaire et grammaire, pp. 97–99
Interactive Tutor, Ch. 9
Online Practice (**go.hrw.com,** Keyword: BD3 CH9)
    ✿ 1.1, 1.2, 1.3, 2.1, 2.2, 3.1

Block 2

OBJECTIVE
Use inversion; Use present participles as adjectives

Core Instruction
Vocabulaire 1, pp. 366–369
• Review **Vocabulaire 1,** pp. 366–369. **10 min.**
• Give **Quiz: Vocabulaire 1. 20 min.**

Grammaire 1, pp. 370–373
• See Teaching **Grammaire,** p. 370. **10 min.**
• Play Audio CD 9, Tr. 2 for Activity 8, p. 370. **5 min.**
• Have students do Activities 9–12, pp. 370–371. **15 min.**
• Present **Flash culture,** p. 371. **5 min.**
• See Teaching **Grammaire,** p. 372. **10 min.**
• Have students do Activities 13–16, pp. 372–373. **15 min.**

Optional Resources
• **Attention!,** p. 371
• Communication (TE), p. 371
• Slower Pace Learners, p. 371 ◆
• Special Learning Needs, p. 371 ●
• French for Spanish Speakers, p. 372
• Communication (TE), p. 373
• Slower Pace Learners, p. 373 ◆
• Special Learning Needs, p. 373 ●

Homework Suggestions
Study for **Quiz: Grammaire 1**
Cahier de vocabulaire et grammaire, pp. 100–101
Cahier d'activités, pp. 81–82
Interactive Tutor, Ch. 9
Online Practice (**go.hrw.com,** Keyword: BD3 CH9)
    ✿ 1.1, 1.2, 4.1, 4.2

Block 3

OBJECTIVE
Use present participles as adjectives; Use si and oui; Learn about francophone culture

Core Instruction
Grammaire 1, pp. 370–373
• Do Bell Work 9.3, p. 372. **5 min.**
• Have students do Activity 17, p. 373. **5 min.**
• Review **Grammaire 1,** pp. 370–373. **10 min.**
• Give **Quiz: Grammaire 1. 20 min.**

Application 1, pp. 374–375
• Have students do Activity 18, p. 374. **5 min.**
• See Teaching **Un peu plus,** p. 374. **5 min.**
• Play Audio CD 9, Tr. 3 for Activity 19, p. 374. **5 min.**
• Have students do Activities 20–23, pp. 374–375. **15 min.**

Culture, pp. 376–377
• See **Lecture culturelle** (TE), p. 376. **10 min.**
• See **Comparaisons et communauté** (TE), p. 376. **10 min.**

Optional Resources
• **Attention!,** p. 374
• Communication (TE), p. 375
• Advanced Learners, p. 375 ▲
• Multiple Intelligences, p. 375
• Prereading Questions, p. 376
• Active Reading Questions, p. 376
• **Vocabulaire supplémentaire,** p. 376
• Bulletin Board Project, p. 377
• Cultures, p. 377
• Communities, p. 377
• Advanced Learners, p. 377 ▲
• Multiple Intelligences, p. 377

Homework Suggestions
Study for **Quiz: Application 1**
Cahier de vocabulaire et grammaire, p. 102
Cahier d'activités, pp. 83–84
Interactive Tutor, Ch. 9
Online Practice (**go.hrw.com,** Keyword: BD3 CH9)
Finish the **Communauté et professions** project, p. 377.
    ✿ 1.1, 1.2, 1.3, 2.1, 2.2, 3.1, 3.2, 4.2, 5.1, 5.2

Block 4

OBJECTIVE
Make suggestions and recommendations; Give an impression

Core Instruction
Application 1, pp. 374–375
• Review **Application 1,** pp. 374–375. **10 min.**
• Give **Quiz: Application 1. 20 min.**

Vocabulaire 2, pp. 378–381
• Present **Vocabulaire 2,** pp. 378–379. See Teaching **Vocabulaire,** p. 378. **15 min.**
• Present **Exprimons-nous!,** p. 379. **5 min.**
• Play Audio CD 9, Tr. 4 for Activity 24, p. 380. **5 min.**
• Have students do Activities 25–26, p. 380. **10 min.**
• See Teaching **Exprimons-nous!,** p. 380. **10 min.**
• Have students do Activities 27–28, p. 381. **10 min.**
• Present **Flash culture,** p. 381. **5 min.**

Optional Resources
• **Cinquain** Poetry, p. 378
• TPR, p. 379
• Teacher to Teacher, p. 379
• Advanced Learners, p. 379 ▲
• Special Learning Needs, p. 379 ●
• Connections, p. 381
• Communication (TE), p. 381
• Slower Pace Learners, p. 381 ◆
• Special Learning Needs, p. 381 ●

Homework Suggestions
Study for **Quiz: Vocabulaire 2**
Cahier de vocabulaire et grammaire, pp. 103–105
Interactive Tutor, Ch. 9
Online Practice (**go.hrw.com,** Keyword: BD3 CH9)
    ✿ 1.1, 1.2, 1.3, 3.1, 4.2, 5.2

Block 5

OBJECTIVE
Use the comparative and superlative; Use demonstrative pronouns

Core Instruction
Vocabulaire 2, pp. 378–381
- Review **Vocabulaire 2,** pp. 378–381. **10 min.**
- Give **Quiz: Vocabulaire 2.** **20 min.**

Grammaire 2, pp. 382–385
- See Teaching **Grammaire,** p. 382. **10 min.**
- Play Audio CD 9, Tr. 5 for Activity 29, p. 382. **5 min.**
- Have students do Activities 30–32, p. 383. **15 min.**
- Present **Flash culture,** p. 384. **5 min.**
- See Teaching **Grammaire,** p. 384. **10 min.**
- Have students do Activities 33–35, pp. 384–385. **15 min.**

Optional Resources
- Communication (TE), p. 383
- Advanced Learners, p. 383 ▲
- Special Learning Needs, p. 383 ●
- **Attention!,** p. 384
- Slower Pace Learners, p. 385 ◆
- Multiple Intelligences, p. 385

Homework Suggestions
Study for **Quiz: Grammaire 2**
Cahier de vocabulaire et grammaire, pp. 106–107
Cahier d'activités, pp. 85–86
Interactive Tutor, Ch. 9
Online Practice (**go.hrw.com,** Keyword: BD3 CH9)
❀ 1.1, 1.2, 1.3

Block 6

OBJECTIVE
*Use demonstrative pronouns; Use **savoir** and **connaître;** Develop listening and reading skills*

Core Instruction
Grammaire 2, pp. 382–385
- Have students do Activities 36–37, p. 385. **10 min.**
- Review **Grammaire 2,** pp. 382–385. **10 min.**
- Give **Quiz: Grammaire 2.** **20 min.**

Application 2, pp. 386–387
- Have students do Activity 38, p. 386. **5 min.**
- See Teaching **Un peu plus,** p. 386. **5 min.**
- Play Audio CD 9, Tr. 6 for Activity 39, p. 386. **5 min.**
- Have students do Activities 40–43, pp. 386–387. **15 min.**

Lecture, pp. 388–391
- See **Lecture** (TE), p. 388. **20 min.**

Optional Resources
- Communication (TE), p. 385
- Communication (TE), p. 387
- Slower Pace Learners, p. 387 ◆
- Special Learning Needs, p. 387 ●
- AP Reading Suggestion, p. 388
- Applying the Strategies, p. 388
- Active Reading Questions, p. 389
- Visualizing a Text, p. 389
- Slower Pace Learners, p. 389 ◆
- Special Learning Needs, p. 389 ●

Homework Suggestions
Study for **Quiz: Application 2**
Cahier de vocabulaire et grammaire, p. 108
Cahier d'activités, p. 87
Interactive Tutor, Ch. 9
Online Practice (**go.hrw.com,** Keyword: BD3 CH9)
❀ 1.1, 1.2, 1.3, 2.2, 4.1

Block 7

OBJECTIVE
Develop listening, reading, and writing skills; Review the chapter

Core Instruction
Application 2, pp. 386–387
- Review **Application 2,** pp. 386–387. **10 min.**
- Give **Quiz: Application 2.** **20 min.**

Lecture, pp. 388–391
- See **Lecture** (TE), p. 390. **10 min.**

L'atelier de l'écrivain, pp. 392–393
- See **L'atelier de l'écrivain** (TE), p. 392. **30 min.**

Prépare-toi pour l'examen, pp. 394–397
- Have students do Activities 1–5, pp. 394–395. **10 min.**
- Play Audio CD 9, Tr. 9 for Activity 6, p. 395. **5 min.**
- Have students do Activity 7, p. 395. **5 min.**

Optional Resources
- Active Reading Questions, p. 390
- Postreading Activity, p. 390
- Connections, p. 391
- Advanced Learners, p. 391 ▲
- Multiple Intelligences, p. 391
- Process Writing, p. 392
- Teaching Suggestion, p. 392
- Connections, p. 392
- **Les pronoms relatifs,** p. 393
- Writing Assessment, p. 393
- Slower Pace Learners, p. 393 ◆
- Special Learning Needs, p. 393 ●
- TPRS, p. 394
- French for Spanish Speakers, p. 394
- Reteaching, p. 394
- Oral Assessment, p. 395
- Cultures, p. 396
- Chapter Review, pp. 396–397
- Game, p. 397

Homework Suggestions
Study for Chapter Test
L'atelier de l'écrivain, Activity 4, p. 393
Cahier d'activités, p. 88
Interactive Tutor, Ch. 9
Online Practice (**go.hrw.com,** Keyword: BD3 CH9)
❀ 1.1, 1.2, 1.3, 2.1, 2.2, 3.1, 3.2, 4.1

Block 8

OBJECTIVE
Prepare for the AP Exam; Review and assess the chapter

Core Instruction
Activités préparatoires, pp. 398–399
- Have students do the **Activités préparatoires,** pp. 398–399. **20 min.**

Chapter Test 50 min.

Révisions cumulatives, pp. 400–401
- Play Audio CD 9, Tr. 11 for Activity 1, p. 400. **5 min.**
- Have students do Activities 2–6, pp. 400–401. **15 min.**

Optional Resources
- Reading Strategy, p. 398
- Writing Strategy, p. 399
- Connections, p. 399
- Slower Pace Learners, p. 399 ◆
- Special Learning Needs, p. 399 ●
- Online Culture Project, p. 400
- Fine Art Connection, p. 401
- **Télé-culture:** Interviews
- **Télé-roman: Camille et compagnie**

Homework Suggestions
Cahier d'activités, pp. 89–90, 118–119
Interactive Tutor, Ch. 9
Online Practice (**go.hrw.com,** Keyword: BD3 CH9)
❀ 1.1, 1.2, 1.3, 2.2, 3.1, 3.2

90-Minute Lesson Plans

Meeting the National Standards

Communication
Communication, pp. 369, 371, 373, 375, 381, 383, 385, 387
À ton tour, p. 401

Cultures
Flash culture, pp. 371, 381, 384
Comparaisons, p. 377
Practices and Perspectives, p. 368
Products and Perspectives, pp. 377, 396

Connections
Language Note, p. 399
Geography Link, p. 367
Music Link, p. 381
Literature Link, p. 391

Comparisons
Comparaisons, p. 377

Communities
Communauté, p. 377
Career Path, p. 377

Using the Photo

Flowers, especially hibiscus and the **tiaré** flower, are a common motif in the art of Tahiti. The **tiaré** flower (Gardenia Tahitensis) with its six to nine white petals, is the emblem of Tahiti. Made into a garland to be placed around a visitor's neck or into a crown during celebrations, the **tiaré** flower is a staple of life. For centuries now, Tahitians have produced Monoï oil, obtained by soaking the **tiaré** flowers in coconut oil. Monoï holds a very important place in Polynesian traditional pharmacopeia and culture. In a three-day celebration in December, Tahitians pay tribute to this flower. Ask students if **tiaré** flowers and/or hibiscus blooms are presented in the painting. The painting is in the naïve, or primitive, style, a style that is often associated with Paul Gauguin and Henri Rousseau. Ask students to compare and contrast the colors, pattern, motif, and theme of this paining to the paintings by Rousseau on pages 169 and 349. 1.1, 3.1

chapitre 9

L'art en fête

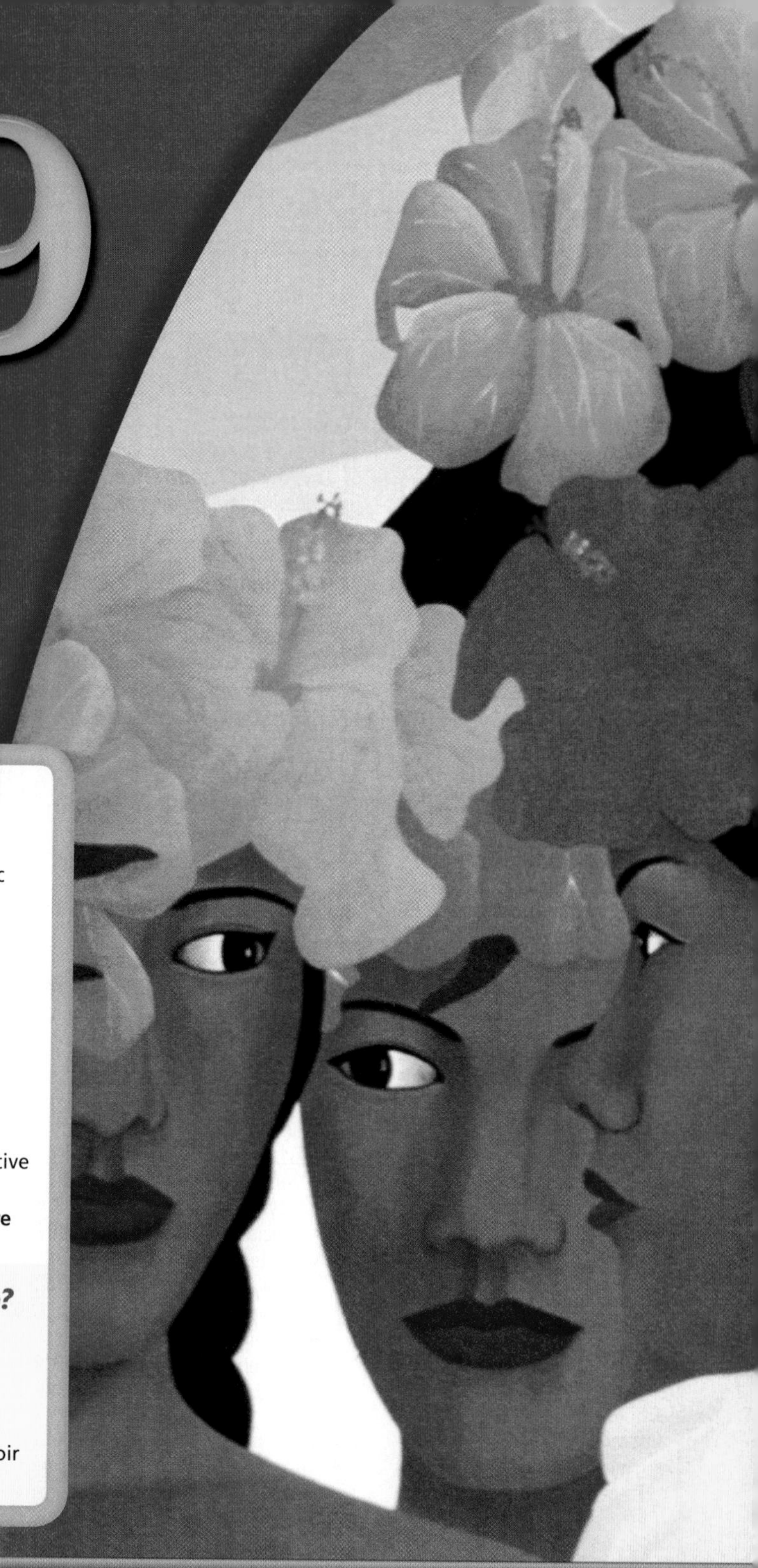

Objectifs

In this chapter, you will learn to
- ask for and give opinions
- introduce and change a topic of conversation
- make suggestions and recommendations
- give an impression

And you will use and review
- inversion
- present participles used as adjectives
- **si** and **oui**
- the comparative and superlative
- demonstrative pronouns
- the verbs **savoir** and **connaître**

Que vois-tu sur la photo?

Qu'est-ce que cette peinture représente?

Qu'est-ce que tu penses de cette peinture?

Et toi, est-ce que tu aimes aller voir des expositions?

Suggested pacing:	Traditional Schedule	Block Schedule
Vocabulaire/Grammaire/Application 1	5 days	2 blocks
Culture	1 day	1 block
Vocabulaire/Grammaire/Application 2	5 days	2 blocks
Lecture	1 day	1/2 block
L'atelier de l'écrivain	1 day	1/2 block
Prépare-toi pour l'examen	1/2 day	1/2 block
Activités préparatoires	1/2 day	1/2 block
Examen	1 day	1/2 block
Révisions cumulatives	1 day	1/2 block

Vocabulaire supplémentaire

Students might use these terms to discuss the photo.

la peinture *painting*
la couleur *color*
le motif *pattern*
le thème *theme*
inspirer *to inspire*
la simplicité *simplicity*
le modèle *pattern*
inspirer *to inspire*

Learning Tips

You may want to show students a photograph or copy of a famous painting at the beginning of each class. Have them discuss the painting using the vocabulary introduced in this chapter and looking up words they want to use but have not yet learned. Ask students to write the new words in a notebook to use as reference in future class discussions about art.

Language Lab

You might want to use your language lab to have students:
• listen to all target vocabulary and phrases in the chapter
• practice pronunciation of vocabulary, using Holt SoundBooth to save their work for evaluation
• complete the listening activities in this chapter

Peinture de Tahiti

LISTENING PRACTICE

Vocabulaire
Activity 2, p. 368, CD 9, Tr. 1
Activity 24, p. 380, CD 9, Tr. 4

Grammaire
Activity 8, p. 370, CD 9, Tr. 2
Activity 29, p. 382, CD 9, Tr. 5

Application
Activity 19, p. 374, CD 9, Tr. 3
Activity 39, p. 386, CD 9, Tr. 6

Language Lab and Classroom Activities

Prépare-toi pour l'examen
Activity 6, p. 395, CD 9, Tr. 9
Télé-culture: Interviews, Chapter 9

Activités préparatoires
Section I, Listening, p. 398, CD 9, Tr. 10
Télé-roman: *Camille et compagnie*, Épisodes 9 et 10

Révisions cumulatives
Activity 1, p. 400, CD 9, Tr. 11

Lecture, pp. 388, 390 CD 9, Trs. 7, 8

Bell Work

Use Bell Work 9.1 in the *Teaching Transparencies,* or write this activity on the board.

Complète les phrases suivantes avec **chacun** ou **chacune**.

1. À la douane, l'employé a demandé à ____ des touristes de montrer son passeport.
2. Il a regardé ____ des photos.
3. Finalement, il a remis leurs papiers à ____ d'entre eux.
4. ____ de ces personnes a pu reprendre ses bagages.

Proverbes

For French proverbs and activities related to the chapter theme and vocabulary, see **Proverbes et expressions,** pp. R6–R7.

Objectifs
- to ask for and give opinions
- to introduce and change a topic of conversation

Vocabulaire
à l'œuvre 1

Un atelier d'artiste

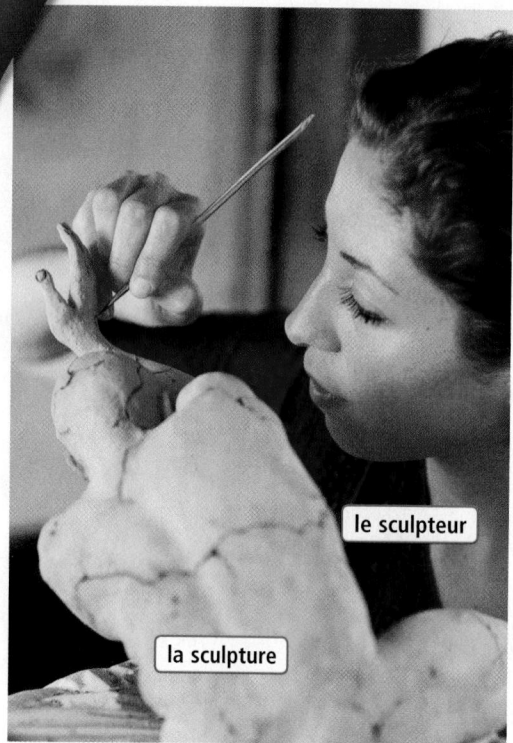

la sculpture · le sculpteur

Le sculpteur **sculpte une statue**.

la potière · une poterie

Les potiers utilisent **un tour** pour faire leurs poteries.

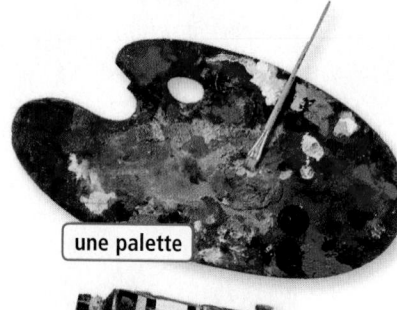

une palette

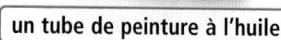

un tube de peinture à l'huile

le modèle · un chevalet · le peintre

Le peintre **peint** des tableaux. Le modèle qui **pose** ne peut pas **bouger**.

Core Instruction

TEACHING VOCABULAIRE

1. Introduce the vocabulary, using transparencies **Vocabulaire 9.1** and **9.2.** Model the pronunciation of each word or expression. **(3 min.)**

2. Ask students to point to and identify various items on the transparency. **Un sculpteur, un modèle, un chevalet (3 min.)**

3. Ask students questions about their artistic abilities.

Est-ce que tu as déjà peint une aquarelle? Tu sais faire de la poterie? (3 min.)

4. Model the expressions in **Exprimons-nous!** Then ask students for their opinion about books, movies, songs, works of art, and so forth. — **Comment trouves-tu le dernier film de James Bond? — Il n'est pas mal. (3 min.)**

Dans une galerie d'art, on peut admirer...

Vocabulaire 1

un paysage

une aquarelle

une peinture abstraite

une nature morte

un (auto)portrait

D'autres mots utiles

un chef-d'œuvre	*master piece*	une peinture naïve	*primitive painting*
un(e) critique d'art	*art critic*	une toile	*painting*
un croquis	*sketch*	un vernissage	*preview*
une exposition	*exhibition*	encadrer	*to frame*
une gravure	*engraving*	exposer	*to exhibit*
une œuvre d'art	*work of art*		

Exprimons-nous!

To ask for opinions	To give opinions
Comment trouves-tu cette sculpture? *How do you like . . . ?*	**Surprenant**(e)/**Émouvant**(e)... *Surprising/Moving. . .*
Cette exposition **t'a-t-elle plu?** *Did you like . . . ?*	**Je l'ai trouvé**(e) **passionnant**(e)! *I found it fascinating.*
Quel est ton avis sur les sculptures de...? *What is your opinion about . . . ?*	**Ce n'est pas mon style.** *It's not my style.*
Qu'est-ce que tu penses de ce tableau? *What do you think about . . . ?*	**Il n'est pas mal.** *It's O.K.*

Interactive TUTOR

Vocabulaire et grammaire, pp. 97–99

Online workbooks

▶ Vocabulaire supplémentaire—Les arts, p. R21

T P R
TOTAL PHYSICAL RESPONSE

Have students respond to these commands.

Lève le doigt si tu aimes les aquarelles.

Assieds-toi si tu préfères encadrer des photos.

Mets la main devant les yeux si les peintures abstraites ne sont pas ton style.

Mets la main sur la bouche si tu fais parfois des croquis en classe.

Dessine une palette.

Then have some students mime the following situations.

Tu es peintre, peins un tableau!

C'est toi le modèle, tu ne peux pas bouger.

Tu fais une sculpture.

Tu fais de la poterie.

Tu es à un vernissage et tu es critique d'art. 🌸 1.2

Connections
Geography Link

The discovery of a distinctively decorated type of pottery, called Lapita, provided the first solid evidence of the general route by which the ancestors of the Polynesians migrated into the Pacific. About 3,300 years ago, there appeared in the New Guinean Bismarck Archipelago a people who could make finely decorated clay pottery. The pottery began turning up in excavations from the islands off the northeast coast of New Guinea to archipelagos at the western edge of Polynesia. Ask students to research the route of the Lapita people and suggest areas from which they may have come orginally. (Southeast Asia) 🌸 3.1

Differentiated Instruction

ADVANCED LEARNERS

Personalization Display paintings of different art styles in the classroom. (You may want to ask the art teacher for paintings). Students should play art critic and comment on the paintings in your "art exhibit." Walking from painting to painting with a partner, they should identify the style of each painting, ask for their fellow art critic's opinion, and give their own opinion. Encourage students to use expressions from **Exprimons-nous!** 🌸 1.1, 3.1

MULTIPLE INTELLIGENCES

Linguistic Have students choose one of the paintings on page 367. Ask them to write a critical essay about it, in French. Students should tell whether or not they like the painting and why they chose that particular painting. Encourage them to note any details in the painting and explain how the painting makes them feel. 🌸 1.3

Cultures

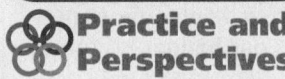

Practice and Perspectives

The carnival traditions of
Martinique and Guadeloupe
include the ancient African tradition of parading in costumes
and masks and moving in circles
through villages. Circling villages
was believed to bring good fortune,
solve problems, and pacify angry
relatives who had passed into the
next world. Carnival traditions also
borrow from the African tradition
of putting together natural objects
(bones, grasses, beads, shells,
fabric) to create sculptures, masks,
or costumes, with each object
representing spiritual forces. Ask
students to research the history of
carnival. Why do Martinique and
Guadeloupe celebrate carnival?

🌼 2.1

❷ Script

See script on p. 363E.

---

❶ L'intrus 🌼 1.2

Lisons/Parlons Trouve le mot qui ne va pas avec les autres dans
chaque liste. Ensuite, donne un terme qui va avec les autres mots.

MODÈLE   un croquis / une gravure / ~~une poterie~~ / une peinture
un tableau

1. un vernissage / une exposition / exposer / un tour de potier
2. un critique d'art / une palette / un chevalet / une toile
3. une statue / un paysage / un modèle / une aquarelle
4. un potier / un paysage / une aquarelle / une peinture abstraite
5. une œuvre d'art / un tableau / un chef-d'œuvre / un modèle

Second part of answers may
vary. Sample answers are given.
1. ~~un tour de potier~~ (une galerie d'art)
2. ~~un critique d'art~~ (un tube de peinture)
3. ~~un modèle~~ (une peinture abstraite)
4. ~~un potier~~ (un autoportrait)
5. ~~un modèle~~ (une toile)

❷ Écoutons   CD 9, Tr. 1   🌼 1.2   1. b 2. c 3. a 4. d

Dis si on parle **a) d'une exposition de natures mortes, b) de
sculptures, c) d'une peinture abstraite** ou **d) d'un potier.**

❸ Des descriptions 🌼 1.3

Parlons/Écrivons Regarde ces photos et dis ce que l'artiste fait.

1.   2.   3.   4.

❹ L'art et toi 🌼 1.3

Lisons/Parlons Réponds aux questions suivantes au sujet de tes
goûts personnels et de tes préférences en ce qui concerne l'art.

1. Comment trouves-tu l'art moderne?
2. Qu'est-ce que tu penses des tableaux de Picasso?
3. Qui est ton peintre préféré? Pourquoi?
4. Est-ce que tu es déjà allé(e) à une exposition d'art?
   T'a-t'elle plu? Pourquoi ou pourquoi pas?
5. Est-ce que tu pratiques un art? Lequel?
6. En sculpture, quel est ton style préféré?
7. Quel est ton avis sur les œuvres des impressionnistes?

Core Instruction

TEACHING EXPRIMONS-NOUS!

1. Model the pronunciation of the phrases in
   Exprimons-nous! Tell students that they
   should pronounce the final "t" of "**au fait**".
   (2 min.)

2. Begin incomplete sentences with the new
   expressions one by one and have the class finish the sentences using, **Entre parenthèses,...**
   Entre parenthèses, ce n'est pas mon style.

3. Ask students to make up sentences beginning
   with these expressions. **(2 min.)**

Exprimons-nous!

To introduce and change a topic of conversation

Au fait, tu as lu cet article?	*By the way . . .*
À propos, tu sais que je suis des cours d'art?	*On that subject, . . .*
Pendant que j'y pense, tu as vu Fabrice?	*While I'm thinking about it, . . .*
Entre parenthèses, c'était nul.	*By the way . . .*

Vocabulaire et grammaire, pp. 97–99 · Online workbooks

⑤ Conversation 🍀1.2

Écrivons Complète la conversation suivante avec les expressions d'**Exprimons-nous!**

ÉMILIE   __1__ tu as été au concert de U2?

SARA   Non, je n'ai pas pu y aller. __2__ de U2, tu pourrais me rendre le CD que je t'ai prêté?

ÉMILIE   Oui, bien sûr. __3__, je ne l'ai pas trouvé si bon que ça.

SARA   Ah non? Moi, je le trouve super, ce CD. Tiens, __4__, est-ce que tu n'aurais pas aussi mon bouquin de recettes japonaises?

⑥ Quel est ton avis? 🍀1.3

Écrivons Deux personnes parlent d'une exposition qu'elles viennent de voir. Une des personnes pose des questions sur l'exposition mais l'autre voudrait parler d'autre chose. Crée leur conversation.

MODÈLE —Comment tu as trouvé cette exposition?
           —Pas mal. Au fait,...

À la française

A graffiti artist in French is called **un tagueur, une tagueuse,** which comes from the English slang **"to tag"**. And the drawing itself is called **un tag.**

Communication

HOLT SoundBooth ONLINE RECORDING

⑦ Opinions personnelles 🍀1.1

Parlons Imagine que tu vas voir une exposition d'art moderne avec un(e) ami(e) français(e). Vous allez à la galerie le jour du vernissage et vous regardez les œuvres qui y sont exposées. Joue cette scène avec un(e) camarade.

MODÈLE —Comment tu trouves cette sculpture, Thomas?
           —Euh... Ce n'est pas mon style. Je n'aime pas les sculptures abstraites.
           —Moi, je...! Tiens, au fait, ...

Planning:

Lesson Planner

 One-Stop Planner

Practice:

Grammar Tutor for Students of French, Chapter 9

Cahier de vocabulaire et grammaire

Differentiated Practice and Assessment CD-ROM

Cahier d'activités

Media Guide

 Teaching Transparencies

Bell Work 9.2

 Audio CD 9, Tr. 2

 Interactive Tutor, Disc 2

Bell Work

Use Bell Work 9.2 in the *Teaching Transparencies*, or write this activity on the board.

Complète les phrases.

1. Le sculpteur...; **2.** Le peintre...; **3.** Ce critique d'art...; **4.** Ce potier...; **5.** Le modèle...

a. a fait connaître beaucoup d'œuvres d'art.

b. pose pour l'artiste.

c. expose ses tableaux dans cette galerie.

d. fait des statues extraordinaires.

e. utilise un tour pour faire ses vases. 🌸1.2

8 Script

See script on p. 363E.

9 Answers

1. Faites-vous aussi de la peinture abstraite?
2. Votre femme fait-elle de la poterie?
3. Êtes-vous déjà allé au musée du Louvre?
4. Comment peint-on avec de la peinture à l'huile?
5. Vos tableaux se vendent-ils bien?
6. Quand votre prochaine œuvre sera-t-elle finie?

Objectifs
• review of inversion
• verbal adjectives (present participles used as adjectives)

 Grammaire à l'œuvre

Révisions Inversion

Interactive TUTOR

1 **Inversion** is a more formal way to ask a question. To ask a question using inversion, reverse the subject pronoun and the verb and add a hyphen between them.

Tu vas au musée?   Vas-tu au musée?   Ne vas-tu pas au musée?

2 If the subject is **il, elle,** or **on** and the verb ends in a vowel, add **-t-** between the verb and subject.

Quand pose-t-il pour le peintre?

3 If a noun is the subject, put the noun first and then invert the appropriate subject pronoun with the verb.

use a pronoun for inversion

Marco expose-t-il ses œuvres dans cette galerie?

4 To make a question using inversion in a compound tense like the **passé composé,** reverse the subject and the helping verb.

Quand sont-ils allés à l'exposition?

Vocabulaire et grammaire, pp. 100–101
Cahier d'activités, pp. 81–83
Online workbooks

Déjà vu!

Do you remember how to form questions in French? The most informal way is to use the intonation.

Tu as vu ce tableau?

Orally or in informal writing, you can add est-ce que to a statement to form a question.

Est-ce qu'il aime ce tableau?

---

8 Écoutons CD 9, Tr. 2 🌸1.2   **1.** b **2.** a **3.** b **4.** a **5.** a **6.** b

Dis si chacune des questions que tu entends **a) utilise l'inversion** ou **b) n'utilise pas l'inversion.**

9 Invitation à un vernissage 🌸1.2

Parlons/Écrivons Lionel est allé à un vernissage avec ses parents et il pose beaucoup de questions au peintre. Utilise l'inversion pour poser ses questions de manière plus formelle.

MODÈLE Est-ce que vous êtes l'auteur de toutes ces œuvres?
Êtes-vous l'auteur de toutes ces œuvres?

1. Est-ce que vous faites aussi de la peinture abstraite?

2. Votre femme fait de la poterie?

3. Est-ce que vous êtes déjà allé au musée du Louvre?

4. Comment est-ce qu'on peint avec de la peinture à l'huile?

5. Est-ce que vos tableaux se vendent bien?

6. Quand est-ce que votre prochaine œuvre sera finie?

Core Instruction

TEACHING GRAMMAIRE

1. Read **Déjà Vu!** aloud with students. **(2 min.)**

2. Go over Points 1–4. Remind students that it is generally better to avoid using inversion when the subject pronoun is **je.** Tell them that inversion with **je** works with some verbs.

Ai-je bien compris? Où suis-je? Que sais-je? It is particularly formal and would be impossible to pronounce with many other verbs. Ask them to try inversion of **Je pose pour le peintre. (4 min.)**

Online Practice
go.hrw.com
Grammaire 1 practice
KEYWORD: BD3 CH9

Chapitre 9
Grammaire 1

⑩ À l'école des Beaux-Arts 🎬1.2

Écrivons Pascale et ses amies parlent pendant leur visite d'une école d'art. Utilise l'inversion.

1. Ce paysage / exister / vraiment
2. Tes parents / avoir fait encadrer / leur tableau
3. Pourquoi / ce potier / utiliser / un tour électrique
4. Comment / cette statue / s'appeler
5. Où / ces aquarelles / avoir été peintes
6. Tes cousins / être allés / à l'exposition van Gogh

⑪ Conversation avec un artiste 🎬1.2

Écrivons/Parlons Christèle a fait la connaissance d'un ami de ses parents qui est artiste. Lis les réponses de l'artiste et imagine les questions que Christèle lui a posées. Utilise l'inversion.

MODÈLE —Comment allez-vous?
—Je vais bien, merci.

1. Je m'appelle Victor Pinseau.
2. Oui, je suis peintre.
3. Non, je n'ai jamais peint d'aquarelles.
4. Je fais des portraits parce que j'aime beaucoup ça.
5. J'expose mes œuvres dans une petite galerie d'art.
6. Non, mes tableaux ne seront jamais au musée du Louvre.
7. Non, petit, je n'aimais pas dessiner.
8. Je peins depuis vingt ans.
9. Le peintre qui m'a le plus inspiré *(inspired)*, c'est van Gogh.

Flash culture

La créativité des Tahitiens s'exprime à travers l'artisanat de bijoux faits de coquillages, de perles, les tissages de paniers ou de chapeaux, les sculptures appelées «tikis» et les tapas qui sont des tissus faits d'écorces *(bark)* de mûriers ou d'hibiscus. Ils sont peints avec des formes stylisées ou géométriques et peuvent servir de décorations ou encore de vêtements de cérémonie. 🎬4.2

Est-ce que ton état est connu pour ses produits artisanaux? Quels sont-ils?

⑩ Answers

1. Ce paysage existe-t-il vraiment?
2. Tes parents ont-ils fait encadrer leur tableau?
3. Pourquoi ce potier utilise-t-il un tour électrique?
4. Comment cette statue s'appelle-t-elle?
5. Où ces aquarelles ont-elles été peintes?
6. Tes cousins sont-ils allés à l'exposition Van Gogh?

⑪ Answers

1. Comment vous appelez-vous?
2. Êtes-vous peintre?
3. Avez-vous déjà peint des aquarelles?
4. Pourquoi faites-vous des portraits?
5. Où exposez-vous vos œuvres?
6. Vos tableaux seront-ils un jour au musée du Louvre?
7. Petit, aimiez-vous dessiner?
8. Depuis combien de temps peignez-vous?
9. Quel peintre vous a-t-il le plus inspiré?

COMMON ERROR ALERT
**/// ATTENTION ! **

When forming inverted questions, students may be reluctant to add '-t-' to the third person singular form of verbs that end in **-ter.** It creates a slight stutter sound that they may think is incorrect, e.g. **visite-t-elle?**

Communication

⑫ Questions personnelles 🎬1.1

Parlons Avec un(e) camarade, posez-vous cinq questions au sujet de cette toile. Utilisez l'inversion dans vos questions.

MODÈLE —À ton avis, quelle scène ce tableau représente-t-il?

HOLT **SoundBooth**
ONLINE RECORDING

Communication

Class Activity: Interpersonal
Have students write a question with inversion that would elicit a response in the **passé composé, imparfait,** or with a **si** clause. Have students circulate and read their statement to classmates, who will try to come up with the question. 🎬1.1

Differentiated Instruction

SLOWER PACE LEARNERS

⑨ ⑩ Building on Previous skills Before students do these activities, ask them to underline the subject in each item. Have them determine whether the subject is a pronoun or a noun and if the verb is a compound tense. Ask them which rule of inversion applies to each item. Referring to the grammar presentation, students should complete these activities.
🎬1.2

SPECIAL LEARNING NEEDS

⑫ Language Impairments Students with language impairments will have difficulty with this activity since they may feel insecure giving oral responses. You might allow students to answer in writing, instead.

Resources

Planning:

Lesson Planner

 One-Stop Planner

Practice:

Grammar Tutor for Students of French, Chapter 9

Cahier de vocabulaire et grammaire

Differentiated Practice and Assessment CD-ROM

Cahier d'activités

Media Guide

 Teaching Transparencies Bell Work 9.3

 Interactive Tutor, Disc 2

Bell Work

Use Bell Work 9.3 in the *Teaching Transparencies,* or write this activity on the board.

Utilise **l'inversion** pour poser ces mêmes questions.

1. Est-ce que tu es allé voir l'exposition de Max?

2. Est-ce que tes parents sont allés avec toi?

3. Est-ce que Max avait exposé toutes ses œuvres?

4. Est-ce que cette exposition vous a plu?

5. Quand est-ce que Max est arrivé?

6. Comment est-ce que tu l'as trouvé? ✿1.2

French for Spanish Speakers

Ask Spanish speakers how present participles are formed in Spanish. (by adding **–ando** to the stem of **–ar** verbs and **–iendo** to the stem of **–ir** and **–er** verbs) Can these present participles then be adjectives as they can in French? (no) ✿4.1

En anglais

In English, present participles end in *-ing.*

They can be used as adjectives:

The dancing clown jumped into the air.

Can you think of another way you use the present participle in English?

In French, present participles end in **-ant.** Present participles are NOT use to show progressive actions. Progressive actions are expressed with the simple present tense.

Elle chante means *She sings* or *She is singing.*

As a verb to show progressive action: he is playing football.

Révisions — Present participles used as adjectives

1 To form the **present participle** (the *-ing* form) of most verbs, drop **-ons** from the present **nous** form of the verb and add **-ant.**

(nous) obéiss**ons**	→	obéiss**ant**
(nous) passionn**ons**	→	passionn**ant**
(nous) impressionn**ons**	→	impressionn**ant**
(nous) émouv**ons**	→	émouv**ant**

2 Present participles are often used as adjectives (des adjectifs **verbaux**). They agree with the noun they modify.

Ce sont **des statues** impressionn**ant**es.   *agrees*

Vocabulaire et grammaire, pp. 100–101
Cahier d'activités, pp. 81–83   **Online** workbooks

13 Différences d'opinion ✿1.2   1. d 2. a 3. b 4. c 5. e

Lisons Jade et Sophie ne sont pas d'accord sur l'exposition qu'elles viennent de voir. Finis les phrases logiquement.

1. Ta réaction est très...
2. Moi, je trouve cette exposition...
3. La visite à pied est un peu...
4. Mais ce sculpteur est vraiment un homme...
5. Ces œuvres sont très...

a. passionnante.
b. fatigante.
c. intéressant.
d. surprenante.
e. impressionnantes.

14 Comment dirais-tu? ✿1.2

Écrivons/Parlons Complète chaque phrase avec l'adjectif verbal du verbe entre parenthèses.

1. En automne, les feuilles ont des couleurs _____. (changer)
2. Les enfants de Laura sont très _____. (amuser)
3. Le café n'est pas une boisson _____. (calmer)
4. Il m'a offert une jolie plante _____. (grimper)
5. J'ai passé des vacances très _____. (relaxer)
6. L'acteur qui joue César est une étoile _____ du cinéma américain. (monter)
7. La cuisine française est très riche et très _____. (nourrir)
8. Quand la soupe est très très chaude, elle est _____. (brûler)
9. Bravo! Tes notes sont très _____. (encourager)

1. changeantes
2. amusants
3. calmante
4. grimpante
5. relaxantes
6. montante
7. nourrissante
8. brûlante
9. encourageantes

Core Instruction

TEACHING GRAMMAIRE

1. Read **En anglais** aloud with students. **(2 min.)**

2. Go over Points 1–2. Point out to students that although every verb has a present participle, not every present participle makes sense as an adjective. **(4 min.)**

3. Call out various verbs and ask students to give you first the **nous** form and then the present participle. **(2 min.)**

15 Au musée d'art contemporain 🎬 1.2

Écrivons Michel visite un musée d'art contemporain avec Christian et son petit frère. Christian est d'accord avec tout ce que Michel dit. Imagine les réponses de Christian.

> MODÈLE —Cette exposition m'intéresse beaucoup.
> —Oui, elle est (très) intéressante.

1. Fais attention, ces sculptures en métal sont dangereuses, elles coupent.

2. Excuse-moi, mais ton petit frère m'énerve vraiment.

3. J'adore regarder ces paysages, ils me reposent.

4. Les croquis humoristiques m'ont amusé.

5. Les explications du guide m'ennuient toujours.

16 Qu'est-ce que tu en penses? 🎬 1.2

Parlons/Écrivons Écris une phrase pour décrire chaque photo. Utilise des adjectifs verbaux.

ennuyer	amuser	relaxer
énerver	intéresser	obéir

MODÈLE   Ce chien est très obéissant.

1.   2.   3.   4.   5.

Communication

17 Opinions personnelles 🎬 1.1

Parlons Avec un(e) camarade, posez-vous au moins cinq questions sur vos goûts personnels au sujet de littérature, de cinéma, etc. Utilisez des adjectifs verbaux.

♻ *Souviens-toi!* The subjunctive, pp. 150, 190, 228, 294

> MODÈLE —**Quel genre de livres aimes-tu lire?**
> —**J'aime les livres qui sont amusants, par exemple, des BD, mais mes parents ne pensent pas que ce soit une lecture très intéressante...**

---

15 Answers

1. Oui, elles sont coupantes.
2. Oui, il est énervant.
3. Oui, ils sont reposants.
4. Oui, ils sont amusants.
5. Oui, elles sont ennuyantes.

16 Possible Answers

1. Ces enfants sont énervants!
2. Ce cours est ennuyant.
3. Cet article est amusant.
4. Ce cours de yoga est relaxant.
5. Cette exposition est intéressante.

Communication

Pair Activity: Interpersonal

Have partners act out a scene in which they are discussing a movie or TV show episode. One student uses **me** as an object pronoun to tell how the movie or or show affected him or her. The other student will respond with a present participle of the verb used by the partner to express agreement or disagreement. 🎬 1.1

MODÈLE
— **Le documentaire sur les baleines m'a beaucoup intéressé.**
— **Ah bon? Je ne l'ai pas trouvé intéressant du tout!**

Differentiated Instruction

SLOWER PACE LEARNERS

Extension Before introducing the grammar presentation, you may want to review the uses of the present participle as verb and gerund. Write the following sentences on the board and ask students for the English equivalents.

Elle est partie en parlant à son ami.

Il ne peut pas parler en étudiant.

Ayant faim, elle a mangé tout le gâteau.

Voici un plan indiquant les endroits de la ville.   🎬 1.2, 4.1

SPECIAL LEARNING NEEDS

13 Students with Learning Disabilities For a learning disabled student, it may be difficult to continue the sentences appropriately with so many choices. You might group beginnings with appropriate endings and allow students to focus on a smaller set of sentences at one time. Suggested beginnings and endings might be 1 – 3 and 4 – 5.

Assess

Assessment Program

Quiz: Grammaire 1

Alternative Assessment

Differentiated Practice and Assessment CD-ROM

Online Assessment
   my.hrw.com

Test Generator

Resources

Planning:

Lesson Planner

 One-Stop Planner

Practice:

Grammar Tutor for Students of French, Chapter 9

Cahier de vocabulaire et grammaire

Differentiated Practice and Assessment CD-ROM

Cahier d'activités

Media Guide

 Teaching Transparencies
Bell Work 9.4

 Audio CD 9, Tr. 3

 Interactive Tutor, Disc 2

Bell Work

Use Bell Work 9.4 in the *Teaching Transparencies* or write this activity on the board.

Tu es d'accord avec tout ce que dit Ahmed et tu lui réponds en utilisant l'adjectif qui correspond au verbe qu'il utilise. Commence tes phrases par **C'est vrai.**

1. **Le dernier roman de cet écrivain me passionne.**
2. **Je suis impressionné par le succès de cette femme.**
3. **Les gens intelligents me fascinent.**
4. **Ses dessins humoristiques ne m'ont pas du tout amusé.**
5. **Mais ses sculptures m'ont surpris.** 🌸1.2

COMMON ERROR ALERT
///ATTENTION !\\\

Students may confuse **si** *(if)* with **si** *(yes,* in response to a negative). Punctuation is essential in order to distinguish **Si je peux...** *(If I can...)* from **Si, je peux** *(Yes, I can!).*

⑲ Script

See script on p. 363E.

Application 1

⑱ **Critique d'art** 🌸1.3

✎ **Écrivons** Choisis un des tableaux suivants et écris un paragraphe pour en faire la critique, bonne ou mauvaise.

MODÈLE La toile que je trouve la plus..., c'est...
Le peintre a vraiment montré...

 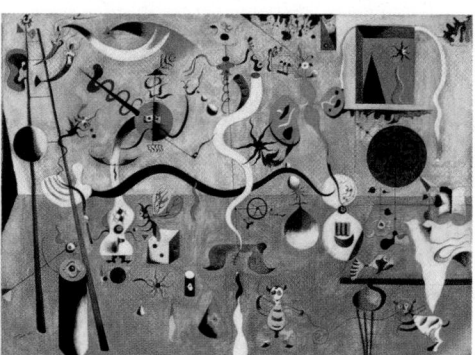 

1. une peinture naïve   2. une peinture moderne   3. une peinture abstraite

Un peu plus

Si and oui

Have you noticed that there are two different words for *yes* in French: **si** and **oui**?

Use **oui** to respond affirmatively to an affirmative question:

—Tu es allée au musée?
—Oui, j'y suis allée hier.

Use **si** to contradict a negative statement or question. Use **Mais si!** for even more emphasis.

—Tu n'aimes pas les tableaux de van Gogh?
—Si! Je les aime beaucoup!

➡ Vocabulaire et grammaire, p. 102
Cahier d'activités, pp. 81–83    **Online** workbooks

⑲ **Écoutons** CD 9, Tr. 3 🌸1.2

🎧 Écoute les conversations suivantes et dis si la personne qui répond **a) contredit** ou **b) ne contredit pas la première personne.** 1. a 2. b 3. a 4. b 5. b

⑳ **Conversation avec Picasso** 🌸1.3

Parlons Imagine les réponses affirmatives du célèbre peintre aux questions suivantes.

1. Vous n'êtes pas d'origine espagnole?
2. Vous avez peint des natures mortes?
3. Vous n'avez pas fait aussi des sculptures?
4. Vous êtes connu dans le monde entier?
5. N'avez-vous pas peint des tableaux abstraits?

Core Instruction

INTEGRATED PRACTICE

1. Have students do Activity 18 to practice previously taught material. **(3 min.)**
2. Introduce **Un peu plus.** (See presentation suggestions at right.) **(4 min.)**
3. Continue with integrated practice Activities 19–23. **(30 min.)**

TEACHING UN PEU PLUS

1. Go over **Un peu plus. (2 min.)**
2. To practice, ask students to answer a few questions with **oui** or **si. Tu ne veux pas que je te donne une bonne note? Si! Tu veux un "A"? Oui! (2 min.)**

Online Practice
go.hrw.com
Application 1 practice
KEYWORD: BD3 CH9

Chapitre 9

Application 1

21 Cours d'art ✿ 1.2, 3.2

Lisons/Écrivons Ahmed est un adolescent qui se passionne pour les arts. Regarde la brochure de cette école d'art, puis réponds aux questions.

Artistes en herbe

Lundi et jeudi :
de 16h à 17h30
Prix: adulte: 85 €
enfant: 55 €

Cours pour adultes. Initiation à la sculpture. *Paul Sequin*

Cours pour adultes. Principes de base de l'aquarelle, préparation de la couleur. *Chantal Leclerc*

Cours d'initiation ou de perfectionnement au tournage. Enfants à partir de 10 ans. *Alexis Legrand*

1. Quel professeur Ahmed doit-il contacter s'il veut apprendre à utiliser un tour?

2. Qui ne prend que des débutants?

3. Quel professeur est-ce qu'il doit choisir s'il s'intéresse au dessin et à la peinture?

4. À quel cours un enfant peut-il s'inscrire?

5. Ahmed voudrait apprendre à faire des statues. Qui va-t-il contacter?

22 Un mécène ✿ 1.3

Écrivons Tu as décidé d'aider un jeune artiste. Écris-lui une note pour lui expliquer ce qu'il devrait faire pour avoir du succès.

♻ *Souviens-toi!* The conditional, p. 330

 **Communication**

 HOLT SoundBooth ONLINE RECORDING

23 Scénario ✿ 1.1

Parlons Tu dois écrire un article pour une revue d'art. Tu interviewes un artiste célèbre joué par un de tes camarades. Pose-lui cinq questions au sujet de ses œuvres et de sa vie. Jouez cette scène devant la classe.

---

20 Answers
1. Si, je suis espagnol.
2. Oui, j'ai peint des natures mortes.
3. Si, j'ai fait aussi des sculptures.
4. Oui, je suis connu dans le monde entier.
5. Si, j'ai peint des tableaux abstraits.

21 Answers
1. Alexis Legrand
2. Paul Sequin, Chantal Leclerc
3. Chantal Leclerc
4. la sculpture, la poterie
5. Paul Sequin

Communication

Group Activity: Interpersonal

In groups of three, have students write two negative questions to their fellow group members. Then have students take turns asking another group member a question. The response can be positive or negative. The third group member should contradict the response with **si** and state a reason for his or her contradiction.

MODÈLE
— **Tu ne fais pas la cuisine?**
— **Non, je ne fais pas la cuisine.**
— **Si, il fait la cuisine. En fait, il fait un bon gâteau!**

✿ 1.1

Differentiated Instruction

ADVANCED LEARNERS

21 Extension After completing this activity, have students create a Web site for a painter who wants to advertise his or her courses in the technique of water color. Students should provide a brief description of the artist's educational background, art exhibits, and teaching experience. They should give the fee for each course, its duration, and the supplies participants will need. Ask students to share their Web sites with the class. ✿ 1.3, 3.1

MULTIPLE INTELLIGENCES

Linguistic Ask students to research the life and work of their favorite painter. They can use the Internet as a research tool; just remind them to evaluate all sources carefully. Ask students to be prepared to present their findings in French to the class. ✿ 3.2

Assess

Assessment Program
Quiz: Application 1
Audio CD 9, Tr. 12 🎧
Alternative Assessment
Differentiated Practice and Assessment CD-ROM
Online Assessment
my.hrw.com
Test Generator

Culture

Lecture culturelle

La Polynésie française est riche en artisanat. Parmi les différentes formes d'artisanat, il y a les colliers de coquillage[1], les objets en nacre[2], les bijoux faits avec des perles noires[3], la vannerie[4] et la sculpture. Les îles Marquises sont réputées pour leurs sculptures sur bois que l'on peut acheter directement à l'artiste ou dans les curios[5] de Tahiti. 2.2

La sculpture, l'âme[6] des Marquises

Les Marquisiens sont d'habiles[7] sculpteurs reconnus en dehors de l'archipel. On compte environ une centaine d'artisans sculpteurs aux Marquises.

Les sculpteurs reproduisent les objets anciens et traditionnels : les tikis (statuettes sculptées à l'image des dieux), les casse-têtes[8] et les lances. Les ustensiles de la vie de tous les jours, plats ronds ou allongés, sont aussi sculptés. Les motifs décoratifs qui ornent les sculptures sont spécifiques à chaque archipel. Ils couvrent en général toute la surface des objets.

La sculpture sur pierre existe toujours mais est rare. Le matériau le plus utilisé est le bois[9]. Le miro ou bois rose et le tou (bois très dur de couleur brune avec de larges veines[10]) sont les bois les plus recherchés. Les artisans utilisent aussi le santal[11], l'acajou[12] et aussi le maru maru[13]. Les noix de coco sont aussi sculptées et peintes.

Compréhension 1.2

1. Pourquoi est-ce que les îles Marquises sont connues?
2. Quel matériau est le plus utilisé pour la sculpture?
3. Quels sont les différents types de sculpture?

1. Elles sont connues pour la sculpture.
2. le bois
3. les tikis, les casse-têtes, les lances, les ustensiles quotidiens

1. *sea shells* 2. *mother-of-pearl* 3. *black pearls* 4. *wickerwork* 5. petits magasins artisanaux 6. *soul* 7. *skilled* 8. *clubs* 9. *wood* 10. *grains (in the wood)* 11. *sandalwood* 12. *mahogany* 13. *type de bois*

Resources

Planning:
Lesson Planner
 One-Stop Planner
Practice:
Cahier d'activités

Prereading Questions

You might ask these questions before students read the selection.

1. **Vas-tu parfois dans des magasins qui vendent des produits faits par des artisans?**
2. **Est-ce que tu as déjà regardé des artisans travailler?**
3. **Est-ce que tu as déjà essayé de peindre, faire une poterie ou créer des bijoux?**
4. **Est-ce que tu aimes bricoler ou travailler avec tes mains?**

Active reading questions

1. **Combien de sculpteurs y a-t-il aux Marquises? (une centaine)**
2. **Quels objets traditionnels ou anciens est-ce que ces sculpteurs reproduisent? (tikis, casse-tête, lances)**
3. **Quels ustensiles reproduisent-ils? (ceux de la vie de tous les jours, des plats)**
4. **Est-ce qu'ils sculptent beaucoup les pierres? (non)**
5. **Qu'est-ce qu'ils font avec les noix de coco? (Ils les sculptent et ils les peignent)**

Vocabulaire supplémentaire

You might use these terms to discuss the selection.

le peintre	*painter*
le potier	*potter*
le tisserand	*weaver*
le cordonnier	*shoe-maker*
le forgeron	*blacksmith*

Core Instruction

LECTURE CULTURELLE

1. Read the introductory paragraph and discuss it with the class. **(3 min.)**
2. Read *La sculpture, l'âme des Marquises* as a class. **(5 min.)**
3. Ask volunteers to answer the questions in **Compréhension. (5 min.)**
4. Ask for students if they know where to find similar crafts in the U.S. (Hawaii) **(2 min.)**

COMPARAISONS ET COMMUNAUTÉ

1. Have students read *Les musées en France* and discuss it in small groups. **(8 min.)**
2. Have students complete the **Et toi?** questions with a partner. **(5 min.)**
3. Go over **Communauté et professions** with students. Ask for volunteers to research how to become an opera singer in the U.S. and what languages are required. **(8 min.)**

Comparaisons

Le musée d'Orsay

Les musées en France. 🏵2.1

Tu viens d'arriver à Paris. C'est lundi, il fait beau.
Tu te promènes et tu découvres la ville.
Le lendemain matin, tu décides d'aller visiter
le musée du Louvre. Tu arrives à la pyramide et

a. tu achètes ton billet d'entrée et tu visites
   les salles.

b. le musée n'est ouvert qu'aux Parisiens le mardi.

c. le musée est fermé.

En France, tous les musées nationaux ferment leurs portes le mardi. Il y
a 34 musées nationaux dans le pays dont 15 à Paris. Le musée du Louvre,
qui est un musée national, est ouvert tous les jours sauf le mardi et les
jours fériés suivants: le 1er janvier, le 1er mai, le 15 août et le 25 décembre.
Les musées nationaux et les musées municipaux ne ferment pas les
mêmes jours. Alors, avant de décider de visiter un musée, vérifie les jours
et les heures d'ouverture.

🏵1.3, 4.2

ET TOI?

1. Est-ce que tu visites souvent des musées? Lesquels as-tu déjà visités?

2. Aux États-Unis, est-ce que les musées sont ouverts tous les jours? Quels jours sont-ils fermés?

Communauté et professions

Le français et la musique 🏵4.2, 5.2

Certains grands opéras, comme *Carmen* de Georges
Bizet, sont en français. Comment devient-on chanteur
d'opéra? En France, chaque année, l'atelier lyrique de
l'Opéra de Paris recrute des jeunes qui doivent passer une
audition: cinq airs[1] d'opéra dans trois langues différentes,
dont le français. Y a-t-il des écoles qui forment les chanteurs
d'opéra aux États-Unis? Quelles langues sont nécessaires pour
devenir un chanteur d'opéra de renommée internationale?
Le français est-il indispensable? Fais des recherches et
présente ce que tu as trouvé à ta classe.

———
1. arias

Affiche de Carmen

Culture

Bulletin Board Project

Have students research the art of French Polynesia. What art forms besides sculpture is prevalent in French Polynesia? Ask groups of students to find one or two photos of French Polynesian art on the Internet or in the library. They should make copies of the photos and write French captions. Ask volunteers to display all captioned photos on a classroom bulletin board. Discuss all entries as a class.
🏵3.2

Cultures

🏵 Products and Perspectives

Paul Gauguin, the famous French painter, spent the last twelve years of his life in Tahiti and in the Marquesas Islands. It was in these exotic islands where he painted his most famous paintings. Have students search for paintings of this artist on the Internet or at the library. 🏵2.2

Communities

Career Path

Have students brainstorm careers related to the arts. Ask if the knowledge of a second language might be useful. For example, would it be important for a guide or an art museum director to speak a foreign language? Why? Suggest that students interested in this field research want ads in French newspapers or magazines online. 🏵5.1

Differentiated Instruction

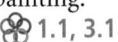

ADVANCED LEARNERS

Extension The leading Post-impressionist painter, Paul Gauguin (1848–1903), was looking for a tropical paradise when he moved to Tahiti and then to the Marquesas Islands where he is buried. One of his famous sayings is, **"L'artiste ne doit pas copier la nature mais prendre les éléments de la nature et créer un nouvel élément."** Show students a copy of one of Gauguin's Polynesian paintings and ask them to discuss how his quote applies to his painting.
🏵1.1, 3.1

MULTIPLE INTELLIGENCES

Artistic Ask students what they recognize as art. Many students will identify painting and drawing as art and a few more might add sculptures. Ask students to name an artist, and some may provide the name of a well-known painter. Create an assignment for students to research a French artist whose field is neither painting nor drawing. Have them tell about the artist's choice of art form. 🏵3.1

Objectifs
- to make suggestions and recommendations
- to give an impression

Vocabulaire *à l'œuvre* **2**

On va au spectacle

une comédie musicale

Les comédies musicales mélangent plusieurs genres: danse, chant et théâtre.

un ballet

un danseur/ une danseuse

une ballerine

un tutu

Les danseurs ont eu beaucoup de succès.

L'orchestre est composé de musiciens.

le chef d'orchestre

les violonistes

Le chef d'orchestre **donne la mesure.**

Les spectateurs applaudissent.

Resources

Planning:

Lesson Planner

 One-Stop Planner

Presentation:

 Teaching Transparencies **Vocabulaire 9.3, 9.4**

Practice:

Cahier de vocabulaire et grammaire

Differentiated Practice and Assessment CD-ROM

Media Guide

 Teaching Transparencies Bell Work 9.5

 Interactive Tutor, Disc 2

Bell Work

Use Bell Work 9.5 in the *Teaching Transparencies,* or write this activity on the board.

Réponds affirmativement aux questions suivantes.

1. Vous n'êtes pas français?
2. Vous connaissez bien Paris?
3. Vous prenez le métro?
4. Alors, vous ne prenez pas le bus?
5. Vous aimez peindre?
6. Vous ne sculptez pas du tout? 🌸 1.2

Cinquain Poetry

Ask students to create a poem with the new chapter vocabulary.

Line 1 One word that is the title
Line 2 Two words
Line 3 Three words
Line 4 Four words
Line 5 One word that relates to the title

Sample answer

**Spectacle
Comédie musicale
Un beau décor
Une scène très comique
Applaudir**

Core Instruction

TEACHING VOCABULAIRE

1. Introduce the vocabulary, using transparencies **Vocabulaire 9.3** and **9.4.** Model the pronunciation of each word or expression. **(3 min.)**

2. Call out new vocabulary words (**l'orchestre, un clown**) and have students point to the illustrations on the transparency. **(2 min.)**

3. Ask students what shows they go to and why.
— **À quels spectacles est-ce que tu vas?**
— **Je vais au cirque.** — **Pourquoi?** — **Parce que j'aime les clowns. (3 min.)**

4. Model the pronunciation of the expressions in **Exprimons-nous!** Have partners write similar sentences about shows and artists of their choice. **(4 min.)**

Allons au cirque!

le chapiteau

la piste

un clown

un jongleur/une jongleuse

un(e) trapéziste

une affiche

D'autres mots utiles

la baguette	*baton*	un(e) pianiste	*piano player*
une chorégraphie	*choreography*	une représentation	*show*
le décor	*set*	un rôle	*part*
une ouvreuse	*usherette*	la scène	*set*
une partition	*music sheet*	une tournée	*tour*

Exprimons-nous!

To make suggestions and recommendations

Interactive TUTOR

Je te **recommande plutôt d'**aller au cirque.
I recommend that you . . . instead.

Ne va surtout pas voir..., il chante **faux!**
Make sure you don't go . . . , . . . out of tune!

Va voir..., **sur scène** il est génial!
Go and see . . . , on the stage . . . !

Ça (ne) vaut (pas) la peine/le coup de réserver. *It is not worth . . .*

Vocabulaire et grammaire, pp. 103–105   **Online** workbooks

▶ Vocabulaire supplémentaire—Les arts, p. R 21

Online Practice
go.hrw.com
Vocabulaire 2 practice
KEYWORD: BD3 CH9

T P R
TOTAL PHYSICAL RESPONSE

Have students respond to these commands.

Lève le pouce si ça vaut la peine d'aller au cirque.

Lève les deux mains si tu aimes les trapézistes.

Lève-toi si ça vaut le coup de voir les clowns.

Lève le doigt si tu sais lire une partition.

Viens ici si tu portes parfois un tutu.

Montre-nous une affiche.

Then have some students mime the following situations.

Tu es chef d'orchestre.

Tu danses comme une ballerine.

Tu chantes faux dans un opéra.

Tu es sur scène comme jongleur.

Le spectacle est fini et tu applaudis. ✿ 1.2

Teacher to Teacher

Sharon Telich
Westside MS
Omaha, NE

This is Sharon's idea to reinforce the concept of **si** versus **oui**.
"Have each student prepare two flashcards, one with **si** written on it and the other with **oui**. Make a list of questions that would be answered "yes" by most of the class. Personalize the questions by using students' names whenever possible. As you read each question aloud, students must answer, "yes" by holding up a card that says **oui** or **si**. After surveying the class for all the answers, have one student give the survey results." ✿ 1.2

Differentiated Instruction

ADVANCED LEARNERS

Extension Have students imagine that they work for their local newspaper as entertainment columnists. Their task is to report on past, current, and future cultural events in their town. Students should write at least three paragraphs, making suggestions and recommendations. Remind students to give their column a title. Ask some students to present their column to the class. ✿ 1.3

SPECIAL LEARNING NEEDS

Students with AD(H)D Ask students to check out a play (drama or comedy) from the school library for the purpose of translation and performance. Form groups and have each group choose a scene from the play to translate into French. Then have groups perform their scenes for the class. ✿ 1.3

Resources

Planning:

Lesson Planner

One-Stop Planner

Presentation:

Teaching Transparencies
Vocabulaire 9.3, 9.4

Practice:

Cahier de vocabulaire et grammaire

Differentiated Practice and Assessment CD-ROM

Media Guide

Audio CD 9, Tr. 4

Interactive Tutor, Disc 2

㉔ Script

1. Oh, là, là! Tu as vu les trapézistes? C'est incroyable, ce qu'ils font! J'ai peur qu'ils tombent, moi!
2. Moi, ce que j'aime le mieux, c'est ce mélange de danse, de théâtre et de chant. Et puis, celle-ci est vraiment drôle!
3. Je te recommande plutôt d'aller voir *Le lac des cygnes.* La chorégraphie et les costumes sont magnifiques!
4. Ne va surtout pas le voir! Les décors sont horribles, l'orchestre est nul et les chanteurs chantent faux!
5. Ça vaut vraiment le coup d'aller voir Gilles Martin sur scène. Il chante super bien et son groupe est génial!

㉖ Possible Answers

1. Va voir ce ballet!
2. Je te recommande plutôt d'aller voir ce spectacle de cirque.
3. Ça vaut la peine de voir cette pièce de théâtre.
4. Ça ne vaut pas le coup de voir ce film.

㉗ Answers

1. surtout pas voir
2. l'impression
3. vaut pas la peine
4. l'air
5. semble
6. recommandes
7. Ça vaut le coup d'y aller.

Entre copains

Ça ne casse pas des briques	*It's not great.*
faire un bide	*to flop*
faire le clown	*to clown around*
faire un tabac	*to be a hit*

㉔ Écoutons CD 9, Tr. 4 ♦1.2

Écoute chaque commentaire et dis de quels types de spectacles ces personnes parlent.

2 **a.** une comédie musicale
b. une pièce de théâtre
3 **c.** un ballet

1 **d.** un spectacle de cirque
5 **e.** un concert de rock
4 **f.** un opéra

㉕ Au spectacle ♦1.2

Lisons/Parlons Lis ces descriptions et dis de qui ou de quoi on parle.

c **1.** C'est l'endroit où la ballerine danse.
e **2.** C'est ce qu'on fait à la fin d'un spectacle qu'on a beaucoup aimé.
b **3.** Les enfants adorent ce personnage au cirque.
d **4.** C'est la personne qui donne des instructions aux musiciens.
g **5.** C'est le vêtement que les danseuses portent.
a **6.** C'est la personne qui vous amène à votre place.

a. l'ouvreuse
b. le clown
c. la scène
d. le chef d'orchestre
e. applaudir
f. l'affiche
g. le tutu

㉖ Des recommandations ♦1.3

Parlons/Écrivons Utilise les expressions d'**Exprimons-nous** pour suggérer ou recommander ces spectacles.

MODÈLE Je te recommande d'aller à ce concert de jazz!

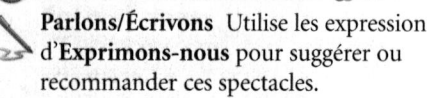

1. un ballet

2. un spectacle de cirque

3. une pièce de théâtre

4. un film

Core Instruction

TEACHING EXPRIMONS-NOUS!

1. Model the pronunciation of each of the expressions in **Exprimons-nous!** (**2 min.**)
2. Point out that the expressions ending in **que** are followed by sentences that could stand alone, whereas the other expressions are an essential part of the sentence. (**2 min.**)
3. Read aloud complete sentences. Students repeat each sentence beginning it with one of the new expressions that ends with **que**.

Then repeat the expressions ending in **de** and **à** and ask students to form complete sentences with them. (**2 min.**)

4. Have partners write similar sentences to give their impression about other things or events. (**3 min.**)

Exprimons-nous!

To give an impression

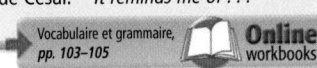

On dirait que c'est le même acteur qui joue les deux rôles. *It looks like . . .*

Il me semble que ce spectacle s'inspire de *Cats*. *It seems to me that . . .*

J'ai l'impression d'avoir déjà vu ça quelque part. *I have the impression that . . .*

J'ai l'impression que cet acteur n'est pas fait pour le rôle. *I have the impression that . . .*

Ils ont l'air de s'amuser sur scène. *They seem to . . .*

Ça me fait penser à une sculpture de César. *It reminds me of . . .*

Vocabulaire et grammaire, pp. 103–105 — Online workbooks

27 Une mauvaise expérience! 🌸1.2

Écrivons Complète la conversation suivante entre Amélie et son copain Alex. Utilise les expressions d'**Exprimons-nous!**

AMÉLIE Ne va ___1___ la dernière comédie musicale de Marcel Candide.

ALEX J'ai ___2___ que tu n'es pas la seule à ne pas avoir aimé ce spectacle! Les critiques sont très mauvaises.

AMÉLIE Pour une fois, je suis d'accord avec elles! Ça ne ___3___ d'y aller. Les danseurs ont ___4___ de s'ennuyer sur scène. Il me ___5___ qu'ils n'aiment pas ce qu'ils font.

ALEX Je suppose que tu me ___6___ plutôt d'aller au concert des *Faux Pas* qui passent en ville?

AMÉLIE Ah oui, alors! Eux, ils sont géniaux ___7___!

Communication

HOLT **SoundBooth** ONLINE RECORDING

28 Scénario 🌸1.1

Parlons En groupes de 3 ou 4, choisissez un spectacle qu'on peut voir dans votre ville ou qui a du succès en ce moment. Des membres du groupe ont vu ce spectacle; les autres ne l'ont pas vu, mais veulent aller le voir. Ils/Elles demandent leurs opinions aux personnes qui ont vu le spectacle. Préparez et jouez cette scène devant la classe.

MODÈLE —Dis, Karen, tu as vu la... qui passe en ville?
—Oui et à mon avis...
—Ah bon? Pourquoi?
—J'ai l'impression...

Flash culture

La tradition musicale est très variée aux Antilles. Dans les années 30, Alexandre Stellis fait découvrir la biguine aux Français. Aujourd'hui, le Zouk, exporté par des groupes célèbres comme Kassav' et Malavoi, est très populaire. À la Guadeloupe, les esclaves ont apporté leurs rythmes battus aux sons des tambours. De nos jours, la musique gwo ka est basée sur ces deux tambours, le boula et le maké.

Quel genre de musique ressemble au Zouk aux États-Unis? 🌸4.2

Connections
Music Link

The people of the Antillean island of Dominica, where music plays an important social and cultural role, have created a form of music called **bouyon**. This music combines elements from several styles and is very popular in Dominica, especially the group WCK (Windward Caribbean Kulture). WCK originated the style by blending the island's traditional music and dance, such as cadence-lypso, jing ping, and other styles of Caribbean music. **Bouyon** is also known as jump-up music in Guadeloupe and Martinique. Students might listen to songs by WCK and identify the different musical styles that the group combines. 🌸3.1, 5.2

Communication

28 Group Activity: Interpersonal

Have students think of a music CD they just bought or a movie they recently saw. Then, in small groups, have them take turns giving their opinions and recommendations. Have the group members add their recommendations, suggestions, and impressions with **Vocabulaire 2** expressions. You might ask for one volunteer from each group to summarize the recommendations for the class. 🌸1.1

Differentiated Instruction

SLOWER PACE LEARNERS

24 Extension Before listening to the recording of this activity, have volunteers use circumlocution to describe the events (a.–f.). Encourage students to ask for clarifications if needed. Then have students complete this activity. 🌸1.2

SPECIAL LEARNING NEEDS

28 Students with Learning Disabilities Students with learning disabilities will need to be carefully distributed among the groups and woven into groups with more advanced communicators. Students with learning disabilities often tend to feel insecure and might better respond to the prompting of classmates to get involved and participate in the group activity.

Assess

Assessment Program
Quiz: Vocabulaire 2
Alternative Assessment
Differentiated Practice and Assessment CD-ROM
Online Assessment
my.hrw.com
Test Generator

Resources

Planning:

Lesson Planner

 One-Stop Planner

Practice:

Grammar Tutor for Students of French, Chapter 9

Cahier de vocabulaire et grammaire

Differentiated Practice and Assessment CD-ROM

Cahier d'activités

Media Guide

Teaching Transparencies Bell Work 9.6

Audio CD 9, Tr. 5

Interactive Tutor, Disc 2

Bell Work

Use Bell Work 9.6 in the *Teaching Transparencies* or write this activity on the board.

Qu'est-ce qu'ils font? Fais des phrases logiques.

1. Le clown...
2. Le chef d'orchestre...
3. Les ballerines...
4. Les spectateurs...
5. L'ouvreuse...

a. dansent sur la scène.
b. fait rire les enfants.
c. amène les spectateurs à leur place.
d. dirige les musiciens.
e. applaudissent à la fin de la représentation. 🌻1.2

Objectifs
- review of comparative and superlative
- review of demonstrative pronouns

Grammaire à l'œuvre 2

Révisions The comparative and superlative

Do you remember how to form the comparative and superlative of adjectives, adverbs, and nouns in French?

COMPARATIVE	SUPERLATIVE
plus moins } [adjective] **que** aussi Cet acteur-ci est **moins** connu **que** celui-là.	*If the adjective precedes the noun:* le la } plus } [adjective] **de** les moins C'est **le plus** connu **des** chanteurs d'opéra. *If the adjective follows the noun:* le le la } [noun] la } plus } [adjective] **de** les les moins C'est le chanteur **le plus** connu **de** tous.
plus moins } [adverb] **que** aussi Il joue **aussi** bien **que** toi.	le } plus } [adverb] moins C'est lui qui chante **le moins** bien.
plus de autant de } [noun] **que** moins de Il a **plus de** succès **qu'**elle.	

Déjà vu!
Bon, bien and **mauvais** have irregular comparative and superlative forms.
Cet acteur est **meilleur** que celui-là.
Je peins **mieux** que toi.
Cet acteur était **pire** que les autres.

Vocabulaire et grammaire, *pp. 106–107*
Cahier d'activités, *pp. 85–87*

Online workbooks

29 Écoutons CD 9, Tr. 5 🌻1.2

🎧 Écoute ces commentaires et complète les phrases suivantes.

1. La pièce de théâtre était _____ que la comédie musicale.
   a. plus amusante   **b.** moins amusante
2. Les jongleurs étaient _____ bons que les trapézistes.
   a. plus   **b.** aussi
3. Le chapiteau de ce cirque était _____ que celui de l'autre cirque.
   a. moins grand   **b.** aussi petit
4. Le premier clown chantait _____ que le deuxième clown.
   a. plus mal   **b.** mieux
5. L'orchestre était _____ que l'orchestre de l'opéra.
   a. meilleur   **b.** aussi bon

29 Script

— Je n'ai pas trouvé la comédie musicale aussi amusante que la pièce de théâtre que nous avons vue la semaine dernière.

— Au cirque, les jongleurs étaient aussi géniaux que les trapézistes.

— Le chapiteau était plus petit que celui de l'autre cirque.

— Le premier clown ne chantait déjà pas très bien, mais alors le deuxième chantait vraiment mal.

— L'orchestre jouait mieux que celui de l'opéra.

Core Instruction

TEACHING GRAMMAIRE

1. Read **Déjà vu!** aloud with students. Tell students that the comparative and superlative forms of adjectives will also agree with the nouns they modify. **(1 min.)**

2. Go over Points 1 and 2. Remind students that adverbs modify verbs and are invariable. Point out that when used with nouns, comparatives indicate greater or lesser quantity, rather than describing qualities of the nouns. **(4 min.)**

30 Comparaisons 1.2

Lisons/Écrivons Philippe et ses amis comparent différents spectacles. Forme des phrases complètes avec les éléments suivants.

MODÈLE   théâtre Rayneau / être / + / petit / l'opéra
Le théâtre Rayneau est plus petit que l'opéra.

1. dans / comédie musicale / la danse / être / = / important / le chant
2. violonistes / sembler / + / calme / chef d'orchestre
3. enfants / aimer / − / jongleurs / clowns
4. cirque / avoir / = / spectateurs / opéra
5. dans / théâtre moderne / scène / être / − / bien décoré / dans / théâtre classique

31 Au théâtre 1.3

Parlons Écris cinq phrases pour décrire cette illustration. Utilise des **superlatifs**.

MODÈLE   **C'est la meilleure pièce de l'année!**

Plus de 50.000 personnes ont déjà applaudi
Axel Trio
dans
Le bouffon
Les critiques sont d'accord :
C'est le chef-oeuvre de l'année !

30 Answers

1. Dans une comédie musicale, la danse est aussi importante que le chant.
2. Les violonistes semblent plus calmes que le chef d'orchestre.
3. Les enfants aiment moins les jongleurs que les clowns.
4. Le cirque a autant de spectateurs que l'opéra.
5. Dans le théâtre moderne, la scène est moins bien décorée que dans le théâtre classique.

Communication

Group Activity: Interpersonal

Have students think of two of their favorite TV shows. Then form small groups and have them discuss these TV shows, the characters, the actors, and so forth. Group members should use the comparative and superlative in the discussion. Remind them to use the appropriate expressions when they want to interrupt and redirect the conversation. 1.1

Communication

HOLT **SoundBooth**
ONLINE RECORDING

32 Interview 1.1

Parlons Demande à un(e) camarade quelle activité il/elle aime le plus et le moins. Ton/Ta camarade te dira aussi quelle activité il/elle fait plus souvent que les autres. Ensuite, échangez les rôles.

MODÈLE   —Qu'est-ce que tu préfères faire le week-end?
—Je préfère jouer au foot, mais je fais plus souvent du skate. Ce que j'aime le moins, c'est faire la vaisselle. Et toi?

Differentiated Instruction

ADVANCED LEARNERS

Variation Ask advanced learners to present the comparative and superlative to the class. They should show how the comparative and superlative are formed and provide examples. Encourage students to use transparencies or to create a PowerPoint® presentation. Encourage all students to ask for clarifications if needed. 1.3

SPECIAL LEARNING NEEDS

31 Students with Language Impairments
Allow students to record a conversation about the scene they see in this activity. Ask them to describe the entire scene in as much detail as possible using as many colorful adjectives as they can. Upon completion, recordings should be shared with the teacher and a speech therapist if one is assigned. 1.3

Resources

Planning:
Lesson Planner

 One-Stop Planner

Practice:
Grammar Tutor for Students of French, Chapter 9

Cahier de vocabulaire et grammaire

Differentiated Practice and Assessment CD-ROM

Cahier d'activités

Media Guide

 Teaching Transparencies Bell Work 9.7

 Interactive Tutor, Disc 2

Bell Work

Use Bell Work 9.7 in the *Teaching Transparencies,* or write this activity on the board.

Compare-les! Forme des phrases complètes avec les éléments suivants.

1. Le clown / être / + / drôle / le jongleur
2. Cette comédie musicale / être / = / bon / cet opéra
3. Cette danseuse / danser / + / bien / moi
4. Il y / avoir / = / spectateurs / au concert / au cirque
5. Cette pièce de théâtre / être / − / long / ce film

🎭 1.2

COMMON ERROR ALERT
///// ATTENTION !

Students may have trouble remembering that the plural of **celui** is **ceux**. It may be helpful to compare them to the disjunctive pronouns **lui** and **eux**.

Flash culture

À Tahiti, les chants et les danses jouent un grand rôle dans la vie sociale. Par exemple, lors des grandes fêtes du Heiva en juillet, on peut assister à des démonstrations de marches sur le feu, à des courses de pirogues, à des spectacles de danses et de chants accompagnés de tambours, de flûtes et d'ukulélés. Les danses traditionnelles peuvent représenter des thèmes aussi variés que des danses guerrières ou des scènes de la vie de tous les jours. 🎭 4.2

À quel état des États-Unis cette culture te fait penser? Pourquoi?

Révisions Demonstrative pronouns

Interactive TUTOR

1 Use a form of **celui** to say *this one, that one, these,* or *those.*

	MASCULINE	FEMININE
SINGULAR	celui	celle
PLURAL	ceux	celles

2 Demonstrative pronouns can be used:

- with **-ci** or **-là** to specify *this/these* or *that/those*
  Tu as parlé avec quel clown? **Celui-ci** ou **celui-là**?

- with **de** plus a noun
  Quelle pièce préfères-tu? **Celle de** Molière ou **celle de** Racine?

- with a relative pronoun
  Ceux qui vont à l'opéra chaque week-end doivent avoir beaucoup d'argent.

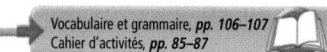
Vocabulaire et grammaire, pp. 106–107
Cahier d'activités, pp. 85–87
Online workbooks

---

33 **De quoi on parle?** 🎭 1.2

Lisons Complète les phrases suivantes avec le bon pronom.

1. Quel spectacle allez-vous voir? (Celui / Celle) que Jonas a recommandé?

2. J'ai offert un poster de clown à mon petit frère. (Celles / Ceux) des acrobates n'étaient pas géniaux.

3. Ces jongleurs sont impressionnants. Ils sont meilleurs que (celles / ceux) que j'ai vus l'année dernière.

4. Cette comédie-ci est plus amusante que (celle-là / celle) dont tout le monde parle!

5. Tu aimes cet acteur ou tu préfères (celui-là / celle-ci)?

34 **Danse et musique** 🎭 1.2

Lisons La mère de Jean-Luc l'emmène régulièrement au spectacle, mais il n'a pas l'air de beaucoup s'amuser. Choisis la réponse de Jean-Luc aux questions de sa mère.

d 1. Quels spectacles préfères-tu?

b 2. Laquelle de ces ballerines danse le mieux?

c 3. Quel décor trouves-tu le plus beau?

e 4. Des trois spectacles, lequel est le meilleur?

a. Celles de L. Weber.

b. Celle qui porte un tutu blanc.

c. Celui de la dernière scène.

d. Ceux qui sont amusants.

e. Celui qu'on a vu la dernière fois.

Core Instruction

TEACHING GRAMMAIRE

1. Go over Point 1. Tell students that **celui/celle/ceux/celles** also means *the one/the ones*. **Celle qui chante faux.** *The one who sings off key.* **(2 min.)**

2. Go over Point 2. You may choose to tell students that in an informal conversation, demonstrative pronouns can be used with prepositions other than **de**.

Quel clown préfères-tu? Celui *avec* le nez rouge. **(2 min.)**

3. To practice, ask students questions to be answered with demonstrative pronouns.

— **Ton livre, c'est lequel?** — **C'est celui-ci / celui qui est devant moi.**

— **C'est le stylo de Susan?** — **Non, c'est celui du prof. (4 min.)**

Grammaire 2

35 Initiation à l'opéra 🎬 1.2 **1.** ceux **2.** Celui-là **3.** celle **4.** Ceux-là **5.** celles **6.** celle

Lisons/Écrivons Jean-Luc a finalement décidé de faire un effort et répète tout ce que sa mère dit. Dans chaque phrase, remplace les mots soulignés par un pronom démonstratif.

MODÈLE Ces places-ci ne sont pas aussi chères que les places qui sont au balcon (*balcony*).
Ces places-ci ne sont pas aussi chères que celles qui sont au balcon.

1. Tous <u>les spectateurs</u> qui ont vu ce ballet l'ont beaucoup aimé.
2. <u>Ce monsieur-là</u>, c'est le chef d'orchestre.
3. La pianiste, c'est <u>la dame</u> qui lui parle.
4. <u>Ces gens-là</u> doivent être les violonistes.
5. Ces partitions, ce sont <u>les partitions</u> des musiciens.
6. Et cette baguette, c'est <u>la baguette</u> du chef d'orchestre.

36 Professionnels du spectacle 🎬 1.2

Parlons/Écrivons Regarde l'image et réponds aux questions. Utilise des pronoms démonstratifs.

MODÈLE —Quel jongleur a des balles?
—**Celui qui a une chemise jaune.**

1. Qui c'est, le chef d'orchestre?
2. Lesquels sont les jongleurs?
3. C'est qui, la ballerine?
4. Qui sont les violonistes?
5. Qui sont les spectateurs?

Communication

Pair Activity: Interpersonal

As a class, compile a list of general items found in a fast-food restaurant, for example, hamburgers, fries, shakes, salads, and so on. Ask students to list the items and note a restaurant next to each. Then have students work with a partner and inquire if the partner likes or dislikes each item at the restaurant listed. Have students interview several partners.

MODÈLE
— **Est-ce que tu aimes les frites?**
— **Oui, j'adore les frites, surtout celles de Burger Hut.** 🎬 1.1, 1.2

Communication

37 Interview 🎬 1.1

Parlons Demande à un(e) camarade ce qu'il/elle aime le plus, puis échangez les rôles. Vous pouvez vous inspirer des mots de la boîte. Utilisez des pronoms démonstratifs dans vos réponses.

les films	les voitures	la musique	les tableaux
les activités	les spectacles	les livres	les professions
les vêtements	les matières	les profs	???

MODÈLE —**Quel genre de films est-ce que tu préfères?**
—**Je préfère ceux où il y a beaucoup d'action.**

HOLT **SoundBooth** ONLINE RECORDING

Differentiated Instruction

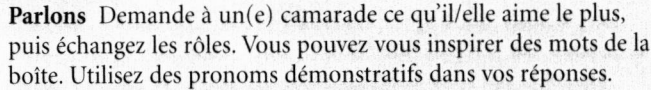

SLOWER PACE LEARNERS

33 Variation Before beginning this activity, ask students to underline the noun that is referred to by the demonstrative pronoun in parentheses. Ask partners to compare their work and encourage them to ask for clarification if needed. 🎬 1.2

MULTIPLE INTELLIGENCES

36 Linguistic The picture in this activity offers the opportunity for a creative writing assignment in French. Ask students to assume a character in the painting and describe the relationships with the other characters depicted. This assignment should be short, fun, and accompanied by personal artwork. Ask volunteers to post the essays on the classroom bulletin board and discuss them as a class. 🎬 1.3

Assess

Assessment Program

Quiz: Grammaire 2

Alternative Assessment

Differentiated Practice and Assessment CD-ROM

Online Assessment

my.hrw.com

Test Generator

Synthèse
• Vocabulaire 2
• Grammaire 2

Application 2

38 À ton avis 🎭1.2

Écrivons Écris un petit paragraphe au sujet d'un spectacle que tu as vu. Dis si tu l'as aimé ou non et pourquoi. Utilise des comparatifs, des superlatifs et des pronoms relatifs.

MODÈLE   **Samedi soir, je suis allé(e) voir... C'était la meilleure représentation de la saison. L'acteur principal était très bon mais celui qui avait le rôle du traître était...**

Un peu plus — Révisions

Review of **savoir** and **connaître**

Use **savoir** to say you
- know a fact
  Je **sais** que Picasso est né en Espagne.
- know how to do something
  Elle **sait** peindre. Elle a étudié les art plastiques à l'université.

Use **connaître** to say you
- know someone or something
  Je **connais** un clown. Il s'appelle Bobo.
- are familiar with a person or place
  Elles **connaissent** bien Nice.

Vocabulaire et grammaire, p. 108
Cahier d'activités, pp. 85–87

Online workbooks

39 Écoutons   CD 9, Tr. 6   🎭1.2

Ton ami t'appelle pour te demander des renseignements au sujet d'un spectacle qu'il veut aller voir. Mais il y a beaucoup de bruit et tu n'entends pas bien. Complète les phrases que tu entends avec le bon verbe.

a. connais	**e.** savoir	**1.** a
b. connaît	**f.** savent	**2.** g
c. sait	**g.** connaissent	**3.** d
d. sais	**h.** connaître	**4.** d
		5. e

40 Un métier difficile 🎭1.2

Lisons/Écrivons Le prof de musique parle du métier de chef d'orchestre. Complète ses phrases avec la forme correcte de **savoir** ou de **connaître**.

1. _____-vous Patrick Botti? C'est un chef d'orchestre français.
2. Vous _____ que ce n'est pas facile, d'être chef d'orchestre?
3. Les chefs d'orchestre _____ communiquer avec les musiciens.
4. Pour être chef d'orchestre, il faut vraiment _____ la musique.
5. Un bon chef d'orchestre _____ donner le rythme.
6. Et puis aussi, il _____ bien les œuvres que l'orchestre joue.

Resources

Planning:
Lesson Planner
 One-Stop Planner

Practice:
Grammar Tutor for Students of French, Chapter 9
Cahier de vocabulaire et grammaire
Differentiated Practice and Assessment CD-ROM
Cahier d'activités
Media Guide
 Teaching Transparencies
   Bell Work 9.8
 Audio CD 9, Tr. 6
 Interactive Tutor, Disc 2

Bell Work

Use Bell Work 9.8 in the *Teaching Transparencies* or write this activity on the board.

Remplace les mots soulignés par le **pronom démonstratif** qui convient.

1. <u>Cette danseuse-ci</u> est la meilleure.
2. Le peintre, c'est <u>l'homme</u> qui a une chemise rouge.
3. Tavernier est <u>le metteur en scène</u> que je préfère.
4. Tous <u>les spectateurs</u> qui ont vu ce spectacle l'ont adoré.
5. Ces sculptures sont <u>les sculptures</u> de Camille Claudel. 🎭1.2

39 Script

See script on p. 363F.

40 Answers

1. Connaissez
2. savez
3. savent
4. connaître
5. sait
6. connaît

Core Instruction

INTEGRATED PRACTICE

1. Have students do Activity 38 to practice previously taught expressions. **(4 min.)**
2. Go over **Un peu plus**. (See presentation suggestions at right.) **(4 min.)**
3. Continue with integrated practice Activities 39–43. **(20 min.)**

TEACHING UN PEU PLUS

1. Review the forms of **savoir** and **connaître**. Point out the **accent circonflexe** in the third-person singular of **connaître**. **(2 min.)**
2. For more practice, call out names of people, places, and activities, or facts related to them. Ask students to respond, using **savoir** or **connaître**. Le prof de maths... Je connais le prof de maths. Où habite Blake... Je ne sais pas où habite Blake. Il va y avoir un examen lundi... Je sais qu'il va y avoir un examen lundi. **(2 min.)**

Online Practice

go.hrw.com

Application 2 practice

KEYWORD: BD3 CH9

41 **Aimez-vous la musique?**  1.2

Écrivons Les personnes suivantes parlent de musique. Forme des phrases complètes pour savoir ce qu'elles disent.

Je	savoir	jouer du piano.
Nous	connaître	cette comédie musicale.
Mes parents		un des musiciens.
Toi, tu		que le violon n'est pas
Mon frère		un instrument facile.
Vous		d'où vient le chef d'orchestre.
		si le spectacle commence
		à huit heures.

Communication

HOLT **SoundBooth**
ONLINE RECORDING

42 **Les connaissances** 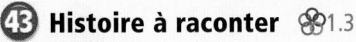 1.2

Parlons Pose des questions à ton/ta camarade pour savoir s'il/elle sait faire ou s'il/elle connaît les choses ou les personnes suivantes.

1. jouer d'un instrument de musique
2. les opéras de Verdi
3. où est le musée d'art moderne
4. le prof de sculpture
5. la dernière chanson à la mode

43 **Histoire à raconter** 1.3

Parlons Regarde les illustrations et explique ce qui s'est passé pendant le spectacle auquel Adrienne a assisté.

Communication

Pair Activity: Interpersonal

Have students make a list of five people or places. Have partners ask each other using **connaître**. Ask them to add some additional facts they know using **savoir que**.

MODÈLE

— **Tu connais New York?**

— **Oui, je connais bien New York. Je sais qu'il y a beaucoup de musées.**

— **Oh, je ne connais pas les musées, mais je sais que Central Park est très beau.** 1.1

Language Examination

PRE-AP PRÉPARATOIRE

To display the drawings to the class, use the Picture Sequences Transparency for Chapter 9.

43 Sample answer

a. **La ballerine a dansé sur scène. Les spectateurs ne l'ont pas du tout aimée.**

b. **Puis le clown a dansé. Il ne savait pas danser et il avait l'air ridicule.**

c. **Les spectateurs ont applaudi le clown. Il a dansé peut-être moins bien que la ballerine, mais c'était lui le plus amusant.**

Differentiated Instruction

SLOWER PACE LEARNERS

43 **Additional Practice** Students may have difficulty remembering the vocabulary they need in order to complete this activity. Have students brainstorm appropriate vocabulary and expressions, and write these on the board. Allow students to refer to the board when talking about the illustrations. 1.2

SPECIAL LEARNING NEEDS

43 **Students with Visual Impairments** For students with visual impairments you might want to copy and enlarge the drawings in this activity. Also, you might ask another student to describe in English each drawing to the visually impaired student.

Assess

Assessment Program

Quiz: Application 2

Audio CD 9, Tr. 13

Alternative Assessment

Differentiated Practice and Assessment CD-ROM

Online Assessment

my.hrw.com

Test Generator

Lecture

AP Reading Suggestion

Remind students not to get caught up on individual words they may not understand. They should rather try to identify the theme of each poem and upon rereading, try to identify details.

Applying the Strategies

For practice with dialoguing with the text, have students use the "Say Something" strategy from the *Reading Strategies and Skills Handbook*.

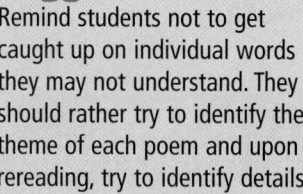

Louis Aragon (1897–1982), poète et écrivain parisien, fonde avec d'autres artistes et écrivains un des mouvements les plus importants du XXᵉ siècle, le surréalisme. À la fin des années 20, Aragon rompt avec les surréalistes et s'engage dans la politique. Après la Deuxième Guerre mondiale, il continue ses activités politiques, mais il retourne aux thèmes plus traditionnels dans ses écrits: la colère, l'amour et l'espérance. Il a écrit entre autres *Le Crève-Cœur* (1941), *Le Fou d'Elsa* (1963) et *Henri Matisse, roman* (1971).

STRATÉGIE pour lire

Dialoguing with the text is a technique you can use to help you understand and analyze the imagery, metaphors, mood, and ultimately, the message or theme of a text. To dialogue with a text, record your reactions and thoughts about what you read as well as any questions you have. For example, you might record how the text makes you feel or what the images in the text bring to mind.

A Avant la lecture 🎴 1.3, 2.2

Le poème suivant s'appelle *Matisse parle*. Est-ce que tu connais l'artiste Henri Matisse? Ses œuvres sont caractérisées par des couleurs vives et des lignes fluides et souples. Regarde le tableau de Matisse sur cette page. Qu'est-ce que tu vois?

Henri Matisse, *Jazz, Le Cauchemar de l'éléphant blanc* (1943)

© 2006 Succession H. Matisse, Paris / Artists Rights Society (ARS), New York

B Answers

1. Matisse
2. le vent, le silence, le parfum, formes passagères, le papier blanc, une feuille, les branches, la lumière
3. l'ouïe
4. optimiste

Core Instruction

LECTURE

1. Read and discuss with students **Stratégie pour lire** and have them do **Avant la lecture**. **(10 min.)**

2. Ask five volunteers to read one stanza each of *Matisse Parle* aloud. Pause regularly to monitor students' comprehension. You may want to point out that each verse of this poem has twelve syllables, a French **alexandrin**.

The last words of every other verse rhyme with each other. You may also want to read the poem to the students so they can hear its rhythm. **(10 min.)**

3. Answer the **Compréhension** questions as a class. **(5 min.)**

CD 9, Tr. 7

Matisse Parle

Je défais dans mes mains toutes les chevelures[1]
Le jour a les couleurs que lui donnent mes mains
Tout ce qu'enfle un soupir[2] dans ma chambre est voilure[3]
Et le rêve durable est mon regard demain

5   J'explique sans les mots le pas qui fait la ronde
J'explique le pied nu qu'a le vent effacé
J'explique sans mystère un moment de ce monde
J'explique le soleil sur l'épaule pensée

J'explique un dessin noir à la fenêtre ouverte
10 J'explique les oiseaux les arbres les saisons
J'explique le bonheur muet[4] des plantes vertes
J'explique le silence habité des maisons

J'explique le parfum des formes passagères
J'explique ce qui fait chanter le papier blanc
15 J'explique ce qui fait qu'une feuille est légère
Et les branches qui sont des bras un peu plus lents

Je rends à la lumière un tribut de justice
Immobile au milieu des malheurs de ce temps
Je peins l'espoir des yeux afin qu'Henri Matisse
20 Témoigne à l'avenir ce que l'homme en attend

Henri Matisse, *Harmonie rouge (La Desserte)* (1908)

© 2006 Succession H. Matisse, Paris / Artists Rights Society (ARS), New York

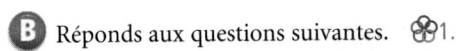

1. *hair* 2. *All that a sigh swells* 3. *sail* 4. *silent*

Compréhension

B Réponds aux questions suivantes. ✿1.2

1. Qui est-ce que *je* représente dans le poème, Matisse ou le poète?
2. Quels mots dans le poème donnent une impression de légèreté?
3. Auxquels des cinq sens (toucher, odorat, vue, goût et ouïe) est-ce que ces mots font penser: *les mots, les oiseaux, muet,* et *le silence*?
4. La vision que Matisse a de l'avenir est plutôt optimiste ou pessimiste? Explique ta réponse.

Active Reading Questions

1. **Quel est le point de vue du poème? (première personne)**
2. **D'après la première strophe, est-ce que Matisse dépeint le monde d'une manière réaliste ou imaginaire? (imaginaire)**
3. **Qu'est-ce que le locuteur explique sans mystère? (un moment)**
4. **Comment le locuteur explique-t-il les choses? (par des images)**
5. **Qu'est-ce que les images de la deuxième strophe symbolisent? (la nature, le silence)**
6. **Quelle qualité ont les images de la quatrième strophe? (la légèreté)**
7. **Quel mot représente la vision de l'avenir communiquée par les tableaux de Matisse? (l'espoir)** ✿1.2

Visualizing a Text

Aragon and Éluard use words to paint remarkable mental images, much as Matisse and Braque created visual images on canvas. Have students reread the poems again, stopping at the end of each line. Ask them to visualize the image(s) mentioned in the line. How do they see each image? What shape and color is it? Can they hear it, smell it, feel it, or taste it? What do they think the image symbolizes? What thoughts and/or feelings does the image evoke in them?

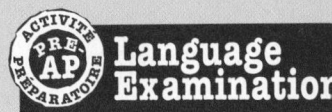

Language Examination

Lecture helps students prepare for Section 1, Part B: **Reading Comprehension.** The audio recording helps them prepare for Part A: **Listening—Short Narratives.**

Differentiated Instruction

SLOWER PACE LEARNERS

Additional Practice Some students may not comprehend the images Aragon and Éluard try to convey in their poems because they do not know words or expressions used by the poets. Ask students to reread the poems and make a list of these words and expressions. You may want to give students the English equivalents of these terms or allow them to look them up in the dictionary. ✿1.2, 4.1

SPECIAL LEARNING NEEDS

Learning Disabilities Provide students with copies of *Matisse Parle.* There should be margins large enough for notes. Underline the important ideas and model the "Dialoguing with the text" strategy for the first two verses. Ask students to follow your model and record their reactions and observations in the margin for the remaining verses.

Active Reading Questions

1. Où se trouve l'oiseau? (au-dessus des nuages)
2. Est-ce que l'oiseau a peur de la lumière? (non)
3. Quel temps fait-il pendant que l'oiseau vole? (Il fait beau/du soleil.)
4. Qu'est-ce que la deuxième strophe décrit? (les champs et les arbres)
5. Qu'est-ce que les feuilles disent? (oui)
6. Est-ce que ce mot est facile ou difficile à dire? (facile)
7. Qui est l'homme décrit dans la dernière strophe? (Braque)
8. Comment est-ce que l'homme regarde le monde? (avec amour)

Postreading Activity

Both of the poems are about twentieth-century artists and, therefore, have some things in common. However, the poems are also quite different from each other. Ask students to compare and contrast the poems. Students might compare and contrast point of view, images, themes, language, and style.

D Possible Answers

1. L'oiseau s'envole.
2. L'oiseau n'a pas peur de la lumière.
3. Le ciel est ensoleillé.
4. Des coquilles de moissons sont cassées.
5. Le poète fait parler les feuilles.
6. On dit « oui » à l'aube.
7. Le poète est l'homme aux yeux légers.
8. Il rassemble la beauté du ciel.

Paul Éluard (1895–1952), poète français, participe au mouvement surréaliste. Il écrit ses premiers poèmes à 18 ans. Ses expériences lui inspirent des idées pacifistes. En 1926, il publie *Capitale de la douleur* qui le propulse au premier plan du monde littéraire. Pendant la Deuxième Guerre mondiale, il participe à des activités clandestines et écrit un de ses plus importants poèmes, *La Liberté* (1942). Parmi ses œuvres, il y a *L'Amour la poésie* (1929) et *Poésie et vérité* (1942).

C Avant la lecture ✿1.3, 2.2

Est-ce que tu connais Georges Braque? Avec Pablo Picasso, il a inventé le cubisme: la nature est réduite aux formes de base. cubes, triangles... Regarde le tableau. Quelles images est-ce que tu vois? Si tu étais poète, quels mots, images ou métaphores utiliserais-tu pour le décrire?

CD 9, Tr. 8

Georges Braque, *La Musicienne* (1917–1918)

Georges Braque, *Les Oiseaux* (1953)

Un oiseau s'envole,
Il rejette les nues[1] comme un voile inutile,
Il n'a jamais craint la lumière,
Enfermé dans son vol,
5   Il n'a jamais eu d'ombre.

Coquilles de moissons brisées[2] par le soleil.
Toutes les feuilles dans les bois disent oui,
Elles ne savent dire que oui,
Toute question, toute réponse
10   Et la rosée[3] coule[4] au fond de ce oui.

Un homme aux yeux légers décrit le ciel d'amour.
Il en rassemble les merveilles
Comme des feuilles dans un bois,
Comme des oiseaux dans leurs ailes
15   Et des hommes dans le sommeil.

1. *clouds* 2. *Shells of ruined harvests/crops* 3. *dew* 4. *runs down/flows*

Core Instruction

LECTURE

1. Read **Avant la lecture** as a class. Have students brainstorm images and metaphors. List their ideas on the board. **(10 min.)**

2. Ask volunteers to read **Georges Braque** aloud. Ask students to do the "Dialoguing with the text" strategy for this poem and then compile a list of student observations on the board for further discussion. **(5 min.)**

3. Answer the **Compréhension** questions and complete **Après la lecture** as a class. What do students think poets and painters have in common? **(15 min.)**

Online Practice
go.hrw.com
Online Edition
KEYWORD: BD3 CH9

Chapitre 9

Lecture

Compréhension 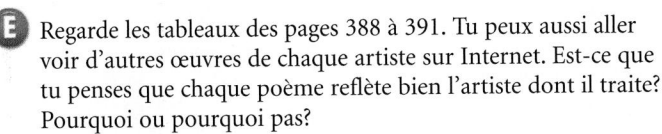1.2

D Réponds aux questions avec des phrases complètes.

1. Qu'est-ce que l'oiseau fait dans la première strophe?
2. De quoi est-ce que l'oiseau a peur?
3. Comment est le ciel où l'oiseau se trouve?
4. Qu'est-ce qui est cassé?
5. Quelle caractéristique humaine est-ce que le poète donne aux feuilles?
6. Quand est-ce qu'on dit «oui» dans la deuxième strophe?
7. Qui est l'homme aux yeux légers?
8. Quelles sont les merveilles que l'homme rassemble?

Après la lecture 1.3

E Regarde les tableaux des pages 388 à 391. Tu peux aussi aller voir d'autres œuvres de chaque artiste sur Internet. Est-ce que tu penses que chaque poème reflète bien l'artiste dont il traite? Pourquoi ou pourquoi pas?

Georges Braque, *Les Deux Poissons* (1953)

Lecture

Connections
Literature Link

Paul Éluard, **nom de plume** of Eugène Grindel, was born in 1895 in Saint-Denis, on the outskirts of Paris. He published his first book of poetry at eighteen, when he was confined to a Swiss sanatorium for tuberculosis. Upon his return to France he joined the army and was injured by exposure to toxic gas. After his war experience, he was briefly involved with the Dada movement, meeting Tristan Tzara, André Breton, Louis Aragon, and other members of surrealist and Dadaist circles. His reputation as a poet was established with the publication of *Capitale de la douleur* in 1926. Éluard had a profound intellectual relationship with Breton and Aragon, although they had different views of communism. Éluard had joined the French Communist Party and eulogized the Soviet dictator Stalin in his political writings. During his lifetime Éluard published over seventy books of poetry and literary and political views. Éluard died in Charenton-le-Pont in 1952. Have students suggest reasons for Éluard's inability to see the reality of the Soviet Union. Why did he admire Stalin as a cultural force for good?

1.1, 3.1

Differentiated Instruction

ADVANCED LEARNERS

Challenge Surrealist poetry often presents itself as a juxtaposition of words that is startling because it is determined by psychological (unconscious) and not logical thought processes. Many surrealist poets rely on automatism, a technique that calls for spontaneous writing without conscious aesthetic or moral self-censorship. Ask students if the poems by Aragon and Éluard have the characteristics of surrealist poetry. Students should provide examples from the poems to support their answers. 3.1

MULTIPLE INTELLIGENCES

Intrapersonal In this chapter students are introduced to several different artists whose artistic presentations vary. In pairs, ask students to research at least two of the artists further via the Internet. Have pairs prepare a short presentation of their findings and share it with the class. 3.2

Assess

Assessment Program

Quiz: Lecture

Online Assessment

my.hrw.com

Test Generator

Resources

Planning:

Lesson Planner

One-Stop Planner

Practice:

Cahier d'activités

Process Writing

Remind students that before they begin taking notes, they should ensure the usefulness of their sources. To determine this, students should ask themselves if each source is relevant and reliable (is accurate; from a reputable and trustworthy publication), and representative (addresses a variety of viewpoints or offers several interpretations).

Teaching Suggestion

Provide students a list of French artists whom they might research, highlighting those who have been featured in *Bien dit!* Encourage each student to choose a different artist. After students have written their report, you might have an art exhibition. Students would post reproductions of their artist's works around the room. Then each student "expert" would give a short talk on an artist and his or her work. You might even serve French snacks as would be done at an exhibit opening.

Connections

Literature Link

Paul Gauguin described his experiences in Tahiti in *Noa Noa*, an autobiographical novel. He wrote, "**J'étais bien loin de ces prisons, les maisons européennes. Une case maorie n'exile, ne retranche point l'individu de la vie, de l'espace, de l'infini.**" Ask students to list other metaphors Gauguin may have used to describe his experiences in Tahiti.

⚘ 3.1

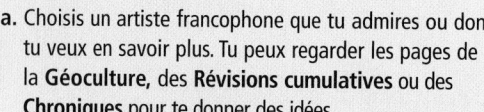

L'atelier de l'écrivain

Interactive TUTOR

Un exposé

Tu viens de lire des poèmes sur deux artistes français. Souvent les artistes ont de l'influence sur les gens et la culture d'une société à travers leurs œuvres et leurs vies. Pour cette activité, tu vas faire des recherches sur la vie et l'œuvre d'un peintre, sculpteur ou autre artiste francophone. Ensuite, tu vas écrire un article qui comprend une courte biographie de l'artiste et une description de quelques-unes de ses œuvres.

1 Plan: l'escalier ⚘1.3

a. Choisis un artiste francophone que tu admires ou dont tu veux en savoir plus. Tu peux regarder les pages de la **Géoculture**, des **Révisions cumulatives** ou des **Chroniques** pour te donner des idées.

b. Fais des recherches sur cette personne et ses œuvres. Tu peux trouver des informations dans des encyclopédies, des livres d'art et des articles de magazines ou de journaux ou encore sur Internet. Prends des notes sur des fiches cartonnées. N'oublie pas de noter tes sources. Ensuite, écris tes impressions sur l'artiste et son œuvre.

c. Organise tes fiches pour qu'elles forment un escalier de trois marches. Sur la première marche, mets les fiches avec les informations sur la vie de l'artiste dans l'ordre chronologique. Sur la deuxième, mets les fiches sur les œuvres de l'artiste dans l'ordre dans lequel tu veux en parler. Puis, sur la troisième marche, organise les fiches avec tes impressions.

Biographie

Henri Matisse
Né : 1869
Mort : 1954

Œuvres

Harmonie Rouge
(1908)

Mes impressions

Ce que j'aime avec Matisse c'est…

STRATÉGIE pour écrire

Note cards Keeping track of information you find while doing research can be a challenge. One solution to this problem is to use note cards. As you conduct your research, write each piece of information in your own words on 4" x 6" cards. Also include where you found the information: the Web site address, book or magazine title, page numbers, etc. When you are ready to begin writing, arrange and rearrange your cards until you find the most logical order in which to present your information. ⚘3.1

Georges Braque, Tête au chignon (1940)

Core Instruction

L'ATELIER DE L'ÉCRIVAIN

1. Discuss the assignment. To help students choose an artist, bring in art books for them to review. Discuss **Stratégie pour écrire.** Work with the class to develop some examples of effective notecards. **(10 min.)**

2. Go over **Vocabulaire à la carte** and **Les pronoms relatifs. (5 min.)**

3. Assign steps 1 and 2 as homework. (You might give students two weeks for research.)

4. Have students work on step 3. Have them work with partners for a second round of proofreading. One checks content and the other checks grammar and spelling. **(25 min.)**

5. Complete step 4 with the class. **(20 min.)**

L'atelier de l'écrivain

Online Practice
go.hrw.com
Online Edition
KEYWORD: BD3 CH9

② Rédaction ❀1.3

Fais un brouillon de ton article. Commence par un bref paragraphe qui explique l'intention de ton article. Ensuite, écris trois ou quatre paragraphes pour le corps de ton article. Suis le plan de la première et de la deuxième marche de ton escalier. Si tu te rends compte que l'ordre n'est pas logique, change-le. Pour finir, écris une conclusion avec tes impressions en suivant le plan de la troisième marche de ton escalier.

③ Correction ❀1.3

Maintenant, relis ton article et pose-toi les questions suivantes:

- Est-ce que j'ai suivi la structure de mon escalier?
- Est-ce que j'ai parlé des faits les plus importants de la vie de cet artiste?
- Est-ce que j'ai parlé des œuvres les plus importantes ou représentatives de l'artiste?
- Est-ce que les détails sont intéressants?
- Est-ce que j'ai donné mes impressions?

Ensuite, relis ton article. Cette fois-ci, vérifie l'emploi des adjectifs et l'accord des verbes et des temps. Assure-toi que tu as utilisé les bons pronoms relatifs. Puis, cherche les mots dans un dictionnaire si tu n'es pas sûr(e) de leur orthographe. Fais les corrections nécessaires et écris ta composition finale.

④ Application ❀1.3

Trouve des photos de l'artiste et des œuvres dont tu as parlées dans ta composition. Illustre ta composition et présente-la à la classe. Ensuite, tes camarades et toi pouvez compiler vos travaux dans un livre de référence sur les artistes francophones.

Henri Matisse

Dans l'article suivant vous allez découvrir la vie et l'œuvre du peintre français Henri Matisse.

Biographie en résumé

Henri Matisse est né le 31 décembre 1869 dans le nord de la France et est mort le 3 novembre 1954 à Nice. Matisse découvre la peinture alors qu'il a déjà une

Vocabulaire à la carte

abstrait(e)	abstract
le contenu	content
exposer	to exhibit
figuratif (-ive)	representational
inspirer	to inspire
la lumière	light
la maquette	mock-up; model
le modèle	model
le rapport	relationship; connection
réaliser	to carry out; to make; to achieve

Les pronoms relatifs

A relative pronoun replaces a noun and introduces a relative clause.

- Use **qui** as the subject of the verb of the relative clause.

  Les artistes qui ont inventé le cubisme sont Picasso et Braque.

- Use **que** as the direct object of the verb of the relative clause.

  Guernica est une œuvre de Picasso que je n'ai jamais vue.

- Use **dont** to say **of whom**.

  L'artiste dont je vais parler est Toulouse-Lautrec.

Les pronoms relatifs

Have students complete the following statements using **que, qui,** or **dont**.

1. **C'est Matisse _____ est associé avec le fauvisme.**
2. **Un bon sujet est quelque chose _____ les artistes ont besoin.**
3. **Avez-vous vu les tableaux _____ Monet a peint à Giverny?**
4. **Yves Klein est l'artiste _____ je t'ai parlé.**

Writing Assessment

To assess **L'atelier de l'écrivain,** you can use the following rubric. For additional rubrics, see the *Assessment Program.*

Writing Rubric	4	3	2	1
Content (Complete—Incomplete)				
Comprehensibility (Comprehensible— Seldom comprehensible)				
Accuracy (Accurate—Seldom accurate)				
Organization (Well-organized—Poorly organized)				
Effort (Excellent effort— Minimal effort)				

18-20: A 14-15: C Under
16-17: B 12-13: D 12: F

Differentiated Instruction

SLOWER PACE LEARNERS

Tell students that when looking up an artist's name in an encyclopedia or an art book, they should search for the artist's last as well as first name. Point out that Philippe Delerm is a famous writer while Vincent Delerm, his son, is a famous composer. When searching for an artist's name on the Internet, students should enter the correct spelling, including accents, of the author's first and last name. ❀1.2

SPECIAL LEARNING NEEDS

Students with AD(H)D As students are preparing their research note cards, ask them to punch a hole in the top, right corner of all the cards. Then have them sort the cards into organizational groups and attach each group to a ring. Once the cards are grouped on rings, students can clip them onto the rings in their binder for safekeeping. ❀1.2

Assess

Assessment Program

Quiz: Écriture

Online Assessment
my.hrw.com

Test Generator

Chapitre 9

Prépare-toi pour l'examen

Interactive TUTOR

Resources

Planning:

Lesson Planner

 One-Stop Planner

Practice:

Cahier d'activités

Media Guide

 Teaching Transparencies
Situation, Chapitre 9
Picture Sequences, Chapter 9

 Audio CD 9, Tr. 9

Interactive Tutor, Disc 2

VIDEO OPTIONS

▶ **Télé-culture: Interviews**

TPRS

You may wish to use the Picture Sequences Transparency that accompanies Activity 7 for a TPRS activity.

② Answers

1. Y a-t-il aussi des cours de danse?
2. Qu'utilise-t-il pour faire ses poteries?
3. Les étudiants utilisent-ils de la peinture à l'huile?
4. Le modèle n'a-t-il pas bougé?
5. À quelle heure les cours commencent-ils?

French for Spanish Speakers

Ask Spanish speakers which verbs in Spanish correspond to **savoir** and **connaître**. (**saber** and **conocer**) Ask students if the rules for the use of these two verbs are the same in Spanish. (Yes, **saber/savoir** both mean to know a fact and **conocer/connaître** both mean to be familiar or acquainted with.) ❀4.1

---

① Ayodele voudrait suivre des cours d'art. Elle visite une école d'art avec sa mère. Décris ce qui se passe sur l'illustration. ❀1.3

① Vocabulaire 1
- to ask for and give opinions
- to introduce and change a topic of conversation
pp. 366–369

② Grammaire 1
- review of inversion
- present participles used as adjectives
Un peu plus
- **si** and **oui**
pp. 370–375

② Ayodele pose des questions à la directrice de l'école. Sa mère voudrait qu'elle soit plus polie. Récris les questions en utilisant l'inversion. ❀1.2

1. Est-ce qu'il y a aussi des cours de danse?
2. Qu'est-ce qu'il utilise pour faire ses poteries?
3. Est-ce que les étudiants utilisent de la peinture à l'huile?
4. Est-ce que le modèle n'a pas bougé?
5. À quelle heure est-ce que les cours commencent?

③ Vocabulaire 2
- to make suggestions and recommendations
- to give an impression
pp. 378–381

③ Lis les phrases et décide si elles sont correctes. Sinon, fais les changements nécessaires. ❀1.2

1. Je suis content que tu viennes au théâtre avec moi pour voir cette exposition.
2. Hier soir, le chef d'orchestre portait un tutu rose.
3. Pour voir une comédie musicale on doit aller au cirque.
4. À l'opéra, il y a toujours un orchestre.
5. Au cirque, on a vu des clowns et des trapézistes.
   Possible answers: 1. incorrect / pièce **2.** incorrect / la ballerine **3.** incorrect / au théâtre **4.** correct **5.** correct

---

Preparing for the Exam

RETEACHING

Review the formation of verbal adjectives. Remind students that the present participle of certain verbs can be used as an adjective and, in most cases, is formed by replacing the **-ons** ending of the **nous** form with **-ant** and modifying the ending to agree with the noun. (**passionnons** – **passionnant(e)(s)**) Call out the infinitives of several verbs and have students tell you the corresponding present participles.

TEST-TAKING STRATEGY

Remind students to recall the chart on demonstrative pronouns on page 384. Demonstrative pronouns are used with **-ci** or **-là**, or with **de** plus a noun, or with a relative pronoun. Making a mental map of the simple chart will help with correct usage of the demonstratives.

Prépare-toi pour l'examen

④ Fais une comparaison pour dire ce que tu préfères. 🍀1.3

   MODÈLE   une nature morte / une peinture abstraite
   **Je trouve les natures mortes plus jolies que
   les peintures abstraites.**

   1. les poteries / les sculptures
   2. une exposition / un spectacle
   3. les jongleurs / les trapézistes
   4. un croquis / un tableau
   5. un opéra / une comédie musicale

⑤ Réponds aux questions suivantes. 🍀2.1, 2.2

   1. Qu'est-ce que c'est, un tapa? Explique.
   2. Qu'est-ce qui se passe pendant les fêtes du Heiva?
   3. Nomme deux danses qui sont originaires des Antilles.

⑥ Écoute ces phrases et dis si on parle a) **d'une exposition** ou
   b) **d'un spectacle.** CD 9, Tr. 9 🍀1.2   **1.** b **2.** b **3.** a **4.** b **5.** a **6.** a

⑦ Adrienne voudrait suivre des cours mais elle ne sait pas lesquels.
   Regarde les illustrations et dis ce qui se passe. 🍀1.3

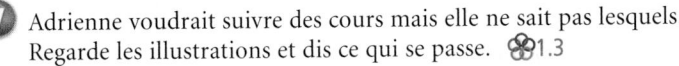

④ **Grammaire 2**
• review of comparative and superlative
• review of demonstrative pronouns
Un peu plus
• **savoir** et **connaître**
pp. 382–387

⑤ **Culture**
• **Comparaisons**
  p. 377
• **Flash culture**
  pp. 371, 381, 384

---

⑤ **Answers**
1. un tissu fait d'écorces et peint
2. On peut assister à des démonstrations de marches sur le feu, à des courses de pirogues et à des spectacles de danse.
3. la biguine, le zouk

⑥ **Script**
1. Le chef d'orchestre donne la mesure aux musiciens.
2. Tu as vu l'affiche à côté du chapiteau?
3. L'artiste a utilisé de la peinture à l'huile pour peindre ce tableau.
4. Les spectateurs ont beaucoup aimé l'acteur principal.
5. Maintenant, c'est un sculpteur, mais il a commencé par faire de la poterie.
6. On n'a pu voir que les œuvres les plus récentes de l'artiste.

PRÉ AP ACTIVITÉ PRÉPARATOIRE **Language Examination**

To display the drawings to the class, use the Picture Sequences Transparency for Chapter 9.

⑦ Sample answer:

a. Adrienne ne sait pas quels cours suivre. Elle aime danser, mais elle aime aussi le cirque.

b. Adrienne visite l'école du cirque. Elle trouve les clowns amusants.

c. Ensuite, elle visite l'école de danse. Elle pense que les danseuses ne sont pas très bonnes. De plus, la directrice a l'air méchante.

d. Adrienne choisit l'école du cirque. Elle est très contente!

Oral Assessment

To assess the speaking activities in this section, you might use the following rubric. For additional speaking rubrics, see the Alternative Assessment section of the *Assessment Program*.

Speaking Rubric	4	3	2	1
Content (Complete—Incomplete)				
Comprehension (Total—Little)				
Comprehensibility (Comprehensible—Incomprehensible)				
Accuracy (Accurate—Seldom Accurate)				
Fluency (Fluent—Not Fluent)				

18-20: A   16-17: B   14-15: C   12-13: D   Under 12: F

Prépare-toi pour l'examen

Grammar Review

For more practice with the grammar topics in this chapter, see the *Grammar Tutor*, the *Interactive Tutor*, or the *Cahier de vocabulaire et grammaire*.

Online Edition

Students might use the online textbook and Holt SoundBooth to practice pronunciation of the **vocabulaire.**

Products and Perspectives

The population of French Guiana (**Guyane**) is ethnically diverse. Each cultural group has enriched the country with its own specific artistic traditions. Woodwork is an essential part of the craft of the Maroons, descendents of escaped African slaves. All of the wooden objects (combs, paddles, furniture, canoes, house doors, and ornaments) have been engraved or painted with special symbols, that have kept alive pan-African aesthetic ideas. The Maroons embroider tablecloths or hammocks with written messages to loved ones. Maroon women make breechcloths, called **kamisas**, as gifts for their husbands. They embroider the **kamisas** with community sayings and stories. Have students research the history and culture of the Maroons in Guiana. ✿2.2

Grammaire 1
- review of inversion
- present participles used as adjectives

Un peu plus
- si and oui
pp. 370–375

Résumé: Grammaire 1

Inversion is a formal way to ask a question. Invert the subject pronoun and the conjugated verb, then insert a hyphen between the two. Add a -t- between the verb and the subject if the verb ends in a vowel and the subject is **on**, **il**, or **elle**.

> **Allez-vous** au théâtre ce soir?
> Ta pièce **a-t-elle reçu** de bonnes critiques?

To form the **present participle** for most verbs, drop the **-ons** from the **nous** form, and add **-ant**. When used as an adjective, it agrees with the noun it modifies.

> agrees
> (nous) émouvons → La pièce est très **émouvante**!

Use **oui** to answer "yes" to an affirmative question. Use **si** to contradict a negative statement or question.

> Tu ne comprends pas?   Si, je comprends!

Grammaire 2
- review of comparative and superlative
- review of demonstrative pronouns

Un peu plus
- savoir and connaître
pp. 382–387

Résumé: Grammaire 2

To form the **comparative** of adjectives and adverbs, use:

> plus/moins/aussi + adjective/adverb + **que**.

To compare nouns, use:

> plus/moins/aussi + **de** + noun + **que**.

To form the **superlative** of adjectives use:

> le/la/les + **plus** or **moins** + adjective + **de**.

If the adjective follows the noun, use:

> le/la/les + noun + le/la/les + **plus/moins** + adjective + **de**.

To form the **superlative** of adverbs use:

> le + **plus/moins** + adverb.

To say *this/that/these/those*, use a form of **celui**:

	MASCULINE	FEMININE
SINGULAR	celui	celle
PLURAL	ceux	celles

Use **savoir** to say you know a fact or how to do something. Use **connaître** to say you know someone or you are familiar with something, a person or a place.

> Je **sais** où il habite, mais je ne le **connais** pas.

Chapter Review

Teacher Management System
Password: admin
For more details, log on to www.hrw.com/CDROMTUTOR.

Create a variety of puzzles to review chapter vocabulary.

DVD Program

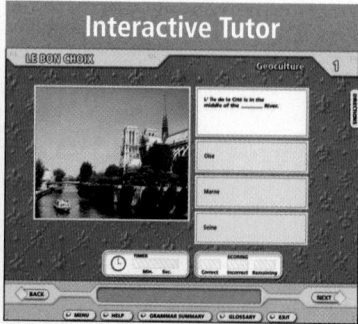

Interactive Tutor

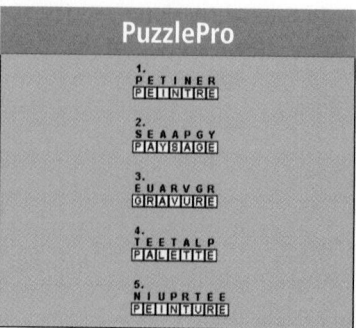

PuzzlePro

Résumé: Vocabulaire 1

HOLT SoundBooth ONLINE RECORDING

Types of fine art

une **aquarelle**	watercolor
un **atelier d'artiste**	art studio
un **(auto)portrait**	(self)portrait
bouger	to move
un **chef-d'œuvre**	master piece
un **chevalet**	easel
un/une **critique d'art**	art critic
un **croquis**	sketch
encadrer	to frame
exposer/une exposition	to exhibit/exhibition
une **galerie d'art**	art gallery
une **gravure**	engraving
le **modèle**	model
une **nature morte**	still life painting
une **œuvre d'art**	work of art
une **palette**	palette
un **paysage**	landscape

le **peintre/peindre**	painter/to paint
une **peinture abstraite/naïve**	abstract/primitive painting
poser	to pose
une **poterie**	pottery
un/une **potier(-ière)**	potter
sculpter/le sculpteur	to sculpt/sculptor
la **sculpture/une statue**	sculpture/statue
un **tableau/une toile**	painting/canvas
un **tour**	wheel
un **tube de peinture à l'huile**	tube of oil paint
un **vernissage**	preview

To ask for and give opinions .... See p. 367

To introduce and change a topic of conversation .... See p. 369

Résumé: Vocabulaire 2

Performing arts

l'**affiche** (f.)	poster
applaudir	to applaud
un **ballet**	ballet
une **ballerine**	ballerina
la **baguette**	baton
le **chapiteau**	big top marquee
le **chef d'orchestre**	conductor
une **chorégraphie**	choreography
le **cirque**	circus
un **clown**	clown
une **comédie musicale**	musical
un/une **danseur(-euse)**	dancer
le **décor**	set
donner la mesure	to set the tempo
un/une **jongleur(-euse)**	juggler
un/une **musicien(-ienne)**	musician
un **opéra**	opera
l'**orchestre** (m.)	orchestra
une **ouvreuse**	usherette
une **partition**	music sheet

un/une **pianiste**	piano player
une **pièce de théâtre**	play
la **piste**	circus ring
une **première**	first night
une **représentation**	performance
un **rôle**	part
la **scène**	stage
un **spectacle**	show
un/une **spectateur(-trice)**	spectator/audience
une **tournée**	tour
un/une **trapéziste**	trapezist
un **tutu**	tutu
un/une **violoniste**	violinist

To make suggestions and recommendations .... See p. 379

To give an impression .... See p. 381

Prépare-toi pour l'examen

Prépare-toi pour l'examen

♟ Game

Il faut que... Start a chain activity by telling what you see in an artist's studio. **Dans l'atelier de l'artiste, je vois une gravure.** Students continue the chain by repeating what you saw and adding another. **Dans l'atelier de l'artiste, je vois une gravure et une peinture.** When a student fails to repeat all the previous items, he or she is out. Start a new chain when someone makes a mistake. The winner is the last one remaining.

🍀 1.1

Online Edition

Transparency: Vocabulaire

Vocabulaire 9.4 — CHAPITRE **9**

Allons au cirque!

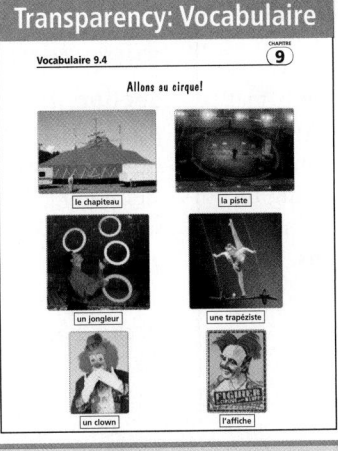

le chapiteau · la piste · un jongleur · une trapéziste · un clown · l'affiche

Transparency: Situation

Situation Des artistes en tout genre — CHAPITRE **9**

Assess

Assessment Program

Examen: Chapitre 9
Audio CD 9, Trs. 14, 15

Examen oral: Chapitre 9
Alternative Assessment
Differentiated Practice and Assessment CD-ROM

Online Assessment
my.hrw.com

Test Generator

Activités préparatoires

Resources

Planning:

Lesson Planner

 One-Stop Planner

Practice:

Cahier d'activités

Cahier de vocabulaire et grammaire

Differentiated Practice and Assessment CD-ROM

 Teaching Transparencies Picture Sequences, Chapter 9

Audio CD 9, Tr. 10

VIDEO OPTIONS

▶ **Télé-culture: Interviews**

The AP French Language Exam

Activités préparatoires provide students with activities similar to those found in the Advanced Placement French Language exam. The activities are based on material taught up to and including this chapter and concentrate on the chapter grammar and vocabulary.

Listening Script

1.
— Que pensez-vous de ces gravures-ci? Ou préférez-vous cette jolie aquarelle?

2.
— Regarde ce clown! Il est drôle!
— Je ne sais pas ce que j'aime mieux: les trapézistes, les clowns, ou les jongleurs.

Reading Strategy

Context Clues Tell students to look for context clues to help narrow down the meaning of unfamiliar words. They should also check if the word might be a derivative of a familiar word.

SECTION I

Listening CD 9, Tr. 10 1.2

🎧 Listen to the dialogues and choose the most appropriate response.

1. A. Je vais acheter une pellicule et un objectif.
  B. Je préfère cette nature morte encadrée.
  C. Je préfère faire autre chose.
  D. Je préférerais que l'on parle d'autre chose.

2. A. J'adore le cirque! C'est chouette!
  B. Ça ne vaut pas la peine de venir.
  C. Cette pièce est très mal jouée.
  D. Il n'y a personne au guichet.

Reading 🌸1.2

Read the following paragraph and answer the questions that follow.

> Jean-Baptiste Poquelin, alias Molière, fut à la fois acteur, dramaturge, metteur en scène et directeur de troupe. Il est l'un des plus grands
> 5 écrivains français, non seulement à cause de la façon dont il maniait ses vers, mais parce qu'il faisait rire aussi. Il était avant tout un auteur comique.
>
> Sa vie fut une série de tourbillons.
> 10 Molière connut de grands succès aussi bien que l'échec total. Il était à la fois adoré par ses amis et détesté par un grand nombre d'ennemis. D'une part, on le comblait de louanges, de l'autre,
> 15 on l'accablait de calomnies.

1. Molière est...
  A. un acteur qui travaillait avec Jean-Baptiste Poquelin.
  B. le meilleur ami de Jean-Baptiste Poquelin.
  C. le nom de théâtre de Jean-Baptiste Poquelin.
  D. le frère de Jean-Baptiste Poquelin.

2. Molière est connu surtout pour...
  A. ses chansons.
  B. ses comédies.
  C. ses opéras.
  D. ses tragédies.

3. La vie de Molière était...
  A. calme.
  B. heureuse.
  C. agitée.
  D. un échec total.

4. Les deux mots qui sont synonymes sont...
  A. calomnies et louanges
  B. succès et échec
  C. adoré et détesté
  D. écrivain et auteur

Preparing for the Exam

ADDITIONAL PRACTICE

Read aloud a sentence containing a verb that can be changed into a verbal adjective (present participle as adjective). **Les chiens m'amusent.** Students agree or disagree with you, using the appropriate form of the verbal adjective in their answer. **Les chiens ne sont pas amusants.**

1.1

TEST-TAKING STRATEGIES

Section I: Listening Tell students not to panic if they do not understand every single word they hear. They should listen for the overall meaning. Details will most likely be repeated several times in the recording.

Section II: Writing When students are asked to supply verb forms, they should look through all the choices first, underlining or highlighting the ones that they recognize as irregular.

The following activities can be used to help you to prepare for the Advanced Placement French Language examination, or to further practice the vocabulary and grammar concepts you have seen in this chapter.

Activités préparatoires

SECTION II

Writing ✿1.2

Complete the sentence by writing the correct form and tense of the verb, based on context. In several instances, you will have to choose between SAVOIR and CONNAÎTRE.

—Est-ce que vous ___1___ bien la musique classique?

—Moi, non. Je ___2___ que Mozart a écrit quelques opéras. Mais c'est tout! Et vous?

—Moi, je trouve l'œuvre de Beethoven ___3___! Vous n'aimez pas l'art non plus?

—Mais si, j'adore les sculptures de Rodin! Elles ___4___ impressionnantes, n'est-ce pas?

—Oui, et j'aime aussi Salvador Dalí.

—Ah, vous ___5___, l'art surréaliste n'est pas très intéressant à mon avis.

—J'aimerais que vous ___6___ avec moi au musée d'art moderne. Je vous ___7___ les tableaux de Dalí et de Magritte aussi.

—D'accord.

1. <u>connaissez</u>
   (savoir/connaître)
2. <u>sais</u>
   (savoir/connaître)
3. <u>émouvante</u>
   (émouvoir)
4. <u>sont</u> (être)
5. <u>savez</u>
   (savoir/connaître)
6. <u>veniez</u> (venir)
7. <u>expliquerai</u>
   (expliquer)

Essay Topic ✿1.3

Write in French a well-organized and coherent composition (10 to 15 lines) on the following topic.

Préférez-vous aller voir un film au cinéma ou aller voir une pièce de théâtre? Expliquez votre réponse.

Speaking ✿1.2

Look at the following drawing, then tell a story about what is occurring in the picture.

Writing Strategy

Encourage students to use transitional words and phrases to lead the reader from one sentence or paragraph to the next. Reading aloud (quietly) to themselves will give them an idea of how well the writing flows.

Language Examination

To display the drawing to the class, use the **Activités préparatoires** Transparency for Chapter 9.

Speaking: Sample Answer

Beaucoup de gens sont allés au vernissage d'un groupe d'artistes. Bien qu'ils aient aimé les tableaux, ils ont surtout trouvé la sculpture intéressante.

You might ask students the following:

Es-tu jamais allé(e) à une exposition d'art? Qu'en pensais-tu?

Connections

Language Note

Molière (1622–1673) was a French playwright, director, actor, and master of comic satire. The names of some of his stock characters have been absorbed by the French language. For example, a **harpagon**, named after the main character of **L'Avare** (1668), is obsessively greedy. A **Don Juan**, a misspelling of the main character of, **Dom Juan ou le festin de pierre** (1665), is a man who seduces women and then abandons them. A **tartuffe** is named after the protagonist in **Tartuffe ou l'imposteur** (1664). Ask students what kind of man is called a **tartuffe**. (a hypocrite, especially a hypocrite who displays affected morality or religious piety) ✿3.1

Differentiated Instruction

SLOWER PACE LEARNERS

Additional Practice Before students create an outline for their essay, have them work with a partner to discuss the pros and cons of seeing a movie at the movie theater and a play at the theater. This will help students develop a comprehensive and logical outline for their essay. ✿1.1

SPECIAL LEARNING NEEDS

Students with Dysgraphia In Section II you might allow students with dysgraphia to record their essay. Students will still be responsible for taking notes in preparation for the assignment so the recording is a final reading of the essay showing evidence of thoughtful organization and coherence. ✿1.3

Resources

Planning:
Lesson Planner
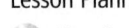 One-Stop Planner

Practice:
Cahier d'activités
Media Guide
 Teaching Transparencies
Fine Art, Chapter 9
 Audio CD 9, Tr. 11
Interactive Tutor, Disc 2

VIDEO OPTIONS

▶ **Géoculture**
▶ **Télé-roman:**
   Camille et compagnie,
   Épisodes 9 et 10

❶ Script

1. Le chef d'orchestre est très connu. Si tu en as l'occasion, je te recommande d'aller le voir.
2. Elle utilise un tour pour créer ses œuvres d'art.
3. Le modèle n'a pas bougé pendant que l'artiste faisait son croquis.
4. Elle aime danser et elle suit des cours de ballet.
5. Personnellement, la partition choisie par l'orchestre m'a beaucoup plu.
6. Il est vraiment doué pour le dessin. Il n'a suivi aucun cours.

❷ Answers

1. oui
2. pendant le vernissage
3. oui
4. Answers will vary.
5. Answers will vary.

chapitres 1-9

Révisions cumulatives

CD 9, Tr. 11   🎧 1.2
1. d 2. b 3. c
4. a 5. d 6. c
❶ Écoute les phrases et dis de quelle photo on parle.

a.   b.   c.   d.

❷ Lis cette affiche pour une exposition d'art et réponds aux questions.   1.2, 3.2

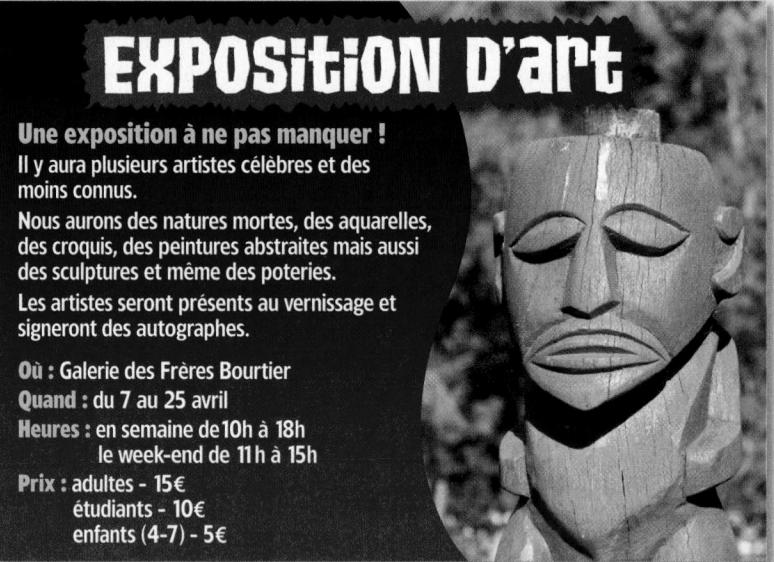

EXPOSITION D'art

Une exposition à ne pas manquer !
Il y aura plusieurs artistes célèbres et des moins connus.
Nous aurons des natures mortes, des aquarelles, des croquis, des peintures abstraites mais aussi des sculptures et même des poteries.
Les artistes seront présents au vernissage et signeront des autographes.

Où : Galerie des Frères Bourtier
Quand : du 7 au 25 avril
Heures : en semaine de 10h à 18h
le week-end de 11 h à 15h
Prix : adultes - 15€
étudiants - 10€
enfants (4-7) - 5€

1. Peut-on rencontrer les artistes qui exposent leurs œuvres?
2. Est-ce que les artistes seront là tout le temps?
3. Quel genre d'œuvres d'art seront exposées?
4. Qui aimerait aller voir cette exposition?
5. Est-ce que cette exposition t'intéresserait? Pourquoi?

Online Culture Project

Imagine that the class is going to visit a local museum whose current exhibit explores the music of the French Antilles. Have students write a short biography of a musician or history of a style of music featured in the museum. Students may research current artists and popular trends in Caribbean music or more traditional styles on the Internet. All work should be completed in French and sources should be carefully documented.   2.2, 3.2

3 Tu aimes bien les peintures. Ton/Ta camarade préfère les sculptures. Chacun explique son point de vue et parle des artistes qu'il préfère et de leurs œuvres. Faites des comparaisons. 🎴1.1

Online Assessment
go.hrw.com
Cumulative Self–test
KEYWORD: BD3 CH9

Révisions cumulatives

FINE ART CONNECTION

Introduction *Le jongleur* was painted by surrealist Marc Chagall, born Moishe Segal in Belarus, in 1887. Chagall left St. Petersburg in 1910 and settled in Paris, but moved back to Russia and became an active participant in the Russian Revolution of 1917. He did not fare well politically under the Soviet system and moved back to Paris in 1923, becoming a French citizen in 1937. With the German occupation of France during World War II and the deportation of the Jews, Chagall fled Paris and arrived in the United States in 1941. In 1946, he returned to Europe. In 1957, he visited Israel, where he created stained-glass windows for a synagogue as well as wall art for the new parliament in Jerusalem. He died at the age of 97 in France.

4 Regarde ce tableau de Chagall et réponds aux questions suivantes. 🎴1.3

1. Quel genre de spectacle est représenté sur ce tableau?

2. Est-ce que tu aimerais assister à ce spectacle? Pourquoi?

3. Combien d'artistes différents est-ce que tu vois sur ce tableau?

4. Si tu devais faire une publicité pour ce spectacle, qu'est-ce que tu dirais?

5. Imagine que tu es critique d'art. Que dirais-tu de ce tableau?

Chagall, Marc. *Le jongleur*, 1943.

Le jongleur de Marc Chagall

Analyzing

Chagall's works are abound with references to his childhood. For example, he often depicts a herring to commemorate his father, who was a herring merchant. You might ask students the following:

1. **À ton avis, que représente l'horloge à pendule?**

2. **Dans le village où Chagall est né, le joueur de violon jouait aux moments critiques de la vie. Peux-tu identifier quelques-uns de ces moments?**

3. **Pourquoi penses-tu que le jongleur a la tête d'un coq?**
🎴3.1

5 Tu es peintre et tu voudrais faire une exposition dans une galerie d'art. Écris une lettre au propriétaire d'une galerie pour le convaincre d'exposer tes œuvres. Explique le genre de tableaux que tu peins. 🎴1.3, 2.2

6 **À ton tour** **À l'affiche!** Avec trois ou quatre camarades créez une affiche pour un spectacle ou pour une exposition. Décrivez le spectacle ou tout ce qui sera présenté à l'exposition. Ensuite, montrez votre affiche à la classe.
🎴1.3

Extension

Before Chagall moved to Paris in 1910, he had a difficult time living as a Jew in Russia. He was even jailed briefly. Ask students to research the life of Jews under tsarist rule. Students should present their research to the class.

 3.1

ACTFL Performance Standards

The activities in Chapter 9 target the communicative modes as described in the Standards.

Interpersonal	Two-way communication using receptive skills and productive skills	**Communication (SE)**, pp. 369, 371, 373, 375, 381, 383, 385, 387 **Communication (TE)**, pp. 369, 371, 373, 375, 381, 383 **À ton tour**, p. 401
Interpretive	One-way communication using receptive skills	**Culture**, pp. 376–377 **Lecture**, pp. 388–391
Presentational	One-way communication using productive skills	**Communication (SE)**, p. 387 **Communication (TE)**, pp. 375, 379, 385

Révisions cumulatives

Planning Guide

Chapter Section		Resources

Vocabulaire 1 — pp. 404–407
- At the airport

Grammaire 1 — pp. 408–411
- Review: Prepositions with places
- Review: The subjunctive

Application 1 — pp. 412–413
- **Un peu plus:**
  Review: Adverb placement

Resources:
- Teaching Transparencies: Vocabulaire 10.1, 10.2; Bell Work 10.1, 10.2, 10.3, 10.4
- Cahier de vocabulaire et grammaire, pp. 109–114
- Grammar Tutor for Students of French
- Cahier d'activités, pp. 91–93
- Media Guide, pp. 37–40

Assessment Program
Quiz: Vocabulaire 1, pp. 275–276
Quiz: Grammaire 1, pp. 277–278
Quiz: Application 1, pp. 279–280

Culture — pp. 414–415
- **Lecture culturelle: A380—Naissance d'un géant**
- **Comparaisons**
- **Communauté et professions**

Resources:
- Cahier d'activités, p. 94

Vocabulaire 2 — pp. 416–419
- Travel by car

Grammaire 2 — pp. 420–423
- Review: The future
- Review: The past perfect

Application 2 — pp. 424–425
- **Un peu plus:**
  Review: The causative **faire**

Resources:
- Teaching Transparencies: Vocabulaire 10.3, 10.4; Bell Work 10.5, 10.6, 10.7, 10.8
- Cahier de vocabulaire et grammaire, pp. 115–120
- Grammar Tutor for Students of French
- Cahier d'activités, pp. 95–97
- Media Guide, pp. 37–40

Assessment Program
Quiz: Vocabulaire 2, pp. 281–282
Quiz: Grammaire 2, pp. 283–284
Quiz: Application 2, pp. 285–286

Lecture — pp. 426–429
- **Un été pour mémoire**

L'atelier de l'écrivain — pp. 430–431
- **Un voyage**

Resources:
- Cahier d'activités, p. 98
- Reading Strategies and Skills Handbook
- Advanced Reader

Assessment Program
Quiz: Lecture, p. 287
Quiz: Écriture, p. 288

Prépare-toi pour l'examen — pp. 432–435
- **Résumé de vocabulaire et grammaire**

Activités préparatoires — pp. 436–437

Révisions cumulatives — pp. 438–439

Resources:
- Teaching Transparencies Picture Sequences, Situation, Ch. 10
- Media Guide, pp. 40, 71–72

Assessment Program
Examen: Chapitre 10, pp. 289–294
Examen oral: Chapitre 10, p. 326

- Teaching Transparencies, Fine Art, Ch. 10
- Cahier d'activités, pp. 99–100

Chroniques — pp. 440–449
- L'impressionnisme
- De l'art naïf au surréalisme
- La sculpture sous toutes ses formes
- Le hit-parade
- Au rythme de l'Afrique

Resources:
- Reading Strategies and Skills Handbook
- Advanced Reader

Planning Guide

Pacing Suggestions

	Essential	Recommended	Optional
Vocabulaire 1 • At the airport • **Flash culture**	✔		
Grammaire 1 • Review: Prepositions with places • Review: The subjunctive	✔		
Application 1 • **Un peu plus:** Review: Adverb placement	✔		
Culture • **Lecture culturelle: A380 - Naissance d'un géant** • **Comparaisons** • **Communauté et professions**		✔	
Vocabulaire 2 • Travel by car • **Flash culture**	✔		
Grammaire 2 • Review: The future • Review: The past perfect • **Flash culture**	✔		
Application 2 • **Un peu plus:** Review: The causative **faire**	✔		
Lecture • **Un été pour mémoire** **L'atelier de l'écrivain** • **Un voyage**		✔	
Prépare-toi pour l'examen		✔	
Activités préparatoires		✔	
Révisions cumulatives			✔
Chroniques			✔

Technology

Bien dit! Online
• Student Edition with multi-media
• SoundBooth recording tool
• Interactive activities with feedback
• Self-tests with feedback
• Cahier d'activités (Interactive workbook)
• Cahier de vocabulaire et grammaire (Interactive workbook)
• Holt Online Assessment

DVD Program
• Télé-roman: Camille et compagnie
• Télé-culture: Interviews

Interactive Tutor
• Interactive practice games
• Writing and recording workshops
• Before You Know It™ Flashcards

Audio Program
• Student Edition Listening Activities
• Assessment listening activities
• Songs

One-Stop Planner
• Complete media and print resources
• ExamView Pro Test Generator
• Holt Calendar Planner

PuzzlePro
• Customizable word games

Differentiated Practice and Assessment CD
For slower pace and advanced learner options, see the Differentiated Practice and Assessment CD.

Planning Guide

Projects

Collage de photos

In this activity, students describe their ideal vacation spot in the Francophone world and make a collage to enhance their presentation.

1.3, 5.2

Suggested Sequence

1. Students decide on a vacation spot to illustrate. Ask students to search for information in reference books or on the Internet. They might also consult travel agencies.

2. Have students gather drawings, photographs, magazine pictures, or small objects for their collage.

3. Have students decide on the final design of their collage. They should outline their presentation and exchange it with a classmate for peer review.

4. Have students present their collage to the class.

Grading the project

Suggested point distribution (100 points total)

College Information . . . . .40 pts.
Creativity. . . . . .20 pts.
Presentation to class . . . . .40 pts.

e-community

e-mail forum:

Post the following questions on the classroom e-mail forum:

> Location: http://french
>
> **Qu'est-ce que tu emportes avec toi en vacances?**
>
> **Combien de valises emporterais-tu pour aller en France?** 5.1

All students will contribute to the list and then share the items.

Partner Class Project

Have students post their collages or photos of them on the student or class Web site. Students should ask the partner class to fill out a questionnaire about the collages posted. The questionnaire should include questions such as the following. Are you familiar with any of these places? If yes, can you provide additional information? How could we improve the collages? Basing your decision on the information and illustrations provided in the collages, would you want to visit any of these places? Why or why not? Students should evaluate the answers of the partner class and present their conclusions to the class.

3.1, 5.1

Game Bank
For game ideas, see pages T60–T63.

La pêche à la Guadeloupe

Fishing is one of Guadeloupe's most time-honored industries. Although coast fishing in modern boats exists, the majority of fishermen continue to use traditional methods, catching several kinds of fish, crustaceans, and mollusks from small, colorful boats, called **saintoises.** All year round they bring their catch to market, providing a mainstay to the island's port economies. Several towns regularly hold **fêtes des marins** and **fêtes du poisson et de la mer** to celebrate their fishermen and the bounty of the sea. The festivals include parades, processions, and dances; however, the most important events are the Mass for the fishermen and the blessing of the sea. Have students research the fishing industry in a region of the United States, such as Louisiana, and compare its methods and customs to those of Guadeloupe. ✿ 3.2, 4.2

La cuisine

Pineapples come from Central America and the Caribbean. They were introduced to Hawaii for the first time in the 18th century. Now, Hawaii is the largest producer of pineapples. Encourage students to prepare **gâteau à l'ananas** in their home economics class or at home. ✿ 3.1, 5.2

Gâteau à l'ananas Pour 6 personnes

1 ananas ou une boîte
   d'ananas
6 œufs
1 ¼ tasse de sucre
2 tasses de farine

½ tasse de noix de coco rapée
¾ tasse de beurre

Mélanger le sucre, les œufs, la farine, la noix de coco et le beurre pour obtenir un mélange homogène. Caraméliser le moule. Couper l'ananas en tranches ou égoutter les tranches d'ananas. Les mettre dans le moule. Verser la pâte dans le moule. Faire cuire au four à 375° F pendant 40 minutes. Démouler et servir froid.

Vocabulaire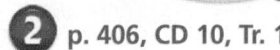

2 p. 406, CD 10, Tr. 1

— Bonjour. Je voudrais faire une réservation pour un billet d'avion, s'il vous plaît.

— Oui. C'est pour un vol intérieur ou international?

— Intérieur. Je voudrais un billet aller-retour Paris-Nice. Départ le 9 avril et retour le 15.

— D'accord... Alors, il y a un vol à 14h30 le 9, mais il y a une escale à Lyon.

— Je préfère un vol direct. C'est possible?

— Attendez... Euh. Oui, départ 14h25, arrivée à Nice à 15h30. Vous avez de la chance, il reste une seule place. Ça vous va?

— Oui, c'est parfait. Et pour le retour?

— Alors, pour le retour, l'avion part de Nice à 13h45. C'est aussi un vol direct. Votre nom?

— Joséphine Nivernais.

— D'accord. Et vous préférez un siège près du hublot ou du côté de l'allée?

— Près du hublot, s'il vous plaît.

— D'accord. N'oubliez pas que tous les passagers doivent arriver une heure en avance pour obtenir leur carte d'embarquement et pour enregistrer leurs bagages.

— On a droit à combien de bagages?

— Deux maximum.

— Bon, très bien. Merci. Au revoir.

Answers to Activity 2
1. à Nice   2. intérieur   3. oui
4. près du hublot   5. une heure   6. deux

Grammaire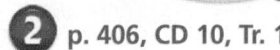

6 p. 408, CD 10, Tr. 2

1. Martine est de Paris, mais elle habite à la Réunion.

2. Maya est mexicaine et elle va en Afrique.

3. Audrey est de Bruxelles et elle va au Texas.

4. Frank était allé à la Guadeloupe, mais il a voulu rentrer chez lui en Suisse après trois semaines.

5. Robert va au Canada, mais il est de Californie.

6. Ahmed vit en Belgique mais cet été, il a rendu visite à sa famille en Algérie.

Answers to Activity 6
1. b   2. a   3. a   4. b   5. b   6. a

Application 1

16 p. 413, CD 10, Tr. 3

1. J'ai demandé un siège près de l'allée comme ça je pourrai regarder le paysage.

2. Les avions vont toujours très lentement sur la piste quand ils vont décoller.

3. J'ai pris un vol direct pour ne pas avoir d'escale.

4. Le commandant de bord nous a montré les consignes de sécurité avant le départ.

5. L'hôtesse de l'air nous a donné l'autorisation d'atterrir.

6. Après avoir atterri, nous avons dû passer la douane.

Answers to Activity 16
1. b   2. b   3. a   4. b   5. b   6. a

Vocabulaire

22 p. 418, CD 10, Tr. 4

1. C'est facile à trouver. Les agences de location de voitures sont toutes à la sortie de l'aéroport.

2. Zut alors! Regarde, on a un pneu à plat! Où est ta roue de secours?

3. Oh, il pleut! Et mes essuie-glaces ne marchent plus!

4. Il y a une station-service à la prochaine sortie. Faisons le plein! Le réservoir est presque vide.

5. Dominique, tu peux nettoyer le pare-brise, s'il te plaît? Il est vraiment sale!

6. Le pauvre! Il est tombé en panne. On s'arrête pour l'aider?

Answers to Activity 22
1. d   2. a   3. e   4. c   5. b   6. a

Grammaire

30 p. 422, CD 10, Tr. 5

1. J'avais passé le volant à un copain.

2. Ma voiture est tombée en panne.

3. Je n'avais pas fait la révision.

4. Le moteur n'a pas voulu démarrer.

5. Heureusement, on n'était pas au milieu de la route.

6. J'ai ouvert le capot, mais je n'ai rien trouvé.

7. J'avais oublié de faire le plein.

Answers to Activity 30
1. a   2. b   3. a   4. b   5. a   6. b   7. a

Application

35 p. 424, CD 10, Tr. 6

1. On rejoindra bientôt l'autoroute.
2. Nous avions pris la sortie numéro 5.
3. C'est toi qui avais trouvé le chemin le plus rapide.
4. Je te passerai le volant à la prochaine station-service.
5. Au carrefour, tu ralentiras pour qu'on puisse lire les panneaux.
6. C'est ici qu'on était tombé en panne, je me souviens.

Answers to Activity 35
1. b   2. a   3. a   4. b   5. b   6. a

Prépare-toi pour l'examen

6 p. 433, CD 10, Tr. 8

1. Cet été, je partirai en vacances avec des amis. On ira à la plage et on fera de la planche à voile.
2. Je serai contente quand on sera arrivé.
3. Je préférais voyager en avion, surtout quand on allait loin.
4. J'achèterai mon billet la semaine prochaine .
5. Un été, j'ai rendu visite à ma grand-mère et elle m'a appris à nager.
6. Nous voyagions souvent en voiture parce que c'était moins cher que l'avion.

Answers to Activity 6
1. a   2. a   3. b   4. a   5. b   6. b

Activités préparatoires

Listening, p. 436, CD 10, Tr. 9

1. — Il y a beaucoup de circulation.
   — Il y a un accident. Je vois un panneau au carrefour là-bas.
2. — Après l'atterrissage à New York, il faut que nous changions de terminal.
   — Et nous n'avons pas beaucoup de temps. Lorsque nous descendrons d'avion, nous devrons prendre un bus.

Answers to Listening Activity
1. C   2. D

Révisions cumulatives  *chapitres 1-10*

1 p. 438, CD 10, Tr. 10

1. Nous avons dû louer une voiture à l'agence parce que Paul n'était pas venu nous chercher à l'aéroport.
2. L'avion a atterri sans problème, mais j'avais quand même un peu peur!
3. Le week-end dernier, j'ai emprunté la voiture de Christian et devine ce qui m'est arrivé... J'ai eu un pneu à plat! Et, bien sûr, il n'avait pas de roue de secours!
4. Cette année, nous n'avons pas eu de vol direct et nous avons dû faire escale sur cette petite île.
5. Je n'aime pas conduire la nuit, surtout quand il pleut!
6. Ce conducteur a eu un pneu à plat. Il va devoir appeler une station-service.

Answers to Activity 1
1. d   2. a   3. b   4. a   5. c   6. b

Listening Activity Scripts

50-Minute Lesson Plans

Bon voyage!

50-Minute Lesson Plans

Day 1

OBJECTIVE
Ask for information

Core Instruction
Chapter Opener, pp. 402–403
• See Using the Photo, p. 402. **5 min.**
• See Chapter Objectives, p. 402. **5 min.**

Vocabulaire 1, pp. 404–407
• Present **Vocabulaire 1,** pp. 404–405. See Teaching **Vocabulaire,** p. 404. **15 min.**
• Present **Exprimons-nous!,** p. 405. **10 min.**
• Do Activity 1, p. 406. **5 min.**
• Play Audio CD 10, Tr. 1 for Activity 2, p. 406. **5 min.**
• Do Activity 3, p. 406. **5 min.**

Optional Resources
• Advanced Learners, p. 405 ▲
• Special Learning Needs, p. 405 ●
• Advanced Learners, p. 407 ▲

Homework Suggestions
Cahier de vocabulaire et grammaire, pp. 109–110

✿ 1.1, 1.2, 1.3, 3.1, 4.2

Day 2

OBJECTIVE
Remind and reassure; Use prepositions with places

Core Instruction
Vocabulaire 1, pp. 404–407
• Do Bell Work 10.1, p. 404. **5 min.**
• Present **Flash culture,** p. 406. **5 min.**
• See Teaching **Exprimons-nous!,** p. 406. **10 min.**
• Have students do Activities 4–5, p. 407. **20 min.**

Grammaire 1, pp. 408–411
• See Teaching **Grammaire,** p. 408. **10 min.**

Optional Resources
• Communication (TE), p. 407
• Multiple Intelligences, p. 407

Homework Suggestions
Study for **Quiz: Vocabulaire 1**
Cahier de vocabulaire et grammaire, p. 111
Online Practice (**go.hrw.com,** Keyword: BD3 CH10)

✿ 1.1, 1.2, 4.2

Day 3

OBJECTIVE
Use prepositions with places

Core Instruction
Vocabulaire 1, pp. 404–407
• Review **Vocabulaire 1,** pp. 404–407. **10 min.**
• Give **Quiz: Vocabulaire 1.** **20 min.**

Grammaire 1, pp. 408–411
• Play Audio CD 10, Tr. 2 for Activity 6, p. 408. **5 min.**
• Have students do Activities 7–9, pp. 408–409. **15 min.**

Optional Resources
• Slower Pace Learners, p. 409 ◆
• Special Learning Needs, p. 409 ●

Homework Suggestions
Cahier de vocabulaire et grammaire, p. 112
Cahier d'activités, p. 91
Online Practice (**go.hrw.com,** Keyword: BD3 CH10)

✿ 1.1, 1.2

Day 4

OBJECTIVE
Use prepositions with places; Use the subjunctive

Core Instruction
Grammaire 1, pp. 408–411
• Do Activity 10, p. 409. **5 min.**
• See Teaching **Grammaire,** p. 410. **10 min.**
• Have students do Activities 11–14, pp. 410–411. **25 min.**

Application 1, pp. 412–413
• Have students do Activity 15, p. 412. **5 min.**
• Play Audio CD 10, Tr. 3 for Activity 16, p. 412. **5 min.**

Optional Resources
• Slower Pace Learners, p. 411 ◆
• Special Learning Needs, p. 411 ●

Homework Suggestions
Study for **Quiz: Grammaire 1**
Cahier de vocabulaire et grammaire, p. 113
Cahier d'activités, p. 92

✿ 1.1, 1.2, 1.3

Day 5

OBJECTIVE
Use adverb placement

Core Instruction
Grammaire 1, pp. 408–411
• Review **Grammaire 1,** pp. 408–411. **10 min.**
• Give **Quiz: Grammaire 1.** **20 min.**

Application 1, pp. 412–413
• See Teaching **Un peu plus,** p. 412. **5 min.**
• Have students do Activities 17–20, pp. 412–413. **15 min.**

Optional Resources
• Communication (TE), p. 413
• Slower Pace Learners, p. 413 ◆
• Special Learning Needs, p. 413 ●

Homework Suggestions
Study for **Quiz: Application 1**
Cahier de vocabulaire et grammaire, p. 114
Cahier d'activités, p. 93

✿ 1.1, 1.2, 3.2

Day 6

OBJECTIVE
Learn about francophone culture

Core Instruction
Application 1, pp. 412–413
• Review **Application 1,** pp. 412–413. **10 min.**
• Give **Quiz: Application 1. 20 min.**

Culture, pp. 414–415
• See **Lecture culturelle** (TE), p. 414. **10 min.**
• See **Comparaisons et communauté** (TE), p. 414. **10 min.**

Optional Resources
• Cultures, p. 415
• Communities, p. 415
• Advanced Learners, p. 415 ▲
• Multiple Intelligences, p. 415

Homework Suggestions
Cahier d'activités, p. 94
Interactive Tutor, Ch. 10
Online Practice (**go.hrw.com,** Keyword: BD3 CH10)
Finish the **Communauté et professions** project, p. 415.

✿ 1.1, 1.2, 1.3, 2.1, 2.2, 3.1, 4.2, 5.1, 5.2

Day 7

OBJECTIVE
Ask for help

Core Instruction
Vocabulaire 2, pp. 416–419
• Do Bell Work 10.5, p. 416. **5 min.**
• Present **Vocabulaire 2,** pp. 416–417. See Teaching **Vocabulaire,** p. 416. **20 min.**
• Present **Exprimons-nous!,** p. 417. **10 min.**
• Have students do Activity 21, p. 418. **5 min.**
• Play Audio CD 10, Tr. 4 for Activity 22, p. 418. **5 min.**
• Have students do Activity 23, p. 418. **5 min.**

Optional Resources
• Advanced Learners, p. 417 ▲
• Multiple Intelligences, p. 417
• Slower Pace Learners, p. 419 ◆

Homework Suggestions
Cahier de vocabulaire et grammaire, pp. 115–116

✿ 1.1, 1.2, 1.3

Day 8

OBJECTIVE
Ask for directions; Use the future

Core Instruction
Vocabulaire 2, pp. 416–419
• See Teaching **Exprimons-nous!,** p. 418. **10 min.**
• Have students do Activities 24–25, p. 419. **15 min.**
• Present **Flash culture,** p. 419. **5 min.**

Grammaire 2, pp. 420–423
• See Teaching **Grammaire,** p. 420. **15 min.**
• Have students do Activity 26, p. 420. **5 min.**

Optional Resources
• Communication (TE), p. 419
• Special Learning Needs, p. 419 ●

Homework Suggestions
Study for **Quiz: Vocabulaire 2**
Cahier de vocabulaire et grammaire, p. 117

✿ 1.1, 1.2

Day 9

OBJECTIVE
Use the future

Core Instruction
Vocabulaire 2, pp. 416–419
• Review **Vocabulaire 2,** pp. 416–419. **10 min.**
• Give **Quiz: Vocabulaire 2. 20 min.**

Grammaire 2, pp. 420–423
• Have students do Activities 27–29, p. 421. **20 min.**

Optional Resources
• Communication (TE), p. 421
• Slower Pace Learners, p. 421 ◆
• Multiple Intelligences, p. 421

Homework Suggestions
Cahier de vocabulaire et grammaire, p. 118
Cahier d'activités, p. 95
Interactive Tutor, Ch. 10
Online Practice (**go.hrw.com,** Keyword: BD3 CH10)

❊ 1.1, 1.2

Day 10

OBJECTIVE
Use the past perfect

Core Instruction
Grammaire 2, pp. 420–423
• Present **Flash culture,** p. 422. **5 min.**
• See Teaching **Grammaire,** p. 422. **10 min.**
• Play Audio CD 10, Tr. 5 for Activity 30, p. 422. **5 min.**
• Have students do Activities 31–34, pp. 422–423. **20 min.**

Application 2, pp. 424–425
• Play Audio CD 10, Tr. 6 for Activity 35, p. 424. **5 min.**
• Do Activity 36, p. 424. **5 min.**

Optional Resources
• Advanced Learners, p. 423 ▲
• Multiple Intelligences, p. 423
• Advanced Learners, p. 425 ▲

Homework Suggestions
Study for **Quiz: Grammaire 2**
Cahier de vocabulaire et grammaire, p. 119
Cahier d'activités, p. 96

❊ 1.1, 1.2, 1.3, 4.1, 4.2

Day 11

OBJECTIVE
*Use the causative **faire***

Core Instruction
Grammaire 2, pp. 420–423
• Review **Grammaire 2,** pp. 420–423. **10 min.**
• Give **Quiz: Grammaire 2. 20 min.**

Application 2, pp. 424–425
• See Teaching **Un peu plus,** p. 424. **5 min.**
• Have students do Activities 37–40, pp. 424–425. **15 min.**

Optional Resources
• Communication (TE), p. 425
• Special Learning Needs, p. 425 ●

Homework Suggestions
Study for **Quiz: Application 2**
Cahier de vocabulaire et grammaire, p. 120
Cahier d'activités, p. 97
Online Practice (**go.hrw.com,** Keyword: BD3 CH10)

❊ 1.1, 1.2

Day 12

OBJECTIVE
Develop listening and reading skills

Core Instruction
Application 2, pp. 424–425
• Review **Application 2,** pp. 424–425. **10 min.**
• Give **Quiz: Application 2. 20 min.**

Lecture, pp. 426–429
• See **Lecture** (TE), p. 426. **20 min.**

Optional Resources
• Slower Pace Learners, p. 427 ◆
• Special Learning Needs, p. 427 ●
• Connections, p. 429

Homework Suggestions
Interactive Tutor, Ch. 10
Online Practice (**go.hrw.com,** Keyword: BD3 CH10)

❊ 1.1, 1.2, 1.3, 3.1, 5.2

Day 13

OBJECTIVE
Develop listening, reading, and writing skills

Core Instruction
Lecture, pp. 426–429
• See **Lecture** (TE), p. 428. **20 min.**

L'atelier de l'écrivain, pp. 430–431
• See **L'atelier de l'écrivain** (TE), p. 430. **30 min.**

Optional Resources
• Advanced Learners, p. 429 ▲
• Special Learning Needs, p. 429 ●
• Advanced Learners, p. 431 ▲
• Special Learning Needs, p. 431 ●

Homework Suggestions
Cahier d'activités, p. 98

❊ 1.1, 1.2, 1.3, 3.1, 3.2, 5.2

Day 14

OBJECTIVE
Review the chapter; Prepare for the AP Exam

Core Instruction
Prépare-toi pour l'examen, pp. 432–435
• Have students do Activities 1–5, pp. 432–433. **25 min.**

Activités préparatoires, pp. 436–437
• Have students do the **Activités préparatoires,** pp. 436–437. **25 min.**

Optional Resources
• Reteaching, p. 432
• Slower Pace Learners, p. 437 ◆
• Special Learning Needs, p. 437 ●
• **Télé-culture:** Interviews

Homework Suggestions
Interactive Tutor, Ch. 10
Online Practice (**go.hrw.com,** Keyword: BD3 CH10)

❊ 1.1 ,1.2, 1.3

Day 15

OBJECTIVE
Review the chapter

Core Instruction
Prépare-toi pour l'examen, pp. 432–435
• Play Audio CD 10, Tr. 8 for Activity 6, p. 433. **10 min.**
• Have students do Activity 7, p. 433. **10 min.**

Révisions cumulatives, pp. 438–439
• Play Audio CD 10, Tr. 10 for Activity 1, p. 438. **5 min.**
• Have students do Activities 2–6, pp. 438–439. **25 min.**

Optional Resources
• Game, p. 435
• Online Culture Project, p. 438
• Fine Art Connection, p. 439
• **Télé-roman: Camille et compagnie**

Homework Suggestions
Study for Chapter Test
Online Practice (**go.hrw.com,** Keyword: BD3 CH10)

❊ 1.1, 1.2, 1.3, 2.2, 3.1, 3.2

Day 16/Test

Core Instruction
Chapter Test 50 min.

Optional Resources
Assessment Program
• Alternative Assessment
• Test Generator
• **Quiz: Lecture**
• **Quiz: Écriture**

Homework Suggestions
Cahier d'activités, pp. 99–100, 120–123
Online Practice (**go.hrw.com,** Keyword: BD3 CH10)

90-Minute Lesson Plans

Block 1

OBJECTIVE
Ask for information; Remind and reassure

Core Instruction
Chapter Opener, pp. 402–403
• See Using the Photo, p. 402. **5 min.**
• See Chapter Objectives, p. 402. **5 min.**

Vocabulaire 1, pp. 404–407
• Present **Vocabulaire 1,** pp. 404–405. See Teaching **Vocabulaire,** p. 404. **20 min.**
• Present **Exprimons-nous!,** p. 405. **10 min.**
• Have students do Activity 1, p. 406. **5 min.**
• Play Audio CD 10, Tr. 1 for Activity 2, p. 406. **5 min.**
• Have students do Activity 3, p. 406. **5 min.**
• Present **Flash culture,** p. 406. **5 min.**
• See Teaching **Exprimons-nous!,** p. 406. **10 min.**
• Have students do Activities 4–5, p. 407. **20 min.**

Optional Resources
• Learning Tips, p. 403
• **Cinquain** Poetry, p. 404
• TPR, p. 405
• French for Spanish Speakers, p. 405
• Advanced Learners, p. 405 ▲
• Special Learning Needs, p. 405 ●
• Connections, p. 406
• Communication (TE), p. 407
• Advanced Learners, p. 407 ▲
• Multiple Intelligences, p. 407

Homework Suggestions
Study for **Quiz: Vocabulaire 1**
Cahier de vocabulaire et grammaire, pp. 109–111
Interactive Tutor, Ch. 10
Online Practice (**go.hrw.com,** Keyword: BD3 CH10)
❀ 1.1, 1.2, 1.3, 3.1, 4.1, 4.2

Block 2

OBJECTIVE
Use prepositions with places; Use the subjunctive

Core Instruction
Vocabulaire 1, pp. 404–407
• Review **Vocabulaire 1,** pp. 404–407. **10 min.**
• Give **Quiz: Vocabulaire 1.** **20 min.**

Grammaire 1, pp. 408–411
• See Teaching **Grammaire,** p. 408. **10 min.**
• Play Audio CD 10, Tr. 2 for Activity 6, p. 408. **5 min.**
• Have students do Activities 7–10, pp. 408–409. **20 min.**
• See Teaching **Grammaire,** p. 410. **10 min.**
• Have students do Activities 11–13, pp. 410–411. **15 min.**

Optional Resources
• **Attention!,** p. 409
• Connections, p. 409
• Communication (TE), p. 409
• Slower Pace Learners, p. 409 ◆
• Special Learning Needs, p. 409 ●
• **Attention!,** p. 410
• Communication, p. 411
• Slower Pace Learners, p. 411 ◆
• Special Learning Needs, p. 411 ●

Homework Suggestions
Study for **Quiz: Grammaire 1**
Cahier de vocabulaire et grammaire, pp. 112–113
Cahier d'activités, pp. 91–92
Interactive Tutor, Ch. 10
Online Practice (**go.hrw.com,** Keyword: BD3 CH10)
❀ 1.1, 1.2, 1.3, 3.1, 4.1

Block 3

OBJECTIVE
Use the subjunctive; Use adverb placement; Learn about franco-phone culture

Core Instruction
Grammaire 1, pp. 408–411
• Do Bell Work 10.3, p. 410. **5 min.**
• Have students do Activity 14, p. 411. **5 min.**
• Review **Grammaire 1,** pp. 408–411. **10 min.**
• Give **Quiz: Grammaire 1.** **20 min.**

Application 1, pp. 412–413
• Have students do Activity 15, p. 412. **5 min.**
• Play Audio CD 10, Tr. 3 for Activity 16, p. 412. **5 min.**
• See Teaching **Un peu plus,** p. 412. **5 min.**
• Have students do Activities 17–20, pp. 412–413. **15 min.**

Culture, pp. 414–415
• See **Lecture culturelle** (TE), p. 414. **10 min.**
• See **Comparaisons et communauté** (TE), p. 414. **10 min.**

Optional Resources
• Communication (TE), p. 413
• Slower Pace Learners, p. 413 ◆
• Special Learning Needs, p. 413 ●
• Prereading Questions, p. 414
• Active Reading Questions, p. 414
• **Vocabulaire supplémentaire,** p. 414
• Bulletin Board Project, p. 415
• Cultures, p. 415
• Communities, p. 415
• Advanced Learners, p. 415 ▲
• Multiple Intelligences, p. 415

Homework Suggestions
Study for **Quiz: Application 1**
Cahier de vocabulaire et grammaire, p. 114
Cahier d'activités, pp. 93–94
Interactive Tutor, Ch. 10
Online Practice (**go.hrw.com,** Keyword: BD3 CH10)
Finish the **Communauté et professions** project, p. 415.
❀ 1.1, 1.2, 1.3, 2.1, 2.2, 3.1, 3.2, 4.2, 5.1, 5.2

Block 4

OBJECTIVE
Ask for help; Ask for directions

Core Instruction
Application 1, pp. 412–413
• Review **Application 1,** pp. 412–413. **10 min.**
• Give **Quiz: Application 1.** **20 min.**

Vocabulaire 2, pp. 416–419
• Present **Vocabulaire 2,** pp. 416–417. See Teaching **Vocabulaire,** p. 416. **15 min.**
• Present **Exprimons-nous!,** p. 417. **5 min.**
• Have students do Activity 21, p. 418. **5 min.**
• Play Audio CD 10, Tr. 4 for Activity 22, p. 418. **5 min.**
• Have students do Activity 23, p. 418. **5 min.**
• See Teaching **Exprimons-nous!,** p. 418. **10 min.**
• Have students do Activities 24–25, p. 419. **10 min.**
• Present **Flash culture,** p. 419. **5 min.**

Optional Resources
• Connections, p. 416
• TPR, p. 417
• Teacher to Teacher, p. 417
• Advanced Learners, p. 417 ▲
• Multiple Intelligences, p. 417
• **Proverbes,** p. 418
• Communication (TE), p. 419
• Slower Pace Learners, p. 419 ◆
• Special Learning Needs, p. 419 ●

Homework Suggestions
Study for **Quiz: Vocabulaire 2**
Cahier de vocabulaire et grammaire, pp. 115–117
Interactive Tutor, Ch. 10
Online Practice (**go.hrw.com,** Keyword: BD3 CH10)
❀ 1.1, 1.2, 1.3, 3.1, 4.1

Block 5

OBJECTIVE
Use the future; Use the past perfect

Core Instruction
Vocabulaire 2, pp. 416–419
- Review **Vocabulaire 2,** pp. 416–419. **10 min.**
- Give **Quiz: Vocabulaire 2.** **20 min.**

Grammaire 2, pp. 420–423
- See Teaching **Grammaire,** p. 420. **10 min.**
- Have students do Activities 26–29, pp. 420–421. **20 min.**
- Present **Flash culture,** p. 422. **5 min.**
- See Teaching **Grammaire,** p. 422. **10 min.**
- Play Audio CD 10, Tr. 5 for Activity 30, p. 422. **5 min.**
- Have students do Activities 31–33, pp. 422–423. **10 min.**

Optional Resources
- Communication (TE), p. 421
- Connections, p. 421
- Slower Pace Learners, p. 421 ◆
- Multiple Intelligences, p. 421
- French for Spanish Speakers, p. 422
- Communication (TE), p. 423
- Advanced Learners, p. 423 ▲
- Multiple Intelligences, p. 423

Homework Suggestions
Study for **Quiz: Grammaire 2**
Cahier de vocabulaire et grammaire, pp. 118–119
Cahier d'activités, pp. 95–96
Interactive Tutor, Ch. 10
Online Practice (**go.hrw.com,** Keyword: BD3 CH10)
    ❀ 1.1, 1.2, 1.3, 3.1, 4.1, 4.2

Block 6

OBJECTIVE
Use the past perfect; Use the causative **faire;** *Develop listening and reading skills*

Core Instruction
Grammaire 2, pp. 420–423
- Have students do Activity 34, p. 423. **10 min.**
- Review **Grammaire 2,** pp. 420–423. **10 min.**
- Give **Quiz: Grammaire 2.** **20 min.**

Application 2, pp. 424–425
- Play Audio CD 10, Tr. 6 for Activity 35, p. 424. **5 min.**
- Have students do Activity 36, p. 424. **5 min.**
- See Teaching **Un peu plus,** p. 424. **5 min.**
- Have students do Activities 37–40, pp. 424–425. **15 min.**

Lecture, pp. 426–429
- See **Lecture** (TE), p. 426. **20 min.**

Optional Resources
- Communication (TE), p. 425
- Advanced Learners, p. 425 ▲
- Special Learning Needs, p. 425 ●
- AP Reading Suggestion, p. 426
- Applying the Strategies, p. 426
- Active Reading Questions, p. 427
- Connecting with the Text, p. 427
- Slower Pace Learners, p. 427 ◆
- Special Learning Needs, p. 427 ●

Homework Suggestions
Study for **Quiz: Application 2**
Cahier de vocabulaire et grammaire, p. 120
Cahier d'activités, p. 97
Interactive Tutor, Ch. 10
Online Practice (**go.hrw.com,** Keyword: BD3 CH10)
    ❀ 1.1, 1.2, 1.3

Block 7

OBJECTIVE
Develop listening, reading, and writing skills; Review the chapter

Core Instruction
Application 2, pp. 424–425
- Review **Application 2,** pp. 424–425. **10 min.**
- Give **Quiz: Application 2.** **20 min.**

Lecture, pp. 426–429
- See **Lecture** (TE), p. 428. **10 min.**

L'atelier de l'écrivain, pp. 430–431
- See **L'atelier de l'écrivain** (TE), p. 430. **30 min.**

Prépare-toi pour l'examen, pp. 432–435
- Have students do Activities 1–5, pp. 432–433. **10 min.**
- Play Audio CD 10, Tr. 8 for Activity 6, p. 433. **5 min.**
- Have students do Activity 7, p. 433. **5 min.**

Optional Resources
- Active Reading Questions, p. 428
- Postreading Activity, p. 428
- Connections, p. 428
- Advanced Learners, p. 429 ▲
- Special Learning Needs, p. 429●
- Process Writing, p. 430
- Teaching Suggestion, p. 430
- **Adjectifs,** p. 431
- Writing Assessment, p. 431
- Advanced Learners, p. 431 ▲
- Special Learning Needs, p. 431●
- TPRS, p. 432
- Reteaching, p. 432
- Oral Assessment, p. 433
- Cultures, p. 434
- Chapter Review, pp. 434–435
- Game, p. 435

Homework Suggestions
Study for Chapter Test
Cahier d'activités, p. 98
Interactive Tutor, Ch. 10
Online Practice (**go.hrw.com,** Keyword: BD3 CH10)
    ❀ 1.1, 1.2, 1.3, 2.2, 3.1, 3.2, 5.2

Block 8

OBJECTIVE
Prepare for the AP Exam; Review and assess the chapter

Core Instruction
Activités préparatoires, pp. 436–437
- Have students do the **Activités préparatoires,** pp. 436–437. **20 min.**

Chapter Test 50 min.

Révisions cumulatives, pp. 438–439
- Play Audio CD 10, Tr. 10 for Activity 1, p. 438. **5 min.**
- Have students do Activities 2–6, pp. 438–439. **15 min.**

Optional Resources
- Reading Strategy, p. 436
- Writing Strategy, p. 437
- Cultures, p. 437
- Slower Pace Learners, p. 437 ◆
- Special Learning Needs, p. 437 ●
- Online Culture Project, p. 438
- Fine Art Connection, p. 439
- **Télé-culture:** Interviews
- **Télé-roman: Camille et compagnie**

Homework Suggestions
Cahier d'activités, pp. 99–100, 120–123
Interactive Tutor, Ch. 10
Online Practice (**go.hrw.com,** Keyword: BD3 CH10)
    ❀ 1.1, 1.2, 1.3, 2.1, 2.2, 3.1, 3.2

90-Minute Lesson Plans

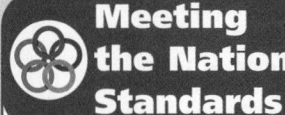

Meeting the National Standards

Communication
Communication, pp. 407, 409, 411, 413, 419, 421, 423, 425

À ton tour, p. 439

Cultures
Flash culture, pp. 406, 419, 422

Comparaisons, p. 415

Practices and Perspectives, pp. 415, 437

Products and Perspectives, p. 434

Connections
Thinking Critically, p. 406

Language-to-Language, p. 409

Language Note, pp. 416, 421

Literature Link, p. 429

Comparisons
Comparaisons, p. 415

Communities
Communauté, p. 415

Career Path, p. 415

Using the Photo
The Arawak probably populated St. Martin from 300 BC until the eighth century when they were pushed out by the Carib people. Columbus landed on the island of St. Martin on November 11, 1493, the feast day of St. Martin of Tours and he decided to name the island in honor of this saint. The island was devided between France and the Netherlands in 1648. Now it is a French overseas possession and forms part of the European Union. Have students research the major industries of St. Martin.

3.1, 4.2

chapitre **10**

Bon voyage!

Objectifs

In this chapter, you will learn to
- ask for and give information
- remind and reassure
- ask for and give help
- ask for directions

And you will review
- prepositions with places
- the subjunctive
- adverb placement
- the future
- the past perfect
- the causative **faire**

▶ Que vois-tu sur la photo?

Où se trouve Saint-Martin?

As-tu visité une des villes mentionnées sur les panneaux?

Et toi, où vas-tu en vacances d'habitude? Où voudrais-tu partir en vacances?

Suggested pacing:	Traditional Schedule	Block Schedule
Vocabulaire/Grammaire/Application 1	5 days	2 blocks
Culture	1 day	1 block
Vocabulaire/Grammaire/Application 2	5 days	2 blocks
Lecture	1 day	1/2 block
L'atelier de l'écrivain	1 day	1/2 block
Prépare-toi pour l'examen	1/2 day	1/2 block
Activités préparatoires	1/2 day	1/2 block
Examen	1 day	1/2 block
Révisions cumulatives	1 day	1/2 block

Vocabulaire supplémentaire

Students might use these terms to discuss the photo.

le panneau	*sign*
la boutique	*boutique*
la ligne électrique	*electric line*
le kilométrage	*distance in kilometers*

Learning Tip

Tell students that often the key to understanding a foreign language is understanding the culture of the country or countries where the language is spoken. Ask students to take a cyberspace tour of Guadeloupe to visit its people and get acquainted with their culture. Encourage students to read the works of the islands' poets and to listen to the music of Guadeloupe. Students should write down terms that are unique to Guadeloupe's culture. 🏵 3.2

Language Lab

You might want to use your language lab to have students:

- listen to all target vocabulary and phrases in the chapter
- use Holt SoundBooth to practice pronunciation of vocabulary and phrases to save their work for evaluation
- complete the listening activities in this chapter

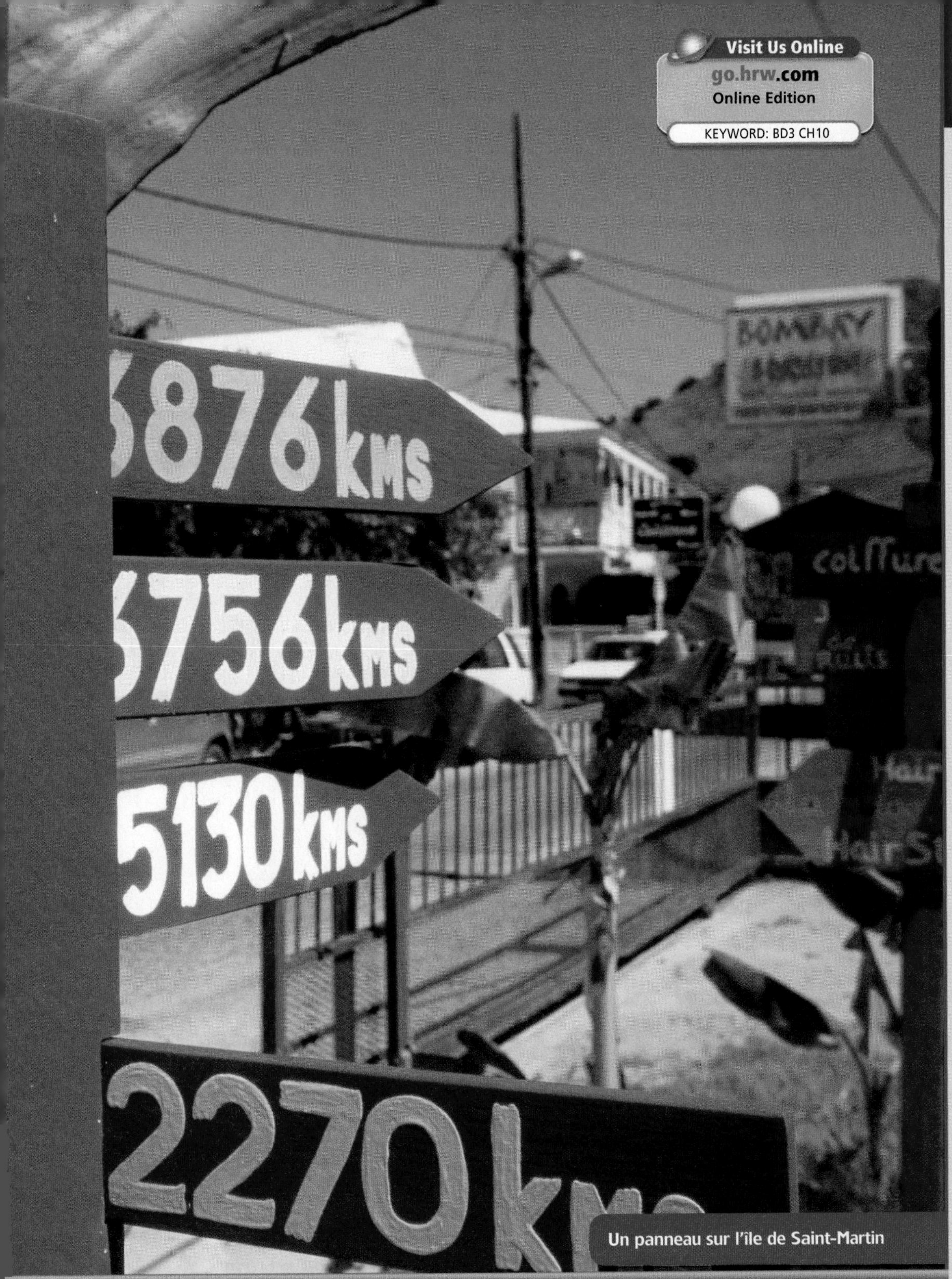

Un panneau sur l'île de Saint-Martin

LISTENING PRACTICE

Vocabulaire
Activity 2, p. 406, CD 10, Tr. 1
Activity 22, p. 418, CD 10, Tr. 4

Grammaire
Activity 6, p. 408, CD 10, Tr. 2
Activity 30, p. 422, CD 10, Tr. 5

Application
Activity 16, p. 412, CD 10, Tr. 3
Activity 35, p. 424, CD 10, Tr. 6

Language Lab and Classroom Activities

Prépare-toi pour l'examen
Activity 6, p. 433, CD 10, Tr. 8
Télé-culture: Interviews, Chapter 10

Activités préparatoires
Section I, Listening, p. 436, CD 10, Tr. 9
Télé-roman: *Camille et compagnie*, Épisodes 11 et 12

Révisions cumulatives
Activity 1, p. 438, CD 10, Tr. 10

Lecture p. 426, CD 10, Tr. 7

Resources

Planning:

Lesson Planner

One-Stop Planner

Presentation:

Teaching Transparencies
Vocabulaire 10.1, 10.2

Practice:

Cahier de vocabulaire et grammaire

Differentiated Practice and Assessment CD-ROM

Media Guide

Teaching Transparencies
Bell Work 10.1

Interactive Tutor, Disc 2

Bell Work

Use Bell Work 10.1 in the *Teaching Transparencies* or write this activity on the board.

Complète les phrases suivantes avec la forme correcte de **connaître** ou **savoir**.

1. **Tu ____ l'opéra de Paris?**
2. **Je n'y suis jamais allé, mais je ____ où il est!**
3. **Ta sœur et toi, vous ____ Carmen, l'opéra de Bizet?**
4. **Bien sûr! Et nous ____ aussi qu'on le joue à l'opéra en ce moment.**
5. **Tu ____ que mes frères jouent dans l'orchestre de l'opéra, non?**

Cinquain Poetry

Have students create a poem with the chapter vocabulary.

Line 1 One noun
Line 2 Two adjectives
Line 3 Three verbs
Line 4 An expression
Line 5 Another word for the noun

Sample answer

Le voyage
Intérieur, international
Décoller, atterrir, annuler
Vous avez de la chance!
Un vol

Objectifs
- to ask for information
- to remind and reassure

Vocabulaire à l'œuvre 1

À l'aéroport

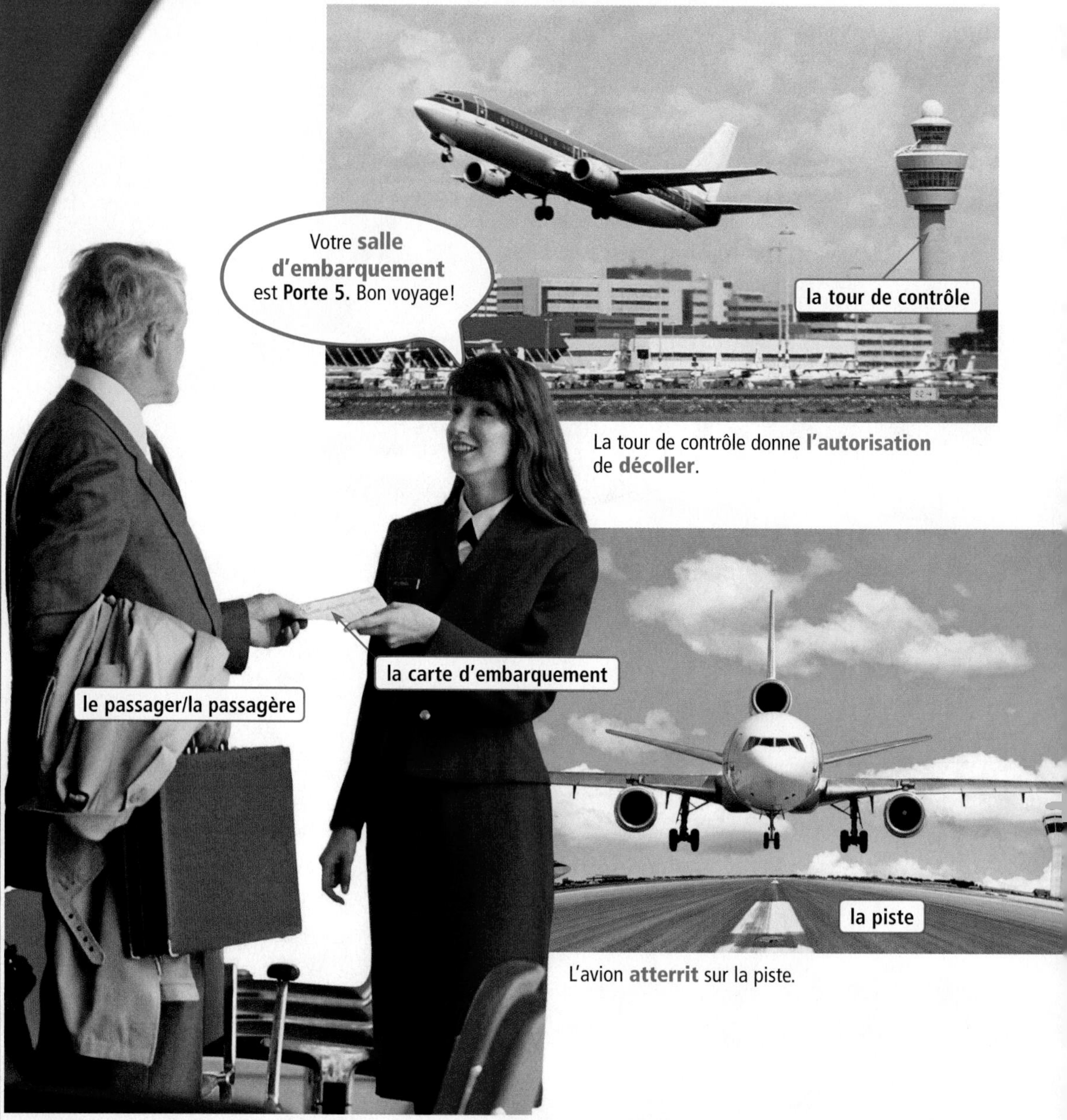
Votre **salle d'embarquement** est **Porte 5.** Bon voyage!
la tour de contrôle
la carte d'embarquement
le passager/la passagère
la piste

La tour de contrôle donne **l'autorisation** de **décoller.**

L'avion **atterrit** sur la piste.

Core Instruction

TEACHING VOCABULAIRE

1. Introduce the vocabulary, using transparencies **Vocabulaire 10.1** and **10.2.** Model the pronunciation of each word or expression. **(3 min.)**
2. Ask students to point to various items on the transparency. **les passagers, l'hôtesse de l'air (3 min.)**
3. Ask students questions about their air travel experiences. **Quel vol est-ce que tu as pris? Où était ton siège? Est-ce que tu as passé la douane?** etc. **(3 min.)**
4. Model the expressions from **Exprimons-nous!** Then have partners make up similar requests for information and clarification and responses. **(3 min.)**

À bord de l'avion

Online Practice
go.hrw.com
Vocabulaire 1 practice
KEYWORD: BD3 CH10

Dans **le cockpit**, il y a **le commandant de bord**.

L'hôtesse de l'air donne **les consignes de sécurité**.

la cabine

le hublot

le siège

D'autres mots utiles

l'allée (f.)	aisle
le décalage horaire	jet lag
l'équipage (m.)	crew
le hall d'arrivée	arrival hall
le vol intérieur/ international	domestic/ international flight
annuler	to cancel
confirmer	to confirm
débarquer	to get off a plane
embarquer	to get on a plane
enregistrer	to check in
passer la douane	to go through customs

Exprimons-nous!

To ask for information	To respond
Est-ce que je peux avoir **une place près du hublot?** *. . . a window seat?*	**Vous avez de la chance, on en a encore deux.** *You are lucky, we have two left!*
On a droit à combien de bagages? *How many bags are we allowed to take?*	Trois **maximum.** *Maximum . . .*
Existe-t-il un vol sans escale pour la Guyane? *Is there a non-stop flight to . . . ?*	Oui, il y a **un vol direct,** mais c'est plus cher. *. . . a direct flight . . .*

Interactive TUTOR

Vocabulaire et grammaire, pp. 109–111

Online workbooks

▶ Vocabulaire supplémentaire—Les voyages en avion, p. R21

Vocabulaire 1

Resources

Planning:
Lesson Planner

 One-Stop Planner

Presentation:
Teaching Transparencies
Vocabulaire 10.1, 10.2

Practice:
Cahier de vocabulaire et grammaire

Differentiated Practice and Assessment CD-ROM

Media Guide

 Audio CD 10, Tr. 1

Interactive Tutor, Disc 2

Connections

Thinking Critically

Martinique is a **département d'outre-mer (DOM)** of France. As part of France, it belongs to the European Union, its currency is the euro, and its people carry EU passports. Ask students if the Martiniquais need a work permit in order to work in Belgium? Do they need a work permit to work in Switzerland? 3.1

❶ Answers

1. passer la douane
2. la tour de contrôle
3. la salle d'embarquement
4. le hall d'arrivée
5. annuler

❷ Script

See script on p. 401E.

❷ Answers

1. à Nice; intérieur
2. oui
3. près du hublot
4. une heure
5. deux

Flash culture

On appelle les régions françaises en dehors de la France les DOM-TOM ou départements et territoires d'outre-mer. Bien qu'on utilise encore souvent le nom DOM-TOM, le statut administratif de ces régions a changé récemment.

Maintenant, on parle officiellement des DROM (département et région d'outre-mer)

Est-ce qu'il existe des territoires rattachés aux États-Unis? Lesquels? Quel est leur status? 4.2

---

❶ En voyage 1.2

Lisons/Parlons Complète les phrases suivantes de façon logique.

1. Quand on arrive dans un pays étranger, on doit _____.
2. C'est _____ qui donne la permission d'atterrir.
3. Notre avion va décoller. Nous devons vite aller à _____.
4. Les passagers débarquent. Allons attendre Léa dans _____!
5. Si on décide de ne plus partir, il faut _____ sa réservation.

❷ Écoutons CD 10, Tr. 1 1.2

Écoute cette conversation et réponds aux questions.

1. Où va Joséphine? Quel genre de vol est-ce que c'est?
2. Est-ce que Joséphine veut un vol sans escale?
3. Où est-ce qu'elle veut s'asseoir dans l'avion?
4. Combien de temps à l'avance doit-elle arriver à l'aéroport?
5. À combien de bagages a-t-elle droit?

❸ À l'aéroport 1.2 1. a 2. b 3. b 4. b 5. a

Parlons/Écrivons Regarde l'illustration et dis si les phrases qui suivent sont a) **vraies** ou b) **fausses**.

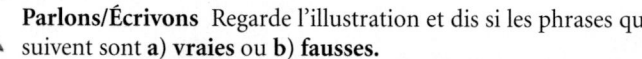

1. Le passager enregistre sa valise.
2. La passagère passe la douane.
3. La jeune femme emporte des bagages en cabine.
4. Le jeune homme vient de débarquer.
5. L'avion décolle.

Core Instruction

TEACHING EXPRIMONS-NOUS!

1. Model the pronunciation of the expressions in **Exprimons-nous!** (2 min.)

2. Ask students questions to remind them of something, using the question starters in **Exprimons-nous!**

Est-ce que tu as pris...? Tu as prévenu...? As-tu bien confirmé...?

Have students use the expressions in **Exprimons-nous!** to reassure you.

3. Have partners ask you similar questions to remind you of something. (3 min.)

Exprimons-nous!

To remind	To reassure
Est-ce que tu as pris ton passeport? *Did you take . . . ?*	**Oui, je l'ai toujours sur moi.** *Yes, I always carry it.*
Tu as prévenu la compagnie aérienne **que** tu étais allergique au poisson? *Have you told . . . that . . . ?*	**Rassure-toi,** j'ai pensé à tout. *Don't worry, . . .*
As-tu bien confirmé ton vol? *Have you confirmed . . . ?*	**Pas encore! Je le fais tout de suite.** *Not yet! I'll do it right away.*

Interactive TUTOR

Vocabulaire et grammaire, pp. 109–111 Online workbooks

④ Le voyage de mamie ✿1.2

Lisons/Écrivons La grand-mère de Loïc va aller aux États-Unis.
Lis les réponses de la grand-mère et imagine les questions de Loïc.

1. —_____?
   —Oui, j'ai téléphoné à l'agence pour le confirmer.

2. —_____?
   —Oui, regarde, il est là, dans mon sac.

3. —_____?
   —Oui, rassure-toi. J'ai demandé un repas végétarien.

4. —_____?
   —Non, j'ai demandé une place près de l'allée.

5. —_____?
   —Oui, on a droit à un bagage dans la cabine.

6. —_____?
   —Pas encore! Je vais téléphoner à l'hôtel tout de suite.

Communication

HOLT **SoundBooth** ONLINE RECORDING

⑤ Scénario ✿1.1

Parlons Tu décides de voyager dans une région française ou
dans un autre pays francophone. Tu vas à l'agence de voyages pour
choisir ta destination et pour faire ta réservation. Joue cette scène
avec un(e) camarade qui va être l'employé(e) de l'agence et te
rappeler ce que tu dois faire, puis échangez les rôles.

♻ *Souviens-toi!* The **conditionnel de politesse**, pp. 64, 330

MODÈLE —**Bonjour. Je peux vous aider?**
—**Oui, je voudrais aller en Suisse...**

---

④ Possible Answers

1. As-tu bien confirmé ton vol?
2. Est-ce que tu as pris ton passeport?
3. Tu as prévenu la compagnie aérienne que tu ne mangeais pas de viande?
4. Tu as demandé une place près du hublot?
5. On a droit à des bagages dans la cabine?
6. As-tu bien confirmé ta réservation d'hôtel?

Communication

Group Activity: Presentational

Ask students to write an account of an unusual plane trip they took. In small groups, have them share their story. Group members should ask questions to get more details.

✿1.3

Differentiated Instruction

ADVANCED LEARNERS

③ Extension After completing this activity, ask partners to write a conversation between the captain and the flight attendant. They should talk about an upcoming flight. Is it an international flight? What is its destination? What is the duration of the flight? Will it be delayed? Is the plane full? Will dinner be served on this flight? You might ask some partners to perform their conversation for the class. ✿1.1, 1.3

MUTIPLE INTELLIGENCES

Spatial Hold a "Best Packer" Contest. Display an open suitcase for all to see. Have each student "fill the suitcase" by writing in French a list of items to be packed. All items must comply with airline regulations and fit inside the suitcase. On the next day, the student with the most items listed, brings all the items and fills the suitcase to prove that they all fit. This student wins a prize for "Best Packer". ✿1.2

Assess

Assessment Program

Quiz: Vocabulaire 1

Alternative Assessment

Differentiated Practice and Assessment CD-ROM

Online Assessment
my.hrw.com

Test Generator

Resources

Planning:

Lesson Planner

 One-Stop Planner

Practice:

Grammar Tutor for Students of French, Chapter 10

Cahier de vocabulaire et grammaire

Differentiated Practice and Assessment CD-ROM

Cahier d'activités

Media Guide

 Teaching Transparencies Bell Work 10.2

🎧 Audio CD 10, Tr. 2

 Interactive Tutor, Disc 2

🖥 Bell Work

Use Bell Work 10.2 in the *Teaching Transparencies* or write this activity on the board.

Joins les phrases logiquement.

1. L'hôtesse de l'air donne...
2. L'équipage accueille...
3. Les avions atterrissent...
4. Quand on débarque à Paris, il faut...
5. L'avion a décollé...
6. Il y a un décalage horaire de...

a. sur la piste.
b. à l'heure en quittant Houston.
c. sept heures entre Paris et Houston.
d. les passagers dans l'avion.
e. les consignes de sécurité.
f. passer la douane. 🌺 1.2

6 Script

1. Martine est de Paris, mais elle habite à la Réunion.
2. Maya est mexicaine et elle va en Afrique.
3. Audrey est de Bruxelles et elle va au Texas.
4. Frank était allé à la Guadeloupe, mais il voulait rentrer en Suisse après trois semaines.
5. Robert va au Canada, mais il est de Californie.

Objectifs

- review of prepositions with places
- review of the subjunctive

Grammaire *à l'œuvre* 1

Révisions Prepositions with places

1 To say *in* or *to* most **cities**, use the preposition **à**.
To say *from* most **cities**, use **de**.

> Le vol 21 arrive à **Paris** à 13h10. Le vol 38 arrive **de Rome** à 8h20.

2 To say *in* or *to* **feminine** **countries** or **states** and **countries** or **states** starting with a vowel, use **en**. Use **au** before masculine **countries** or states, that begin with a consonant, and **aux** before **countries that have plural names**.

> On fera une escale en **Californie**.   Il voudrait aller au **Maroc**.

3 To say *from* **feminine** **countries**, use **de**. Use **du** before masculine **countries**, **d'** before **countries that begin with a vowel**, and **des** before **countries that have plural names**.

> Le vol en provenance d'**Algérie** est arrivé.
> Ils arriveront du **Luxembourg** demain.

Déjà vu!

Remember that country names are either masculine or feminine. Most countries that end in **-e** are feminine (la **France**, la **Belgique**, la **Suisse**, la **Tunisie**, etc.) Countries that end in letters other than **-e** are generally masculine.

le **Maroc**
le **Canada**
le **Niger**

There are *exceptions*, for example le **Mexique** and le **Cambodge**.

Vocabulaire et grammaire, pp. 112–113
Cahier d'activités, pp. 91–93

Online workbooks

---

6 **Écoutons** CD 10, Tr. 2 🌺 1.2 **1.** b **2.** a **3.** a **4.** b **5.** b **6.** a

🎧 Dans les aéroports il y a des gens qui viennent de partout. Écoute et dis si les phrases suivantes sont **a)** **vraies** ou **b)** **fausses.**

1. Martine habite en France.
2. Maya vient du Mexique.
3. Audrey est belge.
4. Frank habite à la Guadeloupe.
5. Robert est canadien.
6. Ahmed ne vit pas en Algérie .

1. à **2.** au **3.** en **4.** des **5.** à **6.** à **7.** en

7 **Itinéraire de vol** 🌺 1.2 **8.** en **9.** de **10.** à **11.** des **12.** au

Lisons/Écrivons Lucas est de Strasbourg et étudie au Texas. Il explique à Ali qui est marocain comment il rentre chez lui. Complète ses phrases.

J'ai étudié pendant un an __1__ Austin, __2__ Texas. Pour rentrer __3__ France __4__ États-Unis, je dois d'abord aller __5__ Dallas. Ensuite, je dois prendre un autre avion pour aller __6__ Bruxelles, __7__ Belgique. Quand j'arrive __8__ Europe, je prends le train __9__ Bruxelles __10__ Strasbourg. Et toi, comment vas-tu __11__ États-Unis __12__ Maroc?

Core Instruction

TEACHING GRAMMAIRE

1. Read **Déjà vu** aloud with students. **(2 min.)**
2. Review Points 1–3. Using a world map with French labels, point to various countries, states, and cities and say, **Je voudrais aller...** Have students finish the sentence with the correct preposition. **(4 min.)**

3. For more practice, ask students a few questions to elicit names of places. **D'où viens-tu? Où habites-tu? C'est où, ça? Dans quel pays aimerais-tu aller en vacances?** Student answers can be short, but should indicate that they have understood the rule for using the appropriate form of the preposition. **(2 min.)**

Online Practice
go.hrw.com
Grammaire 1 practice
KEYWORD: BD3 CH10

Chapitre 10

Grammaire 1

8 Et eux, ils sont d'où? 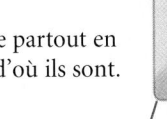1.2

Parlons/Écrivons Ces élèves viennent de partout en Europe. Regarde l'illustration pour dire d'où ils sont. Puis, dis d'où tu es.

MODÈLE Julie est de Bruxelles, en Belgique.

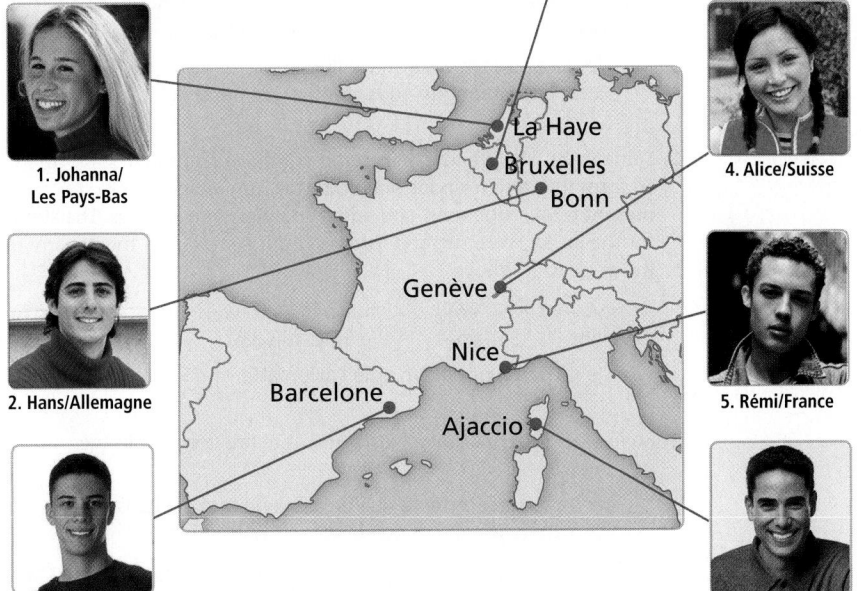

Julie/
Belgique

1. Johanna/
Les Pays-Bas

2. Hans/Allemagne

3. Pablo/Espagne

La Haye
Bruxelles
Bonn
Genève
Nice
Barcelone
Ajaccio

4. Alice/Suisse

5. Rémi/France

6. Sean/Corse

9 Un voyage 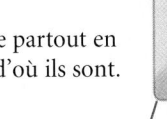1.3

Écrivons Tu as fait un voyage récemment ou tu vas faire un voyage bientôt. Dans quelles villes ou dans quel état est-ce que tu es allée(e) ou tu voudrais aller? Décris ton itinéraire.

MODÈLE Cet été, j'aimerais aller au Colorado et en Californie.

Communication

HOLT SoundBooth
ONLINE RECORDING

10 Questions personnelles 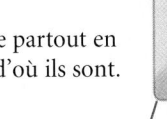1.1

Parlons Demande à un(e) camarade d'où il/elle vient et dans quelles villes il/elle a habité. Ton/Ta camarade te dira aussi où il/elle aimerait habiter plus tard. Ensuite, échangez les rôles.

♻ *Souviens-toi*, The **passé composé**, pp. 22, 26

MODÈLE —D'où viens-tu?
—Je suis né(e) à..., en... Mais j'ai habité à...

Differentiated Instruction

SLOWER PACE LEARNERS

7 Variation Complete this activity as a class. Call for a volunteer to read the first statement with prepositions filled in. Referring to the grammar presentation, students should tell whether the volunteer has used the correct or incorrect prepositions. Then ask for another volunteer to read the second statement. 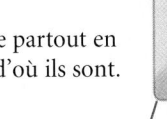1.2

SPECIAL LEARNING NEEDS

7 Students with Language Impairments Students with language impairments will most likely write the correct responses if they have first had the sentences read aloud to them and then say each sentence with the appropriate preposition. You might consider asking another student or a teaching assistant to help with this task. 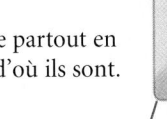1.2

---

8 Answers
1. Johanna est de La Haye aux Pays-Bas.
2. Hans est de Bonn en Allemangne.
3. Pablo est de Barcelone en Espagne.
4. Alice est de Genève en Suisse.
5. Rémi est de Nice en France.
6. Sean est d'Ajaccio en Corse.

COMMON ERROR ALERT
//// ATTENTION ! \\\\

When country names are preceded by **en**, the country's name may be replaced by **y**. Students might assume that it must be replaced by **en**. **Je vais en France** becomes **J'y vais**, never **"J'en vais."**

Connections
Language to Language

The verbs **visiter** (to visit) and **quitter** (to leave) are generally not followed by prepositions. **Le président français a visité la Martinique.** Ask students to create sentences with **quitter** and give the English equivalents.
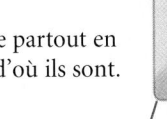3.1, 4.1

Communication
10 Pair Activity: Interpersonal

Have students imagine three cities in different countries they just came from and three countries they will go to in the near future. Ask partners to take turns asking about where the other was and where he or she will be going. Students should also ask what their partners will be doing in the countries they are going to visit.
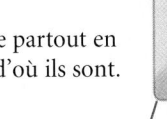1.1

Resources

Planning:

Lesson Planner

 One-Stop Planner

Practice:

Grammar Tutor for Students of French, Chapter 10

Cahier de vocabulaire et grammaire

Differentiated Practice and Assessment CD-ROM

Cahier d'activités

Media Guide

 Teaching Transparencies Bell Work 10.3

 Interactive Tutor, Disc 2

Bell Work

Use Bell Work 10.3 in the *Teaching Transparencies* or write this activity on the board.

Complète les phrases suivantes avec les prépositions **à, de, du, en, au, aux**

1. Coralie habite _____ Laon, _____ France.
2. L'été prochain, elle va venir _____ États-Unis.
3. Son frère préfère voyager _____ Espagne et _____ Portugal.
4. Leur mère est espagnole. Elle est _____ Madrid.
5. Es-tu déjà allé _____ Mexique?
6. Bien sûr! Et justement, je reviens _____ Mexique!

🏵 1.2

COMMON ERROR ALERT
////ATTENTION !////

Students may think they have to change prepositions before cities and countries to show a change in meaning, but such prepositions are invariable. **Il est à Paris.** *(He is in Paris.)* **Il va à Paris.** *(He goes to Paris.)* **Il est en France.** *(He is in France.)* **Il va en France.** *(He goes to France)*

Interactive **TUTOR**

Révisions The subjunctive

1 To conjugate most verbs in the **subjunctive,** take the present tense **ils/elles** form, drop **-ent,** and add the subjunctive endings **-e, -es, -e, -ions, -iez, -ent.**

ils **regardent**	→	**regard-**	→	je **regarde,** tu **regardes**
ils **choisissent**	→	**choisiss-**	→	il/elle **choisisse,** nous **choisissions**
elles **perdent**	→	**perd-**	→	vous **perdiez,** ils/elles **perdent**

Je doute que le vol arrive à l'heure.
Il est important que nous confirmions notre vol.

2 Some verbs, like **prendre, venir,** and **voir** have two subjunctive stems. To form the stem for **nous** and **vous,** take the **nous** form of the present tense, drop **-ons,** and add the subjunctive endings. The stem for the **je, tu, il/elle/on,** and **ils/elles** forms comes from the **ils** form of the present indicative.

| nous **voyons** | → | **voy-** | → | nous voyions, vous voyiez |
| ils **voient** | → | **voi-** | → | je voie, tu voies |

Je ne pense pas qu'on voie l'avion atterrir d'ici.

3 Remember that **aller, avoir, être,** and **faire** are irregular in the subjunctive.

Je ne suis pas certaine que ce vol fasse escale à Paris.
On attend jusqu'à ce que le vol soit prêt à partir.

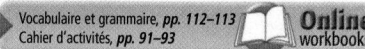
Vocabulaire et grammaire, *pp. 112–113*
Cahier d'activités, *pp. 91–93*
Online workbooks

⑪ Avant le départ 🎞 1.2

Lisons/Parlons M. et Mme Fisson préparent leur voyage. Choisis la bonne forme du verbe pour compléter leurs phrases.

1. Je suis désolée qu'on ne (puisse / peut) pas emmener le chien.
2. Je suis content qu'Alain nous (conduit / conduise) à l'aéroport.
3. Il n'est pas sûr que l'avion (atterrisse / atterrit) à l'heure.
4. Il est possible que tu (as / aies) une place près du hublot.
5. Je doute qu'on (ait / a) droit à cinq valises.
6. J'espère qu'on ne (fera / fasse) pas escale à New York.
7. Tu crois que nous (ayons / avons) tout ce qu'il nous faut?
8. Si tu ne te dépêches pas, je doute qu'on (peut / puisse) arriver à temps!
9. J'ai peur qu'il y (ait / a) un orage pendant notre vol.

Core Instruction

TEACHING GRAMMAIRE

1. Read **Déjà Vu** aloud with students. **(4 min.)**
2. Review Point 1. Point out that **-er** verbs have the same forms in the singular subjunctive and the present. **(2 min.)**

3. Review Points 2 and 3. You may choose to teach students additional irregular verbs. **savoir/que je sache; pouvoir/que je puisse; vouloir/que je veuille. (4 min.)**

12 Conversations d'aéroport 🌼1.2

Écrivons Ces gens sont à l'aéroport et parlent de leur vols. Remplace le verbe souligné par le verbe entre parenthèses et fais tous les changements nécessaires.

1. Je <u>crois</u> que les vols de cette compagnie aérienne sont souvent en retard. (avoir peur)

2. Nous <u>espérons</u> que vous ferez un bon voyage. (souhaiter)

3. Je <u>suis sûre</u> que tu ne pourras pas avoir une place près de moi. (être désolé)

4. Je <u>pense</u> qu'ils viendront nous chercher. (douter)

5. Il <u>est certain</u> que ce vol est annulé. (être possible)

6. Je <u>crois</u> qu'elle pourra trouver une place près du hublot. (il se peut que)

7. Vous <u>êtes sûrs</u> que votre vol est à l'heure. (ne pas être certain)

13 Choses à faire 🌼1.2

Écrivons/Parlons Théo et Pauline vont prendre l'avion pour la Martinique demain. Dis-leur ce qu'il faut qu'ils fassent.

MODÈLE confirmer votre vol aujourd'hui
Il faut que vous confirmiez votre vol aujourd'hui.

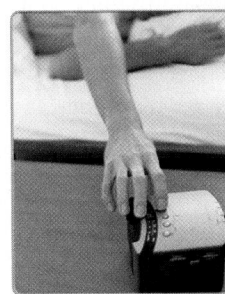   

1. se lever tôt   2. ne pas oublier   3. prendre un taxi   4. arriver à l'avance

Communication  HOLT **SoundBooth** ONLINE RECORDING

14 Scénario 🌼1.1, 1.3

Parlons Ton ami(e) et toi, vous allez partir en vacances. Dites cinq choses qu'il faut que vous fassiez pour préparer votre voyage. Utilisez le subjonctif. Jouez cette scène devant la classe.

Differentiated Instruction

SLOWER PACE LEARNERS

11 Variation Have students use a step-by-step approach to completing each item of this activity. Ask them to write down the correct form of the expression that requires the subjunctive. Next to this expression, students should write the subject of the subordinate clause and then give the correct subjunctive form of the verb. Remind students to connect the main and subordinate clauses with **que**. 🌼1.2

SPECIAL LEARNING NEEDS

13 Students with AD(H)D Simple modifications involving artwork will enhance the activity and keep the attention of students. Distribute copies of the pictures and have students cut out and paste them in chronological order onto a piece of paper with equal space around each picture. Have students write captions in French for each picture to describe what they believe is occurring in each scene. Artwork can be displayed around the classroom. 🌼1.2

---

1. J'ai peur que les vols de cette compagnie aérienne soient souvent en retard.

2. Nous souhaitons que vous fassiez un bon voyage.

3. Je suis désolée que tu ne puisses pas avoir une place près de moi.

4. Je doute qu'ils viennent nous chercher.

5. Il est possible que ce vol soit annulé.

6. Il se peut qu'elle puisse trouver un place près du hublot.

7. Vous n'êtes pas certain que votre vol soit à l'heure.

13 Answers

1. Il faut que vous vous leviez tôt.

2. Il est important que vous n'oubliiez pas vos passeports.

3. Il faut que vous preniez un taxi.

4. Il faut que vous arriviez à l'avance.

Communication

Pair Activity: Interpersonal

Ask partners to act out a conversation between a traveler and an incompetent airline employee. The traveler must get to a certain city by a certain time and tries to negotiate the best price, seat, and the fewest stops. The traveler should use the subjunctive of necessity, desire, and so forth. The employee cannot seem to accommodate the traveler's wishes. The employee should use the subjunctive of doubt, possibility, and negative certainty. You might have partners present their conversations to the class. 🌼1.1

Assess

Assessment Program
Quiz: Grammaire 1
Alternative Assessment
Differentiated Practice and Assessment CD-ROM

Online Assessment
my.hrw.com

Test Generator

Resources

Planning:

Lesson Planner

 One-Stop Planner

Practice:

Grammar Tutor for Students of French, Chapter 10

Cahier de vocabulaire et grammaire

Differentiated Practice and Assessment CD-ROM

Cahier d'activités

Media Guide

 Teaching Transparencies Bell Work 10.4

 Audio CD 10, Tr. 3

 Interactive Tutor, Disc 2

Bell Work

Use Bell Work 10.4 in the *Teaching Transparencies* or write this activity on the board.

Complète les phrases avec la forme correcte des verbes entre parenthèses.

1. Il faut que tu _____ (faire) enregistrer tes bagages.
2. Je doute que l'avion _____ (être) à l'heure.
3. J'aimerais que vous _____ (avoir) une place près du hublot.
4. Je voudrais que vous _____ (voir) la ville en arrivant.

🌸1.2

16 Script

See script on p. 363E.

Synthèse
• Vocabulaire 1
• Grammaire 1

Application 1

15 En campagne 🌸1.3

✏️ **Écrivons** Tu travailles pour une personnalité politique qui doit faire des discours dans trois villes différentes les jours qui viennent. Fais son itinéraire avec les heures de départ et d'arrivée des avions qu'il va prendre.

MODÈLE Mardi, il faudra que vous preniez l'avion qui décolle à 8h45 de Los Angeles en Californie pour arriver à 12h37 à Dallas, au Texas. Mercredi...

16 Écoutons CD 10, Tr. 3 🌸1.2 1. b 2. b 3. a 4. b 5. b 6. a

🎧 Camille parle de son voyage en avion. Dis si ses phrases sont **a) logiques** ou **b) illogiques.**

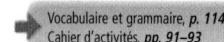 **Un peu plus** **Révisions**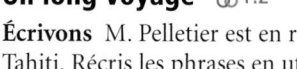

Adverb placement

1. **Adverbs** generally go directly before the adjective or adverb they modify.

   Nous avons passé la douane **très vite**!

2. In a sentence with a simple tense, **adverbs** that modify the verb usually go directly after the verb.

   Notre vol **arrivera tard**.

3. In a sentence with a compound tense, **adverbs** that modify the verb generally go before the **past participle**.

   Est-ce que vous avez **déjà confirmé** votre vol?

4. Longer **adverbs** that tell *when* can go at the beginning or end of the sentence.

   D'habitude, on **embarque** dans l'avion juste avant le départ.

→ Vocabulaire et grammaire, p. 114
Cahier d'activités, pp. 91–93
Online workbooks

17 Un long voyage 🌸1.2

✏️ **Écrivons** M. Pelletier est en route pour Tahiti. Récris les phrases en utilisant des adverbes.

MODÈLE M. Pelletier est en voyage. (actuel)
M. Pelletier est actuellement en voyage.

1. M. Pelletier va à Tahiti au mois de juillet. (habituel)
2. Il aime voyager. (confortable)
3. Cette fois, il a mal dormi dans l'avion. (vrai)
4. Son prochain vol va être en retard. (sûr)
5. Mais il va avoir une place près du hublot. (final)
6. Il regardera le film. (attentif)
7. Dès qu'il arrivera à l'hôtel, il ira dans sa chambre pour se reposer. (direct)

Core Instruction

INTEGRATED PRACTICE

1. Have students do Activities 15–16 to practice previously taught material. **(3 min.)**
2. Go over **Un peu plus.** (See presentation suggestions at right.) **(4 min.)**
3. Continue with integrated practice Activities 17–20. **(30 min.)**

TEACHING UN PEU PLUS

1. Go over **Un peu plus.** Tell students that adverbs of time usually go at the beginning or at the end of the sentence. **Hier, nous sommes arrivés. Nous sommes arrivés hier.** **(4 min.)**
2. To practice, read aloud sentences and adverbs to be added to them. **J'ai dormi dans l'avion.(mal) J'ai mal dormi dans l'avion. J'ai dormi dans l'avion. (aujourd'hui) J'ai dormi dans l'avion aujourd'hui. (2 min.)**

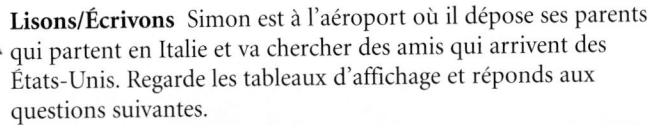

Online Practice
go.hrw.com
Application 1 practice
KEYWORD: BD3 CH10

Chapitre 10

Application 1

18 **Tableaux d'affichage** 1.2

Lisons/Écrivons Simon est à l'aéroport où il dépose ses parents qui partent en Italie et va chercher des amis qui arrivent des États-Unis. Regarde les tableaux d'affichage et réponds aux questions suivantes.

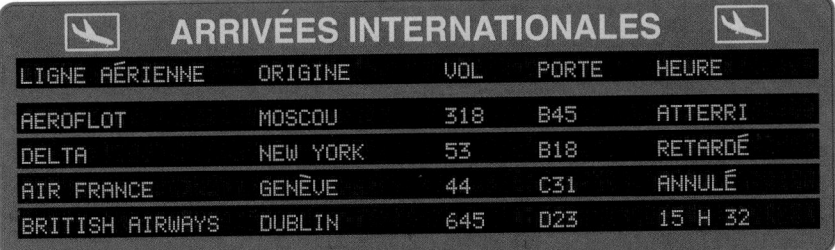

ARRIVÉES INTERNATIONALES				
LIGNE AÉRIENNE	ORIGINE	VOL	PORTE	HEURE
AEROFLOT	MOSCOU	318	B45	ATTERRI
DELTA	NEW YORK	53	B18	RETARDÉ
AIR FRANCE	GENÈVE	44	C31	ANNULÉ
BRITISH AIRWAYS	DUBLIN	645	D23	15 H 32

DÉPARTS INTERNATIONAUX				
LIGNE AÉRIENNE	DESTINATION	VOL	PORTE	HEURE
TRANSMERIDIAN	ATHÈNES	318	A16	EMBARQUEMENT
AIR FRANCE	ROME	53	C44	14 H 08
SWISSAIR	BRUXELLES	44	B12	15 H 54
AMERICAN AIR	DAKAR	120	F54	18 H 41

1. À quelle heure est le vol des parents de Simon?
2. Quel avion va bientôt décoller?
3. D'où vient l'avion qui vient d'atterrir?
4. Quels passagers ne vont pas pouvoir partir?
5. Qu'est-ce qui se passe avec le vol des copains de Simon?

19 **Un e-mail** 1.2

Écrivons Écris un e-mail à un(e) de tes camarades pour lui raconter un de tes voyages en avion ou en train. Utilise au moins cinq adverbes dans ton e-mail.

HOLT SoundBooth
ONLINE RECORDING

20 **Scénario** 1.1

Parlons Tu travailles dans un aéroport et des passagers te demandent ce qu'ils doivent faire pour enregistrer leurs bagages, où aller pour passer la douane, etc. Joue cette scène avec un(e) camarade.

17 Answers

1. Mr. Pelletier va habituellement à Tahiti au mois de juillet.
2. Il aime voyager confortablement.
3. Cette fois, il a vraiment mal dormi dans l'avion.
4. Son prochain vol va sûrement être en retard.
5. Mais il va finalement avoir une place près du hublot.
6. Il regardera attentivement le film.
7. Dès qu'il arrivera à l'hôtel, il ira directement dans sa chambre pour se reposer.

18 Answers

1. à 14 h 08
2. l'avion qui va à Athènes
3. de Moscou
4. ceux qui vont à Genève
5. il est retardé

Communication

20 Pair Activity: Interpersonal

Ask partners to prepare an airport scene to be presented in front of the class. Have them create a conversation between an angry, frustrated traveler who has experienced canceled flights and layovers and an airline employee. The latter asks questions piecing together where the traveler has been and where he or she needs to go. Encourage students to incorporate adverbs and to use as few notes as possible. As the class listens, have them note how often they hear an adverb and the subjunctive. 1.1

Differentiated Instruction

SLOWER PACE LEARNERS

Additional Practice After presenting **Un peu plus,** ask volunteers to provide additional examples of the adverb placement rules. Students should use words and expressions from **Vocabulaire 1.** Have them write the examples in their notebook to use as reference when they do this activity. 1.2

SPECIAL LEARNING NEEDS

Students with Learning Disabilities Students will need an opportunity to view actual airline reservation tables and flight information in French. This can be done by accessing Air France's Web site and choosing the French option to view all flight information in French. Students can select flights, view arrival and departure information, and scroll through vacation packages to gain an understanding of information presented in this format. 3.2

Assess

Assessment Program
Quiz: Application 1
Audio CD 10, Tr. 11
Alternative Assessment
Differentiated Practice and Assessment CD-ROM
Online Assessment
my.hrw.com
Test Generator

Resources

Planning:
Lesson Planner
One-Stop Planner

Practice:
Cahier d'activités

Prereading Questions

You might ask these questions before students read the selection.

1. **Est-ce que tu as déjà pris l'avion?**
2. **Est-ce que tu aimes prendre l'avion?**
3. **Est-ce que tu préfères monter dans un gros avion ou dans un plus petit avion?**
4. **Sais-tu où on construit les Boeing aux États-Unis?**

 1.2

Active Reading questions

1. **Quelle est la longueur de l'A380? (79,8 mètres)**
2. **Quelle est sa hauteur? (24,1 mètres)**
3. **Quel est son poids? (590 tonnes)**
4. **Combien de kilomètres peut-il faire sans escale? (14.400 km)** 1.2

Vocabulaire supplémentaire

You might use these terms to discuss the selection.

l'industrie (f.) *aircraft*
aéronautique *industry*
la ceinture *seatbelt*
de sécurité
l'équipage (m.) *aircrew*

Lecture culturelle

Boeing® et Airbus® sont les deux principaux constructeurs d'avions au monde et sont en constante compétition. Dès les années 80, Airbus a décidé de développer un nouvel avion pour répondre à la demande du traffic aérien qui augmentait de 5% par an environ. Le projet a été lancé officiellement le 23 juin 2000. L'A380 est aussi le résultat de la collaboration entre la France, l'Allemagne, l'Espagne et le Royaume-Uni. Chaque pays construit une partie de l'avion et chaque partie est ensuite assemblée à Toulouse (France) pour former l'avion. 2.2

L'Express

par Bruno D. Cot

A380
Naissance[1] d'un géant

Le monde aéronautique en rêvait, Airbus l'a fait. À la veille de l'assemblage[2] de son premier exemplaire, L'Express retrace[3] les épisodes d'un feuilleton industriel hors du commun[4]: la conception et la construction du plus gros avion civil de tous les temps.

C'est le pari[5] le plus fou de l'histoire aéronautique européenne depuis le Concorde[6]. Si une lettre et trois chiffres suffisent à l'identifier, l'A380 apparaît bien comme l'avion de tous les records. Presque aussi large qu'un terrain de football est long (79,8 mètres), plus haute que l'obélisque de Louksor (24,1 mètres), plus lourde que la Station spatiale internationale (590 tonnes), possédant un des plus grands rayons d'action recensés[7] (14.400 kilomètres) et grâce à une capacité de transport exceptionnelle (de 555 à 800 passagers), la dernière créature d'Airbus ouvre la voie à une nouvelle race ailée[8], celle des paquebots[9] des airs.

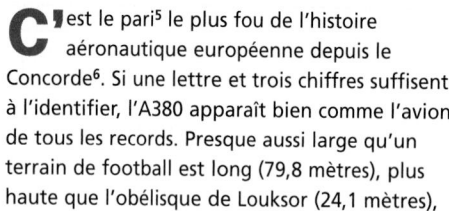

Compréhension 1.2

1. Quel est le nom du nouvel avion d'Airbus?
2. Qu'est-ce qui différencie ce nouvel avion des autres avions?
3. Combien de passagers peuvent embarquer sur l'Airbus A380?

1. L'A380
2. C'est le plus grand avion au monde.
3. L'Airbus A380 peut emmener entre 555 et 800 passagers.

1. le fait d'être né   2. *assembly*   3. raconte   4. le contraire d'ordinaire   5. *bet*   6. avion supersonique qui allait de Paris ou de Londres à New York en 3 heures   7. la plus grande distance   8. *winged*   9. *cruise ships*

Core Instruction

LECTURE CULTURELLE

1. Read the introductory paragraph and discuss it with the class. **(3 min.)**
2. Read *A380, Naissance d'un géant* as a class. **(5 min.)**
3. Ask for volunteers to answer the questions in **Compréhension. (5 min.)**

COMPARAISONS ET COMMUNAUTÉ

1. Have students read *Les autoroutes en France* and discuss it in small groups. Tell students that French toll fees are also based on the size of the vehicle's engine. **(8 min.)**
2. Have students complete the **Et toi?** questions with a partner. **(5 min.)**
3. Go over **Communauté et professions** with students. What are the requirements to become a French flight attendant? **(8 min.)**

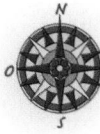

Comparaisons

Péage sur une autoroute en France

Les autoroutes en France 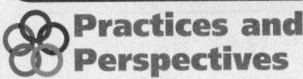 2.1

Tes amis et toi, vous êtes à Paris depuis une semaine. Il ne fait pas beau, alors vous décidez d'aller passer quelques jours en Provence. Vous louez une voiture et prenez l'autoroute. Les autoroutes en France sont...

   a. payantes.
   b. gratuites.
   c. fermées la nuit.

Le système autoroutier français est en grande partie à péage[1]. La construction et l'entretien[2] du réseau autoroutier sont assurés par l'État et par des sociétés privées[3]. Il y a en France environ 10.000 kilomètres d'autoroutes. Les péages sont basés sur un forfait[4] ou sur la distance parcourue. Cela permet aux entreprises privées de pouvoir entretenir les autoroutes existantes et d'en construire de nouvelles.

1.3, 4.2

ET TOI?

1. Est-ce qu'il y a des autoroutes à péage dans ta ville? Dans ta région?

2. Est-ce que tu penses que les autoroutes à péage sont une bonne idée? Pourquoi ou pourquoi pas?

Communauté et professions

Le français et les métiers du tourisme 4.2, 5.2

Être steward ou hôtesse de l'air dans une compagnie aérienne peut être un métier très passionnant[5]. Si tu veux travailler pour une compagnie aérienne internationale, il faut parler au moins une langue étrangère. Selon le ministère du Travail[6] des États-Unis, certaines des grandes compagnies aériennes préfèrent des employés qui parlent deux langues étrangères. Il faut être bien qualifié parce qu'il existe plus de candidats que de postes[7]. Fais des recherches pour savoir ce que les plus grandes compagnies aériennes américaines exigent[8]. Présente les résultats de tes recherches à la classe.

Hôtesse de l'air servant un repas

---

1. *toll*   2. *maintenance*   3. *private companies*   4. *set price*   5. intéressant
6. *Department of Labor*   7. positions   8. demandent

Culture

Bulletin Board Project

Have four groups research the French road system. One group should find a road map of France. Another group should research French traffic signs and create signs out of cardboard. The third group should research the toll road system and make up a fee chart for different cars and trucks. The last group should research how drivers are advised of traffic problems and detours and create a message for drivers. Ask students to collect all materials and display them on a classroom bulletin board. Discuss the French road system as a class.   3.2

Cultures

Practices and Perspectives

Every driver in France knows **Bison futé**, the government agency that gives advice to traveling motorists. **Bison futé** means *smart buffalo,* and the agency's little mascot looks like one! **Bison futé** provides all the information concerning road conditions, road construction, traffic, and the best detour available. You can see and hear **Bison futé** on TV, on the radio, and on the Internet. Ask your students if they have something equivalent in their state.

2.1

Communities

Career Path

Tourism is a major industry in many French-speaking countries. Have students suggest careers related to this industry. Have them select one or two places they would consider for a career in tourism and ask them how speaking French would benefit them. Ask for volunteers to share their thoughts with the class.   5.1

Differentiated Instruction

ADVANCED LEARNERS

Challenge Ask students to imagine that they work as flight attendants on an A380 and a French-speaking passenger wants to know everything about this type of plane. Partners create a conversation between the passenger and the flight attendant. They should use the information provided on p. 414 but might also exaggerate. Have them role-play their conversation for the class. Remind them to use appropriate facial expressions and gestures.   1.1

MULTIPLE INTELLIGENCES

Linguistic Ask students to imagine they are an American flight attendant serving French passengers. They should write a script to welcome the French passengers aboard the flight and give them safety instructions. Flight attendants should also be able to answer questions regarding the location of bathroom facilities, meal and beverage service, and in-flight entertainment. Students should role-play the scene with classmates.   1.3

Resources

Bell Work

Use Bell Work 10.5 in the *Teaching Transparencies* or write this activity on the board.

Récris les phrases en utilisant des adverbes.

1. Laura travaille à la bibliothèque. (habituel)
2. Elle lit son livre. (attentif)
3. Elle apprend ses leçons. (rapide)
4. Elle a envie d'aller à l'université. (vrai)
5. Elle ira à Boston. (sûr)

 1.2

Connections

 Language Note

The verb **klaxonner** is derived from Klaxon, the American trademark for an electromechanical horn. The klaxon has the characteristic "AH-OOOOH-GAH!" sound. The Lovell-McConnell Manufacturing Co. of Newark, New Jersey, bought the rights to the device in 1908. Its founder, F. W. Lovell, coined the name klaxon from the Greek verb **klaz**, *to shriek.* Ask students to brainstorm other verbs in English or French, that are derived from a trademark. (to google, **gougler**) 3.1, 4.1

Objectifs
• to ask for and give help
• to ask for directions

Vocabulaire à l'œuvre 2

Bonne route!

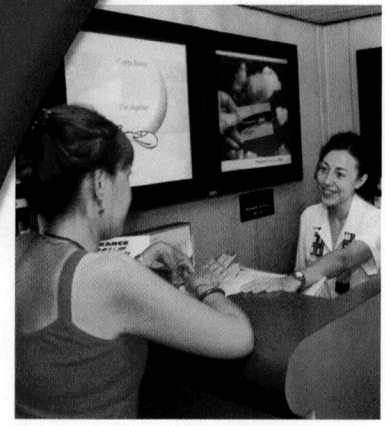

On a réservé une voiture dans **une agence de location** à l'aéroport.

le volant

le rétroviseur

le conducteur

le tableau de bord

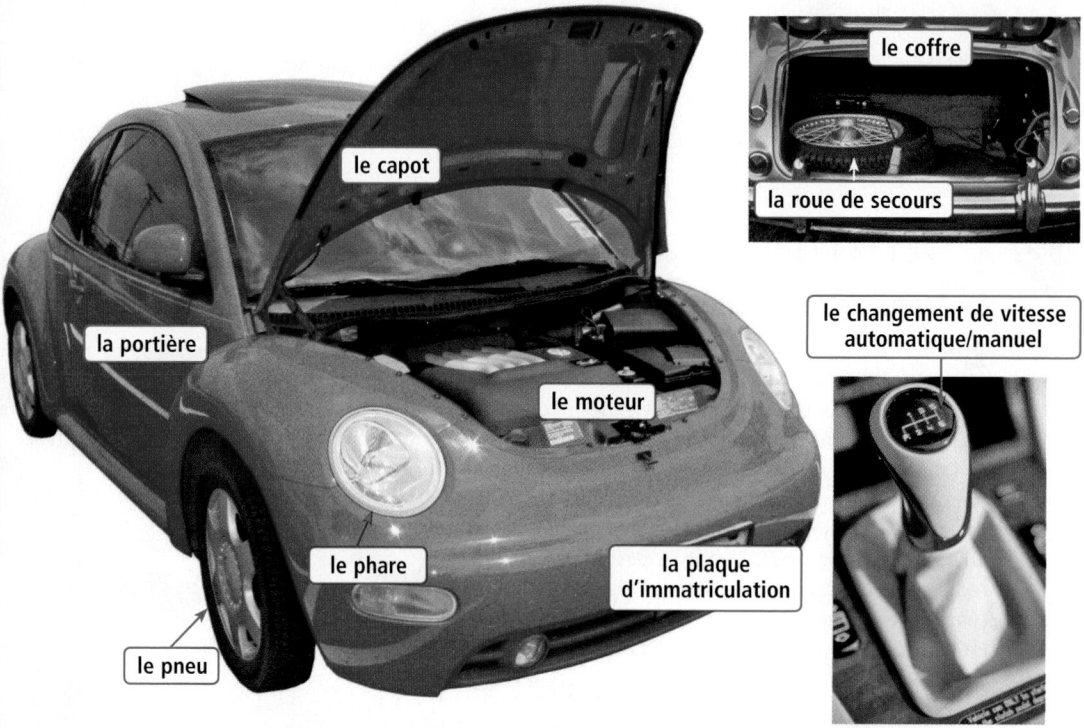

le coffre

la roue de secours

le capot

le changement de vitesse automatique/manuel

la portière

le moteur

le phare

la plaque d'immatriculation

le pneu

Core Instruction

TEACHING VOCABULAIRE

1. Introduce the vocabulary, using transparencies **Vocabulaire 10.3** and **10.4**. Model the pronunciation of each word or expression. **(3 min.)**

2. Have students point to specific items on the transparency as you name them. (**le capot, le volant,** ...) **(2 min.)**

3. Ask students questions about operating a vehicle. **Qu'est-ce qu'on allume la nuit? Où est la roue de secours? Qu'est-ce qu'il y a sous le capot? Qu'est-ce qu'on met dans le réservoir? (4 min.)**

4. Model the pronunciation of the expressions in **Exprimons-nous!** Have partners write similar sentences about different situations. **Je n'arrive pas à allumer la télé/changer de chaîne, tu peux m'aider? Bien sûr, passe-moi la télécommande. (4 min.)**

Pour bien entretenir sa voiture, il faut...

Online Practice
go.**hrw**.com
Vocabulaire 2 practice
KEYWORD: BD3 CH10

avoir une roue de secours

un pneu à plat

faire le plein

la pompe à essence

le réservoir

nettoyer le pare-brise

les essuie-glaces

régler la pression des pneus

D'autres mots utiles

l'essence (f.) sans plomb	unleaded gas	être/tomber en panne	to break down
le frein	brake	changer de vitesse	to shift gears
le gasoil	diesel	faire la révision	to have the car car serviced
le super	regular gas	klaxonner	to honk
accélérer/freiner	to accelerate/ to brake	ralentir	to slow down

Exprimons-nous!

To ask for help	To respond
Je ne sais pas comment changer de vitesse. *I don't know how to shift gears.*	**Appuyez sur la pédale d'embrayage.** *Press the clutch.*
Aide-moi! Je n'y vois rien. *Help me! I can't see anything.*	**Tu ferais mieux de** faire laver le pare-brise. *You'd better . . .*
Je n'arrive pas à me garer. Tu peux m'aider? *I can't manage to park. Can you help me?*	Bien sûr, **passe-moi** le volant. *. . . give me . . .*
Le moteur ne veut pas démarrer. *The engine doesn't want to start.*	**Ouvre le capot,** je vais regarder. *Open the hood, . . .*

Interactive TUTOR

Vocabulaire et grammaire, pp. 115–117

Online workbooks

▶ **Vocabulaire supplémentaire—Les voitures, p. R21**

Vocabulaire 2

T P R
TOTAL PHYSICAL RESPONSE

Have students respond to these commands.

Lève le doigt si tes parents font régulièrement la révision de leurs voitures.

Lève-toi si c'est toi qui nettoies le pare-brise.

Lève la main si tu sais où est la roue de secours.

Assieds-toi par terre si tu as déjà eu un pneu à plat.

Dessine un rétroviseur et des essuie-glaces.

Then have some students mime the following actions.

Ouvre le réservoir et fais le plein.

Règle la pression des pneus.

Klaxonne!

Appuie sur la pédale d'embrayage et change de vitesse.

Mets le frein à main. 🎔 1.2

Teacher to Teacher

Sue DiGiandomenico
Wellesley HS
Wellesley, MA

To practice the new vocabulary, I ask my students to work in pairs to recount an amusing yet troublesome weekend, using PowerPoint®. I have them imagine that they were on a car trip in Martinique for a weekend and I ask them to illustrate (using PowerPoint layout and graphics from the Internet) five to seven slides. They should include their activities, and how they had trouble with the rental car. Students present the project to the class. 🎔 1.3

Differentiated Instruction

ADVANCED LEARNERS

Extension Have partners create a conversation between two driving-school instructors. The instructors reminisce about the worst students they have ever had. For example, one instructor complains about a student who did not know how to shift gears. The instructors try to outdo each other with their stories and exaggerate more and more. Have some pairs present their conversations to the class. 🎔 1.1, 1.3

MULTIPLE INTELLIGENCES

Interpersonal Students can practice giving directions around their hometown in French by taking turns as tourist and tour guide. First, write on a piece of paper well known destinations around town. Next, fold the pieces of paper tightly and throw them into a bin. Partners take turns drawing a slip of paper and asking for and giving directions to the place. 🎔 1.1

21 Associations 🎬1.2

Lisons Indique les parties de la voiture associées à ces actions.

d   **1.** ralentir
a   **2.** mettre ses bagages
f   **3.** faire le plein
b   **4.** regarder derrière
g   **5.** voir la nuit
e   **6.** tourner

a. le coffre
b. le rétroviseur
c. la roue de secours
d. les freins
e. le volant
f. le réservoir
g. les phares

22 Écoutons CD 10, Tr. 4 🎬1.2 **1.** d **2.** a **3.** b **4.** c **5.** b **6.** a

🎧 Écoute chaque commentaire et dis de quoi ces personnes parlent.

a.

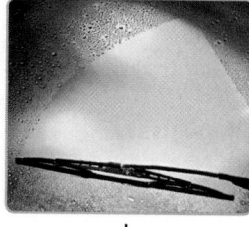
b.

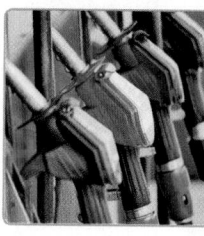
c.

d.

23 Une leçon de conduite 🎬1.2

Lisons/Écrivons Juliane apprend à conduire. Complète la conversation qu'elle a avec son père.

JULIANE   Qu'est-ce que je fais d'abord?

LE PÈRE   Eh bien, d'abord il faut ___1___, bien sûr.

JULIANE   Je n'y arrive pas. ___2___.

LE PÈRE   Attends, je vais aller voir. Ouvre ___3___, s'il te plaît... Bon voilà, ça marche. On peut y aller. Maintenant, regarde bien dans ___4___ avant de démarrer.

JULIANE   Euh... Je ne sais pas comment changer de vitesse.

LE PÈRE   C'est facile. Il faut ___5___.

JULIANE   Ah! D'accord!

LE PÈRE   Il commence à faire nuit. Allume ___6___, c'est plus prudent... Et voilà! Gare-toi ici.

JULIANE   Je n'arrive pas à ___7___, tu peux m'aider s'il te plaît, papa.

LE PÈRE   Bon, d'accord. Passe-moi ___8___!

Entre copains

une bagnole	car
une caisse	car
un chauffard	reckless driver

Core Instruction

TEACHING EXPRIMONS-NOUS!

1. Model the pronunciation of each expression. **(2 min.)**

2. Ask students for directions, using the expressions in **Exprimons-nous!** The answers can be short but should indicate comprehension.

3. To practice, have students ask for directions to places in your town. **Quel est le chemin le plus rapide pour aller au centre commercial? (3 min.)**

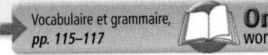
Exprimons-nous!

To ask for directions

Savez-vous où est l'entrée de l'autoroute pour Caen?
Do you know where we can get on the expressway to . . . ?

Quelle sortie faut-il prendre pour visiter le château?
Which exit should I take to . . . ?

Quelle est la route la plus rapide pour Dijon?
What is the quickest way to . . . ?

Comment peut-on rejoindre l'autoroute, s'il vous plaît?
How can we get back on/to . . . ?

Est-ce qu'il existe un chemin qui évite la circulation?
Is there a way that . . . ?

Interactive TUTOR

Vocabulaire et grammaire, pp. 115–117

Online workbooks

24 Demande de renseignements ✿1.2

✎ **Lisons/Écrivons** Ces gens demandent des renseignements. Lis les réponses qu'on leur donne et imagine les questions qu'ils ont posées. Utilise les expressions d'**Exprimons-nous!**

1. L'autoroute pour Marseille? Continuez tout droit et au feu rouge, tournez à droite.

2. Vous voulez reprendre l'autoroute? C'est simple, suivez le panneau A3.

3. Alors, pour éviter la circulation, je vous conseille de prendre les petites routes de campagne.

4. C'est la prochaine sortie. Vous y êtes presque!

5. Ce n'est peut-être pas le chemin le plus court mais c'est le plus rapide!

6. Prenez la première route à droite en sortant du village. Vous verrez l'entrée de l'autoroute pour Dijon.

Flash culture

L'examen du permis de conduire en France est difficile et coûte cher (en moyenne, les candidats paient 1.200 euros). Il y a deux façons d'obtenir son permis: soit on prend des cours de conduite (au moins 20 heures) et on passe le code et l'examen de conduite à 18 ans. Soit, dès 16 ans on peut faire la conduite accompagnée, mais il faut tout de même passer le code et l'épreuve pratique de conduite à 18 ans. Au bout de cinq échecs à l'épreuve pratique, il faut repasser le code.

Comment obtient-on son permis de conduire dans ton état? ✿4.2

AUTO-ECOLE PERMIS

 **Communication**

25 Scénario ✿1.1

HOLT **SoundBooth** ONLINE RECORDING

Parlons Tu voyages en voiture dans le sud de la France avec ta famille. Vous êtes perdus! Quelles questions est-ce que tu poserais à l'employé(e) de l'Office du tourisme pour arriver à destination? Joue cette scène avec un(e) camarade de classe.

MODÈLE —Quel est le chemin le plus rapide pour aller à Arles?
—Alors, pour aller à Arles, vous feriez mieux de prendre l'autoroute A7 et de...

24 Possible Answers

1. Savez-vous où est l'entrée de l'autoroute pour Marseille?
2. Comment peut-on rejoindre l'autoroute, s'il vous plaît?
3. Est-ce qu'il existe un chemin qui évite la circulation?
4. Quelle est la route plus rapide pour Lille?
5. Quelle sortie faut il prendre pour arriver aux grottes?
6. Savez-vous où est l'entrée de l'autoroute pour Dijon?

Communication

25 Group Activity: Interpersonal

In groups of three, have students imagine a car accident. One group member plays the role of a police officer who asks questions and takes the report. The other members play witnesses who detail what happened, using the **passé composé** and the **imparfait**. Encourage students to include vocabulary from **D'autres mots utiles** on p. 417. The police officer should write the report, including the witnesses' comments.
✿1.1

Differentiated Instruction

SLOWER PACE LEARNERS

22 Additional Practice Before playing the recording for this activity, ask for volunteers to describe each photo. If students use expressions from **Vocabulaire 2**, have them write these on the board next to the letter of the photo. Then play the recording and tell students to listen for the expressions that are listed on the board.
✿1.2

SPECIAL LEARNING NEEDS

Students with Learning Disabilities A student with a learning disability will often need to practice language for uncommon or difficult situations prior to their actual occurrence. Have students write a short dialog to practice explaining simple car problems in French. Have partners write a script together and then practice explaining their car trouble to each other.
✿1.1

Bell Work

Use Bell Work 10.6 in the *Teaching Transparencies* or write this activity on the board.

Complète les phrases logiquement avec le vocabulaire de la leçon.

1. Mme Martin a fait des courses et elle met ses achats dans le ____.
2. Jean-Louis a un pneu à plat. Heureusement qu'il a une ____.
3. Mon ____ est vide. Je vais faire ____ à la ____.
4. Quand tu conduis, n'oublie pas de regarder dans ton ____.
5. Zut! Il pleut et mes ____ ne marchent pas. ❁1.2

㉗ Answers

1. appellerai
2. essaieras
3. achèterai
4. devrai
5. verras
6. seras
7. seront
8. deviendra

Objectifs
- review of the future
- review of the past perfect

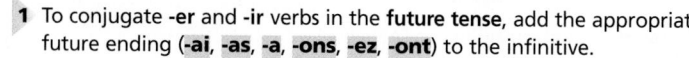 Grammaire à l'œuvre 2

Révisions The future

Interactive TUTOR

1 To conjugate **-er** and **-ir** verbs in the **future tense**, add the appropriate future ending (**-ai, -as, -a, -ons, -ez, -ont**) to the infinitive.

To conjugate **-re** verbs in the **future tense**, drop the **-e** from the infinitive and add the future endings. Notice that all the future stems end in **-r**.

> Nous loue**rons** une voiture à Fort-de-France.
> Cet été, Jacques apprend**r**a à conduire.

2 Many verbs that have a spelling change in the present tense, like **acheter, appeler,** and **essayer,** have the same spelling change in their future stems.

> Nous **achèter**ons un plan de la ville.

3 Some verbs have irregular future tense stems to which you add the future endings. Here are some of these verbs.

aller	→	**ir-**	faire	→	**fer-**
avoir	→	**aur-**	pouvoir	→	**pourr-**
devenir	→	**deviendr-**	savoir	→	**saur-**
devoir	→	**devr-**	venir	→	**viendr-**
envoyer	→	**enverr-**	voir	→	**verr-**
être	→	**ser-**	vouloir	→	**voudr-**

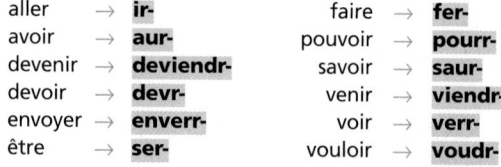 Vocabulaire et grammaire, pp. 118–119
Cahier d'activités, pp. 95–97   Online workbooks

㉖ Un mauvais automobiliste ❁1.2

Lisons/Parlons Thierry n'entretient pas bien sa voiture. Complète ses phrases de manière logique.

1. Je changerai de voiture quand j'(<u>aurai</u> / ai) plus d'argent.
2. Je change de vitesse quand le moteur (<u>fait</u> / fera) beaucoup de bruit.
3. Je nettoierai mon pare-brise quand je ne (vois / <u>verrai</u>) plus rien.
4. Je règle la pression des pneus quand ils (seront / <u>sont</u>) à plat.
5. J'irai à la pompe quand le réservoir (est / <u>sera</u>) vide.
6. Je fais faire l'entretien quand j'y (penserai / <u>pense</u>).
7. Je ferai laver ma voiture quand elle (est / <u>sera</u>) tellement sale qu'on ne (peut / <u>pourra</u>) plus voir de quelle couleur elle est.

Online Practice
go.hrw.com
Grammaire 2 practice
KEYWORD: BD3 CH10

Chapitre 10

Grammaire 2

㉗ Véhicules hybrides ✿1.2

Lisons/Écrivons Elsa parle avec son frère Marc, qui oublie toujours de faire le plein. Complète leur conversation avec **le futur** des verbes entre parenthèses.

MARC   Ma voiture est en panne, j'___1___ (appeler) maman cet après-midi.

ELSA   La prochaine fois, tu ___2___ (essayer) de faire le plein avant de tomber en panne...

MARC   Non, j'___3___ (acheter) une voiture électrique, comme ça je ne ___4___ (devoir) faire le plein.

ELSA   Tu ___5___ (voir), elles sont chères ces voitures, et puis elles sont hybrides, alors tu ___6___ (être) quand même obligé de prendre de l'essence.

MARC   Non, elles ___7___ (être) bientôt moins chères, parce que c'est le soleil qui ___8___ (devenir) la principale source d'énergie.

À la sénégalaise

In Senegal, people refer to **une station-service** as **une essencerie.**

Il a fait le plein dans l'essencerie du coin de la rue.

㉘ Quel travail! ✿1.2

Parlons Ces gens parlent de tout ce qu'ils feront quand ils auront une voiture. Imagine ce qu'ils disent.

MODÈLE   Vous ferez la révision de votre voiture.

vous / faire la révision

1. Albin / nettoyer le pare-brise

2. je / changer de vitesse

3. nous / faire le plein

4. Ludovic et Fanny / prendre la pression des pneus

㉘ Answers
1. Albin nettoiera le pare-brise.
2. J'aurai un changement de vitesse manuel.
3. Nous ferons le plein.
4. Ludovic et Fanny prendront la pression des pneus.

Communication

Pair Activity: Interpersonal
Have students choose a city they would like to visit and imagine what they might want do there. Then have partners ask each other **Où iras-tu?** The answer should be in the future tense. Then they should ask each other about the trip. The answer should be in a compound sentence with the **futur antérieur.**

MODÈLE:
— **Où iras-tu?**
— **J'irai à Nice en France.**
— **Quand est-ce que tu auras assez d'argent pour aller en France?**
— **J'aurai assez d'argent quand j'aurai gagné à la loterie.** ✿1.1

Communication

HOLT **SoundBooth** ONLINE RECORDING

㉙ Scénario ✿1.1

Parlons Ton/Ta camarade va aller à Québec ce week-end et tu lui demandes ce qu'il/elle va faire là-bas. Ton/Ta camarade va mentionner cinq choses qu'il/elle fera.

MODÈLE — **Que feras-tu à Québec?**
— **Je louerai une voiture et j'irai voir les animaux dans les parcs nationaux.**

Connections

Language Note
In English, Quebec refers to the province and Quebec City to its capital. In French, **Québec** refers to the province and **Ville de Québec** or simply **Québec** refers to its capital. The use of gender and prepositions allows French speakers to distinguish between **Québec,** the province, and **Québec,** the city. **Québec,** the province, is one of the seven of Canada's thirteen provinces and territories that are masculine. **Québec,** the city, like most cities and towns, does not bear a gender. Ask students what prepositions they would use with **Québec** the province and what prepositions they would use with **Québec** the city. ✿3.1

Differentiated Instruction

SLOWER PACE LEARNERS

Additional Practice On a sheet of paper write several main clauses (**Gabrielle achètera une voiture. Elle sera heureuse.**) and several subordinate clauses that complement each main clause (**dès qu'elle aura un permis de conduire; quand elle aura un bon travail**). Make one copy for every two students, cut the main and subordinate clauses apart, and distribute the pieces to partners. Have them assemble logical sentences. ✿1.2

MULTIPLE INTELLIGENCES

㉗ Linguistic Assign students the task of continuing the conversation. They may continue it in its current form, or they may change the format to an essay, news report, or magazine article. Conversations or articles can be shared with the class upon completion. ✿1.1, 1.3

Resources

Planning:

Lesson Planner

 One-Stop Planner

Practice:

Grammar Tutor for Students of French, Chapter 10

Cahier de vocabulaire et grammaire

Differentiated Practice and Assessment CD-ROM

Cahier d'activités

Media Guide

 Teaching Transparencies Bell Work 10.7

 Audio CD 10, Tr. 5

 Interactive Tutor, Disc 2

Bell Work

Use Bell Work 10.7 in the *Teaching Transparencies* or write this activity on the board.

Complète les phrases avec la forme correcte des verbes entre parenthèses.

1. Mes amis achèteront une voiture quand ils _____ (aller) en vacances.
2. Quand mon réservoir _____ (être) vide, je ferai le plein.
3. Ralentis quand il _____ (pleuvoir).
4. J'allumerai mes phares quand il _____ (faire) nuit.
5. Vous pourrez venir quand vous _____ (vouloir). 1.2

French for Spanish Speakers

Ask Spanish speakers if they can recall what tense the **plus-que-parfait** corresponds to in Spanish. (**el pluscuamperfecto**) Ask them how they are different. (The **plus-que-parfait** is formed with one of two auxiliary verbs, **avoir** or **être**, whereas the **pluscuamperfecto** has only one auxiliary verb, **haber**.) 4.1

Interactive TUTOR

Révisions The past perfect

1. To say that one event happened further in the past than another event, use the **past perfect** (**plus-que-parfait**).

2. To conjugate verbs in the past perfect, use the **imparfait** of **avoir** or **être** and the past participle of the main verb. Remember, the rules for agreement are the same as for verbs in **passé composé**.

voir	
j'	avais vu
tu	avais vu
il/elle/on	avait vu
nous	avions vu
vous	aviez vu
ils/elles	avaient vu

aller	
j'	étais allé(e)
tu	étais allé(e)
il/elle/on	était allé(e)s
nous	étions allé(e)s
vous	étiez allé(e)(s)
ils/elles	étaient allé(e)s

Papa a dit qu'il avait réservé une voiture.

Maman était partie quand nous sommes arrivés.

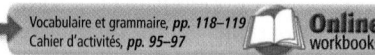  Vocabulaire et grammaire, *pp. 118–119* Cahier d'activités, *pp. 95–97* **Online** workbooks

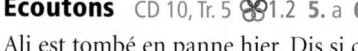 **1.** a **2.** b **3.** a **4.** b

30 Écoutons CD 10, Tr. 5 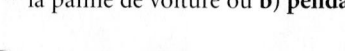1.2 **5.** a **6.** b **7.** a

Ali est tombé en panne hier. Dis si ce qu'il dit s'est passé **a)** **avant** la panne de voiture ou **b)** **pendant et après** la panne.

31 Appel longue distance 1.2

Lisons/Parlons Le frère de Nathalie est à l'étranger et il a eu des nouvelles de la famille grâce à sa tante. Il téléphone chez lui et parle avec sa sœur. Complète ses phrases avec le plus-que-parfait des verbes entre parenthèses.

Tante Alice m'a dit que/qu'…

1. Papa _____ (acheter) une nouvelle voiture.
2. Vous _____ (aller) la choisir avec lui.
3. Maman _____ (se fâcher) parce qu'il voulait une petite voiture de sport.
4. Elle _____ (choisir) une grosse voiture avec l'intérieur en cuir.
5. Ils _____ (discuter) pendant des heures.
6. Papa _____ (accepter) pour faire plaisir à maman.
7. Alors, maman _____ (dire) que papa pourrait choisir la couleur de la voiture.

Flash culture

Le permis de conduire français est un permis à points. Si un conducteur a des contraventions, il perd des points. Le permis n'est plus valable si on perd tous ses points. On obtient d'abord un permis probatoire avec seulement 6 points. Après trois ans de conduite, on obtient son permis à vie avec 12 points. On peut perdre beaucoup de points, par exemple, pour un excès de vitesse *(speeding)*.

Dans ton état, est-ce que tu peux perdre ton permis de conduire pour mauvaise conduite? Comment? 4.2

Core Instruction

TEACHING GRAMMAIRE

Go over this review of the **plus-que-parfait** with students. Remind them that the past perfect is the **passé composé** with the auxiliary in the **imparfait** instead of the present.

Tell students the past perfect is very commonly used in French, even in informal conversation. **(2 min.)**

---

32 Rumeurs 1.2

Écrivons/Parlons Hervé et ses parents viennent de rentrer de vacances, mais Élisabeth sait déjà tout ce qui s'est passé. Récris les phrases suivantes en les commençant par **J'ai entendu dire que...** Mets ses phrases au **plus-que-parfait**.

MODÈLE Tu as passé de bonnes vacances.
   J'ai entendu dire que tu avais passé de bonnes vacances.

1. Tu es parti en vacances avec tes parents.
2. Tes parents ont réservé une voiture dans une agence de l'aéroport.
3. Vous avez eu un pneu à plat.
4. La compagnie de location n'a pas mis de roue de secours dans cette voiture.
5. Vous êtes rentrés à l'hôtel en taxi.

33 Je me rappelle, ce jour-là, ... 1.3

Parlons/Écrivons Tu te souviens du dernier jour de tes vacances et de ce que tes parents et toi aviez encore eu le temps de faire, ce jour-là.

MODÈLE **Ils avaient visité un musée.**

ils

 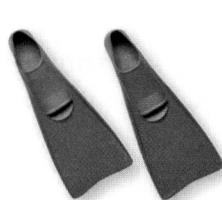  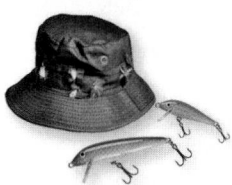

1. ma sœur   2. nous   3. mes parents   4. je

Communication

HOLT **SoundBooth** ONLINE RECORDING

 **34 Interview** 1.1

Parlons Demande à un(e) camarade ce qu'il/elle a fait pendant ses dernières vacances, puis demande-lui cinq choses qu'il/elle avait faites pendant les vacances précédentes. Ensuite, échangez les rôles.

MODÈLE — Qu'est-ce que tu as fait pendant les vacances?
   — Oh... pas grand-chose, je suis resté(e) à la maison.
   — Et pendant les vacances précédentes, qu'est-ce que tu avais fait?

30 Script
See script on p. 401F.

31 Answers
1. avait acheté
2. étiez allés
3. s'était fâchée
4. avait choisi
5. avaient discuté
6. avait accepté
7. avait dit

32 Answers
J'ai entendu dire que...
1. tu étais parti en vacances avec tes parents.
2. tes parents avaient réservé une voiture dans une agence de l'aéroport.
3. vous aviez eu un pneu à plat.
4. la compagnie de location n'avait pas mis de roue de secours dans cette voiture.
5. vous étiez rentrés à l'hôtel en taxi.

Communication

Class Activity: Interpersonal
Have one student start a class chain by making a statement in the **passé composé.** The next student uses the same verb in a **si** clause with the **plus-que-parfait** and a main clause with the **conditionnel passé.** Have the chain continue.

MODÈLE
— **Ma mère a fait un beau gâteau hier.**
— **Si ma mère avait fait un gâteau, il aurait été meilleur que celui de ta mère.** 1.2

Assess

Assessment Program
Quiz: Grammaire 2
Alternative Assessment
Differentiated Practice and Assessment CD-ROM

Online Assessment
my.hrw.com

Test Generator

Differentiated Instruction

ADVANCED LEARNERS

Challenge Call for volunteers to explain the past perfect. They should write on the board the conjugation of verbs in the **plus-que-parfait,** address the rules for agreement of past participles, and discuss the context in which this tense is used. Is it used in the same way in French as it is in English? Students should provide examples. 4.1

MULTIPLE INTELLIGENCE

Interpersonal To practice communicating needs in French, have partners create a conversation between a clerk in a French hotel and a guest whose luggage was lost. The guest will need to request in French all necessary toiletry and comfort items he or she is missing. The hotel clerk will ask questions and expect responses. Ask partners to practice both roles. 1.1

Resources

Planning:

Lesson Planner

 One-Stop Planner

Practice:

Grammar Tutor for Students of French, Chapter 10

Cahier de vocabulaire et grammaire

Differentiated Practice and Assessment CD-ROM

Cahier d'activités

Media Guide

 Teaching Transparencies
Bell Work 10.8

 Audio CD 10, Tr. 6

 Interactive Tutor, Disc 2

Bell Work

Use Bell Work 10.8 in the *Teaching Transparencies* or write this activity on the board.

Complète la phrase avec le plus-que-parfait.

J'ai entendu dire que...

1. ... tes parents t'_____ (offrir) une nouvelle voiture.
2. ... tu _____ (choisir) une petite Peugeot.
3. ... ta mère _____ (vouloir) qu'elle soit rouge.
4. ... ton frère et toi l'_____ (essayer) le soir même.
5. ... la voiture _____ (tomber) en panne.
6. ... vous _____ (devoir) rentrer à pied. ❀1.2

㉟ Script

See script on p. 401F.

㊲ Answers

1. Tu feras faire la révision des 25.000 km.
2. Mireille fera changer une roue.
3. Nous ferons régler nos phares.
4. Vous ferez remplacer vos essuie-glaces.
5. Les parents de Jacques feront vérifier la pression des pneus.
6. Moi, je ferai nettoyer le pare-brise de ma voiture.

Synthèse
• Vocabulaire 2
• Grammaire 2

Application 2

㉟ Écoutons CD 10, Tr. 6 ❀1.2 **1.** b **2.** a **3.** a **4.** b **5.** b **6.** a

Alexandre et ses amis se sont arrêtés au bord de la route pour étudier la carte. Pour chaque phrase, décide si Alexandre a parlé de quelque chose **a) qui s'était passé la dernière fois** qu'ils avaient pris cette route ou **b) qui allait se passer.**

㊱ Une nouvelle voiture ❀1.3

Parlons Réponds aux questions suivantes.

1. Est-ce que tu préfères une voiture à changement de vitesse automatique ou manuel? Pourquoi ou pourquoi pas?
2. Quel genre de voiture tu achèteras plus tard?
3. Est-ce que tu connais quelqu'un qui a une voiture hybride?
4. Est-ce que tes parents louent une voiture quand ils voyagent?
5. Est-ce qu'ils avaient appris à conduire à seize ans?
6. Est-ce que tu sais déjà conduire? Qui t'a appris à conduire?

Un peu plus

The causative **faire**

1. To say that you are *having something done*, use a form of the verb **faire** with the **infinitive** of the main verb.

   Je **fais** **changer** le pneu.

   Il a **fait** **régler** la pression des pneus.

2. If the main verb is **reflexive**, place the **reflexive pronoun** before the conjugated form of **faire**, and use the helping verb **être** in the **passé composé**.

   Je **me** suis **fait** **réveiller** tôt le jour du départ.

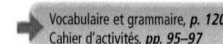 Vocabulaire et grammaire, *p. 120*
Cahier d'activités, *pp. 95–97*  **Online** workbooks

㊲ À la station-service ❀1.2

Lisons/Écrivons Quand on n'est pas bon en mécanique, il faut faire faire le travail par un professionnel. Dis ce que ces gens-là feront faire demain.

MODÈLE Mon frère / faire la vidange *(oil change).*
Mon frère fera faire la vidange.

1. Tu / faire la révision des 25.000 km
2. Mireille / changer une roue
3. Nous / régler nos phares
4. Vous / remplacer vos essuie-glaces
5. Les parents de Jacques / vérifier la pression des pneus
6. Moi, je / nettoyer le pare-brise de ma voiture

Core Instruction

INTEGRATED PRACTICE

1. Have students do Activities 35 and 36 to practice previously taught expressions. **(4 min.)**
2. Introduce **Un peu plus.** (See presentation suggestions at right.) **(4 min.)**
3. Continue with integrated practice Activities 37–40. **(20 min.)**

TEACHING UN PEU PLUS

1. Go over Point 1. Tell students that **faire** can be put into any appropriate tense: **Je/J' fais/faisais/ferai/ferais/ai fait/avait fait/aurais fait laver ma voiture,** even in the subjunctive: **Il faut que je fasse laver ma voiture. (2 min.)**
2. Go over Point 2. Remind students that in a compound tense, the past participle of the causative **faire** never agrees. **Mes sœurs se sont fait couper les cheveux. Le coiffeur les a fait payer. (2 min.)**

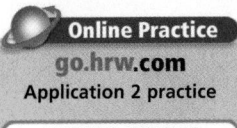

Online Practice
go.hrw.com
Application 2 practice

KEYWORD: BD3 CH10

Chapitre 10
Application 2

38 **Des choses à faire faire** 1.2

 **Parlons/Écrivons** Dis ce que ces personnes font pour préparer leur voyage.

> **MODÈLE** Mes vêtements sont sales.
> **Je dois faire nettoyer mes vêtements.**

1. J'ai besoin d'un vaccin contre la fièvre jaune.
2. Notre caméra ne marche pas.
3. Tes cheveux sont trop longs.
4. Vos passeports ne sont pas en ordre.
5. La voiture de ma mère est en panne.
6. Tu as perdu ta carte d'identité.

Communication

HOLT SoundBooth
ONLINE RECORDING

39 **Travaux récents** 1.1

Parlons Demande à un(e) camarade ce qu'il/elle ou ses parents ont fait faire récemment. Il/Elle te répondra et te posera la même question.

♻ *Souviens-toi,* The disjunctifs pronouns, p. 154

> **MODÈLE** — Qu'est-ce que toi ou tes parents avez fait faire, récemment?
> — Oh... nous avons fait repeindre la maison. Et vous?
> — Moi, j'ai fait...

40 **Histoire à raconter** 1.3

Parlons Sylvie et sa copine Jade partent en vacances. Avec un(e) camarade, parle de ce qui se passe.

---

38 Answers
1. Je dois me faire vacciner...
2. Nous devons faire réparer...
3. Tu dois te faire couper les...
4. Vous devez faire refaire vos...
5. Elle doit faire réparer sa...
6. Tu doit faire faire ta...

PRÉPARATOIRE **AP** **Language Examination**

💻 To display the drawings to the class, use the Picture Sequences Transparency for Chapter 10.

40 Sample answer

a. Sylvie et Jade partent en vacances en voiture.

b. Elles ont un pneu à plat et la voiture tombe en panne. La roue de secours est à plat aussi. Sylvie appelle un mécanicien.

c. Sylvie et Jade font réparer leur voiture à la station-service.

Communication

Pair Activity: Interpersonal
Have partners ask one another which chores they do themselves and which they have done for them. Responses should be in the present tense or should use the causative **faire**. 1.2

Differentiated Instruction

ADVANCED LEARNERS

38 Variation After completing this activity, ask partners to tell each other what kind of travel preparations they usually have to do. Ask them to concentrate specifically on things that they have to have done before a trip. Partners take turns telling each other about their preparations. 1.1

SPECIAL LEARNING NEEDS

Linguistic Ask students to write, in French, a short description of an imaginary road trip they took. They should give details on cities they visit, places of interest and reasons why they've chosen their route. Have volunteers share their road trip with the class. 1.3

Assess

Assessment Program
Quiz: Application 2
Audio CD 10, Tr. 12 🎧
Alternative Assessment
Differentiated Practice and Assessment CD-ROM

Online Assessment
my.hrw.com

Test Generator

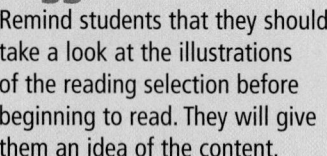

Resources

Planning:

Lesson Planner

 One-Stop Planner

Presentation:

🎧 Audio CD 10, Tr. 7

Practice:

Cahier d'activités

Reading Strategies and Skills
Handbook, Chapter 10

Advanced Reader

AP Reading Suggestion

Remind students that they should take a look at the illustrations of the reading selection before beginning to read. They will give them an idea of the content.

Applying the Strategies

For practice with combining strategies, have students use the "Save the Last Word for Me" strategy from the *Reading Strategies and Skills Handbook.*

READING PRACTICE

Strategy: Save the Last Word for Me

Reading Skill	When can I use this strategy?		
	Prereading	During Reading	Postreading
Comparing and Contrasting			✓
Determining the Main Idea			✓

Strategy at a Glance: Save the Last Word for Me

- After reading a text, students prepare a **Last Word** card: they write their favorite passage from the text on the front of the card; on the back of the card, they write why they like that passage.
- In small groups, students take turns reading their selected passages. The others in the group give their response to the passage.
- After everyone has finished making comments, each student reads his or her comments about the passage, thus having the "last word" about the passage.

Some readers struggle through texts, and when they have finished, they have nothing to say about what they have read. Maybe it's because they never seem to get it right. No one wants to be told continually that their answers are wrong, so rather than speak up in class about what they have read, they just proclaim that they have nothing to say. They either can't answer the question ("What do you want to say about the story?") or they risk an answer, only to discover that their answer is wrong. Eventually, they learn to distrust their own responses, and finally, they don't even bother to form them. When that happens, these readers must be convinced to trust their ability to form responses and to recognize that all readers—including good readers—constantly refine their responses based on what they already know, what they learn from the text, and from others. A strategy that helps readers learn to trust their own responses while learning from others' responses is called **Save the Last Word for Me.** This strategy requires students to choose a portion of a text that they particularly like and to copy that text onto the front of a note card. On the back of the card, they explain what that sentence or passage means to them. Next, students get into small groups and share their passages. The listeners respond to the passage by saying what it means to them. After everyone has finished making comments, the student who wrote the comment turns the card over and shares what he or she has written. At that point, no one can refute, add to, change, or argue with what is said. The last word belongs to that student. Students are willing to participate in **Save the Last Word for Me** because it allows each voice to be heard and, at the same time, gives each participant the opportunity to be the authority.

Philippe Delerm est né en 1950 près de Paris. Il devient enseignant après avoir fait des études de lettres à Nanterre. Il publie son premier roman en 1983 mais ne connaît le succès qu'en 1997. Dans ces livres, Delerm décrit les scènes de la vie de tous les jours. Il parle des petits bonheurs, des malheurs et des choses sans beaucoup d'importance.

Il a écrit entre autres, *La cinquième saison* (1983), *Un été pour mémoire* (1985) et *Enregistrements pirates* (2004)

> **STRATÉGIE pour lire**
>
> **Combining strategies** When you read in your native language, you usually use a combination of strategies to help you understand a text. You can also combine strategies when you read in French. Some helpful prereading strategies you can combine are *activating background knowledge, skimming,* and *making predictions.*

A **Avant la lecture** 🎦1.3

Est-ce que tu as déjà fait un long voyage en voiture la nuit? Quelles sont les images et les impressions qui te viennent à l'esprit?

CD 10, Tr. 7
UN ÉTÉ POUR MÉMOIRE

*Dans cet extrait d'**Un été pour mémoire,** le narrateur voyage en voiture sur l'autoroute. Il raconte son expérience, ses pensées et ses réflexions sur sa vie au cours du voyage.*

J e voyage aujourd'hui par des nuits d'autoroute aux grands soleils phosphorescents. J'aime les tons lunaires des stations-relais, le café du percolateur automatique, et la fraîcheur soudaine de la nuit contre le bruit, cette magie de traverser sans voir, de voyager sur une absence.

En passant à Orléans – mais on ne passe plus, on invente des villes en forme de panneau « Orléans nord, six kilomètres » – j'ai coupé la radio ; j'avais besoin de large, et de vide, et de nuit, de retrouver cette musique un peu

---

Core Instruction

LECTURE

1. Read **Stratégie pour lire** aloud for students and ask students for examples of strategies they have successfully used. **(1 min.)**

2. Do **Avant la lecture** as a class. Ask for volunteers to write students' images and impressions on the board as they recall them. **(10 min.)**

3. Have volunteers take turns reading aloud the first part of *Un été pour mémoire,* to … **que l'aube ne dessine pas encore,** at the top of page 428. Pause regularly to monitor students' comprehension. **(15 min.)**

légère des chagrins[1] d'enfance, et des images au bord de mon chagrin. Tout haut j'ai dit : « Grand-mère est morte à Labastide. » J'aurais voulu que ces mots-là réveillent un peu de terre blonde, l'odeur des prunes écrasées[2] sous le passage des charrettes, tout le coteau de Labastide, et dans le frais d'un chemin creux[3], une silhouette légère. Mais tout de suite j'ai pensé : « Le dernier maillon[4] qui se défait », et le coteau s'est évanoui[5].

On se ménage quelquefois, dans le désert abstrait d'une nuit d'autoroute, une de ces grandiloquentes[6] mises au point, regard de haut sur le destin... Près de cent kilomètres encore avant le péage de Tours, et le regard d'en haut donne un peu le vertige. Morts mes parents sur une route des Ardennes, il y a dix ans. Et morts bien avant eux mes grands-parents de Gandalou – le côté de mon père – et puis grand-père Labastide l'an dernier. La litanie se moque bien des kilomètres, elle chante bien trop vrai ; grand-mère Labastide était comme un dernier regard du temps de mon enfance, et je descends vers elle au fond de la nuit chaude de juillet.

Cafétéria dix kilomètres. Je vais m'arrêter. Dix kilomètres, six minutes... Pourquoi cette vitesse-là ? Le rythme de la nuit, je ne l'invente pas, ces pôles de lumière sur le tableau de bord – bleu vif, orange pâle – le ciel de nuit apprivoisé[7], ce silence capitonné de solitude. Si tout se passe bien, je serai à Bordeaux à trois heures du matin. Si tout se passe... J'aime ce temps-là qui ne fait que passer, que je peux faire semblant de maîtriser, quand tant de choses me dépassent, me ramènent malgré moi sur des chemins d'hier que j'avais refermés.

Je me suis arrêté sur le parking de la station-relais, entre deux caravanes. L'autoroute, la nuit. Ces cathédrales de lumière et de peu de paroles où l'on vous donne de l'essence et du café. Il y a le bruit tout près, mais des cavaliers noirs dorment couchés sur leur moto. Des étrangers, blafards[8] sous le néon, cherchent de la monnaie, fiévreux, devant les appareils automatiques. J'appuie sur les touches glacées : expresso-supplément sucre. Le café n'est pas si mauvais ; j'aime tous les cafés, c'est l'idée – temps arrêté, chaleur – qui compte, et pas le goût. Je me sens presque

1. *tristesse* 2. *squashed* 3. *hollow* 4. *link* 5. *the hill vanished* 6. *pompous* 7. *tamed* 8. *pale*

Active Reading Questions

1. Où est-ce que le narrateur ira le jour suivant? (chez sa grand-mère)

2. Comment était la grand-mère du narrateur? (Elle avait une voix chantante et les yeux bleus. Elle mettait des tabliers pastels.)

3. Pourquoi est-ce que le narrateur veut "encore un peu de nuit, un peu d'autoroute glacée"? (Il ne veut pas éprouver de douleur.)

4. Où se trouve Bordeaux par rapport à Labastide? (loin)

5. Quel temps a-t-il fait près de Châtellerault? (Il a plu.)

6. À quoi est-ce que le narrateur pense? (au passé)

7. Qu'est-ce que le narrateur buvait quand il arrivait chez sa grand-mère? (un verre d'eau parfumé à la fleur d'oranger)

8. Qu'est-ce qui se passe quand le soleil se lève? (Le narrateur n'est plus protégé de son passé.)

1.2

Postreading Activity

Ask students to think of other stories or novels that they have read, or movies that they have seen, about a trip or journey. What did that trip or journey symbolize? What happened to the character(s) on the trip or journey? Then, ask students how *Un été pour mémoire* is similar to or different from those stories. What happens to the narrator in this story? How does he evolve?

bien, dans cette nuit abstraite qui va vers le Midi, qui me conduit du présent vague de Paris à ce passé mal étouffé que l'aube[1] ne dessine pas encore.

[...]

Demain, j'arriverai dans la maison de brique rose et de silence. Dehors, il y aura l'odeur du magnolia. Dans la salle à manger Rouget de Lisle chantera devant le maire de Strasbourg, au dessus de la cheminée. Mais la douceur des tabliers[2] pastel, la voix chantante un peu voilée, mais ce regard humide et bleu posé si lentement sur moi... Sous l'ombre et quel soleil, dans quel jardin perdu à peine évanouis, dans quel chemin d'enfance au vent d'été... Je veux encore un peu de nuit, un peu d'autoroute glacée, un peu de café chaud – sans le sentir glisser vers les vacances d'autrefois, ma peine d'Aquitaine, et dans le frais d'un chemin creux grand-mère en tablier.

Je suis reparti vers Bordeaux, presque content de me savoir encore si loin de Labastide, lumière rassurante du tableau de bord, orage avant Châtellerault, ronron des essuie-glaces[3], et puis la pluie s'arrête, vitre à demi ouverte, bruissement des pneus sur l'asphalte mouillé. Je suis dans le présent de cette nuit, dans les lumières et dans les bruits légers de l'autoroute presque déserte. Je suis dans le présent, mais je me laisse aller ; la nuit est faite aussi d'un vide calme et envoûtant[4] qui recueille le temps – je me laisse aller doucement vers le Midi, vers la mémoire. Demain j'arriverai... Grand-mère m'embrassait à m'étouffer[5]. Dans un petit verre cerclé d'or, elle versait l'eau venue du puits[6], sortait de son placard un flacon[7] bleu profond, avec une étiquette[8] blanche – fleur d'oranger. Dès le flacon ouvert, un bonheur familier s'échappait dans la pièce, un plaisir mesuré à la cuiller, quelques volutes suspendues dans l'eau sucrée du verre. Il n'y avait pas autre chose à boire et ce bonheur unique était le mien, couleur des soifs d'enfance qui s'étanchent[9]...

1. *dawn* 2. *apron* 3. *purring of the windshield wipers* 4. *entrancing, bewitching* 5. *to smother me* 6. *well* 7. *perfume bottle* 8. *label* 9. *quench*

Core Instruction

LECTURE

1. Finish reading *Un été pour mémoire* as a class. Point out the relation between space-travel and time-travel in the text. Do certain places remind students of events from their childhood? What about certain tastes and smells? **(15 min.)**

2. Complete **Compréhension** and **Après la lecture** as a class. Were students' impressions as varied as the narrator's? **(10 min.)**

Online Practice
go.hrw.com
Online Edition

KEYWORD: BD3 CH10

Demain j'arriverai... Je n'ai pas soif ; pour la première fois je ne veux plus gommer[1] la distance et le temps. Déjà la banlieue de Bordeaux. Sur les panneaux, Agen s'annonce bien trop vite ; après, c'est Labastide, la fin de ce voyage à l'abri d'autrefois. Déjà la nuit s'éclaire, se dilue, à chaque nom de ville dépassée me protège un peu moins des étés de lumière.

---
1. effacer

Compréhension ✿1.2

B Réponds aux questions suivantes avec des phrases complètes.

1. Quand est-ce que le narrateur fait son voyage?
2. Où va-t-il? Pourquoi est-ce qu'il va là-bas?
3. Où est-ce qu'il s'arrête sur la route et qu'est-ce qu'il fait?
4. Pourquoi est-ce que le narrateur aime le café?
5. Qu'est-ce que la grand-mère faisait toujours quand le narrateur arrivait chez elle?

C Retrouve dans le texte les mots en gras des phrases suivantes. Ensuite, choisis la réponse qui complète le mieux chaque phrase.

e 1. Les **grands soleils phosphorescents** sont les _____.

b 2. Les mots **tons lunaires** et **voyager sur une absence** donnent l'impression que le narrateur voyage dans _____.

c 3. La **musique... des chagrins d'enfance** fait allusion aux _____.

f 4. Un **maillon** fait partie d'une _____.

a 5. Les **cathédrales de lumière** sont les _____.

d 6. **Je me laisse aller... vers la mémoire** veut dire que le narrateur pense à son _____.

a. stations-relais
b. l'espace
c. souvenirs
d. passé
e. réverbères
f. chaîne

Après la lecture ✿1.3

D As-tu jamais fait un long voyage en voiture, seul(e) ou avec tes parents? Comment c'était? À quoi pensais-tu? Qu'est-ce que ce voyage avait en commun avec celui du narrateur? Comment est-ce qu'il était différent?

Connections

Literature Link

Philippe Delerm is the author of *La première gorgée de bière et autres plaisirs minuscules,* the top bestseller in France in 1997. Prior to the runaway success of the slim, ninety-page book, he had written a dozen books that were critically acclaimed, but not bestsellers. *La première gorgée,* which has sold over 400,000 copies, describes in thirty-four brief chapters some of life's little pleasures and takes one of them as its title. Each chapter is an impassioned ode to one tiny aspect of daily life: the smell of apples, the feeling of a penknife in the pocket, making a call from a public telephone box. In the thirty-five short chapters of *Enregistrements pirates* (2004), Delerm casts an amused glance at daily life in the city. He describes brief encounters, good-byes at the station, scenes in the streets, on the subway, on the beach. An appropriate excerpt from one of the books would give students a good idea of what many French-speakers consider enjoyable popular literature. ✿3.1, 5.2

Assess

Assessment Program

Quiz: Lecture

Online Assessment

my.hrw.com

Test Generator

L'atelier de l'écrivain

Interactive TUTOR

Resources

Planning:

Lesson Planner

 One-Stop Planner

Practice:

Cahier d'activités

Process Writing

Have students make a copy of their work for their partner to review. Then have them read the questions in **Correction** and assign a different color to each question. As students read each other's story, have them underline the information in the story that corresponds to each question with the appropriate color. This will help them see more clearly if the story adequately answers each question. Students should then write comments in the margin, using the color that corresponds to the issue they are addressing. 🎴1.2

Teaching Suggestion

After discussing **Stratégie pour écrire,** form groups of three or four students. Assign each group a "mood." Ask groups to brainstorm words, images, and grammatical constructions that would convey that particular mood. Then have groups write the opening paragraph to a story that uses their ideas. Analyze with the class the effectiveness of the paragraphs in establishing mood. 🎴1.3

Un voyage

Tu viens de lire un texte qui parle d'un voyage. En l'utilisant comme modèle, tu vas écrire une histoire sur un voyage en voiture ou en avion. Tu peux baser ton histoire sur une expérience personnelle ou l'imaginer entièrement. Le narrateur doit parler des événements du voyage: les problèmes expérimentés, les personnes qu'il a rencontrées et ses réactions et pensées. Tu dois aussi créer une ambiance qui évoque une émotion chez le lecteur.

 1 Plan: plan de l'intrigue 🎴1.3

Les histoires naissent souvent de l'expérience personnelle d'un écrivain. Réfléchis un moment aux voyages que tu as faits, seul(e) ou avec ta famille. Essaie de trouver un souvenir qui peut devenir une histoire. Puis, fais un plan. D'abord, pose-toi les questions suivantes:

- Qui est ton personnage principal?
- Quelle sorte de voyage fait-il? Pourquoi?
- Quels sont les obstacles qu'il rencontre?
- Comment réagit-il à ces obstacles?
- Qui ou qu'est-ce qui l'aide à les surmonter?

Écris les réponses à chaque question sur une fiche. S'il y a plus d'une réponse à une question, écris chaque réponse sur une fiche séparée. Ensuite, arrange tes fiches par paragraphe.

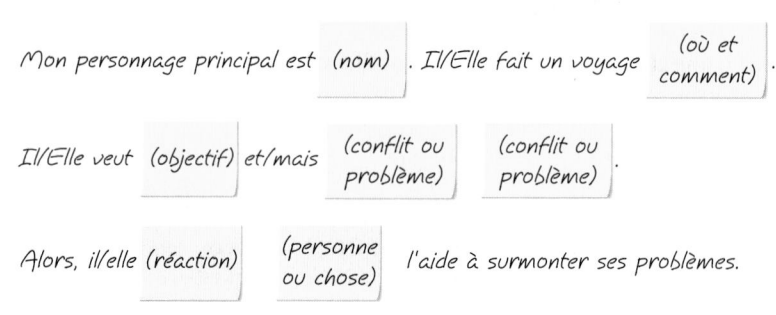

Mon personnage principal est (nom) . Il/Elle fait un voyage (où et comment) .

Il/Elle veut (objectif) et/mais (conflit ou problème) (conflit ou problème) .

Alors, il/elle (réaction) (personne ou chose) l'aide à surmonter ses problèmes.

Core Instruction

L'ATELIER DE L'ÉCRIVAIN

1. Ask for volunteers to talk briefly about a trip they have taken or would like to take. Discuss the assignment and **Stratégie pour écrire.** **(7 min.)**

2. Have students complete step 1. **(13 min.)**

3. Go over the **vocabulaire à la carte** and **Les adjectifs.** Practice forms by giving either the masculine or the feminine form of an adjective and having students supply the form for the other gender. **(5 min.)**

4. Assign step 2 as homework.

5. Have students complete steps 3 and 4. You might post the stories on the school Web site so that others may read them. **(30 min.)**

L'atelier de l'écrivain

② Rédaction ✿1.3

Révise ton plan si nécessaire. Pense à l'ambiance et au ton. Maintenant, fais un brouillon de ton histoire. Raconte-la à la première personne, **je.** Ajoute des détails descriptifs et des images qui évoquent des émotions. Essaie de *montrer* au lieu de *dire* qui sont les personnages, où ils sont et ce qu'ils font.

③ Correction ✿1.3

Échange ton histoire avec celle d'un(e) camarade de classe. Pour t'assurer que ton/ta camarade a bien raconté son histoire, pose-toi les questions suivantes:

- Est-ce que l'histoire est basée sur un conflit pour lequel les personnages doivent trouver une solution?
- Est-ce que l'endroit où l'action se passe est bien décrit?
- Est-ce que l'histoire finit par une résolution du conflit?
- Est-ce que l'histoire évoque une émotion ou une certaine ambiance?
- Est-ce qu'un thème ressort?

Note tes suggestions et rends-la à ton/ta camarade. Ensuite, relis ta propre histoire pour vérifier l'emploi correct du vocabulaire, de la grammaire et de l'orthographe. Assure-toi que l'accord des adjectifs avec les noms qu'ils qualifient, leur orthographe et leur place dans la phrase sont corrects. Fais les corrections nécessaires incorporant les suggestions de ton/ta camarade et écris ta version finale.

④ Application ✿1.3

Avec des camarades de classe, forme un groupe de quatre personnes. Lis ton histoire au groupe. Demande à tes camarades de décrire les émotions qu'ils ressentent pendant la lecture. Quelles sont les images qui les ont impressionnés? Est-ce qu'ils ont aimé ton histoire? Pourquoi ou pourquoi pas?

Quand j'avais onze ans, je voulais absolument aller en colonie de vacances. Tous mes copains allaient en colonie de vacances, alors je voulais faire comme eux. Alors,

Vocabulaire à la carte

à temps	in time
du jour au lendemain	overnight
un endroit	place
un ennui	trouble, worry
par hasard	by chance
plus tard	later on
prévu(e)	planned, forseen
profiter de	to take advantage of

Les adjectifs

- Some adjectives change spelling when in feminine: **-er/-ère, -eur** ou **-eux/-euse, -teur/-trice, -f/-ve.**

  cher/chère, heureux/heureuse

- Adjectives that end in **-el, -il, -en, -et, -on, -as, -os, -sot** double the consonant and add an **e** in the feminine.

  cruel/cruelle, gentil/gentille

  except for: **discret/discrète, complet/complète.**

- A few adjectives don't follow any rules.

  blanc/blanche, sec/sèche, faux/fausse, beau (bel)/belle, vieux (vieil)/vieille, public/publique

---

L'atelier de l'écrivain

Les adjectifs

Have students give the feminine form of the following adjectives: **dernier (dernière), travailleur (travailleuse), joyeux (joyeuse), protecteur (protectrice), destructif (destructive), ancien (ancienne), bon (bonne), gros (grosse), complet (complète), frais (fraîche), vieux (vieille), faux (fausse).**

Writing Assessment

To assess **L'atelier de l'écrivain,** you can use the following rubric. For additional rubrics, see the *Assessment Program.*

Writing Rubric	4	3	2	1
Content (Complete—Incomplete)				
Comprehensibility (Comprehensible—Seldom comprehensible)				
Accuracy (Accurate—Seldom accurate)				
Organization (Well-organized—Poorly organized)				
Effort (Excellent effort—Minimal effort)				

18-20: A   14-15: C   Under
16-17: B   12-13: D   12: F

Differentiated Instruction

ADVANCED LEARNERS

Variation Ask students to write an illustrated story for children about a traveler's journey to a French-speaking country or region. Students should decide as a class on the identity and character of the traveler. While each student will describe a different journey, the traveler's actions and emotions should stay true to his/her character. Remind students to use language and pictures suitable for children. Students should post their story on the school's Web site.

✿3.1

SPECIAL LEARNING NEEDS

Students with Learning Disabilities To help students create mood, feeling, and emotion in their writing, have them recall a movie that made them feel very happy, sad, scared, amused, or angry. Ask them to relate the most intense moment of the movie and then those moments preceding and following. Writing about these emotional moments while recalling them can create the general feeling or mood for a story.

✿1.2

Assess

Assessment Program

Quiz: Écriture

Online Assessment
my.hrw.com

Test Generator

Prépare-toi pour l'examen

Interactive **TUTOR**

Resources

Planning:

Lesson Planner

 One-Stop Planner

Practice:

Cahier d'activités

Media Guide

Teaching Transparencies
Situation, Chapitre 10
Picture Sequences, Chapter 10

🎧 Audio CD 10, Tr. 8

Interactive Tutor, Disc 2

VIDEO OPTIONS

▶ **Télé-culture: Interviews**

TPRS

You may wish to use the Picture Sequences Transparency that accompanies Activity 7 for a TPRS activity. See suggestions in the *Teaching Transparencies.*

❶ Possible Answers

a. Les passagers montent dans l'avion.
b. La tour de contrôle donne la permission à l'avion d'atterrir.
c. L'hôtesse de l'air donne les consignes de sécurité.
d. Les passagers passent la douane.

❷ Answers

1. Il est nécessaire que tu sois à l'heure pour le vol.
2. Il faut que Cédric montre son passeport à la douane.
3. Il faut que nous écoutions l'hôtesse de l'air quand elle donne les consignes de sécurité.
4. Il est nécessaire que vous preniez un taxi pour aller à l'aéroport.
5. Il est possible que la tour de contrôle annule le vol à cause de la tornade.

❶ **Vocabulaire 1**
• to ask for and give information and clarifications
• to remind and reassure
pp. 404–407

❷ **Grammaire 1**
• review of prepositions with places
• review of the subjunctive
Un peu plus
• adverb placement
pp. 408–413

❸ **Vocabulaire 2**
• to ask for and give help
• to ask for directions
pp. 416–419

1. une roue 2. le volant
3. le conducteur/la conductrice
4. les phares 5. les essuie-glaces
6. une agence de location de voitures 7. un permis de conduire
8. Elle est en panne.

❶ Écris une légende pour chaque photo. 🌐1.2

a.

b.

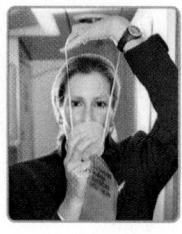
c.

d.

❷ Voici ce qu'il faut faire ou ce qui peut se passer quand on voyage. Fais des phrases correctes en utilisant différentes expressions qui demandent le subjonctif. 🌐1.2

MODÈLE nous / enregistrer les bagages
Il faut que nous enregistrions nos bagages.

1. tu / être à l'heure pour le vol
2. Cédric / montrer son passeport à la douane
3. nous / écouter l'hôtesse de l'air quand elle donne les consignes de sécurité
4. vous / prendre un taxi pour aller à l'aéroport
5. la tour de contrôle / annuler le vol à cause de la tornade

❸ Tu as un ami allemand qui ne parle pas bien français. Il ne trouve pas toujours les mots. De quoi est-ce qu'il parle? 🌐1.2

1. C'est rond et c'est sous la voiture. On doit en avoir une de secours dans le coffre.
2. C'est ce qu'on tourne pour changer de direction.
3. C'est la personne qui conduit la voiture.
4. Ils te permettent de voir la route la nuit ou quand il pleut.
5. Ça va d'un côté à l'autre du pare-brise et tu les utilises quand il pleut ou qu'il neige.
6. C'est là qu'on va quand on veut louer une voiture.
7. C'est le papier qu'il faut pour pouvoir conduire une voiture.
8. C'est ce qu'on dit quand la voiture ne marche pas.

Preparing for the Exam

RETEACHING

To review prepositions with places you might play a map game with a French world map. Beginning a class chain, the first student tells which city, state, and country he or she is from and which city, state, and country he or she would like to go to on vacation. Then he or she will ask another student where that student is from and where he or she wants to go. You might also do this activity in groups of four students.

TEST-TAKING STRATEGY

Tell students that when reviewing adverbs and adverb placement, they should create their own sample sentences for each of the six rules they learned on page 412. Writing the adverb in a different color might help visual learners.

4 Tu vas partir en vacances avec tes parents. Dis ce qui se passera ou ce que vous ferez: 🍀1.3

1. avant de partir
2. dans l'avion
3. à l'arrivée
4. là-bas
5. le dernier jour de vos vacances

5 Réponds aux questions suivantes. 🍀2.1, 2.2

1. Qu'est-ce que c'est un DROM? Donne deux exemples.
2. Qu'est-ce que cela veut dire quand on dit que les autoroutes sont «à péage»?
3. Qu'est-ce que c'est un permis de conduire «à point»?

6 Catherine est contente car elle va bientôt partir en vacances. Elle pense aux vacances qu'elle passait avec ses parents quand elle était petite. Écoute ce qu'elle dit et dis si elle parle **a) de ces vacances-ci** ou **b) de vacances passées.** 🍀1.2
CD 10, Tr. 8 **1.** a **2.** a **3.** b **4.** a **5.** b **6.** b

7 Sylvie et Jade préparent leurs vacances. Regarde les dessins et dis ce qu'elles décident. 🍀1.3

Online Assessment
go.hrw.com
Chapter Self-test
KEYWORD: BD3 CH10

4 Grammaire 2
- review of the future
- review of the past perfect

Un peu plus
- the causative **faire** pp. 420–425

5 Culture
- **Comparaisons** p. 415
- **Flash culture** pp. 406, 419, 422

5 Answers
1. Département et région d'outre-mer (la Guyane française et l'île de la Réunion)
2. Elles sont payantes.
3. On perd des points en recevant une contravention.

6 Script
1. Cet été, je partirai en vacances avec des amis. On ira à la plage et on fera de la planche à voile.
2. Je serai contente quand on sera arrivé.
3. Je préférais voyager en avion, surtout quand on allait loin.
4. J'achèterai mon billet la semaine prochaine.
5. Un été, j'ai rendu visite à ma grand-mère et elle m'a appris à nager.
6. Nous voyagions en voiture parce que c'était moins cher que l'avion.

ACTIVITÉ PRÉPARATOIRE PRÉ-AP

Language Examination

To display the drawings to the class, use the Picture Sequences Transparency for Chapter 10.

7 Sample answer

a. Cet été, Sylvie et Jade iront au bord de la mer. Elles vont se reposer au soleil.

b. Si elles prennent l'avion, ce sera plus rapide mais plus cher.

c. Si elles décident de prendre leur voiture, cela coûtera moins cher mais le voyage sera plus long.

d. Finalement, elles décident de prendre l'avion. Elles montent dans l'avion avec leurs bagages.

Oral Assessment

To assess the speaking activities in this section, you might use the following rubric. For additional speaking rubrics, see the Alternative Assessment section of the *Assessment Program*.

Speaking Rubric	4	3	2	1
Content (Complete—Incomplete)				
Comprehension (Total—Little)				
Comprehensibility (Comprehensible—Incomprehensible)				
Accuracy (Accurate—Seldom Accurate)				
Fluency (Fluent—Not Fluent)				

18-20: A   16-17: B   14-15: C   12-13: D   Under 12: F

Prépare-toi pour l'examen

Grammar Review

For more practice with the grammar topics in this chapter, see the *Grammar Tutor*, the *Interactive Tutor*, or the *Cahier de vocabulaire et grammaire.*

Online Edition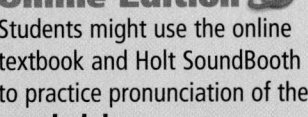

Students might use the online textbook and Holt SoundBooth to practice pronunciation of the **vocabulaire.**

Cultures

Products and Perspectives

The history of aviation in Polynesia began in 1943 with the construction of the first airport in Bora Bora by the American army. Air Polynésie served six destinations in 1970 and eleven in 1972. In 1986, Air Polynésie changed its name to Air Tahiti. In 1987, ATR aircrafts replaced the Fokkers, and more and more islands with modernized, accessible runways were added to the network. Air Tahiti's mission is the development of tourism to Tahiti and her islands. Ask students to research flights from their hometown to Bora Bora. ✿ 2.2

Grammaire 1
- review of prepositions with places
- review of subjunctive

Un peu plus
- adverb placement
pp. 408–413

Résumé: Grammaire 1

Preposition with places;

	cities	feminine country/state	masculine country/state	plural country/state
to/in	à	en	au	aux
from	de	de	du	des

The **subjunctive** in French is used with the following: *expressions of necessity, desire, emotion, disbelief* and *doubt,* most *expressions of possibility, negative expressions of certainty,* and after *conjunctions* like **bien que, jusqu'à,** or **ce que.** To form the subjunctive of most verbs take the present **ils/elles** form and drop the **-ent.** Add the subjunctive endings **-e, -es, -e, -ions, -iez, -ent.**

Adverbs usually go before the adjective or adverb they modify. In a sentence with a simple tense, **adverbs** that modify the verb usually go directly after the verb.
In a sentence with a compound tense, **adverbs** that modify the verb generally go before the past participle.

Grammaire 2
- review of the future
- review of the past perfect

Un peu plus
- the causative **faire**
pp. 420–425

Résumé: Grammaire 2

To form the future of **-er** and **-ir** verbs add the future endings **-ai, -as, -a, -ons, -ez, -ont,** to the infinitive. For **-re** verbs drop the **-e** from the infinitive and then add the future endings. Many verbs which have spelling changes in the present tense keep the same spelling changes in the future tense.

To form the **plus-que-parfait** or past perfect, use the **imparfait** of **avoir** or **être** and the past participle of the main verb. The rules for agreement are the same as the **passé composé.**

voir		aller	
j'	avais vu	j'	étais allé(e)
tu	avais vu	tu	étais allé(e)
il/elle/on	avait vu	il/elle/on	était allé(e)s
nous	avions vu	nous	étions allé(e)s
vous	aviez vu	vous	étiez allé(e)(s)
ils/elles	avaient vu	ils/elles	étaient allé(e)s

To say you are having something done, use a form of the verb **faire** with the infinitive of the main verb. If the main verb is reflexive, place the reflexive pronoun before the conjugated form of **faire,** and use the helping verb **être** in the **passé composé.**

Chapter Review

Teacher Management System
Password: admin
For more details, log on to www.hrw.com/CDROMTUTOR.

Create a variety of puzzles to review chapter vocabulary.

DVD Program	Interactive Tutor	PuzzlePro
	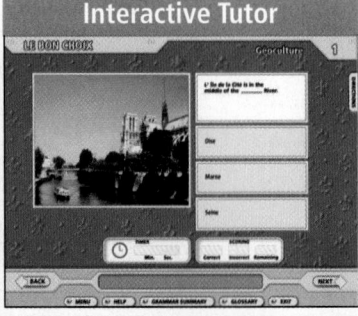	

Résumé: Vocabulaire 1

HOLT **SoundBooth** ONLINE RECORDING

To ask for information and clarifications and respond

à bord	on board	l'hôtesse de l'air (f.)	flight attendant
l'aéroport (m.)	airport	un hublot	window
une allée	alley	le passager/la passagère	passenger
annuler	to cancel	passer la douane	to go through customs
atterrir/décoller	to land/to take off	la piste	runway
l'autorisation (f.)	authorization	la porte d'embarquement	gate
la cabine	cabin	une salle d'embarquement	terminal
une carte d'embarquement	boarding pass	le siège	seat
le cockpit	cockpit	la tour de contrôle	control tower
le commandant de bord	captain	un vol intérieur/international	domestic/international flight
confirmer	to confirm	... un vol sans escale pour...	. . . a non-stop flight for . . .
les consignes de sécurité (f.)	safety instructions	... une place près du hublot	. . . window seat
débarquer/embarquer	to get off/on a plane	maximum	maximum
le décalage horaire	jet lag	On a droit à...	One is allowed . . .
enregistrer	to check in	un vol direct	direct flight
un équipage	crew	Vous avez de la chance, on en a encore deux.	You're lucky, we have two left.
l'escale (f.)	stop		
le hall d'arrivée	arrival hall		

To remind and reassure .... See p. 407

Résumé: Vocabulaire 2

The car

accélérer	to accelerate	le pare-brise	wind shield
une agence de location	rental agency	le phare	headlight
le capot	hood	la plaque d'immatriculation	license plate
le changement de vitesse automatique/manuel	stick shift gear	un pneu (à plat)	(flat) tire
changer de vitesse	automatic/manual gear shift	la pompe à essence	gas pump
le coffre	trunk	la portière	door
le/la conducteur(-trice)	driver	ralentir	to slow down
entretenir	to maintain	régler la pression des pneus	to put air in the tire
l'essence (f.) sans plomb	unleaded gas	le réservoir	gas tank
les essuie-glaces (m.)	windshield wipers	le rétroviseur	side mirror
être/tomber en panne	to break down	la roue de secours	spare tire
faire la révision	to check	le super	regular gas
faire le plein	to fill up the tank	le tableau de bord	dashboard
le frein (à main)	(emergency) brake	le volant	steering wheel
freiner	to brake		
le gasoil	diesel		
klaxonner	to honk		
le moteur	engine		

To ask for help and respond .... See p. 417

To ask for directions .... See p. 419

Game

Il faut que... Start a chain activity by telling what you see in an airport. **Dans l'aéroport, je vois...** Students continue by repeating what you saw and adding others. When a student fails to repeat all the previous items, he or she is out. Start a new chain when someone makes a mistake. The winner is the last one remaining. ✿1.1

Online Edition

Transparency: Vocabulaire

Transparency: Situation

Assess

Assessment Program
Examen: Chapitre 10
Audio CD 10, Trs. 13, 14
Examen oral: Chapitre 10
Alternative Assessment
Differentiated Practice and Assessment CD-ROM

Online Assessment
my.hrw.com

Test Generator

Activités préparatoires

Resources

Planning:

Lesson Planner

 One-Stop Planner

Practice:

Cahier de vocabulaire et grammaire

Differentiated Practice and Assessment CD-ROM

 Teaching Transparencies

Picture Sequences, Chapter 10

Cahier d'activités

 Audio CD 10, Tr. 9

VIDEO OPTIONS

▶ **Télé-culture: Interviews**

The AP French Language Exam

Activités préparatoires provide students with activities similar to those found in the Advanced Placement French Language exam. The activities are based on material taught up to and including this chapter and concentrate on the chapter grammar and vocabulary.

Listening Script

1. — Il y a beaucoup de circulation.
— Il y a un accident. Je vois un panneau au carrefour là-bas.

2. — Après l'atterrissage à New York, il faut que nous changions de terminal.
— Et nous n'avons pas beaucoup de temps. Lorsque nous descendrons d'avion, nous devrons prendre un bus.

Reading Strategy

Formulate an answer Tell students to answer multiple-choice questions, before reading the choices. If none of the choices matches their answer, they should use the process of elimination to narrow down the choices.

SECTION I

Listening CD 10, Tr. 9 1.2

Listen to the dialogues and choose the most appropriate response.

1. **A.** Je ferais mieux de tourner à droite.
   B. Je dois ouvrir le capot.
   C. Tu ferais mieux de regarder la carte afin de chercher un autre chemin.
   D. Je ne trouve pas de place de stationnement.

2. **A.** Rassure-toi. On s'assied près de la sortie de secours.
   B. Ne t'en fais pas. J'ai étiqueté les bagages.
   C. Tu n'as pas entendu les consignes de sécurité?
   D. J'aurais préféré un vol sans escale.

Reading 1.2

Read the following paragraph and answer the questions that follow.

> Pour limiter la circulation automobile à Paris, les Parisiens sont autorisés à laisser garer leur véhicule personnel près de leur domicile, pour une durée
> 5 n'excédant pas 7 jours consécutifs au tarif de 0,5 euro pour une journée ou 2,5 euros pour une semaine, à l'exception des samedis, dimanches, jours fériés et du mois d'août, gratuits.
> 10 Les documents suivants doivent être apposés derrière le pare-brise du véhicule :
> - La carte de stationnement résidentiel, gratuite, délivrée par la
> 15 Mairie de Paris.
> - Le ticket journalier ou hebdomadaire, en cours de validité, délivré par l'horodateur.
> La carte permet le stationnement dans
> 20 une zone autour de votre domicile.

1. Le mot «garé» veut dire...
   A. stationné.
   B. conduit.
   C. ouvert.
   D. vendu.

2. Le mot «domicile» veut dire....
   A. bureau.
   B. maison.
   C. garage.
   D. parc.

3. On permet aux Parisiens de stationner leur voiture près de leur maison...
   A. pour limiter la circulation dans la ville.
   B. pour une journée.
   C. pour 2,5 semaines.
   D. seulement les jours fériés.

4. On obtient la carte de stationnement...
   A. d'un horodateur.
   B. de la Mairie de Paris.
   C. au mois d'août.
   D. dans le journal.

Preparing for the Exam

ADDITIONAL PRACTICE

Make flash cards with the names of various cities, states, countries, provinces, etc. Have students supply the appropriate preposition as they say that they will travel to the place written on the card. To keep their attention, have them repeat all the places named before, and then add their destination to the list. 1.1

TEST-TAKING STRATEGIES

Section I: Listening It may be helpful for students to try to determine the relationship between the speakers. The relationship will determine the type of language people use with one another (**tu/vous,** slang/formal).

Section II: Writing Remind students to include any necessary accent mark when they fill in blanks, especially on past participles of **-er** verbs and on the preposition **à.**

Activités préparatoires

The following activities can be used to help you to prepare for the Advanced Placement French Language examination, or to further practice the vocabulary and grammar concepts you have seen in this chapter.

Online Practice
go.hrw.com
Online Edition
KEYWORD: BD3 CH10

SECTION II

Writing 🎬 1.2

In the following conversation, some words have been omitted. Complete each sentence by choosing the correct word or writing the correct verb form.

—Tu es allé ___1___ Paris?

—Non, pas ___2___ .

—Ah, il faut que tu y ___3___ .

—Oui, je sais. J'ai ___4___ voyagé partout ___5___ États-Unis, même ___6___ Alaska.

—Je ne savais pas que tu y ___7___ .

—Si, en fait, j'___8___ les cinquante états avant d'avoir dix-huit ans.

—Tu as voyagé seul?

—Bien sûr que non! J'étais ___9___ avec mes parents.

—Et tu n'es jamais allé ___10___ France?

—Non, je ne suis ___11___ allé en Europe, mais je ___12___ y aller sans faute cet été.

1. ___à___ (aux/à)
2. ___encore___ (déjà/encore)
3. ___ailles___ (aller)
4. ___déjà___ (toujours/déjà)
5. ___aux___ (en/aux)
6. ___en___ (à/en)
7. ___étais allé___ (aller)
8. ___ai visité___ (visiter)
9. ___toujours___ (toujours/déjà)
10. ___en___ (en/aux)
11. ___pas encore___ (pas encore/déjà)
12. ___vais___ (aller)

Essay Topic 🎬 1.3

Write in French a well-organized and coherent composition (10 to 15 lines) on the following topic.

Préférez-vous conduire en ville ou à la campagne? Pourquoi?

Speaking 🎬 1.3

Look at the drawing, then tell a story about what is occurring in the picture.

Activités préparatoires

Writing Strategy

Remind students that when they proofread, they should consider spelling, fragments, run-on sentences, subject/verb agreement, adjective agreement, past participle agreement, and sequence of tenses.

🅰🅿 Language Examination

🖥 To display the drawing to the class, use the **Activités préparatoires** Transparency for Chapter 10.

Speaking: Sample answer

Les passagers sont en train d'embarquer. L'hôtesse de l'air leur dit où est leur siège. Une des passagères a peur des avions. Son mari la rassure. Un autre passager a emporté ses skis dans la cabine. Il dérange tout le monde.

You might ask students the following.

La première fois que tu as pris l'avion, qu'as-tu ressenti?

Cultures

🌸 Practices and Perspectives

Fort de France, with a population of over 100,000, is the largest city on Martinique. It is a bustling port city with traffic jams that are particularly bad during traditional rush-hour times. Public transportation consists of large passenger buses and eight-passenger taxis known as **taxis collectifs.** Ask students if there are traffic jams in their hometown. If yes, what steps does their community take to avoid traffic congestion?

🌸 2.1

Differentiated Instruction

SLOWER PACE LEARNERS

Additional Practice Some students may have trouble remembering the vocabulary they need in order to tell their story. Ask volunteers to describe only what they see in the drawing without trying to explain why certain actions take place. Write relevant descriptions on the board and encourage students to use these when telling their story. 🌸 1.1, 1.2

SPECIAL LEARNING NEEDS

Learning Disabilities To help students with learning disabilities, have them work with a study partner. Both students should complete the task individually and then share their answers with each other for peer editing.

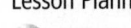

VIDEO OPTIONS

▶ **Géoculture**

▶ **Télé-roman: Camille et compagnie, Épisodes 11 et 12**

❶ Script

1. Nous avons dû louer une voiture à l'agence parce que Paul n'était pas venu nous chercher à l'aéroport.
2. L'avion a atterri sans problème, mais j'avais quand même un peu peur!
3. Le week-end dernier, j'ai emprunté la voiture de Christian et devine ce qui m'est arrivé... J'ai eu un pneu à plat! Et, bien sûr, il n'avait pas de roue de secours!
4. Cette année, nous n'avons pas eu de vol direct et nous avons dû faire escale sur cette petite île.
5. Je n'aime pas conduire la nuit, surtout quand il pleut!
6. Ce conducteur a eu un pneu à plat. Il va devoir appeler une station-service.

❷ Answers

1. oui, de 7h à midi
2. non
3. oui, ils travaillent sur toutes les marques de voitures
4. oui, il y a une campagne cadeau
5. par carte, par chèque, en liquide

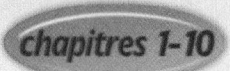
CD 10, Tr. 10 ✿1.2

❶ Choisis l'image qui convient pour chaque phrase.

1. d **2.** a **3.** b **4.** a **5.** c **6.** b

a.   b.   c.   d.

❷ Lis cette brochure pour une station-service, ensuite réponds aux questions. ✿1.2, 3.2

Station-Service Fixetout
Quelques bonnes raisons de choisir notre station-service

- De l'essence de qualité à un prix compétitif
- Des professionnels à votre service
- On travaille sur toutes les marques de voitures étrangères (japonaises, allemandes, américaines, anglaises)
- Une campagne cadeau pour les clients réguliers
- Tout mode de payment accepté

Numéro de téléphone : 02.72.14.65.86
Ouvert : lundi-vendredi : 7h-19h, week-end : 7h-12h

1. Est-ce que la station est ouverte le dimanche?
2. Les mécaniciens sont-ils débutants?
3. Penses-tu qu'ils peuvent réparer une auto à changement de vitesse automatique? Pourquoi?
4. Est-ce qu'il y a un avantage à être un bon client?
5. Comment est-ce qu'on peut les payer?

Online Culture Project

Ask students to put together a photo album with pictures from their summer trip to Guadeloupe. Students should include four photos gathered from the Internet with captions in French that tell the name of each attraction they visited and what they did on the day they visited it. Have students document their sources of information and print their album with typed captions to turn in to you. ✿3.2

Online Assessment
go.hrw.com
Cumulative Self–test
KEYWORD: BD3 CH10

Chapitres 1–10

Révisions cumulatives

Révisions cumulatives

3 Toi et ton ami, vous voudriez aller en vacances. Discutez de l'endroit où vous voudriez aller et de ce que vous ferez là-bas. Parlez de votre itinéraire et expliquez vos projets à la classe. ✿1.1

4 Regarde ce tableau de Matisse et réponds aux questions. ✿1.3, 2.2

1. Où est-ce que cette scène se passe? À quelle période de l'année?

2. Qu'est-ce que cette jeune femme fait?

3. Quelle impression te donne ce tableau?

4. Est-ce que tu aimerais aller en vacances dans cet endroit? Pourquoi ou pourquoi pas?

Matisse, Henri. *The Regattas at Nice*, 1921.

The Regattas at Nice d'Henri Matisse

5 Dessine l'auto du futur. Étiquette *(Label)* toutes les parties en français. Écris un petit paragraphe pour décrire ton auto. ✿1.3

6 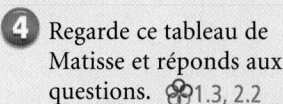 **À l'aéroport** Vous êtes un groupe de passagers et vous attendez dans la salle d'embarquement. L'hôtesse de l'air vous annonce que votre vol a été annulé et que vous devez attendre 5 heures avant le prochain vol. Jouez cette scène devant la classe. ✿1.1

FINE ART CONNECTION

Introduction Henri Matisse, born in 1869 in northern France, is the most important French painter of the twentieth century. He first took up painting while recovering from surgery. In 1891 he studied art briefly at the **Académie Julian** and then at the **École des Beaux-Arts.** Influenced by the Post-impressionists Cézanne, Gauguin, Van Gogh, and Signac, and by Japanese art, he found his own style, characterized by daring, bright colors and broad brush strokes. His preference for bright and expressive colors became more pronounced after he moved to the French Riviera. Matisse became known as a leader of a group of artists called **Les Fauves** ("wild beasts"). He lived in Nice from 1917 until his death in 1954.

Analyzing

The Fauvists emphasized the use of deep color over representational values. They simplified lines, made the subject of the painting easy to read, exaggerated perspectives, and used brilliant but arbitrary colors. Ask students these questions.

1. **Décris la manière dont Matisse utilise les couleurs, les lignes, la perspective et comment il traite du sujet?**

2. **Est-ce que vous diriez que sa peinture est fauviste? Pourquoi ou pourquoi pas?**

Extension

Matisse was a friend as well as a rival of Picasso. Ask students to compare the works of Matisse to those of Picasso. What are the similarities? (Both artists painted women and still life frequently.) What are the differences? (Matisse drew from nature, while Picasso worked from imagination.) ✿1.3, 3.1

ACTFL Performance Standards

The activities in Chapter 10 target the communicative modes as described in the Standards.

Interpersonal	Two-way communication using receptive skills and productive skills	**Communication (SE),** pp. 407, 409, 411, 413, 419, 421, 423, 425 **Communication (TE),** pp. 409, 411, 413, 419, 421, 423 **À ton tour,** p. 439
Interpretive	One-way communication using receptive skills	**Culture,** pp. 414–415 **Lecture,** pp. 426–429
Presentational	One-way communication using productive skills	**Communication (SE),** p. 425 **Communication (TE),** p. 407

CHRONIQUES

Resources

Practice:

Reading Strategies and Skills Handbook

Advanced Reader

Applying the Strategies

You may want to use the "Say Something" strategy from the *Reading Strategies and Skills Handbook* to encourage students to examine the text more closely.

READING PRACTICE

Strategy: Say Something

Prereading

Before you begin this **Chroniques** section, ask students if they enjoy going to art museums and if so, what kind of art and which artists they like. Ask them if they have heard of Impressionism and have volunteers share what they know about this style of art.

PRE-AP Language Examination

The **Chroniques** section helps students prepare for Section I, Part B: **Reading Comprehension**.

CHRONIQUES
L'impressionnisme

La peinture impressionniste est aujourd'hui l'école de peinture française la plus connue et la plus appréciée de l'histoire de l'art moderne. C'est un mouvement artistique qui a marqué le début de la peinture moderne même si, à sa naissance, la grande modernité de ce mouvement a fait scandale.

L'impressionnisme est caractérisé par le désir de ses peintres de rompre avec[1] les conventions et de créer une nouvelle forme d'art réaliste.

Impression soleil levant de Claude Monet (1872)

L'impressionnisme

À l'origine, les impressionnistes sont un petit groupe de jeunes peintres qui sont refusés dans les expositions officielles parisiennes parce que leur conception de l'art s'oppose à la norme de l'époque[2]. Pour eux, le monde n'est pas stable; il est mobile et changeant[3], et chaque artiste est libre d'interpréter la réalité selon sa vision personnelle des choses au moment où il les peint. Leurs sujets ont des formes qui ne sont pas distinctes, mais plutôt suggérées par les couleurs et par les juxtapositions et les contrastes de ces couleurs. Contrairement aux autres[4] peintres de l'époque, les impressionnistes peignent en plein air et la lumière[5] devient l'élément le plus important de leurs tableaux. Ils étudient son effet sur les formes et les couleurs et ils inventent de nouvelles techniques de peinture. Ils utilisent, par exemple, des petites taches[6] de couleur qu'ils posent rapidement sur leurs toiles pour représenter le mouvement de la vie.

1. break away from   2. the norm of the era   3. changing   4. Unlike the other   5. light   6. spots

---

Core Instruction

TEACHING CHRONIQUES

1. Before you begin, have students describe and give their opinion of the paintings featured in this **Chroniques** section. **(3 min.)**

2. Have students read the first section and list the most important characteristics of **l'impressionnisme**. Then have them answer questions 1 and 2 in **Après la lecture.** **(7 min.)**

3. Have students read the other 2 sections. Then make simple statements that describe Monet, Renoir, or both, and have students identify the painter(s) being described. **Il a peint beaucoup de personnages dans des scènes de la vie quotidienne.** (Renoir) **(10 min.)**

4. Finally, have students answer the remaining questions in **Après la lecture.** **(3 min.)**

**Deux grands peintres impressionnistes:
Claude Monet et Auguste Renoir**

Le Déjeuner des canotiers de Pierre-Auguste Renoir (1881)

Auguste Renoir (1841–1919)

C'est le peintre impressionniste le plus connu pour ses représentations de personnages dans des scènes heureuses de la vie de tous les jours. Il s'intéresse surtout à la jeunesse et à la vitalité, comme le montre sa plus grande œuvre impressionniste, *Le Déjeuner des canotiers*[3].

Nympheas de Claude Monet (1916-1919)

Claude Monet (1840–1926)

Il est considéré comme le créateur du mouvement impressionniste. Dans ses tableaux, la lumière est toujours le «personnage principal». Il a pour but de saisir[1] les effets changeants de la lumière à différents moments de la journée. Parmi ses tableaux les plus connus, la série des Cathédrales de Rouen et celle des nymphéas[2] du célèbre jardin de sa maison de Giverny illustrent cette technique.

Le style impressionniste a eu une grande influence sur d'autres mouvements artistiques. En peinture, le néo-impressionnisme et le postimpressionnisme ont leurs racines dans l'impressionnisme. En musique, le terme «impressionniste» décrit un style musical qui s'est développé parallèlement à la peinture impressionniste. Parmi les grands compositeurs impressionnistes, on peut citer, entre autres, Claude Debussy, Maurice Ravel et Érik Satie.

APRÈS ▶ la lecture

🏵1.2, 1.3

1. Qui étaient les impressionnistes et comment voyaient-ils le monde?

2. Quelles sont les caractéristiques principales de l'impressionnisme?

3. Quel est l'élément le plus important dans les tableaux de Monet?

4. Des trois tableaux, choisis celui que tu préfères et décris-le. Ensuite, explique quels éléments dans cette peinture sont typiques de l'impressionnisme.

5. Est-ce que le mot «impressionniste» décrit seulement la peinture? Explique.

1. His goal is to capture   2. water lilies   3. boaters

Connections

Art Link

Bring in photos or reproductions of several other Impressionist paintings. Form small groups and give one image to each group. Have group members prepare a presentation of their painting to be given orally to the class. They should include a detailed description of their painting, identify the Impressionistic elements, and give their opinion of it.   🏵1.3, 3.1

Postreading

Review students' answers to question 2 in **Après la lecture** and write the key characteristics of Impressionism on the board for reference. Show photos of a variety of paintings from different schools and periods to ask them whether or not each one qualifies as an Impressionist work. Have students explain their answers.

Recherches

Have students take a virtual tour of the **musée d'Orsay** (www.musee-orsay.fr) and the **musée Marmottan** (www.marmottan.com). Ask them to find another Impressionist work they like, and have them prepare a short presentation of it. If possible, they should include a photo of the artwork.   🏵1.3, 3.2

Differentiated Instruction

ADVANCED LEARNERS

Have students comment on the following quote by Renoir, **"Pour moi, un tableau doit être une chose aimable, joyeuse et jolie, oui jolie! Il y a assez de choses embêtantes dans la vie pour que nous n'en fabriquions pas encore d'autres."** Ask students if they agree with Renoir and why or why not. Have them carefully look at his painting *Le Déjeuner des canotiers,* and say whether or not it is a good representation of Renoir's philosophy.   🏵1.3, 3.1

MULTIPLE INTELLIGENCES

Musical Bring in a selection of musical pieces by the Impressionist composers Debussy, Ravel, and Satie. Play these selections and ask them to give their opinion of them. Take a vote to see which one students like best, and have volunteers give reasons for their choice.   🏵1.3, 3.1

Applying the Strategies

You may want to use the "Anticipation Guide" strategy from the *Reading Strategies and Skills Handbook* to encourage students to examine the text more closely.

Prereading

Give students a few minutes to look at the four paintings. Ask them to come up with two observations about each one and to share these with the class. Then ask for volunteers to tell which of these paintings they like best and why.

Language Examination

The **Chroniques** section helps students prepare for Section I, Part B: **Reading Comprehension.**

CHRONIQUES

De l'art naïf au surréalisme

La fin du XIXe et le début du XXe siècles ont vu la naissance de plusieurs grands courants[1] artistiques. Voici les descriptions de quelques-uns de ces mouvements et des informations sur les peintres que l'on associe avec eux.

Tigre dans une tempête tropicale d'Henri Rousseau (1891)

L'art naïf: Le Douanier Rousseau (1844–1910)

Dans les années 1870, Henri Julien Félix Rousseau dit le Douanier Rousseau, découvre les grands chefs-d'œuvre[2] de la peinture au musée du Louvre et il commence à peindre. Son art est qualifié de «naïf» car il n'a pas reçu d'éducation artistique formelle. Pour lui, l'art consiste simplement à reproduire ce qu'il voit, c'est-à-dire une réalité très simple. Il ne respecte pas les règles[3] de la perspective et il utilise les couleurs de façon uniforme. L'exotisme et la poésie jouent un rôle important dans son art et il aime reproduire la nature, et plus particulièrement la jungle.

Le fauvisme: Henri Matisse (1869–1954)

Peintre, dessinateur et sculpteur français, Henri Matisse est le grand maître[4] du fauvisme, un courant artistique caractérisé par la simplification des formes (les formes elliptiques sont souvent privilégiées par les peintres fauvistes) et l'utilisation de bandes de couleurs pures, intenses et de contrastes de couleurs qui expriment les émotions de l'artiste. Matisse est aussi célèbre pour ses nombreux collages de papiers peints et pour ses vitraux[5].

La desserte rouge d'Henri Matisse (1908)

1. movements 2. masterpieces 3. rules 4. master 5. stained glass

---

Core Instruction

TEACHING CHRONIQUES

1. Once students have had a chance to look at the paintings, ask simple questions about them. **Est-ce qu'il y a des animaux dans le tableau de Rousseau? Quelle couleur est-ce que Braque utilise surtout dans son tableau? (5 min.)**

2. Have students read the information about the four art movements. Then have them summarize the important facts about each one. **(20 min.)**

3. Finally, have partners answer the questions in **Après la lecture. (8 min.)**

Le Viaduc de L'Estaque de Georges Braque (1908)

Le cubisme: Georges Braque (1882–1963)

En 1907, quelques artistes, dont Georges Braque et Pablo Picasso, s'inspirent des idées et des œuvres de Paul Cézanne pour créer un nouveau style artistique qu'on appellera le cubisme. Ils décident de représenter la nature et le monde avec des formes géométriques: le rectangle, le cercle, le cube et la pyramide. Braque et les cubistes décomposent les paysages et les personnages puis ils les recréent sous une forme différente, toujours géométrique. Braque est célèbre pour ses papiers collés[1] et ses nombreuses natures mortes.

Le surréalisme: René Magritte (1898–1967)

Le surréalisme est un mouvement artistique qui est né après la Première Guerre mondiale. Il s'est manifesté aussi bien en peinture qu'en littérature et en musique. Les surréalistes refusent les conventions sociales, morales et logiques et ils privilégient[2] l'imagination et le rêve[3]. Pour eux, l'art est une expérimentation scientifique. L'artiste doit découvrir l'univers, y compris le monde invisible et explorer l'inconscient. D'après Magritte, un peintre belge surréaliste, la peinture n'est pas un miroir de la réalité. Le peintre ne doit pas représenter un objet réel[4]. Il doit représenter ce qu'il pense de cet objet.

La Condition Humaine de René Magritte (1933)

APRÈS la lecture

🌸 1.2, 1.3

1. Pourquoi est-ce qu'on dit que les tableaux du Douanier Rousseau sont des œuvres naïves?

2. Décris les couleurs et les formes souvent utilisées par les peintres fauvistes.

3. Quelles sont les formes que les cubistes utilisent dans leurs tableaux?

4. Décris la vision surréaliste de l'art en utilisant tes propres mots.

5. Lequel de ces tableaux est-ce que tu préfères? Pourquoi?

1. glued 2. favor 3. dream 4. real

Differentiated Instruction

SLOWER PACE LEARNERS

Before having them answer the questions in **Après la lecture,** give slower pace students a few minutes to reread the sections with which they had trouble and to ask you for clarifications.

MULTIPLE INTELLIGENCES

Visual In addition to the literary version of the **cadavre exquis,** described in the Postreading activity, surrealists also played a graphic version of the game, using art instead of language. Have students work together to create a "surrealist" graphic rendition of the "story" they created in the **cadavre exquis** game they played in the Postreading activity. 🌸 3.1, 5.2

Connections

Art Link

Organize an 'art exhibit' in your class. Ask students to research and bring to class a photo of a painting by a famous Francophone artist. Have each student write a description of their painting and its artist. Display the photos and descriptons in chronological order. Have students discuss the various paintings, art styles, and changes they notice between the various time periods. 🌸 3.1

Postreading

In 1925, surrealist authors invented an experimental game they called **le cadavre exquis** *(exquisite corpse).* This game is played by a group of people who write a "story" in sequence, with each person only allowed to see the end of what the previous person wrote. Have students play a game of **cadavre exquis,** as a class. Start the game by writing a sentence. **Au musée, j'ai remarqué un homme aux cheveux blonds.** Reveal only ...**cheveux blonds.** A student writes the next sentence, revealing only the last words. All students contribute to the story and then discuss it. 🌸 1.2

echerches

Form four groups and have each group research additional information about one of the artistic movements represented in the **Chroniques.** Ask students to make an oral presentation to the class. Remind students to document their sources. 🌸 3.1

Chroniques

Resources

Practice:

Reading Strategies and Skills Handbook

Advanced Reader

Applying the Strategies

You may want to use the "Retellings" strategy from the *Reading Strategies and Skills Handbook* to encourage students to examine the text more closely.

READING PRACTICE

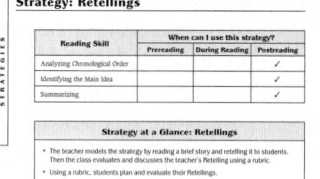

Prereading

In the previous two **Chroniques,** students read about art movements. Before you begin this section, have volunteers summarize what they know about **impressionnisme, art naïf, fauvisme, cubisme,** and **surréalisme.** Then ask them if they are familiar with the works of any famous sculptors (Francophone or other), and have them share what they know with the class.

Language Examination

The **Chroniques** section helps students prepare for Section I, Part B: **Reading Comprehension.**

CHRONIQUES

Voici les portraits de quelques sculpteurs français qui ont révolutionné l'art de la sculpture.

La sculpture sous toutes ses formes

Auguste Rodin
(1840–1917)

est un des maîtres incontestés[1] de la sculpture. Ses œuvres montrent sa capacité[2] à la reproduction fidèle[3] et réaliste, mais gardent une grande liberté de forme et d'expression ainsi qu'une certaine sensualité. On peut admirer ses œuvres, dont *Le Penseur* et *Le Baiser,* au musée Rodin qui est dans l'ancien hôtel Biron à Paris, un endroit où Rodin a habité.

Le Penseur

1. indisputable   2. ability   3. faithful

Camille Claudel (1864–1943)

est une artiste française qui était passionnée de sculpture depuis son enfance. Adulte, elle vient s'installer à Paris pour étudier avec les maîtres. Elle est modèle pour Rodin. Elle devient ensuite une de ses collaboratrices et a une relation amoureuse avec lui.

Femme accroupie

Core Instruction

TEACHING CHRONIQUES

1. Have students look at the illustrations and describe them. Ask for volunteers to give their first impressions of these sculptures. **(4 min.)**

2. Have students work with a partner to read the six sections. Then have volunteers give a short summary of each artist's life and contributions. **(20 min.)**

3. Have the same partners answer the questions in **Après la lecture.** Ask for volunteers to read their answers aloud. **(10 min.)**

Joseph Ferdinand Cheval (1836–1924)

est plus connu sous le surnom du facteur[1] Cheval. C'est un facteur français qui, en 1879, trouve un endroit où il y a des pierres qui ont, d'après lui, une forme étrange. Il a l'idée que si la nature «fait de la sculpture», il va, lui aussi, en faire. Il va alors passer plus de 30 ans de sa vie à construire son *Palais idéal*, fait de ces pierres étranges. C'est considéré aujourd'hui comme un chef-d'œuvre de l'art naïf.

Palais idéal

Arman (1928-2005)

est né à Nice. Il y suit les cours des Arts Décoratifs puis entre à l'École du Louvre. Il crée en 1960 le groupe des Nouveaux Réalistes avec son ami Yves Klein. En 1961, il aborde la *Destruction de l'objet; les Coupes, les Colères* (il coupe, piétine[2] et écrase[3] des violons, saxophones, réveils, meubles, etc. qu'il présente comme des tableaux éclatés). À partir de 1962, il partage sa vie entre Nice et New York. Il a installé plus de 100 monuments publics à travers le monde et ses œuvres figurent aujourd'hui dans les plus grands musées du monde.

Colère de Violon

Marcel Duchamp (1887–1968)

est un peintre et sculpteur français qui va révolutionner l'art du XXe siècle. Son style artistique est difficile à classer car il évoque plusieurs mouvements artistiques différents comme le futurisme, le cubisme, le surréalisme et le mouvement dada. Duchamp a commencé sa carrière artistique par la peinture, puis vers 1913–1915, il se concentre sur la sculpture. Il invente alors le concept des *ready-made*, des objets ordinaires de la vie auxquels il donne une nouvelle signification par la manière[4] dont il les présente en tant que[5] sculptures. Il s'installe aux États-Unis où son art va influencer d'autres mouvements artistiques comme par exemple le pop art.

Roue de bicyclette

Niki de Saint-Phalle (1930–2002)

est d'abord comédienne, puis elle commence à peindre en 1952. En 1960, elle devient membre du mouvement artistique des Nouveaux Réalistes. Plus tard, elle se lance dans la sculpture et crée la série des «Nanas[6]», des sculptures de taille humaine[7] qui représentent des femmes à certains moments importants de leur vie. En collaboration avec son mari, Jean Tinguely, elle a réalisé les sculptures de la fontaine Stravinsky devant le centre Pompidou à Paris.

APRÈS ▶ la lecture

🌸1.2, 1.3

1. Décris *Le Penseur* de Rodin. Que penses-tu de cette sculpture?

2. Comment est-ce que le facteur Cheval a eu l'idée de faire de la sculpture et de construire son *Palais idéal*?

3. Explique le concept du *ready-made* inventé par Duchamp.

4. Décris les «Nanas» de Niki de Saint-Phalle.

5. Laquelle des sculptures représentées ici est-ce que tu préfères? Pourquoi?

1. mailman   2. stomp   3. crush   4. by the way   5. as   6. woman (familiar)   7. lifesize

Connections

Art Link

Form three groups and assign one of the following time periods to each group: 1850–1900; 1900–1950; 1950–today. Have students research famous American sculptors from their period. Ask them to prepare an oral presentation in which they compare and contrast the works of these American sculptors' with those of the Francophone sculptors featured in the **Chroniques**.   🌸3.1

Postreading

Have students rank the sculptures on page 445 according to various criteria: most creative, most interesting, most bizarre, and so forth. Ask them to justify their answers.

Recherches

In addition to his world-renowned sculptures, Rodin's work also includes numerous sketches, paintings, and engravings. Have students go on a virtual tour of the Rodin museum in Paris by visiting its Web site at www.musee-rodin.fr. Ask students to write a journal entry about their visit.   🌸1.3

Differentiated Instruction

ADVANCED LEARNERS

Marcel Duchamp once said: **"Le grand ennemi de l'art, c'est le bon goût."** Have advanced students discuss this quote and consider whether or not the various sculptures featured here are examples of **bon goût**. Ask students to compare Duchamp's quote to that by Renoir on page 441: **"Pour moi, un tableau doit être une chose aimable, joyeuse et jolie, oui jolie!"**   🌸1.2, 1.3

SPECIAL LEARNING NEEDS

Students with Visual Impairments If you have students with visual impairments in your class, you may want to obtain larger photos of the artwork featured in this **Chroniques** section, as well as in the previous two **Chroniques**. Or, if available, you might show slides of this and other relevant artwork.   🌸3.1

Chroniques

Resources

Practice:

Reading Strategies and Skills Handbook

Advanced Reader

Applying the Strategies

You may want to use the "Say Something" strategy from the *Reading Strategies and Skills Handbook* to encourage students to examine the text more closely.

READING PRACTICE

Strategy: Say Something

Prereading

Before you begin the **Chroniques,** ask students what kind of music they enjoy listening to. As a class, discuss popular artists whose work students are familiar with. Then ask if they know any Francophone singers or bands. Ask those who do to share what they know about them with the class.

Language Examination

The **Chroniques** section helps students prepare for Section I, Part B: **Reading Comprehension.**

CHRONIQUES
Le hit-parade

La France a une longue tradition de poésie chantée, mais c'est depuis le milieu du XIXe siècle que la chanson française a, peu à peu, acquis une réputation mondiale avec l'invention du café-concert, puis du music-hall. Depuis la chanson française continue d'évoluer et chaque année, de nouveaux chanteurs et chanteuses contribuent à son évolution.

Les incontournables de la chanson française

Édith Piaf, surnommée la Môme Piaf (1915-1963)

Adolescente, elle commence par chanter dans la rue. En 1935, elle chante dans un cabaret des Champs-Élysées dont le gérant[1] la surnomme «la Môme Piaf» parce qu'elle est petite et chante comme un piaf qui est un petit oiseau. L'année suivante, elle enregistre son premier disque sous le nom d'Édith Piaf. Elle deviendra la chanteuse française la plus renommée dans le monde entier.

Jacques Brel (1929-1978)

Jacques Brel est né dans la banlieue de Bruxelles en Belgique. En 1953, il enregistre un premier disque et un découvreur de talent le fait venir à Paris. Il est engagé dans quelques cabarets parisiens mais le public ne l'apprécie pas beaucoup. Il doit attendre 1958 pour enfin connaître le succès.

En 1964, il crée une de ses chansons les plus connues, *Amsterdam*. En 1966, Jacques Brel est au sommet de sa gloire quand il décide d'abandonner sa carrière de chanteur et de commencer une carrière d'acteur. Il jouera dans huit films. À partir de 1974, sa santé décline et en 1975 il s'installe sur l'île de Hiva-Oa aux Marquises où il meurt et sera enterré aux côtés de Paul Gauguin en 1978.

Yannick Noah

Il s'est reconverti avec succès à la chanson après une carrière de joueur de tennis professionnel (il a gagné le tournoi de Roland Garros en 1983 et il a mené à la victoire l'équipe de France de Coupe Davis en tant que capitaine en 1991). En 1991, il enregistre son premier single *Saga Africa*. En 2003, il sort *Pokahra* puis son sixième album, *Métisse(s)* en 2005. Yannick Noah s'illustre aussi par son soutien[2] à des causes humanitaires. Il a créé **Les enfants de la terre** et **Fête le mur,** deux associations qui viennent en aide aux enfants défavorisés.

1. manager   2. support

Core Instruction

TEACHING CHRONIQUES

1. Ask students to describe the artists in the photos, and have them list the types of music that they might be associated with. Or, if you have some of these artists' CDs, play some short excerpts, making sure the songs you select are appropriate for your class. Ask students to guess who sings each song. **(8 min.)**

2. Ask for a different volunteer to read each section aloud while other students follow along in their books. Pause after each section and ask simple comprehension questions. Then have another volunteer summarize the most important points of each section for the class. **(20 min.)**

3. Have partners answer the questions in **Après la lecture** and share their answers with the class. **(6 min.)**

La musique française d'aujourd'hui

Mylène Farmer

Née à Montréal, elle arrive en France à l'âge de 8 ans. Après une adolescence tumultueuse, elle se lance[1] dans le show business. Elle tourne dans des publicités. En 1984, elle sort sa première chanson *Maman a tort* qui entre au Top 50 et la fait connaître du public. Son second album sort en 1988 se vend à plus de 1.800.000 exemplaires. Après de longues années de silence, elle revient avec un nouvel album en 1999 et une tournée en 2000, le Mylenium Tour. En 2005, elle sort son onzième album, *Avant que l'ombre*.

Le rap français

MC Solaar

MC Solaar est sans doute le rappeur français le plus connu. Alors qu'il poursuit des études de langue à l'université de Jussieu à la fin des années 80, Claude M'Barali, alias MC Solaar, est attiré[2] par la vague de rap américain qui débarque en France. Mais, comme il n'aime pas les paroles qui prônent la violence, il développe son propre style de musique: texte pacifiste et sons empruntés au jazz. Son premier album *Qui sème le vent récolte le tempo* se vend à plus de 400.000 exemplaires. En 2003, il sort *Mach 6*.

Diam's

Elle grandit en écoutant Goldman et Cabrel mais le rap de MC Hammer la séduit[3]. Elle a le coup de foudre pour le rap français de NTM qu'elle verra en concert quand elle n'a que 14 ans. Elle décide de devenir rappeuse. En 1999, elle sort son premier album *Premier mandat*.

Dans ses récents albums *Brut de femme* et *Dans ma bulle*, elle parle de problèmes sociaux comme par exemple de l'enfance maltraitée et de la violence envers les femmes.

APRÈS la lecture

🎞 1.3, 4.2

1. Pourquoi est-ce qu'Édith Piaf était surnommée la môme?

2. Quelle est l'une des chansons les plus connues de Jacques Brel?

3. Pourquoi est-ce que Yannick Noah est connu?

4. Qu'est-ce qui différencie MC Solaar des rappeurs américains?

1. begins   2. attracted   3. charms her

Teaching Suggestion

Once students have answered the questions in **Après la lecture,** have them prepare for a game of Jeopardy. Ask them to reread each section and write two to three Jeopardy-style 'answers' about each singer on a sheet of paper. Form several teams. Collect the papers and read each 'answer', one at a time. The first player to come up with the correct question wins a point for his or her team.
🎞 1.2, 1.3

Postreading

Select an appropriate song by one of the artists featured here. Before class, make copies of the lyrics. (For French lyrics, you might check: www.paroles.net.) Distribute the lyrics and have students follow along, as you play the song. Then, as a class, discuss the music and the lyrics. 🎞 3.2

Recherches

Have students use the Internet to find information about another French singer or band. Have students prepare a short oral report. Be sure to remind them to document their sources.
🎞 3.2

Differentiated Instruction

ADVANCED LEARNERS

Challenge Have students discuss the following well-known proverb: "**La musique adoucit les mœurs.**" 🎞 1.1

MULTIPLE INTELLIGENCES

Musical Have students work together as a class to write the lyrics for a song in French on the theme of their choice. If you have musically-talented students in your class, you might ask them if they would write some music to go with the lyrics. 🎞 1.3, 5.2

Resources

Practice:
Reading Strategies and Skills Handbook
Advanced Reader

Applying the Strategies

You may want to use the "Think aloud" strategy from the *Reading Strategies and Skills Handbook* to encourage students to examine the text more closely.

READING PRACTICE

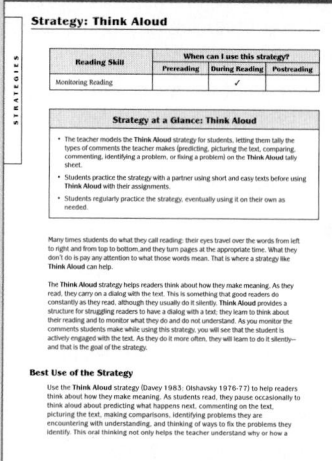

Strategy: Think Aloud

Reading Skill	When can I use this strategy?		
	Prereading	During Reading	Postreading
Monitoring Reading		✓	

Strategy at a Glance: Think Aloud

- The teacher models the Think Aloud strategy for students, letting them tally the types of comments the teacher makes (predicting, picturing the text, comparing, commenting, identifying a problem, or fixing a problem) on the Think Aloud tally sheet.
- Students practice the strategy with a partner using short and easy texts before using Think Aloud with their assignments.
- Students regularly practice the strategy, eventually using it on their own as needed.

Many times students do what they call reading: their eyes travel over the words from left to right and from top to bottom, and they turn pages at the appropriate time. What they don't do is pay any attention to what those words mean. That is where a strategy like Think Aloud can help.

The Think Aloud strategy helps readers think about how they make meaning. As they read, they carry on a dialog with the text. This is something that good readers do constantly as they read, although they usually do it silently. Think Aloud provides a structure for struggling readers to have a dialog with a text: they learn to think about their reading and to monitor what they do and do not understand. As you monitor the comments students make while using this strategy, you will see that the student is actively engaged with the text. As they do it more often, they will learn to do it silently—and that is the goal of the strategy.

Best Use of the Strategy

Use the Think Aloud strategy (Davey 1983; Olshavsky 1976-77) to help readers think about how they make meaning. As students read, they pause occasionally to think about predicting what happens next, commenting on the text, picturing the text, making comparisons, identifying problems they are encountering with understanding, and thinking of ways to fix the problems they identify. This oral thinking not only helps the teacher understand why or how a

Prereading

Bring a large map of Africa to class and put it on the board. Ask students to locate the countries mentioned in the **Chroniques** on the map: **l'Afrique du Nord (la Tunisie, le Maroc, l'Algérie), le Mali,** and **le Sénégal.** Have volunteers share what they already know about these countries with the class. Then ask them what kind of music and they would expect to hear if they traveled there.

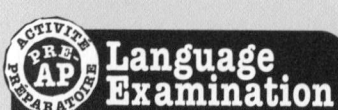

The **Chroniques** section helps students prepare for Section I, Part B: **Reading Comprehension.**

CHRONIQUES
Au rythme de l'Afrique

La musique africaine est très diversifiée. Voici quelques-uns des différents genres qui nous viennent de ce continent.

L'Afrique du Nord

Le raï est un genre littéraire et musical arabe. Dès les années 20, les maîtres du raï traditionnel comme Cheikh Khaldi, Cheikh Hamada ou Cheikha Remitti, ont un répertoire officiel qui célèbre la religion, l'amour et les valeurs morales lors des fêtes, des mariages et la veillée du Ramadan. Ils ont aussi un répertoire chanté seulement dans les souks et les tavernes. Le raï traditionnel était accompagné par la gasba, le gellal, la darbouka, le bendir.

Dans les années 70, de nouveaux instruments comme l'accordéon et la trompette viennent s'ajouter aux flûtes et tambours traditionnels. Ensuite, les guitares électriques, les synthétiseurs et les boîtes à rythmes électroniques apparaissent. De jeunes chanteurs comme Cheb Mami et Khaled, inspiré par Elvis Presley et Johnny Halliday mélangent le raï traditionnel avec les styles rock, pop, funk, reggae, latino, hip-hop et techno. Le raï moderne a connu un grand succès en dehors du monde arabe (par exemple en Europe et en Amérique du nord. Mami a enregistré un disque avec le chanteur anglais Sting en 1999) Alors qu'au début, cette musique a été interdite par les autorites algériennes, elle est maintenant officiellement acceptée comme faisant partie intégrante de la culture.

la darbouka

Le Mali

La culture du Mali est riche et diversifiée à cause du grand nombre d'ethnies qui y vivent et qui ont gardé leur culture spécifique.

Les instruments traditionnels comme le *n'goni* (ancêtre africain du *banjo*), la *cora* (sorte de harpe) ou le *balafon* (xylophone en bois) sont toujours utilisés.

Il y a au Mali de nombreux styles musicaux qui mélangent musique traditionnelle et musique moderne. La chanteuse Oumou Sangaré est considérée comme l'ambassadrice du **wassoulou.** Sa musique est inspirée des musiques et danses traditionnelles de la région. Elle utilise une percussion traditionnelle jouée par les femmes dans les mariages, *la gita*, faite d'une calebasse à laquelle sont attachés des coquillages. Ses chansons s'appuient sur une critique sociale, notamment de la place de la femme dans la société.

Il existe aussi un style hybride, **le blues malien**, mélange de musique arabe et de blues américain, où la guitare électrique a le premier rôle. Ali Farka Touré est le plus célèbre «bluesman» malien.

Core Instruction

TEACHING CHRONIQUES

1. Before class, prepare questions and statements about the music of these African countries based on the information presented in the **Chroniques,** such as, **C'est une genre musical et littéraire arabe,** or **Comment s'appelle le célèbre «bluesman» malien?** Write these questions and statements on the board or on a transparency, and have partners find all the answers as quickly as possible. **(5 min.)**

2. Give students a few minutes to read the questions in **Après la lecture,** and clarify anything they do not understand, before they read the text. **(4 min.)**

3. Have students read the three sections carefully, then answer the questions in **Après la lecture. (20 min.)**

Chroniques

Answers

1. Answers will vary.
2. Elvis Presley, Johnny Halliday
3. Une calebasse à laquelle sont attachés des coquillages.
4. le n'goni, la cora
5. le mbalax, le yella
6. les musiques de Cuba et du Sénégal
7. les calebasses, la cora, le balafon

Le Sénégal

Au Sénégal, la musique et la danse font partie de toutes les occasions traditionnelles où l'on se rassemble autour d'un griot. Les sujets peuvent être l'histoire du village ou d'une famille mais aussi des pamphlets anticolonialistes, des chansons d'amour ou des hommages à de célèbres guerriers. La musique traditionnelle n'emploie que des instruments fabriqués avec des matériaux locaux comme le bois (le sabar, le djembé), des calebasses (la cora, le balafon), du cuir (les peaux de tambours, de luths et de harpes), des cornes de vache et des coquillages.

Un style sénégalais s'est imposé comme référence musicale africaine: **le mbalax**. Le mbalax est sans doute la musique sénégalaise la plus connue, grâce notamment à Youssou N'Dour. Sur un mélange de rythmes traditionnels et modernes, il mêle des instruments européens aux instruments typiquement sénégalais comme le djembé et le tama.

Mais le mbalax n'est qu'un des styles sénégalais modernes. Il y a aussi le **yella**, rythme d'origine pulaar, ethnie du nord du Sénégal, rendu mondialement célèbre par un de ses principaux interprètes, Baaba Maal, qui en fait n'était pas destiné à devenir musicien, n'étant pas issu d'une famille de griots.

Laba Socé et l'Orchestra Baobab ont été les précurseurs de la **salsa**, version sénégalaise, qui mêle les musiques de Cuba et du Sénégal. Et plus récemment, les influences jamaïcaines du reggae, et américaines du hip-hop et du rap, ont entraîné la formation de nombreux groupes qui fusionnent les genres et instruments traditionnels avec l'expression hip-hop et une thématique de problèmes sociaux actuels (en particulier la lutte contre le sida). En décembre 2005, la 5e édition du festival «HIP HOP AWARDS» à Dakar, avait pour thème central la lutte contre la circulation des armes en Afrique.

Oumou Sangaré

la gita

la cora

APRÈS la lecture

1. Pourquoi le raï moderne est-il mieux accepté en Algérie maintenant?
2. Quels musiciens ont inspiré Khaled?
3. Qu'est-ce qu'une *gita*?
4. Cite deux instruments traditionnels africains.
5. Quels sont deux styles de musique sénégalaises?
6. Quels genres de musique est-ce que Laba Socé mélange?
7. Y a-t-il des instruments communs au Sénégal et au Mali?

🌸 1.2, 3.1

Comparisons

Comparing and Contrasting

Have students compare and contrast the music styles of France, (see previous **Chroniques**), those of Africa, presented here, and those that they typically associate with the U.S. Ask them to consider how culture and traditions of an area can affect its music genres.

🌸 4.2

Postreading

If available, bring in CDs by the featured artists and play an appropriate selection of excerpts. Have students try to guess which artist sings each song or what type of music it represents, based on what they read in the **Chroniques.** Then have students discuss the songs and give their opinions of each one. 🌸 3.2

Recherches

Divide the class into groups and have each group research one of the traditional musical instruments mentioned in the **Chroniques.** Have each group prepare a short presentation on their instrument. Remind students to document their sources.

🌸 3.1

Differentiated Instruction

SLOWER PACE LEARNERS

Variation You may want to convert **Après la lecture** to a multiple choice activity. Write the questions, with three possible answers for each one (one correct and two distractors), on the board or on a transparency and call on students to choose the correct answer. 🌸 1.2

SPECIAL LEARNING NEEDS

Students with Learning Disabilities/ Dyslexia To accommodate students with learning challenges in reading, have an advanced student read the text aloud slowly, as the rest of the class follows along. Students with learning disabilities/dyslexia will then be able to focus on understanding the text instead of struggling with the reading. 🌸 1.2

Références

Références

La France

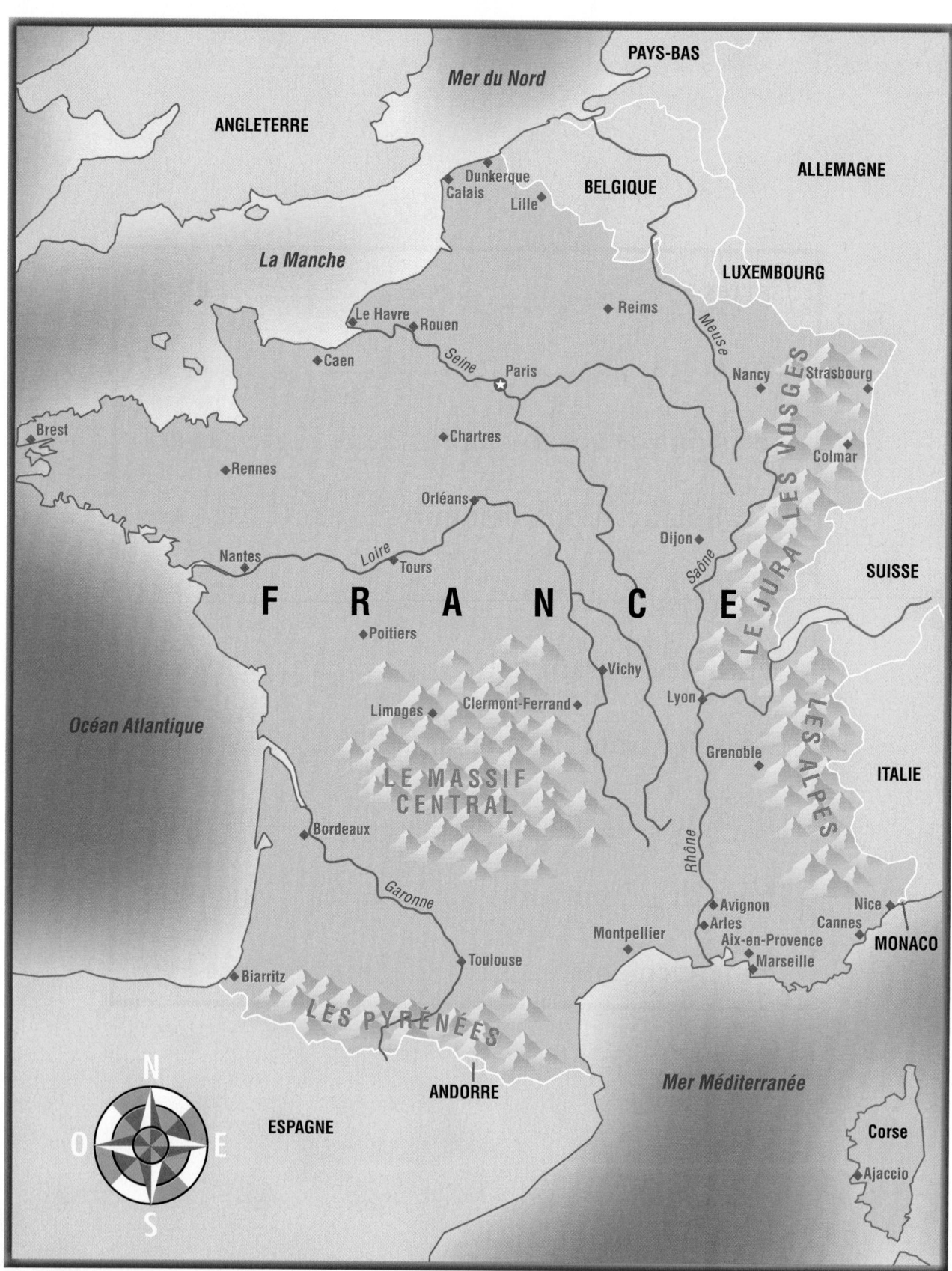

ANGLETERRE
Mer du Nord
PAYS-BAS
BELGIQUE
ALLEMAGNE
Dunkerque
Calais
Lille
La Manche
LUXEMBOURG
Le Havre
Rouen
Reims
Meuse
Nancy
Strasbourg
Caen
Seine
Paris
Brest
Chartres
Colmar
Rennes
Orléans
Dijon
LES VOSGES
Nantes
Loire
Tours
Saône
SUISSE
F R A N C E
LE JURA
Poitiers
Vichy
Clermont-Ferrand
Lyon
Océan Atlantique
Limoges
Grenoble
LES ALPES
ITALIE
LE MASSIF
CENTRAL
Rhône
Bordeaux
Garonne
Avignon
Nice
Arles
Cannes
Montpellier
Aix-en-Provence
MONACO
Toulouse
Marseille
Biarritz
LES PYRÉNÉES
N
O   E
S
ANDORRE
Mer Méditerranée
ESPAGNE
Corse
Ajaccio

L'Europe francophone

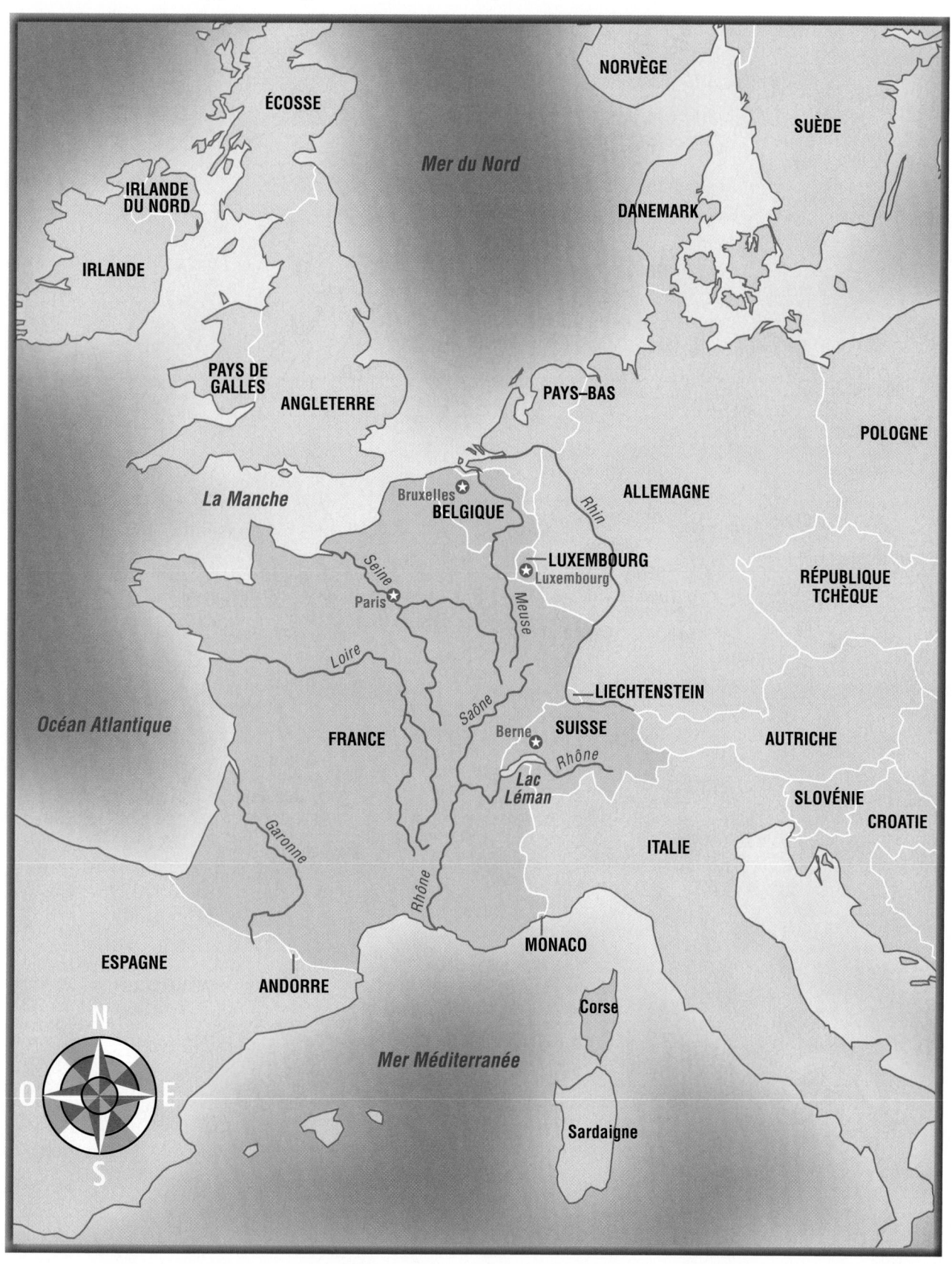

NORVÈGE

ÉCOSSE

SUÈDE

Mer du Nord

IRLANDE DU NORD

DANEMARK

IRLANDE

PAYS DE GALLES

ANGLETERRE

PAYS-BAS

POLOGNE

La Manche

Bruxelles
BELGIQUE

Rhin

ALLEMAGNE

LUXEMBOURG
Luxembourg

RÉPUBLIQUE TCHÈQUE

Seine

Paris

Meuse

Loire

LIECHTENSTEIN

Saône

Océan Atlantique

FRANCE

Berne
SUISSE

Rhône

AUTRICHE

Lac Léman

SLOVÉNIE

Garonne

CROATIE

ITALIE

Rhône

MONACO

ESPAGNE

ANDORRE

Corse

Mer Méditerranée

N
O   E
S

Sardaigne

L'Afrique francophone

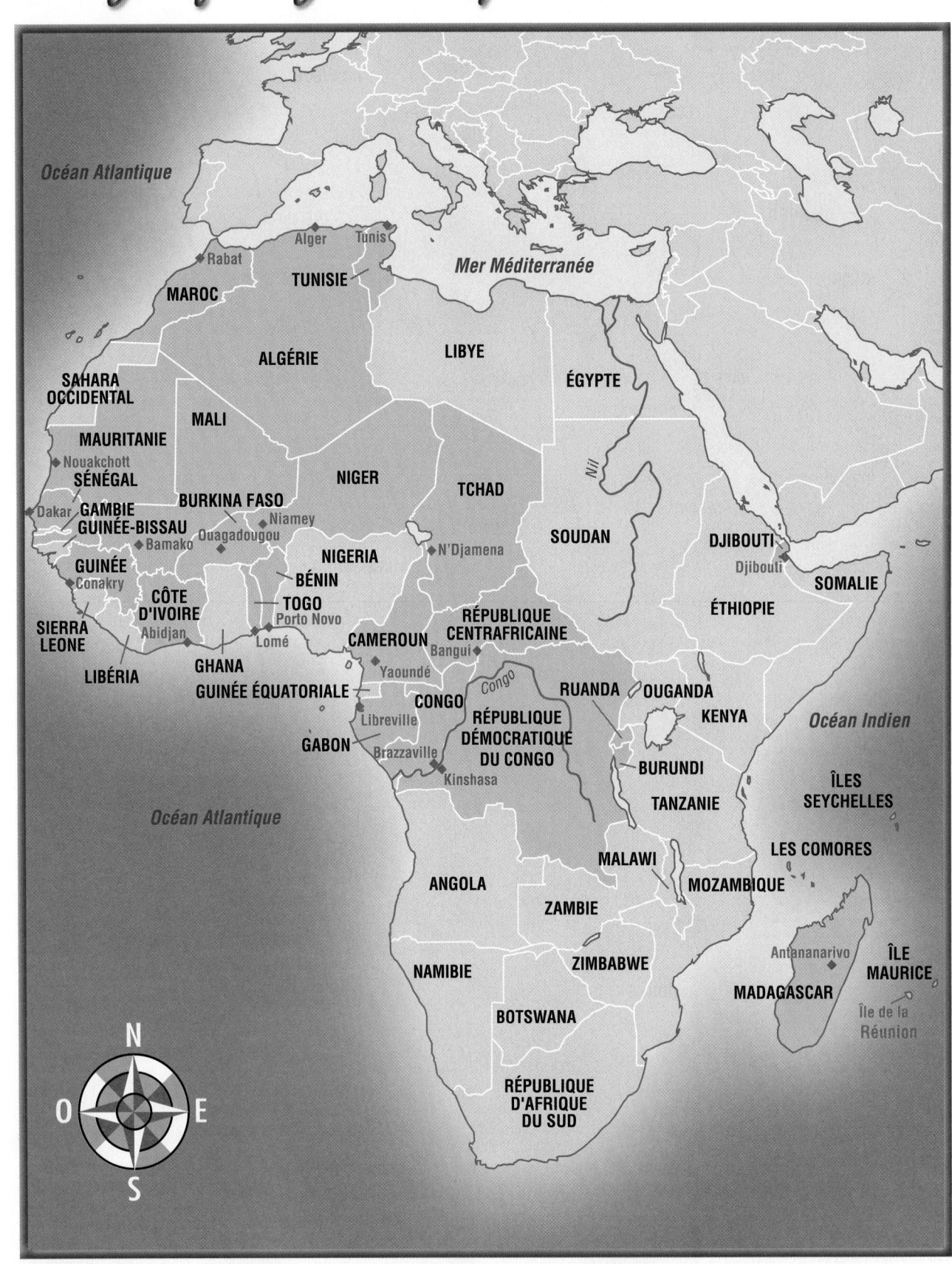

Océan Atlantique

Rabat
Alger
Tunis

MAROC
TUNISIE

Mer Méditerranée

ALGÉRIE
LIBYE
ÉGYPTE

SAHARA OCCIDENTAL
MALI
MAURITANIE
Nouakchott
SÉNÉGAL
NIGER
TCHAD
SOUDAN
DJIBOUTI
Djibouti

Dakar
GAMBIE
BURKINA FASO
Niamey
GUINÉE-BISSAU
Ouagadougou
Bamako
N'Djamena
SOMALIE

GUINÉE
NIGERIA
BÉNIN
ÉTHIOPIE
Conakry
CÔTE D'IVOIRE
TOGO
Porto Novo

SIERRA LEONE
Abidjan
Lomé
CAMEROUN
Bangui
RÉPUBLIQUE CENTRAFRICAINE

LIBÉRIA
GHANA
Yaoundé
Congo

GUINÉE ÉQUATORIALE
CONGO
RUANDA
OUGANDA
KENYA
Océan Indien

Libreville
RÉPUBLIQUE DÉMOCRATIQUE DU CONGO
GABON
Brazzaville
BURUNDI

Kinshasa
ÎLES SEYCHELLES

Océan Atlantique
TANZANIE
LES COMORES

MALAWI
MOZAMBIQUE

ANGOLA
ZAMBIE
Antananarivo
ÎLE MAURICE

NAMIBIE
ZIMBABWE
MADAGASCAR
Île de la Réunion

BOTSWANA

RÉPUBLIQUE D'AFRIQUE DU SUD

N
O
E
S

L'Amérique francophone

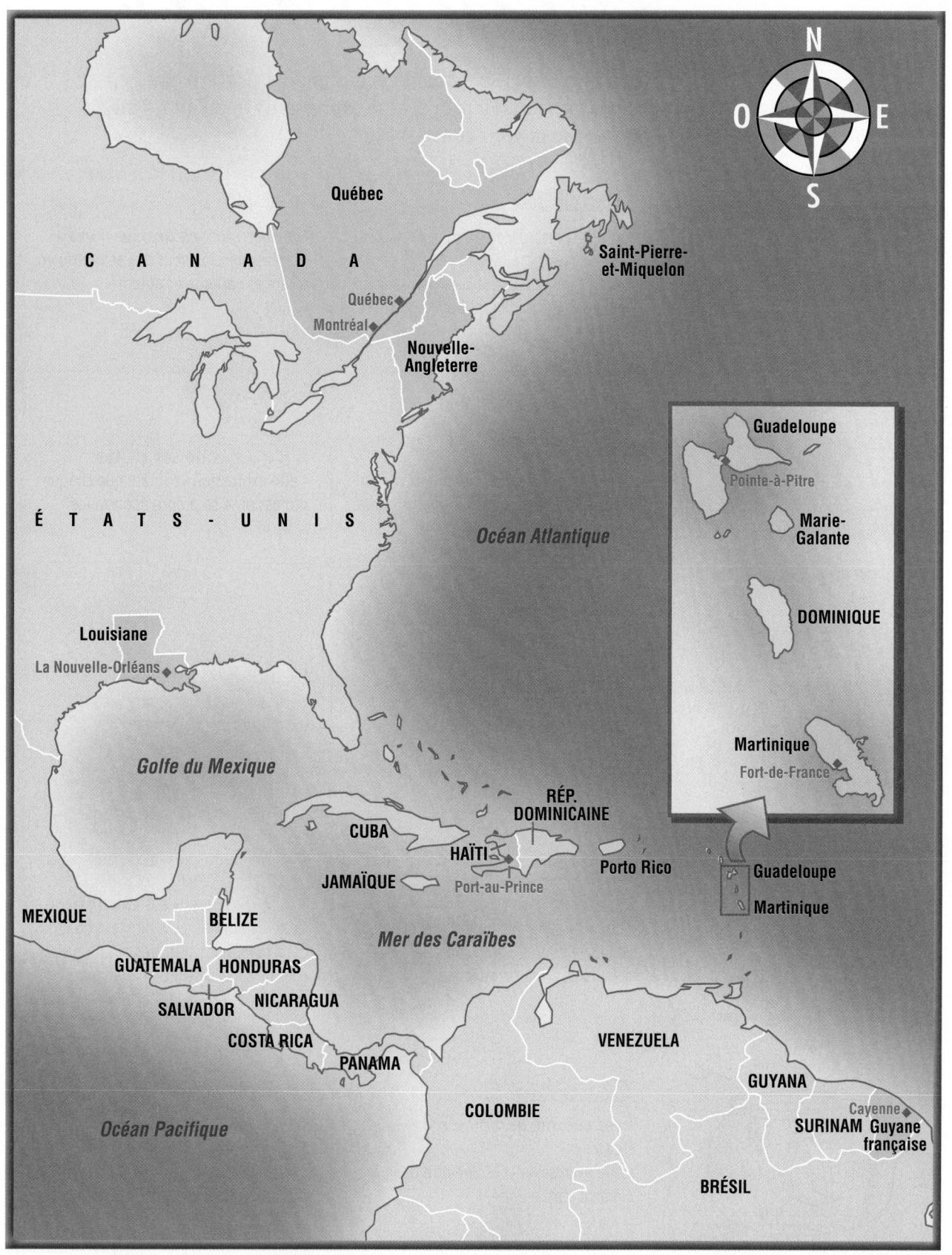

Québec

C A N A D A

Saint-Pierre-
et-Miquelon

Québec ◆
Montréal ◆

Nouvelle-
Angleterre

É T A T S - U N I S

Océan Atlantique

Louisiane

La Nouvelle-Orléans ◆

Golfe du Mexique

CUBA

HAÏTI
Port-au-Prince

RÉP.
DOMINICAINE

Porto Rico

JAMAÏQUE

MEXIQUE

BELIZE

Mer des Caraïbes

GUATEMALA   HONDURAS

SALVADOR   NICARAGUA

COSTA RICA

PANAMA

VENEZUELA

GUYANA

Océan Pacifique

COLOMBIE

Cayenne ◆

SURINAM Guyane
française

BRÉSIL

Guadeloupe
Pointe-à-Pitre

Marie-
Galante

DOMINIQUE

Martinique
Fort-de-France ◆

Guadeloupe

Martinique

Proverbes
et expressions

Like English speakers, the French often use proverbs in their everyday speech. Here are some expressions that you might want to use in your conversations.

Chapitre 1

Parler français comme une vache espagnole
Cette expression est utilisée pour décrire quelqu'un qui parle mal français.

Monter sur ses grands chevaux
Cette expression veut dire se mettre en colère et parler avec autorité.

Chapitre 2

À chacun son métier
Cette expression veut dire que si chacun s'occupe de ses propres affaires, tout ira pour le mieux.

Il n'y a pas de sot métier
Cette expression veut dire que chaque profession a sa propre importance.

Chapitre 3

Aller à pas de géant
Cette expression veut dire faire des progrès rapides.

En raconter de belles
Cette expression veut dire raconter des histoires invraisemblables.

Chapitre 4

L'amour est aveugle
Cette expression veut dire que lorsque l'on est amoureux on ne voit pas les défauts de la personne aimée

Vivre d'amour et d'eau fraîche
Cette expression veut dire que quand deux personnes sont très amoureuses elles ne s'inquiètent de rien d'autre, comme par exemple d'acheter à manger.

Chapitre 5

Être comme un poisson dans l'eau
Cette expression veut dire être dans son élément, être à l'aise.

Il ne faut pas vendre la peau de l'ours avant de l'avoir tué
Cette expression veut dire qu'il ne faut pas promettre quelque chose sans être sûr de pouvoir le faire.

Chapitre 6

Pas de nouvelles, bonnes nouvelles
Cette expression veut dire que quand on n'a pas de nouvelles de quelqu'un, on peut présumer que tout va bien.

Les mauvaises nouvelles ont des ailes
Cette expression veut dire qu'on a plus vite les mauvaises nouvelles que les bonnes nouvelles.

Chapitre 7

Il faut de tout pour faire un monde.
Cette expression veut dire que chaque personne peut avoir ses propres goûts et sa propre personnalité.

Tout est pour le mieux dans le meilleur des mondes
Cette expression est utilisée pour dire que tout pourrait être pire.

Chapitre 8

Plus royaliste que le roi
Cette expression s'utilise pour décrire quelqu'un qui a une opinion encore plus extrême que l'idée qu'il défend.

Diviser pour régner
Cette expression veut dire que pour rester au pouvoir, il faut choisir des subordonnés qui se détestent pour empêcher les alliances.

Chapitre 9

La musique adoucit les mœurs
Cette expression veut dire que la musique rend les personnes plus aimables.

Occuper les devants de la scène
Cette expression veut dire occuper une position importante.

Chapitre 10

À vol d'oiseau
Cette expression est utilisée pour parler de la distance la plus courte. On peut dire que la distance entre Paris et Nice est de 900 km **à vol d'oiseau**. Ce n'est pas une distance exacte.

Les voyages forment la jeunesse
Cette expression veut dire que c'est bien de voyager quand on est jeune, c'est-à-dire qu'on apprend beaucoup en voyageant.

Proverbes et expressions

APRÈS la lecture

🍀 1.1, 4.1

1. Can you think of English equivalents for some of these proverbs and expressions?

2. Pick a proverb that is not illustrated and work in groups of three to create an illustration to explain it.

3. Search the Internet or at the Library to find additional proverbs that use vocabulary and themes you've learned.

4. Work in small groups to create a mini-skit in which you use one or more of these proverbs in context.

Révisions de vocabulaire

This list includes words introduced in Bien dit! Level 2. If you can't find the words you need here, try the French-English and English-French vocabulary sections beginning on page R59.

beginning on page R59.

Les animaux (Animals)

l'âne (m.)	donkey
l'araignée (f.)	spider
le canard	duck
le cheval	horse
la chèvre	goat
le cochon	pig
le flamant rose	flamingo
la grenouille	frog
l'insecte (m.)	insect
le lapin	rabbit
le lézard	lizard
la mouche	fly
le moustique	mosquito
le mouton	sheep
l'oiseau (m.)	bird
le pélican	pelican
la poule	chicken
le serpent	snake
la tortue	turtle
la vache	cow

Le camping (Camping)

aller à la pêche	to go fishing
attraper un poisson	to catch a fish
se baigner	to swim
le bateau	boat
la boîte d'allumettes	box of matches
la boussole	compass
la bouteille isotherme	thermos
le briquet	lighter
camper	to camp out
le camping	camping
la crème solaire	sunscreen
démonter la tente	to take down a tent
le désinfectant	disinfectant
faire un feu de camp	to make a campfire
le fauteuil pliant	folding chair
le gilet de sauvetage	life jacket
la gourde	canteen
la lampe de poche	flashlight
la lanterne	lantern
la lotion anti-moustiques	mosquito repellent
monter la tente	to pitch a tent
la moustiquaire	mosquito net
l'ouvre-boîte (m.)	can opener
se promener	to take a stroll
le réchaud	camping stove

Le corps (Body)

le bras	arm
le cerveau	brain
les cheveux (m.)	hair
la cheville	ankle
le cœur	heart
le corps	body
le cou	neck
le doigt (de pied)	finger (toe)
le dos	back

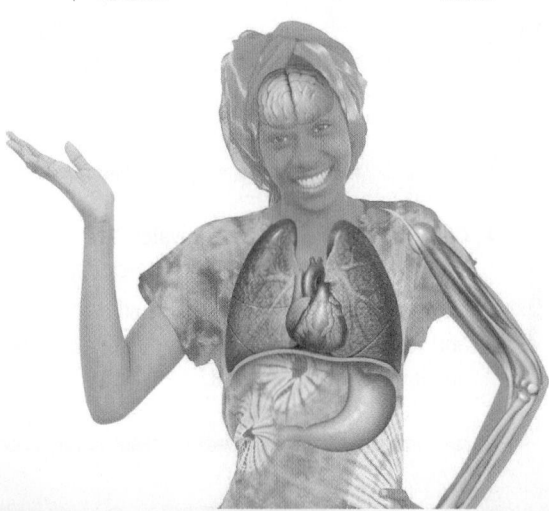

l'épaule (f.)	shoulder	
l'estomac (m.)	stomach	
le front	forehead	
le genou	knee	
la jambe	leg	
la joue	cheek	
la lèvre	lip	
la main	hand	
le muscle	muscle	
l'œil (m.)	eye	
l'os (m.)	bone	
le pied	foot	
le poignet	wrist	
le poumon	lung	
le sourcil	eyebrow	
le visage	face	
les yeux (m.)	eyes	

Les corvées (Chores)

faire les courses	to go grocery shopping
faire le ménage	to do housework
faire la poussière	to dust
ranger la maison	to tidy up the house
ranger ses affaires	to put one's things away
s'occuper (de)	to take care (of)

Les descriptions (Descriptions)

âgé(e)	old
blond(e)	blond(e)
bruyant(e)	noisy
calme	calm
content(e)	happy
court(e)	short
dangereux(-euse)	dangerous
gentil(le)	nice
grand(e)	tall
gros(se)	fat
intelligent(e)	intelligent
long(ue)	long
marrant(e)	funny
mince	slim
obéissant(e)	obedient
pénible	annoying
pollué(e)	polluted
propre	clean
pur(e)	clear
roux (rousse)	red-headed
sale	dirty
sérieux(-euse)	serious
sportif (sportive)	athletic
stressant(e)	stressful

tranquille	peaceful
triste	sad
vert(e)	green
vivant(e)	vibrant

Faire sa toilette
(Washing up)

la baignoire	bathtub
la brosse	brush
la brosse à dents	toothbrush
se brosser les cheveux	to brush one's hair
se brosser les dents	to brush one's teeth
se coiffer	to do one's hair
la crème à raser	shaving cream
le dentifrice	toothpaste
le déodorant	deodorant
la douche	shower
le gel douche	shower gel
faire sa toilette	to clean (oneself) up
le lavabo	sink
se laver les cheveux	to wash one's hair
se laver la figure	to wash one's face

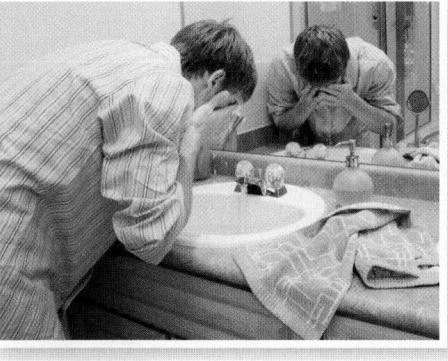

le maquillage	make-up
se maquiller	to put on makeup
le mascara	mascara
le peigne	comb
se peigner (les cheveux)	to comb (one's hair)
le peignoir	robe
prendre un bain	to take a bath
prendre une douche	to take a shower
se préparer	to get ready
se raser	to shave
le rasoir (électrique)	(electric) razor
le rouge à lèvres	lipstick
le savon	soap
le sèche-cheveux	blow-dryer
se sécher les cheveux	to dry one's hair
la serviette de bain	bath towel
la serviette de toilette	hand towel
le shampooing	shampoo

La famille *(Family)*

le chat	*cat*
le chien	*dog*
le/la cousin(e)	*cousin*
le frère	*brother*
la grand-mère	*grandmother*
le grand-père	*grandfather*
la mère	*mother*
l'oncle (m.)	*uncle*
le père	*father*
la sœur	*sister*
la tante	*aunt*

La ferme *(Farm)*

la basse-cour	*barnyard*
la campagne	*countryside*
le champ	*field*
la ferme	*farm*
la grange	*barn*
le paysage	*landscape*
la prairie	*meadow*
le tracteur	*tractor*
le village	*village*

Les fêtes *(Parties/holidays)*

allumer (les bougies)	*to light (the candles)*
les amuse-gueules (m.)	*snacks*
l'anniversaire	*birthday*
le bal populaire	*village dance*
le ballon	*balloon*
la boîte de chocolats	*box of chocolates*
les bougies (f.)	*candles*
le bouquet de fleurs	*bouquet of flowers*
la boum	*party*
la bûche de Noël	*Yule log*
les cadeaux (m.)	*presents*
la carte d'anniversaire	*birthday card*
la carte de vœux	*greeting card*

le chèque-cadeau	*gift card*
choisir la musique	*to choose the music*
les confettis (m.)	*confetti*
les décorations (f.)	*decorations*
décorer la salle	*to decorate the room*
le défilé	*parade*
emballer les cadeaux (m.)	*to wrap presents*
envoyer les invitations (f.)	*to send the invitations*
les fêtes (f.)	*parties/holidays*
la fête des mères	*Mother's Day*
la fête des pères	*Father's Day*
la fête nationale	*national holiday*
le feu d'artifice	*fireworks*
la foule	*crowd*

l'hymne national (m.)	*national anthem*
l'invité(e)	*guest*
le jour de l'an	*New Year's Day*
Noël	*Christmas*
le nouvel an	*New Year's*
organiser une soirée/fête	*to plan a party/mixer*
préparer la maison	*to prepare the house*
remercier	*to thank*
le réveillon	*midnight feast*
le sapin de Noël	*Christmas tree*
la soirée costumée	*costume party*

Les films *(Films)*

l'acteur (m.)	*actor*
l'actrice (f.)	*actress*
le drame	*drama*
le film classique	*classic movie*
le film comique	*a comedy*

le film d'action	action movie
le film d'aventures	adventure movie
le film d'espionnage	spy movie
le film d'horreur	horror movie
le film de guerre	war movie
le film de science-fiction	science-fiction movie
le film étranger	foreign film
l'héroïne (f.)	heroine
le héros	hero
le metteur en scène	director
le personnage principal	main character
le sous-titre	subtitle
la vedette	star
la version originale (V.O.)	original version

La littérature *(Literature)*

l'(auto)biographie (f.)	(auto)biography
le genre	genre/type
la pièce de théâtre	play
le recueil de poésie	poetry collection
le roman d'amour	romance novel
le roman fantastique	fantasy novel
le roman historique	historical novel
le roman policier	mystery novel

Au lycée *(In high school)*

aller au lycée	to go to high school
avoir entraînement	to have practice/training
la cantine	cafeteria
le CDI	library/resource center
une compétition	contest/competition
le complexe sportif	sports complex
le/la conseiller(-ière) d'éducation	school counselor

la cour de récré(ation)	playground
le/la documentaliste	librarian
emprunter (un livre)	to borrow (a book)
être en retenue	to be in detention
faire des recherches	to do research
faire ses devoirs	to do one's homework
faire une expérience	to do an experiment
le gymnase	gymnasium
l'infirmerie (f.)	nurse's office
l'interro(gation) (f.)	quiz
le laboratoire	laboratory
les lunettes (f.) de protection	safety glasses
la note	grade
passer un examen	to take a test
la piste (d'athlétisme)	(athletic) track
préparer son sac	to get one's backpack ready
prendre le bus	to take the bus
rater	to fail (an exam, a class)
rendre (un livre)	to return (a book)
réussir (à)	to pass (an exam, a class)
la salle d'informatique	computer room
suivre un cours	to take a class
le terrain de sport	sports field

La musique *(Music)*

l'animateur (m.)	disc jockey
l'animatrice (f.)	disc jockey
le blues	blues
le country	country
le hip-hop	hip-hop
le jazz	jazz
la pop	pop
le rap	rap
le reggae	reggae
le rock	rock
la techno	techno
le son	sound
le vidéoclip	music video

La nature (Nature)

l'arbre (m.)	tree
le bois	woods
la cascade	waterfall
la fleur	flower
le fleuve	river
la forêt	forest
la nature	nature
la plage	beach
la rivière	river
le sentier	path
le sommet	peak
la toile d'araignée	spider web
la vallée	valley

La nourriture (Food)

l'abricot (m.)	apricot
l'ail (m.)	garlic
ajouter	to add
l'aubergine (f.)	eggplant
la banane	banana
les biscuits (m.)	cookies
la boîte (de conserve)	canned food/ a box (can) of…
du bœuf	beef
les bonbons (m.)	sweets/candy
bouillir	to boil
le brocoli	broccoli
les cacahuètes (m.)	peanuts
le café	café/coffee
la carotte	carrot
la cerise	cherry
le champignon	mushroom
la charcuterie	delicatessen
le chariot	shopping cart
les chips (m.)	chips
le chocolat chaud	hot chocolate
le coca	soda
la courgette	zucchini
couper	to cut
les crevettes (f.)	shrimp
le croque- monsieur	toasted cheese sandwich w/ham
les épices (f.)	spices
faire cuire	to bake, to cook
la farine	flour
le four	oven
la fraise	strawberry
la framboise	raspberry
la fromagerie	cheese market
les fruits (m.)	fruit(s)
les fruits de mer (m.)	seafood

les fruits secs (m.)	dried fruit
le gâteau	cake
la glace	ice cream
les haricots verts (m.)	green beans
l'huile (d'olive) (f.)	(olive) oil
les huîtres (f.)	oyster(s)
le jus de fruit	fruit juice
la laitue	lettuce
les légumes (m.)	vegetables
la limonade	lemon-lime soda
manger	to eat
mélanger	to mix
le melon	melon

l'oignon (m.)	onion
le paquet (m.) de pâtes (f.)	a package of pasta
la pastèque	watermelon
la pâtisserie	pastry shop
la pêche	peach
les petits pois (m.)	peas
la poire	pear
le poivron	bell pepper
la pomme	apple
la pomme de terre	potato
le pot (m.) de confiture (f.)	a jar of jam
le poulet	chicken
le sac en plastique	plastic bag
le sandwich au jambon	ham sandwich
le sucre	sugar
la tarte aux pommes	apple tart
la tomate	tomato
le yaourt	yogurt

L'ordinateur (Computer)

l'accueil	home page
actualiser	refresh (Internet)
l'adresse (f.)	address
l'affichage (m.)	view
arrêter	stop (Internet)
les barres de défilement	scroll bars
le clavier	keyboard

cliquer	*to click*
le courrier	*mail*
le démarrage	*home (Internet)*
démarrer	*to start up*
l'écran (m.)	*screen*
l'édition (f.)	*edit*
les favoris (m.)	*favorites (Internet)*
la fenêtre	*window (Internet)*
le fichier	*file*
graver	*to burn (a CD)*
le graveur de CD/DVD	*CD/DVD burner*
l'imprimante (f.)	*printer*
imprimer	*to print*
s'informer sur Internet	*to find out/to inquire on the Internet*
l'interface (f.)	*interface*
les liens	*links (Internet)*
le logiciel	*software*
le menu déroulant	*pull-down menu*
le moniteur	*monitor*
le navigateur	*browser*
naviguer	*to navigate*
les outils	*tools*
planter	*to crash (a computer)*
la précédente	*back (Internet)*
rechercher	*to research*
retour	*return*
sauvegarder	*to save (a document)*
la souris	*the mouse*
la suivante	*forward (Internet)*
télécharger	*to download*
la touche	*key*
valider	*OK (Internet)*

Les pays et les nationalités
(Countries and nationalities)

à l'étranger	*abroad*
l'Allemagne	*Germany*
allemand(e)	*German*
anglais(e)	*English/British*
l'Angleterre	*England*
la Belgique	*Belgium*
le Danemark	*Denmark*
l'Espagne	*Spain*
espagnol(e)	*Spanish*
la France	*France*

la Grèce	*Greece*
italien(ne)	*Italian*
l'Italie	*Italy*
portugais(e)	*Portuguese*
le Portugal	*Portugal*
la Suisse	*Switzerland*
la Norvège	*Norway*

Les petits commerces
(Small businesses)

le/la boucher(-ère)	*butcher*
la boucherie	*butcher shop*
le/la boulanger(-ère)	*baker*
la boulangerie	*bakery*
le/la caissier(-ière)	*cashier*
la crémerie	*dairy market*
l'épicerie (f.)	*grocery store*
l'épicier(-ière)	*grocer*
le/la poissonnier(-ière)	*fish monger*
la poissonnerie	*fish market*

Les quantités (Quantities)

une bouteille de…	*a bottle of . . .*
une cuillerée à café	*teaspoon*
une cuillerée à soupe	*tablespoon*
une douzaine de…	*a dozen . . .*
un kilo(gramme) de…	*a kilogram of . . .*
un litre de…	*a liter of . . .*
une livre de…	*a pound of . . .*
un morceau de…	*a piece of . .*
une tasse de…	*a cup of . . .*
une tranche de…	*a slice of . . .*

La routine quotidienne
(Daily routine)

aller au travail	*to go to work*
se coucher	*to go to bed*
se déshabiller	*to get undressed*
s'en aller	*to run along*
s'endormir	*to fall asleep*
s'habiller	*to get dressed*
se lever	*to get up / stand up*

la matinée	morning
se mettre au lit	to go to bed
se mettre en pyjama	to put on pajamas
se mettre en chemise de nuit	to put on a nightgown
prendre le petit-déjeuner	to have breakfast
rentrer à la maison	to return to the house
le réveil	alarm
se réveiller	to wake up
sonner	to ring
souhaiter une bonne nuit	to say goodnight

La santé (Health)

avoir de la fièvre	to have a fever
avoir la grippe	to have the flu
avoir un régime équilibré	to have a balanced diet
se blesser	to injure oneself
se brûler	to burn oneself
se casser la jambe	to break one's leg
chez le docteur	at the doctor's office
consommer trop de matières grasses	to consume/eat too many fatty foods
se couper	to cut oneself
le/la dentiste	dentist
éternuer	to sneeze
être en bonne santé	to be healthy
être fatigué(e)	to be tired
faire de la musculation	to lift weights
faire des abdominaux	to do abdominal exercises

faire de l'exercice	to exercise
faire des pompes	to do push ups
faire du yoga	to do yoga
faire un régime	to go on a diet
se faire vacciner	to get vaccinated
se fouler la cheville	to twist one's ankle
se fouler le poignet	to twist one's wrist
fumer	to smoke
manger léger	to eat light
le médecin	doctor
se nourrir	to feed oneself
se peser	to weigh oneself

perdre du poids	to lose weight
prendre des vitamines	to take vitamins
prendre du poids	to gain weight
prendre la température	to take someone's temperature
se priver de sommeil	to deprive oneself of sleep
les produits (m.) bio(logiques)	organic products
se relaxer	to relax
se reposer	to rest
sauter des repas	to skip meals
tousser	to cough
la vie	life

Les souvenirs d'enfance (Childhood memories)

aller au cirque (m.)	to go to the circus
collectionner	to collect
un copain	friend
faire de la balançoire	to swing
faire des châteaux de sable (m.)	to make sandcastles
faire des farces (f.)	to play practical jokes
faire du manège (m.)	to go on a carousel
grimper aux arbres (m.)	to climb trees
jouer au ballon (m.)	to play ball
jouer aux billes (f.)	to play marbles
jouer à chat perché	to play a game similar to tag
jouer aux dames (f.)	to play checkers
jouer à la marelle	to play dolls
jouer aux petites voitures (f.)	to play with matchbox cars
jouer à la poupée	to play dolls
jouer au train électrique (m.)	to play with electric trains
regarder des dessins animés (m.)	to watch cartoons
sauter à la corde	to jump rope

Les sports et les passe-temps (Sports and hobbies)

aller au cinéma	to go to the movies
l'appareil photo (m.) (numérique)	camera (digital)
la balle	(tennis) ball
le caméscope	video camera
faire de la photo	to do photography

faire de la planche à voile	*to windsurf*
faire de la vidéo amateur	*to do amateur videos*
faire de l'escalade	*to mountain climb*
faire du jogging	*to jog*
faire du théâtre	*to do theater/drama*
faire un séjour	*to stay/to sojourn*
faire une randonnée	*to go hiking*
faire une visite guidée	*to take a guided tour*
gagner	*to play chess*
jouer aux échecs	*to win*
jouer au tennis	*to play tennis*
jouer de la batterie	*to play drums*
jouer de la guitare	*to play guitar*
jouer du piano	*to play piano*
lire	*to read*
monter à cheval	*to horseback ride*
la raquette	*racket*
le spectacle son et lumière	*a sound and light show*
voir un film	*to see a movie*

La télé *(T.V.)*

le bulletin météo (rologique)	*weather report*
la chaîne	*station*
le documentaire	*documentary*
l'émission de variétés (f.)	*variety show*
les émissions télé (f.)	*television programs*
en direct	*live*
le feuilleton	*soap opera*
les informations (f.)	*news*
le jeu	*game show*
le présentateur	*newscaster*
la présentatrice	*newscaster*
le reportage sportif	*sports report*
la série	*series*
le soap	*soap opera*
le spot publicitaire	*commercial*
la télécommande	*remote control*

Les voyages *(Trips)*

acheter un guide	*to buy a guidebook*
à la campagne	*in the countryside*
à la montagne	*in the mountains*
aller en colonie de vacances	*to go to summer camp*
au bord de la mer	*at the seashore*
le billet	*ticket*
la brochure	*brochure*
changer de l'argent (m.)	*to change money*
le château	*castle*
les chèques de voyage (m.)	*traveller's checks*
en ville	*in the city*
faire sa valise	*to pack one's suitcase*
faire une demande de visa	*to apply for a visa*
faire une réservation d'avion	*to make an airline ticket reservation*
faire une réservation de billet de train	*to make a train ticket reservation*
faire une réservation d'hôtel	*to make a hotel reservation*
l'itinéraire (m.)	*itinerary/route*
l'office de tourisme (m.)	*tourist center*
le passeport	*passport*
la pièce	*coin*
le permis de conduire	*driver's license*
le plan	*map*
rendre visite à (une personne)	*to visit (a person)*
se renseigner dans une agence de voyages	*to get information at a travel agency*
le site d'une compagnie aérienne	*airline website*
la trousse de toilette	*vanity case*
visiter (un endroit)	*to visit (a place)*

Vocabulaire supplémentaire

This list includes additional vocabulary that you may want to use to personalize activities. If you can't find a word you need here, try the French-English and English-French vocabulary sections, beginning on page R59.

À l'école (At school)

apprendre par cœur	to memorize
le bulletin (le relevé) de notes	report card
le cours facultatif	optional course
le cours obligatoire	required course
la dissertation	paper
l'enseignant(e)	instructor
l'estrade (f.)	podium
l'étude de texte (f.)	text analysis
l'exposé (m.)	oral presentation
faire les révisions (f.)	to review, study for a test
les gradins (m. pl.)	bleachers
l'interro surprise (f.)	pop quiz
l'option (f.)	optional course, elective
le parc à vélos	bicycle parking area
le résumé	summary
réviser	to review, study for a test
le vestiaire	changing room

À la montagne (In the mountains)

le col	pass
la crête	ridge
l'éboulement (m.)	rockslide
le gîte de montagne	mountain cabin
les neiges éternelles (f. pl.)	perpetual snows
le pic	peak
le sommet	summit
le versant	mountain slope

À la mer (At the beach)

le banc de sable	sand bar
le bateau à moteur	motor boat
le bateau pneumatique	inflatable raft
la bouée	floating device, float
la dune	dune
l'écume (f.)	foam
l'îlot (m.)	small island
la jetée	pier
la lagune	lagoon
le matelas pneumatique	float, inflatable mattress
la pêche au gros	deep sea fishing
la vague	wave
le voilier	sailboat
le yacht	yacht

Les métiers (Professions)

l'assistant(e) social(e)	social worker
le/la chercheur(-euse)	researcher
le/la chirurgien(ne)	surgeon
le/la compositeur (-trice)	music composer
l'éleveur (m.)	cattle breeder
l'esthéticien(ne)	beautician, cosmetologist
le/la guide de tourisme	tourist guide
le/la kinésithérapeute	chiropractor
le/la maquilleur(-euse)	makeup artist
le médecin généraliste	general medicine physician

le/la programmeur (-euse)	computer programmer
le/la psychiatre	psychiatrist
le/la psychologue	psychologist
le réparateur	repairman
le/la reporter	journalist, reporter
le/la technicien(ne)	technician

Le monde du travail (Work)

l'assurance-maladie (f.)	health insurance
le/la candidat(e)	job applicant
la carrière	career
le/la chômeur(-euse)	unemployed person
la commission	commission
les congés payés (m. pl.)	paid vacation
les cotisations sociales (f. pl.)	social security/ pension contributions
cotiser pour la retraite	to contribute to one's pension
le déplacement	business trip
l'entretien d'embauche	job interview
être candidat(e) à un poste	to apply for a position
licencier	to lay off
le poste	position (job)
postuler	to apply for a job
les qualifications (f. pl.)	qualifications
la réussite	(financial) success
le salaire de base	base salary

Au téléphone (On the phone)

l'annuaire (m.)	phonebook
l'antenne (f.)	antenna
la commande mémoire	memory button
composer un numéro	to dial a phone number
l'indicatif (m.)	area/country code

l'interlocuteur(-trice)	interlocutor, person one is talking to
l'interrupteur (m.)	power button
la messagerie vocale	voicemail
les pages blanches (f. pl.)	white pages (phonebook)
les pages jaunes (f. pl.)	yellow pages (phonebook)
patienter (en ligne)	to wait, to hold (the line)
le poste	extension
le répertoire téléphonique	telephone index
la touche d'appel	talk key
la touche de fin d'appel	end key
la touche de sélection	selection key

Contes de fées (Fairy tales)

l'arc (m.)	bow
l'armure (f.)	armor
le bal	ball
la bête	beast
le carosse	horse-drawn carriage
le château-fort	fortified castle
la citrouille	pumpkin
la cour	(royal) court
les courtisans (m. pl.)	people of the court
la demoiselle	young lady of the court, damsel
le devoir	duty
le donjon	castle keep, tower
les douves (f. pl.)	moat
empoisonner	to poison
le filtre	magic potion
la flèche	arrow
le gentilhomme	gentleman
la jalousie	jealousy
jaloux(-ouse)	jealous
la lance	spear
la licorne	unicorn
la méchanceté	unkindness, wickedness
le poignard	dagger
le pont-levis	drawbridge
le prétendant	suitor
le souterrain	underground passage

Les conflits (Conflicts)

les armes biologiques (f. pl.)	biological weapons
les armes chimiques (f. pl.)	chemical weapons
les armes nucléaires (f. pl.)	nuclear weapons
attaquer	to attack, engage in battle
battre en retraite	to retreat
la bombe	bomb
les champs de mines (m. pl.)	mine fields
le désarmement	disarmament
les droits de l'homme (m. pl.)	human rights
l'ethnie (f.)	ethnic group
exploser	to explode
faire prisonnier	to take prisoner
la guerre civile	civil war
le missile	missile
le porte-avion	aircraft carrier
le prisonnier de guerre	war prisoner
les rebelles (m. pl.)	rebels
se battre	to fight, combat
la tranchée	trench

La vie (Life)

l'adolescence (f.)	adolescence
l'alliance (f.)	wedding band
la bague de fiançailles	engagement ring
le baptême	baptism
les biens (m. pl.)	assets
la cérémonie civile (religieuse)	civil (religious) ceremony
le cimetière	cemetery
le/la conjoint(e)	spouse
demander en mariage	to ask in marriage
dire une prière	to say a prayer

le domicile conjugal	marital home
l'enterrement (m.)	burial, funeral
enterrer	to bury
les fiançailles (f. pl.)	engagement
fonder une famille	to start a family
le foyer	household
les funérailles (f. pl.)	funerals
la garde des enfants	custody of children
des jeunes mariés (m. pl.)	newlyweds
la lune de miel	honeymoon
le ménage	household, family
la messe	mass
les noces (f. pl.)	wedding
pendre la crémaillère	to have a house warming party
le/la retraité(e)	retiree
la rumeur	rumor, gossip
les seniors (m. pl.)	senior citizens
la tombe	grave
trahir	to betray
le troisième âge	retirement years
tromper	to cheat
verser une pension alimentaire	to pay child support, alimony
le voyage de noces	honeymoon

La faune (Fauna)

l'âne (m.)	donkey
l'antilope (f.)	antelope
le bison	bison
le caméléon	chameleon
le cerf	deer
le chameau	camel
le colibri	hummingbird
le corbeau	raven
la couleuvre	garter snake

Vocabulaire supplémentaire

le crapaud	toad
le flamant (rose)	(pink) flamingo
la girafe	giraffe
le gorille	gorilla
l'hippopotame (m.)	hippopotamus
la libellule	dragonfly
le lièvre	hare
la marmotte	groundhog
le moineau	sparrow
la mouche	fly
la otarie	sea lion
le paon	peacock
la pieuvre	octopus
le porc-épic	porcupine
la puce	flea
le raton laveur	raccoon
le renne	caribou
le sanglier	wild boar
la sauterelle	grasshopper
le scorpion	scorpion
le serpent à sonnette	rattlesnake
le singe	monkey
le tigre	tiger
le vautour	vulture
le zèbre	zebra

Le matériel pour les sports extrêmes
(Extreme sports equipment)

la barre	tiller (boat)
le casque	helmet
la combinaison de ski	ski suit
la dérive	centerboard (boat)
le détendeur	scuba regulator
le gouvernail	rudder
le guidon	handlebar
des lunettes (f. pl.)	goggles
le masque de plongée (de ski)	dive (ski) mask
le mât	mast
la motoneige	snowmobile
des palmes (f. pl.)	fins
le protège-tibia	shin guard

le scooter de mer	jet ski
la selle	seat (bicycle, jet ski, motorcycle, etc.)
le surf des neiges	snowboard
le tuba	snorkel

La presse (The press)

l'abonnement (m.)	subscription
l'article de fond (m.)	in-depth article
l'exemplaire (m.)	copy
l'immobilier (m.)	real estate section
la publicité	advertisement
le sommaire	table of contents

L'actualité (The news)

assassiner	to assassinate
le cambriolage	robbery
la campagne (une vague) de terrorisme	terrorist campaign
les conditions de travail (f. pl.)	work environment
la criminalité	crime
lacrise économique	economic crisis
la délinquance (juvénile)	(juvenile) delinquency
demander une augmentation de salaire	to demand a raise
l'événement (m.)	event
l'insécurité (f.)	lack of safety
le meurtre	murder
la mondialisation	globalization
le taux de criminalité	crime rate
le terrorisme	terrorism
le/la terroriste	terrorist

Les phénomènes naturels
(Natural phenomena)

blesser	to hurt, injure
brûler	to burn
la catastrophe naturelle	natural catastrophe
les consignes de sécurité (f. pl.)	safety instructions
déborder	to overflow
les décombres (m. pl.)	rubble, debris
détruire	to destroy
ensevelir	to bury
la foudre	thunder
le nuage en entonnoir	funnel cloud
l'œil (m.)	eye (of a hurricane)
ordonner l'évacuation	to order evacuation
les secours (m. pl.)	rescuers, emergency workers
s'écrouler	to collapse
la trombe marine	waterspout
le typhon	typhoon

Les problèmes de l'environnement
(Environmental issues)

l'agriculture intensive (f.)	intensive farming
le bac de recyclage	recycling bin
le carton	cardboard
la centrale nucléaire	nuclear power plant
le centre de tri (pour le recyclage)	(recycling) sorting facility
le combustible fossile	fossil fuel
le conteneur	container
la décharge	landfill
les eaux usées (f. pl.)	waste water
l'élevage intensif (m.)	intensive cattle breeding
l'énergie atomique (f.)	nuclear power
les engrais (m. pl.)	fertilizers
le gaz à effet de serre	greenhouse gas

les ordures ménagères (f. pl.)	household waste
les pluies acides (f. pl.)	acid rain
le rayonnement solaire	solar radiation
le réchauffement global	global warming

La politique (Politics)

le centre	center (political)
la conscience politique	political awareness
la droite	right wing (political)
les écologistes (m. pl.)	"green" party, ecologists
la gauche	left wing (political)
l'injustice sociale (f.)	social injustice
la majorité	(political) majority
politisé	having a political slant
le porte-parole	spokesperson
le pouvoir (politique)	(political) power

Les services publics (Public services)

chercher des indices	to search for evidence
la civière	stretcher (ambulance)
commettre une infraction	to break a traffic law
le crime	serious crime, felony
le délit	misdemeanor
l'échelle (f.)	ladder (firefighting equipment)
enquêter	to investigate
faire de la réanimation	to perform CPR
faire une enquête	to conduct an investigation
la faute	fault
la fuite de gaz	gas leak
le gendarme	police officer (similar to a sheriff's deputy)

la preuve	proof
le procès	trial
le tribunal	courthouse

Les arts (The arts)

les accessoires (m. pl.)	stage props
l'acrobate (m./f.)	acrobat
l'artisan (m.)	craftsman
l'artisanat (m.)	arts and crafts
la brosse	brush (painting)
la céramique	ceramic, pottery
les chaussons (m. pl.)	ballet shoes
les costumes (m. pl.)	costumes
le cracheur de feu	fire blower
le four céramique	pottery kiln
la gouache	acrylic paint
huer	to boo
le metteur en scène	director
le/la mime	mime
le pinceau	paintbrush
le salle de spectacle	concert hall, performance hall
le vitrail	stained glass

Les voyages en avion (Air travel)

l'aérogare (m.)	terminal
l'aile (f.)	wing
attacher sa ceinture de sécurité	to fasten one's seat belt
la boutique hors taxe	duty-free shop
le compartiment de première classe	first-class cabin
le compartiment touriste	coach cabin
le comptoir d'enregistrement	baggage check-in counter
le comptoir de renseignements	information counter
le contrôle de sécurité	security check

le contrôle des passeports	passport control
le gilet de sauvetage	life jacket
l'office (m.)	galley (plane)
la passerelle télescopique	skywalk
le poste de pilotage	flight deck
le train d'atterrissage	landing gear
la voie de circulation	taxiway

Les voitures (Cars)

la banquette arrière	rear seat
la batterie	battery
la berline	four-door sedan
les bougies (f. pl.)	spark plugs
le break	station wagon
les câbles de démarrage (m. pl.)	jumper cables
la camionnette	van
le clignotant	turning signal
le cric	jack
la décapotable	convertible
l'embrayage (m.)	clutch
la manivelle	handle (for changing tires)
le pare-chocs	bumper
le pare-soleil	sun visor
la plaque d'immatriculation	license plate
la poignée	handle (door)
le pot d'échappement	muffler
le radiateur	radiator
le sac gonflable	airbag
la serrure	door lock
le siège	seat
le siège pour bébés	child car seat
le toit	roof
le toit ouvrant	moon roof
la trois-portes	hatchback
le véhicule tout-terrain	sport utility vehicle

Liste d'expressions

Functions are probably best defined as the ways in which you use a language for particular purposes. When you find yourself in specific situations, such as interviewing for a job or watching a play, you will want to communicate with those around you. In order to do that you have to "function" in French: you discuss your future plans, express your opinions or talk about what is going on in the world.

Here is a list of the functions presented in this book and the French expressions you'll need to communicate in a wide range of situations. Following each function is the chapter and page number where it is introduced.

Expressing Attitudes and Opinions

Expressing likes, dislikes, and preferences
Ch. 1, p. 7
    Mon/Ma... préféré(e), c'est...
    Ce que j'aime, c'est...
    J'aime bien... , mais je préfère...
    Je déteste... j'adore...

Asking for and giving advice
Ch. 4, p. 137
    Qu'est-ce que tu en penses?
    ... tu ferais mieux de...
    ... à ma place?
    Si j'avais été toi,...
    À ton avis,...?
    Pas nécessairement.
    D'après toi,...?
    Surtout pas!
    Jamais de la vie!

Complaining and offering encouragement
Ch. 5, p. 201
    C'est trop...!
    ... ça en vaut la peine.
    J'ai le vertige!
    Allez, encore un petit effort!
    Je meurs de...
    Tu y es presque!
    Je n'en peux plus!
    Courage,...!

Expressing certainty and possibility
Ch. 6, p. 225
    Je suis sûr(e) que...
    Je suis certain(e) que...
    Il/Elle est persuadé(e) que...
    Il me semble que...
    Il se peut que...
    Il est possible que...
    Il paraît que...

Expressing doubt and disbelief
Ch. 6, p. 226
    Je ne crois pas que...   Je doute que...
    Je ne pense pas que...   Ça m'étonnerait que...

Making predictions and expressing assumptions
Ch. 7, p. 289
    Ça ne m'étonnerait pas que...
    Je parie que...
    ... j'en suis sûr(e).
    Je suis convaincu(e) que...
    Je suppose que...

Expressing and supporting a point of view
Ch. 7, p. 291
    À priori,...
    D'un côté,... , d'un autre,...
    En principe,...
    Ce que je sais, c'est que...

Expressing a point of view
Ch. 8, p. 315
    En ce qui me concerne,...
    Pour ma part,...
    Je ne partage pas ton point de vue.

Speculating
Ch. 8, p. 317

À ce que l'on prétend,...
Il est probable que...
Il y a peu de chance que...
J'ai entendu dire que...
À supposer que ce soit vrai,...
Ça ne m'étonnerait pas que...

Asking for and giving an opinion
Ch. 9, p. 367

Comment trouves-tu...?
Surprenant(e)/Émouvant(e)...
... t'a-t-elle plu?
Je l'ai trouvé(e) passionnant(e)!
Quel est ton avis sur...?
Ce n'est pas mon style.
Qu'est-ce que tu penses de...?
... pas mal.

Making suggestions and recommendations
Ch. 9, p. 379

Je te recommande plutôt de...
Ne va surtout pas voir..., ... faux!
Va voir ..., sur scène...
Ça (ne) vaut (pas) la peine de...
Ça (ne) vaut (pas) le coup de...

Giving an impression
Ch. 9, p. 381

On dirait que...
Il me semble que...
J'ai l'impression de...
J'ai l'impression que...
Ils ont l'air de...
Ça me fait penser à...

Exchanging Information

Asking about plans and responding
Ch. 1, p. 9

Qu'est-ce que tu veux... comme...?
Je n'arrive pas à me décider.
Quel... tu vas...?
Je n'en sais rien.
Pourquoi on ne (n')... pas...?
Bonne idée!
Non, désolé(e), je n'ai pas le temps.

Telling when and how often you did something
Ch. 1, p. 19

... tous les jours...   Le soir,...

Quand...   Tous les deux jours,...

Describing a place in the past
Ch. 1, p. 21

Il y avait...   Il faisait...

... me rappelaient...   C'était...

Asking and telling about future plans
Ch. 2, p. 45

Qu'est-ce que tu as l'intention de...?
Ça me plairait de (d')...
Qu'est-ce que vous comptez faire... comme...?
... travailler dans...
... même... que...
Quels sont tes projets d'avenir?
Aucune idée.

Writing a formal letter
Ch. 2, p. 59

Suite à notre conversation téléphonique, ...
En réponse à votre petite annonce du...
Dans le cadre de ma formation,...
Veuillez trouver ci-joint mon curriculum vitae.
Je vous prie d'agréer, Monsieur/Madame,
    l'expression de mes sentiments distingués.

Setting the scene for a story
Ch. 3, p. 97

Il était une fois...
... dans un pays lointain...
Jadis, dans une tribu reculée,...
On raconte qu'autrefois...

Continuing and ending a story
Ch. 3, p. 99

Le lendemain,...
La veille de...
Le temps a passé et...
... plus tard,...
Ils vécurent heureux et eurent beaucoup
    d'enfants.
Tout est bien qui finit bien.
La morale de cette histoire est que...
Nul ne sait ce qui lui est arrivé.

Relating a sequence of events
Ch. 3, p. 109

Avant de...
À cette époque,...
Par la suite,...
Au moment de...
Après...
Une fois que...

Telling what happened to someone else
Ch. 3, p. 111
... a rapporté que...
... a déclaré que...
... a annoncé que...
Il paraît que...

Saying what happened and responding
Ch. 4, p. 135
J'ai entendu dire que...
Raconte!
Devine...
Je n'en ai pas la moindre idée./Aucune idée.
Figure-toi que...
Tu savais que... toujours...?
Ce n'est pas vrai!
Pas possible!

Sharing good and bad news
Ch. 4, p. 147
À propos,...
Tous mes voeux de bonheur.
Vous savez,...
Toutes mes félicitations!/Félicitations!
Malheureusement,...
Mes sincères condoléances.

Forbidding and giving warning
Ch. 5, p. 189
Il est interdit de...
Prière de ne pas...
Interdiction de...
Défense de...
Fais/Faites attention,...
Prends/Prenez garde...
Méfie-toi/Méfiez-vous des...
Surtout,...

Giving general directions
Ch. 5, p. 199
... dans le nord de...
Au sud de...
Si tu vas plus à l'est,...
... vers l'ouest,...
C'est à environ... de (d')...

Breaking news and responding
Ch. 6, p. 237
Tu as vu...?
Fais voir!
Montre-moi!
Devine...
Tu connais la dernière?
... raconte!
Tu es au courant de...?
..., je t'écoute!
Tu sais quoi?
Tu as entendu parler du /de la / des...?
..., qu'est-ce qui s'est passé?

Asking about information
Ch. 6, p. 239
Qui est-ce qui...?
Qui est-ce que...?
Qu'est-ce qui...?
Qu'est-ce que...?

Cautioning
Ch. 7, p. 277
On prévoit... pour...
Surtout,...
Prenez garde aux...
Méfie-toi de...
... au cas où...

Telling why something happened
Ch. 7, p. 279
C'est pour ça que...
... à cause de...
... dûs à...
Donc,...

Asking for assistance
Ch. 8, p. 327
Vous serait-il possible de contacter mes parents?
À moi!/Au secours!/À l'aide!
Au feu!
Appelez la police!
Au voleur!

Getting information and explaining
Ch. 8, p. 329
On m'a dit de ne... que...
Il m'a expliqué que...
On m'a informé de...
On m'a montré où...
On m'a indiqué comment...

Asking for information and clarifications
Ch. 10, p. 405

... une place près du hublot?
Vous avez de la chance, on en a encore deux.
On a droit à combien de bagages?
... maximum.
Existe-t-il un vol sans escale pour...?
... un vol direct,...

Reminding and reassuring
Ch. 10, p. 407

Est-ce que tu as pris...?
Oui, je l'ai toujours sur moi.
Tu as prévenu... que...?
Rassure-toi,...
As-tu bien confirmé ton vol?
Pas encore! Je le fais tout de suite.

Asking for help and responding
Ch. 10, p. 417

Je ne sais pas comment...
Appuyez sur la pédale d'embrayage.
Aide-moi! Je n'y vois rien.
Tu ferais mieux de...
Je n'arrive pas à me garer, tu peux m'aider?
..., passe-moi le volant.
Le moteur ne veut pas démarrer.
Ouvre le capot,...

Asking for directions
Ch. 10, p. 419

Savez-vous où est l'entrée de l'autoroute pour...?
Quelle sortie faut-il prendre pour...?
Quel est la route la plus rapide pour...?
Comment peut-on rejoindre...?
Est-ce qu'il existe un chemin qui...?

Expressing Feelings and Emotions

Expressing astonishment and fear
Ch. 5, p. 187

Ce n'est pas vrai!
C'est incroyable!
Pas possible!
Je n'en reviens pas!
Quelle horreur!
J'ai peur des...!
J'ai peur que...!
Au secours!/À l'aide!

Persuading

Making polite requests
Ch. 2, p. 47

Te/Vous serait-il posssible de...?
Ça ne te/vous ennuierait pas de...?
Si possible, pourrais-tu/pourriez-vous...

Socializing

Making a phone call and responding
Ch. 2, p. 57

... est-ce que je pourrais parler à...?
Un instant, je vous le/la passe
Vous pouvez rappelez?
C'est de la part de qui/Qui est à l'appareil?
Est-ce que je peux laisser un message?
Je suis bien chez...?
..., vous avez fait le mauvais numéro.
La ligne est occupée.
Ça ne répond pas.

Renewing old acquaintances
Ch. 4, p. 149

Comment va...?
Je ne le vois plus.
Quoi de neuf?
Rien de spécial.
Plein de choses!
Tu n'as pas changé(e)!
Toi non plus.
Je suis ravi(e) de...
... ça fait longtemps que...

Introducing and changing a topic of conversation
Ch. 9, p. 369

Au fait, ...
À propos, ...
Pendant que j'y pense, ...
Entre parenthèses, ...

Liste d'expressions

Synthèse de grammaire

ADJECTIVES

Adjective Agreement

Adjectives are words that describe or modify a noun. Adjectives agree in gender and in number with the nouns they modi fy. To make an adjective feminine, add an **-e** to the masculine singular form. To make an adjective plural, add an **-s** to the singular form.

	SINGULAR	**PLURAL**
MASCULINE	intelligent	intelligents
FEMININE	intelligente	intelligentes

Adjectives ending in *-eux*

If the masculine singular form of the adjective ends in **-eux**, change the **-x** to **-se** to make it feminine.

	SINGULAR	**PLURAL**
MASCULINE	heureux	heureux
FEMININE	heureuse	heureuses

Adjectives ending in *-if*

If the masculine singular form of the adjective ends in **-if**, change the **-f** to **-ve** to create the feminine form.

	SINGULAR	**PLURAL**
MASCULINE	sportif	sportifs
FEMININE	sportive	sportives

Adjectives with Irregular Feminine Forms

The following adjectives have irregular feminine forms.

SINGULAR		**PLURAL**	
MASCULINE	**FEMININE**	**MASCULINE**	**FEMININE**
long	longue	longs	longues
blanc	blanche	blancs	blanches
bon	bonne	bons	bonnes
gros	grosse	gros	grosses

The Irregular Adjectives *beau, nouveau,* and *vieux*

MASCULINE SINGULAR (before a consonant)	MASCULINE SINGULAR (before a vowel)	MASCULINE PLURAL	FEMININE SINGULAR	FEMININE PLURAL
beau nouveau vieux	bel nouvel vieil	beaux nouveaux vieux	belle nouvelle vieille	belles nouvelles vieilles

Adjective Placement

Most French adjectives come **after** the nouns they describe. Adjectives of **beauty, age, number, goodness,** or **size** usually come before the nouns they modify. The following adjectives fall into this group.

CATEGORY	ADJECTIVES
*B*eauty	beau, joli
*A*ge	vieux, jeune
*N*umber	un, deux, trois…
*G*oodness	bon, mauvais
*S*ize	grand, petit

Mme Pasquier est une **belle** dame et elle a des enfants **intelligents.**

If the adjective comes before a plural noun, the word **des** becomes **de.**

Il y a **de** bons films au cinéma ce week-end.

Some French adjectives have a different meaning depending on whether they are placed **before** a noun or **after** a noun. When they are placed after a noun adjectives usually have a more *litteral* meaning:

un **homme grand** is a *tall* man.

If the adjectives are placed before a noun the meaning is more *figurative*:

un **grand homme** is a *great* man.

Possessive Adjectives

Possessive adjectives agree in gender and in number with the nouns they modify. Possessive adjectives agree with the items possessed.

	MASCULINE SINGULAR	FEMININE SINGULAR	PLURAL
my	mon	ma	mes
your	ton	ta	tes
his/her/its	son	sa	ses
our	notre	notre	nos
your	votre	votre	vos
their	leur	leur	leurs

In English, possession can be shown by using **'s.** In French, the preposition **de/d'** is used to show possession.

Le livre **de** Jacqueline est sur la table.

Demonstrative Adjectives

Words like *this*, *that*, *these*, and *those* are called demonstrative adjectives.
There are four demonstrative adjectives in French: **ce, cet, cette,** and **ces.**

MASCULINE SINGULAR	MASCULINE SINGULAR (vowel sound)	MASCULINE PLURAL	FEMININE SINGULAR	FEMININE PLURAL
ce livre	**cet** ordinateur	**ces** livres	**cette** chaise	**ces** chaises

To distinguish between *this* and *that* and *these* and *those*, add **–ci** or
–là to the end of any noun.

J'achète **cette robe-ci** parce que je n'aime pas **cette robe-là**!

Interrogative Adjectives

Certain adjectives in French can be used to form questions. The
interrogative adjective **quel** means *what* and it has four forms.

	SINGULAR	PLURAL
MASCULINE	**Quel** restaurant?	**Quels** restaurants?
FEMININE	**Quelle** classe?	**Quelles** classes?

When a form of **quel** is followed by **est** or **sont**, it agrees in gender and
number with the noun following the verb.

Quelle est ta couleur préférée?

Quel can also be used as an exclamation. Use a form of **quel** plus
a noun to express the idea *"What a…"*

Quelle belle robe!   *What a beautiful dress!*

Adjectives used as Nouns

When used as a noun, the adjective has a definite article in front of it.
Both the adjective and the article will agree in gender and in number
with the noun to which they refer.

—Tu préfères la grande maison ou **la petite?**

—Je préfère **la petite.**

The Adjectives *tout, tous, toute, toutes*

Tout and its forms are used in French to say *all* or *whole*. **Tout** has four
forms and agrees in gender and in number with the noun it modifies.

	SINGULAR	PLURAL
MASCULINE	tout	tous
FEMININE	toute	toutes

Toutes les chemises sont chères!

ADVERBS

Formation of Adverbs

Adverbs modify verbs, adjectives, or other adverbs and tell when, where, why, and to what extent an action is performed. In French, adverbs usually end in **-ment**. To form most adverbs in French, take the feminine form of the adjective and add **-ment**. Common French adverbs are **bien, souvent, de temps en temps, rarement,** and **régulièrement**.

ADJECTIVE (Masculine Singular Form)	ADJECTIVE (Feminine Singular Form)	ADVERB (Feminine Singular Adjective + -ment ending)
sérieux	sérieuse	sérieusement

Paul et Luc étudient **sérieusement** pour leur examen final.

Placement of Adverbs

While adverbs are generally placed near their verbs, they can take other positions in the sentence. Here is a general overview that might help when deciding where to place French adverbs.

TYPE OF ADVERB	EXAMPLES	PLACEMENT IN THE SENTENCE
how much, how often, or how well something is done	**rarement, souvent, bien, mal**	after the verb
adverbs of time	**hier, maintenant, demain**	the beginning or the end of the sentence
some adverbs ending in **-ment**	**normalement, généralement**	the beginning or the end of the sentence

Nous allons **rarement** chez nos cousins.

Patricia a fait du vélo **hier.**

Normalement, je sors avec mes copains après les cours.

Some adverbs are exceptions to these rules and require a special place in the sentence or clause.

ADVERB	PLACEMENT
comme ci comme ça	end of the clause
quelquefois	beginning or end of the clause or after the verb

Paul parle italien **comme ci comme ça.** Il voyage souvent en Italie et **quelquefois** il réussit à communiquer.

The Adverbs *bien* and *mal*

The adjectives **bon** and **mauvais** have irregular adverbs.

ADJECTIVE	ADVERB
bon	bien
mauvais	mal

Ma mère chante **bien,** mais moi, je chante **mal.**

Adverbs with the *passé composé*

The following adverbs are helpful when talking about the past. They can be placed at either the beginning or at the end of a sentence.

hier (matin, après-midi, soir)
yesterday (morning, afternoon, evening)

la semaine dernière/le mois dernier/l'année dernière
last week/last month/last year

soudain *(suddenly)*

Hier, je suis allé au cinéma avec des amis.

Depuis, il y a, ça fait

To say what someone *has been doing* or *for how long* a person has been doing an activity, use **depuis + a time expression.** This expression can also be used to mean **since.**

Nous habitons à Paris **depuis** cinq ans.
*We've been living in Paris **for** 5 years.*

Je travaille **depuis** six heures du matin.
*I've been working **since** 6 a.m.*

You can also use the expressions **il y a** and **ça fait + a time expression** to say *how long something has been going on.* When you use these expressions, they must be followed by the word **que** and usually come at the beginning of the sentence.

Ça fait une semaine **que** nous attendons.
We've been waiting for a week.

Il y a trois mois **que** Marie est malade.
Marie's been sick for three months.

ARTICLES

Definite Articles

There are four definite articles in French.

	MASCULINE (beginning with a consonant)	FEMININE (beginning with a consonant)	MASCULINE OR FEMININE (beginning with a vowel or vowel sound)
SINGULAR	le	la	l'
PLURAL	les	les	les

The definite article contracts with the preposition **à** to express *at the* or *to the.* It contracts with the preposition **de** to express *of the* or *from the.*

DEFINITE ARTICLE	CONTRACTED FORM WITH *À*	CONTRACTED FORM WITH *DE*
le	au	du
les	aux	des
l'	à l'	de l'
la	à la	de la

Je vais **au** café.

Paul répond **aux** questions.

Vous retournez **à la** gare.

Chantal et Paul vont **à l'**école.

Je sors **du** café.

Le père **des** garçons travaille beaucoup.

Le train part **de la** gare.

La porte **de l'**école est grande.

Indefinite Articles

The indefinite articles in French are **un, une,** and **des. Un** and **une** mean *a* or *an* and **des** means *some.* They agree in gender (masculine or feminine) and number (singular or plural) with the nouns they modify.

	SINGULAR	PLURAL
MASCULINE	un livre	des livres
FEMININE	une carte	des cartes

Un, une, and **des** become **de** after a negative.

Chantal a **un** cours de français.

Ils mangent **des** sandwichs.

Chantal n'a pas **de** cours de français.

Ils ne mangent pas **de** sandwichs.

If **de** comes before a noun beginning with a vowel or vowel sound, it changes to **d'.**

The Partitive Articles

The partitive is used in French to express *a part* or *some* of an item.

MASCULINE SINGULAR	FEMININE SINGULAR	BEFORE A NOUN BEGINNING WITH A VOWEL	PLURAL
du café	**de la** salade	**de l'**eau	**des** pommes

Je vais prendre **de l'**eau. Pierre va prendre **du** café.

The partitive will change to **de** after a negative.

Aurélie ne mange pas **de** tarte parce qu'elle ne veut pas grossir.

When speaking about a whole item, use the indefinite articles **un, une,** and **des**.

Tu veux **un** croissant ou **une** orange?

COMPARATIVES AND SUPERLATIVES

Comparing Adjectives

To compare adjectives, use the following expressions. Remember to make your adjectives agree in gender and in number with their noun.

TO SAY	USE
more...than	**plus** + adjective + **que**
as...as	**aussi** + adjective + **que**
less...than	**moins** + adjective + **que**

Marie est **plus** généreuse **que** son frère.

Nous sommes **aussi** fatigués **que** vous.

Les amis de Xavier sont **moins** sportifs **que** les amis de David.

Comparing Nouns

To compare things, persons, places, or ideas, use the following expressions. Use **de** before the noun.

TO SAY	USE
more...than	**plus** + **de** + noun + **que**
as...as	**autant** + **de** + noun + **que**
less...than	**moins** + **de** + noun + **que**

Marie a **plus de** livres **que** son frère.

Nous achetons **autant de** CD **que** vous.

Les amis de Xavier font **moins de** voyages **que** les amis de David.

The Superlative of Adjectives

The superlative is used to convey *the best, the most, the least,* or *the worst.* Make your adjective agree in gender and in number with the noun it modifies. Depending on the adjective, the superlative can come either before or after its noun.

> **C'est + definite article + plus/moins + adjective + noun + de + noun**

C'est la plus jolie fille de la classe.

> **le (l')**
> **C'est + definite article + noun + la (l') + plus/moins + adjective + de + noun**
> **les**

C'est la fille la plus intelligente de la classe.

Irregular Comparatives and Superlatives

The adjectives **bon** and **mauvais** have irregular forms in both the comparative and the superlative.

ADJECTIVE	COMPARATIVE	SUPERLATIVE
bon(s)/bonne(s)	meilleur(s)/meilleure(s) aussi bon(s)/bonne(s) moins bon(s)/bonne(s)	le meilleur/la meilleure les meilleurs/les meilleures
mauvais/mauvaise(s)	pire(s) aussi mauvais/mauvaise(s)	le pire/la pire/les pires

INTERROGATIVES

Inversion

One way of asking questions is by using inversion. The subject and verb switch positions and are connected by a hyphen.

> **Tu aimes** le chocolat? → **Aimes-tu** le chocolat?
> **Vous parlez** français? → **Parlez-vous** français?

If your subject is **il, elle,** or **on** and if your verb ends with a vowel, insert **-t-** between the verb and the subject.

> **Elle va** au cinéma ce soir? → **Va-t-elle** au cinéma ce soir?

When you have a noun as the subject, such as a person's name, use the subject and then invert with the corresponding pronoun.

> Est-ce que **Paul** préfère le vert? → **Paul, préfère-t-il** le vert?

NEGATIVE EXPRESSIONS

Negative Expressions

The most common negative expression is **ne... pas**. To make a sentence negative, put **ne... pas** around the conjugated verb.

Vous travaillez bien! → Vous **ne** travaillez **pas** bien!

In the **passé composé**, the negative comes around the helping verb.

Ils **ont mangé** ensemble. → Ils **n'**ont **pas mangé** ensemble.

Here are more negative expressions in French.

NEGATIVE EXPRESSION		EXAMPLE
ne... pas encore	*not yet*	Ils **n'**ont **pas encore** mangé.
ne... plus	*no longer*	Elle **ne** mange **plus** de croissants.
ne... ni... ni	*neither nor*	Je **n'**aime **ni** les bananes **ni** les pommes.
ne... jamais	*never*	Tu **ne** viens **jamais** au parc avec nous.
ne... personne	*no one*	Danièle **n'**entend **personne** au téléphone.
ne... rien	*nothing*	Nous **ne** faisons **rien** ce soir.
ne... que	*only*	Je **n'**aime **que** le chocolat suisse.

When used as subjects, both **rien** and **personne** come before **ne**.

Rien n'est impossible! **Personne n'**écoute Charles!

In the past tense **ne... personne** works differently. Put the **ne** before the helping verb, but position the word **personne** after the past participle.

—Hier soir, vous avez vu **Marie** au théâtre ?

—Non je **n'**ai vu **personne** au théâtre.

The negative expressions **ne... rien, ne... personne**, and **ne... que** are often used with the expressions **quelque chose** (*something*) and **quelqu'un** (*someone*).

Two other negative expressions are **ne... aucun(e)** (*no, not any*) and **ne... nulle part** (*nowhere*).

EXPRESSION	CORRESPONDING NEGATIVES
quelque chose	ne... rien; ne... que
quelqu'un	ne... personne, ne... que

Tu veux **quelque chose?**
Do you want something?

Je **ne** veux manger **que** la salade.
I only want the salad.

Vous attendez **quelqu'un?**
Are you waiting for someone?

Non, nous **n'**attendons **personne**.
No, we aren't waiting for anyone.

Je **n'**attends **que** mes parents.
*I'm **only** waiting for my parents.*

NOUNS

Feminine form of nouns

Nouns referring to people's professions may be made feminine in a number of ways.

Leave the masculine form unchanged, but change the preceding article.
(**un** journaliste / **une** journaliste)

Add **–e** to the masculine form of the noun.
(un avocat / une avocat**e**)

Change the ending of the masculine form of the noun as follows:

	MASCULINE	**FEMININE**
ien / ienne	un musicien	une musicienne
eur / euse	un serveur	une serveuse
teur / trice	un acteur	une actrice
er / ère	un boulanger	une boulangère
ier / ière	un fermier	une fermière

Add **-sse** to the masculine form of some nouns.
un prince / une prince**sse**   un maître / une maître**sse**

Make no change at all.
un professeur   un juge   un ministre

PRONOUNS

Subject Pronouns

Here are the subject pronouns in French.

PERSON	SINGULAR PRONOUNS		PLURAL PRONOUNS	
1ST	je (j')	*I*	nous	*we*
2ND	tu	*you*	vous	*you*
3RD	il/elle/on	*he/she/one, we*	ils/elles	*they*

Tu and **vous** both mean *you*. Here are the rules for using them.

TU	VOUS
• someone your own age	• someone older than you
• someone younger than you	• someone you've just met
• family members	• someone in authority
• friends	• groups
• someone called by his/her first name	

When referring to a group with both masculine and feminine nouns (people or things), use **ils.**

Disjunctive (stress) pronouns

Disjunctive pronouns, also called stress pronouns, correspond to the following subject pronouns:

je	moi	nous	nous
tu	toi	vous	vous
il	lui	ils	eux
elle	elle	elles	elles

Direct Object Pronouns

A **direct object** is the person or thing that receives the action of a verb. A direct object can be either a noun or a pronoun. Direct objects can be replaced by **direct object pronouns**.

DIRECT OBJECT PRONOUNS	
me (m') *me*	**nous** *us*
te (t') *you (fam)*	**vous** *you (formal, plural)*
le/la (l') *him/her, it*	**les** *them*

Direct object pronouns come before the conjugated verb or infinitive.

> Paul et Sophie **nous** invitent au restaurant.

> Tu veux regarder **la télévision**? → Oui, je veux **la** regarder.

When using a direct object pronoun with a negative, place the negative expression around the direct object pronoun and its verb.

> Pierre **n'**entend **pas ses amis.** → Pierre **ne les** entend **pas.**

In the **passé composé,** the direct object pronoun will come before the helping verbs **avoir** or **être.**

> Tu **as** regardé **le film français** hier? → Tu **l'as** regardé hier?

In the **passé composé** with **avoir,** the past participle doesn't agree with the subject. It will agree with a preceding direct object.

> Michel a écouté **la radio**. → Michel **l'**a écoutée.

> Nicole n'a pas aimé **les croissants**. → Nicole ne **les** a pas aimés.

Indirect Object Pronouns

An **indirect object** is the person who benefits from the action of the verb. Indirect objects indicate *to whom* or *for whom* something is done. In French, the indirect object is usually preceded by the preposition **à** and is often used with verbs of giving (**donner, offrir, envoyer**) and of communication (**parler, écrire, dire, téléphoner**).

> Nous allons écrire une carte postale **à nos parents**.

INDIRECT OBJECT PRONOUNS	
me (m') *to me*	**nous** *to us*
te (t') *to you*	**vous** *to you (formal, plural)*
lui *to him, to her*	**leur** *to them*

Indirect object pronouns come before the verb. In the present tense, place the object before the conjugated verb.

> Paul et Sophie **nous** envoient une lettre.

If there is an infinitive in the sentence, place the indirect object pronoun in front of the infinitive.

> Tu veux parler <u>à ta mère?</u> → Oui, je veux **lui** parler.

When using an indirect object pronoun with a negative, place the negative expression around the indirect object pronoun and its verb.

> Pierre **ne** téléphone **pas à ses amis**. → Pierre **ne leur** téléphone **pas**.

In the **passé composé,** the indirect object pronoun will come before the helping verbs **avoir** or **être**.

> J'ai dit <u>à ma cousine</u> de venir ce soir. → Je **lui** ai dit de venir ce soir.

The Pronoun *en*

The pronoun **en** replaces **de** + noun. **En** is best understood to mean *some, any, of it,* or *of them*.

> Tu prends **du café?**   *Do you want some coffee?*
>
> Oui, j'**en** veux bien.   *Yes, I'd really like some.*

You can use the pronoun **en** to replace nouns that follow numbers or expressions of quantity.

> D'habitude, j'achète **beaucoup de pain.** D'habitude, j'**en** achète **beaucoup**.
>
> Tu as combien **de sœurs?** J'**en** ai **une**.

If there is an infinitive in the sentence, the pronoun **en** comes before the infinitive.

> Je peux **en** manger.

In the **passé composé,** the pronoun **en** comes before the helping verb **avoir** or **être**.

> Nous avons fait **des gâteaux.** Nous **en** avons fait.

A negative expression comes around the pronoun **en** and its verb.

> Paul ne veut pas **de glace?** Non, il **n'en** veut **pas**.

The Pronoun *y*

The pronoun **y** replaces the names of places that start with prepositions like **à, dans, en, chez, sur,** and **sous.**

> Monique travaille **au musée?** → Oui, elle **y** travaille.

If there is an infinitive in the sentence, the pronoun **y** comes before the infinitive.

> Vous voulez voyager **en Italie** l'année prochaine?
>
> Oui, je veux **y** voyager l'année prochaine.

In the **passé composé,** the pronoun **y** comes before the helping verb **avoir** or **être.**

> Nous avons dîné **au restaurant.** → Nous **y** avons dîné.
>
> Elles sont allées **à la bibliothèque.** → Elles **y** sont allées.

Object Pronouns

It is possible to have both a **direct object** and an **indirect object** in the same sentence. When this occurs, place the pronouns before the verb in the following order.

me					
te	le (l')				
se	→ la (l') →	lui →	y →	en →	verb
nous	les	leur			
vous					

J'envoie **la lettre à mes parents.**	*I am sending my parents the letter.*
Je **leur** envoie la lettre.	*I am sending **them** the letter.*
Je **la leur** envoie.	*I am sending **it to them.***

The Relative Pronouns *qui, que, dont*

To refer to something or someone already mentioned in conversation, use the relative pronouns **qui** and **que** *(that, which, who,* or *whom).*

Qui, meaning *that, which,* or *who,* is used as the subject of the second clause and is always followed by a verb.

> C'est un étudiant **qui est** très sérieux.

Que, meaning *that, which, whom,* is the object of the second clause and is followed by a subject and a verb.

> Paul est un ami **que nous aimons** beaucoup.

If the **passé composé** follows **que,** the past participle agrees in gender and number with the noun to which **que** refers.

> **La maison que** vous avez achetée est très grande!

Use the relative pronoun **dont** *(that, whom, whose)* to replace a prepositional phrase beginning with **de.**

> Tu parles **de Céline?** Elle travaille à la boulangerie.
>
> La fille **dont** tu parles travaille à la boulangerie.

Relative pronouns with ce

Ce qui, **ce que** and **ce dont** are relative pronouns that may translate as "*what*" meaning "*the thing(s) that.*"

Ce qui acts as the subject of a dependent clause and is usually followed by a verb.

Tu sais **ce qui** est arrivé?   Do you know *what* happened?

Ce que acts as the direct object of a dependent clause and is usually followed by a subject+verb.

Tu sais **ce que** j'aime?   Do you know *what* I like?

Ce dont replaces a prepositional phrase introduced by **de**

Il a envie de quelque chose.   Tu sais **ce dont** il a envie?
He wants something.   Do you know *what* he wants?

Interrogative Pronouns

To ask *which one* or *which ones*, use the appropriate form of the interrogative adjective **lequel**. It refers back to someone or to something already mentioned and agrees in gender and in number with its noun.

	MASCULINE	**FEMININE**
SINGULAR	lequel	laquelle
PLURAL	lesquels	lesquelles

Voici un sandwich au jambon et un sandwich au poulet.
Lequel veux-tu?

Les chaussures noires ou les chaussures blanches? **Lesquelles** achètes-tu?

Contractions with lequel

The interrogative pronoun **lequel** may also be used as a relative pronoun. It combines with the prepositions **à** and **de** exactly as the definite articles (**le/la/les**) do.

à + **lequel** = **auquel**   de + **lequel** = **duquel**

à + **laquelle** = **à laquelle**   de + **laquelle** = **de laquelle**

à + **lesquels** = **auxquels**   de + **lesquels** = **desquels**

à + **lesquelles** = **auxquelles**   de + **lesquelles** = **desquelles**

Tu connais le café en face **duquel** il habite?

Voici les voitures **auxquelles** il s'intéresse.

Demonstrative Pronouns

The **demonstrative pronoun** is used to refer back to the person(s) or thing(s) already mentioned. Demonstrative pronouns agree in gender and in number with the nouns they replace.

	MASCULINE	**FEMININE**
SINGULAR	celui	celle
PLURAL	ceux	celles

Cette affiche est jolie.

Laquelle? **Celle** qui est sur la table.

To make a distinction between *this one* and *that one,* and to separate *these* from *those,* use **-ci** and **-là**.

Je veux des bananas. **Celles-ci** sont bonnes mais **celles-là** sont mauvaises.
I want some bananas. These are good but those are bad.

VERBS

Present Tense of regular *-er* verbs

Regular verbs ending in **-er** are formed by dropping the **-er** from the verb and adding the appropriate endings.

aimer *(to love/tolike)*	
j'	aime
tu	aime**s**
il/elle/on	aime
nous	aim**ons**
vous	aim**ez**
ils/elles	aim**ent**

Tu **aimes** chanter avec la radio, n'est-ce pas?

Verbs ending in *-ger* and *-cer*

Verbs ending in **-ger** or **-cer** have a slightly different conjugation pattern. Verbs ending in **-ger**, like **manger**, follow the regular pattern except for the **nous** form. Verbs ending in **-cer**, like **commencer**, also change in the **nous** form.

	manger *(to eat)*	**commencer** *(to begin)*
je	mange	commence
tu	manges	commences
il/elle/on	mange	commence
nous	mangeons	commençons
vous	mangez	commencez
ils/elles	mangent	commencent

Regular -re verbs

Regular verbs ending in -re are formed by dropping the -re ending and adding the appropriate endings.

attendre (to wait for)	
j'	attends
tu	attends
il/elle/on	attend
nous	attendons
vous	attendez
ils/elles	attendent

Regular -ir verbs

Regular verbs ending in -ir are formed by dropping the -ir ending from the verb and adding the appropriate endings.

finir (to finish)	
je	finis
tu	finis
il/elle/on	finit
nous	finissons
vous	finissez
ils/elles	finissent

Stem-changing verbs

Some -er verbs, like **préférer** and **acheter**, change their stems in the **je**, **tu**, **il/elle/on**, and **ils/elles** forms of the verb.

préférer (to prefer)		acheter (to buy)	
je préfère	nous préférons	j'achète	nous achetons
tu préfères	vous préférez	tu achètes	vous achetez
il/elle/on préfère	ils/elle préfèrent	il/elle/on achète	ils/elles achètent
Verbs like préférer:		**Verbs like acheter:**	
espérer, répéter		amener, emmener, lever, promener	

Tu **préfères** le café.   Elles **achètent** de belles bananas au marché.

Other verbs like **appeler** (to call) change their stems by doubling a consonant. Verbs ending in -**yer**, like **nettoyer** (to clean), change the -y to -**i.**

appeler (to call)		nettoyer (to clean)	
j'appelle	nous appelons	je nettoie	nous nettoyons
tu appelles	vous appelez	tu nettoies	vous nettoyez
il/elle/on appelle	ils/elles appellent	il/elle/on nettoie	ils/elles nettoient
Verbs like appeler:		**Verbs like nettoyer:**	
jeter, épeler, rappeler		balayer, envoyer, essayer (de), payer	

J'**appelle** mon frère souvent.

Laurence ne **nettoie** jamais sa chambre!

The Irregular Verbs *avoir*, *être*, *aller*, and *faire*

The verbs **avoir**, **être**, **aller**, and **faire** are all irregular.

	avoir *(to have)*	**être** *(to be)*	**aller** *(to go)*	**faire** *(to make, to do)*
je/j'	ai	suis	vais	fais
tu	as	es	vas	fais
il/elle/on	a	est	va	fait
nous	avons	sommes	allons	faisons
vous	avez	êtes	allez	faites
ils/elles	ont	sont	vont	font
Past Participle	eu	été	allé	fait

The Irregular Verbs *vouloir*, *pouvoir*, and *devoir*

The verbs **vouloir**, **pouvoir**, and **devoir** are all irregular. They do not follow the normal conjugation pattern like regular **-ir** verbs.

	vouloir *(to want)*	**pouvoir** *(to be able to)*	**devoir** *(must, to have to)*
je	veux	peux	dois
tu	veux	peux	dois
il/elle/on	veut	peut	doit
nous	voulons	pouvons	devons
vous	voulez	pouvez	devez
ils/elles	veulent	peuvent	doivent

The Irregular Verb *prendre*

prendre *(to take, to have food or drink)*			
je	prends	nous	prenons
tu	prends	vous	prenez
il/elle/on	prend	ils/elles	prennent

Other verbs that follow the conjugation of **prendre** are: **apprendre**, **comprendre**, and **reprendre**.

The Verbs *dormir*, *sortir*, and *partir*

The verbs **dormir**, **sortir**, and **partir** follow a different conjugation pattern than regular **-ir** verbs.

	dormir *(to sleep)*	**partir** *(to leave)*	**sortir** *(to go out)*
je	dors	pars	sors
tu	dors	pars	sors
il/elle/on	dort	part	sort
nous	dormons	partons	sortons
vous	dormez	partez	sortez
ils/elles	dorment	partent	sortent

The Irregular Verbs *boire* and *voir*

The verbs **boire** and **voir** are both irregular.

	boire *(to drink)*	**voir** *(to see)*
je	bois	vois
tu	bois	vois
il/elle/on	boit	voit
nous	buvons	voyons
vous	buvez	voyez
ils/elles	boivent	voient

The Verbs *manquer* and *plaire*

When used with a direct object, **manquer** means *to miss*.

Il a **manqué** le bus.   He *missed* the bus.

When used with an indirect object and a noun referring to a person, **manquer** means that the person *is missed by someone*.

Mon ami me **manque**.   I *miss* my friend.
(My friend *is missed by* me).

Tu nous **manques**.   We *miss* you. (You *are missed by* us).

When used with an indirect object, **plaire** means *to please someone*.

Ce livre me **plaît**.   This book *pleases* me. (I *like* this book)

The reflexive verb **se plaire** means *to enjoy oneself*.

Je **me suis plu** au parc.   I *enjoyed myself* at the park.

The reciprocal verb **se plaire** means *to like each other*.

Ils **se sont plu** tout de suite.   They *liked each other* right away.

The Verbs *savoir* and *connaître*

Both **savoir** and **connaître** mean *to know* and they are irregular verbs.

savoir *(to know)*		**connaître** *(to know; to be acquainted with)*	
je sais	nous savons	je connais	nous connaissons
tu sais	vous savez	tu connais	vous connaissez
il/elle/on sait	ils/elles savent	il/elle/on connaît	ils/elles connaissent
Past participle: su		**Past participle:** connu	

Savoir means *to know about something*. It is used to express general knowledge, facts, and also means to know how to do something.

Nous **savons** l'heure. Il est trois heures et demie.

Connaître means *to know* as in the sense of being *acquainted with*. It is used with people, places, works of art, and literature.

Je **connais** bien cet hôtel.

Vous **connaissez** Martin?

The verb **paraître** means to appear, to be published. It is conjugated like **connaître**. Its past participle is **paru**.

The Irregular Verb *mettre*

The verb **mettre** is an irregular verb. Its past participle is **mis**.

mettre *(to put, to put on clothes)*	
je mets	nous mettons
tu mets	vous mettez
il/elle/on met	ils/elles mettent

Tu **mets** un pull bleu? Chantal **met** le CD dans son sac.

The Irregular Verb *conduire*

The verb **conduire** is an irregular verb in the present tense. Its past participle is **conduit**.

conduire *(to drive)*	
je conduis	nous conduisons
tu conduis	vous conduisez
il/elle/on conduit	ils/elles conduisent
passé composé: conduit	

The Irregular Verb *courir*

The verb **courir** is irregular. Its past participle is **couru**.

courir *(to run)*	
je cours	nous courons
tu cours	vous courez
il/elle/on court	ils/elles courent

The Verbs *ouvrir* and *offrir*

The verbs **offrir** and **ouvrir** end in **-ir,** but are conjugated like **-er** verbs.

ouvrir *(to open)*	**offrir** *(to offer)*
j' offre	j' ouvre
tu offres	tu ouvres
il/elle/on offre	il/elle/on ouvre
nous offrons	nous ouvrons
vous offrez	vous ouvrez
ils/elles offrent	ils/elles ouvrent

The Verb *recevoir*

The verb **recevoir** is irregular. Its past participle is **reçu**.

recevoir *(to receive, to get)*	
je reçois	nous recevons
tu reçois	vous recevez
il/elle/on reçoit	ils/elles reçoivent

Synthèse de grammaire

The Irregular Verb *suivre*

The verb **suivre** is irregular. You can use this verb to say which courses you are taking this year.

suivre *(to follow)*	
je suis	nous suivons
tu suis	vous suivez
il/elle/on suit	ils/elles suivent

The Irregular Verb *vaincre*

Vaincre is an irregular verb in the present tense. Its singular forms are regular, but all of its plural forms change -**c** to -**qu** before adding the usual endings.

vaincre *(to to vanquish, to conquer)*	
je vaincs	nous vainquons
tu vaincs	vous vainquez
il/elle/on vainc	ils/elles vainquent
passé composé: vaincu	

The *passé composé* with *avoir*

The **passé composé** tells what happened in the past. The **passé composé** has two main parts, a helping verb (usually the verb **avoir**) and a past participle.

To form the past participle of an -**er** verb, take off the -**er** and add -**é.** To form the past participle of an -**ir** verb, take off the -**r.** For -**re** verbs, drop the -**re** and add a -**u** to form its past participle.

INFINITIVE	PAST PARTICIPLE
écouter	écouté
choisir	choisi
perdre	perdu

	écouter *(to listen to)*	**choisir** *(to choose)*	**perdre** *(to lose)*
j'	ai écouté	ai choisi	ai perdu
tu	as écouté	as choisi	as perdu
il/elle/on	a écouté	a choisi	a perdu
nous	avons écouté	avons choisi	avons perdu
vous	avez écouté	avez choisi	avez perdu
ils/elles	ont écouté	ont choisi	ont perdu

To make the **passé composé** negative, put **ne** and **pas** around the helping verb.

Vous **n'**avez **pas** écouté le professeur.

Past Participles of Irregular Verbs

Here is a list of some irregular verbs and their past participles.

INFINITIVE	PAST PARTICIPLE	INFINITIVE	PAST PARTICIPLE
être	**été**	faire	**fait**
avoir	**eu**	pleuvoir	**plu**
vouloir	**voulu**	connaître	**connu**
boire	**bu**	devoir	**dû**
lire	**lu**	dire	**dit**
voir	**vu**	écrire	**écrit**
mettre	**mis**	pouvoir	**pu**
prendre	**pris**	savoir	**su**

The *passé composé* with *être*

Some verbs, mainly verbs of motion like **aller,** use **être** instead of **avoir** as a helping verb in the **passé composé.** For these verbs, the past participle agrees with the subject.

aller *(to go)*	
je suis **allé(e)**	nous sommes **allé(e)s**
tu es **allé(e)**	vous êtes **allé(e)s**
il est **allé**	ils sont **allés**
elle est **allée**	elles sont **allées**

Les professeurs **sont arrivés** en retard pour leurs cours.

Here is a list of verbs that take **être** in the **passé composé.**

VERB	PAST PARTICIPLE	VERB	PAST PARTICIPLE
arriver	**arrivé**	partir	**parti**
descendre	**descendu**	rester	**resté**
entrer	**entré**	tomber	**tombé**
sortir	**sorti**	mourir	**mort**
retourner	**retourné**	naître	**né**
monter	**monté**	venir	**venu**

Verbs with *être* or *avoir* in the *passé composé*

Some verbs can take either **être** or **avoir** to form the **passé composé.**
When these verbs have a direct object, the past participle agrees with the direct object if it comes before the past participle.

Anne **est sortie** hier soir avec ses amies.
Anne went out last night with her friends.

Anne **a sorti la poubelle** après le dîner.
Anne took out the trash after dinner.

Anne **l'a sortie** après le dîner.
Anne took it out (the trash) after dinner.

C'est versus il/elle est

Use C'est With	Use Il/Elle est With
• someone's name • an article/possessive adjective + a noun • an article + a noun + an adjective	• an adjective by itself • a profession

C'est **Pierre**. Il est **dentiste**. C'est **un restaurant italien**.

Venir and the passé récent

The verb **venir** means *to come* and is an irregular verb.

venir *(to come)*	
je viens	nous venons
tu viens	vous venez
il/elle/on vient	ils/elles viennent

A form of **venir** plus the preposition **de** plus an infinitive can be used to express an action that has just occurred.

> Nous **venons de finir** nos devoirs.
> *We have just finished our homework.*

The Imperative

To give a command in French, use the imperative. The imperative form comes from the **tu, nous,** and **vous** forms. In **-er** verbs, the **-s** is dropped from the **tu** form.

	tu	nous	vous
écouter	écoute	écoutons	écoutez
finir	finis	finissons	finissez
attendre	attends	attendons	attendez

To make a command negative, put **ne** and **pas** around the verb.

> **Donne** le livre à Monique! → **Ne donne pas** le livre à Monique!

Reflexive Verbs

Reflexive verbs are used when the same person does and receives the action of the verb. These verbs use reflexive pronouns.

se laver *(to wash oneself)*	
je me lave	nous nous lavons
tu te laves	vous vous lavez
il/elle/on se lave	ils/elles se lavent

Marie **se lave** les cheveux chaque soir et elle **se brosse** les dents.

Reflexive Pronouns with Infinitives

When you use the reflexive verb in the infinitive form, the reflexive pronoun will agree with the subject.

> **Nous** n'allons pas **nous** ennuyer à la plage!

Reflexive Verbs in the *passé composé*

All reflexive verbs use **être** to form the **passé composé**.

> Paul **s'est déshabillé** et puis il **s'est couché.**

In the **passé composé** of reflexive verbs, the past participle usually agress in gender and number with the reflexive pronoun.

se coucher *(to go to bed)*	
je me suis **couché(e)**	nous nous sommes **couché(e)s**
tu t'es **couché(e)**	vous vous êtes **couché(e)(s)**
il/elle/on s'est **couché(e)**	il/elles se sont **couché(e)s**

The past participle agrees with the reflexive pronoun only if the pronoun is a direct object. The reflexive pronoun, however, is not always a direct object.

> Monique **s'est lavée.** Monique **s'est lavé les mains.**

Commands with Reflexive Verbs

When you make an affirmative command with a reflexive verb, connect the reflexive pronoun to the verb with a hyphen.

> **Couche-toi!**   *Go to bed!*

If the command is negative, however, the reflexive pronoun comes before the verb and **ne... pas**, comes around the whole structure.

> **Ne te** couche **pas!**   *Don't go to bed!*

Reciprocal Verbs

Reflexive verbs may be used in their plural forms (**nous/vous/ils/elles**) to express reciprocal actions. When used in this manner, they express the idea of *one another* or *each other.*

Sometimes only context will let you know whether a verb is being used as a **reciprocal** or simply as a **plural reflexive**.

> **Ils** se sont lavé les mains.   *(plural reflexive)*
> *They washed their (own) hands.*

> Ils se sont parlé.   *(reciprocal)*
> *They talked to each other.*

> Nous nous sommes regardés   *(plural reflexive or reciprocal; depends on context)*
> *We looked at ourselves (in a mirror).*   *We looked at each other.*

In the **passé composé**, reciprocal verbs are conjugated with **être** and follow all rules dealing with agreement of past participles.

The *imparfait*

The **imparfait** is used to describe events in the past or to emphasize that certain actions were done habitually. To form the imperfect, drop the **-ons** from the **nous** form of the verb and add the endings. The **only** verb that has an irregular stem is **être: ét-**.

	parler	**finir**	**vendre**
je	parlais	finissais	vendais
tu	parlais	finissais	vendais
il/elle/on	parlait	finissait	vendait
nous	parlions	finissions	vendions
vous	parliez	finissiez	vendiez
ils/elles	parlaient	finissaient	vendaient

Remember that **-ger** verbs, like **manger** and **-cer** verbs, like **commencer** have a different stem in the **nous** form than in the other forms of the verb.

	manger	**commencer**
je	mangeais	commençais
tu	mangeais	commençais
il/elle/on	mangeait	commençait
nous	**mangions**	**commencions**
vous	**mangiez**	**commenciez**
ils/elles	mangeaient	commençaient

The past perfect

Form the **plus-que-parfait** exactly as you do the **passé composé**, but put the appropriate helping verb (**avoir** or **être**) in the **imparfait**. Follow all rules dealing with agreement of past participles.

> **passé composé:** Elles se sont regardées.
>
> **plus-que-parfait:** Elles s'étaient regardées

Use the past perfect (**plus-que-parfait**) to say that one past action preceded another.

> Son fils lui a dit qu'il **avait fini** ses devoirs.
> (second action)   (first action)
> Her son told her that he *had finished* his homework.

The Future

The future tense in French is used to tell what will happen. To form the future tense, use the infinitive as the stem and add the future endings. Drop the **-e** from **-re** verbs before you add the future endings.

	parler	**finir**	**vendre**
je	parlerai	finirai	vendrai
tu	parleras	finiras	vendras
il/elle/on	parlera	finira	vendra
nous	parlerons	finirons	vendrons
vous	parlerez	finirez	vendrez
ils/elles	parleront	finiront	vendront

While the endings for the future are the same for all three types of verbs, several verbs have irregular future stems.

aller	ir-	j'irai	tu iras
avoir	aur-	j'aurai	tu auras
devoir	devr-	je devrai	tu devras
être	ser-	je serai	tu seras
faire	fer-	je ferai	tu feras
pouvoir	pourr-	je pourrai	tu pourras
vouloir	voudr-	je voudrai	tu voudras
venir	viendr-	je viendrai	tu viendras
voir	verr-	je verrai	tu verras
envoyer	enverr-	j'enverrai	tu enverras
courir	courr-	je courrai	tu courras
mourir	mourr-	je mourrai	tu mourras

Verbs like **appeler, acheter, lever,** and **préférer** that have spelling changes in the present tense also have spelling changes in the future.

The Future Perfect

Form the future perfect (**futur antérieur**) exactly as you do the **passé composé**, but put the appropriate helping verb in the **futur**.

passé composé: J'ai répondu.

futur antérieur: J'aurai répondu.

passé composé: Elle est arrivée.

futur antérieur: Elle sera arrivée.

Use the **futur antérieur** along with the future to say that one future action will precede another.

J'y travaillerai quand **j'aurai fini** mes études.
  (second action)   (first action)
  I will work there when *I (will) have finished* my studies.

Synthèse de grammaire

The Conditional

The conditional (**le conditionnel**) is used to tell what *would* happen. To form the conditional, use the infinitive as the stem (same as the future stem) and add the endings from the **imparfait**.

	parler	finir	vendre
je	parlerais	finirais	vendrais
tu	parlerais	finirais	vendrais
il/elle/on	parlerait	finirait	vendrait
nous	parlerions	finirions	vendrions
vous	parleriez	finiriez	vendriez
ils/elles	parleraient	finiraient	vendraient

The conditional can also be used to make polite requests.

Est-ce que **tu pourrais** m'aider?   *Could you help me?*

The Past Conditional

Form the **conditionnel passé** exactly like the **passé composé**, but put the helping verb in the **conditionnel**. Follow all rules of past participle agreement.

J'ai fini.   Elle est revenue.   Ils se sont habillés.

J'aurais fini...   Elle serait revenue...   Ils se seraient habillés...

The past conditional **conditionnel passé** is used to express what would have happened in the past if certain conditions had been met.

Use the **plus-que-parfait** in the if clause and **conditionnel passé** in the result clause. The order of the two clauses does not matter.

Je **aurais répondu** si j'avais su la réponse.
I *would have replied* if I had known the answer.

Si elle m'avait invité, **je serais allé** au cinéma avec elle.
If she had invited me, I *would have gone* to the movies with her.

Use the **conditionnel passé** of pouvoir to say that something could have happened but did not.

Il aurait pu mourir.   *He could have died.*

Si clauses

To express what you would do if circumstances were different, use two different types of clauses, an "if" clause and a "result" clause. The if clause will be in either the present or the **imparfait** and the result clause will be in either the present, the future, or the conditional.

Si tu étudies beaucoup, **tu réussis**.
If you study a lot, you succeed.

Si tu étudies beaucoup, **tu réussiras**.
If you study a lot, you will succeed.

Nous viendrions si nous avions le temps.
We would come if we had the time.

You can also use a **si** clause to make an invitation. To do this, you will use *si + on + imparfait*.

Si on allait à la plage ce week-end?
How about going to the beach this weekend?

The *passé composé* versus the *imparfait*

Both the **imparfait** and the **passé composé** can be used to talk about the past.

The **imparfait** is generally used to talk about things that happened over and over again in the past or how things used to be.

Quand Nicole **était** petite,   *When Nicole was little, her family*
sa famille **rendait** visite à   *used to visit her grandparents*
ses grands-parents en été.   *every summer.*

The **imparfait** can also be used to give descriptions of the weather, people, or places.

Hier, il **faisait** mauvais. Il **pleuvait**.
Yesterday, the weather was bad. It was raining!

The **passé composé** is used to tell what happened at a specific moment in the past.

Ce matin, **j'ai téléphoné** deux fois à Max mais il **n'a pas répondu**!
This morning I called Max two times but he didn't answer!

USE THE IMPARFAIT TO:	USE THE PASSÉ COMPOSÉ TO:
give background information	tell what happened on a particular occasion
set the scene and explain the circumstances in a story	tell the sequence of events in a story (d'abord, ensuite, puis, après)
explain what used to happen repeatedly	indicate a sudden change or the reaction to something
Key words: **souvent, tous les jours, d'habitude, le lundi (mardi, jeudi…etc.)**	Key words: **soudain, à ce moment-là, au moment où, une fois, deux fois…**

The passé simple

The **passé simple** is a past tense that is often used in place of the **passé composé** in historical or literary texts.

Form the **passé simple** by replacing the infinitive ending with **passé simple** endings.

> **-er verbs:**   -ai/ -as / -a / -âmes / -âtes / -èrent
>
> **–re and –ir verbs:**   -is / -is / -it / -îmes / -îtes / -irent

The verbs avoir, être, faire, mourir, naître and venir are irregular in the passé simple.

avoir	eus / eus / eut / eûmes / eûtes / eurent
être	fus / fus / fut / fûmes / fûtes / furent
faire	fis / fis / fit / fîmes / fîtes / firent
mourir	mourus / mourus / mourut / mourûmes / mourûtes / mourûrent
naître	naquis / naquis / naquit / naquîmes / naquîtes / naquirent
venir	vins / vins / vint / vînmes / vîntes / vinrent

Some other irregular verbs base their stem on their past participle.

boire (bu)	bus / bus /but / bûmes / bûtes / burent
mettre (mis)	mis / mis / mit / mîmes / mîtes / mirent
dire (dit)	dis / dis / dit / dîmes / dîtes / dirent
vivre (vécu)	vécus / vécus / vécut / vécûmes / vécûtes / vécurent

Sequence of tenses in indirect discourse

Use indirect discourse to relate what people have said without quoting them directly. There is a sequence of tenses that must be followed.

MAIN CLAUSE	DEPENDENT CLAUSE
Présent *He says that...*	**Présent** *he is doing...* **Futur** *he will do...* **Passé composé/Imparfait** *he did... he was doing...*
Passé composé *He said that...*	**Imparfait** *he was doing...* **Conditionnel** *he would do...* **Plus-que-parfait** *he had done...*

The Subjunctive of Regular Verbs

The present tense, the **passé composé,** and the future tense are in the indicative mood. There is another mood in French called the **subjunctive** mood that is used after certain expressions like **il faut que.** The subjunctive is used to express emotion, desire, and doubt.

Il faut que nous nous **dépêchions.**
We have to hurry!

Ma mère **est heureuse que** je **finisse** mes devoirs.
My mother is happy that I am finishing my homework.

Use the **subjunctive** with the following expressions:

Il faut que…	**Je veux que…**
Il est important que…	**Je suis content(e) que…**
Il est nécessaire que…	**Je suis triste que…**
Il est bon que….	

To form the subjunctive, drop the **-ent** from the **ils/elles** present tense form of the verb and add the following endings: **-e, -es, -e, -ions, -iez, -ent**

	parler **ils** par**lent**	**finir** **ils** finiss**ent**	**vendre** vend**ent**
que je	parle	finisse	vende
que tu	parles	finisses	vendes
qu'il/elle/on	parle	finisse	vende
que nous	parl**ions**	finiss**ions**	vend**ions**
que vous	parl**iez**	finiss**iez**	vend**iez**
qu'ils/elles	parl**ent**	finiss**ent**	vend**ent**

The Subjunctive of Irregular Verbs

Some verbs in the subjunctive are irregular because they have different stems for the **nous** and **vous** forms of the verb.

boire	que je boive	que nous buvions
devoir	que je doive	que nous devions
prendre	que je prenne	que nous prenions
venir	que je vienne	que nous veniez
voir	que je voie	que nous voyions

	aller	**être**	**avoir**	**faire**
que je (j')	aille	sois	aie	fasse
que tu	ailles	sois	aies	fasses
qu'il/elle/on	aille	soit	ait	fasse
que nous	allions	soyons	ayons	fassions
que vous	alliez	soyez	ayez	fassiez
qu'ils/elles	aillent	soient	aient	fassent

Synthèse de grammaire

Subjunctive after conjunctions

Certain conjunctions in French must be followed by the **subjonctif**.

Some examples are:

à condition que *(provided that)*	en attendant que *(while, until)*
à moins que *(unless)*	jusqu'à ce que *(until)*
afin que *(so that)*	malgré que *(in spite of the fact that)*
avant que *(before)*	pour que *(so that)*
bien que *(although)*	pourvu que *(provided that)*
de sorte que *(so that)*	sans que *(without)*

Other conjunctions must be followed by the **indicatif**.

Some examples are:

parce que (because)	quand (when)
pendant que (while)	lorsque (when)
depuis que (since)	dès que (as soon as)

If both clauses in a sentence have the same subject, sometimes you can use a preposition+infinitive instead of a **conjunction+subjonctif**.

Some examples are:

Conjunction	**Preposition**
à moins que	à moins de
afin que	afin de
avant que	avant de
pour que	pour
sans que	sans
à condition que	à condition de
en attendant que	en attendant de

Il travaille afin que sa famille ait de l'argent.

Il travaille afin d'avoir de l'argent.

Past subjunctive

Form the past subjunctive exactly as you form the **passé composé**, but use the present subjunctive form of the helping verb (**avoir** or **être**).

All rules dealing with past participle agreement apply. All of the expressions and conjunctions that require the subjunctive may also be followed by the past subjunctive to talk about actions that happened or may have happened in the past.

The past infinitive

Form the past infinitive by using the infinitive of the appropriate helping verb, (**avoir** or **être**) followed by the past participle of the main verb.

Use the **past infinitive** to say that one action occurred before another.

Compare the following examples:

Present Infinitive:

Je suis ravi de la voir.
I am delighted *to see* her.   (*simultaneous actions*).

Past Infinitive:

Je suis ravi de l'avoir vue hier.
(second action) (first action)
I am delighted *to have seen* her yesterday.

All rules involving agreement of past participles apply to past infinitives as well.

Après s'être levée, elle a fait le lit.

Passive voice

Use passive voice when the subject of the sentence is receiving the action rather than performing the action.

Actif: **Les cyclones détruisent les maisons.**
Hurricanes destroy houses.

Passif: **Les maisons sont détruites par les cyclones.**
Houses are destroyed by hurricanes.

To form passive voice, use a form of **être** followed by the past participle of the main verb. The past participle acts as an adjective and must agree with the subject of the sentence.

Use a phrase introduced by **par** if you want to name the "agent", that is, the person or thing performing the action.

Causative faire

To say that someone has something done by someone else instead of doing it himself, use the causative **faire**.

Form the causative **faire** by using the appropriate form and tense of **faire** followed by the infinitive of the action being performed.

Je fais tondre la pelouse.
I <u>have</u> the lawn mowed.

Tu as fait couper les cheveux.
You <u>had</u> your hair cut.

Ils feront réparer la voiture.
They <u>will have</u> their car repaired.

To tell who did the action, you may add a phrase introduced by **par**.

Je fais tondre la pelouse **par un voisin**.
I have the lawn mowed <u>by a neighbor</u>.

Present Participles

Form the **present participle** of French verbs by taking off the **-ons** from the nous form and add the ending **-ant**.

VERB	NOUS FORM	PRESENT PARTICIPLE
sortir	sortons	sortant
aller	allons	allant
attendre	attendons	attendant
finir	finissons	finissant
prendre	prenons	prenant
vouloir	voulons	voulant
dormir	dormons	dormant
faire	faisons	faisant

The present participles for **avoir, être,** and **savoir** are irregular.

VERB	PRESENT PARTICIPLE
être	étant
avoir	ayant
savoir	sachant

Use **en** or **tout en** + **present participle** to indicate that someone is doing one thing while another is going on. It can also show two activities that occur at the same time.

> J'ai répondu au téléphone **en mangeant** un croissant.
> *I answered the phone while eating a croissant.*

The present participle can also be used as an adjective. Remember to make it agree in gender and in number with its noun.

> C'est une maison **charmante**!

Glossaire français–anglais

This vocabulary includes almost all of the words presented in the textbook, both active (for production) and passive (for recognition only). An entry in **boldface** type indicates that the word or phrase is active. Active words and phrases are practiced in the chapter and are listed in the **Résumé** pages at the end of each chapter. You are expected to know and be able to use active vocabulary.

All other words are for recognition only. These words are found in activities, in optional and visual material, in the **Géoculture**, **Comparaisons, Lecture, Écriture,** and the **Chroniques.** Many words have more than one definition; the definitions given here correspond to the way the words are used in *Bien dit!*

The number after each entry refers to the chapter where the word or phrase first appears or where it is presented as an active vocabulary word. Active words and phrases from Level 1 and Level 2 are indicated by the Roman numerals I and II.

l' (auto)biographie, (f.) *(auto)biography,* II
à *to/at/in* + *city,* I, II; **À bientôt.** *See you soon.,* I; **à bord** *aboard,* 10; **à cause de** *because of,* 7; **à ce moment-là** *at that moment,* II; **À ce que l'on prétend...** *Allegedly,* 8; **à cette époque** *during that time,* 3; **à côté de** *next to,* I; **À demain.** *See you tomorrow.,* I; **à destination de** *heading for,* I; **à droite de** *to the right of,* I; **à gauche de** *to the left of,* I; à haute voix *aloud,* 5; à l' *at/to,* II; **À l'aide!** *Help!,* 5; **à la** *at/to,* II; à l'abri de *sheltered,* 10; **à l'attention de** *to the attention of,* 2; à l'avenir *in the future,* 9; **à l'étranger** *abroad,* II; **à l'heure** *on time,* I; à la suite de *following,* 8; à l'instant *immediately,* 8; **à ma place** *in my place,* 4; **À moi!** *Help!,* 3; à moins de *unless,* 4; **à mon avis** *in my opinion,* I; à mon compte *self-employed,* 2C; à part *on its own,* 8C; **à peine** *barely,* II; **à peu près** *about,* II; **à pied** *by foot,* I; **À plus tard.** *See you later.,* I; **à point**

medium, I; **a priori** *at first glance,* 7; **À propos,...** *By the way,* ... 4; À quatre reprises,... *Four times,* ... 9G; **À quel nom?** *Under what name?,* I; **à quelle heure** *at what time,* I; **À quelle heure tu as...?** *At what time do you have ...?* I; à ras bord *full to the brim,* 7; **À supposer que ce soit vrai...** *If what they say is true ...,* 8; **À ton avis,...** *In your opinion,* ... 4; **À tout à l'heure.** *See you later.,* I; à travers *through,* 7G; **à vélo** *by bicycle,* I; **À votre service.** *You're welcome.,* I
s' **abattre (sur)** *to swoop down (on),* 6
abattre *to break down,* 8
les **abdominaux,** (m. pl.) *abdominal muscles,* II
l' **abeille,** (f.) *bee,* 5
abîmer *to damage,* 7
abolir *abolish,* 1G
s' **abonner** *to subscribe,* 6
aborder *to land,* 2
aborigène *native/aboriginal* 5G
l' **abricot,** (m.) *apricot,* II
abriter *to shelter,* 3G
absolument *absolutely,* II
abstrait(e) *abstract,* 9
accabler *to crush,* 9
l' acajou, (m.) *mahogany,* 9
accélérer *to accelerate,* 10
l' **accès (handicapé),** (m.)

(handicapped) access, I
les **accessoires** (m. pl.) *accessories,* I
l' **accident,** (m.) *accident,* 6; **l'accident de la circulation** *traffic accident,* 8
l' **accord,** (m.) *agreement,* 3
accorder *to grant,* 3; **accorder des souhaits** *to grant wishes,* 3
s' accorder *to agree,* 4
accrocher *to hang,* 7
l' **accueil,** (m.) *home page,* II
accueillir *to greet, to welcome, to receive,* 7G
l' **accumulation,** (f.) *accumulation,* 7
l' achat, (m.) *purchase,* 5G
acheter *to buy,* II
achever *to finish,* 7
l' **acteur,** (m.) *actor,* II
l' **activité,** (f.) *activity,* I
l' **actrice,** (f.) *actress,* II
actualiser *refresh,* II
l' **actualité,** (f.) *current events,* 6; **actualité internationale,** *international news,* 6
actuellement *currently,* 2
l' **addition,** (f.) *bill,* I
additionner *to add,* 2
adhérer *to join,* 9
adopter *to adopt,* 4
adorer *to love/to adore,* 1
l' **adresse,** (f.) *address,* II; **l'adresse e-mail** *e-mail address,* I
s' **adresser** *to address,* I; **Adressez-vous...** *Ask ...,* I
aérien(ne) *air/air-related,* II

l' **aérobic,** (f.) *aerobics,* I
aéronautique *aeronautic,* 10
l' **aéroport,** (m.) *airport,* 10
les affaires, (f. pl.) *business,* 4
l' **affichage,** (m.) *view,* II
l' **affiche,** (f.) *poster,* 9; **l'affiche électorale** *campaign poster* 8
l' **afficheur,** (m.) *caller ID,* 2
afin de *in order to,* 2
africain(e) *African,* 3
l' **Afrique de l'Ouest,** (f.) *West Africa,* 3
l' **âge,** (m.) *age,* I
âgé(e) *elderly,* II; *old,* 4
l' **agence de location** (f.) *rental agency,* 10
l' **agence de voyages,** (f.) *travel agency,* II
s' agrandir *to grow larger, to expand,* 9G
agricole *agricultural,* IG
l' **agriculteur/ l'agricultrice** *farmer,* 2
Ah, mais si! J'ai oublié. *Ah, yes! I forgot.,* II
l' **aide,** (m.) *aid,* 8
l' **aide,** (f.) *help,* II
Aide-moi. *Help me.,* 10
aider *to help,* I
les aïeux, (m. pl.) *ancestors,* 5
l' **aigle,** (m.) *eagle,* 5
l' **ail,** (m.) *garlic,* II
l' aile, (f.) *wing,* 1
ailé(e) *winged,* 10
ailleurs *somewhere else,* 3
aimer *to like/to love,* II; **aimer bien** *to like,* I; **aimer mieux** *to like better/to prefer,* I
ainsi *this way,* 2C
l' **air** (m.) *air,* 7
l' air d'opéra (m.) *aria,* 9
aisément *easily,* 8
ajouter *to add,* II
l' **album photos,** (m.) *photo album,* 4
les alentours, (m. pl.) *surroundings,* 1
l' **alerte,** (f.) *alert,* 7
l' **Algérie,** (f.) *Algeria,* 3
alimentaire *food,* 2
l' **allée,** (f.) *aisle,* 10
l' **Allemagne,** (f.) *Germany,* II
l' **allemand** (m.) *German (language),* I
allemand(e) *German (adj.),* II
aller *to go,* II; **aller à la pêche** *to go fishing,* 1; **aller au cinéma** *to go to the movies,* 1; **s'en aller** *to run along,* II; **aller de travers** *to go wrong,* II
l' **aller simple** (m.) *one way ticket,* I
l' **aller-retour** (m.) *round-trip ticket,* I

Allô. *Hello.,* 2
Allez au tableau! *Go to the board!,* I; **Allez tout droit jusqu'à...** *Go straight until . . .,* I; **Allez, encore un petit effort!** *Come on, one last effort!,* 5
l' alliance, (f.) *wedding ring,* 4
l' **alligator,** (m.) *alligator,* 5
allongé(e) *oblong,* 9
l' **allume-gaz** (m.) *gas lighter,* II
allumer *to light,* II
allumer (les bougies) *to light (the candles)*
les **allumettes** (f.) *matches,* II
l' allumeur de réverbères, (m.) *lamplighter,* 2
alors *so, well/then,* II; **alors que** *while,* II
l' **alpinisme,** (m.) *mountain climbing,* 5
l' **aluminium,** (m.) *aluminum,* 7
l' amateur (de), (m.) *lover (of sth.),* IG
l' **ambulance,** (f.) *ambulance,* 8
l' **ambulancier/l'ambulancière** *paramedic,* 8
l' âme, (f.) *soul,* 9
s' **améliorer** *to improve,* 7
amener *to bring someone along,* I
américain(e) *American,* I
l' amertume, (f.) *bitterness,* 10
l' **ami(e)** *friend,* I
l' **amitié,** (f.) *friendship,* 4
l' **amour,** (m.) *love,* 4
amoureux(-euse) *in love,* 4
amusant(e) *funny/amusing,* II
les **amuse-gueules,** (m. pl.) *snacks,* II
s' **amuser** *to have fun,* II
Amuse-toi bien... *Have fun...,* II
l' ancêtre, (m.) *ancestor,* 5G
ancien(ne) *former,* 1G; l'ancien, (m.) *elder,* 4
l' **âne,** (m.) *donkey,* II
anéantir *to annihilate, to destroy,* 8
l' **anglais,** (m.) *English (language),* 1
anglais(e) *English/British,* II
l' **Angleterre,** (f.) *England,* II
l' **animal,** (m.) *animal,* I; **l'animal domestique** *pet,* 2; **l'animal sauvage** *wild animal,* 5; **les animaux,** (m. pl.) *animals,* I
l' **animateur/l'animatrice** *disc jockey,* II
s' animer *to come to life,* 9
l' anneau, (m.) *ring,* 3
l' année, (f.) *year,* 1G; l'année scolaire, (f.) *school year,* 1
l' **anniversaire,** (m.) *birthday,* II
l' **annonce,** (f.) *ad,* 2
annoncer (que) *to announce (that),* 3

annuel(le) *annual, yearly,* 5
annuler *to cancel, stop,* II
l' **anorak,** (m.) *winter jacket,* I
les Antilles, (f. pl.) *West Indies,* 9G
août *August,* 5
apparaître *to appear,* 3
l' appareil, (m.) *machine,* 10
l' **appareil photo (numérique),** (m.) *(digital) camera,* II
l' **appartement,** (m.) *apartment,* I
appeler *to call,* 2; **s'appeler** *to be named,* I
applaudir *to applaud,* 9
apporter *to bring,* 5
apposer *to affix, to place,* 10
apprendre *to learn,* I; apprendre sur le tas *to learn, to train on the job,* 3
l' **apprentissage,** (m.) *apprenticeship,* 2
apprivoiser *to tame,* 10
appuyer *to press,* 10
après *after,* 1; **après ça** *after that, afterwards,* II
après-demain *day after tomorrow,* II
l' **après-midi** *afternoon,* I
l' **aquarelle,** (f.) *watercolor,* III
l' **araignée,** (f.) *spider,* II
l' arbitre, (m.) *mediator,* 3
l' **arbre,** (m.) *tree,* II
l' archipel, (m.) *archipelago*
l' **architecte,** (m./f.) *architect,* 2
l' **architecture,** (f.) *architecture,* 2
l' **argent,** (m.) *silver,* I; *money,* I
l' **armée,** (f.) *army,* I
l' **armoire,** (f.) *wardrobe,* I
l' **arrêt,** (m.) *stop,* I; **l'arrêt de bus** *bus stop,* I; l'arrêt de mort *death sentence,* 4
arrêter *to stop,* II
l' **arrivée,** (f.) *arrival,* I
arriver *to arrive,* II; **arriver (à quelqu'un)** *to happen (to someone),* II
l' arrosage, (m.) *watering,* 7
arroser *to water,* I
l' **article,** (m.) *article,* 6
l' artisan, (m.) *artisan, craftsman,* 9
l' artisanat, (m.) *craft industry,* 9
l' **artiste,** *artist,* 9
les **arts plastiques,** (m. pl.) *visual arts,* 1
l' **ascenseur,** (m.) *elevator,* I
l' **aspirateur,** (m.) *vacuum cleaner,* I
aspirer *to suck up,* 7
l' assemblage, (m.) *assembly,* 10
assembler *to assemble,* 10
s' asseoir *to sit,* 4
Asseyez-vous! *Sit down!,* I
assez *quite,* I; *pretty/rather,* II; **Assez bien.** *Pretty well.,* 2

l' **assiette,** (f.) *plate,* I
assis(e) *seated,* 4
l' assistance, (f.) *company, all present,* 8
assurer *to enforce, to secure,* 3G
l' **atelier,** (m.) *studio, workshop,* 9; **l'atelier d'artiste** *art studio,* 9
l' **athète,** (m./f.) *athlete,* 6
l' **athlétisme,** (m.) *track and field,* I
l' **atmosphère,** (f.) *atmosphere,* 7
l' **atout,** (m.) *asset,* 2; l'atout maître *master trump,* 5
attendre *to wait,* II
l' **attentat,** (m.) *terrorist attack,* 6
l' attention, (f.) *attention, care,* 8
atterrir *to land,* 10
attraper *to catch,* 1
au *to/at the; to/at + masculine country,* II; **au bord de la mer** *seashore,* II; **au bout de** *at the end of,* II; **au cas où** *in case,* 7; au cours *during,* 7G; au-dessus *above,* 7; **Au fait,...** *By the way...,* 9; **Au feu!** *Fire!,* 8; **au fond de** *at the end of,* I; *at the bottom of,* 4; **au milieu de** *in the middle of,* II; **au moment de** *at the time of,* 3; **au moment où** *at the time (when)/as,* II; **au plus tard** *at the latest,* II; **Au revoir.** *Goodbye.,* I; **Au secours!** *Help!,* 5; au sein de *within,* 4; **au sud de** *south of,* 5; **Au voleur!** *Stop thief!,* 8
l' **aube,** (f.) *dawn,* 10
l' **aubergine,** (f.) *eggplant,* II
Aucune idée. *I have no idea.,* 2
l' **augmentation,** (f.) *raise,* 6
aujourd'hui *today,* I
auprès de *next to,* 5
l' **aurore australe,** (f.) *aurora australis,* 7; l'aurore boréale *aurora borealis,* 7; l'aurore polaire *aurora polaris,* 7
aussi *also,* 1
aussitôt *immediately,* 7
autant que *as much as,* II
l' **auteur** *author,* 5
l' **automne,** (m.) *fall,* I
l' **automobile,** (f.) *automobile,* 7
l' **autonomie,** (f.) *autonomy,* 3
l' **autoportrait,** (m.) *self-portrait,* 9
l' **autorisation,** (f.) *authorization,* 10
l' **autoroute,** (f.) *highway,* 6
autour de *around,* II
autrefois *in the past,* 3
aux *to /at,* I
l' **avalanche,** (f.) *avalanche,* 6
avancer *to go forward,* I
avant de *before,* 3
l' avarice, (f.) *greed,* 8
avec *with,* I; **Avec qui...?** *With whom...?,* I; **avec vue** *with a view,* I
avertir *to warn,* 3
l' **avion,** (m.) *airplane,* II
l' **avis,** (m.) *opinion,* 9
l' **avocat(e)** *lawyer,* 2
avoir *to have,* II; **avoir besoin de** *to need,* II; **avoir chaud** *to be hot,* I; **avoir de la chance** *to be lucky,* 10; **avoir de la fièvre** *to have a fever,* II; **avoir de la patience** *to have patience,* 5; **avoir de l'expérience** *to have experience,* 2; **avoir entraînement** *to have practice/ training,* II; **avoir envie de** *to feel like,* I; **avoir faim** *to be hungry,* I; **avoir froid** *to be cold,* I; **avoir intérêt à** *to be in one's best interest,* I; **avoir l'air** *to seem,* II; **avoir le temps** *to have time,* II; **avoir les yeux...** *to have...eyes,* I; **avoir lieu** *to take place,* 3; **avoir mal (à)** *to hurt/ache,* II; **avoir raison** *to be right,* II; **avoir soif** *to be thirsty,* I; avoir tort *to be wrong,* 7
avouer *to admit,* 4
avril *April,* I

le **bac à sable** *sandbox,* 5
le **bacon** *bacon,* I
les **bagages (à main),** (m. pl.) *(carry-on) luggage,* I
le **bagnard** *convict,* 9G
le **bagne** *convict prison,* 9G
la **bague** *ring,* I; la bague de fiançailles *engagement ring,* 4
la **baguette** *loaf of French bread,* I; **la baguette magique** *magic wand,* 3
la baignade *bath, dipping,* 1
se **baigner** *to swim,* II
la **baignoire** *bathtub,* II
la **baisse** *drop,* 6
le **bal populaire** *village dance,* II
le **baladeur** *walkman,* I
la balançoire *swing,* 5
balayer *to sweep,* I
le **balcon** *balcony,* I
la **baleine** *whale,* 5
la **balle** *ball,* II
le **ballet** *ballet,* 9
la **ballerine** *ballerina,* 9
le **ballon** *ball, balloon,* II
banal(e) *commonplace*
la **banane** *banana,* II

le banc *bench,* 5
bancal(e) *lame,* 6
la **bande dessinée (BD)** *comic strip,* II
la **banderille** *banderilla,* 6
la **banlieue** *suburb,* 1
la **banque** *bank,* I
la barbe *beard,* 3
barbouillé(e) *smeared,* 1
la barre *rail,* 6
la **barre de défilement** *scroll bar,* II
bas(se) *low,* I
le **base-ball** *baseball,* I
le **basket-ball** *basketball,* I, II
les **baskets (f. pl.)** *tennis shoes,* I
la **basse-cour** *barnyard,* II
la **bataille** *battle,* 3
le **bateau** *boat,* II
la **batte** *bat,* I
la **batterie** *drums,* II
le **bayou** *bayou,* 5
beau *handsome/beautiful,* I, II
beaucoup *a lot / much,* 4; **beaucoup (de)** *a lot (of),* 1
le **beau-père** *stepfather,* II
le **bébé** *baby*
la **Belgique** *Belgium,* II
belle *beautiful,* II
la **belle-mère** *stepmother,* II
la berge *bank,* 5
le besoin *need,* 2
la bête *animal,* 1
le **beurre** *butter,* I
la **bibliothèque** *library,* I
la **biche** *doe,* 1
le bidon *can,* 7
le bien *property,* 8
bien *well,* I; **bien cuit(e)** *well-done,* I; **bien entendu** *of course,* I; **bien mûr(e)** *well ripe,* II; **bien sûr** *of course,* I; **Bien sûr que non.** *Of course not.,* II
bientôt *soon,* II
le **bijou** *jewel,* 9
la **bijouterie** *jewelry,* I
le **bijoutier/la bijoutière** *jeweler,* I
bilingue *bilingual,* 3
le **billet** *bill/ticket,* II; **le billet d'avion** *plane ticket,* I; **le billet de train** *train ticket,* II
la **biologie** *biology,* 1
bio(logique) *organic,* 7
le **biscuit** *cookie,* II
le **bison** *buffalo,* 5
la blague *hoax, trick,* 1L
blafard(e) *pale,* 10
blanc(he) *white,* I
le **blé** *wheat,* 7
blessé(e) *injured,* 6
se **blesser** *to injure oneself,* II; blesser *to hurt,* 6

bleu(e) *blue*, II
le **bloc-notes** *scratch pad*, 6
blond(e) *blond(e)*, II
la **blouse** *smock/lab coat*, II
le **blues** *blues*, II
le **bocal** *jar*, 1
le **bœuf** *beef*, II
boire *to drink*, II
le **bois** *woods*, II
la **boisson** *drink*, I
la **boîte** *box*, II; la **boîte d'allumettes** *box of matches*, II; **la boîte de chocolats** *box of chocolates*, II; **la boîte de conserve** *canned food*, II
le **bol** *bowl*, II
bon(ne) *good*, I; **Bonne année!** *Happy New Year.*, II; **Bon anniversaire!** *Happy birthday!*, II; **bon appétit** *enjoy your meal*, I; **Bonne idée!** *Good idea!*, 1; **bon marché(e)** *inexpensive*, I; **Bonne route!** *Have a good (road) trip!*, 10; **Bonne soirée!** *Have a good evening!*, II
le **bonbon** *sweets/candy*, II
le **bonheur** *happiness*, 9
Bonjour. *Hello./Good morning.*, I
Bonsoir. *Hello./Good evening.*, I
le **bord** *edge*, II
le **bord de la mer** *seashore*, 1
borner *to bound, to limit*, 8
le **bossu** *hunchback*, 7
la **botte** *boot*, I
la **bouche** *mouth*, I
bouche bée *with opened mouth, agape*, 1
le **boucher/la bouchère** *butcher*, II
la **boucherie** *butcher shop*, II
le **bouclage** *sealing off*, 6
la **boucle d'oreille** *earring*, I
bouger *to move*, 9
la **bougie** *candle*, II
bouillir *to boil*, II
le **boulanger/la boulangère** *baker*, II
la **boulangerie** *bakery*, II
le **bouleversement** *upheaval*, 4
le **bouquet de fleurs** *bouquet of flowers*, II
la **boussole** *compass*, II
la **bouteille d'eau** *bottle of water*, II; **la bouteille de plongée** *scuba tank*, 5; **la bouteille isotherme** *thermos*, II
la **boutique** *shop*, I
le **bracelet** *bracelet*, I
la **branche** *branch*, II
branlant(e) *shaky*, 1L
le **bras** *arm*, II
bref *in short*, II
briller *to shine*, 4

la **brique** *brick*, 10
le **briquet** *lighter*, II
brisé(e) *broken, ruined*, 9
la **brochure** *brochure*, II
le **brocoli** *broccoli*, II
la **brosse** *brush*, II; **la brosse à dents** *toothbrush*, II
se **brosser les cheveux** *to brush one's hair*, II; **se brosser les dents** *to brush one's teeth*, II
le **bruissement** *rumbling*, 10
le **bruit** *noise*, II
brûlé(e) *burnt*, 1
se **brûler** *to burn oneself*, II
la **brume** *mist*, 7
brun(e) *brown(-haired)*, I
bruyant(e) *noisy*, II
la **bûche de Noël** *Yule log*, II
le **bulletin de vote** *ballot paper*, 8; **le bulletin météo(rologique)** *weather report*, II
le **bureau** *desk*, I; **le bureau de change** *currency exchange office*, I; **le bureau de vote** *polling station*, 8
le **bus** *bus*, I
le **but** *goal*, 3
le **buveur** *drinker*, 2

C'est à environ... de... *It's about . . . from . . .*, 5; **C'est avec...** *It's with . . .*, II; **C'est avec qui?** *Who's in it?*, II; **C'est basé sur une histoire vraie.** *It's based on a true story.*, II; **c'est bon** *it's fine*, II; **C'est complet.** *It's booked.*, I; **c'est compliqué** *it's complicated*, II; **C'est facile de faire...?** *Is it easy to make . . . ?*, II; **C'est incroyable!** *It's incredible!*, 5; **C'est l'heure de...** *It's time to . . .*, II; **C'est pas génial.** *It's not great.*, II; **C'est pas mal, sans plus.** *It's not bad, that's all.*, II; **Ce n'est pas vrai!** *You're kidding*, 4; *It can't be true!*, 5; **C'est possible.** *It's possible.*, II; **C'est pour ça que...** *That's why . . .*, 7; **c'est tout pour aujourd'hui** *that's all for today*, II; **c'est très simple** *it's very simple*, II; **C'est trop...** *It's too . . .*, 5; **C'est... le kilo.** *It's . . . per kilo.*, II
c'est-à-dire *i.e.*, 3
C'était... *It was...*, 1
ça *this/that*, I; **Ça commence à**

quelle heure? *At what time does it begin?*, II; **Ça dépend** *That depends*, II; **Ça en vaut la peine.** *It's worth the trouble.*, 5; **ça fait** *since/ago/for*, II; **Ça fait combien (en tout)?** *How much is it (total)?*, I; **Ça fait longtemps...** *It's been a long time . . .*, 4 ; **Ça fait...** *It's . . . (euros).*, I; **Ça m'énerve!** *How annoying!*, II; **Ça m'étonnerait que...** *It would surprise me that . . .*, 9 ; **Ça me fait penser à...** *That reminds me of . . .*; **Ça me plairait d'être...** *I'd like to be a . . .*, 2; **Ça me plaît beaucoup.** *I really like it.*, I; **Ça n'a pas l'air d'aller.** *I seem not to be doing well.*, II; **Ça n'a rien à voir avec le roman.** *It has nothing to do with the novel.*, II; **Ça ne m'étonnerait pas que...** *I wouldn't be surprised . . .*, 7; **Ça ne vaut pas la peine de...** *It's not worth . . .*, 9; **Ça ne vaut pas le coup de...** *It's not worth the effort . . .*, 9; **Ça ne vous ennuierait pas de...?** *Would you mind . . . ?*, 2; **Ça parle d'un petit garçon qui...** *It's about a little boy who . . .*, II; **Ça passe où?** *Where is it playing?*, II; **ça se trouve où?** *where is it found?*, II; **Ça s'écrit...** *It is spelled . . .*, I; **Ça t'ennuie de...?** *Would you mind . . . ?*, II; **Ça te/vous dit de...?** *Do you feel like . . . ?*, II; **Ça te plaît,...?** *Do you like . . . ?*, I; **Ça va?** *How are you? (informal)*, I; **Ça va aller mieux.** *It's going to get better.*, II; **Ça, ce sont...** *These are . . .*, I; **Ça, c'est...** *This is . . .*, I
la **cabine** *cabin*, 10; **la cabine téléphonique** *telephone booth*, I
le **cabinet** *office*, 2; *cabinet*, 8
la **cacahuète** *peanut*, II
le **cadeau** *present*, II
le **cadet/la cadette** *younger, junior*, 3
le **cadre** *environment*, 8
le **cadi** *Mohammdan judge*, 8
le **café** *coffee house*, I; *coffee*, II; **le café au lait** *coffee w/milk*, I
le **cahier** *notebook*, I
la **caisse** *checkout/cash register*, II
le **caissier/la caissière** *cashier*, II
la **calculatrice** *calculator*, I
calé(e) *propped*, 6
le **calife** *caliph*, 3
le **calme** *calm*, 2
le **Cameroun** *Cameroon*, 3
le **caméscope** *video camera*, II
le **camion** *truck*, 8; **le camion des pompiers** *firetruck*, 8

la campagne *countryside*, 1; **la campagne électorale** *electoral campaign*, 8
camper *to camp out*, 1
le camping *camping*, II
le canard *duck*, II
le candidat/la candidate *candidate*, 8
la canne à pêche *fishing rod*, 1
le canoë *canoe*, 5
la cantine *cafeteria*, II
capable *capable, qualified*, 8
capitonné(e) *padded*, 10
le capot *hood*, 10
la caravane *caravan*, 10
la carotte *carrot*, II
le carreau *small square*, 2
le carrefour *intersection, crossroads*, I
la carrière *career*, 2
la carte *map*, I; **la carte routière** *road map*, 10; **la carte** *menu*, I; **la carte** *card*, I; **la carte bancaire** *bank card*, I; **la carte d'anniversaire** *birthday card*, II; **la carte d'embarquement** *boarding pass*, 10; **la carte d'identité** *I.D. card*, 8; **la carte de vœux** *greeting card*, II; **la carte d'embarquement** *boarding pass*, I; **la carte géographique** *geographic map*, 3; **la carte postale** *postcard*, 1; **la carte téléphonique** *calling card*, I
la cascade *waterfall*, II
la case *hut, cabin*, 1L
la caserne des pompiers *fire station*, 8
le casque *helmet*, I
la casquette *cap*, I
casser *to break*, 6; **se casser la jambe** *to break one's leg*, II
le casse-tête *club*, 9
le castor *beaver*, 5
la catastrophe *catastrophe*, 6
causer *to cause*, 7
le cavalier *rider*, 1
le CD *CD*, I
le CDI (centre de documentation et d'information) *library*, II
ce *this*, I; **Ce n'est pas grave.** *It's not serious.*, II; **Ce n'est pas mon style.** *It's not my cup of tea.*, 9; **ce qui** *what (before verb)*, II; **Ce sera tout?** *Will that be all?*, II
la ceinture *belt*, I
célibataire *single*, 4
la cendre *ash*, 7
cent *one hundred*, I; **cent un** *one hundred and one*, I
des centaines de milliers *hundreds of thousands*, 5

le centre aéré *outdoor center*, I; **le centre commercial** *mall*, I; **le centre-ville** *downtown*, I
cependant *however*, 3
cerclé(e) *rimmed*, 10
les céréales, (f. pl.) *cereal*, I
le cerf *deer*, 5
le cerf-volant *kite*, I
la cerise *cherry*, II
certain(e) *some*, 9
certes *most sertainly, to be sure*, 5
le cerveau *brain*, II
ces *these*, I
cesser *to cease*, 8
le cessez-le-feu *ceasefire*, 3
C'est *It's*, I; **C'est chouette!** *Splendid!*, 8; **C'est combien (pour)...?** *How much is (it) . . . ?*, I; **C'est tout à fait toi.** *It's totally you.*, I; **C'est une bonne affaire!** *It's a good deal!*, I; **C'est... arobase... point...** *It's . . . @ . . . dot . . .*, I
cet(te) *this*, I
chacun(e) *each one*, 8
le chagrin *sorrow, disappointment*, 10
la chaîne *chain*, I, *station*, II; **la chaîne stéréo** *stereo system*, I
la chaise *chair*, 1
la chaleur *heat*, 6
chamarré(e) *embroidered*, 3
la chambre *bedroom*, I; **la Chambre** *house (government)*, 8; **la chambre avec vue** *room with a view*, I
le champ *field*, II
le champignon *mushroom*, II
le champion/la championne *champion*, 6
le changement de vitesse automatique/manuel *automatic/manual transmission*, 10; **changer (en)** *to change (into)*, I; **changer de l'argent** *to exchange money*, II; **changer de vitesse** *to shift gears*, 10
le chant *singing*, 9
chanter *to sing*, I
le chanteur/la chanteuse *singer*, 2
le chapeau *hat*, I
le chapiteau *circus tent*, 9
chaque *each/every*, II
la charcuterie *delicatessen*, II
le chariot *shopping cart*, II
le charmeur de serpents *snake charmer*, 3G
la charrette *cart*, 10
chassé(e) de *expelled, driven out*, 7G
chasser *to chase away*, 3
le chat *cat*, II
châtain(s) *light brown(-haired)*, I

le château *castle*, II
chaud(e) *hot*, I
le chauffeur *driver*, 2
la chaussette *sock*, I
la chaussure *shoe*, 1; **les chaussures de randonnée,** (f. pl.) *hiking shoes*, 1
la chauve-souris *bat*, 5
chavirer *to capsize*, 1
le chef *head*, 8; **le chef de l'état** *head of state*, 8; **le chef-d'œuvre** *master piece*, 9; **le chef d'orchestre** *conductor*, 9;
le chemin *path / way*, 3
la chemise *man's shirt*, I
le chemisier *woman's blouse*, I
le chèque *check*, I; **le chèque-cadeau** *gift card*, II; **le chèque de voyage** *traveler's check*, II
cher/chère *expensive*, I
chercher *to look for*, I
le chercheur *researcher*, 3
chétif/chétive *puny*, 3
le cheval *horse*, II
le chevalet *easel*, 9
le chevalier *knight*, 3
la chevelure *hair*, 9
les cheveux (m. pl.) *hair*, II
la cheville *ankle*, II
la chèvre *goat*, II
chez *at the house of*, II; **chez moi** *at (my) home*, I
le chien *dog*, II
le chiffre *figure*, 6
la chimie *chemistry*, 1
les chips, (f. pl.) *chips*, II
le chocolat *chocolate*, I; **le chocolat chaud** *hot chocolate*, II
choisir *to choose*, II
le chômage *unemployment*, 6
le chômeur/la chômeuse *unemployed person*, 6
la chorégraphie *choreography*, 9
la chose *thing*, I
chrétien(ne) *Christian*, 1G
le christianisme *Christianity*, 1G
cibler *to target*, 6
le ciel *sky*, 5; **les cieux,** (pl.) *heaven*, 5
la cigale *cicada*
la cigogne *stork*, 5
le cinéaste *film director*, 7
le cinéma *movie theater*, 1
cinq *five*, I
cinquante *fifty*, I
cinquième *fifth*, 2L
la circulation *traffic*, 8
le cirque *circus*, 9
la citerne *tank*, 7
le citoyen/la citoyenne *citizen*, 9G
la citoyenneté *citizenship*, 9G
la citrouille *pumpkin*, 3

clair(e) *light*, I
la classe *classroom*, 1
  classer *to file*, 7G
le classeur *binder*, I
  classique *classical*, I
le clavier *keyboard*, II
le climat *climate*, 7
la climatisation *air conditioning*, I
  cliquer *to click*, II
le clown *clown*, 3
le club (de tennis, de foot) *(sports) club*
le coca *soda, Coke*, II
le cochon *pig*, II
le cockpit *cockpit*, 10
le code postal *zip code*, I
le cœur *heart*, II
le coffre *trunk*, 10
se coiffer *to do one's hair*, II
le coiffeur/la coiffeuse *hairdresser*, 2
  coincé(e) *stuck*, 4
la colère *anger*, 6
le colis *package*, I
la collection *collection*, 6
  collectionner *to collect*, II
le collier *necklace*, I
le colon *settler, colonist*, 5G
la colonie *colony*, 3; **la colonie de vacances** *summer camp*, II
la colonisation *colonization*, 3
le combat *fight*, 3
  combattre *to fight*, 3
  combien (de) *how much/how many*, I; **Combien vous en faut-il?** *How many do you need?*, II
la combinaison de plongée *wetsuit*, 5
le combiné *receiver*, 2
  combler *to shower*, 9
la comédie *comedy*, II; **la comédie musicale** *musical*, 9
le commandant de bord *captain*, 10
la commande *order*, 2
le commencement *beginning*, 3
  commencer *to begin*, II
  comment *how*, II; **Comment allez-vous?** *How are you? (formal)*, I; **Comment ça s'écrit?** *How do you write that?*, I; **Comment ça va?** *How are you? (informal)*, I; **Comment c'est,...?** *How is ... ?*, I; **Comment dit-on... en français?** *How do you say ... in French?*, I; **Comment est ton cours de...?** *How is your ... class?*, I; **Comment est...?** *How is ... ?*, I; **Comment est-ce qu'on fait pour...?** *What do you do to ...?*, II; **Comment est-ce qu'on fait...?** *How do you make ...?*, II; **Comment il/elle s'appelle?** *What's his/her name?*, I;

Comment peut-on rejoindre...? *How do you meet up with ...?*, 10; **Comment s'est passé(e)...?** *How did ... go?*, II; **Comment sont...?** *How are ...?*, I; **Comment trouves-tu...?** *How do you like ...?*, 9; **Comment tu épelles...?** *How do you spell ...?*, I; **Comment tu t'appelles?** *What is your name?*, I; **Comment tu t'appelles?** *What's your name?*, II; **Comment tu trouves...?** *What do you think of ...?*, I; **Comment va...?** *How is ...?*, 4
le **commerçant/la commerçante** *retailer*, 8C
le commissariat de police *police station*, 8
la commode *chest of drawers*, I
la **commune** *town*, 7C
la compagnie *company*, II; **la compagnie aérienne** *airline company*, 10
le compartiment *compartment*, I
la compétition *contest/competition*, II
  complet (complète) *booked/full*, I
  complètement *completely*, II
le complexe sportif *sports facilities*, 1
  compliqué(e) *complicated*, II
  composter *to punch (a ticket)*, I
  comprendre *to understand*, I
le comprimé *compress/tablet*, I
la **comptabilité** *accounting*, 2
le comptable/la comptable *accountant*, 2
le comptoir *trading post*, 3
le **concours** *competitive exams*, 6
le conducteur/la conductrice *driver*, 10
  conduire *to drive*, 8
la conduite *behavior / comportment*, 3
les **confettis,** (m. pl.) *confetti*, II
  confier *to entrust*, 8
  confirmer *to confirm*, 10
la confiture *jam*, I
le conflit *conflict*, 3
  conjointe *joint*, 4C
  conjurer *to beg*, 3
  connaître *to know*, II
  conquérir *to conquest*, 3G
la conquête *conquest*, 3
  consacré(e) *devoted*, 6
le **conseil** *advice*, 3
  conseiller *to advise*, I
le conseiller/la conseillère d'éducation *school counselor*, 1; **le conseiller familial** *family counselor*, 4
  consentir *to agree, to consent*, 4
la conséquence *consequence*, 7

la conservation *preservation*, 7
  conserver *to keep*, 6
la consigne *baggage locker*, I; *order*, 2; **les consignes de sécurité,** (f. pl.) *safety procedures*, 10
  consommer *to consume/eat*, II
le constat *report*, 8
le constructeur *builder*, 10
  construire *to build*, 1G
  contacter *to contact*, 8
le conte *tale*, 3
  contenir *to contain*, 7
  content(e) *happy*, II
le **conteur** *storyteller*, 3g
  continuer *to continue*, I
la contravention *fine*, 8
  contre *against*, 8
le contrôleur *ticket collector*, I
  convaincre *to convince*, 7
  convenir *to agree*, 3
se **convertir** *to become converted*, 3G
le copain/la copine *friend*, 1
le **coquillage** *sea shell*, 9
la coquille *shell*, 9
le corail *coral*, 5
la corde *rope*, 5
le corps *body*, II
la correspondance *connecting flight / connection*, I
  corriger *to correct*, I
la **Corse** *Corsica*, 1G
la corvée *chore*, I
le costume *suit*, I
la côte *coast*, 7
le **coteau** *hill*, 10
le coton *cotton*, I
le cou *neck*, II
se **coucher** *to go to bed*, II
le coucher de soleil *sunset*, 2
la couchette *sleeping car*, I
le **couillon** *idiot*, 1
la coulée de lave *lava flow*, 7
  couler *to run/to drip, to flow* II
la couleur *color*, I
le **couloir** *hallway*, 7
la country *country music*, II
le **coup** *blow*, 6; **le coup d'état** *hostile take over*, 3; **le coup de foudre** *love-at-first-sight*, 4
  coupable *guilty*, 3
  couper *to cut*, II; **couper (les cheveux)** *to cut (hair)*, 2; **se couper** *to cut oneself*, II
le coupe-vent *windbreaker*, I
la cour de récré(ation) *schoolyard*, II
  Courage,... *Cheer up,...*, 5
le courant *currant*, 7
la courge *gourd*, 7
la courgette *zucchini*, II

courir *to run*, II
couronner *to crown*, 1G
le courrier *mail*, 6; **le courrier des lecteurs** *letters to the Editor*, 6
le cours *class(es)*, 1
court(e) *short (length)*, II
le cousin/la cousine *cousin*, II
le couteau *knife*, I
coûter *to cost*, I
le couturier/la couturière *fashion designer*, 2
le couvert *table setting*, I
la couverture *cover*, 6
la couverture *blanket*, 7
couvrir *to cover*, 3G
craindre *to fear*, 5
la crainte *fear*, 8
le cratère *crater*, 3G
la cravate *tie*, I
le crayon *pencil*, I
le crayon (de couleur) *(colored) pencil*, I
créatif(-ive) *creative*, I
créer *to create*
la crème à raser *shaving cream*, II; **la crème solaire** *sunscreen*, II
la crémerie *dairy market*, II
creuser *to dig*, 7C
creux/creuse *empty, hollow*, 10
la crevette *shrimp*, II
la critique *critic*, 6; **le/la critique d'art** *art critic*, 9
le crocodile *crocodile*, 5
croire (à) *to think/to believe (in)*, II; **croire que** *to think that*, 7
la croisade *crusade*, 1G
le croissant *croissant*, I
le croque-monsieur *toasted ham and cheese sandwich*, II
le croquis *sketch*, 9
la croyance *belief*, 3
la cruauté *cruelty*, 8
cube *cubic*, 7
cueillir *to pick/to gather*, 5
la cuillère *spoon*, I
la cuillerée à café *teaspoon*, II; **la cuillerée à soupe** *tablespoon*, II
le cuir *leather*, I
la cuisine *cooking, kitchen* I
le cuisinier/la cuisinière *cook*, 2
culinaire *culinary*, 1G
Culture *Arts page*, 6
le curriculum vitæ *resumé*, 2
le cybercafé *Internet café*, I
le cyclone *hurricane*, 7

d'abord *first*, I
D'accord. *Okay.*, II
d'ailleurs *besides*, 4
D'après toi,... *In your opinion, . . .*, 4
D'un côté... d'un autre... *On one hand . . . on the other hand . . .*, 7
le **Danemark** *Denmark*, II
le **danger** *danger*, 3; **en danger** *in danger*, 3
dangereux(-euse) *dangerous*, II
danois(e) *Danish*, II
dans *in/inside*, II; **dans le cadre de** *in the context of*, 2; **dans le nord de** *in the north of*, 5; **dans un pays lointain** *in a far away country*, 3; **Dans..., il y a...** *In . . ., there is . . .*, I
la **danse** *dancing*, 9
le **danseur/la danseuse** *dancer*, 9
danser *to dance*, I
d'après moi *according to me*, I
le **dauphin** *dolphin*, 5
de *of/from + city, feminine country*, I; **de bonne heure** *bright and early*, II; **de bonne/mauvaise humeur** *in a good/bad mood*, 4; **de la/l'** *of the*, I; **de la/l'** *some, from*, II; **De quelle couleur sont...?** *What color are . . . ?*, II; **De quoi ça parle?** *What's it about?*, II; **De quoi tu as besoin?** *What do you need?*, I; **de temps en temps** *from time to time*, I
débarquer *to disembark*, 10
débarrasser *to clear (something)*, I; **débarrasser la table** *to clear the table*, I
le **débat télévisé** *televised debate*, 8
le **déboire** *difficulty*, 3
débutant(e) *beginner*, 2
le **décalage horaire** *jet lag*, 10
décembre *December*, I
le **déchet** *waste*, 10
décidé(e) *determined*, 4
déclarer (que) *to declare (that)*, 3
décoller *to take off*, 10
la **décolonisation** *decolonization*, 3
le **décor** *scenery/set*, 9
le **décorateur/la décoratrice** *interior designer*, 2
décoratif(-ive) *ornamental, decorative*, 9

la **décoration** *decoration*, II
décorer *to decorate*, II; **décorer la salle** *to decorate the room*, II
découvrir *to discover*, 5G
le **décret** *executive order*, 9G
décrire *to describe*, 9G
décrocher *to pick up*, 2
déçu(e) *disappointed*, 4
la **déesse** *goddess*, 3
défaire *to undo*, 9
défendre *to protect, to defend*, 5G
Défense de... *You musn't . . .*, 5
déferler *to break (waves)*, 1L
le **défilé** *parade*, II
définir *to define*, 8
la **déforestation** *deforestation*, 7
les **dégâts,** (m. pl.) *damage*, 7
dehors *outside*, 10
déjà *already*, II
le **déjeuner** *lunch*, I
Délicieux(-euse)! *Delicious!*, I
le **deltaplane** *hang gliding*, 5
délivrer *to rescue*, 3
demain *tomorrow*, I
se **demander** *to wonder*, II; **demander un prêt** *to apply for a loan*, 4
se démarquer *to differentiate oneself from*, 2C
démarrage *home (Internet)*, II
démarrer *to start up*, II
déménager *to move (location), to move out*, 3
demeurer *to stay*, 3; *to remain*, 6
demi(e) *half*, I
le **demi-frère** *half-brother*, I
la **demi-pension** *room with breakfast and one meal*, 1
la **demi-sœur** *half-sister*, I
démissionner *to resign*, 8
la **démocratie** *democracy*, 8
démonter la tente *to take down a tent*, II
la dentelle *lace*, 7G
le **dentifrice** *toothpaste*, II
le **dentiste** *dentist*, II
les **dents,** (f. pl.) *teeth*, II
le **déodorant** *deodorant*, II
le **départ** *departure*, I
dépasser *to pass beyond*, 3
se **dépêcher** *to hurry*, I
Dépêche-toi! *Hurry up!*, II
dépendre *to depend*, II
dépenser *to spend*, 7
déposer *to deposit*, I
la **dépouille** *skin*, 8
déprimant(e) *depressing*, II

depuis *since/ago* II
le député/la députée *congressman/ congresswoman*, 8
déranger *to disturb*, I
dernier(-ière) *last/latest*, II
derrière *behind*, I
des *of the*, I; *some, from*, II
dès *as early as*, 7
le désastre *disaster*, 3
descendre *to go down/to get out*, II; **descendre des rapides** *to shoot the rapids*, 5
le désert *desert*, 7
se déshabiller *to get undressed*, II
le désinfectant *disinfectant*, II
désirer *to want*, I
désolé(e) *sorry*, I
Désolé(e), je n'ai pas le temps. *Sorry, I don't have the time.*, II
despotique *tyrannical*, 8
le dessin *drawing*, I; **le dessin humoristique** *cartoon*, 6
dessiner *to draw*, I
le destin *destiny*, 10
la destination *destination*, I
destiné(e) *aimed*, 6
détenir *to hold/to be in possession of*, 6
détester *to hate*, II
détruire *to destroy*, 6
le DEUG *diploma obtained after 2 years of college*, 1
deux *two*, I
deux cent un *two hundred and one*, I
deux cents *two hundred*, I
deuxième *second*, I; **la deuxième classe** *second class*, I; **la Deuxième Guerre mondiale,** *World War II*, 3
devant *in front (of)*, I
développer *to develop*, 6
devenir *to become*, 1G
Devine... *Guess...*, 4
deviner *to guess*, 4
la devise *motto*
devoir *to have to/must*, II
le devoir *duty*, 4; **le devoir,** *homework*, 1
d'habitude *usually*, I
le diamant *diamond*, 4
la dictature *dictatorship*, 8
le dictionnaire *dictionary*, I
le dicton *old saying, maxime*, 7
le dieu *god*, 3
différent(e) de *different from*, II
difficile *difficult*, I
diffusé(e) *distributed*, 6
digne *worth*, 4
se diluer *to become diluted*, 10
dimanche *Sunday*, I

dîner *to have dinner*, I
le diplôme *diploma*, 2
dire *to say/to tell*, II
direct(e) *live*, II
diriger *to lead/to be in charge of*, 2
le discours *speech*, 8
discuter (avec des amis) *to talk (with friends)*, I
Dis-moi,... *Tell me, ...,* II
disparaître *to disappear*, 3
disponible (pour) *available (for)*, I
se disputer *to argue (with one another)*, 4
les distinctions (f. pl.) *honors*, 8
distraire *to entertain*,
le distributeur d'argent *cash machine*, I; **le distributeur de billets** *ticket machine*, I
dites-moi *tell me*, I
diviser *to divide*, 3G
divorcer *to divorce*, 4
dix *ten*, I
dix-huit *eighteen*, I
dix-neuf *nineteen*, I
dix-sept *seventeen*, I
le docteur/la doctoresse *doctor*, 2
le document *document*, II
le documentaire *documentary*, II
le documentaliste/la documentaliste *librarian*, II
le doigt *finger*, II; **le doigt de pied** *toe*, II
le domicile *residence*, 10
dominer *to master*, 3; *to overlook*, 8
le don *gift*, 6
donc *therefore*, 7
donner *to give*, I; donner carte blanche à quelqu'un *to give someone free choice*, 4; donner la mesure *to set the tempo*, 9; **se donner rendez-vous** *to make a date (with one another)*, 4
Donnez-moi... *Give me...,* I
dormir *to sleep*, II
le dos *back*, II
la douane *customs*, 10
le doublage *dubbing, doubling*, 3
le doubleur/la doubleuse *dubber*, 3
doucement *slowly*, 10
la douceur *softness*, 10
la douche *shower*, II
la douzaine d'œufs *a dozen eggs*, II
douze *twelve*, I
le dramaturge *playwright*, 9
le drame *drama*, II
le drap *cloth*, 3; *sheet*, 7
le drapeau *flag*, 3
le dressage *training*, 1C
dresser *to draw up*, 8; **dresser un**

constat *to draw up a report*, 8
le droit *right*, 8; **le droit de vote** *right to vote*, 8
la droite *right*, I
drôle *funny*, II
du *of the*, I; **du** *some, from*, II
dû(e) à *due to*, 7
du... au *from the ... to the ...,* I
le duo *duet*, 3
dur(e) *hard*, 6
durable *lasting*, 9
la durée (de) *period (of)*, 2
durer *to last*, 6
du reste *moreover*, 2C
le DVD *DVD*, I

l' **eau,** (f.) *water*, I; **l'eau minérale,** (f.) *mineral water*, I
échanger *to exchange*, 4
échapper *to escape*, 8
l' **écharpe,** (f.) *winter scarf*, I
l' échec, (m.) *failure*, 9
les **échecs,** (m. pl.) *chess*, I
l' **éclair,** (m.) *lightning flash*, 7
s' éclairer *to light up*, 10
l' éclat, (m.) *shine*, 7
éclater *to burst / to erupt*, 3
l' **école,** (f.) *school*, I
l' **écologiste,** (m./ f.) *environmentalist*, 7
l' **Économie** (f.) *business page*, 6
écouter *to listen*, I; **écouter de la musique** *to listen to music*, I
les **écouteurs,** (m. pl.) *headphones*, I
Écoutez! *Listen!*, I
l' **écran,** (m.) *screen*, II
écrasé(e) *squashed*, 10
s' écraser *to crash*, 2
l' **écrevisse,** (f.) *crawfish*, 5
écrire *to write*, II
écrit(e) *written*, 6
l' écriture, (f.) *writing*, 6
l' écrivain, (m.) *writter*, 9G
l' **écureuil,** (m.) *squirrel*, 5
édicter *to enact, to edict*, 6
l' édifice, (m.) *building*, 7G
l' **édition,** (f.) *edition*, 6
l' **éducation musicale,** (f.) *music education*, I
effacer *to erase*, 9
effectuer *to carry out*, 6; **effectuer (une année d'études)** *to complete (a year of studies)*, 2
l' **effet,** (m.) *effect*, 7; **l'effet de serre, (m.)** *greenhouse effect*, 7
effrayer *to scare*, 8
l' égalité *equality*

l' **église,** (f.) *church,* I
l' **électeur/l'électrice** *voter,* 8
l' **élection,** (f.) *election,* 8
electoral(e) *electoral,* 8
l' **électricien/l'électricienne** *electrici* *an,* 2
électriser *to thrill,* 6
l' **électroménager,** (m.) *appliances,* 7
élégant(e) *elegant,* I
l' **élevage,** (m.) *breeding,* 1
l' **élève,** (m./f.) *student,* 1
élevé(e) *high,* 3G
élire *to elect,* 3
elle *she,* I; **Elle est comment,...?** *How is . . . ?,* I
elles *they (fem),* I
élu(e) *elected,* 8
l' **e-mail,** (m.) *e-mail,* I
s' **émanciper** *to free oneself*
emballer *to wrap,* II; **emballer les cadeaux** *to wrap the presents,* II
embarquer *to board,* 10
emboutir *to crash into,* 6
embrasser *to kiss, to hug,* 10
émigrer *to emigrate,* 5G
l' **émission de variétés,** (f.) *variety show,* II
les **émissions télé,** (f. pl.) *television programs,* II
emménager *to move in,* 4
emmener *to lead, to take,* 8
empêcher *to prevent,* 9G
l' **empereur,** (m.) *emperor,* 3
l' **empire,** (m.) *empire,* 3
empirer *to worsen,* 7
l' **emploi,** (m.) *job,* 2; **l'emploi du temps** *schedule,* 1
l' **employé(e),** (m./f.) *employee,* I
emporter *to take (with),* II
l' **empreinte,** (f.) *print,* 1
l' **emprunt,** (m.) *loan,* 4
emprunter *to borrow,* 1; **emprunter (des livres)** *to borrow (books),* 1
en *to/at + feminine country,* I; **en** *in/to,* II; **en** *some of it (them)/any of it (them),* II; **en argent** *(of) silver,* I; **en avance** *early,* I; **en baisse** *dropping,* 6; **en bas** *downstairs,* I; **en bus** *by bus,* I; **En ce qui me concerne...** *As far as I'm concerned . . . ,* 8; **en colère** *angry,* 6; en dehors *outside,* 9; **en face de** *across from,* I; **en grève** *on strike,* 6; **en haut** *upstairs,* I; **en jean** *(of) denim,* I; **en laine** *(of) wool,* I; **en lin** *(of) linen,* I; **en même**

temps (que) *at the same time (as),* II; **en métro** *by subway,* ; **en or** *(of) gold,* I; **en premier** *first/firstly,* II; **en principe** *theoretically,* 7; **en provenance de** *from,* I; **en quel mois** *which month,* I; **En quelle saison...?** *In which season . . . ?,* I; **en quête de** *in pursuit of,* 3; **en retard** *late,* I; en route *on the way,* 5C; **en solde** *on sale,* I; **en taxi** *by taxi,* I; **en train de** *in the process of,* II; **en voiture** *by car,* I
encadrer *to frame,* 9
enchaîner *to continue,* 2
enchanté(e) *enchanted,* 3; **Enchan té(e)!** *Delighted!,* I
encore *more,* I; *yet/again,* I
encourager *to encourage,* I
endommager *to damage,* 7
s' **endormir** *to fall asleep,* II
endurant(e) *enduring, resistant*
l' **énergie,** (f.) *energy,* 7
énervé(e) *annoyed,* 4
énerver *to annoy,* II; **s'énerver** *to get annoyed,* 4
l' **enfance,** (f.) *childhood,* 4
l' **enfant,** (m./f.) *child,* I
enfermer *to shut, to confine,* 9
enfler *to swell,* 9
englober *to include,* 2C
engloutir *to swallow,* 1L
l' **enjambée,** (f.) *step,* 2
enlever *to remove,* 6; **enlever ses vêtements** *to take off one's clothes,* II
l' **ennemi(e)** *enemy,* 3
ennuyeux(-euse) *boring,* II
enregistrer *to record,* 6; *to check in,* 10
s' **enrouler** *to wrap (oneself),* 3
enseigner *to teach,* 7
ensemble *together,* 4
l' **ensemble** *whole,* 4
ensuite *then/next,* II
entendre *to hear,* I; **entendre parler de** *to hear about,* 6
l' **entraînement,** (m.) *training,* 1
entre *between,* I; **Entre parenthèses,...** *Incidentally, . . . ,* 9; **entre... et** *between . . . and (in between),* I
l' **entrée** (f.) *entry hall,* 7
entreprendre *to undertake,* 2
entre autres *among others,* 4
entrer *to enter,* II
entretenir *to take care of,* 10
l' **entretien,** (m.) *interview,* 2; *maintenance,* 10
l' **entrevue,** (f.) *interview,* 2
l' **enveloppe,** (f.) *envelope,* I

environ *approximately,* II
l' **environnement,** (m.) *environment,* 7
l' **envol,** (m.) *taking flight,* 1
s' **envoler** *to take off,* 9
envoûtant(e) *entrancing, bewitching,* 10
envoyer *to send,* II; **envoyer des e-mails** *to send e-mails,* I; **envoyer les invitations** *to send the invitations,* II
l' **éolienne,** (f.) *windmill,* 7
épaissir *to thicken,* 5
l' **épaule,** (f.) *shoulder,* II
l' **épée,** (f.) *sword,* 3
épeler *to spell,* I
l' **épicerie,** (f.) *grocery store,* II
les **épices,** (f. pl.) *spices,* II
l' **épicier/l'épicière** *grocer,* II
éponger *to wipe (the sweat),* 2
l' **épouse** (f.) *spouse,* 4
épouser *to marry,* 7G
l' **EPS (éducation physique et sportive),** (f.) *Physical education (P.E.),* I
l' **épreuve,** (f.) *test,* 1
l' **épuration,** (f.) *purification,* 7C
l' **équilibre** *balance,* 6
équilibré(e) *balanced,* II
l' **équipage,** (m.) *crew,* 10
l' **équipe,** (f.) *team,* 6
l' **équipement,** (m.) *equipment,* 5
équiper *to equip,* 7
l' **équitation,** (f.) *horse riding*
l' **équité,** (f.) *equity,* 3
l' **errance,** (f.) *wandering,* 3
l' **éruption,** (f.) *eruption,* 7
l' **escalade,** (f.) *mountain climbing,* II
l' **escale,** (f.) *stopover, layover,* 10
l' **escalier,** (m.) *staircase,* I
l' **esclavage,** (m.) *slavery*
l' **esclave,** (m.) *slave*
l' **Espagne,** (f.) *Spain,* 10
espagnol(e) *Spanish,* II
l' **espèce,** (f.) *species,* 5
l' **espérance,** (f.) *hope,* 9
espérer *to hope,* II
l' **esprit** (m.) *spirit,* 4
les **essais nucléaires** (m.) *nuclear testings,* 9G
essayer *to try (on),* I
l' **essence,** (f.) *gasoline,* 7; **l'essence sans plomb,** (f.) *unleaded gasoline,* 10
les **essuie-glaces,** (m. pl.) *windshield wipers,* 10
est-ce que *is it that/does,* II
estimer *to estimate,* 7; **s'estimer** *to have a high opinion of oneself,* 8
l' **estomac,** (m.) *stomach,* II
Es-tu en forme? *Are you in shape?,* II

l' estuaire, (m.) *estuary*, 5
et *and*, I; **Et toi?** *How about you?*
  (informal), I; **Et vous?** *How*
  about you? (formal), I
établir *to establish*, 3
l' **étage**, (m.) *floor*, I
l' **étagère**, (f.) *bookshelf*, I
l' étalage, (m.) *display*, 7
étancher *to quench*, 10
l' **état**, (m.) *state*, 8
l' **été**, (m.) *summer*, II
éteindre *to extinguish*, 8
s' **étendre** *to spread, to stretch*, 3G
éternuer *to sneeze*, II
l' étiquette, (f.) *label*, 10
étiqueter *to label*, 10
l' étoile, (f.) *star*, 2
étonner *to surprise*, 7
étouffer *to smother*, 10
étranger(-ère) *foreign*, II
étrangler *to strangle*, 3
être *to be*, II; **être amoureux(-**
  euse) *to be in love*, 4; **être au**
  chômage *to be unemployed*, 2;
  être au courant de *to be*
  aware of, 6; être d'accord *to*
  agree, 4; **être en baisse** *to be*
  falling, 6; **être en colère** *to be*
  angry, 6; **être en forme** *to be*
  in shape/healthy, II; **être en**
  retard *to be late*, II; **être en**
  retenue *to be in detention*, II;
  être engagé(e) *to be hired*, 2;
  être fatigué(e) *to be tired*, II;
  être fiancé(e) *to be engaged*, 4;
  être licencié(e) *to be fired*, 2
étroit(e) *tight*, I
l' **étudiant/l'étudiante** *student*, 2
étudier *to study*, I
évacuer *to evacuate*, 7
s' **évanouir** *to vanish*, 10
l' évasion, (f.) *escape*, 9G
éventuel(le) *possible*, 4
évidemment *obviously*, II
éviter *to avoid*, 6
évoluer *to move around*, 5
s' **exalter** *to grow excited*, 7
Excellent(e)! *Excellent!*, II
Excusez-moi *Excuse me*, I
exécuter *to execute, to carry out*, 8
l' **exercice**, (m.) *activity*, I;
  exercise, II
exiger *to require*, 10
existant(e) *existing*, 10
expliquer *to explain*, 9
l' **explorateur**, (m.) *explorer*, 3
explorer *to explore*, 3
exposer *to unfold*, 7; *to exhibit*, 9
l' **exposition**, (f.) *exhibit*, 6
exprimer *to express*, 5
expulser *to expel*, 5G
l' extrait, (m.) *excerpt*, 2

l' **extraterrestre**, (m./
  f.) *extraterrestrial*, 6

la **fable** *fable*, 3
fâché(e) *angry*, 4
facile *easy*, I
la façon *manner*, 6
le **facteur** *mail carrier*, I
  faire *to do/to make*, II;
    faire (la France) *to visit*
    (France), I; **faire cuire** *to*
    cook/to bake, II; **faire de**
    l'alpinisme *to mountainn*
    climb, 5; **faire de l'escalade** *to*
    mountain climb, II; **faire de**
    la balançoire *to swing*, II;
    faire de la musculation *to*
    lift weights, II; **faire de la**
    photo *to do photography*, 1;
    faire de la planche à voile *to*
    windsurf, II; **faire de la**
    plongée sous-marine *to go*
    scuba diving, 5; **faire de la**
    randonnée *to go hiking*, 1; **faire**
    de la vidéo amateur *to make*
    amateur videos, II; **faire de la**
    voile *to go sailing*, II; **faire des**
    activités *to do activities*, 1;
    faire des châteaux de sable *to*
    make sandcastles, II; **faire des**
    clés *to make keys*, 2; **faire**
    des études *to study*, 2; **faire**
    des farces *to play practical*
    jokes, II; **faire des heures**
    supplémentaires
    to work overtime, 2; **faire**
    du skate *to skateboard*, 1;
    faire du canoë-kayak *to go*
    canoeing/kayaking, 5; **faire du**
    deltaplane *hang glinding*, 5;
    faire du manège *to go on a*
    carousel, II; **faire du parachut**
    isme *parachuting*, 5; **faire du**
    rafting *to go rafting*, 5; **faire du**
    sport *to play sports*, I; **faire du**
    théâtre *to do theater/drama*, II;
    faire escale *to make a*
    stopover, I; ; faire la connaissance
    de *to meet so./to get acquainted*
    with so., 2; **faire la cuisine** *to*
    cook, I; **faire la fête** *to party*, I;
    faire la lessive *to do the*
    laundry, I; **faire la poussière** *to*
    dust, II; **faire la queue** *to stand*
    in line, I; **faire la révision** *to*
    have one's car checked, 10; **faire**
    la sieste *to take a nap*, II; **faire**
    la vaisselle *to do the dishes*, I;

faire le ménage *to clean the*
  house, II; **faire le plein** *to*
  fill up, 10; **faire le tour du**
  monde *to take a world tour*, II;
  faire le tour du monde à la voile
  to sail around the world, 5;
  faire les courses *to go*
  grocery shopping, II; **faire les**
  magasins *to go shopping*, 1;
  faire les valises *to pack the*
  bags, I; faire mouvoir *to put in*
  motion, 8; **faire naufrage** *to*
  wreck, 7; faire partie de *to be*
  part of, 7G; **faire sa toilette** *to*
  clean (oneself) up, II; faire
  semblant *to pretend*, 10;
  faire ses devoirs *to do one's*
  homework, II; **faire son lit** *to*
  make one's bed, I; **faire un**
  apprentissage *to train/to have*
  an apprenticeship, 4; **faire un**
  emprunt *to apply for a loan*, 4;
  faire un feu de camp *to make*
  a campfire, II; **faire un pique-**
  nique *to go on a picnic*, I; **faire**
  un séjour *to stay/to sojourn*, II;
  faire un stage *to be in training/*
  to do an internship, 2; **faire un**
  voyage *to take a trip*, I; **faire**
  un voyage organisé *to take*
  an organized trip, II; **faire une**
  demande de visa *to apply for a*
  visa, II; **faire une expérience** *to*
  do an experiment, II; **faire une**
  randonnée *to go hiking*, II;
  faire une recherche *to*
  do a Web search, II; **faire**
  une réservation *to make*
  a reservation, II; **faire une**
  visite guidée *to take a guided*
  tour, II; **se faire vacciner** *to get*
  vaccinated, II
les **faits divers**, (m. pl.) *miscellaneous*
  news, 6
  falloir *to have to/to be necessary*, II
la **famille** *family*, II
  fantastique *fantastic / fantasy*, 3
le **fantôme** *ghost*, 3
la **farine** *flour*, II
  fascinant(e) *fascinating*, I
  fatigué(e) *tired*, 7
la fatuité *self-conceit*, 3
la **faune~** *fauna*, 5
le **fauteuil** *armchair*, I; **le fauteuil**
  pliant *folding chair*, II
  faux *off-key*, 9
  faux(fausse) *false*, 8
les **favoris**, (m. pl.) *favorites*
  (Internet), II
  fécond(e) *fertile/fruitful*, 5
la **fée** *fairy*, 3
  féliciter *to congratulate*, 7

féminin(e) *feminine/female,* 6
la femme *wife,* I; *woman,* 4
la fenêtre *window,* II
le fer *iron*
la ferme *farm,* II
fermer *to close,* I
le fermier/la fermière *farmer,* 2
le festin *banquet,* 3
la fête *party / holiday,* II; **la fête des mères** *Mother's Day,* II; **la fête des pères** *Father's Day,* II; **la fête nationale** *national holiday,* II
fêter *to celebrate,* 1G
le feu *traffic light,* I; **le feu** *fire,* 7; **le feu de camp** *campfire,* 7
la feuille *sheet,* I; *leaf,* II; **la feuille de papier** *piece of paper,* I
le feuilleton *television series,* II
les feux d'artifice, (m. pl.) *fireworks,* II
février *February,* I
se fiancer *to get engaged,* 4
le fichier *file,* II
fidèle *faithful,* 2
fiévreux(-euse) *feverish,* 10
se figurer *to imagine,* 4
Figure-toi que *Imagine that,* II
la fille *girl, daughter,* I; **la fille unique** *only daughter,* I
le film *film/movie,* II; **le film classique** *classic movie,* II; **le film d'action** *action movie,* II; **le film d'aventures** *adventure movie,* II; **le film d'espionnage** *spy movie,* II; **le film d'horreur** *horror movie,* II; **le film de guerre** *war movie,* II; **le film de science-fiction** *science-fiction movie,* II; **le film étranger** *foreign film,* II
le fils *son,* I; **le fils unique** *only son,* I
la fin *end,* 3
fin(e) *slender,* 6
finalement *finally,* II
finir *to finish,* II
le flacon *perfume bottle, flask,* 10
le flamant rose *flamingo,* II
flamboyant(e) *blazing,* 7
flatteur(-euse) *flattering,* 6
la fleur *flower,* II
le fleuriste *flower shop,* I
le fleuve *river,* II
la flore *flora,* 5
le flot *wave, flood, tide,* 5
flotter *to float,* 7
la fois *time,* I; **...fois par...** *. . . times a . . . ,* II
foncé(e) *dark,* I
le fonctionnaire *civil servant,* 8
fonder *to found,* 6
les fonds marins, (m. pl.) *sea floor,* 9G
le football *soccer,* I

la force *force/strength,* 7
la forêt *forest,* II
le forfait *set price,* 10
la formation *training,* 2
la formule *incantation/phrase,* 3
fort(e) *stout strong,* I
fou(folle) *crazy,* 10
le foulard *scarf,* I
la foule *crowd,* II
se fouler la cheville/le poignet *to twist one's ankle/wrist,* II
le four *oven,* II
la fourchette *fork,* I
fournir *to supply,* 1
la fourniture *supply,* I; **les fournitures scolaires** (f. pl.) *school supplies,* I
le foyer *home,* 3
la fraîcheur *coolness/chilliness,* 10
frais (fraîche) *cool,* 4
la fraise *strawberry,* II
la framboise *raspberry,* II
le français *French (language),* 1
français(e) *French,* 1
la France *France,* II
franchement *honestly,* I
frappant(e) *striking*
la fraternité *brotherhood*
le frein à main *hand brake,* 10
freiner *to brake,* 10
frénétiquement *with frenzy, madly,* 7
le frère *brother,* II
friable *friable, crumbly,* 7
les frites, (f. pl.) *fries,* I
froid(e) *cold,* I
le fromage *cheese,* I
la fromagerie *cheese market,* II
le front *forehead,* II
la frontière *border,* 7G
le fruit *fruit,* II; **les fruits de mer,** (m. pl.) *seafood,* II; **les fruits secs** *dried fruit,* II
la fumée *smoke,* 7
fumer *to smoke,* II
furieux(-euse) *furious,* 4
la fusée *rocket,* 5

gagner *to win,* II; **gagner de l'argent** *to earn money,* 2
la galerie d'art *art gallery,* 9
le gant *glove,* I
le garage *garage,* I
le garçon *boy,* I
le garde-manger *pantry,* 3
garder des enfants *to babysit,* II
la gare *train station,* I
garer *to park,* 10

le gasoil *diesel,* 10
gaspiller *to waste,* 7
le gâteau *cake,* 2
la gauche *left,* 8
gaulois(e) *Gallic, of Gaul,* IG
le gaz *natural gas,* 7
le géant/la géante *giant,* 3
le gel douche *shower gel,* II
la gêne *constraint,* 8
gêné(e) *embarassed,* 4
généreux(-euse) *generous,* I
génial(e) *great,* I
le génie *genie,* 3
génial(e) *genius,* 2
le genou *knee,* II
le genre *genre,* 9
gentil(le) *sweet,* II
la géographie *geography,* I
le gibier *game,* 3
gigoter *to kick,* 1
le gilet de sauvetage *life jacket,* 5
la glace *ice cream,* II
glacé(e) *icy,* 10
la glacière *ice cooler,* I
la glissade *slip, slide,* 5
le glissement de terrain *landslide,* 7
glisser *to slide, to slip,* 10
la gomme *eraser,* 4
gommer *to erase,* 10
gonfler *to grow,* 7
la gorge *throat,* II
le goudron *tar* 10
la gourde *canteen,* 1
le goût *taste,* 6
le gouvernement *government,* 8
gouverner *to rule,* 1G
grâce à *thanks to,* 6
grand(e) *big/tall,* II
la grande surface *superstore,* I
grandiloquent(e) *pompous,* 10
grandir *to grow (up),* I
la grand-mère *grandmother,* II
le grand-parent *grandparent,* I
le grand-père *grandfather,* II
la grange *barn,* II
gratuit(e) *free,* 6
grave *serious,* 4
graver *to burn (a CD),* II
le graveur de CD/DVD *CD/DVD burner,* II
gravir *to climb,* 6
la gravure *etching,* 9
grec(grecque) *Greek,* II
la Grèce *Greece,* II
la grêle *hail,* 7
la grenadine *pomegranate syrup,* II
la grenouille *frog,* 5
grésiller *to chirp,* 7
la grève *strike,* 6
la griffe *label, signature,* 6
grimper aux arbres *to climb trees,* II

grincer *to grate,* 10
gris(e) *gray,* I
gros(se) *fat,* I
le (gros) titre *headline,* 6
grossir *to gain weight,* II
la grotte *cave,* 5
la guêpe *wasp,* 5
la guerre *war,* 1G
le guichet *window/counter/ticket office,* I
le guide *guidebook,* II, *guide,* 5
guidé(e) *guided,* II
guillotiner *to guillotine*
la guitare *guitar,* II
le gymnase *gymnasium,* II

habile *skilled,* 9
s' habiller *to get dressed,* II
l' **habit** (m.) *clothes,* 3
habiter *to live,* I
le hall *lobby,* I; **le hall d'arrivée** *arrival hall,* 10
la halte *stop,* 5
Hanoukkah *Hanukkah,* II
les haricots verts, (m. pl.) *green beans,* II
la hâte *haste,* 7
hâtif(-ive) *hasty, hurried,* 5
haut(e) *high,* I
la haute couture *high fashion,* 2
l' **hebdomadaire,** (m.) *weekly publication,* 6
l' herbe (f.) *grass, herb* 7
le hérisson *hedgehog,* 3
l' **héroïne,** (f.) *heroine,* 3
héroïque *heroic,* 3
le héron *heron,* 5
le héros *hero,* 3
l' **heure,** (f.) *hour,* I; **des heures supplémentaires** *overtime,* 2
heureusement *fortunately,* II
heureux(-euse) *happy,* 4
hier *yesterday,* I
le hip-hop *hip-hop,* II
l' **histoire,** (f.) *history,* I; *story,* 3
l' **hiver,** (m.) *winter,* I
le hockey *hockey,* I
l' honneur (m.) *honor,* 8
l' **hôpital,** (m.) *hospital,* I
l' **horaire,** (m.) *schedule,* I
l' horloge, (f.) *clock,* 7
l' horlogerie, (f.) *clock trade,* 7
l' horodateur, (m.) *parking stub machine,* 10
horrible *horrible,* I
hors *apart,* 10
l' **hôtel,** (m.) *hotel,* 1

l' **hôtesse,** (f.) *stewardess,* I, **l'hôtesse de l'air,** (f.) *flight attendant,* 10
le hublot *window,* 3
l' **huile (d'olive),** (f.) *(olive) oil,* II
huit *eight,* I
l' **huître,** (f.) *oyster,* II
humain(e) *human,* 3
l' **humeur,**(f.) *mood,* 4; **de bonne/ mauvaise humeur** *in a good/ bad mood,* 4
hybride *hybrid,* 7
l' **hymne national,** (m.) *national anthem,* II

l' **identité,** (f.) *identification,* 8
l' **iguane,** (m.) *iguana,* 5
il *he,* I; **Il/Elle coûte combien,...?** *How much does . . . cost?,* I; **Il/Elle coûte...** *It costs . . . ,* I; **Il/Elle est brun(e)** *He/She has brown hair.,* I; **Il/Elle est comment...?** *How is . . . ?,* I; **Il/Elle est horrible.** *It's horrible.,* I; **Il/Elle est très...** *He/ She is very . . . ,* I; **Il/Elle me va,...?** *How does . . . fit me?,* I; **Il/Elle n'est ni... ni...** *He/She is neither . . . nor . . . ,* I; **Il/Elle s'appelle...** *His/Her name is . . . ,* I; **Il/Elle te plaît,...?** *Do you like . . . ?,* I; **Il aime...** *He likes . . . ,* II; **Il en a déjà plein.** *He already has plenty of them.,* II; **Il est bon/Elle est bonne,...?** *Is the . . . good?,* I; ; **Il est deux heures dix.** *It is ten past two.,* I; **Il est deux heures.** *It is two o'clock.,* I; **Il est deux heures et demie.** *It is two thirty.,* I; **Il est deux heures et quart.** *It is a quarter past two.,* I; **Il est génial!** *It's great!,* II; **Il est important que tu le désinfectes.** *It is important that you disinfect it.,* II; **Il est interdit de...** *It is forbidden to . . . ,* 5; **Il est midi.** *It is noon.,* I; **Il est minuit.** *It is midnight.,* I; **Il/Elle est persuadé(e) que...** *He/She's convinced that . . . ,* 6; **Il est possible/probable que...** *It's possible that . . . ,* 6; **Il est probable que...** *It's likely that . . . ,* 8; **Il est temps de...** *It's time to . . . ,* II; **Il est trois heures moins le quart.** *It is quarter till three.* ; **Il est trois heures moins**

vingt. *It is twenty till three.;* **Il est une heure.** *It is one o'clock.;* **Il était une fois...** *Once upon a time . . . ,* 3; **Il faisait...** *The temperature was . . . ,* 1; **Il fait beau.** *It's nice outside.,* I; **Il fait chaud.** *It's hot.,* I; **Il fait froid.** *It's cold.,* I; **Il fait mauvais.** *It's bad weather.,* I; **Il faudrait que tu fasses du yoga.** *You should do yoga.,* II; **Il faudrait que...** *It would be necessary for . . . to . . . ,* 2; **il faut** *it is necessary,* II; **Il faut que je me fasse vacciner avant de partir au Sénégal.** *I have to get vaccinated before going to Senegal.,* II; **Il faut que tu achètes un médicament.** *You need to buy medicine.,* II; **Il m'a expliqué que...** *He explained to me that . . . ,* 8; **Il me faut...** *I need . . . ,* II; **Il me semble que...** *It seems to me that . . . ,* 6; **Il n'est pas mal.** *It's not bad.,* 9; **Il n'y a pas d'histoire.** *There's no story.,* II; **Il ne faut surtout pas oublier nos chèques de voyage.** *We especially must not forget our traveler's checks.,* II; **Il neige.** *It's snowing.,* I; **Il n'y en a pas.** *There aren't any.,* I; **Il pleut.** *It's raining.,* I; **Il se peut que...** *It might . . . ,* 6; **Il te faut autre chose?** *Do you need anything else?,* II
il y a *since/ago/for,* II; *There is/are...,* II; **Il y a beaucoup de suspense.** *There's a lot of suspense.,* II; **il y a bien longtemps** *a long time ago,* 3; Il y a des nuages. *It's cloudy.,* I; **Il y a du soleil.** *It's sunny.,* I; **Il y a du vent.** *It's windy.,* I;
Il y avait... *There were . . . ,* II;
Il y en a... *There are . . . of them.,* I
Il/Elle est... *He/She is . . . ,* II; **Il/ Elle est comment, ton ami(e)?** *What is your friend like?,* II
Il/Elle ne te va pas du tout. *It doesn't suit you at all.,* I
l' **île,** (f.) *island,* 5
illustrer *to illustrate,* 2
l' **îlot,** (m.) *small island,* 9G
ils *they (masc),* I
Ils/Elles sont comment,...? *What are . . . like?,* I; **Ils/Elles sont soldé(e)s à...** *They are on sale for . . . ,* I; **Ils ont l'air de...** *They seem . . . ,* 9; **Ils sont...** *They are . . . ,* II

Ils vécurent heureux et eurent beaucoup d'enfants. *They lived happily ever after and had many children.*, 3
l' **iguane,** (m.) *iguana*, 5
l' **immeuble,** (m.) *apartment building* , I
l' **immigrant(e)** *immigrant*, 8
immobile *motionless, unmoved*, 9
l' **imperméable,** (m.) *raincoat*, I
importuner *to bother*, 3
l' **impôt,** (m.) *tax*, 1G
impressionnant(e) *impressive*
impressionner *to impress*, 4
l' **imprimante,** (f.) *printer*, II
imprimer *to print*, II
l' **imprimerie** (f.) *printing*, 8
les **impuretés,** (f. pl.) *impurities*, 7
l' **inégalité,** (f.) *inequality*, 4
inamovible *irremovable*, 8
l' **incendie,** (m.) *fire*, 7
l' **inconvénient,** (m.) *disadvantage*, 7
l' **Inde,** (f.) *India*
l' **indépendance,** (f.) *independence*, 3
indifférent(e) *indifferent*, 4
l' **indigène,** (m.) *native*, 5G
l' **infirmerie,** (f.) *nurse's office*, II
l' **infirmier/l'infirmière** *nurse*, 2
l' **informaticien(ne)** *computer scientist*, 2
les **informations,** (f. pl.) *news*, II
l' **informatique,** (f.) *computer science*, II
s' **informer** *to find out*, II;
s'informer sur Internet *to find out/to inquire on the Internet*, II
l' **ingénieur,** (m.) *engineer*, 2
l' **inimitié,** (f.) *enmity*, 3
l' **inondation,** (f.) *flood*, 7
inquiet(-iète) *worried*, 4
inscrire *to write down*, 6
l' **insecte,** (m.) *insect*, II
insistant(e) *strong*, 7
inspirer *to inspire*, 1
installer *to install*, 2;
s'installer *to settle, to move to* 4
instamment *earnestly*, 3
l' **instituteur/l'institutrice** *elementary school teacher*, 2
intellectuel(le) *intellectual*, II
intelligent(e) *intelligent / smart*, II
Interdiction de... *. . . is not allowed*, 5
interdir *to forbid*, 5
intéressant(e) *interesting*, I
l' **intérêt,** (m.) *interest*, I
l' **interface,** (f.) *interface*, II
intérieur(e), (m.) *domestic*, 10
international(e) *international*, 6
l' **Internet,** (m.) *Internet*, I
l' **interprète,** (m./f.) *interpreter*, 2
l' **interro(gation),** (f.) *quiz*, II

l' **interrupteur,** (m.) *switch*, 7
intervertir *to reverse*, 6
intriguer *to plot*, 3
inutile *useless*, 9
l' **invasion,** (f.) *invasion*, 3
l' **invention,** (f.) *invention*, 7
l' **invité(e)** *guest*, II
l' **Irlande, (f.)** *Ireland*, 1
irréel(le) *unreal*, 3G
issu(e) *born of*, 1
l' **Italie, (f.)** *Italy*, II
italien(ne) *Italian*, II
l' **itinéraire, (m.)** *itinerary / route*, II

J'adore... *I love . . .*, I
J'ai... ans. *I am . . . years old.*, II
J'ai besoin de... *I need to . . .*, II;
J'ai besoin de faire... *I need to have . . .*, 2; **J'ai complètement oublié!** *I completely forgot!*, II;
J'ai entendu dire que... *I heard that . . .*, 4; **J'ai grossi.** *I gained weight.*, II; **J'ai l'impression de/que...** *I have the feeling that . . .*, 9; **J'ai le nez qui coule.** *I have a runny nose.*, II; **J'ai le vertige!** *I'm dizzy!*, 5; **J'ai mal au cœur.** *I'm nauseated.*, II; **J'ai mal aux dents/à la tête/à l'estomac.** *I have a toothache/ headache/stomachache.*, II; **J'ai mal partout.** *I ache everywhere.*, II; **J'ai peur des/ que...!** *I'm afraid of/that . . .!*, 5; **J'ai sommeil.** *I'm sleepy.*, II
J'aime bien... *I like...*, I; **J'aime bien..., mais je préfère...** *I like . . ., but I prefer . . .*, 1; **J'aime mieux...** *I like . . . better.*, I
J'aimerais... *I would . . .* II
J'en suis sûr(e) *I'm sure of it.*, 7
J'espère que tu vas passer... *I hope that you have...*, II
jadis *long ago*, 3
J'adore... *I love...*, II
jamais *never*, II; **Jamais de la vie!** *Not in a million years!*, 4
la **jambe** *leg*, II
le **jambon** *ham*, I
janvier *January*, I
le **jardin** *yard/garden*, I
jaune *yellow*, I
le **jazz** *jazz*, II
je *I*, I; **Je cherche...** *I'm looking for . . .*, I; **Je cherche... pour mettre avec...** *I am looking for . . . to wear with . . .*, I; **Je déteste... j'adore...** *I hate . . .*

I love . . ., 1; **Je dois...** *I must . . .*, II; **Je dois faire...** *I need to have . . .*, 2; **Je doute que...** *I doubt that . . .*, 6; **Je fais...** *I do . . .*, I; **Je fais du...** *I wear a size . . .*, I; **Je joue...** *I play . . .*, I; **Je l'ai trouvée passionnant(e)!** *I found it fascinating!*, 9; **Je l'ai gagnée.** *I won it.*, II; **Je le/la trouve...** *I think he/she is . . .*, I; **Je m'appelle...** *My name is...*, II; **Je me demande si...** *I wonder if . . .*, II; **Je me sens mal.** *I feel ill.*, II; **Je me suis coupé le doigt.** *I cut my finger.*, II; **Je meurs de...!** *I'm dying of . . .!*, 5; **Je n'arrive pas à me décider.** *I can't decide.*, 1 ;**Je n'arrive pas à me garer, tu peux m'aider?** *I can't manage to park; can you help me?*, 10; **Je n'en ai pas la moindre idée.** *I haven't the least idea.*, 4; **Je n'en peux plus!** *I can't do anymore!*, 5; **Je n'en reviens pas!** *I can't get over it!*, 5; **Je n'en sais rien.** *I have no idea.*, 1; **Je n'ai pas de... mais...** *I don't have any . . . but . . .*, I; **Je n'aime pas beaucoup...** *I don't like . . . very much.*, II; **Je ne comprends pas.** *I don't understand.*, I; **Je ne crois pas que...** *I don't think that . . .*, 6; **Je ne fais rien.** *I'm not doing anything.*, I; **Je ne joue pas...** *I don't play . . .*, I; **Je ne le vois plus.** *I don't see him anymore.*, 4; **Je ne me sens pas très bien.** *I don't feel very well.*, II; **Je ne partage pas ton point de vue.** *I don't share your point of view.*, 8; **Je ne pense pas que...** *I don't think that . . .*, 6; **Je ne sais pas comment...** *I don't know how . . .*, 10; **Je ne sais pas quoi faire!** *I don't know what to do!*, II; **Je ne sais pas quoi prendre.** *I don't know what to take.*, I; **Je ne te conseille pas ce reportage. Il est nul.** *I don't recommend this report. It's worthless.*, II; **Je n'en sais rien.** *I don't know anything about it.*, II; **Je parie que...** *I bet that . . .*, II; ; **Je peux essayer...?** *May I try on . . .?*, I; **Je peux vous aider?** *May I help you?*, I; **Je peux vous montrer...?** *May I show you . . .?*, I; **Je préfère...** *I prefer . . .*, I; **Je suis certain(e) que...** *I'm certain that . . .*, 6;

Je suis convaincu(e) que... *I'm convinced that . . .*, 7; **Je suis fatigué(e). *I'm tired.*, II; **Je suis ravi(e) que... *I'm delighted that . . .*, 4; **Je suis stressé(e).** *I'm stressed.*, II; **Je suis sûr(e) que...** *I'm sure that . . .*, 6; **Je suis trop occupé(e),** *I'm too busy,* II; **Je suppose que...** *I suppose that . . .*, 7; **Je t'écoute!** *I'm listening!*, 6; **Je te/vous présente...** *Let me introduce you to . . .*, I; **Je te conseille de...** *I advise you to . . .*, I; **Je te plains.** *I feel sorry for you.*, II; II; **Je te recommande plutôt de...** *You should . . . instead of . . .*, 9; **Je te/vous souhaite...** *I wish you . . .*, II; **Je trouve ça...** *I think it's . . .*, I; **Je vais...** *I am going to . . .*, I; **Je vais prendre...** *I will have . . .* I; **Je voudrais...** *I would like . . .*, I; **Je voudrais faire le tour du monde.** *I would like to take a world tour.*, II; **Je voudrais quelque chose pour...** *I would like something for . . .*, I
le jean *jeans,* I
J'en ai... *I have . . . of them.*
jeter *to throw,* I
le jeu *game,* II
le jeu vidéo *video game,* I
jeudi *Thursday,* I
le jeune *young man,* II
les **jeunes gens,** (m. pl.) *young men,* 4
le jogging *jogging,* I
le jongleur/la jongleuse *juggler,* 9
la joue *cheek,* II
jouer *to play,* II; **jouer à chat perché** *[similar to tag],* II; **jouer à des jeux vidéo** *to play video games,* I; **jouer à la marelle** *to play hopscotch,* II; **jouer à la poupée** *to play dolls,* II; **jouer au ballon** *to play ball,* II; **jouer au base-ball** *to play baseball,* I; **jouer au basket-ball** *to play basketball,* 1; **jouer au football** *to play soccer,* I; **jouer au tennis** *to play tennis,* II; **jouer au train électrique** *to play with electric trains,* II; **jouer au volley-ball** *to play volleyball,* 1; **jouer aux billes** *to play marbles,* II; **jouer aux cartes** *to play cards,* I; **jouer aux dames** *to play checkers,* II; **jouer aux échecs** *to play chess,* I; **jouer aux petites voitures** *to play*

with toy cars, II; **jouer de la guitare** *to play guitar,* 1
le joueur *player,* 5
le jour *day,* I; **le jour de l'an** *New Year's Day,* II; **le jour férié** *public holiday,* 10
le journal *newspaper,* I
le journaliste/la journaliste *journalist,* 2
Joyeux Noël *Merry Christmas,* II
le juge *judge,* 2
juillet *July,* I
juin *June,* I
les **jumeaux/les jumelles** *twins,* 4
les **jumelles,** (f. pl.) *binoculars,* 7
la **jument** *mare,* 1
la **jupe** *skirt,* I
jurer *to swear,* 3
juridique *judicial,* 4
le jus *juice,* I; **le jus de fruit** *fruit juice,* II; **le jus de pomme** *apple juice,* I; **le jus d'orange** *orange juice,* I
Jusqu'à quelle heure...? *Until what time . . . ?,* I

le kilo(gramme) *kilogram,* II
le kiosque *stand,* 6; **le kiosque à journaux** *newspaper stand,* 6
klaxonner *to honk,* 10

la *the,* I; *her/it,* II
là *here/there,* I; **Là, c'est...** *Here is . . .,* I
le laboratoire *laboratory,* 1
le lac *lake,* II
lâcher *to release,* 6
la **laine** *wool,* I
laissé(e) *left,* 10
laisser *to leave,* 10
laisser les mains libres *to let decide,* 4
le lait *milk,* I
le lambeau *shred,* 7
la lampe *lamp,* I; **la lampe de poche** *flashlight,* II
la **lance** *spear,* 9
lancer *to throw,* I; *to launch,* 6
la lanterne *lantern,* II
la **langue** *language,* 5G; **la langue maternelle** *birth tongue,* 2
le lapin *rabbit,* II
la **plupart (de)** *most (of),* 5G

large *loose,* I; *wide,* 10
le large *space, room,* 10
le lavabo *sink,* II
la lave *lava,* 7
laver *to wash,* I
se laver la figure *to wash one's face,* II; **laver la voiture** *to wash the car,* I; **se laver les cheveux** *to wash one's hair,* II
le lave-vaisselle *dishwasher,* I
le *the,* I; *him/it,* II; **Le lundi,...** *On Mondays, . . .,* II; **Le soir,...** *Every evening, . . .,* 1
la leçon *lesson,* 3; **la leçon de conduite** *moral,* 3
le lecteur *reader,* 6; **le lecteur de CD/DVD** *CD/DVD player,* I
la légende *legend,* 3; *caption,* 6
léger(-ère) *light,* II
le légume *vegetable,* II
le lendemain *the next day,* 3
lent(e) *slow,* 9
lequel/laquelle/lesquels *which,* II
les *the,* I; *them,* II
la lessive *laundry,* I
la lettre *letter,* I
leur *their,* I
leur *(indirect object) (to) them,* II
lever *to raise,* I; **se lever** *to get up/stand up,* II
la lèvre *lip,* II
le lézard *lizard,* II
la liberté *freedom,* 5
le libraire *bookseller,* 2
la librairie *bookstore,* I
libre *free,* I
le lien *link (Internet),* II
lié(e) *linked,* 5
le lieu *location, place,* 1G
la limonade *lemon-lime soda,* II
le lin *linen,* I
le liquide (argent) *cash,* I
lire *to read,* I
le lit *bed,* I; **le lit double** *double bed,* I; **le lit simple** *single bed,* I
le litige *litigation*
le litre *liter,* II; **le litre de jus d'orange** *liter of orange juice,* II
littéraire *literary,* II
le livre *book,* I
la livre (f) *pound of,* II; **la livre de cerises** *pound of cherries,* II
livrer *to deliver,* 2
le livreur *delivery boy,* 2
loger *to lodge, to accommodate,* 2
le logiciel *software,* II
la loi *law,* 8
loin de *far from,* I
lointain(e) *far away,* 9
le loisir *leisure, spare time,* 10
le lombric *worm,* 7C
long(ue) *long,* II

longtemps *a long time,* 3
lors de *during,* 8
lorsque *when,* 8
la lotion anti-moustiques *mosquito repellent,* 1
la louange *praise,* 9
louer *to rent,* 4
le loup *wolf,* 5
lourd(e) *heavy,* 10
la lueur *glimmer,* 7
lui *(indirect object)(to) him/her,* II
la lumière *light,* II
lunaire *lunar,* 10
lundi *Monday,* I
la lune *moon,* 3G
les lunettes, (f. pl.) *glasses,* I; **les lunettes de soleil,** (f. pl.) *sunglasses,* II
la lutte *fight,* 8
le lutteur *fighter,* 4
le lycée *high school,* 1

ma *my,* I
la machine à calculer *calculator,* 2
le maçon *mason,* 4
madame *Mrs.,* I; **Madame,..., s'il vous plaît?** *Ma'am, . . ., please?,* II
mademoiselle *Miss,* I
le magasin *shop/store,* I
le magazine *magazine,* I; **le magazine féminin** *womenn's magazine,* 6
le Maghreb *Maghreb,* 3
le magicien/la magicienne *magician,* 3
la magie *magic,* 3
magique *magic,* 3
la magistrature *magistracy,* 8
se magner *(slang) to hurry,* II
mai *May,* I
maigre *skinny,* 4
maigrir *to lose weight,* II
le maillon *link,* 10
le maillot de bain *swimsuit,* I
la main *hand,* I
maintenant *now,* I
se maintenir *to last,* 8
le maire *mayor,* 10
la mairie *city hall,* 8
mais *but,* I; **Mais oui!** *But of course!,* II
le maïs *corn,* 7
la maison *house,* II; **la Maison des jeunes et de la culture (MJC)** *recreation center,* I
le maître *master,* 7
la maîtrise *control,* 6; *master degree,* 8

maîtriser *to control*
mal *badly,* I; *evil,* 3
malade *sick,* II
maléfique *evil,* 3
malgré *despite,* 3
malhabile *clumsy,* 5
le malheur *misfortune,* 7
Malheureusement,... *Unfortunately,...,* 4
le Mali *Mali,* 3
le mandat *money order,* I
manger *to eat,* II
le manguier *mango tree,* 1
la manie *obsession,* 6
manier *to wield,* 8
la manière *manner,* 5
la manifestation *protest,* 8
manquer *to miss,* I
le manteau *coat,* I
le maquillage *make-up,* II
se maquiller *to put on makeup,* II
le marais *marsh, swamp,* 5G
la marâtre *evil stepmother,* 3
le marchand/la marchande *vendor,* 6; **le marchand de journaux** *newspaper vendor,* 6
le marché *open air market,* I
marcher *to work / run,* II
mardi *Tuesday,* I
la marée *tide,* 5G; **la marée noire** *oil slick,* 7
le mari *husband,* I
se marier *to get married,* 4
la marmaille *gang of kids,* 1
le Maroc *Morocco,* 3
la maroquinerie *leather goods* I
la marque *brand,* 2
la marraine *godmother,* 3
marrant(e) *funny,* II
marron *brown,* II
mars *March,* 1
le mascara *mascara,* II
le masque de plongée *diving mask,* I; 5
le massif de fleurs *flowerbed,* 5
le matériau *material,* 9
les mathématiques (les maths), (f. pl.) *mathematics,* I
la matière *school subject,* 1; **les matières grasses,** (f. pl.) *fatty substances,* II, les matières premières, (f. pl.) *raw materials,* 7G
le matin *morning,* I
la matinée *morning,* II
mauvais(e) *bad,* I
me (m') *(direct object)* me, *(indirect object) (to)* me, II
le mécanicien/la mécanicienne *mechanic,* 2
méchant(e) *mean,* 1

la médaille *medal,* 6; **la médaille d'or** *gold medal,* 6
le médecin *doctor,* II
les médias (m. pl.) *media,* 6
le médicament *medicine,* I
la méduse *jellyfish,* 5
se méfier *to beware,* I; **Méfie-toi des...** *Look out for . . .,* 5
mélanger *to mix,* II
mêler *to mix,* 5
le melon *melon,* II
même *even,* 1G
menacer *to threaten,* 7
se ménager *to spare oneself,* 10
mener *to lead,* 1G; mener à bien *to manage successfully,* 4
le mensuel *monthly,* 6
la menthe *mint,* I
la mer *sea,* II
merci *thank you,* I
mercredi *Wednesday,* I
la mère *mother,* II
la mémoire *memory,* 10
mépriser *to despise,* 2
la merveille *mavel, wonder,* 9
mes *my,* I; **Mes sincères condoléances.** *My deepest sympathies.,* 4
la mesquinerie *pettiness,* 3
la mesure *beat,* 9
la Météo *weather page,* 6
le métier *job,* 2
le métro *subway,* I
le metteur en scène *producer,* 9
mettre *to set,* I; *to put, to wear,* II; **se mettre** *to put on,* II; mettre en cause *to implicate,* 6; **se mettre en pyjama/en chemise de nuit** *to put on pajamas/ nightgown,* II; **mettre la table/ le couvert** *to set the table,* I; mettre au courant *to inform,* 3
le meuble *furniture,* 1
le meurtrier *murderer,* 6
le Mexique *Mexico,* 1G
le Mexicain *Mexican,* 1G
midi *noon,* I
le Midi *south of France,* 10
mignon(ne) *cute,* I
migrateur *migratory,* 5G
le million *million,* 7
mince *thin,* II
la mine *appearance,* II
mineur(e) *minor,* 4
le ministre *secretary,* 6; *minister,* 8; **le ministre du travail** *Secretary of Labor,* 6
minuit *midnight,* I
la minuterie *automatic time switch,* 7
le miroir *mirror,* II
la mise au point *fine tuning, adjustment,* 10

la misère *poverty*, 5
le mobile *cell phone*, I
le modèle *model*, 9
modéré(e) *moderate*, 8
moderne *modern*, I
moi *me*, I; **Moi aussi.** *Me, too.*, II; **Moi non plus.** *Me neither.*, II; **Moi si.** *I do.*, II; **Moi, j'aime... Et toi?** *I like . . . And you?*; **Moi, je n'aime pas...** *I don't like . . .*, II
moindre *least*, 4
moins *minus*, I; **moins... que** *less . . . than*, II
le mois *month*, I; **le mois dernier** *last month*, I
moisir *to mold*, 7
la moisson *harvest, crop*, 9
le moment *moment*, I
mon *my*, I; mon for intérieur *my mind* 4; **Mon/Ma pauvre.** *Poor thing.*, II; **Mon rêve, ce serait de...** *My dream would be to . . .*, II; **Mon... préféré, c'est...** *My favorite . . . is . . .*, 1
la monarchie *monarchy*, 3
le monde *world*, 7
mondial(e) *world-wide*, 7G
le moniteur/la monitrice *instructor*, 2
la monnaie *change (coins)*, I
le monsieur *gentleman* I
le monstre *monster*, 3
la montagne *mountain*, 1
monter *to go up*, II; **monter à cheval** *to go horseback riding*, II; **monter la tente** *to pitch a tent*, II
la montre *watch*, I
Montre-moi! *Show me!*, 6
se moquer *to mock*, 10
le morale *morality*, 3
le morceau *piece*, II; **le morceau de fromage** *piece of cheese*, II
mordre *to bite*, 5
la morsure *bite*, 6
la mort *death*
mort(e) *dead*, 3
le moteur *engine*, 10
le motif *motif, pattern, ornament*, 9
mou(molle) *soft, weak*, 6
la mouche *fly*, II
le mouchoir *handkerchieft*, 2
mouillé(e) *wet*, 10
mourir *to die*, 4
le moustique *mosquito*, II
le mouton *sheep*, II
le moyen *means*, 7
le Moyen-Âge *Middle-Age*, 7G
les moyens de transport (m. pl.) *means of transportation*, 7
le Moyen-Orient *Middle East*, 3

le MP3 *MP3*, I
muet(te) *silent*, 9
le mulet *mule*, 3
multiplier *to multiply*, 2
muni(e) *fitted*, 7
le mur *wall*, 5
mûr(e) *ripe*, II
le muscle *muscle*, II
le musée *museum*, I
le musicien/la musicienne *musician*, 2
la musique *music*, II
la mutinerie *mutiny*, 9G

la nacre *mother-of-pearl*, 9
nager *to swim*, I
le nain/la naine *dwarf*, 3
la naissance, *birth*, 1G
naître *to be born*, 4
la nappe *table cloth*, I
natal(e) *native*, 2
la natte *mat*, 4
la nature *nature*, II; **la nature morte** *still life*, 9
naturel(le) *natural*, 7
le naufrage *shipwreck*, 7
le navigateur *browser*, II
naviguer *to navigate*, II
ne... jamais *never*, I; **ne... pas** *not*, I; **ne pas avoir le temps** *not to have the time*, II; **ne... pas encore** *not yet*, I; **ne... personne** *no one*, I; **ne... plus** *no longer*, I; **ne... que** *only*, 8; **ne... rien** *nothing*, I; **Ne t'en fais pas!** *Don't worry!*, II; **Ne va surtout pas voir..., il chante faux!** *Don't go see . . . He sings off-key!*, 9
la neige *snow*, 7
neiger *to snow*, I
le nerf *nerve*, 4
nettoyer *to clean*, 2
neuf(neuve) *nine*, I
neutre *neutral*, 7G
le neveu *nephew*, I
le nez *nose*, I
la nièce *niece*, I
le niveau *level*, 1
la noblesse *nobility*, 8
Noël *Christmas*, II
noir(e) *black*, I
la noix de coco *coconut*, 9
le nom *name*, I
nombreux(-euse) *numerous*, 6
nommer *to name*, 8

non *no*, I
non-fumeur *non-smoking*, I
nos *our*, I
notamment *in particular, among others*, 4
la note *grade*, II
notre *our*, I
N'oublie pas... *Don't forget . . .*, II
se **nourrir** *to feed oneself*, II
nous *we*, I; *(to) us*, II
Nous sommes... *There are... of us.*, I; **Nous sommes...** *Today is...*, I
nouveau(nouvelle) *new*, II
les **nouvelles**, (f. pl.) *news*, 6
novembre *November*, I
nu(e) *naked*, 9
le nuage *cloud*, I
la nuance *shade*, 2
les **nues**, (f. pl.) *clouds*, 9
la nuit *night*, I
le numéro *number*, I; **le numéro précédent** *previous issue*, 6; **le numéro de téléphone** *phone number*, I

l' objectif, (m.) *lens*, 9
l' objet, (m.) *objective*, 2
obliger *to bind, to compel*, 8
obséder *to obsess*, 6
observer *to watch*, 5
obtenir *to obtain*, 3
occupé(e) *busy*, II
s' **occuper (de)** *to take care (of)*, II
octobre *October*, I
l' odeur, (f.) *smell*, 2
l' odorat, (m.) *smell*, 2
l' œil, (m.) *eye*, II
l' œuf, (m.) *egg*, I
l' œuvre, (f.) *work, masterpiece*, 6; **l'œuvre d'art,** work of art, 9
l' office de tourisme, (m.) *tourist center*, II
offrir *to offer*, II
l' ogre/l'ogresse *ogre*, 3
l' oie, (f.) *goose*, 5
l' oignon, (m.) *onion*, II
l' oiseau, (m.) *bird*, II
olfactif(-ive) *olfactory*, 2
l' olive, (f.) *olive*, II
l' olivier, (m.) *olive tree*, 7
l' ombre, (f.) *shadow*, 7
l' omelette, (f.) *omelet*, I
on *one/we*, I, **On a...** *We have . . .*, I; **On a droit à... maximum.** *You are allowed up to...*, 10; **On a rapporté que...** *It was reported that .*

..., 3; On dirait que... *You would say that . . .,* 9; **On fait...?** *Shall we do...?,* I; **On m'a dit de...** *I was told to . . .,* 8 **;On m'a indiqué comment...** *I was told how . . .,* 8 ;**On m'a informé de...** *I was informed of . . .,* 8 ;**On m'a montré où...** *I was shown where . . .,* 8; **On pourrait...** *We could . . .,* I ; **On prévoit... pour...** *They are predicting . . . for . . .,* 7 ; **On raconte qu'autrefois...** *It is said that, in times past, . . .,* 3; **On va...?** *How about going to . . .?,* I

l' **oncle,** (m.) *uncle,* II
ondulant(e) *flowing,* 7
onze *eleven,* I
l' **opéra,** (m.) *opera,* 9
l' **opposition,** (f.) *opposition,* 8
l' **or,** (m.) *gold,* I
l' **orage,** (m.) *thunderstorm,* 7
orange *orange,* I
l' **orchestre,** (m.) *orchestra,* 9
l' **ordinateur,** (m.) *computer,* I; **l'ordinateur (portable),** (m.) *(laptop) computer,* II
ordonner *to command,* 4
l' **oreille,** (f.) *ear,* I
organisé(e) *organized,* II
organiser *to plan / to organize,* II; organiser une soirée/fête *to plan a party,* II
l' **orignal,** (m.) *moose,* 5
orner *to decorate,* 9
l' **orphelin(e)** *orphan,* 4
l' **os,** (m.) *bone,* II
oser *to dare,* 2
ou *or,* I
où *where,* II; **Où ça?** *Where?,* I; Où est...? *Where is . . .?,* I; Où est-ce que je pourrais trouver...? *Where could I find . . .?,* II; Où se trouve...? *Where is . . .?,* I
oublier *to forget,* II
oui *yes,* I
l' **ouïe** (m.) *hearing,* 9
l' **ouragan,** (m.) *hurricane,* 7
l' **ours,** (m.) *bear,* 5
l' **outil,** (m.) *tool,* II
l' **ouverture,** (f.) *opening,* 4
l' **ouvreuse,** (f.) *usher,* 9
ouvrir *to open,* II; **ouvrir une session** *to open a session,* II

pacifiquement *peacefully,* 3
la **page** *page,* I
le **pain** *bread,* I
la **paix** *peace,* 3
le **palais** *palace,* 3
la **palette** *palette,* 9
les **palmes,** (f. pl.) *flippers,* I
le **pamplemousse** *grapefruit,* I
la **panne** *break down,* 10
le **panneau** *sign/panel,* 7; **le panneau solaire** *solar panel,* 7
le **pansement** *bandage,* I
le **pantalon** *pair of pants,* I
la **pantoufle** *slipper,* 3
le **pape** *pope,* 1G
la **papeterie** *stationery store,* I
le **papier** *paper,* I; **les papiers d'identité,** (m. pl.) *personal documents (ID),* 8
le **papillon** *butterfly,* 5
le **paquebot** *liner/cruise ship,* 10
le **paquet** *package,* II; **le paquet de pâtes** *package of pasta,* II
par la suite *afterwards,* 3
le **parachute** *parachute,* 5
le **parachutisme** *sky diving,* 5
par ailleurs *moreover,* 2
par terre *on the floor,* 4
paraître *to appear, to be published* 6
le **parapluie** *umbrella,* I
le **parc** *park,* I; **le parc naturel** *nature reserve,* 5
parcourir *to go over, to wander through,* 5
parcouru(e) *covered,* 10
pardon *excuse me,* I; **Pardon, savez-vous où est...?** *Excuse-me, do you know where . . . is?,* I
le **pare-brise** *windshield,* 10
le **parent** *parent,* I
parer *to dress up,* 3
paresseux(-euse) *lazy,* I
parfois *sometimes,* 3
le **parfum** *perfume,* 9
le **parfumeur** *perfumer,* 1
le **pari** *bet,* 10
parier *to bet,* 7
le **parking** *parking lot,* I
le **parlement** *parliament,* 8
parler *to speak,* II; **se parler** *to speak (to one another),* 4

parmi *among,* 3
la **parole** *word,* 10
partager *to share,* 8
le **parti politique** *political party,* 8
participer (à) *to participate in,* 8
le **particulier** *private person,* 8
partir *to leave,* 1; **partir en vacances** *to leave on vacation,* 1; **partir en voyage** *to go on a trip,* II
la **partition** *score/sheet music,* 9
partout *everywhere,* 2
parvenir *to reach,* 3; parvenir à *to manage to,* 2; **parvenir à son but** *to reach one's goal,* 3
le **pas** *step,* 7
pas de *not any,* II; **pas de problème** *no problem,* II; **pas du tout** *not at all,* I; **pas encore** *not yet,* 10; **Pas grand-chose.** *Not much.,* I; **Pas maintenant. Je dois d'abord...** *Not now. First, I have to . . .,* II; **Pas mal.** *Not bad.,* I; **Pas mauvais.** *Not bad.,* I; **Pas moi.** *Not me./I don't.,* II; **Pas nécessairement.** *Not necessarily.,* 4; **Pas possible!** *Really?!,* 4; *Impossible!,* 5; **Pas question!** *Out of the question!,* I
le **passage secret** *secret passage,* 3
le **passager/la passagère** *passenger,* 10
passager(ère) *transitory,* 9
le **passeport** *passport,* II
passer (à un endroit) *to stop by,* I; **passer (quelqu'un)** *to transfer,* 2; **se passer** *to happen,* II; passer *to spend,* 1G; passer de... à *to go from . . . to . . .,* 1G; se passer de *to do without,* 4; **passer la douane** *to go through customs* 10; **passer l'aspirateur** *to vacuum,* I
passible *liable,* 3
passionnant(e) *exciting,* II; *fascinating,* 9
passionner *to fascinate/to excite,* 6
la **pastèque** *watermelon,* II
les **pâtes,** (f. pl.) *pasta,* I
le **patin à glace** *ice-skating,* I
le **patineur/la patineuse** *(ice) skater*
la **patinoire** *ice-skating rink,* I
la **pâtisserie** *pastry shop,* II

le pâtissier/la pâtissière *baker*, 2
le patrimoine *estate*, 8
    payant(e) *which must be paid for*, 10
    payer *to pay*, I; **payer avec une carte** *to pay with a credit card*, I; **payer en liquide** *to pay cash*, I; **payer par chèque** *to pay by check*, I
le pays *country*, 1G
le paysage *landscape*, 9
le paysan *peasant*, 7G
la pêche *peach*, II
le péage *toll*, 10
la pédale d'embrayage *clutch*, 10
le peigne *comb*, II
le peignoir *(bath)robe*, II
    peindre *to paint*, 9
le peintre *painter*, 9
la peinture *painting*, 9; **la peinture abstraite** *abstract painting*, 9; **la peinture à l'huile** *oil paint*, 9; **la peinture naïve** *primitive painting*, 9
le pélican *pelican*, 5
la pelouse *lawn*, I
la pellicule *film*, 9
    pendant *during*, II; **pendant les vacances** *during vacation*, II; pendant que *while/during*, II; **Pendant que j'y pense,...** *While I'm thinking about it, . . .*, 9
    pendre *to hang*, 7
    pénétrant(e) *penetrating*, 7
    pénétrer *to enter*, 9G
    pénible *tiresome/difficult*, I; *annoying*, II
la pénombre *semi-darkness*, 4
    penser *to think*, II
la pension complète *room with three meals included*, 1
    perdre *to lose*, II; **se perdre** *to get lost*, 5
le père *father*, II
    perfectionner *to perfect*, 6
la période *period (of time)*, 3
le périodique *periodical*, 6
les péripéties (f. pl.) *change of fortune, ups and downs*, 3
le périple *tour*, 5
la perle *pearl*, 9
    permettre *to allow*, 7G
le permis de conduire *driver's license*, 8
    pernicieux(euse) *pernicious, injurious, harmful*, 8
    persan(ne) *Persian*, 8
le personnage (principal) *(main) character*, II
    personne *nobody*, II
le personnel *staff*, 4
    personnifié(e) *personified*, 3

pesant(e) *heavy*, 6
se peser *to weigh oneself*, II
le pesticide *pesticide*, 7
    petit(e) *little, small*, II
le petit-déjeuner *breakfast*, I
la petite-fille *granddaughter*, I
les petits-enfants *grandchildren*, I
les petites annonces, (f. pl.) *classifieds*, 6
le petit-fils *grandson*, I
les petits pois, (m. pl.) *peas*, II
le pétrolier *oil tanker*, 7
le peuple *nation/people*, 3
la peur *fear*, 4
le phare *head/taillight*, 10
la pharmacie *pharmacy*, I
le pharmacien/la pharmacienne *pharmacist*, 2
le phénomène *phenomenon*, 7
la photo *photo*, 5, **la photo d'identité** *I.D. photo*, 8
la physique *physics*, 1
le pianiste/la pianiste *pianist*, 9
le piano *piano*, II
la pièce *room*, I; *coin*, II; **la pièce de théâtre** *play*, II
le pied *foot*, II
la pierre *stone*, 3
les pierreries *precious stones, gems*, 3
le pilote *pilot*, I
le piment mûr *ripe pimento*, 4
le pin *pine tree*, 7
le pinceau *brush*, 5
le pique-nique *picnic*, I
    piquer *to sting*, 5
le pire *the worst*, 6
la piscine *swimming pool*, I
la piste *circus ring*, 9; *runway*, 10; **la piste (d'athlétisme)** *track*, II
la pizza *pizza*, II
le placard *closet/cabinet*, 8
la place (assise) *seat*, I
    placer *to place*, I
la plage *beach*, II
    plaire *to like/to appeal*, 9; **se plaire** *to please (one another)*, 4
le plan *map*, II
la planche *plank, board*, 1; **la planche à voile** *windsurf*, 1; **la planche de surf** *surfboard*, I
la planète *planet*, 7
la plante *plant*, I
    planter *to crash (a computer)*, II
le planteur *grower of vegetable*, 7
    plat(e) *flat*, 10
le plat *dish*, 9
    plein(e) *full/plenty*, II
le plein *full*, 10
le plein air *open air/outdoors*, II; de plein gré *own free will*, 4
    pleurer *to cry*, 7

pleuvoir *to rain*, II
le plombier *plumber*, 2
la plongée *scuba diving*, 9G; **la plongée sous-marine** *scuba diving*, 5
la pluie *rain*, 7
    plus *no longer*, I; **plus de ... que** *more of . . . than*, II; **Plus ou moins.** *More or less.*, I; **plus tard** *later on*, 2; *later*, 3; **plus... que** *more . . . than*, II
    plusieurs *several*, IG
    plutôt *rather*, 9
le pneu *tire*, 10; **le pneu à plat** *flat tire*, 10
le poids *weight*, 8
le poignet *wrist*, II
le poing *fist*, 7
la pointure *shoe size*, I
la poire *pear*, II
les pois chiches, (m. pl.) *chick peas*
le poisson *fish*, 1
la poissonnerie *fish market*, II
le poissonnier/la poissonnière *fish monger*, II
le poivre *pepper*, I
le poivron *bell pepper*, II
la police *police*, 8
le policier *police officer*, 8
la politique *politics*, 8
    polluant(e) *polluting*, 7
    pollué(e) *polluted*, II
    polluer *to pollute*, 7
la pollution *pollution*, 7
la pomme *apple*, II; **la pomme de terre** *potato*, II
la pompe à essence *gasoline pump*, II
les pompes, (f. pl.) *push ups*, II
le pompier *fireman*, 8
le pont *bridge*, I
la pop *pop*, II
le porc *pork*, I
le portable *cell phone*, I; **le portable** *laptop*, I
la porte *door*, I; **la porte d'embarquement** *boarding gate*, I
le porte-bagages *luggage carrier / rack*, I
le portefeuille *wallet*, I
le porte-monnaie *change purse*, I
    porter *to wear*, I; *to carry*, 7; **porter secours** *to bring aid*, 7
le porteur *carrier, bearer*, 6
la portière *car door*, 10
le portrait *portrait*, 9
    portugais(e) *Portuguese*, II
le Portugal *Portugal*, II
    poser *to pose*, 9; **poser sa candidature** *to apply for a job*, 4; poser (une question) *to ask*, 6

posséder *to possess,* 1
la poste *post office,* I
le poste *position,* 10
le poster *poster,* I
le pot *jar,* II; **le pot de confiture** *jar of jam,* II
la poterie *pottery,* 9
le potier/la potière *potter,* 9
la potion *potion,* 3
la poubelle *trash,* I
la poule *hen,* II
le poulet *chicken,* II
le poumon *lung,* II
pour lors... *so . . ., then . . .,* 8
Pour ma part... *As for me . . .,* 8
pour une fois *for once,* II
pourquoi *why,* II; **Pourquoi pas?** *Why not?,* II
Pourriez-vous...? *Could you . . .?,* 2
la poussière *dust,* 7
poursuivre *to pursue, to continue,* 2
pouvoir *to be able to/can,* II
le pouvoir *power,* 3; **les pouvoirs magiques** *magic powers,* 3
la prairie *meadow,* II
la précaution *precaution,* 7
précédent(e) *previous,* 6; **précédente** *back (Internet),* II
précieux(-euse) *precious,* 4
précipiter *to rush,* 5
préféré(e) *favorite,* I
préférer *to prefer,* II
premier/première *first,* I
le premier étage *second floor,* I
le premier ministre *prime minister,* 8
le premier plan *limelight, forefront,* 9
la première *first night,* 9
la première classe *first class,* I
la première page *front page,* 6
prendre *to take,* II; **prendre garde à** *to watch out for,* 7; **prendre la température** *to take someone's temperature,* II; **prendre le bus** *to take the bus,* II; **prendre le petit-déjeuner** *to have breakfast,* II; **prendre sa retraite** *to retire,* 4; **prendre un bain** *to take a bath,* II; **prendre une douche** *to take a shower,* II
Prends garde à... *Pay attention to...,* 5
Prenez... *Take...,* I
le préparateur *preparer, maker,* 2
préparer *to prepare,* II; **se préparer** *to get ready,* II; **préparer les amuse-gueules** *to prepare the snacks,* II; **préparer son sac** *to get one's backpack ready,* II
prépondérant(e) *main,* 6C

près de *next to,* I
le présentateur/la présentatrice *newscaster,* II
présenter *to introduce,* II; **se présenter** *to run as a candidate,* 8
le président *president,* 3
presque *almost,* 1
la presse (spécialisée) *(specialized) press,* 6; **la presse à sentation** *tabloids,* 6
presser *to squeeze,* 6; presser le pas *to hurry,* 5
la pression *pressure,* 10
prêt(e) *ready,* II
le prêt-à-porter *ready-to-wear,* 2
prêter *to lend,* I
prévenir *to warn,* 10
prévoir *to foresee,* 6; *to predict,* 7
Prière de ne pas... *Please don't...,* 5
le prince/la princesse *prince/princess,* 4
le principe *principle,* 7
le printemps *spring,* II; le printemps pourri *rainy spring,* 7
la prison *prison,* 8
prisonnier(-ière) *imprisoned,* 3
se priver *to deprive oneself,* II
la probité *integrity,* 8
le problème *problem,* 7
le procédé *process,* 7
prochain(e) *next,* II; **la prochaine fois** *next time,* II
proche *close to,* 1
proclamer *to proclaim,* 4
produire *to produce,* 7; **se produire** *to take place,* 6
le produit bio(logique) *organic product,* 7
le professeur/la professeur *teacher/professor,* 2
la profession *profession,* 2
Profite bien de... *Enjoy...,* II
profiter *to make the most of/to enjoy,* II
le programme télé *t.v. program,* II
promener *to take for a walk,* I; *to walk (a dog),* I; **se promener** *to take a stroll,* II
promettre *to promise,* 3
prononcer *to pronounce,* I
propre *clean,* II; *own,* 3
le propriétaire *owner,* 7
prospérer *to flourish,* 7
le protecteur *protector,* 8
le protectorat *protectorate,* 3
protéger *to protect,* 7
provoquer *to produce/to provoke,* 7
le public *public,* 6
publier *to publish,* 6
puis *then,* I

la puissance *power,* 5
le puits *well,* 10
le pull *sweater,* II
pur(e) *clear,* II
le pur-sang *thoroughbred horse,* 1

Qu'est-ce que *What,* I; Qu'est-ce qu'elle est bien, cette pub! *What a good commercial!,* II; Qu'est-ce qu'il vous faut? *What do you need?,* II; Qu'est-ce qu'il y a dans...? *What's in . . .?,* II; Qu'est-ce qu'on joue au cinéma? *What's playing at the movie theater?,* II; Qu'est-ce que ça raconte? *What's it about?,* II; Qu'est-ce que je pourrais offrir à...? *What could I get for . . .?,* II; Qu'est-ce que tu aimes faire? *What do you like to do?,* I; Qu'est-ce que tu aimes faire pendant les vacances? *What do you like to do during vacation?,* II; Qu'est-ce que tu aimes regarder à la télé? *What do you like to watch on TV?,* II; Qu'est-ce que tu as l'intention de faire...? *What do you intend to do . . .?,* 2; Qu'est-ce que tu as lu d'intéressant récemment? *What have you read lately that's interesting?;* Qu'est-ce que tu as? *What's wrong?,* II; Qu'est-ce que tu en penses? *What do you think?,* 4; Qu'est-ce que tu fais...? *What are you doing on . . .?,* I; Qu'est-ce que tu fais comme sport? *What sports do you play?,* I; Qu'est-ce que tu feras plus tard? *What will you do later on?,* 2; Qu'est-ce que tu penses de...? *What do you think of . . .?,* 9; Qu'est-ce que tu utilises comme...? *What do you use as . . .?,* II; Qu'est-ce que tu veux... comme...? *What . . . do you want to . . .?,* 1; Qu'est-ce que vous comptez... comme...? *What are you planning on . . . as . . .?,* 2; Qu'est-ce que vous me conseillez? *What do you recommend?,* I; Qu'est-ce qui s'est passé? *What happened?,* 6; Qu'est-ce qui...? *What . . .?,* 6
le quai *platform,* I

quand *when,* 1; **Quand est-ce que tu as...?** *When do you have . . . ?,* I; **Quand est-ce que...?** *When . . . ?,* I; **Quand j'aurai fini mes études,...** *When I'm done with my studies, . . .* 2; **Quand j'avais... ans,...** *When I was . . . years old, . . .,* II; **Quand j'étais petit(e),...** *When I was little, . . .,* II; **Quand j'étais plus jeune,...** *When I was younger, . . .,* II

quarante *forty,* I

le quart *quarter,* I

quatorze *fourteen,* I

quatre *four,* I

quatre-vingt-dix *ninety,* I

quatre-vingt-onze *ninety one,* I

quatre-vingts *eighty,* I

quatre-vingt-un *eighty one,* I

que (qu') *what,* II

quel(quelle) *which,* I; **Quel est le chemin le plus rapide pour...?** *What is the fastest way to . . . ?,* 10; **Quel est ton avis sur...?** *What is your opinion of . . . ?,* 9; **Quel jour sommes-nous?** *What day is today?,* 1; **Quel temps fait-il?** *What is the weather like?,* 1; **Quel... tu vas...?** *What . . . are you going to . . . ?,* 1; **Quelle est ton adresse e-mail / mail?** *What is your e-mail address?,* I; **Quelle heure est-il?** *What time is it?,* I; **Quelle horreur!** *How horrible!,* 5; **Quelle pointure faites-vous?** *What shoe size do you wear?,* I; **quelle qu'elle soit** *whatever it may be,* 3; **Quelle sorte de/d'...?** *What type of . . . ?,* II; **Quelle sortie faut-il prendre pour...?** *Which exit do you take for . . . ?,* 10; **Quelle taille faites-vous?** *What size do you wear?,* I

quelles *which,* I; **Quelles sont tes activités préférées?** *What are your favorite activities?,* I

quelque part *somewhere,* 2

Quelque temps après,... *Some time later,...,* 3

quelqu'un *someone,* II

quels *which,* I

se quereller *to quarrel,* 3

la quête *quest,* 3

la queue *line,* I

qui *who,* II; **Qui c'est, ça?** *Who is that?,* I; **Qui est-ce que/qui...?** *Who...?,* 6

la quiche *quiche,* I

quinze *fifteen,* I

se quitter *to leave (one another),* 4

Quoi de neuf? *What's new?,* 4

le quotidien *daily paper,* 6

la raclée *hiding,* 1

Raconte! *Tell me!,* 4

raconter *to tell,* 3

raccourcir *to make shorter,* 6

raccrocher *to hang up,* 2

la radio *radio,* I

le rafia tressé *braided palm,* 4

rajouter *add,* 6

la raison *reason,* IG

ralentir *to slow down,* 10

rallumer *to relight,* 2

ramener *to bring back,* 10

la ramure *foliage,* 7

la randonnée *hike,* 1

le rang *rank,* 8

ranger *to put away/to tidy up,* II; **se ranger** *to agree,* 4; **ranger la maison** *to tidy up the house,* II; **ranger sa chambre** *to pick up one's bedroom,* I; **ranger ses affaires** *to put one's things away,* II

le rap *rap,* II

rapide *fast,* 10

les rapides *rapids,* 5

rappeler *to remind,* II; **se rappeler** *to recall/to be reminded,* 1

Rapporte-moi... *Bring me back...,* II

rapporter *to bring back,* II

la raquette *racket,* II

rarement *rarely,* II

se raser *to shave,* II

le rasoir (électrique) *(electric) razor,* II

se rassasier *to satisfy one's hunger,* 3

rassembler *to gather,* 9

rassurer *to reassure,* 10

Rassure-toi. *Don't worry.,* 10

rater *to miss,* I; *to fail (an exam, a class),* II

le raton laveur *raccoon,* 5

ravager *to ravage/to destroy,* 7

ravauder *to mend,* 6

le rayon *department,* I; **le rayon d'action** *range (aircraft),* 10; **le rayon bijouterie** *jewelry department,* I; **le rayon maroquinerie** *leather goods department,* I; **le rayon plein air** *outdoor goods department,* I

le raz-de-marée *cyclone,* 7

le rebondissement *twist,* II

recenser *to register,* 7

la réception *reception,* I

la réceptionniste *receptionist,* I

la recette *recipe,* 5

recevoir *to receive/to get,* II

le réchaud *camping stove,* II

le réchauffement *warming,* 7

la recherche *research,* 7

rechercher *to search,* II

le récit *story,* 3

réclamer *to claim,* 5

recommander *to recommend,* I

la récompense, *reward,* 8

récompenser *to reward,* 7

se réconcilier *to make up,* 4

la reconnaissance *recognition,* 2

reconnaître *to recognize,* 3G

le record *record,* 6

recouvrir *to cover,* 7

la récré(ation) *break,* I

recruter *to recruit,* 9

le recueil de poésie *anthology of poems,* II

recueillir *to collect,* 10

reculé(e) *remote,* 3

le recyclage *recycling,* 7

recycler *to recycle,* 7

le rédacteur/la rédactrice en chef *editor-in-chief,* 6

la rédaction *editorial,* 6C

redevable *indebted,* 6

redire *to say again,* 5

réduire *to reduce,* 7

refermer *to close,* 10

refléter *to reflect,* 3

regagner *to go back*

le regard *look, glance,* 9

regarder *to look at, to watch,* I; *to concern,* 4; **regarder des dessins animés** *to watch cartoons,* II; **regarder la télé** *to watch TV,* I; **Regardez (la carte)!** *Look (at the map)!,* I

le reggae *reggae,* II

le régime *diet,* II; **le régime politique** *political regime,* 8

la région (sinistrée) *(stricken) region,* 7

la règle *ruler,* I; *rule,* 4

régler *to tune/to adjust,* 10; *to regulate,* 8 **régler la pression des pneus** *to adjust the tire pressure,* 10

le règne *reign,* 3G

regretter *to regret, to be sorry* 4

régulièrement *regularly,* I

la reine *queen,* 3

rejeter *to throw back,* 9

rejoindre *to meet up,* 10

se réjouir *to delight,* 6

relâcher *to loosen,* 8

se relaxer *to relax,* II

relier *to link,* 4

se **remarier** *to remarry,* I
remercier *to thank,* II
remettre *to put back,* 6
la remise *shed,* 7
remonter *to date, to go back to,* 6
remplacer *to replace,* 2
remporter *to take back/to win,* 6
la reprise *repeat, rerun,* 6
le renard *fox,* 5
renarrer *to tell again,* 3
la rencontre *connection, meeting,* 3
se **rencontrer** *to meet (one another),* 4
le rendez-vous *date,* 4; *place of meeting,* IG
rendre *to give back,* I; **rendre (un livre)** *to return (a book),* II; **rendre visite (à une personne)** *to visit (a person),* 1
la renommée *fame,* 7G
se **renseigner** *to become informed,* II
la rentrée *beginning of classes/first day of classes,* 1
rentrer *to return (home),* II; **rentrer à la maison** *to return home,* II
répandre *to pour out, to spill,* 5
réparateur *refreshing,* 6
réparer (les voitures) *to fix (cars),* 2
repartir *to leave,* 7
le repas *meal,* I
repasser le linge *to iron,* 2
repeindre *to repaint (the house),* 2
répéter *to repeat,* I
Répétez! *Repeat!,* I; **Répétez, s'il vous plaît?** *Could you please repeat that?,* I
répondre (à) *to answer,* I
le reportage *report,* II; **le reportage sportif** *sports report,* II
le repos *rest,* 2
se **reposer** *to rest,* II
reprendre *to have more,* I; *to go over,* 6
la représentation *performance,* 9
la reprise *repeat, rerun,* 6
reproduire *to reproduce,* 9
la république *republic,* 3
réputé(e) *well-known, famous,* 3G
requérir *to require,* 1
le requin *shark,* 5
la réservation *reservation,* II
réserver *to book/to reserve,* 10
le réservoir *tank,* 10
résider *to reside, to live,* 1G
ressembler *to be like, lo look like,* 3G
ressentir *to feel* 4
le ressort *spring,* 6
les ressources naturelles, (f. pl.) *natural resoources,* 7
rester *to stay,* II; **rester chez**

soi *to stay at home,* II
se **rétablir** *to recover,* 8
retirer *to withdraw,* I
rétorquer *to retort,* 3
le retour *return,* 1
retourner *to return,* II; **Retournez à vos places!** *Go back to your seats!,* I
retracer *to recount,* 10
se **retrouver** *to find/to meet (one another),* 4
le rétroviseur *rearview mirror,* 10
la réunion *meeting,* 5C
réussir (à) *to pass (an exam)/to succeed,* I
le rêve *dream,* II
le réveil *alarm,* II; *awakening,* 1G
se **réveiller** *to wake up,* II
le réveillon *midnight feast,* II
la revendication *demand,* 4
revenir *to come back,* 5
rêver (de) *to dream (of,* 5
le réverbère *street light,* 2
la révision *tune up,* 10
se **revoir** *to see (one another) again,* 4
la revue *journal,* 6
le rez-de-chaussée *first floor,* I
le rhume *cold,* I
rien *nothing,* II; **Rien de spécial.** *Nothing special.,* 4; **rien ne marche** *nothing is working,* II
rigoureux(-euse) *harsh,* 9G
la rigueur *rigor, harshness,* 2
rire *to laugh,* 9
la rive *bank,* 5
la rivière *river,* II
le riz *rice,* I
la robe *dress,* I
le robinet *faucet,* II
le rocher *rock,* II
le roi *king,* 3
le rôle *part,* 7
le roman *novel,* II; **le roman d'amour** *romance novel,* II; **le roman fantastique** *fantasy novel,* II; **le roman historique** *historical novel,* II; **le roman policier** *mystery novel,* II
rompre *to break,* 4
rond(e) *round,* 9
la ronde *rounds, patrol,* 9
le ronron *purring,* 10
la rose *pink,* I
la rosée *dew,* 9
la roue à dents *cogged wheel,* 2; **la roue de secours** *spare tire,* 10
rouge *red,* I
le rouge à lèvres *lipstick,* II
la rouille *rust,* 1
la route *road,* 10

roux/rousse *red-head(ed),* II
le royaume *kingdom,* 3; le Royaume-Uni *United Kingdom,* 10
la rubrique *column,* 6
la rue *street,* I
le ruisseau *stream,* II

sa *his/her,* I
le sable *sand,* 7
le sac à dos *backpack,* I; **le sac à main** *purse,* I; **le sac de couchage** *sleeping bag,* 1; **le sac de voyage** *travel bag,* 1; **le sac en plastique** *plastic bag,* II
la sagesse *wisdom,* 4
saignant(e) *rare,* I
la Saint-Sylvestre *New Year's Eve,* II
la saison *season,* I
la salade *salad,* I
le salaire *salary,* 2
sale *dirty,* II
la salle *room,* I; **la salle à manger** *dining room,* I; **la salle d'embarquement** *departure lounge,* 10; **la salle d'informatique** *computer room,* 1; **la salle de bain** *bathroom,* I; **la salle de classe** *classroom,* 1
le salon *living room,* I
saluer *to greet, to bow,* 2
Salut. *Hi./Goodbye.,* I
samedi *Saturday,* I
la sandale *sandal,* I
le sandwich *sandwich,* I; **le sandwich au jambon** *ham sandwich,* II
le sang *blood,* 5
le sanglier *wild boar,* 5
sans *without,* I; **sans doute** *without a doubt,* II; **sans fil** *cordless,* 2
la santé *health,* II
le sapeur-pompier *fireman,* 8
le sapin de Noël *Christmas tree,* II
le saucisson *salami,* I
le saut *jump,* 5
sauter à la corde *to jump rope,* II; **sauter des repas** *to skip meals,* II
sauvage *wild,* 5
sauvegarder *to save (a document),* II
sauver *to rescue,* 3
Savez-vous...? *Do you know . . . ?,* I
savoir *to know,* II
le savon *soap,* II
le scénariste/la scénariste *screenwriter,* 6

la scène *stage*, 9
  scolaire *scholastic*, I
  sculpter *to sculpt*, 9
le sculpteur *sculptor*, 6
la sculpture *sculpture*, 9
  se déplacer *to move/to travel*, 3
  se réjouir *to rejoice*, 6
  se terminer *to come to an end*, 3
la séance *showing*, II
  sec(sèche) *dry*, 7
le sèche-cheveux *blow-dryer*, II
se sécher les cheveux *to dry one's hair*, II
la sécheresse *drought*, 7
la Seconde Guerre mondiale *World War II*, 3
  secouer *to shake*, 7
le secours *help / aid*, 7
le secrétaire/la secrétaire *secretary*, 2
  séculaire *something that has existed for centuries*, 4
  seize *sixteen*, I
le séjour *stay / sojourn*, II
le sel *salt*, I
le self *cafeteria*, 1
  selon *according to*, 4
la semaine *week*, 1; la semaine dernière *last week*, I
le sénateur/la sénatrice *senator*, 8
le sens *interpretation, meaning*, 8
la sentence *decision, verdict*, 3
le sentier *path*, II
  se sentir *to feel*, 2
  se séparer *to separate, to part (from)*
  sept *seven*, I
  septembre *September*, I
la séquelle *after-effects*, 6
la série *series*, II
  sérieux(-euse) *serious*, II
le serment *oath*, 8
le serpent *snake*, II
  serré(e) *tight*, I
le serveur/la serveuse *waitperson*, 2
le service *service*, 2; le service public *government service*, 8
la serviette *napkin*, I; la serviette de bain *bath towel*, II; la serviette de toilette *hand towel*, II
  se servir *to use*, 2
  ses *his/her*, I
  seul(e) *only*
le shampooing *shampoo*, II
le short *a pair of shorts*, I
  si *if*, II; *yes (to negative question)*, II
le siècle *century*, 3
le siège *seat*, 10
  siéger *to hold a seat*, 8
  la sieste *nap*, II
la signature *signature*, 8
  signer *to sign*, 3

s'il te plaît *please*, I
s'il vous plaît *please*, II
Silence! *Quiet!*, I
le sillon *furrow*, 5
  simple *simple*, II
  simulé(e) *fictitious*
  sinistré(e) *stricken*, 7
la sirène *siren*, 8
le sirop *syrup*, I; le sirop d'érable *maple syrup*, 5; le sirop de menthe *mint syrup*, II
  sirupeux(-euse) *sirupy*, 6
le sitcom *sitcom*, II
le site *website*, II; le site d'une compagnie aérienne *airline website*, II
  situé(e) *located* 6
  six *six*, I
le skate(board) *skateboarding*, I
le ski *skiing / skis*, I
le slogan publicitaire *advertising slogan*, 2
le SMS *instant message*, I
le soap *soap opera*, II
la société *company*, 2; *society*, 8; la société privée *private company*, 10
la sœur *sister*, II
le sofa *couch*, I
la soie *silk*, I
la soif *thirst*, 10
  soigner *to care for*, 2
le soin *care*, 4
le soir *evening*, I
la soirée *party / mixer*, II; la soirée costumée *costume party*, II
  soixante *sixty*, I
  soixante et onze *seventy one*, I
  soixante-dix *seventy*, I
  soixante-douze *seventy two*, I
le sol *ground*, 7; le sol en terre battue *mud floor*, 4
  solaire *solar*, 7
le soldat *soldier*, 3
les soldes (f.) *sale*, I
le soleil *sun*, I
  solitaire *solo*, 5
le sommeil *sleep*, II
le sommet *peak*, II
  son *his/her*, I
le son *sound*, II
le sondage *survey*, 8
  songer *to dream, to think*, 1
  sonner *to ring*, II
la sonnerie *ringing*, 2
le sorcier *sorcerer*, 3
la sorcière *witch*, 3
le sort *spell*, 3
la sorte *type*, II
la sortie *dismissal*, I; *exit*, 10; la sortie de secours *emergency exit*, 10

  sortir *to go out*, II; *to take out*, 10; sortir la poubelle *to take out the trash*, I
  soudain(e) *sudden, unexpected*, 8
  souffler *to blow*, 7
le souhait *wish*, 3
  souhaiter *to wish*, II; souhaiter une bonne nuit *to say good night*, II
  soumettre *to keep under*, 4
  soumis(e) *subjected*, 8
le soupir *sigh*, 9
  souple *supple, flexible*, 9
la source *spring*, 3G; la source d'énergie *energy source*, 7
le sourcil *eyebrow*, II
  sourd(e) *deaf*, 3
la souris *mouse*, II
  sous *under*, I
les sous, (m. pl.) *money*, 1
le sous-produit *by-product*, 6
les sous-titres, (m. pl.) *subtitles*, II
  soustraire *to subtract*, 2
  soutenir *to support*, 8
  souterrain(e) *underground*, 3G
  se souvenir *to remember*, 7G
  souvent *often*, 3
le souverain *monarch* 3
la souveraineté *sovereignty*, 5G
  spécialisé(e) *specialized*, 6
le spectacle *show*, II; le spectacle son et lumière *sound and light show*, II
le spectateur/la spectatrice *spectator/ audience*, 9
la spéléologie *caving / spelunking*, 5
le sport *sports*, I; les sports extrêmes *extreme sports*, 5; les Sports, (m. pl.) *sports page*, 6
  sportif(-ive) *athletic*, II;
le spot publicitaire *commercial*, II
le stade *stadium*, I
le stage *internship*, 2
la station de métro *subway station*, I
la station-relais *relay station*, 10
la station-service *gas station*, 10
le stationnement *parking*, 10
la statue *statue*, 9
la statuette *statuette*, 9
le steak *steak*, I
  stressant(e) *stressful*, II
le stewart *flight attendant*, 10
  stimuler *to stimulate*, 7
le style *style*, 9
le stylo *pen*, I
  subir *to suffer, to undergo*, 3
le substrat *substratum*, 7
le succès *success*, 6
le sucre *sugar*, II
  sucré(e) *sweetened*, 10

la **Suède** *Sweden,* II
suggérer *to suggest,* 3
la **Suisse** *Switzerland,* II
suivant(e) *following,* 9
suivante *forward (Internet),* II
suivre *to follow,* II; **suivre un cours** *to take a class,* II
le **sultan** *sultan,* 3
le **super** *regular gas,* 10
superflu(e) *superfluous, unnecessary,* 6
supposer *to suppose,* 7
supprimer *to exterminate,* 4; *to delete,* 6
sur *on,* I; **sur le point de** *about to,* II
sûr(e) *certain,* 7
le **surf** *snowboarding,* I
surfer *to surf,* I; **surfer sur Internet** *surf the Net,* I
surnommer *to nickname*
surprenant(e) *surprising,* 9
surtout *above all, especially,* 5; **Surtout pas!** *Certainly not!,* 4
surveiller *to observe,* 5
suspendu(e) *hanging,* 10
le **suspense** *suspense,* II
les **SVT** *natural sciences,* 1
le **sweat-shirt** *sweat-shirt,* I
sympa(thique) *nice,* I
le **syndicat** *union,* 2

ta *your (informal f.),* I
la **table** *table,* I; **la table basse** *coffee table,* I; **la table de nuit** *night stand,* I
le **tableau** *board,* I; **le tableau** *painting on canvas,* 6; **le tableau d'affichage** *information board,* I; **le tableau de bord** *dashboard,* 10
le **tablier** *apron,* 10; *hood (of a fireplace)*
les **tâches ménagères,** (f. pl.) *housework,* 4
la **taille** *clothing size,* I
le **taille-crayon** *pencil sharpener,* I
le **tailleur** *woman's suit,* I
talentueux(-euse) *talented,* 2
tandis que *while,* 2
le **tangage** *pitching,* 1
tant que *as much as,* 5; **Tant que j'y suis,...** *As long as I'm here, ...,* 9
la **tante** *aunt,* II
tape-à-l'œil *flashy,* I
le **tapis** *rug,* I; **le tapis volant** *flying carpet,* 3

tard *late,* II
tardif(-ive) *late, tardy,* 7
le **tarif** *fee,* I; **le tarif réduit** *reduced fee/discount,* I
la **tarte** *pie,* I; **la tarte aux pommes** *apple pie,* II
la **tartine** *bread with butter or jam,* I
la **tasse** *cup,* II
le taureau *bull,* 1G
le **taxi** *taxi,* I
te (t') *te,* II; *(to) you,* II
la **techno** *techno music,* II
le **tee-shirt** *t-shirt,* I
teindre les cheveux *to dye hair,* 2
la **teinturerie** *dry cleaner's,* 2
le **teinturier/la teinturière** *dry cleaner,* 2
la **télé(vision)** *television,* I
télécharger *to download,* II
la **télécommande** *remote control,* II
le **téléphone** *telephone,* I
téléphoner (à des amis) *to call (friends),* I; **se téléphoner** *to telephone (one another),* 4
tellement *so, so much/really,* II
témoigner *to witness,* 6
le **témoin** *witness,* 8
la **température** *temperature,* 6
la **tempête** *storm,* 7; **la tempête de neige/sable** *snow/sand storm,* 7
le **temps** *weather,* I; *time,* I; **le temps libre** *free time,* I
tenir *to hold,* 5; tenir une réunion *to hold a meeting,* 4; se tenir au courant *to be kept informed* 3
le **tennis** *tennis,* I
la **tente** *tent,* 1
le **terminal** *terminal,* I
se **terminer** *to end,* 3
le **terrain** *land,* 7; **le terrain de sport** *sports field,* II
la terreur *terror,* 5G
le terrier *burrow,* 3
tes *your (informal pl.),* I
la **tête** *head,* I
le **texto** *instant message,* I
le **théâtre** *drama,* I; *theater,* 9
le **ticket** *ticket,* I
Tiens. *Here.,* I
le tiers *third,* 6C
la tige *stem,* 7
le **timbre** *stamp,* I
timide *shy,* I
tiqueté(e) *speckled,* 1
tirer *to pull,* 2
le **titre** *title,* 6; **le (gros) titre** *headline,* 6
le **toast** *toast,* I
toi *you,* I; **Toi non plus.** *You, neither!,* 4

la **toile** *canvas,* 9; **la toile d'araignée** *spider web,* II; **la toile de jute** *jute cloth,* 7
les **toilettes,** (f. pl.) *restroom,* I
la **tomate** *tomato,* II
la **tombe** *tomb, grave,* 1
tomber *to fall,* I; **tomber amoureux(-euse)** *to fall in love,* 4; **tomber en panne** *to break down,* 10; **tomber malade** *to get sick,* 4
ton *your (informal m.),* I
tondre *to mow,* I; **tondre la pelouse** *to mow the lawn,* I
le **tonnerre** *thunder,* 7
la **tornade** *tornado,* 7
tôt *early,* II
la **touche** *key,* II
le **toucher** *feel, touch,* 9
toujours *always,* I
la **tour** *tower,* 3; **la tour de contrôle** *control tower,* 10
le **tour** *tour,* II; *potter's wheel,* 9
le **tourbillon** *whirlwind,* 9
le **tourisme** *tourism,* II
la **tournée** ~ *tour,* 9
tourner *to turn,* I; **Tournez au/à la prochain(e)...** *Turn at the next...,* I
tous les deux jours *every other day,* 1; **tous les jours** *every day,* 1; **tous les mercredis** *every Wednesday,* II; **Tous mes vœux de bonheur.** *I wish you all the best.,* 4
tousser *to cough,* II
tout(toute) *all,* I; **tout à coup** *suddenly,* 7; **tout à fait** *totally/absolutely,* I; **tout à l'heure** *very soon,* II; **tout de suite** *right away/immediately,* I; **tout droit** *straight ahead,* I; **tout près** *right next to,* II; **toute la nuit** *all night,* I; **Toutes mes félicitations!** *Congratulations!,* 4
toutefois *however,* 6;
la **toux** *cough,* I
le **tracteur** *tractor,* II
le **traducteur/la traductrice** *translator,* 2
trahir *to betray,* 7
le **train** *train,* II
le **traîneau** *sleigh,* 5
traîner *to trail behind/dawdle,* II
le **traité (de paix)** *(peace) treaty,* 3
le **traitement** *treatment,* 7
traiter *to talk about,* 9
le **traître** *traitor,* 3
la **tranche** *slice,* II; *bracket,* 6; **la tranche de jambon** *slice of ham,* II

la vitre *window,* 10
  vivant(e) *vibrant,* II; *alive,* 4
  vivement *deeply,* 4
  vivre *to live,* 4
le vizir *vizier,* 3
  voici *here is,* 1
la voie *track,* I; *way, road,* 10
  voilà *here is . . . ,* I; *here,* II
la voile *sail,* II
le voile *veil,* 9
  voir *to see,* II
le voisinage *neighborhood, proximity,* 3
la voiture *car,* I; **la voiture de sport** *sports car,* I
le vol *flight,* I; *theft,* 6; **le vol direct** *direct flight,* 10; **le vol intérieur** *domestic flight,* 10; **le vol international** *international flight,* 10; **le vol sans escale** *non-stop flight,* 10
le volant *steering wheel,* 10
le volcan *volcano,* 7

voler *to steal,* 6
le voleur/la voleuse *thief,* 6
le volley *volleyball,* I
la volonté *will,* 4
la volute bleutée *bluish smoke,* 7
la variété *variety, diversity,* 9G
la voilure *aerofoil, sail,* 9
  vos *your (formal pl.),* I
  voter *to vote,* 8
  votre *your (formal),* I
  vouloir *to want,* II
  vous *you,* II; *(to) you,* II; **Vous serait-il possible de contacter mes parents?** *Would it be possible for you to contact my parents?,* 8
la voûte *vault,* 7
le voyage *trip,* II
  voyager *to travel,* II
le voyageur *traveler,* 8
  vrai(e) *true,* 6
  vraiment *really,* 4
le VTT *mountain bike,* I
la vue *view,* I; *sight,* 9

le wagon *(railroad) car,* I; **le wagon-restaurant** *buffet car,* I
le week-end *weekend,* II

y *there,* II
le yaourt *yogurt,* II
les yeux, (m. pl.) *eyes,* II
le yoga *yoga,* II

zéro *zero,* I
le zoo *zoo,* I

Glossaire français–anglais

Glossaire anglais–français

This vocabulary includes all of the words presented in to the **Vocabulaire** sections of the chapters. These words are considered active—you are expected to know them and be able to use them. French nouns are listed with the definite article. Expressions are listed under the English word you would most likely reference. The number after each entry refers to the chapter in which the word or phrase is introduced. Words and phrases from Level 1 and Level 2 are indicated by the Roman numerals I and II.

To be sure you are using French words and phrases in their correct context, refer to the chapters listed. You may also want to look up French phrases in the **Liste d'expressions,** pages R22–R25.

a little bit too… *un peu trop…,* I; **a long time** *longtemps,* 3; **a long time ago** *il y a bien longtemps,* 3; **a lot (of)** *beaucoup (de),* 1; **a lot/much** *beaucoup,* 4; **a pair of shorts** *le short,* I
abdominal muscles *les abdominaux, (m. pl.),* II
aboard *à bord,* 10
about *à peu près,* II; **about to** *sur le point de,* II
above all, especially *surtout,* 5
abroad *à l'étranger,* II
absolutely *absolument,* II
abstract *abstrait(e),* 9
to **accelerate** *accélérer,* 10
access *l'accès, (m.),* I
accessories *les accessoires (m. pl.),* I
accident *l'accident, (m.),* 6
according to me *d'après moi,* I
accumulation *l'accumulation, (f.),* 7
across from *en face de,* I
action movie *le film d'action,* II
activity *l'activité, (f.),* I; *l'exercice, (m.),* I
actor *l'acteur, (m.),* II
actress *l'actrice, (f.),* II
to **add** *ajouter,* II
address *l'adresse, (f.),* II
to **address** *adresser (s'),* I
to **adjust the tire pressure** *régler la pression des pneus,* 10
to **adopt** *adopter,* 4
adventure movie *le film d'aventures,* II
to **advise** *conseiller,* I

aerobics *l'aérobic, (f.),* I
African *africain(e),* 3
after *après,* 1
afternoon *après-midi,* I
afterwards *par la suite,* 3; *après ça,* II
age *l'âge, (m.),* I
aid *l'aide, (f.),* 8
air *l'air, (m.)* 7; **air/air-related** *aérien(ne),* II; **air conditioning** *la climatisation,* I
airline website *le site d'une compagnie aérienne,* II
airport *l'aéroport, (m.),* 10
aisle *l'allée, (f.),* 10
alarm *le réveil,* II
alert *l'alerte, (f.),* 7
Algeria *l'Algérie, (f.),* 3
all night *toute la nuit,* I
Allegedly… *À ce que l'on prétend…,* 8
alligator *l'alligator, (m.),* 5
already *déjà,* II
also *aussi,* 1
aluminum *l'aluminium, (m.),* 7
always *toujours,* I
amateur film-making *le vidéo amateur,* II
ambulance *l'ambulance, (f.),* 8
American *américain,* I
among *parmi,* 3
and *et,* I
anger *la colère,* 6
angry *fâché(e),* 4; *en colère,* 6
animal(s) *l'animal, (m.), les animaux, (m. pl.),* I
ankle *la cheville,* II
to **announce (that)** *annoncer (que),* 3

to **annoy** *énerver,* II; **annoyed** *énervé(e),* 4; **annoying** *pénible,* II
to **answer** *répondre (à),* I
apartment *l'appartement, (m.),* I; **apartment complex** *l'immeuble, (m.),* I
to **appear** *apparaître,* 3; **to appear** *paraître,* 6
appearance *la mine,* II
to **applaud** *applaudir,* 9
apple *la pomme,* II; **apple juice** *le jus de pomme,* I; **apple pie** *la tarte aux pommes,* II
to **apply for a job** *poser sa candidature,* 4; **to apply for a visa** *faire une demande de visa,* II
approximately *environ,* II
apricot *l'abricot, (m.),* II
April *avril,* I
to **argue (with one another)** *disputer (se),* 4
arm *le bras,* II
armchair *le fauteuil,* I
army *l'armée, (f.),* I
arrival *l'arrivée, (f.),* I; **arrival hall** *le hall d'arrivée,* 10; **to arrive** *arriver,* II
art critic *le critique d'art,* 6; **art gallery** *la galerie d'art,* 9
article *l'article, (m.),* 6
artist *l'artiste, (m.),* 9
Arts page *Culture,* 6
as much as *autant que,* II
ash *la cendre,* 7
Ask… *Adressez-vous…,* I
at/to *à, à l', à la, au, aux,* II; **at first glance** *a priori,* 7; **at (my) home** *chez moi,* I;

at that moment *à ce moment-là*, II; **at the end of** *au fond de*, I; *au bout de*, II; **at the house of** *chez*, II; **at the latest** *au plus tard*, II; **at the same time (as)** *en même temps (que)*, II; **at the time (when)/as** *au moment où*, II; **at the time of** *au moment de*, 3; **at what time** *à quelle heure*, I

athletic *sportif(-ive)*, II

atmosphere *l'atmosphère*, *(f.)*, 3

attention *à l'attention de*, 2

August *août*, 5

aunt *la tante*, II

authorization *l'autorisation*, *(f.)*, 10

(auto)biography *l'(auto)biographie*, *(f.)*, II

automatic transmission *le changement de vitesse automatique*, 10

automobile *l'automobile*, *(f.)*, 7

autonomy *l'autonomie*, *(f.)*, 3

available (for) *disponible (pour)*, I

avalanche *l'avalanche*, *(f.)*, 6

to **babysit** *garder des enfants*, II

back (Internet) *précédente*, II

backpack *le sac à dos*, 1; *le sac (à dos)*, I

bacon *le bacon*, I

bad *mauvais(e)*, I; **badly** *mal*, I

baggage locker *la consigne*, I

baker *le boulanger*, *la boulangère*, II

bakery *la boulangerie*, II

balanced *équilibré(e)*, II

balcony *le balcon*, I

ball, balloon *le ballon*, II; **ball** *la balle*, II

ballerina *la ballerine*, 9

ballet *le ballet*, 9

ballot box *l'urne*, *(f.)*, 8

ballot paper *le bulletin de vote*, 8

banana *la banane*, II

bandage *le pansement*, I

bank *la banque*, I; **bank card** *la carte bancaire*, I

barely *à peine*, II

barn *la grange*, II

barnyard *la basse-cour*, II

baseball *le base-ball*, I

basketball *le basket-(ball)*, I

bat *la chauve-souris*, 5; **bat** *la batte*, I

bath towel *la serviette de bain*, II

bathroom *la salle de bain*, I

bathtub *la baignoire*, II

battle *la bataille*, 3

bayou *le bayou*, 5

to **be** *être*, II; **to be able to/can** *pouvoir*, II; **to be aware of** *être au courant de*, 6; **to be born** *naître*, 4; **to be cold** *avoir froid*, I; **to be hot** *avoir chaud*, I; **to be hungry** *avoir faim*, I; **to be in detention** *être en retenue*, II; **to be in one's best interest** *avoir intérêt à*, I; **to be in shape/healthy** *être en forme*, II; **to be in training/to do an internship** *faire un stage*, 2; **to be late** *être en retard*, II; **to be located** *trouver (se)*, II; **to be lucky** *avoir de la chance*, 10; **to be named** *appeler (s')*, I; **to be right** *avoir raison*, I; **to be thirsty** *avoir soif*, I; **to be tired** *être fatigué(e)*, II; **to be unemployed** *être au chômage*, 2

beach *la plage*, II

bear *l'ours*, *(m.)*, 5

beat *la mesure*, 9

beautiful *beau/belle*, II

beaver *le castor*, 5

because of *à cause de*, 7

to **become informed** *renseigner (se)*, II

bed *le lit*, I

bedroom *la chambre*, I

bee *l'abeille*, *(f.)*, 5

beef *le bœuf*, II

before *avant de*, 3

to **begin** *commencer*, II

beginning *le commencement*, 3

behavior/comportment *la conduite*, 3

behind *derrière*, I

Belgium *la Belgique*, II

belief *la croyance*, 3

bell pepper *le poivron*, II

belt *la ceinture*, I

to **bet** *parier*, 7

between *entre*, I; **between… and (in between)** *entre... et*, I

to **beware** *méfier (se)*, I

big/tall *grand(e)*, II

bike *le vélo*, I

bill/ticket *le billet*, II; **bill** *l'addition*, *(f.)*, I

binder *le classeur*, I

binoculars *les jumelles*, *(f. pl.)*, 7

bird *l'oiseau*, *(m.)*, II

birthday *l'anniversaire*, *(m.)*, II; **birthday card** *la carte d'anniversaire*, II

to **bite** *mordre*, 5

black *noir(e)*, I

blond(e) *blond(e)*, II

blow-dryer *le sèche-cheveux*, II

blue *bleu(e)*, II; **blues** *le blues*, II

board *le tableau*, I

to **board** *embarquer*, 10

boarding gate *la porte d'embarquement*, I; **boarding pass** *la carte d'embarquement*, I, 10

boat *le bateau*, II

body *le corps*, II

to **boil** *bouillir*, II

bone *l'os*, *(m.)*, II

book *le livre*, I

to **book/to reserve** *réserver*, 10

booked/full *complet*, I

bookseller *le libraire*, 2

bookshelf *l'étagère*, *(f.)*, I

bookstore *la librairie*, I

boot *la botte*, I

boring *ennuyeux(-euse)*, II

to **borrow (books)** *emprunter (des livres)*, 1

bottle of water *la bouteille d'eau*, II

bouquet of flowers *le bouquet de fleurs*, II

bowl *le bol*, II

box *la boîte*, II; **box of chocolates** *la boîte de chocolats*, II; **box of matches** *la boîte d'allumettes*, II

boy *le garçon*, I

bracelet *le bracelet*, I

brain *le cerveau*, II

to **brake** *freiner*, 10

branch *la branche*, II

bread *le pain*, I; **bread with butter or jam** *la tartine*, I

break *la récréation*, I; **break down** *la panne*, 10; **to break down** *tomber en panne*, 10; **to break one's leg** *casser la jambe (se)*, II

breakfast *le petit-déjeuner*, I

bridge *le pont*, I

bright and early *de bonne heure*, II

to **bring** *apporter*, 5; **to bring aid** *porter secours*, 7; **to bring back** *rapporter*, II; **to bring someone along** *amener*, I

broccoli *le brocoli*, II

brochure *la brochure*, II

brother *le frère*, II

brown *le marron*, II; **brown(-haired)** *brun(e)*, I

browser *le navigateur*, II

brush *la brosse*, II

to **brush one's hair** *brosser les cheveux (se)*, II

to **brush one's teeth** *brosser les dents (se)*, II

buffalo *le bison*, 5

buffet car *le wagon-restaurant*, I

to **burn (a CD)** *graver*, II

to burn oneself *brûler (se)*, II
to burst/to erupt *éclater*, 3
bus *le bus*, I; **bus stop** *l'arrêt de bus*, *(m.)*, I
business page *l'Économie (f.)*, 6
busy *occupé(e)*, II
but *mais*, I
butcher *le boucher, la bouchère*, II; **butcher shop** *la boucherie*, II
butter *le beurre*, I
butterfly *le papillon*, 5
to buy *acheter*, II; **to buy a guidebook** *acheter un guide*, II
by bicycle *à vélo*, I
by bus *en bus*, I
by car *en voiture*, I
by foot *à pied*, I
by subway *en métro*, I
by taxi *en taxi*, I

cabin *la cabine*, 10
cabinet *le cabinet*, 8
cafeteria *le self*, 1; *la cantine*, II
cake *le gâteau*, 2
calculator *la calculatrice*, I
caliph *le calife*, 3
to call (friends) *téléphoner (à des amis)*, I; **to call** *appeler*, 8
calling card *la carte téléphonique*, I
calm *le calme*, 2
Cameroon *le Cameroun*, 3
to camp out *le camper*, 1
campaign *la campagne*, 8
camping *le camping*, II; **camping stove** *le réchaud*, II
to cancel *annuler*, 10
candidate *le candidat, la candidate*, 8
candle *la bougie*, II
canned food *la boîte de conserve*, II
canoe *le canoë*, 5
canteen *la gourde*, 1
canvas *la toile*, 9
cap *la casquette*, I
captain *le commandant de bord*, 10
caption *la légende*, 6
car *la voiture*, I; **car (in a train)** *le wagon*, I; **car door** *la portière*, 10
card *la carte*, I
to care for *soigner*, 2
career *la carrière*, 2
carrot *la carotte*, II
to carry *porter*, 7
(carry-on) luggage *les bagages (à main)*, *(m. pl.)*, I
cartoon *le dessin humoristique*, 6

cash *le liquide (argent)*, I; **cash machine** *le distributeur d'argent*, I
cashier *le caissier, la caissière*, II
castle *le château*, II
cat *le chat*, II
catastrophy *la catastrophe*, 6
to catch (a fish) *attraper (un poisson)*, 1
to cause *causer*, 7
cave *la grotte*, 5
caving/spelunking *la spéléologie*, 5
CD *le CD*, I; **CD/DVD player** *le lecteur de CD/DVD*, I; **CD/DVD burner** *le graveur de CD/DVD*, II
ceasefire *le cessez-le-feu*, 3
cell phone *le mobile*, I; *le portable*, I
century *le siècle*, 3
cereal *les céréales*, *(f. pl.)*, I
chain *la chaîne*, I
chair *la chaise*, 1
champion *le champion(-ne)*, 6
change (coins) *la monnaie*, I
change of gear *le changement de vitesse*, 10
change purse *le porte-monnaie*, I
to change (into) *changer (en)*, I; **to change gear** *changer de vitesse*, 10; **to change money** *changer de l'argent*, II
check *le chèque*, I
to check in *enregistrer*, 10
checkout/cash register *la caisse*, II
cheek *la joue*, II
cheese *le fromage*, I; **cheese market** *la fromagerie*, II
chemistry *la chimie*, 1
cherry *la cerise*, I
chess *les échecs*, *(m.pl.)*, I
chest of drawers *la commode*, I
chicken *le poulet*, II
child *l'enfant*, *(m./f.)*, I; **childhood** *l'enfance*, *(f.)*, 4
chips *les chips*, *(f. pl.)*, II
chocolate *le chocolat*, I
to choose (the music) *choisir (la musique)*, II
chore *la corvée*, I
choregraphy *la chorégraphie*, 9
Christmas *Noël*, II; **Christmas tree** *le sapin de Noël*, II
church *l'église*, *(f.)*, I
circus *le cirque*, 9; **circus ring** *la piste*, 9; **circus tent** *le chapiteau*, 9
city *la ville*, II; **city hall** *la mairie*, 8
civil servant *le fonctionnaire, la fonctionnaire* 8
class(es) *le(s) cours*, 1
classic movie *le film classique*, II

classical *classique*, I
classifieds *les petites annonces*, *(f. pl.)*, 6
classroom *la classe*, 1
clean *propre*, II
to clean *nettoyer*, 2; **to clean (oneself) up** *faire sa toilette*, II; **to clean the house** *faire le ménage*, II
clear *pur(e)*, II
to clear (something) *débarrasser*, I; **to clear the table** *débarrasser la table*, I
to click *cliquer*, II
to climb trees *grimper aux arbres*, II
to close *fermer*, I
closet/cabinet *le placard*, 8
clothe *le vêtement*, I
clothing size *la taille*, I
cloud *le nuage*, I
clown *le clown*, 3
clutch *la pédale d'embrayage*, 10
coast *la côte*, 7
coat *le manteau*, I
cockpit *le cockpit*, 10
coffee *le café*, II; **coffee house** *le café*, I; **coffee table** *la table basse*, I; **coffee with milk** *le café au lait*, I
coin *la pièce*, II
cold *froid(e)*, I; *le rhume*, I
to collect *collectionner*, II
collection *la collection*, 6
colonization *la colonisation*, 3
colony *la colonie*, 3
color *la couleur*, I
(colored) pencil *le crayon (de couleur)*, I
column *la rubrique*, 6
comb *le peigne*, II;
to comb (one's hair) *peigner (les cheveux) (se)*, II
to come *venir*, II
to come to an end *se terminer*, 3
comedy *la comédie*, II
comic strip *la bande dessinée (BD)*, II
commercial *le spot publicitaire*, II
company *la compagnie*, II
compartment *le compartiment*, I
compass *la boussole*, II
to complete (a year of studies) *effectuer (une année d'études)*, 2
completely *complètement*, II
complicated *compliqué(e)*, II
compress/tablet *le comprimé*, I
computer *l'ordinateur*, *(m.)*, I; **computer room** *la salle d'informatique*, 1, II; **computer science** *l'informatique*, *(f.)*, II; **computer scientist** *l'informaticien, l'informaticienne*, 2

to dry one's hair *sécher les cheveux (se)*, II
dry cleaner's *la teinturerie*, 2
duck *le canard*, II
due to *dû à*, 7
during *pendant*, II; **during that time** *à cette époque*, 3; **during vacation** *pendant les vacances*, II
to dust *faire la poussière*, II
DVD *le DVD*, I
to dye hair *teindre les cheveux*, 2

each/every *chaque*, II
eagle *l'aigle, (m.)*, 5
ear *l'oreille, (f.)*, I
early *en avance*, I; *tôt*, II
earring *la boucle d'oreille*, I
earth/ground/dirt *la terre*, 7
earthquake *le tremblement de terre*, 7
easel *le chevalet*, 9
easy *facile*, I
to eat *manger*, II
edge *le bord*, II
edition *l'édition, (f.)*, 6
editor-in-chief *le rédacteur en chef, la rédactrice en chef*, 6
effect *l'effet, (m.)*, 7
egg *l'œuf, (m.)*, I
eggplant *l'aubergine, (f.)*, II
eight *huit*, I
eighteen *dix-huit*, I
eighty *quatre-vingts*, I; **eighty-one** *quatre-vingt-un*, I
elderly *âgé(e)*, II
to elect *élire*, 3
election *l'élection, (f.)*, 8
electoral *électoral*, 8; **electoral campaign** *la campagne électorale*, 8; **electoral poster** *l'affiche électorale, (f.)*, 8
(electric) razor *le rasoir (électrique)*, II
electrician *l'électricien, (m.), l'électricienne, (f.)*, 2
elegant *élégant(e)*, I
elementary school teacher *l'instituteur, l'institutrice*, 2
elevator *l'ascenseur, (m.)*, I
eleven *onze*, I
e-mail *l'e-mail, (m.)*, I; **e-mail address** *l'adresse e-mail, (f.)*, I
embarassed *gêné(e)*, 4
emergency room *les urgences, (f. pl.)*, 8
emperor *l'empereur, (m.)*, 3
empire *l'empire, (m.)*, 3
employee *l'employé(e)*, I

to empty *vider*, I; **to empty the dishwasher** *vider le lave-vaisselle*, I
enchanted *enchanté(e)*, 3
to encourage *encourager*, I
end *la fin*, 3
energy *l'énergie, (f.)*, 7
engine *le moteur*, 10
England *l'Angleterre, (f.)*, II
English/British *anglais(e)*, II
enjoy your meal *bon appétit*, I
Enjoy… *Profite bien de...*, II
enemy *l'ennemi(e)*, 3
to enter *entrer*, II
envelope *l'enveloppe, (f.)*, I
environment *l'environnement, (m.)*, 7;
environmentalist *l'écologiste, (m.)*, 7
to equip *équiper*, 7
equipment *l'équipement, (m.)*, 5
eraser *la gomme*, 4
eruption *l'éruption, (f.)*, 7
to establish *établir*, 3
etching *la gravure*, 9
to evacuate *évacuer*, 7
evening *le soir*, I
every day *tous les jours*, 1; **every other day** *tous les deux jours*, 1; **every Wednesday** *tous les mercredis*, II
evil *mal*, 3; *maléfique*, 3; **evil stepmother** *la marâtre*, 3
to exchange *échanger*, 4
exciting *passionnant(e)*, II
excuse-me *pardon*, I
exercise *l'exercice, (m.)*, II
exhibit *l'exposition, (f.)*, 6
to exhibit *exposer*, 9
exit *la sortie*, 10
expensive *cher/chère*, I
experiments *travaux pratiques*, 1
to explore *explorer*, 3
explorer *l'explorateur, l'exploratrice*, 3
explosion *l'explosion, (f.)*, 6
to extinguish *éteindre*, 8
extreme sport(s) *le(s) sport(s) extrême(s)*, 5
eye *l'œil, (m.)*, II; **eyes** *les yeux, (m. pl.)*, II
eyebrow *le sourcil*, II

fable *la fable*, 3
face *le visage*, II
factory *l'usine, (f.)*, 7
to fail (an exam, a class) *rater*, II
fairy *la fée*, 3

fall *l'automne, (m.)*, I
to fall *tomber*, I; **to fall asleep** *endormir (s')*, II; **to fall in love** *tomber amoureux (-euse)*, 4; **to fall sick** *tomber malade*, 4
family *la famille*, II
fantastic/fantasy *fantastique*, 3
fantasy novel *le roman fantastique*, II
far away *lointain(e)*, 9
far from *loin de*, I
farm *la ferme*, II
farmer *l'agriculteur, l'agricultrice*, 2
to fascinate/to excite *passionner*, 6
fascinating *passionnant(e)*, 9; *fascinant(e)*, I
fast *rapide*, 10
fat/big *gros(se)*, II, I
father *le père*, II
Father's Day *la fête des pères*, II
fatty substances *les matières grasses, (f. pl.)*, II
faucet *le robinet*, II
favorite *préféré(e)*, I; **favorites (Internet)** *les favoris, (m. pl.)*, II
February *février*, I
fee *le tarif*, I
to feed oneself *nourrir (se)*, II
to feel like *avoir envie de*, I
feminine/female *féminin(e)*, 6
field *le champ*, II
fifteen *quinze*, I
fifth *cinquième*, 2L
fifty *cinquante*, I
fight *le combat*, 3
to fight *combattre*, 3
figure *le chiffre*, 6
file *le fichier*, II
to fill up *faire le plein*, 10
film/movie *le film*, II
finally *finalement*, II
to find/to like *trouver*, 9
to find/to meet (one another) *retrouver (se)*, 4
to find/to think *trouver*, I
to find out/to inquire on the Internet *informer sur Internet (s')*, II
to find out *informer (s')*, II
fine *la contravention*, 8
finger *le doigt*, II
to finish *finir*, II
Fire! *Au feu!*, 8; **fire** *l'incendie, (m.)*, 7; *le feu*, 8
fireman *le pompier*, 8
fire station *la caserne des pompiers*, 8
firetruck *le camion des pompiers*, 8
fireworks *les feux d'artifice, (m. pl.)*, II

first *d'abord*, I; **first** *premier*, I; **first/firstly** *en premier*, II; **first class** *la première classe*, I; **first floor** *le rez-de-chaussée*, I; **first-aid kit** *la trousse de premiers soins*, II

fish *le poisson*, 1; **fish market** *la poissonnerie*, II; **fish monger** *le poissonnier, la poissonnière*, II

fishing rod *la canne à pêche*, 1

five *cinq*, I

to fix (cars) *réparer (les voitures)*, 2

flag *le drapeau*, 3

flamingo *le flamant rose*, II

flashlight *la lampe de poche*, II

flashy *tape-à-l'œil*, I

flat *plat(e)*, 10; **flat tire** *le pneu crevé*, 10

flight *le vol*, I; **flight attendant** *l'hôtesse de l'air, (f.)*, 10

flippers *les palmes, (f. pl.)*, I

flood *l'inondation, (f.)*, 7

floor *l'étage, (m.)*, I

flora and fauna *la flore et la faune*, 5

flour *la farine*, II

flow *la coulée*, 7

flower *la fleur*, II

flower shop *le fleuriste*, I

fly *la mouche*, II

flying carpet *le tapis volant*, 3

folding chair *le fauteuil pliant*, II

to follow *suivre*, II

foot *le pied*, II

for once *pour une fois*, II

force/strength *la force*, 7

forehead *le front*, II

foreign *étranger(e)*, II; **foreign film** *le film étranger*, II

to foresee *prévoir*, 6

forest *la forêt*, II

to forget *oublier*, II

fork *la fourchette*, I

fortunately *heureusement*, II

forty *quarante*, I

forward (Internet) *suivante*, II

four *quatre*, I; **fourteen** *quatorze*, I

fox *le renard*, 5

to frame *encadrer*, 9

France *la France*, II

free *gratuit(e)*, 6; *libre*, I; **free time** *le temps libre*, I

freedom *la liberté*, 5

French *français(e)*, 1

Friday *vendredi*, I

friend *l'ami, (m.)*, I; *l'amie, (f.)*, I; *la copine*, II; *le copain*, 1

friendship *l'amitié, (f.)*, 4

fries *les frites, (f. pl.)*, I

frog *la grenouille*, 5

from *en provenance de*, I; *de*, II; **from the… to the…** *du… au*, I; **from time to time** *de temps en temps*, I

front page *la une*, 6

fruit *le fruit*, II; **fruit juice** *le jus de fruit*, II

full *le plein*, 10; **full/plenty** *plein(e)*, II; **full-board** *la pension complète*, 1

funny *drôle*, II; *marrant(e)*, II

funny/amusing *amusant(e)*, II

furious *furieux(-euse)*, 4

to gain weight *grossir*, II

game *le jeu*, II

garage *le garage*, I

garlic *l'ail, (m.)*, II

gas *l'essence, (f.)*, 7; *le gaz*, 7; **gas leak** *la fuite de gaz*, 6; **gas station** *la station-service*, 10

gasoline pump *la pompe à essence*, 10

gate *la porte*, 10

generous *généreux(-euse)*, I

genie *le génie*, 3

genre *le genre*, 9

geographic map *la carte géographique*, 3

geography *la géographie*, I

German *allemand(e)*, II

Germany *l'Allemagne, (f.)*, II

to get dressed *habiller (s')*, II

to get information in a travel agency *renseigner dans une agence de voyages (se)*, II

to get married *marier (se)*, 4

to get one's backpack ready *préparer son sac*, II

to get ready *préparer (se)*, II

to get undressed *déshabiller (se)*, II

to get up/stand up *lever (se)*, II

to get vaccinated *faire vacciner (se)*, II

ghost *le fantôme*, 3

gift card *le chèque-cadeau*, II

girl, daughter *la fille*, I

to give *donner*, I; **to give back** *rendre*, I

glass *le verre*, 7; **glasses** *les lunettes, (f. pl.)*, I

glove *le gant*, I

to go *aller*, II; **to go down/to get out** *descendre*, II; **to go fishing** *aller à la pêche*, 1; **to go forward** *avancer*, I; **to go grocery shopping** *faire les courses*, II; **to go hiking** *faire la randonnée*, 1; *faire une randonnée*, II; **to go on a carousel** *faire du manège*, II; **to go on a picnic** *faire un pique-nique*, I; **to go on vacation** *partir en voyage*, II; **to go out** *sortir*, II; **to go rafting** *faire du rafting*, 5; **to go sailing** *faire de la voile*, II; **to go scuba diving** *faire de la plongée sous-marine*, 5; **to go shopping** *faire les magasins*, 1; **to go through customs** *passer la douane*, 10; **to go to a coffee shop** *aller au café*, I; **to go to bed** *coucher (se)*, II; **to go to summer camp** *aller en colonie de vacances*, II; **to go to the circus** *aller au cirque*, II; **to go to the movies** *aller au cinéma*, 1; **to go to the pool** *aller à la piscine*, I; **to go to work** *aller au travail*, II; **to go up** *monter*, II; **to go windsurfing** *faire de la planche à voile*, 1; **to go wrong** *aller de travers*, II

goal *le but*, 3

goat *la chèvre*, II

god *le dieu*, 3; **goddess** *la déesse*, 3; **godmother** *la marraine*, 3

gold *l'or, (m.)*, I; **gold medal** *la médaille d'or*, 6

good *bon/bonne*, I

Good idea! *Bonne idée!*, 1

Goodbye. *Au revoir.*, I

government *le gouvernement*, 8; **government service** *le service public*, 8

grade *la note*, II

grandchild *le petit-enfant*, I

granddaughter *la petite-fille*, I

grandfather *le grand-père*, II

grandmother *la grand-mère*, II

grandparent *le grand-parent*, I

grandson *le petit-fils*, I

to grant *accorder*, 3; **to grant wishes** *accorder des souhaits*, 3

grapefruit *le pamplemousse*, I

gray *gris(e)*, I

great *génial(e)*, I

Greece *la Grèce*, II

Greek *grec/grecque*, II

green *vert(e)*, II; **green beans** *les haricots verts, (m. pl.)*, II; **greenhouse effect** *l'effet de serre, (m.)*, 7

greeting card *la carte de vœux*, II

grocer *l'épicier, (m.), l'épicière, (f.)*, II

grocery store *l'épicerie, (f.)*, II

to grow (up) *grandir*, I

to guess *deviner*, 4

guest *l'invité(e)*, II

guidebook *le guide*, II
guided *guidé(e)*, II
guitar *la guitare*, II
gymnasium *le gymnase*, II

hail *la grêle*, 7
hair *les cheveux (m. pl.)*, II;
    hairdresser *le coiffeur, la*
    coiffeuse 2
half *demi(e)*, I; **half-board**
    la demi-pension, 1; **half-brother**
    le demi-frère, I; **half-sister**
    la demi-sœur, I
ham *le jambon*, I; **ham**
    sandwich *le sandwich au*
    jambon, II
hand *la main*, I; **hand brake**
    le frein à main, 10; **hand towel**
    la serviette de toilette, II
handicap access *l'accès handicapé,*
    (m.), I
handsome/beautiful *beau/*
    belle, I, II
hang gliding *le delta-plane*, 5
Hannukkah *Hanoukkah*, II
to happen *passer (se)*, II
to happen (to someone) *arriver*
    (à quelqu'un), II
happy *heureux(-euse)*, 4;
    heureuse, I; *content(e)*, II
Happy birthday! *Bon*
    anniversaire!, II
Happy New Year *bonne année*, II
hat *le chapeau*, II
to hate *détester*, II
to have *avoir*, II; **to have a**
    fever *avoir de la fièvre*, II;
    to have breakfast *prendre*
    le petit-déjeuner, II; **to have**
    dinner *dîner*, I; **to have…**
    eyes *avoir les yeux…*, I; **to have**
    fun *amuser (s')*, II; **to have just**
    (done something) *venir de*, II;
    to have more *reprendre*, I; **to**
    have one's car checked *faire la*
    révision, 10; **to have practice/**
    training *avoir entraînement*, II;
    to have time *avoir le temps*, II; **to**
    have to/must *devoir*, II; **to have**
    to/to be necessary *falloir*, II
he *il*, I
head *le chef*, 8; **head (body)**
    la tête, I; **head of state** *le chef*
    de l'état, 8; **head/taillight**
    le phare, 10
headline *le gros titre*, 6
heading for *à destination de*, I
headphones *les écouteurs,*
    (m. pl.), I

to hear *entendre*, I; **to hear**
    about *entendre parler de*, 6
health *la santé*, II
heart *le cœur*, II
heat *la chaleur*, 6; **heat wave** *la*
    vague de chaleur, 6
helmet *le casque*, I
help/aid *le secours*, 7; **Help!**
    À moi!, 3; *À l'aide!*, 5, 8;
    Au secours!, 5; **help** *l'aide, (f.)*, II
to help *aider*, I
hen *la poule*, II
her/it *la*, II
here/there *là*, I
here *voilà*, II
Here. *Tiens.*, I
here is *voici*, 1
hero *le héros*, 3
heroic *héroïque*, 3
heroine *l'héroïne, (f.)*, 3
heron *le héron*, 5
high *haut(e)*, I; **high school**
    le lycée, 1; **highway** *l'autoroute,*
    (f.), 6
hike *la randonnée*, 1
hiking shoes *les chaussures de*
    randonnée, (f. pl.), 1
him/it *le*, II
hip-hop *le hip-hop*, II
his/her *sa, ses, son*, I
historical novel *le roman*
    historique, II
history/geography *l'histoire-géo,*
    (f.), 1
history/story *l'histoire, (f.)*, 3, I
hockey *le hockey*, I
to hold/to be in possession of
    détenir, 6
to hold a seat *siéger*, 8
home (Internet) *démarrage*, II
home page *l'accueil, (m.)*, II
homework *les devoirs, (m. pl.)*, 1
honestly *franchement*, I
to honk *klaxonner*, 10
hood *le capot*, 10
to hope *espérer*, II
horrible *horrible*, I
horror movie *le film d'horreur*, II
horse *le cheval*, II
hospital *l'hôpital, (m.)*, I
hot *chaud*, I; **hot chocolate**
    le chocolat chaud, II
hotel *l'hôtel, (m.)*, 1
hour *l'heure, (f.)*, II
house *la maison*, II
house coat *le peignoir*, II
house (government) *la chambre*, 8
how *comment*, II
how many/how much *combien*
    de (d'), II; **how much/how**
    many *combien*, I
however *cependant*, 3

human *humain(e)*, 3
to hurry *dépêcher (se)*, II;
    magner (se), II; **Hurry**
    up! *Dépêche-toi!*, II
to hurt/ache *avoir mal (à)*, II
husband *le mari*, I
hybrid *hybride*, 7

I *je*, I
I.D. card *la carte d'identité*, 8
I.D. photo *la photo d'identité*, 8
i.e. *c'est-à-dire*, 3
ice cooler *la glacière*, I
ice cream *la glace*, II
ice skater *le patineur, la*
    patineuse, 6
ice-skating *le patin à glace*, I
ice-skating rink *la patinoire*, I
identification *l'identité, (f.)*, 8
if *si*, II
iguana *l'iguane, (m.)*, 5
to imagine *figurer (se)*, 4; **Imagine**
    that *Figure-toi que*, II
immigrant *l'immigrant(e)* 8
Impossible! *Pas possible!*, 5
imprisonment *l'emprisonnement,*
    (m.), 6
to improve *améliorer (s')*, 7
in/inside *dans*, II; **in/to** *en*, II;
    in a far away country *dans*
    un pays lointain, 3; **in a good/**
    bad mood *de bonne/mauvaise*
    humeur, 4; **in case** *au cas où*, 7;
    in front (of) *devant*, I; **in love**
    amoureux(-euse), 4; **in my**
    opinion *à mon avis*, I; **in my**
    place *à ma place*, 4; **in pursuit**
    of *en quête de*, 3; **in short**
    bref, II; **in the context of** *dans*
    le cadre de, 2; **in the middle of**
    au milieu de, II; *en train de*, II;
    in the north of *dans le nord*
    de, 5; **in the past** *autrefois*, 3
incantation/phrase *la formule*, 3
independence *l'indépendance,*
    (f.), 3
indifferent *indifférent(e)*, 4
inexpensive *bon marché(e)*, I
information board *le tableau*
    d'affichage, I
to injure oneself *blesser (se)*, II
injured *blessé(e)*, 6
insect *l'insecte, (m.)*, II
to install *installer*, 2
instant message *le SMS*, I;
    le texto, I
intellectual *intellectuel(le)*, II
intelligent/smart *intelligent(e)*, II

interest *l'intérêt, (m.),* I
interesting *intéressant(e),* I
interface *l'interface, (f.),* II
international *international(e),* 6; **international flight** *le vol international,* 10; **international news** *l'actualité internationale, (f.)* 6
Internet *l'Internet, (m.),* I; **Internet café** *le cybercafé,* I
interpretation, meaning *le sens,* 8
intersection, crossroads *le carrefour,* I
to introduce *présenter,* II
invasion *l'invasion, (f.),* 3
invention *l'invention, (f.),* 7
Ireland *l'Irlande, (f.),* 1
iron *le fer*
to iron *repasser le linge,* 2
is it that/does *est-ce que,* II
issue *le numéro,* 6
it is necessary *il faut,* II
Italian *italien(ne),* II
Italy *l'Italie, (f.),* II
itinerary/route *l'itinéraire, (m.),* II

jacket *la veste,* I
jam *la confiture,* I
January *janvier,* I
jar *le pot,* II; **jar of jam** *le pot de confiture,* II
jazz *le jazz,* II
jeans *le jean,* I
jet lag *le décalage horaire,* 10
jewel *le bijou,* 9; **jewelry** *la bijouterie,* I; **jewelery department** *le rayon bijouterie,* I
job *le métier,* 2
jogging *le jogging,* I
journal *la revue,* 6
juggler *le jongleur, la jongleuse* 9
juice *le jus,* I
July *juillet,* I
to jump rope *sauter à la corde,* II
June *juin,* I

key *la touche,* II
keyboard *le clavier,* II
kilogram *le kilo(gramme),* II
king *le roi,* 3
kingdom *le royaume,* 3
kitchen *la cuisine,* I
kite *le cerf-volant,* I

knee *le genou,* II
knife *le couteau,* I
to know (to be familiar with) *connaître,* II; **to know (a fact)** *savoir,* II

laboratory *le laboratoire,* 1
lake *le lac,* II
lamp *la lampe,* I
land *le terrain,* 7
to land *atterrir,* 10
landscape *le paysage,* 9
landslide *le glissement de terrain,* 7
lantern *la lanterne,* II
laptop *le portable,* I; **(laptop) computer** *l'ordinateur (portable), (m.),* II
last/latest *le dernier, la dernière* II; **last month** *le mois dernier,* I; **last week** *la semaine dernière (la),* I
to last *durer,* 6
late *en retard,* I; **late** *tard,* II
later *plus tard,* 3; **later on** *plus tard,* 2
laundry *la lessive,* I
lava *la lave,* 7; **lava flow** *la coulée de lave,* 7
law *la loi,* 8
lawn *la pelouse,* I
lawyer *l'avocat, (m.), l'avocate, (f.),* 2
lazy *paresseux(-euse),* I
leaf *la feuille,* II
leak *la fuite,* 6
to learn *apprendre,* I
leather *le cuir,* I; **leather department** *le rayon maroquinerie,* I; **leather goods** *la maroquinerie,* I
to leave *partir,* 1; **to leave (one another)** *quitter (se),* 4; **to leave on vacation** *partir en vacances,* 1
left *la gauche,* 8
leg *la jambe,* II
legend *la légende,* 3
lemon-lime soda *la limonade,* II
to lend *prêter,* I
less... than *moins... que,* II
lesson *la leçon,* 3
letter *la lettre,* I; **letters to the Editor** *le courrier des lecteurs,* 6
librarian *le documentaliste, la documentaliste* II
library *la bibliothèque,* I; **library** *le CDI (centre de documentation et d'information),* II

license *le permis,* 8
life *la vie,* II; **life jacket** *le gilet de sauvetage,* 5
to lift weights *faire de la musculation,* II
light (adj.) *clair(e),* I; **light (weight)** *léger(ère),* II; **light (n.)** *la lumière,* II; **light brown (-haired)** *châtain(s),* I
to light (the candles) *allumer (les bougies),* II
lighter *le briquet,* II
lightning flash *l'éclair, (m.),* 7; **to like/to appeal** *plaire,* 9; **to like/to love** *aimer,* II; *aimer bien,* I
to like better/to prefer *aimer mieux,* I
line *la queue,* I
linen *le lin,* I
link (Internet) *le lien,* II
lip *la lèvre,* II; **lipstick** *le rouge à lèvres,* II
to listen *écouter,* I; **to listen to music** *écouter de la musique,* I
liter *le litre,* II; **liter of orange juice** *le litre de jus d'orange,* II
literary *littéraire,* II
little, small *petit(e),* II
live *direct(e),* II
to live *vivre,* 4; *habiter,* I
living room *le salon,* I
lizard *le lézard,* II
loaf of French bread *la baguette,* I
lobby *le hall,* I
long *long(ue),* II; **long ago** *jadis,* 3
to look at, to watch *regarder,* I
to look for *chercher,* I
loose *large,* I
to lose *perdre,* II
love *l'amour,* 4
to love/to adore *adorer,* 1
love-at-first-sight *le coup de foudre,* 4
low *bas,* I
luggage carrier/rack *le porte-bagages,* I
lunch *le déjeuner,* I
lung *le poumon,* II

magazine *le magazine,* I
Maghreb *le Maghreb,* 3
magic *la magie,* 3; **magic** *magique,* 3; **magic wand** *la baguette magique,* 3

magician *le magicien, la magicienne* 3

mail *le courrier,* 6; **mail carrier** *le facteur,* I

main character *le personnage principal,* II

to make amateur videos *faire de la vidéo amateur,* II; **to make a campfire** *faire un feu de camp,* II; **to make a date (with one another)** *donner rendez-vous (se),* 4; **to make keys** *faire des clés,* 2; **to make one's bed** *faire son lit,* I; **to make a reservation** *faire une réservation,* II; **to make sandcastles** *faire des châteaux de sable,* II; **to make a stopover/layover** *faire escale,* I; **to make a stopover** *faire escale,* I; **to make the most of/to enjoy** *profiter,* II; **to make up** *réconcilier (se),* 4

make-up *le maquillage,* II

Mali *le Mali,* 3

mall *le centre commercial,* I

man's shirt *la chemise,* I

manual transmission *le changement de vitesse manuel,* 10

map *la carte,* I; *le plan,* II

maple syrup *le sirop d'érable,* 5

March *mars,* 1

mascara *le mascara,* II

math *les maths, (f. pl.),* 1

mathematics *les mathématiques, (f. pl.),* I

May *mai,* I

me *moi,* I

meadow *la prairie,* II

meal *le repas,* I

mean *méchant(e),* 1

means *le moyen,* 7

means of transportation *le moyen de transport,* 7

mechanic *le mécanicien, la mécanicienne* 2

medal *la médaille,* 6

media *les médias,* 6

medicine *le médicament,* I

medium *à point,* I

to meet (one another) *rencontrer (se),* 4

to meet up *rejoindre,* 10

melon *le melon,* II

menu *la carte,* I

Merry Christmas *Joyeux Noël,* II

Middle East *le Moyen-Orient,* 3

midnight *minuit,* I; **midnight feast** *le réveillon,* II

milk *le lait,* I

mineral water *l'eau minérale, (f.),* I

minister *le ministre,* 8

minor *mineur(e),* 4

mint *la menthe,* I; **mint syrup** *le sirop de menthe,* II

minus *moins,* I

mirror *le miroir,* II

miscellaneous news *les faits divers, (m. pl.),* 6

Miss *mademoiselle,* I

to miss *manquer,* I; *rater,* I

to mix *mélanger,* II

model *le modèle,* 9

modern *moderne,* I

moment *le moment,* I

monarch/sovereign *le souverain,* 3

monarchy *la monarchie,* 3

Monday *lundi,* I

money *l'argent, (m.),* I; **money order** *le mandat,* I

monster *le monstre,* 3

month *le mois,* I

monthly *le mensuel,* 6

moose *l'orignal, (m.),* 5

moral *le morale,* 3

more *encore,* I; **more… than** *plus... que,* II

morning *le matin,* I; *la matinée,* II

Morocco *le Maroc,* 3

mosquito *le moustique,* II; **mosquito repellent** *la lotion anti-moustiques,* 1

mother *la mère,* II

Mother's Day *la fête des mères,* II

mountain *la montagne,* 1; **mountain bike** *le VTT (le vélo tout terrain),* 5, I

to mountain climb *faire de l'escalade,* II

mountain climbing *l'alpinisme, (m.),* 5; *l'escalade, (f.),* II

mouse *la souris,* II

mouth *la bouche,* I

to move *bouger,* 9; **to move (location), to move out** *déménager,* 3; **to move/to travel** *se déplacer,* 3

movie premiere *la première,* 9; **movie star** *la vedette,* II; **movie theater** *le cinéma,* 1

to mow (the lawn) *tondre (la pelouse),* I

MP3 *le MP3,* I

Mr. *monsieur (M.),* I

Mrs. *madame (Mme),* I

murderer *le meurtrier, la meurtrière* 6

muscle *le muscle,* II

museum *le musée,* I

mushroom *le champignon,* II

music *la musique,* II; **music education** *l'éducation musicale, (f.),* I; **music video** *le vidéoclip,* II

musical *la comédie musicale,* 9

my *ma, mes, mon,* I

mystery novel *le roman policier,* II

name *le nom,* I

nap *la sieste,* II

napkin *la serviette,* I

national anthem *l'hymne national, (m.),* II

national holiday *la fête nationale,* II

natural *naturel(le),* 7; **natural gas** *le gaz,* 6; **natural sciences** *les SVT,* 1

nature *la nature,* II; **nature reserve** *le parc naturel,* 5

to navigate *naviguer,* II

neck *le cou,* II

necklace *le collier,* I

to need *avoir besoin de,* II

nephew *le neveu,* I

never/not ever *ne...jamais,* I, II; **never** *jamais,* II

new *nouveau, nouvelle,* II; **New Year's Day** *le jour de l'an,* II; **New Year's Eve** *la Saint-Sylvestre,* II

news *les informations, (f. pl.),* II

newscaster *le présentateur/ la présentatrice,* II

newspaper *le journal,* I; **newspaper stand** *le kiosque à journaux,* 6; **newspaper vendor** *le marchand /la marchande de journaux,* 6

next *prochain(e),* II; **next time** *la prochaine fois,* II; **next to** *à côté de,* I; **next to** *près de,* I

nice *sympathique,* I

niece *la nièce,* I

night *la nuit,* I

nightgown *la chemise de nuit,* II

night stand *la table de nuit,* I

nine *neuf,* I; **nineteen** *dix-neuf,* I

ninety *quatre-vingt-dix,* I; **ninety-one** *quatre-vingt-onze,* I

no *non,* I; **no longer** *ne... plus,* I; **no longer** *plus,* I; **no more/no longer/not anymore** *ne... plus,* II; **no one** *ne... personne,* I; **no problem** *pas de problème,* II

nobody *personne,* II; **nobody/no one** *ne...personne,* II

noise *le bruit,* II

noisy *bruyant(e),* II

non-smoking *non-fumeur,* I

non-stop flight *le vol sans escale,* 10

noon *midi*, I
nose *le nez*, I
not *ne... pas*, I; II; **not any** *pas de*, II; **not at all** *pas du tout*, I; **not yet** *pas encore*, 10; **not yet** *ne... pas encore*, I; II
to **not have the time** *ne pas avoir le temps*, II
notebook *le cahier*, I
nothing/not anything *ne...rien*, I, II; *rien*, II
nothing is working *rien ne marche*, II
novel *le roman*, II
November *novembre*, I
now *maintenant*, I
number *le numéro*, I
nurse *l'infirmier, l'infirmière* 2
nurse's office *l'infirmerie, (f.)*, II

objective *l'objet, (m.)*, 2
to obtain *obtenir*, 3
obviously *évidemment*, II
October *octobre*, I
of/from + city, feminine country *de*, I
of course *bien entendu*, I; *bien sûr*, I
(of) denim *(en) jean*, I
(of) gold *(en) or*, I
(of) linen *(en) lin*, I
(of) silver *(en) argent*, I
of the *de l', de la, des, du*, I
(of) wool *(en) laine*, I
offended *vexé(e)*, 4
to offer *offrir*, II
off-key *faux*, 9
often *souvent*, 3
ogre *l'ogre, (m.)*, 3
ogress *l'ogresse, (f.)*, 3
oil paint *la peinture à l'huile*, 9
oil slick *la marée noire*, 7
oil tanker *le pétrolier*, 7
OK (Internet) *valider*, II
Okay. *D'accord*, II
old *âgé(e)*, 4; *vieux, vieille*, II
olive *l'olive, (f.)*, II; (olive) oil *l'huile (d'olive), (f.)*, II
omelet *l'omelette, (f.)*, I
on *sur*, I; **on sale** *en solde*, I; **on strike** *en grève*, 6; **on time** *à l'heure*, I
once *une fois que*, 3
one *un/une*, I; **one hundred** *cent*, I; **one hundred and one** *cent un*, I;
one/we *on*, I
one way *aller simple*, I

onion *l'oignon, (m.)*, II
only *ne... que*, 8; *unique*, I; **only daughter** *la fille unique*, I; **only son** *le fils unique*, I
to open *ouvrir*, II; **to open a session** *ouvrir une session*, II
open air/outdoors *le plein air*, II
open air market *le marché*, I
opera *l'opéra, (m.)*, 9
opinion *l'avis, (m.)*, 9
opposition *l'opposition, (f.)*, 8
or *ou*, I
orange *orange*, I; **orange juice** *le jus d'orange*, I
orchestra *l'orchestre, (m.)*, 9
organic *bio(logique)*, 7; **organic product** *le produit bio(logique)*, 7
organized *organisé(e)*, II
original version *la version originale (VO)*, II
orphan *l'orphelin, l'orpheline*, 4
our *nos, notre*, I
outdoor center *le centre aéré*, I
outdoor goods department *le rayon plein air*, I
oven *le four*, I
own *propre*, 3
oyster *l'huître, (f.)*, II

to **pack one's suitcase** *faire sa valise*, II
to **pack the bags** *faire les valises*, I
package *le colis*, I; *le paquet*, II; **package of pasta** *le paquet de pâtes*, II
page *la page*, I
painter *le peintre*, 9
painting *la peinture*, 9; *le tableau*, I; **painting on canvas** *le tableau*, 9
pair of pants *le pantalon*, I
pajamas *le pyjama*, II
palace *le palais*, 3
palette *la palette*, 9
paper *le papier*, I
parachute *le parachute*, 5
parade *le défilé*, II
paramedic *l'ambulancier, l'ambulancière*, 8
parent *le parent*, I
park *le parc*, I
to park *garer*, 10
parking *le parking*, I
parliament *le parlement*, 8
party/holiday *la fête*, II; **party/mixer** *la soirée*, II
to party *faire la fête*, I

to **pass (an exam, a class)** *réussir (à un examen)*, II; **to pass/to succeed** *réussir (à)*, I
passenger *le passager*, 10
passport *le passeport, la passagère* II
pasta *les pâtes, (f. pl.)*, I
pastry shop *la pâtisserie*, II
path *le sentier*, II
path/way *le chemin*, 3
to pay *payer*, I; **to pay by check** *payer par chèque*, I; **to pay cash** *payer en liquide*, I; **to pay with a credit card** *payer avec une carte*, I
peace *la paix*, 3
peaceful *tranquille*, II; **peacefully** *pacifiquement*, 3
peach *la pêche*, II
peak *le sommet*, II
peanut *la cacahuète*, II
pear *la poire*, II
peas *les petits pois, (m. pl.)*, II
pelican *le pélican*, 5
pen *le stylo*, I
pencil *le crayon*, I; **pencil case** *la trousse*, I; **pencil sharpener** *le taille-crayon*, I
people (population) *le peuple*, 3
pepper *le poivre*, I
performance *la représentation*, 9
period (of) *la durée (de)*, 2; **period (of time)** *la période*, 3
periodical *le périodique*, 6
personified *personnifié(e)*, 3
pesticide *le pesticide*, 7
pet *l'animal domestique, (m.)*, 2
pharmacist *le pharmacien, la pharmacienne*, 2
pharmacy *la pharmacie*, I
phenomenon *le phénomène*, 7
phone number *le numéro de téléphone*, I
photo *la photo*, 5; **photo album** *l'album photos, (m.)*, 4; **photo camera** *l'appareil photo, (m.)*, II
Physical education (P.E.) *l'EPS (éducation physique et sportive), (f.)*, I
physics *la physique*, 1
piano *le piano*, II
to **pick up one's bedroom** *ranger sa chambre*, I
picnic *le pique-nique*, I
pie *la tarte*, I
piece *le morceau*, II; **piece of cheese** *le morceau de fromage*, II; **piece of paper** *la feuille de papier*, I
pig *le cochon*, II
pilot *le pilote*, I

pink *la rose*, I
to pitch a tent *monter la tente*, II
pizza *la pizza*, I
to place *placer*, I
to plan/to organize *organiser*, II
to plan a party *organiser une soirée/ fête*, II
plane *l'avion*, *(m.)*, II; **plane ticket** *le billet d'avion*, I
planet *la planète*, 7
plant *la plante*, I
plastic bag *le sac en plastique*, II
plate *l'assiette*, *(f.)*, I
platform *le quai*, I
play *la pièce de théâtre*, II
to play *jouer*, II; **to play ball** *jouer au ballon*, II; **to play baseball** *jouer au base-ball*, I; **to play cards** *jouer aux cartes*, I; **to play checkers** *jouer aux dames*, II; **to play chess** *jouer aux échecs*, I; **to play dolls** *jouer à la poupée*, II; **to play guitar** *jouer de la guitare*, 1; **to play hopscotch** *jouer à la marelle*, II; **to play marbles** *jouer aux billes*, II; **to play "off-ground" tag** [similar to tag] *jouer à chat perché*, II; **to play practical jokes** *faire des farces*, II; **to play soccer** *jouer au football*, I; **to play sports** *faire du sport*, I; **to play tennis** *jouer au tennis*, II; **to play video games** *jouer à des jeux vidéo*, I; **to play with electric trains** *jouer au train électrique*, II; **to play with matchbox cars** *jouer aux petites voitures*, II
playground *la cour de récré(ation)*, II
please *s'il te plaît*, I; *s'il vous plaît*, II
to please (one another) *plaire (se)*, 4
to plot *intriguer*, 3
plumber *le plombier*, 2
poetry collection *le recueil de poésie*, II
police officer *le policier*, 8
police station *le commissariat de police*, 8
political *la politique*, 8; **political party** *le parti politique*, 8
polling station *le bureau de vote*, 8
to pollute *polluer*, 7
polluted *pollué(e)*, II
pollution *la pollution*, 7
pomegranate syrup *la grenadine*, II
pop *la pop*, II

pork *le porc*, I
portrait *le portrait*, 9
Portugal *le Portugal*, II
Portuguese *portugais(e)*, II
to pose *poser*, 9
post office *la poste*, I
postcard *la carte postale*, 1
poster *l'affiche*, *(f.)*, 9; **poster** *poster*, I
potato *la pomme de terre*, II
potion *la potion*, 3
potter *le potier*, 9
pottery *la poterie*, 9
pound (of cherries) *la/une livre (de cerises)*, II; **pound of** *la livre (f.)*, II
power *le pouvoir*, 3
precaution *la précaution*, 7
precious *précieux/précieuse*, 4
to predict *prévoir*, 7
to prefer *préférer*, II
to prepare *préparer*, II; **to prepare the snacks** *préparer les amuse- gueules*, II
present *le cadeau*, II
preservation *la conservation*, 7
president *le président*, 3
to press *appuyer*, 10
press *la presse*, 6
pressure *la pression*, 10
pretty/rather *assez*, II
previous *précédent(e)*, 6
prime minister *le premier ministre*, 8
prince *le prince*, 3
princess *la princesse*, 3
principle *le principe*, 7
to print *imprimer*, II
printer *l'imprimante*, *(f.)*, II
prison *la prison*, 8
private viewing *le vernissage*, 9
problem *le problème*, 7
to produce *produire*, 7; **to produce/ to provoke** *provoquer*, 7
to pronounce *prononcer*, I
protectorate *le protectorat*, 3
protest *la manifestation*, 8
public *le public*, 6
published *publié(e)*, 6
to punch (a ticket) *composter*, I
puny *chétif/chétive*, 3
purple *violet(te)*, I
purse *le sac (à main)*, I
push ups *les pompes*, *(f. pl.)*, II
to put away/to tidy up *ranger*, II
to put on *mettre (se)*, II; **to put on makeup** *maquiller (se)*, II; **to put on pajamas/nightgown** *mettre en pyjama/en chemise de nuit (se)*, II

to put one's things away *ranger ses affaires*, II
to put, to wear *mettre*, II

quarter *le quart*, I
queen *la reine*, 3
quest *la quête*, 3
quiche *la quiche*, I
Quiet! *Silence!*, I
quite *assez*, I
quiz *l'interro(gation)*, *(f.)*, II

rabbit *le lapin*, II
raccoon *le raton laveur*, 5
racket *la raquette*, II
radio *la radio*, I
to rain *pleuvoir*, II
raincoat *l'imperméable*, *(m.)*, I
to raise *lever*, I
rap *le rap*, II
rapids *les rapides*, *(m. pl.)*, 5
rare *saignant(e)*, I; **rarely** *rarement*, II
raspberry *la framboise*, II
rather *plutôt*, 9
to ravage/to destroy *ravager*, 7
to reach *parvenir*, 3; **to reach one's goal** *parvenir à son but*, 3
to read *lire*, I
reader *le lecteur, la lectrice* 6
ready *prêt(e)*, II
Really?! *Pas possible!*, 4
rearview mirror *le rétroviseur*, 10
to reassure *rassurer*, 10
to recall/to be reminded *rappeler (se)*, 1
to receive/to get *recevoir*, II
reception *la réception*, I
receptionist *le réceptionniste, la réceptionniste*, I
to recommend *recommander*, 9
record *le record*, 6
to record *enregistrer*, 6
recreation center *la Maison des jeunes et de la culture (MJC)*, I
recycling *le recyclage*, 7
red *rouge*, I; **red-head(ed)** *roux/rousse*, I
to reduce *réduire*, 7
reduced fee/discount *le tarif réduit*, I
to reflect *refléter*, 3
refresh *actualiser*, II

sister *la sœur,* II
sitcom *le sitcom,* II
six *six,* I
sixteen *seize,* I
sixty *soixante,* I
skateboarding *le skate(board),* I
sketch *le croquis,* 9
skiing/skis *le(s) ski(s),* I
to skip meals *sauter des repas,* II
skirt *la jupe,* I
sky diving *le parachutisme,* 5
sleep *le sommeil,* II
to sleep *dormir,* II
sleeping bag *le sac de couchage,* 1; sleeping car *la couchette,* I
slice *la tranche,* II; slice of ham *la tranche de jambon,* II
slide *le glissement,* 7
slipper *la pantoufle,* 3
to slow down *ralentir,* 10
smock/lab coat *la blouse,* II
smoke *la fumée,* 7
to smoke *fumer,* II
snacks *les amuse-gueules, (m. pl.),* II
snake *le serpent,* II
to sneeze *éternuer,* II
snorkel *le tuba,* I
snow *la neige,* 7
to snow *neiger,* I
snowboarding *le surf,* I
so, so much/really *tellement,* II; so, well/then *alors,* II
soap *le savon,* II; soap opera *le soap,* II
soccer *le football,* I
society *la société,* 8
sock *la chaussette,* I
soda, Coke *le coca,* II
software *le logiciel,* II
solar *solaire,* 7; solar panel *le panneau solaire,* 7
soldier *le soldat,* 7
solo *solitaire,* 5
some, from *de l', de la, des, du,* II; some of it(them)/any of it(them) *en,* II
someone *quelqu'un,* II
sometimes *parfois,* 3
son *le fils,* I
soon *bientôt,* II
sorcerer *le sorcier,* 3
sorry *désolé(e),* I
sound *le son,* II; sound and light show *le spectacle son et lumière,* II
source *la source,* 7
south of *au sud de,* 5
Spain *l'Espagne, (f.),* II
Spanish *espagnol(e),* II
spare tire *la roue de secours,* 10

to speak *parler,* II; to speak (English) *parler (anglais),* I; to speak (French) *parler (français),* I; to speak (to one another) *parler (se),* 4
specialized press *la presse spécialisée,* 6; specialized press *spécialisé(e),* 6
species *l'espèce, (f.),* 5
speckled *tiqueté,* 1
speed *la vitesse*
to spell *épeler,* I
spices *les épices, (f. pl.),* II
spider *l'araignée, (f.),* II; spider web *la toile d'araignée,* II
spoon *la cuillère,* I
sports *le sport,* I; sports car *la voiture de sport,* I; (sports) club *le club (de tennis, de foot),* I; sports facilities *le complexe sportif,* 1; sports field *le terrain de sport,* II; sports page *les Sports, (m. pl.),* 6; sports report *le reportage sportif,* II
spring *le printemps,* II
spy movie *le film d'espionnage,* II
squirrel *l'écureuil, (m.),* 5
stadium *le stade,* I
stage *la scène,* 9
staircase *l'escalier, (m.),* I
stamp *le timbre,* I
stand *le kiosque,* 6
to stand in line *faire la queue,* I
to start up *démarrer,* II
state *l'état, (m.),* 8
station *la chaîne,* II
stationary store *la papeterie,* I
statue *la statue,* 9
stay/sojourn *le séjour,* II
to stay *rester,* II; to stay/to sojourn *faire un séjour,* II; to stay at home *rester chez soi,* II
steak *le steak,* I
steering wheel *le volant,* 10
stepfather *le beau-père,* II
stepmother *la belle-mère,* II
stereo system *la chaîne stéréo,* I
stewardess *l'hôtesse, (f.),* I
still life *la nature morte,* 9
to sting *piquer,* 5
stomach *l'estomac, (m.),* II
stone *la pierre,* 3
stop *l'arrêt, (m.),* I
to stop (Internet) *arrêter/annuler,* II
to stop by *passer (à un endroit),* I
stopover, layover *l'escale, (f.),* 10
stork *la cigogne,* 5
storm *la tempête,* 7
story *le récit,* 3
stout/strong *fort(e),* I
straight ahead *tout droit,* I

strawberry *la fraise,* II
stream *le ruisseau,* II
street *la rue,* I
stressful *stressant(e),* II
stricken *sinistré(e),* 7
strike *la grève,* 6
student *l'élève, (m.),* 1
studio *l'atelier, (m.),* 9
to study *faire des études,* 2; to study *étudier,* I
style *le style,* 9
to subscribe *abonner (s'),* 6
subtitles *les sous-titres, (m. pl.),* II
subway *le métro,* I; subway station *la station de métro,* I
sugar *le sucre,* II
to suggest *suggérer,* 3
suit *le costume,* I
suitcase *la valise,* I
sultan *le sultan,* 3
summer *l'été, (m.),* II; summer camp *la colonie de vacances,* II
sun *le soleil,* I
Sunday *dimanche,* I
sunglasses *lunettes de soleil, (f. pl.),* II
sunscreen *la crème solaire,* II
superstore *la grande surface,* I
supply *la fourniture,* I
to suppose *supposer,* 7
to surf *surfer,* I; to surf the Net *surfer sur Internet,* I
surfboard *la planche de surf,* I
to surprise *étonner,* 7
surprising *surprenant,* 9
survey *le sondage,* 8
suspense *le suspense,* II
swarming *polluant,* 7
sweater *le pull,* II
sweat-shirt *le sweat-shirt,* I
Sweden *la Suède,* II
to sweep *balayer,* I
sweet *gentil(le),* II
sweets/candy *le bonbon,* II
to swim *nager,* I; *baigner (se),* II
swimming pool *la piscine,* I
swimsuit *le maillot de bain,* I
to swing *faire de la balançoire,* II
Switzerland *la Suisse,* II
to swoop down (on) *abattre (s') (sur),* 6
syrup *le sirop,* I

t.v. program *le programme télé,* II
table *la table,* I; table cloth *la nappe,* I; table setting *le couvert,* I; tablespoon *la cuillerée à soupe,* II

to take *prendre*, II; **to take (with)** *emporter*, II; **to take a bath** *prendre un bain*, II; **to take a class** *suivre un cours*, II; **to take a guided tour** *faire une visite guidée*, II; **to take a nap** *faire la sieste*, II; **to take a shower** *prendre une douche*, II; **to take a stroll** *promener (se)*, II; **to take a trip** *faire un voyage*, I; **to take a world tour** *faire le tour du monde*, II; **to take an organized trip** *faire un voyage organisé*, II; **to take back/ to win** *remporter*, 6; **to take care (of)** *occuper (de) (s')*, II; **to take down a tent** *démonter la tente*, II; **to take for a walk** *promener*, I; **to take off one's clothes** *enlever ses vêtements*, II; **to take off** *décoller*, 10; **to take out the trash** *sortir la poubelle*, I; **to take place** *avoir lieu*, 3; *produire (se)*, 6; **to take someone's temperature** *prendre la température*, II; **to take the bus** *prendre le bus*, II

tale *le conte*, 3

to talk (with friends) *discuter (avec des amis)*, I

tank *le réservoir*, 10

taste *le goût*, 6

taxi *le taxi*, I; **taxi driver** *le chauffeur de taxi*, 2

teacher/professor *le professeur, la professeur*, 2

team *l'équipe, (f.)*, 6

teaspoon *la cuillerée à café*, II

techno *techno*, II

telephone *le téléphone*, I; **telephone booth** *la cabine téléphonique*, I

to telephone (one another) *téléphoner (se)*, 4

television *la télé(vision)*, I; **television programs** *les émissions télé, (f. pl.)*, II

to tell *raconter*, 3

tell me *dites-moi*, I

ten *dix*, I

tennis *le tennis*, I; **tennis shoes** *les baskets (f. pl.)*, I

tent *la tente*, 1

terminal *le terminal*, I

terrorist attack *l'attentat , (m.)*, 6

to thank *remercier*, I

thank you *merci*, I

the *la, (l'), le (l'), les*, I; **the next day** *lendemain*, 3; **the night before** *la veille*, 3

theater *le théâtre*, 9

theft *le vol*, 6

their *leur(s)*, 3

them *les*, II

then *puis*, I; **then/next** *ensuite*, II

theoretically *en principe*, 7

there *y*, II

therefore *donc*, 7

thermos *la bouteille isotherme*, II

these *ces*, I

they (fem) *elles*, I; **they (masc)** *ils*, I

thief *le voleur, la voleuse*, 6

thin *mince*, II

thing *la chose*, I

to think *penser*, II; **to think/ believe** *croire*, II; **to think that** *croire que*, II

thirteen *treize*, I

thirty *trente*, I; **thirty-one** *trente et un*, I

this *ce, cet, cette*, I; **this/that** *ça*, I

to threaten *menacer*, 7

three *trois*, I

throat *la gorge*, II

to throw *jeter*, I; *lancer*, I

thunder *le tonnerre*, 7; **thunderstorm** *l'orage, (m.)*, 7

Thursday *jeudi*, I

ticket *le ticket*, I; **ticket collector** *le contrôleur*, I; **ticket machine** *le distributeur de billets*, I

to tidy up the house *ranger la maison*, II

tie *la cravate*, I

tight *étroit(e)*, I; **tight** *serré(e)*, I

time *la fois*, I; *le temps*, I

times a week *fois par semaine*, II; **times per...** *fois par...*, I

tire *le pneu*, 10

tiresome/difficult *pénible*, I

title *le titre*, 6

to /at + city *à*, I; **to/at + feminine country** *en*, I; **to/at + masculine country** *au*, I; **to/at the** *au, aux*, I

(to) him/her *lui*, II

(to) me *me (m')*, II

to the left of *à gauche de*, I

to the right of *à droite de*, I

(to) them *leur*, II

(to) us *nous*, II

(to) you *te (t')*, II; **(to) you** *vous*, II

toast *le toast*, I

toasted ham and cheese sandwich *le croque-monsieur*, II

today *aujourd'hui*, I

toe *le doigt de pied*, II

together *ensemble*, 4

tomato *la tomate*, II

tomorrow *demain*, I

too/too much *trop*, II

tool *l'outil, (m.)*, II

toothbrush *la brosse à dents*, II

toothpaste *le dentifrice*, II

tornado *la tornade*, 7

totally/absolutely *tout à fait*, I

tour *le tour*, II; **tour** *tourné*, II

tourism *tourisme*, II

tourist center *l'office de tourisme, (m.)*, II

towards the west *vers l'ouest*, 5

track *la voie*, I; *la piste (d'athlétisme)*, II

track and field *l'athlétisme, (m.)*, I

tractor *le tracteur*, II

trading post *le comptoir*, 3

traffic *la circulation*, 8

traffic light *le feu*, I

to trail behind/dawdle *traîner*, II

to train/to have an apprenticeship *faire un apprentissage*, 4

train *le train*, II; **train station** *la gare*, I; **train ticket** *le billet de train*, II

training *la formation*, 2

traitor *le traître*, 3

to transform *transformer*, 3

translator *le traducteur, la traductrice*, 2

transportation *le transport*, 7

trash *la poubelle*, I

to travel *voyager*, II

travel agency *l'agence de voyages, (f.)*, II

travel bag *le sac de voyage*, 1

traveler's check *le chèque de voyage*, II

tree *l'arbre, (m.)*, II

trip *le voyage*, II

tropical *tropical(e)*, 5

truck *le camion*, 8

trunk *le coffre*, 10

to try (on) *essayer*, I

t-shirt *le tee-shirt*, I

tube *le tube*, 9

Tuesday *mardi*, I

to tune/to adjust *régler*, 10

tune up *la révision*, 10

Tunisia *la Tunisie*, 3

to turn *tourner*, I

turtle *la tortue*, II

tutu *le tutu*, 9

twelve *douze*, I

twenty *vingt*, I; **twenty-eight** *vingt-huit*, I; **twenty-five** *vingt-cinq*, I; **twenty-four** *vingt-quatre*, I; **twenty-nine** *vingt-neuf*, I; **twenty-one** *vingt et un/vingt et une*, I; **twenty-seven** *vingt-sept*, I; **twenty-six** *vingt-six*, I; **twenty-three** *vingt-trois*, I; **twenty-two** *vingt-deux*, I

twin *le jumeau, la jumelle*, 4

to twist one's ankle/wrist *fouler la cheville/le poignet (se)*, II
twist *le rebondissement*, II
two *deux*, I; **two hundred** *deux cents*, I; **two hundred and one** *deux cent un*, I
type *sorte*, II

umbrella *le parapluie*, I
uncle *l'oncle, (m.)*, II
under *sous*, I
to understand *comprendre*, I
to undo *défaire*, 9
Unfortunately,... *Malheureusement,...*, 4
union *le syndicat*, 2
unleaded gas *l'essence sans plomb, (f.)*, 10
upstairs *en haut*, I
usher *l'ouvreuse, (f.)*, 9
to use *utiliser*, I
usually *d'habitude*, I

vacation *les vacances, (f. pl.)*, I
vacationist *le vacancier, la vacancière*, 6
to vacuum *passer l'aspirateur*, I
vacuum cleaner *l'aspirateur, (m.)*, I
valley *la vallée*, II
vanity case *la trousse de toilette*, II
variety show *l'émission de variétés, (f.)*, II
vegetable *le légume*, II
vendor *le marchand, la marchande*, 6
very *très*, II; **very badly** *très mal*, I; **very soon** *tout à l'heure*, II; **very well** *très bien*, I
veterinarian *le vétérinaire, la vétérinaire*, 2
vibrant *vivant(e)*, II
victim *la victime*, 3
victory *la victoire*, 6
video camera *le caméscope*, II
video game *le jeu vidéo*, I
view *la vue*, I
view (Internet) *l'affichage, (m.)*, I
village *le village*, II
village dance *le bal populaire*, II
violent *violent(e)*, 6
visa *le visa*, I
visit/tour *la visite*, II

to visit (a person) *rendre visite (à une personne)*, 1; **to visit (a place)** *visiter (un endroit)*, II; **to visit (France)** *faire (la France)*, I
visual arts *les arts plastiques, (m. pl.)*, 1
vitamin *la vitamine*, II
vizier *le vizir*, 3
volcano *le volcan*, 7
volleyball *le volley*, I
to vote *voter*, 8
voter *l'électeur, l'électrice*, 8

to wait *attendre*, II
waitperson *le serveur, la serveuse*, 2
to wake up *réveiller (se)*, II
to walk (the dog) *promener (le chien)*, I
walkman *le baladeur*, I
wallet *le portefeuille*, I
to want *désirer*, I; *vouloir*, II
war movie *le film de guerre*, II
wardrobe *l'armoire, (f.)*, I
warming *le réchauffement*, 7
to warn *prévenir*, 10
to wash *laver*, I; **to wash one's face** *laver la figure (se)*, II; **to wash one's hair** *laver les cheveux (se)*, II; **to wash the car** *laver la voiture*, I
wasp *la guêpe*, 5
waste *les déchets, (m. pl.)*, 10
watch *la montre*, I
to watch cartoons *regarder des dessins animés*, II; **to watch out for** *prendre garde à*, 7; **to watch TV** *regarder la télé*, I
water *l'eau, (f.)*, I
to water (the plants) *arroser (les plantes)*, I
watercolor *l'aquarelle, (f.)*, III
waterfall *la cascade*, II
watermelon *la pastèque*, II
wave *la vague*, 6
we *nous*, I
to wear *porter*, I
weather *le temps*, I
weather page *la Météo*, 6
weather report *les prévisions météorologiques, (f. pl.)*, 6; *le bulletin météo(rologique)*, II
website *le site*, II
Wednesday *mercredi*, I
week *la semaine*, 1
weekend *le week-end*, II
weekly *l'hebdomadaire, (m.)*, 6
to weigh oneself *peser (se)*, II
well *bien*, I; **well-done** *bien cuit*, I; **well ripe** *bien mûr(e)*, II

West Africa *l'Afrique de l'Ouest, (f.)*, 3
wetsuit *combinaison de plongée*, 5
whale *la baleine*, 5
what *que (qu')*, II; **what (before verb)** *ce qui*, II
wheel *le tour de potier*, 9
when *quand*, 1
where *où*, II
which *quel, quelle, quels, quelles*, I; **which month** *en quel mois*, I; **which one(s)** *lequel, laquelle, lesquels, lesquelles*, II
while *alors que*, II; **while/during** *pendant que*, II
white *blanc(he)*, I
who *qui*, II
why *pourquoi*, II
widow *la veuve*, 4
widower *le veuf*, 4
wife *la femme*, I
wild animal *l'animal sauvage, (m.)*, 5
wild boar *le sanglier*, 5
to win, *gagner* II
wind *le vent*, I
windbreaker *le coupe-vent*, I
windmill *l'éolienne, (f.)*, 7
window/counter/ticket office *le guichet*, I
window (seat on a plane) *le hublot*, 3; **window** *la fenêtre*, II
windshield *le pare-brise*, 10
windshield wipers *les essuie-glaces, (m. pl.)*, 10
to windsurf *faire de la planche à voile*, II
windsurfing *la planche à voile*, 1
winter *l'hiver, (m.)*, I
winter jacket *l'anorak, (m.)*, I
winter scarf *l'écharpe, (f.)*, I
wish *le souhait*, 3
to wish *souhaiter*, II
witch *la sorcière*, 3
with *avec*, I; **with a view** *avec vue*, I; **with whom** *avec qui*, I
to withdraw *retirer*, I
without *sans*, I; **without a doubt** *sans doute*, II
wolf *le loup*, 5
woman's blouse *le chemisier*, I
woman's suit *le tailleur*, I
to wonder *demander (se)*, II
woods *le bois*, I
wool *la laine*, I
to work *travailler*, I; **to work/run** *marcher*, II; **to work half-time** *travailler à mi-temps*, 2; **to work in** *travailler dans*, 2; **to work overtime** *faire des heures supplémentaires*, 2; **to work part-time** *travailler à temps partiel*, 2

work, masterpiece *l'œuvre,*
(f.), 6
work of art *l'œuvre d'art, (f.),* 9
world *le monde,* 7
World War II *la Seconde Guerre*
mondiale, 3
worried *inquiet(-iète),* 4
to worsen *empirer,* 7
to wrap *emballer,* II; **to wrap**
the presents *emballer les*
cadeaux, II
wrist *le poignet,* II
to write *écrire,* II
written *écrit(e),* 6

yard/garden *le jardin,* I
yellow *jaune,* I
yes *oui,* I; **yes (to negative**
question) *si,* II
yesterday *hier,* I
yet/again *encore,* I
yoga *le yoga,* II
yogurt *le yaourt,* II
you *toi,* I; *tu,* I; *vous,* II
young *le jeune,* II
your (formal) *vos,* I;

your (formal) *votre,* I;
your (informal) *ta,* I;
your (informal) *tes,* I;
your (informal) *ton,* I
Yule log *la bûche de Noël,* II

zero *zéro,* I
zip code *le code postal,* I
zoo *le zoo,* I
zucchini *la courgette,* II

Glossaire anglais–français

Index de grammaire

Page numbers in boldface type refer to the first presentation of the topic. Other page numbers refer to the grammar topic in subsequent presentations or in *Bien dit!* features. The Roman numeral I preceding page numbers indicates Level 1; the Roman numeral II indicates Level 2; the Roman numeral III indicates Level 3. For more grammar references, see the **Synthèse grammaticale** on pages R26–R57.

à I: **56,** 118, 334; II: **102;** III: **230,** 284, 408
à: combined with **le** to form **au** I: **56,** 334; II: **102;** III: **318,** 408, see also contractions, see also prepositions
à: combined with **les** to form **aux** I: **56,** 334; II: **102;** III: **318,** 408, see also contractions, see also prepositions
à: with **commencer** I: **118**
à: with countries and cities I: **334;** III: **408,** see also prepositions
à: with the verb **croire** III: **230,** see also prepositions
à condition que III: **294,** see also conjunctions
à moins que III: **294,** see also conjunctions
acheter: present tense I: **128;** II: **22**
acheter: spelling changes in the future tense II: **252;** III: **48,** 330, 420
adjectives I: **84,** 86, 130, 226, 228; II: **12,** 14, 164, 210, 212, 214; III: **62,** 104, 280, 372, 382
adjectives: agreement I: **84,** 86, 130, 132, 226, 228; II: **12,** 14, 210, 212, 214; III: **372**
adjectives: as nouns I: **130**
adjectives: collective adjectives **tout, tous, toute, toutes** II: **164**
adjectives: demonstrative adjectives **ce, cet, cette, ces** I: **226**
adjectives: ending in **-el** and **-ng** II: **12**
adjectives: ending in **-eux** and **-if** I: **84;** II: **12**
adjectives: feminine forms I: **84,** 86, 130, 132, 226, 228; II: **12,** 14, 210, 212, 214; III: **372**
adjectives: interrogative adjectives **quel, quelle, quels, quelles** I: **228**
adjectives: irregular adjectives **beau, nouveaux, vieux** I: **86;** II: **14**
adjectives: irregular feminine forms I: **84,** 86
adjectives: **marron** II: **12**
adjectives: masculine forms ending in **-s** I: **84**
adjectives: masculine forms ending in unaccented **-e** I: **84;** II: **12**
adjectives: placement I: **84,** 86, 226, 228; II: **14**
adjectives: plural forms I: **84,** 86, 226, 228; II: **12,** 14
adjectives: placed before the noun I: **84,** 86, 226, 228; II: **14**
adjectives: possessive adjectives I: **94**
adjectives: present participles used as adjectives II: **316;** III: **62,** 372
adjectives: whose meaning changes based on placement III: **104**

adjectives: with the comparative II: **210,** 214; III: **280,** 382
adjectives: with the superlative II: **212,** 214; III: **280,** 382
adorer II: **22**
adverbs: **comme ci comme ça, de temps en temps, quelquefois** II: **202;** III: **412**
adverbs: **dès que, lorsque, quand** III: **292**
adverbs: ending in **-ent** or **-ant** III: **322**
adverbs: ending in **-i** or **-e** III: **322**
adverbs: general formation I: **158;** III: **322,** 412
adverbs: general placement II: **202;** III: **232,** 412
adverbs: irregular adverbs **beaucoup** and **trop** III: **322,** 412
adverbs: irregular adverbs **bien** and **mal** I: **158;** III: **322**
adverbs: **quelque part** and **quelquefois** III: **232,** 412
adverbs: **souvent, de temps en temps, rarement, regulièrement** I: **158;** III: **412**
adverbs: superlative of adverbs III: **280,** 382
adverbs: with the **passé composé** I: **242;** III: **412**
afin que III: **294,** see also conjunctions
aimer: **aimer** + **infinitive** I: **46**
aimer: future tense III: **48**
aimer: present-tense I: **46;** III: **10**
aller: **aller** + infinitive (**futur proche**) I: **167;** II: **178;** III: **14**
aller: **passé simple** III: **100**
aller: irregular conditional stem II: **286;** III: **330**
aller: irregular future tense stem II: **252;** III: **48,** 420
aller: irregular imperative forms I: **202**
aller: irregular subjunctive forms II: **276;** III: **150,** 410
aller: present tense I: **167,** 310; III: **12**
aller: with the **passé composé** I: **274,** 346; III: **22**
amener I: **128**
amener: vs. **apporter** III: **202**
appeler: present tense I: **332**
appeler: spelling changes in the future tense II: **252;** III: **48,** 330, 420
apporter: vs. **amener** III: **202**
apprendre I: **200,** 310
après III: **284,** see also prepositions
arriver: past participle I: **274;** II: **60**
arriver: with the **passé composé** I: **274,** 346; II: **60**
articles: definite articles I: **44;** II: **318**
articles: indefinite articles I: **24,** 188, 314; II: **318**
articles: partitive articles I: **188,** 314; II: **86**
articles: with professions and nationalities II: **318**
attendre: future tense III: **48**
attendre: present participle II: **316**
attendre: present tense I: **116,** 310; III: **10**

la: definite article I: **44,** 130, see also articles
la: direct object pronoun II: **46,** 350; III: **240,** see also pronouns
lancer I: 118
le: before days of the week to express routine actions I: **120**
le: definite article I: **44,** 120, 130, see also articles
le: direct object pronoun II: **46,** 350; III: **240,** see also pronouns
le: with **moins, mieux,** or **plus** to form superlative of adverbs III: **280,** 382, see also superlative
le/la/les plus/moins + adjective + **de** II: **212,** 330; III: **382,** see also superlative
lequel, laquelle, lesquels, lesquelles II: **326,** III: **318,** see also pronouns
lever I: 128
les: definite article I: **44,** 130, see also articles
les: direct object pronoun II: **46,** 350; III: **240,** see also pronouns
lire: irregular past participle I: **240,** 344; III: **22**
leur: indirect object pronoun II: **48,** 350, see also pronouns
loin de III: **284,** see also prepositions
lorsque III: **292,** see also adverbs
lui: disjunctive pronoun III: **154,** see also pronouns
lui: indirect object pronoun II: **48,** 350; III: **240,** see also pronouns

maigrir I: **190,** 310; II: **24**
mais I: **58,** see also conjunctions
mal I: **158,** see also adverbs
malgré que III: **294,** see also conjunctions
manger: present tense I: **118**
manger: stem changes in the **imparfait** II: **198**
manquer III: **142**
manquer: with a direct object III: **142**
manquer: with an indirect object III: **142**
mauvais: irregular adverb **mal** I: **158,** see also adverbs
mauvais: irregular comparative and superlative forms II: **214,** 330
me: direct object pronoun II: **46,** 350; III: **240,** see also pronouns
me: indirect object pronoun II: **48,** 350; III: **240,** see also pronouns
me: reflexive pronoun II: **162,** see also pronouns
meilleur(e) II: **214,** 330; III: **280,** 382, see also comparative, see also superlative
mettre: future tense stem II: **250**
mettre: idiomatic expressions III: **206**
mettre: irregular past participle I: **240,** 344; II: **58;** III: **22**
mettre: present tense I: **230,** 310
mieux: irregular comparative of **bien** III: **280,** 382
mieux: with **le** to form superlative of adverbs III: **280,** 382
moi: disjunctive pronoun III: **154,** 240, see also pronouns
moins: with **le** to form superlative of adverbs III: **280,** 382
moins + adjective + **que** II: **210,** 330; III: **280,** 382, see also comparative

moins bon(ne)(s) II: **214,** see also comparative, see also superlative
moins de II: **210;** III: **280,** 382, see also comparative
monter: past participle I: **274;** II: **60**
monter: with a direct object in the **passé composé** II: **242**
monter: with the **passé composé** I: **274,** 346; II: **60,** 242
mourir: past participle I: **274;** II: **60**
mourir: with the **passé composé** I: **274,** 346; II: **60**

naître: past participle I: **274;** II: **60**
naître: with the **passé composé** I: **274,** 346; II: **60**
ne: contraction to **n'** before vowel sound I: **26,** 202, 238, 264
ne... que II: **124**
negatives I: **26,** 202, 238, 264, 302, 344; II: **10,** 62, 124, 162, 176; III: **10,** 22, 240, 244
negatives: **ne... aucun(e)** III: **244**
negatives: **ne... jamais** I: **264;** II: **62;** III: **244**
negatives: **ne... ni... ni...** I: **264;** III: **244**
negatives: **ne... nulle part** III: **244**
negatives: **ne... pas** I: **26,** 202, 238, 264, 302, 344; II: **10,** 62, 162; III: **10,** 240, 244
negatives: **ne... pas encore** I: **264;** II: **62;** III: **244**
negatives: **ne... pas** with the **passé composé** I: **238,** 344; III: **22**
negatives: **ne... pas** with reflexive verbs II: **162**
negatives: **ne... personne** I: **264;** II: **124;** III: **244**
negatives: **ne... personne** as the subject of a sentence II: **124**
negatives: **ne... plus** I: **264;** II: **62;** III: **244**
negatives: **ne... rien** I: **264;** II: **62,** 124; III: **244**
negatives: **ne... rien** as the subject of a sentence II: **124**
negatives: with commands I: **202,** 302; II: **176;** III: **240**
negatives: with indefinite articles I: **24,** see also articles
negatives: with reflexive verbs I: **238,** 264, 344; II: **162,** 176
negatives: with the **passé composé** I: **238,** 264, 344; III: **22,** 244
negatives: without complete sentences II: **62**
nettoyer: present tense I: **276,** 310
nouns: as direct objects II: **46**
nouns: as subjects I: **12,** 312
nouns: ending in -**al** I: **48**
nouns: ending in -**eau/-eu** I: **48**
nouns: determining masculine and feminine I: **44**
nouns: feminine forms III: **50**
nouns: feminine forms ending in -**e** III: **50**
nouns: feminine forms ending in -**esse** III: **50**
nouns: irregular plural forms I: **24,** 48
nouns: masculine and feminine forms III: **50**
nouns: proper nouns in inversion questions I: **312**
nouns: plurals I: **24,** 48
nouns: replaced by pronouns I: **12,** 26, 312; II: **46,** 48
nous I: 12, 14, see also pronouns
nous: direct object pronoun II: **46,** 350; III: **240,** see also pronouns
nous: disjunctive pronoun III: **154,** see also pronouns
nous: indirect object pronoun II: **48,** 350; III: **240,** see also pronouns
nous: reflexive pronoun II: **162,** see also pronouns
nous: with reciprocal verbs III: **138**
nouveau: irregular adjective I: **86;** II: **14,** see also adjectives

Index de grammaire

Remerciements

ACKNOWLEDGMENTS

Grateful acknowledgment is made to the following sources for permission to reproduce copyrighted materials:

"M6 bouleverse le Code de la famille: Des nouveaux droits pour les Marocaines" by Olivia Marsaud from *Afrique sur l'Internet* Web site, accessed August 14, 2006, at http://www.afrik.com/article6670.html. Copyright © 2006 by **Afrik.com.** Reproduced by permission of the copyright holder.

"Designer olfactif" by Jean-Baptiste François from Phosphore, June 2005, No. 288. Copyright © 2005 by **Bayard Presse.** Reproduced by permission of the publisher.

"La littérature maghrébine en français" by Hafsa Benmchich from *Ecrit-vains* Web site, accessed August 25, 2006, at http://ecrits-vains.com/points_de_vue/hafs_benmchich.htm. Copyright © by **Hafsa Benmchich.** Reproduced by permission of the author.

Le fils d'Agatha Moudio by Francis Bebey. Copyright © 1968 by **Éditions CLE.** Reproduced by permission of the publisher.

From "Jean de Florette" by Marcel Pagnol from *Marcel Pagnol: Œuvres complètes III, Souvenirs et romans* Copyright © 1955 by Marcel Pagnol. Reproduced by permission of **Éditions de Fallois.**

From Chapter XIV from *Le Petit Prince* by Antoine de Saint-Exupéry. Copyright 1943 by **Harcourt, Inc.;** copyright renewed © 1971 by Consuelo de Saint-Exupéry. Reproduced by permission of Harcourt, Inc. and electronic format by permission of **Éditions Gallimard.**

"Georges Braque" from *Capitale de la douleur* by Paul Eluard. Copyright © 1925 by **Éditions Gallimard.** Reproduced by permission of **Éditions Gallimard, www.gallimard.fr.**

"Matisse parle" from *Le nouveau Crève-coeur* by Louis Aragon. Copyright © 1948 by **Éditions Gallimard.** Reproduced by permission of **Éditions Gallimard, www.gallimard.fr.**

Un été pour mémoire by Philippe Delerm. Copyright © 2000 by **Éditions du Rocher.** Reproduced by permission of the publisher.

Un papillon dans la cité by Gisèle Pineau. Copyright © 1996 by **Éditions Sépia.** Reproduced by permission of the publisher.

"Naissance d'un géant" by Bruno D. Cot from *L'Express*, May 3, 2004. Copyright © 2004 by **L'Express.** Reproduced by permission of the publisher.

"Les origines de l'inimitié entre l'homme et les animaux" by Najima Thay Thay from *Aux origines du monde: Contes et légendes du Maroc.* Copyright © 2001 by **Flies France.** Reproduced by permission of the publisher.

"L'écriture" by Françoise Giroud from *Profession journaliste: Conversations avec Martine de Rabaudy.* Copyright © 2001 by **Hachette littératures.** Reproduced by permission of the publisher.

"Les oies voyageuses: Des allers-retours à ne pas manquer" from Bonjour Québec Web site, accessed June 14, 2006, at http://www.bonjourquebec.com/qc-fr/oiseaux.html. Copyright © 2006 by Ministère du Tourisme and Bell Canada. Reproduced by permission of the **Ministère du Tourisme, Québec.**

"Dépollution par le lombric" by Fabien Gruhier from *Le Nouvel Observateur,* No 2113, May 11, 2005. Copyright © 2005 by Le Nouvel Observateur. Reproduced by permission of the publisher.

"Je viens d'une île de soleil" from *Points cardinaux.* Copyright © 1966 by **Anthony Phelps.** Published by Holt, Rinehart and Winston, Montréal,1966. Reproduced by permission of the author.

"Chevaux de polo" by Ariane Bavelier from *Le Figaro*, April 7, 2004 Copyright © by **Le Figaro.** Reproduced by permission of the publisher.

PHOTOGRAPHY CREDITS

All images by HRW Photo unless otherwise noted.

FRONTMATTER: T6 (l), Sam Dudgeon/HRW; T6 (r, b), Victoria Smith/HRW; T22 (tl), Royalty-Free/CORBIS; T23 (cl), Royalty-Free/CORBIS; T23 (tl), Brand X Pictures; T23 (bl), Medioimages; T24 (tl), Goodshoot; T24 (bl), Brian Atkinson/Alamy; T24 (cl), Victoria Smith/HRW; T24 (bl), PhotoDisc/Getty Images; T25 (cl, bl), Victoria Smith/HRW; T25 (tl), Sam Dudgeon/HRW; T26 (bl), Victoria Smith/HRW; T26 (tl), Royalty-Free/CORBIS; T27 (bl), Victoria Smith/HRW; T27 (cl, tl), Sam Dudgeon/HRW; T28 (bl), Sam Dudgeon/HRW; T28 (cl), Sam Dudgeon/HRW; T28 (tl), Victoria Smith/HRW; T29 (bl, tl), Victoria Smith/HRW; T30 (bl), Edge Productions/HRW; T30 (tl), Victoria Smith/HRW; T31 (bl, cl), Sam Dudgeon/HRW; T31 (tl), Glen Allison/PhotoDisc/Getty Images; T32 (bl), Mark Antonan/HRW; T32 (tl), Sam Dudgeon/HRW; T33 (tl), Cindy Verheyden/HRW; T33 (bl), Marty Granger/HRW; T33 (cl), Marty Granger/HRW; T44 (tl), image100; T45 (br), Sam Dudgeon/HRW; T46 (tl), COMSTOCK, Inc.; T47 (br), Sam Dudgeon/HRW; T52 (b), Victoria Smith/HRW; T53 (b), BananaStock Ltd.; T60 (t), Sam Dudgeon/HRW/SCRABBLE® is a trademark of Hasbro in the United States and Canada. 2002 Hasbro, Inc. All Rights Reserved.; T60 (b), Victoria Smith/HRW; T61 (b), Sam Dudgeon/HRW; T62 (cr), Victoria Smith/HRW; T63 (cr), PhotoDisc/Getty Images; T63 (br), Sam Dudgeon/HRW; vi (tl), Neil Setchfield/Getty Images; vi (tc), Agence Images/Alamy; vi (tr), Royalty-Free/CORBIS; vii (tr); vii (tl), Richard Bouhet/Imaz Press Reunion/Gamma Press Images; viii (l), Image Source Limited; viii (t), Look GMBH/eStock Photo; ix (tl), photographer/Alamy; ix (tc), Royalty-Free/CORBIS; x (l), Philip Coblentz, Brand X Pictures; x (t), Image Ideas, Inc.; xi (tl), Owaki-Kulla/CORBIS; xi (tc), Royalty Free/CORBIS; xiii (tc), Victoria Smith/HRW; xiii (tl), Copyright Image Source Limited; xiv (l), Sam Dudgeon/HRW; xv (tc), Royalty-Free/CORBIS; xix (tr), PhotoDisc/Getty Images; xix (tc), Sam Dudgeon/HRW; xix (tl), Sam Dudgeon/HRW; xx (r), PhotoDisc/Getty Images; xx (r), PhotoDisc/Getty Images; xxi (l), Sam Dudgeon/HRW; xxi (l), Sam Dudgeon/HRW; xxi (r), SW Productions/gettyimages.

CHAPTERS 1 & 2 GÉOCULTURE: xxii (cr), Bettmann/CORBIS; xxii (b), Copyright Image Source Limited; xxiii (t), Bob Krist/CORBIS; 1 (br), Agence Images/Alamy; 1 (bl), Stephen Bardens/Alamy; 1 (tr), Neil Setchfield/Getty Images; 1 (tl), Art Kowalsky/Alamy; 1 (cl), Homer Sykes/Alamy; 2 (tl), Bettmann/CORBIS; 2 (bl), Pictor International/ImageState/Alamy; 2 (tr), Summerfield Press/CORBIS; 2 (br), Erich Lessing/Art Resource, NY; 3 (tl), Scala/Art Resource, NY; 3 (c, bl), Bettmann/CORBIS; 3 (r), Royalty-Free/CORBIS.

CHAPTER 1: 3A (t), Neil Setchfield/Digital Vision/Getty Images; 3B (b), Victoria Smith/HRW; 3D (t), Andy Christiansen/HRW; 3D (b), Louise Lister/Getty Images; 3C (t), Photodisc/gettyimages; 4–5 (all), Victoria Smith/HRW Photo; 6 (tl), Sam Dudgeon/HRW; 9 (1), Victoria Smith/HRW Photo; 9 (2), Sam Dudgeon/HRW Photo; 9 (3), Royalty-Free/Corbis; 9 (4), Creatas; 10 (b), Victoria Smith/HRW; 11 (2, 4), Sam Dudgeon/HRW Photo; 11 (1), Justin Kase/Alamy; 11 (3), SW Productions/PhotoDisc/gettyimages; 11 (Sylvestre), BE&W agencja fotograficzna Sp. z o.o./Alamy; 12 (b), Sam Dudgeon/HRW; 14 (Je), Victoria Smith/HRW Photo; 14 (1), Royalty Free/CORBIS; 14 (2), Royalty Free/CORBIS; 14 (3), Royalty Free/CORBIS; 14 (4), Sam Dudgeon/HRW Photo; 16 (r), James

D. Morgan/Rex USA; 17 (t), Owen Franken/Corbis; 17 (b), Jeff Greenberg/NewsCom; 18 (bl), PhotoDisc/Getty Images; 18 (bc), STEEF HANEMAAIJER/FOTO NATURA/Minden Pictures; 18 (br), Goodshoot/PunchStock; 19 (tl), PhotoDisc/Getty Images; 19 (tr), Bob Krist/CORBIS; 19 (cl), Nacivet/Getty Images; 19 (cr), Victoria Smith/HRW Photo; 21 (tr), Gareth McCormack/Alamy; 21 (5), Jean-Luc Armand/Photononstop; 21 (3), Sarkis Images/Alamy; 21 (1), image100/Alamy; 21 (6), Comstock/Punchstock; 21 (2), Blend Images/Alamy; 21 (4), Victoria Smith/HRW Photo; 25 (Lucien), Cindy Bland Verheyden; 25 (1), Hulton|Archive/Getty Images; 25 (2), Ben Kopilow/Acclaim Stock Photography; 25 (3), Royalty Free/CORBIS; 25 (4), Steve Skjold/Alamy; 28 (t), BASSOULS SOPHIE/CORBIS SYGMA; 29 (t), Thomas Eckerle/Jupiterimages; 29 (b), Robert Fried/Alamy; 30 (b), Robert Fried/Robert Fried Photography; 30 (t), Walter Bibikow/DanitaDelimont.com; 32 (r, bl), Royalty Free/CORBIS; 33 (br), Anneliese Villiger/zefa/Corbis; 34 (1, 2), Royalty Free/CORBIS; 34 (4), PunchStock; 34 (3), PhotoDisc/Getty Images; 40 (a.), StockShot/Alamy; 40 (b.), Sam Dudgeon/HRW Photo; 40 (c.), Peter Van Steen/HRW; 40 (d.), Victoria Smith/HRW Photo; 41 (c), The Granger Collection, New York.

CHAPTER 2: 40 (b), Victoria Smith/HRW; 41C (tl), David Buffington/PhotoDisc/gettyimages; 41D (tr), Stefano Rellandini/Reuters/CORBIS; 41D (bl), J-C Valliant/Photononstop; 42–43 (all), Victoria Smith/HRW Photo; 44 (all), Victoria Smith/HRW Photo; 45 (t), Paul Almasy/CORBIS; 45 (r), Eric Futran/Foodpix/Photo; 45 (b), PhotoDisc/gettyimages; 46 (Serge), Rob Crandall/Stock Connection/Alamy; 46 (1), PhotoDisc/gettyimages; 46 (3, 4, 5), Royalty Free/CORBIS; 46 (6), Annebique Bernard/CORBIS Sygma; 46 (2), AMET JEAN PIERRE/CORBIS SYGMA; 47 (r), Joe Baraban/Alamy; 48 (b), Victoria Smith/HRW; 49 (Alexandra), L. Langemeier/A. B./zefa/CORBIS; 49 (1), PunchStock; 49 (2), Baumgartner Olivia/Corbis Sygma; 49 (3), Tom Stewart/CORBIS; 49 (4), Lester Lefkowitz/CORBIS; 54 (r), Charlie Abad/Photononstop; 54 (c), PunchStock; 55 (t), Alain Le Bot/Gamma Press Images; 55 (b), AP Photo/Michel Lipchitz; 56 (tl), Emely/zefa/CORBIS; 56 (r), Victoria Smith/HRW; 56 (bl), Victoria Smith/HRW; 57 (t), Emely/zefa/CORBIS; 58 (c., d.), PunchStock; 58 (a.), Jack Star/Photodisc Green/gettyimages; 61 (c.), Dennis Galante/CORBIS; 61 (3), PunchStock; 61 (1), Royalty Free/CORBIS; 61 (2), David De Lossy/Photodisc Green/Getty Images; 61 (4), PunchStock; 66 (t), Bettmann/CORBIS; 66 (b), Photo by Sam Dudgeon/HRW Photo. All rights reserved; 67–68 (all), Photo by Sam Dudgeon/HRW Photo. All rights reserved; 70 (r), PunchStock; 72 (a.), Mark Andersen/Jupiterimages; 72 (b.), imagebroker/Alamy; 72 (c.), Giry Daniel/Dorbis Sygma; 72 (d.), Bonnie Kamin/PhotoEdit, Inc.; 78 (1), Royalty Free/CORBIS; 78 (3), PunchStock; 78 (4), Peter Casolino/Alamy; 78 (5), Patrick Ramsey/Imagestate; 78 (inset), Michael Prince/Corbis; 78 (2), Larry Williams/CORBIS; 78 (b), Royalty-Free/CORBIS; 79 (l), Erich Lessing/Art Resource, NY.

CHRONIQUES: 80 (t), Photononstop/SuperStock; 81 (cl), Peter Dazeley/Getty Images; 81 (tr), Vacances Far-West Enfants, www.farwest-enfants.com; 82 (tl), David Frazier/Photo Edit; 84 (cl), Pierre Perrin/Sygma/Corbis; 84 (cr), Roger Viollet/Getty Images; 84 (bl), Roger Viollet/Getty Images; 85 (tl), NASA; 85 (cr), GIRAUD PHILIPPE/CORBIS SYGMA; 85 (br), Graziano Arici/age fotostock; 86 (c, r), Photo by Jim and Mary Whitmer; 86 (b), Robert Harding Picture Library Ltd/Alamy; 87 (cl, inset), Ian Cumming/Axiom/Aurora Photos; 87 (tr), SuperStock, Inc./SuperStock; 88 (tl), Hulton-Deutsch Collection/CORBIS; 88 (cr), POPPERFOTO/Alamy; 88 (bl), Royalty-free; 89 (t), Dr. Dennis Kunkel/Visuals Unlimited; 89 (tr), Dave Starrett; 89 (tr), David Boag/Alamy; 89 (cr), LUMIERE/THE KOBAL COLLECTION; 89 (bl), Getty Images; 89 (bl), DK Limited/CORBIS.

CHAPTERS 3 & 4 GÉOCULTURE: 89A (t), HBJ/HRW; 89B (b), PhotoDisc/Getty Images; 90 (t), GILLES NICOLET/Peter Arnold, Inc.; 90 (b), David Jones/Alamy; 90 (cr), Eric Meola/Getty Images; 91 (bl), FRANCES STÉPHANE/MONDE/Hémisphères Images; 91 (br), Look GMBH/eStock Photo; 91 (cl), Sylvain Grandadam/Robert Harding Picture Library Ltd/Alamy; 91 (cr), Steve Lewis/Getty Images; 91 (t), Frans Lemmens/Getty Images; 91 (br), Look GMBH/eStock Photo; 92 (l), Sandro Vannini/CORBIS; 92 (b), HIP/Art Resource, NY; 92 (cr), A. Van Zandbergen/BRUCE COLEMAN INC./Alamy; 93 (t), The Bombardment of Algiers by the Royal Navy, 1816, engraved by J. Bailey for 'The Naval Chronology of Great Britain' by J. Ra by Whitcombe, Thomas (c.1752–1824) Private Collection/The Stapleton Collection/The Bridgeman Art Library Nationality/copyright status: English/out of copyright; 93 (bl), Topham/The Image Works; 93 (cr), Bettmann/CORBIS; 93 (br), HIRB/Index Stock Imagery, Inc.

CHAPTER 3: 95C (tl), Peter Adams/zefa/CORBIS; 95D (tr), Sam Dudgeon/HRW; 95D (b), Brian Hagiwara/Jupiter Images/Foodpix/NewsCom; 94–95 (all), Martin Harvey/CORBIS; 96 (bl), Victoria Smith/HRW Photo; 100 (b), Black Star/Alamy; 102 (b), Victoria Smith/HRW; 103 (2), Myron Jay Dorf/CORBIS; 103 (inset, 1), PunchStock; 103 (1), PunchStock; 103 (3), Hermann/Starke/CORBIS; 103 (4), B.S.P.I./CORBIS; 106 (r), Victoria Smith/HRW; 107 (all), Victoria Smith/HRW Photo; 108 (bl), Victoria Smith/HRW Photo; 108 (c), Stefano Bianchetti/CORBIS; 108 (t), CORBIS; 108 (br), Roger-Viollet/The Image Works; 109 (c), AP/Wide World Photos; 109 (t), AFP/Getty Images; 110 (map), Royalty Free/CORBIS; 110 (2), AP Photo/Visar Kryeziu; 110 (3), Réunion des Musées Nationaux/Art Resource, NY; 110 (4), Robert van der Hilst/CORBIS; 110 (1), Bettmann/CORBIS; 112 (b), Victoria Smith/HRW; 113 (cat), Cindy Bland Verheyden; 113 (1, 2, 3), Sam Dudgeon/HRW; 113 (4), Digital Vision/gettyimages; 119 (t), Stephanie Friedman/HRW; 122 (r), Ann Ronan Picture Library/Heritage-Images/The Image Works; 122 (border), Sam Dudgeon/HRW; 130 (a.), Tim Graham/AP/Wide World Photos; 130 (b.), AP Photo/Michel Gangne; 130 (c.), The Art Archive/Private Collection/Marc Charmet; 130 (d.), Royalty Free/CORBIS; 130 (e.), Archive Holdings, Inc./Getty Images; 130 (inset), Images.com/CORBIS; 130 (l), Comstock; 131 (c), The Granger Collection, New York.

CHAPTER 4: 131C (t), Don Couch/HRW; 131D (t), Craig Aurness/CORBIS; 131D (b), Brand X Pictures; 132–133 (all), MANAUD JEAN-LUC/HOA-QUI/Groupe Hachette Filipacchi Photos; 134–135 (all), Sam Dudgeon/HRW Photo; 138 (all), Victoria Smith/HRW; 139 (all), Don Couch/HRW; 144 (r), Moroccan Government/AP/Wide World Photos; 145 (t), PunchStock; 145 (b), Sam Dudgeon/HRW; 146 (tr), Tim Mannakee/Alamy; 146 (cr), Tom Stoddart Archive/Getty Images; 146 (br), David Turnley/CORBIS; 146 (l), Sam Dudgeon/HRW Photo; 147 (tl, tr), Sam Dudgeon/HRW; 147 (cl), World Religions Photo Library/Alamy; 148 (modéle), Zoran Steiner/AAI/Age Fotostock America; 148 (1), VStock/Alamy; 148 (2), PunchStock; 148 (3), CORBIS; 148 (4), Paul Barton/CORBIS; 148 (cr), Orit Allush/Alamy; 151 (c, 4), Sam Dudgeon/HRW Photo; 151 (1), Victoria Smith/HRW; 151 (2), Royalty Free/CORBIS; 151 (3), Brand X Pictures; 153 (Lubin), Victoria Smith/HRW Photo; 153 (3), Steve Hamblin/Alamy; 153 (2), Stockdisc/gettyimages; 153 (4), Royalty Free/CORBIS; 153 (1), MedioImages/gettyimages; 156 (t), Pierre Rene-Worms; 156 (b), Eric Travers/Gamma; 157 (c), Robert Harding Picture Library Ltd./Alamy; 158 (t), Yvan Travert/Photonoctop; 160 (r), Archive Films/Getty Images; 160 (r), Sam Dudgeon/HRW; 168 (b., cl, cr), PunchStock; 168 (a.), PunchStock; 168 (c.), Photononstop/Photolibrary; 168 (d.), AP Photo/Jalil Bounhar; 168 (e., bc), Royalty Free/CORBIS; 168 (b), HRW Photo/Louis Boireau; 169 (cr), On-page credit.

CHRONIQUES: 170 (l), Photo by Sam Dudgeon/HRW. All rights reserved; 170, ANNEBICQUE/ CORBIS SYGMA; 172 (bl), Roger Viollet/Getty Images; 172 (br), The Granger Collection, New York; 173 (t), Christie's Images/CORBIS; 174 (cl), Richard Melloul/Sygma/Corbis; 174 (br), Content Mine International/Alamy; 175 (t), Bruno Calvo/Warner Bros/Bureau L.A. Collection/Corbis; 175 (cr), Content Mine International/Alamy; 176 (tl), AFP/Getty Images; 176 (tl), AFP/Getty Images; 176 (tr); 176 (cr), BananaStock/Alamy; 177 (tr), Bruno Barbey/Magnum Photos; 177 (tl), RubberBall/Alamy; 177 (br), Nik Wheeler/CORBIS; 178 (inset), Bettmann/CORBIS; 178 (t), Portraits of Louis XVI (1754–93) and Marie Antoinette (1755–93), British Library, London, UK, Calmann & King Ltd/The Bridgeman Art Library; 178 (b), Robert Fried/Alamy; 179 (t), The Art Archive/Musée du Château de Versailles/Dagli Orti (A); 179 (bl), Alain Nogues/CORBIS SYGMA.

CHAPTERS 5 & 6 GÉOCULTURE: 179A (t), PhotoDisc/Getty Images; 179B (b), Victoria Smith/HRW; 180 (cr), Erwin Bud

Remerciements

gettyimages; 417 (cr), Kathy deWitt/Alamy; 418 (a.), Royalty Free/CORBIS; 418 (b.), photographer-or-collection/CORBIS; 418 (c.), ImageState/Alamy; 418 (d.), Victoria Smith/HRW; 419 (r), Jean-Marc Romain/photononstop; 421 (vous), PhotoDisc/Getty Images; 421 (1), Brian Elliott/Alamy; 421 (2), Transtock Inc./Alamy; 421 (3), PunchStock; 421 (4), David J. Green/Alamy; 423 (ils), Manchan/gettyimages; 423 (1), Artville/Getty Images; 423 (3), Dinodia Images/Alamy; 423 (2), PhotoDisc/Getty Images; 423 (je), C Squared Studios/Photodisc Green/gettyimages; 423 (1), PhotoDisc/Getty Images; 423 (3), Chuck Eckert/Alamy; 423 (4), Siede Preis/Photodisc Green/gettyimages; 426 (t), Eric Fougere/CORBIS SYGMA; 430 (r), Design Pics Inc./Alamy; 432 (a.), Robert Fried/Alamy; 432 (b.), Roger Tully/Getty Images; 432 (c.), PunchStock; 432 (d.), Victoria Smith/HRW Photo; 438 (a.), Leonid Serebrennikov/Alamy; 438 (b.), PunchStock; 438 (c.), George Logan/Getty Images; 438 (d.), Victoria Smith/HRW Photo; 438 (b), PhotoDisc/Getty Images; 439 (r), Lefevre Fine Art Ltd., London/Bridgeman Art Library.

CHRONIQUES: 440 (c), Impression: Sunrise, Le Havre, 1872 (oil on canvas), Monet, Claude (1840–1926)/Musee Marmottan, Paris, France, Giraudon/The Bridgeman Art Library; 441 (cl), Christie's Images/CORBIS; 441 (tr), Francis G. Mayer/CORBIS; 442 (l), The Granger Collection, New York; 442 (b), Alinari Archives/CORBIS; 443 (tl), Viaduct at L'Estaque, 1908 (oil on canvas), Braque, Georges (1882–1963)/Musee National d'Art Moderne, Centre Pompidou, Paris, France, Lauros/Giraudon/The Bridgeman Art Library; 443 (cr), Archivo Iconografico, S.A./CORBIS; 444 (t), Richard Cummins/CORBIS; 444 (bl), The Thinker (Le Penseur) (bronze), Rodin, Auguste (1840–1917)/Private Collection, Giraudon/The Bridgeman Art Library; 444 (br), Banque d'Images, ADAGP/Art Resource, NY; 445 (tc), Erich Lessing/Art Resource, NY; 445 (tc), Colere de Violon, 1974 (mixed media), Arman (Armand Fernandez), (b.1928)/Musee Cantini, Marseille, France, Giraudon/The Bridgeman Art Library; 445 (cr), Cameraphoto/Art Resource, NY; 445 (bl), Norman Parkinson Limited/Corbis; 446 (tl), Mary Evans Picture Library/Alamy; 446 (bl), Pierre Vauthey/CORBIS SYGMA; 446 (c), Royalty Free; 446 (r), Edward Boone/For Picture/Corbis; 447 (tr), Marianne Rosenstiehl/Sygma/Corbis; 447 (cl), AMET JEAN PIERRE/CORBIS; 447 (br), Stephane Cardinale/People Avenue/Corbis; 448 (l), Lawrence Migdale/Getty Images; 448 (r), Lebrecht Music and Arts Photo Library/Alamy; 449 (tl), Lindsay Hebberd/CORBIS; 449 (cl, c), Photgraphy by DrumSkull Drums.

BACKMATTER: r8 (bl, tr, bc), Sam Dudgeon/HRW; r8 (c), ImageState; r9 (b), Artville/Getty Images; r9 (tc), Alan Bailey/Rubberball/Alamy; r9 (tr, cr), Victoria Smith/HRW; r10 (tl, cr), Victoria Smith/HRW; r10 (tr), Ingram Publishing; r10 (c), PhotoDisc/Getty Images; r11 (l), Victoria Smith/HRW; r11 (t), Stephanie Friedman/HRW; r11 (br), Sam Dudgeon/HRW; r12 (r), Sam Dudgeon/HRW; r12 (t), PhotoDisc/Getty Images; r13 (cr), Victoria Smith/HRW; r13 (l), Comstock; r13 (br), Sam Dudgeon/HRW; r13 (tr), Dougal Waters/Getty Images; r14 (l), Sam Dudgeon/HRW; r14 (br), Victoria Smith/HRW; r15 (l), Brand X Pictures; r15 (tr), Book Cover: Quebec: Guides Bleus Evasion, Courtesy of Hachette Livre, 2000, All rights reserved; r15 (br), Victoria Smith/HRW; r16 (tr, tc), Sam Dudgeon/HRW; r16 (cr, bl), Royalty-Free/CORBIS; r16 (br), PhotoDisc/Getty Images; r17 (br, cr, c), Ingram Publishing; r17 (bl, tl), PhotoDisc/Getty Images; r17 (tr), Digital Vision/gettyimages; r18 (cl), The Stocktreck Corp/Brand X Pictures/gettyimages; r18 (giraffes, br), Royalty-Free/CORBIS; r18 (br), COMSTOCK, Inc.; r18 (bl, c, tr), PhotoDisc/Getty Images; r19 (tr), Index Stock; r19 (monkey, br), PhotoDisc/Getty Images; r19 (tl), Royalty-Free/CORBIS; r19 (le monde), Sam Dudgeon/HRW; R20 (tc), Royalty-Free/CORBIS; r20 (cl), COMSTOCK, Inc.; r20 (tr, cr), PhotoDisc/Getty Images; r20 (br), Copyright Image Source Limited; r21 (l, c), Royalty Free/CORBIS; r21 (b, cr), PhotoDisc/Getty Images.

Staff Credits

David Alvarado, Sara Anbari, Jeffrey Atkins, Kimberly Barr, Sally Bess, Ed Blake, Marion Bermondy, Priscilla Blanton, Kristina Bigelow, Jeremy Brady, Konstanze Alex Brown, Stacy Cooper, Lynda Cortez, Lana Cox, Nina Degollado, Yamilé Dewailly, Michelle Dike, Lydia Doty, Mila Escamilla, Shawn Farris, James Foster, José Garza, Kristin Hay, Rebecca Jordan, Marta Kimball, Kadonna Knape, Cathy Kuhles, Liann Lech, Sean McCormick, Richard Metzger, Erin Miller, Cathy Murphy, Mercedes Newman, Amber Nichols, Nanda Patel, Paul Provence, Mike Rinella, Marleis Roberts, Annette Saunders, Glenna Scott, Kay Selke, Chris Smith, Sara Stavchansky, Jeff Streber, Stephanie Swope, Jeannie Taylor, Géraldine Touzeau-Patrick, David Trevino, Vickie Tripp, Jaishree Venkatesan, Cindy Verheyden, Karen Vigil, Holly Whittaker.